Praise for *1,000 Jewish Recipes*
by Faye Levy

"It's a joy! It's a miracle! This magnum opus chronicles 5,760 years of Jewish nourishment, and then some. More than a cookbook, it is a celebration of community and continuity at the Jewish table, written with integrity and love. *B'tayavon* (good appetite) 1,000 times to Faye Levy."

—Rozanne Gold, award-winning chef and author of *Little Meals,
Recipes 1-2-3, Recipes 1-2-3 Menus,* and *Entertaining 1-2-3*

"This may well be the most comprehensive book on Jewish cooking ever written, and as I thumb through its pages, I'm convinced that no one knows more about Jewish cooking than Faye Levy. Neophytes will find here enough great recipes for a lifetime and even seasoned Jewish cooks will discover dishes they never dreamed of. Use it for holiday feasts or everyday cooking. *1,000 Jewish Recipes* is a true tour de force by one of the most authoritative writers in the business. Run, don't walk, to your local bookstore and buy a copy for yourself, your children, and your friends."

—Steven Raichlen, award-winning author of *The Barbecue Bible,
Miami Spice,* and *Healthy Jewish Cooking*

"*1,000 Jewish Recipes* is the ultimate and complete Jewish cookbook. It covers the holidays from Sukkot to Shavuot, and every other day as well. Sephardic (Eastern Jewish) and Ashkenazic (Western Jewish) recipes are there from appetizers to desserts. If only my mother, God rest her soul, had this cookbook when I was a child! I highly recommend it!"

—Ed Koch, radio show host, author, and former New York City mayor

"This book is a treasure trove, spanning the gamut of Jewish cooking from traditional to 'trendy,' from Eastern Europe Ashkenazic to North African and Middle Eastern. With her broad culinary knowledge, her fluency with Jewish culture, and her clear voice, Faye Levy is the perfect person to write this definitive work. I can't wait to use it!"

—Mollie Katzen, bestselling author of the *Moosewood Cookbook,* and public television host

"*1,000 Jewish Recipes* is not only a masterful collection of delicious recipes, it is also chock-full of information on Jewish holiday and daily ritual and traditions. The book is a 'must-have' for every Jewish family and it is destined to become a classic."

—Nina Simonds, award-winning author of *A Spoonful of Ginger*

"You don't have to be Jewish to love Faye Levy's *1,000 Jewish Recipes.*"

—Kemp Minifie, senior food editor of *Gourmet* magazine

"Faye Levy is one of the most gifted recipe writers I know. Her work always shines with a kind of inspired simplicity, yet the finished dishes are so delicious. Recipes like that can only come from years in the kitchen. Her experience can be enjoyed on every page of this authoritative yet very personal book honoring centuries of Jewish cooking."

—Russ Parsons, food editor of *The Los Angeles Times*

"*1,000 Jewish Recipes* tells everything there is to know about Jewish cooking—from old-world Eastern European traditions to North African delicacies. Faye Levy provides hundreds of ideas and tips that put this book at the vanguard of cooking in the 21st century."

—Carl Schrag, managing editor of *The Jerusalem Post*

1,000 JEWISH *Recipes*

1,000 JEWISH Recipes

BY FAYE LEVY

IDG Books Worldwide, Inc.
An International Data Group Company

Foster City, CA • Chicago, IL • Indianapolis, IN • New York, NY

IDG BOOKS WORLDWIDE, INC.
An International Data Group Company
919 E. Hillsdale Boulevard
Suite 400
Foster City, CA 94404

The IDG Books Worldwide logo is a registered trademark under exclusive license to
IDG Books Worldwide, Inc., from International Data Group, Inc.
For general information on IDG Books Worldwide's books in the U.S.,
please call our Consumer Customer Service department at 800-762-2974.
For reseller information, including discounts and premium sales,
please call our Reseller Customer Service department at 800-434-3422.
Library of Congress Cataloging-in-Publication Data
Levy, Faye.
1,000 Jewish Recipes / Faye Levy.
    p. cm.
Includes index.
ISBN 0-02-862337-1 (hardcover)
1. Cookery, Jewish. I. Title.

TX724 .L4125 2000
641.5'676—dc21

99-055743

Cover and Book Design by Michele Laseau
Cover Illustration by Elizabeth Traynor

Manufactured in the United States of America
10 9 8 7 6 5 4 3 2 1

Dedication

This book is dedicated with love to my mother,

Pauline Kahn Luria

And in loving memory of my father, Louis Kahn, and my

mother- and father-in-law, Rachel and Zechariah Levy

Contents

Acknowledgments

When you're as passionate about a subject as I am about Jewish cooking, inspiration comes from a great variety of people. Growing up in an Orthodox Ashkenazic home in Washington, D.C. and being part of a close-knit Jewish community was, in a sense, the beginning of my education for this book. My active research into Jewish cooking began thirty years ago when I lived in Israel, and all along the way people have been so kind and generous with their recipes and insights on how they cook and the part food plays in their lives.

This book was my biggest undertaking ever. The challenge of researching, cooking for, and writing a book with 1,000 Jewish recipes seemed daunting. It turned out to be a pleasure and has enriched my life on many levels.

Ideas for the book came from so many sources, from people to publications to radio and television shows to the Internet, that I cannot begin to list them all. I learned from lucky encounters at Seders, parties, and markets. Relatives and strangers told me about their special herb mixtures, their beloved versions of Passover haroset, or the best grocery stores to buy treasured spices. The fondness with which people I had just met described their favorite foods and their mealtime memories fueled my enthusiasm and made for many enjoyable, interesting experiences. Many even invited me into their kitchens. I would like each person to know how much I appreciate the information he or she gave me.

I have gained so much from the questions and suggestions of students in my Jewish cooking classes and of readers of my cooking column. A warm "thank you" also goes to my immediate and my extended family as well as my husband's, and to my friends, neighbors, teachers, colleagues, and acquaintances, who contributed their knowledge of Jewish culture and cuisine. I value all I have learned about cooking and Jewish life from my mother, Pauline Kahn Luria, who emigrated as a young child from Warsaw to the United States and has lived in Jerusalem for the last thirty years. She taught me not only the secrets of tasty Ashkenazic cooking but also how to make just about any recipe kosher.

During the past three decades I have gained invaluable insights into the Yemenite Jewish lifestyle and cooking from my mother-in-law, Rachel Levy, who was born in Yemen and lived in the Tel Aviv area for most of her adult life.

I would like to thank my brother, Tzvi Kahn, who was happy to join me in such endeavors as searching for the best challah for Shabbat in his neighborhood in Jerusalem, of which he has been a proud resident for the past thirty years. No one could evoke our childhood memories as well as he. With his lifelong fascination with Jewish culture and history, he has helped me to keep apprized of new food customs becoming popular in Israel.

Each of my sisters-in-law and brothers-in-law taught me wonderful recipes and cooking tips from the meals our families shared over the years: Mati Kahn, Tzvi's wife, an immigrant to Israel from India; Hedva and Dudu Cohen, Nirit and Yahalom Levy, and Etti and Prachya Levy.

I am grateful to my husband's relatives in Israel for their tips about Sephardic cooking and the warmth of their hospitality, especially his Aunt Mazal Cohen, his cousin Sara Boni, and to Saida Avraham; his cousin Cohava Cohen in New York and his relative Dvora Cohen in Paris.

My special gratitude goes to my aunt Sylvia Saks, my late uncle Herman Saks and their children, Marilyn Saks McMillion, Marlene Oliver and Michael Saks, for their support, ideas, and enthusiasm for my work over the years. Thanks also to my cousin Mildred Greenberg for her cooking tips.

Of our friends in Los Angeles, I especially appreciate everything I have learned from Valerie and Chaim

Alon, a couple dedicated to celebrating Jewish life and good Jewish cooking with their four children. They are the best neighbors anyone could have. Thanks also to my friend Shulamit Wilder and her mother Perla Abergel for their Moroccan-Jewish specialties; and to my professional chef friend Teri Appleton, who is full of delicious ideas on every dish from hummus to cheesecake.

I also learned much from my friend in Jerusalem, Ronnie Venezia, from wonderful desserts to tasty Lebanese-Israeli cooking, and from her late mother Suzanne Elmaleh, who taught me her authentic Lebanese Jewish specialties in Ronnie's kitchen.

From Jaklyn Cohen of Holon, Israel, I learned to prepare kubbeh and other dishes of the Jews of Iraq. From Ninette Bachar of Givatayim, Israel, I learned Tunisian Jewish Shabbat dishes. Paule Tourdjman, a friend in Paris, introduced me to many dishes and traditions of Moroccan Jews. My friend Greg Dinner in London, England, a writer and food lover, encouraged me always and shared his family's traditional holiday recipes with me.

As a newlywed living in Bat Yam, Israel, I learned much from my neighbors, who patiently explained to me how they cook their heirloom dishes, and from colleagues, friends, and fellow students from many ethnic traditions, whom I met during my studies and work at Hebrew University in Jerusalem and at Tel Aviv University.

Ruth Sirkis, Israel's best-known cookbook author, was my mentor and later my first Hebrew cookbook publisher. I appreciate all she taught me about cooking, food writing, and recipe testing during the two years I worked as her sole assistant.

Over the past decade I have been given a terrific opportunity to write regular newspaper cooking columns and thereby further explore and freely present culinary customs and recipes. In Los Angeles thanks go to Jim Burns, my editor at the *Los Angeles Times Syndicate*, and in Israel to Carl Schrag, Faye Bittker, Haim Shapiro and Batsheva Tsur, my editors at the *Jerusalem Post*.

Many other food editors of magazines and newspapers encouraged me throughout my career by their words of encouragement and by publishing my articles and recipes. I would especially like to thank Zanne Stewart and Kemp Miles Minifie of *Gourmet* magazine; Barbara Fairchild and Kristine Kidd of *Bon Appétit* magazine; Larry Levine of *Western Chef Magazine*; Russ Parsons of the *Los Angeles Times*, formerly of the *Los Angeles Herald Examiner*; and Susan Puckett of the *Atlanta Journal and Constitution*, and former food editors Charles Britton of Copley Los Angeles Newspapers and Kit Snedaker of the *Los Angeles Herald Examiner*.

When I was growing up in Washington, D.C., my teachers at the Hebrew Academy and at Midrasha Hebrew High School enlightened me about the Jewish heritage. In Paris during six delightful years, Anne Willan and my chef-instructors and colleagues at La Varenne Cooking School, especially Fernand Chambrette, Albert Jorant and Claude Vauguet, taught me the art of fine cuisine.

I owe a big debt of gratitude to my editor, Linda Ingroia, for her thorough reading and creative suggestions that improved the book, as well as for her good humor while gently pushing me to do my best. I also appreciate the work of Michele Laseau, Trudy Coler, and Holly Wittenberg, the designers; of Melissa Moyal and Mark Steven Long, the production editors; of Amy Gordon, the copy editor; and of recipe tester Elaine Koshrova. Thanks also to Maureen and Eric Lasher for their support and for finding a good home for my book.

Most of all, thanks to Yakir, for helping me with shopping, cooking, and eating all my renditions of gefilte fish, honey cakes, and countless other dishes, and for making it possible for me to embark on (and for sharing with me) an amazing culinary adventure that had spanned three decades and continents.

Introduction

Growing up in a traditional Jewish family means living in a cycle of celebration. The rhythm of life is dictated by the next upcoming event or holiday and Jews everywhere enjoy celebrating each one with traditional festive dishes. Food, in fact, is one of the most important elements of Jewish culture.

As children, my brother and I knew that at the end of every week there would be special dishes for Shabbat, the Sabbath—the day of rest that begins Friday at sunset and ends Saturday after sunset. We could expect to enjoy aromatic homemade chicken soup with light matzo balls, a beautiful braided challah, a golden brown roast chicken, noodle kugel with mushrooms and onions, and my mother's scrumptious chocolate applesauce cake. There were honey cakes and plenty of other sweets for Rosh Hashanah, cheesecakes for Shavuot, triangular filled pastries called hamantaschen for Purim, and a whole week of special food during Passover. In other Jewish families some of the dishes were different but all were following the same schedule of feasting.

The customs of the Jewish festivals are a major influence on Jewish cooking. Because cooking is prohibited on the Sabbath and on certain holidays, Jews around the world have created a variety of slow-cook and make-ahead main courses. Since bread is not eaten on Passover, every community has developed matzo casseroles, stuffings, and other matzo specialties.

The special element that colors Jewish food traditions is *kashrut*, the rules of keeping kosher. These regulations are not simply lists of permitted foods, but constitute a guideline for menu and recipe planning, not just for the holidays, but for 365 days a year. Keeping meat and dairy foods separate leads to an ongoing search for tasty dairy-free sauces and accompaniments to serve at meat meals. Avoiding nonkosher meats and shellfish leads to an emphasis on developing delicious dishes of fish, chicken, and kosher meat.

Like American cooking, Jewish cooking is multicultural. I first noticed the richness of the Jewish culinary culture when I lived in Israel. Growing up on such Ashkenazic specialties as gefilte fish, chopped liver, and blintzes, I assumed that these foods were what all Jews ate. I was completely unaware of Sephardic phyllo-dough *bourekas*, Moroccan couscous, and Yemenite meat soup. Discovering these dishes and their new flavors was a true awakening for me. They inspired me to explore new realms of Jewish cooking and to expand my knowledge of my own Polish-Jewish cooking background as well.

All my life I had been learning about Jewish food as part of my culture. During my college years in Israel, my passion for Jewish cooking was aroused and I began trying to learn as much as I could about my rich culinary heritage.

Fortunately, educating myself in this direction proved easy. Living in Israel for more than seven years, I was surrounded by Jews from all over the world, even from places that I had never heard of like Kurdistan and Bulgaria. My new relatives by marriage were from Yemen, Morocco, and India. I had neighbors from Tunisia and Iraq. I even found quite a few old acquaintances from my elementary and junior high school, the Hebrew Academy of Washington, D.C., who had also become motivated to move to the Jewish state. They had plenty to teach me about Russian and Hungarian-Jewish food. I continued to discover many more Jewish specialties during my years of living in two other major Jewish centers: Paris and Los Angeles.

I also went back to my mother, who has always been known in our family as an excellent cook and baker. When I was younger, I had been too busy with school to learn how to cook, but now my mother and I find great pleasure cooking together whenever we can. I encourage all parents and grandparents to follow the time-honored Jewish tradition of cooking with their children and grandchildren, as this time spent together and the knowledge gained are priceless treasures.

Like other styles of cooking in the modern world, Jewish cuisine has evolved over time. Few people cook dishes today exactly as they were prepared two hundred years ago. For example, our health concerns lead us to make chopped liver with less chicken fat than our grandmothers used, or perhaps with none at all. Sometimes we might even make vegetarian "chopped liver," but this appetizer still retains its identity with the characteristic flavor of deeply browned onions. From time to time we might add asparagus to our potato kugel, because many more fresh vegetables are available to us year round than could be found years ago in central Europe. Many of us bake our blintzes instead of frying them because today homes have ovens.

Actually, this way of creating new dishes is not new. Over the ages, it too has been part of the development of cuisine. As ingredients became available, people used them. If this had not happened, there never would have been potato latkes for Hanukkah. The dish was created in eastern Europe but potatoes come from the New World. A few hundred years ago, Ashkenazic Jews in Europe had not heard of them.

Israeli food also has had a pronounced influence on Jewish cooking. Thus we find Israeli salads, pastries, and stews in Jewish homes and restaurants from Paris to Los Angeles. Perhaps this modern Israeli style could be defined as a fusion of Mediterranean cooking with traditional Jewish foods from many lands. Because so many Jews live together and exchange ideas, Israeli home cooks are creating their own distinct version of Jewish cooking.

The increasing prominence of Israeli "cuisine" makes perfect sense. The eastern Mediterranean is not only the birthplace of kosher laws and Jewish culture, it is also where oil has always been the main cooking fat, not butter or animal fat, and where meat is rarely cooked with cream. With the increasing involvement in cultural traditions of Jews both young and old, and with the widespread interest in healthful eating, Israel is now becoming a center for the renaissance of Jewish cooking.

Even with this great diversity, a kernel of flavor remains in our group memory and food culture. We all cook dishes we remember from our childhood, especially for the holidays. This is a chain that links us to our culinary past. Recreating these unique dishes and tastes is a celebration of Jewish life.

The recipes in this book preserve the traditional tastes of the different Jewish communities and also represent the type of food that is cooked today in Jewish homes around the world. The dishes benefit from the wealth of fresh ingredients available and reflect our desire that what we eat be mostly healthful and simple to prepare.

All the recipes in this book are kosher. To make them easy to use in kosher menus, I have labeled each recipe with M for Meat, D for Dairy, or P for Pareve.

I hope that cooking from these recipes and savoring these dishes will give you some of the joy that I feel when I cook and eat with my family. And so, from our home to yours, I propose a toast: "Le'Chaim"—To life!

Faye Levy

The World of Jewish Cooking

Throughout most of their history, the Jews have been a diverse people. The Torah relates that the Jews were a people of ten tribes, descended from the sons of Jacob. Jews have lived in many different countries of the world and this has greatly influenced their cuisine.

The majority of Jews in North America are of Ashkenazic, or central and eastern European, extraction. For this reason most of the dishes familiar to Americans as "Jewish" are Ashkenazic. This style is one of the two major branches of Jewish culture and cuisine.

The other major grouping of Jewish communities is the Sephardic, comprising Jews of Mediterranean and Middle Eastern origin. The Sephardic style of cooking is prominent on the Israeli culinary scene. As part of the healthful Mediterranean diet, it is gaining favor among American Jews as well.

Neither branch is homogeneous. Polish gefilte fish, for example, is quite different from Russian. Russian Jews from Georgia cook in a much different manner than those from areas bordering the Ukraine. The food of Jews from India bears little resemblance to that of Jews from Greece, although both groups are categorized under the Sephardic umbrella.

In addition, there is plenty of intermingling of ideas and recipes. Jews have moved to many different areas of the world. There are Sephardic and Ashkenazic communities in South and Central America, western Europe, and South Africa. Many families, like mine, include both Ashkenazic and Sephardic members. Of course, neighbors, friends, and colleagues actively exchange recipes. Thus, a sort of multicultural fusion Jewish cuisine is being continuously created. This is not a new trend; Jews have always learned from each other and from people of other religions. In modern days this tendency has been accelerated because people, foods, and ideas move more freely.

The signature dishes of each community and their numerous regional variations are described in the introductions to those recipes. Here is a general overview of the foods and flavors of the major branches of Jewish cooking.

Ashkenazic Jews

"Ashkenaz" is a medieval Hebrew name for Germany. Originally it referred to Jews from that country but was broadened to include those born in central and eastern Europe and their descendants. Thus it also comprises Jews from Austria, Hungary, Poland, and much of Russia.

Sephardic Jews, or Communities of the East

Similarly, "Spharad" is the Hebrew word for Spain; Sephardic refers loosely to Jews whose ancestors lived in Spain but in fact includes Jews from a vast area that stretches from the western Mediterranean all the way to India.

When the Jews of Spain were expelled in 1492, they were scattered throughout the Mediterranean region. Some traveled as far as Holland and eventually to the New World. The members of the resulting communities became known as Sephardic Jews. However, in some of the countries in which these Spanish Jews arrived, the other Jews were not from Spain.

A large migration of Jews occurred much earlier, from ancient Israel eastward. In the eighth century B.C. the Assyrians conquered Israel and exiled some Jews to ancient Babylon (now Iraq), and from there some moved to what is now Iran.

Historians are not sure where the Jews from Yemen, Ethiopia, and India came from. Their origins are not traced to Spain.

All these groups are commonly referred to as Sephardic. Because many did not originate in Spain, some feel it is more accurate to call this category "Edot Hamizrach" or "the communities of the East."

The Ashkenazic Culinary Style

In general, Ashkenazic cooks use fewer spices than Sephardic ones and season their food with a lighter hand. Sautéed onions are the main flavoring of many dishes. Often the onions are cooked until they are deeply browned and give a rich taste and color to such dishes as braised chicken and noodle kugels. In traditional recipes the onions are sautéed in chicken fat or goose fat for meat meals and in butter for dairy menus, and these cooking fats contribute their unique flavors.

For deeper color, the onions might be browned with sweet paprika, a favorite seasoning for meats and vegetables. In Hungarian homes, hot paprika is also used and cooking from this region can be quite spicy.

Garlic is used in the Ashkenazic kitchen, but in smaller amounts than in Sephardic dishes. Parsley, dill, and bay leaves are the favorite herbs. Cinnamon is well liked in desserts. A distinctive condiment liked by Ashkenazic Jews is horseradish, especially with fish. Sweet and sour dishes of fish, meat, and vegetables appear in many Ashkenazic pots and are a departure from the otherwise delicate cooking style.

Chicken is often roasted, and beef and veal are pot-roasted, braised, or stewed. Many of the fish dishes are made of fresh-water fish, the ones from the lakes and rivers of the region. Smoked and cured fish are popular for appetizers and light meals.

The vegetables that appear most often in Ashkenazic recipes are carrots, potatoes, celery, cabbage, cauliflower, beets, beans, peas, cucumbers, and mushrooms, ingredients traditionally available in eastern and central Europe. This selection is supplemented with fruit, both fresh and dried, which appears not only in desserts but is also used in soups and is stewed with meats and vegetables. Hungarians also use plenty of peppers. Romanian Jews prepare some spicy eggplant and other vegetable dishes resembling those of their Sephardic neighbors farther south in Bulgaria and Turkey.

Dairy foods and dairy-based *milchig* meals, as they are called in Yiddish, are well liked in Ashkenazic homes. Sour cream and soft fresh cheeses like cottage cheese, farmer's cheese, and cream cheese are widely used, notably in such specialties as blintzes and noodle dishes.

Noodles frequently appear on the Ashkenazic table, especially as egg noodles and filled kreplach in soup. Equally loved are noodle kugels, for which the noodles are combined with sautéed mushrooms, apples, or other ingredients, both savory and sweet. Dumplings are sometimes made of potatoes but the favorite ones are matzo balls. Pearl barley and kasha (buckwheat) are frequently served grains especially among Jews from Poland and Russia, and corn meal is commonly served by those from Romania. The favorite breads are rich braided challah, bagels, rye bread, and pumpernickel. Poppy seeds and caraway seeds are used to flavor breads.

Ashkenazic Jews excel in dessert making and have developed a wide range of cakes, cookies, and pastries. The Hungarian and Austrian desserts are held in high esteem and are the basis for many of the most popular desserts in Israeli as well as in American Jewish bakeries. These include fruit and cheese blintzes, cheesecakes, strudels, tortes, honey cakes, and breakfast breads.

The Sephardic Culinary Style

The most distinguishing characteristic of Sephardic food is that spices and herbs are used more liberally than in the Ashkenazic kitchen. This does not mean that all Sephardic food is hot or heavily spiced, as delicate dishes are made as well.

Garlic and lemon are popular flavorings, and olive oil is the favored cooking fat, although vegetable oil is also used.

Like Ashkenazic Jews, many Sephardic Jews love dill. It perfumes the foods of the Jews of Greece, Turkey, Iraq, and even India, and is also popular in Israel today. Cilantro and Italian parsley are widely used throughout much of the Sephardic community, most notably south of the Mediterranean and in the Middle East. Moroccan Jews use mint to flavor tea and Lebanese Jews use it in cooking.

Cumin is a favorite spice and appears in the cuisines of Jews from Morocco all the way to India, although it is used somewhat less along the northern rim of the Mediterranean Sea. It is a hallmark of Yemenite cooking, and it has become a favorite in modern Israeli cooking. Turmeric is used in the same areas.

Like Ashkenazic Jews, Sephardic Jews use paprika extensively. They like cinnamon too and use it not only in sweets but to subtly accent meat and chicken casseroles as well. Ginger is used in its dried form by Jews from North Africa to season their stews and by those from Yemen to flavor their coffee.

The cuisines of the Jews of Morocco, Libya, Algeria, and Yemen are known for their fiery dishes. Cooks from these countries love chiles, both fresh and dried, for making condiments and for adding to a variety of braised and stewed dishes and salads. Cayenne pepper and hot paprika are also favorites.

The sesame seed is important as a flavoring for breads, and it is also turned into two favorites of the cuisine: tahini (sesame sauce), and halvah, a rich sesame sweet.

Chicken and beef are the most-used meats, and lamb is also a favorite. For home cooking, the meats are usually stewed or made into soups, but for special occasions, grilled meats and fish are popular. Most Sephardic fish recipes call for salt-water fish.

Among Jews from Middle Eastern countries, pita is the bread generally found on the table. Pita is not always in the form of the familiar pocket bread but varies from one region to another. Sometimes it is much broader or much flatter and the food is placed on top and rolled instead of being slipped into a pocket. Bread flavorings, in addition to sesame seeds—the general favorite—include anise seeds, popular with Moroccan Jews, and black caraway seeds or *nigella*, a Yemenite staple.

Rice is by far the most-loved grain and is used extensively in the Sephardic kitchen. In North Africa, couscous is the main grain-based dish.

Vegetables are central to the Sephardic kitchen and provide a substantial part of menus. The most commonly used ones are Mediterranean vegetables: tomatoes, peppers, eggplant, and zucchini, but many others are used according to their seasons, notably artichokes, okra, chard, and fava beans. All sorts of dried beans are used but chickpeas (garbanzo beans) are the top choice. Besides being used in soups, stews, and side dishes, vegetables are great favorites as salads, both cooked and raw, as pickles, and as appetizers. Olives are also loved as an appetizer throughout much of the Sephardic world and are used in a variety of preparations.

In general, Sephardic Jews use dairy products less extensively than in the Ashkenazic kitchen. They don't usually build a meal around a dairy main course they way Ashkenazic Jews do with blintzes or noodle kugels. However, yogurt is popular in some Sephardic communities in salads and as an accompaniment for pareve dishes of legumes or grains. Turkish, Greek, and Bulgarian Jews love feta cheese, on its own, in salads, and in phyllo pastries. Like other Mediterranean peoples, Sephardic Jews don't make as many desserts of sour cream or whipped cream as do those from central Europe. Sephardic Jews do use milk to prepare puddings, especially of rice.

Desserts are traditionally less important than in Ashkenazic meals. To end the meal, Sephardic Jews often serve fresh fruit and nuts. When sweets are served, cakes and pastries are flavored with nuts (especially almonds, pistachios, pine nuts, and walnuts), sesame seeds, lemon and orange juice and rind, orange flower water, cinnamon, dates, figs, and raisins. Phyllo dough is used by Jews from Eastern Mediterranean countries to make desserts that are often sweetened with honey or sugar syrup.

A Guide to Keeping Kosher

All the recipes in this book are kosher. For many Jews, keeping kosher is a way of life. To the newcomer, it may appear complicated but it's easy once a person gets used to it. After a while, it becomes second nature and is part of the general attitude towards selecting and preparing food.

Keeping kosher is a cornerstone in observing Judaism. Orthodox Jews believe that keeping kosher is a divine command. *Kashrut* is the body of laws, outlined in the Torah, that describes what is kosher and how to keep kosher. Over the years, the laws have been interpreted and spelled out by the overseeing rabbis in Jewish communities around the world.

More and more couples are interested in *kashrut*, as part of a general trend of exploring their roots and respecting Jewish customs. Some Jews, even if they do not follow all the rules of Orthodox Judaism, choose to keep kosher at home so that any Jew would feel comfortable eating at their table, knowing the food is kosher.

The regulations for keeping kosher involve choices of meats, fish, and dairy products, shopping guidelines for foods, special preparation of foods, menu planning regarding what foods may be eaten together, and use of dishes and utensils for cooking and for eating.

Meats and Fish

The Torah defines kosher animals as the ones that have split hooves and chew their cud. Therefore, beef, veal, lamb, and goat are kosher, but pork and rabbit are not. Poultry—chicken, turkey, duck, goose, and Cornish hens—is also kosher. Game birds like quail can be kosher if they are properly slaughtered, not shot in the wild.

Fish must have scales and fins in order to be kosher. This excludes all shellfish but includes most familiar fish, except for such scale-less fish as monkfish and eel.

Special Preparation of Meats and Poultry

Besides choosing the proper meats, other steps are necessary to make meats and poultry kosher before they can be cooked. First, the animals must be slaughtered by a qualified kosher butcher, according to the laws that govern this process. For example, a knife must be used rather than a gun, and therefore shooting game animals or birds is not permitted. Venison can be kosher if it is properly slaughtered. If there is a kosher label on the meat or poultry, people know that this step has been done properly.

Only certain cuts of meat are kosher—those from the fore quarter of the animal. In order for cuts of meat from the hind part of animals to be kosher, the sciatic nerve must be removed. Few butchers do this, so these cuts of meat are not sold at kosher butchers in the United States. In Israel this nerve is removed, and therefore you can sometimes find kosher beef tenderloin and other hind quarter cuts in kosher markets there.

Next, meats and poultry must be salted or "koshered" to remove as much blood as possible, as blood is not kosher. The salt used is coarse salt, also known as kosher salt.

When I was growing up, my mother had to kosher all the meat and poultry at home. Today it has often been done already by the packager or at the kosher butcher shop. If in doubt, ask whether the meat has been salted. For instructions in koshering meat at home, see page xxii.

Dairy Products

Many hard cheeses are made with rennet, which is an animal product. Kosher cheeses are made without animal rennet.

Soft dairy products such as yogurt and ice cream are sometimes made with gelatin. If gelatin is used, it should be kosher gelatin, which generally comes from non-animal sources and may contain such ingredients as seaweed-based carageenan or agar-agar; nonkosher gelatin is made from animal bones and, in the kosher kitchen, cannot be combined with dairy foods.

Kosher dairy products are found not only at kosher grocery stores and the kosher sections of supermarkets, but also at vegetarian and natural foods stores.

Some foods are labeled "dairy" even though they do not contain dairy foods because the company cooks them in pans that are used for other foods that are dairy.

Other Foods

Wine is a special ingredient because it is used in blessings and must be certified as kosher.

All fresh produce is kosher.

Processed foods can be kosher if they are prepared in a kosher fashion—made with kosher foods and prepared with kosher utensils and pots. There is a wide array of packaged food products—from breakfast cereals to canned beans—that have kosher certification.

Shopping

Keeping kosher requires reading labels of processed products to see if they have kosher certification or to find out if they contain dairy or meat foods that are not obvious, such as whey, which is dairy, or meat broth.

Food companies have their products reviewed for kosher certification, allowing them to add symbols to the labels that make kosher products easy to recognize. A U with a circle around it, the most widely accepted symbol, represents certification from the Union of

Orthodox Jewish Congregations. K is another widely used symbol for *Kosher*. The letter K is often used as part of a kosher symbol such as K inside a circle, a triangle, or a star. The best known is K with a circle around it, from the Organized Kashrut Laboratories in Brooklyn, New York. Used alone, the letter K does not belong to a specific certifying organization; it is printed on the package by the food producer. Other kosher symbols come from regional rabbinical boards, such as R.C.C., which stands for the Rabbinical Council of California. You can obtain a list of local types of certification from a rabbi.

Kosher products from Israel may have different kosher symbols. The name of the rabbi certifying the product may appear, sometimes only in Hebrew.

Some foods also are labeled D for *Dairy*, M for *Meat*, or P for *Pareve* next to their kosher symbol.

With so many kosher symbols and origins of certification, many people decide which to follow based on their personal preference, background, or advice from their rabbi.

Supermarkets increasingly carry many foods with kosher labels, usually in a designated kosher foods section. Some people, though, feel that the best way to ensure that all their food is kosher is to buy it at a kosher grocery store, in which all the foods are kosher. For more on specific kosher ingredients, see Stocking the Jewish Pantry, page xxv.

Menu Planning

The basic principle of kosher menu planning is keeping meat products and dairy products completely separate. Meals that contain meat or poultry are called *fleishig* in Yiddish or *bsari* in Hebrew; dairy meals are *milchig* in Yiddish or *halavi* in Hebrew.

Rabbis through the ages have developed the laws that govern this separation, which is derived from the biblical command in Exodus and in Deuteronomy that prohibits cooking a young goat in its mother's milk. Thus, dairy foods and meat foods require separate sets of dishes and other kitchen equipment.

Cooking Kosher Foods

Meats and Poultry

Because kosher meats and poultry are salted during koshering, it has a salty taste. For dry-heat cooking methods like roasting and grilling, little or no additional salt is needed. For soups and stews some salt can be added to season the other ingredients; it is best to add only a little and to taste before adding more.

Some people find that poultry and meat taste better because they have been salted. It is a similar effect to soaking them in brine, a process done to meat and poultry in some recipes before they are cooked.

The amount of saltiness can vary depending on the size and shape of the piece of meat. If you find kosher meat or poultry too salty, soak it in cold water for thirty minutes before cooking the next time. Some people do this on a routine basis in order to reduce the sodium content in the meat. (Keep in mind that soaking may diminish flavor.)

In the kosher kitchen steaks and burgers are never served rare. Because blood is not kosher, meat is cooked until it is well done.

Fish

There are no special rules for preparing or cooking fish. It can even be served raw, as sushi, if you like.

When fish is included in a menu that contains meat, fish is usually the first course. Fish is not served on the same plate as meat.

Eggs

Eggs that have blood spots are not kosher and must be discarded. In making cake batters and other mixtures that contain several eggs, cooks break each egg into a separate dish before adding it to the mixture in order to inspect it.

Vegetables

Greens, cauliflower, and broccoli must be rinsed and inspected thoroughly before being used to ensure there are no bugs inside. Insects would make the vegetable not kosher. In Israel some lettuces are sold wrapped with a label indicating they are guaranteed to be free of bugs.

A third category of neutral foods called *pareve* are neither dairy nor meat and can be served with either one. These include eggs, vegetables, fruits, breads, grains, and oils. Fish is also pareve but has some special rules for serving it with other foods.

Keeping dairy and meat foods separate means that they are not combined in the same dish or on the same menu. Many Orthodox Jews wait for six hours after eating meat before eating dairy foods, and thirty minutes after eating dairy foods before eating meat. In some communities, the waiting times vary.

Kitchen Utensils

A kosher kitchen has two sets of dishes, flatware, pots, and other mixing and cooking implements. One set is for meat and one is for dairy foods. Two additional sets are reserved for Passover meals. (See Passover, page 1). Meat and dairy dishes must be cleaned with separate sponges and towels, and set on separate dish racks. Those who can afford it have two separate sinks. The soap used to wash dishes and hands should be kosher.

Stocking the Jewish Pantry

Because Jewish cooking is so diverse, you are likely to find a different selection of pantry ingredients in each home, depending on the family's background. Still, some pantry items are widely used by many Jews and they are the ones discussed here.

There is additional information about ingredients in each chapter. The favorite flavorings of the different Jewish communities are covered in The World of Jewish Cooking on pages xvii–xix. Specific foods and holiday foods are explained in their respective chapters. For example, important grains are discussed in the grains chapter and Passover ingredients are detailed in the section devoted to the holiday.

Many of the special ingredients used in Jewish cooking relate to keeping kosher. In recent years this category of ingredients has been growing at a dizzying pace, as kosher products become in greater demand.

As a child in the 1950s and '60s, I never saw kosher boxed cake mixes or canned or packaged soups or sauces. We bought all our challah and other kosher bread at a kosher bakery. Kosher chicken was available at the kosher butcher shop and not at the supermarket.

Today many supermarkets have kosher food sections and bakery items like kosher challah, prepared soups and sauces, and a variety of cake, brownie, and cookie mixes. In the freezer there are kosher knishes, pizza, and other baked goods. It's pretty easy to find frozen kosher chicken and sometimes fresh as well. The supermarket also carries kosher cheeses, both fresh and slicing cheeses, wines, and deli meats. There is a variety of prepared fish, from lox and smoked whitefish to herring and gefilte fish.

Naturally, there is a large number of kosher foods in supermarkets in cities with substantial Jewish populations. Still, the most extensive array of kosher foods can be found in kosher or Jewish markets. The selection differs from one market to another, depending on whether they emphasize Ashkenazic or Sephardic products or both. At the Ashkenazic Jewish stores all the ingredients can be found to serve the signature dishes of that culinary style: gefilte fish, noodles, noodle kugels, potato pancakes, lox, bagels, blintzes, and cheesecake. At Sephardic markets, there are many kinds of pita bread, olives, feta cheeses, basmati rice, bulgur wheat, many kinds of dried beans, frozen savory phyllo turnovers called *bourekas,* and Yemenite *jahnoon*, a flaky rolled pastry. Israeli markets often have both kinds of kosher products as well as special foods from Israel, notably cheeses, a mild yogurt called *leben*, and other dairy products, spices, soup mixes, and cookies.

As Jewish cooks become increasingly interested in each other's cooking, more and more of these stores are carrying foods for both major styles of Jewish cooking. It is no longer uncommon to find layered Yemenite pancake-like pastries called *malawah* and Iraqi Jewish *kubeh* (crisp stuffed bulgur wheat appetizers) in the freezer next to Ashkenazic gefilte fish mix. In the deli section, Polish horseradish stands next to Yemenite *zehug* (hot pepper chutney). And of course, all kosher stores carry matzo, kosher cheeses, and usually fresh challah bread for Shabbat and holidays.

Meats

Many supermarkets carry frozen kosher chickens and turkeys as well as kosher frankfurters, salami, and other prepared meats.

Kosher beef, lamb, veal, ducks, and geese tend to be available only at kosher markets and butcher shops. In these shops there is also a greater variety of cold cuts and other prepared meats and more cuts of chicken and turkey.

Cheeses and Other Dairy Products

Kosher cheeses must be made without animal-based rennet or gelatin. Soft cheeses such as cottage cheese, ricotta, farmers cheese, pot cheese, and cream cheese are especially popular, as are sour cream and other cultured dairy products. Grating and slicing cheeses like mozzarella, Swiss cheese, Muenster, Parmesan, Edam, other Dutch-style cheeses, and reduced-fat kosher cheeses are available in a much wider selection at kosher stores than in supermarkets. Feta and goat cheese, often from Israel, is also available. Kosher cheeses also can be found at natural foods stores because many vegetarians want their cheeses free of animal-based rennet.

Kosher-certified milk can also be found at some Jewish grocery stores.

Pareve Foods

The array of pareve foods has greatly expanded in recent years, thanks in part to the growing interest in healthy and in natural foods. Some of these are available at kosher grocery stores and many in vegetarian and natural foods shops.

Margarine has long been important in the kosher kitchen, especially pareve margarine, which is used instead of butter for such dishes as mashed potatoes if they will be served with meat. Many kosher cooks make most of their cakes, cookies, and pastries with pareve margarine, in case anyone in the family feels like eating them after a meat meal. (Today, many health-conscious cooks may substitute oil.)

Some margarines contain dairy products, and so buyers who keep kosher always check the label to see whether the margarine is pareve.

Dairy-Like Pareve Foods

Pareve "milk" is made from a variety of ingredients. Soy and rice milk are the most common. Some stores also carry almond milk and multigrain milk.

Some of these pareve beverages come in different flavors, like vanilla, chocolate, and carob.

Nondairy "cheeses" are made from tofu or from rice, as is pareve ice cream.

Meat-Like Pareve Foods

There is also a large selection of pareve foods designed to look and taste like meat. They are made from soy beans, wheat, or a combination of these. There is meatless ground "meat" as well as burgers, frankfurters, and sliced deli "meats".

Some of these foods also come in dry form, either as granules or as chunks, which can be rehydrated and cooked in sauces similar to those used for meat.

Fish

As most common fish are kosher, Jewish cooks often buy the ones they are familiar with at the supermarket. Some supermarkets carry wrapped fish that are certified kosher and have been handled with kosher knives. A greater array of kosher fish can be found at kosher fish stores in some Jewish neighborhoods.

Prepared kosher fish such as lox, whitefish, herring, and gefilte fish are easy to find at the supermarket. They are popular ingredients in the Ashkenazic pantry.

Wine

It's a common misconception that Jewish wine must be sweet because sweet wine has traditionally been used for blessings. This is a matter of taste, however, not law. Now there is a variety of kosher wines made from many different grapes and styles of wine making, in the United States, Israel, and France.

Baked Goods and Baking Ingredients

Bread, Cake, and Pastry

Kosher bakeries carry a wide variety of breads, cakes, and pastries. Some specialize in pareve baking, while some have both pareve and dairy sweets. These baked goods can also be found at Jewish grocery stores and some supermarkets.

The reason for buying kosher breads, pastries, and desserts is to be sure they do not contain nonkosher fats, cheeses, or animal-based gelatin.

Crackers and Other Snack Foods

As with breads and other baked goods, Jewish cooks who keep kosher check to make sure these do not contain nonkosher fats, cheeses, or animal-based gelatin.

Other Ingredients

Kosher salt, or coarse salt, is for sprinkling on meats and poultry in the process of koshering them (page xxii). In recent years kosher salt has also become a "gourmet" ingredient. Many chefs prefer its flavor for seasoning food because it's purer and has no additives.

Kosher gelatin is vegetable-based instead of being made with meat bones. It is often made from a seaweed base called agar-agar.

Menus

❧

Following are some holiday menus that I particularly enjoy preparing. These are flexible guidelines. Adapt them to suit your own taste, substituting other favorite dishes where you like. Prepare more or fewer dishes according to the time you wish to spend preparing the meal.

Before shopping and cooking, check the number of portions in each recipe and multiply them according to your needs.

A Passover Seder of Mediterranean Flavors

Sephardic Haroset with Matzo
Tovah's Trout with Paprika Oil and Cilantro
Springtime Israeli Salad
Artichokes with Spicy Lemon-Herb Dressing
Moroccan Beef Stew with Cumin, Potatoes, and
    Peppers
Syrian Squash with Carrots
Walnut Cocoa Layer Cake, Orange Frosting
Almond Macaroons

An Old-Fashioned Passover Seder, Ashkenazic Style

Ashkenazic Haroset with Matzo
Whitefish Gefilte Fish
Nirit's Sweet Beet Salad
Passover Chicken Soup with Matzo Balls
Old-Fashioned Roast Chicken
Mushroom and Matzo Kugel
Roasted Potatoes
Toasted Hazelnut Cake
Strawberry Sauce

Shavuot Gathering, French-Jewish Style

Braided Challah
Spinach Salad with Goat Cheese, Walnuts, and
    Peppers
Herb Blintzes with Duxelles Filling

Broccoli Gratin with Light Cheese Sauce
Sweet Cheese Tart
Raspberry Sauce

Israeli Rosh Hashanah Celebration

Round Challah
Apples and Honey
Sea Bass in Saffron–Tomato Sauce
Adi's Kibbutz Honey Chicken
Rosh Hashanah Sweet Potato Casserole
Sweet Carrot Coins
Rosh Hashanah Fruit Salad
Cocoa-Orange Honey Cake

Make-Ahead Rosh Hashanah Dinner

Round Challah
Apples and Honey
Carrot Salad with Cranberries and Mint
Hungarian Halibut
Traditional Meat Tzimmes
Potato Kugel with Mushrooms and Peas
Apple and Honey Cake

Yom Kippur Feast Before the Fast

Round Challah
Ashkenazic Green Bean and Carrot Salad
Roman Fish with Pine Nuts and Raisins
Light Chicken Soup with Noodles
Whole Poached Chicken with Vegetables
Herbed Rice
Sephardic Almond Honey Squares

Break-The-Fast Menu After Yom Kippur

Bagels
Israeli Salad, California Style
Smoked Whitefish Spread
Lox and Eggs with Asparagus
Old-Fashioned Coffeecake

Sukkot Pot Luck

Apricot-Pecan Challah with Raisins
Mediterranean Chopped Salad with Capers and
  Olives
Italian-Jewish Halibut in Tomato Celery Sauce
Hungarian-Jewish Stuffed Peppers
Basmati Rice Pilaf with Sunflower Seeds
Zucchini Pistou Puree
Pauline's Carrot Cake

Sukkot Harvest Celebration

Sweet and Fruity Challah
Grilled Eggplant and Pepper Salad with Sun-Dried
  Tomatoes
Harvest Soup
Whole Stuffed Zucchini with Turkey, Raisins, and
  Pecans
Carrots and Potatoes with Chard
Green Beans with Tomatoes and Herbs
Apple Strudel

My Hanukkah Party Cooking Class Meal

Classic Potato Latkes
Mushroom Latkes with Dill
Creamy Dill Topping
Chunky French Applesauce
Eggplant Salad with Garlic and Coriander
Sea Bass in Saffron–Tomato Sauce
Traditional Cinnamon-Walnut Rugelach

A Family Hanukkah Feast

Red Cabbage Slaw with Walnuts and Citrus
  Fruits
Brisket with Chickpeas and Zucchini
Baked Potato Latkes
Old-Fashioned Applesauce
Israeli Doughnuts (Soofganiygot)
Homemade Hanukkah Gelt

A Purim Box of Treats

Hamantaschen with Pareve Poppyseed-Walnut
  Filling
Chocolate Hamantaschen
Hamantaschen with Date Filling
Haman's Fingers

Chocolate-Apricot Wine Balls
Purim Pinwheels

Friday Night Dinner From My Childhood

Braided Challah
Chopped Liver the Way My Mother Makes It
Shabbat Salad
Friday Night Chicken
Lukshen Kugel with Mushrooms and Onions
Glazed Carrots
Chocolate-Pecan Chiffon Cake

Shabbat Midday Menu in the Sephardic Spirit

Braided Challah
Israeli Olive and Tomato Salad
Dvora's Bright-and-Easy Pepper Salad
Chicken Cholent with Wheat Berries and
  Chickpeas
Savory Red Chard with Garlic
Fresh Tomato Salsa, Yemenite Style
Salad of First Fruits

Springtime Shabbat Dinner

Mediterranean Chopped Salad with Capers and
  Olives
Red Trout and Asparagus with Lemon-Parsley
  Sauce
Rosemary Roast Chicken
Carrots and Potatoes with Chard
Low-Fat Chocolate Applesauce Cake
Strawberry Sauce

Light and Summery Shabbat Lunch

Cucumber and Pepper Salad with Fresh Mint
Cod in Green Olive–Tomato Sauce
Saffron Basmati Rice
Pareve Almond Cake
Mango Sauce

Shabbat Menu With Autumn Flavors

Shabbat Salad
Light Eggplant Caponata
Chicken Soup with Noodles, Leeks, and Winter
  Squash
Chicken Baked with Tzimmes and Kneidel

Jewish Apple Cake with Walnuts and Dried
   Cranberries

Hearty Winter Shabbat Dinner

   Red Cabbage Salad with Apples and Pecans
   Moroccan Carrot Salad
   Hamin for Shabbat, Yemenite Style
   The Cantor's Compote

Sunday Brunch

   Smoked Whitefish Spread
   Creamy Cucumber Salad with Lox
   Avocado and Arugula Salad with Tomatoes and
      Cucumbers
   Main Course Cheese Blintzes
   Apple-Cinnamon Noodle Kugel with Sour Cream
   Chocolate Chip Sweet Rolls

Thanksgiving with A Difference

   Red Cabbage Slaw with Walnuts and Citrus
      Fruits
   Spiced Roast Turkey
   Challah Stuffing (double recipe)
   Savory Sweet Potato Kugel
   Tangy Tunisian Mashed Pumpkin
   Carrots and Green Beans Gremolata
   Fall Fruit in White Wine
   Streusel Apple Pie

Potluck Pareve Supper

   My Favorite Vegetarian Chopped Liver
   Grilled Eggplant and Red Pepper Salad
   Couscous Salad with Tomatoes, Pine Nuts, and
      Mint
   Cauliflower Kugel with Sautéed Onions
   Stuffed Small Squashes with American Rice
      Pilaf
   Tu Bishvat Date Bars with Macadamia
      Nuts

Barbecue with the Kids

   Everyday Israeli Salad
   Our Family's Favorite Grilled Chicken Legs
   Glazed Carrots
   Oven-Fried Potatoes
   Valerie's Two-Way Shabbat Rice
   Crisp Chocolate Chip Cookies with Pecans

My Family's Fish Feast

   Mediterranean Marinated Peppers
   Savory Mushroom Sauté
   Yemenite Fish with Tomatoes and Spices
   Easy Baked Salmon Fillet
   Basil Cream with Diced Tomatoes
   Israeli Rice Pilaf
   My Favorite Cheesecake

Passover

Haroset
6

Ashkenazic Haroset

Sephardic Haroset

Yemenite Haroset

Haroset with Orange Juice

Haroset Truffles

Persian Pear and Banana Haroset

Passover Pyramids

Salads and Soups
9

Beet and Baby Lettuce Salad
with Jicama

Artichokes with Spicy Lemon-
Herb Dressing

Springtime Green Salad with
Passover Nuts

Passover Vinaigrette

Passover Chicken Soup with
Matzo Balls

Zucchini Soup with Passover
Croutons

Passover Soup "Nuts"

Main Courses
12

Spiced Salmon with Asparagus

Sea Bass with Mushrooms,
Lettuce, and Warm Vinaigrette

Spring Chicken

Rosemary Roast Chicken

Passover Turkey Schnitzel

Passover Spinach Stuffing

Farfel Stuffing with Leeks and
Carrots

Tunisian Passover Lamb Stew
(Msouki)

Roast Lamb with Matzo-Onion
Stuffing

Moroccan Beef Stew with
Cumin, Potatoes, and Peppers

The springtime festival of Passover takes place in late March or in April and lasts for eight days. The Seder, the ceremonial holiday dinner, is prepared on the first and second nights of the holiday, except in Israel, where there is a Seder only on the first night.

Perhaps the best-known passage about the holiday is the question recited by all Jewish children as part of the Seder, "Why is this night different from all other nights?" The standard response delineated in the Haggadah, the Seder book of readings, prayers, and songs, is that Passover commemorates the liberation of the ancient Hebrews from slavery in Egypt.

A more offhand answer to this question might be, "because the food is different." The kitchen, and indeed the entire house, undergoes extensive preparation and cleaning for the holiday. Certain foods are avoided during the holiday or even completely removed from the house.

Naturally, in observant families, food for Passover must be kosher. In addition, it has to be Kosher-for-Passover. The Hebrew word for food that is not kosher for the holiday is *hametz*, or leavening, because the Torah prohibits eating leavened bread during the holiday to recall the flat bread the Hebrews ate during their flight from Egypt, when they could not wait for their bread to rise.

This flat bread was the first matzo. It has become the symbol of Passover and is served not only as bread, but is also used to make a variety of other foods, from dumplings to cakes.

Matzo is ground and made into matzo meal, which is used in cooking and baking instead of raw wheat flour, which can leaven naturally when combined with liquid and is thus not allowed during the holiday. Cake meal, a finer version of matzo meal, is used to make sponge cakes and other light cakes.

In Ashkenazic and some Sephardic communities, other types of grains and beans are avoided as well. These are grouped under the term *kitniyot*, Hebrew for legumes, which is used in a broad sense to include corn, rice, other grains, beans, peas, and sesame and sunflower seeds. Other foods derived from these are also not used, including cornstarch and corn oil.

Despite these restrictions, Passover is not at all an occasion for deprivation. The opposite is true; in the recipe repertoires of many families, the greatest number of favorite dishes and desserts are Passover ones.

When I was growing up, the number of Passover foods was limited. Now markets feature a dizzying array of foods with Kosher-for-Passover labels. This is true not only of kosher grocery stores but also supermarkets in neighborhoods with a substantial number of Jewish residents.

Old-fashioned macaroons, once known only in classic almond or coconut flavors, come in many new varieties like chocolate-mint and cinnamon-pecan. Also, now, not only macaroons are sold and served at Passover, but also biscotti and chocolate chip cookies, plus a great variety of cakes and cookies, including coffee cake, rugelach, and cinnamon rolls— things we never used to have for the holiday. There are Passover noodles and even pizza dough mix. Passover equivalents of popular breakfast cereals are also available, instead of just farfel, the little squares of matzo we ate as cereal as children.

I still love farfel for breakfast, and I understand those friends of mine who feel that using the new foods takes away from the special taste of the holiday. I am glad to have the choice, however. There is still plenty of cooking and baking to be done for that homemade taste, and it can be convenient to keep a few prepared foods on hand in case extra treats are needed.

Passover Preparations

Before the holiday, to get the kitchen ready, the oven, burners, refrigerator, and sink need to be cleaned thoroughly. Passover sets of dishes, flatware, cooking utensils, and pots, one for meat and one for dairy foods, replace the ones used during the rest of the year. Some utensils can be *kashered*, or made suitable for Passover by being scalded with boiling water; specifics on this procedure can be obtained from a rabbi.

Food staples that are *hametz*, or not kosher for Passover, are handled in differerent ways. Some people use up these foods before the holiday. *Hametz* products may also be locked in a cabinet for the duration of the holiday. The local rabbi symbolically "sells" this food to a person who is not Jewish and "buys back" the food after the holiday. Some families officially authorize the sale and purchase of the food, while in other families it is understood that the rabbi handles the transaction for them.

Finally the house is checked to be sure there are no bread crumbs. In a ceremony known as "inspecting for *hametz*," on the night before Passover, the head of the household checks the house for bread crumbs with a candle. If he finds any, the next morning they are burned, outdoors, in areas where local laws allow this. Some people might also include in the burning some *hametz* foods such as bread or cereal for this symbolic ritual.

Special Seder Foods

The day before Passover is spent cooking for the Seder and preparing the symbolic items for the Seder plate. This plate is often beautifully decorated and contains labeled sections for each food. The best known of these is the tasty haroset, a sweet and spicy spread made of fruits and nuts, of a reddish-brown color to represent the mortar and bricks the Hebrew slaves made in ancient Egypt. To recall the bitter lives led by the slaves, there is *Maror*, or bitter herbs, which can be fresh horseradish or bitter greens.

Beitza, a roasted hard boiled egg, and *Zeroah*, a roasted lamb bone or poultry neck, appear on the plate to recall the animals brought to the High Priest at the Holy Temple in Jerusalem in ancient Israel for the Passover sacrifice. *Karpas*, a celery stalk or a parsley sprig, reminds us that Passover is the Festival of Spring.

A separate plate contains the three matzos that will be eaten during the ceremonial part of the Seder. They are covered with a decorative matzo cloth.

The Tasting Ceremony During the Seder

Four glasses of wine is the traditional portion served to each person to drink during the Seder. The wine can be sweet or dry but must be kosher for Passover. In some families grape juice is substituted. When I was growing up, we always had sweet wine but our glasses were very small.

Following the instructions in the Haggadah, the first food to be tasted is *Karpas*, celery or parsley dipped in salt water. Then a small piece of matzo is tasted. The bitter herbs are tasted alone, then combined with some haroset and matzo.

Just before the meal, hard boiled eggs are dipped in salt water and tasted. After the meal is served, the children look for the *afikoman* or *afikomen*, a Greek-derived Hebrew word meaning a piece of matzo that the head of the household has hidden or that a child has stolen and hidden; the one who finds it gets a present. There are numerous explanations of what this broken matzo and its hidden half represent—the extreme poverty of the slaves in Egypt, the messiah who is yet to come, and the future redemption of the unfree, are a few. Some attribute a more practical rationale for hiding the matzo—this game keeps the children awake during the Seder. Tasting the *afikoman* is the last food of the Seder.

Cooking for the Seder

The Seder is a multi-course feast. After sitting at the dinner table and reading the Haggadah, which can take several hours, everyone is really hungry! Since you can't always know exactly how long the reading and chanting will take, it's convenient to plan a Seder menu of dishes that can be prepared ahead. For this reason, soups and braised dishes are traditional choices.

Chicken soup with matzo balls is a Passover favorite in many Ashkenazic families. In my family we love very light matzo balls made without chicken fat.

For a main course, I like to serve roasted or braised chicken or turkey. When I make a sauce or gravy, I thicken it with potato starch, the most important "flour" allowed for Passover for thickening sauces. Matzo stuffing is a popular accompaniment in our family.

I like to balance these hearty, old-fashioned foods with light, healthy fresh ones, including plenty of salads. Asparagus often finds its way into our menus as a side dish. This is in keeping with the theme that Passover is the "Festival of Spring."

Despite the restrictions on flour, Jewish cooks have developed an incredible variety of Passover desserts over the ages. Cakes, cookies, brownies, and pies are made using special Passover products. They don't taste exactly like those made during most of the year, but that is part of the reason they are appreciated.

The best known cakes are flourless nut cakes and sponge cakes. Macaroons and meringues are the traditional cookies. I love making these at home, although they are widely available in cans. To me, the flavor of these homemade treats is much better.

For specific Passover menu suggestions, see Menus, page xviii.

New Passover Celebrations

Celebrating Passover is very much a part of modern Jewish life. In some homes, celebrating the holiday has evolved into a time to get together for a family vacation. When I was in Paris, travel company advertisements proposed that families return to their Jewish roots in Morocco and Spain to celebrate Seders in those countries. American Jews might travel to such resort destinations as Las Vegas or participate in a Hawaiian "Passover in Paradise." In Israel several of my family members celebrate with a week-long Passover vacation in a luxurious hotel. The timing makes perfect sense; after all, Israeli children are on vacation during the holiday.

✿ Haroset

Haroset is a sweet mixture of fruit, nuts, and spices prepared for the Seder, the ceremonial Passover dinner that commemorates the exodus of the Israelites from Egypt. It is one of the special foods that appears on the ritual Seder plate. Haroset has a reddish-brown color to recall the mortar and bricks which the Hebrew slaves were forced to make during the days of the Pharaohs. During the Seder, the haroset is tasted along with grated fresh horseradish, of which the bitter taste is a reminder of the harshness of slavery.

In spite of these somber memories, haroset happens to be delicious and is the best-loved of the Seder foods. Children look forward to it as one of the treats of the holiday.

As an essential element of the Seder plate, haroset is one of the few dishes made by Jews around the world. Different Jewish communities and families within these groups have different recipes.

The Ashkenazic haroset recipe is a mixture of apples, walnuts, and wine. Sephardic (Mediterranean and Middle Eastern) Jews tend to favor dried fruits, especially dates, which give the haroset a rich texture and intense fruit taste. Jews from Iran add bananas. Popular nuts among Sephardic Jews are almonds and pine nuts.

Ashkenazic Haroset

Makes 8 servings   **P**

When I was growing up, we made our haroset like this, with plenty of apples and walnuts and a touch of sugar, wine, and cinnamon. It is light-textured and very tasty. Be sure to use good-quality fresh walnuts. Serve haroset with matzos.

³/₄ to 1 cup walnuts

2 to 3 tablespoons sugar

2 or 3 large apples, peeled, halved, and cored

1 teaspoon ground cinnamon

2 to 4 tablespoons sweet red wine

1. Grind walnuts with 2 tablespoons sugar in a food processor until fairly fine, leaving a few small chunks. Transfer to a bowl.

2. Grate apples on large holes of a grater. Add to nut mixture. Stir in cinnamon. Gradually stir in enough wine to make a thick spread. Add more sugar if desired.

3. Spoon into a serving bowl. Serve at room temperature or cold, as a spread with matzos.

Sephardic Haroset

Makes about 8 servings   **P**

Dates give Sephardic haroset its characteristic flavor and color, but dried apricots or other dried fruit might be included. The haroset often contains a small amount of apple as well, as in this version, but the apple is not as dominant as in Ashkenazic style haroset. Sugar is not needed because there is enough natural sweetness in the dates, apple, and wine.

8 ounces pitted dates, coarsely chopped

¹/₂ cup almonds, coarsely chopped

1 sweet apple such as Golden Delicious or Gala, peeled, halved, and cored

1 teaspoon ground cinnamon

2 to 4 tablespoons sweet red wine

¹/₂ cup toasted pine nuts (optional)

1. Halve dates and remove any pits or pit fragments. Put dates and almonds into a medium bowl.

2. Grate apple on large holes of a grater. Add to date mixture. Stir in cinnamon, then gradually stir in enough wine to make a thick spread. Spoon into a serving bowl. If using, garnish with toasted pine nuts. Serve at room temperature or cold, as a spread with matzos.

Note: Toasting nuts at home is easy. For small amounts, a toaster oven is most convenient. To toast pine nuts, preheat oven or toaster oven to 350°F. Toast pine nuts in oven 3 minutes or until lightly browned. Remove to a plate.

Yemenite Haroset

Makes 10 to 12 servings

Like most Yemenites, my mother-in-law always has a jar of "coffee spice," a mixture of cinnamon, ginger, cloves, and cardamom, for adding to dark Turkish coffee. These same spices also give an exotic taste to Yemenite haroset. Sweet and concentrated, it is made primarily of dates, other dried fruits, and nuts and does not contain apples or other fresh fruits. Some people add toasted sesame seeds.

1/2 cup almonds

1/3 cup walnuts

8 ounces pitted dates

1/2 cup raisins

1 1/2 teaspoons ground cinnamon

Pinch of ground cloves

1/4 teaspoon ground ginger

1/4 teaspoon ground cardamom

Pinch of freshly ground pepper

2 to 4 tablespoons sweet red wine or water

Finely chop almonds and walnuts in a food processor almost to a powder. Remove nut powder from the processor, then finely chop dates and raisins. Combine chopped nuts with chopped fruit in a bowl. Stir in spices. Gradually stir in enough wine or water to make a thick spread. Serve at room temperature or cold, as a spread with matzos.

Haroset with Orange Juice

Makes 8 servings

This is a chunky, sweet, fresh-tasting haroset, made of chopped apples and two kinds of nuts. To give it an Israeli accent, you can also add chopped dates, diced bananas—a secret of Israeli mothers to ensure that the haroset will appeal to the children—and a touch of cinnamon.

1/2 cup hazelnuts

1/2 cup walnuts or pecans

3 to 4 tablespoons sugar

2 large apples, peeled, halved, and cored

3 tablespoons sweet red wine

2 tablespoons orange juice

Grated rind of 1/2 orange

Grind hazelnuts and walnuts with sugar in a food processor until fairly fine, leaving a few small chunks. Transfer to a bowl. Chop apples in food processor or with a knife until fine. Add them to nut mixture. Stir in wine, orange juice, and grated rind. Serve at room temperature or cold, as a spread with matzos.

Haroset Truffles

Makes 10 to 12 servings of a few truffles each

When I attended a Seder in Paris, where most of the guests were of Moroccan origin, the haroset was served in little balls, rather like chocolate truffles. These are good not only at the Seder but also as a tasty, natural treat with a rich, slightly spicy flavor.

8 ounces pitted dates

1/2 cup pecans

1/2 cup almonds

About 3 tablespoons sweet red wine

1 teaspoon ground cinnamon

1/2 teaspoon ground ginger

1 sweet apple such as Golden Delicious or Gala, peeled and cored

1. Halve dates and remove any pits or pit fragments. Finely chop pecans and almonds in a food processor and remove to a bowl. Add dates, 3 tablespoons wine, and spices to processor and grind until fairly smooth. Mix with nuts. Grate apple on large holes of a grater. Stir into date mixture. If mixture is dry, add more wine by teaspoons.

2. Roll haroset between your palms into small balls of about 3/4- or 1-inch diameter. Serve in foil or paper candy cups.

Persian Pear and Banana Haroset

Makes 8 servings

Like many Sephardic Jews, Iranian Jews like their haroset flavored with dates. Some add bananas and pears as well. Seasonings are exotic, and might include saffron or cardamom.

$^1/_2$ cup pecans

2 to 3 tablespoons sugar

1 apple, peeled, halved, and cored

2 to 3 tablespoons sweet red wine

$^3/_4$ teaspoon ground cinnamon

$^1/_2$ teaspoon ground ginger

$^1/_4$ teaspoon ground nutmeg

$^1/_4$ teaspoon ground cardamom (optional)

$^1/_2$ cup almonds, coarsely chopped

12 pitted dates, coarsely chopped

1 pear

1 banana

Pine nuts (for garnish)

1. Grind pecans with 2 tablespoons sugar in a food processor until fine. Grate apple on large holes of a grater into a bowl and add 2 tablespoons wine. Stir in ground nuts, spices, almonds, and dates. Peel and finely dice pear and banana and add to bowl. Taste and add more sugar or wine, if desired.

2. To serve, spread on a flat dish and decorate with pine nuts. Serve at room temperature or cold, as a spread with matzos.

Passover Pyramids

Makes 16 little pyramid sandwiches

These are pyramids of matzo and haroset. In the Seder, haroset serves as a reminder of the mortar that the slaves used to build the pyramids. In this recipe the haroset is the mortar that holds together the miniature matzo pyramids. Eating a sandwich of matzo and haroset is a custom of the Seder. This is a new and fun way to present these sandwiches. The haroset in this recipe is also delicious on its own.

12 ounces pitted dates

$^3/_4$ cup almonds

$^3/_4$ cup walnuts

About 6 tablespoons sweet red wine

$1^1/_2$ teaspoons ground cinnamon

$1^1/_2$ teaspoons ground ginger

Small pinch ground cloves

2 small sweet apples such as Golden Delicious or Gala, peeled, halved, and cored

12 square matzos

16 toasted almonds or walnuts (for garnish)

1. Halve the dates and remove any pit fragments. Finely chop almonds and walnuts in food processor, then remove to a bowl. Add dates, 4 tablespoons wine, and spices to processor and grind until fairly smooth. Mix with nuts. Grate apples on large holes of a grater and stir into mixture. Gradually add wine by teaspoons, if necessary, to make a mixture that is spreadable but still thick.

2. To make 16 pyramids, briefly dip 4 matzos one by one in a pan of cold water. With a sharp knife, cut these matzos in 3-inch squares. Put them on a plate. Dip 3 matzos in water and cut them in 2-inch squares. Then, dip 2 matzos in water and cut them in $1^1/_2$-inch squares. Put them on a plate. Last, dip 2 more matzos in water and cut them in 1-inch squares. Put them on a plate. You will need 16 of each size of squares. Let squares stand for a few minutes to dry slightly so they become easier to handle.

3. Spread squares gently with haroset. For each pyramid, use a 3-inch square as a base, top with a 2-inch square, then a $1^1/_2$-inch, and finally a 1-inch square. Top each pyramid with a toasted almond or walnut.

❧ Salads and Soups

Beet and Baby Lettuce Salad with Jicama

Makes 4 servings

Beets are a favorite on the Passover menu in many homes. We love serving them this way, in a salad with baby greens, and an added California touch—sweet crunchy jicama and a lime juice dressing.

2 large beets, rinsed

2 quarts mixed baby lettuces, washed and dried

3 cups peeled diced jicama

2 tablespoons lime juice

2 to 4 tablespoons walnut oil or vegetable oil

Salt and freshly ground pepper, to taste

1/3 cup toasted mixed nuts

1. Put beets in a pan, cover with water, and bring to a boil. Cover and simmer over low heat 40 to 50 minutes or until tender. Let cool. Run beets under cold water and slip off the skins. Cut beets into wedges.

2. In a large bowl combine lettuces and jicama, and toss. In a small bowl, whisk lime juice, oil, salt, and pepper until blended. Pour over greens mixture and toss thoroughly. Taste and adjust seasoning. Serve greens topped with beets and sprinkled with nuts.

Artichokes with Spicy Lemon-Herb Dressing

Makes 4 servings

Artichokes are a Passover favorite in the French-Jewish and Sephardic kitchens. This is an easy, flavorful way to serve them.

4 medium or 8 small artichokes

2 tablespoons strained fresh lemon juice

Salt and freshly ground pepper, to taste

5 or 6 tablespoons extra-virgin olive oil

2 teaspoons fresh thyme or 1 teaspoon dried

1/2 to 1 teaspoon minced jalapeño pepper, or to taste

1 to 2 tablespoons chopped fresh Italian parsley

1. To trim artichokes: cut off top 1 inch of large artichokes or 1/2-inch of small ones. Trim spikes from tips of leaves with scissors.

2. Put artichokes in a large saucepan of boiling salted water and cover with a lid of slightly smaller diameter than that of the pan to keep them submerged. Cook over medium heat until a leaf can be easily pulled out; medium artichokes will need about 30 minutes and small ones 15 to 20 minutes.

3. To make dressing: whisk lemon juice with salt and pepper. Whisk in oil, thyme, and jalapeño pepper. Taste and adjust seasoning. Before using, whisk dressing and add chopped parsley.

4. Using tongs, remove artichokes from water, turn them upside down, and drain thoroughly. Either cover to keep warm or let cool and serve at room temperature or chilled. Serve dressing on the side.

Springtime Green Salad with Passover Nuts

Makes 4 servings

When my husband was growing up in Israel, hazelnuts were known as "Passover nuts," and he still often refers to them by this name. A sprinkling of hazelnuts lends a festive touch to this salad. We toast the hazelnuts for richer flavor but you can use them raw in the salad if you like.

For the greens, I often use chopped romaine lettuce hearts mixed with tender butter lettuce or crunchy iceberg lettuce. Another terrific choice is mixed baby greens. Sliced red radishes and thin slivers of mild onions—either sweet onions or red onions—give pleasing accents of taste and color.

1/4 cup hazelnuts

4 cups romaine lettuce

2 cups butter lettuce (Boston lettuce)

1 cup iceberg lettuce

4 to 6 baby radishes, cut into thin slices

1/4 sweet onion, cut into thin slivers

3 to 4 tablespoons Passover Vinaigrette (page 10)

1. To toast the hazelnuts, preheat oven to 350°F. Toast hazelnuts in a shallow baking pan in oven about 8 minutes or until skins begin to split. Transfer to a strainer. Rub hot hazelnuts with a towel against strainer to remove some of skins. Cool nuts on a plate.

2. Tear or cut lettuces into bite-size pieces or larger. Mix lettuces, radishes, and onion in a serving bowl. Just before serving, add dressing, and toss until greens are moistened. Taste and adjust seasoning. Serve salad sprinkled with nuts.

Passover Vinaigrette

Makes 7 or 8 tablespoons

Olive oil is the best choice for vinaigrette, and not only for reasons of taste. Many vegetable oils are not kosher for Passover, as they might contain corn oil, soy oil, or other types of oil that are avoided during the holiday. Wine vinegar that is kosher for Passover is widely available in supermarkets and at kosher markets.

2 tablespoons red or white wine vinegar
Salt and freshly ground pepper, to taste
5 to 6 tablespoons extra-virgin or other olive oil

Whisk vinegar with salt and pepper in a small bowl. Whisk in olive oil. You can multiply this dressing as you like and keep it in a jar in the refrigerator. Shake or whisk before using.

Passover Chicken Soup with Matzo Balls

Makes 6 to 8 servings

Matzo ball soup undoubtedly originated as a Passover specialty, because the kneidelach, *or dumplings, are made from matzo meal. It became so popular that it is a standard on the Shabbat table in many homes. Our family enjoys it not only for Shabbat, but also for most holidays. Indeed, some people want to be able to feast on this savory soup any day of the year and therefore it is one of the best-loved items on deli menus.*

Passover matzo balls are made without baking powder because no leavening is allowed. I like to give the soup a springtime accent with plenty of fresh parsley from my garden and occasionally some baby carrots or asparagus.

2 pounds chicken pieces
10 cups cold water
1 whole onion, peeled
2 ribs celery, including leafy tops
1 bay leaf
5 sprigs fresh parsley
Salt and freshly ground pepper, to taste
1/2 pound baby carrots, peeled
3 large eggs
1 cup matzo meal
About 2 quarts salted water (for simmering the matzo balls)
3 tablespoons chopped fresh parsley

1. Combine chicken, water, onion, celery, bay leaf, parsley sprigs, and a pinch of salt in a large saucepan and bring to a boil. Skim thoroughly. Partially cover and simmer 1 1/2 hours, skimming occasionally. Add carrots and simmer about 15 minutes or until tender. Skim off excess fat. Chicken soup can be kept 3 days in refrigerator; skim fat again and reheat before serving. Add pepper and taste for seasoning.

2. To make matzo balls: Lightly beat eggs in a small bowl. Add matzo meal and a pinch of salt and pepper and stir with a fork until smooth. Gradually stir in 2 to 4 tablespoons chicken soup, adding enough so mixture is just firm enough to hold together in rough-shaped balls.

3. Bring salted water to a bare simmer. With wet hands, take about 2 teaspoons of matzo ball mixture and roll it between your palms into a ball. (Mixture will be very soft.) Gently drop matzo ball into simmering water. Continue making balls, wetting hands before shaping each one. Cover and simmer over low heat 30 minutes. Cover to keep them warm until ready to serve.

4. When serving, skim fat again from soup. Discard onion, celery, bay leaf, and parsley sprigs. Reheat to a simmer. Remove from heat and add chopped parsley.

5. For each serving, remove 2 or 3 matzo balls from their cooking liquid with a slotted spoon, add them to soup bowls, and ladle hot soup over them. Serve hot.

Note: If the soup is hot, skim the fat from its surface with a large spoon. To remove the last bits of fat, you can dab the surface with a double thickness of paper towels; this must be done quickly so the towels won't disintegrate into the soup. The fat can be skimmed off most easily if the soup is first refrigerated. As the soup cools, the fat rises to the top and solidifies. The fat can be scraped off the cold soup's surface with a spoon.

Zucchini Soup with Passover Croutons

Makes 4 servings

Instead of being thickened with flour, this light, thyme-scented soup gains its body from a puree of zucchini and onion. The croutons are made of toasted matzo farfel rather than bread.

1 cup matzo farfel

2 tablespoons plus 2 teaspoons vegetable oil

Salt and freshly ground pepper, to taste

Pinch of paprika

1 large onion, halved and cut into thin slices

1¹/₂ pounds zucchini, unpeeled and sliced

1 large sprig fresh thyme or ¹/₂ teaspoon dried thyme

1 bay leaf

1¹/₂ cups vegetable broth or water

¹/₂ cup milk

¹/₃ cup whipping cream or additional milk

Pinch of cayenne pepper

1. To make croutons: Preheat oven to 350°F. Mix farfel with 2 teaspoons oil and a pinch of salt and pepper in a bowl. Spread on a baking sheet and sprinkle with paprika. Bake, stirring once or twice, about 12 minutes or until lightly browned.

2. Meanwhile, heat 2 tablespoons oil in a medium saucepan over low heat. Add onion and cook over medium heat, stirring occasionally, about 10 minutes or until soft but not brown. Add zucchini, thyme, bay leaf, salt, and pepper. Stir over low heat for 2 minutes. Add broth and bring to a boil. Cover and cook over low heat about 10 minutes or until zucchini are very tender. Discard bay leaf and fresh thyme sprig.

3. Let soup cool slightly. Pour into blender. Puree soup until smooth. Return soup to pan and bring to boil, stirring. Stir in milk and bring to a simmer. Stir in cream and return to simmer. Add cayenne pepper, taste and adjust seasoning. Serve hot soup with croutons.

Passover Soup "Nuts"

Makes 8 to 10 servings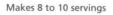

These delicately spicy baked soup nut-like croutons are sometimes called mandeln, *the Yiddish word for almonds, because they are somewhat crunchy. They are good in chicken or vegetable soup.*

¹/₃ cup water

3 tablespoons vegetable oil

¹/₂ teaspoon salt

²/₃ cup matzo meal

¹/₄ teaspoon ground cumin

Pinch of cayenne pepper

2 large eggs

1. Preheat oven to 375°F. Generously oil a baking sheet. Combine water, oil, and salt in a small saucepan. Bring to a boil. Remove from heat and add matzo meal all at once. Mix well. Add cumin and cayenne pepper. Return pan to low heat and cook, stirring, for 1 minute. Remove from heat and cool about 5 minutes.

2. Beat in 1 egg. When mixture is completely smooth, beat in second egg.

3. With a pastry bag or a teaspoon, drop batter by quarter teaspoons onto greased baking sheet, allowing about ¹/₂-inch between them. Bake 20 to 30 minutes or until golden brown and firm.

❧ Main Courses

Spiced Salmon with Asparagus

Makes 4 servings Ⓟ

*My favorite way to welcome spring is to serve a salmon
and asparagus dinner. In this season when gardens are
blooming in a burst of fresh colors and fragrances, I
crave a colorful, fresh, light entree. Since Passover is
the festival of spring, I love to serve this roasted salmon
with asparagus, either for the Seder or for another festive dinner during the holiday.*

1¼ pounds salmon fillet, preferably tail section, about
    1 inch thick
1 tablespoon plus ½ teaspoon strained fresh lemon juice
1 tablespoon plus 1 teaspoon extra-virgin olive oil
1 teaspoon ground cumin
1 teaspoon ground coriander
½ teaspoon paprika
½ teaspoon dried thyme
Salt and freshly ground pepper, to taste
Cayenne pepper, to taste
1 pound medium-width asparagus, spears peeled, trimmed,
    and cut into 3 pieces

1. Preheat oven to 450°F.

2. Set salmon in a heavy roasting pan. Sprinkle fish
with 1 tablespoon lemon juice and 1 tablespoon oil and
rub over fish. Sprinkle fish with cumin, coriander,
paprika, and thyme and lightly rub in spices. Last,
sprinkle evenly with salt, pepper, and cayenne. Roast
salmon uncovered about 12 minutes or until the flesh
just flakes and has changed color in its thickest part.

3. Meanwhile, cook asparagus in a saucepan of boiling salted water about 3 minutes or until crisp-tender.
Drain and toss with remaining ½ teaspoon lemon
juice, 1 teaspoon olive oil, salt, and pepper.

4. Arrange salmon on a platter and spoon asparagus
around it. Serve hot.

Sea Bass with Mushrooms, Lettuce, and Warm Vinaigrette

Makes 4 servings Ⓟ

*For Passover you can sauté fish with a coating of
matzo meal instead of flour, or for a lighter alternative, you can omit the coating completely as in this
quick dish. It makes a light and tasty entree during
Passover or for any festive spring menu. Serve steamed
new potatoes as an accompaniment and for dessert,
ripe strawberries. The sea bass is also great served cold
or room temperature as a first course for Shabbat.*

1 large clove garlic, peeled
⅓ cup firmly packed sprigs fresh parsley
1¼ to 1½ pounds sea bass fillets, ¾- to 1 inch thick,
    cut into 4 pieces
Salt and freshly ground pepper, to taste
3 to 4 tablespoons olive oil
One 6-ounce package sliced mushrooms (3 cups)
1 quart butter lettuce or mixed baby lettuces
2 tablespoons tarragon vinegar mixed with 1 tablespoon
    water

1. Mince garlic in a small food processor or with a
large knife. Add parsley and mince together.

2. Sprinkle fish with salt and pepper. Heat 3 tablespoons oil in a large, heavy nonstick skillet over medium-high heat. Add fillets. Sauté about 4 minutes on
each side or until the flesh flakes and the color has
changed in the thickest part of the fish; if oil begins to
brown, reduce heat to medium. Transfer fish to a platter, arrange pieces side by side, and keep warm.

3. If pan is dry, add 2 or 3 teaspoons oil and heat
it over medium-high heat. Add mushrooms, salt, pepper, and garlic-parsley mixture and sauté, tossing often,
until mushrooms are just tender, about 2 minutes.
Spoon mushroom mixture over fish. Add lettuce
to platter.

4. Remove pan from heat and pour vinegar mixture
into hot pan. Swirl it around pan, and pour it evenly
over fish and lettuce.

Spring Chicken

Makes 4 servings

I love this colorful Passover entree of braised chicken with carrots and asparagus. The herb-accented sauce is flavorful and light. It is thickened with a little potato starch, as flour-thickened sauces cannot be made during the holiday.

2¹/₂ pounds chicken pieces, patted dry

Salt and freshly ground pepper, to taste

2 tablespoons vegetable oil

¹/₂ cup dry white wine

¹/₂ cup chicken stock

3 medium carrots, quartered and cut into 2-inch lengths

1 teaspoon potato starch

1 tablespoon water

1¹/₄ pounds medium-width asparagus, spears peeled, trimmed, and cut into 3 pieces

1 tablespoon chopped fresh parsley

2 teaspoons chopped fresh chives

1. Sprinkle chicken lightly with pepper. Heat oil in large, heavy skillet over medium heat. In batches, lightly brown chicken pieces in oil. Transfer each batch to a plate, using tongs.

2. Return all chicken pieces to skillet. If they don't fit in one layer, arrange leg and thigh pieces on bottom of pan and place breasts on top. Add wine, stock, and chicken juices from plate. Bring to a boil. Cover and cook over low heat about 15 minutes or until breast pieces are tender. Transfer breast pieces to a platter, cover and keep them warm. Continue cooking remaining pieces 10 minutes more or until tender. Add them to platter; cover.

3. Meanwhile, put carrots in a medium saucepan, cover with water and add a pinch of salt. Bring to a boil. Cover and simmer 10 minutes.

4. Skim excess fat from chicken cooking liquid. Bring liquid to a simmer. Mix potato starch with 1 tablespoon water in a small cup. Whisk this mixture into the simmering liquid over medium heat. Cook 1 to 2 minutes or until thickened.

5. Add asparagus pieces to carrots and simmer uncovered for 3 minutes or until asparagus is just tender. With a slotted spoon, transfer vegetables to sauce; reserve their cooking liquid for other uses. Heat vegetables in sauce for 1 or to 2 minutes. Stir in parsley and chives. Taste and adjust seasoning.

6. Drain any fat from platter of chicken. Spoon vegetables and sauce over chicken and serve.

Rosemary Roast Chicken

Makes 4 servings

This simple, Italian style roast chicken is great for Passover or for Shabbat. The rosemary gives the chicken and its juices a wonderful aroma. Serve the chicken with a separately baked stuffing, such as Farfel Stuffing with Leeks and Carrots (page 15) or with Passover Spinach Stuffing (page 14). If you like, arrange some halved new potatoes around the chicken in the pan so they absorb flavor from the roasting juices.

One 3- to 3¹/₂-pound chicken, rinsed, giblets removed

6 sprigs fresh rosemary, plus a few more for garnish

1 or 2 tablespoons extra-virgin olive oil

Salt (optional) and freshly ground pepper, to taste

1. Preheat oven to 400°F. Pull out fat from inside chicken. Set chicken in a small roasting pan. Stuff chicken with 3 rosemary sprigs. Pour oil over chicken and sprinkle it with salt, if using, and with a little pepper. Rub oil and seasonings into chicken. Add 3 more rosemary sprigs to pan, tucking them under chicken.

2. Roast chicken uncovered, basting once or twice, about 1 hour or until chicken juices run clear when thickest part of thigh is pierced with a thin knife or skewer.

3. Remove cooked rosemary from chicken and from pan. Carve chicken and put pieces on a platter. Garnish with fresh rosemary sprigs. Skim excess fat from roasting juices. Taste juices and adjust seasoning. When serving, spoon a little of pan juices over chicken.

Passover Turkey Schnitzel

Makes 4 servings

Turkey schnitzel, an Israeli favorite, is usually prepared by dipping thin slices of turkey breast in flour, egg, and bread crumbs, then frying them.

For Passover, matzo meal is used instead of flour and crumbs and the result is very tasty. I learned this technique from the Israeli army. When my husband was in the service, his unit went on a camping trip to the southern resort town of Eilat and the men were allowed to bring their wives. Everyone took turns cooking, and when it was our turn, our job was to dip turkey breasts to make schnitzel. Although it wasn't Passover, we were instructed to use matzo meal for the coating and we liked the result.

1¼ pounds turkey breast slices (about 8 slices), about ¼-inch thick

½ teaspoon salt

¼ teaspoon freshly ground pepper

Pinch of cayenne pepper

About 1 cup matzo meal

2 large eggs

⅓ cup vegetable oil

Lemon wedges (optional)

1. Pound any thick turkey slices between 2 pieces of plastic wrap to an even thickness of ¼ inch, using a flat meat mallet or rolling pin. Arrange turkey in one layer on plate. Mix salt, black pepper, and cayenne in a small bowl. Sprinkle mixture evenly on both sides of turkey slices.

2. Divide matzo meal onto 2 plates. Beat eggs in shallow bowl. Lightly coat a turkey slice with matzo meal on both sides. Tap and shake slice to remove excess. Dip slice in egg. Last, dip both sides in matzo meal from the second plate, coating turkey completely; pat and press lightly so matzo meal adheres. Repeat with remaining slices. Set pieces side by side on a large plate. (Handle turkey lightly.)

3. Heat oil in large, heavy skillet over medium-high heat. Add enough turkey to make one layer. Sauté about 1 minute per side, until golden brown on both sides. Turn carefully using two wide spatulas. If oil begins to brown, reduce heat to medium. Set turkey slices side by side on ovenproof platter and keep them warm in a low oven (275°F) while sautéing remaining slices. Garnish with lemon wedges, if using. Serve hot.

Passover Spinach Stuffing

Makes about 8 servings, or enough for 2 chickens

Spoon this savory stuffing inside chicken before roasting, or bake it as in the recipe below as a separate stuffing casserole to serve with roasted poultry or meat. If you wish to serve it with fish or at a dairy meal, substitute vegetable broth for the chicken stock.

4 matzos, crumbled

1 cup hot chicken stock

3 to 4 tablespoons vegetable oil

2 medium onions, finely chopped

Salt and freshly ground pepper, to taste

3 large cloves garlic, minced

3 pounds fresh spinach, stems removed, or two 10-ounce bags rinsed spinach leaves

Freshly grated nutmeg, to taste

3 large eggs, beaten

1. Put crumbled matzo in a large bowl and pour chicken stock over it. Mix well. Let stand about 15 minutes. Heat 2 to 3 tablespoons oil in a large skillet and add onions, salt, and pepper. Sauté over medium heat, stirring often, about 10 minutes or until softened. Add garlic and cook 30 seconds.

2. Preheat oven to 350°F. Grease a 2-quart casserole dish. Set aside.

3. Meanwhile, rinse spinach well, especially if using a bunch of spinach. Cook spinach uncovered in a large saucepan of boiling salted water over high heat about 3 minutes or until tender. Rinse with cold water, drain, and squeeze out liquid by handfuls. Chop with knife or in food processor.

4. Add onions and spinach to matzo mixture and season with salt, pepper, and nutmeg. Add eggs and mix well.

5. Spoon stuffing into casserole dish. Spoon remaining oil over top. Bake for about 45 minutes or until set. Serve hot.

Farfel Stuffing with Leeks and Carrots

Makes 6 to 8 servings

Matzo farfel, or little squares of lightly baked matzo, is convenient for using in stuffings and kugels because there's no need to break it into pieces. This delicate farfel stuffing is delicious with Old-Fashioned Roasted Chicken (page 346) or with roast lamb or veal. I also like it as a side dish with fish or as an accompaniment for baked eggplant.

1½ cups hot vegetable stock

5 cups matzo farfel

2 tablespoons plus 2 teaspoons vegetable oil

1 large or 2 medium leeks, rinsed and thinly sliced

Salt and freshly ground pepper, to taste

2 large carrots, coarsely grated

2 large eggs, beaten

Pinch of paprika

1. Preheat oven to 350°F. Lightly oil a 2-quart casserole dish. Set aside. Pour vegetable stock over farfel in a large bowl. Let stand to soften.

2. Meanwhile, heat 2 tablespoons oil in a large skillet. Add leeks, salt, and pepper and sauté over medium heat, stirring often, for 5 minutes. Cover and cook over low heat, stirring often, about 5 minutes or until tender. Remove from heat and stir in carrots. Add vegetable mixture to bowl of farfel and let cool. Taste and adjust seasoning. Stir in eggs.

3. Spoon stuffing into casserole dish. Sprinkle with remaining oil, then with paprika. Bake about 45 minutes or until firm.

Note: To prepare leeks: split leeks twice lengthwise and dip them repeatedly in a large bowl of water to rinse, then cut the white and green parts as needed.

Tunisian Passover Lamb Stew
Msouki

Makes 6 servings

Made of lamb or beef, cooked with plenty of vegetables, and thickened with matzo, this stew is prepared for Passover in Tunisian and Algerian Jewish homes. I first tasted it at a North African Jewish restaurant called Douieb in the Sephardic section of Paris near rue Montmartre. In Paris they use thick, round Tunisian matzo decorated with a lacy pattern to both add to the stew as well as to accompany it.

Some people use only spring vegetables like artichokes and fava beans in their msouki. Others omit the meat and simply cook a hearty vegetable stew and thicken it with matzo. Flavored abundantly with herbs, the stew is aromatic and delicious.

2 pounds lamb shoulder, excess fat removed, cut into
    1-inch pieces

Salt and freshly ground pepper, to taste

1 teaspoon paprika

1 tablespoon olive oil

2 cups water

1 tablespoon tomato paste

2 large sweet onions, halved and sliced

4 large cloves garlic, chopped

3 carrots, diced

1 medium turnip, peeled and diced

2 ribs celery, trimmed and diced

One 10-ounce bag of rinsed spinach leaves

1½ pounds fresh fava beans, shelled, or 2 cups frozen fava
    beans or lima beans

2 zucchini, diced

1 pound fresh peas, shelled, or 1 cup frozen

⅓ cup chopped fresh Italian parsley

⅓ cup chopped fresh cilantro

Harissa, other hot pepper sauce, or cayenne pepper, to taste

Freshly grated nutmeg, to taste

2 matzos, broken into 1-inch pieces

1. Sprinkle lamb lightly with pepper and paprika.

2. Combine oil, water, and tomato paste in a large enamel-lined casserole or stew pan and whisk to blend.

Bring to a simmer over low heat. Add onions, garlic, carrots, turnip, celery, salt, and pepper, and mix well. Set seasoned lamb pieces on top. Raise heat and bring to a boil. Cover and cook over low heat, stirring from time to time, for 30 minutes. Add spinach, fava beans, and zucchini and return to a boil. Cover and cook 30 minutes or until meat is tender. Add peas and cook 5 to 10 minutes or until tender.

3. Taste stew and adjust seasoning. Reserve 1 tablespoon parsley and 1 tablespoon cilantro for garnish. Add remaining parsley and cilantro to stew and cook 3 minutes. Add harissa and nutmeg. Taste and adjust seasoning. Put matzo pieces on top, stir gently, cover, and let stand 1 to 2 minutes to soften. Sprinkle with reserved parsley and cilantro and serve.

Roast Lamb with Matzo-Onion Stuffing

Makes 8 to 10 servings

A touch of Yemenite spices—cumin and turmeric—liven up the stuffing. Serve this savory lamb with glazed carrots, zucchini in tomato sauce, or an eggplant stew.

4 matzos

1 cup hot chicken soup or stock

1/4 cup vegetable oil

2 large onions, chopped

Salt and freshly ground pepper, to taste

2 teaspoons ground cumin

1/2 teaspoon ground turmeric

2 large eggs, beaten

5 1/2 to 6 pounds lamb shoulder, boned, with a pocket cut for stuffing (about 4 1/2 pounds after boning)

1. For stuffing: Crumble matzos into a bowl and pour chicken soup over them. Heat oil in a skillet and add onions, salt, pepper, 1 teaspoon cumin and the turmeric. Sauté over medium heat, stirring often, until onions are tender and golden brown. Add onions to matzo mixture and let cool. Taste and adjust seasoning. Stir in eggs.

2. For roast: Preheat oven to 450°F. Stuff pocket in lamb shoulder with stuffing, packing it in firmly; you

will need about half the stuffing. Close pocket with skewers or sew it closed with trussing needle and kitchen string. Set lamb in a medium sized roasting pan. Sprinkle lamb with remaining cumin and with a little pepper. Roast 15 minutes to sear lamb. Reduce oven temperature to 350°F and continue roasting lamb 1 1/4 hours.

3. After lamb has roasted for 1 1/2 hours, spoon remaining stuffing into a greased deep 4- to 5-cup baking dish and put it in the oven. Continue baking 30 to 45 minutes or until stuffing is set and lamb is very tender; a meat thermometer inserted in lamb should register 160°F.

4. Transfer meat to a cutting board and let rest for 15 minutes. Carve into about 1/2 to 3/4 inch slices, using a very sharp large knife. With a small knife, cut any excess fat from each slice. Use a broad spatula to transfer slice to each plate. Serve extra stuffing separately.

Moroccan Beef Stew with Cumin, Potatoes, and Peppers

Makes 4 servings

Peppers, both hot and sweet, are used extensively in the Moroccan Jewish kitchen. This stew is moderately spicy; increase the number of jalapeño peppers or be generous with the cayenne if you want it to be hot.

2 pounds boneless beef chuck, excess fat trimmed, cut into 1 1/4- to 1 1/2-inch pieces

2 to 3 tablespoons vegetable oil

1 large onion, chopped

Approximately 3 cups water

4 large cloves garlic, minced

1 or 2 jalapeño peppers, seeds and ribs discarded, minced (see Note), or cayenne pepper, to taste

1 tablespoon ground cumin

1 teaspoon paprika

Salt and freshly ground pepper, to taste

1 3/4 pounds small red skinned potatoes

2 red or green bell peppers, cut into lengthwise strips

3 tablespoons chopped fresh cilantro (optional)

1. Pat beef dry. Heat oil in 4- to 5-quart Dutch oven or heavy casserole. Add beef in batches and brown cubes on all sides over medium-high heat. Transfer cubes to a plate as they brown.

2. Add onion to pan and cook over low heat, stirring often, about 7 minutes or until softened. Return meat to pan, with any juices on plate. Add enough water to barely cover beef. Add garlic, jalapeño pepper, cumin, paprika, salt, and pepper. Bring to boil, stirring often. Cover and cook, stirring occasionally, 1¹/₄ hours. If pan appears dry or sauce is too thick, stir in more water. Peel potatoes if you like. Quarter potatoes, add to stew, and push down into liquid. Cover and cook, stirring occasionally, 30 to 40 minutes or until beef and potatoes are just tender when pierced with tip of knife. Add peppers and cook over low heat about 10 minutes or until tender.

3. If sauce is too thick, stir in a few tablespoons water. If it is too thin, carefully remove beef and vegetables with a slotted spoon, boil sauce, uncovered, stirring often, until lightly thickened, and then return beef and vegetables to pan. Stir in half the cilantro, if using. Taste and adjust seasoning. Serve stew, sprinkled with remaining cilantro, if using, from casserole or deep serving dish.

Note: Wear rubber gloves when handling hot peppers.

❧ Side Dishes

Passover Rolls

Makes 18 to 20 rolls

In our family these rolls have long been a favorite. Although we like matzo, these fit the bill when we start to miss having bread on the table.

1 cup water
7 tablespoons vegetable oil
1 teaspoon salt
1¹/₂ cups matzo meal
5 large eggs

1. Preheat oven to 400°F. Grease 2 baking sheets and set aside. Combine water, oil, and salt in a medium saucepan, and bring to a boil. Remove from heat and add matzo meal all at once. Mix well. Return pan to low heat and cook, stirring, 1 minute. Remove from heat and cool about 5 minutes.

2. Beat in 1 egg. When mixture is completely smooth, beat in a second egg. Continue adding eggs, one at a time, beating thoroughly after each addition.

3. Drop batter by heaping portions of about 2 tablespoons each onto baking sheets, allowing about 1¹/₂ inches between them. Bake about 40 minutes or until golden brown and firm.

Savory Passover Noodle Kugel

Makes 6 to 8 servings

This recipe may be a surprise, considering it is made with noodles, but you can buy pasta that is kosher for Passover. Made of matzo meal and potato starch, they are available as egg noodles and yolk-free noodles. Their taste is similar to that of noodles made with flour.

This kugel is flavored with plenty of sautéed onions. As it is pareve, you can serve it with meat, poultry, or fish or as part of a vegetarian meal.

8 ounces Passover noodles

4 to 5 tablespoons vegetable oil

2 large onions, chopped

Salt and freshly ground pepper, to taste

1 teaspoon paprika, plus a little more for sprinkling

2 large eggs, beaten

1. Preheat oven to 350°F. Cook noodles uncovered in a large pot of boiling salted water over high heat about 3 minutes or until nearly tender but firmer than usual. Drain, rinse with cold water, then drain well again. Transfer to a large bowl.

2. Heat 3 to 4 tablespoons oil in a large skillet over medium-low heat. Add onions and sauté about 15 minutes or until very tender and light brown. Add salt, pepper, and 1 teaspoon paprika, and sauté about 5 minutes or until well browned. Cool slightly.

3. Stir onion mixture into noodles. Adjust seasoning; mixture should be seasoned generously. Add eggs and mix well. Oil a 2-quart baking dish and add noodle mixture. Sprinkle with remaining tablespoon oil, then dust with paprika. Bake uncovered 1 hour or until set. Serve from baking dish.

Savory Carrot Kugel

Makes 4 to 6 servings

Most carrot kugels contain sugar to accentuate the carrots' sweetness. This one is different—it's flavored with onion, herbs, and chicken stock. It's a good accompaniment for chicken or lamb. You can also make the kugel with vegetable broth and serve it at a meatless dinner.

3 cups coarsely grated carrots

2 large eggs, beaten

1/3 cup minced onion

1/2 teaspoon paprika, plus a little for sprinkling

1/2 teaspoon dried dill

1/2 teaspoon salt

1/4 teaspoon freshly ground pepper

2 tablespoons vegetable oil

1 cup chicken stock

1 tablespoon chopped fresh Italian parsley

2/3 cup matzo meal

Preheat oven to 350°F. Oil a 6-cup baking dish. Mix carrots with eggs, onion, paprika, dill, salt, pepper, oil, stock, and parsley in a medium bowl. Stir in matzo meal. Pour mixture into prepared dish. Bake for about 40 minutes or until firm. Serve hot.

Grated Potato Kugel

Makes 6 to 8 servings

Potato kugel is popular for Passover because it is substantial and helps satisfy your hunger when bread is not allowed. There are two basic ways to prepare potato kugel: one is from mashed boiled potatoes and the other is from grated raw potatoes, which then bake with eggs as a casserole. Grated raw onions are the standard flavoring. I prefer to sauté the onions so they have a sweeter, more mellow taste.

Kugel made of grated potatoes has a slightly crisp crust. To help the crust to form on the bottom and sides of the kugel, the baking dish is oiled and heated in the oven before the potato mixture is spooned into it.

3 to 4 tablespoons vegetable oil

2 large onions, chopped

2 pounds baking potatoes, peeled

3 large eggs, beaten

1 teaspoon salt

1/2 teaspoon freshly ground pepper

1/4 cup matzo meal

1. Preheat oven to 350°F. Heat 2 or 3 tablespoons oil in a skillet, add onions, and sauté over medium-low heat about 10 minutes or until light golden. Transfer to a large bowl.

2. Coarsely grate potatoes, put in large strainer and squeeze out excess liquid. Add to bowl of onions. Add eggs, salt, pepper, and matzo meal.

3. Generously grease a 7-cup baking dish. Heat in oven for 5 minutes. Remove dish from oven and carefully spoon potato mixture into dish. Sprinkle with remaining tablespoon oil. Bake about 1 hour or until kugel is browned and set.

Mushroom and Matzo Kugel

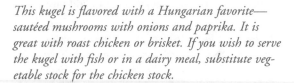

Makes about 6 to 8 servings

This kugel is flavored with a Hungarian favorite—sautéed mushrooms with onions and paprika. It is great with roast chicken or brisket. If you wish to serve the kugel with fish or in a dairy meal, substitute vegetable stock for the chicken stock.

8 matzos

1 1/2 cups hot chicken stock

3 tablespoons vegetable oil

2 large onions, chopped

1 rib celery, cut into thin slices

8 ounces mushrooms, sliced

Salt and freshly ground pepper, to taste

1 teaspoon sweet or mild paprika, plus a pinch for sprinkling

2 medium yellow squash, grated

Pinch of hot paprika or cayenne pepper

2 large eggs, beaten

1. Preheat oven to 350°F. Crumble matzos into a large bowl and pour hot chicken stock over them.

2. Heat 2 tablespoons oil in a large skillet. Add onions and celery and sauté over medium heat, stirring often, about 7 minutes or until onions begin to turn golden. Add 2 teaspoons oil, then mushrooms, salt, pepper, and sweet paprika, and sauté 3 minutes or until tender. Remove from heat and stir in squash. Add mushroom mixture to matzo mixture and let cool. Add hot paprika, then adjust seasoning. Stir in eggs.

3. Lightly oil a 2-quart casserole dish, then spoon kugel mixture into dish. Sprinkle with remaining teaspoon oil, then with sweet paprika. Bake for 45 minutes or until firm.

Baked Broccoli with Walnuts and Cheese

Makes 4 servings

Matzo meal can replace bread crumbs in casseroles and other baked dishes, as in this easy accompaniment. Serve it with fish or at vegetarian meals. If you prefer to omit the cheese, increase the walnuts to 1/3 cup.

1 1/2 pounds broccoli, divided into medium florets

2 tablespoons olive oil, vegetable oil, or melted butter

2 tablespoons matzo meal

3 tablespoons coarsely chopped walnuts

1/3 to 1/2 cup coarsely grated Swiss or other firm cheese

1. Preheat oven to 400°F. Cook broccoli in a large saucepan containing enough boiling salted water to generously cover florets. Boil uncovered about 4 minutes or just until tender. Drain broccoli gently, rinse with cold running water until cool, then drain well again.

2. Oil a shallow 5-cup baking dish. Arrange broccoli in one layer in prepared dish, stems pointing inward. Sprinkle with 1 tablespoon oil. Mix matzo meal, walnuts, and cheese in a bowl. Sprinkle evenly over broccoli. Drizzle with remaining oil.

3. Bake about 10 minutes or until cheese melts. If you like, broil for about 30 seconds to lightly brown top. Serve hot.

❧ Desserts, Cakes, and Cookies

Matzo Kugel with Apples, Almonds, and Raisins

Makes about 8 servings   **P**

This cinnamon-flavored kugel makes a scrumptious dessert. If you wish to serve it with a main course such as chicken, use tart apples and reduce the amount of sugar to 4 or 5 tablespoons.

4 matzos

1/2 cup whole unblanched almonds

7 tablespoons sugar

1/3 cup raisins

4 large eggs, separated

1 teaspoon ground cinnamon

2 large sweet apples such as Golden Delicious, peeled, cored, and thinly sliced

2 to 3 tablespoons vegetable oil

1. Preheat oven to 350°F. Grease a 7- to 8-cup deep baking dish and set aside. Break matzos into small pieces and put in a medium bowl. Cover with boiling water and let stand 2 minutes. Drain matzos and squeeze out as much water as possible.

2. In a food processor, grind almonds with 2 tablespoons sugar until fine. Add to bowl of matzos. Add raisins.

3. In a medium bowl, beat egg yolks with cinnamon and 3 tablespoons sugar until lightened. Stir in matzo mixture, apples, and oil.

4. Beat egg whites until just stiff. Add remaining 2 tablespoons sugar and beat at high speed another 30 seconds or until glossy. Gently fold egg whites into matzo mixture.

5. Spoon mixture into greased dish. Bake in preheated oven about 40 minutes or until browned and firm. Serve hot or warm.

Matzo and Cottage Cheese Pudding

Makes 6 servings   **D**

This scrumptious dessert could be considered a "bread pudding" for Passover. It consists of a cottage cheese custard flavored with raisins, pecans, and cinnamon baked between layers of matzo. It makes a delicious brunch or lunch dish or can be served as dessert after a fish, dairy, or vegetarian supper. If you like, top each serving with sour cream.

4 matzos

1 pound cottage cheese

3 large eggs, beaten

1/2 teaspoon ground cinnamon

6 tablespoons sugar

1/2 cup chopped pecans

1/3 cup raisins

1/4 cup (1/2 stick) butter, melted

1. Preheat oven to 325°F. Soak whole matzos in cold water to cover 1 or 2 minutes until slightly softened. Drain well and set aside. Mix together cottage cheese, eggs, cinnamon, sugar, pecans, and raisins in a medium bowl.

2. Coat an 8- or 9-inch square baking dish or cake pan with about 2 tablespoons melted butter. Set 1 whole matzo in pan, filling in any spaces with pieces from another matzo. Spread half the cheese mixture in pan. Cover with another layer of matzo. Spread remaining cheese mixture in pan. Top with a layer of matzo. Drizzle remaining melted butter on top. Bake for about 1 hour or until set and top is browned.

3. Cut into squares and serve hot or lukewarm.

Shulamit's Pecan-Glazed Carrot Soufflé

Makes about 6 servings **D** or **P**

My friend Shulamit Wilder, an Israeli married to an American, gave me the recipe for this sweet soufflé. Unlike classic French soufflés, there's no need to separate the eggs, so it is very easy to make, like a kugel. When Shulamit makes it for Passover, she uses matzo cake meal, while the rest of the year she makes it with flour. For dairy dinners for company, she uses butter, sometimes up to a full stick, but to keep the soufflé pareve she uses nondairy margarine. For family meals she often reduces the margarine or butter to ¹/₄ cup.

1 pound carrots

Pinch of salt

6 tablespoons (³/₄ stick) margarine or butter

¹/₂ cup plus 2 tablespoons sugar

3 large eggs

3 tablespoons matzo cake meal or matzo meal

Freshly grated nutmeg, to taste

1 teaspoon vanilla extract or vanilla sugar

3 to 4 tablespoons chopped pecans

1. Preheat oven to 350°F. Grease a 6-cup baking dish. Set aside. Put carrots in a saucepan, cover with water, and add salt. Bring to a boil, cover, and cook over medium-low heat about 15 minutes or until very tender. Drain well. (You can reserve cooking liquid for a vegetable stock.)

2. Puree carrots in a food processor until smooth. Add 4 tablespoons margarine, ¹/₂ cup sugar, eggs, cake meal, nutmeg, and vanilla. Puree until well blended.

3. Transfer carrot mixture to prepared baking dish. Bake 30 to 40 minutes or until set.

4. In a small saucepan, melt remaining 2 tablespoons margarine. Remove from heat and stir in pecans and remaining 2 tablespoons sugar. Spoon pecan mixture over top of soufflé. Return to oven and bake about 5 minutes or until top is lightly glazed.

Toasted Hazelnut Cake

Makes 8 servings

This flavorful cake is delicious on its own but you can also dress it up with a light drizzling of Sweet Chocolate Glaze (page 25). If you're not glazing the cake, you might like to serve each slice with Strawberry Sauce (page 580) and a garnish of fresh kiwi slices, or with Bittersweet Chocolate Sauce (page 579). Other great pareve accompaniments are Fresh Raspberry Sorbet or Orange Sorbet (pages 560–561).

For the freshest flavor, bake this cake within a day of serving it. Keep it covered at room temperature or in the refrigerator.

1²/₃ cups hazelnuts

¹/₄ cup cake meal or matzo meal

1 cup sugar

4 large eggs, separated

1 teaspoon grated lemon rind

Pinch of salt

1. Preheat oven to 350°F. Toast hazelnuts in a shallow baking pan in oven about 8 minutes or until skins begin to split. Transfer to a strainer. (Leave oven on.) Rub hot hazelnuts energetically with a towel against strainer to remove some of skins. Cool nuts completely. Grease 9-inch springform pan with margarine and set aside.

2. Grind hazelnuts with cake meal and ¹/₄ cup sugar in food processor until fine; set aside. Beat egg yolks with ¹/₂ cup sugar in a large bowl with an electric mixer at high speed until batter is light and fluffy. Beat in lemon rind just until blended. Set aside.

3. Whip egg whites with pinch of salt in a medium clean bowl until soft peaks form. Gradually beat in remaining ¹/₄ cup sugar, beating until egg whites are stiff and shiny.

4. Alternately fold whites and nut mixture into yolk mixture, each in 3 batches. Transfer to prepared pan. Bake about 35 minutes or until a cake tester inserted in center of cake comes out clean. Cool 5 minutes. Run a metal spatula gently around cake and remove sides of springform pan. Cool on a rack. Cake will sink slightly.

5. Serve cake at room temperature.

Passover Sponge Cake With Apples

Makes 8 to 10 servings

This is a traditional light Passover sponge cake with a surprise—ripples of cinnamon-sprinkled apple slices running through the cake. My mother taught me how to make it fairly recently, when she came from Jerusalem to celebrate Passover at my house.

1/2 cup matzo cake meal

1/4 cup potato starch

6 large eggs, separated

3/4 cup sugar

1 teaspoon strained fresh lemon juice

1 teaspoon finely grated lemon zest

Pinch of salt

2 Golden Delicious apples (10 to 11 ounces), peeled, cored, and cut into 1/8-inch slices

2 teaspoons ground cinnamon mixed with 1 tablespoon sugar

1. Preheat oven to 325°F. Have ready a 9-inch spring-form pan; do not grease it.

2. Sift cake meal with potato starch into a bowl. Beat egg yolks in a large bowl with an electric mixer. Beat in 1/2 cup sugar. Whip at high speed about 5 minutes or until mixture is pale and very thick. Stir in lemon juice and zest.

3. In another large clean bowl, beat egg whites and salt with a mixer until soft peaks form. Gradually beat in remaining 1/4 cup sugar. Beat at high speed until whites are stiff and shiny but not dry.

4. Fold cake meal mixture into yolks. Lightly fold in whites in 3 batches, just until batter is blended.

5. Lightly spoon about one third of the batter in prepared pan. Gently cover with half the apples. Sprinkle them with 2 1/2 teaspoons cinnamon mixture. Top with half the remaining batter, then with the remaining apples, and sprinkle them with the remaining cinnamon mixture. Spoon remaining batter over apples and spread gently.

6. Bake about 1 hour or until top is firm and a cake tester inserted in cake's center comes out clean. Cool in pan on a rack 10 minutes. Run a metal spatula carefully around cake. Remove sides of pan. Cool completely. (Cake can be kept, covered, 2 days in refrigerator.)

Rich Chocolate Almond Cake

Makes 8 servings **D** or **P**

Like many Passover cakes, this one is made with potato starch instead of flour. For vegetarian or fish dinners, I like to prepare the cake with butter rather than margarine. The cake is luscious enough to be served on its own but if you're serving it after a meatless meal, you might like to top each portion with a spoonful of whipped cream.

1 cup blanched almonds

1/2 cup sugar

5 ounces semisweet chocolate, chopped

1/2 cup (1 stick) unsalted margarine or butter, cut into pieces

2 tablespoons water

4 large eggs, separated, at room temperature

2 tablespoons potato starch

1. Preheat oven to 325°F. Lightly grease an 8 × 2 1/2-inch springform pan with margarine and line its base with parchment paper or foil and grease. Set aside.

2. Grind almonds with 2 tablespoons sugar in a food processor until almost a powder. Transfer to a bowl and set aside. (Note: Process in pulses to prevent heat from making the nuts a paste instead of a powder.)

3. Combine chocolate, margarine, and water in a large bowl set above a pan of hot water over low heat. Stir until smooth. Remove bowl of chocolate mixture from pan of water.

4. Whisk egg yolks to blend in a small bowl. Gradually add yolks to chocolate mixture, whisking vigorously. Stir in 1/4 cup sugar, followed by almonds and potato starch. Mix well.

5. Whip egg whites in a large bowl until soft peaks form. Gradually beat in remaining 2 tablespoons sugar.

Whip at high speed until whites are stiff and shiny but not dry. Gently fold whites into chocolate mixture in 3 batches, folding just until blended.

6. Transfer batter to prepared pan and spread evenly. Bake about 1 hour or until a cake tester inserted in center of cake comes out clean.

7. Cool in pan on a rack for 10 minutes. Run a knife or metal spatula carefully around cake. Turn cake onto rack, gently release spring, and remove sides and base of pan. Carefully remove liners and cool cake completely. Invert cake onto another rack, then onto a platter so that smoothest side of cake faces up.

Walnut Cocoa Layer Cake

Makes 12 servings   **D** or **P**

With its orange frosting and garnish of toasted nuts, this cake makes a festive finale to the Seder. If you're serving it after a meatless meal, you might like to make the frosting with butter instead of margarine.

3¹/₂ cups walnuts

1¹/₂ cups sugar

5 tablespoons matzo cake meal or sifted matzo meal

2 tablespoons unsweetened cocoa powder

6 large eggs, separated, at room temperature

Passover Orange Frosting and Filling (this page)

3 tablespoons toasted walnuts, coarsely chopped

1. Preheat oven to 350°F. Using margarine, grease two 9-inch round cake pans, about 1¹/₂ inches deep. Line base of each with parchment paper or foil and grease liner. Use a little matzo cake meal to flour sides of pans and lined bases, tapping to remove excess. Set pans aside.

2. Grind 1³/₄ cups walnuts with ¹/₄ cup sugar in a food processor to a fine powder. Transfer to a bowl. Repeat with remaining walnuts and another ¹/₄ cup sugar, and add to first nut mixture. Sift cake meal with cocoa. Add to nut mixture and stir until blended.

3. Beat egg yolks with ¹/₂ cup sugar in a large bowl with an electric mixer, about 5 minutes or until mixture is pale yellow and very thick.

4. In another large clean bowl, beat egg whites with a mixer until soft peaks form. Gradually add remaining ¹/₂ cup sugar and whip at high speed about 30 seconds or until whites are very stiff and shiny but not dry.

5. Sprinkle ¹/₃ of nut mixture over yolks and fold gently until nearly blended. Spoon ¹/₃ of whites on top and fold gently. Repeat until all of nut mixture and whites are added. Fold just until blended.

6. Pour into prepared pans and spread quickly. Bake about 30 minutes or until a cake tester inserted in center of cakes comes out clean. Set a rack on each pan, turn over and leave upside down for 10 minutes, with pan still on each cake. Turn back over. Run a metal spatula around sides of each cake. Turn out onto racks, carefully peel off liner, and let cool completely.

7. Spread about ¹/₃ of frosting on one cake layer. Set second layer on top. Carefully trim top layer to make it flat, if necessary, using a serrated knife. Spread frosting in thin layer on cake sides, then on top. Smooth frosting with a long metal spatula. Sprinkle with chopped walnuts. Refrigerate for at least 2 hours, or for up to 2 days. Remove from refrigerator about 30 minutes before serving.

Passover Orange Frosting and Filling

Makes enough to fill and frost a 9-inch two layer cake   **D** or **P**

Frostings for Passover are made with granulated or superfine sugar rather than confectioner's sugar. (Confectioner's sugar usually contains cornstarch, a derivative of corn, a grain not allowed during the holiday.)

1 cup (2 sticks) unsalted margarine or butter, softened

¹/₂ cup superfine or granulated sugar

1 tablespoon finely grated orange rind

¹/₄ cup strained fresh orange juice

Beat margarine and sugar in a bowl with an electric mixer until smooth. Stir in grated orange rind, then gradually beat in juice. Beat batter until smooth and fluffy. Spread on cake immediately.

Passover Cheesecake

Makes 8 to 10 servings

Instead of the standard graham cracker crust, this luscious, creamy cheesecake has a tasty, two-ingredient macaroon crust. (You can use leftover dry Almond Macaroons, page 27, or any other variety.) The cheese filling is flavored with fresh lemon rind instead of vanilla extract. Many kosher cooks avoid vanilla because the extract is usually made with grain-based alcohol, which is not kosher for Passover.

6 tablespoons (³/4 stick) unsalted butter, melted

1¹/4 cups macaroon crumbs (see Note)

1 pound block cream cheese, cut into pieces and softened

2 cups sour cream

³/4 cup plus 3 tablespoons sugar

3 large eggs

Grated rind of 1 large lemon

1. Preheat oven to 350°F. Lightly butter a 9-inch springform pan and set aside. Add melted butter to macaroon crumbs and mix well. Press macaroon mixture in an even layer on bottom of prepared pan and about 1 inch up sides of pan. Bake 5 minutes. Let cool completely. Leave oven at 350°F.

2. Beat cream cheese with ¹/2 cup sour cream in a large bowl with an electric mixer at low speed until very smooth. Gradually beat in ³/4 cup sugar. Beat in eggs, one by one. Beat in lemon rind. Carefully pour filling into cooled crust and bake about 45 minutes or until firm in center. Remove from oven and cool 15 minutes. Raise oven temperature to 425°F.

3. To make topping: mix remaining 1¹/2 cups sour cream with 3 tablespoons sugar. Carefully spread topping on cake, in an even layer, without letting it drip over crust. Return cake to oven and bake 7 minutes. Remove from oven and cool to room temperature. Refrigerate at least 2 hours before serving. Remove sides of springform pan just before serving.

Note: To make macaroon crumbs, process macaroons in a food processor to fine crumbs. Alternately, put them in a bag and crush them with a rolling pin; then measure needed amount into a bowl.

Chocolate Macaroon Cake

Makes 8 to 10 servings **P**

Macaroon cakes are becoming Passover traditions in many homes. Like classic macaroons, these cakes are made of a flourless mixture of coconut or ground nuts, sugar, and egg whites. Some of the egg whites are whipped to make the cake lighter than macaroon cookies. This is my favorite version, made with almonds and melted chocolate. It is moist and rich tasting, with a chewy, brownie-like crust. Serve it on its own, accompanied by sliced oranges or strawberries or, for dairy meals, with whipped cream.

4 ounces bittersweet or semisweet chocolate, chopped

2 cups whole blanched almonds

³/4 cup sugar

8 large egg whites (divided into two bowls, 4 in each)

1 teaspoon grated orange rind

1. Preheat oven to 325°F. Lightly grease an 8-inch springform pan. Line base and side of pan with parchment paper or wax paper; generously grease liner. Melt chocolate in a medium bowl over a pan of nearly simmering water. Stir until smooth. Remove bowl of chocolate from water; let cool.

2. Grind almonds with 2 tablespoons sugar in a food processor to a fine powder. Add 2 egg whites (half those in one bowl) and ¹/4 cup sugar; process 10 seconds or until smooth. Add another 2 egg whites and ¹/4 cup sugar; process again. Transfer to a medium bowl. Stir in orange rind.

3. Beat remaining egg whites in a large clean bowl until soft peaks form. Gradually beat in remaining 2 tablespoons sugar. Beat at high speed until whites are stiff and shiny but not dry.

4. Slowly stir cooled chocolate into almond mixture. Gently fold about ¹/4 of whites into chocolate mixture until nearly blended. Fold in remaining whites in 3 batches. Chocolate mixture will not mix easily with whites, so continue folding until batter is blended.

5. Spread batter in prepared pan. Bake about 40 minutes or until cake springs back when pressed lightly.

Cool in pan on a rack 5 minutes. Invert cake onto rack. Gently release spring and remove sides and base of pan. Carefully peel off liner; cool cake completely. Turn cake onto another rack, then onto a platter so smooth side of cake faces up. Serve at room temperature.

Pecan Torte with Strawberries and Cream

Makes about 10 servings

A wonderful welcome to spring, this cake gains its richness from pecans and contains no butter or oil. It's most beautiful and delicious when coated with whipped cream and garnished with sliced strawberries. If you do frost the cake, serve it within an hour or two so the whipped cream won't soften. If you want to keep the cake pareve or to serve it several times, leave it unfrosted.

1³/₄ cups pecans

3¹/₂ tablespoons matzo cake meal or sifted matzo meal

1 cup plus 3 tablespoons sugar

7 large eggs, separated

Grated rind of ¹/₂ lemon

1 tablespoon strained fresh lemon juice

Tiny pinch of salt

1¹/₂ cups heavy cream or whipping cream, well chilled

Strawberries, sliced lengthwise

1. Place rack in center of oven and preheat oven to 350°F. Have ready a 10 × 4¹/₈-inch tube pan (not a non-stick pan) with a removable bottom; do not grease pan.

2. Grind pecans with cake meal and 3 tablespoons sugar in a food processor to a fine powder, pulsing machine on and off. Transfer mixture to a bowl.

3. Reserve 5 tablespoons of sugar for beating into whites and 1 tablespoon for adding to whipped cream. Beat yolks in a large bowl with an electric mixer until blended. Gradually beat in remaining ¹/₂ cup plus 2 tablespoons sugar. Beat 5 minutes or until yolk mixture is very thick and light in color. Beat in lemon rind. Gradually beat in lemon juice.

4. Whip whites with a pinch of salt in another large bowl with a mixer until soft peaks form. Gradually beat in reserved 5 tablespoons sugar. Whip at high speed about 30 seconds until glossy.

5. Lightly and quickly fold ¹/₃ of nut mixture, then ¹/₃ of whites into egg yolk mixture. Continue with remaining egg whites and nut mixtures, adding last batch of whites before nuts are completely blended in.

6. Transfer batter immediately to pan and smooth top. Bake in center of oven about 1 hour and 10 minutes or until a cake tester inserted into cake comes out clean. Turn cake upside down in pan on a rack and leave about 2 hours or until completely cool.

7. To remove from pan, run a metal spatula around sides of cake. Push up bottom and remove sides of pan. Slide spatula or a thin knife around tube, then very carefully under cake. Turn cake over onto a large platter.

8. For whipped cream: chill a large bowl and beaters from a mixer. Up to half a day before serving, whip cream with 1 tablespoon sugar in chilled bowl until stiff. (If not using immediately, chill, covered, in the refrigerator.) Spread over top and sides of cake. Garnish top of cake with sliced strawberries. Serve chilled.

Sweet Chocolate Glaze

Makes enough for a 9-inch cake, about 8 servings **D** or **P**

Drizzle this easy-to-make glaze over Toasted Hazelnut Cake (page 21). Make it with butter for dairy meals or with unsalted nondairy margarine if you want to keep it pareve.

3 ounces semisweet or bittersweet chocolate

3 tablespoons orange juice or water

3 tablespoons unsalted butter or margarine

3 tablespoons sugar

1. Combine all ingredients in a small, heavy saucepan. Cook over low heat, stirring constantly, until smooth. Let cool slightly.

2. To use: Spoon glaze slowly over cake and allow it to drip down sides. Refrigerate briefly so glaze sets.

Passover Chocolate Cream Puffs

Makes 10 servings ⓓ

This delicious dessert is perfect for teatime or after a meatless Passover meal. To make the dessert even more glamorous, serve the cream puffs (made with Passover Rolls) with fresh Raspberry Sauce or Strawberry Sauce (page 580).

10 Passover Rolls (page 17)

1 cup milk

3 large egg yolks

5 tablespoons sugar

2 tablespoons potato starch

3 ounces semisweet or bittersweet chocolate, finely chopped

1. Prepare Passover Rolls. Let cool.

2. Bring milk just to a simmer in a small, heavy saucepan; remove from heat and set aside.

3. Whisk egg yolks and sugar in a medium bowl until smooth. Gently stir in potato starch, using whisk. Gradually add hot milk, whisking quickly. Return mixture to saucepan. Cook over medium-low heat, whisking constantly, until mixture comes just to a boil. Continue cooking over low heat, whisking constantly, for 1 minute. Remove from heat. Add chocolate all at once and whisk until melted. Transfer to a bowl. Cool to room temperature, stirring often to prevent a skin from forming. Refrigerate at least 1 hour or up to 2 days.

4. Just before serving, fill puffs: Whisk chocolate mixture, cut puffs nearly in half and spoon chocolate mixture inside.

Passover Brownies with Chocolate-Wine Glaze

Makes 16 to 20 brownies ⓟ

These orange-scented brownies are topped with a luscious glaze flavored with chocolate, cocoa, and sweet red wine.

6 ounces bittersweet or semisweet chocolate, chopped

1/2 cup (1 stick) unsalted margarine, cut into pieces

3 large eggs

1 cup sugar

1/8 teaspoon salt

2 teaspoons grated orange zest

3/4 cup matzo cake meal

3/4 cup coarsely chopped walnuts

Chocolate Wine Glaze

3 tablespoons sugar

2 tablespoons unsweetened cocoa powder

1/3 cup sweet red wine

2 ounces bittersweet or semisweet chocolate, chopped

6 tablespoons (3/4 stick) unsalted margarine, chilled, cut into pieces

16 to 20 walnut halves or pieces

1. Position rack in center of oven and preheat to 350°F. Line base and sides of a 9- to 9 1/2-inch square baking pan with a single piece of wax paper or foil and cover with a little margarine. Melt chocolate with margarine in a medium bowl set over a larger bowl of hot water, stirring until smooth. Remove bowl of chocolate mixture from bowl of water; cool 5 minutes.

2. Beat eggs lightly in a medium bowl with an electric mixer. Add sugar and salt; whip at high speed about 5 minutes or until batter is thick and light. Add chocolate mixture in 3 batches, beating at low speed until blended after each addition. Stir in orange zest, followed by cake meal and chopped walnuts.

3. Transfer batter to prepared pan; carefully spread to corners of pan in an even layer. Bake about 30 minutes or until a wooden pick inserted 1/2 inch from center of mixture comes out nearly clean. Cool in pan on a rack

to room temperature. Turn out onto a tray; remove paper or foil.

4. For the glaze: Whisk sugar with cocoa and wine in a small saucepan until blended. Bring to a boil over medium-high heat, whisking. Simmer over low heat 2 minutes, whisking occasionally. Add chocolate and stir until melted. Off heat, stir in margarine until blended in. Refrigerate, stirring occasionally, about 45 minutes or until spreadable. Stir glaze until smooth.

5. Spread glaze over brownies. Top with walnut pieces, spacing them evenly. Refrigerate about 30 minutes or until glaze sets.

Easy Passover Cocoa Brownies

Makes 20 to 24 brownies

This recipe comes from a woman who used to work at my neighborhood supermarket. She often told me about these Passover brownies, so recently, I finally baked some. Now I know why she was so enthusiastic; they're terrific! The brownies are especially popular with children, who love the sweet chocolate taste and nut-free texture. For serving after meatless meals, I make the brownies with butter.

1 cup (2 sticks) margarine, butter, or half butter and half vegetable oil, softened

2 cups sugar

4 large eggs

1 cup unsweetened cocoa powder, preferably Dutch process

²/3 cup matzo cake meal

1. Preheat oven to 350°F. Grease a square 9-inch cake pan and set aside. Beat margarine with sugar and eggs in a large bowl with an electric mixer until very light and fluffy. Add cocoa and cake meal. Beat slowly to combine, then beat at higher speed until mixture is fluffy.

2. Spoon batter into pan. Bake 30 to 35 minutes until the color has changed evenly on top and a cake tester or toothpick inserted 2 inches from center comes out dry. Do not overbake. Serve at room temperature.

Almond Macaroons

Makes about 30 macaroons

I find home-baked macaroons much more enticing and flavorful than packaged ones. At the cooking school in Paris where I studied, I learned the secret to keeping them moist: bake them on a paper-lined baking sheet and pour a little water under the paper before removing the cookies from the sheet.

These macaroons are great as an accompaniment for fresh fruit salad or with coffee, tea, or milk. If you like, flavor them with vanilla sugar, which you can find in kosher grocery stores and gourmet stores.

2¹/4 cups whole or slivered blanched almonds

1¹/2 cups sugar

3 large egg whites

1 packet vanilla sugar (optional)

1. Position rack in upper third of oven and preheat to 350°F. Line 2 baking sheets with parchment paper or wax paper; grease liner lightly with margarine.

2. Grind almonds with ¹/4 cup sugar in food processor until mixture forms fine, even crumbs. Add egg whites and vanilla sugar, if using, and process until smooth, about 20 seconds. Add remaining sugar in 2 additions and process about 10 seconds after each or until smooth.

3. With moistened hands, roll about 1 tablespoon mixture between your palms to a smooth ball. Put on prepared baking sheet. Continue shaping macaroons, spacing them 1 inch apart.

4. Press each macaroon to flatten it slightly so it is about ¹/2 inch high. Brush entire surface of each macaroon with water. If both baking sheets don't fit on rack, bake them one at a time. Bake macaroons 18 to 20 minutes or until very lightly but evenly browned; centers should still be soft. Remove from oven.

5. Lift one end of paper and pour about 2 tablespoons water under it, onto baking sheet; water will boil on contact with hot baking sheet. Lift other end of paper and pour about 2 tablespoons water under it. When water stops boiling, remove macaroons carefully from paper. Transfer to a rack to cool. Keep them in airtight containers.

Chocolate Macaroons

Makes about 40 macaroons

These brownie-like macaroons have a deep chocolate flavor. They are much richer tasting than store-bought versions. You can bake them a week ahead and keep them in airtight containers.

3 ounces bittersweet or semisweet chocolate, coarsely chopped
1 cup (about 4 ounces) blanched almonds
²/₃ cup sugar
2 large egg whites

1. Position rack in center of oven and preheat to 325°F. Line 2 baking sheets with parchment paper or wax paper; grease liner lightly with margarine.

2. Melt chocolate in a medium bowl set over pan of nearly simmering water. Stir until smooth. Let chocolate cool but do not let it harden.

3. Grind almonds with 2 tablespoons sugar in food processor until mixture forms fine, even crumbs. Add egg whites and remaining sugar alternately, each in 2 batches, processing about 10 seconds after each addition or until smooth. Transfer to bowl. Gradually add cooled chocolate, stirring until mixture is smooth.

4. Transfer mixture to a pastry bag fitted with a medium sized plain tip (¹/₂ inch in diameter, #6); pipe mixture onto prepared baking sheets in mounds of about 1 inch diameter, spacing them about 1 inch apart. If necessary, flatten points of cookies with a lightly moistened finger, so they have a smooth, round shape.

5. Bake macaroons 5 minutes. Wedge open oven door slightly with handle of wooden spoon and bake for 7 to 8 more minutes or until they are just firm to the touch; centers should be soft. Remove from oven.

6. Lift one end of paper under cookies and pour about 2 tablespoons water under it, onto baking sheet; water will boil on contact with hot baking sheet. Lift other end of paper and pour 2 tablespoons water under it. When water stops boiling, carefully remove macaroons from paper with a metal spatula. Transfer to a rack to cool. Keep them in airtight containers.

Note: If 2 baking sheets won't fit on one rack, bake them on two racks. Half way through their baking time, switch the positions of the baking sheets from the lower to the upper racks so all the macaroons bake evenly; or if you prefer, bake them one sheet at a time.

Parisian Passover Coconut Macaroons

Makes 50 to 60 macaroons

I enjoyed these at Sephardic bakeries in Paris. The secret to keeping them moist and light is to make them with Italian meringue, a mixture of egg whites beaten with boiling sugar syrup. Buy finely grated unsweetened coconut, which is available at natural foods stores, fine supermarkets, and some ethnic markets. When making this for Passover, dust the baking sheets with matzo cake meal. You can use flour at other times of the year.

Matzo cake meal for dusting
1¹/₄ cups sugar
³/₄ cup water
3 large egg whites
3 cups (8 ounces) unsweetened grated coconut

1. Position 2 racks in oven and preheat oven to 325°F. Grease then dust 2 or 3 baking sheets with matzo meal, shaking off excess.

2. Prepare Italian meringue: Combine sugar and water in a small, heavy saucepan. Cook over low heat, stirring occasionally, until sugar dissolves. Bring to a boil and boil without stirring, 3 minutes. Begin whipping egg whites in a large clean bowl with an electric mixer at low speed and continue whipping until stiff.

3. Meanwhile, boil syrup until it reaches the soft ball stage (238°F on a candy thermometer). Gradually pour hot syrup in a thin stream onto stiff egg whites, beating constantly at high speed. (Be careful not to let syrup touch metal beaters or bowl sides or the syrup will harden.) Continue beating mixture until cooled to room temperature. Stir in coconut.

4. Using a pastry bag fitted with a large star tip (about ¹/₂ inch diameter, #4), pipe mixture onto prepared baking sheets in rosettes or peaked mounds of about 1 inch diameter, spacing them about 1 inch apart. Alternately, moisten your fingers and shape the mixture in peaked mounds of about 1 inch diameter.

5. Bake until ridges or peaks of macaroons turn light brown, but rest of surface remains pale in color, 12 to 13 minutes; they should be just firm enough so they can be removed from baking sheet without losing their shape. Half way through baking time, switch positions of baking sheets from lower to upper racks so all bake evenly. Using a metal spatula, very carefully remove macaroons from baking sheet and transfer to a rack to cool.

Chocolate Chip Meringues

Makes about 36 meringues

Kosher-for-Passover chocolate chips are available at many supermarkets. If you can't find them, you can cut bittersweet or semisweet chocolate into very small cubes to make these crunchy cookies.

Matzo cake meal for dusting pan
6 large egg whites
Pinch of salt
1^1/2 cups sugar
1 cup semisweet chocolate chips
^{3}/4 cup coarsely chopped walnuts

1. Preheat oven to 275°F. Lightly grease corners of 2 baking sheets with margarine and line them with foil. Grease and lightly dust foil with matzo cake meal, tapping baking sheet to remove excess.

2. Whip egg whites with salt in a large bowl with an electric mixer until stiff. Gradually beat in ^{3}/4 cup sugar at high speed and whip until whites are very shiny.

3. As quickly as possible, gently fold in remaining ^{3}/4 cup sugar in 2 batches. Quickly fold in chocolate chips and walnuts. Spoon mixture in irregular mounds onto prepared baking sheets, using 1 mounded tablespoon for each and spacing them about 1^1/2 inches apart.

4. Bake 30 minutes. Reduce oven temperature to 250°F. Bake 30 minutes more or until meringues are firm to touch, dry at bases, and can be easily removed from foil. They will be light beige.

5. Transfer meringues to a rack to cool. Put them in airtight containers as soon as they are cool.

❧ Breakfast and Brunch

Classic Matzo Brei

Makes 4 or 5 servings

D or **P**

This breakfast favorite, also known as fried matzo with eggs, could be considered a Passover version of French toast because many dip the matzo in egg and fry it the way bread is prepared for the American breakfast classic. Most families serve it at least once during the holiday. Indeed, it has become so well-liked that it is a staple on many deli menus all year round. It is definitely one of the easiest dishes to prepare. This recipe is how we always made it when I was growing up—more like scrambled eggs with matzos. I still make it this way. I like matzo brei on its own, but many people like to sprinkle it with sugar or top it with jam.

You can vary the taste by using different kinds of matzos, such as egg matzos or whole wheat or onion matzos.

5 matzos
5 large eggs
^{1}/4 to ^{1}/2 teaspoon salt
3 to 4 tablespoons butter or vegetable oil

1. Soak matzos in cold water for about 10 minutes and drain. Break them into bite size squares and place in large bowl. Beat eggs with salt and pour over matzos. Stir until matzos are coated.

2. Melt butter in a heavy skillet. Add the matzo mixture. Cook over low heat, stirring, until the eggs are scrambled and done to your taste. Serve at once.

Onion Matzo Brei

Makes 4 or 5 servings

Matzo brei gains a new dimension when flavored with sautéed onions. If you like, you can double the flavor impact and make it with onion matzo. This recipe is cooked like a flat omelet rather than like scrambled eggs. Top this matzo brei with sour cream, if you like, and sprinkle with chives; or serve it with sliced tomatoes.

5 matzos
1/4 cup (1/2 stick) butter or vegetable oil
1 large onion, chopped
1/2 teaspoon paprika
4 large eggs
1/4 to 1/2 teaspoon salt
Freshly ground pepper, to taste

1. Soak matzos in cold water for about 10 minutes and drain. Break them into bite size squares and place in large bowl.

2. Heat 2 tablespoons butter or oil in a heavy skillet. Add onion and paprika and sauté over low heat, stirring often, about 10 minutes or until lightly browned.

3. Meanwhile, beat eggs with salt and pepper and pour over matzos. Stir until matzos are coated. Add sautéed onions and stir again.

4. Melt remaining butter in skillet over medium heat. Add matzo mixture. Cook, without stirring, occasionally pushing egg mixture from edge of pan to inside, until eggs are set and bottom of matzo brei "cake" browns. Slide onto a plate, turn over onto another plate, and return to pan. Sauté until second side browns. Serve at once.

Farfel Muesli

Makes 1 serving

When I was growing up, there were no kosher-for-Passover breakfast cereals and so my brother and I ate matzo farfel (little squares) with bananas as our breakfast cereal. We liked it so much that we always hoped some would be left over after Passover so we could continue starting our day with it. The cereal slightly resembles Swiss muesli, with farfel instead of oats. You can add dried fruits and nuts.

1 to 1 1/2 cups matzo farfel
1/2 to 1 cup milk
1 small banana, sliced
Sugar or raisins (optional)
1 tablespoon diced toasted pecans (optional)

Mix farfel with milk and banana. Sprinkle with sugar or raisins and toasted pecans, if using.

Shavuot

Salads and Appetizers
34

Valerie's Shavuot Salad

Spinach Salad with Goat Cheese, Walnuts, and Peppers

Israeli Salad with Early Summer Herbs

Mediterranean Green and White Bean Salad

Barley Tabbouleh

Corn, Green Bean, and Zucchini Salad with Tomatoes

Tomato Pasta Salad with Avocado and Mozzarella Cheese

Green Bean and Feta Cheese Salad with Walnut Oil Dressing

Goat Cheese and Cucumber Canapés

Cold Tomato-Cucumber Soup with Yogurt and Herbs

Savory Blintzes and Pastries
38

Broccoli Blintzes

Main Course Cheese Blintzes

Cheese Bourekas

Potato and Cheese Filling for Bourekas

Fresh Spinach Tart

Shell for Savory Tarts

Main Courses
41

Broiled Salmon with Green Beans and Roasted Garlic Vinaigrette

Rice Casserole with Sea Bass and Asparagus

Striped Vegetable Terrine

Chickpea and Summer Vegetable Stew

Lima Beans with Spinach Sauce

Creamy Onion Soufflé

The two-day holiday of Shavuot falls in late May or June and takes place seven weeks after Passover. (Shavuot means "weeks" in Hebrew.) It honors the receiving of the Torah by Moses and the Hebrews at Mount Sinai. Originally an agricultural festival timed according to the harvest, it later developed into a celebration of the Mount Sinai revelation and of the Torah, according to some scholars. Shavuot is called the Feast of Weeks in Deuteronomy 16, which instructs to count the seven weeks from "when the sickle is first put to the standing grain."

Like many other holidays, the observation of Shavuot also has seasonal significance. In ancient Israel, Shavuot marked the beginning of a new agricultural season as well as the end of the grain harvest. Thus the holiday came to be known as "The Feast of the First Fruits" and the "Festival of the Harvest." To give thanks for both, the early fruits of the season and loaves of bread from the just-harvested grains were brought to the Holy Temple in Jerusalem.

In many Jewish communities it is the custom to celebrate Shavuot with dairy foods and thus, without meat. The origin of this practice is said to be that the Israelites avoided meat the day before they received the Torah. Some say it's because when the Israelites received the Torah, which included the laws of *kashrut*, they realized that their meat and their pots were not kosher. Since they did not have time to prepare kosher meat and pots, they ate uncooked dairy dishes so they didn't need to use any pans. Others relate this custom to seasonal considerations, as this is the time when cows, goats, and sheep give plenty of milk and much of it is turned into cheese. One custom is to eat dairy foods with honey because of a phrase in the Song of Songs "Honey and milk are under your tongue," which biblical sages interpret as describing the sweetness of the Torah.

For lovers of cheesecake and blintzes, this is a holiday that is eagerly anticipated. There are plenty of other treats to enjoy as well. Sour cream noodle kugels, both sweet and savory, have always been favorites in my family. Sephardic Jews from Greece, Turkey, Syria, and Lebanon prefer savory cheese *bourekas* made of phyllo or puff pastry. In Alsace many Jews enjoy such luscious French dishes as cheese soufflés and quiches with creamy vegetable or cheese fillings.

During the years when my husband and I lived in Paris, celebrating Shavuot was a real feast. There were so many delightful French dairy dishes and products to enjoy at the holiday, it was hard to decide what not to include on the menu. I love vegetable gratins baked in bechamel sauce, a smooth, nutmeg-flavored white sauce, and browned with a sprinkling of cheese. Pasta, vegetables, and fish are especially wonderful when served with a French mushroom sauce enriched with cream. It's impossible to resist the tarts with buttery crusts, from savory spinach and cheese tarts to strawberry tarts with vanilla pastry cream and shiny jam glaze.

At home, I try to space out the treats over the two days of the holiday and add generous amounts of vegetables and fruits to celebrate the "first fruits" aspect of the holiday. In Israel, where Shavuot lasts for one day only, there is a lot of eating to do!

Salads and Appetizers

Valerie's Shavuot Salad

Makes 4 servings   **D**

When we celebrated Shavuot recently at the home of our neighbors Valerie and Chaim Alon in Woodland Hills, California, this is the delicious salad that began the dinner. Made of colorful greens and thin cucumber slices tossed with a light lemon dressing and topped with olives and feta cheese, it's too delicious to serve only once a year.

6 cups mixed baby greens, rinsed and dried thoroughly
1¹/₂ cups cucumber, preferably hothouse or Japanese,
    halved lengthwise and sliced thin
1 tablespoon strained fresh lemon juice
2 to 3 tablespoons extra-virgin olive oil
Salt and freshly ground pepper, to taste
¹/₃ cup good-quality black olives, such as Kalamata,
    pitted
¹/₂ to 1 cup coarsely crumbled feta cheese

Place greens in a bowl. Add cucumber, lemon juice, 2 tablespoons oil, salt, and pepper. Toss thoroughly. Taste, and add more oil if desired. Scatter olives and cheese over the top and serve.

Spinach Salad with Goat Cheese, Walnuts, and Peppers

Makes 4 servings   **D**

This easy-to-make salad is a perfect first course in a festive Shavuot meal, followed by a main course of kugel or blintzes. The colorful, tasty salad is seasoned with just a touch of herb vinaigrette. For the most delicate flavor, use baby spinach.

¹/₂ red bell pepper
¹/₂ yellow bell pepper
6 cups rinsed spinach leaves, regular or baby, medium packed
1¹/₂ to 2 tablespoons extra-virgin olive oil
2¹/₄ teaspoons herb vinegar or tarragon vinegar
¹/₄ teaspoon dried thyme
Salt and freshly ground pepper, to taste
¹/₄ cup walnut pieces, toasted
¹/₄ to ¹/₂ cup crumbled goat cheese

1. Cut peppers into strips about ¹/₃ inch wide; cut in half if long. Combine with spinach in a large bowl.

2. Whisk oil with vinegar and thyme in a small bowl. Toss with bell peppers and spinach. Season with salt and pepper. Top with walnuts and goat cheese and serve.

Israeli Salad with Early Summer Herbs

Makes 4 servings   **P**

At Shavuot time the garden is bursting with the aromas of fresh herbs. I love to add herbs from my garden to my Shavuot version of Israeli salad, or chopped salad. Fresh chives give the salad a more delicate taste than the customary onion. Tarragon lends its flavor as part of tarragon vinegar. I also like the savory accent of young oregano. The salad is so flavorful that you can omit the oil if you wish, for a fat-free appetizer or accompaniment. The best tomatoes for this salad are ripe but firm.

3 ripe medium tomatoes, cut into small dice
¹/₂ long cucumber, hothouse or Japanese, cut into small dice
2 tablespoons chopped or sliced fresh chives
1 tablespoon chopped fresh oregano
2 to 3 teaspoons extra-virgin olive oil or vegetable oil
2 to 3 teaspoons tarragon vinegar
Salt and freshly ground pepper, to taste

Mix together diced tomatoes, cucumber, chives, and oregano in bowl. Add oil, vinegar, salt, and pepper. Serve cold or at room temperature.

Mediterranean Green and White Bean Salad

Makes 4 servings

Ripe tomatoes, black olives, and fresh herbs give this beautiful salad its charm. Be sure to use crisp green beans and to cook them briefly so they keep their vivid color. It's a terrific complement to all the cheesy dishes that are likely to be on your Shavuot menus.

3/4 pound green beans, ends removed, halved

3 to 4 tablespoons extra-virgin olive oil

1 large onion, halved and sliced thin

2 cups cooked white beans or one 15-ounce can white beans, drained

3/4 pound ripe tomatoes, diced

1/3 cup black olives, or Kalamata olives, halved and pitted

3 tablespoons coarsely chopped fresh basil or oregano

1 to 2 tablespoons strained fresh lemon juice

Salt and freshly ground pepper, to taste

1. Add green beans to a large saucepan of boiling salted water and boil uncovered over high heat 5 minutes or until crisp-tender. Drain in a colander, rinse with cold water, and drain well again.

2. Heat 2 tablespoons oil in a medium skillet. Add onion and sauté over medium-low heat, stirring often, about 7 minutes or until tender but not brown.

3. Combine white beans, green beans, onion with oil, tomatoes, olives, and basil in glass bowl and toss lightly.

4. Whisk lemon juice with 1 tablespoon oil and salt and pepper to taste in a bowl; salt lightly because olives are salty. Add to salad and toss until ingredients are coated. Taste and adjust seasoning. Add remaining oil if desired and toss again. Serve at room temperature.

Barley Tabbouleh

Makes 4 to 6 servings

One aspect of Shavuot is reading the Book of Ruth, whose events took place at harvest time, and celebrating the new crop of grain. I like to add barley to the holiday menu, as it is a biblical grain.

We tend to think of barley in hearty soups, but for the warm weather of Shavuot, which takes place in late May or in June, a salad is more appropriate. Instead, I like to turn it into a fresh-tasting, colorful salad—a new variation of the Middle Eastern favorite, tabbouleh. Usually tabbouleh is made with bulgur wheat, but unlike bulgur, pearl barley is easy to find in any market. Barley's nutty taste is a fine complement for the tabbouleh's traditionally generous amounts of Italian parsley, mint, and fresh vegetables.

2 1/2 cups water

1 cup pearl barley

2 tablespoons strained fresh lemon juice

2 to 3 tablespoons extra-virgin olive oil

Salt and freshly ground pepper, to taste

6 ripe plum tomatoes, cut into small dice

1/2 cucumber or 1/3-long cucumber, hothouse or Japanese, peeled if desired and cut into small dice

4 green onions, thinly sliced

2 cups small sprigs fresh Italian parsley, rinsed, patted dry, and coarsely chopped

1/3 cup fresh mint leaves, coarsely chopped

1. In a heavy saucepan, bring water to a boil with a pinch of salt. Add barley, cover and simmer over low heat about 40 minutes or until barley is tender. Transfer barley to a large bowl and let cool.

2. Add lemon juice, olive oil, salt, and pepper to barley. Add tomatoes, cucumbers, and green onions and toss. Lightly stir in parsley and mint. Taste and adjust seasoning. Serve cool or at room temperature.

Corn, Green Bean, and Zucchini Salad with Tomatoes

Makes 4 servings (P)

Shavuot is a celebration of the season's new produce. Serving this light, colorful salad of the first young, tender summer vegetables is a healthful way to commemorate this aspect of the holiday. You can make it ahead but if you do, add the lemon juice at the last minute to keep the color of the green beans bright.

1 pound green beans, ends removed, halved

1/2 pound zucchini, cut into 1-inch dice

2 cups fresh or frozen corn kernels

2 to 3 teaspoons extra-virgin olive oil

2 teaspoons chopped fresh oregano or 1/2 teaspoon dried

Salt and freshly ground pepper, to taste

3/4 pound ripe tomatoes, diced

1 tablespoon strained fresh lemon juice (optional)

Add green beans to a saucepan of boiling salted water. Boil uncovered 5 minutes. Add zucchini and corn and return to a boil over high heat. Cook 3 minutes or until vegetables are crisp-tender. Drain in a colander or strainer. Transfer to a bowl. Add olive oil, oregano, salt, and pepper. Toss to combine. Add tomatoes and toss again. Add lemon juice, if using. Serve warm, room temperature, or cold.

Tomato Pasta Salad with Avocado and Mozzarella Cheese

Makes 4 servings (D)

A celebration of late spring and summer, this tricolor salad combines fresh mozzarella cheese, fresh tomatoes, tomato-flavored pasta, and avocado cubes for a delightful warm-weather main course. If you prefer, you can substitute diced feta cheese for the mozzarella. You can also add grilled or marinated peppers or mushrooms.

1 tablespoon strained fresh lemon juice or herb vinegar

Salt and freshly ground pepper, to taste

4 to 5 tablespoons extra-virgin olive oil

1/4 cup chopped green onion

2 tablespoons chopped fresh parsley

1 tablespoon chopped fresh oregano or 1 teaspoon dried

8 ounces tomato (or plain) pasta spirals

3/4 to 1 pound ripe tomatoes, diced

1/3 to 1/2 cup diced fresh mozzarella cheese

1 ripe avocado

1. For the dressing: Combine lemon juice, salt, and pepper in a large bowl. Whisk in oil. Stir in green onion, parsley, and oregano.

2. Cook pasta in a large pot of boiling salted water uncovered over high heat, stirring occasionally, about 7 minutes or until tender but firm to the bite. Drain, rinse with cold water, and drain well again. Add to dressing and mix well. Add tomatoes and cheese. A short time before serving, cut avocado into small dice. Add to salad. Adjust seasoning.

Green Bean and Feta Cheese Salad with Walnut Oil Dressing

Makes 4 servings

Serve this tasty, attractive salad at a Shavuot buffet along with a tomato or red pepper salad.

4 teaspoons tarragon vinegar

Salt and freshly ground pepper, to taste

3 tablespoons walnut oil

1 tablespoon sliced fresh chives

1 1/2 pounds green beans, ends removed

1/2 cup crumbled feta cheese

1/3 cup walnut halves or pieces, toasted and chopped

1 large hard boiled egg, chopped

1. Whisk vinegar, salt, and pepper in a small bowl. Whisk in oil, then chives. Adjust seasoning and set aside.

2. Cook beans in a large pan of boiling salted water about 4 minutes or until crisp tender. Rinse under cold running water until cool and drain thoroughly. Gently pat dry.

3. Transfer beans to a large round platter, with all beans pointing to center. Whisk dressing and spoon it evenly over beans. Sprinkle feta cheese over center, covering ends of beans where they meet. Sprinkle walnuts in a circle around feta. Sprinkle chopped hard boiled egg in a circle around walnuts. Allow ends of green beans to show. Serve at room temperature.

Goat Cheese and Cucumber Canapés

Makes 10 to 12 canapés

Good quality Israeli goat cheese is easy to find not only in Jerusalem and Tel Aviv but in many American markets as well. Mix goat cheese with chives as a delicious spread for these easy canapés, which make tasty hors d'oeuvres at a party. You can serve them as a first course at a Shavuot dinner, accompanied by sliced tomatoes or roasted peppers.

4 ounces creamy goat cheese, at room temperature

3 to 4 tablespoons sour cream

2 tablespoons minced fresh Italian parsley

2 tablespoons snipped fresh chives

Salt (optional) and freshly ground pepper, to taste

1/2 seedless cucumber, such as hothouse or Japanese

10 to 12 thin slices baguette or other good quality bread

1. Remove any dark rind from goat cheese by scraping gently with a knife. Beat cheese with 2 tablespoons sour cream in a bowl with a wooden spoon until smooth. Stir in enough of remaining sour cream to obtain a spreadable consistency. Stir in parsley and 1 tablespoon chives. Add a pinch of pepper; taste before adding any salt.

2. Peel cucumber if you like, and remove center with a corer. Cut cucumber into thin slices; they will be ring-shaped. Spread them on paper towels to absorb excess moisture.

3. If bread slices are large, use a round pastry cutter of about same diameter as cucumber slices to cut bread into circles. Spread bread with goat cheese mixture and set cucumber slices on top. Sprinkle remaining tablespoon chives in center of rings.

Cold Tomato-Cucumber Soup with Yogurt and Herbs

Makes 6 servings

This refreshing first course is perfect for Shavuot, when the weather is usually warm. Garlic gives the soup a subtle kick that is balanced by the fresh flavor of the herbs.

Be sure to use good-quality cucumbers; the small, thin-skinned Middle Eastern type is ideal. They are sometimes labeled Israeli, Middle Eastern, or Persian cucumbers. Japanese and hothouse cucumbers also are very good in this dish. Nonfat yogurt gives good results but you can use any yogurt you like.

1 small clove garlic, pressed or minced fine

1/2 teaspoon salt, or to taste

6 cups plain yogurt

Pinch of cayenne pepper

1/2 pound cucumbers, halved lengthwise and sliced thin

1/2 pound ripe tomatoes, cut into small dice, about 1/3 cup reserved

1 tablespoon chopped fresh dill

2 tablespoons minced fresh Italian parsley

2 tablespoons chopped fresh chives or garlic chives

1. Mash garlic with salt in a large bowl, using the back of a spoon. Add yogurt and cayenne pepper. Stir to blend thoroughly.

2. Add cucumbers and a larger amount of diced tomatoes. Fold vegetables gently into yogurt. Adjust seasoning. Refrigerate at least 15 minutes or up to 6 hours before serving.

3. A short time before serving, stir in dill, parsley, and half the chives. Serve soup garnished with reserved diced tomato and remaining chives.

Savory Blintzes and
Pastries

Broccoli Blintzes

Makes 6 servings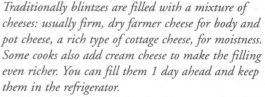

These blintzes with their creamy vegetable filling make a delicious Shavuot main course. You can fill them a day ahead and have them in their baking dishes, ready to heat in the oven.

12 Basic, Whole-Wheat, or Pareve Buckwheat Blintzes
    (pages 300 and 302)

$^1/_4$ cup ($^1/_2$ stick) butter

2 tablespoons all-purpose flour

$1^1/_4$ cups milk

Salt and freshly ground white pepper, to taste

Freshly grated nutmeg, to taste

$^1/_3$ cup heavy cream

Pinch of cayenne pepper

3 to $3^1/_2$ cups coarsely chopped cooked broccoli

1. Prepare blintzes, stack them and cover them with a kitchen towel.

2. Melt 2 tablespoons butter in a heavy saucepan over low heat. Add flour and cook, whisking constantly, about 2 minutes, or until foaming but not browned. Remove from heat and gradually stir in milk. Bring to boil over medium-high heat, whisking constantly. Add a small pinch of salt, white pepper, and nutmeg. Reduce heat to low and cook, whisking often, 3 minutes. Add cream and bring to a boil. Reduce heat to low and cook, whisking often, about 5 minutes or until thick. Add cayenne pepper. Stir in broccoli. Adjust seasoning.

3. Preheat oven to 400°F. Butter one large shallow baking dish or two small shallow baking dishes. Spoon $2^1/_2$ to 3 tablespoons filling onto brown side of each blintz near edge of blintz closest to you. Fold over edges of blintz to right and left of filling so that each covers about half of filling; roll up, beginning at edge with filling.

4. Arrange blintzes in one layer in baking dish. Cut remaining butter into small pieces and put 2 pieces on each blintz. Bake about 20 minutes or until hot and lightly browned. Serve immediately.

Main-Course Cheese Blintzes

Makes 4 to 6 servings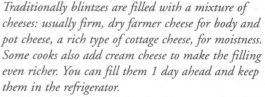

Traditionally blintzes are filled with a mixture of cheeses: usually firm, dry farmer cheese for body and pot cheese, a rich type of cottage cheese, for moistness. Some cooks also add cream cheese to make the filling even richer. You can fill them 1 day ahead and keep them in the refrigerator.

My mother always bakes her blintzes and so do I. Some people prefer their blintzes fried. If you wish to fry them, see the note at the end of the recipe.

Serve these for brunch, lunch, or supper. The filling is delicately sweet and does not contain as much sugar as dessert blintzes.

12 Basic Blintzes, 8 inches in diameter (page 300)

2 cups farmer cheese (about 15 ounces)

$^1/_3$ cup pot cheese or whole-milk cottage cheese

2 large egg yolks

3 tablespoons sugar, or to taste

$^1/_4$ teaspoon ground cinnamon, or to taste

Pinch of salt

2 to 3 tablespoons butter, cut into small pieces

Sour cream or yogurt

1. Prepare blintzes, stack them and cover with a kitchen towel.

2. Mash farmer cheese with pot cheese in a large bowl. With a wooden spoon, beat in egg yolks, sugar, cinnamon, and salt until mixture is well blended.

3. Preheat oven to 400°F. Spoon $2^1/_2$ to 3 tablespoons filling onto brown side of each blintz near edge of blintz closest to you. Fold over edges of blintz to right and left of filling so that each covers about half of filling; roll up, beginning at edge with filling.

4. Arrange blintzes in one layer in a shallow buttered baking dish. Dot each with 2 small pieces of butter. Bake about 20 minutes or until heated through and lightly browned. Serve blintzes hot, with sour cream or yogurt.

Note: To fry blintzes, heat 1 tablespoon vegetable oil and 2 to 3 tablespoons butter in a heavy skillet. Add blintzes seam side down. Fry over low heat 3 to 5 minutes on each side or until golden; do not let them burn.

Cheese Bourekas

Makes about 30 pastries

These savory pastries, Sephardic favorites for Shavuot, come in several shapes—triangular, half-moon shaped, and even ring-shaped. Some people make them with a dough resembling pie dough, others use puff pastry. But the most popular is phyllo dough. (For this recipe, I often have handy more than the 15 sheets I need, in case the phyllo tears or becomes brittle.) Feta is a traditional Sephardic choice to flavor the filling. Often it's mixed with other cheeses for a milder flavor.

1 pound phyllo dough (about 20 sheets)

¹/₄ cup farmer cheese or ricotta

³/₄ cup finely crumbled feta cheese (about 4 ounces)

2 large eggs, beaten lightly

1 cup grated Swiss cheese (about 3 ounces)

Salt and freshly ground pepper, to taste

¹/₂ to ³/₄ cup (1 to 1¹/₂ sticks) butter or margarine, melted

2 teaspoons sesame seeds

1. If phyllo dough is frozen, thaw it in refrigerator 8 hours or overnight. Remove dough from refrigerator 2 hours before using; leave it in its package.

2. For cheese filling: Mash farmer cheese with feta in a bowl to blend well. Add eggs and Swiss cheese and mix until smooth. Add salt and pepper.

3. Remove phyllo sheets from package and unroll them on a dry towel. With a sharp knife, cut stack in half lengthwise, to form two stacks of sheets 16 × 7 inches. Cover sheets immediately with wax paper, then

with a damp towel. Work with only one sheet at a time and always keep remaining sheets covered with paper and towel, so they don't dry out.

4. Remove a phyllo sheet from pile. Brush it lightly with melted butter and fold it in half lengthwise, so its dimensions are about 16 × 3¹/₂ inches. Dab it lightly with butter. Place about 2 teaspoons cheese filling at one end of strip. Fold end of strip diagonally over filling to form a triangle, and dab it lightly with butter. Continue folding it over and over, keeping it in a triangular shape after each fold, until you reach end of strip. Set triangular pastry on a buttered baking sheet. Brush it lightly with butter. Shape more pastries with reserved phyllo sheets and filling. (Pastries can be shaped 1 day ahead and refrigerated on baking sheets or on plates. Cover them tightly with plastic wrap.)

5. Preheat oven to 350°F. Just before putting pastries in the oven, brush them again lightly with melted butter and sprinkle with sesame seeds. Bake 20 to 25 minutes or until golden brown. Serve warm (not hot) or at room temperature.

Potato and Cheese Filling for Bourekas

Makes about 1 to 1¹/₄ cups

Bourekas enclosing a potato filling are popular in many Sephardic homes and are widely available at bakeries. The potato can be mixed with a zesty cheese like kashkaval or feta. For a pareve filling, it can be flavored instead with sautéed onions. Follow the instructions in Cheese Bourekas (this page) to shape and bake the pastries.

¹/₂ pound boiling potatoes

¹/₂ cup finely crumbled feta cheese

¹/₄ cup chopped green onions

Salt and freshly ground pepper, to taste

1 large egg, beaten

1. Put potatoes in a saucepan with water to cover and a pinch of salt and bring to a boil. Cover and simmer over low heat about 30 minutes or until very tender. Drain and leave until cool enough to handle.

2. Peel potatoes. Cut each into a few pieces, place in a bowl, and mash with a potato masher. Lightly stir in feta cheese and green onions. Season filling with salt and pepper. Stir in beaten egg. Refrigerate in a covered container until ready to use.

Fresh Spinach Tart

Makes 6 servings   Ⓓ

This tart has a delicious shell of flaky pastry and a creamy, bright green spinach filling. Be sure to season the filling well with freshly grated nutmeg, a great partner for spinach. Prepare the pastry shell at least a few hours before baking the tart to allow enough time to chill it thoroughly. You can bake the tart a day ahead and keep it covered in the refrigerator. Before serving, warm it in a 300°F oven.

9- to 10-inch Shell for Savory Tarts (this page)

Dry beans or rice (for weighting pie shell)

2¹/₂ pounds fresh spinach

2 large eggs

1 large egg yolk

¹/₄ cup sour cream

Salt and freshly ground pepper, to taste

Freshly grated nutmeg to taste

³/₄ cup heavy cream

¹/₄ cup grated Gruyere or Swiss cheese

1. Prepare pastry shell. Then, position rack in lower third of oven and preheat to 425°F. Line pastry shell with parchment paper or foil and fill with dry beans or rice. Set shell on a baking sheet and bake 10 minutes. Carefully remove beans or rice and liner, and bake shell 8 to 10 minutes more or until lightly browned. Transfer tart pan to a rack and let shell cool. Move baking sheet to center of oven. Reduce oven temperature to 350°F.

2. Remove stems of spinach and wash leaves thoroughly. In a large saucepan of boiling salted water, cook spinach uncovered over high heat, pushing leaves down into water often, about 3 minutes or until very tender. Drain, rinse with cold water, and drain well again. Squeeze out liquid by handfuls. Chop finely in food processor or with a knife.

3. Whisk eggs with yolk, sour cream, and pinches of salt, pepper, and nutmeg in a bowl. Stir in heavy cream and chopped spinach.

4. Return pastry shell to baking sheet in oven. Ladle spinach mixture slowly into shell. Sprinkle with Gruyere. Bake 30 minutes or until filling is set. Let cool on a rack for 10 minutes. Serve warm or at room temperature.

Shell for Savory Tarts

Makes an 8-inch tart shell   Ⓓ or Ⓟ

Use this shell for quiches and for tarts and pies such as Fresh Spinach Tart (this page) and Chard and Onion Pie (page 296). If you wish to make the dough with pareve margarine, choose a firm stick margarine, not a soft tub margarine.

1 large egg yolk

2 to 3 tablespoons ice water

1¹/₃ cups all-purpose flour

¹/₄ teaspoon salt

7 tablespoons cold unsalted butter or margarine, cut into small pieces

1. Whisk egg yolk with 2 tablespoons ice water in a small bowl. Set aside.

2. Combine flour and salt in a food processor and process briefly to blend. Scatter butter pieces over flour. Mix with brief pulses until mixture resembles coarse meal. Pour egg yolk mixture evenly over mixture in processor. Process with brief pulses, scraping down the sides occasionally, until dough forms sticky crumbs that can easily be pressed together (but before dough comes together in a ball). If crumbs are dry, sprinkle ¹/₂ teaspoon water and process with brief pulses until dough forms sticky crumbs. Add more water in same way, ¹/₂ teaspoon at a time, if crumbs are still dry.

3. Using a rubber spatula, transfer dough to a sheet of plastic wrap, wrap up dough, and push it together. Shape dough into a flat disk. Refrigerate dough 1 hour or up to overnight.

4. Butter an 8-inch fluted tart pan with removable rim. Roll dough on a lightly floured surface to a round about 1/8-inch thick. Roll dough loosely around rolling pin and unroll it over tart pan. Gently ease dough into pan. Using your thumb, gently push dough down slightly all around the top edge of the pan, making top edge of dough thicker than remaining dough. Roll rolling pin across pan to cut off excess dough. With your finger and thumb, press dough gently against pan so that it rises 1/4-inch above the pan's rim. Prick bottom of shell lightly with a fork. Refrigerate for 30 minutes or up to 2 days.

Note: Use these ingredients to make a 9- to 10-inch tart shell, following directions above:

2 large egg yolks

2 tablespoons ice water

1 1/2 cups all-purpose flour

3/8 teaspoon salt

1/2 cup (1 stick) cold unsalted butter or margarine

❧ *Main Courses*

Broiled Salmon with Green Beans and Roasted Garlic Vinaigrette   Ⓟ

Makes 4 servings

You might like to plan your holiday menu around this lovely, festive entree. Serve the salmon hot or cold with a simple cucumber salad or an Israeli salad. You can serve more roasted garlic cloves separately so each person can squeeze some more sweet, smoky garlic on his or her portion. This will make a festive but light dinner, so you'll have room for a creamy noodle kugel, a cheesecake, or another rich Shavuot treat.

If you like, use the slim French haricots verts instead of the usual green beans, or serve asparagus instead. Whichever green vegetable you choose, its color will remain most vivid if you toss it with the dressing just before serving. If you don't have roasted garlic on hand and want a quicker dressing for this dish, serve Chive-Caper Vinaigrette (page 594) instead.

5 cloves Roasted Garlic (page 456)

2 tablespoons white wine vinegar

Salt and freshly ground pepper, to taste

5 tablespoons plus 2 teaspoons extra-virgin olive oil

1 tablespoon chopped fresh parsley

1 1/4 pounds salmon fillet, preferably tail section, about 1-inch thick

1 tablespoon strained fresh lemon juice

1/2 teaspoon dried thyme

1 pound green beans, ends removed

Lemon wedges

1. Prepare roasted garlic. Then, squeeze garlic pulp out of the skins into a blender or small food processor. Add vinegar, salt, and pepper. Process until blended. With motor running, slowly add 5 tablespoons oil in a thin, steady stream. Transfer to a bowl, then stir in parsley. Adjust seasoning. Set aside.

2. Sprinkle salmon with lemon juice and the remaining 2 teaspoons oil and rub over fillet. Sprinkle fish evenly with thyme, salt, and pepper.

3. Boil green beans uncovered in a large saucepan of enough boiling salted water to generously cover them over high heat 5 to 7 minutes or until crisp-tender. Drain, rinse with cold water, and drain well again. (If you are cooking green beans ahead, and you want to serve them hot, you can put them back in a pan of boiling water for 30 seconds, then drain and serve them.)

4. Line broiler rack with foil if you like, or brush it lightly with oil. Preheat broiler. Set salmon on broiler rack and broil 4 minutes. Turn salmon over and broil 4 to 5 minutes more. To check whether fish is done, make a small cut with a sharp knife in thickest part; color of flesh should have changed all the way through.

5. To serve, toss green beans with 2 or 3 tablespoons dressing and salt and pepper. Spoon onto a platter. Put fish on platter and spoon remaining vinaigrette over it. Garnish with lemon wedges.

Rice Casserole with Sea Bass and Asparagus

Makes 4 servings   Ⓓ

This meal-in-one pot is a delicious dish to serve for Shavuot or Sukkot. Subtly scented with fresh tarragon in the French style, the rice is mixed lightly with poached sea bass and asparagus. It gains additional flavor from cooking in the herbed fish poaching liquid. The only accompaniment you need is a colorful salad, such as Israeli Salad, California Style (page 239).

3 cups Fish Stock (page 600), vegetable stock, or broth
6 fresh tarragon stems (without leaves)
5 fresh parsley stems (without leaves)
1 large sprig fresh thyme or 1/4 teaspoon dried thyme
1 bay leaf
1 1/4 to 1 1/2 pounds sea bass steaks or fillets, rinsed
Salt and freshly ground pepper, to taste
3 tablespoons butter or vegetable oil
3/4 cup minced onion
1 1/2 cups long grain white rice
3/4 pound thin asparagus, trimmed, spears cut into 3 pieces
1/4 to 1/3 cup heavy cream, whipping cream, or sour cream, at room temperature
3 tablespoons minced fresh tarragon leaves
2 tablespoons chopped fresh parsley

1. Combine stock, tarragon stems, parsley stems, thyme, and bay leaf in a saucepan. Bring to a simmer. Add sea bass, salt, and pepper and return to simmer. Cover and cook over low heat, turning once, 8 to 10 minutes or until color of fish turns opaque.

2. With slotted spatula transfer fish to a plate. Discard herb sprigs and bay leaf. Measure liquid and add enough water to make 3 cups. Return liquid to saucepan, cover, and keep warm.

3. Preheat oven to 350°F. Heat 2 tablespoons butter or oil in a large ovenproof sauté pan or deep skillet. Add onion and cook over low heat, stirring, about 7 minutes or until soft but not brown. Add rice and sauté over medium heat, stirring, about 4 minutes or until grains begin to turn milky white.

4. Bring fish poaching liquid to boil over high heat. Pour over rice and stir once.

5. Add salt and pepper. Bring to boil. Remove from heat and cover tightly. Bake in oven, without stirring, 18 to 20 minutes. Taste rice; if it is too chewy or if liquid is not absorbed, bake 3 to 5 minutes more and taste again. Reduce oven temperature to 300°F.

6. Meanwhile, dice sea bass, discarding any liquid. Put asparagus in a medium saucepan of boiling salted water. Return to boil. Boil uncovered about 3 minutes or until asparagus is just tender. Drain well again. Return to dry saucepan, add 1 tablespoon butter and reserve.

7. When rice is cooked, pour cream quickly and evenly over it; do not stir. Top with diced sea bass. Cover pan, return to oven, and bake for 5 minutes or until cream is absorbed and fish is hot. Heat asparagus with its butter and a pinch of salt and pepper over medium heat, tossing.

8. Use fork to fluff rice and to gently stir in diced fish, chopped tarragon, and half of asparagus. Adjust seasoning. Serve topped with remaining asparagus and sprinkled with parsley.

Striped Vegetable Terrine

Makes 8 servings   Ⓓ

This beautiful vegetable loaf à la française *makes a wonderful dish for a Shavuot buffet. The terrine is made of alternating layers of carrot and spinach purees baked as a loaf, then served sliced to show the striped pattern. Be sure to season each layer well so the terrine will not be bland. Serve it French style with a rich sauce such as Basil Cream with Diced Tomatoes (page 464) or, for a lighter option, with a vinaigrette such as Tomato Dressing (page 64).*

3 pounds fresh spinach in bunches (or two 10-ounce bags spinach leaves), stemmed and rinsed

2 pounds carrots, cut into 1/2-inch slices

1 2/3 cups heavy cream

Salt and freshly ground pepper, to taste

Freshly grated nutmeg to taste

6 large eggs

1 large egg yolk

1. Cook spinach in large saucepan of boiling salted water uncovered over high heat, pushing leaves down into water often, about 3 minutes or until very tender. Drain, rinse with cold water, and drain well again. Squeeze out liquid by handfuls. Puree in a food processor until very smooth.

2. Put carrots in a large saucepan, cover with water, add a pinch of salt, and bring to boil. Cover, reduce heat to medium, and cook about 35 minutes or until very tender. Drain thoroughly. Puree in a food processor until very smooth.

3. Preheat oven to 375°F. Generously butter an 8 × 4-inch loaf pan. Line base and sides of pan with parchment paper, letting paper extend slightly above edge of pan, and butter liner. Butter a sheet of foil to cover pan.

4. Cook spinach puree in a medium, heavy, wide saucepan over low heat, stirring often, for 5 minutes, to evaporate excess moisture. Stir in 2/3 cup cream. Bring to boil over high heat. Cook over medium heat, stirring often, until cream is absorbed and mixture is reduced to 2 cups. (Precise measuring is important.) Transfer to a bowl. Season with salt, pepper, and nutmeg.

5. Cook carrot puree in a large, heavy, wide saucepan over low heat, stirring often, for 5 minutes, to evaporate excess moisture. Stir in remaining 1 cup cream. Bring to boil over high heat. Cook over medium heat, stirring often, until cream is absorbed and mixture is reduced to 3 1/3 cups. Transfer to a second bowl. Season with salt and pepper.

6. For spinach layers: Whisk 2 eggs with 1 yolk in a large bowl until blended. Gradually whisk in spinach mixture. For carrot layers: Whisk 4 eggs in a large bowl, then whisk in carrot mixture.

7. Bring a small kettle of water to boil. Spread half of carrot mixture evenly in loaf pan. Tap on counter to pack mixture down. Spoon all of spinach mixture over carrot layer and spread smooth. Spoon remaining carrot mixture evenly on top. Smooth gently. Set the loaf pan in a roasting pan and transfer to oven. Add enough boiling water to roasting pan to come halfway up sides of loaf pan. Set sheet of buttered foil atop pan.

8. Bake about 2 1/2 hours or until terrine is firm to the touch when pressed gently and cake tester inserted into center comes out clean. During baking, add hot water to roasting pan occasionally so that it does not become dry. If water comes close to a boil, add a few tablespoons cold water.

9. Carefully remove loaf pan from water bath. Cool terrine in the loaf pan on a rack at least 1 hour. Carefully run a metal spatula around edge of loaf. Set oval or rectangular platter atop loaf pan and invert both. Gently lift off pan and peel off paper. Slice very gently with the point of a thin, sharp knife in 3/4-inch slices. With aid of a spatula, set each slice on a plate. Serve cool or cold.

Chickpea and Summer Vegetable Stew

Makes 4 servings (P)

Shavuot dishes tend to be delicate in flavor because they're often rich in dairy products. Here is a lively and lean vegetarian main course seasoned in the Yemenite tradition that is a perfect foil for the holiday's creamy dishes. It's great accompanied by couscous or brown rice or in a menu that includes a kugel or blintzes.

2 tablespoons vegetable oil

1 medium onion, coarsely chopped

4 large cloves garlic, minced

1 jalapeño pepper, minced, or 2 teaspoons diced canned roasted jalapeño peppers

4 teaspoons ground cumin

1 teaspoon ground turmeric

1/4 teaspoon hot red pepper flakes, or to taste

1 medium eggplant, unpeeled and cut into small dice

Salt and freshly ground pepper, to taste

1 pound ripe tomatoes, diced, or one 141/2-ounce can diced tomatoes with their juice

1 tablespoon tomato paste

One 15-ounce can chickpeas (garbanzo beans), drained, or 11/2 to 2 cups cooked chickpeas

2 medium zucchini, diced

2 tablespoons coarsely chopped fresh cilantro

1. Heat oil in a heavy, wide stew pan, add onion, and sauté over medium-low heat 5 minutes or until beginning to brown. Add garlic, jalapeño pepper, cumin, turmeric, and pepper flakes and cook, stirring, 1 minute.

2. Add eggplant, sprinkle with salt, and stir over low heat until eggplant is coated with spices. Add tomatoes and bring to boil over high heat. Mix tomato paste with 1/2 cup water and stir into mixture. Cover and simmer over low heat, stirring often, 20 minutes. Add chickpeas and zucchini and simmer 10 to 20 minutes more or until vegetables are tender and stew is thick. Taste and adjust seasoning. Serve hot, sprinkled with cilantro.

Lima Beans with Spinach Sauce

Makes 4 main-course servings (P)

On the day before the Israelites in the desert received the Torah, they abstained from eating any meat. This is why meatless meals are a custom for the holiday. Here is a light and easy vegetarian entree that is welcome on a rich Shavuot menu. For a dairy meal, you can serve it accompanied by feta cheese or yogurt. Since it's pareve on its own, it can also be good for other meals as a partner for chicken or meat.

2 tablespoons olive oil

1 medium onion, chopped

2/3 cup long-grain rice

31/2 cups vegetable stock

Two 10-ounce packages frozen lima beans

10 large cloves garlic, chopped

3 cups coarsely chopped fresh spinach

2 tablespoons minced fresh dill or 1 teaspoon dried

Salt and freshly ground pepper, to taste

1. Heat 1 tablespoon oil in a heavy saucepan, add onion, and sauté over medium-low heat, stirring often, 7 minutes or until golden. Add rice, then 3 cups stock, and bring to simmer. Cover and cook over low heat 10 minutes. Add beans and 1/2 cup stock, shake pan and bring to boil. Cover and cook 5 minutes or until rice and beans are barely tender.

2. Heat remaining oil in a medium, heavy skillet. Add garlic and sauté 15 seconds. Add spinach and sauté over medium heat, stirring, 2 minutes. Stir in dill. Puree spinach mixture in food processor.

3. Add spinach mixture to beans and stir gently. Add salt and pepper to taste. Cook uncovered over medium heat 2 minutes or until beans and rice are tender. Serve hot, in bowls.

Creamy Onion Soufflé

Makes 4 servings Ⓓ

Like most classic soufflés, these must be baked just before they are served, but you can prepare the base a day ahead, refrigerate it, and reheat it. The slowly stewed onions become sweet as they cook and impart a lovely flavor to the creamy soufflés.

1 tablespoon vegetable oil

3 tablespoons butter

1¹/₄ pounds white-, yellow-, or brown-skinned onions, halved and thinly sliced

Salt and freshly ground pepper, to taste

2 tablespoons plus 1 teaspoon all-purpose flour

²/₃ cup milk

3 large egg yolks

5 large egg whites

¹/₄ teaspoon cream of tartar (optional)

1. Heat oil and 1 tablespoon butter in a medium sauté pan. Add onions, salt, and pepper. Cover tightly and cook over low heat, stirring occasionally, about 30 minutes or until onions are very soft. If liquid remains in pan, uncover and cook over medium heat, stirring, until onions are dry.

2. Butter four 1 to 1¹/₄ cup soufflé dishes; butter rims well. Position rack in lower third of oven and preheat to 425°F.

3. Melt remaining 2 tablespoons butter in a small, heavy saucepan. Add flour and cook over low heat, whisking, 2 minutes or until foaming but not brown. Remove from heat. Pour in milk, whisking constantly. Bring to a boil over medium-high heat, continuing to whisk. Add a small pinch of salt and pepper. Cook over low heat, whisking often, for 5 minutes. Off heat, stir in onions. Bring to a boil, stirring.

4. Remove from heat and vigorously whisk in egg yolks, one by one. Cook over low heat, whisking constantly, about 3 minutes or just until thickened. Do not overcook or boil, or yolks may curdle. Adjust seasoning. (If not baking soufflé, refrigerate mixture in a covered container.)

5. Have four heatproof plates ready near oven. Put soufflé dishes on a baking sheet. If soufflé base is cold, heat it in a small saucepan over low heat, whisking, until just warm. Remove from heat.

6. Beat egg whites with cream of tartar, if using, in a large bowl with an electric mixer at medium speed until soft peaks form. Then beat briefly at high speed until whites are stiff but not dry. Quickly fold about ¹/₄ of whites into onion mixture. Spoon this over remaining whites and fold in lightly but quickly, until just blended.

7. Transfer to prepared soufflé dishes and smooth tops. Bake about 12 minutes or until puffed and browned; when you gently move oven rack, soufflés should shake very slightly in center. Do not overbake or soufflés may burn on top and may shrink. Set soufflé dishes on heatproof plates and serve immediately.

❧ Vegetable Side Dishes

Eggplant with Tomatoes and Yogurt

Makes 4 servings ⒟

This savory dish is inspired by an elaborate creation—a charlotte—I learned to prepare at La Varenne Cooking School in Paris. Fried eggplant slices lined a mold that was filled with layers of eggplant, tomato sauce, and yogurt, baked, and then unmolded. I always loved the combination of flavors. They are delicious in this dish, which is low in fat, easy to make, and perfect for Shavuot.

1¹/₂ tablespoons olive oil

1 medium onion, chopped

1³/₄ pound Japanese or small Italian eggplants, unpeeled and cut crosswise into ³/₈-inch slices

Salt and freshly ground pepper, to taste

One 14¹/₂-ounce can stewed tomatoes, preferably Italian style (with basil, garlic, oregano), with their juice

1 to 2 tablespoons shredded fresh basil

About 1 cup nonfat plain yogurt

1. Heat oil in a large, heavy sauté pan or wide casserole, add onion, and sauté over medium heat 2 minutes. Add eggplant, sprinkle with salt, and stir over heat until eggplant is coated with onion mixture. Cover and cook 5 minutes, stirring once or twice.

2. Stir in tomatoes and bring to a boil. Cover and cook over medium-low heat, stirring occasionally, 15 to 20 minutes or until eggplant is tender. Stir in basil and pepper. Serve hot or cold, topped with yogurt.

Zucchini Baked in Parmesan Sauce

Makes 4 servings ⒟

Old-fashioned vegetable gratins are not for every day but these creamy dishes make delectable offerings for Shavuot. Serve these zucchini to accompany a baked or grilled fish or with some light, simple vegetable dishes. Classically, the sauce contains 2 egg yolks to help give the gratin a deeper golden color but I usually omit them. Do try to use freshly grated nutmeg, however; it gives the sauce an essential flavor.

12 to 14 ounces small zucchini, halved crosswise and cut into 2-inch pieces

1¹/₂ tablespoons butter

1¹/₂ tablespoons all-purpose flour

1 cup milk

Salt and white pepper, to taste

Freshly grated nutmeg, to taste

¹/₄ cup plus 2 tablespoons freshly grated Parmesan cheese

1. Preheat oven to 425°F. Put zucchini pieces in a saucepan of boiling salted water and boil uncovered about 4 minutes or until barely tender. Drain, rinse with cold running water until cool and drain thoroughly.

2. Melt butter in a small, heavy saucepan over low heat. Add flour and cook, whisking constantly, about 2 minutes or until foaming but not browned. Remove from heat. Whisk in milk. Bring to boil over medium-high heat, whisking often. Add a small pinch of salt, white pepper, and nutmeg. Cook over low heat, whisking often, 5 minutes. Remove from heat and whisk in ¹/₄ cup cheese. Adjust amounts of salt, pepper, and nutmeg.

3. Butter a heavy 5-cup gratin dish or other shallow baking dish. In prepared dish, arrange zucchini in one layer. Spoon sauce carefully over them to coat completely. Sprinkle evenly with remaining 2 tablespoons cheese.

4. Bake until sauce begins to bubble, 7 to 10 minutes. If top is not brown, transfer dish to broiler and broil about 1 minute or just until cheese is lightly browned. Serve hot, from baking dish.

Fresh Corn with Cumin Butter

Makes 6 servings

Corn was not one of the crops of ancient Israel; it comes from the New World. However, since part of the message of Shavuot is to be thankful for the year's first grains, for modern celebrations, because fresh corn is also becoming plentiful at this time of year, it's a terrific food to include on holiday menus.

Instead of serving the corn with plain butter, I like to prepare a seasoned butter that includes the beloved Israeli spice, cumin, along with fresh parsley and a hint of lemon juice and cayenne pepper. If you prefer, substitute olive oil for the butter.

6 tablespoons (³/₄ stick) butter, softened

1 teaspoon ground cumin

2 teaspoons minced fresh Italian parsley

¹/₂ teaspoon strained fresh lemon juice

Pinch of cayenne pepper

Salt and freshly ground pepper, to taste

6 fresh ears of corn, shucked

1. In a small bowl, beat butter until smooth. Stir in cumin, parsley, lemon juice, cayenne pepper, salt, and black pepper. Let stand 1 hour or refrigerate in a covered container up to 1 day to blend flavors.

2. Just before serving, bring the seasoned butter to room temperature. Bring a large pot of water to a boil, add the corn, and cook it 5 to 10 minutes or until it's done to your taste. With tongs remove the corn, drain, and transfer to a platter or to plates.

3. Serve the corn hot with the seasoned butter.

Sugar Snap Peas and Carrots

Makes 4 servings D or P

This colorful, lively combination is a new take on the old-fashioned pair, peas and carrots. Sugar snap peas, a cross of snow peas with green peas, are a wonderful vegetable treat. They are fast-cooking and there's no need to shell them, as you eat the whole pods. The bright green pea pods with the vivid orange carrot sticks make a beautiful side dish. It is a terrific light partner for all those creamy, cheesy Shavuot specialties. To best appreciate the vegetables' freshness, be careful to cook them only until they are crisp-tender.

2 or 3 large carrots (8 to 12 ounces), cut into 2-inch matchsticks

8 to 12 ounces sugar snap peas, rinsed, ends removed

2 to 3 teaspoons butter or vegetable oil

Salt and freshly ground pepper, to taste

1. Put carrots in a medium saucepan with a pinch of salt and water to cover. Bring to a boil, cover, and simmer 3 minutes. Add sugar snap peas and boil uncovered over high heat 2 to 3 minutes or until peas are crisp-tender. Drain in a colander.

2. Heat butter or oil in the saucepan, add vegetables, and toss until combined. Add salt and pepper and toss until vegetables are coated. Serve hot.

Broccoli and Red Pepper Sauté

Makes 3 or 4 servings (P)

This quick, colorful vegetable medley is flavored with a popular Sephardic combination—garlic and Italian parsley. The broccoli is briefly cooked in water so it retains its bright color before being sautéed with the peppers and flavorings. It's a great partner for a savory Shavuot kugel such as My Mother's Milchig Mushroom Noodle Kugel (page 51).

1 pound broccoli, peeled and thick stems removed

1 or 2 tablespoons olive oil

2 red bell peppers, cut into strips

2 large cloves garlic, chopped

2 tablespoons chopped fresh Italian parsley

2 tablespoons water

Salt and freshly ground pepper, to taste

1. Divide broccoli into medium florets. Add broccoli to a sauté pan of boiling salted water and boil uncovered 3 minutes to partially cook. Drain in a colander or strainer, rinse under cold water, and drain well again.

2. Heat oil in the same pan. Add peppers and sauté over medium heat for 3 minutes. Cover and cook over low heat, stirring often, about 5 minutes or until nearly tender. Add garlic and parsley and sauté, stirring, about 15 seconds. Add broccoli and 2 tablespoons water. Sprinkle vegetables with salt and pepper. Cover and cook over medium-low heat, stirring often, about 2 minutes or until broccoli is crisp-tender. Serve hot.

❧ Grains

Bulgur Wheat with Asparagus and Tarragon

Makes 4 servings (P) or (D)

Besides the main theme of receiving the Torah, Shavuot is also a holiday of thanks. The ancient Israelites expressed their appreciation for the bounty of their early-season crop of grains. This festive recipe makes use of bulgur wheat, an ancient Middle Eastern grain that's still a favorite.

2 tablespoons vegetable oil, olive oil, or butter

1 medium onion, chopped

2 cloves garlic, minced

3/4 cup medium bulgur wheat

1 1/2 cups vegetable stock or water

Salt and freshly ground pepper, to taste

1 pound asparagus, ends removed, spears cut into
      3 pieces

2 to 3 teaspoons chopped fresh tarragon

2 tablespoons chopped fresh Italian parsley

1. Heat oil in medium, heavy saucepan over medium heat. Add onion and cook, stirring often, about 5 minutes or until softened. Add garlic and cook 1 minute. Add bulgur and sauté, stirring, 2 minutes. Add stock, salt, and pepper and bring to boil. Reduce heat to low, cover, and cook about 15 minutes or until water is absorbed. Adjust seasoning.

2. Add asparagus pieces to a saucepan of boiling water and simmer uncovered 3 minutes or until asparagus is just tender.

3. Fluff bulgur wheat with a fork and lightly stir in tarragon and parsley. Set aside a few asparagus tips for garnish. Gently stir remaining asparagus into bulgur wheat. Taste and adjust seasoning. Serve topped with remaining asparagus tips.

Saffron Rice Pilaf with Artichokes and Almonds

Makes 4 to 6 servings

Although many of us like to think of Shavuot as the holiday of dairy delights, nobody claims that the ancient Hebrews ate cheesecake or blintzes in the desert! We are told simply that they did not eat meat the day before receiving the Torah. Since Shavuot commemorates this event, another way to celebrate is to serve a vegetarian meal. Try this tasty entree, for example, of a colorful rice pilaf with Mediterranean flavors. Of course, if you like, for a dairy dish you can serve some feta cheese or grated kashkaval or Swiss cheese on the side.

4 medium cooked artichoke hearts or Artichoke Bottoms and Stems (page 589)

5 parsley stems (without leaves)

1 sprig fresh thyme or 1/4 teaspoon dried thyme

1 bay leaf

2 cups boiling water

1/4 teaspoon crushed saffron threads (2 pinches)

3 tablespoons olive oil

1/2 cup minced onion

1 cup long grain white rice

Salt and freshly ground pepper, to taste

2 ripe medium tomatoes, peeled, seeded, and cut into small dice

1/4 cup slivered almonds

2 small zucchini, cut into thin strips 1 1/2 inches long

2 tablespoons chopped fresh parsley

1. Cook artichoke hearts. Cut each into 1/2-inch dice and drain on paper towels.

2. Preheat oven to 350°F. To make bouquet garni, wrap parsley stems, thyme, and bay leaf in cheesecloth and tie the ends to form a seasoning bag. Set aside. Combine boiling water and saffron in small saucepan. Cover and keep warm over low heat.

3. Heat 1 1/2 tablespoons oil in an ovenproof sauté pan or deep skillet over low heat. Add onion, and cook, stirring, about 7 minutes or until soft but not brown. Raise heat to medium, add rice, and sauté, stirring, about 4 minutes or until grains begin to turn milky white.

4. Bring saffron water to boil over high heat. Pour over rice and stir once. Add bouquet garni and submerge it in liquid. Add 1/4 teaspoon salt and pinch of pepper. Raise heat to high and bring mixture to boil. Cover with tight lid. Place in oven and bake without stirring 18 minutes.

5. Meanwhile, put tomatoes in strainer and leave to drain.

6. Toast almonds in small baking dish in oven alongside pilaf about 4 minutes or until they are light brown. Transfer them to a plate.

7. Taste rice; if it is too chewy or if liquid is not absorbed, bake 2 minutes more. Discard cheesecloth bag.

8. Heat 1 1/2 tablespoons olive oil in a skillet. Add zucchini, salt, and pepper. Sauté over medium heat about 1 1/2 minutes, or until barely tender.

9. When rice is cooked, scatter diced artichokes and tomatoes on top. Cover and let stand 5 to 10 minutes. With a fork, fluff rice and gently stir in tomatoes and artichokes. Add zucchini with its oil and minced parsley. Stir gently. Taste and adjust seasoning. Serve sprinkled with almonds.

Pesto Brown Rice with Summer Squash

Makes 4 servings

Easy, festive, and with just a touch of cheese, home-made pesto made with fresh basil is an ideal Shavuot seasoning. Use its sprightly flavor to enhance pasta in the traditional way, or try it in this healthful dish with brown rice and vegetables. Serving brown rice and early summer vegetables like squashes or sugar snap peas also helps commemorate Shavuot's theme of celebrating the grain and produce harvest.

To make this dish very easy to prepare, use quick-cooking brown rice, which is ready in 10 minutes.

2 teaspoons olive oil

8 ounces yellow summer squash or zucchini, cut into
    $^1/_2$-inch dice

2 cups quick-cooking brown rice

1$^3/_4$ cups water

1 pound ripe tomatoes, diced, or one 14$^1/_2$-ounce can diced
    tomatoes, drained

Classic Pesto (this page)

Salt and freshly ground pepper, to taste

1. Heat oil in a medium saucepan. Add squash and sauté over medium heat 2 minutes. Add rice and water and stir once. Bring to boil over high heat. Reduce heat to low, cover tightly, and simmer, without stirring, 5 minutes.

2. Lightly stir in tomatoes and heat to simmer. Cover, remove from heat and let stand 5 minutes. Fluff rice gently with a fork, then with the fork, stir in 2 table-spoons pesto. Season with salt and pepper. Spoon remaining pesto over rice in small dollops, or serve it separately.

Classic Pesto

Makes $^1/_2$ to $^2/_3$ cup

Pesto is great for celebrating the holiday of Shavuot with a touch of dairy because the holiday falls just when fresh basil is becoming plentiful at the market. You can keep pesto 2 days in a covered container in

the refrigerator. Although traditional Italian pesto requires crushing ingredients in a mortar with a pestle, the food processor eases the job considerably.

2 large cloves garlic, peeled

2 tablespoons pine nuts

1 cup packed fresh basil leaves (1 bunch of about 1 ounce)

$^1/_2$ cup freshly grated Parmesan cheese (about 1$^1/_2$ ounces)

$^1/_3$ cup extra-virgin olive oil

With blade of food processor turning, drop garlic cloves one by one through feed tube and process until finely chopped. Add pine nuts, basil, and cheese and process until basil is chopped. With blade turning, gradually add olive oil through feed tube. Scrape down sides and process until mixture is well blended. Transfer to a small bowl. Either use immediately or refrigerate for 2 days. Serve at room temperature.

Couscous with Milk and Honey

Makes 4 servings

In some homes it is a custom to serve honey, or cakes made with honey, along with dairy-based breakfast dishes on the first day of Shavuot. In the Song of Songs the Torah is compared to milk and honey, and Shavuot is a celebration of the receiving of the Torah.

2 cups water

1 to 2 tablespoons honey

4 to 6 tablespoons butter, room temperature, cut into pieces

One 10-ounce package couscous

$^1/_2$ cup raisins

2 cups hot milk

1. Bring water, honey, and 1 tablespoon butter to a boil in a medium saucepan. Stir in couscous and raisins and return to a boil. Remove from heat, cover, and let stand 5 minutes. Add remaining butter and mix lightly with a fork.

2. Serve couscous in bowls. Serve hot milk separately in a pitcher.

❧ Noodle Kugels

My Mother's Milchig Mushroom Noodle Kugel

Makes 4 to 6 serving　Ⓓ

In our family this is a favorite of three generations—my mother, her children, and her grandchildren. It's a simple dish, made of noodles and sautéed mushrooms and onions, and enriched with cottage cheese, sour cream, and eggs.

When my mother and I make this kugel together, she always emphasizes that the secret to its good taste is to brown the onions and mushrooms well. To do this, use a frying pan that is large enough so the vegetables are not piled too high and crushing each other, as that makes them watery. Another tip: be sure to use fresh mushrooms, as old ones tend to give off a lot of liquid.

4 to 5 tablespoons butter or vegetable oil

1 large onion, chopped

12 ounces mushrooms, stemmed, halved, and cut into thick slices

Salt and freshly ground pepper, to taste

1 teaspoon paprika, plus a little for sprinkling

7 to 8 ounces medium egg noodles

1 cup cottage cheese

$^1/_2$ to $^3/_4$ cup sour cream

2 large eggs, beaten

1. Preheat oven to 350°F. Heat 3 or 4 tablespoons butter or oil in a large skillet over medium-low heat. Add onion and sauté 10 minutes or until very tender. Add mushrooms, salt, pepper, and 1 teaspoon paprika and sauté 10 minutes or until mushrooms are tender and onions are browned. If liquid remains in pan, cook over high heat, stirring, 2 minutes until it evaporates.

2. Cook noodles uncovered in a large pot of boiling salted water over high heat 4 minutes or until nearly tender but firmer than usual. Drain, rinse with cold water, and drain well again. Transfer to a large bowl.

3. Add mushroom mixture to bowl of noodles and mix well. Add cottage cheese and sour cream; mix well. Adjust seasoning; mixture should be seasoned generously. Stir in eggs.

4. Grease a 2-quart baking dish and add noodle mixture. Sprinkle with remaining tablespoon oil or dot with remaining butter. Sprinkle lightly with paprika. Bake uncovered 50 minutes or until set. Serve from baking dish.

Macaroni and Cheese Kugel

Makes 6 servings　Ⓓ

Macaroni and cheese has a lot in common with kugel. When I was growing up, both were my favorite dishes. My mother always made them from scratch. Here I have combined them for a savory Shavuot kugel. It's much easier to make than macaroni and cheese because there's no need to make a separate sauce. I like to cook broccoli florets at the last minute as an accompaniment.

3 tablespoons butter

1 large onion, minced

3 cups small elbow macaroni

1 cup cottage cheese

$^1/_2$ cup sour cream

$^1/_4$ teaspoon Tabasco or other hot sauce

Salt and freshly ground pepper, to taste

Freshly grated nutmeg to taste

1 to 1$^1/_4$ cups grated Swiss or other firm grating cheese

4 large eggs, beaten

1. Preheat oven to 400°F. Melt butter in a large skillet over medium-low heat. Add onion and sauté 7 minutes or until tender.

2. Cook macaroni uncovered in a large pot of boiling salted water over high heat, stirring occasionally, 5 minutes or until nearly tender but firmer than usual. Drain, rinse with cold water, and drain well again. Transfer to a large bowl. Gently stir in onions.

3. Mix cottage cheese with sour cream, Tabasco, salt, pepper, and nutmeg in a medium bowl. Add mixture to macaroni and mix gently. Add all but $^1/_4$ cup of the grated cheese and mix gently. Adjust seasoning; mixture should be generously seasoned. Fold in eggs.

4. Grease a 2-quart baking dish and add noodle mixture. Sprinkle with remaining ¼ cup grated cheese. Bake about 35 minutes or until set. Let stand 5 minutes before serving. Serve from the baking dish.

Healthful Spinach, Cottage Cheese, and Noodle Kugel

Makes 4 servings

This noodle kugel is reduced in fat but is creamy and delicious. If you would like to reduce the fat further, use egg substitute instead of the eggs. Serve each portion topped with nonfat yogurt or sour cream.

One 10-ounce bag rinsed spinach leaves, stemmed

7 or 8 ounces medium egg noodles

2 tablespoons vegetable oil

1 large onion, chopped

Salt and freshly ground pepper, to taste

1 cup nonfat sour cream

¾ cup nonfat cottage cheese

Freshly grated nutmeg, to taste

Cayenne pepper, to taste

2 large eggs, beaten

1. Preheat oven to 350°F. Cook spinach in a medium saucepan of boiling water about 2 minutes or until just wilted. Drain, rinse with cold water, and drain well again. Chop coarsely.

2. Cook noodles in a large saucepan of boiling salted water over high heat 4 minutes or until nearly tender but firmer than usual. Drain, rinse with cold water, and drain well again. Transfer to a large bowl.

3. In a skillet, heat 1 tablespoon plus 2 teaspoons oil. Add onion and sauté over medium heat, stirring, 5 minutes or until onions begin to turn golden. Remove from heat. Add spinach, sprinkle with salt and pepper, and mix well.

4. Add sour cream and cottage cheese to noodles and mix well. Add spinach mixture and mix again. Season to taste with nutmeg, salt, pepper, and cayenne. Stir in eggs.

5. Lightly grease a 2-quart baking dish with oil spray and add noodle mixture. Sprinkle with remaining teaspoon oil. Bake uncovered 40 minutes or until set. Serve from the baking dish.

Apple-Cinnamon Noodle Kugel with Sour Cream

Makes 8 servings

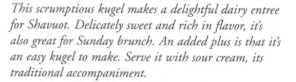

This scrumptious kugel makes a delightful dairy entree for Shavuot. Delicately sweet and rich in flavor, it's also great for Sunday brunch. An added plus is that it's an easy kugel to make. Serve it with sour cream, its traditional accompaniment.

14 ounces medium egg noodles

¼ cup (½ stick) butter, melted

Pinch of salt

1 cup sour cream

4 large eggs

6 tablespoons sugar

1 teaspoon vanilla extract

3 Golden Delicious apples (about 1½ pounds), halved, cored, and thinly sliced

1½ teaspoons ground cinnamon

1. Preheat oven to 350°F. Grease a 13 × 9 × 2-inch baking dish. Cook noodles in a large pot of boiling salted water until barely tender, about 5 minutes. Drain, rinse with cold water, and drain well again.

2. Transfer noodles to a large bowl. Separate noodles with your fingers. Add 3 tablespoons melted butter and a pinch of salt and mix well. Stir in sour cream, eggs, 2 tablespoons sugar, and vanilla. Mix half the apples with the noodle mixture.

3. In a small bowl, mix remaining sugar with 1 teaspoon cinnamon. Add half of noodle mixture to baking dish. Top with remaining apples in an even layer and sprinkle them with the cinnamon mixture. Top with remaining noodle mixture and spread gently to cover apples. Sprinkle with ½ teaspoon cinnamon, then with remaining melted butter. Cover dish and bake 30 minutes. Uncover and bake 15 to 20 minutes or until set. Serve hot or warm.

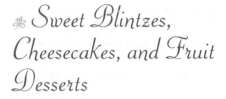

Sweet Blintzes, Cheesecakes, and Fruit Desserts

Creamy Raspberry Blintzes

Makes 4 to 6 servings Ⓓ

Prepare these elegant blintzes when you can get fresh raspberries. Additional fresh raspberries make a pretty garnish. For an even more impressive presentation and great flavor, serve the hot blintzes with a cool Raspberry Sauce (page 580). I prefer these as dessert blintzes but you can serve them as a brunch dish.

To save time, you can prepare blintzes bletels ("crepes" in Yiddish) ahead and keep them in your freezer. In some markets you can purchase them ready-made, and then all you need to do is add the easy-to-make filling.

12 to 15 Basic Blintzes (page 300), about 8 inches
    in diameter

2 cups farmer cheese (about 15 ounces)

$^1/_4$ cup cottage cheese

1 large egg

$^1/_3$ cup sugar, or to taste

$^1/_2$ teaspoon vanilla extract

1 cup fresh raspberries, plus more for garnish

2 tablespoons butter, melted

1. Prepare blintzes, stack them and cover them with a kitchen towel. Preheat oven to 400°F.

2. To make filling: Mash farmer cheese in a medium bowl with a fork until fairly smooth. Stir in cottage cheese, egg, sugar, and vanilla. Beat with spoon until well blended. Lightly stir in raspberries.

3. Spoon $2^1/_2$ tablespoons filling onto brown side of each blintz near one edge. Fold over edges of blintz to right and left of filling so that each covers about half of filling. Roll up blintz, beginning at edge with filling.

4. Arrange blintzes in one layer in a shallow, lightly buttered baking dish. Lightly brush blintzes with melted butter. Bake for about 20 minutes, or until heated through and lightly browned.

5. Serve blintzes garnished with fresh raspberries.

Cheese Cannelloni Blintzes with Blueberry Sauce

Makes 4 to 6 servings Ⓓ

There is no need to make crepes for these blintzes; the sweet, lemon-scented cheese filling is wrapped in cannelloni. The cheeses needed—cottage cheese, ricotta, and cream cheese—are easy to find in any supermarket. Use cream cheese in block form, not in a tub. You can fill the cannelloni a day ahead and keep them in the covered baking dish in the refrigerator.

Blueberry Sauce (page 580)

8 ounces cream cheese, softened

$^1/_2$ cup ricotta cheese

$^1/_4$ cup cottage cheese, drained in a strainer

2 large egg yolks

3 tablespoons sugar

$^1/_2$ teaspoon vanilla extract

1 teaspoon grated lemon rind

$^1/_2$ teaspoon strained fresh lemon juice

12 dried cannelloni tubes

4 to 6 tablespoons ($^1/_2$ to $^3/_4$ stick) butter, melted

2 tablespoons powdered sugar

Sour cream or plain yogurt, for serving

Fresh blueberries for garnish

1. Prepare blueberry sauce and refrigerate. Butter a 13 × 9 × 2-inch baking dish. For filling: Mash cream cheese in a medium bowl with a fork until smooth. Beat in ricotta, cottage cheese, egg yolks, and sugar. Stir in vanilla and grated lemon rind and juice. Refrigerate 15 minutes.

2. Cook cannelloni uncovered in a large pot of boiling salted water over high heat, stirring occasionally, about 6 minutes or until just tender but firm to the bite. Drain well. Transfer to a large bowl of cold water.

3. Preheat oven to 400°F. Remove 1 cannelloni from water and put it on a work surface. Slit it lengthwise with a knife, open it flat, and pat it dry. Put 3 tablespoons filling along 1 long side. Roll up in cigar shape and put in baking dish. Fill remaining cannelloni, placing them in one layer, side by side in the dish.

4. Brush cannelloni with butter. Cover dish with foil. Bake about 20 minutes or until heated through. Baste cannelloni with butter from their dish. Sprinkle with powdered sugar, return to oven and bake 3 minutes.

5. With a slotted spatula, remove cannelloni from dish, leaving excess butter behind. Serve hot, topped with sour cream and blueberries. Serve cold blueberry sauce separately.

Pecan Streusel Cheesecake

Makes 10 servings

This scrumptious cheesecake has a creamy lemon-scented filling, a wonderful pecan crumble topping, and a rich pastry base.

Sweet Pastry Base and Streusel (this page)
1 pound cottage cheese
1 pound cream cheese, softened
³/₄ cup sugar
2 large eggs
2 large egg yolks
¹/₂ cup whipping cream
1 teaspoon vanilla extract
1 tablespoon grated lemon rind
¹/₃ cup diced pecans

1. Prepare Sweet Pastry Base and Streusel.

2. Preheat oven to 350°F. Push cottage cheese through a strainer. In a large bowl with an electric mixer, beat cream cheese with sugar until smooth. Beat in eggs one by one, then beat in yolks. Stir in cottage cheese, cream, vanilla, and grated lemon rind.

3. Pour filling into prepared pastry in springform pan. Crumble reserved streusel mixture between your fingers and sprinkle on top of filling. Sprinkle pecans over crumbs. Pat gently so topping adheres to filling.

4. Set springform pan on a baking sheet. Bake about 1 hour and 15 minutes or until set. If topping is not brown, broil about 30 seconds, checking very often, until golden brown. Cool completely on a rack. Refrigerate at least 2 hours before serving. Serve cold.

Sweet Pastry Base and Streusel

Makes a base for a 9-inch cheesecake

This two-in-one recipe creates both a rich, sweet pastry and a delectable buttery crumble topping called streusel. Both are made from a pastry dough resembling French pâte sucrée, *a sweet, buttery pie dough used for fruit tarts, that can be easily made in the food processor. Use it for cheesecakes or, if you use pie pans instead of a springform pan, for fruit pies.*

2¹/₂ cups all-purpose flour
¹/₂ cup sugar
Pinch of salt
1 cup (2 sticks) cold butter or margarine, cut into small pieces
1 large egg, beaten
2 teaspoons grated lemon rind

1. To prepare streusel: Lightly butter a 9-inch springform pan. Combine flour, sugar, and salt in a food processor and process briefly to blend. Scatter butter pieces over mixture. Process with brief pulses until mixture resembles coarse meal. Pour egg evenly over mixture. Sprinkle with grated rind. Process with brief pulses, scraping down the sides occasionally, until dough forms sticky crumbs; do not allow dough to come together in a ball.

2. To prepare pastry base: Sprinkle 3 cups of crumbs evenly in pan. Put rest of crumbs in a bowl in freezer. With floured hands press crumbs together and pat them 2 inches up sides of pan. Chill pastry base in freezer while preparing filling.

My Favorite Cheesecake

Makes 8 to 10 servings

This is the version of the popular American-style cream cheese cake with a sour cream topping that I love best. Mine is creamier and less solid than most because I stir some sour cream into the filling instead of using all cream cheese.

Almond-Graham Cracker Crust (this page)

1 pound cream cheese, cut into pieces and softened

2 cups sour cream

³/₄ cup plus 3 tablespoons sugar

3 large eggs

2 teaspoons grated lemon rind

2 teaspoons vanilla extract

1. Prepare crust.

2. Preheat oven to 350°F. Bake crust 10 minutes, then let cool completely. Leave oven at 350°F.

3. Beat cream cheese with ¹/₂ cup sour cream in a large bowl with an electric mixer at low speed until very smooth. Gradually beat in ³/₄ cup sugar. Beat in eggs, one by one. Stir in lemon rind and 1 teaspoon vanilla. Carefully pour filling into cooled crust. Bake about 45 minutes or until center is just firm. Remove from oven and cool on a rack for 15 minutes. Raise oven temperature to 425°F.

4. To make topping: Mix together remaining 1¹/₂ cups sour cream, 3 tablespoons sugar, and 1 teaspoon vanilla in a medium bowl with a spoon. Carefully spread topping on cake, in an even layer, without letting it drip over crust. Bake cake 7 minutes to set topping. Remove from oven and cool on a rack to room temperature. Refrigerate at least 2 hours. Remove sides of pan just before serving.

Almond–Graham Cracker Crust

Makes enough for one 9-inch cheesecake, about 8 to 10 servings

When I make cheesecake using a simple cracker crust, I often add chopped nuts to the crust for extra interest. I especially like the delicate taste of blanched almonds with the rich creamy fillings. Macadamia nuts and pecans are also good. Often I chop some extra nuts of the same kind I use in the crust for sprinkling on top of the finished cake just before I serve it.

My mother, who lives in Jerusalem and doesn't usually have graham crackers, makes this crust from simple plain cookies and omits the sugar. I love that version too!

¹/₄ cup slivered almonds

3 tablespoons sugar

5 ounces graham crackers (for 1¹/₄ cups crumbs)

¹/₃ cup butter, melted

1. Lightly butter a 9-inch springform pan and set aside.

2. Finely grind almonds with sugar in a food processor. Transfer to a medium bowl. Process graham crackers in food processor to fine crumbs. Measure 1¹/₄ cups, add to almond crumbs, and mix well. Add melted butter and mix well.

3. Press mixture in an even layer on bottom and about 1 inch up sides of prepared pan.

My Mother's Low-Fat Cheesecake

Makes 8 to 10 servings Ⓓ

I have tasted many low-fat cheesecakes and this one remains my favorite. My mother and I often prepare it for Shavuot as an alternative to a rich one, and this is the one many of our guests prefer. We are always amazed at how delicious it turns out, even though we use ingredients such as nonfat ricotta cheese and nonfat sour cream, that frankly we are not fond of on their own.

If you would like to cut the fat and calories even further, omit the sugar and oil from the crust; simply sprinkle the graham cracker crumbs on the base of the pan and over the top of the cake instead of making a crust.

Crumb Crust

5 ounces graham crackers, preferably low-fat
    (for 1¹/₄ cups crumbs)

1¹/₂ tablespoons sugar

3¹/₂ tablespoons vegetable oil

Cheese Filling

One 15-ounce container nonfat ricotta cheese (1³/₄ cups)

³/₄ cup nonfat sour cream

³/₄ cup sugar

2 large eggs, separated

2 tablespoons all-purpose flour

2 teaspoons grated orange rind

1 teaspoon vanilla extract

Yogurt Topping

¹/₂ cup plain nonfat yogurt

1 cup nonfat sour cream

3 tablespoons sugar

1 teaspoon vanilla extract

1. To prepare crust: Preheat oven to 350°F. Lightly grease a 9-inch springform pan

2. Grind crackers in a food processor to fine crumbs. Measure 1¹/₄ cups and mix crumbs with sugar in a large bowl. Add oil and mix well. Press crumb mixture in an even layer on bottom and about 1 inch up sides of prepared pan. Bake 8 minutes. Let cool completely on a rack. Leave oven at 350°F.

3. To prepare cheese filling: Beat ricotta with sour cream in a large bowl with an electric beater at low speed until very smooth. Gradually beat in sugar. Beat in egg yolks, flour, orange rind, and vanilla. Whip egg whites in a medium bowl with an electric beater until stiff. Fold them into cheese mixture. Carefully pour filling into cooled crust. Bake about 50 minutes or until top center is just firm but still shakes when you gently move the pan, and top begins to crack. Remove from oven and cool 15 minutes on a rack. Raise oven temperature to 425°F.

4. To make topping: Pour off any watery liquid from top of yogurt. Mix yogurt with sour cream, sugar, and vanilla. Spoon topping evenly over cake. Carefully spread topping in an even layer on cheesecake, without letting it drip over edge of crust. Bake cake 7 minutes or until edge of topping sets. Remove from oven and cool to room temperature. Cover and refrigerate at least 2 hours.

5. Just before serving, carefully run a metal spatula around cake and remove side of pan. When serving, free each slice from underneath to remove crust from pan. For neat slices, rinse knife after each cut.

White Chocolate Cheesecake with Raspberry Sauce

Makes 12 servings D

When it comes to chocolate cheesecake, white chocolate gets my vote. Its delicate taste goes well with cream cheese and makes the cake even more rich and creamy. Brilliant red, fresh raspberry sauce is the ideal accompaniment. If you like, garnish the cake with fresh raspberries as well.

Cocoa Crumb Crust

5 ounces graham crackers (for 1¼ cups crumbs)

3 tablespoons sugar

2 tablespoons unsweetened cocoa powder

5 tablespoons butter, melted

White Chocolate-Cheese Filling

6 ounces fine-quality white chocolate, finely chopped

¾ cup whipping cream

1 pound cream cheese, at room temperature, cut into pieces

¾ cup plus 2 tablespoons sugar

4 large eggs

2 teaspoons grated lemon rind

1 teaspoon vanilla extract

Topping and Garnish

1½ cups sour cream

3 tablespoons sugar

1 teaspoon vanilla extract

About ⅛ ounce semisweet chocolate (optional)

Raspberry Sauce (page 580)

1. To prepare crust: Preheat oven to 350°F. Lightly grease a round 9 × 3-inch springform pan and set aside.

2. Grind crackers in a food processor to a fine powder. Measure 1¼ cups and mix crumbs with sugar in a large bowl. Sift in cocoa; stir until blended. Add melted butter; mix well with a fork. Using a spoon, press mixture in an even layer on base and 1¼ inches up side of pan. Bake 10 minutes, then cool completely on a rack. Leave oven at 350°F.

3. To prepare filling: Melt chocolate and ½ cup whipping cream in a medium bowl over nearly simmering water, stirring often. Remove from water and let cool. If necessary, whisk until smooth. Beat cream cheese with remaining ¼ cup cream in a large bowl with an electric mixer at low speed until perfectly smooth. Gradually beat in sugar. Add eggs, one at a time and beat until perfectly smooth. Stir in cooled chocolate, lemon rind, and vanilla until well blended.

4. Carefully pour filling into crust. Bake 1 hour 5 minutes or until top center is just firm but still shakes when you gently move the pan, and top begins to crack. Remove from oven; cool 15 minutes on a rack. Increase oven temperature to 425°F.

5. To prepare topping: Mix sour cream, sugar, and vanilla in a medium bowl. Carefully spread topping in an even layer on cheesecake without letting it drip over crust. Bake cake 7 minutes or until edge of topping sets. Remove from oven and cool completely on a rack. Grate semisweet chocolate, if using, over cake. Cover and refrigerate at least 1 day.

6. Just before serving, carefully run a metal spatula around cake and remove side of pan. When serving, free each slice from underneath to remove crust from pan. For neat slices, rinse knife after each cut. Spoon a little raspberry sauce around base of each slice.

Quick Couscous Pudding with Strawberries

Makes 4 servings   **D**

Creamy like rice pudding, this dessert is ideal for Shavuot. It's bursting with fresh strawberries, which are at their peak during this holiday. Best of all, this luscious treat is very fast and simple to prepare and requires almost no cooking.

1¼ cups strawberries, halved and sliced

3 tablespoons sugar

1 cup milk

½ cup couscous

½ teaspoon grated lemon rind

¾ cup whipping cream, well chilled

½ teaspoon vanilla

Small whole or halved strawberries (for garnish)

1. Put strawberries in a medium bowl and sprinkle with 1 tablespoon sugar. Toss gently and refrigerate. Chill a bowl for whipping cream.

2. Bring milk and 1 tablespoon sugar to a simmer in a small saucepan, stirring until sugar is dissolved. Stir in couscous, cover pan, and remove from heat. Let stand 15 minutes or until milk is absorbed. Transfer couscous to a large bowl and stir with a fork to separate grains. Let cool to room temperature, then stir in lemon rind.

3. Whip cream in chilled bowl until it holds soft peaks. Add remaining sugar and vanilla and whip cream until just stiff. Gently fold whipped cream into couscous, followed by sliced strawberries and their liquid. Spoon mixture into 4 custard cups, small ramekins, or other dessert dishes. Cover and refrigerate at least 2 hours or overnight. Serve cold, garnished with strawberries.

Light Strawberry Parfait

Makes 4 servings   **D**

This easy dessert makes a delightful and healthful Shavuot treat. You simply puree strawberries to make a fresh sauce, then mix it with sliced berries and spoon it into glasses, alternating it with spoonfuls of vanilla yogurt. If you like, you can use other flavors of yogurt, like lemon, lime, or strawberry. You can even use softened frozen vanilla yogurt, to turn this into an ice cream parfait.

1 cup Strawberry Sauce (page 580)

¾ cup sliced ripe strawberries

1 pint vanilla yogurt, nonfat or low-fat

4 small ripe strawberries, cut into fan shape

1. Prepare strawberry sauce.

2. Chill 4 parfait glasses, wine glasses, or other glasses of about 1 cup volume.

3. Mix ¾ cup strawberry sauce with sliced berries. Spoon 3 tablespoons strawberry mixture into each glass. Top each with ¼ cup vanilla yogurt. Spread to an even layer to edges of glass. Chill about 10 minutes in freezer.

4. Divide remaining strawberry mixture among glasses, using about 3 tablespoons for each. Top with remaining yogurt, using about ¼ cup for each. Chill in freezer 5 minutes. Spoon remaining ¼ cup strawberry sauce on top. Garnish each with a strawberry and serve.

Salad of First Fruits

Makes 4 to 6 servings

Shavuot is known as the Festival of the First Fruits, because of the harvest of early fruits in ancient Israel. I like to prepare a salad of the first fruits in our markets. My husband and I have young peach, apricot, and nectarine trees and raspberry vines in our back yard. We look forward to when they will bear fruit so we can celebrate the holiday with our own first fruits.

This salad is terrific on its own or as a fresh, colorful accompaniment for cheesecake.

3 peaches or nectarines, sliced into wedges

3 apricots (optional), sliced into wedges

1 pint strawberries, quartered lengthwise

1 cup blackberries

1 cup raspberries

2 to 3 tablespoons sugar

2 tablespoons clear raspberry brandy or 1 tablespoon
strained fresh lemon juice

1. Put peach slices and apricot slices, if using, in a bowl. Add strawberries, blackberries, and raspberries.

2. Sprinkle fruit with sugar and brandy. With a rubber spatula, mix ingredients as gently as possible. Serve immediately, or cover and refrigerate for 30 minutes.

Peaches and Melon with Spirited Syrup

Makes 4 servings

Serve this refreshing, nonfat dessert as an accompaniment for Shavuot cheese blintzes, with frozen yogurt, or as a healthful sweet on its own.

1 tablespoon apple or orange juice

1 tablespoon peach or cherry liqueur or kirsch

1 tablespoon sugar or honey (optional)

2 large ripe peaches or nectarines, sliced into wedges

2 cups cantaloupe or honeydew melon balls or dice,
or 1 cup of each

Mix juice, liqueur, and sugar, if using, in a small cup. In a large bowl, gently mix the peaches with the cantaloupe. Pour syrup over the fruit and mix gently again. Refrigerate 30 minutes or longer. Serve cold.

Rosh Hashanah and Yom Kippur

Rosh Hashanah
62

Salads, Appetizers, and Soups

Corn, Sweet Pepper, and Green Bean Salad

Carrot Salad with Cranberries and Mint

Beet Salad with Apples and Orange Juice

Tomato Dressing

Quinces in Cinnamon Syrup

Whitefish Gefilte Fish

Sea Bass in Saffron-Tomato Sauce

Hungarian Halibut

Wine-Poached Trout with Tarragon Sauce

Chicken Soup with Sweet Vegetables and Matzo Balls

Old-Fashioned Chicken Soup with Kreplach

Meat Tzimmes and Other Main Courses

Traditional Meat Tzimmes

Rosh Hashanah Couscous with Meat and Vegetables

Veal Tzimmes with Apricots and Prunes

Turkey Tzimmes with Sweet Potatoes

Adi's Kibbutz Honey Chicken

Side Dishes

Sweet Carrot Coins

Quick-Braised Butternut Squash with Ginger and Onion

Leek Compote

Zucchini in Israeli Tomato Sauce

Rosh Hashanah Sweet Potato Casserole

Sephardic Spinach Cakes

Black-Eyed Peas with Browned Onions and Tomatoes

Carrots and Potatoes with Chard

Traditional Steamed Couscous

Rice Pilaf with Golden Raisins and Pistachios

P = *Pareve*   D = *Dairy*   M = *Meat*

Yom Kippur
84

Honey Cakes and Other Desserts

Cocoa-Orange Honey Cake

Light Honey Cake with Candied Ginger

Sephardic Almond Honey Squares

Apple Cake with Honey

Chocolate Chip Honey Cake

Cocoa Applesauce Cake with Honey Frosting

Honey Buttercream

Honey Ganache

Fresh Plum Sauce

Red Wine and Pear Sauce

Hazelnut Walnut Tayglach

Rosh Hashanah Fruit Salad

Rashi's Figs

Before the Fast

Roman Fish with Pine Nuts and Raisins

Whole Poached Chicken with Vegetables

Chicken with Forty Cloves of Garlic

Noodle Kugel with Carrots and Apples

Chocolate Chip Mandelbrot

After the Fast

Moroccan Lentil, Chickpea, and Meat Soup (Harira)

Smoked Whitefish Spread

Creamy Cucumber Salad with Lox

Old-Fashioned Coffeecake

Rosh Hashanah— The Jewish New Year

Rosh Hashanah is celebrated for two days in September or October. It occurs on the first days of Tishrei, the first month of the Jewish calendar. This date not only inspires a theme of hope for a great year, but because it also coincides with the beginning of the agricultural year in ancient Israel, Rosh Hashanah is a celebration of the season's bounty, with wishes for a plentiful harvest.

In the holiday meal, these two themes are seen in the emphasis on sweet foods (for a sweet year) and in the important role vegetables and fruits play.

Jews throughout the world begin the Rosh Hashanah dinner with a tasting of apple wedges that are dipped in honey. In some Moroccan, Greek, and Turkish homes, sweet cinnamon-scented quinces also begin the meal.

Preference is given to sweet vegetables. Sweet potatoes, winter squashes, and beets are popular. Perhaps the best loved of all are carrots; not only are they sweet, but when sliced in rounds, they resemble coins—symbols of prosperity.

For modern cooks, plenty of other naturally sweet vegetables can be applied to this Rosh Hashanah theme. Sweet corn and red and yellow bell peppers are just two examples. They don't appear in old holiday recipes from Europe or the Mediterranean because these vegetables originated in the New World.

Even onions and leeks are appropriate for holiday dishes because, although they are sharp when raw, they become mellow and sweet when cooked slowly in oil because their natural sugars caramelize. The same thing happens to cooked parsnips and turnips.

Fruit is also essential on the Rosh Hashanah table. During the celebration, a special blessing is said over a new fruit that is tasted for the first time in the year, often a pomegranate, date, or fig, because these are fruits of ancient Israel.

Another sweet food that is tasted at the beginning of the meal is challah, the traditional Jewish holiday bread, which many people dip in honey. Bakeries as well as home bakers prepare a different kind of challah for Rosh Hashanah; instead of the common braid, it has a round or dome shape and often is sweetened with raisins.

On most tables a fish course appears as an appetizer, to represent abundance and fertility. A fish served with its head intact is another symbolic food: "Rosh" in Rosh Hashanah means "head" and the fish head represents a favorite Hebrew expression that "we would rather be a head than a tail." After the fish, most families enjoy a chicken or meat entree.

With honey such an important holiday ingredient, it's not surprising that it is used to sweeten Rosh Hashanah desserts. Honey cake, originally a Rosh Hashanah favorite among Ashkenazic Jews, now appears on most tables. Sampling a slice of honey cake is a much-loved way to express the traditional holiday greeting, "Have a Good and Sweet New Year."

In addition to food customs shared by most Jews, different communities have special foods and flavors they cherish. Although the custom of beginning the Rosh Hashanah feast with apples and honey seems to be just about universal, cooking sweet dishes for the rest of the menu is emphasized more in Ashkenazic homes. Recipes accentuate the sweetness of vegetables by cooking them with honey or sugar. Vegetables are cooked with fruits in an Eastern European Jewish casserole called tzimmes, which includes carrots, prunes, sweet potatoes, honey, or sugar, and sometimes beef as well.

Specific foods have other symbolic roles on Sephardic menus. Spinach and Swiss chard, long-time favorites on the Sephardic table, stand for the hope for plenty of vegetables at the harvest. Rice and black-eyed peas stand for abundance. The Hebrew names for leeks (*krayshah*) and beets (*selek*) recall divine protection from our enemies, and those vegetables appear on many tables. In some homes, small portions of these foods are tasted in a ceremony, with a blessing said before each, similar to the Passover Seder.

Salads, Appetizers, and Soups

Corn, Sweet Pepper, and Green Bean Salad

Makes 4 servings

The sweetness of fresh corn and red bell peppers makes these vegetables ideal additions to the traditional Rosh Hashanah sweet foods list. Together with green beans, they make a colorful, tasty appetizer salad.

1¹/₂ pounds green beans, ends removed, halved

2 cups fresh (2 large ears) or frozen kernels

2 large red or orange bell peppers, cut into strips

¹/₄ cup minced green onion

2 or 3 tablespoons vegetable oil or olive oil

Salt and freshly ground pepper, to taste

1 tablespoon fresh lime or lemon juice or dry white wine (optional)

1. Cook beans and corn in a saucepan of boiling salted water about 5 minutes or until beans are crisp-tender. Rinse under cold water until cool and drain well. Transfer to a large bowl. Add red pepper, green onion, and oil. Season with salt and pepper. Refrigerate until ready to serve.

2. A short time before serving, add lime juice, if using, and add more seasoning if necessary. Serve cold or at room temperature.

Carrot Salad with Cranberries and Mint

Makes 4 to 6 servings

A light and lively change from the familiar mayonnaise-dressed carrot and raisin salad often served at Rosh Hashanah, this colorful salad pairs the carrots with dried cranberries. The dressing is mostly orange juice mixed with a little vegetable oil, which you can omit to make the salad fat free. The salad is pretty on its own, or spooned onto a bed of tender lettuce.

1 pound carrots (about 6 medium), coarsely grated

¹/₄ cup dried cranberries

¹/₄ cup strained fresh orange juice

1 to 2 tablespoons vegetable oil

1 tablespoon chopped fresh mint or 1 teaspoon dried

2 to 3 teaspoons sugar, or to taste

Salt to taste

Put carrots and cranberries in a bowl. Add orange juice, oil, mint, sugar, and salt, and mix well. Serve cold.

Beet Salad with Apples and Orange Juice

Makes 4 servings

Grated freshly cooked beets are so flavorful that they don't need much seasoning. Tart apples provide the perfect balance to their sweetness. Moisten the salad with a little orange or lemon juice and, if you wish, a drizzle of oil. Depending on the sweetness of the beets and the apples, you can add a touch of sugar also.

Beets are easiest to peel after they are cooked. Rinse cooked beets under cold running water and the peel will slip off easily. Be careful with beets because they stain clothes easily.

8 to 10 beets of 1¹/₂ inch diameter (about 1 pound, without greens)

2 tart apples, such as Granny Smith, peeled and coarsely grated

2 to 3 tablespoons orange juice

1 tablespoon vegetable oil (optional)

1 teaspoon sugar (optional)

Salt and freshly ground pepper, to taste

1. Cover beets with water and cook in a medium saucepan, covered, 45 minutes to 1 hour or until tender when pierced with a sharp knife. Rinse and peel.

2. Grate beets on large holes of grater and place in large bowl. Mix apples with beets, then add orange juice. Taste, and add oil and sugar, if using. Season with salt and pepper. Serve cold.

Tomato Dressing

Makes about 8 servings

In addition to eating sweet foods for the Jewish New Year, some people avoid such sour ingredients as vinegar and lemon juice. Here is a salad dressing that doesn't require either. It takes advantage of the season's wonderful ripe tomatoes. True, tomatoes do have some acidity, but because it's balanced by their natural sweetness, tomatoes are not considered sour ingredients. The dressing is good with salads of greens, potatoes, pasta, or fish.

This is a delicate dressing flavored with herbs. If you like, you can add a little minced shallot or garlic. You can prepare the dressing a day ahead.

1¹/₂ pounds ripe tomatoes
Salt and freshly ground pepper, to taste
³/₄ cup extra-virgin olive oil
1 tablespoon minced fresh tarragon or basil
1 tablespoon minced fresh Italian parsley

1. To peel tomatoes, cut out their cores, turn tomatoes upside down and slit skins in an X-shaped cut. Fill a large bowl with cold water. Put tomatoes in a saucepan of enough boiling water to cover them. Boil about 10 seconds or until skin begins to pull away from flesh. Remove tomatoes with a slotted spoon and put them in the bowl of cold water. Leave for a few seconds. Remove tomatoes and pull off skins.

2. Cut each tomato in half and squeeze out its seeds. Cut each half into quarters, salt them lightly, and put them in a strainer. Let stand 15 minutes to drain.

3. Finely chop tomato pieces and put them in a bowl. Add salt and pepper and whisk until smooth. Slowly and gradually whisk in olive oil. Add herbs, then adjust seasoning. Refrigerate until almost ready to serve. Serve at room temperature.

Quinces in Cinnamon Syrup

Makes 8 servings

A Sephardic specialty, this delicious dish is sampled in many homes before the Rosh Hashanah dinner as a taste of a sweet New Year.

3¹/₂ pounds large quinces (about 6), peeled
1 strip of lemon peel
1³/₄ cups sugar
4 teaspoons ground cinnamon

1. Cut quinces in eighths and cut out core section from each piece. Put them in a large, heavy saucepan or stew pan. Add lemon peel and water just to cover the quinces. Bring to a boil. Cook uncovered over medium heat, carefully turning pieces over from time to time, about 50 minutes or until quinces are tender and about half the water has evaporated. Discard lemon peel.

2. Add sugar and cinnamon to pan. Swirl pan to dissolve the sugar but try not to stir the quinces, so they hold their shape. Cook over medium-low heat, gently basting quinces from time to time, about 20 minutes. Quinces should be very tender and appear shiny and glazed; syrup should taste concentrated. Spoon quinces and their syrup into serving dishes. Serve cold.

Whitefish Gefilte Fish

Makes 16 to 18 pieces, 8 or 9 servings

Gefilte fish is the quintessential Jewish holiday appetizer. (The dish's name comes from the Yiddish for filled fish, because the mixture used to be put back into the fish skin before cooking.)

In old-fashioned Eastern European recipes, gefilte fish was made with a mixture of carp, pike, and whitefish. The reason is simple: these freshwater fish were the ones available. Today, cooks use a variety of fish. I started making it with whitefish and halibut when I couldn't find pike or carp, and it was so good that this is the way I usually make it. (The gefilte fish is more subtly flavored.) Serve it with horseradish, its traditional accompaniment, store-bought or prepared as on page 339.

If you have the whitefish filleted at the store, ask for the bones and head of the fish so you can make the stock for cooking the gefilte fish. This dish can be prepared up to 3 days ahead.

6 to 8 cups Fish Stock for Gefilte Fish (page 601)

One 3-pound whitefish (including bones and head), filleted, bones and heads reserved

3/4 pound sea bass or halibut fillets

2 large eggs

2 medium onions, finely chopped

2 teaspoons salt

1/2 teaspoon freshly ground pepper, preferably white

1 small carrot, finely grated (optional) plus 2 large carrots, sliced

2 tablespoons matzo meal

Leaves of tender lettuce, such as Boston lettuce

1. Prepare fish stock. Pour strained stock into a large, deep pot.

2. If whitefish fillets have their skin on, remove it: Set fillets on a board, skin side down. Slip blade of a flexible knife between flesh and skin and use it to remove skin of fish, sliding knife away from you with one hand and pulling off skin with other. Run your fingers carefully over fish fillets and remove any small bones remaining in flesh. Remove any skin or bones in the sea bass fillets. Cut fish into large pieces.

3. Grind both types of fish in a food processor in 2 batches until very fine. (Move first batch to a large bowl.) Leave second batch in food processor and add 1 egg, half the chopped onions, 1 teaspoon salt, and 1/4 teaspoon pepper. Process to thoroughly mix. Transfer to another large bowl. Repeat with the first batch of fish, egg, onion, salt, and pepper. Transfer to bowl with other batch and mix. Stir in grated carrot, if using, and matzo meal.

4. Add sliced carrots to strained stock and bring to a simmer. With moistened hands, shape fish mixture into ovals or balls, using about 1/3 cup mixture for each. Carefully drop fish balls into simmering stock. If necessary, add enough hot water to just cover them, pouring it carefully into stock near edge of pan, not over fish. Return to a simmer, cover, and let simmer over low heat for 1 hour. Let fish cool in stock. Refrigerate fish and carrots in stock for at least 4 hours before serving. (It can be kept 3 days in the refrigerator.)

5. To serve, remove fish pieces carefully from stock and set them on a bed of lettuce. Garnish each with a carrot slice.

Sea Bass in Saffron-Tomato Sauce

Makes 4 main course
or about 6 fish-course servings

If you're looking for a terrific, easy-to-make Rosh Hashanah fish course, try this Sephardic style dish. The fish simmers right in the sauce and can be served hot or cold. You can prepare the sauce ahead and refrigerate or freeze it.

1/8 teaspoon saffron threads

3 tablespoons extra-virgin olive oil

1 medium onion, chopped

1/2 cup diced red bell pepper

1 1/2 pounds ripe tomatoes, peeled, seeded, and pureed, or one 28-ounce and one 14-ounce can plum tomatoes, drained and pureed

Salt and freshly ground pepper, to taste

1 1/2 to 1 3/4 pounds sea bass fillets, about 1 inch thick

3 tablespoons chopped fresh basil or Italian parsley

1. Slightly crush saffron with your fingers and soak it in the oil in a small cup about 20 minutes. Transfer saffron oil to a large sauté pan or skillet and cook briefly over low heat. Add onion and bell pepper and sauté over medium-low heat about 5 minutes or until onion begins to turn golden. Add tomatoes, salt, and pepper and cook over medium-high heat, stirring often, 8 to 10 minutes or until thick.

2. Add sea bass in one layer to sauce and sprinkle with salt and pepper. Cover and cook over medium-low heat, spooning sauce over fish from time to time, about 10 minutes or until thickest part of fish becomes opaque inside; check with a sharp knife. Taste sauce and adjust seasoning. Stir 2 tablespoons basil gently into sauce. Serve hot or cold, sprinkled with remaining basil.

Hungarian Halibut

Makes 6 main-course
or 8 to 10 appetizer servings

For this savory first course, the fish bakes in a Hungarian green pepper sauce. For Rosh Hashanah it's more likely to be served as a cold appetizer but it's also good hot. You can prepare it a day ahead and keep it in the refrigerator. In fact, the fish continues to gain flavor as it chills. If you like, substitute haddock, cod, or sea bass or other delicate, white-fleshed fish for the halibut.

2 tablespoons vegetable oil

1 medium onion, halved and sliced thin

1 pound green bell peppers (or mixed green, red, and yellow) cut into strips 1/2-inch wide and 2 inches long

2 teaspoons paprika

1 pound ripe tomatoes, peeled, seeded, and diced, or one 28-ounce can diced tomatoes, drained

Salt and freshly ground pepper, to taste

Pinch of hot paprika or cayenne pepper (optional)

2 pounds halibut fillets, about 1 inch thick

1. Heat oil in a medium skillet. Add onion and sauté over medium-low heat 5 minutes or until onion begins to turn golden. Add peppers and sauté, stirring occasionally, 15 minutes. Add paprika and sauté 1 minute, stirring.

2. Add tomatoes, salt, and pepper. Cover and simmer, stirring occasionally, about 15 minutes or until peppers are tender and mixture is thick. Adjust seasoning, adding hot paprika, if using. (If not serving immediately, store pepper sauce in a covered container in the refrigerator.)

3. When ready to prepare fish, preheat oven to 425°F. Lightly oil a shallow baking dish large enough to hold fish in a single layer. Reheat pepper sauce, if necessary. Spread half of sauce in dish. Arrange halibut fillets on top, in one layer. Season them lightly with salt and pepper. Spread remaining sauce over fish.

4. Bake uncovered about 15 minutes or until thickest part of fish becomes opaque inside; check with a sharp knife. Serve hot or chilled.

Wine-Poached Trout with Tarragon Sauce

Makes 4 servings **P**

French Jews prepare dishes like this as holiday first courses. The sauce of mayonnaise, shallot, and herbs is easy to make but you should use fresh tarragon rather than dried. If you prefer, choose a low-fat mayonnaise for the sauce.

1 carrot, sliced about $1/4$-inch thick

1 onion, halved and sliced about $1/4$-inch thick

4 sprigs fresh tarragon, stems and leaves separated

1 bay leaf

1 teaspoon salt

$1/4$ teaspoon black peppercorns

5 cups water

$1/2$ cup dry white wine

4 small trout (about 8 ounces each)

Salt and white pepper, to taste

$2/3$ cup mayonnaise

1 small shallot, finely minced

1 tablespoon chopped fresh parsley

Fresh parsley and tarragon sprigs (for garnish)

1. Combine carrot, onion, tarragon stems, bay leaf, salt, peppercorns and water in a large saucepan. Bring to a boil. Cover and simmer over low heat 20 minutes. Strain into a bowl and add wine.

2. Preheat oven to 400°F. Using sturdy scissors, snip fins of fish. Rinse fish inside and out, removing any scales, and pat dry. Leave on heads and tails. Season fish inside and out with salt and pepper.

3. Set fish in one layer in a large, heavy, flameproof baking dish. Pour enough of wine mixture over fish to cover. Bring to a simmer. Cover with foil. Transfer to oven and bake about 12 minutes or until a thin skewer inserted into thickest part of fish comes out hot to touch. Uncover fish and let cool in liquid until lukewarm.

4. For the sauce, chop enough tarragon leaves to make 1 tablespoon. Use either fish poaching liquid or water to thin the mayonnaise. If using poaching liquid, strain a few tablespoons of it. Gradually whisk 1 tablespoon strained poaching liquid or water into mayonnaise. If necessary, whisk in a little more liquid until sauce reaches desired thickness. Stir in shallot, tarragon, and parsley. Add salt and white pepper if needed.

5. With 2 slotted spatulas, transfer fish carefully to a plate lined with paper towels. Remove skin of each fish by scraping gently with paring knife; leave skin on head and tail. Cover and refrigerate fish until ready to serve. Refrigerate sauce in a separate covered dish. Serve fish garnished with parsley and tarragon sprigs. Serve sauce separately.

Chicken Soup with Sweet Vegetables and Matzo Balls

Makes about 6 servings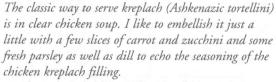

At my house we love chicken soup with lots of vegetables in it. For this one I add a piece of banana squash, some yellow crookneck squash, and a few sugar snap peas; they contribute a sweet flavor and lovely bright color. You can blanch the sugar snap peas ahead but it's best to heat them in the soup at the last moment so they stay bright green and retain their texture. Generally I opt for Extra-Light Matzo Balls (page 280) for copious holiday meals but you can add any type of matzo balls you like.

2 pounds chicken thighs, drumsticks, or wings

8 to 10 cups water

1 medium onion, diced

2 ribs celery, diced

1 large carrot, diced

1 large clove garlic, chopped

Salt and freshly ground pepper, to taste

One 1-pound piece banana squash, peeled and diced

2 medium yellow crookneck squash, diced

Matzo Balls (pages 279–282)

1/4 to 1/2 pound sugar snap peas

2 tablespoons chopped fresh dill or parsley

1. Put chicken in a soup pot, cover with the water, and bring to a boil. Skim foam. Add onion, celery, carrot, garlic, and salt. Cover and cook over low heat 1 hour. Add banana squash and simmer 30 minutes or until chicken is tender and soup is well flavored. Remove chicken. Add yellow crookneck squash to soup and simmer 5 minutes or until barely tender. Refrigerate soup. Thoroughly skim fat from soup.

2. Prepare matzo balls.

3. Before serving, reheat matzo balls in their cooking liquid. Bring soup to a simmer. If you like, remove some of chicken meat from bones, return meat to soup and heat through. With a slotted spoon, add matzo balls to soup. Add sugar snap peas and simmer 3 to 5 minutes or until just tender. Adjust seasoning. Serve sprinkled with chopped dill or parsley.

Old-Fashioned Chicken Soup with Kreplach

Makes about 6 servings

The classic way to serve kreplach (Ashkenazic tortellini) is in clear chicken soup. I like to embellish it just a little with a few slices of carrot and zucchini and some fresh parsley as well as dill to echo the seasoning of the chicken kreplach filling.

If you don't feel like making kreplach, you can prepare this soup with frozen kreplach. You can find these in kosher grocery stores and some supermarkets.

2 pounds chicken thighs, drumsticks, or wings

8 to 10 cups water

1 medium onion, whole

2 ribs celery, whole

2 large carrots, 1 whole and 1 sliced

4 fresh sprigs dill (optional)

Salt and freshly ground pepper, to taste

Chicken Kreplach (page 491)

2 small zucchini, halved and sliced thin

2 tablespoons chopped fresh parsley

1 to 2 tablespoons chopped fresh dill or 1 to 2 teaspoons dried

1. Put chicken in a soup pot, cover with the water, and bring to a boil. Skim foam. Add onion, celery, whole carrot, dill sprigs if using, and salt. Cover and cook over low heat 1 1/2 hours or until chicken is very tender and soup is well flavored. Remove onion, celery, whole carrot, and dill sprigs. Remove chicken; reserve for other uses. Refrigerate soup. Thoroughly skim fat from soup.

2. Prepare kreplach.

3. Before serving, bring soup to a simmer. Add sliced carrot and simmer 10 minutes. Add kreplach and zucchini and simmer 5 minutes or until kreplach are hot and zucchini is just tender. Stir in half the parsley and half the dill. Season soup with salt and pepper. Serve sprinkled with remaining parsley and dill.

Meat Tzimmes and Other Main Courses

Traditional Meat Tzimmes

Makes 4 to 6 servings

When I was a child, my mother usually made this hearty tzimmes (Ashkenazic stew with sweet vegetables) for our family's Rosh Hashanah dinners. She made it the old-fashioned way, with beef, sweet potatoes, and prunes.

You can prepare the stew 1 or 2 days ahead and keep it in the refrigerator. Reheat it in a covered pan over low heat or in a 300°F oven.

1 tablespoon vegetable oil

2 pounds beef chuck, cut into 1-inch cubes, or beef for stew

2 large onions, chopped

4 large carrots, cut into 1-inch chunks

¹/₂ teaspoon salt

3 to 4 cups water

1¹/₂ pounds orange-fleshed sweet potatoes or yams, peeled and diced

¹/₄ cup brown sugar or honey

Pinch of freshly ground pepper

¹/₂ pound pitted prunes

1 tablespoon all-purpose flour

1. Heat oil in a Dutch oven or heavy casserole over medium heat. Add meat in batches and brown well on all sides. Remove from pan. Add onions and sauté until they brown thoroughly. Return meat to pan and add carrots, salt, and enough water to just cover. Bring to a boil, skimming occasionally. Cover and simmer over low heat, skimming once or twice, for 1 hour.

2. After stew has cooked 1 hour, add sweet potatoes, sugar, and pepper and mix gently. Push vegetables into liquid. Bring to a boil. Partially cover and simmer over low heat 30 minutes. Meanwhile, soak prunes in enough hot water to cover for about 30 minutes.

3. Gently stir stew once. Remove prunes from their liquid, reserving liquid, and add prunes to pan. Uncover and simmer 30 minutes more or until meat is very tender. Occasionally stir very gently.

4. Mix flour with 2 tablespoons prune soaking liquid in a small bowl. Gradually stir in about 1 cup of stew

broth. Add this mixture to stew, stir very gently, and simmer about 5 minutes or until thickened. Adjust seasoning. Serve hot, from a deep serving dish.

Rosh Hashanah Couscous with Meat and Vegetables

Makes about 6 servings

A tradition in Moroccan homes is to serve couscous with seven vegetables for Rosh Hashanah, because seven is thought to be a lucky number. The vegetables vary among different communities but usually include orange winter squash, carrots, chickpeas, and leeks or onions. The couscous is also embellished with raisins for sweetness for the New Year.

Generally the vegetables are cooked in a delicately seasoned broth with meat—either lamb, beef, or chicken. On other occasions the couscous and stew is served with harissa, *a spicy pepper paste, but many families avoid it for Rosh Hashanah.*

If you wish to cook couscous the traditional way, steam it above the simmering broth; set the couscous in its steamer on top of the broth pot.

1 cup dried chickpeas (garbanzo beans), sorted, or one 15-ounce and one 8-ounce can, drained

1 or 2 beef soup bones

2 large onions, sliced

¹/₄ teaspoon saffron threads or ground turmeric

Salt and freshly ground pepper, to taste

2 quarts water

2 pounds beef chuck, excess fat removed, cut into 1¹/₂-inch cubes

2 large leeks, split, cleaned, and cut into 2-inch pieces

One 14¹/₂-ounce can diced tomatoes, drained

³/₄ pound butternut squash, banana squash, or other winter squash, peeled and cut into 1-inch dice (about 2 cups)

4 medium (³/₄ pound) carrots, halved lengthwise and cut into 1-inch pieces

3 ribs celery, cut into 1-inch pieces

1 small turnip, peeled and cut into 1-inch pieces

2 medium (¹/₂ pound) zucchini, cut into 1-inch pieces

Pinch of ground cinnamon

³/₄ cup raisins

1 pound (2¹/₂ cups) Traditional Steamed Couscous (page 76), or quick-cooked according to package directions

1. Rinse dried chickpeas, if using. Cover them with cold water in a large saucepan and soak them overnight.

2. Drain soaked chickpeas. Return to saucepan. Add 1 quart cold water and bring to a boil. Cover and simmer about 1 1/2 hours, adding hot water occasionally to keep them covered with water. Add a pinch of salt and continue simmering 30 to 45 minutes more or until tender.

3. Meanwhile, put beef bones in a large pot and add onions, saffron, salt, and pepper. Cover and heat 5 minutes over low heat, stirring. Add the water and bring to a boil. Cover and simmer over low heat 30 minutes. Add beef chuck and simmer 1 1/2 hours.

4. Add leeks, tomatoes, butternut squash, carrots, celery, turnip, and cooked or canned chickpeas to broth. Bring to a boil. Simmer 20 minutes, add zucchini, then continue to simmer 10 more minutes or until meat and vegetables are tender. Discard bones. Add cinnamon to broth. Adjust seasoning.

5. Transfer 1 cup broth to a small saucepan. Add raisins and simmer for 10 minutes or until tender. Cover and keep them warm.

6. Prepare couscous.

7. To serve, mound couscous in a cone shape on a large platter. Garnish top with raisins and a few chickpeas. Spoon some of meat and vegetables onto platter around couscous. Serve broth with remaining meat and vegetables from a tureen. Serve couscous in shallow bowls, and spoon meat, vegetables, and broth over it.

Veal Tzimmes with Apricots and Prunes

Makes 4 servings   Ⓜ

Prunes are traditional in tzimmes because they are a common dried fruit in Eastern Europe, where the stew originated. They lend a delicate sweetness to the red wine sauce in this tzimmes. Today, cooks take advantage of the many dried fruits available to flavor their tzimmes. I find that dried apricots are a perfect complement for veal tzimmes because of their lively color and flavor. Serve the dish with rice pilaf or boiled potatoes.

1 tablespoon vegetable oil

2 pounds boneless veal, cut into 1-inch cubes

1 large onion, chopped

2 large carrots, diced

1 rib celery, diced

1 tablespoon all-purpose flour

1 cup dry red wine

1 tablespoon tomato paste

1 cup veal or chicken stock

1/4 teaspoon ground allspice

1/4 teaspoon ground cinnamon

1 bay leaf

1 cup dried apricots

3/4 cup small pitted prunes

1/2 teaspoon sugar, or more to taste

Salt and freshly ground pepper, to taste

1. Heat oil in Dutch oven over medium heat. Add veal and sauté lightly in 2 batches, removing to a plate as it changes color.

2. Add onion, carrot, and celery to pot and sauté about 5 minutes. Stir in flour and cook 30 seconds, stirring, until bubbling. Add wine, stirring until smooth and scraping in brown juices. Bring to a simmer. Stir in tomato paste. Add stock, allspice, cinnamon, and bay leaf. Mix well.

3. Return veal to pan. Cover and cook over low heat, stirring occasionally, 30 minutes. Add apricots and prunes and simmer about 30 minutes or until veal is tender when pierced with a knife. Remove bay leaf. Skim as much fat as possible from sauce.

4. Add sugar to sauce. Adjust seasoning, adding salt, pepper, or more sugar if needed. Serve hot.

Turkey Tzimmes with Sweet Potatoes

Makes 4 to 6 servings

Classic tzimmes recipes call for beef but I often celebrate Rosh Hashanah with a lighter twist on the traditional Ashkenazic specialty by making it with turkey. Another bonus—the cooking time of the dish is shorter.

1 tablespoon vegetable oil

2 pounds boneless turkey fillets, cut into 1-inch cubes

2 onions, chopped

1 tablespoon all-purpose flour

1²/₃ cups turkey or chicken stock, or broth mixed with water

5 large carrots, cut into 1-inch chunks

1/2 teaspoon salt

2 large boiling potatoes, peeled and cut into large dice

1 pound orange-fleshed sweet potatoes or yams, peeled and cut into large dice

1/4 cup honey

1/2 teaspoon ground cinnamon

Pinch of freshly ground pepper

1/2 pound pitted prunes

1. Heat oil in Dutch oven over medium heat. Add turkey and sauté lightly in 2 batches, removing each to a plate as it changes color. Cover and set aside.

2. Add onions, cover, and sauté about 10 minutes, stirring often, until light brown. Stir in flour and cook 30 seconds, stirring often. Add stock, stirring until smooth and scraping in brown juices. Bring to a simmer.

3. Add carrots, salt, and enough water to just cover. Bring to a boil, skimming occasionally. Cover and

simmer over low heat, skimming once or twice, for 10 minutes.

4. Add boiling potatoes and sweet potatoes to pan. Add honey, cinnamon, and pepper, and mix gently. Push vegetables into liquid. Bring to a simmer. Partially cover and simmer for 30 minutes.

5. Gently stir stew once. Add turkey cubes and prunes. Cover and cook over low heat for about 30 minutes or until turkey pieces are tender when pierced with a knife. Shake pan occasionally to prevent sticking but avoid stirring so as not to break up ingredients. (Stew can be made 1 day ahead; reheat in a covered pan over low heat, stirring often, or in a 300°F oven.)

6. Serve from a deep serving dish.

Adi's Kibbutz Honey Chicken

Makes 4 servings

My niece Adi Levy, who grew up at Kibbutz Ein Harod in northern Israel, learned this dish when she worked in the kibbutz kitchen. The chicken was partially roasted, then finished cooking with a sauce of honey, dry wine, and soy sauce—now a popular seasoning in Israel—which formed a sweet glaze. At the kibbutz they prepared this dish for Rosh Hashanah. With the chicken they served rice, potatoes, carrots, and many salads. I like it with Sweet Carrot Coins (page 72) or with Carrot Puree (page 161), and with Rice Pilaf with Golden Raisins and Pistachios (page 77).

One 3¹/₂- to 4-pound chicken

1/4 cup honey

1/4 cup dry white wine

3 tablespoons soy sauce

Salt and freshly ground pepper, to taste

1¹/₂ cups chicken stock, broth, or water

1 teaspoon potato starch or cornstarch, dissolved in 2 tablespoons cold water

1. Preheat oven to 400°F. Reserve chicken neck and giblets. Pull out fat from inside chicken. Truss chicken if desired.

2. Set chicken on a rack in a heavy roasting pan. Roast chicken for 20 minutes. Meanwhile, mix 3 tablespoons honey with the wine, soy sauce, and pepper in a small bowl. Remove chicken from oven and brush all over with honey mixture. Add ¹/₂ cup stock to roasting pan.

3. Roast chicken 20 more minutes. Turn chicken over. If it's browning too fast, cover it with foil. If pan is dry, add a few tablespoons stock. Roast 10 to 20 minutes longer or until it is done. Juices should run clear when thickest part of thigh is pierced with thin knife or skewer; if juices are pink, roast a few more minutes and test again. Transfer chicken to a board, cover and keep warm.

4. To make sauce, remove roasting rack from pan. Skim fat from roasting juices in pan. Set roasting pan on a burner over medium heat. Add remaining stock and bring to a simmer, scraping browned juices into stock. Remove from heat. Strain juices into a medium saucepan. Skim fat again.

5. Bring juices to a simmer. Whisk potato starch mixture and gradually pour into simmering juices, whisking constantly. Return to a boil, whisking. Simmer 1 or 2 minutes until thickened. Remove from heat and stir in remaining tablespoon honey. Season with salt and pepper.

6. Carve chicken and serve with sauce.

❧ Side Dishes

Sweet Carrot Coins

Makes 8 servings

P

Everyone loves these carrots, including children, because of their appealing sweetness. I first learned to prepare sweet glazed carrots in France, where they are made with white sugar and butter. I add honey for Rosh Hashanah and I cook the carrots with oil, to keep the holiday meal kosher, since it usually includes meat or poultry.

A friend of mine from Morocco adds a pinch of cinnamon, which is also a delicious addition. She cooks the carrots for a long time over low heat until they are brown on the edges and beginning to caramelize.

2 pounds carrots, sliced

2 cups water

Pinch of salt

2 tablespoons honey

3 tablespoons brown or white sugar

3 tablespoon vegetable oil

¹/₄ teaspoon ground cinnamon (optional)

Combine carrots, water, and salt in a large saucepan. Bring to a boil. Simmer uncovered over medium-low heat 10 minutes. Add honey, sugar, oil, and cinnamon, if using. Continue cooking over medium-low heat, stirring occasionally, until carrots are very tender and liquid is absorbed, about 15 minutes. Watch so mixture does not burn. Serve hot.

Quick-Braised Butternut Squash with Ginger and Onion

Makes about 4 servings

In Sephardic homes sweet winter squash is a customary vegetable on the Jewish New Year menu. For this easy dish, I streamline the usual braising technique by using the microwave. It not only shortens the cooking time, but it also saves me the trouble of cutting the skin off the squash, and is especially useful if you want to substitute one of the ridged squashes like sweet dumpling or acorn. I simply scoop out the cooked pulp and braise it briefly with the flavorings.

2¹/₂ pounds butternut squash

1 to 2 tablespoons vegetable oil

1 medium onion, minced

1 tablespoon minced peeled fresh ginger

¹/₄ cup vegetable broth or water

¹/₂ teaspoon ground ginger

Pinch of sugar (optional)

Salt and freshly ground pepper, to taste

1. Halve squash and remove seeds and strings. Put squash halves cut-side down in a microwave-safe baking dish, add 2 tablespoons water and cover with wax paper. Microwave on high power about 15 minutes or until tender; check by piercing squash in its thickest part with a fork. Remove squash pulp from peel. Roughly dice pulp.

2. Heat oil in a large skillet or sauté pan. Add onion and sauté over medium heat, stirring often, 7 minutes. Add minced ginger and sauté over low heat 30 seconds. Add squash pieces, ¹/₄ cup broth, ground ginger, sugar if using, salt, and pepper. Cover and cook, stirring often, about 5 minutes or until squash is coated with flavorings and is heated through. (Don't worry if squash pieces fall apart.) Serve hot.

Leek Compote

Makes 4 to 6 servings   Ⓜ or Ⓟ

Leek compote is a delicious and simple French specialty. Basically it is leeks cooked until tender with only delicate seasoning, so you really enjoy the flavor of the vegetable. I find it's perfect for Rosh Hashanah, especially because leeks are one of the traditional vegetables on the Sephardic holiday table.

The leeks are a wonderful accompaniment for chicken or fish. If you're serving them at a vegetarian or fish dinner, you can cook them with butter instead of oil and use vegetable stock. For this dish, use the white and light- to medium-green parts of leeks. Reserve very dark green parts for making soups and stocks (you can freeze them).

2 pounds leeks, rinsed, halved, and thinly sliced

2 or 3 tablespoons vegetable oil or olive oil

Salt and freshly ground pepper, to taste

1¹/₂ teaspoons fresh thyme or ¹/₂ teaspoon dried

¹/₄ cup chicken or vegetable stock

1. Put sliced leeks in a bowl of cold water and separate the pieces. Let stand about 5 minutes. Lift leeks out of water. Put them in a colander to drain. If water is sandy, soak and drain them again.

2. Heat oil in a heavy casserole or stew pan. Add leeks, salt, and pepper. Cover and cook over low heat, stirring occasionally, 5 minutes. Add thyme and stock. Cover and cook, stirring from time to time, about 15 minutes or until leeks are tender. If mixture is soupy, uncover and cook, stirring often, to evaporate the excess liquid. Adjust seasoning. Serve hot.

Zucchini in Israeli Tomato Sauce

Makes 4 servings

Israelis often have a multicultural approach to tomato sauce. They take cumin, turmeric, and plenty of garlic—favorite flavors in Middle Eastern tomato sauces—and match them with those loved by Eastern European Jews—dill and a pinch of sugar. The result is a wonderful sauce that turns a common vegetable into a rich tasting side dish. It's a very good accompaniment for roasted or grilled chicken.

For this dish the zucchini are usually cooked until very tender. If you prefer them al dente, simmer them only a few minutes in the tomato sauce.

4 to 5 tablespoons olive oil or vegetable oil

1 medium onion, minced

3 large cloves garlic, minced

1¹/₂ teaspoons ground cumin

³/₄ teaspoon paprika

¹/₄ teaspoon ground turmeric

2 pounds ripe tomatoes, peeled, seeded, and chopped, or two 28-ounce cans plum tomatoes, drained and chopped

1 tablespoon tomato paste

Salt and freshly ground pepper, to taste

¹/₄ teaspoon sugar, or to taste

Pinch of cayenne pepper

1¹/₄ to 1¹/₂ pounds zucchini, halved and cut into ³/₈-inch slices

2 tablespoons snipped fresh dill

1. Heat 2 tablespoons oil in large saucepan. Add onion and sauté over medium-low heat about 7 minutes or until soft and golden. Add garlic, cumin, paprika, and turmeric and cook, stirring, 30 seconds. Add tomatoes, tomato paste, salt, and pepper and stir well. Bring to boil over medium-high heat. Cook uncovered over medium-low heat, stirring occasionally, 20 to 30 minutes or until tomatoes become a thick, chunky sauce. Add sugar and cayenne pepper, and adjust seasoning.

2. Heat 2 to 3 tablespoons olive oil in large, heavy skillet. Add zucchini, salt, and pepper. Sauté over medium heat, stirring often, about 3 minutes or until nearly tender. Add sauce and simmer 5 to 10 minutes or until zucchini are done to your taste. Taste and adjust seasoning. Stir in dill. Serve hot or at room temperature.

Rosh Hashanah Sweet Potato Casserole

Makes 6 to 8 servings

When I was growing up, this sweet potato casserole was a family favorite. The mashed sweet potatoes were lightly sweetened with brown sugar and flavored with orange and sweet spices. It was enriched with pareve margarine but you could substitute oil, or, for meatless meals, use butter. Sometimes my mother garnished it with maraschino cherries but I prefer to omit these.

2 pounds medium orange-fleshed sweet potatoes

2 tablespoons soft margarine or butter or vegetable oil

2 to 4 tablespoons brown sugar

¹/₄ cup orange juice

2 teaspoons grated orange rind

¹/₂ teaspoon ground cinnamon

Pinch of cloves

Salt to taste

1 large egg

Corn flakes, lightly crushed

1. Put sweet potatoes in a large saucepan with water to cover and a pinch of salt and bring to a boil. Cover and simmer over low heat about 30 minutes or until tender. Drain and let cool.

2. Preheat oven to 350°F. Peel potatoes. Mash them with a potato masher. Stir in 1 tablespoon margarine, 2 tablespoons brown sugar, orange juice, orange rind, cinnamon, cloves, and salt. Taste, and add more sugar if you like. Stir in egg.

3. Grease a 1¹/₂- to 2-quart casserole. Add potato mixture. Sprinkle with corn flakes. Dot with remaining margarine or drizzle remaining oil. Bake about 40 minutes or until top is firm and light golden at edges.

Sephardic Spinach Cakes

Makes about 6 appetizer servings

To represent the wish for a year with plenty of produce, Sephardic Jews serve greens such as spinach. Often the greens appear in flat omelets, which are cut into wedges and served as an appetizer, or in these savory cakes.

Two 10-ounce bags rinsed spinach leaves, large stems removed

3 to 5 tablespoons vegetable oil

2 cloves garlic, chopped

Salt and freshly ground pepper, to taste

1/2 cup all-purpose flour

2 large eggs

1. Cook spinach in a large pan of boiling salted water 2 minutes or until just tender. Rinse with cold water. Squeeze spinach to remove excess liquid. Chop finely.

2. Heat 1 tablespoon oil in a medium skillet. Add garlic and sauté over medium-low heat, stirring, about 30 seconds. Add spinach and sauté about 2 minutes, stirring. Season with salt and pepper.

3. Mix flour, eggs, and 1/4 teaspoon salt in a medium bowl to a thick batter. Add spinach mixture and mix well.

4. Heat 3 tablespoons oil in a heavy skillet over medium heat. For each cake, drop 2 or 3 tablespoonsful spinach mixture to pan and flatten to form a cake. Fry about 2 minutes or until golden brown on each side. Transfer to paper towels to drain. Stir batter from time to time and add more oil to pan if needed. Serve hot.

Black-Eyed Peas with Browned Onions and Tomatoes

Makes about 8 servings

Black-eyed peas are popular as a Rosh Hashanah food in many Sephardic homes and can sometimes be found fresh in their pods in Israel. Finishing cooked beans with well-browned onions is a technique I learned from Lebanese-born Suzanne Elmaleh of Jerusalem. For Rosh Hashanah the beans are served as a side dish with chicken or meat, but for other meals they're delicious accompanied simply by hot, cooked rice.

For this dish you can use dried black-eyed peas, the form in which they are most commonly available. If your market carries the frozen kind, you can use them to save time; simply cook them according to the package directions.

1 pound dried black-eyed peas

10 cups water

1 pound ripe tomatoes, peeled, seeded, and diced, or one 14-ounce can diced tomatoes, drained

2 large cloves garlic, chopped

1 1/2 teaspoons ground cumin

Salt and freshly ground pepper, to taste

1 tablespoon tomato paste

3 or 4 tablespoons olive oil

2 large onions, chopped

1/4 cup chopped fresh Italian parsley

1. Pick over dried peas, discarding pebbles and broken or discolored peas. Put them in a large saucepan and add the water. Bring to a simmer. Cover and cook over low heat about 1 hour or until just tender.

2. Drain peas, reserving 1 cup of cooking liquid. Put peas in a saucepan. Add tomatoes, garlic, cumin, salt, and pepper to peas. Mix tomato paste with 1/3 cup reserved cooking liquid and add to pot. Bring to a simmer. Cook over low heat for 10 minutes to blend flavors.

3. Heat oil in a heavy skillet. Add onions and sauté over medium heat, stirring often, about 10 minutes or until deeply browned. Add onion mixture to pot of peas. Cover and heat gently 3 minutes. Stir in 3 tablespoons parsley. Adjust seasoning. Serve hot, sprinkled with remaining parsley.

Carrots and Potatoes with Chard

Makes 4 servings

In this colorful Middle Eastern stovetop casserole, the chard leaves cook with garlic to form a sauce for the other vegetables. Chard is a traditional vegetable on the Sephardic Rosh Hashanah table. You can also serve this as a winter side dish for a Shabbat roast chicken or with braised beef. It reheats beautifully.

2 tablespoons olive oil

4 large cloves garlic, chopped

6 cups rinsed finely chopped red or green chard leaves

1 medium onion, chopped

2 cups thin slices red or green chard stems

3/4 pound carrots, cut into 3/4-inch dice

3/4 pound baking potatoes, peeled and cut into 3/4-inch dice

1 1/2 cups vegetable or chicken stock or broth

Salt and freshly ground pepper, to taste

1. Heat 1 tablespoon oil in a large, deep nonstick skillet or sauté pan. Add garlic and sauté 15 seconds over medium-low heat. Add chard leaves with liquid clinging to them and sauté about 30 seconds. Cover and cook for 2 minutes or until wilted. Remove mixture from pan.

2. Add remaining 1 tablespoon oil to pan. Add onion and sauté over medium heat about 3 minutes or until beginning to turn golden. Add chard stems, carrots, and potatoes and sauté, stirring, 2 minutes. Add stock, salt, and pepper and bring to boil. Cover and simmer over low heat for 15 minutes.

3. Return chard-garlic mixture to pan and cook for 10 minutes or until vegetables are tender, adding a few tablespoons water if pan becomes dry. Taste and adjust seasoning. Serve hot.

Traditional Steamed Couscous

Makes about 6 servings   **P**

Steaming couscous above a savory meat and vegetable broth, such as in Rosh Hashanah Couscous with Meat and Vegetables (page 69), is the traditional way to prepare it. I learned how to steam couscous from my mother-in-law's neighbor, Hannah, who was born in Tunisia and now lives in Givatayim, Israel.

To steam couscous, you need a couscous cooker called a couscoussier *or* couscoussiere, *in which the stew simmers in the bottom pot and the couscous cooks in the steamer above it. Steaming is necessary to cook the raw couscous, which can be purchased in bulk at some Middle Eastern stores. Most of the packaged couscous is precooked but you can steam it if you wish, so it will have a more delicate texture; many people prefer its flavor.*

1 pound (2 1/2 cups) couscous

1/2 cup water

1 teaspoon salt

1/4 to 1/3 cup vegetable oil

1. Rinse couscous in a bowl and drain in a fine strainer. Transfer to a shallow bowl and rub grains to be sure they are separated. Let dry for 15 or 20 minutes.

2. Put couscous in steamer part of couscous cooker. Tie a damp towel around base of steamer part so steam won't escape from sides. Steam couscous uncovered above a simmering stew for 1/2 hour.

3. Remove couscous, put it in a large bowl and let cool. Mix the water with salt. Sprinkle couscous lightly with salted water, rubbing and tossing it between your fingers to prevent grains from sticking together.

4. About 1/2 hour before serving, return couscous to steamer and set it above simmering broth from main recipe. Steam uncovered about 30 minutes or until steam comes through couscous. Transfer to a large bowl.

5. Sprinkle oil over couscous in bowl. Slowly add 1/4 cup of stew broth. Mix lightly with a fork or with your fingers. Serve hot, accompanied by stew.

Rice Pilaf with Golden Raisins and Pistachios

Makes 4 servings

M or **P**

Rice appears on the Sephardic Rosh Hashanah table as a symbol of plenty. For the holiday it's prepared in an especially festive way, such as this lovely pilaf studded with toasted pistachios and raisins and delicately flavored with orange.

2 or 3 tablespoons vegetable oil

1 small onion, minced

1 cup long-grain rice

2 cups hot chicken stock or water

1 bay leaf

Salt and freshly ground pepper, to taste

1/2 cup golden raisins

1 teaspoon finely grated orange rind

1/3 to 1/2 cup shelled toasted pistachios

1. Heat oil in a deep skillet or sauté pan, add onion, and cook over low heat about 5 minutes or until tender. Add rice and sauté over medium heat, stirring, about 2 minutes. Add hot stock, bay leaf, salt, and pepper and bring to a boil. Stir once. Cover and cook over low heat 10 minutes. Add raisins without stirring. Cover and cook about 8 minutes or until rice is just tender. Let stand off heat, covered, 10 minutes.

2. Fluff rice lightly with a fork. Using fork, lightly stir in orange rind. Taste and adjust seasoning. Serve pilaf in a shallow bowl, garnished with pistachios.

🍁 Honey Cakes and Other Desserts

Cocoa-Orange Honey Cake

Makes about 10 servings

P

Although honey cake began as an Ashkenazic sweet, now Jews of every origin enjoy it as the traditional Rosh Hashanah dessert. This honey cake is dark, rich, studded with walnuts, and, as is the custom in many Israeli homes, flavored with cocoa.

Honey cake keeps well; if wrapped in foil, this one tastes fresh for two weeks or more. Because of this, in many families it's a custom to serve honey cakes made for Rosh Hashanah after Yom Kippur and on Sukkot as well. For best flavor, bake this cake at least one or two days ahead.

1 1/2 cups all-purpose flour

2 tablespoons unsweetened cocoa powder

1 1/2 teaspoons baking powder

1/2 teaspoon baking soda

1/2 teaspoon ground cinnamon

1/2 teaspoon ground ginger

2 large eggs

1/2 cup sugar

1/2 cup honey

1/2 cup vegetable oil

1 tablespoon grated orange rind

1/4 cup water

1/2 cup walnuts, coarsely chopped

1. Preheat oven to 325°F. Lightly grease an 8 × 4-inch loaf pan, line it with parchment paper or foil and grease the liner. Sift flour with cocoa, baking powder, baking soda, cinnamon, and ginger into a bowl.

2. Beat eggs lightly in a large bowl with an electric mixer. Add sugar and honey and beat until mixture is very smooth and lightened in color. Gradually add oil and beat until blended. Beat in orange rind. Stir in flour mixture alternately with water, each in two batches. Last, stir in walnuts.

3. Pour batter into prepared pan. Bake about 1 hour or until a cake tester inserted in cake comes out clean. Cool in pan for about 15 minutes. Turn out onto rack and carefully peel off liner. Wrap in foil when completely cool. (If tightly wrapped, cake keeps 2 weeks at room temperature.) Serve in thin slices.

Light Honey Cake with Candied Ginger

Makes 8 to 10 servings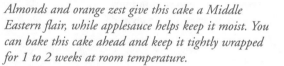

My family loves candied ginger as a sweet with tea. It's also terrific in honey cakes and gives much more zip than ginger powder, which is a common honey cake spice.

With less oil and sugar than most honey cakes, this one is lighter in fat and calories, but it still has great taste.

To turn honey cake into a more sophisticated dessert, I like to serve each thin slice with a few spoonfuls of Red Wine and Pear Sauce (page 81) and to garnish the plate with a few thin wedges of fresh ripe pear. The pear should be cut at the last minute so it doesn't discolor.

1¹/₂ teaspoons instant coffee granules

6 tablespoons hot water

1¹/₂ cups all-purpose flour

1 teaspoon baking powder

¹/₂ teaspoon baking soda

¹/₂ teaspoon ground cinnamon

Small pinch of cloves

2 large eggs

¹/₂ cup sugar

¹/₂ cup honey

¹/₃ cup vegetable oil

¹/₄ cup very finely chopped crystallized ginger

¹/₃ to ¹/₂ cup pecans, coarsely chopped

1. Preheat oven to 325°F. Lightly grease an 8 × 4-inch loaf pan, line it with parchment paper or wax paper and grease liner.

2. Dissolve coffee granules in the hot water in a cup. Let cool. Sift flour with baking powder, baking soda, cinnamon, and cloves in a medium bowl.

3. Beat eggs lightly in a large bowl with an electric mixer. Add sugar and honey and beat until mixture is very smooth and lightened in color. Gradually add oil and beat until blended. Stir in flour mixture alternately with coffee, each in two batches. Last, stir in crystallized ginger and pecans.

4. Pour batter into prepared pan. Bake 50 to 55 minutes or until a cake tester inserted in cake comes out clean. Cool in pan for about 15 minutes. Turn out onto rack and carefully peel off liner. Wrap in foil when completely cool. (If tightly wrapped, cake keeps 1 week at room temperature.) Serve in thin slices.

Sephardic Almond Honey Squares

Makes 12 servings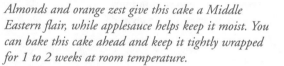

Almonds and orange zest give this cake a Middle Eastern flair, while applesauce helps keep it moist. You can bake this cake ahead and keep it tightly wrapped for 1 to 2 weeks at room temperature.

2¹/₄ cups all-purpose flour

2¹/₄ teaspoons baking powder

³/₄ teaspoon baking soda

¹/₂ teaspoon ground cinnamon

¹/₂ teaspoon ground ginger

3 large eggs

³/₄ cup sugar

1 cup honey

³/₄ cup vegetable oil

1¹/₂ teaspoons grated orange rind

¹/₂ cup unsweetened applesauce

³/₄ cup blanched almonds, chopped

1. Preheat oven to 350°F. Lightly grease a 9-inch square pan, line it with parchment paper or wax paper and grease the liner.

2. Sift flour with baking powder, baking soda, cinnamon, and ginger into a bowl.

3. Beat eggs lightly in a large bowl with an electric mixer. Add sugar and honey and beat until mixture is smooth and lightened in color. Gradually add oil and beat until blended. Add orange rind and beat briefly.

On low speed, beat in flour mixture alternately with applesauce, each in a few portions. Add almonds and beat just until blended.

4. Pour batter into prepared pan. Bake about 55 minutes or until a cake tester inserted in cake comes out clean. Cool in pan about 15 minutes. Turn out onto rack and carefully peel off paper. Wrap with foil when completely cool. Serve at room temperature. Cut into squares.

Apple Cake with Honey

Makes 9 or 10 servings

Apples dipped in honey are delicious on Rosh Hashanah. The pair also makes a wonderful flavoring combination for holiday cakes. This moist cake flavored with cinnamon and lemon is not a honey cake, as the honey is a flavor accent instead of the dominating taste.

$3/4$ cup plus 1 tablespoon sugar

1 teaspoon ground cinnamon

2 large eggs

$1/4$ cup honey

$1/2$ cup vegetable oil

2 teaspoons finely grated lemon rind

$1^1/2$ cups all-purpose flour

$1^1/4$ teaspoons baking powder

$1/4$ teaspoon baking soda

$1/4$ teaspoon salt

2 tablespoons strained fresh lemon juice

2 tablespoons water

$1/2$ cup diced or coarsely chopped pecans (optional)

2 large sweet apples, such as Golden Delicious (total $3/4$ pound), peeled, cored, and sliced paper-thin

1. Preheat oven to 350°F. Lightly grease an 8-inch square pan, then flour pan lightly. Mix 1 tablespoon sugar with the cinnamon in a small bowl and set aside.

2. Beat eggs with $3/4$ cup sugar in a large bowl with an electric mixer on medium speed. Add honey, oil, and lemon rind, and beat to blend. In a medium bowl, sift flour, baking powder, baking soda, and salt. Add about half of flour mixture to egg batter and blend together at low speed. Mix lemon juice and water in a small bowl and add to batter. Slowly blend in remaining flour mixture. Add pecans and blend on low speed.

3. Spoon $1/4$ of batter into prepared pan and spread evenly. Arrange $1/3$ of apple slices on batter and sprinkle evenly with $1/3$ of cinnamon mixture (about 1 heaping teaspoon). Spoon another $1/4$ of the batter in dollops over apples and spread very gently. Repeat with 2 more layers of apples, cinnamon, and batter, ending with batter. (Top layer of apples may not be completely covered.)

4. Bake 40 to 45 minutes or until a tester inserted in cake's center comes out clean. Cool cake in pan on a rack about 20 minutes. Run a metal spatula carefully around cake and turn out onto rack. Let cool. Serve at room temperature.

Chocolate Chip Honey Cake

Makes 9 to 12 servings

Everyone loves chocolate chips. Even children who won't eat honey cake will be glad to celebrate Rosh Hashanah with this easy-to-make cake.

$2^1/4$ cups all-purpose flour

$2^1/4$ teaspoons baking powder

$3/4$ teaspoon baking soda

$3/4$ teaspoon ground cinnamon

$1/2$ teaspoon ground ginger

3 large eggs

1 cup brown sugar

$3/4$ cup honey

$2/3$ cup vegetable oil

$1/2$ cup unsweetened applesauce

$3/4$ cup semisweet chocolate chips

1. Preheat oven to 350°F. Lightly grease a 9-inch square pan, line it with parchment paper or wax paper and grease the liner. Sift the flour with the baking powder, baking soda, cinnamon, and ginger into a bowl.

2. Beat the eggs lightly in a large bowl with an electric mixer on medium speed. Add the sugar and honey and beat until the mixture is smooth and lightened in color. Gradually add the oil and beat until blended. On low speed, beat in the flour mixture alternately with the applesauce, each in two batches. Last, beat in the chocolate chips.

3. Pour the batter into the prepared pan. Bake about 55 minutes or until your finger does not leave an indentation when you press lightly on top of cake, and a cake tester inserted in the cake comes out clean. Cool in the pan on a rack about 15 minutes. Turn out onto rack and carefully peel off the liner. Wrap in foil when completely cool. Serve at room temperature. Cut into squares or bars.

Cocoa Applesauce Cake with Honey Frosting

Makes about 16 to 20 servings

This is a new twist on my mother's chocolate applesauce cake. It's the same cake, but she usually frosts it with chocolate melted with a little margarine. For Rosh Hashanah I like to make a frosting from the favorite holiday sweetener, honey. I use either Honey Buttercream (this page) or a chocolate-based Honey Ganache (page 81). For garnish, a simple sprinkling of chopped pecans is perfect. If you're using the Honey Buttercream, you can sprinkle grated chocolate instead, as it complements the light beige color of the frosting. Either version makes our family's beloved cake into a wonderful dessert.

3 cups all-purpose flour

2/3 cup unsweetened cocoa powder

1 tablespoon ground cinnamon

2 teaspoons baking soda

1 cup vegetable oil

2 cups sugar

2 large eggs

2 cups unsweetened applesauce

1/2 cup chopped pecans, plus extra for garnish if desired

Honey Buttercream frosting (this page) or Honey Ganache (page 81)

1. Preheat oven to 350°F. Grease and flour a 13 × 9 × 2-inch baking pan. Sift flour with cocoa, cinnamon, and baking soda into a medium bowl.

2. Beat oil with sugar and eggs in a large bowl with an electric mixer until pale and fluffy. Stir flour mixture alternately with applesauce into egg mixture and mix well, either on low speed of mixer or with a wooden spoon. Stir in the chopped pecans.

3. Transfer batter to prepared pan. Bake 35 to 45 minutes or until a cake tester inserted in cake's center comes out clean. Cool in pan on a rack about 20 minutes or until just warm. Turn out onto a rack or leave in the pan; cool completely.

4. Prepare frosting or ganache. Then, spread in a thin layer over top of cake. Sprinkle top with pecans if using for garnish.

5. Refrigerate cake about 2 hours before serving.

Honey Buttercream

Makes about 1³/4 cups, enough for a 13 ×9 ×2-inch cake

Honey is the only flavoring in this frosting, so be sure to use a kind of honey you like. It's great on chocolate cakes, spice cakes, and cakes made with fruit. Use butter for dairy meals or nondairy margarine to keep the cake pareve.

1 cup (2 sticks) unsalted butter or margarine

2 large eggs

1/2 cup honey

1. Soften butter slightly but keep it cool.

2. Beat eggs in a large bowl with an electric mixer until smooth. Bring honey to a boil in a small saucepan. Gradually pour honey onto eggs, whisking constantly. Whip at high speed about 5 minutes or until completely cool and thick.

3. Cream butter in another large bowl with the mixer until smooth and fluffy. Beat in honey mixture gradually, beating thoroughly after each addition.

Honey Ganache

Makes about 1½ cups, enough for
the top of a 13 × 9 × 2-inch cake or

*This luscious frosting is great on chocolate cakes or
on brownies.*

½ cup whipping cream, nondairy creamer, or nondairy
    rice milk

6 ounces semisweet chocolate, finely chopped

6 tablespoons (¾ stick) unsalted butter or margarine,
    slightly softened

3 tablespoons plus 1 teaspoon honey

1. Bring cream to a boil in a small, heavy saucepan. Remove from heat and immediately add chopped chocolate. Using a small whisk, stir quickly until chocolate is completely melted and mixture is smooth. Transfer to a bowl. Cool to room temperature. Using an electric mixer, whip mixture at high speed about 3 minutes.

2. Cream butter in a large bowl with an electric mixer until very soft and smooth. Beat in chocolate mixture in 3 batches. Beat well until frosting is smooth. Gradually beat in honey until blended.

Fresh Plum Sauce

Makes 5 or 6 servings

Red-fleshed plums give this sauce a beautiful color. Turn a slice of honey cake into an elegant dessert by surrounding it with a ribbon of this sauce and accompanying it with a few wedges of fresh fruit. It's also good with sponge cake or angel food cake.

Another way to use plum sauce is in savory dishes. Omit the powdered sugar, and you can serve this dish with roast chicken or duck, instead of applesauce.

¾ cup sugar

3 cups water

1 vanilla bean (optional)

1 pound ripe plums, preferably red-fleshed, halved
    and pitted

5 to 6 tablespoons powdered sugar, sifted

1 to 2 teaspoons plum brandy (optional)

1. Combine sugar, water, and vanilla bean, if using, in a heavy saucepan. Cook over low heat, stirring gently, until sugar dissolves. Bring to boil over high heat. Add plums. Cover and cook plums over low heat about 12 minutes or until tender when pierced with sharp knife. Cool in syrup. Refrigerate for 30 minutes.

2. Remove plums from their poaching syrup; reserve syrup. Puree plums with 5 tablespoons of poaching syrup in food processor or blender. Add 5 tablespoons powdered sugar and puree until smooth. Strain into a bowl, pressing gently on pulp in strainer. Use rubber spatula to scrape remaining sauce from underside of strainer.

3. Whisk sauce until smooth. If sauce is too thick, gradually whisk in 1 or 2 tablespoons more syrup. Taste and add more powdered sugar if needed. Whisk sauce thoroughly to blend in sugar. Strain sauce again if necessary. Cover and refrigerate until ready to serve. Stir in plum brandy, if using. Serve cold.

Red Wine and Pear Sauce

Makes about 1 cup sauce, about 4 to 6 servings (P)

This sauce requires advance planning to prepare, but it's worth it: with its rosy wine color, it is great with cakes, especially in autumn. Serve it with homemade or bakery honey cake, vanilla ice cream, or pear sorbet.

Only part of the delicious wine syrup is needed for the sauce. Save the rest and use it to moisten fruit salads. Or make a quick fruit compote: Bring the syrup to a simmer, add dried fruit, and let it steep in the syrup off the heat until tender.

½ cup sugar

2 cups dry red wine

1 vanilla bean

¾ pound ripe pears, peeled, halved, and cored

2 tablespoons powdered sugar, sifted

1. Combine sugar, wine, and vanilla bean in medium, heavy saucepan and cook over low heat, stirring gently, until sugar dissolves. Raise heat to high and bring to boil. Add pears. Cover with a lid slightly smaller than diameter of saucepan to keep fruit submerged. Cook pears over low heat 30 minutes to 1 hour or until tender when pierced with sharp knife; cooking time varies with ripeness.

2. Cool in syrup, still covered, to room temperature. Refrigerate in syrup for 8 hours or overnight so that pears absorb color and flavor from syrup.

3. With a slotted spoon remove pears from syrup, reserving syrup.

4. Puree pears with 3 tablespoons of poaching syrup in a food processor or blender. Add powdered sugar and puree until smooth. Strain into a bowl, pressing on pulp in strainer. Use rubber spatula to scrape sauce from underside of strainer. Whisk sauce until smooth and sugar is completely blended in. If a thinner sauce is desired, gradually whisk in up to 2 tablespoons more syrup. Strain again if any lumps of sugar remain. Cover and refrigerate 30 minutes. Stir before serving. Serve cold.

Hazelnut Walnut Tayglach

Makes about 30 pieces

If you like gooey, sticky sweets, tayglach are for you. This old-fashioned Ashkenazic confection of pastry balls and nuts simmered in honey is a Rosh Hashanah specialty. Just before the holiday, tayglach are featured at Jewish bakeries, where the shiny sweets are often shaped in mounds, set in cupcake papers, and garnished with candied cherries. Be sure to serve them with strong unsweetened coffee or tea.

Tayglach keep very well wrapped in plastic and stored in airtight containers. (The plastic prevents them from sticking to the container.) You can either wrap the tayglach mixture and cut it when you need it, or cut it into squares and wrap each one.

1 cup hazelnuts

1/2 cup small walnut halves

1 1/3 cups all-purpose flour

2 teaspoons ground ginger

1/4 teaspoon baking powder

1/4 teaspoon salt

2 large eggs

2 large egg yolks

2 tablespoons vegetable oil

1 cup honey

1 cup sugar

1. Preheat oven to 350°F. Put hazelnuts in a baking pan. Toast them in oven about 8 minutes or until their skins begin to split. Transfer hazelnuts to a strainer. While they are hot, remove most of skins by rubbing hazelnuts energetically with a towel against strainer. Let nuts cool on a plate. Add walnuts to hazelnuts. Leave oven on.

2. Grease 2 large baking sheets. Sift flour with 1/2 teaspoon ginger, baking powder, and salt in a medium bowl. Make a well in center. Add eggs, egg yolks, and oil to well. Stir until combined. Knead on a lightly floured surface about 3 minutes or until it becomes a soft, smooth dough. If dough is very sticky, knead in about 1 tablespoon more flour. If dough is very dry, add 1 tablespoon water.

3. Cut dough into 8 pieces with floured knife. Using both hands, roll a piece of dough on a lightly floured surface into a thin rope of 1/2-inch diameter. With a floured, heavy knife, cut rope into 1/2-inch lengths. Repeat with remaining dough.

4. Place dough pieces on baking sheets without letting them touch each other. Bake about 10 minutes or until their bottoms are light brown. Remove from oven. Line another large baking sheet with foil and oil the foil.

5. Combine honey, sugar, and remaining 1 1/2 teaspoons ginger in large, heavy saucepan. Cook over low heat, stirring occasionally, until sugar dissolves. Bring to a boil over medium heat; be careful, as mixture boils over easily. Cook over low heat about 5 minutes or until syrup reaches the hard-ball stage, 260°F on a candy thermometer.

6. Carefully add tayglach, hazelnuts, and walnuts to syrup. Cook over medium-low heat, stirring occasion-ally, about 10 minutes or until tayglach are golden brown.

7. Stir tayglach mixture to distribute nuts evenly. Spoon mixture onto foil-lined baking sheet. Flatten it so that tayglach form a thin layer; let cool completely.

8. Turn tayglach over onto a board. Carefully peel off foil. Cut into 1-inch squares. To store, wrap in plastic wrap. Keep in shallow, airtight containers at room temperature until ready to serve. Serve in candy papers.

Rosh Hashanah Fruit Salad

Makes 4 servings

During this season, plums are plentiful and make a lovely addition to fresh fruit salads. Choose two different types to make a good mix of color. They make a pretty and delicious combination with yellow nectarines and green or red grapes. For Rosh Hashanah, make a light, easy dressing from honey, wine, and mint.

If you like, serve the fruit salad with Fresh Plum Sauce (page 81) instead of making the honey dressing. Or, if Rosh Hashanah falls on a hot day, serve the fruit salad in bowls and top each with a scoop of fruit sorbet.

6 ripe plums, preferably 3 red-fleshed and 3 yellow-fleshed, cut into wedges

1⅓ cups green or red seedless grapes

3 ripe nectarines

2 tablespoons honey

2 tablespoons dry red or white wine or orange juice

2 teaspoons chopped fresh mint

Fresh mint sprigs for garnish

Put plum wedges in a large bowl. Add grapes, nectarines, honey, wine, and mint. Serve cold, garnished with mint sprigs.

Rashi's Figs

Makes about 8 servings

As a child and teenager I studied at the Hebrew Academy of Washington, D.C. Many of the lessons in our Torah classes required reading the writings of Rashi, the most famous Torah commentator, who lived in France in the eleventh century.

Rashi believed that the fruit of the Garden of Eden wasn't apples, but figs. He pointed out that apples didn't grow in that part of the world and that Adam and Eve covered themselves with fig leaves.

Rashi was not only a great scholar but a winemaker too. I have to admit, I don't know if he really poached fresh figs in wine syrup, but it's certainly plausible. I learned the recipe from one of his twentieth century countrymen, Master Chef Fernand Chambrette.

If you want more delicately textured figs, remove the skins gently with a vegetable peeler, as French chefs do. I skip this step when using Mission figs from my tree.

1¼ cups sugar

4 cups dry red wine

Rind of ½ lemon

2 pounds fresh figs

1. Heat the sugar, wine, and lemon rind in a medium saucepan over low heat, stirring gently until the sugar dissolves. Bring the syrup to a boil and add the figs. Bring the syrup to a simmer. Reduce the heat to low and poach the figs uncovered about 15 minutes or until they are just tender but retain their shape.

2. Let figs cool in the syrup. With a slotted spoon remove them carefully and put them in a deep dish. Discard the lemon rind pieces.

3. Boil the syrup without stirring until it is reduced to about 2 cups. Let syrup cool, then pour it over the figs. Refrigerate 1 hour or longer. Serve cold.

Yom Kippur, the Day of Atonement, is the most solemn holiday, a day of fasting and repentance for sins. It takes place in late September to early October, ten days after Rosh Hashanah, the Jewish New Year. No food or drink is allowed. The entire day is spent in prayer.

Before The Fast

Food customs on the eve of Yom Kippur are designed to minimize thirst (and discomfort) during the fast. Foods are delicately spiced dishes; people cook with less salt and other seasonings than in most meals. (Also, some people gradually reduce the amount of coffee they drink during the week preceding Yom Kippur to prevent caffeine headaches during the fast.)

The dinner before the fast is generous but fairly simple. Generally a chicken entree is served. Many cooks poach a chicken with vegetables and serve its flavorful soup as a first course. In Ashkenazic homes, the soup often contains matzo balls or kreplach, which resemble tortellini. Sephardic families tend to opt for rice.

As with the Jewish New Year, the bread is usually a round challah. Desserts vary with each family but tend to be simple. When I was growing up, we had a slice of sponge cake or chiffon cake. Some serve honey cake because they baked an extra one at Rosh Hashanah.

Roman Fish with Pine Nuts and Raisins

Makes 4 servings

This dish is customary in the before-fast meal of Italian Jews. Usually it's made with whole fish but in this version I use fillets to make it easier to prepare and eat.

1¹/₂ pounds sea bass steaks or fillets

3 tablespoons olive oil

3 tablespoons white wine vinegar

Salt and freshly ground pepper, to taste

¹/₃ cup pine nuts

¹/₃ cup raisins

1 tablespoon chopped fresh Italian parsley (optional)

Preheat oven to 400°F. Oil a heavy baking dish and arrange fish fillets inside. Mix oil and vinegar and spoon it over fish. Sprinkle fish lightly with salt and pepper. Scatter pine nuts and raisins over fish. Cover with foil and bake 15 to 20 minutes or until thickest part of fish becomes opaque inside; check with a sharp knife. Serve hot or cold, sprinkled with parsley, if using.

Whole Poached Chicken with Vegetables

Makes about 6 servings

Also known as chicken in the pot, chicken in soup, or boiled chicken, this is a favorite main course for the meal before the fast. Generally it's made with carrots, onions, and celery but I like to add a greater variety of vegetables and serve them with the chicken. A stewing hen is the traditional choice but I use a large roasting or frying chicken as it's easier to find.

The broth from cooking the whole chicken makes the best chicken soup. Serve it as a first course in the pre-Yom Kippur dinner with kreplach, kneidel, noodles, or rice.

One 3¹/₂- to 4-pound chicken

1 large onion, whole

2 ribs celery, including leafy tops

1 parsnip or parsley root (optional)

2 large cloves garlic, coarsely chopped

2 bay leaves

Salt and freshly ground pepper, to taste

2 quarts water

1 pound banana squash or other winter squash

4 boiling potatoes, quartered

4 medium carrots, cut into 1-inch slices

4 medium zucchini, cut into thick slices

8 ounces mushrooms, quartered

3 to 4 tablespoons chopped fresh Italian parsley

1. Remove excess fat from chicken. Put chicken in a large stew pan or pot, allowing room for vegetables. Add onion, celery, parsnip if using, garlic, bay leaves, and a pinch of salt. Add the water to cover. Bring to a boil. Skim foam from surface. Cover and cook over low heat 1¹/₂ hours.

2. Cut peel from banana squash and cut meat into 1-inch cubes. Add to pot. Add potatoes and carrots. Cover and cook over low heat 20 minutes. Add zucchini and mushrooms. Cook 10 to 15 minutes or until chicken and vegetables are tender. Season broth with salt and pepper.

3. Remove chicken pieces and cool slightly. Remove skin from chicken. Cut chicken into serving pieces and return them to soup. Skim fat from broth. (If time permits, chill soup so fat is easier to skim.)

4. To serve: if chilled, reheat chicken in soup and add chopped parsley. Serve chicken in fairly shallow bowls with pieces of banana squash, carrots, potato, zucchini, and mushrooms. Moisten each serving with a few spoonfuls of soup.

Chicken with Forty Cloves of Garlic

Makes 4 servings

It might surprise you to find this Provençal specialty on a pre-Yom Kippur menu, given that subtle seasonings are the norm to avoid provoking thirst. But it is a perfect choice, especially when you want a change from the usual boiled chicken. Cooks in southern France discovered that long, gentle cooking of garlic mellows it and gives it a delicate sweetness. The garlic imparts a lovely aroma to the chicken and to its juices.

Best of all, it's easy to make. Don't picture yourself peeling all that garlic; it cooks in its peel. You serve the individual cloves so you can squeeze the soft, delicious garlic onto your portion of chicken or, if you like, onto the accompanying vegetables. You don't even have to count to 40; you can just use two garlic heads. Be sure the garlic is fresh and firm.

In France the mellow garlic is spread on oven-toasted slices of baguette or French bread. You could use toasted pita wedges, but to my taste, not sweet challah.

I like to serve the chicken with Sweet Potato Puree, Miami Style (page 200) or Rosh Hashanah Sweet Potato Casserole (page 74). Herbed Rice (page 500) is another good choice for soaking up the delicious chicken juices.

In traditional French recipes, you make a paste of flour and water and smear it between the lid and the casserole to keep it tightly closed. I use a heavy casserole dish with a tight cover and skip this step.

One 3-pound chicken, cut into 8 pieces
Salt and freshly ground pepper, to taste
2 to 4 tablespoons olive oil
2 ribs celery, cut into thin slices
1 large sprig fresh thyme or 1 teaspoon dried thyme
1 bay leaf
2 tablespoons chopped fresh Italian parsley
40 medium cloves garlic, unpeeled
1/4 cup brandy

1. Preheat oven to 350°F. Sprinkle the chicken pieces lightly with salt and pepper. In a deep, heavy, enamel-coated cast iron casserole with a tight-fitting lid, or in a Dutch oven, mix oil with celery, thyme, bay leaf, and 1 tablespoon parsley. Add chicken pieces and stir well to coat them with the mixture.

2. Separate the garlic cloves from the heads and remove any loose skin. Add the garlic and brandy to the casserole. Cover tightly. Bake chicken for 1 hour 15 minutes. To check whether chicken is done, insert a skewer into thickest part of thigh; juices that run from chicken should be clear. If juices are pink, continue baking chicken a few more minutes and check again. Keep it warm, covered, until ready to serve.

3. If you like, bring the casserole to the table so everyone enjoys the aroma. Discard bay leaf and thyme sprig. Sprinkle chicken with remaining parsley. Serve chicken pieces with garlic cloves and a spoonful of the juices.

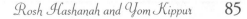

Noodle Kugel with Carrots and Apples

Makes 8 to 10 servings

Noodle kugel has long been a treasured accompaniment on our family's before-the-fast dinner menu. Many people make their noodle kugel with either fruit or vegetables, but for this one I like to combine both. Since carrots are sweet, they harmonize well with the apples, and provide flecks of pretty color. Actually, it's not such a wild combination; some people make carrot and apple tzimmes.

This kugel does not contain much sugar. Seasoned with a touch of cinnamon and ginger, the sweet-savory kugel is delicious with roast chicken or tzimmes.

1 pound wide egg noodles

3 large carrots, coarsely grated

3 large apples, sweet or tart, peeled and coarsely grated

4 tablespoons vegetable oil

2 to 3 tablespoons sugar

1/2 teaspoon salt, or to taste

Freshly ground pepper, to taste

1/2 teaspoon ground cinnamon

1/2 teaspoon ground ginger

4 large eggs, beaten

1. Preheat oven to 350°F. Grease a 3 1/2- to 4-quart baking dish or two smaller baking dishes and set aside.

2. Cook noodles in a large pot of boiling salted water uncovered over high heat, stirring occasionally, about 4 minutes or until nearly tender but firmer than usual, since they will be baked. Drain, rinse with cold water, and drain well again. Transfer to a large bowl.

3. Add carrots, apples, 3 tablespoons oil, 2 tablespoons sugar, salt, pepper, cinnamon, and ginger to noodles. Taste and adjust seasoning; add remaining sugar if you like. Add beaten eggs and mix well Add noodle mixture to prepared baking dish. Sprinkle with remaining tablespoon oil.

4. Bake 45 to 55 minutes or until set; kugel will bake faster in shallow dishes than in deep ones. Serve hot, from baking dish.

Chocolate Chip Mandelbrot

Makes about 36 cookies

The traditional Ashkenazic version of these crunchy cookies is made with almonds (see Orange Mandelbrot, page 578) but they're good with all sorts of nuts. Adding chocolate chips is an American innovation.

3 large eggs

1 1/4 cups sugar

1 cup vegetable oil

1 teaspoon grated lemon rind

1 teaspoon vanilla extract

4 cups all-purpose flour

1 1/2 teaspoons baking powder

1/4 teaspoon salt

1 1/2 cups semisweet or bittersweet chocolate chips

3/4 cup pecans, chopped

1. Preheat oven to 350°F. Grease 2 to 3 baking sheets. Beat eggs, sugar, and oil in a large bowl with an electric mixer until blended. Beat in lemon rind and vanilla. Sift flour with baking powder and salt into a medium bowl. Add to egg mixture and stir on low speed of mixer just until blended. Stir in chocolate chips and pecans on low speed.

2. Shape dough into 4 log-shaped rolls, each about 2 inches in diameter; their shape will not be very even, as dough is sticky. Place on a baking sheet. Refrigerate 30 minutes. Use spatula to smooth dough and to push again into log shape, as it will have relaxed and spread a bit.

3. Bake logs 30 minutes or until lightly browned and set. Transfer carefully to a cutting board and let stand until cool enough to handle. With a sharp knife, carefully cut in diagonal slices about 1/2 inch thick; dough will be slightly soft inside. Return slices to cleaned baking sheets in one layer; you will need 2 to 3 baking sheets.

4. Bake about 7 minutes per side or until lightly toasted so they are beige and dotted in places with golden brown; side of cookie touching baking sheet will brown first. Watch carefully so cookies don't brown throughout. Cool on a rack. Keep in airtight containers.

After the Fast

When Yom Kippur is over, after a night and day spent in prayer and remorse for sins (and, occasionally, dreaming about food), the mood is festive. Finally the time has arrived to break the fast.

In our family and in many others, this means eating comfort food. What is eaten depends on each family's traditions. Some serve a *fleishig* meal with a main course of meat. When my husband was growing up in the Tel Aviv suburb of Givatayim, his family usually had a hearty bowl of spicy Yemenite meat soup, accompanied by dark bread and *zehug* (hot pepper chutney), followed by fresh fruit.

In my childhood home in Washington, D.C., my mother prepared a *milchig*, or dairy-based, supper. She felt that a light meal was best after fasting. We were delighted, as this was the food we loved best: scrambled eggs and brunch-type foods like bagels with lox and cream cheese.

A caterer friend of mine in Los Angeles offers a very popular menu in this style. Her clients feast on smoked salmon, herring in cream sauce, tuna salad, egg salad, and Muenster cheese, along with challah, bagels, and raisin pumpernickel bread. For dessert, there is a choice between cheese cake and carrot cake.

In most homes, where the meal is home cooked, the menu is composed of dishes that are quick or that have been made ahead because cooking is prohibited during Yom Kippur. Sometimes my mother made a savory or sweet kugel the day before Yom Kippur and put it in the oven to reheat as soon as we returned home from the prayers at *shul* (Yiddish for "synagogue").

Of course, a taste of something sweet is often a favorite way to break the fast.

Moroccan Lentil, Chickpea, and Meat Soup

Harira

Makes 4 to 6 servings

My neighbor, Valerie Alon, prepares this hearty soup for the break-the-fast meal after Yom Kippur. It's a tradition in her husband's family and in many other Moroccan homes. Valerie makes her delicious version with beef, saffron, and aromatic vegetables. Some people make it with lamb and some with chicken. Tomatoes and lemon juice give the soup a tasty tang. Serve it as a main course with good crusty bread.

1 cup lentils

2 to 4 tablespoons olive oil

1 pound beef chuck or stew meat, diced small

1/2 onion, chopped fine

3 ribs celery, chopped fine

4 large cloves garlic, chopped fine

1/2 teaspoon ground turmeric

1/2 teaspoon freshly ground pepper

1/4 teaspoon ground cinnamon

6 cups chicken stock mixed with water (about equal parts)

Pinch of saffron

4 ripe tomatoes, peeled and chopped, or a 141/2-ounce can diced tomatoes, drained

1/2 cup chopped fresh Italian parsley

One 15-ounce can chickpeas (garbanzo beans), drained

1 tablespoon all-purpose flour

1 to 3 tablespoons strained fresh lemon juice

2 to 4 tablespoons coarsely chopped fresh cilantro

1. Spread lentils on a plate, pick through them carefully, rinse and drain them.

2. Heat oil in a large saucepan and add beef, onion, celery, garlic, turmeric, pepper, and cinnamon. Sauté over medium heat, stirring often, about 10 minutes or until beef cubes change color.

3. Add stock mixture, saffron, lentils, tomatoes, parsley, and chickpeas. Bring to a boil. Cover and cook over low heat 30 minutes. If soup is too thick, add 1 to 2 cups boiling water. Cook 45 minutes more or until meat and lentils are tender.

4. Spoon flour into a small bowl and stir in 1 tablespoon water and 1 tablespoon lemon juice. Stir until smooth. Gradually blend in 1 cup liquid from soup. Pour mixture into pot of soup, stirring. Return to a simmer, stirring. Simmer 1 minute. Season soup to taste with salt, pepper, and more lemon juice if needed.

5. Serve hot, sprinkled with cilantro.

Smoked Whitefish Spread

Makes about 6 servings

In many homes smoked fish is a favorite food on the break-the-fast table, and so are bagels. This spread is a perfect topping for bagels, but is also good on rye bread or on crackers that aren't very salty such as water crackers.

8 ounces whipped cream cheese

1/3 cup flaked smoked whitefish

2 teaspoons chopped fresh chives

2 to 3 tablespoons sour cream (optional)

Freshly ground pepper to taste

Cayenne pepper to taste

Mix cream cheese with whitefish and chives in a small bowl. If spread is too stiff, stir in sour cream, a tablespoon at a time. Season with pepper and cayenne. Refrigerate until ready to serve.

Creamy Cucumber Salad with Lox

Makes 6 to 8 servings

Cucumbers and smoked fish are traditional partners because the mild, refreshing cucumber flavor is the ideal foil for the concentrated, salty taste of the fish. To lend a festive air to this salad, you can garnish it with a few teaspoons of red caviar.

1 cup sour cream

2 cups plain yogurt

1 green onion, white and green parts, finely chopped (1 tablespoon reserved for garnish)

2 tablespoon chopped fresh dill or 1 teaspoon dried

Salt and freshly ground pepper, to taste

Cayenne pepper to taste

2 large hothouse cucumbers, thinly sliced

4 ounces lox or smoked salmon, cut into thin strips (a few reserved for garnish)

1. Mix sour cream and yogurt in a bowl. Add unreserved green onion, dill, salt, pepper, and cayenne pepper. Mix well.

2. Put cucumber in a shallow serving bowl. Add sour cream mixture and blend gently. Stir in the larger amount of lox. Taste and adjust seasoning. Serve cold, garnished with reserved lox and green onion.

Old-Fashioned Coffeecake

Makes 10 to 12 servings   Ⓓ

This is the type of coffeecake my mother often made when I was growing up. Enriched with sour cream and swirled with cinnamon and sugar, it is the perfect, after-the-fast treat. In fact, it's great at any time! Now, for a lighter treat, my mother and I often use half sour cream and half yogurt, as in this version, and it's still delicious, but you can use all sour cream if you prefer. You can bake it 2 to 3 days ahead, wrap it, and keep it at room temperature or in the refrigerator.

1¹/₂ teaspoons ground cinnamon

1 cup plus 3 tablespoons sugar

1³/₄ cups all-purpose flour

1¹/₂ teaspoons baking powder

¹/₂ teaspoon baking soda

³/₄ cup sour cream

³/₄ cup plain yogurt, regular, low-fat, or nonfat

1 teaspoon vanilla extract

¹/₂ cup unsalted butter

3 large eggs

1. Position rack in center of oven and preheat to 350°F. Generously grease a 9¹/₂ × 4-inch Bundt pan, kugelhopf mold, or fluted tube pan, taking care to butter tube and each fluted section. Mix cinnamon with 3 tablespoons sugar in a small bowl. Sift flour, baking powder and baking soda into a medium bowl. In another bowl mix sour cream, yogurt, and vanilla.

2. Cream butter in a large bowl with an electric mixer until light. Add 1 cup sugar and beat until smooth and fluffy. Beat in eggs, one by one. At low speed, stir in flour mixture alternately with sour cream mixture, each in 2 portions.

3. Pour slightly less than ¹/₂ the batter into prepared pan. Sprinkle with ¹/₂ the cinnamon sugar. Gently spoon dollops of batter over mixture, using just enough to cover it. Sprinkle with remaining cinnamon sugar. Gently add remaining batter in dollops over it. Spread gently to cover mixture. Bake about 55 minutes or until a cake tester inserted in cake's center comes out clean. Cool in pan on a rack 10 minutes. Run a thin-bladed flexible knife around tube but not around sides of pan. Invert cake onto a rack and cool completely. Serve at room temperature.

Breaking The Fast—Sweetly

In many Jewish homes, a favorite way to break the Yom Kippur fast is with a taste of something sweet. It might be a slice of honey cake that's still around from Rosh Hashanah. (Honey cake keeps very well.) Other frequent choices are a slice of sponge cake or a piece of almond bread called *mandelbrot* in Yiddish.

Another popular custom is to break the fast with breakfast pastries and cakes; after all, the word "breakfast" has "break the fast" in it! Cinnamon rolls are loved, and so are coffeecakes.

When it comes to coffeecakes, there are two distinct types. My brother and I have always preferred my mother's sour cream coffeecake. Other families opt for the Old World style of coffeecakes, which rise from the action of yeast.

My mother's coffee cake belongs to the relatively modern style—it can be made quickly and rises from the action of baking powder. It tends to be sweeter than the old-fashioned cakes like *kugelhopf*, a delicate, yeast-leavened cake usually studded with raisins and almonds. That probably explains why we, as children, liked the modern type of cake the best.

Besides being delicious and giving us a sense that we were pampering ourselves, the sweet indulgence custom may have a practical reason, too. Sugar is a quick source of energy, and most people definitely need a boost by the time the fast finally reaches its end.

Sukkot

Salads and Appetizers
93

Dvora's Bright and Easy
Pepper Salad

Mediterranean Chopped Salad
with Capers and Olives

Grilled Eggplant and Pepper
Salad with Sun-Dried Tomatoes

Green Salad with Smoked Fish

Tomatoes Stuffed with
Sole Salad

Red Cabbage Relish with Kiwi

Mushroom Croûtes

Bruschetta with an Israeli Touch

Harvest Soup

Pareve Creamy Carrot Soup

Main Courses
99

Coriander Roasted Sea Bass

Italian-Jewish Halibut in Tomato
Celery Sauce

Grilled Marinated Salmon,
Moroccan Style

Indian-Jewish Salmon and
Rice Casserole

Sephardic Chicken Lentil Soup

Baked Chicken with Potatoes,
Peppers, and Sage

Savory Sweet Chicken
with Quinces

Quick Turkey and Couscous

North African Lamb Tajine with
Jerusalem Artichokes

Kosher Moussaka

Ground Lamb Stew with Pine
Nuts

Lecso Pizza

Stuffed Vegetables
105

Old-Fashioned Stuffed Cabbage

Meat and Rice Stuffing

Artichokes with Tomato Stuffing

Spinach Stuffed Mushrooms

Spicy Stuffed Eggplant
with Turkey

Yemenite Turkey Stuffing

Sweet and Sour Stuffed Onions

Chicken Stuffing with Pecans
and Cranberries

P = *Pareve*   **D** = *Dairy*   **M** = *Meat*

Side Dishes
109

Rachel's Spiced Cauliflower
with Chickpeas

Zucchini Pistou Puree

Layered Chard and Bell
Pepper Gratin

Green Beans with Tomatoes
and Herbs

Potatoes with Onions,
Sephardic Style

Hungarian Noodles with
Slow-Cooked Cabbage

Basmati Rice Pilaf with
Sunflower Seeds and Vegetables

Sauces
112

Pineapple-Papaya Salsa

Fresh Red Onion, Tomato,
and Sweet Pepper Relish

Jalapeño Tomato Sauce

Desserts
114

Apple Strudel

Jewish Apple Cake with Walnuts
and Dried Cranberries

Pauline's Carrot Cake

Chocolate Pudding Cake

Creamy Cinnamon-Honey
Sauce

Fall Fruit in White Wine

Persimmon, Pear, and Kiwi Salad

*C*elebrated in early fall, Sukkot lasts for one week and is known as the Feast of Tabernacles. The Sukkah, or tabernacle in Hebrew, is a hut with a leafy roof that gives the holiday its name. It symbolizes the temporary shelters in which the ancient Israelites had to live during their flight from Egypt.

Spending much of the holiday in the Sukkah is the most important custom. Most people dine and receive visitors in the Sukkah, and some sleep there as well.

Sukkot is one of the harvest holidays, which include Shavuot and Rosh Hashanah, and produce plays a prominent role in its celebration. Pieces of fruit hang from the roof of the Sukkah for decoration. A prayer ceremony involves a fragrant citrus fruit called a citron (*etrog* in Hebrew), palm fronds, and other branches.

Building and decorating the Sukkah is a popular family activity, traditionally begun shortly after Yom Kippur. When I was growing up, we tied pears, bananas, and grape clusters to strings that my parents hung from the branches that formed the roof of our sukkah. My husband's family had a more elaborate sukkah that won awards from the city (Givatayim, Israel) for its beauty. He and the other children made artistic paper decorations and hung in their Sukkah pomegranates as well as guavas and citrus fruit from the trees in their yard.

Sukkot foods emphasize the harvest theme. Stuffed vegetables are traditional highlights of the menu, especially in Israel, where stuffed peppers, eggplant, and zucchini are special favorites. (These vegetables are plentiful during this season.) Desserts made of fruit are popular. Apple strudel appears on Ashkenazic tables and quince preserves as well as pumpkin- and squash-filled phyllo pastries on Sephardic ones.

A practical consideration also influences the Sukkot menu. Dishes need to be easy to carry and serve, as the distance from the kitchen to the dinner table is farther than usual and involves going outside. Thus casseroles and stews are favorites. When I was growing up, the fruit and vegetable casserole called tzimmes was often on our Sukkot table, as in many other Ashkenazic homes, and so was a big pot of stuffed cabbage.

Immediately after Sukkot are two more holidays, Shmini Atzeret, the Eighth Day of Assembly, and Simhat Torah, the Rejoicing of the Torah. In Israel both festivals are celebrated on the same day. On Shmini Atzeret a special prayer for rain is said, as the rainy season in Israel is about to begin. On Simhat Torah the year-long cycle of weekly Torah readings ends and the next one begins.

❋ Salads and Appetizers

Dvora's Bright and Easy Pepper Salad

Makes 4 to 6 servings

Jews from North Africa have numerous ways of utilizing peppers, and this is a particularly good one. I first tasted it at a Shabbat dinner during Sukkot at the home of Dvora Cohen, a relative of my husband. An excellent cook, Dvora was born in Morocco and now lives in Paris.

This simple salad showcases the pure flavors of the peppers. To prepare it, you don't need to grill or peel the peppers. All you do is cook a medley of sweet and hot peppers together in oil. Dvora likes plenty of hot peppers but you can use any proportion of sweet and hot peppers you prefer. She often makes this with green peppers but you can use red also.

4 to 6 tablespoons vegetable oil or olive oil

4 large red, green, or yellow bell peppers, cut into 1/3-inch-wide strips

3 or 4 jalapeño or 6 to 8 serrano peppers, seeds and ribs removed, finely diced (see Note)

Salt, to taste

Heat oil in a large skillet or sauté pan. Add bell peppers and sauté over medium-low heat, stirring occasionally, about 15 minutes or until peppers are nearly tender; reduce heat if necessary so that peppers do not brown. Add jalapeño peppers and cook over low heat, stirring often, about 5 minutes or until bell peppers are completely tender. If hot peppers begin to brown, add 2 to 3 tablespoons water. Season with salt. Serve cold.

Note: Wear rubber gloves when handling hot peppers.

Mediterranean Chopped Salad with Capers and Olives

Makes 4 servings

For this Provençal twist on the Israeli standard chopped salad, I like to use a dressing accented with both lemon juice and a little grated lemon zest.

5 plum tomatoes (about 1/2 pound), diced

1/2 long European cucumber or 1 common cucumber, diced

1/4 red onion, chopped

2 tablespoons extra-virgin olive oil

1 tablespoon strained fresh lemon juice

1 teaspoon fresh thyme or 1/4 teaspoon dried

1/2 teaspoon finely grated lemon zest

Salt and freshly ground pepper, to taste

2 tablespoons chopped fresh Italian parsley

1/4 cup to 1/3 cup good-quality black olives, pitted

1 tablespoon capers

Mix tomato, cucumber, and onion in a shallow bowl. Whisk oil, lemon juice, thyme, lemon zest, salt, and pepper in a small bowl. Add to salad and mix well. Add parsley, olives, and half the capers, then adjust seasoning. Serve sprinkled with remaining capers.

Grilled Eggplant and Pepper Salad with Sun-Dried Tomatoes

Makes about 6 servings

Ⓟ

Eggplants and many varieties of peppers are at the peak of their seasons on Sukkot and are popular for the holiday. If you're grilling the rest of your meal outdoors, prepare the vegetables for this festive salad on the barbecue; or grill the vegetables one day and keep them for the next. Otherwise, use a ridged stove-top grill pan or broil them. I like to toss the grilled vegetables with flavorful greens like spinach, romaine lettuce, or a mixture of both.

2 Japanese, Chinese, or small Italian eggplants, unpeeled and cut crosswise into 1/4-inch slices

3 tablespoons extra-virgin olive oil, plus a little for brushing

Salt and freshly ground pepper, to taste

1 red bell pepper, halved and cored

1 yellow or green bell pepper, halved and cored

8 cups spinach leaves

1 1/2 to 2 tablespoons strained fresh lemon juice

1 teaspoon fresh thyme or 1/2 teaspoon dried

2 tablespoons slivered fresh basil (optional)

6 oil-packed sun-dried tomatoes, halved

1. Brush eggplant lightly with oil on both sides and sprinkle with salt and pepper. Grill or broil 5 to 7 minutes on each side or until tender. Remove and let cool.

2. Set peppers on grill or broiler with their skin side facing the heat. Grill or broil about 5 minutes or until pepper skins begins to blister. Put peppers in a bowl, cover, and let stand 10 minutes; pull off skins.

3. Cut peppers into strips about 1/3-inch wide. Dice eggplants. Combine with spinach in a large bowl.

4. Whisk 3 tablespoons oil with lemon juice, thyme, salt, and pepper in a small bowl. Add to salad mixture and toss gently. Add basil, then adjust seasoning. Top with sun-dried tomatoes.

Green Salad with Smoked Fish

Makes 4 servings

Ⓟ

As in many other holidays, a cold fish appetizer is popular for Sukkot as it is convenient to prepare ahead and have ready to bring right to the Sukkah table. For this festive, easy salad, the fish tops a colorful mixture of romaine lettuce and red cabbage dressed with a light Asian vinaigrette. For another variation, try barbecued cod in place of the smoked fish.

4 ounces smoked whitefish, salmon, or cod

1 tablespoon Asian sesame oil

2 teaspoons vegetable oil

1 tablespoon rice vinegar

1/2 teaspoon soy sauce

Several drops hot sauce, or to taste

3 cups romaine lettuce, torn into bite-size pieces

1 cup shredded red cabbage

1. If using whitefish or cod, flake fish, discarding any bones. If using salmon, cut it into thin strips.

2. Whisk sesame oil with vegetable oil, vinegar, soy sauce, and hot sauce in a small bowl. Mix lettuce and cabbage in a serving bowl, add dressing and toss. Adjust seasoning, adding more soy sauce or hot sauce if you like. Serve greens topped with fish.

Tomatoes Stuffed with Sole Salad

Makes 6 light main course or 12 appetizer servings

Although hot stuffed vegetables are the custom for Sukkot, I also like to serve cold ones. These richly flavored tomatoes subtly seasoned with basil and curry make a delectable main course. Or you can serve half a tomato as a first course.

This is a simplified version of a dish I learned from Master Chef Fernand Chambrette in Paris. It appeared in the book we wrote together, La Cuisine du Poisson. *He used two kinds of fish and poached them in court bouillon, a quick broth made of aromatic vegetables and herbs cooked in wine and water, but I use sole and cook it in canned vegetable broth to save time. If you have already cooked fish or canned red salmon, you can substitute it for the sole.*

1 tablespoon vegetable oil

1 small onion, minced

1 teaspoon curry powder

1 cup long-grain rice

Salt and freshly ground pepper, to taste

2 cups boiling water

12 ounces sole fillets

2 cups vegetable broth or broth mixed with water,
    or 1 cup dry white wine and 1 cup broth

1 rib celery, peeled and finely diced

1 to 2 tablespoons shredded fresh basil plus 12 small basil
    leaves for garnish

1/2 green or red bell pepper, halved, cored, and diced

1/4 to 1/3 cup mayonnaise

6 large tomatoes

1. Heat oil in a heavy sauté pan. Add onion and cook over medium-low heat, stirring often, about 7 minutes or until soft but not brown. Add curry powder and rice and sauté, stirring, about 2 minutes or until rice is coated with onion mixture. Add salt, pepper, and the boiling water and stir once. Cover and cook over low heat without stirring about 18 minutes or until rice is tender. Let stand, covered, off heat, about 10 minutes. Fluff with a fork, transfer to a bowl and let cool.

2. Run your fingers over sole fillets to check for bones; pull out any bones using tweezers or a sharp paring knife. Sprinkle sole on both sides with salt and pepper. Fold each fillet in half. In a small sauté pan or medium saucepan wide enough to hold sole in one layer, bring vegetable broth to a simmer. Add sole. Cover and cook over low heat about 3 minutes or until fillets become opaque. Uncover and let stand in broth 2 minutes. Remove with a slotted spoon and let cool. (You can freeze the broth and save it for soups.)

3. Put sole in a bowl and flake it. Add rice, celery, basil, and peppers. Mix gently. Add just enough mayonnaise to moisten the filling. Adjust seasoning. Refrigerate until ready to serve.

4. To serve: Halve tomatoes horizontally. Remove interior with a teaspoon, leaving a layer of pulp attached to skin to form a shell. Fill tomato halves with salad, mounding filling. Refrigerate up to 1 hour. Garnish each with a small basil leaf and serve.

Red Cabbage Relish with Kiwi

Makes 4 servings **P**

This colorful vegetable and fruit medley is a good way to use kiwis that refuse to ripen. Their tart flavor and firm texture are perfect with the cabbage and the sweet vegetables—red bell pepper and jicama. Of course, you can make it with ripe kiwis too.

The relish is a good, fat-free accompaniment for grilled chicken or for Garlic-Scented Turkey Patties (page 367). It lends a lively note to the plate when served with Lebanese Lentil and Rice Casserole (page 502).

2 tablespoons red or white wine vinegar

1 teaspoon sugar

Salt and freshly ground pepper, to taste

4 cups shredded red cabbage

1 red bell pepper, halved, cored, and diced

2 cups diced peeled jicama

1¹/₂ cups coarsely chopped romaine lettuce or romaine
mixed with iceberg lettuce

2 kiwi, peeled, quartered, and sliced

1 tablespoon sliced fresh chives

Whisk vinegar with sugar, salt, and pepper in a large bowl. Add cabbage and mix well, until it is evenly moistened. Add red pepper, jicama, and lettuce and toss well. Add kiwi and chives to salad and toss. Adjust seasoning, adding more vinegar or sugar if you like.

Mushroom Croûtes

Makes 4 or 8 servings **P** or **D**

These crisp mushroom toasts resemble Italian crostini. To make them, you spread oven-toasted bread with a savory French mushroom topping called duxelles. *They make appealing hors d'oeuvres or snacks to serve to visitors who come during the week of Sukkot. They're also good as appetizers. For dairy meals, you can sprinkle them with cheese.*

8 ounces mushrooms, rinsed and patted dry

1 tablespoon olive oil, plus a little more for brushing
and drizzling

1 small shallot, minced

1¹/₂ teaspoons chopped fresh oregano or ¹/₂ teaspoon dried

Salt and freshly ground pepper, to taste

8 slices challah or French or Italian bread, ¹/₄-inch thick,
or 16 thin slices baguette

3 tablespoons bread crumbs or freshly grated Parmesan
cheese

1. Chop mushrooms in a food processor with pulsing motion so they are chopped into fine pieces but are not pureed. Heat 1 tablespoon oil in a medium skillet over low heat, add shallot, and sauté about 30 seconds until soft but not brown. Add mushrooms and oregano and sprinkle with salt and pepper. Cook over high heat, stirring, 3 to 5 minutes or until mixture is dry. Adjust seasoning.

2. Preheat oven to 425°F. Lightly brush both sides of bread slices with olive oil and put them on a baking sheet. Bake 5 minutes. Turn slices over and bake 3 more minutes.

3. Spread mushroom mixture on bread slices. Sprinkle with bread crumbs or cheese. If using bread crumbs, drizzle lightly with olive oil. Return to oven and bake 7 minutes or until hot. Serve hot.

Bruschetta with an Israeli Touch

Makes 4 servings

Bruschetta are trendy Italian appetizers often served at restaurants, but they're extemely easy to prepare at home. They're simply garlic toast with a fresh tomato-basil topping. I like to add the popular Israeli hot pepper chutney, zehug, to give it extra zip. Sometimes I substitute cilantro, which many Jews of Middle Eastern descent prefer to basil.

These hors d'oeuvres are terrific for serving in the Sukkah. You can bring them on a tray or simply bring a plate of toast and a bowl of topping, and your family and guests will make their own. If you prefer, you can skip the step of brushing the bread with oil and simply toast it in a toaster instead of in the broiler.

1/2 teaspoon Zehug (page 592), hot salsa, or hot sauce, or to taste

2 cups diced fresh tomatoes

3 tablespoons thin strips fresh basil or chopped cilantro

2 to 3 tablespoons extra-virgin olive oil

Salt and freshly ground pepper, to taste

8 slices Italian bread or 16 slices baguette or other slim crusty bread

2 large cloves garlic, peeled and halved

1. Prepare Zehug.

2. Mix tomatoes with Zehug, 2 tablespoons basil, and 2 tablespoons olive oil in a medium bowl. Season with salt and pepper.

3. Lightly brush bread with olive oil. Broil it until lightly toasted; turn over, brush with oil and lightly toast second side. Watch carefully; they burn easily. Rub both sides of toast with cut garlic while bread is still hot.

4. Serve toast topped with tomato-basil mixture.

Harvest Soup

Makes 4 servings

Celebrating the late summer harvest at the beginning of autumn has become a trend. Everyone who loves food seems to be in on it—restaurant chefs, farmers' market vendors, specialty nursery growers, and of course, home cooks and gardeners. It's a delightful way to entertain and a joyous reason to get together. Of course, this is not a completely new craze. Honoring the bounty of produce has long been a prominent theme in Sukkot menus.

Since this soup's cooking time is very brief—only about 10 minutes—it's convenient not only for the holiday menu, but for those days when you're short on time. As a basis, I begin with Mexican tortilla soup, a chile-flavored tomato soup garnished with fried tortillas. To make it simpler, I use packaged tortilla strips or chips, usually the low-fat kind. I add plenty of colorful vegetables, including corn kernel, to echo the flavor of the corn tortillas. Cilantro is the traditional herb but if I still have fresh basil in my garden I add some in.

Instead of canned mild chiles, you can add 1 or 2 chopped fresh jalapeño peppers.

1 tablespoon vegetable oil

1 medium onion, chopped

1 bell pepper (red, yellow, orange, or green) halved, cored, and diced

2 large cloves garlic, chopped (optional)

One 4-ounce can diced mild green chiles, drained (see Note)

One 28-ounce can diced tomatoes, drained

1 3/4 cups vegetable or chicken broth

2 cups hot water

3 medium zucchini or yellow crookneck squash, diced

1 cup fresh or frozen corn kernels

2 cups diced fresh tomatoes, red, yellow, orange, or a mixture

1/4 cup coarsely chopped fresh basil or cilantro

Salt to taste (optional)

Pure chili powder or cayenne pepper, to taste

3 to 4 cups tortilla chips, regular, baked, or oil-free, lightly crushed

Heat oil in a large saucepan. Add onion and bell pepper and sauté over medium heat 3 minutes. Stir in garlic, if using, and chiles, then canned tomatoes, broth, and water. Bring to a boil. Add zucchini and corn and return to a boil. Cover and simmer over medium-low heat 5 minutes or until vegetables are just tender. Add fresh tomatoes and 2 tablespoons basil. Season with salt, if using, and chili powder. Serve soup sprinkled with remaining basil. Sprinkle each bowl with tortilla chips or pass them separately.

Note: In some markets canned mild chiles are labeled simply "green chiles." If you're not sure how hot they are, before you cook with them, taste a bit; if they seem hot, add only half while preparing the soup, then add more to the finished soup if you like.

Pareve Creamy Carrot Soup

Makes 4 servings

With its wonderful delicate taste and lovely color, this soup is great comfort food and is a good choice for serving as a smooth, delicate first course before a traditional Sukkot meat casserole. Rice milk is great in carrot soup. It gives the soup a creamy feel without adding any dairy products. It adds a hint of sweetness that is perfect with the carrots. You can buy it in low-fat or nonfat versions. Before I discovered rice milk, I used to cook rice in my carrot soup and puree them together.

If you like your soups with a crunchy garnish, serve the soup with easy-to-make Baked Croutons (page 283).

1 tablespoon vegetable oil
1 onion, chopped
1¼ pounds carrots, diced
2¼ cups vegetable broth or water
Salt and freshly ground pepper, to taste
¼ teaspoon dried thyme, crumbled
1 bay leaf
1 to 1¼ cups rice milk (nondairy rice beverage)
Pinch of sugar (optional)
1 tablespoon chopped fresh Italian parsley

1. Heat oil in a heavy saucepan. Add onion and carrots and sauté over medium-low heat, stirring often, 5 minutes. Add broth, salt, pepper, thyme, and bay leaf and bring to a boil. Cover and cook over low heat about 20 minutes or until carrots are very tender. Remove bay leaf.

2. Puree soup in a blender or food processor until very smooth. If using a food processor, use a slotted spoon to transfer vegetables from soup to processor, and puree them; with machine running, gradually pour in cooking liquid. Return puree to saucepan.

3. Simmer soup over low heat 5 minutes, stirring often. Add 1 cup rice milk and bring to a boil, stirring. Add more milk if necessary to thin soup to desired consistency. Bring again to a boil, stirring. Adjust seasoning, adding sugar if needed. Serve garnished with parsley.

Main Courses

Coriander-Roasted Sea Bass

Makes 4 servings

Ground coriander seeds give a wonderful, delicate flavor to fish. For this simple but savory recipe, the fish is smeared with a quick spice rub and baked at high heat. I love it with fresh Chilean sea bass, as the spices subtly season but do not overpower the great taste of the fish, but other kinds of sea bass are good too.

It's a terrific entree for entertaining during Sukkot as its cooking time is very brief. As guests sit down to eat, have the oven preheated and the fish in its pan in the refrigerator. Then roast the fish just after you serve the first course. (For easier cleanup, line the roasting pan with foil.) If it's more convenient, you can even roast it just before the dinner and serve it at room temperature. Everyone will appreciate that this dish is low in fat and it's a good alternative entree when you want a main course that's less rich than many of the customary casseroles served during the holiday.

For accompaniments, I love Zucchini in Israeli Tomato Sauce (page 74) and Basmati Rice Pilaf with Sunflower Seeds and Vegetables (page 112).

1¼ to 1½ pounds sea bass fillet, about 1 inch thick

1 tablespoon strained fresh lemon juice

2 to 3 teaspoons extra-virgin olive oil

1½ teaspoons ground coriander

½ teaspoon paprika

¼ teaspoon dried thyme

Pinch of cayenne pepper

Salt and freshly ground pepper, to taste

Lemon wedges

1. Preheat oven to 450°F. Set fish in a heavy roasting pan. Sprinkle fish with lemon juice and oil and rub over fish. Mix coriander, paprika, thyme, and cayenne in a small bowl. Sprinkle the mixture over the fish on both sides and lightly rub in the spices. Then sprinkle fish evenly with salt and pepper.

2. Roast fish in oven 10 to 12 minutes or until the thickest part of the fish becomes opaque inside; check with a sharp knife. Serve fish with lemon wedges.

Italian-Jewish Halibut in Tomato Celery Sauce

Makes 6 to 8 first course or 4 main-course servings

Serving a cold fish in this savory tomato sauce is traditional on Sukkot for the Jews of Italy. The sauce is flavored with a few anchovies but you don't notice them in the finished dish; they simply contribute a pleasing accent.

2 to 3 tablespoons olive oil

3 ribs celery, cut into thin slices

4 anchovies, diced

1 cup or one 8-ounce can tomato sauce

1 cup water

1½ pounds halibut fillets or steaks, about 1 inch thick

Salt and freshly ground pepper, to taste

1 tablespoon strained fresh lemon juice, or to taste

Lemon wedges

1. Heat oil in a large sauté pan or skillet. Add celery and sauté over medium-low heat for 5 minutes or until celery begins to turn golden. Add anchovies and sauté 30 seconds. Add tomato sauce and the water and mix well. Bring to a simmer.

2. Add fish in one layer and sprinkle with salt and pepper. Cover and cook over low heat for 5 minutes. Turn fish over carefully. Cook 5 more minutes or until thickest part of the fish becomes opaque inside; check with a sharp knife. With a slotted spatula, carefully transfer fish to a serving dish deep enough to hold the sauce.

3. If sauce is too thin, cook it uncovered over medium heat, stirring often, for 2 or 3 minutes to thicken it. Stir in lemon juice and heat gently for 30 seconds. Adjust seasoning. Spoon sauce over fish. Serve fish cold, with lemon wedges.

Grilled Marinated Salmon, Moroccan Style

Makes 4 servings ℗

Moroccan Jewish cooks have many wonderful fish recipes. This is one of my favorites. Salmon's flavor stands up well to the pesto-like marinade blend of cilantro, garlic, cumin, and olive oil. For this recipe, I like to reserve some of the marinade and use it as a savory topping for the fish.

This fish is delicious whether grilled on an outdoor barbecue or a stovetop grill pan, or simply cooked in the broiler. We love it during Sukkot week because the weather in Southern California is usually perfect for outdoor barbecuing, which we can do, conveniently, next to the Sukkah.

Moroccan Marinade (page 341)
Salt and freshly ground pepper, to taste
4 small salmon steaks, about 1 inch thick
Pinch of cayenne pepper
Lemon wedges
Fresh cilantro sprigs

1. Prepare marinade.

2. Spoon half the marinade into a bowl and season to taste with salt; cover and refrigerate to use as sauce. Pour remaining marinade over salmon steaks. Rub into both sides of fish. Marinate 30 minutes.

3. Preheat barbecue, stovetop grill pan, or broiler. If using broiler, set rack about 4 inches from heat source. Line broiler pan with foil, if you like.

4. Lightly oil barbecue, grill pan, or broiler pan. Remove extra marinade (sauce) from refrigerator to let it come to room temperature. Remove fish from marinade. Scrape off pieces of herbs and garlic adhering to fish. Sprinkle fish on both sides with salt and pepper. Sprinkle lightly with cayenne pepper.

5. Set fish on grill or broiler rack and grill or broil 4 minutes. Turn over and grill or broil 4 to 5 more minutes. Fish is done when the thickest part of the fish becomes opaque inside; check with a sharp knife near bone.

6. To serve, spoon a little of reserved sauce on each steak. Serve hot, with lemon wedges and cilantro sprigs.

Indian-Jewish Salmon and Rice Casserole

Makes 4 servings ℗

Unlike many Indian dishes, the spicing in this layered casserole of fish, vegetables, and rice is subtle. It relies on fresh cilantro, onions, and garlic for its flavor. The casserole works well with salmon cooked any way—poached, broiled, grilled, or even microwaved. If you don't have fresh salmon, you can use canned. The casserole keeps hot for a while and is convenient to serve in the Sukkah. If you would like to double the recipe, bake it in 2 casseroles instead of 1 large one as the layers will bake more evenly.

4 tablespoons vegetable oil
2 large onions, sliced
3 large cloves garlic, chopped
6 cups water
1^1/$_3$ cups long grain rice
1 large carrot, halved and sliced
2 yellow squash or zucchini, diced
1 cup frozen peas
^{1}/$_2$ teaspoon ground turmeric
Salt and freshly ground pepper, to taste
Cayenne pepper, to taste
2 cups flaked cooked fish, preferably salmon
^{1}/$_4$ cup coarsely chopped fresh cilantro or Italian parsley
^{1}/$_2$ cup hot water

1. Preheat oven to 350°F. Heat 3 tablespoons oil in large saucepan, add onions, and sauté over medium heat, stirring often, about 7 minutes or until onions begin to turn golden. Add garlic and sauté a few seconds. Transfer onion and garlic to a platter.

2. In same pan bring the water to a boil with a pinch of salt. Add rice and sliced carrot and boil uncovered 7 minutes. Add squash and peas, return to a boil, and boil uncovered 3 minutes. Drain rice and vegetables, rinse with cold water, and drain well again. Rice will be partially cooked.

3. In a large bowl mix rice and vegetables with turmeric. Season with salt, pepper, and cayenne. Lightly mix in fish.

4. Spoon half of onion mixture into a 2-quart casserole. Top with half the rice and half the cilantro. Repeat layers. Spoon remaining tablespoon oil over top. Pour 1/2 cup hot water around edge of casserole. Cover and bake 45 minutes or until rice is tender and water is absorbed.

Sephardic Chicken Lentil Soup

Makes 8 servings

Light but satisfying, this makes an all-in-one main course that's convenient to serve in the Sukkah. Unlike many lentil soups, it's colorful because it contains winter squash, carrots, and plenty of parsley. Serve the soup with rice, couscous, or pita bread.

If you wish to keep the broth and lentils lean, pull the skin off the chicken pieces before cooking them.

3 1/2 pounds chicken pieces

2 large onions, cut into thick slice

3 quarts water

Salt and freshly ground pepper, to taste

2 cups lentils, stones removed, rinsed

3/4-pound piece banana squash, peeled and cut into 1-inch cubes

2 large carrots, cut into thick slices (about 1/2-inch)

6 large cloves garlic, chopped

1 1/2 teaspoons ground cumin

1 teaspoon paprika

1 teaspoon dried oregano

1/4 to 1/2 teaspoon hot red pepper flakes

1/2 cup chopped fresh Italian parsley

1. Combine chicken pieces, onions, water, and a little salt in a large stew pan or soup pot. Bring to a boil. Skim foam and fat. Simmer 30 minutes.

2. Add lentils to soup. Add squash cubes, carrots, garlic, cumin, paprika, oregano, and pepper flakes. Cover and simmer over low heat 1 hour or until lentils are tender. Remove chicken from the pot. If you left skin on chicken, remove it now. Either leave chicken in pieces, or remove it from bone, dice it, and return to soup; or reserve chicken for other uses.

3. Skim fat from surface of soup. Adjust seasoning. Stir in parsley a short time before serving.

Baked Chicken with Potatoes, Peppers, and Sage

Makes 6 servings

An easy baked chicken dish is one of my favorite entrees for Sukkot, especially one baked with its accompaniments so it's simple to serve and to carry to the Sukkah.

3 pounds boiling potatoes, peeled and sliced, about 3/8-inch thick

Salt and freshly ground pepper, to taste

10 fresh sage leaves

3 to 3 1/4 pounds chicken pieces

2 large onions, halved and sliced

1 red bell pepper, cored and quartered lengthwise

1 green bell pepper, cored and quartered lengthwise

1 tablespoon finely chopped fresh sage

1 tablespoon chopped fresh Italian parsley (optional)

1. Preheat oven to 400°F. Lightly oil a roasting pan. Add potatoes and sprinkle with salt and pepper. Toss so all are coated. Top with sage leaves, then with chicken pieces. Season chicken on both sides with pepper. Top with sliced onions. Cover with foil and bake 30 minutes.

2. Remove chicken pieces. Discard sage leaves. Put pepper pieces on potatoes. Turn chicken pieces over and return to pan with onions underneath them. Cover and bake chicken 15 minutes. Uncover and bake 15 minutes or until chicken is tender and light brown and juices are no longer pink when thickest part of thigh is pierced. Remove chicken pieces. If potatoes are not tender, cover and bake 10 more minutes.

3. Serve chicken on bed of potato-pepper mixture. Sprinkle with sage and parsley, if using.

Savory Sweet Chicken with Quinces

Makes 4 to 6 servings

M

Quinces look like large apples and resemble them somewhat in flavor but are always cooked. They are especially plentiful in markets around Rosh Hashanah and Sukkot, and appear in Sephardic menus for both holidays. Their cooking time varies from 30 to 60 minutes, so check them occasionally as you cook them.

For this festive entree, the chicken and quinces are braised with a touch of honey, a cinnamon stick, some fresh ginger, and saffron, and garnished with toasted sesame seeds. The chicken is wonderful with couscous or rice. Green beans make a good accompaniment.

3 large quinces (about 1¹/₂ to 2 pounds total), cut into
    eighths, core and seeds removed

3 pounds chicken pieces, patted dry

2 large onions, chopped

Large pinch of saffron threads (about ¹/₈ teaspoon)

1 cup chicken stock, broth, or water

2 tablespoons vegetable oil (optional)

One 2-inch cinnamon stick

Salt and freshly ground pepper, to taste

1 tablespoon chopped peeled fresh ginger

2 tablespoons honey

2 tablespoons toasted sesame seeds

1. Put quince pieces in a large stew pan or casserole dish. Add chicken, onions, saffron, stock, oil if using, cinnamon stick, and a pinch of salt. Bring to a boil. Cover and simmer over low heat, gently turning chicken and quince pieces occasionally, about 35 minutes. Check quinces and remove if they are tender. Simmer 10 more minutes or until chicken is tender and juices are no longer pink when thickest part of thigh is pierced. Transfer chicken pieces to a plate. If quinces are still in pan, check them again; if they are not tender, simmer them 10 more minutes. Remove quinces.

2. Add ginger and honey to casserole and cook uncovered over medium heat, stirring occasionally, 5 minutes. Adjust seasoning, then discard cinnamon stick.

3. Return chicken and quinces to casserole and turn gently to coat with sauce. Cover and cook over low heat 5 minutes. Serve garnished with sesame seeds.

Quick Turkey and Couscous

Makes 4 servings

M

For an easy, mid-week dinner in the Sukkah, prepare this tasty dish. North African Jews often make quick couscous dishes for the middle of the week using couscous they steamed for Shabbat or for a holiday. Our easiest solution is to use packaged couscous, which is ready in five minutes. Cooked green beans or Fresh Red Onion, Tomato, and Sweet Pepper Relish (page 113) is a good accompaniment.

2 tablespoons olive oil

1 to 1¹/₄ pounds turkey breast fillets, cut into 1-inch dice

1¹/₂ teaspoons ground cumin

Salt and freshly ground pepper, to taste

1 small red bell pepper, cut into strips, or ¹/₂ cup strips of
    bottled roasted red bell peppers

2 large cloves garlic, chopped (optional)

1 teaspoon paprika

2¹/₂ cups chicken or turkey broth, or mixed broth and water

Hot sauce to taste

2 green onions, sliced

One 10-ounce package couscous (1²/₃ cups)

1. Heat oil in a large, heavy sauté pan. Add turkey and sprinkle with cumin and pepper. Sauté over medium heat for 3 minutes. Stir in bell pepper, garlic if using, and paprika and sauté 30 seconds. Add ¹/₂ cup broth. Stir and bring to a simmer over high heat. Cover and cook over medium-low heat about 5 minutes or until meat turns opaque inside; cut a thick piece to check. Add hot sauce and salt if needed. Cover and keep warm.

2. Bring remaining broth to a boil in a small saucepan. Stir in green onions and couscous and remove from heat. Cover and let stand 5 minutes. Taste and adjust seasoning. Serve couscous in bowls and top with turkey and its sauce.

North African Lamb Tajine with Jerusalem Artichokes

Makes 4 servings

Moroccan stews called tajines, *which are traditionally cooked and served in conical casserole dishes, are ideal Sukkot entrees. They can be made ahead and reheated and are easy to carry to the Sukkah. Tomatoes, saffron, and black olives make this one very appealing. Ground ginger is traditionally used in the sauce but I love the zip that fresh ginger contributes. Serve the tajine with couscous or rice.*

Jerusalem artichokes, also called sunchokes, are not really artichokes but tubers with a light, slightly crunchy texture and a mild flavor. If you don't find them, substitute diced yellow squash.

2 pounds boneless lamb shoulder, excess fat trimmed, cut into 1-inch pieces and patted dry

1 medium onion, cut into thin slices

3 large cloves garlic, chopped

2 teaspoons minced peeled fresh ginger or $^3/_4$ teaspoon ground ginger

6 tablespoons chopped fresh cilantro

Salt and freshly ground pepper, to taste

1 pound ripe tomatoes, peeled, seeded, and chopped, or one 28-ounce can plum tomatoes, drained and chopped

$^1/_4$ teaspoon saffron threads, crushed (optional)

2 pounds Jerusalem artichokes (sunchokes), scrubbed

$^1/_2$ cup pitted black olives, drained

1. Combine lamb, onion, garlic, ginger, and 2 tablespoons chopped cilantro in a heavy stew pan. Sprinkle with salt and pepper and cook over low heat, stirring, 3 minutes. Add tomatoes and bring to a boil, stirring. Add saffron, if using, and $1^1/_2$ cups water, and bring to a boil. Cover and cook, stirring occasionally, for 1 to $1^1/_4$ hours, or until lamb is just tender when pierced with a knife. Skim fat from sauce.

2. Peel Jerusalem artichokes with a paring knife. Put them in a bowl of water. Cut large ones into 1-inch chunks; leave small ones whole. Return them to water.

3. When lamb is tender, rinse and drain Jerusalem artichokes and add to casserole. Cover and simmer for 20 minutes or until just tender but not falling apart.

Remove lamb and vegetables with slotted spoon. Boil sauce, stirring, until reduced to $1^1/_3$ cups. Return lamb and vegetables to sauce, add olives, and heat gently for 2 minutes. Stir in remaining cilantro. Adjust seasoning, and serve.

Kosher Moussaka

Makes 6 to 8 servings

Moussaka is a popular Greek casserole composed of layers of eggplant, meat sauce, and a topping of white sauce and cheese. Sephardic Jews originating from Greece and nearby countries prepare their own version, without the cheese and with a light tomato topping instead of the white sauce. I bake the eggplant slices instead of frying them, not only to save on calories but because it's simpler. In the oven all the eggplant cooks at once. To absorb the savory sauce and make the moussaka easier to serve, I mix the meat with penne (quill-shaped pasta).

Ground Lamb Stew with Pine Nuts (page 104)

1 large eggplant (about $1^1/_2$ pounds), unpeeled and cut crosswise into $^1/_4$-inch slices

2 tablespoons olive oil

Salt and freshly ground pepper, to taste

1 pound penne rigate or plain penne

3 large cloves garlic, minced

1 large egg, beaten

2 tablespoons tomato paste

$^1/_2$ cup beef, chicken, or vegetable broth

1. Prepare lamb stew.

2. Preheat oven to 450°F. Arrange eggplant on a foil-lined baking pan. Brush lightly with oil and sprinkle with salt and pepper. Bake 8 to 10 minutes per side or until tender.

3. Cook penne in a large pot of boiling salted water over high heat, stirring occasionally, about 9 minutes or until nearly tender but a bit firmer than usual. Drain, rinse briefly with cold water, and drain well again. Transfer to a large bowl. Add lamb stew and half the minced garlic and toss. Adjust seasoning. Stir in the egg.

4. Preheat oven to 350°F. Oil a 13 × 9 × 2-inch baking dish. Make 1 layer of eggplant slices in the dish.

Cover with about half the pasta and lamb mixture. Cover with another layer of eggplant. Spread remaining pasta mixture on top. Top with a layer of remaining eggplant.

5. To make the topping: Put the tomato paste in a small bowl and whisk in the broth. Add the remaining garlic and a pinch of salt and pepper. Pour mixture over the moussaka.

6. Bake uncovered 50 minutes. Cover after 30 minutes if top appears to be getting dry. Let stand about 10 minutes before serving.

Ground Lamb Stew with Pine Nuts

Makes 6 to 8 servings

Ⓜ

Lamb and pine nuts are favorite Sephardic recipe ingredients. They flavor this easy-to-make meat and tomato stew. Use it to make Kosher Moussaka (page 103) or simply serve it over spaghetti, rice, or couscous.

2 tablespoons olive oil

1 large onion, minced

3 large cloves garlic, minced

1¼ pounds ground lamb

2 pounds ripe tomatoes, peeled, seeded, and chopped, or two 28-ounce cans tomatoes, drained and chopped

½ teaspoon dried oregano

Salt and freshly ground pepper, to taste

½ cup pine nuts

½ cup chopped fresh Italian parsley

Heat oil in a large skillet or sauté pan over medium-low heat. Add onion and cook about 10 minutes or until tender. Add garlic and lamb and cook over medium heat, crumbling with a fork, until it changes color, about 7 minutes. Add tomatoes, oregano, salt, and pepper and cook over medium heat about 35 minutes or until sauce is very thick. Add pine nuts and cook 2 more minutes. Add parsley, then adjust seasoning.

Lecso Pizza

Makes 2 pizzas, total 6 to 8 servings

Ⓓ

The Hungarian pepper stew called lecso *makes a delicious pizza topping. I find it's a perfect dish for midweek during Sukkot, as it's easy to serve in the Sukkah and a welcome surprise when you serve it to friends who drop by during the holiday.*

You can make it pareve or sprinkle it with a little cheese for a dairy version. Either way it tastes great.

Pizza Dough (page 546)

2 cups Lecso (page 459)

1 to 2 tablespoons olive oil

6 tablespoons freshly grated Parmesan cheese or ½ cup coarsely shredded Swiss cheese or other firm kosher cheese (optional)

1. Make dough and let rise. Cook lecso uncovered in a skillet over medium heat until it is very thick. Let cool.

2. Lightly oil 2 baking sheets. Knead dough briefly, divide into 2 pieces, and put each on a baking sheet. With oiled hands, pat each portion of dough into a 10-inch circle, with rims slightly higher than centers.

3. Spread lecso evenly over pizzas, leaving a ½-inch border. Brush dough edges lightly with oil; sprinkle remaining oil over filling. Sprinkle with cheese, if using.

4. Preheat oven to 425°F. Let pizzas rise for about 15 minutes. Bake pizzas about 18 minutes or until dough is golden brown and firm. Serve hot.

❧ *Stuffed Vegetables*

Old-Fashioned Stuffed Cabbage

Makes 6 servings

A time-honored Sukkot entree, this stuffed cabbage has a sweet and sour sauce. When my Aunt Sylvia makes it, she uses the juice of Meyer lemons from her tree to flavor the sauce. Because these lemons are less acidic, she adds less sugar or supplements the lemons' acidity with sour salt, which is powdered citric acid extracted from lemons. In fact, sour salt, now found in kosher grocery stores, is the real sour agent used in old recipes. After all, this dish is a specialty of Jews of Poland, where fresh citrus fruits were not plentiful. Today many people prefer to use lemon juice.

Meat and Rice Stuffing (this page)

One 3-pound head of cabbage, cored

1 tablespoon vegetable oil

1 medium onion, minced

3 cups beef stock or broth, or half broth and half water

2 tablespoons tomato paste

3 tablespoons raisins

1 tablespoon strained fresh lemon juice

1 to 2 teaspoons sugar

Salt (optional) and freshly ground pepper, to taste

1. Prepare stuffing and set aside.

2. Carefully remove 12 to 16 large outer cabbage leaves by cutting them from core of cabbage. Put leaves in a large pot of boiling water and boil 5 minutes. Transfer them carefully to a colander and rinse gently with cold water. Pat dry with a towel. Coarsely chop remaining cabbage.

3. Heat oil in a large, heavy casserole dish or stew pan. Add onion and sauté over medium-low heat, stirring often, 5 minutes or until softened but not brown. Remove from heat. Add the chopped cabbage.

4. Trim thick ribs of each cabbage leaf slightly so you can bend leaf easily. Put 2 tablespoons stuffing on stem end of a leaf and fold stem end over it. Fold sides over

stuffing to enclose it. Beginning at stem end, roll up leaf to a neat package. If any leaves are torn, patch with a piece of another leaf on the inside. Place roll, seam end down, in the casserole dish containing the onions and chopped cabbage. Continue with remaining leaves and stuffing. Arrange stuffed cabbage rolls tightly, side by side in the casserole dish. Chop any remaining blanched leaves and add to casserole.

5. Add 2¹/₂ cups stock to casserole. Mix tomato paste with remaining stock until blended. Add to casserole. Bring to a simmer. Cover and simmer over low heat 1 hour and 15 minutes. Add raisins, lemon juice, and sugar and simmer 5 minutes. Season with salt, if using, and pepper. Serve stuffed cabbage in deep dishes with plenty of sauce.

Meat and Rice Stuffing

Makes 2 to 2¹/₂ cups, enough for 6 to 8 servings

Use this easy-to-make stuffing to roll in cabbage leaves or to stuff peppers, onions, or tomatoes. Because the beef is not cooked before the stuffing is put in the vegetable, be sure to bake or simmer the stuffed vegetable long enough to cook the beef completely.

¹/₂ cup white rice, short- or long-grain

3 cups boiling water

1 tablespoon vegetable oil

1 medium onion, minced

1 teaspoon paprika

¹/₂ pound lean ground beef

¹/₄ teaspoon salt

¹/₄ teaspoon freshly ground pepper

¹/₄ teaspoon cayenne pepper (optional)

Cook rice uncovered in a saucepan of boiling salted water for 10 minutes; it should be partially cooked. Rinse with cold water and drain well. Transfer to a bowl. Heat oil in a skillet, then add onion and cook over medium-low heat, stirring often, 5 minutes or until soft. Add paprika and cook, stirring, 1 minute. Transfer mixture to bowl of rice and let cool completely. Add beef, salt, pepper, and cayenne pepper, if using. Knead with clean hands to blend ingredients thoroughly. Refrigerate in a covered container until ready to use.

Artichokes with Tomato Stuffing

Makes 4 servings

Stuffed artichokes are a favorite on the Sephardic holiday table. Meat stuffing is common but for a change of pace for Sukkot, I like this colorful filling made of the season's ripe tomatoes.

4 large or 8 small cooked Artichoke Bottoms and Stems, fresh (page 589) or canned

2 tablespoons olive oil or butter

2 shallots or 1 small onion, minced

1¹/₂ pounds ripe tomatoes, peeled, seeded, and chopped, or two 28-ounce cans whole tomatoes, halved, drained well, and chopped

Salt and freshly ground pepper, to taste

1 sprig of fresh thyme or ¹/₂ teaspoon dried thyme

1 bay leaf

5 parsley stems

1 tablespoon chopped fresh basil (optional)

1. Prepare artichoke bottoms.

2. Heat oil in a sauté pan. Add shallots and cook over low heat, stirring often, until softened but not brown. Add tomatoes, salt, and pepper. Tie thyme sprig, bay leaf, and parsley stems together with string or in a piece of cheesecloth and add to tomatoes. Cook over medium heat, stirring often, about 20 minutes or until mixture is very thick. Discard tied herbs. Add basil, if using, and adjust seasoning.

3. Preheat oven to 375°F. Lightly oil a baking dish and set artichoke bottoms in it. Sprinkle them with salt and pepper. Spoon tomato filling into each artichoke. Bake 10 minutes to heat through.

Note: An equal weight of canned (a 16-ounce and an 8-ounce can) tomatoes can be substituted for fresh ones. Drain them, remove as many seeds as possible, and chop.

Spinach Stuffed Mushrooms

Makes 4 to 6 servings **D**

Stuffed mushrooms are often bland and not very colorful when they're made mostly of bread crumbs and a few mushroom stems. This one has lots of flavor from the nutmeg-scented spinach and cheese filling, and a vivid green color. You can serve these as a Sukkot appetizer for a dairy or pareve dinner or as an accompaniment for baked fish.

3¹/₂ pounds spinach bunches, leaves rinsed well, or three 10-ounce bags rinsed spinach leaves, stemmed

3 tablespoons butter

2 large shallots, minced

Salt and freshly ground pepper, to taste

¹/₄ cup heavy cream or milk

¹/₂ cup ricotta cheese (4 ounces)

6 to 8 tablespoons freshly grated Parmesan cheese

Freshly grated nutmeg to taste

1 pound large mushrooms, stemmed, rinsed, and dried

1. Add spinach to a large pot of enough boiling salted water to cover it generously, and cook uncovered over high heat about 2 minutes or until spinach wilts. Drain, rinse with cold water, and drain well again. Squeeze out as much liquid as possible. Puree in food processor or chop with large knife until very fine.

2. Melt 2 tablespoons butter in a large skillet. Add shallots and cook over low heat about 2 minutes or until tender. Add spinach and a pinch of salt and pepper and cook 2 minutes. Stir in cream and heat until it is absorbed by spinach. Transfer to a medium bowl and let cool. Stir in ricotta and 4 tablespoons Parmesan cheese. Season to taste with salt, pepper, and nutmeg.

3. Preheat oven to 375°F. Put mushroom caps, rounded side down, in a lightly oiled shallow baking dish. Sprinkle them lightly with salt and pepper. Fill with spinach filling. Sprinkle with remaining cheese.

4. Bake stuffed mushrooms for 10 to 15 minutes, or until mushrooms are tender and filling is hot. Serve hot.

Spicy Stuffed Eggplant with Turkey

Makes 4 to 6 servings

To make the stuffing for these eggplants, I sauté the inside of the vegetable with extra garlic and add the mixture to Yemenite Turkey Stuffing.

Yemenite Turkey Stuffing (this page)

2¹/2 pounds small or medium eggplants, stemmed and halved lengthwise

Salt and freshly ground pepper, to taste

2 tablespoons olive oil

6 large cloves garlic, minced

2 tablespoons tomato paste

1 teaspoon ground cumin

¹/2 teaspoon ground turmeric

Fresh cilantro sprigs

1. Prepare stuffing and set aside.

2. If eggplant is fresh, there is no need to peel it. With a spoon, scoop out eggplant centers, leaving boat-shaped shells. Sprinkle eggplant shells with salt. Put them in a colander upside down and let drain for 30 minutes. Chop eggplant centers.

3. Preheat oven to 425°F. Heat 1 tablespoon oil in a skillet, add chopped eggplant, and sprinkle with salt and pepper. Sauté over medium-low heat, stirring often, about 10 minutes or until tender. Stir in half the garlic. Adjust seasoning. Let mixture cool. Mix sautéed eggplant with turkey stuffing.

4. Rinse eggplant shells, pat them dry, and put them in a baking dish. Fill them with stuffing. Mix tomato paste with ¹/4 cup water and spoon mixture over eggplant. Add enough water to dish to cover eggplant by one third. Add remaining garlic, cumin, and turmeric to dish. Spoon 1 tablespoon oil over eggplant. Cover and bake 15 minutes. Reduce oven temperature to 350°F and bake 15 more minutes. Uncover and bake, basting occasionally, 30 minutes or until eggplant is very tender. Serve hot, garnished with cilantro.

Yemenite Turkey Stuffing

Makes 2 to 2¹/2 cups, enough for 6 to 8 servings

When I am using turkey as a basis for my stuffing for vegetables, I like to use Yemenite flavors to give the lean meat plenty of zip. Use this stuffing in Spicy Stuffed Eggplant with Turkey (this page), or for cabbage leaves or zucchini.

¹/2 cup long-grain rice

3 cups boiling water

2 tablespoons olive oil

1 medium onion, minced

2 large cloves garlic, minced

1 jalapeño pepper, seeds removed, chopped, or 1 teaspoon Zehug (page 592)

1 teaspoon ground cumin

¹/2 teaspoon ground turmeric

¹/2 pound ground turkey

2 teaspoons tomato paste

2 tablespoons minced fresh cilantro

¹/4 teaspoon salt

³/4 teaspoon freshly ground pepper

1. Cook rice uncovered in a saucepan of boiling salted water for 10 minutes; it should be partially cooked. Rinse with cold water and drain well. Transfer to a bowl.

2. Heat oil in a skillet, add onion, and cook over medium-low heat, stirring often, 7 minutes or until golden. Add the garlic, jalapeño pepper, cumin, and turmeric and cook, stirring, 1 minute. Transfer mixture to bowl of rice and let cool completely. Add turkey, tomato paste, cilantro, salt, and pepper. Knead with clean hands to blend ingredients thoroughly. Refrigerate in a covered container until ready to use.

Sweet and Sour Stuffed Onions

Makes about 6 servings

To prepare this dish, you don't really stuff whole onions. Instead, you cook onions and remove outside layers, which become thin shells for stuffing. White onions are best because they are a bit more delicate, but you can also use yellow onions. I like to flavor the sauce with dried cranberries, which also appear in the stuffing. They're delicious not only for Sukkot, but also for Thanksgiving. Stuffing the onions takes some time but they can be cooked ahead and reheated.

Chicken Stuffing with Pecans and Cranberries (this page)
3 large white onions (about 2 pounds)
1¹/₂ cups chicken stock or broth or water
Salt and freshly ground pepper, to taste
¹/₄ cup dried cranberries
2 tablespoons strained fresh lemon juice
Pinch of sugar (optional)

1. Prepare stuffing. Then, set an onion on cutting board, root side down. Put the tip of knife at top core of onion and cut once to root core, making a slit in onion. Repeat with remaining onions. Put onions in a saucepan of boiling salted water and simmer for about 20 minutes or until it is easy to separate them in layers. Drain and leave until cool enough to handle. Cut off top and bottom of onions. Carefully remove as many layers as possible from onions.

2. Put about 1 teaspoon stuffing at one end of an onion piece and roll it up tightly, following the shape of the onion piece. Cut any large onion pieces in two, to make two stuffed onion pieces.

3. Put stuffed onions in a sauté pan, arranging them in a tight layer with seam side down. Add 1 cup stock, or enough to just cover them. Sprinkle with salt and bring to a simmer. Cover and cook over low heat about 1 hour or until onions are very tender, adding a little stock from time to time if pan gets dry; check them often, as the onions burn easily. Add cranberries and lemon juice and cook 5 more minutes. Season sauce with salt, pepper, and sugar, if using.

Chicken Stuffing with Pecans and Cranberries

Makes about 2 cups,
enough for 4 to 6 servings

This savory stuffing is made of ground chicken and bulgur wheat and is accented with grated lemon, toasted pecans, and dried cranberries. I like it for stuffing onions or zucchini.

¹/₂ cup medium or fine-grain bulgur wheat
1 cup boiling water
3 tablespoons dried cranberries
¹/₄ pound ground chicken
3 tablespoons diced pecans, lightly toasted
¹/₂ teaspoon grated lemon rind
¹/₄ teaspoon ground allspice
¹/₂ teaspoon salt
¹/₂ teaspoon freshly ground pepper
1 tablespoon vegetable oil

1. In a bowl combine bulgur wheat and the boiling water. Let stand until mixture is cool. If any water is left, drain bulgur thoroughly. Put bulgur in a dry bowl.

2. If cranberries are very dry, soak them in a little hot water for 5 minutes. Drain well. Add to bulgur wheat.

3. Add chicken, pecans, lemon rind, allspice, salt, pepper, and oil. Knead to mix well. Refrigerate in a covered container until ready to use.

❧ Side Dishes

Rachel's Spiced Cauliflower with Chickpeas

Makes 4 to 6 servings

My mother-in-law, Rachel Levy, prepares a wonderful dish of cauliflower with the popular Yemenite spice combination of cumin and turmeric, which give the cauliflower a lovely hue and flavor. She usually fries the cauliflower, then simmers it in tomato sauce. I have adapted the recipe to be more healthful by omitting the step of frying the cauliflower. I've made the dish easy to prepare too, by cooking the cauliflower directly in the sauce.

My new version of the dish is always a hit. It's great with basmati rice, as a vegetarian entree, or as an accompaniment for chicken or fish.

1 tablespoon olive oil

1 large onion, quartered and sliced

1 large head cauliflower, divided into medium florets

Salt and freshly ground pepper, to taste

1 teaspoon ground cumin

$^1/_2$ teaspoon ground turmeric

3 large cloves garlic, chopped

One 14$^1/_2$-ounce can diced tomatoes, drained

One 8-ounce can tomato sauce

One 15-ounce can chickpeas (garbanzo beans), drained

1. Heat oil in a large, heavy stew pan over medium heat. Add onion and sauté, stirring often, about 5 minutes or until softened but not brown. Add cauliflower florets with stems touching bottom of pan. Sprinkle with salt, pepper, cumin, and turmeric. Cover and cook over medium-low heat 5 minutes, checking once or twice to be sure onions don't burn.

2. Add garlic, tomatoes, and tomato sauce. Stir very gently but keep cauliflower florets with their stems facing down. Cover and cook over medium heat 10 minutes. Add chickpeas without stirring. Cover and cook 5 to 10 minutes or until cauliflower is tender; check by piercing thick part of stems with a knife. Adjust seasoning. Serve hot.

Zucchini Pistou Puree

Makes 4 servings

Pistou is a Provençal version of pesto that often doesn't have cheese. For this simple recipe the pistou flavors simply cooked zucchini, a popular Sukkot vegetable. Serve the zucchini with chicken, fish, or vegetarian meals, or toss it with spaghetti.

1$^1/_2$ pounds small zucchini

3 tablespoons extra-virgin olive oil

3 large cloves garlic, minced

$^1/_2$ cup fresh basil leaves

Salt and freshly ground pepper, to taste

Pinch of cayenne pepper

1. Cook zucchini whole in a saucepan of boiling salted water about 10 minutes or until they are tender enough to be easily pureed. Cut zucchini into 1-inch pieces and put them in a colander or large strainer. Crush them lightly with spoon. Let stand to drain 15 minutes.

2. Heat 2 tablespoons oil in a medium skillet, add garlic, and sauté over low heat, stirring, 30 seconds. Add zucchini and cook over medium heat, stirring often, 5 minutes. Let cool slightly.

3. Combine zucchini mixture and basil in a food processor and process until pureed. With motor running, slowly add remaining olive oil.

4. Reheat puree gently in saucepan. If it is too thin, cook over medium heat, stirring, until thickened. Season with salt, pepper, and cayenne pepper. Serve hot.

Layered Chard and Bell Pepper Gratin

Makes about 6 servings   Ⓟ

This is a Mediterranean style gratin made with a tomato sauce rather than a cheesy one. Chard is a mild flavored tender green that is easy to find at the market. You can serve this hearty dish as a main course accompanied by a grain dish, such as the Romanian polenta dish called Mamaliga (page 522). It's also delicious with roasted or grilled chicken.

1¹/₂ pounds Swiss chard, rinsed thoroughly

5 tablespoons olive oil

1 small onion, minced

1³/₄ pounds ripe tomatoes, peeled, seeded, and finely chopped, or two 28-ounce cans whole tomatoes, drained well and finely chopped

1¹/₂ teaspoons fresh thyme or ¹/₂ teaspoon dried

2 large cloves garlic, minced

Salt and freshly ground pepper, to taste

1 large red or yellow bell pepper, cut into ¹/₄-inch-wide strips

1 medium green bell pepper, cut into ¹/₄-inch-wide strips

3 tablespoons unseasoned bread crumbs

3 tablespoons slivered almonds, chopped

1. Preheat oven to 400°F. Cut chard leaves from stems. Peel stems if they are stringy. Pile chard leaves, cut them in half lengthwise and then crosswise in strips ¹/₂-inch wide. Keep them separate from stems. In a saucepan of boiling salted water, cook stems uncovered 5 minutes. Add leaves and cook about 3 minutes or until just tender. Drain thoroughly. Squeeze chard by handfuls to remove excess moisture.

2. Heat 2 tablespoons oil in a large skillet. Add onion and cook over medium heat about 5 minutes or until soft but not brown. Stir in tomatoes. Cook over high heat, stirring very often, about 12 minutes or until mixture is dry. Stir in thyme and garlic. Season with salt and pepper.

3. Heat 2 more tablespoons oil in large skillet. Add bell peppers, salt, and pepper, and cook over medium-low heat, stirring often, about 7 minutes or until tender.

4. Lightly oil a heavy 5-cup gratin dish or other shallow baking dish. Spread chard in dish and sprinkle with salt and pepper. Spoon tomato mixture over chard and spread it smooth. Spoon pepper mixture evenly over tomatoes.

5. Sprinkle top with bread crumbs, then with almonds, and finally with remaining 1 tablespoon olive oil. Bake about 15 minutes, or until gratin is hot and beginning to bubble at bottom of dish. If top is too light, broil about 1 minute, or just until lightly browned; check often and turn dish if necessary. Serve hot, warm, or at room temperature.

Green Beans with Tomatoes and Herbs

Makes 4 servings   Ⓟ

Green beans slow-cooked in tomato sauce is a favorite dish in the Sephardic kitchen and is a standard side dish on the Sukkot menus of my sister-in-law Etti Levy who lives in Givatayim, Israel. Here is a quicker version that makes use of diced fresh tomatoes. It's great for showcasing the flavor of good tomatoes from the season's harvest. You can use equal parts yellow beans (wax beans) and green beans for a more colorful dish. The beans keep their bright color best if you serve this dish as soon as it's cooked.

2 pounds green beans, ends removed, halved

1 to 2 tablespoons olive oil

Salt and freshly ground pepper, to taste

Cayenne pepper to taste (optional)

1 pound tomatoes, diced

1 tablespoon chopped fresh oregano or ¹/₂ teaspoon dried

1¹/₂ teaspoons fresh thyme or ¹/₂ teaspoon dried

2 tablespoons chopped fresh Italian parsley

Add beans to a large saucepan of boiling salted water and boil 5 to 7 minutes or until crisp-tender. Drain in a colander or strainer. Transfer to a bowl and toss with oil, salt, pepper, and cayenne, if using. Add tomatoes and herbs and toss again. Serve hot or at room temperature.

Potatoes with Onions, Sephardic Style

Makes 4 servings

For this simple but savory dish, sliced cooked potatoes are sautéed with onions in olive oil so the dish will be pareve and will be a good accompaniment for a simple Sukkot roast chicken. When I studied in France, we used to prepare a similar dish called potatoes Lyonnaise, so named because the area of Lyon is known for its onions. The French version used butter and was seasoned simply with salt and pepper.

1¹/2 pounds boiling potatoes

3 to 4 tablespoons olive oil

3 medium onions, sliced into thin rings

Salt and freshly ground pepper, to taste

1 teaspoon paprika, plus more for sprinkling

¹/4 teaspoon cayenne pepper, or to taste

1. Put whole potatoes in a large saucepan, cover with water, and add salt. Cover, bring to a boil, and cook over medium heat about 25 minutes, or until just tender. Drain well. Peel potatoes if you wish. Cut them into fairly thin rounds. Set aside.

2. Heat 2 tablespoons oil in a large, heavy skillet. Add onions and sauté over medium-low heat until they are tender and lightly golden. Transfer onions to a plate.

3. Heat another tablespoon oil in the skillet. Add potatoes and sauté, carefully turning them over occasionally, until lightly browned. Add more oil during sautéing if necessary. Add half the onions and mix gently with potatoes. Season with salt, pepper, paprika, and cayenne. Transfer mixture to a platter and top with remaining onions. Sprinkle lightly with more salt and paprika.

Hungarian Noodles with Slow-Cooked Cabbage

Makes 6 servings

Stewing the cabbage over low heat is the secret to this old-fashioned dish that remains popular. The cabbage acquires a sweetness from the slow cooking. Some cooks enhance it with several spoonfuls of sugar, while others add a little or a lot of onions, which also turn sweet as they cook with the cabbage. I like to use plenty of onion and just a little sugar.

The pasta used is generally broad egg noodles, square noodles, or bow-ties. Hungarian cooks use a generous amount of chicken fat, goose fat, or butter to cook the cabbage; some American Jewish cooks use margarine, while Israeli cooks tend to favor vegetable oil. The choice is yours. In this recipe I have reduced the oil but the dish is still rich in flavor. Serve it as a side dish with chicken, beef, or fish.

2 pounds green cabbage (about ³/4 of a large head), cored and shredded

Salt and freshly ground pepper, to taste

¹/4 cup vegetable oil

2 large onions, diced

1 to 2 teaspoons sugar

8 ounces square noodles or broad noodles

1. Put cabbage in a large bowl and sprinkle with 1 teaspoon salt. Toss to combine. Let stand 30 minutes. Squeeze cabbage by handfuls to remove excess liquid.

2. Heat oil in a large skillet or stew pan. Add onion, cabbage, and pepper. Sauté over medium heat, 5 minutes. Add 1 teaspoon sugar. Cover and cook over low heat, stirring often, 30 minutes or until very tender. Check often; if vegetables brown too fast or pan becomes very dry, add a few tablespoons boiling water.

3. When vegetables are tender, if they are not yet brown, uncover and cook over medium-high heat, stirring, until lightly browned. If you like, add another teaspoon sugar and cook vegetables another 2 or 3 minutes to blend it in.

4. Cook noodles in a large pot of boiling salted water 7 minutes or until just tender. Drain well and add to cabbage. Toss over low heat for 1 or 2 minutes. Taste for seasoning; season generously with pepper. Serve hot.

Basmati Rice Pilaf with Sunflower Seeds and Vegetables

Makes 6 to 8 servings

Serve this colorful, easy-to-make dish as an accompaniment for a vegetable stew or for braised or roasted chicken. I love it with aromatic basmati rice but you can substitute long-grain rice.

To speed up preparation, buy sunflower seeds shelled and pre-roasted. You can also use roasted pepitas, the green Mexican squash seeds.

2 tablespoons vegetable oil

1 medium onion, chopped

1 large carrot, cut into small dice

2 cups white basmati rice, rinsed and drained

Salt and freshly ground pepper, to taste

4 cups hot vegetable or chicken stock or water

1 bay leaf

1 sprig fresh thyme or 1/2 teaspoon dried thyme

1 cup frozen peas, thawed

1 cup frozen corn, thawed

1/3 cup roasted sunflower seeds

1. Heat oil in a large sauté pan. Add onion and carrot, and sauté over medium-low heat, stirring often, 5 minutes. Add rice, salt, and pepper and sauté, stirring, 1 minute. Pour hot stock over rice and stir once. Add bay leaf and thyme. Bring to a boil over high heat. Reduce heat to low, cover tightly, and simmer, without stirring, 15 minutes.

2. Scatter peas and corn over top of rice in thin layer. Cover and simmer 2 or 3 minutes or until rice is just tender, liquid is absorbed, and corn and peas are hot. Let stand off heat 10 minutes. Discard bay leaf and thyme sprig. Fluff rice with a fork and gently mix in half the sunflower seeds. Adjust seasoning. Serve garnished with remaining sunflower seeds.

❧ *Sauces*

Pineapple-Papaya Salsa

Makes 6 to 8 servings

P

It's hard to believe this tasty, multicolored salsa is fat free! I learned to prepare it when I went to a culinary camp at the Marriott Resort in Palm Desert, California. It was a real winner among the students. The chef-instructor noted that you can prepare it with mango, papaya, or both. He served it with corn fritters. The salsa is perfect for Sukkot because it's full of colorful fruit and vegetables. It makes a savory-sweet topping for grilled chicken or fish. I also like it for Hanukkah with potato latkes, sweet potato latkes, and Cajun corn latkes.

To save time, you can use 3 cups ready-diced fresh pineapple, which is available in the salad bar section of many supermarkets.

1 large fresh pineapple

1 medium papaya

1 red bell pepper, diced

1/2 green bell pepper, diced

1 cup finely chopped red onion

3 green onions, finely chopped

3 tablespoons chopped fresh cilantro

2 tablespoons strained fresh lime juice, preferably from Mexican or Key limes

1/8 teaspoon cayenne pepper or hot sauce, to taste

Salt and freshly ground pepper, to taste

1. Cut peel from pineapple. Slice pineapple and cut out core from center of each slice. Dice pineapple. Halve papaya and scoop out seeds. Remove papaya flesh with a spoon and dice it.

2. In a large non-aluminum bowl, combine all ingredients. Mix gently, then adjust seasonings. Refrigerate until ready to serve. The salsa is best on the day it is made. Serve cold.

Fresh Red Onion, Tomato, and Sweet Pepper Relish

Makes 4 to 6 servings

Like a salsa, this fat-free, easy-to-make relish requires no cooking, but it is not hot. The relish is terrific with chicken or fish, either grilled or roasted. I also love it as a fresh accompaniment for simple grain and pasta dishes and for Indian-Jewish Salmon and Rice Casserole (page 100).

¹/₂ cup finely chopped red onion

1 small yellow or green bell pepper, halved, cored, and finely diced

³/₄ to 1 pound ripe tomatoes, seeded and diced

1 to 2 tablespoons strained fresh lemon juice

Several drops hot sauce, or to taste

¹/₄ cup chopped fresh Italian parsley

Salt and freshly ground pepper, to taste

Combine onion, pepper, tomatoes, lemon juice, and hot sauce in a bowl. Cover and refrigerate 30 minutes or up to 1 day. A short time before serving, add parsley and season with salt, pepper, and more hot sauce, if desired. Serve cold.

Jalapeño Tomato Sauce

Makes 8 to 10 servings

I first tasted this sauce at a family picnic birthday party during Sukkot, where it was served cold with grilled beef kebabs and was very popular. Each person spooned the sauce over meat kebab pieces that were fitted into pita bread. You can also serve it with grilled chicken, or if you like to serve spicy dips with chips as an appetizer, it's good for that, too. You can also serve the sauce hot.

The recipe came from a Moroccan-Israeli friend of the family who lives in California. It's easy to make, but she cautions that you should stir the sauce often as it simmers so the tomatoes don't burn. Moroccan cooks love hot chiles and make use of a variety of them. In this sauce, she uses jalapeño peppers, as they are easy to find in the United States.

If you would like the sauce to be less spicy, remove the seeds and membranes from the jalapeño peppers.

10 jalapeño peppers, green or red, chopped or sliced (see Note)

Two 28-ounce cans crushed tomatoes, with their liquid

6 large cloves garlic, chopped

1 to 2 tablespoons olive oil or vegetable oil

Salt and freshly ground pepper, to taste

Put jalapeño peppers in a large saucepan. Add tomatoes, garlic, and oil. Bring to a simmer, stirring. Cook uncovered over low heat, stirring often, 30 minutes to 1 hour or until the sauce is as thick as you would like it. Season with salt and pepper. Serve hot or cold.

Note: Wear rubber gloves when handling hot peppers.

Desserts

Apple Strudel

Makes about 12 servings **D** or **P**

With plenty of just-harvested apples in season, it's no wonder apple strudel is a time-honored Sukkot dessert. You can find it at most Jewish bakeries but it's so much better with a fresh-tasting homemade filling. Strudel is easy to make with prepared phyllo sheets, which are often also labeled "strudel dough." Be sure the walnuts you use in the strudel are very fresh. Serve the strudel on its own, or with regular or pareve vanilla ice cream.

1¹/₂ pounds sweet tender apples such as Golden Delicious,
    peeled, halved, cored, and sliced paper-thin
¹/₂ cup sugar
1 tablespoon strained fresh lemon juice
1 teaspoon grated lemon rind
2 teaspoons ground cinnamon
¹/₄ cup apricot preserves
²/₃ cup golden raisins
1 cup walnuts, chopped
8 phyllo or strudel sheets, thawed if frozen
¹/₂ cup (1 stick) butter or margarine, melted, or vegetable oil
¹/₂ cup dry cookie crumbs or plain bread crumbs
Powdered sugar (optional)

1. Put apples in a large bowl. Add sugar, lemon juice, lemon rind, cinnamon, and apricot preserves and mix well. Stir in raisins and walnuts.

2. Preheat oven to 375°F. Lightly grease a baking sheet.

3. Remove phyllo sheets from their package and unroll them on a dry towel. Cover phyllo immediately with a piece of wax paper, then with a damp towel.

4. Lay 1 phyllo sheet on a large sheet of wax paper. Keep remaining phyllo sheets covered. Brush with melted butter and sprinkle with 1 tablespoon cookie crumbs. Top with a second sheet of phyllo. Brush with butter and sprinkle with 1 tablespoon crumbs.

5. Put one fourth of filling near one end of top sheet, arranging it in a log shape and leaving a 1-inch border. Starting with that end, carefully roll up dough as for a

jelly roll, using the paper to help support dough. End with seam of dough on the bottom. Transfer to baking sheet. Brush top with butter.

6. Make 3 more strudels, using remaining filling and remaining dough sheets. Roll remaining phyllo sheets up, wrap tightly, and return them to freezer.

7. Bake strudels 25 minutes or until golden. Serve warm, sprinkled with powdered sugar, if using.

Jewish Apple Cake with Walnuts and Dried Cranberries

Makes 12 to 15 servings **P**

Apple cakes with an oil-based batter are often called Jewish apple cake, probably because the oil makes them pareve, and they are a popular Sukkot dessert. This one is studded with diced apples, walnuts, and bright red dried cranberries. You can substitute raisins for the cranberries for a more traditional taste, or use half cranberries and half golden raisins to make the cake more colorful. Often the apple slices are layered with the batter. You can do that with this cake too but I usually dice them and mix them in. It's quicker, easier, and just as delicious.

You can use just about any apple you like in this cake—tart apples like Pippin or Granny Smith, medium-tart ones like McIntosh or Jonathan, or sweet ones like Golden Delicious.

2 teaspoons ground cinnamon
1 cup sugar
1¹/₂ pounds apples, peeled, halved, cored, and diced
2 large eggs
²/₃ cup vegetable oil
2 cups all-purpose flour
1¹/₂ teaspoons baking powder
1 teaspoon vanilla extract
¹/₂ cup dried cranberries
¹/₂ cup walnuts, coarsely chopped

1. Preheat oven to 350°F. Lightly grease a 13 × 9 × 2-inch cake pan, line base and sides of pan with a sheet of foil and grease foil.

2. Mix cinnamon and ¹/₃ cup sugar in a large bowl. Add apples and toss to combine.

3. Beat eggs with remaining ⅔ cup sugar in a large bowl with an electric mixer on medium speed until light. Add oil and beat until blended. Sift flour with baking powder in a medium bowl and stir into egg mixture. Stir in vanilla, cranberries, walnuts, and apple mixture. Spread in prepared cake pan. Smooth top. Bake for about 40 minutes or until a cake tester or toothpick inserted in center of cake comes out dry. Cool in pan on a rack about 20 minutes or until just warm. Turn out onto a rack. Cool to room temperature. Serve cold or at room temperature.

Pauline's Carrot Cake

Makes about 12 servings

My brother and I often enjoyed this cake whenever my mother, Pauline Kahn, baked it, especially if she made it without nuts. Today I think it tastes even better with chopped pecans or walnuts. Carrot cake has long been popular on Jewish holiday menus because most recipes call for oil, not butter, and so the cake is pareve and convenient to serve after meat entrees. You may want to save a few pieces of it for a meatless meal and enjoy it with Creamy Cinnamon-Honey Sauce (page 116).

I especially like it for Sukkot because the carrots tie in with the harvest theme. The cake is easy to make and is moist and flavorful enough that it needs no frosting.

2 cups all-purpose flour

1 teaspoon ground cinnamon

1 teaspoon baking powder

1 teaspoon baking soda

1 teaspoon salt

1 cup vegetable oil

2 cups sugar

4 large eggs

2 cups finely grated carrots

½ to 1 cup chopped pecans or walnuts (optional)

1. Preheat oven to 350°F. Grease and flour a 13 × 9 × 2-inch baking pan.

2. Sift flour with cinnamon, baking powder, baking soda, and salt in a medium bowl. In a large bowl, beat oil and sugar until well blended. Beat in eggs, one by one. Stir flour mixture and grated carrots alternately

into batter. Mix well. Stir in chopped nuts, if using. Batter will be thick. Spoon into prepared pan. Bake about 45 minutes or until a cake tester inserted in cake comes out clean. Turn out onto a rack or leave in the pan; cool completely.

Chocolate Pudding Cake

Makes 8 or 9 servings **D** or **P**

This moist, rich, chocolatey dessert is halfway between a cake and a pudding. It's best served lukewarm but it's good at room temperature too. You can bake it three days ahead and keep it covered tightly at room temperature. If you like, serve a bowl of softly whipped cream as an accompaniment. The dessert is also delicious with regular or pareve coffee ice cream, which complements the coffee flavor in the cake.

5 ounces semisweet chocolate, chopped

3 tablespoons water

1½ teaspoons instant coffee powder or granules

½ cup (1 stick) plus 2 tablespoons unsalted butter or pareve margarine, cut into pieces, room temperature

4 large eggs, separated

½ cup plus 2 tablespoons sugar

¼ teaspoon cream of tartar

⅓ cup all-purpose flour, sifted

1. Preheat oven to 325°F. Lightly grease an 8-inch square baking pan. Line base with parchment paper or wax paper; grease, then flour the lined pan.

2. Melt chocolate with water and coffee in a medium bowl set over a pan of simmering water. Stir until smooth. Add butter pieces; stir until blended. Remove from pan of water; let cool.

3. Beat egg yolks in a large bowl with an electric mixer, then beat in ½ cup sugar. Whip at high speed about 5 minutes or until mixture is pale and very thick.

4. Beat egg whites with cream of tartar in a large dry bowl with the mixer until soft peaks form. Gradually beat in remaining 2 tablespoons sugar. Whip at high speed until whites are stiff and shiny but not dry.

5. Gently stir chocolate mixture into yolk mixture. Sift flour over chocolate mixture and fold it in gently. Gently fold in whites in 3 batches. Pour batter into prepared pan. Bake about 40 minutes or until a cake tester inserted in center of cake comes out clean. Cool cake in pan on a rack until lukewarm; center of cake will settle slightly.

6. Cut cake into squares while in pan. Serve lukewarm or at room temperature.

Creamy Cinnamon-Honey Sauce

Makes 4 servings (D)

This easy-to-make sauce is delicious with carrot cake, sponge cake, or angel food cake. You can also dip apples or bananas in it as a light snack. You can use the low-fat or nonfat versions of yogurt and sour cream if you like.

¹/₂ cup plain yogurt

¹/₂ cup sour cream

2 tablespoons honey

¹/₂ teaspoon ground cinnamon

Mix yogurt, sour cream, honey, and cinnamon in a bowl. Serve cold.

Fall Fruit in White Wine

Makes 6 to 8 servings (P)

Pears, plums, and prunes in citrus-scented wine make a delicious treat. The fruits gain flavor from the wine and impart their own fruity taste to it. Both the plums and the prunes give the wine a lovely color. Serve these fruit in their wine syrup as a light dessert, as an accompaniment for honey cake, sponge cake, or pound cake, or as a topping for ice cream. You can remove the citrus zest strips and vanilla bean at serving time or leave them in, as they look interesting.

3 cups dry white wine, such as Chardonnay

³/₄ cup sugar

Strip of orange zest

Strip of lemon zest

1 vanilla bean (optional)

4 ripe but firm medium pears (about 1¹/₂ pounds)

1 pound ripe plums, halved and pitted

4 ounces pitted prunes

1. Combine wine, sugar, orange zest, lemon zest, and vanilla bean, if using, in medium, heavy saucepan. Cook over low heat, stirring gently, until sugar dissolves. Raise heat to high and bring to boil. Remove from heat and cover.

2. Peel, halve, and core pears. Bring wine syrup to boil. Add pear halves. Cover with a lid slightly smaller than diameter of saucepan to keep pears submerged. Return to simmer. Reduce heat to low and cook pears about 30 minutes or until tender when pierced with sharp knife. Carefully remove pears with slotted spoon. Add plums and prunes and poach over low heat about 12 minutes or until they are tender. Remove from heat.

3. Return pears to syrup. Cover fruit with a small lid to keep it submerged. Cool fruit in syrup. Refrigerate fruit in syrup for at least 4 hours so they absorb flavor from syrup. Serve cold, in deep dishes.

Persimmon, Pear, and Kiwi Salad

Makes 4 to 6 servings (P)

This colorful fruit salad makes use of the luscious, bright orange persimmons that are plentiful in the fall. Choose carefully: If you have the pointy, Hachiya persimmon, it must be very soft and mushy, or else it will taste unpleasantly astringent. If you have the round Fuyu type, it should not be hard but it can be firm like an apple or, if you prefer, soft.

2 persimmons, peeled and sliced

2 kiwis, peeled, halved, and sliced

1 to 2 tablespoons strained fresh lemon juice

1 to 2 tablespoons sugar

2 ripe pears

Put persimmons and kiwi in a serving bowl. In a small cup mix lemon juice and sugar. A short time before serving, core and slice pears; add to serving bowl. Add lemon juice mixture and toss. Taste, and add more lemon juice or sugar if you like.

Hanukkah

Potato Latkes, Pancakes, and Fritters
120

Classic Potato Latkes

Baked Potato Latkes

Uncle Herman's Potato Latkes

French Potato Fritters

Parisian Hanukkah Crepes

Vegetable Latkes
124

Leek Latkes

Spiced Pumpkin Pancakes

Curried Cauliflower Pancakes

Cajun Corn Latkes

Mushroom Latkes with Dill

Saint Louis Carrot Latkes

Spinach Latkes with Nutmeg Cream

Zucchini-Potato Latkes

Sweet Potato Pancakes

Aunt Sylvia's Sweet Potato Patties

Latke Toppings and Accompaniments
131

Savory Mushroom Sauté

Sephardic Salsa

Creamy Dill Topping

Shallot, Herb, and Yogurt Topping

Mustard-Tarragon Topping

Onion Marmalade

Tomato-Garlic Topping

Old-Fashioned Applesauce

Chunky French Applesauce

Raspberry Applesauce

Apple-Apricot Sauce

Cranberry Applesauce

Salads and Appetizers
136

Hanukkah Party Salad

Red Cabbage Slaw with Walnuts
and Citrus Fruits

Nirit's Sweet Beet Salad

Spinach Salad with Red Beans

Hanukkah Party Tomato-and-
Herbed Cheese Sandwiches

Easy Bean and Vegetable Soup

Main Courses
139

Roasted Fish with Rosemary

Chicken and Split Pea Soup
with Rice and Vegetables

Onion-Smothered Chicken

Chicken Breast Schnitzel

Caper-Lemon Salsa

Veal Stew in the Style of
Osso Buco

Brisket with Chickpeas
and Zucchini

Fruit Desserts
147

Citrus Salad with Home-
Candied Orange Peel

Pears in Vanilla Syrup

Russian-Style Prune Compote
with Tea

Pear Cake with Honey

Soofganiyot and Other Treats
143

Israeli Doughnuts (Soofganiyot)

Soofganiyot with Jam

Dreidel Cookies

Crisp Chocolate Chip Cookies
with Pecans

Homemade Hanukkah Gelt

On the Jewish calendar, the eight-day holiday of Hanukkah is the main winter celebration and occurs in December or at the end of November. Hanukkah is celebrated with parties, songs, and games rather than prayers. It is not a biblical holiday but rather commemorates an historic event. More than two thousand years ago the Jews drove the pagan army out of Jerusalem and rekindled the eternal light in the holy temple with oil. Enough ritually pure oil for only one day could be found, but a miracle occurred: the oil lasted for eight days. The Syrian rulers had been trying to deny the Jews the right to practice Judaism, and rekindling the eternal light was an expression of a return to religious freedom.

To recall the miracle, candles are lit in a decorative Hanukkiah, a Hanukkah candelabrum, giving Hanukkah its name—the Festival of Lights. On the menu, oil is used to fry the two favorite holiday treats—potato latkes, or pancakes, and *soofganiyot*, or doughnuts without holes, often filled with red jam.

My mother taught me how to prepare potato latkes, and we enjoy making them when we are together for Hanukkah. Since we both enjoy experimenting and tasting new foods, we also make a variety of latkes from other vegetables besides potatoes. After all, the Hanukkah miracle involved oil, not potatoes, which didn't even exist in Israel at that time. The potato tradition came centuries afterwards, from eastern and central Europe. Pumpkin, spinach, corn, and cauliflower all make tasty latkes. Sweet potato latkes are definitely a hit. When my family wants a lighter holiday treat, we make low-calorie zucchini latkes and eat them with yogurt.

Potato pancakes are generally served on their own at Hanukkah parties. Sour cream and applesauce are the time-honored toppings. My relatives and I also serve low-fat sour cream or yogurt.

I like to serve an array of other toppings in addition to the customary ones, from sweet to savory to hot, including pesto, salsa, relishes, and sautéed mushrooms.

Israeli home cooks prepare two types of *soofganiyot*, the "classic" type made with yeast and a quick version with baking powder. At Hanukkah time, the yeast version is also widely available at the stores. It's sold fresh by all the bakeries as well as many supermarkets and grocery stores.

The remaining dishes served for Hanukkah are usually winter favorites. Brisket or roast chicken are often served. On Ashkenazic tables, goose and duck are old-fashioned entrees still savored by some families, sometimes with latkes as accompaniments.

Potato Latkes, Pancakes, and Fritters

Classic Potato Latkes

Makes 8 to 10 servings

This is my mother's potato latke recipe. I have already published it in a previous cookbook but since everyone is always asking for the recipe for these delicious latkes, I thought I'd offer it here as well.

A friend of mine who is a caterer said my mother's recipe saved her when she needed to prepare latkes for hundreds of people because my mother and I figured out how to avoid having to fry them at the last minute. My friend simply fried them a few days before the party and froze them. I often prepare them ahead too. I refrigerate or freeze the fried latkes on a cookie sheet. Once they are frozen, I put them in a freezer bag. I partially thaw frozen ones, and reheat them in a preheated 450°F oven for about 5 minutes. It may seem surprising, but I like them even better this way. To me it seems they come out crisper. But maybe I like them more because with make-ahead latkes, I'm able to enjoy the party!

Potato latkes have become very popular with chefs of fancy restaurants. They crown them with caviar or smoked salmon for appetizers, or they serve main course foods like veal or fish on top of a potato pancake. I like the creative appetizers but when a latke is under a substantial piece of meat coated in a sauce, it often turns out soggy and I wish it were served on the side, the old-fashioned way.

For Hanukkah, most cooks follow tradition and serve potato latkes with bowls of sour cream, sugar, and applesauce. Of course, fresh homemade Old-Fashioned

Applesauce or Chunky French Applesauce (page 134) is the best, or try a new variation made with apples and apricots (page 135).

2¹/₂ pounds potatoes (about 8 large)—or, baking, boiling, or Yukon Gold

2 medium onions

2 large eggs

1¹/₂ teaspoons salt

¹/₂ teaspoon ground white pepper

¹/₄ cup all-purpose flour

About ³/₄ cup vegetable oil (for frying)

1. Preheat oven to 250°F. Line a tray with paper towels for draining latkes and have a baking sheet ready for keeping latkes warm.

2. Peel and grate potatoes and onions on the large holes of a grater or with a food processor fitted with a coarse grating disk, alternating onion and potato. Transfer grated onion and potato to a colander. Squeeze mixture by handfuls to remove as much liquid as possible.

3. Put potato-onion mixture in a bowl. Add egg, salt, pepper, and flour and mix well.

4. Heat ¹/₂ cup oil in a deep, large, heavy skillet. For each latke, drop about 2 tablespoons of potato mixture into pan. Flatten with back of a spoon so each pancake is 2¹/₂ to 3 inches in diameter. Do not crowd them in pan. Fry over medium heat 4 to 5 minutes on each side, or until crisp and golden brown. Turn carefully with 2 slotted spatulas so oil doesn't splatter. Transfer to paper towels. Stir batter before frying each new batch. Add more oil to the pan as necessary, and heat it before adding more latkes. After frying about half the batter, put latkes on baking sheet and keep warm in oven.

5. Pat tops of latkes with paper towels before serving. Serve hot or warm.

Baked Potato Latkes

Makes 4 to 6 servings

You'll discover that these latkes, which are baked in muffin pans, have an appealing flavor even though they use much less fat than fried latkes. Serve them with applesauce (preferably homemade, see page 134) or, for a milchig meal, with fat-free or low-fat sour cream or yogurt or with Creamy Dill Topping (page 132) made using the lighter versions of the dairy products. I have found it useful to try different brands, as the taste varies greatly from one to another. Some are tangier, some more creamy. If you like to get creative with your accompaniments, buy one of the new flavors of applesauce, like apple-apricot or apple-blackberry, or top the latkes with sweet and savory Pineapple-Papaya Salsa (page 112).

2 tablespoons plus $^3/_4$ teaspoon vegetable oil

2 medium onions, chopped

$^3/_4$ teaspoon dried thyme

1$^1/_4$ teaspoons paprika, plus more for sprinkling

1$^3/_4$ pounds baking potatoes

2 large eggs

1 teaspoon salt

$^1/_2$ teaspoon freshly ground pepper

1$^1/_2$ cups applesauce (optional), for serving

1. Preheat oven to 400°F. Heat 1 tablespoon plus $^3/_4$ teaspoon oil in a heavy nonstick skillet. Add onions and sauté over medium low heat until softened, about 10 minutes; if pan becomes dry during sautéing, add $^1/_2$ tablespoon water. Add thyme and 1$^1/_4$ teaspoons paprika and sauté 30 seconds, stirring. Let cool.

2. Peeled and coarsely grate potatoes on the large holes of grater or using a food processor fitted with a coarse grating disk. Transfer grated potatoes to a colander and squeeze out excess liquid. Put potatoes in a bowl. Add sautéed onions, eggs, salt, and pepper.

3. Grease a 12-cup nonstick muffin pan, making sure to grease bases well, especially at the point where the base meets the sides. Add scant $^1/_3$ cup potato mixture to each muffin tin. Smooth tops lightly. Spoon $^1/_4$ teaspoon oil over each, then shake a little paprika on top. Bake about 45 minutes or until brown at edges and firm.

4. Remove from oven and run a small sturdy rubber spatula around edges of latkes to release them. You can then leave them in pan 15 to 30 minutes to keep hot. Serve latkes hot, accompanied by applesauce, if using.

Uncle Herman's Potato Latkes

Makes 8 to 10 servings

Herman Saks, my Uncle Herman, who was born in Russia, was the family's latke-maker when I was growing up, and every year he patiently and expertly fried numerous latkes at the family's big Hanukkah parties. His secret technique? He made his batter in a blender. This method is convenient, especially when making large quantities of latkes; you can quickly whip up batches of batter as you need them. Uncle Herman gave me his recipe just a few weeks before he passed away at the age of 91.

2 large eggs

1$^1/_2$ teaspoons salt

About $^1/_3$ cup matzo meal, more if needed

$^1/_2$ teaspoon baking powder

8 large potatoes

1 onion, cut into chunks

$^3/_4$ cup canola oil (for frying)

1. Preheat oven to 250°F. Line a tray with paper towels for draining the latkes and have a baking sheet ready for keeping latkes warm.

2. Put eggs, salt, matzo meal, and baking powder in a blender. Peel and cut potatoes into small chunks. Add potato and onion chunks a few at a time and process until potatoes and onions are chopped small and batter is blended well. Scrape batter down occasionally.

3. Pour batter into a bowl. If it is very thin, stir in another tablespoon or two of matzo meal.

4. Heat $^1/_2$ cup oil in a deep, large, heavy skillet. For each latke, drop 2 to 3 tablespoons of potato mixture into pan. Do not crowd them in pan. Fry over medium heat 4 to 5 minutes on each side or until crisp and golden brown. Turn carefully with 2 slotted spatulas so oil doesn't splatter. Transfer to paper towels. Stir batter before frying each new batch. Add more oil to the pan as necessary, and heat it before adding more latkes. After frying about half the batter, put latkes on baking sheet and keep warm in oven.

5. Pat tops of latkes with paper towels before serving. Serve hot or warm.

French Potato Fritters

Makes 6 to 8 servings Ⓓ

If you have a fear of frying, you'll overcome it if you try potato beignets. They're easy and forgiving even if you're not sure of the temperature of the oil. And they're delicious! Creamy on the inside and delicately crisp on the outside, they're one of the favorite potato dishes of France, where they are served at elegant dinners. I find they're perfect for Hanukkah.

1¹/₂ pounds boiling potatoes, peeled and cut into 2 or 3 pieces

¹/₃ cup milk

¹/₄ cup (¹/₂ stick) plus 2 tablespoons butter

Salt and white pepper, to taste

Freshly grated nutmeg to taste

¹/₂ cup plus 1 tablespoon all-purpose flour

¹/₂ cup water

2 large eggs

Vegetable oil for deep-frying (at least 6 cups)

1. Put potatoes in a saucepan with enough water to cover them and add a pinch of salt. Bring to a boil, cover and simmer over medium heat 20 to 25 minutes or until potatoes are very tender. Drain well.

2. Puree potatoes in a food mill or mash with a potato masher. Return them to saucepan. Add milk, 2 tablespoons of the butter, and salt, white pepper, and nutmeg. Stir over low heat until mixture is smooth. Remove from heat; let cool.

3. Sift flour onto a piece of wax paper. Heat water, ¹/₄ teaspoon salt, and ¹/₄ cup butter in a medium saucepan until butter melts. Raise heat to medium-high

and bring to a boil. Remove from heat. Add flour immediately and stir quickly with a wooden spoon until mixture is smooth. Set pan over low heat and beat mixture for about 30 seconds. Remove from heat; cool for a few minutes. Add 1 egg and beat it into mixture. Beat in second egg. Stir in potato puree.

4. Preheat oven to 300°F. Line baking sheets with paper towels. Pour oil into a deep fryer or deep, heavy saucepan. Do not fill pan more than halfway with oil. Heat oil to about 370°F on a frying thermometer. If thermometer is not available, test by putting a drop of potato mixture into oil; when oil is hot enough, it should bubble energetically.

5. Take a rounded teaspoonful of batter. With a second teaspoon, slide it gently into oil, forming a rounded fritter. Do not crowd pan; fritters need room to puff. Fry them, turning them occasionally, 2 to 3 minutes or until they are golden brown on all sides. Don't let them brown too fast, as batter needs time to cook through. Transfer to paper towels. Keep in oven while frying remaining mixture. Serve as soon as possible.

Safety Tips For Deep Frying

- Fill the pan no more than half full of oil.
- When adding foods to the oil, hold the food near the oil's surface and add it gently. Do not drop food from high above the oil because it will splash the hot oil.
- Be careful not to crowd the pan, as the oil might bubble up and over the top.
- Regulate the heat as necessary to keep the oil at the right temperature.
- Never leave the pan unattended while frying. Give frying your full attention.
- Let the pan of oil cool before moving it.

Parisian Hanukkah Crepes

Makes 16 small pancakes, 4 or 5 servings

I started making these delectable potato crepes during the years that I celebrated the Festival of Lights in the City of Lights. Pureed baked potatoes paired with cooked leeks give the crepes wonderful flavor. French cooks developed potato crepes to use up leftover baked potatoes, but they became very popular in fine restaurants as side dishes. Although they're called crepes in France, they are thicker than traditional ones (but not as thick as American pancakes). Serve them topped with crème fraîche, sour cream, or Savory Mushroom Sauté (page 131).

1¼ pounds baking potatoes (2 large), scrubbed

1 pound large leeks

2 tablespoons butter

½ cup plus 1 or 2 tablespoons milk

1½ teaspoons salt

Freshly ground pepper, to taste

Freshly grated nutmeg, to taste

3 large eggs

2 tablespoons all-purpose flour

⅓ cup vegetable oil

1. Preheat oven to 425°F. Pierce potatoes with a fork. Bake on a rack in oven about 1 hour or until tender.

2. Use white and light green parts of leeks only; save dark green parts for soups and stocks. Halve leeks lengthwise, rinse well and cut into ¼-inch slices. Put sliced leeks in a bowl of cold water and separate the pieces. Soak them 5 minutes to remove any sand. Lift leeks into colander, rinse, and drain well.

3. Melt butter in medium, heavy skillet. Add leeks. Cook over medium heat, stirring very often, about 10 minutes or until leeks are soft but not brown. If any liquid remains in pan, cook leek mixture over medium-high heat, stirring, until it evaporates. Transfer leek mixture to a bowl; let cool.

4. Halve hot potatoes and scoop out pulp. Puree in a food mill or mash with a potato masher until very fine. Transfer to a bowl. Stir in ½ cup milk, salt, pepper, and nutmeg.

5. Let cool. Stir in leeks. Add more salt, pepper, and nutmeg if needed. Stir in eggs one by one, stirring well after each addition. Stir in flour.

6. Preheat oven to 250°F. Heat ¼ cup oil in a large, heavy skillet over medium heat. Using a large tablespoon, add a spoonful of batter to oil and flatten slightly to make a small pancake of 2- to 2½-inch diameter. Mixture should spread but pancake does not need to be very thin. If mixture is too thick to spread at all, add a little milk to batter. If pancakes do not hold together, add 1 tablespoon more flour to batter.

7. Make more pancakes of same size and fry about 5 minutes or until they are golden brown on both sides; turn them carefully with 2 slotted spatulas. Transfer to paper towels on an ovenproof tray. Keep warm in oven while frying rest of pancakes. Stir batter occasionally; add more oil to skillet as needed.

8. The pancakes are best if served right away, but they can be kept warm about 30 minutes. You can also make them 1 day ahead and refrigerate them; heat in 1 layer on a baking sheet in a 250°F oven.

❧ Vegetable Latkes

Veggie Burgers—The New Latkes

There has been a mushrooming of vegetable burgers at the supermarket recently. They are found at various places at the store—in the deli department, in the natural foods section, and next to the frozen vegetables. They have even invaded the meat shelf, and are displayed between the bacon and the beef.

Many are creatively spiced and contain a variety of ingredients, from mushrooms to water chestnuts to black beans. Their new popularity and prominence is undoubtedly due to people's desire to incorporate more vegetables into their diet. Their advantage over meat burgers is that many contain little or no saturated fat or cholesterol.

Whether they're called meatless burgers, veggie patties, or pancakes, they seemed familiar to me when I sampled them. After I tasted a few, I realized why—my mother has been making them for years, especially around Hanukkah. But she calls them latkes!

Latkes made of grated potatoes are the best known to many of us. But latke in Yiddish simply means a sautéed cake or patty. Latkes are in fact made of many different foods, from fish to noodles to apples. Modern cooks often make them of vegetables, singly or as mixtures. They use either grated raw vegetables, such as carrots, onions, or sweet potatoes, or with mashed, pureed, or chopped cooked ones.

I've never met a vegetable that doesn't like becoming a latke. From asparagus to zucchini, I've made latkes with just about every vegetable. A woman I met shopping told me that her husband, a rabbi, makes latkes by simply cooking and mincing whatever frozen vegetables they happen to have.

My mother, the expert latke maker in our family, pointed out that you can make latkes out of any food, as long as you add egg or egg white to moisten it, plus flour, bread crumbs, or matzo meal to hold it together, and salt and pepper to flavor it.

To turn latkes into protein-rich entrees like some of the prepared meatless patties, you can add canned chickpeas (garbanzo beans), red beans, or other legumes. Other options are soy granules (sometimes labeled "TVP" for textured vegetable protein), soy ground meat substitute, or cooked whole grains.

The seasonings can vary from onions, salt, and pepper as in potato latkes, to herbs, garlic, or any spice blend you like. You can even add such flavorings as Chinese black bean paste or plum sauce. Serve vegetable latkes with the traditional toppings of sour cream and applesauce or with whatever sauces you have on hand. I serve fruit-based salsa, tomato sauce, and curry sauce, as well as ketchup for kids who request it.

Chefs might include wild mushrooms in their latkes and top them with caviar or smoked salmon, but latkes excel particularly as a down-to-earth, economical treat. They are a legacy of home cooks over the ages who made tasty holiday treats out of potatoes and other humble foods.

Leek Latkes

Makes 4 to 6 servings

These delicate latkes are delicious and elegant when topped with a dollop of sour cream and a small spoonful of caviar. Another tasty option is serving them with Mustard-Tarragon Topping (page 132).

6 large leeks (about 3 pounds)

5 to 6 tablespoons vegetable oil

Salt and freshly ground pepper, to taste

1/2 cup all-purpose flour

2 large eggs

1/4 teaspoon ground white pepper

Freshly grated nutmeg, to taste

1. Preheat oven to 250°F. Line a tray with paper towels to drain latkes and have a baking sheet ready for keeping latkes warm.

2. Discard the root ends of the leeks. Cut off the dark green part and save for making soups, stocks, or sauces. Halve the leeks lengthwise, rinse them, and cut into thin slices crosswise. Put slices in a bowl of cold water, separate them and let stand 5 minutes. Lift leek slices out of water and put them in a strainer to drain well.

3. Heat 2 tablespoons oil in a large, heavy saucepan, add leeks, and sprinkle with salt and pepper. Cover and cook over low heat, stirring occasionally, 5 minutes or until tender. Transfer to a large bowl. Adjust seasoning.

4. Mix flour, eggs, white pepper, nutmeg, and 1/4 teaspoon salt in a medium bowl until to a very thick batter. Add batter to bowl of leeks and mix very well.

5. Heat 3 tablespoons oil in a deep, heavy skillet over medium heat. Add leek mixture by tablespoonfuls and flatten each after adding it. Do not crowd pan. Fry about 2 minutes or until golden brown on each side. Turn carefully with 2 slotted spatulas so oil doesn't splatter. Transfer to paper towels. Stir batter before frying each new batch. Add more oil to the pan as necessary, and heat it before adding more latkes. After frying about half the batter, put latkes on baking sheet and keep warm in oven.

6. Pat tops of latkes with paper towels before serving. Serve hot or warm.

Spiced Pumpkin Pancakes

Makes 4 to 6 servings

In some Sephardic families pumpkin pancakes are served for Rosh Hashanah. They also make a nice change from potato latkes for Hanukkah. Make them either with sugar pumpkins, sometimes sold as "pie pumpkins," or with sweet winter squash such as butternut, acorn, or carnival squash. I usually microwave the squash to cook it quickly but you can poach it or steam it if you wish.

For meatless meals I like these gently spiced pancakes topped with yogurt and sprinkled very lightly with brown sugar. Served this way, they make a tasty brunch entree.

2 pounds pumpkin or winter squash, halved, seeded, then halved again

1/2 cup plus 1 tablespoon all-purpose flour

2 large eggs

1/2 teaspoon ground cinnamon

1/4 teaspoon ground ginger

1/4 teaspoon ground allspice

1/2 teaspoon sugar

1/4 teaspoon salt

1/4 teaspoon ground white pepper

About 1/4 cup vegetable oil (for frying)

Yogurt or sour cream (optional, for dairy meals)

Brown sugar (for sprinkling)

1. Preheat the oven to 250°F. Line a tray with paper towels to drain the pancakes and have a baking sheet ready for keeping pancakes warm.

2. Put the pumpkin or squash cut side down in a casserole dish and add about 1/4 inch water. Cover and microwave on high 8 to 10 minutes or until tender when pierced with a fork.

(To poach the pumpkin, cut it into 6 or 8 pieces. Add to a large saucepan with enough boiling salted water to cover it halfway. Return to a boil, cover, and simmer over medium-low heat, turning once or twice, 15 to 20 minutes or until tender.)

3. Remove cooked pumpkin to a plate and let cool slightly. Scoop out pulp. Cut pulp into pieces and mash it with a fork. Press pulp gently in a strainer to remove excess liquid. Transfer pulp to a bowl.

4. Mix flour, eggs, cinnamon, ginger, allspice, sugar, salt, and white pepper in a medium bowl until it becomes a very thick batter. Add to mashed pumpkin and mix very well.

5. Heat oil in a deep, heavy skillet over medium heat. Fry pumpkin mixture by tablespoonfuls, flattening each after adding, about 2 minutes or until golden brown on each side. Turn carefully with 2 slotted spatulas so oil doesn't splatter. Transfer to paper towels. Stir batter before frying each new batch. Add more oil to the pan as necessary, and heat it before adding more pancakes. After frying about half the batter, put pancakes on baking sheet and keep warm in oven.

6. Pat tops of pancakes with paper towels before serving. Serve hot or warm. Top with yogurt, if using, and sprinkle with brown sugar.

Curried Cauliflower Pancakes

Ⓟ

Makes 6 servings

These golden pancakes are great with grilled fish, lamb, or chicken. If you prefer to serve them as an appetizer or as part of an assortment of latkes, top them with sour cream or yogurt and garnish them with a sprig of cilantro. For a pareve meal, accompany them, instead, with mild or medium salsa.

The secret to the flavor of these latkes is lightly sautéing the cumin and curry powder with the onions.

1 large head cauliflower (about 2 pounds), divided into medium florets

5 to 6 tablespoons vegetable oil, or more if needed

1 medium onion, finely chopped

1 teaspoon curry powder

$^{1}/_{2}$ teaspoon ground cumin

Salt and freshly ground pepper, to taste

6 tablespoons unseasoned bread crumbs

2 large eggs

1. Preheat oven to 250°F. Line a tray with paper towels to drain pancakes and have a baking sheet ready for keeping pancakes warm.

2. Cook cauliflower in a large pan of boiling salted water uncovered over high heat about 12 minutes or until very tender. Meanwhile, heat 2 tablespoons oil in a large, heavy skillet, add onion, and cook over medium-low heat about 10 minutes or until soft and golden brown. Add curry powder and cumin and sauté, stirring, 30 seconds.

3. Drain cauliflower well. Mash it with a fork or chop it in a food processor, leaving some small pieces. Transfer to a bowl. Stir in sautéed onion mixture. Season to taste with salt and pepper. Add bread crumbs and eggs and mix well.

4. Preheat oven to 300°F. Heat 3 tablespoons oil in a large, heavy skillet. Take 1 heaping tablespoon cauliflower mixture in your hand and press to make it compact. Flatten it to a cake about $^{1}/_{2}$-inch thick and add to pan. Make 4 or 5 more cakes and add them to the pan. Fry over medium heat about 3 minutes on each side or until brown. Turn carefully with 2 slotted spatulas so oil doesn't splatter. Transfer to paper towels. Stir batter before frying each new batch. Add more oil to the pan as necessary, and heat it before adding more pancakes. After frying about half the batter, put pancakes on baking sheet and keep warm in oven.

5. Pat tops of pancakes with paper towels before serving. Serve hot or warm.

Cajun Corn Latkes

Makes 4 appetizer or side-dish servings **P**

Corn and bell peppers, a popular Louisiana combination for stews and salads, also make terrific latkes. These pancakes have just a hint of spice. If you'd like them hotter, add more cayenne to the batter or serve the latkes with hot sauce. If you like, top each latke with a spoonful of Sephardic Salsa (page 131) or savory-sweet Pineapple-Papaya Salsa (page 112).

2 cups frozen corn kernels, cooked, drained, and cooled, or canned corn kernels

$1/3$ cup finely diced red or green bell pepper

$1/4$ cup chopped celery

Salt and freshly ground pepper, to taste

Pinch of cayenne pepper

$1/2$ teaspoon ground cumin

3 tablespoons all-purpose flour

1 large egg

About $1/4$ cup vegetable oil (for frying)

1. Line a tray with paper towels to drain latkes. Puree $1/2$ cup of the cooked corn in a food processor; a few chunks may remain. Mix pureed corn with bell pepper, celery, salt, pepper, cayenne, cumin, and flour. Adjust seasoning. Stir in egg, then the $1^1/2$ cups remaining corn kernels.

2. Heat $1/4$ cup oil in a deep, large, heavy skillet. For each pancake, drop 1 heaping tablespoon of corn mixture into the pan. Flatten pancakes slightly with back of a spoon. Fry over medium heat 2 to 3 minutes on each side or until golden brown. Turn carefully with 2 slotted spatulas so oil doesn't splatter. Transfer to paper towels. Stir batter before frying each new batch. Add more oil to the pan as necessary, and heat it before adding more latkes.

3. Pat tops of latkes with paper towels before serving. Serve hot.

Mushroom Latkes with Dill

Makes 4 to 5 appetizer or side-dish servings **P**

You can serve these pancakes for Hanukkah or for Passover. They're a tasty accompaniment for broiled sea bass or salmon or roasted chicken. If you serve them as an appetizer, top them with Leek Compote (page 73) and a sprinkling of fresh dill. For dairy meals, I like them with Creamy Dill Topping (page 132) or garnished with a dollop of sour cream and a few strips of lox.

$1/4$ pound small mushrooms

3 tablespoons vegetable oil

1 medium onion, finely chopped

$1/4$ cup chopped celery

1 tablespoon snipped fresh dill

Salt and freshly ground pepper, to taste

2 large eggs, slightly beaten

2 to 3 tablespoons matzo meal

About $1/4$ cup vegetable oil (for frying)

1. Line a tray with paper towels to drain the latkes. Separate mushroom stems from caps; halve caps and stems lengthwise and cut into thin slices. Heat 3 tablespoons oil in a large skillet. Add onion and sauté over medium-low heat for 5 minutes. Add mushrooms and celery and sauté 8 minutes or until vegetables are tender. Let cool. Transfer to a bowl. Add dill, salt, pepper, eggs, and 2 tablespoons matzo meal. Mix well; if mixture appears watery, add another tablespoon matzo meal.

2. Heat $1/4$ cup oil in a deep, large, heavy skillet. For each pancake, drop 1 heaping tablespoon of mixture into pan. Flatten them slightly with back of a spoon. Fry over medium heat 2 to 3 minutes on each side, or until golden brown. Turn carefully with 2 slotted spatulas so oil doesn't splatter. Transfer to paper towels. Stir batter before frying each new batch. Add more oil to the pan as necessary, and heat it before adding more latkes.

3. Pat tops of latkes with paper towels before serving. Serve hot.

Saint Louis Carrot Latkes

Makes about 4 servings

When I visited Saint Louis, I learned that carrot latkes are a specialty of the restaurant at the city's Jewish Community Center. The latkes have a delicate sweetness and an eye-catching orange hue. I like to season them with a little ginger and to serve them with Onion Marmalade (page 133).

1¼ pounds carrots

½ small onion

1 large egg

½ teaspoon salt

½ teaspoon ground ginger

¼ teaspoon white pepper (optional)

3 tablespoons all-purpose flour

About ½ cup vegetable oil (for frying)

1. Preheat oven to 250°F. Line a tray with paper towels to drain latkes.

2. Grate carrots and onion, using the large holes of a grater or a food processor fitted with a coarse grating disk. Transfer to a large bowl. Beat egg with salt, ginger, and pepper, if using, in a small bowl and add to carrot mixture. Add flour and mix well.

3. Heat ¼ cup oil in a heavy 10- to 12-inch skillet, preferably nonstick. For each latke, drop about 2 tablespoons of carrot mixture into pan. Flatten with back of a spoon so each pancake is about 2½ inches in diameter. Do not crowd pan. Fry over medium heat 4 minutes on each side, or until light golden. Turn carefully with 2 slotted spatulas so oil doesn't splatter. Transfer to paper towels. Stir batter before frying each new batch. Add more oil to the pan as necessary, and heat it before adding more latkes. After frying about half the batter, put latkes on baking sheet and keep warm in oven.

4. Pat tops of latkes with paper towels before serving. Serve hot or warm.

Spinach Latkes with Nutmeg Cream

Makes 4 to 6 servings

Spinach and nutmeg are classic partners in European cooking, and they complement each other well in these shallot-accented pancakes. They make a colorful addition to a platter of potato latkes or a good accompaniment for baked fish.

Three 10-ounce bags rinsed spinach leaves

2 tablespoons butter or vegetable oil

2 medium shallots, chopped

Salt and freshly ground pepper, to taste

Cayenne pepper, to taste

Freshly grated nutmeg, to taste

½ cup all-purpose flour

2 large eggs

2 tablespoons milk

1 cup sour cream (regular, low-fat, or nonfat)

Ground white pepper, to taste

About ¼ cup vegetable oil (for frying)

1 tablespoon chopped fresh chives

1. Line a tray with paper towels to drain the latkes. Cook spinach in a large pan of boiling salted water 3 minutes or until tender. Rinse with cold water. Squeeze spinach to remove excess liquid. Chop fine with a knife.

2. Melt butter in a medium skillet. Add shallots and sauté over medium heat 1 minute. Add spinach and cook about 2 minutes, stirring. Season with salt, pepper, cayenne pepper, and nutmeg. Transfer to a large bowl.

3. Mix flour, eggs, milk, ¼ teaspoon salt, and a pinch of nutmeg in a small bowl until it becomes a thick batter. Add batter to spinach and mix well.

4. To make nutmeg cream topping: Mix sour cream with nutmeg, salt, white pepper, and cayenne pepper to taste.

5. Heat oil in a heavy skillet over medium heat. Fry spinach mixture by tablespoonfuls, flattening each after adding it, about 2 minutes per side or until golden browned. Do not crowd pan. Turn carefully with 2 slotted spatulas so oil doesn't splatter. Transfer to paper towels. Stir batter before frying each new batch. Add more oil to the pan as necessary, and heat it before adding more latkes.

6. Pat tops of latkes with paper towels before serving. Serve hot, with a small dollop of topping and a sprinkling of chives.

Zucchini-Potato Latkes

Makes about 4 appetizer servings

You can make pancakes from zucchini alone but the latkes come out a little crisper when the zucchini are paired with potatoes. These light latkes are flavored with onion and garlic and taste good with veal chops, roast chicken, or baked halibut. As an appetizer, they're good with Sephardic Salsa.

1/2 medium onion

1 large baking potato (about 5 ounces)

3 medium zucchini (about 12 ounces)

1 tablespoon chopped garlic

1 tablespoon chopped fresh Italian parsley

1 egg, lightly beaten

3/4 teaspoon salt

1/4 teaspoon white pepper

3 tablespoons all-purpose flour

About 1/4 cup vegetable oil (for frying)

1. Line a tray with paper towels to drain latkes. Peel and grate onion and potato using large holes of a grater or a food processor fitted with a coarse grating disk, alternating onion and potato. Transfer them to a colander. Squeeze mixture by handfuls to remove as much liquid as possible. Put potatoes and onions in a bowl. Grate zucchini the same way and squeeze out excess liquid. Add to bowl of potato and onion. Add garlic, parsley, egg, salt, pepper, and flour and mix well.

2. Heat oil in a deep, large, heavy skillet. For each pancake, drop 1 heaping tablespoon of zucchini mixture into the pan. Flatten them slightly with back of a spoon. Fry over medium heat 2 to 3 minutes on each side or until golden brown. Turn very carefully with 2 slotted spatulas so the oil doesn't splatter. Transfer to

paper towels. Stir batter before frying each new batch. Add more oil to the pan as necessary, and heat it before adding more latkes.

3. Pat tops of latkes with paper towels before serving. Serve hot.

Sweet Potato Pancakes

Makes about 4 servings

One Hanukkah my mother and I made new latkes from all sorts of vegetables, a different one each night. My favorites were those we prepared on the seventh night—sweet potato latkes, with a subtle sweet flavor and a lovely orange color. They're great with Chunky French Applesauce (page 134), Creamy Dill Topping (page 132), or, for an unusual touch, Pineapple-Papaya Salsa (page 112).

Use a nonstick skillet and be especially careful when frying these latkes, as the high sugar content of sweet potatoes can cause them to burn easily. You can make these ahead and reheat them on a cookie sheet in a 400°F oven about 7 minutes; but watch them so their edges don't scorch.

1 1/2 pounds orange-fleshed sweet potatoes, peeled

1 medium onion

2 large eggs

3/4 teaspoon salt

1/4 teaspoon ground white pepper

5 tablespoons all-purpose flour

About 1/2 cup vegetable oil (for frying)

1. Line a tray with paper towels to drain pancakes. Grate sweet potatoes and onion using large holes of a grater or a food processor fitted with a coarse grating disk. Transfer to a large bowl. Beat eggs with salt and white pepper in a small bowl and add to potato mixture. Add flour and mix well.

2. Heat 1/4 cup oil in a heavy 10- to 12-inch skillet, preferably nonstick. Fill a 1/4-cup measure with mixture, pressing to compact it, and turn it out in a mound into skillet. Quickly form 3 more mounds. Flatten each with back of a spoon so each cake is 2 1/2 to 3 inches in diameter, pressing to compact it. Fry over medium heat 3 minutes; turn carefully with 2 slotted spatulas and fry second side about 2¹/₂ minutes or until golden brown and crisp. Transfer to paper towels. Stir potato mixture before frying each new batch. Add more oil to the pan as necessary, and heat it before adding more latkes.

3. Pat tops of latkes with paper towels before serving. Serve hot.

Aunt Sylvia's Sweet Potato Patties

Makes 6 to 8 servings   Ⓟ

For as long as I can remember, these easy-to-make patties have been a Thanksgiving tradition at the table of my aunt Sylvia Saks. For Hanukkah, she serves them alongside my Uncle Herman's Potato Latkes (page 121). The sweet potatoes are mixed with pineapple, shaped into patties, given a crunchy coating of corn flakes, and a candied cherry garnish and are baked. Aunt Sylvia does not add sugar; the sweet potatoes and pineapple provide enough sweetness. She used to make them with potato chips instead of corn flakes, and people liked the contrast of the salty chips with the sweet potatoes, but she no longer uses them because many people are salt conscious. (But you can still try it if you like.)

Aunt Sylvia often doubles the recipe and bakes part of it as a casserole instead of making it into patties,

because some family members prefer it that way. For the casserole, she sprinkles the corn flakes on top. If you like, dot the top with marshmallows in addition to candied cherries.

2 pounds medium orange-fleshed sweet potatoes, scrubbed

One 8-ounce can crushed pineapple

Salt, to taste

About 2 cups corn flakes

Candied cherries, halved

1. Put sweet potatoes in a large saucepan with enough water to cover and a pinch of salt and bring to a boil. Cover and simmer over low heat about 30 minutes or until tender. Drain and let cool.

2. Preheat oven to 350°F. Grease a baking sheet. Peel potatoes. Mash them with a potato masher. Drain pineapple, reserving liquid. Stir pineapple and salt into potatoes. If mixture is dry, gradually add enough pineapple liquid to moisten it, but don't make it wet.

3. Put corn flakes in a bowl and crush lightly. For each patty, drop about ¹/₄ cup of potato mixture into bowl of corn flakes. Turn with 2 spoons to coat potato. Transfer to baking sheet and shape in a patty. Make an indentation in each patty and put a candied cherry half inside.

4. Bake patties about 15 minutes or until heated through. Serve hot.

Latke Toppings and Accompaniments

Savory Mushroom Sauté

Makes 4 servings

This flavorful medley of exotic and button mushrooms is a delicious topping for potato latkes or for Parisian Hanukkah Crepes (page 123). It's also wonderful as an appetizer or an accompaniment for fish, pasta, rice, or Mamaliga, either soft or Oven-Toasted (page 522). If you make the sauté without butter, you can serve it with chicken, turkey, or veal. This is best with exotic mushrooms such as chanterelle, shiitake, or portobello, but you can make it with only button mushrooms; it will still taste very good.

¹/₄ pound fresh exotic mushrooms
1 tablespoon vegetable oil
2 tablespoons butter or additional vegetable oil
¹/₄ pound button mushrooms, rinsed, dried, and quartered
Salt and freshly ground pepper, to taste
2 medium shallots, finely chopped
2 tablespoons chopped fresh Italian parsley

1. Clean exotic mushrooms very gently with damp paper towel. If using shiitake mushrooms, cut off stems, which are tough. Cut any large mushrooms into bite-size pieces, following the mushroom's shape.

2. Heat oil and butter in a heavy skillet over medium-high heat. Add exotic and button mushrooms, salt, and pepper. Sauté about 3 minutes. Add shallots and sauté, tossing often, 2 to 3 minutes or until mushrooms are lightly browned and tender and any liquid in pan has evaporated. Be careful; shallots burn easily. Add parsley. Adjust seasoning. Serve hot.

Sephardic Salsa

Makes about 2¹/₂ cups, 8 to 10 servings

Flavored with herbs, garlic, and lemon juice, this chunky, medium-hot salsa makes a fresh, pareve topping for all sorts of latkes. I especially like it with Cajun Corn Latkes (page 127) and Curried Cauliflower Pancakes (page 126).

2 medium jalapeño peppers (see Note)
2 large cloves garlic, peeled
¹/₄ cup sprigs fresh cilantro
¹/₄ cup sprigs fresh Italian parsley
1 pound ripe tomatoes, finely diced
¹/₄ cup minced onion
1 to 2 tablespoons strained fresh lemon juice
1 tablespoon olive oil (optional)
1 teaspoon ground cumin
Salt and freshly ground pepper, to taste
1 to 2 tablespoons water, if needed

Core jalapeño peppers; remove seeds and ribs if you want them to be less hot. Put jalapeño peppers and garlic in food processor and chop finely. Add cilantro and parsley and chop finely. Transfer to a medium bowl. Add tomatoes, onion, lemon juice, olive oil if using, and cumin. Season with salt and pepper. Add water if salsa is too thick. Refrigerate salsa in a covered container until ready to serve. Serve cold.

Note: Wear rubber gloves when handling hot peppers.

Creamy Dill Topping

Makes about 6 servings

This topping is great on Classic Potato Latkes (page 120) or on Mushroom Latkes with Dill (page 127). But don't stop with latkes. I love it on plain baked potatoes, boiled fresh beets, and briefly cooked zucchini. Use sour cream and yogurt in the richness you prefer—regular, low-fat, or nonfat.

^{1}/$_2$ **cup sour cream**

1 cup yogurt

1 tablespoon snipped fresh dill

Salt and freshly ground pepper, to taste

Cayenne pepper to taste

Mix sour cream, yogurt, and dill in a bowl. Season with salt, pepper, and cayenne. Refrigerate until ready to serve.

Shallot, Herb, and Yogurt Topping

Makes 4 servings

Like onions, shallots become sweet when they are lightly sautéed. In this topping the shallots add a hint of sweetness to the tangy yogurt. I like it on carrot, sweet potato, and zucchini latkes.

2 to 3 teaspoons olive oil

2 large shallots, minced

^{1}/$_4$ **cup vegetable broth**

1 cup plain yogurt (regular, low-fat, or nonfat)

Salt, to taste

Cayenne pepper, to taste

2 teaspoons fresh thyme or 1 teaspoon dried, crumbled

1 tablespoon chopped fresh Italian parsley

2 teaspoons finely sliced fresh chives

1. Heat oil in a very small skillet. Add shallots and cook over low heat, stirring often, about 3 minutes or until they are tender but not brown. Add broth and bring to a simmer, stirring. Cook over medium-low heat until shallots absorb broth. Transfer to a small bowl and let cool.

2. Add yogurt to shallot mixture. Season to taste with salt and cayenne. Stir in thyme, parsley, and half the chives. Adjust seasoning. Serve cold. Serve in a bowl, sprinkled with remaining chives, or spoon a little onto each latke and then sprinkle it with chives.

Mustard-Tarragon Topping

Makes about 1 cup, about 6 servings

A dollop of this creamy sauce is the perfect complement to Leek Latkes (page 125). Make it with regular or reduced-fat sour cream, yogurt, and mayonnaise.

^{1}/$_2$ **cup sour cream**

^{1}/$_4$ **cup yogurt**

^{1}/$_4$ **cup mayonnaise**

2 tablespoons Dijon mustard, or to taste

1 to 2 teaspoons tarragon vinegar or herb vinegar

2 tablespoons chopped green onions

2 tablespoons chopped fresh tarragon

1 tablespoon chopped fresh Italian parsley

Salt and freshly ground pepper, to taste

Mix sour cream, yogurt, mayonnaise, and mustard in a bowl until smooth. Stir in 1 teaspoon vinegar, followed by green onions, tarragon, and parsley. Add more mustard and vinegar if you like and season with salt and pepper. Cover and refrigerate until ready to serve.

Onion Marmalade

Makes 8 to 10 servings

Onions cooked until they are sweet and soft are often called onion marmalade. Usually they are tangy and sweet, like in this recipe, which is made with sweet onions, dry red wine, wine vinegar, cranberry juice, and a little brown sugar. How sweet to make it depends on your taste and on the sweetness of the onions. If you like, add more sugar or vinegar to the finished marmalade and simmer a minute to blend them in.

Chefs often serve onion marmalade as a savory-sweet accompaniment for meats. I find it's a great complement to latkes too, especially those that are flavored with a little onion. It's a delectable topping for potato latkes, whether fried (page 120) or baked (page 121), Saint Louis Carrot Latkes (page 128), and Sweet Potato Pancakes (page 129). Sweet onion marmalade is also good in cold chicken or turkey sandwiches.

2 tablespoons olive oil

2¹/₂ pounds red onions, white onions, or other sweet
    onions, halved and sliced thin

Salt and freshly ground pepper, to taste

1 to 2 tablespoons brown sugar

¹/₃ cup red wine vinegar

²/₃ cup dry red wine

¹/₄ cup cranberry apple juice

1. Heat oil in a large sauté pan or stew pan. Add onions. Sauté over medium heat, stirring often, 5 minutes. Sprinkle with salt and pepper. Cover and cook over medium-low heat, stirring often, 5 minutes or until onions are golden brown; reduce heat if they are browning too fast.

2. Add 1 tablespoon sugar to onions, stir, and cook 1 minute to dissolve sugar. Add vinegar and bring to a boil, stirring. Add wine and bring to a boil. Cook uncovered over medium heat, stirring often, about 5 minutes or until most of liquid evaporates. Add cranberry apple juice and cook, stirring often, until it is absorbed and onions are very tender. Adjust seasoning. If you like, add remaining sugar and cook another minute, stirring. Serve hot or cold.

Tomato-Garlic Topping

Makes enough topping for 4 or 5 servings

If you're able to get good tomatoes at Hanukkah time, prepare this savory topping to serve with your latkes. The tomatoes may be expensive but you need just a little bit of topping to add a lively color to your plate of latkes. You can serve the latkes with only this topping, or with a yogurt or sour cream topping in addition. If you can't find ripe tomatoes, you can use good quality canned ones. I like this topping with any latkes, but especially with those made of potato, zucchini, or cauliflower.

1 tablespoon olive oil

2 medium cloves garlic, minced

2 tablespoons chopped fresh Italian parsley

2 medium ripe tomatoes (about 1 pound), diced (see Note)

Salt and freshly ground pepper, to taste

1. Heat 1 tablespoon oil in a large, heavy skillet. Add garlic and sauté over medium heat 30 seconds. Add parsley and toss over heat a few seconds. Remove from heat and stir in tomatoes. Season with salt and pepper.

2. To serve, spoon topping over center of each latke. Serve hot or at room temperature.

Note: If fresh tomatoes are not available, use a 14¹/₂-ounce can whole tomatoes. Drain well, dice, and drain again.

Old-Fashioned Applesauce

Makes 8 to 12 servings

Like many good cooks, my mother makes applesauce this way, for Hanukkah or any time. All the parts of the apple, including the peel and core, contribute their flavor to this applesauce. If the peel is red, it adds a little color too. You save time peeling the apples but then you do need to work the applesauce through a food mill.

If you don't have a food mill, you can still make this applesauce. Simply peel and core the apples, then puree the applesauce in a blender or food processor. It might come out thicker but you can adjust the thickness with water.

Use any apples that are good for cooking. Recipes often call for tart apples such as Pippin or Granny Smith, but I also like medium-tart ones like Jonathan or sweet apples such as Golden Delicious or Gala. Besides, if you use sweet apples, you need less sugar.

This applesauce is plain and simply highlights the taste of the apples. There are many ways to flavor the applesauce: you can simmer a cinnamon stick or a vanilla bean with the apples or you can flavor the finished applesauce with all sorts of seasonings: a pinch of ground cinnamon, nutmeg or cloves, or grated lemon rind or vanilla extract. If you prefer, cook the apples with equal amounts of brown sugar or honey instead of white sugar, then taste and adjust sweetener if necessary. Applesauce keeps 3 or 4 days in a covered container in the refrigerator.

4 pounds apples, quartered

1/2 cup sugar, or more if needed

1/2 cup water

1 to 2 tablespoons strained fresh lemon juice (optional)

1. Combine apples, sugar, and water in a large saucepan. Bring to a boil. Cover and cook over medium-low heat, 10 minutes. Uncover and cook, stirring often, about 15 minutes or until apples are very tender. Let cool.

2. If any liquid remains in pan, use a slotted spoon to transfer the apples to a food mill fitted with the coarse grating disk. Puree the apples in the food mill. Return puree to the saucepan. Simmer a few more minutes, stirring, until applesauce is as thick as you like it.

Add lemon juice, if using, or more sugar, if needed. If adding sugar, simmer applesauce 1 minute, stirring, to blend it in.

Chunky French Applesauce

Makes 8 to 10 servings

In our house this applesauce is the favorite topping for potato and sweet potato latkes. In France some call this mixture apple compote, while others refer to it as apple marmalade. It is actually a thick, chunky version of applesauce. This mixture is said to originate in Normandy, the French province famous for apples, butter, and a powerful apple brandy called Calvados, which some cooks like to slip into their applesauce for extra zest. French cooks do not add water so the apple flavor will be intense.

Chunky applesauce is easier to make than most versions because you don't need to strain it through a food mill, which is messy to clean. The apples cook quickly because they are cut into thin slices. This delicious applesauce keeps for several days.

When making it, start with the smaller amount of sugar and add more if you wish, according to the sweetness of the apples and, of course, to your taste. If you prefer unsweetened applesauce, use Golden Delicious apples, which are naturally sweet, and omit the sugar. You can make the applesauce with oil instead of butter so it will be pareve.

2 to 4 tablespoons butter or 2 to 3 tablespoons vegetable oil

3 pounds Golden Delicious, Pippin, or Granny Smith apples, peeled, halved, cored, and thinly sliced

2 teaspoons strained fresh lemon juice

Grated rind of 1 lemon (optional)

3 to 6 tablespoons sugar, or to taste

1. Heat butter in a heavy stew pan or Dutch oven. Add apples and sauté over medium heat, turning pieces over often, 2 minutes or until they are coated with butter. Add lemon juice and grated lemon rind, if using. Cover tightly and cook over low heat, stirring often, 25 to 30 minutes or until apples are very tender. As the apples cook, check the pan from time to time; if it looks dry, add 1 or 2 tablespoons water.

2. Stir in 3 tablespoons sugar. Cook over medium heat, stirring, until mixture is thick and most of the liquid in the pan evaporates. Add more sugar if desired; heat briefly to dissolve it. Serve warm or cold.

Raspberry Applesauce

Makes about 2½ cups, about 8 servings

This is a beautiful new type of applesauce. The raspberries give the applesauce wonderful flavor and color. Serve this sauce with potato or sweet potato latkes or sweeten it a bit more and serve it with fruit, sweet cheese blintzes, or with cake for dessert.

2 cups Chunky French Applesauce (page 134)

10- to 12-ounce package frozen unsweetened or lightly
    sweetened raspberries, thawed

½ cup powdered sugar, or more to taste, sifted

1. Prepare applesauce. Puree applesauce in a food processor or blender until smooth. Transfer to a bowl.

2. Put raspberries in processor or blender and puree them. Add ½ cup powdered sugar and process until very smooth. Strain into a bowl, pressing on pulp in strainer; use rubber spatula to scrape mixture from underside of strainer.

3. Mix raspberry puree with applesauce. Taste sauce, and whisk in more powdered sugar if you like. Whisk to blend well. If sauce is too thick, whisk in a little water, 1 tablespoon at a time. Refrigerate in a covered container for 30 minutes or until ready to serve. Stir before serving. Serve cold.

Apple-Apricot Sauce

Makes 8 to 10 servings

Today cooks are making many new versions of applesauce. For serving with potato latkes, I particularly like applesauce with dried apricots. The apricots contribute a delicious, slightly tangy taste and a pleasing texture to the sauce.

½ pound dried apricots

2 tablespoons vegetable oil

2½ pounds Golden Delicious, Pippin, or Granny Smith
    apples, peeled, halved, cored, and thinly sliced

2 teaspoons strained fresh lemon juice

2 tablespoons water

3 to 6 tablespoons sugar, or to taste

1. Soak apricots in hot water to cover for about 10 minutes or until tender. Remove from water and cut into small dice.

2. Heat oil in a heavy stew pan or Dutch oven. Add apples and sauté over medium heat, turning pieces over often, 2 minutes. Add lemon juice. Cover tightly and cook over low heat, stirring often, 15 minutes.

3. Add apricots and water. Cover and cook 10 to 15 more minutes or until apples are very tender, adding 1 or 2 tablespoons more water if needed.

4. Stir in 3 tablespoons sugar. Cook sauce over low heat, stirring, 1 to 2 minutes or until sugar dissolves. Add more sugar if desired; heat briefly to dissolve it. Serve warm or cold.

Cranberry Applesauce

Makes about 8 servings

This colorful sauce is made of fresh cranberries cooked in wine and apple juice syrup, combined with applesauce. It's good not only with potato latkes but also with roast turkey, chicken, duck, and goose.

1¹/₂ cups dry red wine

¹/₂ cup apple juice

²/₃ cup sugar, or more to taste

1 cinnamon stick

12 ounces (3 cups) fresh or frozen cranberries, rinsed

2 cups applesauce

Combine wine, apple juice, sugar, and cinnamon stick in a medium saucepan. Bring to a boil, stirring. Add cranberries, cover, and simmer over low heat 6 to 7 minutes or until tender. Discard cinnamon stick. Stir in applesauce. Add more sugar if needed. Heat, stirring, until sugar dissolves.

Salads and Appetizers

Hanukkah Party Salad

Makes 8 servings

Serving a salad before the latkes is a great idea. A salad I enjoyed at a Hanukkah party in Los Angeles inspired me to create this one. It was a colorful mixed salad and everyone was delighted to have such a fresh, light dish before "attacking" the latkes.

10 cups mixed salad greens, such as green leaf lettuce, escarole, and romaine, or mixed baby lettuces

2 cups finely shredded red cabbage

1 large red pepper, halved, cored, and cut into thin strips

¹/₄ red onion, very thinly sliced

2 tablespoons red wine vinegar

Salt and freshly ground pepper, to taste

¹/₄ cup extra-virgin olive oil

1 tablespoon chopped fresh oregano or 1 teaspoon dried

2 cups sliced white mushrooms

1. Combine salad greens, red cabbage, red pepper, and red onion in a large bowl. Mix well.

2. Whisk vinegar with salt and pepper in a small bowl. Whisk in olive oil, then add oregano. Put sliced mushrooms in a medium bowl, add 1¹/₂ tablespoons of the dressing, and toss to combine.

3. Add remaining dressing to salad mixture and toss to moisten salad evenly. Add mushrooms and toss. Adjust seasoning.

Red Cabbage Slaw with Walnuts and Citrus Fruits

Makes about 8 servings

Before serving latkes, put this colorful, easy-to-make cole slaw on the table as a light appetizer. Be sure to use fresh walnuts. If you're in a hurry, you can use packaged shredded red cabbage and carrots.

8 cups shredded red cabbage

1 medium carrot, shredded

2 ribs celery, thinly sliced

1 tablespoon red wine vinegar

2 tablespoons orange juice

1/4 cup vegetable oil

Salt and freshly ground pepper, to taste

2 oranges

1 red or pink grapefruit

1/2 cup walnut pieces, lightly toasted

1. Mix cabbage, carrot, and celery in a large bowl. Add vinegar, orange juice, oil, salt, and pepper and mix until vegetables are evenly moistened. Adjust seasoning. Refrigerate 30 minutes or up to 1 day.

2. Just before serving, peel the oranges and grapefruit and divide them into segments. Cut half the grapefruit segments in 2 or 3 pieces and add them to the salad. Add half the orange segments and toss. Adjust seasoning. Serve topped with remaining orange and grapefruit segments and with toasted walnuts.

Nirit's Sweet Beet Salad

Makes 4 servings

This tasty salad is seasoned very delicately, to highlight the natural flavor of the beets. The salad has a hint of vinegar but should be more sweet than sour. My sister-in-law Nirit Levy finds that it's a good way to get children to eat a vegetable. She prepares it for holiday meals, as part of an array of vegetable salads.

8 to 10 beets of 1 1/2-inch diameter (about 1 pound, without greens)

Pinch of salt

2 to 3 teaspoons sugar

1 to 2 teaspoons vinegar

1. Rinse the beets, taking care not to pierce their skins.

2. Put 1 inch of water in a steamer and bring to a boil. Place the beets on a steamer rack above the boiling water. Cover tightly and steam 50 minutes to 1 hour or until tender, adding boiling water occasionally if the water evaporates. Cool beets slightly. Run them under cold water briefly and slip off their skins.

3. Grate beets on large holes of grater or with a food processor fitted with a coarse grating disk. Transfer to bowl. Add salt, sugar, and vinegar. Adjust seasonings. Serve cold.

Spinach Salad with Red Beans

Makes about 8 servings

Salads tend to be scarce on Hanukkah menus and my family misses them when attending the round of Hanukkah parties. I try to make a point of including salads at the meals we eat at home, and to keep on hand ingredients that enable me to have salad ready at a moment's notice. Some of my winter favorites are washed, ready-to-eat spinach, lettuce mix, and canned beans.

1 small red onion, very thinly sliced

1 large yellow bell pepper

8 cups spinach leaves, rinsed

2 cups iceberg lettuce mix

One 15-ounce can red beans, drained

3 to 4 tablespoons extra-virgin olive oil

4 to 6 teaspoons balsamic vinegar

1/2 teaspoon dried thyme

1/2 teaspoon dried oregano

Salt and freshly ground pepper, to taste

1. Separate onion slices into rings. Quarter pepper lengthwise around core. Cut pepper pieces into crosswise strips about 1/3-inch wide; cut in half if long. Combine with spinach, lettuce mix, and beans in a large bowl.

2. Whisk oil with vinegar, thyme, and oregano in a small bowl. Add to salad and toss. Season with salt and pepper.

Hanukkah Party Tomato-and-Herbed Cheese Sandwiches

Makes 20 to 25 canapes (D)

These colorful appetizers disappear in no time and are very easy to prepare. Inspired by my favorite childhood cream cheese and tomato on rye bread sandwiches, they feature an herb-accented cheese spread topped with sun-dried tomatoes. They make great buffet sandwiches for Hanukkah, so that guests can nibble on them while they're waiting for the latkes. Best of all, they can be made ahead and kept, covered with plastic wrap, in the refrigerator.

1/4 pound cream cheese, at room temperature

3 to 4 tablespoons sour cream

3 tablespoons minced fresh Italian parsley

1 tablespoon snipped fresh chives

2 teaspoons chopped fresh tarragon, or 3/4 teaspoon dried

Salt (optional) and freshly ground pepper, to taste

20 to 25 slices cocktail-size rye or pumpernickel bread

20 to 25 oil-packed sun-dried tomato halves, drained well

20 to 25 Israeli or Kalamata olives, pitted

1. Using a wooden spoon, beat cheese with 2 tablespoons sour cream in a bowl until smooth. Stir in enough of remaining sour cream to obtain a spreadable consistency. Stir in parsley, chives, and tarragon. Add a pinch of pepper. Taste spread before adding salt. If you like, cover and refrigerate overnight.

2. Spread bread with cheese mixture and top with tomato halves and olives, pressing them into cheese. Serve cold or at room temperature.

Easy Bean and Vegetable Soup

Makes 6 servings (P)

Hearty bean soups have long been winter favorites in the Jewish kitchen, both Ashkenazic and Sephardic. Bean soup mix, made from a medley of whole dried beans, has long been a staple in my mother's kitchen and it is in mine too. During the busy week of Hanukkah, I make a big pot of the soup with the mix and add fresh vegetables. This gives us a satisfying soup ready to serve before the latkes.

2 cups vegetable stock or water

2 quarts water

One 6-ounce package bean soup mix (3/4 to 1 cup dry mix)

3 ribs celery, sliced, plus leafy tops

2 large onions, diced

1 medium turnip, peeled and diced

2 large potatoes, peeled and diced

3 large carrots, sliced

1 tablespoon tomato paste

4 medium zucchini, halved and sliced

1/4 cup chopped green onion

1/3 cup chopped fresh Italian parsley

Salt (optional) and freshly ground pepper, to taste

Cayenne pepper to taste (optional)

1. Bring stock and water to a boil and add soup mix. Cover soup and begin to simmer it over low heat.

2. Plan soup's cooking time according to package directions. During the last 45 minutes of cooking, add leafy celery tops (but not sliced ribs), onions, turnip, and potatoes. Cover and simmer 15 minutes. Add carrots and sliced celery and simmer soup 20 minutes. Mix tomato paste with 2 tablespoons water and stir gently into soup. Add zucchini and simmer for 10 minutes or until beans and vegetables are tender.

3. Just before serving, stir in green onion and parsley. Season with salt, if using, pepper, and cayenne, if using. Serve hot.

❦ Main Courses

Roasted Fish with Rosemary

Makes 4 servings

*When you're busy preparing latkes and you want a
light and easy main course, this one is perfect. Besides,
since it's meatless, you can enjoy your latkes topped
with sour cream.*

*My choice is usually a rich, flavorful fish such as
salmon or sea bass that stands up to the robust tastes
of the rosemary and the garlic. You can also use cod
or halibut.*

1 teaspoon minced fresh rosemary or $^1/_4$ teaspoon dried

1 medium clove garlic, minced

$^1/_2$ teaspoon paprika

Cayenne pepper to taste

1 to 2 tablespoons extra-virgin olive oil

Salt and freshly ground pepper, to taste

$1^1/_4$ pounds sea bass fillets or steaks, about 1 inch thick

Lemon wedges

Preheat broiler with rack about 4 inches from heat
source. Mix rosemary, garlic, paprika, cayenne, and oil
in a small bowl. Sprinkle fish lightly with salt. Spoon
half the garlic mixture over fish and rub it in. Arrange
fish on broiler rack. Broil 5 minutes. Turn fish over,
sprinkle second side with salt, and rub with remaining
garlic mixture. Broil 4 or 5 more minutes or until thickest part of fish becomes opaque inside; check with a
sharp knife. Serve hot, with lemon wedges.

Chicken and Split Pea Soup with Rice and Vegetables

Makes 6 main-course servings

*This substantial, warming dish can be considered a
thick soup or a soupy stew. The split peas are not
pureed, but are part of the colorful selection of vegetables. The flavorful soup-stew makes a good choice for
serving during the week of Hanukkah.*

2 pounds chicken drumsticks or thighs

1 large onion, sliced

1 cup split peas, sorted and rinsed

11 cups water

Salt and freshly ground pepper, to taste

12-ounce piece banana squash or other winter squash,
        peeled, seeded, and cut into 1-inch cubes

2 large carrots, sliced

2 ribs celery, sliced

1 teaspoon ground turmeric

1 teaspoon ground cumin

1 cup long-grain rice

4 large cloves garlic, chopped

$^1/_4$ cup chopped fresh Italian parsley

2 tablespoons chopped fresh dill

Cayenne pepper, to taste

1. Combine chicken with onion, peas, water, and a
pinch of salt in large saucepan. Bring to a boil. Cover
and simmer for 1 hour. Add squash, carrots, celery,
turmeric, and cumin and cook 15 minutes or until split
peas and chicken are tender.

2. Skim fat from soup. Season soup with salt and
pepper. Remove chicken pieces and discard skin and
bones. Cut meat into strips and set aside.

3. Return soup to a simmer. Add rice and garlic.
Cover and simmer 15 minutes or until rice and vegetables are tender. Gently stir in chicken and half the parsley and dill. Adjust seasoning; add cayenne pepper.
Serve soup sprinkled with remaining parsley and dill.

Onion-Smothered Chicken

Makes 4 servings

This slowly cooked, gently spiced chicken with its rich onion sauce is wonderful with potato or vegetable latkes.

3 pounds chicken pieces, patted dry

Salt and freshly ground pepper, to taste

2 tablespoons olive oil

3 large onions, halved and thinly sliced

1 teaspoon ground cumin

1 teaspoon ground coriander

1 teaspoon paprika

4 large cloves garlic, chopped

3/4 cup chicken stock

1. Sprinkle chicken pieces with pepper on both sides.

2. Heat oil in deep large sauté pan or stew pan. Lightly brown chicken pieces in 2 batches over medium heat. Remove with tongs to a plate. Add onions and cook over medium-low heat 10 minutes or until softened. Return chicken to pan and add any juices from plate. Add cumin, coriander, paprika, garlic, and stock. Cover and simmer, turning pieces once or twice, about 30 minutes for breast pieces and about 35 minutes for leg and thigh pieces.

3. Remove chicken pieces from pan but leave in onion. Skim fat from cooking liquid. Adjust seasoning. Return chicken to pan. Cover and warm over low heat about 3 minutes. Serve hot.

Chicken Breast Schnitzel

Makes 4 servings

In almost every Israeli home chicken schnitzel (pan-fried cutlets) appears frequently on the menu, for both holiday and casual meals. It's a good choice for Hanukkah because it's a favorite of children. Besides, it cooks quickly and leaves plenty of time for preparing latkes. I like to rub the chicken with garlic before coating it, for extra flavor.

Caper-Lemon Salsa (page 141) is a lively accompaniment. If you're serving the schnitzel to children, serve the salsa in a separate dish.

Caper-Lemon Salsa (page 141) or lemon wedges (for serving)

1 to 1 1/4 pounds boneless skinless chicken breasts, patted dry

2 or 3 cloves garlic, crushed

Salt and freshly ground pepper, to taste

1/3 cup all-purpose flour

1 or 2 large eggs

2/3 cup dry bread crumbs

About 1/3 cup vegetable oil

1. Prepare salsa, if using. Preheat oven to 275°F.

2. Rub chicken pieces all over with crushed garlic, then discard garlic pieces. Sprinkle chicken with pepper.

3. Spread flour in a large plate and mix it with a pinch of salt. Beat 1 egg in a shallow bowl. Spread bread crumbs in another large plate. Lightly coat 1 chicken piece with flour on both sides. Tap and shake to remove excess flour. Dip piece in egg. Dip in bread crumbs, completely coating both sides; pat lightly so crumbs adhere. Set on a large plate. Repeat with remaining chicken. If necessary, beat another egg. Set coated pieces on plate side by side.

4. Heat oil in a large, heavy skillet. Add enough chicken to make one layer. Sauté over medium-high heat about 3 minutes per side or until golden brown. Turn carefully using two slotted spatulas, so oil doesn't splatter. If oil begins to brown, reduce heat to medium. If you like, set schnitzels on paper towels to absorb excess oil.

5. Set cooked chicken pieces side by side on an ovenproof platter and keep them warm in the oven. Top each portion with a small spoonful of Caper-Lemon Salsa or a lemon wedge.

Caper-Lemon Salsa

Makes 4 to 6 servings

Capers grow in Jerusalem and are delicious with Hanukkah dishes such as Chicken Breast Schnitzel (page 140) or with fried fish. If you're serving it with broiled fish or chicken, you might like to add a tablespoon of olive oil. This salsa is tangy rather than peppery. It's perfect for wintertime as it doesn't require out-of-season produce. Serve this salsa in small spoonfuls; a little goes a long way.

1 lemon

¹/₂ cup finely chopped red, white, or sweet yellow onions

1 tablespoon strained fresh lemon juice

¹/₄ teaspoon dried oregano

Tiny pinch of salt

2 tablespoons capers, rinsed

Cayenne pepper, to taste

1 tablespoon extra-virgin olive oil (optional)

2 tablespoons chopped fresh Italian parsley

1. Use a small serrated knife to remove skin and all white pith from lemon. Hold lemon over bowl to catch juice and cut segments: cut inside the membrane on each side of a section. Cut to release the section from the lemon. Fold back membrane. Continue with remaining segments. Cut lemon segments into tiny dice.

2. Combine onions, 1 tablespoon lemon juice, oregano, and a pinch of salt in a bowl. Let stand 5 minutes.

3. Add diced lemon to bowl of onions. Add capers, cayenne pepper, and olive oil, if using. A short time before serving, add parsley. Mix well. Adjust seasoning.

Veal Stew in the Style of Osso Buco

Makes 4 to 6 servings

Osso buco, a cut of veal shank meat with marrow bones used to make an Italian stew of the same name, is not easy to find at kosher butcher shops. Still, veal stew meat used in the classic osso buco recipe style results in a delicious entree. The stew is garnished with the traditional gremolata, made of minced garlic, parsley, and grated lemon rind. Serve the veal for Hanukkah, accompanied by Classic Potato Latkes (page 120), Baked Potato Latkes (page 121), or Zucchini-Potato Latkes (page 129). The stew is also wonderful for Sukkot or Shabbat, with a side dish of orzo or other pasta, or of pareve saffron risotto, which tastes great with the rich sauce.

2 pounds boneless veal shoulder, cut into 1-inch pieces and patted dry

Salt and freshly ground pepper, to taste

¹/₄ cup all-purpose flour

¹/₄ cup olive oil

1 medium onion, finely chopped

1 medium carrot, chopped

1 medium rib celery, chopped

2 sprigs fresh Italian parsley

3 sprigs fresh thyme or ³/₄ teaspoon dried thyme, crumbled

1 bay leaf

¹/₂ cup dry white wine

3 large cloves garlic, minced

1¹/₂ pounds ripe tomatoes, peeled, seeded, and chopped, or one 28-ounce and one 14¹/₂-ounce can tomatoes, drained and chopped

1¹/₂ cups brown veal stock or chicken stock or broth

1 tablespoon tomato paste

Gremolata

1 teaspoon finely grated or finely chopped lemon rind

1 medium clove garlic, very finely minced (¹/₂ teaspoon)

¹/₄ cup minced fresh Italian parsley

1. Preheat oven to 350°F. Sprinkle veal lightly with salt and pepper. Spread flour on plate.

2. Heat oil in a heavy enameled cast-iron stew pan or Dutch oven over medium heat. Meanwhile, dredge half the veal pieces on all sides in flour. Pat off excess flour. Add floured veal to hot oil and brown it lightly on all sides. Transfer veal pieces as they brown to a plate. Reduce heat so oil in pan doesn't burn. Dredge and brown remaining veal and transfer to the plate.

3. Immediately reduce heat to low. Add onion, carrot, and celery to pan and scrape up brown bits. Cook, stirring, until vegetables soften, about 7 minutes. In a piece of cheesecloth, tie parsley sprigs, thyme, and bay leaf to make an herb bag, and add to pan. Add wine and garlic. Bring to a boil over high heat, stirring. Boil, stirring, until wine evaporates and pan is nearly dry.

4. Return veal to pan with any juices on plate. Add tomatoes and stock and bring to a boil, stirring. Push down herb bag to immerse it in liquid. Cover and braise veal in oven about 1 hour and 15 minutes or until veal is tender when pierced with a sharp knife.

5. Transfer veal to a plate with a slotted spoon or tongs. Discard herb bag. Stir tomato paste into sauce. Bring to a boil, stirring. Boil, stirring often, until sauce is thick enough to lightly coat a spoon. Add pepper, and adjust seasoning. Return veal to pan of sauce and spoon sauce over to coat. Cover and keep warm. If making veal ahead, refrigerate in a covered container.

6. To make gremolata: Combine lemon rind, garlic, and parsley in a small bowl. Mix thoroughly with a fork. If not using immediately, cover.

7. Just before serving, bring veal stew to a simmer. Sprinkle gremolata evenly over veal. Cover and cook over low heat 2 minutes. Serve hot.

Brisket with Chickpeas and Zucchini

Makes 4 to 6 servings

(M)

Beef brisket is a favorite Hanukkah entree. We tend to think of brisket for braising in one piece, but this cut also makes good beef stew and this way is easier to serve. Here the brisket cooks gently in a richly flavored Mediterranean style sauce of tomatoes, rosemary, and garlic.

³/4 cup dried chickpeas (garbanzo beans), rinsed and sorted (see Note)

2 tablespoons vegetable oil

2 pounds beef brisket, cut into 1¹/4-inch pieces, trimmed of fat, and patted dry

1 large onion, chopped

1 tablespoon all-purpose flour

1 cup water

One 28-ounce can diced tomatoes, drained

1 serrano or small jalapeño pepper, seeds and ribs discarded, minced

1 tablespoon minced fresh rosemary or 1 teaspoon dried

Salt, to taste

8 medium cloves garlic, minced

1 tablespoon tomato paste

1 pound zucchini, cut into ¹/2-inch cubes

1. Place chickpeas in a bowl and soak in enough water to cover 8 hours or overnight. Drain chickpeas and rinse. Put in medium saucepan and cover with fresh water. Bring to boil. Reduce heat to low, cover, and simmer until tender, about 1 hour and 15 minutes. Reserve chickpeas in their liquid.

2. Heat oil in large heavy enameled cast-iron or stainless-steel stew pan over medium-high heat. Brown beef in 2 batches, removing it with a slotted spoon to a plate.

3. Add onion to pan and cook over low heat, stirring often, about 7 minutes or until softened. Return meat to pan, reserving any juices on plate, and sprinkle meat with flour. Toss lightly to coat. Cook over low heat, stirring often, 5 minutes.

4. Stir in 1 cup liquid from the cooked chickpeas or 1 cup water. Add reserved meat juices from plate, tomatoes, hot pepper, rosemary, salt, and 1 tablespoon of the garlic. Bring to boil, stirring often. Cover and cook over low heat, stirring and turning beef cubes over occasionally, 3 1/2 hours.

5. Stir tomato paste into stew. Drain chickpeas and add them. Cover and cook about 30 more minutes or until beef is very tender; when a piece is lifted with a sharp knife, it should fall from knife. If you would like a thicker sauce, uncover pan and simmer over low heat, stirring occasionally, very gently, about 5 minutes.

6. Add zucchini, cover, and simmer until it is tender, about 5 minutes. Stir in remaining garlic and simmer, uncovered, 30 seconds Adjust seasoning. Serve hot.

Note: You can substitute 1 1/2 cups canned chickpeas for the dried ones. Add them to stew at same time as the tomato paste.

❧ Soofganiyot and Other Treats

Israeli Doughnuts

Soofganiyot

Makes about 12 large doughnuts
(not including the scraps)

For many Israeli children soofganiyot, or doughnuts without holes, are the most anticipated Hanukkah treat. During Hanukkah they are everywhere—sold at bakeries, supermarkets, and even at the corner grocery store. (In the United States, look for them in Jewish bakeries.) Some are filled with red jam; others are plain. Many Israelis also make them at home and serve them sprinkled with powdered sugar. Most use a traditional yeast dough but some prepare quicker versions from batters lightened by baking powder or eggs.

Although this recipe can be made by hand, it is easier made with an electric mixer fitted with a dough hook.

3/4 cup lukewarm water

2 envelopes dry yeast (each 1/4 ounce)

1/4 cup sugar

4 cups all-purpose flour, or more if necessary

2 large eggs, at room temperature

2 large egg yolks, at room temperature

6 tablespoons (3/4 stick) butter or margarine, at room temperature, cut into bits

1 teaspoon vanilla extract

Grated rind of 1 lemon

2 teaspoons salt

About 6 cups vegetable oil (for deep-frying)

Powdered sugar

1. Pour 1/2 cup lukewarm water into a small bowl. Sprinkle yeast on top and add 1 teaspoon sugar. Let stand 10 minutes or until yeast is foamy.

2. Spoon 4 cups flour into the large bowl of an electric mixer fitted with a dough hook. Make a well in center of flour. To the well add remaining sugar, eggs, yolks, butter, vanilla, grated lemon rind, remaining water, and salt. Mix the ingredients in the well until blended. Add yeast mixture. Mix until the ingredients come together to form a dough.

3. Knead with dough hook at medium speed, scraping down the dough occasionally, 5 minutes. If the dough is very sticky, add 2 tablespoons flour. Knead 5 more minutes or until very smooth. Put dough in a clean, oiled bowl and turn to coat it with oil. Cover with a damp cloth and let rise in a warm place 1 to $1^{1}/_{2}$ hours or until doubled in volume.

4. Lightly coat a large tray with flour. Roll out half the dough on a floured surface until it is $^{1}/_{2}$-inch thick, flouring dough occasionally. With a $2^{1}/_{2}$- to 3-inch cutter or a glass of similar diameter, cut dough into rounds. Transfer rounds to tray, placing them $^{1}/_{2}$-inch apart. Continue with remaining dough. Cover rounds with a damp cloth and let rise in a warm place about 30 minutes. Knead the scraps of dough, put them in an oiled bowl, cover with a damp cloth, and let rise for about 30 minutes.

5. Line a tray with paper towels. Pour oil into a deep fryer or deep, heavy saucepan. Do not fill pan more than halfway with oil. Heat oil to 350°F; if a deep-fat thermometer is not available, test by adding a small piece of dough to oil; oil is hot enough when it bubbles gently around dough. Add 4 or 5 doughnuts; do not crowd them. Fry doughnuts about 3 minutes on each side or until golden brown. If they brown too quickly, reduce heat so they have a chance to cook through. Drain on paper towels. Pat the tops gently with paper towels to absorb excess oil.

6. If you like, make more doughnuts with the scraps; they won't be as light but will still be good.

7. Put soofganiyot on a serving dish and sift powdered sugar over them. Serve hot, warm, or at room temperature.

Soofganiyot with Jam

Makes about 14 large doughnuts
(not including the scraps)

Israeli filled soofganiyot *usually feature red jam or preserves, but you can use any kind you like. I think apricot preserves taste very good. These doughnuts are rolled thinner than plain* soofganiyot. *They are cut into rounds, which are then sandwiched with the filling. Some people inject thick ones with the jam instead of sandwiching thin ones.*

Ingredients for Israeli Doughnuts (page 143)
About $^{1}/_{4}$ cup strawberry or apricot preserves

1. Prepare dough for soofganiyot and let it rise.

2. Lightly coat a large tray with flour. Roll out half the dough on a floured surface until it is $^{1}/_{4}$-inch thick, flouring dough occasionally. With a $2^{1}/_{2}$- to 3-inch cutter or a glass of similar diameter, cut dough into rounds. Put 1 teaspoon apricot or strawberry preserves on the center of half the number of rounds. Brush the rim of one round lightly with water. Set a plain round on top. With floured fingers, press edges of round firmly all around to seal it. Transfer this "sandwich" immediately to tray. If it has stretched out to an oval, plump it gently back into a round shape. Continue with remaining rounds and remaining dough, placing each $^{1}/_{2}$ inch apart on the tray. Cover them with a damp cloth and let rise in a warm place about 30 minutes.

3. Knead the scraps of dough, put them in an oiled bowl, cover with a damp cloth, and let rise about 30 minutes.

4. Line a tray with paper towels. Pour oil into a deep fryer or deep, heavy saucepan. Do not fill pan more than halfway with oil. Heat oil to 350°F; if a deep-fat thermometer is not available, test by adding a small piece of dough to oil; oil is hot enough when it bubbles gently around dough. Add 4 doughnuts; do not crowd them. Fry doughnuts about 3 minutes on each side or until golden brown. If they brown too quickly, reduce heat so they have a chance to cook through. Drain on paper towels. Pat the tops gently with paper towels to absorb excess oil.

5. If you like, make more doughnuts with the scraps; they won't be as light but will still be good.

6. Put soofganiyot on a serving dish and sift powdered sugar over them. Serve warm or at room temperature. Do not serve these immediately because the jam is boiling hot.

Dreidel Cookies

Makes 15 to 20 cookies

A dreidel is a spinning top with Hebrew letters used by children for playing games on Hanukkah. The Hebrew letters on Israeli dreidels—Nun, Gimmel, Hay, and Pay—stand for "Nes Gadol Haya Poh," "a great miracle happened here." Outside of Israel, the last letter is "Shin" instead of "Pay" to replace "here" with "there." The reference is to the Hanukkah miracle. To cut these cookies, use dreidel-shaped cookie cutters. You can find them at Judaic gift shops.

2 large eggs

1 large egg yolk

1/2 cup sugar

1/4 teaspoon salt

2 teaspoons grated orange rind

1/2 cup (1 stick) unsalted butter or firm margarine, well-chilled and cut into 16 pieces

11/2 cups all-purpose flour

1 to 2 tablespoons cold orange juice or water (optional)

1. Combine eggs, egg yolk, sugar, salt, orange rind, and butter in a food processor. Process using 10 brief pulses, then process continuously about 5 seconds or until nearly blended. Add flour; process 2 seconds. Scrape down and process about 3 seconds or until dough begins to form sticky crumbs but does not come together in a ball. If crumbs are dry, add juice or water and process using brief pulses just until blended.

2. Transfer dough to a work surface. Blend dough further by kneading it lightly: push about 1/4 of dough away from you and press it with the heel of your hand against the work surface. Continue with remaining

dough in 3 batches. Repeat if dough is not yet well blended. With a rubber spatula, transfer dough to a sheet of plastic wrap. Push pieces together. Wrap dough loosely and press into a flat disk. Wrap well and refrigerate dough at least 6 hours or up to 2 days.

3. Position rack in center of oven and preheat to 375°F. Lightly butter 2 baking sheets. Roll out half of dough on a cold, lightly floured surface until about 1/4-inch thick. Cut cookies using a dreidel-shaped cookie cutter. Transfer to buttered baking sheets, spacing about 1 inch apart. Refrigerate 15 minutes. Repeat with remaining dough. Gently press trimmings together. Wrap and refrigerate trimmings 30 minutes or until firm enough to roll. Roll out dough and cut more cookies.

4. Bake cookies about 10 minutes or until very lightly golden at edges. Transfer cookies to racks to cool. Keep them in a cookie tin or airtight container up to 5 days.

Crisp Chocolate Chip Cookies with Pecans

Makes about 4 dozen

When I was growing up, we never heard of soofganiyot, *the Israeli jelly doughnuts. Our Hanukkah treats at the end of a meal were my mother's chocolate chip cookies.*

If you like, you can make mini cookies and dip them in chocolate to make Homemade Hanukkah Gelt (page 146).

1 cup all-purpose flour

1/2 teaspoon salt

1/2 teaspoon baking soda

1/2 cup (1 stick) butter or margarine, slightly softened

1/4 cup firmly packed brown sugar

1/2 cup granulated sugar

I large egg

1/2 teaspoon vanilla extract

3/4 cup semisweet or bittersweet chocolate chips

3/4 cup diced pecans

1. Preheat oven to 350°F. Lightly grease 2 baking sheets. Sift flour, salt, and baking soda into a medium bowl.

2. Cream butter in a large bowl with an electric mixer. Add both types sugar; beat until smooth and fluffy. Add egg; beat until smooth. Add vanilla; beat until blended. Stir in flour mixture until blended. Stir in chocolate chips and pecans.

3. Push batter from a teaspoon with a second teaspoon onto buttered baking sheets, using about 1 1/2 teaspoons batter for each cookie and spacing them about 2 inches apart. Flatten each cookie by pressing it firmly with the bottom of a fork dipped in water.

4. Bake about 7 minutes or until lightly golden. With a metal spatula, carefully transfer cookies to racks; cool completely. Before baking more cookies, cool baking sheets; clean off any crumbs and grease sheets again. Keep cookies in a cookie tin or an airtight container up to 1 week.

Note: To make mini chocolate chip cookies, use about 1 teaspoon batter for each. Check them for doneness after 5 minutes.

Homemade Hanukkah Gelt

Makes 40 to 50 dipped cookies   Ⓓ or Ⓟ

Chocolate treats are traditional on Hanukkah. Usually they are in the form of coin-shaped chocolates called "Hanukkah gelt" or Hanukkah money, following an old custom of giving children a little money as a holiday gift.

I like to make Hanukkah gelt by dipping small round cookies in chocolate. They don't exactly look like coins because the part of the cookie that you hold doesn't get coated. But they are delicious. You can use any type of small, flat cookie you like, home baked or store-bought. Don't use crumbly cookies because they will break apart when you're dipping them. I like to use Crisp Chocolate Chip Cookies with Pecans (page 145) as the centers for my Hanukkah gelt. Nobody will say there isn't enough chocolate in these treats!

Crisp Chocolate Chip Cookies with Pecans (page 145) or 40 to 50 small cookies of your choice

8 ounces fine-quality bittersweet or semisweet chocolate, chopped

1. Prepare homemade cookies, if using.

2. Melt chocolate in a small deep bowl over a pan of nearly simmering water. Stir until smooth. Remove from water. Let chocolate cool to 88 to 90 degrees, or until it feels neither hot nor cold to the touch. Line 2 or 3 trays with foil or wax paper.

3. Dip half to three-fourths of a cookie in chocolate, moving it back and forth in chocolate until cookie is well coated. Remove and gently shake several times so excess chocolate drips into bowl. Set cookie on lined tray. Continue dipping more cookies. When chocolate becomes too thick for dipping, gently reheat it by setting bowl above a pan of hot water. Remove it from water before dipping more cookies.

4. Refrigerate dipped cookies about 15 minutes or until set. Gently remove from paper. You can dip the cookies ahead and keep them in airtight shallow containers about 4 days in the refrigerator.

Note: It's easiest to dip the cookies when you have more than enough chocolate. Let extra chocolate cool and harden. Store wrapped tightly in foil. You can melt it again to use in cakes, frostings, and desserts, but not for more dipping.

Fruit Desserts

Citrus Salad with Home-Candied Orange Peel

Makes 4 to 6 servings

Jaffa oranges, named for the port city in Israel from which they were originally shipped, have long been renowned, and citrus fruits enter the Israeli menu in many ways. They are plentiful at Hanukkah time. This festive salad provides a refreshing dessert to balance all the rich holiday foods.

5 large oranges, preferably seedless
Candied Orange Peel (page 583)
2 small or 1 large grapefruit
2 to 3 tablespoons syrup from Candied Orange Peel
3 tablespoons orange or grapefruit juice, or a mixture of both
1 to 2 tablespoons Grand Marnier
Fresh mint sprigs (optional)

1. Pare rind from oranges. Use the rind from 2 of them to make Candied Orange Peel. Reserve candied peel in its syrup.

2. With a serrated knife, cut peel and white pith from oranges and grapefruit. Hold fruit over a bowl while peeling to catch any juice. Slice oranges crosswise in rounds. Cut grapefruit same way. If grapefruit slices are large, cut them in half. Put fruit in a glass bowl and mix gently.

3. Pour 2 tablespoons syrup from candied peel into a small bowl. Stir in 3 tablespoons orange or grapefruit juice and 1 tablespoon Grand Marnier. Add more syrup or Grand Marnier if you like. Pour over fruit and mix gently. With a fork, remove strips of candied peel from their syrup, using 3 or 4 tablespoons. Scatter over salad. Serve cold, garnished, with mint sprigs, if using.

Pears in Vanilla Syrup

Makes 4 servings

Pears in syrup make a refreshing, delicate dessert on its own or accompanied by vanilla ice cream. For Hanukkah, Shabbat, or other festive occasions you might like to serve this as a partner for Pear Cake with Honey (page 148).

³/₄ cup sugar
3 cups water
1 vanilla bean
3 or 4 strips of lemon rind (optional)
1¹/₂ pounds ripe, fairly firm pears
¹/₂ lemon
2 tablespoons strained fresh lemon juice
1 teaspoon vanilla extract (optional)

1. Combine sugar, water, and vanilla bean, and lemon rind, if using, in a medium saucepan. Bring to a boil, stirring gently to dissolve sugar. Remove from heat.

2. Peel pears. Rub them well with cut side of lemon half, squeezing lemon a little so some juice comes out on pears. Cut pears in half lengthwise. With point of peeler, remove flower end and core of each pear, including long, stringy part that continues to stem.

3. Return syrup to a boil and add pear halves and lemon juice. Reduce heat to low. Cover with a lid that is a bit too small for saucepan, to keep pears submerged. Cook about 12 minutes or until pears are very tender when pierced with a sharp knife.

4. Let pears cool in their syrup. Taste syrup; if you would like a stronger vanilla flavor, add vanilla extract. Serve pears warm, room temperature, or cold, with a little syrup spooned over them.

Russian-Style Prune Compote with Tea

Makes 6 to 8 servings

Tea-flavored desserts have become fashionable in recent years but Russian Jews have long used tea for cooking their compotes of dried fruit, which were traditional cold weather desserts. Choose any tea you like. Earl Grey is good with its tangy bergamot flavor. For a more delicate taste, choose oolong tea. This makes a light, refreshing finale to a copious Hanukkah dinner.

1 pound prunes (with pits)

3¹/₂ cups light brewed tea

¹/₂ cup sugar

1 lemon

1. Put prunes and tea in glass bowl. Cover with a plate to keep prunes submerged. Let soak 8 hours or overnight at room temperature.

2. Gently transfer prunes and their soaking liquid to a medium saucepan. Add enough water to just cover fruit. Add sugar. Cook over low heat, stirring very gently, until sugar dissolves. Cover and cook over low heat 25 minutes.

3. Cut lemon into thin rounds, discarding ends. Remove any seeds. Add lemon slices to saucepan. Continue cooking about 5 minutes or until prunes are tender. Transfer to a bowl and let cool. Serve cold.

Pear Cake with Honey

Makes about 12 servings

We always tend to associate honey with apples but pears and honey are a great combination too. Be sure to use good, sweet, ripe pears. I like it for Hanukkah, Sukkot, Rosh Hashanah, or before or after the Yom Kippur fast. It's also great for Shabbat. Serve the cake plain, garnished with a few ripe pear slices, or accompanied by Pears in Vanilla Syrup (page 147) or by Red Wine and Pear Sauce (page 81).

1 cup (2 sticks) butter or margarine

1 cup sugar

¹/₃ cup honey

3 large eggs

1 teaspoon vanilla extract

3 cups all-purpose flour

2¹/₂ teaspoons baking powder

2 teaspoons finely grated lemon rind

2 pounds ripe pears, peeled, halved, cored, and finely diced

1. Preheat oven to 350°F. Lightly grease a 13 × 9 × 2-inch cake pan, line base and sides of pan with a sheet of foil and grease foil.

2. Beat butter in a large bowl with an electric mixer until smooth. Add sugar and beat until fluffy. Beat in honey. Add eggs one by one, beating well after each addition. Add vanilla. Mix flour with baking powder and stir mixture into egg mixture. Stir in grated rind. Last, stir in pears.

3. Spread batter in prepared cake pan. Smooth top. Bake 45 minutes or until a cake tester inserted in cake's center comes out clean. Cool in pan on a rack about 20 minutes or until just warm. Turn out onto a rack. Cool to room temperature.

Purim

Salads, Appetizers, and Soups
152

Broccoli and Cauliflower Salad
with Capers

Beet Salad with Dill Dressing

Queen Esther's Salad

Persian Spinach Salad

North African Carrot Salad
with Peas and Corn

Eggplant Salad with Garlic
and Coriander

Freshly Cooked Chickpeas

Chickpeas with Cumin
and Garlic

Cauliflower Cream Soup

Split Pea Soup with Leeks

Main Courses
156

Turkey in Pepper Sauce

Turkey Legs with Mushrooms,
Carrots, and Egg Noodles

Turkey Breasts in Garlic Sauce

Roast Turkey with Pear-Pecan
Stuffing

Pear-Pecan Stuffing

Alsatian-Jewish Sauerkraut
with Meat

Side Dishes
160

Vegetable Kugel with Dill

Carrot Puree

Aromatic Parslied Potatoes

Brown Rice Pilaf with
Mushrooms and Asparagus

$\mathcal{P}$urim takes place in late February or March. Like Hanukkah, its origin is not in the Torah but in an historic event in the life of the Jewish people. Purim's story is recounted in the Book of Esther. It tells of the Persian King Ahasueros who married Esther, a Jewish woman, and made her the queen. When the king's evil advisor, Haman, plotted to destroy the Jewish community, Esther interceded with the king and saved the Jews.

Purim is celebrated with costumes. Children dress up as Queen Esther, King Ahasueros, and other characters from the Purim story, or as their favorite movie heroes. Adults also often attend costume parties. At the synagogue, children are encouraged to make lots of noise when the name "Haman" is mentioned during the reading of the Book of Esther.

Holiday pastries and other foods celebrate the defeat of the wicked Haman and his evil plan. Three-cornered, filled cookies called *hamantaschen* are the main Purim treats. In Yiddish the name means "Haman's pockets" although some say the cookie recalls the shape of his hat. The Hebrew name for these treats are *oznei Haman* or "Haman's ears," which is also the name for certain Sephardic fried pastries served on the holiday. When I was growing up, poppy seed and prune were the only fillings for hamantaschen. I was surprised to discover that in Israel, date filling rivals poppy seed in popularity.

The Purim feast is accompanied by wine. For the main course, many people—particularly in Israel and France—serve turkey. Although the source of this tradition is unclear, the Book of Esther says that King Ahasueros ruled from India to Ethiopia. The word for turkey is expressed as "India bird" in Hebrew and French, so to Jews on this holiday the turkey represents Ahasueros. (Another theory is that the turkey is considered a foolish bird and Ahasueros a foolish king, but that may just be a cultural joke.) Most people celebrate Purim with vegetarian foods, and beans, chickpeas (garbanzo beans), nuts, and dried fruits are on the menu in many homes. Jews in Tunisia serve hard boiled eggs with fava beans. Other Jews in North Africa serve couscous garnished with raisins. Ashkenazic Jews sprinkle poppy seeds on their noodles.

The story behind the vegetarian customs is that Esther became a vegetarian when she married the king, in order to avoid eating meat that was not kosher. Even today, her solution of following a vegetarian diet is often the choice of Orthodox Jews who are traveling or who are in situations in which kosher food is difficult to find.

A popular Purim custom is exchanging sweets—hamantaschen, cookies, chocolates, candies, and bite-size pieces of cake. Most are homemade but busy people combine some homemade treats with some purchased ones. Children in costume often bring them arranged in pretty boxes to friends, neighbors, and relatives.

Salads, Appetizers, and Soups

Broccoli and Cauliflower Salad with Capers

Makes 8 servings Ⓟ

Broccoli and cauliflower are available all year but they are at their peak during the cold months. This salad will liven up your Purim or Hanukkah table with plenty of freshness, whether you are serving a fleishig, milchig, *or pareve meal. You can cook the vegetables and make the dressing ahead, but put the salad together a short time before serving so the broccoli keeps its bright color.*

One 1-pound-head cauliflower, divided into medium florets

1 pound broccoli, stalk peeled and sliced and divided into florets

Chive-Caper Vinaigrette (page 594)

1/2 red onion, sliced thin, slices divided into slivers

8 to 10 cups iceberg lettuce mix (iceberg lettuce, carrot, and red cabbage) or bite-size pieces of any tender lettuce

1 large hard boiled egg, chopped

1/2 red bell pepper, finely diced (optional)

Paprika, to taste

1. Add cauliflower to a large saucepan of boiling salted water and boil uncovered over high heat about 6 minutes or until florets are crisp-tender. With a slotted spoon put florets in a colander. Rinse them with cold water and drain well. Transfer to a large bowl.

2. Reheat water to a boil. Add broccoli and boil uncovered over high heat 4 or 5 minutes or until florets are crisp-tender. Drain in colander, rinse gently with cold water and drain well. Add to bowl of cauliflower.

3. Prepare vinaigrette. Then lightly mix red onion with lettuce in another bowl. Add about 3 tablespoons dressing, or enough to just moisten. Toss, then adjust seasoning. Transfer to a platter.

4. Add 2 to 3 tablespoons dressing to bowl of cauliflower and broccoli. Mix very gently and add more if needed. Spoon mixture over center of lettuce. Sprinkle broccoli mixture with chopped egg, diced bell pepper if using, and paprika.

Beet Salad with Dill Dressing

Makes 4 to 6 servings Ⓟ

For a festive beginning to your Purim dinner, serve this salad of beets spooned over a bed of lettuce and embellished with walnuts. For the best flavor, buy small beets and steam them. And of course, use fresh dill.

8 to 10 small beets (about 1 1/2 inches in diameter), gently rinsed

2 tablespoons white wine vinegar

Salt and freshly ground pepper, to taste

1/4 cup walnut oil or vegetable oil, or 2 tablespoons of each

2 to 3 teaspoons chopped fresh dill

3 to 4 cups strips of romaine lettuce leaves

1/3 to 1/2 cup walnuts

1. Bring at least 1 inch of water to a boil in base of steamer. Boiling water should not reach holes in top part of steamer.

2. Place beets on steamer rack above boiling water. Cover tightly and steam 50 minutes to 1 hour or until beets are tender, adding boiling water occasionally if water evaporates. Let cool. Peel beets while holding them under cold running water.

3. Whisk vinegar with salt, pepper, and oil in a small bowl. Adjust seasoning. Stir in half the dill.

4. Put lettuce in a large bowl, add 3 tablespoons dressing, and toss. Transfer to a serving dish. Slice beets and put in bowl. Add remaining dressing and toss gently.

5. Adjust seasoning. Spoon beet mixture over lettuce. Just before serving, sprinkle salad with remaining dill and with walnuts.

Queen Esther's Salad

Makes 4 servings P

This salad commemorates Queen Esther's fare when she lived at the Persian king's palace. Her diet is believed to have consisted of nuts, seeds, and legumes. If you like, add Freshly Cooked Chickpeas (page 154) to the salad. It's so tasty that you'll want to serve it not just for Purim, but during the rest of the year.

6 cups mixed baby lettuces, rinsed and dried thoroughly

2 teaspoons white or red wine vinegar

2 tablespoons extra-virgin olive oil

Salt and freshly ground pepper, to taste

2 or 3 tablespoons toasted sunflower seeds

1/4 cup toasted walnuts or mixed toasted nuts

Put greens in a large bowl. Add vinegar, oil, salt, and pepper. Toss thoroughly. Serve sprinkled with sunflower seeds and toasted nuts.

Persian Spinach Salad

Makes 4 servings D

This easy, aromatic salad of cooked spinach originated in ancient Persia, now Iran, where the Purim story took place. The spinach is flavored with sautéed white onions, garlic, and yogurt. Serve the salad with other appetizers and with fresh flat bread at a meatless Purim meal.

4 cups tightly packed spinach leaves, rinsed and chopped

2 to 3 tablespoons olive oil or vegetable oil

2 white onions, halved and thinly sliced

3 large cloves garlic, chopped

1 cup nonfat or low-fat plain yogurt

Salt and freshly ground pepper, to taste

Cayenne pepper, to taste

1. Bring about 1 inch of water to a boil in a sauté pan. Add spinach, cover, and return to a boil. Cook over medium heat, stirring often, about 3 minutes or until wilted. Drain in a colander, rinse with cold water, and drain well again. Squeeze gently to remove excess water.

2. Dry sauté pan, add oil, and heat. Add onion and sauté over medium-low heat about 7 minutes or until golden. Add garlic and sauté 1 minute. Stir in spinach and sauté 2 minutes. Transfer mixture to a bowl and let cool.

3. Stir yogurt in a bowl until smooth. Add spinach and mix gently. Season with salt, pepper, and cayenne. Serve cold.

North African Carrot Salad with Peas and Corn

Makes 4 to 6 servings P

To celebrate Purim, take a cue from Mediterranean Jewish cooks and present an array of savory salads. You can serve them either as appetizers or as a light buffet for a Purim party, followed by hamantaschen. This salad is classically made with carrots but I often stir in frozen peas and corn for additional color with practically no effort. I use frozen vegetables because fresh aren't as reliable during this winter holiday.

1 1/2 pounds carrots (about 7 medium), sliced

1 1/2 cups frozen peas

1 1/2 cups frozen corn kernels

1 or 2 tablespoons vegetable oil

1 medium onion, halved and thinly sliced

1/2 teaspoon caraway seeds

1/2 teaspoon paprika

1/2 teaspoon ground cumin

Pinch of salt

2 tablespoons strained fresh lemon juice

Cayenne pepper, to taste

1. In a saucepan cover carrots with water and add salt. Bring to a boil and simmer over medium heat about 15 minutes or until nearly tender. Add peas and corn and return to a boil. Simmer 2 minutes or until tender.

2. Heat oil in a large skillet. Stir in onions and sauté over medium heat 7 minutes or until softened. Add 1/4 cup vegetable cooking liquid, caraway seeds, paprika, cumin, and a pinch of salt. Bring to a boil, stirring. Reduce heat to low.

3. Drain vegetables and add to skillet. Simmer, uncovered, 5 minutes or until sauce is reduced and coats vegetables. Serve hot, warm, or cold. Add lemon juice, then cayenne, just before serving.

Eggplant Salad with Garlic and Coriander

Makes 4 servings

P

Seasoned with sautéed garlic and ground coriander in the Middle Eastern style, this salad is delicious served warm or cold, with fresh or toasted pita bread. Since you can make it ahead, it's convenient for Shabbat, Purim, and other holiday occasions. Make extra and keep some in the refrigerator as an alternative spread for bread instead of butter.

3¹/2 pounds eggplant (3 medium)

4 or 5 tablespoons extra-virgin olive oil

8 large cloves garlic, finely chopped

2 teaspoons ground coriander

1¹/2 teaspoons ground cumin

Cayenne pepper, to taste

Salt and freshly ground pepper, to taste

Fresh Italian parsley sprigs

Pita bread, cut into wedges

1. Prick eggplants a few times with fork. Either grill eggplants above medium-hot coals about 1 hour, broil them about 40 minutes, turning often, or bake them at 400°F about 1 hour. When done, the eggplant flesh should be tender and eggplants should look collapsed. Let stand until cool enough to handle.

2. Cut off stems of eggplants and halve lengthwise. Drain off any liquid from inside eggplants. Scoop out pulp with a spoon and chop it with a knife.

3. Heat 4 tablespoons oil in a heavy, large skillet or sauté pan. Add garlic and cook over low heat, stirring, 1 minute. Stir in coriander and cumin. Add eggplant and mix well. Cook over low heat 5 minutes to thicken. Season with cayenne, salt, and pepper. Add more oil if needed. Serve hot or cold, garnished with parsley and surrounded with pita wedges.

Freshly Cooked Chickpeas

Makes 4 servings

P

Chickpeas appear on many tables for the Purim feast to honor Esther's becoming a vegetarian when she moved into the king's palace. Often they are cooked fresh and served plain, as one of several appetizers.

1¹/2 cups dried chickpeas (garbanzo beans)

6 cups cold water

Salt and freshly ground pepper, to taste

1. Sort chickpeas and soak overnight in a bowl generously covered with cold water. Drain, and put in a saucepan. Add the water and bring to a boil. Cover and simmer about 1¹/2 hours, adding hot water occasionally to keep chickpeas covered. Add a pinch of salt and continue simmering 30 to 45 minutes or until tender. (Reserve cooking liquid for soups, if you like.)

2. Drain and serve hot, sprinkled with salt and pepper.

Chickpeas with Cumin and Garlic

Makes 4 servings

P

Plain boiled chickpeas are a popular item on many Purim menus but I like to prepare them with cumin and garlic, which give the beans an enticing aroma. If you wish, serve cucumber slices on the side for a refreshing accent. This is a very quick and easy recipe if you use canned chickpeas.

1 tablespoon olive oil

1 large onion, sliced

4 large cloves garlic, chopped

1 teaspoon ground cumin

3¹/2 to 4 cups cooked chickpeas (garbanzo beans)
    or two 15-ounce cans, drained

¹/4 cup water

Salt and freshly ground pepper, to taste

¹/2 teaspoon hot red pepper flakes, or more to taste

3 tablespoons chopped fresh cilantro or Italian parsley
    (optional)

Heat oil in a medium sauté pan. Add onion and sauté over medium heat 5 minutes. Add garlic and cumin and stir over low heat 1 minute. Add chickpeas, water, salt, pepper, and pepper flakes. Stir and bring to boil. Cover and simmer 5 to 7 minutes or until onions are tender. Add cilantro, if using. Adjust seasoning. Serve hot.

Cauliflower Cream Soup

Makes 4 servings

During Purim, the weather usually is still cold, so there's nothing as welcome as a warm, soothing soup. This luscious soup is perfect for a vegetarian Purim party. It's also great as a first course, followed by a fish entree.

2 small heads cauliflower (about 2¹/₂ pounds total), stalks peeled and sliced, separated into florets

2 tablespoons butter or vegetable oil

2 tablespoons all-purpose flour

2 to 3 cups milk

Salt and white pepper, to taste

Freshly grated nutmeg, to taste

¹/₃ cup whipping cream (optional)

1 tablespoon chopped fresh chives or parsley

1. Add cauliflower to a large pan of boiling salted water and return to a boil.

2. Melt butter in a heavy, medium saucepan over low heat. Add flour and cook over low heat, whisking, for 2 minutes. Remove from heat. Whisk in 1¹/₂ cups milk. Cook over medium-high heat, whisking constantly, until mixture thickens and comes to boil. Add a pinch of salt, white pepper, and nutmeg.

3. Add cauliflower and another ¹/₂ cup milk. (Liquid will not cover cauliflower.) Bring to boil. Reduce heat to low. Cover and simmer over low heat, stirring often and occasionally crushing cauliflower with spoon, about 25 minutes or until cauliflower is very tender.

4. Using a slotted spoon, remove cauliflower and puree it (in batches if necessary) in a blender or food processor. With machine running, gradually add rest of soup to puree. Puree until very smooth. Return soup to saucepan and bring to a boil, stirring.

5. Add enough of remaining milk to bring soup to desired consistency. Bring to a boil, stirring. Add cream,

if using, and bring to a boil again, stirring. If necessary, simmer 1 to 2 minutes to desired consistency. Adjust seasoning; soup should be generously seasoned with salt, pepper, and nutmeg. Serve hot, garnished with chives or parsley.

Split Pea Soup with Leeks

Makes 4 to 6 servings

An Alsatian Jewish custom is to begin the Purim menu with split pea soup, followed by a big platter of sauerkraut topped with an array of smoked and cured meats. If you're serving such a menu, it's a good idea to serve this soup in small bowls. For other occasions, a good-size bowl of this soup is substantial enough to be a meal in itself.

Alsatian cooks like to flavor their split pea soup with onions, garlic, and plenty of leeks. Polish cooks add parsley root or diced peeled kohlrabi to the usual onions and carrots. If you would like a fleishig version, many cooks prepare this soup with beef or chicken broth instead of water, or add sliced beef frankfurters for the last 10 minutes of cooking.

2 large leeks

2 tablespoons vegetable oil

1 large onion, halved and sliced

2 quarts water

1 pound green split peas, sorted and rinsed

4 large cloves garlic, chopped

Salt and freshly ground pepper, to taste

1. Use all of leek for this dish. Trim off a little from tops. Cut each leek into a few pieces. Halve each piece lengthwise. Slice leek pieces and put in a large bowl of cold water. Separate slices with your fingers. Let them soak for 5 minutes so that any sand goes to bottom of bowl. Lift into a colander, rinse well, and drain.

2. Heat oil in a large saucepan. Add onion and leeks and sauté over medium-low heat, stirring often, about 7 minutes or until soft but not brown. Add water and split peas and bring to a boil. Cover and cook over low heat 45 minutes. Add garlic, salt, and pepper and cook 15 to 30 more minutes or until split peas are very soft. Adjust seasoning. Serve hot.

❊ Main Courses

Turkey in Pepper Sauce

Makes 4 servings

Israelis love turkey for Purim, and turkey breast in this savory green and red pepper sauce makes the center-piece for a healthful holiday feast. The sauce is prepared in the Hungarian fashion, a favorite cooking style in Israel. Thoroughly browning the onions gives the sauce a rich brown hue. Hungarian-Israeli food can be pretty spicy, so if you like it hot, feel free to add extra hot paprika or cayenne. Whichever spice you choose, add it gradually, to your taste.

1 boneless turkey breast roast (1¹/₂ pounds)
Salt and freshly ground pepper, to taste
2 to 3 tablespoons vegetable oil
2 large onions, sliced
³/₄ cup chicken stock or broth
1 large green bell pepper, diced (³/₄ to 1 inch)
1 large red bell pepper, diced (³/₄ to 1 inch)
3 large cloves garlic, chopped
1 tablespoon sweet paprika
¹/₄ to ¹/₂ teaspoon hot paprika or cayenne pepper, or to taste
One 14¹/₂-ounce can diced tomatoes, drained

1. Sprinkle turkey with salt and pepper. Heat oil in a large, heavy stew pan over medium heat. Add turkey breast and brown lightly on all sides. Remove to a plate.

2. Add onions to pan and sauté over medium heat about 15 minutes or until browned; add a few table-spoons of the stock if the onions begin to stick. Stir in bell peppers and sauté 3 minutes. Stir in garlic, sweet paprika, and hot paprika, and sauté 1 minute. Add tomatoes and remaining stock and bring to a simmer.

3. Return turkey to pan and add juices from plate. Cover and cook over low heat, turning once, about 40 minutes or until thermometer inserted in thickest part of turkey registers 170°F.

4. Remove turkey to a plate. Boil sauce to reduce until thick and well flavored, 3 to 4 minutes. Adjust seasoning; add more hot paprika if desired. Cut turkey into thin slices and serve with sauce.

Turkey Legs with Mushrooms, Carrots, and Egg Noodles

Makes 6 to 8 servings

Like their counterparts in Israel, the Jews of Alsace like to serve turkey for Purim, due to a play on the Hebrew and French words for turkey, meaning "India bird." Here turkey legs are cooked in the typical Alsatian method, braised gently with wine, fresh and dried mush-rooms, and aromatic herbs and served with another favorite in the region—fresh noodles. The turkey comes out moist and tender, and the sauce is richly flavored.

2 tablespoons vegetable oil
2 large onions, 1 whole and 1 sliced
1 rib celery, sliced
5 cloves garlic, chopped
3¹/₂ pounds turkey drumsticks (2 large)
1 pound carrots, cut into ¹/₂-inch slices
1³/₄ cups chicken stock or broth
4 whole cloves
3 cups dry white wine
2 large sprigs fresh thyme or 2 teaspoons dried thyme
1 bay leaf
Salt and freshly ground pepper, to taste
1 ounce dried cepes, porcini, or shiitake mushrooms
Cayenne pepper, to taste
8 ounces button mushrooms, cut into bite-sized pieces
3 tablespoons potato starch, arrowroot, or cornstarch
5 tablespoons water
5 tablespoons chopped fresh Italian parsley
1 pound medium egg noodles

1. Heat oil in a Dutch oven or heavy stew pan over medium heat. Add sliced onion and sauté 10 minutes or until lightly golden. Add celery and garlic and sauté 1 minute. Add turkey, carrots, and stock. Bring to boil, cover and cook 5 minutes. Stick cloves in whole onion and add to casserole. Add wine, thyme, bay leaf, salt, and pep-per and bring to a boil. Cover and simmer over low heat, turning turkey over from time to time, for 1¹/₂ hours.

2. Soak dried mushrooms in enough hot water to cover them for 30 minutes. Remove mushrooms and rinse them. If using shiitake mushrooms, discard stems. Cut mushrooms into bite-size pieces.

3. Add soaked dried mushrooms (but not fresh mushrooms) to pan and cook about 30 more minutes or until turkey is very tender when pierced in thickest part with a sharp knife. Uncover and cool about 15 minutes.

4. Remove turkey from liquid. Remove skin with aid of a paring knife. Discard bones, cartilage, and visible fat from turkey. Pull or cut meat into wide strips and set aside. Skim fat from liquid. Discard whole onion, thyme sprigs, and bay leaf. Season liquid to taste with salt, pepper, and cayenne.

5. Add fresh mushrooms to pan and cook 10 minutes or until tender. Remove vegetables to a plate with slotted spoon.

6. Mix potato starch with the water in small bowl until blended. Bring turkey cooking liquid to a simmer. Gradually whisk in potato starch mixture and simmer 1 minute or until thickened. Adjust seasoning. Return turkey and vegetables to sauce and heat gently. Stir in 4 tablespoons parsley.

7. Cook egg noodles in a large pot of boiling water about 5 minutes or until just tender. Drain well. Serve noodles topped with turkey and sauce, and sprinkled with remaining parsley.

Turkey Breasts in Garlic Sauce Ⓜ

Makes 4 servings

Two heads of garlic might seem like an enormous amount, but slowly poaching whole garlic cloves to mellow them is a trick that has long been known to Jewish cooks from North Africa. The garlic becomes delicious and imparts a terrific flavor to the sauce of the lean turkey breasts. For a Purim feast, serve them with couscous or basmati rice and with Quick-Braised Butternut Squash with Ginger and Onion (page 73).

2 medium heads of garlic

2 pounds boneless turkey breast fillets

Salt and freshly ground pepper, to taste

2 tablespoons olive oil

1 medium onion, chopped

1 1/2 cups turkey or chicken stock

1 small dried chile, such as chile arbol

1/2 teaspoon dried thyme

1 bay leaf

3 tablespoons cold water

2 teaspoons tomato paste

1 tablespoon cornstarch or potato starch

1/4 cup chopped fresh Italian parsley

Several drops strained fresh lemon juice (optional)

1. Separate garlic heads into cloves. Place each clove under the flat side of a wide knife (blade facing away from you) and hit knife with the heel of your hand. Remove loosened peel.

2. Pat turkey dry and sprinkle with pepper. Heat oil in a heavy stew pan or Dutch oven. Add turkey and brown lightly over medium heat on all sides. Remove to a plate. Add onion to stew pan and sauté, stirring often, until golden brown.

3. Add stock, chile, thyme, and bay leaf to pan. Bring to a boil. Add turkey and garlic and return to a simmer. Cover and simmer over low heat about 30 minutes or until turkey is tender when pierced with a sharp knife. Remove turkey to a board and keep it warm. Discard bay leaf.

4. Whisk water into tomato paste in a small bowl. Add cornstarch and whisk to a smooth paste. Gradually whisk mixture into simmering sauce. Return to a boil, stirring. On the cutting board, slice turkey. If necessary, reheat very gently in sauce. Add parsley to sauce. Taste sauce and add lemon juice, if using; adjust seasoning. Serve turkey with garlic sauce spooned over it.

Roast Turkey with Pear-Pecan Stuffing

Makes 8 servings

Turkey is the most popular meat for the Purim feast in Israeli homes. Combine it with pecans, a favorite nut in Israel, for a tasty entree.

Pear-Pecan Stuffing (this page)

3¹/₄ cups Turkey Stock (pages 598–599), chicken stock, or broth

One 10- to 12-pound fresh or thawed frozen turkey

Salt and freshly ground pepper, to taste

2 tablespoons vegetable oil

¹/₄ cup dry white wine

¹/₄ cup all-purpose flour

1. Prepare stuffing and prepare turkey stock, if using. Remove top rack and preheat oven to 425°F. Sprinkle turkey inside and out with salt and pepper. Spoon some stuffing into neck cavity. Fold neck skin under body and fasten with a skewer. Pack body cavity loosely with stuffing and cover opening with a crumpled piece of foil. Truss turkey if desired. Spoon remaining stuffing into an oiled 4- to 6-cup baking dish and refrigerate.

2. Put turkey breast-side-up on a rack in a large roasting pan. Spoon oil slowly over turkey breast. Roast turkey 30 minutes, basting twice.

3. Reduce oven temperature to 350°F. Roast turkey 1¹/₂ hours, basting with pan juices every 15 minutes. If pan becomes dry, add ¹/₄ cup of stock.

4. Put dish of extra stuffing in oven and baste with turkey juices. Cover with foil; bake 45 minutes. Meanwhile, continue roasting turkey, basting every 15 minutes, until juices run clear when thigh is pricked, or thermometer inserted into thickest part of thigh registers 180°F, 20 to 45 minutes; cover turkey with foil if it browns too fast.

5. Transfer turkey to platter or large board. Discard strings and skewers. Baste once with pan juices, and cover turkey.

6. Pour roasting juices into measuring cup. Pour off fat and reserve it. Return juices to pan. Add wine and ³/₄ cup stock and bring to a boil, stirring and scraping to dissolve any brown bits in pan. Strain into a bowl.

7. Heat ¹/₄ cup reserved fat in a saucepan over low heat. Add flour and cook, over low heat, whisking, about 4 minutes or until bubbling. Add remaining 2¹/₄ cups stock and liquid used to deglaze roasting pan. Bring to a boil, whisking. Simmer, whisking occasionally, about 5 minutes or until thick enough to coat a spoon. Adjust seasoning.

8. Carve turkey and arrange on platter. Spoon stuffing onto platter or into a serving dish. Reheat sauce briefly. Pour into a sauceboat and serve alongside turkey.

Pear-Pecan Stuffing

Makes 8 to 9 cups, 6 to 8 servings;
enough for one 10- to 12-pound turkey
or two 4-pound chickens

Fresh and dried pears and raisins combine with the pecans to give this stuffing a wonderful flavor. Bake the stuffing inside a turkey for Purim or Thanksgiving, or use it to stuff chickens. It also makes a tasty side-dish casserole baked on its own.

You can make the stuffing ahead and refrigerate it up to 1 day in a covered container, but to prevent harmful bacteria from developing, do not stuff a bird until just before roasting it.

1 cup pecans

1 cup finely diced (¹/₄-inch dice) dried pears

¹/₄ cup raisins

¹/₂ cup dry white wine

8 to 10 ounces day-old or stale white bread or challah, cut into ¹/₂-inch cubes

3 to 4 tablespoons vegetable oil

1 large onion, finely chopped

1 cup chopped celery

2¹/₂ cups peeled and finely chopped pears

Salt and freshly ground pepper, to taste

¹/₈ teaspoon ground cloves

1 teaspoon minced fresh thyme or ¹/₄ teaspoon dried, crumbled

1 teaspoon minced fresh sage or ¹/₄ teaspoon dried, crumbled

4 to 6 tablespoons turkey or chicken stock or broth

1. Preheat oven to 350°F. Toast nuts until lightly browned, about 5 minutes. Let nuts cool, then coarsely chop them.

2. Combine dried pears, raisins, and wine in a small saucepan and mix well. Bring to a simmer. Cover, remove from heat and let stand 30 minutes, stirring occasionally.

3. Reduce oven temperature to 275°F. Put bread cubes on a large baking sheet. Bake until crisp and dry, stirring frequently, about 20 minutes. Cool and transfer to a large bowl.

4. Heat oil in large skillet over medium heat. Add onion, celery, pears, and a pinch of salt and pepper. Cook, stirring occasionally, until onion is soft but not brown, about 10 minutes. Add cloves, thyme, and sage and stir until blended. Remove from heat.

5. Add onion mixture, nuts, and dried fruit mixture with its liquid to bread and toss lightly until blended. Gradually add 2 tablespoons stock, tossing lightly. Mixture may appear dry, but will become much moister from juices in bird. Adjust seasoning. (Stuffing can be refrigerated up to 1 day in covered container.)

6. To stuff turkey, spoon stuffing lightly into neck and body cavities; for chickens, spoon stuffing lightly into body cavity. Do not pack stuffing in tightly. Fold skin over stuffing; truss or skewer closed. Roast as desired.

Notes:

- If there is extra stuffing, add a little more stock, if necessary, so most of bread is very lightly moistened. Grease casserole dish of same or slightly larger volume than amount of extra mixture and spoon stuffing into it. Dot with margarine. Cover and refrigerate until about 1 hour before roast is done. If roasting poultry or meat at 375°F or lower, bake stuffing during last hour of roasting, basting stuffing with 2 to 3 tablespoons stock every 15 or 20 minutes. If baking less than 4 cups stuffing, bake only 45 minutes. If roasting poultry at higher temperature, bake extra stuffing separately at 325°F.
- To bake all of stuffing separately, preheat oven to 325°F. Grease a 2½-quart casserole dish and spoon stuffing into it. Dot stuffing with margarine and cover casserole dish. Bake 20 minutes. Baste stuffing by pouring ¼ cup stock evenly over top. Bake 20 more minutes and repeat with another ¼ cup stock. Bake 20 more minutes; uncover for last 10 minutes for crisper top. Serve hot.

Alsatian-Jewish Sauerkraut with Meat

Makes 4 to 6 servings

Alsatian Jews serve choucroute garnie, *or sauerkraut with meat, for Purim and sometimes for Hanukkah. In France, Alsatian-style sauerkraut is esteemed because it is delicate in flavor. Cooks first rinse their sauerkraut thoroughly so it will not be aggressively acidic. Instead of adding apples and sugar to obtain a sweet and sour taste, they simmer the sauerkraut gently in dry Riesling wine. Some Alsatians partially cook the meat separately, so that the sauerkraut does not become too greasy. The meat finishes cooking with the sauerkraut to promote an exchange of flavors.*

The Jews of Alsace have a long history of developing their own delicious kosher sauerkraut recipes. The traditional flavoring for their sauerkraut is goose fat. The sauerkraut may be a quick dish made with simple beef frankfurters, or it might cook for longer with a substantial piece of cured beef like pastrami or corned beef. They serve it with mustard and with hot boiled potatoes, or with Aromatic Parslied Potatoes (page 161).

Sauerkraut is easy to find at delicatessens and in the Jewish deli products section of the supermarket. It is best to purchase refrigerated sauerkraut in a jar or plastic pouch rather than in a can, so it has a fresher flavor.

This easy version of sauerkraut makes use of meats that you can readily find in the supermarket and has less fat than in traditional recipes. If you have fat from roasting a goose or duck, you can use it for a more authentic Alsatian taste. You can add a few slices of corned beef at the same time as the pastrami, or use turkey versions of these meats instead of beef.

4 pounds uncooked sauerkraut

3 tablespoons chicken fat or vegetable oil

2 onions, sliced

1 bay leaf

3 whole cloves

6 juniper berries (optional)

6 coriander seeds

6 peppercorns

6 cloves garlic, peeled

2 cups Riesling or other dry white wine

12 good quality beef frankfurters

12 ounces sliced pastrami

Salt and freshly ground pepper, to taste

4 to 6 hot boiled potatoes, such as red, white,
     or Yukon Gold

Dijon mustard

1. Drain sauerkraut in a colander. Rinse thoroughly under cold running water, drain again, squeezing out excess liquid.

2. Heat fat in a large casserole dish, add onions, and cook over medium-low heat, stirring, about 7 minutes or until soft but not brown. Wrap bay leaf, cloves, juniper berries if using, coriander seeds, peppercorns, and garlic with cheesecloth and tie into a seasoning bag. Add sauerkraut, cheesecloth bag, and wine to casserole. Bring to a boil. Cover and simmer over low heat 45 minutes. If sauerkraut is very soupy, simmer it uncovered for a few minutes to evaporate excess liquid. Discard cheesecloth bag.

3. Heat frankfurters in a pan of simmering water for about 5 minutes. Remove from liquid. Add them to casserole dish, pushing them inside sauerkraut. Put pastrami slices on top. Cover and cook over low heat for 10 minutes. Taste sauerkraut and adjust seasoning. Spoon sauerkraut onto a platter and arrange frankfurters, pastrami, and potatoes over it. Serve mustard separately.

❧ *Side Dishes*

Vegetable Kugel with Dill

Makes 6 to 8 servings

A mixture of grated vegetables gives this kugel good taste as well as good nutrition. To prepare the vegetables quickly, you can use the coarse grater of the food processor. Serve it with braised turkey breast, roast chicken, or broiled salmon, or as a hot entree in a vegetarian buffet.

3 tablespoons plus 1 teaspoon vegetable oil

1 large onion, chopped

3 large carrots, coarsely grated

1/2 pound zucchini, coarsely grated

1/2 pound yellow squash, coarsely grated

2 large baking potatoes, peeled and coarsely grated

3 large eggs

1 teaspoon salt

1/4 teaspoon freshly ground pepper

1 to 2 tablespoons chopped fresh dill or 1 teaspoon dried

1 teaspoon paprika, plus a little more for sprinkling

1/4 cup bread crumbs

1. Preheat oven to 350°F. Heat 2 tablespoons oil in a skillet, add onion, and sauté over medium-low heat until softened, about 10 minutes. Transfer to a large bowl and let cool. Add grated carrots.

2. Put zucchini, yellow squash, and potatoes in large strainer and squeeze out excess liquid. Add to bowl of vegetables. Add eggs, salt, pepper, dill, paprika, and bread crumbs.

3. Put 1 tablespoon oil in a 7- or 8-cup baking dish and brush a little of the oil on sides of dish. Heat dish in oven 5 minutes. Add vegetable mixture to hot dish. Sprinkle with 1 teaspoon oil, then shake a little paprika on top. Bake about 1 hour or until brown and set.

Carrot Puree

Makes 4 servings

This colorful accompaniment brightens a plate of Purim turkey and is delicious, especially when you can get really sweet carrots. Carrot puree is especially good with Roast Turkey with Pear-Pecan Stuffing (page 158). If you're celebrating Purim with a meatless dinner, you can add butter instead of oil when heating the puree.

1 pound carrots, cut into 1/2-inch slices

1 or 2 tablespoons vegetable oil

1/2 teaspoon sugar

Salt, to taste

Pinch of ground white pepper (optional)

1. Put carrots in a medium saucepan with enough water to cover and a pinch of salt. Bring to a boil. Cover and simmer about 20 minutes or until carrots are very tender when pierced with a sharp knife.

2. Drain carrots. Put them in a food processor or blender and puree until very smooth.

3. Return puree to saucepan and stir briefly over low heat to dry. Add oil, sugar, salt, and white pepper, if using, and stir over low heat until blended and puree is very hot. Adjust seasoning. Serve hot.

Aromatic Parslied Potatoes

Makes 4 servings

Flavored with shallots, garlic, and parsley, these potatoes sometimes accompany sauerkraut with meat instead of the usual plain boiled potatoes. Traditionally they are cooked with goose fat rather than vegetable oil. You could use chicken fat if you like.

3 tablespoons vegetable oil

1 1/2 pounds fairly small white or red-skinned potatoes, peeled and quartered

6 shallots, sliced

6 cloves garlic, chopped

1/3 cup chopped fresh Italian parsley

Salt and freshly ground pepper, to taste

1. Heat oil slightly in a large, heavy sauté pan. Add potatoes, shallots, garlic, and half the parsley. Sprinkle with salt and pepper. Add enough water to just cover. Bring to a boil. Cover and cook over medium heat 10 minutes.

2. Uncover and cook over medium-high heat, stirring occasionally, about 15 minutes or until potatoes are tender and most of liquid evaporates. If liquid evaporates before potatoes are tender, add a few tablespoons more water and reduce heat. Adjust seasoning. Serve sprinkled with remaining parsley.

Brown Rice Pilaf with Mushrooms and Asparagus

Makes 4 servings **P**

This dish is delicious as an accompaniment for Purim turkey or with an entree of chickpeas or beans, if you're preparing a vegetarian holiday feast.

If you have time, you can cook the asparagus before the rice, and use the asparagus cooking liquid as part of the vegetable stock for cooking the rice.

3 tablespoons vegetable oil or olive oil

1 large onion, chopped

1^1/2 cups long-grain brown rice

3 cups hot vegetable stock or water

Salt and freshly ground pepper, to taste

1 bay leaf

1 large sprig fresh thyme or ^{1}/2 teaspoon dried thyme

12 ounces asparagus, peeled if more than ^{1}/4-inch thick

6 to 8 ounces sliced mushrooms

2 tablespoons chopped fresh parsley

1. Heat 2 tablespoons oil in a large sauté pan or wide casserole. Add onion and cook over low heat, stirring, about 7 minutes or until soft but not brown. Add rice and sauté, stirring, about 2 minutes.

2. Add stock, salt, pepper, bay leaf, and thyme. Stir once with a fork and cover. Cook over low heat, without stirring, for 40 minutes. Taste rice; if not yet tender, simmer 2 more minutes. Discard bay leaf and thyme sprig. Add more salt and pepper if needed. Cover and let stand for 10 minutes.

3. Cut asparagus tips from stems. Cut stems into 2 or 3 pieces, discarding tough ends (about ^{1}/2-inch from end). Add all of asparagus to a medium saucepan of boiling salted water. Boil uncovered until asparagus is just tender when pierced with a small sharp knife, 2 to 3 minutes. Drain, rinse with cold running water until cool, and drain well again.

4. Just before serving, heat remaining tablespoon oil in a medium skillet. Add mushrooms and sauté over medium heat about 3 minutes or until tender. Add asparagus, salt, and pepper and sauté about 1 minute. Gently fluff rice with a fork. Stir in parsley. Adjust seasoning. Gently stir in asparagus-mushroom mixture. Serve hot.

Hamantaschen

Basic Hamantaschen

Makes about 32 hamantaschen

No matter what dough or filling you use to make these three-cornered filled Purim cookies, homemade or purchased, you shape hamantaschen the same way. Use cookie dough, knish dough, rugelach dough, or yeast dough. You can even make hamantaschen from extra challah dough.

Hamantaschen made with yeast dough are best when warm. Wrap them in foil and heat them in the oven.

Eastern European Cookie Dough or Refrigerator Yeast Dough (page 163)

Prune or Poppy Seed Filling (page 165) or other homemade fillings

1 large egg, beaten with a pinch of salt, for glaze (optional)

1. Grease 2 baking sheets. Cut dough in four pieces. Roll out one piece on a lightly floured surface until about ^{1}/8-inch thick. Using a 3-inch cookie cutter, cut dough into rounds. Brush edges lightly with water. Put 1 teaspoon filling in center of each round. (Avoid the temptation to use extra filling, or it may ooze out during baking.) Pull up edges of circle in 3 arcs that meet in center above filling. Close them firmly. Pinch edges to seal. With a spatula, transfer to baking sheet, placing them 1 inch apart, and refrigerate. Wrap and refrigerate scraps at least 30 minutes.

2. Roll remaining dough and shape more hamantaschen. Do the same with the scraps. Refrigerate at least 30 minutes or overnight before baking to firm dough. If using yeast dough, cover chilled hamantaschen with plastic wrap or a slightly damp cloth and let rise at room temperature about 15 minutes.

3. Position rack in the center of the oven and preheat oven to 350°F. Brush hamantaschen with egg glaze, if using. Bake hamantaschen about 14 minutes or until they are lightly golden at edges and golden on the bottom. Transfer to a rack to cool.

Eastern European Cookie Dough

Makes about 1½ pounds dough,
enough for 3 dozen hamantaschen
(including scraps); or 2 dozen
hamantaschen, if scraps are not used

*Favored among Jews of Polish and Hungarian descent,
this dough makes crisp, delicious hamantaschen. In
countries where the metric system is used, it is also
known as One, Two, Three Dough because it has 100
grams sugar, 200 grams butter, and 300 grams flour,
with enough liquid to hold the dough together. The
liquid can be water, juice, milk, beaten egg, or any
combination. I use powdered sugar instead of granulated to make the dough easier to roll out.*

2¾ cups all-purpose flour

1 cup powdered sugar

1 teaspoon baking powder

Pinch of salt

1 cup (2 sticks) cold butter or firm margarine, cut into
    small pieces

1 teaspoon vanilla extract

1 large egg, beaten

1 to 3 tablespoons water

1. Combine flour, powdered sugar, baking powder,
and salt in a food processor and process briefly to blend.
Scatter butter pieces over mixture. Process with brief
pulses until mixture resembles coarse meal. Add vanilla
to beaten egg. Pour mixture evenly over mixture in
processor. Process with brief pulses, scraping down the
sides occasionally, until dough just begins to come
together in a ball. If crumbs are dry, sprinkle with
1 tablespoon water and process briefly; repeat if crumbs
are still dry.

2. Transfer dough to a work surface. Knead lightly to
blend. With a rubber spatula, transfer dough to a sheet
of plastic wrap, wrap, and push it together. Shape
dough into a flat disk. Refrigerate at least 3 hours or up
to 3 days.

3. Remove dough from refrigerator 30 minutes
before using.

Note: This amount of dough needs about 1 cup filling.

Refrigerator Yeast Dough

Makes enough for 2½ to 3 dozen
hamantaschen

*Jewish bakers enjoy using a variety of yeast doughs for
making hamantaschen, from challah dough to sour
cream dough to ultra-rich, buttery brioche made by
French Jews.*

*This is a quick and easy yeast dough to make
because it doesn't require rising and waiting. The
dough is sometimes called "crisp" or "cold" yeast dough,
because it is mixed and refrigerated, much like pie
pastry. This is not just for convenience; letting the
dough rise less (it rises slightly in the refrigerator) helps
to make the hamantaschen somewhat crisp, rather
than bread-like. Besides, chilling the dough makes it
easier to roll out. The dough is richer than many yeast
doughs, so the hamantaschen stay fresh-tasting for
longer. The yeast gives them a special texture, different
from cookie-dough hamantaschen.*

*Use water for the milk and nondairy margarine or
vegetable oil if you want these to be pareve.*

¼ cup lukewarm water

1 envelope dry yeast

⅓ cup sugar

3 to 3¼ cups all-purpose flour

½ cup (1 stick) soft butter or margarine or 7 tablespoons
    vegetable oil

1 large egg

2 teaspoons grated lemon rind

½ teaspoon salt

About ½ cup lukewarm milk or additional water

1. Pour ¼ cup of water into small bowl. Sprinkle
yeast over water. Sprinkle 1 teaspoon of sugar over
yeast. Let stand until foamy, about 10 minutes. Stir if
not smooth.

2. Sift 3 cups of flour into bowl of an electric mixer
fitted with dough hook. Make a large, deep well in center. Add butter, remaining sugar, egg, grated lemon
rind, and salt. Mix with dough hook to blend liquid
ingredients thoroughly; most of flour will remain on
edges of well.

3. To well, add yeast mixture and milk or water. Mix at medium-low speed, pushing flour in from sides of bowl and scraping dough down occasionally from bowl and hook, until dough just begins to cling to hook, about 7 minutes. If dough is too soft to cling to hook, gradually beat in more flour. Knead by mixing at medium speed, scraping down twice, until dough is smooth, partially clings to hook, and almost cleans sides of bowl, about 5 more minutes. Dough should be soft and smooth.

4. Wrap dough in plastic wrap and put it on a plate. Refrigerate 8 hours or overnight.

5. Remove dough from refrigerator 30 minutes before using.

Oil-Based Dough

Makes enough dough for 2 dozen
hamantaschen (including scraps) Ⓟ

Hamantaschen made with this dough have a pleasing sweet taste and slightly crunchy texture. This dough is made with healthful canola oil instead of butter or margarine. The dough is pareve so the hamantaschen can be served after any kind of meal.

2 cups all-purpose flour

³/₄ teaspoon baking powder

Pinch of salt

¹/₂ cup sugar

1 large egg

6 tablespoons canola oil

1 teaspoon grated orange rind

2 to 3 tablespoons strained fresh orange juice

1. Combine flour, baking powder, salt, and sugar in the food processor and process to blend. Beat egg with oil in a small bowl and add to processor. Add orange rind. Pulse until dough is the texture of coarse meal.

2. Add juice 1 tablespoon at a time, pulsing after each addition, until dough becomes sticky crumbs. Transfer to a bowl and press together. Wrap in plastic wrap and refrigerate 4 hours or overnight.

3. Remove dough from refrigerator 30 minutes before using.

Note: This amount of dough needs about ²/₃ cup filling.

Pareve Poppy Seed–Walnut Filling

Makes about 1¹/₄ cups Ⓟ

Poppy seed is the classic filling for hamantaschen. Combining the seeds with honey and walnuts is a Polish-Jewish favorite. If possible, buy fresh seeds in Jewish, Polish, or Middle Eastern grocery stores. Leave them whole for a slightly crunchy filling or grind them in a spice grinder for a finer consistency.

³/₄ cup poppy seeds (¹/₄ pound)

¹/₂ cup water

6 tablespoons sugar

3 tablespoons honey

2 tablespoons margarine

¹/₃ cup finely chopped walnuts

Combine poppy seeds, water, sugar, and honey in small saucepan and bring to a simmer. Cook over low heat, stirring often, 15 to 20 minutes or until thick. Add margarine and stir over low heat until it melts. Remove from heat. Stir in walnuts. Cover and chill about 1 hour before using.

Creamy Poppy Seed Filling with Raisins

Makes about 1 cup

Milk and honey give this filling its rich flavor, which is further embellished with raisins and butter. Milk softens the slightly bitter taste of poppy seeds. If you like, grind poppy seeds in a spice grinder.

3/4 cup poppy seeds (1/4 pound)

1/2 cup milk

1/3 cup sugar

3 tablespoons honey

1/3 cup raisins

3 tablespoons butter

1 teaspoon vanilla extract

Combine poppy seeds, milk, sugar, and honey in small saucepan and bring to a simmer. Cook over low heat, stirring often, 15 to 20 minutes or until thick. Add raisins and butter and stir over low heat until butter melts. Remove from heat and stir in vanilla. Chill about 1 hour before using.

Prune Filling

Makes about 1 cup filling

Ever since I was a child, I have loved hamantaschen with prune filling. Prunes make a luscious, flavorful filling with little embellishment other than a few chopped almonds or other nuts and some prune or plum jam, also known respectively as lekvar *or* povidl *in Yiddish. If you don't have plum jam, you can use straw- berry or raspberry jam. Many people cook the prunes, but soaking them is enough to make them tender.*

8 ounces pitted prunes

3 tablespoons chopped blanched almonds

1/4 cup plum jam or jelly

1 teaspoon grated lemon rind

1. Put prunes in a small bowl. Pour enough boiling water over prunes to cover them. Let them soak 15 minutes.

2. Grind almonds to a fine powder in food processor; transfer to a bowl. Drain prunes and chop finely or puree in food processor. Mix prune puree with almonds, jam, and lemon rind.

Date Filling

Makes about 1 cup

In Israel date filling for hamantaschen is nearly as popular as poppy seed. With their natural sweetness and luscious texture, dates do make a wonderful filling.

2 tablespoons diced pecans

3/4 pound pitted dates, cut into pieces

2 to 3 tablespoons plum jam or orange marmalade

Chop pecans finely in food processor and remove. Add dates to processor and puree them. Add pecans and 2 tablespoons jam and process to blend. Transfer to a bowl. Add remaining jam if desired.

Fig Filling

Makes about 1 cup

Figs are loved in Israel for filling cookies, and they are great in hamantaschen. You can also use this tasty, sweet mixture in Purim Pinwheels (page 168) or in Middle Eastern filled pastries or cookies.

1/4 pound dried black Mission figs or other dried figs, stems removed, halved

1/2 cup raisins

1/2 cup walnuts, chopped

1/4 cup thick jam, such as fig jam or plum jam

1 tablespoon orange juice

1/2 teaspoon grated orange rind

2 tablespoons flaked coconut (optional)

Combine figs and raisins in food processor. Chop them together. Transfer to a bowl and stir in walnuts, jam, orange juice, orange rind, and coconut, if using.

Chocolate Hamantaschen

Makes about 32 hamantaschen

Although these are not traditional, whenever I make them, children love them best. They feature a buttery, tasty sour cream dough and a very easy-to-make chocolate filling. Use fine quality chocolate for the best flavor. If you're short on time, choose the type that is easy to cut into small pieces.

1 large egg

2 to 4 tablespoons sour cream or yogurt

2¹/₂ cups all-purpose flour

¹/₂ cup powdered sugar, plus more for dusting if desired

1 teaspoon baking powder

¹/₄ teaspoon salt

³/₄ cup (1¹/₂ sticks) cold butter or margarine, cut into small pieces

1 pound semisweet or bittersweet chocolate, cut into ¹/₂-ounce pieces

1. Beat egg with 2 tablespoons sour cream in a small bowl. Combine flour, powdered sugar, baking powder, and salt in a food processor and process briefly to blend. Scatter butter pieces over mixture. Process with brief pulses until mixture resembles coarse meal. Pour egg mixture evenly over mixture. Process with brief pulses, scraping down the sides occasionally, until dough just begins to come together in a ball. If mixture is dry, add more sour cream by tablespoons, dropping small dollops over mixture, and process briefly again.

2. Transfer dough to a work surface. Knead lightly to blend. With a rubber spatula, transfer dough to a sheet of plastic wrap, wrap, and push together. Shape dough into a flat disk. Refrigerate at least 2 hours before using.

3. Grease a baking sheet. Cut dough into 4 pieces. Roll one piece on a lightly floured surface until about ¹/₈ inch thick. With a 3-inch cookie cutter, cut dough into circles. Brush edges lightly with water. Put 1 chocolate piece in center of each. Pull up edges of circle in 3 arcs that meet in center above filling. Close them firmly. Pinch edges to seal. Put on baking sheet and refrigerate. Wrap and refrigerate scraps at least 30 minutes.

4. Roll remaining dough, then the scraps, and shape more hamantaschen. Refrigerate hamantaschen 1 hour to firm dough, or up to overnight.

5. Preheat oven to 375°F. Bake hamantaschen about 14 minutes or until they are lightly golden at edges and golden on the bottom. Serve dusted with powdered sugar, if using.

Chocolate-Almond Phyllo Hamantaschen

Makes about 36 pastries

Phyllo dough is becoming popular as the pastry for hamantaschen because you can buy it ready-made. It's easy to fold in triangles, which approximate the hamantaschen shape. In addition, you can regulate the richness of these treats according to how much butter or margarine you brush on the pastry. Chocolate matched with ground almonds, orange zest, and orange liqueur makes a delicious new filling.

1 pound phyllo sheets (about 20 sheets)

2 ounces bittersweet or semisweet chocolate, chopped

1 cup whole blanched almonds

7 tablespoons sugar

1 large egg, beaten

2 tablespoons plus 2 teaspoons orange liqueur

2 teaspoons grated orange rind

³/₄ to 1¹/₄ cups (1¹/₂ to 2¹/₂ sticks) unsalted butter or margarine, melted and cooled

About 2 teaspoons sesame seeds

1. If phyllo dough is frozen, thaw in refrigerator 8 hours or overnight. Remove package from refrigerator 2 hours before using.

2. Melt chocolate in a medium bowl over a pan of nearly simmering water. Stir until smooth. Remove bowl from the pan; let cool.

3. Grind almonds with 2 tablespoons sugar in a food processor to a fine powder. Add remaining 5 tablespoons sugar and egg; process until blended. Add chocolate; process until blended. Add liqueur; process until blended. Transfer to a bowl. Stir in orange rind.

4. Preheat oven to 350°F. Line 2 baking sheets with parchment or grease them. Remove phyllo sheets from their package and unroll them on a dry towel. With a sharp knife, cut stack in half lengthwise to form 2 stacks of sheets, about 16 × 7-inch. Cover phyllo immediately with a piece of wax paper, then with a damp towel. Work with only 1 sheet at a time; keep remaining sheets covered with paper and towel so they don't dry out.

5. Carefully remove 1 phyllo sheet from stack. Brush it lightly with melted butter; fold in half lengthwise so dimensions are about 16 × 3 1/2-inch. Place about 1 1/2 teaspoons filling at 1 end of strip. Fold end of strip diagonally over filling to form a triangle. Fold it over and over, keeping it in a triangular shape after each fold, until end of strip is reached. Before last fold, brush sheet lightly with butter to seal triangle together. Set triangle on a baking sheet and brush lightly with butter. Cover with plastic wrap. Make pastries with remaining phyllo sheets and filling. (Pastries can be kept, covered tightly, 1 day in refrigerator.)

6. Just before baking, brush pastries again lightly with melted butter. Sprinkle with sesame seeds. Bake about 25 minutes or until golden brown. If baking on 2 racks, switch their positions halfway through baking time. Serve warm or at room temperature.

❧ Other Sweet Treats and Desserts

Haman's Fingers

Makes about 30 pastries

A Purim tradition among Sephardic Jews from Turkey and Greece, Haman's fingers are made with a spiced almond or walnut filling. To cut their preparation time, I like to make them from phyllo dough.

1/2 pound phyllo dough (1/2 package)

1 1/2 cups almonds

3 tablespoons sugar

1 teaspoon ground cinnamon

1 teaspoon grated orange rind

6 to 8 tablespoons (3/4 to 1 stick) margarine, melted

Powdered sugar

1. If phyllo dough is frozen, thaw it in the refrigerator 8 hours or overnight. Remove package from refrigerator 2 hours before using.

2. Chop almonds with sugar in food processor, leaving some pieces; do not grind finely. Transfer to a bowl and stir in cinnamon and grated orange rind.

3. Preheat oven to 350°F. Line 2 baking sheets with parchment paper or grease them. Remove phyllo sheets from their package and unroll them on a dry towel. With a sharp knife, cut stack in half lengthwise, then in half crosswise. Cover phyllo immediately with a piece of wax paper, then with a damp towel. Work with only 1 sheet at a time, keeping remaining sheets covered so they don't dry out.

4. Carefully remove one pastry square from stack. Brush it lightly with melted margarine. Put about 2 teaspoons filling at one end of a phyllo square so it extends all along the edge. Fold the two ends of dough in, slightly over filling, then roll up tightly to form a thin finger. Transfer to baking sheet. Make more phyllo fingers with remaining dough and filling.

5. Bake pastries 15 to 20 minutes or until very lightly golden. Transfer to a rack to cool. Serve dusted with powdered sugar.

Purim Pinwheels

Makes about 24 cookies

My family always makes pinwheel cookies for Purim. We don't usually make a special dough and filling; we simply use our hamantaschen dough and fillings in a different, easier shape. After we have made enough hamantaschen, we quickly shape and bake some pinwheel cookies, often out of dough scraps. We find they're attractive alongside the hamantaschen in Purim gift boxes. You can make them with homemade or purchased dough, sweetened or not sweetened, and any thick filling.

2 cups all-purpose flour

1/3 cup powdered sugar (optional)

1 teaspoon baking powder

1/2 teaspoon salt

1/2 cup (1 stick) plus 2 tablespoons unsalted butter or firm margarine, cut into small pieces

1 large egg, beaten

Fig Filling (page 165)

1. Combine flour, powdered sugar if using, baking powder, and salt in a food processor and process briefly to blend. Scatter butter pieces over mixture. Process with brief pulses until mixture resembles coarse meal. Pour beaten egg evenly over mixture. Process with brief pulses, scraping down the sides occasionally, until dough just begins to come together in a ball. If mixture is dry, add water by tablespoons, and process briefly after each addition.

2. Transfer dough to a work surface. Knead lightly to blend. With a rubber spatula, transfer dough to a sheet of plastic wrap, wrap, and push together. Shape dough into a flat disk. Refrigerate at least 1 hour or up to overnight.

3. Prepare filling. Then, lightly grease 2 baking sheets. Cut dough into 2 pieces. Roll one into a rectangle about 1/8-inch thick. Spread with half the filling, leaving a 1/2-inch border. Beginning at a long side, roll up tightly like a jelly roll. Cut into slices about 1/2-inch thick. Put each slice on baking sheet with its less-open side (the side that was cut second) facing down. Refrigerate slices. Repeat with remaining dough and filling. Refrigerate pinwheels at least 30 minutes or up to overnight.

4. Preheat oven to 375°F. Bake pinwheels about 12 minutes or until they are light golden at edges and golden on the bottom. Transfer to racks to cool.

Brazil Nut and Raisin Cookies

Makes about 48 cookies

These cookies are crisp and easy to make. They're a perfect item to include along with hamantaschen in Purim gift cookie boxes. If you like, you can substitute chopped dried apricots for the raisins, or use dark or white chocolate chips.

1 cup all-purpose flour

1/2 teaspoon salt

1/2 teaspoon baking soda

1/2 cup (1 stick) unsalted butter or firm margarine, slightly softened

1/2 cup firmly packed brown sugar

1/4 cup granulated sugar

1 large egg

1 teaspoon grated lemon rind

1 cup coarsely chopped unsalted Brazil nuts

1/2 cup raisins

1. Preheat oven to 350°F. Lightly grease 2 baking sheets. Sift flour, salt, and baking soda into a medium bowl.

2. Cream butter in a large bowl with an electric mixer; add sugars and beat until smooth and fluffy. Add egg; beat until smooth. Add lemon rind; beat until blended. Stir in flour mixture until blended. Stir in nuts and raisins.

3. Push batter from a teaspoon with a second teaspoon onto baking sheets, using about 1 1/2 teaspoons batter for each cookie and spacing them about 2 inches apart. Flatten each cookie by pressing it firmly with the bottom of a fork dipped in water.

4. Bake about 8 minutes or until lightly browned. Using a metal spatula, carefully transfer cookies to racks; cool completely. Cool baking sheets; clean off any crumbs then grease sheets again. Bake remaining cookies. Cookies can be kept 1 week in an airtight container at room temperature.

Poppy Seed Cookies

Makes 20 to 24 cookies

The dough for these crisp cookies is easily made in the food processor. Since they take only a few minutes to bake, you can shape them and keep them 1 or 2 days in the refrigerator, ready to pop in the oven, for a treat of just-baked cookies for Purim guests.

1 large egg

1 large egg yolk

$1/2$ cup sugar

Pinch of salt

2 tablespoons poppy seeds, plus more for sprinkling

Grated rind 1 orange

$1/2$ cup (1 stick) plus 1 tablespoon unsalted butter or firm margarine, well-chilled and cut into small pieces

2 cups all-purpose flour

1 to 2 tablespoons orange juice or water (optional)

1. Combine egg, egg yolk, sugar, salt, 2 tablespoons poppy seeds, orange rind, and butter in a food processor. Process using 10 brief pulses, then process continuously 5 seconds until nearly blended. Add flour; process 2 seconds. Scrape down sides and process about 3 seconds or until dough begins to form sticky crumbs but does not come together in a ball. If crumbs are dry, add juice or water and process using brief pulses just until blended. With a rubber spatula, transfer dough to a sheet of plastic wrap, wrap, and push together. Shape dough into a flat disk. Refrigerate dough at least 4 hours or up to 2 days.

2. Lightly grease 2 baking sheets. Roll out $1/2$ of dough on a cold, lightly floured surface until about $1/4$-inch thick. Using a round $2^1/2$-inch cutter, cut dough into circles. Sprinkle each with $1/8$ to $1/4$ teaspoon poppy seeds, according to your taste. Press lightly to make them adhere to dough. Put cookies on baking sheets and refrigerate. Gently press scraps together, wrap them, and refrigerate 30 minutes or until firm enough to roll.

3. Roll remaining dough to shape more cookies. Do the same with the scraps. Refrigerate cookies at least 30 minutes before baking to firm dough. (They can be kept, covered, overnight in refrigerator.)

4. Preheat oven to 375°F. Bake cookies 8 to 9 minutes or until they are very light golden at the edges and golden on the bottom. Transfer cookies to racks to cool.

Chocolate-Apricot Wine Balls

Makes about 30 candies

From the time of the Talmud, it has been a custom to enjoy wine for Purim as part of the spirit of celebration, and sometimes wine finds its way into candies as well. In these treats, sweet wine provides a pleasing complement to the chocolate and the dried apricots. When I was growing up, we prepared a variety of easy sweets like this to add to the cookie boxes for our friends. We made them by mixing chocolate, dried fruit, and wine with cake or cookie crumbs, then rolling them in chopped nuts or coconut.

$1/2$ cup diced dried apricots

$1/2$ cup sweet wine or orange juice

4 ounces bittersweet or semisweet chocolate, chopped

2 tablespoons unsweetened cocoa powder

2 tablespoons sugar

6 tablespoons ($3/4$ stick) butter or margarine, at room temperature and cut into pieces

$3/4$ to 1 cup cookie crumbs

About $1^1/2$ cups chopped blanched almonds

1. Combine apricots and wine in a jar and cover. Shake, then let stand about 1 hour. Remove apricots, reserving wine.

2. Heat chocolate, cocoa, sugar, and reserved wine in a medium, heavy saucepan over low heat, stirring often, until chocolate melts. Remove from heat and add butter. Stir until melted. Stir in cookie crumbs and apricots. Mix well. Refrigerate 30 to 45 minutes or until firm enough to shape.

3. Put almonds in a shallow bowl or tray. Shape chocolate mixture into balls, using about 2 teaspoons for each. Roll balls in almonds. Set candies on plates. Refrigerate 1 hour before serving. Serve in foil or paper candy cups.

Easy Chocolate Truffles

Makes about 20 truffles of about 1-inch diameter

When I appeared on Israel's popular TV morning show, "Boker Tov Yisrael" ("Good Morning Israel"), to prepare treats for Purim, these were everyone's favorites. They contain only three ingredients (chocolate and heavy cream—called ganache in French when blended together—plus nuts), and are fun to make. In fact, making them is a great family project. But they're main attraction is that they are so delicious!

Be sure to use fine chocolate for these truffles. You can make them ahead and keep them up to 5 days in an airtight container in the refrigerator, or you can freeze them.

8 ounces fine quality semisweet or bittersweet chocolate, very finely chopped

³/₄ cup heavy cream

²/₃ cup finely chopped walnuts or unsalted macadamia nuts

1. Put chocolate in heatproof medium bowl. Heat cream in small, heavy saucepan over medium-high heat, whisking, until it comes to a full boil. Pour cream over chocolate all at once. Whisk until chocolate is completely melted and mixture is smooth. Let cool to room temperature, occasionally stirring gently.

2. Cover bowl of ganache and refrigerate, stirring occasionally, until very thick and firm enough to scoop out in mounds but not hard, about 45 minutes.

3. Using 2 teaspoons, spoon mixture in ³/₄-inch mounds onto a foil-lined tray, using about 2 teaspoons of mixture for each. Cover and refrigerate until firm enough to handle, about 15 minutes.

4. Press each mound into a rough ball and return to tray. Then roll each between your palms to a smooth ball and return to tray. Work quickly so they do not soften too much. If truffles become very soft, refrigerate or freeze to slightly firm them.

5. Put nuts in a shallow bowl. Roll each truffle in nuts, pressing so nuts adhere and truffle is well coated. Place on foil-lined tray. Cover and refrigerate until firm, about 2 hours. Serve cold or at room temperature, in foil or paper candy cups.

Baba Cupcakes

Makes 16 cupcakes

Popular in Alsace for Purim, babas are traditional French cakes baked in small bucket-shaped molds. Here, I use cupcake or muffin tins because they're more common in most kitchens. These taste great on their own but you can serve them with Vanilla Whipped Cream (page 581) if you like.

Unlike most yeast cakes, babas are light and airy. They are dipped in syrup to keep them moist. In classic recipes, they are sprinkled with rum just before being served but you can use other spirits that you like. If you're serving them to children, simply leave out the spirits; the cake has good flavor without them and is plenty moist from the syrup. Finally, the cakes are frosted with apricot glaze. If you like, you can decorate each with red candied cherries and sliced almonds just after brushing on the glaze, as bakeries often do.

If you want to prepare these ahead, the best stage to keep them is before they are dipped. Then you can store them in an airtight container for 3 days at room temperature. You can keep the glazed babas in a covered dish in the refrigerator for about 3 more days, but after a day, they start to lose their rum flavor and to become a bit soggy. That doesn't matter in our house—they're still delicious!

²/₃ cup dark raisins

1 tablespoon rum or water

1 package active dry yeast

¹/₄ cup warm water (110°F)

1 tablespoon plus 1 teaspoon sugar

2 cups all-purpose flour

4 large eggs

1 teaspoon salt

7 tablespoons unsalted butter or margarine, cut into 14 pieces, at room temperature

Syrup and topping

1¹/₄ cups sugar

2 cups water

Apricot Glaze (page 582)

7 to 9 tablespoons rum or other spirits

1. Put raisins in a small jar and add rum or water. Cover tightly and shake to combine. Let stand while making the dough.

2. Sprinkle yeast over $1/4$ cup warm water in a small bowl and add 1 teaspoon sugar. Let stand 10 minutes or until foamy. Sift the flour into the bowl of an electric mixer fitted with a dough hook, then add 2 eggs, salt, and 1 tablespoon sugar. Mix at low speed until a few tablespoons of flour are drawn into egg mixture. Add yeast mixture and remaining 2 eggs. Mix at low speed, occasionally scraping down dough, about 10 minutes or until dough is soft and smooth. Beat at medium speed about 12 minutes or until dough is very smooth and most of it comes away from side of bowl. Dough will be soft and very sticky.

3. Lightly oil a medium bowl and place dough in it. Put butter pieces in one layer on dough. Cover bowl with a slightly damp towel or plastic wrap. Let dough rise in a warm, draft-free place about 1 hour or until doubled in bulk. Transfer to clean mixer bowl. Beat in butter with dough hook at low speed, scraping down often, about 3 minutes or until blended. Drain raisins, reserving rum if using, and stir into dough, with a cutting and folding motion of wooden spoon.

4. Generously butter 16 muffin cups. Add about 2 tablespoons dough to each cup. Cover with plastic wrap and let rise in warm, draft-free place 20 minutes. Remove covering; let rise to top of molds, about 15 more minutes.

5. Preheat oven to 400°F. Put a little water in any empty muffin cups. Bake babas about 12 minutes or until dough comes away from sides of pan, top is browned, and cake tester inserted into a cake comes out clean; test 2 or 3 to be sure. Unmold onto a rack and let cool completely.

6. To make syrup: Heat sugar and water in a medium, heavy saucepan over low heat, stirring gently until sugar dissolves. Bring to a boil over high heat. Remove from heat.

7. Set a cake rack above a rimmed tray. Lift one baba on a slotted skimmer or slotted spoon, dip it in hot syrup and leave a few seconds. Ladle syrup over baba several times until it is moist but not soggy. Roll baba quickly around in syrup to encourage it to absorb more syrup. Cake should absorb plenty of syrup so that no part of it remains dry. Lift cake using slotted spoon. Touch it to check that it is well moistened and softened; if there are any firm parts, ladle syrup over cake a few more times. Remove carefully with slotted spoon and set on prepared rack. Continue dipping babas. Reheat syrup occasionally. If any syrup remains, slowly spoon it over cakes. Drain cakes 30 minutes on rack.

8. Prepare glaze. Then, put babas on plates or on tray with their tops facing down. A short time before serving, spoon 7 to 9 tablespoons rum very slowly over each baba, rolling cake so it absorbs rum evenly.

9. Turn babas over and set on rack with their tops facing up. Heat glaze in a small saucepan until just beginning to bubble. Stir in reserved rum. Brush on all sides of cakes. Let stand about 10 minutes before serving.

Note: If you don't have a dough hook, make the dough in a food processor: Put yeast mixture, 1 tablespoon sugar, and eggs in food processor; process about 5 seconds or until blended. Sift in flour and salt; process 30 seconds without stopping machine. If dough is not smooth, transfer to a medium bowl, lift dough up, and slap it down in bowl a few times to knead it. Let dough rise with butter pieces on top, as above. With a wooden spoon, stir butter into dough with a cutting and folding motion. Gently slap dough a few times in bowl to blend in butter completely. Continue with recipe.

Kugelhopf

Makes 12 to 16 servings

The quintessential coffeecake, kugelhopf is a favorite among Alsatian Jews for Purim and is great for Shabbat morning too. It's a popular treat throughout Alsace. Made of an easy, yeast-leavened batter, kugelhopf is baked in a traditional fluted tube pan (also known as a kugelhopf *pan) and has a lovely golden crust with an almond studded in each ridge. If you like, dust the whole cake with powdered sugar before serving it.*

1/2 cup dark raisins

1/2 cup light raisins

3 tablespoons kirsch or cherry brandy

1 cup lukewarm milk (110°F)

2 (1/4-ounce) packages active dry yeast (about 2 tablespoons)

2/3 cup sugar

3 1/2 cups all-purpose flour

1 1/2 teaspoons salt

3 large eggs

1 cup (2 sticks) unsalted butter, cut into 16 pieces, at room temperature

16 to 18 whole blanched almonds

Powdered sugar (optional)

1. Put raisins in a small jar or bowl and add kirsch. Cover tightly; shake to mix. Let soak at least 4 hours or overnight in refrigerator.

2. Pour 1/2 cup warm milk into a small bowl; sprinkle with yeast and 1/4 teaspoon sugar. Let stand 10 minutes or until foamy. Put 1/2 cup flour in a medium bowl. Add yeast mixture and 1/4 cup milk; stir to combine. A few lumps may remain. Cover with slightly damp towel or plastic wrap; let stand about 15 minutes.

3. Spoon remaining 3 cups flour into a large bowl of an electric mixer; make a well in center of flour. Add salt, remaining sugar, and remaining 1/4 cup milk. With wooden spoon, mix ingredients in well briefly. Add eggs and 8 butter pieces to well. Using dough hook, mix at low speed, scraping bowl occasionally, until dough is smooth. Gradually beat in remaining butter, followed by yeast mixture. Beat on medium speed about 10 minutes or until dough is very smooth. Cover and set in a warm, draft-free place 30 minutes or until dough begins to rise but does not double in bulk.

4. Generously butter a 9 1/2 × 4-inch kugelhopf mold, fluted tube pan, or bundt pan, taking care to butter tube and each ridge. Put 1 almond in base of each ridge. Stir raisins and kirsch into risen batter. Carefully transfer batter to pan, without moving almonds. Smooth top. Cover and let rise in warm place 40 minutes.

5. Preheat oven to 400°F. Uncover dough and let rise about 20 minutes or until it nearly reaches top of pan. Bake kugelhopf in center of oven for 10 minutes.

Reduce oven temperature to 350°F. Bake about 45 minutes longer or until a cake tester inserted in cake comes out clean. If kugelhopf browns enough on top before it is done, cover it with foil.

6. Cool in pan on a rack about 10 minutes. Invert cake onto rack; cool completely. Dust with powdered sugar, if using, just before serving.

Apples in Spiced Wine

Makes 4 servings

Ⓟ

Flavored with cinnamon and cloves, the red wine syrup in which these apples poach recalls the mulled wine that's often prepared for New Year's. You can serve the apples in their aromatic syrup warm or cold, on their own or as an accompaniment for unfrosted cakes. I like them for Purim, as a fruit dessert to serve before the hamantaschen. On Hanukkah they make a good partner for potato or sweet potato latkes.

3/4 cup sugar

3 cups dry red wine

1 cinnamon stick

2 whole cloves

1 vanilla bean (optional)

1 1/4 pounds Golden Delicious, Pippin, or Granny Smith apples (4 medium), peeled, halved, and cored

1. Combine sugar, wine, cinnamon stick, cloves, and vanilla bean, if using, in a medium saucepan. Bring to a boil, stirring gently to dissolve sugar. Remove from heat.

2. Cut each apple half in two. Return syrup to a boil and add apple quarters. Reduce heat to low. Cover with a lid that is a bit too small for saucepan, to keep apples submerged. Cook 15 to 20 minutes or until apples are very tender when pierced with point of a knife.

3. With a slotted spoon, carefully transfer apples to a bowl. Simmer syrup uncovered over medium heat for about 5 minutes to thicken slightly. Pour over apples. Let apples cool in their syrup. Remove cloves before serving, but leave vanilla bean, if using, for a pretty presentation. Serve apples warm or cold.

Shabbat

Appetizers and Soups
176

Mock Liver with Cashews

Lentil Liver

Shabbat Salad

Broccoli and Carrot Salad with
Water Chestnuts

Light Eggplant Caponata

Alphabet Chicken Soup

Chicken Soup with Noodles,
Leeks, and Winter Squash

Meaty Bean Soup with Saffron
and Cilantro

Fish Courses
180

Traditional Gefilte Fish

Sole Salad for Shabbat

Smoked Whitefish and
Couscous Salad

Spicy Moroccan Fish Stew

Sweet and Sour Salmon

Baked Halibut with French
Spinach-Watercress Sauce

Poultry Main Courses
184

Friday Night Chicken

Chicken Baked with Tzimmes
and Kneidel

Savory Chicken with Olives

Pineapple Roast Chicken

Chicken with Fig, Bulgur
Wheat, and Toasted Almond
Stuffing

Fig, Bulgur Wheat, and Toasted
Almond Stuffing

Cornish Hens with Orzo
and Apricot Stuffing

Orzo Stuffing with Apricot
and Cashews

Shabbat, the Sabbath, is the weekly holiday, taking place from sundown on Friday to nightfall on Saturday. It is a day of rest and no cooking is permitted. Shabbat is a festive day, for relaxing, enjoying good food, and visiting friends.

Shabbat is the high point of the week on the Jewish calendar. People save the best foods and new clothes for Shabbat. Preparation begins on Wednesday or Thursday, when shopping is done for the holiday. Many people also do preliminary food preparation such as baking cakes.

Because no cooking or turning on the stove is permitted after sunset on Friday and during Saturday, Jewish cooks throughout the ages have created special dishes for Shabbat. Foremost among them is a category of dishes called *cholent* in Yiddish or *hamin* in Hebrew. It is basically a casserole of meat, usually combined with beans, potatoes, or both, that is put in the oven before sunset on Friday, cooks in low heat overnight, and is served for lunch on Saturday. Cooks from the different Jewish communities prepare their own versions of this dish and it is the standard Shabbat main course in many homes. It is so popular that it also appears on the tables of people who do not observe the Shabbat rules.

Other hot foods for Shabbat are either kept warm or refrigerated and reheated, depending on the family's custom. Even if the food is reheated, the stove is not turned on during Sabbath; the food is set on a hot plate or in a low oven that was turned on before the holiday.

Meals for Shabbat are more festive than during the rest of the week, calling for the best dishes and flatware. The table is covered with a decorative tablecloth and adorned with fresh flowers and the Shabbat candles. Challah is the bread for Shabbat and is covered with a special cloth called a challah cover.

The two main Shabbat meals take place on Friday evening and on Saturday at midday. Appetizers are usually foods that are best served cold, such as marinated vegetables, chopped liver, or a cold fish dish. Roast chicken is a favorite main course, especially for the Friday night dinner. It is served with rice pilaf in Sephardic homes, noodle kugel in Ashkenazic ones, or with roasted potatoes in either. When I was growing up, my mother always baked a cake for Shabbat dessert, and often more than one so we could have a choice. Many people also indulge in cakes or pastries for Shabbat breakfast.

Late in the morning on Shabbat, there is often a light meal in the synagogue after services called a *kiddush*. This Hebrew word means a blessing over wine but its meaning is expanded to include snacks or a light meal served at the same time. Often there is herring, small gefilte fish balls, crackers, and honey cake. When I was growing up, the spread was a bit more substantial if someone was having a bar mitzvah—the celebration of a boy's passage into adulthood—including bagels, lox, cream cheese, tuna salads, molded fruit salads, and sheet cakes.

My husband's family attended a Sephardic synagogue in Israel and for the kiddush they might have savory phyllo pastries called *bourekas* if there was a bar mitzvah in a Bulgarian or a Turkish family. In Jerusalem the tradition is to serve small pieces of warm Jerusalem Kugel (page 479).

Mock Liver With Cashews

Makes 8 to 10 servings

Traditional chopped liver is a popular opening for many Shabbat dinners but if the meal is bountiful, I often opt for a meatless starter. (For more chopped liver recipes see the "Appetizer" chapter, pages 204–234.)

I got the idea for this dish from Aviva Mandl of Jewish Food Online. She makes her vegetarian chopped liver with fresh green beans and enriches it with cashews. For this rich version of mock liver, I like to combine toasted cashews with other nuts and to add a few cashews for garnish.

3/4 pound green beans, ends removed, halved

3 to 4 tablespoons vegetable oil

2 large onions, chopped

One 15-ounce can peas, drained

1/4 cup walnuts, toasted or raw

1/4 cup pecans, toasted or raw

1/3 cup toasted cashews plus 15 to 20 more for garnish

1 or 2 large hard boiled eggs, chopped

Salt and freshly ground pepper, to taste

Green leaf lettuce leaves

Cherry tomatoes or wedges of ripe tomatoes

1. Cook green beans in a large pan of boiling salted water about 10 minutes or until very tender. (They should be more tender than usual so you can chop them easily.) Rinse beans with cold water and drain well.

2. Heat 3 tablespoons oil in a large, heavy skillet, add onions, and sauté over medium heat, stirring often, for 10 minutes or until golden brown.

3. Chop green beans in a food processor. Then add peas, walnuts, pecans, 1/3 cup cashews, and sautéed onions with their oil. Process until smooth. If you would like the pâté to be more moist, add a little more oil and process until blended. Transfer to a bowl. Lightly stir in chopped hard boiled eggs. Season with salt and pepper.

4. To serve, line a platter with lettuce leaves. Mound the mock liver in the center. Arrange tomatoes on the lettuce. Garnish the mock liver with toasted cashews.

Lentil Liver

Makes 6 to 8 servings **M** or **P**

Lentils, the ingredient in the biblical pottage for which Esau sold his birthright to his brother Jacob, are still popular today in the land of the Bible. One tasty, creative way to use them is in this spread. It is inspired by a recipe I received from Nechama Alpert of Haifa, a reader of my Jerusalem Post *food column. Her family and friends feel this easy-to-make, health-ful pâté tastes like real chopped liver. She uses only 1 teaspoon vegetable oil and a full cup of walnuts and makes her stock from bouillon cubes or powder. I increased the oil a bit to make the onions easier to sauté. Usually I have a jar of vegetable cooking liquid in my refrigerator and I use this broth as vegetable stock.*

1 cup lentils, picked through, rinsed, and drained

2 cups vegetable or chicken stock

1 tablespoon vegetable oil

1 large onion, chopped

3/4 cup walnuts

Salt and freshly ground pepper, to taste

1. Combine lentils and stock in a medium saucepan. Cover and cook about 30 minutes or until tender; during cooking add a little hot water if necessary so pan will not become dry, but for best flavor do not add too much so lentils don't become soupy. When lentils are tender, drain off excess liquid.

2. Heat oil in a heavy nonstick skillet. Add onion and sauté over medium-low heat about 5 minutes or until translucent. If pan becomes too dry, add 1 or 2 table-spoons water so onions don't burn.

3. Puree lentils, onion, and walnuts in a food proces-sor until desired consistency, either smooth or slightly chunky. Season with salt and pepper. Refrigerate 2 or 3 hours before serving.

Shabbat Salad

Makes 4 servings

During the week most of our salads are Israeli salads or green salads. This festive, colorful salad combines the best of both. Serve it in a glass bowl to show it off to its best advantage.

1¹/₂ to 2 cups strips of romaine lettuce

1 medium cucumber, peeled and diced

¹/₂ red bell pepper, diced

8 small very white fresh mushrooms, quartered

¹/₂ cup finely shredded red cabbage (optional)

2 medium or large tomatoes, diced

1 green onion, white and green parts, chopped

1 to 2 tablespoons extra-virgin olive oil

1 to 2 tablespoons strained fresh lemon juice

Salt and freshly ground pepper, to taste

Combine lettuce, cucumber, bell pepper, mushrooms, and cabbage, if using, in a bowl and mix. Add tomato and onion and mix gently. A short time before serving, add olive oil, lemon juice, salt, and pepper. Mix gently but thoroughly.

Broccoli and Carrot Salad with Water Chestnuts

Makes 8 servings

It's not easy to serve broccoli at its bright-green best on Shabbat because the vegetable tends to lose its vivid color if cooked ahead and reheated. Rinsing it with cold water immediately after cooking and serving it cold helps to keep its bright green color. This recipe for a colorful salad with a lively fresh ginger dressing is a tasty solution. Keep the cooked broccoli in a separate container and add it to the salad just before serving; otherwise the vinegar in the dressing can discolor the broccoli.

2 large carrots, cut into ¹/₄-inch diagonal slices

8 cups medium broccoli florets

2 teaspoons finely grated peeled fresh ginger

3 to 4 tablespoons soy sauce

¹/₄ cup rice vinegar

2 teaspoons sugar

3 tablespoons water

Hot sauce to taste

3 to 4 tablespoons vegetable oil

Salt, to taste

One 8-ounce can whole water chestnuts, drained and quartered

1. Cook carrots in a large saucepan of water to cover. Bring to a boil and simmer about 4 minutes or until crisp-tender. Remove with a slotted spoon and drain well.

2. Bring a large saucepan of water to boil. Add salt and broccoli. Boil uncovered over high heat 3 to 5 minutes or until broccoli is crisp-tender. Drain in a colander and immediately rinse under cold water until completely cold.

3. In a small bowl, mix grated ginger, 3 tablespoons soy sauce, vinegar, sugar, water, hot sauce, and 3 tablespoons oil. Whisk to blend. Adjust seasoning; add more soy sauce, hot sauce, or oil if you like.

4. Combine water chestnuts in a bowl with carrot slices. Add about half the dressing and toss lightly. If not serving immediately, refrigerate broccoli, salad, and reserved dressing separately.

5. A short time before serving, bring salad to room temperature, then add broccoli and remaining dressing to salad. Toss lightly and serve.

Light Eggplant Caponata

Makes 6 servings

A favorite of Italian Jews, this colorful, tangy salad is perfect as a Shabbat appetizer. It uses readily available ingredients, most of which are probably in your pantry. Make up a batch during a cool time of the day and have it on hand for a festive summer appetizer or sandwich. Caponata keeps for 4 or 5 days in the refrigerator.

In its simplest version, caponata is made of eggplant cooked in tomato sauce accented with onions, celery, wine vinegar, a touch of sugar, and capers. If you like, add 2 tablespoons raisins at the same time as the pine nuts that enhance this rendition.

Usually caponata contains a large amount of oil. This version is quite low in fat but if you prefer a richer caponata, use 4 or 5 tablespoons olive oil.

2 to 3 tablespoons olive oil

1 medium onion, halved and thinly sliced

2 ribs celery, thinly sliced

1 1/2 pounds eggplant, preferably small Italian or Japanese, unpeeled and cut into 1/4-inch dice

Salt and freshly ground pepper, to taste

One 8-ounce can tomato sauce

One 14 1/2-ounce can diced tomatoes, drained

1 to 2 tablespoons red wine vinegar

1 to 2 teaspoons sugar

1/3 to 1/2 cup pitted green olives, halved

2 tablespoons capers, rinsed

1 to 2 tablespoons pine nuts

Heat oil in a large, heavy nonstick skillet or sauté pan. Add onion and celery and sauté over medium heat 5 minutes. Add eggplant, salt, and pepper and sauté over medium-high heat, stirring, for 2 minutes. Add tomato sauce and tomatoes and bring to a simmer. Cover and cook over medium-low heat 10 minutes. Add vinegar, 1 teaspoon sugar, olives, capers, and pine nuts. Cover and simmer over low heat, stirring often, 10 minutes or until eggplant is tender. Adjust seasoning and add remaining sugar if needed. Serve cold or at room temperature.

Alphabet Chicken Soup

Makes about 6 servings

Whenever I see packages of alphabet noodles, they bring back fond memories of Shabbat from my childhood. My mother often made chicken soup with alphabet noodles to encourage us to eat soup. Naturally, my brother and I enjoyed finding the letters of our names in the soup. Sometimes we even had Hebrew alphabet noodles.

Recently I bought some alphabet noodles that came in soup mix with green and yellow split peas and barley. This combination is also attractive and tasty in chicken soup.

2 1/2 pounds chicken wings or legs

1 large onion, peeled

3 large carrots, cut into thick slices

3 ribs celery, with leafy tops

1 bay leaf

Salt and freshly ground pepper, to taste

8 to 10 cups water

1 1/2 cups alphabet noodles

2 tablespoons chopped fresh parsley (optional)

1. Put chicken in a large casserole or pot. Add onion, carrots, celery, bay leaf, salt, and pepper. Cover ingredients with water. Bring to a boil. Skim foam from surface. Cover and cook over low heat 1 1/2 hours or until chicken and vegetables are tender.

2. Cook noodles in a large pan of boiling salted water about 7 minutes or until just tender. Drain well. Reserve in a bowl.

3. Discard onion, celery, and bay leaf. Thoroughly skim off fat. If preparing soup ahead, refrigerate, then skim fat. Reserve chicken for other uses; or remove meat from bones, shred enough meat to obtain about 1 cup, and return it to soup.

4. Reheat soup before serving. Add noodles and parsley, if using. Adjust seasoning. Serve hot.

Chicken Soup with Noodles, Leeks, and Winter Squash

Makes about 6 servings (M)

When I lived in Israel, I learned that many cooks use large leeks to flavor their chicken soup. Often they add a piece of orange winter squash to their soup as well. These were new ideas to me, as I grew up with chicken soup flavored with onion, carrot, and celery. I now really enjoy the delicate tastes they contribute to the soup.

2 large leeks, split lengthwise and rinsed thoroughly

2¹/₂ pounds chicken wings or legs

1 large onion, peeled

1 parsley root or parsnip (optional)

1 bay leaf

Salt and freshly ground pepper, to taste

¹/₂ teaspoon ground cumin

8 to 10 cups water

2 medium carrots, cut into 1-inch slices

One ³/₄-pound piece winter squash, peeled and diced

1¹/₂ cups very fine noodles (soup noodles)

2 tablespoons chopped fresh Italian parsley (optional)

1. Leave 1 leek as is; slice second leek and reserve. Put chicken in a large casserole or pot. Add onion, parsley root if using, whole leek, bay leaf, salt, pepper, and cumin. Cover ingredients with water. Bring to a boil. Skim foam from surface. Cover and cook over low heat 1 hour. Discard onion, parsley root, and whole leek. Add carrots, sliced leek, and squash. Bring to a simmer, cover and cook 30 minutes or until chicken and vegetables are tender.

2. Cook noodles in a large pot of boiling salted water about 7 minutes or until just tender. Drain well. Reserve in a bowl.

3. Discard bay leaf. Thoroughly skim off fat. If preparing soup ahead, refrigerate, then skim fat. Reserve chicken for other uses, or remove meat from bones and return to soup.

4. Reheat soup before serving. Adjust seasoning. Serve soup with carrot and leek slices and squash pieces. Add noodles and parsley, if using, to each bowl of hot soup.

Meaty Bean Soup with Saffron and Cilantro

Makes 6 to 8 servings (M)

Perfect for winter, this meaty soup in the Sephardic style is thick and satisfying. For a festive touch, some cooks add eggs in their shells to the soup during the last hour of simmering; the shelled eggs are served on top of each portion of soup.

1 pound dried white beans (about 2¹/₂ cups), sorted

1 tablespoon vegetable oil

2 large onions, diced

1¹/₂ pounds beef with bones, such as beef shank

3 large cloves garlic, chopped

1 teaspoon paprika

¹/₄ teaspoon saffron

¹/₂ cup chopped fresh cilantro

6 to 8 cups water

One 14¹/₂-ounce can diced tomatoes, with their juice

4 large eggs in shells, rinsed (optional)

Salt, to taste

Cayenne pepper, to taste

1. Generously cover beans with cold water in a large bowl and soak overnight. Or, for a quicker method, cover beans with 2 quarts water in a large saucepan, bring to a boil, and boil 2 minutes; cover and let stand off heat 1 hour.

2. Rinse beans and drain. Heat oil in large saucepan over medium heat, add onions and sauté about 10 minutes. Add beef, beans, garlic, paprika, saffron, ¹/₄ cup cilantro, and 6 cups water and bring to a boil. Cover and cook over low heat 1 hour. Stir tomatoes into soup and gently add eggs, if using. Cover and cook, adding hot water if soup becomes too thick, 1 hour more or until meat is very tender.

3. Skim excess fat from soup. (If preparing soup ahead, refrigerate, then skim off fat.) Season with salt and cayenne. Remove beef. Dice any meat, discarding bones, and add meat to soup along with 2 tablespoons cilantro.

4. Shell eggs and halve them lengthwise. Serve soup hot, topped with egg halves and sprinkled with remaining cilantro.

Fish Courses

Traditional Gefilte Fish

Makes about 12 servings

The term "gefilte" fish means "filled" fish in Yiddish. Originally a ground fish mixture was used as a stuffing for whole fish. Today gefilte fish is usually made into balls or oval shapes. It is poached in fish stock made from the heads and bones of the fish.

A mixture of carp, pike, and whitefish is the most common choice for making gefilte fish. Using several fish gives a more complex taste than a single fish. Adding carp also helps to jell the cooking liquid, and this aspic (savory jelled sauce) is prized in some families. Some cooks use cod, haddock, sea bass, or even salmon. In Israel carp is often mixed with mullet or hake.

When I was growing up, my mother filleted the fish, ground it in a grinder, and then chopped it in a wooden chopping bowl. It was a lot of work but she still made it quite often. Now making gefilte fish is easy. You can have the fish filleted at the store; just be sure to ask for the head and bones. Some stores will even grind the fish for you, or you can grind it in a food processor.

There are different styles of seasoning gefilte fish. Many people add sugar, and you can also find gefilte fish flavored with sugar in jars. My mother never adds sugar. I still prefer gefilte fish that is not too sweet, but this version does taste good with a little sugar added to the stock and to the fish mixture.

Serve gefilte fish the traditional way, accompanied by horseradish prepared with beets. If you like, prepare your own horseradish (page 339).

2 pounds whitefish (including bones and head), filleted, skin removed, bones and head reserved

2 pounds carp (including bones and head), filleted, skin removed, bones and head reserved

2 pounds pike (including bones and head), filleted, skin removed, bones and head reserved

Fish Stock for Gefilte Fish (page 601)

3 large eggs

1/4 cup cold water

2 to 3 tablespoons matzo meal

2 large onions, finely chopped

2 1/2 teaspoons salt

3/4 teaspoon ground pepper, preferably white

1 teaspoon sugar (optional)

2 large carrots, sliced

1. Use heads and bones of fish to make fish stock. If skin of fish has not been removed at the store, remove it: Set a fillet on a board, skin side down. Slip blade of a flexible knife between flesh and skin at tail end. Remove skin, sliding knife away from you with one hand and pulling off skin with other. Run your fingers over fish fillets and remove any small bones remaining in flesh. Cut fish into large pieces.

2. Grind fish in batches in a food processor until very fine. Transfer to a large bowl. Add eggs, water, 2 tablespoons matzo meal, onion, salt, pepper, and 1/4 teaspoon sugar, if using. Mix very well. If mixture is too soft to be formed into balls, add another tablespoon matzo meal. Mix well.

3. Add carrots and remaining 3/4 teaspoon sugar, if using, to strained stock and bring to a simmer. If you would like to taste the fish mixture for seasoning, shape a teaspoonful of it into a small ball and poach it for 5 minutes in the stock; remove it with a slotted spoon and taste it. Add more salt and pepper to the mixture if you like. Mix well.

4. With moistened hands, shape fish mixture into ovals or balls, using 1/4 to 1/3 cup mixture for each one. Carefully drop fish balls into simmering stock. If necessary, add enough hot water to barely cover them, pouring it carefully near edge of pan, not over fish. Return to a simmer, cover, and simmer over low heat about 1 hour. Let gefilte fish cool in stock. Refrigerate fish and carrots in stock for at least 4 hours before serving.

5. Serve each fish ball topped with a carrot slice. If you like, serve a little of the jelled stock on the side.

Sole Salad for Shabbat

Makes 4 main-course or
6 to 8 first-course servings

Serve this delicate salad of steamed sole with a lemon-mint vinaigrette as a first course. For Shabbat lunch in the summertime, it makes a refreshing main course. If you're serving it for other occasions, try serving the sole warm; it makes a pleasant contrast with the cool vegetables.

Lemon-Mint Vinaigrette (page 594)

1^1/4 to 1^1/2 pounds sole fillets

Salt and freshly ground pepper, to taste

2 tablespoons chopped fresh mint

6 cups of bite-size pieces green or red-tipped leaf lettuce or mixed baby lettuces, rinsed and dried thoroughly

1 red bell pepper, cored and cut into thin strips

1 yellow bell pepper, cored and cut into thin strips

2 tablespoons chopped fresh Italian parsley

^{1}/2 cup pitted black olives

1 lemon, halved and thinly sliced

1. Prepare vinaigrette. Then, bring at least 1 inch of water to a boil in a steamer. Boiling water should not reach holes in top part of steamer.

2. Run your fingers over sole fillets to check for bones; pull out any bones using tweezers or a sharp paring knife.

3. Sprinkle sole on both sides with salt and pepper. Sprinkle with mint, using a total of about ^{1}/2 tablespoon. Fold each fillet in half. Sprinkle top with remaining ^{1}/2 tablespoon mint. Set sole on top portion of a steamer over boiling water, cover, and cook over high heat about 2 minutes or until fillets become opaque. Transfer them to a plate.

4. Mix lettuce with red and yellow peppers, mint, and parsley in a bowl. Whisk dressing. Add about ^{1}/4 cup dressing to salad and toss to combine well. Add more dressing if needed. Adjust seasoning.

5. To serve, transfer salad to a platter. Arrange sole fillets on top. Whisk dressing again and spoon a little dressing over sole. Garnish with olives. Arrange lemon slices around outer edge of platter. Serve cold.

Smoked Whitefish and Couscous Salad

Makes 4 servings

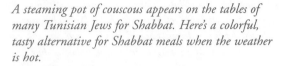

A steaming pot of couscous appears on the tables of many Tunisian Jews for Shabbat. Here's a colorful, tasty alternative for Shabbat meals when the weather is hot.

^{1}/4 cup slivered almonds

1 cup quick-cooking couscous

3 tablespoons strained fresh lemon juice

2 to 3 tablespoons vegetable oil

Salt (optional) and freshly ground pepper, to taste

^{1}/2 red onion, chopped fine

1 small red bell pepper, diced

^{1}/2 pound smoked whitefish, skinned and boned

^{1}/3 long (hothouse) cucumber, large seeds removed, diced

^{1}/4 cup chopped fresh Italian parsley

1. Preheat toaster oven or oven to 350°F. Toast almonds in oven about 3 minutes or until lightly browned. Transfer to a plate.

2. Meanwhile, bring 1^1/4 cups water to a boil in a medium saucepan. Stir in couscous and return to boil. Remove from heat, immediately cover pan tightly, and let stand for 5 minutes. Transfer couscous to a bowl. Fluff with fork. Let cool.

3. Whisk lemon juice with 2 tablespoons oil in a small bowl. Add pepper to taste. Drizzle dressing over couscous and mix gently with a fork. Add red onion, bell pepper, whitefish, cucumber, and parsley. Toss salad gently. Season with pepper; add salt if needed. If you like, add another tablespoon oil. Serve sprinkled with almonds.

Spicy Moroccan Fish Stew

Makes 4 main course or 6 appetizer servings

There are many versions of this tasty Moroccan-Jewish Shabbat specialty. Most combine tomatoes with hot pepper in some form, either as fresh or dried chiles or as hot red pepper flakes. Cumin, garlic, and parsley usually appear, often with onions and cilantro. For a more substantial version, some cooks add potatoes. The dish can be made with whole fish, fish steaks, or fillets.

1 teaspoon ground cumin

8 large cloves garlic, minced

1/2 cup chopped fresh Italian parsley

Salt and freshly ground pepper, to taste

Cayenne pepper, to taste (optional)

2 pounds halibut, cod, or sea bass steaks or fillets,
    1-inch thick

1 onion, halved and thinly sliced

3 jalapeño peppers, seeded and chopped, or more if you like
    (see Note)

1 1/2 pounds ripe plum tomatoes, thinly sliced

3 to 4 tablespoons extra-virgin olive oil

1. Combine cumin, half the garlic, and half the parsley in a small bowl. Add salt, pepper, and a pinch of cayenne, if using. Put fish on a plate. Spread spice mixture over the fish on both sides. Let stand to marinate while preparing vegetables.

2. Put onion and jalapeño peppers in a large sauté pan. Top with a layer of tomatoes. Sprinkle with salt and pepper. Top with fish in one layer and add any spice mixture remaining on the plate. Top fish with any remaining tomato slices. Pour oil evenly over top. Sprinkle with remaining garlic and 2 tablespoons of remaining parsley.

3. Bring liquid barely to a simmer. Cover and cook over low heat about 15 minutes or until fish can be easily flaked with a fork.

4. If you would like sauce to be thicker, remove fish and vegetables with a slotted spatula. Boil liquid to reduce it until slightly thickened. Adjust seasoning. Spoon sauce over fish. Serve fish hot or cold, sprinkled with remaining parsley.

Note: Wear rubber gloves when handling hot peppers.

Sweet and Sour Salmon

Makes 8 first-course or 4 main-course servings

Salmon in a sweet-and-sour sauce has become a favorite on the American Jewish table. Originally prepared with carp by Jews in Eastern Europe, it is now preferred by many in this newer version. It's light, colorful, and easy to make.

3 pounds salmon steaks, 1 inch thick

Salt and freshly ground pepper, to taste

2 large onions, sliced

2 large carrots, sliced into rounds

2 bay leaves

1 sprig fresh thyme or 1/2 teaspoon dried thyme

1 1/2 cups dry white wine

3 cups water

3 sprigs fresh tarragon

3 large shallots, chopped

3 tablespoons white wine vinegar

1 or 2 tablespoons sugar

1 teaspoon ground ginger

1/4 cup golden raisins

1/4 cup currants

3 tablespoons chopped fresh tarragon (from above sprigs)

6 tablespoons chopped fresh parsley

1/4 cup toasted diced pecans

1. Sprinkle salmon lightly with salt and pepper and set aside.

2. Combine onions, carrots, bay leaves, thyme, salt, pepper, wine, and water in a shallow stew pan in which fish can fit in a single layer. Remove leaves from tarragon stems and reserve for chopping; add stems to pan. Bring to a boil. Cover and simmer 20 minutes.

3. Add salmon to pan and return to a simmer. Cover and cook over low heat 10 to 12 minutes or until fish is tender; check near bone—flesh should have turned a lighter shade of pink. Transfer salmon carefully to a deep serving dish.

4. Boil cooking liquid about 7 minutes or until it is reduced to 3 1/2 cups. Strain, reserving a few carrot slices for garnish, and return strained liquid to pan. Add shallots, vinegar, sugar, and ginger. Simmer, stirring, for 1 minute. Add raisins and currants and simmer 1 minute. Add 2 tablespoons tarragon and 5 tablespoons parsley. Adjust seasoning. Pour sauce over fish.

5. Serve fish cold. When serving, spoon a little of the liquid over fish, with the raisins and currants. Sprinkle with remaining tarragon, parsley, and with the pecans. Garnish with a few carrot slices.

Baked Halibut with French Spinach-Watercress Sauce

Makes about 8 first-course or
5 or 6 main-course servings

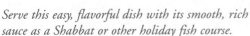

Serve this easy, flavorful dish with its smooth, rich sauce as a Shabbat or other holiday fish course.

2 pounds halibut steaks or fillets, about 1-inch thick

1 tablespoon olive oil or vegetable oil

Salt and freshly ground pepper, to taste

$1/2$ teaspoon dried thyme

2 tablespoons water

2 cups spinach leaves, stems removed and leaves rinsed thoroughly

$1/3$ cup watercress leaves

$1/3$ cup small sprigs fresh Italian parsley

1 cup mayonnaise

$1/2$ teaspoon Dijon mustard (optional)

2 tablespoons strained fresh lemon juice, or to taste

watercress sprigs for garnish

1. Preheat oven to 400°F. Lightly oil a baking dish in which fish fits easily in one layer. Put fish in dish and sprinkle it with oil, salt, pepper, and thyme. Add the water to dish. Cover lightly with foil and bake 10 to 12 minutes or until thickest part of fish becomes opaque inside; check with a sharp knife.

2. Add spinach and watercress to a medium saucepan of boiling water. Return to a boil. Immediately drain in a colander. Rinse under cold running water and drain well. Squeeze to remove excess liquid.

3. Puree spinach, watercress, and parsley in a food processor until smooth. If necessary, add 2 to 3 tablespoons mayonnaise to help make a smoother mixture.

4. Add remaining mayonnaise and process until smooth. Add salt and pepper if needed. Transfer to a bowl. Beat in mustard, if using. Gradually beat in lemon juice. If sauce is too thick, beat in 1 or 2 tablespoons warm water, 1 teaspoon at a time, until sauce is just thin enough to be poured. Season with salt and pepper.

5. Serve fish hot or cold, garnished with watercress sprigs. Put a small dollop of sauce on each portion, or serve sauce separately.

❧ Poultry Main Courses

Friday Night Chicken

Makes 6 servings

Golden brown baked chicken is the most popular main course in our family for our Friday night dinner. This is the way my sisters-in-law and I usually prepare it. Often we use chicken pieces rather than roasting a whole chicken so there's no last minute carving. Flavored with plenty of spice but not hot, this chicken appeals to everyone, and a spoonful of the savory roasting juices makes a delicious addition to rice or potatoes.

1 tablespoon ground cumin

1 teaspoon paprika

1 teaspoon ground turmeric

$^1/_2$ teaspoon freshly ground pepper

$^1/_4$ teaspoon salt (optional)

3 to 3$^1/_2$ pounds chicken pieces

1 pound onions, halved and cut into thick slices

1. Preheat oven to 400°F. Mix together cumin, paprika, turmeric, pepper, and salt, if using. Rub mixture into chicken. Lightly oil a heavy roasting pan and add onions. Top with chicken. Bake uncovered 30 minutes.

2. Reduce heat to 375°F. Turn chicken pieces over with tongs. Bake uncovered 10 minutes to brown second side. Cover with foil and bake 10 to 20 minutes longer or until chicken is tender. Cut to check; juices should no longer be pink when thickest part of thigh is pierced with a sharp knife.

Chicken Baked With Tzimmes And Kneidel

Makes 4 servings

My mother loves to make tzimmes (or stew) with matzo balls and this beautiful new main course is her idea. She devised it during a holiday visit to California a few years ago, when we were cooking Shabbat dinner together shortly before Hanukkah.

The deep brown roasted chicken pieces bake with sweet potatoes, carrots, and prunes. Their slightly sweet sauce complements the chicken wonderfully and gains a rich taste from it during the baking. The kneidel, or matzo balls, turn golden and absorb flavor from the sauce.

The dish is a complete entree in itself but we also like to serve it with briefly cooked broccoli. If you wish to prepare it ahead, reheat it, covered with foil, at 300°F for about 30 minutes.

1$^1/_4$ pounds orange-fleshed sweet potatoes, peeled, halved, and sliced $^1/_2$-inch thick

$^3/_4$ pound carrots, sliced $^1/_2$-inch thick

4 ounces pitted prunes

5 cups water

2 tablespoons brown sugar

1 large egg, beaten

$^1/_3$ cup matzo meal

$^1/_8$ teaspoon baking powder

Salt and freshly ground pepper, to taste

2 to 2$^1/_2$ pounds chicken leg pieces (drumstick with thigh attached), skinned

$^1/_2$ teaspoon onion powder

$^1/_2$ teaspoon paprika

1. Combine sweet potatoes, carrots, prunes, water, and brown sugar in a medium saucepan. Bring to a simmer. Simmer over low heat 5 minutes.

2. Meanwhile make kneidel mixture: Put the egg in a medium bowl. Stir in matzo meal, baking powder, salt, and pepper. Mixture should be just firm enough to hold together in roughly shaped balls. If mixture is too firm, gradually beat in 1 or 2 tablespoons liquid from the simmering tzimmes.

3. Turn heat very low under tzimmes so liquid no longer bubbles.

4. Keep a glass of water handy and wet your hands. Take about 2 teaspoons kneidel mixture and with your wet hands, shape it very gently into a soft ball, rolling it lightly from one hand to the other. Put ball in tzimmes. Continue making balls, wetting hands before shaping each one.

5. Bring tzimmes to a simmer. Cover and simmer over low heat 15 minutes. Turn matzo balls over. Simmer 5 to 10 more minutes or until vegetables and prunes are tender.

6. Preheat oven to 350°F. Put chicken in a 13-inch square baking pan. Sprinkle with onion powder and paprika. Roast 45 minutes.

7. Reserve 1 cup of liquid from sweet potato mixture. Spoon mixture with all of remaining liquid around chicken. Baste chicken. Bake uncovered 20 minutes. Add reserved tzimmes liquid and bake 10 minutes more. If making ahead, cover to keep it warm. Serve hot.

Savory Chicken with Olives

Makes 4 servings

This delicious dish appears as the star of the Friday night dinner of a Moroccan friend of mine who now lives in Los Angeles. Her mother cooks the lavish meal and invites her children and grandchildren, and a few friends as well.

Everyone loves the chicken in its slightly spicy tomato sauce made a bit tangy by the green olives. My friend serves it with a festive version of rice pilaf topped with pecans and raisins. You can make it like

Rice Pilaf with Golden Raisins and Pistachios (page 77) but substitute toasted pecans for the pistachios and use dark raisins.

2 tablespoons olive oil

1 large onion, chopped

2¹/₂ pounds chicken pieces, patted dry

Salt and freshly ground pepper, to taste

6 large cloves garlic, minced

1 jalapeño pepper, chopped

¹/₄ cup chopped fresh cilantro or Italian parsley

2 pounds ripe tomatoes, peeled, seeded, and chopped, or
    two 28-ounce cans tomatoes, drained and chopped

¹/₄ teaspoon hot red pepper flakes

¹/₂ teaspoon ground cumin

¹/₂ cup water

³/₄ cup pitted green olives

Several drops strained fresh lemon juice (optional)

1. Heat oil in a large stew pan. Add onion and sauté over medium heat about 5 minutes or until softened. Add chicken pieces, sprinkle with pepper, and sauté with onion, turning chicken pieces often, about 5 minutes or until onion begins to brown.

2. Add garlic, jalapeño pepper, and half the cilantro to pan and sauté a few seconds. Stir in tomatoes, pepper flakes, cumin, and water. Bring to a boil. Cover and simmer over low heat 45 to 50 minutes or until chicken is tender. Skim fat from sauce.

3. Add olives and 1 tablespoon cilantro to sauce and cook over low heat for 5 minutes. Adjust seasoning; add lemon juice, if using. Serve hot, sprinkled with remaining cilantro.

Pineapple Roast Chicken

Makes 4 servings

Chicken with pineapple is a popular combination on many Jewish tables. It probably started with the well-known Jewish love for Chinese food, which seems to have begun as a New York Jewish custom of going out to Chinese restaurants. Some say the reason is that Jews wanted food that was exotic and a complete change from what they ate at home. The sweet and sour dishes may have also appealed to many who were of Ashkenazic origin who found this taste familiar to dishes in their own cuisine.

With that idea in mind, my sister-in-law Nirit prepares her pineapple chicken with honey and soy sauce.

In other families, the seasonings used are not necessarily Asian. A friend of mine bakes the chicken and pineapple in a savory sauce of onions, garlic, cumin, and tomato.

For this easy version, the chicken is seasoned simply with curry and roasted. After being carved, it's baked briefly with fresh pineapple slices sautéed with gently spiced pears. It's convenient for Shabbat because you can assemble the chicken and fruit in the baking dish and heat it in the oven when you need it. Serve it with a colorful accompaniment, such as Glazed Carrots (page 199), Carrot Puree (page 161) or Sweet Potato Puree (page 200).

3¹/2- to 4-pound chicken

1 tablespoon curry powder

Salt (optional) and freshly ground pepper, to taste

2 to 3 tablespoons vegetable oil

2 large pears, ripe but firm, peeled, halved, cored, and
    quartered

¹/2 teaspoon ground allspice

¹/2 teaspoon ground ginger

8 slices fresh pineapple, cored and halved

1 to 2 tablespoons chopped fresh chervil or parsley

1. Preheat oven to 400°F. Pull out fat from inside chicken. Mix curry powder, pepper, and 1 tablespoon oil in a small bowl. Rub chicken all over with mixture. Set chicken on a rack in a roasting pan. Roast chicken, basting occasionally, about 1 hour or until juices no longer run pink when thickest part of thigh is pierced with a sharp knife. If juices are pink, roast chicken a few more minutes.

2. Meanwhile, heat remaining oil in a large skillet. Add pears, allspice, and ginger and sauté over medium heat about 3 minutes on each side, or until nearly tender. Add pineapple slices and sauté together, turning pineapple once or twice, about 3 more minutes or until fruit is tender. Season lightly with pepper.

3. Transfer chicken to a carving board. Reduce oven temperature to 350°F. Let chicken stand 5 to 10 minutes. Carve chicken into four or eight pieces and put them in a shallow casserole dish. Add spiced fruit. Bake uncovered about 10 minutes or until heated through. (If you're refrigerating chicken before serving it, reheat it, covered, at 300°F for about 40 minutes or until completely hot.)

4. Sprinkle chicken and fruit with chervil before serving.

Chicken With Fig, Bulgur Wheat, and Toasted Almond Stuffing

Makes 4 servings

Middle Eastern favorites—bulgur wheat, almonds, and figs—flavor the stuffing of this chicken. Ground coriander, allspice, and ginger, which are popular in the region, season both the chicken and its stuffing.

If you have extra stuffing, put it in a small oiled baking dish, cover it tightly, and bake it alongside the chicken for 10 to 15 minutes or until heated through.

Serve this festive bird for Shabbat. It's also great for Sukkot, when fresh figs are often available. (You can use some figs as a holiday garnish for the platter of chicken.)

Fig, Bulgur Wheat, and Toasted Almond Stuffing (this page)

1 teaspoon ground coriander

1 teaspoon ground ginger

1/2 teaspoon ground allspice

1/2 teaspoon freshly ground pepper

1/4 teaspoon salt (optional)

One 3 1/2- to 4-pound chicken

1 to 1 1/2 tablespoons vegetable oil

Fresh parsley sprigs

1. Prepare stuffing. Let cool completely before stuffing chicken.

2. Preheat oven to 400°F. Mix coriander, ginger, allspice, pepper, and salt, if using. Rub chicken with about 1 tablespoon oil and sprinkle it evenly with spice mixture. Rub spices into chicken.

3. Spoon enough stuffing into chicken to fill it, without packing it tightly; reserve any extra stuffing in the refrigerator.

4. Set chicken on a rack in a roasting pan and roast about 1 hour or until juices no longer run pink when thickest part of thigh is pierced with a sharp knife. If juices are pink, continue roasting chicken a few more minutes. Transfer chicken to a carving board. Let stand 5 to 10 minutes before serving.

5. Serve chicken and its stuffing on a platter. Garnish with parsley sprigs.

Fig, Bulgur Wheat, and Toasted Almond Stuffing

Makes about 3 1/2 cups, enough for 1 chicken **M** or **P**

This savory stuffing with a touch of sweetness is delicious in chicken but don't limit it to poultry dinners. Use it to stuff acorn squash for a lovely vegetarian entree, or simply serve it on its own as an accompaniment for grilled lamb chops, braised beef, or roasted vegetables.

1/2 cup slivered almonds

2 or 3 tablespoons vegetable oil

1 medium onion, finely chopped

1 cup medium bulgur wheat

2 cups chicken stock, vegetable stock, or water

1 teaspoon ground coriander

1 teaspoon ground ginger

1/2 teaspoon ground allspice

Salt and freshly ground pepper, to taste

1 cup dried small dark figs (Mission figs), stems removed, quartered

1. Preheat oven or toaster oven to 400°F. Toast almonds in a baking dish in oven, stirring occasionally, until lightly browned, about 5 minutes. Transfer to a bowl and let cool.

2. Heat oil in heavy saucepan over high heat. Add onion and sauté over medium heat, stirring often, about 7 minutes or until onion begins to turn golden. Add bulgur and sauté, stirring, 2 minutes. Add stock, coriander, ginger, allspice, salt, and pepper and bring to a boil. Cover and cook over low heat 10 minutes. Add figs without stirring. Cover and cook about 5 more minutes or until water is absorbed. Gently stir in almonds. Adjust seasoning.

3. Let cool before stuffing chicken.

Cornish Hens with Orzo and Apricot Stuffing

Makes 4 servings   **M**

Cornish hens are delicious with a fruit stuffing and make a beautiful holiday entree, whether it's for Rosh Hashanah, Sukkot, or Shabbat. Combining poultry with fruit is traditional in both the Persian and the Moroccan culinary styles.

I like to poach some extra dried apricots in wine and use them to garnish the hens as well. The hens make an impressive presentation when you serve them whole but are easier to eat if you cut them in half.

1 cup dried apricots

1/2 cup dry white wine

1/2 cup water

Orzo Stuffing with Apricots and Cashews (page 189)

4 medium Cornish hens (each about 1 1/4 to 1 1/2 pounds)

1/2 teaspoon freshly ground pepper

1 teaspoon ground ginger

1 teaspoon soy sauce

1 teaspoon vegetable oil

2 tablespoons plus 2 teaspoons honey

1. Combine apricots, wine, and the water in a bowl. Put a small plate on top to keep apricots in liquid. Let them soak while you prepare the other ingredients.

2. Prepare stuffing. Then, preheat oven to 400°F. Discard excess fat from hens. Mix pepper, ginger, soy sauce, oil, and 2 teaspoons honey in a small bowl. Rub hens all over with honey mixture.

3. Spoon 1/3 to 1/2 cup stuffing into each hen, packing it in gently. Reserve remaining stuffing in the refrigerator.

4. Set hens in a roasting pan or shallow baking dish just large enough to contain them. Roast hens, basting occasionally and adding a few tablespoons hot water to pan juices if they brown, for 45 minutes or until drumstick is tender and juices no longer run pink when the thickest part of the drumstick is pierced with a sharp knife. If juices are pink, continue roasting hens for a few more minutes and check again. Stuffing should be hot inside.

5. Gently put apricots and their soaking liquid in a saucepan. Add remaining 2 tablespoons honey and enough water to barely cover fruit. Very gently stir over low heat until honey blends in to liquid. Cover and cook over low heat about 20 minutes or until apricots are tender.

6. Spoon 2 to 3 tablespoons of pan juices into a medium skillet. Add reserved refrigerated stuffing and cook over medium-low heat, stirring gently with a fork, about 5 minutes or until hot. Spoon into a serving dish.

7. To serve hens, add stuffing from hens to serving dish with extra stuffing. Serve hens whole or, if you like, divide them by cutting each in half lengthwise with poultry shears. Garnish with poached apricots.

Orzo Stuffing with Apricots and Cashews

Makes 3½ to 4 cups, enough for
1 chicken or 4 Cornish hens

(M)

A stuffing with fruit and nuts turns an ordinary chicken dinner into a celebration. Use this vibrant melange to stuff Cornish hens or a chicken. I also like it in acorn squash or zucchini, or as a side dish instead of as a stuffing. For meatless meals I make it with vegetable stock instead of chicken stock.

¼ cup vegetable oil

¼ cup chopped green onions

1½ cups orzo or riso (rice-shaped pasta), about 12 ounces

½ cup diced dried apricots

3 cups hot chicken stock

1 teaspoon ground ginger

⅔ cup toasted cashews

⅓ cup chopped fresh parsley

Salt (optional) and freshly ground pepper, to taste

1. Heat oil in a medium saucepan. Add green onions and sauté over medium heat, stirring, 1 minute. Add orzo and cook over low heat, stirring, 3 minutes. Scatter diced apricots on top. Add stock and ginger and bring to a boil. Cover and cook over low heat about 14 minutes or until orzo is just tender.

2. Fluff mixture with a fork to break up any lumps in orzo. Add cashews and parsley and toss mixture to combine. Season with salt, if using, and pepper. Let stuffing cool before spooning into poultry.

Cholents

Cholent with Brisket

Makes about 8 servings

(M)

There are many variations to this hearty Ashkenazic style cholent *(slow-cooking meat stew). Smoked beef or salami are favorites of Hungarian cooks, in addition to the fresh beef, to lend flavor to the beans. Any long-cooking cut of beef is good: Brisket, short ribs, flanken, chuck, or stew meat. If the meat is boneless, many cooks add a few marrow bones or other beef bones for extra richness.*

Dried lima beans or other large white beans are most popular, although many favor a mixture of beans. Potatoes and a cup or two of barley are often included. Some cooks, especially those of Polish or Russian extraction, add kasha (buckwheat groats) instead of barley. If you're adding kasha, use the largest size grain.

Onions are the most popular flavoring and sometimes are sautéed in schmaltz (chicken fat) before being put in the pot. Many cooks add a few garlic cloves also. Spicing is generally simple—salt, pepper, and, in the case of cooks from Hungary, good quality Hungarian paprika. You can use sweet or hot paprika, or a little of each.

More elaborate versions of cholent *include a kneidel, a savory kugel made of challah or flour; a stuffed kishke; or a stuffed chicken or goose neck.*

1 pound dried lima beans, Great Northern beans, or other white beans

2 large onions, cut into large cubes

2 tablespoons vegetable oil or chicken fat (optional)

3 pounds beef brisket

2 teaspoons salt

½ teaspoon freshly ground pepper

1 tablespoon sweet paprika

½ teaspoon hot paprika or cayenne pepper, or to taste (optional)

8 boiling potatoes, peeled and quartered

4 large cloves garlic, coarsely chopped (optional)

1. The night before you will make the cholent, sort through and rinse the beans. Put them in a bowl and cover generously with water. Soak overnight in the refrigerator.

2. Preheat oven to 200°F (or lowest number setting that isn't "keep warm"). If you want to sauté the onions, heat oil or chicken fat in a large, heavy stew pan or Dutch oven. Add onions and sauté over medium-high heat about 5 minutes or until onions begin to turn golden. Remove from heat. Transfer onions to a plate.

3. Trim excess fat from beef. Place beef in stew pan. Season on both sides with salt, pepper, and sweet and hot paprika if using.

4. Drain soaked beans and add to stew pan. Add potatoes, onions, and garlic, if using. Add about 2 quarts water, or enough to cover ingredients by about 2 inches. Bring to a boil. Simmer uncovered over low heat for 20 minutes.

5. Cover tightly and transfer to oven. Bake cholent, without stirring, about 10 hours or overnight.

Hamin for Shabbat, Yemenite Style

Makes about 8 servings

Ⓜ

Hamin *is the Hebrew word for* cholent, *the meat stew that cooks slowly overnight for Shabbat and is made by Jews throughout the world. This version is spiced the way my mother-in-law taught me, with garlic, cumin, and turmeric. The long cooking with the spices gives the beef, beans, and potatoes a wonderful flavor.*

The custom of putting eggs in their shells on top of the hamin *so the eggs become brown and creamy inside is popular among Sephardic Jews. The eggs are absolutely delicious.*

In some homes 1 or 1 1/2 cups of whole wheat berries are added to the hamin. *Either they are mixed with the other ingredients or put in a separate bag or cheesecloth so they stay together and steam in the stew's*

juices. You can find them at natural foods stores and Middle Eastern grocery stores.

The traditional way to cook hamin *is to put it in a low oven or on a heating plate set on low just before sundown on Friday and to leave it until it is served on Saturday for an early lunch. Since sundown's time changes from summer to winter, the stew's cooking time varies also.*

Because of the long cooking time, most cooks start with a generous amount of water to be sure the hamin *doesn't burn. Depending on the pot that is used, more or less water will evaporate. On Shabbat, cooks do not add more water and do not boil the liquid to thicken it. If the stew turns out too soupy, they simply begin with less water the next time.*

2 1/2 pounds beef chuck

2 cups dried medium lima beans or other white beans, picked over and rinsed

8 small boiling potatoes, peeled

2 large onions, cut into thick slices

8 cloves garlic, coarsely chopped

2 teaspoons salt

1/2 teaspoon freshly ground pepper

2 tablespoons ground cumin

4 teaspoons ground turmeric

8 large eggs in shells, rinsed

1. Preheat oven to 200°F (or lowest number setting that isn't "keep warm"). Trim excess fat from beef and cut meat into 2-inch pieces.

2. Combine meat, beans, potatoes, onions, and garlic in a large, heavy stew pan or Dutch oven. Sprinkle with salt, pepper, cumin, and turmeric; mix well. Add 2 quarts water. Bring to a boil. Simmer uncovered for 20 minutes. Remove from heat. Set eggs gently on top and push them slightly into liquid.

3. Cover tightly and bake mixture, without stirring, about 10 hours or overnight. If you wish to cook it faster, bake it at 250°F for 5 hours.

4. Shell and halve eggs. Serve stew from the stew pan or a deep serving dish, garnished with eggs.

Chicken Cholent with Wheat Berries and Chickpeas

Makes 6 to 8 servings

When I first ate chicken cholent, I thought it was a recent development because of the interest in eating lighter food. However, I learned that chicken cholent has been a tradition for many years in some families. Actually, this makes perfect sense. The custom is to save the best food for the Shabbat dinner to make it festive. Since meat was expensive and therefore a rare luxury, it was used when people could get it. Sometimes poultry was available rather than meat and so chicken or goose was used.

This cholent follows the Sephardic fashion in the spicing and use of chickpeas. Some people soak the chickpeas but I find it is not necessary. The dark meat of turkey is also very good when prepared this way.

4 pounds chicken quarters (legs with thighs attached), excess fat removed

1 teaspoon paprika

1 teaspoon ground cumin

1/2 teaspoon ground coriander

1/2 teaspoon ground allspice

1/2 teaspoon freshly ground pepper

3 cups dried chickpeas (garbanzo beans), sorted and rinsed

1 1/2 pounds boiling potatoes, peeled and halved if large

1 cup wheat berries (available at natural foods shops), rinsed

1 large onion, cut into thick slices

8 large cloves garlic, coarsely chopped

1/2 teaspoon salt

1 tablespoon tomato paste

1/4 cup water

6 to 8 large eggs in shells, rinsed

1. Preheat oven to 200°F (or lowest number setting that isn't "keep warm"). Remove chicken skin, if you like. Put chicken in a large stew pan or Dutch oven. Mix paprika, cumin, coriander, allspice, and pepper in a small bowl. Sprinkle spices over chicken on all sides.

2. Add chickpeas and potatoes to casserole. Add wheat berries, onion, and garlic. Sprinkle with salt. Add enough water to cover ingredients by 2 inches. Mix tomato paste with 1/4 cup water until smooth. Add to casserole. Bring to a boil. Cover and cook over very low

heat 30 to 45 minutes. Set eggs gently on top of stew and push them slightly into liquid.

3. Cover tightly and bake mixture, without stirring, overnight. Serve hot.

My Mother's Chicken and Barley Cholent

Makes 6 to 8 servings

My mother has lived in Jerusalem for many years. Like many cooks in Israel, over time her way of making cholent has changed to a hybrid of Ashkenazic and Sephardic styles. Sometimes she adds a touch of cumin to the basic Ashkenazic seasoning mixture of salt, pepper, and paprika. She has also adopted the Sephardic custom of putting eggs on top so they brown "because Israelis like it that way."

To make good cholent, she feels it's important to include both white and brown beans and barley. Generally she makes her cholent with chicken but occasionally she uses beef. Often she browns the onion so it will add more flavor.

When I asked her if you could cook the cholent ahead for 2 or 3 hours or until everything is tender, refrigerate it, and reheat it in a low oven, she answered, "Why would you want to do that? Cholent tastes much better when it cooks very slowly all night."

If you like, remove the skin from the chicken before cooking the cholent. The chicken will stay moist because of all the liquid in the pot. However, leaving the skin on and removing it before serving will give you a richer tasting cholent because some of the fat from the chicken skin will blend in.

4 pounds chicken pieces, excess fat removed

1 to 2 tablespoons vegetable oil

2 large onions, cut into thick slices

1 teaspoon paprika

1/2 teaspoon ground cumin (optional)

1/4 teaspoon freshly ground pepper

3/4 cup navy beans or other white beans, sorted and rinsed

3/4 cup brown beans or red kidney beans, sorted and rinsed

1 cup barley, sorted and rinsed

6 to 8 fairly small boiling potatoes

1/2 teaspoon salt

6 to 8 large eggs in shells, rinsed

1. Preheat oven to 200°F (or lowest number setting that isn't "keep warm"). Remove chicken skin, if you like. Heat oil in a large stew pan or Dutch oven. Add onions and sauté over medium-high heat, stirring often, about 5 minutes until onions begin to brown; they don't need to soften. Remove from heat. Add chicken to stew pan or Dutch oven and sprinkle with paprika, cumin if using, and pepper. Mix well.

2. Add the beans and barley to the casserole. Peel potatoes, if you like. Add to pan and sprinkle with salt. Add enough water to cover ingredients by 2 inches. Bring to a boil. Cover and cook over very low heat 20 to 30 minutes. Set eggs gently on top of stew and push them slightly into liquid.

3. Cover tightly and bake mixture, without stirring, overnight. Serve hot.

Nirit's Garlic-Scented Hamin

Makes 8 to 10 servings

My husband's sister-in-law Nirit Levy adds a whole head of garlic to her pot of hamin, *or* cholent. *The flavor of the garlic slowly infuses into the* hamin. *The garlic cloves become meltingly tender and taste very good. There is no need to peel the garlic; you simply squeeze the skin and the garlic comes out.*

Nirit follows the Sephardic custom of using a mixture of beans and chickpeas in her hamin. *She also adds barley and arranges it and each kind of bean in a separate section of the pot for easy serving. She prefers bone-in skinless chicken thighs and for seasoning, she likes our mother-in-law's mixture of cumin, turmeric, and black pepper.*

An important element in cholent *is the water. There is always a lot of discussion regarding how much to add. You can't let the* cholent *dry but you don't want it to be too soupy either. How much evaporates depends on the shape of the pot used, how tight the lid is, how low the heat is, and even the age of the* beans. *Nirit soaks the beans and barley overnight and cooks them for 5 minutes before putting them in the* cholent *pot. This eliminates much of the guesswork because the beans and barley have already absorbed most of the water they need.*

1 pound dried white beans such as Great Northern
    (about 2¼ cups), sorted and rinsed

1 cup dried chickpeas (garbanzo beans), sorted and rinsed

½ cup pearl barley, sorted and rinsed

2 pounds small boiling potatoes, peeled

1 large onion, quartered

1 large head of garlic

4½ to 5 pounds chicken thighs, skin removed

1 teaspoon salt

½ teaspoon freshly ground pepper

2 tablespoons ground cumin

4 teaspoons ground turmeric

8 to 10 large eggs in shells, rinsed

1. The night before you make the hamin, put the beans, chickpeas, and barley in separate bowls and cover generously with water. Soak them overnight in the refrigerator.

2. The next day, drain white beans. Put them in a saucepan, cover with water, and bring to a boil. Simmer 5 minutes. Drain and rinse. Repeat with chickpeas and barley.

3. Preheat oven to 200°F (or lowest number setting that isn't "keep warm"). Spoon white beans, chickpeas, and barley in separate piles into a very large stew pan or casserole. Add potatoes, onion, garlic, and chicken. Sprinkle with salt, pepper, cumin, and turmeric. Add 2 quarts water or enough to just cover the ingredients. Bring to a boil. Cover and cook over very low heat 20 minutes. Set eggs gently on top of stew and push them slightly into liquid.

4. Cover tightly and bake mixture, without stirring, 10 hours or overnight. Serve hot.

Pareve Cholent

Makes 6 to 8 servings

A meatless or vegetarian cholent *is a popular item for serving at synagogue lunches following the Shabbat morning service. There are several practical reasons for this. Not everyone will eat meat but almost all will be glad to have a taste of* cholent. *Often the kitchen at the synagogue has utensils and equipment for serving dairy or pareve food but not meat.*

When I was discussing vegetarian cholent *with a cook who prepared it every week for a synagogue, he mentioned that he had trouble making it come out brown. I suggested browning the onions and adding soy sauce. He tried it and was pleased with the result.*

Pareve Cholent can be just as tasty as one made with meat. When I was at a festive synagogue lunch after a bar mitzvah, the Iranian caterer prepared three vegetarian cholents: *one made with rice, tomatoes, and whole baby carrots; one with large chunks of sweet potatoes, sautéed onions, and whole-wheat berries; and one with chickpeas, plenty of garlic, and curry-like seasonings. All tasted great and together they were a good demonstration of the many possibilities of vegetarian* cholent.

If you like, you can add textured vegetable protein, which is available dry at natural foods stores. It comes in several sizes; choose one that is in $^1/_2$- *to 1-inch cubes that resemble pieces of meat.*

3 to 4 tablespoons olive oil or vegetable oil

3 large onions, sliced thick

8 large cloves garlic, coarsely chopped

One 28-ounce can diced tomatoes, with their juice

1 teaspoon dried thyme

1 teaspoon dried oregano

$^3/_4$ cup dried white beans such as Great Northern, sorted and rinsed

$^3/_4$ cup dried pinto beans, sorted and rinsed

$^3/_4$ cup dried chickpeas (garbanzo beans), sorted and rinsed

1 cup dry chunks of textured vegetable protein (optional)

4 large carrots, cut into 3-inch pieces

1 pound large mushrooms, halved

1 pound large boiling potatoes, peeled and quartered

3 tablespoons soy sauce

1 teaspoon sugar

Salt and freshly ground pepper, to taste

6 to 8 large eggs in shells (optional), rinsed

1. Preheat oven to 200°F (or lowest number setting that isn't "keep warm"). Heat oil in a large stew pan or Dutch oven. Add onions and sauté over medium-high heat, stirring often, about 7 minutes or until onions begin to turn golden; there is no need for them to soften. Stir in garlic, followed by tomatoes, thyme, and oregano. Add beans, textured vegetable protein if using, carrots, mushrooms, potatoes, soy sauce, sugar, salt, and pepper.

2. Add enough water to cover ingredients by 2 inches. Bring to a boil. Cover and cook over very low heat 20 minutes. Set eggs, if using, on top and push them gently into liquid. Cover and bake in low oven overnight. Serve hot.

Kneidel for Cholent

Makes 8 servings   Ⓜ or Ⓟ

A popular addition to Ashkenazic style cholent *is a* kneidel, *or dumpling. You can add it as small balls like for matzo ball soup, but instead many cooks add it as one large ball and slice it for serving. As it cooks gently all night, it absorbs flavor from the meat and* cholent *seasonings. Matzo meal* kneidel *is the most popular but some cooks use cracker meal or flour instead. Hungarian cooks season it with paprika.*

Add the kneidel *when you bring* cholent *to a simmer.*

2 large eggs
1 tablespoon vegetable oil or chicken fat (optional)
1/2 teaspoon salt
1/2 teaspoon paprika (optional)
Freshly ground pepper, to taste
2/3 cup matzo meal
2 tablespoons water

1. Beat eggs with oil if using, salt, paprika if using, and pepper in a small bowl. Stir in matzo meal. Mixture should be just firm enough to hold together in a roughly shaped ball. If mixture is too firm, gradually beat in 1 or 2 tablespoons water.

2. With wet hands, shape kneidel mixture into a ball and add to cholent.

Moroccan Cholent

Schinah or Dafina

Makes about 8 servings   Ⓜ

Many Moroccan Jews call their rich and filling all-night Shabbat stew schinah, *from the Hebrew word* shchinah, *which means divine presence, which is said to descend on the home that serves this dish for Shabbat.*

There is great variety in the recipes for this dish, from simple to very elaborate. Most are made of beef, chickpeas, potatoes, and hard boiled eggs in a savory sauce. Some also include other beans, lentils, or bulgur wheat. Sweet potatoes are another popular ingredient, instead of or in addition to white potatoes, as in this version from Moroccan-born Dvorah Alon, my neighbor's mother. Some cooks spice their dafina *with*

saffron, turmeric, or cumin, and some accent it with a hint of sweetness, using honey, jam, sugar, dates, dried apricots, or prunes to mellow the flavor of the sauce.

Rice steamed in the meat's juices is a favorite addition. Mrs. Alon sometimes adds lentils or dried black-eyed peas to the rice. Traditionally the rice or rice-bean mixture is tied in a piece of cloth. Today many cooks put it in a roasting bag and pierce a few holes in the bag for the steam.

2 cups dried chickpeas (garbanzo beans) or white beans, sorted and rinsed
2 to 2 1/2 pounds beef chuck, brisket, or short ribs, trimmed of excess fat and cut into large chunks or 2-inch pieces
2 marrow bones (optional)
8 small boiling potatoes, peeled and left whole
1 1/2 pounds small sweet potatoes
3 medium onions, peeled and left whole
1 head garlic, unpeeled and left whole
1 teaspoon paprika (optional)
1 to 2 teaspoons salt, or to taste
1/2 teaspoon freshly ground pepper
1/2 teaspoon ground turmeric or 1/4 teaspoon saffron threads
8 large eggs in shells, rinsed
1 cup rice, rinsed well
2 tablespoons vegetable oil

1. Put chickpeas in a bowl, cover generously with water, and soak overnight. Drain and rinse chickpeas, then put them in a large, heavy stew pan or Dutch oven.

2. Add meat and marrow bones, if using, to pan. Add potatoes, sweet potatoes, onions, and garlic. Sprinkle with paprika if using, 1 1/2 teaspoons salt, 1/4 teaspoon pepper, and half the turmeric or all the saffron; mix well. Add enough water to cover ingredients by 2 inches. Bring to a boil. Simmer uncovered 20 minutes. Remove from heat. Set eggs gently on top and push them slightly into liquid.

3. Put rinsed rice in a piece of cheesecloth or a roasting bag with oil, 1/2 teaspoon salt, 1/4 teaspoon pepper, and 1/4 teaspoon turmeric. Tie cheesecloth or close bag. Pierce a few holes in bag. Set bag in stew pan.

4. Preheat oven to 200°F. Cover casserole tightly. Bake mixture, without stirring, overnight. If you wish to cook it faster, bake it at 250°F for 5 or 6 hours.

5. Serve from stew pan; or, serve potatoes, meat with beans, rice, eggs, and juices in separate serving dishes.

Beef Sausage for Dafina

Makes enough for about 8 servings

Adding a well-seasoned meatloaf-type mixture rolled in a sausage shape is a popular way to enrich dafina *(Moroccan cholent). The ground beef might be mixed with rice or, for a sweet stuffing, with nuts, sugar, and ginger.*

I first learned about it from Miriam, a college-age Moroccan woman who lives in Paris. Although she is still single, she makes a big pan of dafina *every weekend. She speaks lovingly of her "daf" and her friends enthusiastically agree with her, as they are the ones who benefit. She prefers meat that is not too lean so it won't become dry in the course of the long cooking. The meat sausage cooks gently in the flavorful beef and vegetable juices.*

Some cooks wrap the mixture in cloth or foil, others in beef casings. Occasionally it is used as a stuffing for whole zucchini, which are placed in the casserole. I've also liked it in small, firm, round winter squashes like sweet dumpling or carnival, as they are delicious, hold their shape, and make attractive servings. Their delicately sweet flesh complements the texture of the stuffing.

Prepare this mixture when dafina *is nearly ready to be put in oven.*

1¼ cups rice, rinsed

½ pound ground beef

2 large eggs

2 tablespoons vegetable oil (if beef is fairly lean)

½ teaspoon salt

½ teaspoon freshly ground pepper

½ teaspoon ground mace or freshly grated nutmeg

¼ teaspoon ground turmeric (optional)

1. Combine rice and beef in a bowl. Beat eggs with oil if using, salt, pepper, mace, and turmeric, if using, in a small bowl. Add to rice and beef. Mix very well. Spoon mixture onto a piece of cheesecloth and pat it to a salami shape. Roll cheesecloth to enclose it. Tie ends. Tie 1 or 2 strings around center to keep shape more even. Refrigerate if dafina is not yet ready.

2. When adding to dafina, place the meat and rice sausage gently near the top.

Spiced Bulgur Wheat for Dafina

Makes about 8 servings

Madeleine, my next-door neighbor when I lived in Bat-Yam, Israel, always added spiced wheat to her dafina *(Moroccan cholent). Occasionally she used whole wheat kernels but most of the time, like many cooks, she used cracked wheat or bulgur. Israeli and Middle Eastern markets carry bulgur in several sizes; it's best to use the largest size you can find for this long cooked dish.*

The wheat steams in the casserole in a cloth, bag, or heatproof bowl. Some people instead put it in the oven in a separate small, heavy pan, cover it, and remove it from the oven when the wheat has absorbed all the liquid.

1½ cups bulgur wheat, rinsed and drained

4 cloves garlic, coarsely chopped

2 or 3 tablespoons vegetable oil

1 teaspoon paprika

¼ to ½ teaspoon cayenne pepper or 2 small dried chiles such as chiles japones

1 teaspoon ground cumin

½ teaspoon salt

½ teaspoon freshly ground pepper

1. Mix wheat with garlic, oil, paprika, cayenne, cumin, salt, and pepper. Put wheat mixture on a piece of cheesecloth and shape as a square packet; fold cheesecloth to enclose mixture and tie it with a few strings. Or put mixture in a roasting bag and pierce a few holes in bag. If you wish to steam mixture in a bowl, choose a heavy heatproof one and add 3 cups water to the mixture.

2. When adding to dafina, place the wrapped wheat mixture or the bowl at the top of the casserole.

Baked Cracker Stuffing
Modern Kishke

Makes about 8 servings

Kishke *is a time-honored Ashkenazic stuffing specialty traditionally made in beef casings like sausage. The word* kishke *is Yiddish for "intestines." Traditionally, they were stuffed with a mixture of flour, chicken fat, aromatic vegetables, and spices and often cooked inside a pot of* cholent. *At some delis you can buy it made this way.*

In modern home cooking, kishke *underwent a transformation—foil replaced the beef casing. Now* kishke *is much more convenient. It has changed from a complicated and time-consuming food to a very easy dish.*

Today, people often make an oil- or margarine-based mixture instead of using chicken fat and bake the kishke *in the oven. All or part of the flour is frequently replaced by crushed crackers, bread, or even corn flakes. Matzo meal is another favorite, for Passover and year round. I like to use crackers as they make it easy to vary the taste, according to which cracker you use. Whole wheat are my favorite. The standard seasonings are salt, pepper, sugar, and paprika but I like to add thyme also. Some people grate the vegetables, some grind them in a meat grinder, but most chop them fine in a food processor or blender.*

Kishke is served sliced as a side dish. Some cooks like to bake* kishke *ahead and freeze it unsliced, then place it whole in a pot of* cholent *before putting the* cholent *in the oven. This way the* kishke *can slowly absorb flavors from the stew.*

8 ounces plain crackers
1/2 teaspoon salt (if crackers are unsalted)
1/2 teaspoon freshly ground pepper
1/2 teaspoon sugar
1 teaspoon paprika
1/2 teaspoon dried thyme
2 large onions, cut into eighths
2 ribs celery, strings removed and cut into chunks
2 large carrots, cut into chunks
1/4 to 1/3 cup vegetable oil
2 to 3 tablespoons chicken broth, vegetable broth, or water (optional)

1. Preheat oven to 350°F. Process the crackers in a food processor to fine crumbs. Remove to a bowl. Add salt if using, pepper, sugar, paprika, and thyme.

2. Put onions in the processor and chop finely with brief pulses. Add celery to processor. Add carrots and process to chop. Add oil and process to blend.

3. Add vegetable mixture to bowl of crackers. Mix very well. If mixture is too dry to hold together, add broth, water, or a few teaspoons oil. Adjust seasoning.

4. Make 2 strips of foil, each about 15 inches long and 10 inches wide. Arrange kishke mixture in 2 long rolls of about 1 1/2- to 2- inch diameter on center of each piece of foil. Wrap tightly in foil. Set the rolls on a baking sheet. Bake for about 1 hour. Serve hot, in slices.

Kugels and Side Dishes

Asparagus and Potato Kugel

Makes about 6 servings

The recipe for this festive casserole is adapted from a family favorite of my dear friend Gregory Dinner, who lives in London. It's based on a specialty of his grandmother, whose family came to the United States from Poland. Serve the kugel for Shabbat, Passover, or any special occasion.

Gregory prefers to make his kugel with schmaltz (rendered chicken fat, see page 602) the traditional way. Prepared this way, it's a good accompaniment for meat meals. For dairy dinners, it tastes great with butter. I generally use vegetable oil so there is less saturated fat and the casserole is pareve.

2^1/4 pounds boiling potatoes (about 6 large), unpeeled

1^1/2 pounds thick or medium asparagus, peeled and cut into 1-inch pieces

4 to 6 tablespoons vegetable oil, schmaltz, or butter

2 large onions, chopped

Salt and freshly ground pepper, to taste

1 large egg, beaten

Paprika (for sprinkling)

1. Put potatoes in a large saucepan, add enough water to cover and a pinch of salt, and bring to a boil. Cover and simmer over low heat 35 to 40 minutes or until very tender. Drain and leave until cool enough to handle.

2. Boil asparagus in a saucepan of boiling salted water to cover 3 minutes or until tender. Remove asparagus with slotted spoon, reserving cooking liquid. Rinse asparagus with cold water and drain it well.

3. Heat 2 tablespoons oil in a large skillet, add onions, and sauté over medium heat until golden brown, about 20 minutes. Remove ^{1}/2 cup sautéed onions for mixing with potatoes. To onions in skillet add asparagus, sprinkle with salt and pepper, and toss over low heat 2 minutes.

4. Preheat oven to 350°F. Peel potatoes while still fairly hot. Mash them with a potato masher or food mill, not in a food processor. Add remaining oil and stir until blended. Add reserved ^{1}/2 cup of fried onion. If using the smaller amount of fat, add 2 tablespoons of the reserved asparagus cooking liquid. Add salt and pepper; mixture should be seasoned generously. Add egg and mix well.

5. In a greased 2-quart casserole dish, layer half of potato mixture (about 2^1/2 cups), top with all of asparagus mixture, then with remaining potatoes. Smooth top.

6. Sprinkle casserole lightly with paprika and bake uncovered about 50 minutes or until top is firm and lightly golden at edges. Let stand about 10 minutes before serving. Use a spoon to serve.

Cauliflower Kugel with Sautéed Onions

Makes 4 to 6 servings **P**

This is a favorite of my mother's and mine for Shabbat. It's great with chicken prepared any way, whether poached, braised, or roasted. Since Shabbat meals can be rich and fattening (although always delicious), we sometimes use egg substitute in this dish for a more healthful twist.

1 large head cauliflower (2 pounds), divided into medium florets, stalks peeled and sliced

2 to 3 tablespoons vegetable oil

1 medium onion, chopped

2 large eggs, or 1 large egg and equivalent of 1 egg in egg substitute

1 tablespoon matzo meal

Salt and freshly ground pepper, to taste

About ^{1}/2 teaspoon paprika (optional)

1. Place rack in the upper third of the oven and preheat oven to 375°F. Boil cauliflower in a large saucepan of boiling salted water 8 to 10 minutes or until stalk slices are very tender. Drain well and cool. Mash with potato masher, leaving a few small chunks. Transfer to a bowl.

2. Heat 1 to 2 tablespoons oil in medium nonstick skillet, add onion and sauté over medium-low heat 7 minutes or until onion begins to turn golden.

3. Add eggs and matzo meal to cauliflower mixture. Season well with salt and pepper. Lightly stir in onion mixture and any oil in pan.

4. Grease a shallow 8-inch square baking dish. Add cauliflower mixture. Sprinkle 1 tablespoon oil over top. Sprinkle with paprika, if using. Bake 40 minutes or until set and very lightly browned on top. Remove from oven and run a knife around edges. Let stand about 5 minutes before serving. Serve hot, cut carefully into squares. Use a spoon to remove portions.

Savory Zucchini Kugel

Makes 6 to 8 servings

This kugel makes a good accompaniment for a Shabbat roast chicken or for baked or grilled fish. For a meatless meal you can serve it as a light entree and top each serving with a dollop of Garlic-Yogurt Sauce (page 462).

2 pounds medium zucchini

4 tablespoons olive oil

1 large onion, chopped

4 large cloves garlic, minced

1/4 cup chopped fresh Italian parsley

1/4 cup dry bread crumbs

Salt and freshly ground pepper, to taste

Cayenne pepper, to taste

4 large eggs, beaten

1. Preheat oven to 375°F. Grate zucchini on large holes of grater. Put in a strainer and squeeze firmly to remove excess liquid. Transfer zucchini to a bowl.

2. Heat 2 tablespoons oil in a medium skillet. Add onion and sauté over medium heat, stirring often, about 7 minutes or until onion begins to turn golden. Remove from heat and stir in garlic. Cool slightly, then add mixture to zucchini. Let cool.

3. Add parsley and bread crumbs to zucchini mixture. Season well with salt, pepper, and cayenne so mixture will not be bland. Add eggs and mix well.

4. Heat 1 tablespoon oil in a shallow 8-inch square baking dish in oven for about 3 minutes. Add zucchini mixture to hot dish. Sprinkle with remaining tablespoon oil. Bake about 50 minutes or until set. Remove from oven and run a knife around edges. Let stand about 5 minutes before serving. Serve hot, cut carefully into squares. Use a spoon to remove portions.

Lukshen Kugel with Mushrooms and Onions

Makes 8 to 10 servings

P

This noodle kugel has long been a Shabbat tradition in our family. When my brother and I were children, if my mother made another kugel, we clamored for this one. Now her grandchildren react the same way. My mother always calls it lukshen *kugel, using the Yiddish word for noodles.*

Since this is a large kugel, I sauté the onions and mushrooms separately so they will cook evenly, then I finish sautéing them together. If you crowd the mushrooms in the pan, they often become watery.

6 or 7 tablespoons vegetable oil

2 large onions, minced

1 pound small white mushrooms, quartered

Salt and freshly ground pepper, to taste

1 1/2 teaspoons paprika

1 pound medium egg noodles

4 large eggs, beaten

1. Preheat oven to 350°F. Heat 4 tablespoons oil in a large, heavy skillet. Add onions and sauté over medium-low heat, stirring often, about 15 minutes or until golden brown. Remove onions to a plate. Add 1 or 2 tablespoons oil to skillet and heat it. Add mushrooms, salt, and pepper and sauté over high heat about 7 minutes or until tender. Return onions to skillet and sprinkle with 1 teaspoon paprika. Sauté over medium-high heat, stirring often, about 5 minutes or until onions and mushrooms are well browned.

2. Cook noodles uncovered in a large pot of boiling salted water over high heat about 4 minutes or until nearly tender but firmer than usual. Drain, rinse with cold water, and drain well again. Transfer to a large bowl.

3. Add mushroom-onion mixture to noodles and mix well. Adjust seasoning; mixture should be seasoned generously. Add eggs and mix well. Oil a large baking dish or two medium ones. Add noodle mixture. Sprinkle with remaining tablespoon oil, then dust with remaining paprika. Bake uncovered for 1 hour or until set. Serve from baking dish.

Spinach with Garlic

Makes 4 servings

My Sephardic neighbors often serve this tasty spinach dish for Shabbat to accompany a main course of chicken or fish.

3 pounds fresh spinach

2 tablespoons olive oil

3 large cloves garlic, minced

1 tablespoon strained fresh lemon juice

Salt and freshly ground pepper, to taste

Cayenne pepper, to taste

Lemon wedges

1. Rinse spinach thoroughly by submerging it in a large bowl of cold water, then lifting spinach out and putting it in a colander. If sand remains at the bottom of the bowl, rinse spinach again. Repeat as necessary until spinach is completely clean. Remove any thick stems from spinach.

2. Add spinach to a saucepan of boiling salted water and cook over high heat 2 minutes or until just wilted. Drain spinach; reserve a few tablespoons of the cooking liquid.

3. Heat oil in the saucepan, add garlic and sauté over low heat 30 seconds. Add spinach and heat through, stirring gently. Add 2 or 3 tablespoons cooking liquid if spinach is dry. Add lemon juice and heat through. Season with salt, pepper, and cayenne. Serve in a bowl, with lemon wedges.

Glazed Carrots

Makes 4 to 6 servings

It's amazing that cooked carrots can become so delicious with so little effort. These reheat beautifully too. Serve them with roast chicken for Shabbat, with roast lamb for Passover, or with rice, kasha, or bulgur wheat for a vegetarian dinner.

1¹/₂ pounds long, thin, straight carrots

Salt, to taste

1 to 2 teaspoons white or brown sugar

2 tablespoons vegetable oil or butter

1. Cut carrots into 2-inch lengths. Quarter any wide pieces lengthwise.

2. Put carrots in a sauté pan and add enough water to cover them. Add salt, sugar, and oil. Bring to a boil. Simmer uncovered over medium heat about 25 minutes or until the thickest carrot pieces are very tender. After the first 5 minutes, avoid stirring; instead, shake the pan gently from time to time to turn the carrots.

3. If too much liquid remains in pan, continue cooking uncovered over medium-low heat, shaking pan often, 2 or 3 more minutes or until it thickens to your taste.

Sweet Potato Puree, Miami Style

Makes about 6 servings

I love to serve this easy-to-make, comforting dish with a Friday night roast chicken dinner. It complements chicken well and gives bright color to the plate. For the feast preceding the Yom Kippur fast, it's also great, as an accompaniment for Chicken with Forty Cloves of Garlic (page 85).

It's different than other sweet potato purees because it includes a trick I learned at a Miami restaurant— it's flavored with vanilla! Either I add a little vanilla extract or, if I have a vanilla bean, I infuse it in a little pareve soy milk and beat the milk into the sweet potatoes. For a meatless meal, you can use dairy milk.

2¹/₂ pounds medium orange-fleshed sweet potatoes
    (sometimes labeled yams), unpeeled
1 vanilla bean or 1 teaspoon vanilla extract
³/₄ cup dairy milk or soy milk (if using a vanilla bean)
1 to 2 tablespoons brown or white sugar (optional)
Salt and freshly ground pepper, to taste

1. Put sweet potatoes in a large saucepan, add enough water to cover, and a pinch of salt, and bring to a boil. Cover and simmer over low heat about 30 minutes or until tender.

2. If using a vanilla bean, split it lengthwise and put it in a small saucepan. (Do not add vanilla extract). Add milk. Bring to a simmer. Cover and let stand off the heat while sweet potatoes are cooking.

3. Drain sweet potatoes, let cool, and peel them. Put in a large bowl, cut each into a few pieces, and mash.

4. Return sweet potatoes to dry saucepan. Heat, stirring often, to dry them slightly. Remove vanilla bean from milk. Gradually beat ¹/₂ cup milk into sweet potatoes, stirring. Continue heating until milk is absorbed and puree has thickened to your taste. If you like, beat in remaining milk and heat it until it is absorbed. Beat in sugar, if using. Heat over low heat, stirring, about 1 minute. Season puree with salt and pepper. If using vanilla extract and not vanilla bean, stir it in now.

Roasted Potatoes

Makes 4 servings

A trick I learned from my mother to help potatoes roast more quickly and evenly is to first blanch them briefly. We like these simply cooked potatoes with roast chicken for Shabbat.

8 medium potatoes, peeled and halved
3 to 4 tablespoons vegetable oil
Salt and freshly ground pepper, to taste
About ¹/₂ teaspoon paprika

1. Preheat oven to 375°F. Put potato halves in saucepan with enough water to cover and bring to a boil. Cover and cook over medium-low heat 10 minutes. Drain gently.

2. Heat half of oil in a small, heavy roasting pan or heavy baking dish in oven for 5 minutes. Add potatoes and sprinkle them with salt, pepper, paprika, and remaining oil. Bake uncovered in oven, turning two or three times, about 45 minutes or until tender. Serve hot.

Saffron Basmati Rice

Makes about 4 servings

Jews from Iran are especially fond of seasoning their rice with saffron. The aromatic long-grained basmati rice from India is their top choice. In recent years this wonderful type of rice has become generally popular in Sephardic cooking both in Israel and in the United States.

¹/₄ teaspoon crushed saffron threads (2 pinches)
¹/₄ cup boiling water
1¹/₂ cups basmati rice
2 tablespoons vegetable oil
1 medium onion, minced
2¹/₄ cups water
Salt and freshly ground pepper, to taste

1. In a small cup, combine saffron and ¹/₄ cup boiling water. Cover and let stand. Meanwhile, rinse rice in several changes of water. Drain well.

2. Heat oil in a large saucepan. Add onion and cook over low heat, stirring occasionally, about 7 minutes or until onion is soft and begins to turn golden. Add rice, water, saffron water, salt, and pepper. Bring to a boil. Cover and cook over low heat, without stirring, 18 to 20 minutes or until rice is tender and liquid is absorbed. Remove from heat and let stand, covered, 10 minutes. Fluff with a fork. Serve hot.

Rice with Butternut Squash

Makes 4 servings

Italians are famous for their risotto with pumpkin but they are not the only ones who love rice with members of the winter squash family. Jews from Iraq and from Kurdistan cook rice with all sorts of squash. This simple dish is prepared with either orange winter squash or with zucchini or other summer squash. The rice gains a delicate flavor from the natural sweetness of the squash. It makes an attractive accompaniment for Friday Night Chicken (page 184), Savory Chicken with Olives (page 185), or Pineapple Roast Chicken (page 186).

2 tablespoons vegetable oil

1 medium onion, minced

1¹/₂ pounds butternut or other winter squash, peeled, halved, seeded, and cut into 1-inch cubes

Salt and freshly ground pepper, to taste

2 cups water

1 cup long-grain rice

1. Heat oil in a large, heavy saucepan, add onion, and sauté 5 minutes over low heat. Add squash, salt, and pepper. Cover and cook over low heat, stirring occasionally, 10 minutes; add 1 to 2 tablespoons water if necessary so juices do not burn.

2. Add water, more salt and pepper and bring to a boil. Add rice and stir once. Cover and cook over low heat about 20 minutes or until squash and rice are tender. Adjust seasoning. Serve hot.

❧ *Cakes and Pastries*

Light Cinnamon-Apple Cake

Makes 8 to 12 servings

This fast, one-bowl cake is a good one to make in winter, when time is short on Friday, to get the Shabbat meal ready before sundown. There's no need to layer apples with batter, to separate any eggs, or even to cream fat with sugar; all the ingredients are quickly mixed and spooned into the pan.

1 large egg

1 large egg white or ¹/₄ cup egg substitute

²/₃ cup sugar

¹/₃ cup vegetable oil

1¹/₂ cups all-purpose flour

1¹/₂ teaspoons ground cinnamon

1¹/₄ teaspoons baking powder

¹/₄ teaspoon baking soda

¹/₃ cup orange juice

1 pound sweet apples, such as Golden Delicious or Jonagold, peeled, halved, cored, and finely diced (2¹/₄ cups total)

1. Preheat oven to 350°F. Lightly grease and flour a square 9-inch cake pan. Beat egg, egg white, sugar, and oil in a large bowl with an electric mixer until blended. Sift flour with cinnamon, baking powder, and baking soda into a medium bowl. Stir half of flour mixture into egg mixture on low speed. Stir in orange juice. Stir in remaining flour. With a wooden spoon, stir in diced apples.

2. Spread batter in prepared cake pan. Smooth top. Bake about 40 minutes or until a cake tester inserted in cake's center comes out clean. Cool in pan on a rack. Serve cut into squares.

Chocolate Chip Cake

Makes 8 to 10 servings

My mother used to make this cake with grated chocolate because the regular-size chocolate chips sank during baking. Now she often uses mini-chocolate chips. If you use grated chocolate, keep the chocolate cool. Hold it with plastic wrap while you grate it so it won't melt from the heat of your hands.

1 cup all-purpose flour
1¹/₂ teaspoons baking powder
¹/₄ teaspoon salt
3 large eggs, separated
³/₄ cup plus 2 tablespoons sugar
¹/₂ cup vegetable oil
1 teaspoon vanilla extract
6 tablespoons water
1 cup mini-semisweet chocolate chips or 6 ounces grated semisweet or bittersweet chocolate

1. Preheat oven to 325°F. Have ready an 8-inch tube pan with a removable tube; do not grease it. Sift flour with baking powder and salt into a medium bowl.

2. Beat egg yolks with ³/₄ cup sugar in a large bowl with an electric mixer until light and fluffy. Beat in oil. Add vanilla. Lightly stir in flour mixture in 3 batches, alternating with water in 2 batches.

3. Beat egg whites in a clean large or medium bowl with the mixer until soft peaks form. Gradually beat in remaining 2 tablespoons sugar. Beat at high speed until whites are stiff and shiny but not dry. Fold about ¹/₄ of whites into yolk mixture until nearly blended. Gently fold yolk mixture into remaining whites. When nearly blended, sprinkle chocolate chips over batter and fold in lightly.

4. Transfer batter to prepared pan. Bake 50 minutes to 1 hour or until a cake tester inserted in cake's center comes out clean. Invert pan on its "feet" or on a heat-proof funnel or bottle; let stand about 1¹/₂ hours or until completely cool. Run a metal spatula gently around side of cake. Push up tube to remove side of pan. Run a thin-bladed knife around tube. Run metal spatula carefully under cake to free it from base; turn out carefully onto a platter.

Orange Jelly Roll with Raspberry Filling

Makes 8 to 10 servings

Jelly rolls have long been favorites in Jewish homes because they are pareve and the ingredients are usually at hand. The baking time is brief and so the cake can be whipped up in no time.

Usually, jelly rolls are made from sponge cakes. This one is instead a variation of the French genoise, a classic cake that is easier to make than other sponge cakes because there is no need to separate the eggs. The extra yolks in the batter help the cake to be more flexible so there is little chance of it cracking when you roll it.

Brushing the cake with syrup before rolling it is another trick I learned in France. The syrup keeps sponge cakes moister and adds good flavor. If you would prefer an alcohol-free syrup, substitute orange juice syrup.

Raspberry Brandy Syrup (page 582) or orange liqueur syrup
6 tablespoons all-purpose flour
¹/₄ cup cornstarch
4 large eggs
3 large egg yolks
7 tablespoons sugar
1 teaspoon grated orange rind
³/₄ cup good quality raspberry preserves
Powdered sugar (optional)

1. Prepare syrup and let cool. Position rack in center of oven and preheat to 400°F. Lightly grease the corners of a 17 × 11-inch rimmed baking sheet. Line pan with foil or parchment paper. Sift flour and cornstarch into a bowl.

2. Beat eggs and yolks in a large bowl with an electric mixer. Add sugar and beat at high speed about 5 minutes or until mixture is very thick. Fold in orange rind. Sift about ¹/₃ of flour mixture over batter; fold in as gently as possible. Repeat with remaining flour mixture in 2 batches.

3. Transfer batter to prepared baking sheet; spread evenly but lightly. Bake about 7 minutes or until cake is just firm and springy to touch and beginning to brown. Transfer cake with its liner to a rack. Pull liner gently from sides of cake. Cool to room temperature. Fill cake as soon as possible, so it will not be dry. Cover with a towel if not using immediately.

4. Using a brush, dab syrup generously on cake. Spread preserves evenly over cake. Beginning with a long side, roll up cake carefully, unsticking liner. Use liner to help roll cake. At the end, use the edge of the liner to roll the cake towards you. Cover tightly and refrigerate 30 minutes before serving. Sprinkle with powdered sugar, if using. To serve, use a serrated knife to gently slice cake.

Yemenite Breakfast Pastries

Jahnoon

Makes 6 to 8 servings

Eating jahnoon, *also spelled* jihnoon, *a pastry that bakes all night, is a Shabbat tradition in most Yemenite homes. In fact, this flaky pastry has caught on in Israel, and now many Jews of all origins enjoy it for a leisurely Shabbat brunch. In Israel, and in some Israeli and kosher grocery stores in the United States, you can buy the dough frozen, shaped, and ready to bake. The pastries are served on their own, with sugar for sprinkling, or accompanied by hard boiled eggs or Brown Eggs (page 313). Another favorite accompaniment is Fresh Tomato Salsa, Yemenite Style (page 234), as well as a bowl of freshly grated tomatoes for children and for those who don't want the fire of salsa. Some people serve slow-cooked red beans on the side.*

The sweetness and richness of the dough varies with the person making it. Some versions are made with large amounts of sugar, while others contain just a touch of sugar or honey. The dough is spread with margarine or samneh, *the Yemenite clarified butter resembling Indian ghee, then folded to make it flaky.*

4 cups all-purpose flour

1/4 cup sugar

1 teaspoon baking powder

1 1/2 teaspoons salt

1 large egg

About 1 1/3 cups water

1/2 to 3/4 cup (1 to 1 1/2 sticks) margarine or butter, cut into 6 to 8 pieces

1. Combine flour, sugar, baking powder, and salt in food processor and process to blend. Add egg and 1 cup water and process with brief pulses to mix. With motor running, gradually add enough of remaining water so mixture comes together to a smooth, fairly stiff dough. It will be sticky.

2. Remove dough from processor. Knead dough well by slapping it vigorously on the work surface. Divide into 6 to 8 pieces and knead each one with a slapping motion until smooth. Roll each in your palm to a ball. Put on an oiled plate or tray, cover with plastic wrap, and refrigerate at least 4 hours or overnight.

3. Grease working surface and rolling pin. Let margarine stand at room temperature until very soft. Roll out 1 ball of dough on oiled surface to a very thin square. To help stretch dough, pull it gently from time to time by hand, until very thin. If dough tears, simply press it together. Brush dough with one of the pieces of soft margarine. Fold dough in half, then in half again to make a long strip. Roll up strip from a short side into a tight cylinder. Put in a greased, shallow square baking dish. Cover with foil and a lid and refrigerate at least 2 or up to 8 hours.

4. Preheat oven to 200°F. Bake pastries in their covered dish overnight or 13 to 14 hours or until golden brown. Serve hot.

Appetizers

P = *Pareve*   **D** = *Dairy*   **M** = *Meat*

$\mathcal{A}$ppetizers are an important part of Shabbat and holiday dinners. The best known of Jewish appetizers is probably chopped liver. This is primarily an Ashkenazic specialty and is probably the favorite beginning for a *fleishig* meal (one containing meat). As a child, I remember having it very often. Today my mother and I often make vegetarian or "mock" chopped liver instead. A delicious appetizer in its own right, it is made in numerous variations.

Although some Sephardic Jews also serve chopped liver, they prepare cooked vegetable appetizers more often. Especially popular are tomato dips, which may be moderately spicy or very hot, as well as salads and spreads based on grilled or broiled peppers and eggplants seasoned with olive oil or tahini.

Festive meals, whether meat or dairy, often begin with an appetizer or first course of fish. For Shabbat it's usually a home-cooked fresh fish. For other occasions, like a festive brunch, it's more likely to be smoked or pickled fish or lox purchased from a deli. To make a dinner even more festive, many cooks like to serve several appetizers by adding a few simple salads to the table along with the fish or chopped liver. Olives and pickles are an easy addition to the array of appetizers.

Everyone loves savory filled pastries, from Ashkenazic knishes to Sephardic *bourekas*, from Russian *piroshki*, to fried Moroccan cigars. In most families, homemade pastries are prepared for special occasions and sometimes for Shabbat. For some of these recipes, many buy pastry dough so they're easier to make and the family can enjoy them more often.

Perhaps the most famous Israeli appetizer is falafel, or chickpea (garbanzo bean) croquettes. Falafel is not served for Shabbat or other holidays. Instead it is a casual appetizer, party snack, or quick meal.

In Israel, an assortment of appetizers might be served as a light meal or party menu. There might be hummus, tahini, or cheese or vegetable spreads. Other elements on the table are cut vegetables and perhaps some sliced cheeses or, if there's no cheese, some sliced cold meats. The breads are chosen according to the type of appetizer—pita is the natural choice for serving with hummus, tahini, or marinated eggplant slices, while challah or rye bread is a favorite with chopped liver.

❋ Chopped Liver Variations

Chopped Liver the Way My Mother Makes It

Makes 6 to 8 appetizer servings

This is a most popular appetizer in Jewish cooking and can be found in almost every deli. But it's very easy to make at home. The secret is to brown the onions thoroughly and to season the chopped liver well. My mother and I use oil for sautéing the onions but you can substitute chicken fat if you like.

At some delis beef liver is used, but in my family we always make it with chicken liver. The liver is broiled, not sautéed, because broiling is necessary to remove the blood to make it kosher, instead of simply salting, as with other meats.

Some people prefer their chopped liver to be chunky rather than smooth, and so they either chop the mixture with a knife or grind it in a meat grinder. If you like it smooth, simply use a food processor.

Serve the liver with any bread or cracker you like. Traditional choices are rye bread, challah, or, on Passover, matzo.

1 pound chicken livers

Kosher salt

3 tablespoons vegetable oil

2 medium onions, chopped

2 large hard boiled eggs, coarsely grated

Salt and freshly ground pepper, to taste

Lettuce leaves and tomato slices for serving (optional)

1. Preheat broiler with rack about 3 inches from heat source. Rinse livers and pat dry on paper towels; cut off any green spots. Put livers on foil-lined broiler rack and sprinkle with kosher salt. Broil 3 minutes or until livers brown lightly on top. Turn them over, sprinkle second side with salt, and broil 3 to 4 more minutes or until cooked through and color is no longer pink; check by cutting with a sharp knife. Discard juices from foil. Cool livers slightly.

2. Heat oil in large, heavy skillet. Add onions and sauté over medium-low heat, stirring often, about 15 minutes or until tender and well browned.

3. Chop the liver in a food processor. Add onions and chop with brief pulses until blended in. Transfer to a bowl and lightly mix in eggs. Season well with salt and pepper. Refrigerate, covered, until ready to serve, up to 2 days. Serve cold, in scoops on lettuce leaves and garnished with tomato slices, if using.

Chopped Chicken Liver with Chickpeas

Makes about 8 servings

When I was trying to find a way to reduce the fat in chopped liver but still enjoy the authentic flavor, I experimented with blending in various ingredients, including baked eggplant and sautéed mushrooms. Then I thought of adding chickpeas to the liver. My family and I were delighted with this new version. It is truly delicious, easy to make, and, in our house, it is the chopped liver recipe we eat most often.

8 to 10 ounces chicken livers

Kosher salt

1 to 3 tablespoons vegetable oil

2 large onions, chopped

4 to 7 tablespoons chicken stock

One 15-ounce can chickpeas (garbanzo beans), rinsed, or 1²/₃ cups cooked chickpeas

1 large hard boiled egg, grated, or whites of 2 large hard boiled eggs, chopped

Salt (optional) and freshly ground pepper, to taste

1. Preheat broiler with rack about 3 inches from heat source. Rinse livers and pat dry on paper towels; cut off any green spots. Put livers on foil-lined broiler rack and sprinkle with kosher salt. Broil 3 minutes or until livers brown lightly on top. Turn them over, sprinkle second side with salt, and broil 3 to 4 more minutes or until cooked through and color is no longer pink; check by cutting with a sharp knife. Discard juices from foil. Cool livers slightly.

2. Heat oil in large, heavy skillet. Add onions and sauté over medium-low heat, stirring often, about 15 minutes or until well browned; add 1 or 2 tablespoons stock during sautéing if pan becomes dry.

3. Grind chickpeas and 4 tablespoons broth in a food processor until mixture is smooth. Transfer to a bowl. Chop the liver in food processor. Add onions and chop with brief pulses until blended in. Return chickpeas to processor and pulse to blend, adding 1 tablespoon broth if needed. Transfer to a bowl. Lightly mix in egg. Add salt if needed; season generously with pepper. Serve cold.

French-Jewish Chopped Liver

Makes about 6 servings

Also known as liver pâté, this rich spread is seasoned in the French style with thyme, garlic, shallots, and a hint of cognac and white wine. To make it kosher, it is enriched with margarine rather than butter; you can substitute chicken fat or goose fat if you want. Another step done for the purpose of kashrut (kosher laws): the livers are broiled until thoroughly cooked.

This dish is great for special occasions. You present it in individual portions by serving it in ramekins. Serve the pâté with thin slices of French bread or toasted pita wedges.

8 ounces chicken livers

Kosher salt

1 tablespoon Cognac or brandy

1/4 cup dry white wine

1 teaspoon dried thyme, crumbled

3 tablespoons olive oil or chicken fat

4 medium shallots, chopped

1 medium clove garlic, chopped

Pinch of freshly grated nutmeg

5 tablespoons margarine, softened, or chicken fat

Salt and freshly ground pepper, to taste

1. Preheat broiler with rack about 3 inches from heat source. Rinse livers and pat dry on paper towels; cut off any green spots. Put livers on foil-lined broiler rack and sprinkle with kosher salt. Broil 3 minutes or until livers

brown lightly on top. Turn them over, sprinkle second side with salt, and broil 3 to 4 more minutes or until cooked through and color is no longer pink; check by cutting with a sharp knife. Discard juices from foil. Cool livers slightly.

2. Transfer livers to a bowl. Spoon cognac, wine, and 1/2 teaspoon thyme over them. Cover and marinate 30 minutes to 1 hour in refrigerator.

3. Heat oil in a small skillet. Add shallots and garlic and sauté over low heat 1 minute or until softened. Transfer shallot mixture to a bowl and let cool.

4. Transfer livers to a food processor, discarding marinade. Puree livers in a food processor until smooth. Add shallot mixture, remaining thyme, nutmeg, and margarine and process until well blended. Adjust seasoning.

5. Spoon into ramekins and refrigerate at least 1 hour before serving.

Easy Mock Chopped Liver

Makes 8 to 10 servings (P)

My mother and many of her friends make vegetarian "liver" pâté this way. It's easy because the only cooking necessary is sautéing the onions. The well-browned onions are combined with canned peas and chopped nuts. My mother feels that pecans are the best nut to use. And she insists that for the best texture, a meat grinder rather than a food processor should be used to blend the mixture.

Serve this pâté on a bed of lettuce garnished with tomato wedges and radishes, with fresh bread or crackers.

3 tablespoons vegetable oil

1 large onion, chopped

Two 15-ounce cans peas, drained

1/2 cup pecans

1 large hard boiled egg

Salt and freshly ground pepper, to taste

1. Heat oil in a large skillet, add onions and sauté over medium heat until golden brown, about 10 minutes.

2. Grind peas, pecans, and sautéed onions with their oil in a meat grinder or food processor. If using a meat grinder, grind egg with the other ingredients. If using a food processor, coarsely grate the egg, then lightly stir it into the mixture in a bowl. Season with salt and pepper. Serve cold.

My Favorite Vegetarian Chopped Liver

Makes 8 to 10 servings

My mother and I have an ongoing debate about the best way to make mock chopped liver. She uses green peas and pecans (see page 208), while I prefer chickpeas, green beans, and walnuts.

This version is light, as I substitute vegetable stock for part of the oil and use only a small amount of nuts. When I prepare it in cooking demonstrations, everyone loves it. By the way, I don't think it has the same flavor as chopped liver; I simply like it as a delicious appetizer. However, some of my students find it tastes just like chopped liver. One tasted it and called it "a miracle on a plate."

Serve it with fresh bread, toast, crackers, or matzo, or with a green salad.

3/4 pound green beans, ends removed, halved

1 1/2 to 3 tablespoons vegetable oil

2 large onions, chopped

Two 15-ounce cans chickpeas (garbanzo beans) or 3 cups cooked chickpeas

1/4 cup walnuts

1/4 cup vegetable stock or broth, or more if needed

1 large hard boiled egg or the whites of 2 large hard boiled eggs, coarsely grated

Salt and freshly ground pepper, to taste

1. Cook green beans in a large pan of boiling salted water about 10 minutes or until very tender. They should be more tender than usual so you can chop them easily. Rinse beans with cold water and drain well.

2. Heat oil in a large, heavy skillet, add onions, and sauté over medium heat 5 minutes. If using the smaller amount of oil, cover onions so they won't burn. Continue to sauté, stirring often, about 5 more minutes, or until golden brown.

3. Chop green beans in a food processor. Drain chickpeas and add to processor. Add walnuts, 1/4 cup stock, and sautéed onions with their oil. Process until smooth. If you would like the pâté to be more moist, add more broth by tablespoons, processing after each addition. Transfer to a bowl. Lightly stir in hard boiled egg. Season with salt and pepper. Serve cold.

Vegetarian Chopped Liver, Israeli Style

Makes 6 to 8 servings

Eggplant, mushrooms, and plenty of sautéed onions give this spread great flavor. Serve it in scoops or oval spoonfuls on a bed of mixed baby lettuces and garnish with cherry tomatoes, or serve it as a spread with fresh or toasted pita bread.

3 to 4 tablespoons vegetable oil

2 large onions, chopped

1 1/2 pounds eggplant, peeled and cut into 1/2-inch dice

Salt and freshly ground pepper, to taste

6 to 8 ounces mushrooms, diced

Cayenne pepper, to taste

1 or 2 large hard boiled eggs, chopped or grated

1. Heat oil in a large skillet. Add onions and sauté over medium-low heat 8 minutes or until onions are soft and begin to brown. Add eggplant, salt, and pepper. Sauté 5 minutes over medium heat. Cover pan and cook over low heat, stirring often, about 15 minutes or until eggplant is tender. Add mushrooms. Cover and cook, stirring often and mashing vegetables occasionally with a wooden spoon, 15 minutes or until vegetables are very tender. If you would like a finer-textured spread, puree mixture in a food processor.

2. Transfer mixture to a bowl and let cool. Add a pinch of cayenne. Adjust seasoning. Lightly stir in hard boiled eggs. Serve cold.

Lox Pâté

Makes 8 to 12 servings   Ⓓ

This pâté is adapted from a creation of French Master Chef Fernand Chambrette, who was my teacher and mentor in Paris for nearly six years. He combined smoked salmon, poached fresh salmon, and butter and garnished the finished pâté with salmon caviar. When it was spread on good quality baguette, it was one of the best appetizers imaginable.

I now use half butter and half cream cheese instead of all butter. You can even use reduced-fat cream cheese. The pâté will still be delicious, sumptuous, and very rich. A little goes a long way. For such a tasty appetizer, it's very easy to make.

You can serve the pâté with slices of very fresh, crusty French baguette. It's also good with thin slices of small-loaf rye or pumpernickel bread, with simple crackers that are not salty, or even on bagel chips.

¹/₄ cup dry white wine

¹/₂ cup water

5 parsley stems

1 bay leaf

1 small sprig fresh thyme or ¹/₄ teaspoon dried thyme

One 10-ounce piece fresh salmon fillet or steak

¹/₂ pound lox or smoked salmon, cut into pieces

¹/₂ cup (1 stick) unsalted butter, softened and cut into pieces

4 ounces cream cheese, softened and cut into pieces

Freshly ground pepper, to taste

Pinch of freshly grated nutmeg

About 2 tablespoons salmon caviar or 1 tablespoon snipped chives

Slices of fresh French or sourdough baguette, rye bread, or pumpernickel

1. Combine wine, water, parsley, bay leaf, and thyme in a sauté pan. Bring to a simmer. Add fresh salmon. Return to a simmer. Cover and poach over low heat about 5 minutes for fillet or 9 to 10 minutes for steak or until salmon is just tender when pierced with a sharp knife. Uncover and let cool in the poaching liquid.

2. Remove salmon from the liquid. (You can save the liquid for use as a light fish stock.) Discard salmon skin and any bones.

3. Combine poached salmon and lox in a food processor. Process until finely ground. Add butter and process until blended. Add cream cheese and process to blend. Add a pinch of pepper and nutmeg. Spoon into small serving dishes or ramekins and chill thoroughly.

4. Just before serving, top pâté with salmon caviar or chives. Serve cold, with bread.

Cream Cheese and Lox Spread

Makes 8 to 12 servings   Ⓓ

You can buy this ready-made but it's better, fresher, and more economical if you make it yourself. And it's one of the easiest recipes around. At some fish markets you can buy inexpensive lox trimmings and they're perfect for this spread. Whether the smoked fish is labeled "lox" or "smoked salmon," it will be delicious.

Use any kind of soft cream cheese you like— regular, low-fat, or nonfat. If you're using a firm block of cream cheese, soften it at room temperature and stir in a few tablespoons sour cream to give it a spreadable consistency. Of course, it's perfect on bagels but there's no need to stop there. I also love it on rye bread, pumpernickel, water crackers, and matzo.

For a pretty and easy hors d'oeuvre, you can spread it on crackers or cocktail bread and top each one with a blanched asparagus tip.

1 pound whipped cream cheese

2 to 4 ounces lox or smoked salmon, finely chopped

5 teaspoons chopped fresh chives or green onion

Freshly ground pepper, to taste

Salt, to taste (optional)

Mix cheese with lox and chives in a small bowl. Season with pepper. Taste for seasoning (you will probably not need salt).

Alsatian Herring Salad with Apples, Walnuts, and Crème Fraîche

Makes 6 to 8 servings

Herring has long been an Ashkenazic Jewish favorite for buffets, Shabbat kiddush, (snacks after synagogue service) and for Yom Kippur after the fast. It is served pickled or as a salad or spread.

Some recipes begin with salted herrings that need to be soaked or pickled. Today many cooks instead use pickled herrings from a jar, which is readily available at the supermarket. When prepared this way, the spread or salad is ready in no time.

Many herring salads and spreads include apples and onions to balance the sweet and sour taste of the pickled herring. This version from the Alsatian Jewish kitchen makes use of pickled cucumbers and crème fraîche to balance the sweetness of the pickled herring. You can either dice the ingredients fine and serve the herring salad with boiled potatoes or you can blend them to a spread and serve it with bread.

One 16-ounce jar marinated herring or herring in
    wine sauce

1 apple, peeled and finely diced

1/4 cup finely diced pickles

2 shallots, minced, or 1/3 cup chopped red or white onion

1/4 cup chopped walnuts

1/4 to 1/2 cup crème fraîche or sour cream, or to taste

1 tablespoon strained fresh lemon juice

1 teaspoon mustard

2 tablespoons chopped fresh parsley

Remove herring pieces from jar; reserve liquid. Cut herring into small dice. Combine herring, apple, pickles, shallots, and walnuts in a bowl. In a small bowl, mix crème fraîche with lemon juice and mustard. Add to salad and mix well. If necessary, add liquid from the herring to moisten the salad; or add more crème fraîche. Sprinkle with chopped parsley.

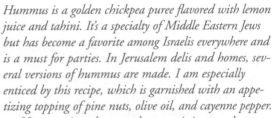

Hummus and Other Vegetable Dips and Spreads

Jerusalem Hummus

Makes 8 to 12 servings

Hummus is a golden chickpea puree flavored with lemon juice and tahini. It's a specialty of Middle Eastern Jews but has become a favorite among Israelis everywhere and is a must for parties. In Jerusalem delis and homes, several versions of hummus are made. I am especially enticed by this recipe, which is garnished with an appetizing topping of pine nuts, olive oil, and cayenne pepper.

Hummus is such a popular treat it is now also widely available prepackaged—in Israel and even in the United States. Here hummus has quickly gone from a specialty item relegated to Israeli and Middle Eastern grocery stores to being available at the supermarket. Still, there's no comparing store-bought to homemade.

Serve this festive dip with fresh pita bread, or keep it on hand for sandwiches. You can store it for 4 to 5 days in the refrigerator.

1 pound dried chickpeas (garbanzo beans), about 21/2 cups

3 large cloves garlic, peeled

1/2 cup tahini (sesame paste), stirred before measuring

1/2 cup strained fresh lemon juice

About 11/4 cups water

Salt, to taste

Cayenne pepper, to taste

Extra-virgin olive oil

2 to 3 tablespoons pine nuts, lightly toasted

1. Pick over chickpeas, discarding any pebbles and broken or discolored peas. In a large bowl, generously cover chickpeas with water and soak 8 hours or overnight.

2. Drain chickpeas and rinse. Put them in a large saucepan and generously cover with water. Bring to a simmer. Cover and cook over low heat about 2 hours or until very tender. Drain well. Cool slightly.

3. Mince garlic in food processor. Add chickpeas and process to chop. Add tahini, lemon juice, and 1/2 cup water and puree until finely blended. Transfer to a bowl.

Stir in enough water so that mixture has consistency of a smooth spread. Season with salt and cayenne. Refrigerate in a covered container until ready to serve.

4. To serve, spread hummus on a serving plate. Drizzle with olive oil. Sprinkle hummus very lightly with cayenne, then with pine nuts.

Low-Fat Hummus

Makes about 8 servings

Hummus is actually a healthy spread. You can spread it on bread instead of butter or cream cheese. My mother often uses it in sandwiches instead of mayonnaise.

This version is incredibly quick and easy to prepare, as it's made from canned chickpeas. You can buy low-salt chickpeas if you prefer. It keeps about 4 days in the refrigerator in a covered container.

If serving the hummus as an appetizer, spread it on plates and sprinkle it with chopped parsley and with paprika or cayenne pepper.

3 medium cloves garlic, peeled

Two 15-ounce cans chickpeas (garbanzo beans), drained and rinsed

3 tablespoons tahini (sesame paste), stirred before measuring

1/4 cup strained fresh lemon juice, or more to taste

About 1/2 cup water

Salt, to taste

Cayenne pepper, to taste

1. Mince garlic in food processor. Add chickpeas and process to chop.

2. Add tahini to food processor. Add 1/4 cup lemon juice and 1/4 cup water and puree until finely blended. Add more lemon juice if you like. Add more water if necessary so that mixture has consistency of a smooth spread. Season with salt and cayenne.

Country-Style Hummus

Makes about 8 servings

This rich type of hummus is chunky rather than smooth. You can either cook your own chickpeas and make your own sauce, or, for a quick version, buy prepared, ready-to-eat tahini sauce (not the paste, which is designed for making your own tahini) and canned chickpeas.

Serve this hummus in bowls for dipping, or for spooning over pita bread. It's saucy and is not a thick spread. It's also good served as a salad on a bed of lettuce.

1/2 to 3/4 cup Tahini Dip (page 214)

2 large cloves garlic, peeled

1/2 teaspoon ground cumin

1/4 to 1/2 teaspoon hot red pepper flakes

1 tablespoon strained fresh lemon juice, or to taste

Two 15-ounce cans chickpeas (garbanzo beans), drained and rinsed

Salt and freshly ground pepper, to taste

Cayenne pepper, to taste

4 tablespoons chopped fresh Italian parsley or cilantro

1. Prepare Tahini Dip. Then, combine 1/2 cup tahini sauce, garlic, cumin, and pepper flakes in blender or food processor. Processor until garlic is finely minced and sauce is well blended.

2. Transfer sauce to a bowl. Stir in 1 tablespoon lemon juice.

3. Coarsely chop half the chickpeas in food processor. Add chopped and whole chickpeas to sauce. Season with salt, pepper, and cayenne. If you would like it more saucy, stir in remaining tahini sauce. Add more lemon juice, salt, pepper, or cayenne if needed. Just before serving, stir in 3 tablespoons parsley or cilantro. Serve sprinkled with remaining parsley or cilantro.

Roasted Red Pepper Hummus

Makes about 8 servings

Today hummus is made in a variety of flavors. I especially love this one, with the rich taste and light salmon color it gains from roasted red bell peppers. Either roast your own peppers or, to save time, use roasted peppers from a jar.

2 large red bell peppers

3 medium cloves garlic, peeled

Two 15-ounce cans chickpeas (garbanzo beans), drained and rinsed

2 to 4 tablespoons tahini (sesame paste), stirred before measuring

4 to 6 tablespoons strained fresh lemon juice

4 to 6 tablespoons water

Salt and freshly ground pepper, to taste

Cayenne pepper, to taste

1. Broil or grill peppers, turning them often, until their skins blister all over, about 15 minutes. Transfer to a bowl and cover tightly; or put in a plastic bag and close bag. Let stand 10 minutes. Peel peppers using paring knife and remove seeds.

2. Mince garlic in food processor. Add red peppers and chickpeas and process to chop.

3. Add 2 tablespoons tahini to food processor. Add 4 tablespoons lemon juice and 4 tablespoons water and puree until finely blended. Add more tahini and lemon juice if you like. Add more water if necessary so that mixture has consistency of a smooth spread. Season with salt, pepper, and cayenne.

Spicy Tomato Hummus

Makes about 8 servings

Make this hummus as hot as you like. Roasted jalapeño peppers give it a terrific flavor, but if you want a quicker option, flavor it to taste with Zehug or Harissa (page 592) if you have some, or simply add your favorite hot sauce. Another option is to season the hummus with dried chili flakes or cayenne pepper. Try to use a tomato sauce that doesn't contain sugar.

2 large cloves garlic, peeled

Two 15- to 16-ounce cans chickpeas (garbanzo beans), drained and rinsed

1 1/2 teaspoons ground cumin

3 tablespoons extra-virgin olive oil

1/4 cup tomato sauce

2 tablespoons strained fresh lemon juice, or to taste

About 1/4 cup water

2 or 3 jalapeño peppers, roasted and peeled (page 588), see Note, or about 2 teaspoons hot sauce

Salt and freshly ground pepper, to taste

1. Mince garlic in food processor. Add chickpeas and process to chop. Add cumin, oil, tomato sauce, 2 tablespoons lemon juice, and 1/4 cup water and puree until finely blended. Add more water if necessary so that mixture has consistency of a smooth spread.

2. Mince jalapeño peppers. Stir jalapeño peppers or hot sauce into chickpea mixture. Add salt and pepper. Add more lemon juice, hot sauce, salt, or pepper if needed.

Note: Wear rubber gloves when handling hot peppers.

Basil–Black Bean Dip

Makes about 8 servings

This is a take-off on hummus and, in some American delis and natural food stores, this type of dip would be labeled "black bean hummus." To Israelis, this label does not make sense because the word "hummus" in Hebrew does not mean dip, but means chickpeas. So you cannot make hummus with any other bean. Whatever you call it, this dip is tasty and easy to make. It's also useful to keep on hand as an alternative to butter for spreading on bread or on tortillas.

If you don't have fresh basil, substitute cilantro or parsley.

2 large cloves garlic, peeled

1/3 cup fresh basil leaves

2 to 3 tablespoons extra-virgin olive oil

Two 15-ounce cans black beans, drained

2 tablespoons strained fresh lemon or lime juice, or to taste

About 1/2 cup water

Salt and freshly ground pepper, to taste

Pure chili powder (not the spice blend) or cayenne pepper, to taste

Shredded fresh basil or basil sprigs

Combine garlic, basil, and olive oil in food processor. Process until garlic and basil are minced. Add beans and process to chop. Add 2 tablespoons lemon juice and 1/4 cup water and puree until finely blended. Add more water if necessary so that mixture has consistency of a smooth spread. Season with salt, pepper, and chili powder. Stir in a little more lemon juice if you like. Serve garnished with basil.

Tahini Dip

Makes about 2 cups, 10 to 12 servings

Tahini, or sesame paste, is a popular ingredient for making sauces and dips in the Sephardic kitchen as it gives them lots of flavor and a creamy texture. It's very thick and is always diluted with water before being used, and usually with lemon juice as well. It can be made into a sauce or a dip.

Serve this dip with fresh pita bread. It's usually served at parties alongside hummus (chickpea dip). People often spoon a little of each into their pita, so the tahini dip acts like a sauce for the thicker hummus. I also like serving tahini dip with raw vegetables such as carrot, cucumber, and jicama sticks.

For this recipe buy tahini paste and not the prepared, ready-to-eat tahini sauce. Stir the tahini gently before measuring it.

1 cup tahini (sesame paste), stirred before measuring

About 1 cup plus 2 tablespoons water

1/2 teaspoon salt, or to taste

4 to 5 tablespoons strained fresh lemon juice

5 large cloves garlic, minced

1/2 teaspoon ground cumin (optional)

Cayenne pepper or paprika, to taste

Extra-virgin olive oil (optional)

2 to 3 tablespoons chopped fresh Italian parsley

1. Stir tahini to blend in its oil in a medium bowl. Stir in 1 cup water. Add salt, 4 tablespoons lemon juice, garlic, cumin if using, and cayenne. If sauce is too thick, gradually stir in more water. Taste, and add more salt or lemon juice if desired. Refrigerate in a covered container until ready to serve.

2. Before serving, gradually stir in a little more water if tahini has become too thick. (It thickens on standing.) Spread tahini on a deep serving plate or in shallow bowl. If desired, make a small hollow in center and spoon in a little olive oil. Sprinkle tahini lightly with paprika or cayenne and with chopped parsley.

Low-Fat Sesame Dip

Makes 4 servings

Serve this tasty dip with grilled falafel or with other dishes in which you would like a quicker, lighter alternative to tahini. I also like it for dunking vegetables. It is based on yogurt and therefore is not kosher with meat dishes.

¾ cup low-fat or nonfat yogurt

¼ cup fat-free sour cream or additional yogurt

1 teaspoon minced garlic

2 teaspoons minced cilantro mixture, reserved from making falafel (page 219), or minced fresh cilantro

1 teaspoon Asian sesame oil

Salt and freshly ground pepper, to taste

Cayenne pepper, to taste

Mix yogurt, sour cream, garlic, cilantro mixture, and sesame oil in a small bowl. Season with salt, pepper, and cayenne. Serve cool.

Grilled Eggplant and Red Pepper Salad

Makes 6 servings

A favorite among Jews from Yugoslavia and Bulgaria, this delicious salad is also sold in jars as a spread called ajvar. Traditionally the eggplant and peppers should be chopped very finely with a knife so they keep their texture, then stirred together very well so the peppers impart a reddish color to the whole mixture. To save time you can use a food processor.

I like to use a generous proportion of red peppers. They give the salad such a wonderful sweet flavor that it's even good without oil. This version is mildly spiced. If you like, follow the custom of some cooks and make it hot by adding 2 or 3 grilled peeled jalapeño peppers or cayenne pepper to taste.

2 long, fairly slender eggplants (about 2 pounds total)

1½ to 2 pounds red bell peppers

2 medium cloves garlic, minced

Salt and freshly ground pepper, to taste

1 tablespoon extra-virgin olive oil (optional), see Note

1 tablespoon vinegar (optional), any kind

1. Prick eggplants a few times with fork. Grill eggplants on barbecue at medium-high heat about 1 hour, or broil about 40 minutes; in either case, turn eggplants from time to time, until skin blackens. When done, flesh should be tender and eggplants should look collapsed.

2. Broil or grill or peppers, turning them often, until their skins blister all over, about 15 minutes. Transfer to a bowl and cover tightly; or put in a plastic bag and close bag. Let stand 10 minutes. Peel peppers using paring knife and remove seeds. Dice peppers.

3. Leave eggplants until cool enough to handle. Cut off eggplant caps. Cut eggplants in half and drain off any liquid from inside eggplant. With a spoon, scoop flesh from peel; discard peel. Chop eggplant and peppers very finely, either with a knife or in a food processor. Transfer to a bowl and add garlic, salt, and pepper. Mix very well. Add oil and vinegar, if using. Adjust seasoning. Serve cold or at room temperature.

Note: If you omit the oil, omit the vinegar.

Grilled Eggplant Dip with Garlic

Makes 6 to 8 servings

A favorite in Israel as well as most of the Middle East, this is the most basic form of eggplant dip, seasoned simply with minced garlic, olive oil, and lemon juice. For best results, be sure the garlic is very fresh and in very tiny pieces because it's added to the salad raw.

Serve the eggplant mixture either as a dip for pita wedges or crackers, or as a sandwich filling. It makes a tasty sandwich combined with thin turkey slices or, for a vegetarian sandwich, with roasted peppers and pitted olives.

Traditionally the dip is made with large eggplants but I like it even better with small Chinese or Japanese eggplants, which take only 15 to 20 minutes in the broiler. If you use them, you can make the salad with less oil, since the flavor of Asian eggplants is more delicate.

2 medium eggplants (total about 2¹/₂ pounds)

1 large clove garlic, finely minced

1¹/₂ to 3 tablespoons extra-virgin olive oil, plus extra for drizzling

1 to 3 tablespoons strained fresh lemon juice

2 tablespoons chopped fresh Italian parsley

Salt and freshly ground pepper, to taste

Cayenne pepper, to taste

1 large ripe tomato, very finely diced (optional)

Fresh parsley sprigs

1. Prick eggplants a few times with fork. Grill eggplants on barbecue at medium-high heat about 1 hour, or broil about 40 minutes; in either case, turn eggplants from time to time, until skin blackens. When done, flesh should be tender and eggplants should look collapsed.

2. Leave eggplants until cool enough to handle. Cut off caps. Cut eggplants in half and drain off any liquid from inside. With a spoon, scoop flesh from peel; discard peel. Chop flesh finely with knife.

3. Transfer eggplant to a bowl. Add garlic and mix well. Stir in 1¹/₂ tablespoons olive oil, lemon juice, and parsley. Season generously with salt, pepper, and cayenne. Refrigerate 1 hour in a covered container to blend flavors.

4. Just before serving, stir in tomato, if using, and adjust seasoning.

5. Taste, and add more oil if needed. To serve, spoon into a shallow bowl and garnish with parsley sprigs. Drizzle with a little olive oil.

Creamy Eggplant Dip

Makes 6 to 8 servings

When I lived in Israel, this dip was the item I bought most often at delis, before I realized how easy it is to make at home. The mayonnaise-enriched dip probably came to Israel with Russian immigrants; it's not common in other Middle Eastern countries.

I love the dip's rich flavor and smooth texture. Serve it with pita bread wedges or crackers. It also makes delicious spreads for sandwiches, for example with smoked turkey or chicken breast.

If you prefer, you can grill or broil the eggplant instead of baking it. Follow the instructions in Grilled Eggplant Dip with Garlic (this page).

2 medium eggplants (total about 2¹/₂ pounds)

1 large clove garlic, minced

1 tablespoon minced onion

¹/₃ cup mayonnaise

1 tablespoon strained fresh lemon juice, or to taste

Salt and freshly ground pepper, to taste

Cayenne pepper, to taste (optional)

Fresh parsley sprigs

1. Preheat oven to 400°F. Pierce each eggplant a few times with a fork to prevent them from bursting. Bake whole eggplants on a large baking sheet lined with foil 30 minutes. Turn eggplants over and bake them 30 to 40 more minutes, or until they are very tender. Leave eggplants until cool enough to handle. Holding cap, peel off skin of each eggplant. Let eggplants drain in a colander 1 hour.

2. Cut off eggplant caps. Cut eggplants in half and drain off any liquid from inside eggplant. With a spoon, scoop flesh from peel; discard peel. Chop flesh finely with knife.

3. Transfer eggplant to a bowl. Add garlic and onion and mix well. Stir in mayonnaise, lemon juice, and salt, pepper, and cayenne, if using, and mix well; mixture should be highly seasoned. Refrigerate in a covered container 30 minutes to blend flavors.

4. Spoon dip into a shallow bowl or plate and garnish it with parsley sprigs. Serve cold.

Sephardic Eggplant Dip with Tahini

Makes 6 to 8 servings

This is the most popular eggplant dip in Israel. In the United States, it's often sold by its Arabic name, baba ghanouj, but in Israel it's known by its Hebrew name, salat hatzilim im tahina, or eggplant salad with tahini. Although it's called "salad," it's really a dip for scooping up with pita wedges.

Charring over a flame is an ancient method for cooking eggplant that has long been a favorite in the Middle East because the eggplant gains an appealing smoky flavor. I try to always have a few eggplants on hand to put on the barbecue whenever I am grilling other foods. The eggplant is flexible when it comes to the heat of the barbecue. You can use high, medium, or low and you don't have to worry about overcooking it as long as it doesn't burn.

The broiler works well too, but if your broiler compartment is small, be sure the eggplants are slender enough to fit. One other method: my neighbors in Israel set their eggplants directly on the gas burners of their stove. (For safety, turn eggplants with tongs.)

2 medium eggplants (total about 2¹/₂ pounds)

¹/₂ cup tahini (sesame paste), stirred before measuring

6 tablespoons strained fresh lemon juice

2 tablespoons water

2 or 3 large cloves garlic, minced

1 teaspoon ground cumin

Salt and freshly ground pepper, to taste

2 tablespoons chopped fresh cilantro or Italian parsley (optional)

Paprika or cayenne pepper, to taste

Extra-virgin olive oil

1. Prick each eggplant a few times with fork. Cook eggplants on grill at medium-high heat about 1 hour, or broil about 40 minutes; in either case, turn eggplants from time to time, until skin is blackened. When done, flesh should be tender and eggplants should look collapsed.

2. Cut off caps. Cut eggplants in half and drain off any liquid from inside. With a spoon, scoop flesh from peel; discard peel. Chop flesh finely with knife. Transfer eggplant to a bowl.

3. Stir tahini until blended in another bowl. Add lemon juice and water, stirring tahini until smooth. Add garlic and cumin. Add tahini mixture to eggplant and mix well. Season with salt and pepper. Refrigerate in a covered container until ready to serve.

4. To serve, spread on a plate and sprinkle with cilantro or parsley, if using. Then, sprinkle very lightly with paprika or cayenne, and drizzle with olive oil.

Avocado Garlic Dip

Makes about 1 cup

Israelis use avocado in a variety of savory recipes, most often as dips or spreads. I love this rich dip with a variety of crunchy vegetables, such as carrot sticks, cucumber spears, and cauliflower florets. You can also serve it with pita bread or crackers. Make it quickly in the food processor, but no more than 2 hours before serving so the avocado keeps its green color. Omit the Parmesan if you want the dip to be pareve.

2 medium cloves garlic, halved

1 cup packed fresh Italian parsley leaves

2 tablespoons pine nuts

2 tablespoons freshly grated Parmesan cheese (optional)

1 ripe medium avocado, preferably Haas (¹/₂ pound)

4 to 6 tablespoons vegetable oil or olive oil

Salt and freshly ground pepper, to taste

Cayenne pepper, to taste

1 tablespoon strained fresh lemon juice (optional)

1. With blade of food processor turning, drop garlic cloves, one at a time, through feed tube and process until finely chopped. Add parsley, pine nuts, and cheese, if using, and process until parsley is chopped.

2. Peel and pit avocado and cut into a few chunks. Add to mixture in processor and puree it. With blade turning, gradually add oil through feed tube. Scrape down sides and process until mixture is well blended. Season with salt, pepper, and cayenne. Add lemon juice, if using. Transfer dip to a bowl. If making it ahead, cover dip by pressing plastic wrap directly on its surface; refrigerate until ready to serve.

Sephardic Roasted Vegetable Spread

Makes 4 to 6 servings (P)

Sephardic Jews from all around the Mediterranean and the Middle East enjoy spreads made from vegetables. This spread is made from a medley of vegetables that are roasted together in the oven—eggplant, potatoes, peppers, tomatoes, garlic, and onions. It's easy to make because the vegetables are roasted whole. The vegetables are pureed in a food processor (except for the potato, which would become gluey) and the puree is seasoned with lemon juice and olive oil. Serve it with pita bread, toast, or with French or sourdough bread. It also makes a light and pretty appetizer spread on cucumber slices.

2 baking potatoes (total 1 pound)

3 Japanese eggplants or 1 small Italian eggplant
    (total 3/4 pound)

2 large red bell peppers

4 ripe plum tomatoes (total 1/2 pound)

1 small onion, unpeeled

4 large cloves garlic, unpeeled

3 tablespoons extra-virgin olive oil

1 tablespoon strained fresh lemon juice

Salt and freshly ground pepper, to taste

Cayenne pepper, to taste (optional)

1. Preheat oven to 400°F. Rinse vegetables and pat dry. Prick potatoes and eggplant a few times with a fork and put in a roasting pan. Add peppers, tomatoes, onion, and garlic. Bake vegetables until tender— tomatoes, onions, and garlic 30 minutes, peppers 45 to 50 minutes, eggplants 50 minutes to 1 hour, and potatoes about 1 hour and 10 minutes; turn vegetables once during roasting.

2. When done, peel tomatoes, onion, and garlic. When pepper is done, transfer to a bowl and cover tightly (or close in a plastic bag). Let stand 10 minutes. Peel with aid of a paring knife. Halve and drain liquid from inside peppers. Remove core. Cut into pieces. Peel eggplant with aid of paring knife. Puree the vegetables (not potatoes) in food processor until smooth.

3. Scoop out pulp from potatoes into a bowl. Mash with a potato masher or in a food mill. Mix with remaining vegetables. Stir in oil, lemon juice, salt, pepper, and cayenne, if using; season generously. Serve cold or at room temperature.

Zesty Moroccan Pepper Dip

Makes 6 to 8 servings (P)

This rich and flavorful medley of hot and sweet peppers cooked with tomatoes is a favorite in Israel. It's usually served cold as a dip with pita bread. I also like it hot or cold as a sauce or accompaniment for meat, fish, or grains.

This version is medium-hot; increase the amount of jalapeño peppers or leave in their seeds and ribs if you would like it hotter. Another way to adjust the heat is to add a pinch or two of cayenne pepper to the finished mixture.

3 or 4 tablespoons olive oil

2 large green bell peppers, diced (1/2-inch dice)

2 large red bell peppers or 1 red and 1 yellow, halved, cored,
    and diced

2 1/2 pounds ripe tomatoes, peeled, seeded, and diced,
    or two 28-ounce cans diced tomatoes, drained

Salt, to taste

6 large cloves garlic, chopped

3 jalapeño peppers, seeds and ribs removed, chopped
    (see Note)

1 teaspoon ground cumin (optional)

1/2 cup small sprigs fresh cilantro, chopped

1. Heat oil in a large, wide, deep pan, such as a Dutch oven. Add both types bell peppers and sauté over medium-low heat about 10 minutes or until softened. Remove peppers with slotted spoon.

2. Add tomatoes to the pan, sprinkle with salt, and bring to boil. Cook uncovered over medium heat, 20 minutes. Add sautéed peppers, garlic, jalapeño peppers, and cumin, if using, and cook over medium heat, stirring often, about 10 minutes or until bell peppers are tender and mixture is thick. Add cilantro and cook 2 minutes. Adjust seasoning. Serve hot, cold, or at room temperature. Stir before serving.

Note: Wear rubber gloves when handling hot peppers.

Quick-and-Spicy Garlic Dip

Makes 6 to 8 servings

Serve this tasty pareve dip with raw or cooked vegetables as an appetizer or to accompany cooked fish. Be sure to use very fresh garlic. Generally I use fresh jalapeño pepper to flavor the dip but you can use other fresh chiles or omit them if you prefer.

4 medium cloves garlic, peeled

1/2 small red or green jalapeño pepper, seeds and ribs discarded

1 cup mayonnaise

About 1 tablespoon strained fresh lemon juice

1 tablespoon extra-virgin olive oil

Salt and freshly ground pepper, to taste

Mince garlic and jalapeño in a mini food processor or with a knife. Mix mayonnaise with garlic, jalapeño pepper, 1 tablespoon lemon juice, and olive oil in a bowl. Adjust seasoning, and add more lemon juice if desired.

Falafel and Fritters

Rachel's Falafel

Makes 4 or 5 dozen,
about 12 appetizer servings

This is the way my mother-in-law, Rachel Levy, made falafel. Serve falafel as an appetizer with an assortment of dips and salads, with a plate of Everyday Israeli Salad (page 238) or as a sandwich in very fresh pita bread cut in half. If you're serving it as a sandwich, add a few spoonfuls of Israeli salad, some tahini sauce, and a drizzle of hot sauce.

My mother-in-law used a meat grinder to prepare the falafel mixture. I use a food processor because it's easier. If you like, you can prepare the mixture ahead and refrigerate it in a covered container up to 2 days.

1 pound dried chickpeas (garbanzo beans), about 2²/₃ cups

3 medium heads of garlic (about 30 medium cloves), peeled

1 thick slice stale white bread, crusts removed

1 large onion, minced

1/3 cup small sprigs fresh cilantro, chopped

2¹/₂ tablespoons ground coriander

2¹/₂ tablespoons ground cumin

1 tablespoon salt

2¹/₂ teaspoons prepared black pepper

1/4 cup all-purpose flour

1 teaspoon baking powder

About 6 cups vegetable oil (for frying)

1. Soak chickpeas overnight or 8 to 12 hours in cool water to generously cover; drain in colander and rinse. Note: The chickpeas are soaked but are not boiled—the frying cooks them enough.

2. Mince garlic in food processor; remove. Sprinkle bread with about 1 tablespoon water; squeeze dry. Grind chickpeas and bread in processor in batches. Transfer to a bowl. Add minced onion, garlic, chopped cilantro, coriander, cumin, salt, pepper, flour, and baking powder. Mix well. Knead thoroughly with hands to mix very well.

3. To shape the falafel, take 1 tablespoon of mixture and squeeze to compact it. Then press it to a ball. Roll lightly between your palms to give it a smooth round shape.

4. Heat oil in a deep fryer or heavy saucepan to about 350°F. Add about one sixth of the falafel balls. Do not drop them into oil from high up or oil will splash. Fry about 2 minutes or until falafel balls are deep golden brown and crisp. Drain briefly on paper towels. Serve hot.

Grilled Falafel

Makes 4 servings, 8 patties

Sometimes I like to prepare falafel in a non-traditional way. I shape the patties as burgers and grill them on a barbecue. My grilled falafel is easier to prepare than the original because you don't have to deal with a deep fat fryer and sizzling oil. Naturally, my falafel's fat content is greatly reduced as well. My recipe drew smiles from my mother-in-law, who is a falafel expert, but she agreed that falafel's main appeal is its spicing. Generous amounts of cumin, garlic, and black pepper are what give falafel its unique flavor. Usually falafel contains cilantro too but you can substitute Italian parsley.

To make falafel even more quickly, I use canned chickpeas so I don't have to soak dried chickpeas overnight. I chop the chickpeas and other ingredients in a food processor instead of working them through a meat grinder. Serve the grilled falafel like fried falafel (see Box and Recipe, Falafel). Instead of tahini, I sometimes prepare a simple, low-fat sesame sauce.

6 large cloves garlic, peeled

1/3 cup small sprigs fresh cilantro or Italian parsley

1 medium onion, peeled and quartered

Two 15- or 16-ounce cans chickpeas (garbanzo beans), drained

2 1/2 teaspoons ground cumin

2 teaspoons ground coriander

1/2 teaspoon salt

1/2 teaspoon freshly ground pepper

Pinch of cayenne pepper

2 tablespoons bread crumbs

1 large egg white

Falafel

On the day that Israel commemorates its independence, many in the crowd celebrating in the streets feast on the Middle Eastern specialty that has been informally crowned as "Israel's national dish"—falafel.

Like the American hamburger, "falafel" describes a sandwich and the food that gives the sandwich its name. Chickpea (garbanzo bean) batter is shaped into small balls, then fried and placed inside a pita pocket, with chopped vegetables and zesty condiments.

Flavorful, inexpensive falafel are so ubiquitous on Israeli streets that it is now unquestioningly associated, in the minds of both natives and tourists, with Israel. It is a favorite pick-me-up for children on their way home from school, for adults on their lunch break, and for families enjoying a stroll in big cities like Jerusalem or Tel Aviv. Israelis did much to popularize these vegetarian burgers by opening falafel restaurants abroad, thus giving it an Israeli identity in Europe and in the United States.

The first time I ate falafel was in Israel when I was seventeen. It was quite a surprise because I had never eaten spicy-hot food before. I bit into the falafel and immediately had to ask for a glass of water. I didn't manage to finish the whole sandwich.

Several years later my mother-in-law opened a falafel café in Givatayim, a suburb of Tel Aviv. She made falafel every day by grinding soaked chickpeas with fresh garlic and spices. After frying the falafel balls in vegetable oil, she served them the favorite Israeli way: inside a split, very fresh pita with several spoonfuls of Israeli salad. For those who wanted it, she added shredded green or red cabbage, hot sauce, pickles, and tahini (sesame paste) sauce. I tasted her falafel and understood why everyone loved it. The combination of sizzling hot, just-fried falafel balls, crisp cooling vegetables, fiery hot pepper sauce, and smooth, rich tahini sauce was irresistible.

1. Mince garlic and cilantro in food processor. Add onion to mixture in processor and mince it by pulsing. Add chickpeas, cumin, coriander, salt, pepper, cayenne, and bread crumbs. Process with brief pulses to a chunky puree, scraping down sides occasionally. Add egg white and process until blended. Transfer to a bowl. Mix well.

2. Shape mixture in 8 smooth patties. Pack mixture firmly when shaping so that falafel holds together.

3. Heat grill and brush with oil. Grill falafel patties over medium heat about 5 minutes per side or until slightly firm on top, turning patties over carefully with 2 spatulas. Serve hot.

Golden Zucchini and Onion Patties

Makes 12 small patties,
about 4 appetizer or side-dish servings   Ⓟ

These tasty patties can play a variety of roles on holiday or special occasion menus. They can be a Sukkot side dish for fish, meat, or chicken or, in vegetarian meals, for rice or the Romanian cornmeal dish called mamaliga. You can also serve them as a new type of latke for Hanukkah. The patties also make tasty appetizers topped with Caper-Lemon Salsa (page 141) or served with Spiced Yogurt (page 460) or Sephardic Salsa (page 131) as a dipping sauce.

2¹/₂ cups coarsely grated golden zucchini, yellow crookneck squash, or green-skinned zucchini (about 2 or 3 medium, total 10 ounces)

1 medium onion, coarsely grated

1 tablespoon chopped garlic

Salt and freshly ground pepper, to taste

1 large egg, lightly beaten

3 tablespoons all-purpose flour

About ¹/₄ cup vegetable oil (for frying)

1. Line a tray with paper towels to drain the patties. Combine zucchini and onion in a colander. Squeeze to remove excess liquid. Transfer to a bowl. Add garlic, salt, and pepper. Add beaten egg and stir in lightly. Stir in flour.

2. Heat oil in a deep, large, heavy skillet. For each patty, drop 1 heaping tablespoon of zucchini mixture into pan. Flatten them slightly with back of a spoon. Fry over medium heat 2 to 3 minutes on each side, or until golden brown. Turn carefully with 2 slotted spatulas so oil doesn't splatter. Transfer to paper towels. Stir batter before frying each new batch. Add more oil to the pan as necessary, and heat it before adding more latkes.

3. Pat tops of patties with paper towels before serving. Serve hot or warm.

Fried Eggplant with Herbed Tomatoes

Makes 4 to 6 servings   Ⓟ

This old-fashioned dish is a popular appetizer in Israel for weddings and other festive occasions. The eggplant can be served on its own or accompanied by a hot sauce. I like it with a simple topping of tomatoes, garlic, and herbs. If you prefer a lighter dish, prepare Broiled Eggplant (page 445) and serve it with the topping.

Fried eggplant is also used for other preparations, for example, to prepare marinated eggplant (see page 224).

When I have Chinese or Japanese eggplants, I skip the step of salting them.

1 large eggplant (1 to 1¹/₂ pounds), unpeeled

Salt and freshly ground pepper, to taste

7 to 8 tablespoons olive oil

2 large cloves garlic, minced

2 tablespoons chopped fresh Italian parsley

1¹/₄ pounds ripe tomatoes, diced

2 tablespoons chopped fresh cilantro

¹/₂ teaspoon dried oregano

Zehug (page 592), hot sauce, or cayenne pepper, to taste

1. Cut eggplant into ³/₈-inch slices crosswise. To salt eggplant, sprinkle the slices lightly but evenly with salt on both sides and put on a rack. Let stand to drain 1 hour, turning slices over after 30 minutes. Thoroughly pat dry with paper towels.

2. Heat 2 tablespoons olive oil in a large, heavy skillet over medium heat. Quickly add enough eggplant slices to make one layer; if you add them too slowly, the first ones soak up all the oil. Sauté eggplant 2 to 3 minutes per side or until tender when pierced with a fork. Transfer to a plate with a slotted spatula.

3. Add 2 tablespoons oil to pan, heat, and sauté second batch of eggplant in same way. Repeat with another 2 tablespoons oil and remaining eggplant. Add more oil if necessary during frying. Transfer fried eggplant to paper towels and pat to absorb excess oil. Transfer them to a serving plate.

4. Heat 1 tablespoon oil in pan over medium-high heat. Add garlic and sauté 30 seconds. Add parsley and toss over heat a few seconds. Remove from heat and stir in tomatoes, cilantro, and oregano. Season with salt, pepper, and zehug. Spoon tomato mixture over eggplant slices. Serve at room temperature.

Sephardic Fried Cauliflower

Makes 4 to 6 servings   **P**

Jews from Mediterranean and Middle Eastern countries often prepare cauliflower this way. This spicy, deep golden version is my mother-in-law's, and it is irresistible. She also liked to simmer the fried cauliflower in tomato sauce but members of the family usually snatched many of the just-fried florets before she had a chance to do this. You can serve these florets as an appetizer with tomato sauce for dipping, or as a side dish with Spicy Beef Patties (page 394).

1 medium head cauliflower (about 2 pounds)
1 teaspoon ground cumin
1/2 teaspoon ground turmeric
1/2 teaspoon salt
1/4 teaspoon freshly ground pepper
Pinch of cayenne pepper
1/2 cup all-purpose flour
2 large eggs or 3 large egg whites
About 2 tablespoons water
About 1/3 cup vegetable oil
Fresh Tomato Sauce or Tomato Sauce with Mild Chiles
    (pages 585 and 587), optional

1. Divide cauliflower into fairly large florets with stems attached. Cook cauliflower uncovered in a large pan of boiling salted water 2 minutes; it should be only partly tender. Drain and rinse gently until cool.

2. Mix cumin, turmeric, salt, pepper, cayenne, and flour in a medium bowl. Sprinkle cauliflower florets lightly with part of the spice-flour mixture. Add eggs and 2 tablespoons water to remaining spice mixture. Gently stir with whisk until blended to a thick batter. Dip a floret in batter; it should coat floret lightly. If batter sticks to floret in a thick layer, stir in 1 teaspoon water.

3. Heat 1/3 cup vegetable oil in a large skillet, preferably with a nonstick surface, over medium heat. Holding a floret by its stem end, dip flower and part of stem in batter and add gently to oil. Dip 5 or 6 more florets. Fry dipped florets about 10 minutes or until golden brown. Drain on paper towels. Continue with remaining cauliflower. Serve as soon as possible, with hot tomato sauce.

❦ *Marinated Vegetables*

Greek Marinated Mushrooms

Makes 4 servings   Ⓟ

For quick summer suppers, an easy way to have vegetables ready is to cook them during a cool part of the day. Instead of plain boiled veggies, I prepare marinated vegetables, which keep for several days. They make a zesty, cold, and refreshing first course for Shabbat meals, served in a bowl or spooned over a bed of salad greens. You might also like to serve them with Brown Eggs (page 313), a traditional Shabbat first-course of the Jews of Greece. Although the members of this community of Sephardic Jews are now few in number in Greece, their roots date back more than 2000 years.

This dish is also good as an accompaniment for barbecued chicken breasts, fish fillets, or cold cuts for weekday meals.

This version is lighter in oil than classic marinated mushrooms. You can also use the marinade of dry wine, olive oil, lemon juice, herbs, and coriander seeds with other vegetables, such as zucchini, cauliflower, baby onions, celery, carrots, and cucumbers.

1 large sprig fresh thyme or ¹/₂ teaspoon dried thyme

1 bay leaf

¹/₃ cup dry white wine, such as Sauvignon Blanc

1 to 2 tablespoons extra-virgin olive oil

¹/₂ cup water

2 tablespoons tomato sauce or 1 tablespoon tomato paste

1 tablespoon whole coriander seeds

Salt and freshly ground pepper, to taste

Juice of ¹/₂ lemon

1 pound small whole mushrooms, rinsed briefly

1. Combine the thyme, bay leaf, wine, oil, water, tomato sauce, coriander seeds, salt, pepper, and lemon juice in a sauté pan. Stir and bring to a boil.

2. Add mushrooms to pan. Cook uncovered over high heat, gently stirring occasionally, about 7 minutes or until mushrooms are just tender. Transfer to a shallow dish, discarding the thyme sprig and bay leaf. Adjust seasoning. Serve cool or cold.

Mediterranean Marinated Peppers

Makes 6 servings   Ⓟ

A specialty of the Sephardic kitchen, this simple dish is one of the best ways to make use of the late-summer abundance of sweet peppers. It makes a terrific appetizer for Shabbat, Sukkot, or for any festive meal. This version is from my sister-in-law Mati Kahn who adds a touch of cumin to give the marinade a distinctive taste.

8 large red bell peppers, or 4 red and 4 green

2 tablespoons extra-virgin olive oil

1¹/₂ to 2 tablespoons strained fresh lemon juice

¹/₂ teaspoon ground cumin

Salt and freshly ground pepper, to taste

Pinch of cayenne pepper

3 large cloves garlic, halved

1. Grill and peel peppers (see page 588). Remove cores. Cut peppers into wide strips. Pat dry.

2. Put peppers in shallow serving dish. Whisk olive oil with lemon juice, cumin, salt, pepper, and cayenne in a small bowl. Pour mixture over peppers and add garlic. Let stand at room temperature, turning occasionally, 30 minutes, or refrigerate overnight. Remove garlic. Serve peppers at room temperature.

Israeli Marinated Eggplant

Makes 4 to 6 servings

Garlic, chiles, and cilantro flavor this summer appetizer, which is usually served with fresh pita wedges. It also makes a pleasant accompaniment for cold chicken or turkey. I use one or two jalapeño or seeded serrano chiles but you can use more chiles if you like it hotter. If you prefer, substitute parsley for the cilantro. Garnish the eggplant with tomato wedges, roasted peppers, or sun-dried tomatoes in olive oil.

2 medium eggplants (2 pounds), unpeeled

2 teaspoons salt, plus extra for seasoning

$2/3$ cup plus 2 tablespoons olive oil

3 large cloves garlic, minced

1 to 2 fresh jalapeño or 2 serrano peppers, halved lengthwise, seeds removed if desired (see Note)

1 teaspoon ground cumin

$1/4$ cup white wine vinegar

$1/4$ cup finely chopped fresh cilantro

Freshly ground pepper, to taste

Fresh cilantro sprigs

1. Cut eggplants into $1/2$ inch slices crosswise. Arrange slices in 1 layer on a rack set over a tray. Sprinkle evenly with 1 teaspoon salt on each side. Let slices drain 1 hour. Thoroughly dry them with several paper towels.

2. Heat 3 tablespoons oil in a large, heavy skillet over medium heat. Quickly add enough eggplant slices to make 1 layer. Sauté eggplant about $2^1/2$ minutes on each side or until tender when pierced with a fork. Transfer to a plate. Add 3 tablespoons oil to skillet, heat, and sauté remaining eggplant in batches, adding more oil between batches as necessary. Transfer eggplant to a large shallow serving dish or baking dish.

3. To prepare the marinade: Heat 2 tablespoons oil in a small saucepan, add chopped garlic and halved chiles and cook over low heat 2 minutes. Stir in cumin, a small pinch of salt, and vinegar. Bring to a boil and cook over low heat 1 minute. Remove marinade from heat and discard chiles. Add chopped cilantro.

4. Pour marinade evenly over eggplant slices and sprinkle them with pepper. Turn eggplant slices over so that marinade coats all of them. Let stand at room temperature 30 minutes before serving; or refrigerate in a covered container up to 3 days.

5. Serve eggplant cold or at room temperature, garnished with cilantro sprigs.

Note: Wear rubber gloves when handling hot peppers.

Israeli Olive and Tomato Salad

Makes about 4 servings as an appetizer
or 8 servings as an accompaniment

Olives have been a product of the land of Israel since biblical times, and today Israel exports several varieties of olives as well as olive oil. They appear very often on the table as a condiment and are used in many dishes, especially Sephardic ones.

Serve this salad as an appetizer or as a savory topping for baked fish, beans, or rice. Be sure to use good quality olives. Leave them whole or cut them in half. If you're making the salad ahead, try to add the parsley close to serving time so it will stay bright green.

2 tablespoons strained fresh lemon juice

$1/4$ teaspoon hot red pepper flakes, or to taste

$1/2$ teaspoon dried thyme

1 cup black olives, pitted

1 cup green olives, pitted

1 pound ripe tomatoes, finely diced

$1/4$ cup chopped green onion

$1/4$ cup chopped fresh Italian parsley

Freshly ground pepper, to taste

Combine lemon juice, pepper flakes, and thyme in a serving bowl. Add olives, tomatoes, green onion, and parsley. Season with pepper. Refrigerate in a covered container until ready to serve.

❧ Pastries and Snacks

Knishes

Makes 36 to 40 small knishes

(depending on filling)

These pillows of dough enclosing a savory filling are time-honored specialties of the Ashkenazic kitchen. Knishes filled with meat, potatoes, and kasha are the most traditional and are available at many delis. In recent years home cooks and deli chefs have created many new flavors. I've sampled spinach knishes, turkey knishes, and broccoli and cheddar knishes. There are even knishes with sweet fillings. To stuff these knishes with a meat filling, use pareve margarine. For vegetable or cheese fillings, you can use either margarine or butter, or make the knishes with sour cream dough.

2¹/2 cups all-purpose flour
Scant ³/4 teaspoon salt
³/4 cup (1¹/2 stick) unsalted firm margarine or butter,
    well chilled and cut into small pieces
5 to 7 tablespoons ice water
1¹/4 cups filling for knishes (see following recipes)
1 large egg, beaten with pinch of salt (for glaze)

1. Combine flour and salt in food processor and process briefly to blend. Add margarine and process with brief pulses until mixture resembles small crumbs. With blades turning, add ice water gradually, until dough begins to clump together. Knead dough very lightly and briefly just until it holds together. Wrap dough in plastic wrap, press together to form a ball, and flatten to a disc. Refrigerate dough at least 1 hour or up to 2 days before using it.

2. Prepare filling. Cut dough into 4 pieces. Take first piece and roll dough on a lightly floured surface until as thin as possible, at most ¹/8-inch thick. With a 3-inch cutter, cut dough into rounds. Put about 1¹/2 teaspoons filling in center of each. Moisten edges about half way around circle and fold in half, bringing unmoistened side over to moistened side. Pinch edges together to seal them. Put them on a greased baking sheet. Continue making knishes from remaining dough and scraps left from cutting. Refrigerate knishes 30 minutes or up to overnight.

3. Preheat oven to 375°F. Brush knishes with beaten egg. Make 2 or 3 slits in pastry with a small sharp knife so steam can escape. Bake knishes 20 to 25 minutes or until they are light brown. Serve warm.

Kasha-Walnut Filling for Knishes

Makes about 2 cups   Ⓜ or Ⓟ

Fillings of kasha, also called buckwheat groats or roasted buckwheat kernels, have long been popular among knish mavens. Some cooks add nuts as well, and I like the way their flavor complements that of the kasha and the browned onions. Fine kasha is the best for making fillings but you can use medium kasha if your market does not carry the finely ground type. You can find kasha with the kosher products in many supermarkets.

2 large eggs
Salt and freshly ground pepper, to taste
¹/2 cup kasha, preferably fine
1 cup hot beef, chicken, or vegetable stock or water
3 tablespoons vegetable oil
1 large onion, peeled and chopped
¹/4 cup finely chopped walnuts

1. Beat 1 egg with a pinch of salt in a wide bowl. Combine kasha with beaten egg and stir with a fork until grains are thoroughly coated. Add mixture to a dry, heavy skillet and heat over medium heat, stirring constantly to keep grains separate, 3 minutes. Meanwhile, bring hot stock to a boil in a small saucepan. Add boiling stock to kasha and stir. Cover and cook over low heat 15 minutes or until all the water is absorbed. Fluff with a fork.

2. Heat oil in a skillet, add onion, and sauté over medium-low heat, stirring occasionally, about 10 minutes or until soft and golden brown. Add to kasha. Transfer mixture to a bowl. Add walnuts and stir with a fork. Season with salt and pepper; kasha benefits from generous seasoning. Cool slightly. Stir in remaining egg. Cool completely. Refrigerate in a covered container until ready to use.

Note: Extra kasha filling can be made into small casseroles: Mix filling lightly with an equal volume of cooked rice or pasta such as orzo. Spoon mixture into small greased ramekins and bake at 350°F 20 to 30 minutes or until surface is hot and egg is cooked.

Potato Filling for Knishes

Makes about 1¹/₃ cups

Well-browned onions give potato filling good flavor. Schmaltz is traditionally used to sauté the onions but I use oil instead. If you wish to use Schmaltz, see page 602.

6 small (³/₄ pound) boiling potatoes
1 to 2 tablespoons vegetable oil
1 small onion, chopped (²/₃ cup)
Salt and freshly ground pepper, to taste
1 large egg, beaten

1. Put potatoes in a saucepan with water to cover and a pinch of salt and bring to a boil. Cover and simmer over low heat about 30 minutes or until very tender. Drain and leave until cool enough to handle.

2. In a medium skillet heat oil, add onion, and sauté over medium heat, stirring often, 10 to 12 minutes or until tender and browned.

3. Peel potatoes. Cut each into a few pieces, put in a bowl, and mash with a potato masher. Lightly stir in onion mixture. Season filling with salt and pepper; it should be seasoned generously. Stir in beaten egg. Refrigerate in a covered container until ready to use.

Broccoli-Cheddar Filling for Knishes

Makes 2 to 2¹/₂ cups

Innovative fillings are appearing inside knish pastry on many Jewish-American tables. This one is inspired by a broccoli cheddar knish that I sampled at a deli in St. Louis. Make knishes with this filling using the method in Knishes (page 225).

¹/₂ pound boiling potatoes
1 pound broccoli
Salt and freshly ground pepper, to taste
¹/₂ cup grated cheddar cheese
1 large egg, beaten

1. Put potatoes in a saucepan with water to cover and a pinch of salt and bring to a boil. Cover and simmer over low heat about 30 minutes or until very tender. Drain and leave until cool enough to handle.

2. Peel and slice thick broccoli stem. Divide rest of broccoli into medium florets. Cook broccoli in a saucepan of boiling salted water about 7 minutes or until very tender. Drain, rinse with cold water, and drain well. Chop finely with a knife; or puree in a food processor, leaving a few chunks. Return chopped broccoli to saucepan, sprinkle it with salt and pepper, and heat over medium heat, stirring often, to evaporate excess water.

3. Peel potatoes. Cut each into a few pieces, put in a bowl, and mash with a potato masher. Stir in broccoli puree and cheddar cheese. Season filling to taste with salt and pepper. Stir in beaten egg. Refrigerate in a covered container until ready to use.

Note: Extra broccoli filling can be made into small casseroles: Mix filling lightly with an equal volume of cooked rice or pasta such as orzo. Spoon mixture into small greased ramekins and bake at 350°F 20 to 30 minutes or until hot inside and egg is cooked.

Three-Cheese Knishes

Makes about 16 small knishes

Knishes made with cheese fillings are becoming as popular as those with potato or meat. Some knish-bakers are even coming up with sweet fillings. A friend of mine who works at a knish bakery in Brooklyn, New York, told me her favorite filling in their array is a sweet cheese-chocolate blend.

I make these savory cheese knishes with a rich sour cream dough. For shaping them I like to use the slice-and-bake method, which is much easier than the usual way of cutting and folding individual circles or squares. The result is attractive pinwheel knishes.

1¹/₂ cups all-purpose flour
1 teaspoon baking powder
¹/₂ teaspoon salt
¹/₂ cup (1 stick) unsalted butter, cut into small pieces
¹/₃ cup sour cream
Three-Cheese Filling for Knishes (page 227)

1. Combine flour, baking powder, salt, and butter in a food processor. Process with brief pulses until mixture resembles coarse meal. Spoon sour cream fairly evenly over mixture. Process with brief pulses until dough just holds together and forms sticky crumbs, adding 1 teaspoon water if necessary. Knead dough lightly on work surface until it comes together. Wrap dough with plastic wrap and flatten to a square. Refrigerate 2 hours or up to overnight.

2. Prepare filling. Lightly grease a baking sheet. Divide dough into 2 pieces. Roll one to an 8 × 10-inch rectangle, slightly under ⅛-inch thick. Spread with half the filling, leaving a ½-inch border. Beginning at a long side, roll up tightly like a jelly roll. Cut into slices 1 inch thick. Put each slice on baking sheet with its less open side (the side that was cut second) facing down. Refrigerate slices. Repeat with remaining dough and filling. Refrigerate knishes at least 30 minutes or up to overnight.

3. Preheat oven to 400°F. Bake knishes 15 to 18 minutes or until lightly browned. Serve hot or warm.

Three-Cheese Filling for Knishes

Makes about 1⅓ cups, enough for about 16 small knishes

Farmer cheese is a fresh cheese that is much drier than cottage cheese and leaner than cream cheese. You can find it at kosher food shops and some supermarkets. Kashkaval, a grating cheese loved in Israel, is available at Israeli and Eastern European markets.

4 ounces farmer cheese

2 tablespoons cream cheese, diced and softened

1 cup shredded Swiss cheese, or ½ cup Swiss and ½ cup Kashkaval cheese

Salt (optional) and freshly ground pepper, to taste

Hot paprika or cayenne pepper, to taste (optional)

1 large egg

Mash farmer cheese and mix with cream cheese in a bowl. Add Swiss cheese and mix with a fork. Season mixture with pepper, and salt and hot paprika if using. Beat egg and, using fork, blend with cheese mixture. Refrigerate in a covered container until ready to use.

Mati's Mushroom Bourekas

Makes about 40 small pastries, about 10 servings

In the home kitchen, bourekas are made with puff pastry more often than with phyllo dough. My sister-in-law Mati Kahn, who lives in Jerusalem, serves these bourekas with a Mushroom Sauce (page 234) for festive Shabbat meals. Mati has been making her own puff pastry since she was a teenager and finds it easy to do. Many other Israelis buy the pastry instead. It's easy to find pareve puff pastry in kosher grocery stores.

If you wish to make these ahead, you can freeze them either baked or unbaked. Bake them frozen, adding about 5 minutes to baking time; or reheat baked ones in a 325°F oven.

½ pound boiling potatoes

2 tablespoons vegetable oil

1 small onion, chopped

¼ pound mushrooms, rinsed, halved, and thinly sliced

Salt and freshly ground pepper, to taste

2 large eggs

2 pounds puff pastry, well chilled

2 teaspoons sesame seeds

1. Put potatoes in a saucepan with water to cover and a pinch of salt and bring to a boil. Cover and simmer over low heat about 30 minutes or until very tender. Drain and leave until cool enough to handle.

2. Heat oil in a medium skillet, add onion, and sauté over medium-low heat, stirring often, 5 minutes or until onions just begin to turn golden. Add mushrooms, salt, and pepper and sauté over medium-high heat, stirring, about 3 minutes or until tender.

3. Peel potatoes. Cut each into a few pieces, put in a bowl, and mash with a potato masher. Lightly stir in mushroom mixture. Season filling with salt and pepper; it should be seasoned generously. Beat 1 egg and stir into filling. Refrigerate in a covered container until ready to use.

4. Sprinkle 2 baking sheets with water. Beat 1 egg with a pinch of salt.

5. Roll out half of dough on a cool, lightly floured surface until about 1/8-inch thick. Using a 3-inch round cutter, cut rounds of dough. Separate rounds from rest of dough, reserving scraps. Roll each round to elongate it slightly to an oval. Put 1 teaspoon mushroom filling in center of each oval. Brush half of oval, around a narrow end, with beaten egg. Fold oval in half to enclose filling, joining second side to egg-brushed side. Press to seal well. Set turnovers on a prepared baking sheet. Refrigerate at least 30 minutes. Shape more pastries from remaining pastry and filling. Refrigerate scraps at least 30 minutes and use them also.

6. Preheat oven to 425°F. Brush pastries with beaten egg. Sprinkle with sesame seeds.

7. Bake pastries about 10 minutes. Reduce oven temperature to 375°F and bake about 12 minutes more or until pastries are puffed and brown. Serve warm or at room temperature.

Yemenite Pastry Pancakes
Malawah

Makes 6 rounds, about 12 appetizer servings

The Jews of Yemen brought malawah—*this specialty of pan-fried cakes of rich, flaky pastry—to Israel. They are very popular at cafés and for making at home. You can make the dough ahead and keep it in the refrigerator or freezer.*

When I was a newlywed, I often sat with my mother-in-law at the table of her home in Givatayim, a city near Tel Aviv, and watched her make these. She expertly rolled the dough very thin, folded it gently, rolled it in spirals, and flattened them with her knuckles. I thought I would never learn to make them properly but I was pleased to find out that even my clumsy first attempts turned out tasty.

These pancakes are served hot for supper, plain, or with Brown Eggs (page 313) or sliced cheese and Fresh Tomato Salsa, Yemenite Style (page 234). Some people serve them sprinkled with sugar or drizzled with honey. My father-in-law liked his with an egg pan-fried together

with the pancake. Because malawah *are rich, I like to cut them into wedges and serve them as an appetizer.*

3³/₄ cups all-purpose flour

1 teaspoon baking powder

1¹/₂ teaspoons salt

1 teaspoon sugar (optional)

1 large egg

About 1¹/₄ cups water

¹/₂ cup (1 stick) margarine, cut into 6 pieces, softened

About 2 tablespoons vegetable oil or margarine (for frying)

1. Combine flour, baking powder, salt, and sugar, if using, in food processor and process to blend. Add egg and 1 cup water and process with brief pulses to mix. With motor running, gradually add remaining water, about 1/4 cup, adding enough so mixture comes together to a smooth, fairly stiff dough. It will be sticky.

2. Remove dough from processor. Knead dough well by slapping it vigorously on a work surface. Divide it into 6 pieces and knead each one with a slapping motion until smooth. Roll each in your palm to a ball. Put on an oiled plate or tray, cover, and refrigerate at least 4 hours or overnight.

3. Grease work surface and rolling pin. Roll out 1 ball of dough as thin as possible, so you can almost see through the sheet, to about a 12-inch square. If dough tears, press it together. Spread dough with one piece of the soft margarine. Roll up as for a jelly roll. Tap the resulting roll with your knuckles to flatten it. Roll it up in a spiral. Put spiral on a plate, cover, and refrigerate overnight or up to 2 days; or wrap it well and freeze it. (If freezing dough, thaw before cooking it.)

4. Just before serving, set a ball of dough on a lightly oiled plate and flatten it with your lightly oiled hands into a round as large as the skillet. Heat 1 teaspoon oil or margarine in a heavy 9-inch skillet. Add round of dough. Cover and fry over medium-high heat 30 seconds, then over medium-low heat about 5 minutes per side or until well browned on both sides and cooked through. Cut each into 4 wedges with a sturdy knife and serve hot.

Roasted Garlic and Tomato Toasts

Makes 4 servings

Once you've roasted the garlic, or if you have roasted garlic on hand, these fresh colorful appetizers are ready in a few moments. Use either garlic heads that you have roasted whole, or individual roasted garlic cloves. Serve these tasty hors d'oeuvre for Shavuot or Sukkot, at parties, or to begin a light Saturday night meal.

2 or 3 heads roasted garlic or 30 roasted garlic cloves
    (page 456)

16 thin slices French or sourdough baguette or other slim
    crusty bread

2 or 3 teaspoons olive oil

Salt and freshly ground pepper, to taste

2 ripe small plum tomatoes

16 small fresh basil leaves

1. Prepare garlic. Then, preheat oven to 425°F. Arrange bread on a lightly oiled baking sheet and brush it lightly with olive oil. Toast bread lightly on both sides, 3 to 4 minutes per side.

2. If using garlic heads, cut them in half crosswise and squeeze out the pulp. If using individual roasted cloves, simply squeeze them or crush each clove with a fork to remove the pulp from the skin. Spread the garlic pulp on the toasted bread. Sprinkle with salt and pepper.

3. Cut tomatoes in half lengthwise. Cut into thin slices. Arrange slices on garlic toasts. Garnish each with a small basil leaf. Serve at room temperature.

Chopped Liver Appetizer Puffs

Makes about 12 servings

I first tasted this appetizer years ago at my brother's wedding in Jerusalem. For the wedding the pastries were formed into little swans. I laughed when I saw them because I had just learned to prepare such swan-shaped pastries at cooking school in Paris, where they are always filled with sweet whipped cream! But as soon as I tried them, I had to admit that they were delicious.

I shape the choux pastry puffs in mounds rather than swans, so they are easy to make. You can also buy the

unfilled puffs at some Jewish bakeries. For good flavor, it is important that they be fresh. You can keep them for a day in an airtight container or you can freeze them, but they really do taste best on the day they are made.

Don't fill them too generously, so they won't be too substantial. After all, these are appetizers.

As a variation, you could fill these with vegetarian or mock chopped liver (pages 207–209).

1/2 cup water

1/4 teaspoon salt

1/4 cup (1/2 stick) margarine, cut into pieces

1/2 cup plus 1 tablespoon all-purpose flour, sifted

3 large eggs

Pinch of salt

Chopped Liver the Way My Mother Makes it (page 207)

Fresh parsley sprigs (for garnish)

1. Position rack in lower third of oven and preheat to 400°F. Lightly grease 2 baking sheets. Combine water, salt, and margarine in a small, heavy saucepan. Cook over low heat, stirring constantly, until margarine melts. Bring to a boil; remove from heat. Immediately add flour all at once; stir quickly with a wooden spoon until mixture is smooth. Set pan over low heat; beat mixture about 30 seconds.

2. Remove from heat; cool about 3 minutes. Add 1 egg; beat thoroughly into mixture. Add second egg; beat mixture until smooth. Beat third egg in a small bowl. Gradually beat 1 or 2 tablespoons of this egg into dough, adding enough so dough becomes very shiny and is soft enough so it just falls from the wooden spoon. Add a pinch of salt to remaining egg; beat until blended. Reserve as glaze.

3. Using a pastry bag and medium plain tip, or 2 teaspoons, shape mounds of dough about 1 1/4 inches in diameter, spacing them about 2 inches apart on baking sheets. Brush them with remaining beaten egg, gently pushing down any points.

4. Bake 28 minutes or until dough is puffed and browned. With a serrated knife, carefully cut off top half of each puff; set aside as a "hat." Cool puffs on a rack.

5. Just before serving, spoon a little chopped liver into each puff, then top with "hat." Garnish with parsley sprigs.

Piroshki with Cabbage and Mushrooms

Makes about 3 dozen *piroshki*

In areas where Russian Jews live, whether in Russia, Israel, or in Brooklyn, New York, you see small filled turnovers called piroshki *everywhere. Some are fried and some are baked. Yeast dough is most common, although some people make their* piroshki *with a pastry resembling pie dough. If you don't have time to make your own dough, you can use prepared bread dough or pie dough. Favorite fillings are meat, chicken, buckwheat, and cabbage. I like to enhance my cabbage filling with some dried mushrooms. (Look for "Polish mushrooms" in kosher grocery stores; other names are porcini or cèpes.) Polish Jews prepare* piroshki *also; they are made of noodle dough and resemble kreplach (tortellini).*

Serve piroshki *as an appetizer or a festive partner for hearty vegetable or meat soups. If serving with meat meals, omit the sour cream and use vegetable oil rather than butter. For dairy meals, use vegetable broth. They are best when freshly baked and served warm. You can bake them a day ahead, refrigerate in a container, and reheat; or you can freeze them.*

Yeast Dough for Piroshki (page 231)

1 ounce dried Polish mushrooms or shiitake mushrooms

1¼ pounds green cabbage (about ½ large), cored, rinsed, and finely chopped

2 tablespoons butter or vegetable oil

Salt and freshly ground pepper, to taste

¼ cup vegetable or chicken broth

2 tablespoons sour cream (optional)

1 large egg beaten with a pinch of salt (for glaze)

1. Prepare dough the day before baking.

2. Soak mushrooms in a bowl of hot water 30 minutes. Remove from water. If using shiitake mushrooms, remove stems. Chop mushrooms.

3. Boil cabbage in a large pan of boiling salted water 2 minutes or until wilted. Drain, rinse with cold water, and drain well. Squeeze out excess liquid.

4. Melt butter in a large skillet. Add cabbage, salt, and pepper. Cover and cook over low heat 10 minutes. Add dried mushrooms and broth and cook uncovered over medium heat, stirring occasionally, about 5 minutes or until mixture is thick. Transfer mixture to a bowl and cool to room temperature. Stir in sour cream, if using. Adjust seasoning. Refrigerate 15 minutes.

5. Lightly grease 2 or 3 baking sheets. Cut dough into 4 pieces; return 3 pieces to refrigerator. Shape fourth piece into a round. Roll it on a lightly floured surface until it is about ⅛-inch thick. With a 3-inch cutter, cut out rounds; reserving scraps.

6. Brush each round of dough lightly with egg glaze. Place 1½ teaspoons filling in center of each round. Shape filling in an oval across center of round, leaving a ⅜-inch border at each end. Bring up 2 long opposite edges around filling and mold dough around it to a boat-like shape, joining two edges at the top, over filling. Pinch edges together along top, fluting them neatly. Arrange piroshki 1½ inches apart on baking sheets. Cover with a lightly dampened towel and let rise in a warm place 15 minutes. Continue with remaining dough and filling.

7. Preheat oven to 400°F. Brush piroshki with more egg glaze. Bake 15 minutes or until golden brown.

8. Knead dough scraps together and refrigerate 2 hours. Refrigerate remaining filling. Prepare more piroshki. Serve them warm.

Yeast Dough for Piroshki

Makes enough for about 3 dozen piroshki **D** or **P**

This dough is easiest to roll if you make it a day ahead and refrigerate it. If you're using a meat or poultry filling or serving the piroshki *in a* fleishig *dinner, make the dough with water and either margarine or vegetable oil. For instructions on shaping* piroshki, *see* Piroshki with Cabbage and Mushrooms *(page 230).*

1/4 cup lukewarm water

1 envelope dry yeast (1/4-ounce or 2 teaspoons)

1 tablespoon sugar

About 3 1/4 cups all-purpose flour

1 1/2 teaspoons salt

1/2 cup lukewarm milk or water, or more if needed

7 tablespoons melted butter or pareve margarine
    or vegetable oil

2 large eggs

1. Pour lukewarm water into a small bowl. Sprinkle with yeast and 1 teaspoon sugar. Let mixture stand 10 minutes, or until it is foamy.

2. Combine 3 cups flour with salt in a large bowl, or in bowl of mixer if you have a dough hook. Mix flour with salt and make a well in center. To well add yeast mixture, 1/2 cup milk, butter, eggs, and remaining 2 teaspoons sugar. Mix ingredients with a dough hook or with you hands until they come together to a soft dough, adding more milk or water by tablespoons if needed.

3. If using mixer, beat dough at medium speed about 10 minutes or until smooth, adding more flour as necessary if dough is too sticky.

4. If making dough by hand, knead on a lightly floured surface, adding more flour as necessary to keep it from sticking, 10 to 15 minutes or until smooth.

5. Form dough into a ball, put it in an oiled bowl, and turn to coat it with oil. Cover with plastic wrap. Let rise in a warm place 1 to 1 1/2 hours or until it is double in bulk. Punch it down and knead again lightly. Cover and refrigerate overnight.

Spicy Moroccan Cigars

Makes about 24 bite-size hors d'oeuvres **M**

Moroccan Jews serve these tasty pastry appetizers at dinners celebrating special occasions. The filling might be of potatoes (page 232) or chicken, but the most popular one is of beef spiced with cumin, chiles, and garlic.

A traditional way to make these pastries is to use "brik" wrappers, also called ouarka *leaves, which are very thin, delicate crepe-like rounds made of flour and water. They are not widely available and are difficult to use. Pastry cigars are sometimes made using phyllo sheets cut in rectangles of about 8 by 3 inches. Perla Abergel, a friend of mine in California, gave me the great idea of using won ton wrappers, and they work very well.*

1 1/4 cups diced cooked beef

1 large clove garlic, minced

1/2 teaspoon finely minced jalapeño pepper, or cayenne
    pepper to taste

1/2 teaspoon ground cumin

1/4 teaspoon paprika

Salt and freshly ground pepper, to taste

1 large egg white

One-half 12-ounce package won ton wrappers

Vegetable oil for frying, about 1 inch deep

1. Put beef in food processor with garlic and jalapeño and chop together to blend well. Transfer to a bowl. Add cumin, paprika, salt, and pepper and mix well. Add 1 1/2 to 2 teaspoons egg white, or enough to moisten lightly.

2. Remove 1 won ton wrapper from package. Take 1 slightly rounded teaspoon filling and put it along longer side of wrapper, 1/4-inch from edge nearest you, leaving 1/2-inch of pastry free at each side. Press to compact filling in finger shape. Fold 2 pastry edges, at left and right, over filling. Brush edge of dough farthest from you with remaining egg white. Roll up dough with filling, from edge nearest you to opposite edge, to form cigar shape. Press to seal to egg-brushed dough.

3. In deep, heavy saucepan, heat 1 inch oil to 340°F or 350°F on a frying thermometer. Fry pastries in batches 2 to 2 1/2 minutes or until golden brown. Transfer to paper towels. Serve hot.

Potato Filling for Cigars

Makes about 1 cup

Potato fillings are almost as popular as meat fillings for Moroccan cigars and they have the advantage of being pareve, thus suitable for serving with any other food. These crisp, bite-size pastries make tasty appetizers. To shape and fry the pastries, see Spicy Moroccan Cigars (page 231). If you like, serve a small amount of spicy salsa such as Sephardic Salsa (page 131) or Cilantro Salsa (page 341) as an accompaniment.

1/2 pound boiling potatoes

1 to 2 tablespoons vegetable oil

1 small onion, chopped

1 large clove garlic, minced

1/2 teaspoon finely minced jalapeño pepper, or cayenne pepper to taste

1/2 teaspoon paprika

Salt and freshly ground pepper, to taste

1 large egg white

1. Put potatoes in a saucepan with water to cover and a pinch of salt and bring to a boil. Cover and simmer over low heat about 30 minutes or until very tender. Drain and leave until cool enough to handle.

2. Heat oil in a small skillet, add onion, and sauté over medium-low heat, stirring often, about 5 minutes or until tender and golden brown. Add garlic, jalapeño pepper, and paprika and sauté over low heat, stirring, 1 minute.

3. Peel potatoes. Cut each into a few pieces, put in a bowl, and mash with a potato masher. Lightly stir in onion mixture. Season filling with salt and pepper; it should be seasoned generously. Stir in 2 teaspoons egg white, or enough to moisten lightly. Refrigerate in a covered container until ready to use.

Baked Cheese Puffs

Makes about 6 servings

Serve these savory pastries with vegetable soups, vegetables in sauce, or on their own as an appetizer. They're easy to make and a great dairy choice for Shavuot.

1/2 cup plus 1 tablespoon all-purpose flour

1/2 cup water

1/4 teaspoon salt

1/4 cup (1/2 stick) butter, cut into 8 pieces, or 2 tablespoons butter and 2 tablespoons vegetable oil

Pinch of cayenne pepper

Freshly grated nutmeg to taste

3 large eggs

2 ounces Swiss cheese, coarsely grated

1 large egg, beaten with a pinch of salt (for glaze)

1. Preheat oven to 400°F. Lightly butter 2 baking sheets. Sift flour onto a piece of wax paper.

2. Heat water, salt, and butter in a small, heavy saucepan until butter melts. Raise heat to medium-high and bring to a boil. Remove from heat. Add flour immediately and stir quickly with a wooden spoon until mixture is smooth. Set pan over low heat and beat mixture about 30 seconds. Remove, stir in cayenne and nutmeg, and let cool a few minutes.

3. Transfer dough to food processor and process 5 seconds. Add 2 eggs and process about 15 seconds or until mixture is smooth. Reserve 2 tablespoons of shredded cheese for sprinkling on top. Add remaining cheese to dough and process just until blended. (To make without a food processor, beat eggs one by one into dough with a wooden spoon, then beat in cheese.)

4. Transfer dough to a bowl. Beat third egg in a small bowl with a fork. Gradually beat enough of this egg into dough until dough becomes very shiny and is soft enough so it just falls from spoon.

5. With a pastry bag and small plain tip, or with 2 teaspoons, shape small mounds of dough, spacing them about 1 1/2 inches apart on baking sheets. Brush them with egg glaze. Sprinkle them with remaining cheese. Bake about 15 minutes or until dough is puffed and browned. Serve warm or at room temperature.

Chicken Kubeh

Makes about 6 appetizer portions (M)

Kubeh are pastries made of a crunchy case and a meat or chicken filling. Usually the case is made of bulgur wheat but variations abound, made with potatoes, rice, semolina, or matzo meal. Making them is a tradition of Jews born in many Middle Eastern countries. People from Iraq are especially fond of them. Serve the kubeh with Tahini Dip (page 214).

Kubeh are traditionally formed in a football shape but this takes practice. I use the easier method below and shape them into disks.

3 cups cold water

1 cup bulgur wheat, finest grind

Chicken Filling for Kubeh (this page)

2 tablespoons fine dry bread crumbs

3 tablespoons all-purpose flour

1 teaspoon salt

1/2 teaspoon ground turmeric

3 to 4 tablespoons water

About 1 cup vegetable oil (for frying)

1. Pour water over bulgur wheat and let stand about 1 hour or until softened. Make filling.

2. Drain wheat in strainer. Squeeze out excess water. Return wheat to bowl. Add bread crumbs, flour, salt, and turmeric. Mix well. Gradually add water by tablespoons, kneading mixture with your hands; add enough water so that mixture is just moist enough to form a stiff dough; it will be sticky. Adjust seasoning; it should be well seasoned.

3. Take about 2 tablespoons dough and squeeze together in a patty shape between both hands about 15 times, pressing to make dough compact. Then roll between your palms to a smooth ball. Put balls on a plate.

4. With moistened hands, flatten a ball of dough into a disk. Press to flatten it further in your palm. Cup your palm so there is a hollow in the middle of the dough. Put about 1 1/2 teaspoons filling in the hollow. Bring dough around filling. Press to join edges to completely enclose filling. Pat again to a disk. Set on prepared baking sheet. Continue with remaining dough and remaining filling. Refrigerate, uncovered, 1 hour or up to overnight.

5. Heat oil in a large, deep, heavy skillet over medium-high heat; when oil is hot enough, it should sizzle when the end of a *kubeh* is touched to it. Fry *kubeh* in batches, without crowding, about 4 minutes per side or until deep golden brown; reduce heat if they brown too fast. Stand back while frying, as oil tends to splatter. Use 2 slotted spatulas to turn them carefully. Drain well on several layers of paper towels. Serve hot, warm, or at room temperature.

Chicken Filling for Kubeh

Makes enough for 6 servings (M)

Use this spicy filling with a bulgur wheat shell to make kubeh *(this page).*

2 tablespoons vegetable oil

1 medium onion, chopped

6 ounces ground chicken

1 teaspoon ground cumin

1/2 teaspoon ground turmeric

1/2 teaspoon paprika

1/2 teaspoon dried dill

2 tablespoons water

Salt and freshly ground pepper, to taste

Heat oil in medium, heavy skillet over medium heat. Add onion and sauté about 10 minutes or until well browned. Add chicken, cumin, turmeric, paprika, dill, water, salt, and pepper. Sauté, stirring often, about 10 minutes or until chicken changes color and is cooked through. Transfer to a bowl. Adjust seasoning. Refrigerate until ready to use.

Sauces

Fresh Tomato Salsa, Yemenite Style

Makes 1⅓ cups, 6 to 8 servings

The traditional way to make this easy salsa is by grating some ripe tomatoes, then stirring in enough fiery hot pepper chutney called zehug *to flavor the tomatoes to the desired degree of hotness. This salsa is a favorite accompaniment for Shabbat pastries, breads, and hard boiled eggs. It is usually made at the last minute so the tomatoes are as fresh as possible.*

You can make your own zehug, *buy it at Israeli markets, or substitute another thick hot sauce. If you prefer, puree the tomatoes in a blender or food processor instead of grating them.*

1 to 2 tablespoons Zehug (page 592), or hot sauce, or to taste
½ pound ripe tomatoes
Salt, to taste

Prepare Zehug. Then, grate tomatoes using large holes of grater. Transfer to a bowl. Stir in zehug and salt. Serve cold.

Mushroom Sauce for Bourekas

Makes 8 to 10 servings as
accompaniments or appetizers (M) or (P)

Serve this sauce with Mati's Mushroom Bourekas (page 227) or, if you like, with meat-filled knishes. To avoid making the pastry soggy, either serve the sauce separately, or spoon it on the plate, not over the bourekas, *at serving time.*

If you wish to serve this sauce with bourekas *or knishes containing dairy products, make it with vegetable stock.*

¼ cup vegetable oil or margarine
1 medium onion, minced
8 ounces mushrooms, halved and sliced
Salt and freshly ground pepper, to taste
1 teaspoon sweet paprika
¼ cup all-purpose flour
2 cups chicken, beef, veal, or vegetable stock
1 tablespoon tomato paste
1 teaspoon dried thyme
Hot paprika or cayenne pepper, to taste
2 tablespoons chopped fresh Italian parsley (optional)

1. Heat oil in a large sauté pan or skillet, add onion and sauté over medium heat 5 minutes or until onions are tender and begin to turn golden. Add mushrooms, salt, and pepper. Sauté over medium heat about 3 minutes, then over medium-high heat about 2 minutes, or until mushrooms and onions are light brown.

2. Transfer mushroom mixture to a medium saucepan. Heat over low heat. Add sweet paprika and flour and sauté mixture, stirring constantly, 1 minute. Remove from heat and stir in 1¾ cups stock. Return to heat and bring to a boil, stirring.

3. Blend remaining stock with tomato paste in a small bowl and stir into sauce. Add thyme. Bring to a simmer, stirring. Simmer sauce 5 minutes or until thickened to taste. Add hot paprika. Adjust seasoning. Stir in parsley, if using, just before serving. Serve hot.

Salads

Israeli Vegetable Salads
238

Everyday Israeli Salad

Israeli Breakfast Salad with
Bulgarian Cheese

Springtime Israeli Salad

Creamy Israeli Salad

Israeli Salad with Tahini

Israeli Salad, California Style

Other Raw Vegetable Salads
240

Lettuce and Tomato Salad with
Garlic-Cumin Dressing

Colorful Spinach Salad with
Feta Cheese

Polish Cucumbers in
Sour Cream

Avocado and Arugula Salad with
Tomatoes and Cucumbers

Cucumber and Pepper Salad
with Fresh Mint

Sour-Sweet Cucumbers

Polish Carrot Salad with Apples
and Horseradish

Carrot Salad with Spicy Orange
Juice Dressing

Cole Slaw with Creamy Dressing

Red Cabbage Salad with Apples
and Pecans

Radish and Carrot Salad

Fat-Free Cole Slaw

Cooked Vegetable Salads
244

Beet and Cucumber Salad with
Hazelnut Oil Dressing

Garlicky Beet Salad

Ashkenazic Green Bean
and Carrot Salad

Sephardic Artichoke Salad
with Roasted Peppers

Three-Bean Salad, North
African–Jewish Style

Mediterranean Chickpea Salad
with Fresh Basil

Fava Beans with Carrots
and Zucchini

Moroccan Carrot Salad

Roasted Pepper Salad with
Tomatoes and Garlic

Moroccan Zucchini Salad

Egyptian Jewish Okra Salad

Cauliflower Salad with
Red Pepper

Salad of Sweet Vegetables with
Lemon-Mint Vinaigrette

P = Pareve   **D** = Dairy   **M** = Meat

Serving an array of salads of cooked and raw vegetables is a delightful Sephardic way of beginning holiday menus. In fact, salads have always been popular on Jewish menus and play an even more prominent role today. I learned to appreciate them more than ever when I lived in Israel, where salad is an integral part of most meals, both for holidays and for everyday cooking, often even for breakfast.

The most popular salad is generally called Israeli salad and is in fact prepared in many Mediterranean and Middle Eastern countries, from Lebanon to Iran. It is made of small cubes of tomatoes and cucumbers mixed with chopped onion, and appears on most menus, whether the main course is meat, fish, eggs, or legumes. I love this healthful custom and I usually make this pretty salad or a variation of it every day.

Other favorite vegetables for making uncooked salads in the Jewish kitchen are carrots and red and green cabbage. These are not only made into the sweet carrot salads and cole slaw familiar to Americans, but also into lemony carrot and tangy cabbage salads.

Potato salads are much loved in the Jewish kitchen. There are creamy potato salads like the type typically found in delis, although in home kitchens the dressing tends to be made of mayonnaise rather than a sweet and sour boiled dressing. These salads are not just for casual meals. For entertaining, potato salad might be attractively presented on a bed of greens and garnished with toasted pecans.

Salads of grilled eggplant, peppers, and other Mediterranean vegetables seasoned with olive oil are esteemed in the Sephardic kitchen and have become generally popular on Israeli tables. Cooked beets and carrots are often made into salads with a tangy vinaigrette dressing of oil and either vinegar or lemon juice.

Israeli Vegetable Salads

Everyday Israeli Salad

Makes 4 servings

(P)

Beyond a national flag or song, Israelis have a "national" salad. Originally a Middle Eastern salad, it has become a standard on the tables of Israelis, no matter what their ethnic origin. This is the traditional way to prepare it.

4 medium tomatoes, cut into 1/2-inch dice

1/2 long (hothouse) cucumber or 1 medium cucumber, peeled (optional) and cut into 1/2-inch dice

1/4 cup minced green onion

1 to 2 tablespoons extra-virgin olive oil or vegetable oil

1 to 2 tablespoons strained fresh lemon juice

Salt and freshly ground pepper, to taste

Mix together tomatoes, cucumber, and green onion in a bowl. Add oil, lemon juice, and salt and pepper. Serve at cool or room temperature.

Israeli Breakfast Salad with Bulgarian Cheese

Makes 4 servings

(D)

In Israeli homes when there's time for a relaxed breakfast, a salad of fresh vegetables is a welcome item. Usually it also includes a savory cheese. A popular choice is Bulgarian cheese, which somewhat resembles feta cheese but in Israel is also available in tasty low-salt and low-fat versions. In the United States, you can find it in some markets that carry Israeli cheeses. Feta cheese makes a good substitute. The cheese adds so much richness and flavor to the salad that no oil or seasoning may be needed; it's a matter of taste.

4 ripe plum tomatoes, cut into small dice

1/2 long (hothouse) cucumber, cut into small dice

1/4 cup chopped green onion

2 tablespoons chopped fresh Italian parsley

4 ounces Bulgarian or feta cheese, diced or crumbled into large crumbs

2 to 3 teaspoons extra-virgin olive oil (optional)

2 to 3 teaspoons strained fresh lemon juice (optional)

Salt and freshly ground pepper, to taste (optional)

Mix together diced tomatoes, cucumber, green onion, and parsley in a bowl. Add cheese to salad and mix gently. Add oil, lemon juice, and salt and pepper if using. Serve cold or at room temperature.

Springtime Israeli Salad

Makes 8 servings

(P)

Sweet onions, baby radishes, and plenty of parsley add their fresh touch to the standard mix of cucumbers and tomatoes. If you don't have sweet white onions, use spring onions or green onions. I also like to add a small amount of arugula or other spring greens. This salad is perfect for Passover.

4 medium tomatoes or 8 to 12 plum tomatoes, cut into small dice

1 long (hothouse) cucumber or 2 medium cucumbers, peeled and cut into small dice

8 small red radishes, cut into small dice

1/4 to 1/2 sweet white onion, minced

1/3 cup chopped fresh Italian parsley

1 cup coarsely chopped arugula (optional)

2 to 3 tablespoons extra-virgin olive oil

1 to 2 tablespoons strained fresh lemon juice

Salt and freshly ground pepper, to taste

Mix tomatoes, cucumber, radishes, onion, parsley, and arugula, if using, in a glass bowl. Add olive oil, lemon juice, salt, and pepper. Serve cool or cold.

Creamy Israeli Salad

Makes 4 to 6 servings

Occasionally Israelis dress the usual salad of diced tomatoes and cucumbers with a creamy dressing instead of the more common oil and lemon juice. It's good for the holiday of Shavuot. When I lived in Israel, I often made it for breakfast.

A favorite way to make the dressing in Israel is with eshel or leben, both of which resemble mild-flavored whole-milk yogurt. In the United States, I use yogurt.

Naturally, the yogurt you choose determines how rich the dressing will be. Whole-milk yogurt, alone or mixed with a little sour cream, gives the most luscious result. Yet the salad also tastes great when made with nonfat yogurt, which is the way I usually make it. For leaner versions made with nonfat or low-fat yogurt, you can also stir in some nonfat sour cream.

1 to 1½ cups plain yogurt, regular, low-fat, or nonfat,
Salt and freshly ground pepper, to taste
Pinch of cayenne pepper (optional)
2 cups finely diced cucumber (¼-inch dice)
8 ripe plum tomatoes, diced
2 tablespoons chopped green onion
2 tablespoons chopped fresh Italian parsley
Paprika for sprinkling

Mix yogurt with salt, pepper, and cayenne, if using, in a bowl. Lightly stir in cucumber, tomato, green onion, and parsley. Adjust seasoning. Refrigerate until ready to serve. Serve in a shallow bowl. Sprinkle with paprika just before serving.

Israeli Salad with Tahini

Makes 4 servings

I first tasted this salad in a Yemenite restaurant in Israel. Its rich sesame dressing is creamy but has no dairy products. Thus it's perfect for a meal that includes meat or poultry.

Either make your own tahini dip or buy it prepared. Do not use plain tahini paste on its own as the dressing; it is too thick and concentrated.

½ cup Tahini Dip (page 214)
2 cups finely diced cucumber (¼-inch dice)
6 ripe plum tomatoes, diced
⅓ cup finely chopped onion
3 tablespoons chopped fresh Italian parsley
Salt and freshly ground pepper, to taste
1 tablespoon strained fresh lemon juice (optional)
Paprika for sprinkling

Prepare dip. Then, combine cucumber, tomato, onion, and 2 tablespoons parsley in a shallow bowl. Mix lightly. Add tahini dip, salt, and pepper. Add lemon juice, if using. Serve sprinkled with paprika and with remaining parsley.

Israeli Salad, California Style

Makes 4 servings

This is the way I often prepare Israeli salad at home, for entertaining as well as for quick meals. To the traditional trio of tomatoes, cucumbers, and onions, I add jicama and sweet bell peppers. Their delicate sweetness complements the other vegetables perfectly. This salad is beautiful as well as delicious and is always a hit. If you like, substitute ½ Japanese cucumber or 4 Middle Eastern or pickling cucumbers for the one listed.

½ long (hothouse) cucumber, cut into small dice
8 plum tomatoes or 4 medium tomatoes, cut into small dice
½ cup chopped red, white, or sweet onion
1 small red, orange, or yellow bell pepper, cut into small dice
1 cup finely diced peeled jicama
3 to 4 tablespoons chopped fresh Italian parsley
1 to 2 tablespoons extra-virgin olive oil
1 to 2 tablespoons strained fresh lemon juice
Salt and freshly ground pepper, to taste

Mix together cucumbers, tomato, onion, peppers, jicama, and parsley in a bowl. Add oil, lemon juice, and salt and pepper. Serve cold or at room temperature.

Other Raw Vegetable Salads

Lettuce and Tomato Salad with Garlic-Cumin Dressing

Makes 4 to 6 servings   **P**

The aromatic Moroccan style dressing transforms even a simple dinner salad into a tasty appetizer. Use any type of lettuce you have, from baby lettuces to basic iceberg or romaine.

1 small clove garlic, finely minced

1/2 teaspoon ground cumin

1/2 teaspoon paprika

3 tablespoons extra-virgin olive oil

1 tablespoon strained fresh lemon juice

Salt and freshly ground pepper, to taste

Cayenne pepper, to taste

4 to 6 cups lettuce, in bite-size pieces

1/2 cup quarter slices red or white onion, pulled apart into slivers

1/4 cup chopped fresh Italian parsley (optional)

2 large or 4 medium tomatoes, cut into wedges

1. Combine garlic, cumin, paprika, oil, lemon juice, salt, pepper, and cayenne in a small bowl. Whisk ingredients until blended.

2. Combine lettuce, onion slivers, and parsley, if using, in a bowl. Add about three quarters of dressing and toss gently. Transfer to a platter and top with tomato wedges. Sprinkle with remaining dressing and serve.

Colorful Spinach Salad with Feta Cheese

Makes 4 servings   **D**

This salad in the style of the Jews of Greece makes a delicious first course before a main course of grilled or baked fish. It also makes a lively accompaniment for an entree of brown rice or beans.

3/4 pound fresh spinach (1 medium bunch) or a 10-ounce bag rinsed spinach leaves

2 thin slices red onion, halved and separated into half moons

1/2 small bulb of fennel (optional), very thinly sliced, then cut into thin sticks

1/3 long (hothouse) cucumber, halved and cut into thin slices

2 or 3 tablespoons extra-virgin olive oil

2 tablespoons strained fresh lemon juice

Salt and freshly ground pepper, to taste

2 medium tomatoes, cut into eight wedges

1/2 cup crumbled feta cheese

8 to 12 Kalamata olives, pitted if desired

1. If using a bunch of spinach, remove stems and any wilted leaves and wash remaining leaves thoroughly. Dry spinach well in salad spinner or towel. Tear any large leaves into two or three pieces.

2. In a large bowl combine spinach, red onion, fennel if using, and cucumber. Toss to combine. Add olive oil, lemon juice, salt, and pepper and toss. Adjust seasoning. Spoon salad onto a platter or shallow serving dish. Arrange tomato wedges around edge of salad. Scatter feta cheese over center. Garnish with olives.

Polish Cucumbers in Sour Cream

Makes 4 servings **D**

A hint of sweet-and-sour flavor characterizes this specialty of the Polish Jewish kitchen. If you wish, make it with low-fat or nonfat sour cream.

In traditional recipes the cucumber is salted so that it gives off liquid, then is rinsed, but I like to make this with crisp hothouse cucumbers and to omit that step.

3 tablespoons sour cream

2 tablespoons white wine vinegar

2 tablespoons cold water

1 tablespoon sugar

1 long (hothouse) cucumber, cut into thin slices

Salt, to taste

Spoon sour cream into a serving bowl. Slowly stir in vinegar, water, and sugar. Stir in cucumber slices. Season with salt. Serve cold.

Avocado and Arugula Salad with Tomatoes and Cucumbers

Makes 4 servings **P**

The avocado is as popular in Israel as it is in California and is used in a variety of ways. Here it adds a luscious flavor and texture to Israeli style chopped salad. Choose avocado that is ripe but not too soft so you can dice it. I prefer the black-skinned Haas variety because of its buttery texture. With such a rich addition, you may find you don't need to add any oil. This salad is a lovely accompaniment for broiled or grilled salmon.

4 medium tomatoes, cut into small dice

1/2 to 2/3 long (hothouse) cucumber, cut into small dice

1 cup coarsely chopped arugula

1 cup shredded romaine lettuce or bok choy leaves

1 or 2 ripe avocados, preferably Haas

Salt and freshly ground pepper, to taste

1 tablespoon strained fresh lemon juice (optional)

1 tablespoon extra-virgin olive oil (optional)

Combine tomatoes, cucumber, arugula, and romaine in a bowl and toss lightly. Just before serving, halve avocado, remove pit, scoop out meat, and dice. Add to salad and toss lightly. Sprinkle with salt and pepper and toss again. Add lemon juice and olive oil if using. Serve as soon as possible.

Cucumber and Pepper Salad with Fresh Mint

Makes 4 servings **P**

Jews from Morocco, Algeria, and Tunisia use fresh mint extensively, not just to flavor their tea but also in their salads. This light and easy summertime salad is a great foil for the cheesy dishes of Shavuot. It's also a refreshing addition to any warm weather Shabbat lunch.

1 small clove garlic, pressed or finely minced

1 tablespoon strained fresh lemon juice

1 to 2 tablespoons extra-virgin olive oil

Salt and freshly ground pepper, to taste

Cayenne pepper, to taste

1 long (hothouse) cucumber, halved and thinly sliced

1 red bell pepper, cut into strips

1 green or yellow bell pepper, cut into strips

3 tablespoons coarsely chopped fresh mint

Fresh mint sprigs

1. Prepare dressing: Combine garlic, lemon juice, oil, salt, pepper, and cayenne in a small bowl.

2. Mix cucumber slices and pepper strips in a shallow serving bowl. Whisk dressing, add to salad, and mix well. Just before serving, add mint and toss lightly. Serve garnished with mint sprigs.

Sour-Sweet Cucumbers

Makes 4 servings

P

This refreshing salad is fat-free and very simple. It's traditional in Ashkenazic cooking and appears on the tables of Jews from Poland, Hungary, Austria, and Germany as an accompaniment for cold meats. The dressing is simply a mixture of vinegar, water, and a little sugar in amounts that vary from one cook to another. Some also add sliced onions. Not everyone adds dill but I love the freshness it contributes. The old-fashioned way of preparing it is to salt the cucumber, let it stand for about an hour, and squeeze out the juices. In this quick version I simply add a little salt to the dressing.

1 long (hothouse) cucumber, peeled (optional) and thinly sliced

1/4 red or white onion, cut into very thin slices

Salt and freshly ground pepper, to taste

1/4 cup white wine vinegar

1/4 cup water

2 teaspoons sugar

3 tablespoons snipped fresh dill

Combine all ingredients except dill in a bowl. Mix well. Refrigerate at least 15 minutes so salad is well chilled. Add dill just before serving. Serve cold, in deep dishes.

Polish Carrot Salad with Apples and Horseradish

Makes 2 or 3 servings

D

Horseradish is a beloved condiment in Polish Jewish cooking, most notably as an accompaniment for gefilte fish. But it's used in other ways as well, like in this salad, where it gives zip to the medley of grated carrots and apples enriched with sour cream. Make it with any kind of sour cream you like.

1 tablespoon cider vinegar or other mild vinegar

1 teaspoon bottled white horseradish or finely grated fresh horseradish

2 to 3 teaspoons sugar

Salt, to taste

2 medium apples

3 large carrots, coarsely shredded (about 3 1/2 cups)

2 to 3 tablespoons sour cream, regular, low-fat, or nonfat

Mix vinegar with horseradish, 2 teaspoons sugar, and a pinch of salt in a bowl. Peel apples and coarsely grate them. Add to dressing. Add carrots and mix. Stir in sour cream. Adjust seasoning; add more sugar if needed. Serve cold.

Carrot Salad with Spicy Orange Juice Dressing

Makes 4 servings

P

Salads of grated carrots with orange juice are popular in Israel. Mothers often add sugar to entice their children to eat carrots. Here is an adult version, flavored with a touch of hot pepper and garlic. Be sure to use garlic that is very fresh

1 pound carrots (about 6 medium), coarsely grated

1/4 cup strained fresh orange juice

1 tablespoon strained fresh lemon juice

1 to 2 tablespoons extra-virgin olive oil

1 medium clove garlic, pressed or finely minced

1/2 teaspoon hot pepper sauce, or to taste

Salt, to taste

Cayenne pepper, to taste (optional)

Put carrots in a bowl. Add orange juice, lemon juice, oil, garlic, hot pepper sauce, and salt and mix well. Adjust seasoning; add cayenne, if using. Serve on a flat plate.

Cole Slaw with Creamy Dressing

Makes 4 to 6 servings **D**

Shred the cabbage with a knife or in a food processor, or, quickest of all, buy an 8-ounce package of cole slaw mix. Use any kind of mustard and vinegar that you like.

4 cups shredded green cabbage

1 large carrot, coarsely shredded

$^1/_2$ cup sour cream, regular, low-fat, or nonfat

1 to 3 tablespoons mayonnaise

1 tablespoon mustard

1 teaspoon vinegar or strained fresh lemon juice

1 teaspoon sugar

2 teaspoons water

Salt and freshly ground pepper, to taste

Combine cabbage and carrot in a large bowl. Mix sour cream with mayonnaise, mustard, vinegar, sugar, and water in a small bowl until blended. Toss with cabbage mixture. Season with salt and pepper.

Red Cabbage Salad with Apples and Pecans

Makes 4 servings **P**

I love the red cabbage salad served in Israeli restaurants and delis with its tangy dressing. My favorite way to prepare it at home is to toss it with finely diced crisp apples and to embellish it with toasted pecans. Serve this salad with grilled chicken or with cold sliced turkey.

2 to 3 tablespoons red or white wine vinegar

2 tablespoons vegetable oil

1 teaspoon sugar

Salt and freshly ground pepper, to taste

4 cups shredded red cabbage, or an 8-ounce package

1 rib celery, sliced thin

1 large apple (tart or sweet)

$^1/_4$ cup pecan pieces

Whisk 2 tablespoons vinegar with oil, sugar, salt, and pepper in a large bowl. Add red cabbage and celery and mix well, until cabbage is evenly moistened. Peel apple and cut into $^1/_2$-inch dice. Add to salad and toss. Adjust seasoning; add remaining tablespoon vinegar if you like. Serve salad topped with pecans.

Radish and Carrot Salad

Makes 4 to 6 servings **P**

Kurdish Jews serve this salad as an accompaniment for grilled meats. Use any large radish that you like. I generally choose the mild, white Asian daikon radish that is widely available at the market. Use black radishes or sharper ones if you prefer. You can either mix the vegetables or dress each one separately and serve them side by side.

For an eye-catching salad, when preparing the radish and carrots I hold them almost parallel to the grater to get attractive long shreds.

2 cups coarsely grated peeled daikon radish

2 cups coarsely grated carrot

1 green onion, white and green parts, chopped

2 to 3 tablespoons olive oil

2 tablespoons strained fresh lemon juice

Salt and freshly ground pepper, to taste

With a fork, lightly mix grated vegetables with green onion, oil, and lemon juice in a bowl. Season with salt and pepper. Serve cold or at room temperature.

Fat-Free Cole Slaw

Makes about 4 servings

Cole slaw is such an important accompaniment to sandwiches with cold cuts and other meats. It's now easy to find turkey pastrami and low-fat versions of smoked meats, and if you're serving these, you probably don't want the cole slaw to be high in fat.

This salad is crunchy and has the appealing sweetness of jicama. Flavored with horseradish, it's more like a relish than a salad and is terrific with all kinds of cold meats. For meatless meals, if you want it to have the creamy quality of cole slaw, add 1/4 cup nonfat sour cream and 1/4 cup nonfat yogurt. I like to add toasted sunflower seeds or pepitas (pumpkin seeds) to this salad, but if you want it completely fat-free, you can omit them.

3 cups shredded napa cabbage

1 cup shredded red cabbage

1 large carrot, coarsely shredded

1/2 cup finely diced cucumber

1 cup peeled, finely diced jicama

1 tablespoon white horseradish, or to taste

1 tablespoon cider vinegar, or to taste

1 teaspoon sugar

2 teaspoons water

Salt and freshly ground pepper, to taste

1/2 cup bean sprouts (optional)

3 tablespoons toasted sunflower seeds or pepitas

Combine napa cabbage, red cabbage, carrot, cucumber, and jicama in a large bowl. Mix horseradish with vinegar, sugar, and water in a small bowl until blended. Toss with cabbage mixture. Season with salt and pepper. Serve topped with bean sprouts, if using, and toasted seeds.

✾ Cooked Vegetable Salads

Beet and Cucumber Salad with Hazelnut Oil Dressing

Makes 4 servings

Borscht made of beets is one of the best-known specialties of the Ashkenazic kitchen. But beets are used in many other ways in Jewish cooking. A favorite in many homes is beet salad. You can use canned or ready-cooked packaged beets, but home-cooked beets make the salad truly delicious.

Vegetable oil is commonly used but I like to update the recipe by flavoring the dressing with hazelnut oil. You can substitute walnut or vegetable oil, if you like. Nut oil will keep for several months if stored in the refrigerator.

2 large beets

4 large romaine leaves, cut into strips

4 cups iceberg lettuce mix

1 medium cucumber, peeled, quartered lengthwise, and sliced

1/3 small jicama, peeled, thinly sliced, and cut into sticks

2 tablespoons strained fresh lemon juice

2 tablespoons hazelnut oil (also called filbert oil)

Salt and freshly ground pepper, to taste

1. Rinse beets, taking care not to pierce their skins. Put in a pan, cover with water, and bring to a boil. Cover and simmer over low heat 40 to 50 minutes or until tender. Let cool. Run beets under cold water and slip off the skins. Halve beets, place cut side down and slice them.

2. Combine romaine strips, iceberg lettuce mix, cucumber slices, and jicama in a bowl. Toss to mix. Add lemon juice, hazelnut oil, salt, and pepper and mix well. Serve topped with sliced beets.

Garlicky Beet Salad

Makes 8 servings

My sister-in-law Nirit often includes this bright red, zesty salad on her Seder menu, as it's very popular with our family and friends. I like it for Purim too, especially if I'm celebrating it with a turkey dinner. Any leftover salad is great with cold cooked or smoked turkey or chicken.

2 pounds of beets of about 1¹/₂-inch diameter

3 to 4 large cloves garlic, pressed or finely minced

1 white, red, or other mild onion, grated

2 tablespoons cider vinegar

1 tablespoon vegetable oil

Salt and freshly ground pepper, to taste

1. Rinse beets, taking care not to pierce their skins. Put in a large saucepan, cover with water, and bring to a boil. Cover and simmer over low heat for 40 to 50 minutes or until tender. Let cool. Run beets under cold water and slip off their skins.

2. Grate beets on large holes of grater. Add garlic, onion, vinegar, oil, salt, and pepper. Cover and refrigerate overnight so that flavors blend. Adjust seasoning. Serve cold.

Ashkenazic Green Bean and Carrot Salad

Makes about 6 servings

Eastern European Jewish green bean salads often feature more vinegar than oil, unlike those of France which customarily are dressed with 3 parts oil to 1 part vinegar. For a colorful medley, I like to combine the beans with carrots. The sweetness of the carrots also balances the tart dressing. You can let the vegetables marinate in the dressing for a few hours for more flavor but their colors will be brightest if you serve them right away.

1 pound carrots

1¹/₂ pounds green beans, ends removed, cut into 3-inch lengths

3 tablespoons citrus, cider, or rice vinegar

1 teaspoon sugar

1 to 2 tablespoons vegetable oil

Salt and freshly ground pepper, to taste

¹/₄ cup chopped fresh parsley

Cut carrots into 2-inch lengths. Slice each piece lengthwise, then cut it into sticks about ¹/₃-inch thick. Add carrots and green beans to a large saucepan of boiling salted water and boil uncovered over high heat 7 minutes or until the vegetables are crisp-tender. Drain in a colander, rinse with cold water, and drain well. Transfer to a bowl. Add vinegar, sugar, 1 tablespoon oil, salt, and pepper. Add more oil if you like. Add parsley just before serving.

Sephardic Artichoke Salad with Roasted Peppers

Makes 4 servings

Artichokes are used liberally in Sephardic homes both as hot dishes and as salads, like this colorful one that I savored in Jerusalem. If you use roasted sweet red peppers from a jar and canned or frozen artichokes, it's quick and easy to make.

4 large artichokes, one 9-ounce package frozen artichoke heart pieces, or one 14-ounce can artichoke hearts or bottoms, drained

1 red bell pepper, roasted and peeled (page 588), or two roasted red bell pepper halves from a jar

1 medium clove garlic, pressed or very finely minced

1¹/₂ tablespoons strained fresh lemon juice

2 to 3 tablespoons extra-virgin olive oil

1 tablespoon chopped fresh Italian parsley

Hot pepper sauce to taste

Salt and freshly ground pepper, to taste

12 Kalamata olives, pitted if desired

1. If using fresh artichokes, prepare and cook artichoke bottoms (page 589). If using frozen artichokes, cook them according to package directions. Drain fresh, frozen, or canned artichokes well. Quarter artichoke bottoms or hearts.

2. Cut roasted peppers into thin strips. Combine peppers and artichokes in a bowl.

3. Mix garlic, lemon juice, oil, parsley, hot sauce, and salt and pepper in a small bowl. Add to salad and toss. Serve garnished with olives.

Three-Bean Salad, North African–Jewish Style

Makes 4 servings

Unlike the familiar sweet and sour American three-bean salad, this colorful vegetable medley is brightened with the fresh flavors of the southern Mediterranean—ripe tomatoes, capers, cilantro, lemon juice, and a touch of olive oil.

One 10-ounce package frozen lima beans

8 ounces green beans or yellow beans (wax beans), ends removed, cut in half

One 15-ounce can chickpeas (garbanzo beans), drained and rinsed

3 ripe plum tomatoes, diced

1/3 cup finely chopped red onion or sweet onion

2 or 3 tablespoons extra-virgin olive oil

1 1/2 tablespoons strained fresh lemon juice

2 tablespoons chopped fresh cilantro

Salt and freshly ground pepper, to taste

1 tablespoon capers, rinsed

1. Add lima beans to a medium saucepan of boiling salted water, cover, and bring to a boil. Cook 5 minutes. Add green beans and return to a boil. Cook uncovered over high heat about 5 minutes or until both types of beans are tender. Drain, rinse with cold water, and drain well.

2. Combine cooked beans with chickpeas, tomatoes, and onions in a bowl. Add oil, lemon juice, half the cilantro, salt, and pepper and mix well. Adjust seasoning. Sprinkle with remaining cilantro and with capers. Serve cold or at room temperature.

Mediterranean Chickpea Salad with Fresh Basil

Makes 4 appetizer servings

This colorful medley is satisfying and very easy to prepare. Serve it as a Shabbat appetizer or even as a light summertime main course. If you wish, you can omit the oil.

One 15-ounce can chickpeas (garbanzo beans), drained and rinsed

1/2 teaspoon dried oregano

1 tablespoon extra-virgin olive oil

1 to 2 tablespoons strained fresh lemon juice

1 1/2 cups finely diced cucumber

1 red, yellow, orange, or green bell pepper, diced

8 ripe plum tomatoes, diced

1/3 cup chopped red onion

2 tablespoons shredded fresh basil

Salt and freshly ground pepper, to taste

Cayenne pepper, to taste

Mix chickpeas with oregano, oil, and 1 tablespoon lemon juice in a bowl. Add cucumber, bell pepper, tomatoes, onion, and basil. Season with salt, pepper, and cayenne. Add remaining lemon juice if needed. Serve cold or at room temperature.

Fava Beans with Carrots and Zucchini

Makes 4 servings

Fresh fava beans are a highlight of the Sephardic table, especially during Passover. Often they are prepared very simply as in this recipe so their natural character can be appreciated.

The beans are more beautiful and pleasant to eat when their second skin is removed, although some cooks omit this step because it is time consuming. To remove this skin, blanch the beans, then when cool enough to touch, press on one side of each bean, and the bean comes out like an almond. To save time, you can use frozen fava beans, which have been removed from their pods but still have their second skins. You can find them at Israeli and Middle Eastern markets.

1/2 pound fairly thin carrots, quartered lengthwise and cut into 3-inch pieces

3/4 pound zucchini, quartered lengthwise and cut into 3-inch pieces

2 pounds fava beans in pods (about 2 1/2 cups shelled)

1/4 red onion, cut into thin slices and separated into slivers

2 tablespoons extra-virgin olive oil

1 to 2 tablespoons strained fresh lemon juice

Pinch of cayenne pepper

Salt and freshly ground pepper, to taste

1/3 cup chopped fresh Italian parsley

1. Cook carrots in a saucepan of boiling water for 5 minutes, add zucchini, and cook 3 minutes or until vegetables are just tender. Drain, rinse with cold water, and drain well.

2. Boil the fava beans in a saucepan of boiling water 4 to 5 minutes or until tender. Drain the beans and let them cool until they can be handled. If you wish, peel off and discard the tough outer skins.

3. Combine zucchini, carrots, fava beans, and red onion in a shallow bowl. Whisk oil, lemon juice, cayenne, and salt and pepper in small bowl. Add to salad and toss gently. Adjust seasoning. Add parsley, toss gently, and serve.

Moroccan Carrot Salad

Makes 4 to 6 servings (P)

A perennial favorite in the delis of Jerusalem and Tel Aviv as well as Israeli delis in the United States, this spicy salad flavored with hot red pepper flakes, garlic, and lemon juice turns carrots into a wonderful savory dish. If you're used to carrots always being flavored with sweet seasonings, this salad will be a pleasant surprise.

2 to 3 tablespoons strained fresh lemon juice

1 small clove garlic, pressed or finely minced

2 to 3 tablespoons extra-virgin olive oil or vegetable oil

Salt, to taste

1/4 teaspoon hot red pepper flakes

1 teaspoon paprika

1/2 teaspoon ground cumin

1 1/2 pounds medium carrots, sliced into 1/4-inch-thick rounds

1/4 cup chopped fresh Italian parsley

Cayenne pepper, to taste

1. Combine lemon juice, garlic, oil, salt, pepper flakes, paprika, and cumin in a medium bowl. Whisk to blend.

2. Put carrots in a saucepan, cover with water, add salt, and bring to a boil. Simmer about 7 minutes or until carrots are just tender. Drain carrots (reserve their cooking liquid to use as a vegetable broth). Transfer warm carrots to bowl of dressing and mix gently.

3. Add parsley a short time before serving. Adjust seasoning, adding more salt and cayenne if needed. Serve hot, warm, or cold.

Roasted Pepper Salad with Tomatoes and Garlic

Makes 4 to 6 servings (P)

For this favorite North African appetizer, many cooks like to marinate the peppers in the dressing for a few hours before serving them. The garlic can be added finely chopped, as in this version, or in whole cloves that are removed before the salad is put on the table.

4 bell peppers, green, red, orange, or a mixture, roasted and peeled (page 588)

2 to 3 teaspoons strained fresh lemon juice or vinegar

2 to 3 tablespoons extra-virgin olive oil

1 small clove garlic, pressed or finely minced

Salt and freshly ground pepper, to taste

2 large tomatoes, cut into wedges

1. Cut each roasted pepper into 4 to 6 pieces lengthwise, each about 3/4- to 1 inch wide. Halve pieces if peppers are long. Put peppers in a bowl.

2. Combine lemon juice, oil, garlic, salt, and pepper in small bowl. Whisk to combine. Spoon dressing over peppers. Cover and refrigerate 30 minutes or up to 2 days.

3. Arrange peppers on platter, alternating them with tomato wedges. Spoon dressing over vegetables. Serve at room temperature.

Moroccan Zucchini Salad

Makes 4 or 5 servings

The Moroccan Jewish kitchen is noted for its array of salads made from just about every vegetable. It's the seasonings that turn the vegetables into tasty appetizers. In this easy-to-make salad, the zucchini cook in a spicy tomato-garlic dressing, then are crowned with fresh cilantro.

1¹/₂ pounds zucchini, quartered lengthwise and diced

2 large cloves garlic, minced

¹/₄ teaspoon hot red pepper flakes (optional)

2 tablespoons extra-virgin olive oil

¹/₄ cup water

Salt and freshly ground pepper, to taste

1 tablespoon tomato paste

1 teaspoon ground cumin

Cayenne pepper, to taste

1 green onion, chopped

1 to 2 tablespoons strained fresh lemon juice

1 to 2 tablespoons chopped fresh cilantro

Put zucchini in a large skillet or sauté pan with garlic, pepper flakes if using, oil, and water. Sprinkle with salt and pepper. Bring to a boil. Cook uncovered over medium-high heat, stirring often, about 5 minutes or until zucchini is crisp-tender and most of liquid has evaporated. Add tomato paste, cumin, and cayenne and stir over low heat 30 seconds. Remove from heat, add onion and lemon juice. Adjust seasoning. Serve warm or cool, sprinkled with cilantro.

Egyptian Jewish Okra Salad

Makes 4 servings

Jews from Egypt are real fans of okra and use it in many creative ways. Unlike other vegetables, that are usually cooked in plenty of water before being made into salad, I find that okra tastes better sautéed, then cooked slowly with a little water. Then it needs only a simple dressing, like this one of lemon juice, coriander seed, garlic, and cilantro.

3 tablespoons extra-virgin olive oil

1 pound fresh, small, tender okra, rinsed and patted dry, caps trimmed

Salt and freshly ground pepper, to taste

¹/₄ cup water

¹/₄ cup chopped red onion

2 tablespoon strained fresh lemon juice

1 medium clove garlic, very finely minced

¹/₄ teaspoon ground coriander

Cayenne pepper, to taste

2 tablespoon chopped fresh cilantro

1. Heat 2 tablespoons oil in a large sauté pan. Add okra and sauté 2 minutes over medium heat, stirring lightly. Sprinkle with salt and pepper. Add water, cover, and cook over low heat, shaking pan occasionally and adding water only if needed, about 7 minutes or until just tender. Remove okra gently to a shallow serving dish. Add onion and mix gently.

2. Combine remaining tablespoon oil, lemon juice, garlic, coriander, cayenne, salt, and pepper in a bowl. Pour dressing over okra. Sprinkle with cilantro. Serve at room temperature or cold.

Cauliflower Salad with Red Pepper

Makes 4 servings

In Israel, I learned that cooked cauliflower can be the basis of a tasty salad, like this one, redolent of the flavors of North Africa—cumin, cilantro, and a touch of hot pepper. Be sure to cook the cauliflower so it is crisp-tender, not mushy. This colorful salad makes a good pre-latke salad at a Hanukkah party. If your family isn't fond of cilantro, substitute Italian parsley.

2 pounds cauliflower

2 tablespoons strained fresh lemon juice

2 teaspoons ground cumin

$^1/_2$ teaspoon paprika

Cayenne pepper, to taste

1 tablespoon water

3 tablespoons olive oil

1 red bell pepper, diced

$^1/_3$ cup chopped red onion

$^1/_4$ cup chopped fresh cilantro

Salt and freshly ground pepper, to taste

1. Divide cauliflower into medium florets. Peel stem and slice it. Cook cauliflower in a large pan of boiling salted water uncovered over high heat about 7 minutes or until crisp-tender. Drain, rinse with cold water, and drain well.

2. In a bowl large enough to contain cauliflower, whisk lemon juice with cumin, paprika, cayenne, and water. Add olive oil and whisk again.

3. Add cauliflower to bowl. Add bell pepper, onion, and 3 tablespoons cilantro. Gently fold to mix. Season with salt and pepper. Serve at room temperature, sprinkled with remaining chopped cilantro.

Salad of Sweet Vegetables with Lemon-Mint Vinaigrette

Makes 6 to 8 servings

Lemon-mint dressing lends a Sephardic taste to this colorful salad, which makes a lovely first course or a good accompaniment for broiled or roasted chicken. It's a good choice for Passover, when beets, carrots, and potatoes are favorite menu item. To the cooked vegetables I like to add a crunchy raw one—diced jicama, which contributes its delightful texture as well as its delicate sweetness.

Lemon-Mint Vinaigrette (page 594)

14 small beets (about 1$^1/_2$ inches in diameter)

4 large boiling potatoes, cut into 1-inch chunks

6 large carrots, diagonally sliced $^1/_4$-inch thick

Salt and freshly ground pepper, to taste

$^1/_2$ large jicama

1 tablespoon chopped fresh mint

1. Prepare vinaigrette. Then, rinse beets, taking care not to pierce skin. Put 1 inch of water in a steamer and bring to a boil. Place beets on steamer rack or on another rack or in a colander above boiling water. Cover tightly and steam 50 minutes to 1 hour or until tender, adding boiling water occasionally if water evaporates. Let cool. Rinse beets with cold water and slip off skins. Dice beets.

2. Meanwhile, put potatoes in a large saucepan with enough water to generously cover them. Add a pinch of salt and bring to a boil. Cover and cook over medium-low heat 5 minutes. Add carrots and return to a boil. Cover and cook over medium-low heat about 20 minutes or until vegetables are tender. Drain well. Transfer to a bowl. Add dressing and mix gently. Adjust seasoning. If making salad ahead, refrigerate it, covered. Refrigerate beets in a separate covered dish.

3. Just before serving, peel and dice jicama. Add beets and half of jicama to salad and mix very gently. Sprinkle with reserved jicama, then with mint.

❧ Potato and Pasta Salads

Low-Fat Potato Salad with Creamy Cumin Dressing

Makes 4 servings

The Jews of India lived primarily in Bombay and Cochin until the late 1940s, when many moved to Israel and England. They use cumin not only as a component of curries and other stews but also to flavor sauces like this yogurt dressing, in which a touch of ground cumin lends a subtle flavor. For garnish, the salad is sprinkled with toasted whole cumin seeds. Serve this tasty, refreshing salad as an alternative to the many rich dairy dishes served at the holiday of Shavuot. When you're having a fish barbecue, this light salad makes a good accompaniment instead of the usual high-fat potato salads.

2 pounds red-skinned potatoes of uniform size, scrubbed but not peeled

1 cup low-fat or nonfat plain yogurt

1/4 teaspoon paprika

1/4 teaspoon ground cumin

Pinch of cayenne pepper (optional)

1 teaspoon chopped fresh cilantro

Salt, to taste

1 small green onion, green and white parts, chopped

1 cup cooked peas

1 teaspoon whole cumin seeds

1. Put potatoes in large saucepan, cover with water by about 1/2-inch, and add a pinch of salt. Bring to boil. Cover and simmer over low heat about 25 minutes or until tender enough that a knife pierces center of largest potato easily; do not overcook, or potatoes will fall apart when cut.

2. Drain potatoes in colander and peel while warm. Cut into medium dice. Put potatoes in a large bowl. Let cool to room temperature

3. Mix yogurt with paprika, ground cumin, cayenne if using, cilantro, and salt. Pour over potatoes. Fold gently to mix, separating any potato pieces that are stuck together. Fold in green onion and peas. Adjust seasoning. Cover and refrigerate for 1 to 2 hours. Remove from refrigerator about 30 minutes before serving.

4. Toast cumin seeds in a small, heavy skillet over medium heat 2 minutes, stirring often; be careful not to let them burn. Just before serving, sprinkle toasted cumin seeds over salad.

Israeli Potato Salad

Makes 4 servings **P**

Potato salad dressed with mayonnaise and studded with peas, carrots, and diced pickles is the type often made in Israeli homes. Unlike American potato salad, the dressing is not sweet and sour.

2 pounds red-skinned potatoes of uniform size, scrubbed but not peeled

1 1/2 cups diced cooked carrots

1 cup cooked peas

1/4 cup chopped onion

1 dill pickle, diced small

3 tablespoons chopped fresh Italian parsley

3/4 to 1 1/4 cups mayonnaise

Salt and freshly ground pepper, to taste

1. Put potatoes in large saucepan, cover with water by about 1/2-inch, and add salt. Bring to boil. Cover and simmer over low heat about 25 minutes or until tender enough that knife pierces center of largest potato easily. Do not overcook, or potatoes will fall apart when cut.

2. Drain potatoes in colander and peel while warm. Cut into medium dice. Put potatoes in large bowl. Add carrots, peas, onion, pickle, and parsley. Add mayonnaise and fold it in gently. Season with salt and pepper. Refrigerate until ready to serve.

Potato Salad with Capers and Tarragon

Makes 4 servings

During a walk with my mother around her neighborhood in Jerusalem, she pointed out the caper plants that were growing wild. Although I knew that capers are widely used in Mediterranean cooking, seeing the healthy plants in their native setting was a vivid illustration of the reason for their popularity. They're best known as a condiment for fish but they also lend a lively touch to salads, like this potato salad with fresh herbs, seasoned with a vinaigrette dressing instead of mayonnaise. Although tarragon is not traditional, I love its taste with potatoes. You can substitute Italian parsley, dill, or cilantro, which are more commonly used in Jerusalem. Serve this with grilled chicken.

2 tablespoons dry white wine

Salt and freshly ground pepper, to taste

2 pounds boiling potatoes of uniform size, scrubbed but not peeled

¼ cup minced red onion

2 tablespoons tarragon vinegar or white wine vinegar

5 or 6 tablespoons vegetable oil

2 tablespoons minced fresh tarragon

1 tablespoon plus 1 teaspoon capers, rinsed

1. Combine wine, salt, and pepper in small bowl and stir to blend.

2. Put potatoes in large saucepan, cover with water by about ¹/₂-inch, and add a pinch of salt. Bring to boil. Cover and simmer over low heat about 25 minutes or until tender enough that knife pierces center of largest potato easily; do not overcook, or potatoes will fall apart when cut.

2. Drain potatoes in colander and peel while warm. Cut into medium dice. Put potatoes in a large bowl. Add wine mixture and fold gently into mix, separating any potato pieces that are stuck together. Fold in onion. Cool to room temperature.

3. Meanwhile, prepare dressing: whisk vinegar with salt and pepper in a medium bowl; whisk in oil. Adjust seasoning. Add dressing to potato mixture and fold it in

gently with rubber spatula. Adjust seasoning. A short time before serving, fold in tarragon and 1 tablespoon capers. Serve salad at room temperature, sprinkled with remaining capers.

Potato Salad with Yemenite Flavors

Makes 4 servings

Some scholars date the ancient Jewish community of Yemen back to the time of the Queen of Sheba's visit to King Solomon in Jerusalem. She brought some of his advisers and their families back to her country, which many claim was Yemen. Most of the Jews from Yemen now live in Israel. They came primarily from Yemen's capital city of Sana and the coastal area of Aden. The exuberant seasonings favored by the Jews of Yemen make for tasty salads like this light and easy potato salad. Turmeric added to the cooking water gives the potatoes an attractive yellow hue.

2 pounds boiling potatoes, scrubbed but not peeled

¹/₂ teaspoon ground turmeric

Salt and freshly ground pepper, to taste

2 tablespoons strained fresh lemon juice

1 teaspoon ground cumin

1 or 2 jalapeño peppers, minced

1 tablespoon water

2 to 3 tablespoons extra-virgin olive oil

¹/₃ cup chopped green onions

¹/₄ cup chopped fresh cilantro

Cayenne pepper to taste (optional)

4 plum tomatoes, cut into small dice

1. Put potatoes in large saucepan, cover with water by about ¹/₂-inch, and add turmeric and salt. Bring to boil. Cover and simmer over low heat about 25 minutes, or until a knife can pierce center of largest potato easily and potato falls from knife when lifted; do not overcook, or potatoes will fall apart when cut.

2. Meanwhile, prepare dressing: In a bowl large enough to contain potatoes, whisk lemon juice with a pinch of salt, pepper, cumin, chopped jalapeño peppers, and water. Add 2 tablespoons olive oil and whisk again.

3. Drain potatoes in colander and peel while warm. Cut into medium dice. Add to bowl. Fold gently but thoroughly with dressing. Let cool. Fold in green onions and cilantro. Adjust seasoning; add cayenne, if using, and another tablespoon oil if desired. Gently fold in tomatoes. Serve at room temperature.

Potato Salad with Fresh Herbs and White Wine Dressing

Makes 4 servings (P)

This salad is made without vinegar or lemon juice and is good for Rosh Hashanah if your family avoids these acidic ingredients for the holiday, or anytime— because the lively flavor from the wine, thyme, chives, and parsley is always satisfying.

1/4 cup dry white wine

Salt and freshly ground pepper, to taste

2 pounds boiling potatoes of uniform size, scrubbed but not peeled

1 medium carrot, diced

1/4 cup minced sweet or white onion

5 or 6 tablespoons vegetable oil

2 teaspoons chopped fresh thyme or 3/4 teaspoon dried

2 tablespoons snipped fresh chives

3 tablespoons chopped fresh Italian parsley

1. Combine 2 tablespoons wine, salt, and pepper in small bowl and stir to blend.

2. Put potatoes in large saucepan, cover with water by about 1/2-inch and add a pinch of salt. Bring to boil. Cover and simmer over low heat for 15 minutes. Add carrot and cook about 10 minutes or until potatoes and carrot are tender enough that knife pierces center of largest potato and carrot easily; do not overcook, or potatoes will fall apart when cut.

3. Drain potatoes and carrot in colander. Peel potatoes while warm and cut into medium dice. Put potatoes and diced carrot in a large bowl. Add wine mixture and fold gently to mix. Fold in onion. Cool to room temperature.

4. To make dressing, whisk remaining 2 tablespoons wine with salt and pepper in a medium bowl. Whisk in 5 tablespoons oil and add thyme. Adjust seasoning.

Add dressing to potato mixture and fold it in gently with rubber spatula. Add remaining oil if needed. Adjust seasoning. A short time before serving, fold in 1 tablespoon chives and 2 tablespoons parsley. Serve salad at room temperature, sprinkled with remaining chives and parsley.

Couscous Salad with Tomatoes, Pine Nuts, and Mint

Makes 4 servings (P)

The colorful salad features the popular Eastern Mediterranean flavor combination of toasted pine nuts, fresh mint, green onions, and lemon juice loved in Israel and Lebanon. The salad needs no cooking at all; you simply pour boiling water over the couscous and wait a few minutes until it softens. Serve the salad as an appetizer or accompaniment for cold chicken for a summertime Shabbat lunch.

2 tablespoons strained fresh lemon juice

Salt and freshly ground pepper, to taste

3 to 5 tablespoons extra-virgin olive oil

1 cup plain or whole-wheat couscous

1 cup boiling water

2 tablespoons pine nuts

6 ripe plum tomatoes, diced

1 green onion, finely chopped

3 tablespoons chopped fresh mint

Green or red leaf lettuce leaves

Red, yellow, or orange cherry tomatoes

1. Whisk lemon juice with a pinch of salt and pepper in a medium bowl. Whisk in 3 tablespoons oil.

2. Combine couscous with a pinch of salt in a medium saucepan. Shake saucepan to spread couscous in an even layer. Pour boiling water evenly over couscous, immediately cover saucepan tightly, shake it to distribute water evenly, and let stand 5 minutes. Whisk dressing again and drizzle 2 tablespoons of dressing over couscous. Cover and let stand 2 minutes. Transfer couscous to a bowl and break up any lumps with a fork. Let cool completely.

3. Toast pine nuts in a small skillet over medium heat, shaking skillet often, until lightly browned, about 3 minutes. Transfer to a bowl and cool.

4. Whisk remaining dressing, drizzle it over cous-cous, and toss gently with a fork. Add diced tomatoes, green onion, and mint and toss salad gently. Cover and refrigerate 1 hour.

5. Add pine nuts and toss salad. Adjust seasoning. Add 1 to 2 more tablespoons oil if needed. To serve, make a bed of lettuce on a platter. Spoon couscous mixture in a mound in center. Garnish with cherry tomatoes.

Shabbat Pasta Salad with Tomatoes and Fresh Oregano

Makes 8 appetizer servings

Long before they were trendy, pasta salads played a role on the Shabbat menus of Jews from Italy because in observant homes everything for Shabbat is cooked ahead. Cold dishes are often served for the midday meal on Saturday.

I love the taste of fresh oregano in this simple salad but you can use basil or Italian parsley instead.

1 pound ripe plum tomatoes, cut into small dice

6 to 7 tablespoons extra-virgin olive oil

1 medium clove garlic, pressed or finely minced

Salt and freshly ground pepper, to taste

1 pound medium or large pasta shells (about 6 cups)

Cayenne pepper, to taste

1/4 cup coarsely chopped fresh oregano, basil, or Italian parsley

1. Combine tomatoes, 4 tablespoons oil, garlic, salt, and pepper in a large bowl.

2. Cook pasta uncovered in a large pot of boiling salted water over high heat, stirring occasionally, 5 to 8 minutes or until tender but firm to bite. Drain well and add to tomato mixture. Add 2 or 3 tablespoons olive oil and mix well. Season to taste with salt, pepper, and cayenne. Cover and refrigerate. About 30 minutes before serving remove from refrigerator. Add fresh herbs a short time before serving.

Fish Salads

Sardine and Spaghetti Salad with Tomatoes and Spinach

Makes 4 or 5 servings

I learned to appreciate sardines when I lived in Israel. My neighbors often created a quick, easy lunch of canned sardines in a spicy tomato sauce, accompanied by a salad of cucumbers, onions, and diced tomatoes, some dark bread, and a little yogurt. At the time I didn't know how healthful this light meal was. In recent years I've learned that sardines are rich in omega-3 fatty acids, which are important to a heart-healthy diet. Canned sardines are also a very convenient product for busy cooks. I like to use very small Brislings from Norway, esteemed as the finest sardines.

This pareve salad is satisfying enough to be served as a main course or can be a first course in either a meat or dairy meal. If you like, you can garnish the salad with a couple tablespoons of toasted pine nuts.

1 pound ripe tomatoes, diced

2 medium cloves garlic, minced

1/2 teaspoon dried oregano, crumbled

Salt and freshly ground pepper, to taste

2 to 4 tablespoons extra-virgin olive oil

12 ounces spaghetti, spaghettini, or vermicelli

2 cups coarsely chopped fresh spinach leaves

3 to 4 tablespoons chopped fresh Italian parsley

Two 3- or 4-ounce cans sardines, preferably Brislings, drained

1 tablespoon strained fresh lemon juice (optional)

1. Put tomatoes in a large bowl. Add, garlic, oregano, salt, pepper, and 2 tablespoons oil. Let stand at room temperature while pasta cooks.

2. Cook pasta uncovered in a large pot of boiling salted water over high heat, separating strands occasionally with fork, 6 to 8 minutes or until tender but firm to the bite. Drain well, rinse briefly with cold water, and drain again. Add to tomato mixture. Toss well using tongs. Add spinach and parsley.

3. If using Brisling sardines, leave them whole; cut other sardines into bite-size pieces. Leave a few sardines or sardine pieces for garnish. Add remaining sardines to salad and toss. Just before serving, add lemon juice, if using. Taste salad and adjust seasoning; add 1 to 2 more tablespoons olive oil if desired. Serve salad with reserved sardines.

Spinach Salad with Lox and Walnuts

Makes 4 servings

Orange-colored lox on bright green spinach makes for a pretty salad. Walnuts add a festive note, as does the walnut oil dressing. This salad makes a light and color-ful beginning for a Hanukkah latke party or for a Sunday brunch that features a noodle kugel as an entree.

3 cups rinsed dried spinach leaves, preferably baby spinach

2 cups iceberg lettuce mix

1 long (hothouse) cucumber, halved and sliced

1 or 2 tablespoons walnut or hazelnut oil

1 tablespoon strained fresh lemon juice

Salt and freshly ground pepper, to taste

¼ cup toasted walnut pieces

1 or 2 ounces lox, cut into thin strips

Toss spinach with lettuce, cucumber, oil, lemon juice, salt, and pepper in a salad bowl. Adjust seasoning. Serve sprinkled with walnuts and topped with lox strips.

Tunisian Tuna and Pepper Salad

Makes 2 or 3 main-course or 6 appetizer servings

Jews from Tunisia cook many delicious fish specialties. Here is a simple dish from the Tunisian kitchen that turns everyday tuna into a tasty appetizer. You can also serve it as a main course or use it as a delicious filling for a sandwich. If you use roasted peppers from a jar, it can be made very quickly.

4 red or green bell peppers, or 2 of each, roasted and peeled (page 588), or 8 roasted red pepper halves from a jar

One 6-ounce can tuna, preferably in olive oil

1 tablespoon strained fresh lemon juice

1 to 2 tablespoons extra-virgin olive oil

Salt and freshly ground pepper, to taste

2 tablespoons chopped fresh Italian parsley

2 tablespoons chopped green onion

2 teaspoons capers, rinsed

1. Prepare peppers.

2. Cut each pepper into wide strips and arrange them on a platter. Top them with chunks of tuna.

3. Combine lemon juice, oil, salt, and pepper in small bowl. Whisk to combine. Spoon over peppers and tuna. Sprinkle with parsley, onion, and capers. Serve at room temperature.

❧ Chicken and Turkey Salads

Chicken Salad with Brown Rice, Water Chestnuts, and Kiwi

Makes 3 or 4 main-course or 6 appetizer servings

Chicken salad is a favorite in many homes and for good reason— salad is a good dish to make out of the extra cooked chicken from Shabbat. Instead of the usual mayonnaise, try a sprightly ginger and orange dressing and add water chestnuts for a bit of delicate crunch. Fruit lends a festive touch, and you can even use kiwis that are still firm and tart.

3 cups chicken stock

1¹/₂ cups long-grain brown rice

1¹/₂ tablespoons red wine vinegar

2 tablespoons orange juice

3 or 4 tablespoons vegetable oil

Salt and freshly ground pepper, to taste

2 teaspoons grated peeled fresh ginger

¹/₂ teaspoon grated orange rind

3 cups cooked chicken, diced or in strips

¹/₃ cup chopped red onion

One 8-ounce can water chestnuts, drained and sliced

¹/₄ cup chopped fresh parsley

4 kiwi, quartered lengthwise and sliced

1¹/₂ cups diced papaya (optional)

1. Bring stock to a boil in a large, heavy saucepan. Add rice, cover, and cook over low heat 40 to 45 minutes or until just tender. Transfer to a large bowl, fluff with fork, and cool.

2. While rice is cooking, whisk together vinegar, orange juice, oil, salt, pepper, ginger, and orange rind in a bowl. Add 3 tablespoons of this dressing to chicken. Add onion and mix well.

3. Toss chicken mixture with rice and remaining dressing. Add water chestnuts, parsley, and kiwi and mix lightly. Adjust seasoning. Garnish with kiwi half slices and papaya, if using.

Turkey and Rice Salad with Cranberries and Pecans

Makes 6 servings

Make this salad using leftover turkey from Shabbat or from Thanksgiving. It's colorful, festive, light, and easy. If you happen to have 4 or 5 cups cooked white or brown rice, it's even easier.

2¹/₂ to 3 cups shredded or diced cooked turkey

1 to 1¹/₂ tablespoons herb vinegar or white wine vinegar

3 to 4 tablespoons vegetable oil

Salt and freshly ground pepper, to taste

2 quarts water

1¹/₂ cups white rice

2 cups diced carrots

1¹/₂ cups frozen peas

¹/₃ cup minced red onion

¹/₄ cup dried cranberries

¹/₄ cup pecans

¹/₄ cup chopped fresh Italian parsley

1. Put turkey in a large bowl. Whisk 1 tablespoon vinegar with 3 tablespoons oil, the salt, and pepper in a small bowl. Add to turkey and mix well.

2. Boil about 2 quarts water in a large saucepan and add a pinch of salt. Add rice and boil uncovered 12 to 14 minutes or until tender; check by tasting. Drain, rinse with cold water, and drain well.

3. Put carrots in medium saucepan and add enough water to generously cover them. Bring to boil. Simmer 2 minutes. Add peas and return to a boil. Simmer uncovered over medium heat for 3 minutes or until vegetables are crisp-tender. Drain in a colander, rinse with cold water, and drain well.

4. Add rice to bowl of turkey and mix well. Add carrots, peas, onion, cranberries, and pecans and mix gently. Add parsley. Adjust seasoning; add more oil or vinegar if desired.

Wild Rice and Turkey Salad

Makes 4 servings

If you have served wild rice and roast turkey for Shabbat or for a holiday, this easy, colorful salad is convenient to make afterwards. Simply cook extra wild rice and turkey when you're preparing the first meal. If you don't have cooked turkey, you can use cooked chicken or substitute smoked turkey.

3 to 4 tablespoons extra-virgin olive oil

1 tablespoon red or white wine vinegar

1 small clove garlic, finely minced

1/2 teaspoon dried oregano

2 to 2 1/2 cups strips of cooked turkey

8 ripe plum tomatoes, diced small

1/4 cup chopped fresh parsley

Salt and freshly ground pepper, to taste

One 10-ounce package frozen lima beans

4 cups cooked wild rice, or mixed wild rice and white rice

1/4 cup chopped green onions

1. Combine 3 tablespoons oil with vinegar, garlic, and oregano in a large bowl. Add turkey, tomatoes, 2 tablespoons parsley, and salt, and pepper. Let stand 5 minutes.

2. Cook lima beans according to package directions and drain. Add to salad. Add wild rice and green onions and toss. Adjust seasoning. Add remaining tablespoon olive oil if you like. Serve sprinkled with remaining parsley.

Sephardic Chicken and Pasta Salad with Marinated Artichokes

Makes 4 main-dish servings

Black olives, lemon juice, olive oil, and herbs add a terrific flavor to this salad. It's an easy, tasty way to use any chicken left over from Shabbat.

Oregano–Red Onion Dressing (page 596)

2 to 3 cups diced roast chicken

Salt and freshly ground pepper, to taste

8 ounces medium pasta shells (about 3 cups)

One 6-ounce jar or 1 cup drained marinated artichokes, quartered

1/2 cup Niçoise or other black olives, halved and pitted

1/3 cup chopped fresh Italian parsley

2 tablespoons slivered fresh basil or sage

3 ripe small tomatoes, diced

1. Prepare dressing. Add chicken to dressing; adjust seasoning. Cover and marinate, stirring occasionally, about 1 hour in refrigerator.

2. Cook pasta uncovered in a large pot of boiling salted water over high heat, stirring occasionally, 5 to 8 minutes or until tender but firm to the bite. Drain, rinse with cold water, and drain well. Add to bowl of chicken. Add artichokes, olives, parsley, basil, and tomatoes to salad and toss gently. Adjust seasoning.

Soups

Chicken Soups
260

Chicken in the Pot, Yemenite Style

Moroccan Chicken Soup with Tomatoes and Rice

Sabbath Soup

My Mother-in-Law's Spicy Chicken Soup

Light Chicken Soup with Noodles

Chicken Soup with Chickpeas and Chard

Quick Chicken Vegetable Soup with Orzo

Five-Minute Chicken and Silver Noodle Soup

Chicken Soup with Herb-Blintz Strips

Curried Chicken Soup with Spinach, Mushrooms, and Rice

Turkey Soups
266

Turkey and Bean Soup with Cilantro, Dill, and Vegetables

Easy Turkey Soup with Tomatoes and Vegetables

Bok Choy and Turkey Soup with Bean Threads and Mushrooms

Persian Split Pea Soup with Turkey and Rice

Meat Soups
268

Meat and Vegetable Borscht

Sephardic Beef and Bean Soup

Persian Chickpea Meatball Soup

Bean and Grain Soups
269

Split Pea Soup with Egg White Matzo Balls

Easy Split Pea Soup with Mushrooms

Moroccan Minestrone

Pareve Bean, Barley, and Vegetable Soup

Vegetarian Bean Soup with Meatless Sausages

Pressure Cooker Bean and Vegetable Soup with Dill

Hungarian White Bean Soup

Yemenite Lentil Soup

Hungarian Mushroom-Barley Soup

Fast Fat-Free Barley Soup

*M*ention chicken soup, and everyone thinks of Jewish cooking. Indeed, it may be the dish most identified with the Jewish kitchen. In many homes, it is a must for every *fleishig* (meat-based) menu for Shabbat and for holidays. This wonderful comfort food is very easy to make and can be served simply as a clear broth with a few carrot slices or as a hearty main course with chicken pieces and lots of vegetables.

Kneidel, or matzo balls, are the best known embellishment for chicken soup. Because they are a staple of deli mènus, they have become very familiar in American cities. They are, in fact, an Ashkenazic recipe, although many Sephardic Jews make them as well. Kreplach, which resemble tortellini, are also specialties of Eastern European Jews, and are nearly always served in clear soup. Egg noodles and rice are other popular additions to chicken soup.

Homemade soups play a major role in Jewish cooking and there are a great many others besides chicken soup. Jews from Yemen are famous for their savory whole-meal meat soups, redolent of cumin and turmeric and served with fresh pita bread and hot salsa. Polish Jews are famous for their sweet and sour borscht made of beets or cabbage and for their mushroom-barley soup. Bean soups, both vegetarian and meat based, are prepared by Jews of many origins.

When it comes to vegetable soups, many cooks who keep kosher have two separate recipes. When the soup will be served at a dairy meal, it might be made with vegetable stock or broth and finished with milk. If it will be served at a meat meal, the base will be chicken or meat stock and, of course, will not include any dairy products.

❧ Chicken Soups

Chicken in the Pot, Yemenite Style

Makes 6 servings

In many Yemenite families the midday meal during the week often revolves around a big pot of golden, aromatic chicken soup. This is a flavorful, whole-meal soup that I like to prepare often. Potatoes are traditional but I add plenty of other vegetables according to the season: carrots and zucchini all year, yellow crookneck squash and green beans in summer, green peas in spring, butternut squash and sometimes mushrooms in the winter. Serve it Yemenite style, with fresh pita bread and the spicy Yemenite chutney called zehug *on the side.*

2¹/₂ to 3 pounds chicken pieces, fat and skin removed

Salt and freshly ground pepper, to taste

5 teaspoons ground cumin

2 teaspoons ground turmeric

1 large onion, whole or sliced

6 medium carrots, cut into 2-inch lengths

4 large cloves garlic, coarsely chopped

About 2 quarts water

6 medium boiling potatoes

6 medium zucchini, halved and cut into 1-inch slices

1. Put chicken in a large stew pan or pot. Sprinkle with salt, pepper, cumin, and turmeric. Add onion, carrots, garlic, and water. Bring to a boil. Cover and cook over low heat, skimming foam occasionally 1 hour.

2. Peel potatoes, if desired. Halve them, add to soup, and simmer 20 minutes. Add zucchini and bring to a simmer. Cover and cook over low heat 15 minutes or until vegetables are tender. Skim off fat. (If making soup ahead, refrigerate, then skim off fat.) Adjust seasoning; season generously with pepper. Remove chicken, discard skin, cut meat from bones, discard bones, and return meat to soup. Serve soup in fairly shallow bowls with chicken and vegetables.

Moroccan Chicken Soup with Tomatoes and Rice

Makes 6 servings

Use homemade chicken stock or broth for the best flavor in this aromatic, gently spiced soup. If you make it ahead, add a little water when reheating it, as it thickens over time.

2 tablespoons olive oil or vegetable oil

2 medium onions, chopped

1 pound ripe plum tomatoes, peeled and diced

1 quart chicken stock or broth

3 cups water

1 rib celery, cut into thin crosswise strips

¹/₄ teaspoon ground turmeric

¹/₂ cup long-grain rice

¹/₃ cup coarsely chopped fresh cilantro

Salt and freshly ground pepper, to taste

Heat oil in a large, heavy stew pan. Add onions and sauté over medium heat about 7 minutes or until golden. Add tomatoes and sauté lightly. Add stock, water, celery, and turmeric and bring to a simmer. Cover and simmer 10 minutes, skimming fat occasionally. Add rice. Stir once, cover and cook over low heat 15 minutes or until rice is tender. Add cilantro. Taste soup; season generously with pepper. Serve hot.

Sabbath Soup

Makes 6 to 8 servings

Since some people prefer their chicken soup with noodles, while others like matzo balls, one solution is to serve both. Then you really have the best of both worlds. You can prepare the soup and matzo balls ahead and reheat them when you need them.

2 pounds chicken pieces

10 cups cold water

1 whole onion, peeled

2 ribs celery, including leafy tops

1 small leek, cleaned and left whole

1 bay leaf

Salt and freshly ground pepper, to taste

1/2 pound carrots, sliced

My Mother's Matzo Balls (page 279) or Extra-Light Matzo Balls (page 280)

1 cup very fine noodles (soup noodles)

2 tablespoons chopped fresh dill or Italian parsley

1. Combine chicken, water, onion, celery, leek, bay leaf, and a pinch of salt in a large saucepan and bring to a boil. Skim thoroughly. Partially cover and simmer 11/2 hours, skimming occasionally. Add carrots and simmer about 15 minutes or until tender. Skim off excess fat. Add pepper. Refrigerate soup. Thoroughly skim fat from soup.

2. Prepare matzo balls. Then, skim fat again from soup. Discard onion, celery, bay leaf and leek. Reheat to a simmer. Cover and keep hot.

3. Cook noodles in a large pan of boiling salted water about 7 minutes or until just tender. Drain well.

4. Add dill to soup. For each serving, remove 2 or 3 matzo balls from their cooking liquid with a slotted spoon, add them to soup bowls and ladle hot soup over them. Add noodles and a few carrot slices to each bowl. Serve hot.

My Mother-In-Law's Spicy Chicken Soup

Makes 4 to 6 servings

This is the traditional chicken soup made by Jews from Yemen. Its wonderful golden color and aroma come from the popular Yemenite spice blend known simply as "soup spice," a mixture of ground cumin seeds, turmeric, and plenty of black pepper. Some cooks add sliced summer squash or whole potatoes to the soup, while others prefer to cook the chicken without vegetables.

Usually the soup is served in shallow bowls with pieces of chicken and some potatoes or rice. My mother-in-law often cooks rice in a separate pan as pilaf, using some of the chicken soup as the cooking liquid. This results in wonderfully flavorful rice!

21/2 pounds chicken pieces

5 teaspoons ground cumin

2 teaspoons ground turmeric

Salt and freshly ground pepper, to taste

7 cups boiling water

1 large onion, peeled

1 large tomato

3 zucchini or other summer squash, cut into thick slices (optional)

1. Put chicken in a large, heavy stew pan or Dutch oven. Sprinkle with cumin, turmeric, salt, and pepper. Heat over low heat about 7 minutes, turning pieces occasionally, so they are coated with spices.

2. Add water, onion, and tomato to stew pan. Bring to a boil. Skim foam from surface. Cover and cook over low heat 1½ hours. Add zucchini, if using, and cook 30 minutes or until soup is well flavored and zucchini is very tender. Skim excess fat. Discard onion and tomato. Adjust seasoning. Serve hot, in shallow bowls.

Light Chicken Soup with Noodles

Makes 4 servings **(M)**

This economical soup needs only a small amount of chicken and is convenient when you need only a few servings. It does not have the intense flavor of broth made with a whole bird but is practical to make when you are preparing a main course of roasted or braised chicken and you don't need to cook another whole chicken.

10 to 12 ounces chicken legs or thighs

1 medium onion, quartered

1 large carrot, cut into thin slices

2 ribs celery, sliced, with leafy tops

3 sprigs fresh cilantro or Italian parsley

1 bay leaf

Salt to taste

About 6 cups water

1 cup very fine noodles (soup noodles)

2 tablespoons chopped fresh cilantro or Italian parsley

1. Remove skin from chicken, if desired. Put chicken in a saucepan and add onion, carrot, celery, cilantro sprigs, bay leaf, and salt. Add 6 cups water or enough to generously cover. Bring to a boil. Skim foam. Cover and simmer over low heat for 45 minutes to 1 hour or until just tender. Remove chicken and reserve for other uses.

2. Continue simmering soup 15 minutes or until it is well flavored. Discard celery tops, cilantro, and bay leaf. Refrigerate soup. Thoroughly skim fat from soup.

3. Cook noodles in a large pan of boiling salted water about 7 minutes or until just tender. Drain well.

4. Reheat soup before serving. Serve soup with a few carrot and celery slices and chicken strips, if using. Add noodles to each bowl of hot soup and sprinkle with chopped cilantro.

Chicken Soup with Chickpeas and Chard

Makes 4 to 6 main-course servings **(M)**

Flavored with garlic, chiles, cumin, turmeric, and cilantro, this is the kind of soup that Jews from Middle Eastern countries prepare for hearty winter meals.

1^1/2 cups dried chickpeas (garbanzo beans), about 10 ounces

2 large onions, sliced

2 small dried chiles, such as chiles japones, or ^{1}/4 to ^{1}/2 teaspoon hot red pepper flakes

2 to 2^1/2 pounds chicken pieces

10 cups water

6 large cloves garlic, chopped

1 teaspoon ground cumin

^{1}/2 teaspoon ground turmeric

Salt and freshly ground pepper, to taste

1 pound green or red chard, rinsed well

^{3}/4 cup long-grain white rice

^{1}/3 cup chopped fresh cilantro or Italian parsley

1. Sort chickpeas, discarding any broken ones and any stones. Soak chickpeas in a large bowl in cold water to generously cover overnight.

2. Rinse chickpeas, drain, and put them in a stew pan or large pot. Add onions, chiles, chicken, and the water and bring to a boil. Skim foam from surface. Cover and cook over low heat 1 hour or until chicken is tender. Remove chicken. Add garlic, cumin, turmeric, and salt and cook 30 minutes to 1 hour or until chickpeas are tender. Skim fat from soup. (If you like, refrigerate soup at this point, then skim fat.)

3. Peel chard stems if they have thick ribs. Cut stems into thin strips. Chop leaves; keep them separate from stems.

4. Remove chicken and discard skin and bones. Cut meat into strips and reserve.

5. Add chard stems and rice to soup, stir once, cover and cook over low heat 20 minutes or until rice is tender. Add chard leaves and chicken strips and bring to a simmer. Cook 5 minutes or until chard is tender. Add half the cilantro. Adjust seasoning. Sprinkle with remaining cilantro when serving.

Quick Chicken Vegetable Soup with Orzo

Makes 4 servings

Long noodles aren't the only type of pasta that is great in chicken soup. The pasta called orzo or riso has long been used in Israel because of its appealing rice shape.

This simple but savory soup can be made quickly if you already have chicken soup or if you use good quality prepared broth. If you prefer, make it pareve and use vegetable broth. To make it more substantial, heat 1½ to 2 cups strips of cooked chicken or turkey in the soup.

2 tablespoons olive oil

1 onion, chopped

1½ cups orzo or riso (rice-shaped pasta)

6 large cloves garlic, chopped

Salt and freshly ground pepper, to taste

7 cups chicken stock or broth

2 medium carrots, diced

2 medium yellow crookneck squash or zucchini, halved and sliced

8 ounces mushrooms, quartered

1½ cups frozen peas (optional)

½ teaspoon paprika, either sweet or hot

½ teaspoon ground turmeric

2 tablespoons chopped fresh cilantro

1. Heat oil in a medium saucepan, add onion, and sauté 5 minutes over medium heat. Add orzo and half the garlic and sauté over low heat, stirring often, 2 minutes. Add salt, pepper, and 3 cups chicken stock. Stir and bring to a boil. Cover and cook over low heat about 12 minutes or until orzo is just tender. Fluff with a fork.

2. Meanwhile, bring remaining stock to a simmer with carrots in another saucepan. Cover and simmer 5 minutes. Add squash, mushrooms, peas if using, paprika, turmeric, and remaining garlic. Bring to a boil. Simmer 5 minutes or until vegetables are just tender. Adjust seasoning.

3. Just before serving, add cilantro. Serve orzo in a separate bowl, for adding to soup.

Five-Minute Chicken and Silver Noodle Soup

Makes 4 servings

For chicken soup with a difference, try the light bean threads known on Thai menus as "silver noodles" because they become transparent when cooked. (In stores, they may be labeled as bean vermicelli, cellophane noodles, or transparent noodles.) These light noodles, made from mung beans, have another plus— very thin ones cook in only two minutes. Thus they are perfect for quick soups like this one. They don't even need an extra pot.

1 quart chicken soup or chicken stock

1 cup water

1 cup shredded carrots

1 or 2 cups shredded cooked chicken (optional)

One 3½-ounce package very thin bean threads

¼ cup fresh cilantro, Italian parsley, or watercress leaves

¼ cup chopped green onions

Salt, to taste

Bring soup and water to a simmer in a medium saucepan. Add carrots, chicken if using, and bean threads. Cook over low heat about 2 minutes or until bean threads are just translucent. Stir in cilantro and green onions. Add salt if needed. Serve using tongs and a ladle.

Simple Soups From Extra Chicken or Turkey

The last thing I want to do the day after a big cooking-and-feasting marathon, whether for Passover, Sukkot, or Thanksgiving, is to spend a lot of time in the kitchen or have another copious meal. So I break with traditional recipes for using leftovers. I stay away from classic American chicken and turkey casseroles, as they tend to be high in fat and calories and often require washing several pans.

Instead I prepare a soothing bowl of soup. I don't mean a huge production that entails chopping the carved bird's carcass and simmering it for hours. I prefer to make a quick vegetable soup and enhance it with strips of chicken or turkey. Even with brief cooking, the turkey makes the soup delicious. This meal-in-a-bowl is welcome a day or two after the holiday, or, if you freeze some of the bird, several weeks later. It's also a great way to use extra roast chicken after Shabbat and also works well with extra brisket.

A chicken or turkey vegetable soup demands little effort and time. You have great flexibility in terms of calories and fat too. For a light soup, don't add much chicken. If you want something heartier, add more. You can even add chicken or turkey to each bowl according to the taste of each person in your household—more turkey or less, dark or white meat. Then microwave each bowl of soup to heat the turkey.

Most of the time I make the soup from a few aromatic vegetables—onions, carrots, and celery. I don't bother to chop them into tiny dice. It's amazing how quickly a roughly cut onion or a thickly sliced carrot can cook in soup. Ten or fifteen minutes is usually enough.

Beyond my soup trio, the choice of vegetables is wide open. Sliced, packaged mushrooms top my list of valuable vegetables—those with lots of taste and nutrients for little toil. Cleaned spinach from a bag is a close second. Green beans and turnips add good flavor, and a small amount needs only minutes to prepare.

For a more substantial soup, I throw in a few diced boiling potatoes. I don't bother peeling them—rinsing and scrubbing them with a brush is enough. Even easier to add is rice or pasta. Either I simmer it right in the soup or I add some already cooked grains or noodles if I have any in my refrigerator or freezer.

Today we can make a tasty soup without cutting up a single vegetable. For the basics, if you like, use packaged carrot and celery sticks, peeled baby carrots, or bagged refrigerated or frozen diced onions. Simpler still, purchase a package of frozen stew vegetables. To them add more of your favorites from the freezer, as single vegetables or as a mixture. I like corn, green beans, and peas, or medleys that include broccoli or beans.

Canned tomatoes or beans from my pantry are an excellent last-minute addition. If I don't think of adding beans, my husband, whose partial to them, might slip some in the pot, generally chickpeas (garbanzo beans) or white beans and sometimes even black beans.

Chicken Soup with Herb-Blintz Strips

Makes 6 servings

Blintzes, or crepe-like wrappers, cut into strips make a lovely addition to clear soups. They resemble noodles but are even richer tasting. Serve this soup as a holiday first course or any time you have extra blintz wrappers. If your blintzes are dairy, make the soup with vegetable stock.

6 Herb Blintzes for Meat Fillings (page 301)

6 cups chicken soup or chicken stock

1 cup water

1½ cups sliced carrots

Salt and freshly ground pepper, to taste

¼ cup chopped fresh Italian parsley

¼ cup chopped green onions

1. Prepare blintzes. Then, bring soup and water to a simmer in a medium saucepan. Add carrots and cook over low heat about 10 minutes or until carrots are tender. Season with salt and pepper.

2. Halve blintzes and cut them into thin strips, about ½-inch wide. Just before serving, bring soup to a simmer and add blintz strips. Return to a simmer, or cover soup so blintz strips heat through. Stir in parsley and green onions and serve.

Curried Chicken Soup with Spinach, Mushrooms, and Rice

Makes about 4 servings

My in-laws from India often serve soup with rice spooned into each bowl. It's a delicious and satisfying way to enjoy soups, whether of vegetables, lentils, or chicken.

If you already have extra cooked chicken, soup, and rice from a Shabbat dinner, this hearty soup can be an easy-to-make meal-in-a-bowl for a Sunday lunch or supper. If you don't have leftovers, the soup can still be prepared in no time. Simply use prepared stock, roasted chicken from a deli, and, instead of pilaf, use packaged quick-cooking rice. I cook the vegetables briefly in the soup so they retain their fresh flavor.

2 cups Israeli Rice Pilaf (page 499)

6 cups chicken or vegetable stock, or stock mixed with water

1 small onion, diced

1 small turnip, peeled and diced

2 large carrots, diced

Salt and freshly ground pepper, to taste

1 teaspoon curry powder

¼ head cabbage, shredded

6 ounces sliced fresh mushrooms

2 cups diced cooked chicken

One 10-ounce bag rinsed spinach leaves

1. Prepare rice. Then, combine stock, onion, and turnip in a large saucepan and bring to a boil. Add carrots, salt, pepper, and curry powder. Return to a simmer. Cover and cook for 15 minutes. Add cabbage and simmer 5 minutes. Add mushrooms and chicken and bring to a simmer. Add spinach and cook for 2 minutes over low heat.

2. If not freshly cooked, heat rice in a container in the microwave. Ladle soup into bowls and top each with a few spoonfuls of rice pilaf.

❧ Turkey Soups

Turkey and Bean Soup with Cilantro, Dill, and Vegetables

Makes about 4 servings (M)

The perfect time to make this hearty, healthful soup is after Thanksgiving, when you have cooked turkey and turkey or chicken stock on hand. It's also a good way to use cooked chicken and soup from Shabbat. Flavored with two popular herbs in Israeli soup pots—cilantro and dill—the soup is both refreshing and satisfying. When I happen to have the pale green dried French beans called flageolets, I'll add those—I love the color and delicate flavor they contribute, but the soup is good with white beans too.

1 cup dried flageolets or white beans, sorted

6 cups turkey or chicken stock, or half stock and half water

1 large onion, diced

2 sprigs fresh thyme or 1/2 teaspoon dried thyme

5 sprigs fresh parsley (optional)

3 fresh dill stems plus 1 to 2 tablespoons chopped leaves, reserved (or 1 teaspoon dried)

3 fresh cilantro stems plus 3 to 4 tablespoons chopped leaves, reserved

1 bay leaf

One 1-pound package frozen mixed vegetables (carrots, corn, green and lima beans, peas)

2 to 3 cups thin strips of cooked turkey (dark or light meat or both)

1. If you wish to shorten cooking time, soak beans in a large bowl generously covered with water overnight. Drain and rinse. In a large pot combine beans with stock, onion, thyme, parsley, dill, cilantro stems, and bay leaf. Bring to a boil. Cover and simmer over low heat for 1 1/2 to 2 hours or until tender. Remove herb sprigs.

2. Add frozen vegetables to pot and bring to a simmer. Cover and cook about 10 minutes or until tender. Stir in turkey and heat through. Add chopped dill and cilantro just before serving.

Easy Turkey Soup with Tomatoes and Vegetables

Makes about 4 servings (M)

In addition to the vegetables mentioned in Simple Soups from Extra Chicken or Turkey (see page 264), I usually add a zucchini or two if I find them in my refrigerator. While the soup is cooking, I cut the zucchini into cubes, and add it a few minutes before we eat. If I have some extra chopped herbs from the holiday meal, I add them at the last minute. Almost any herb will do; parsley, basil, tarragon, sage, dill, and cilantro are all fine.

3 1/2 cups homemade or canned chicken or vegetable broth

3 cups water

1 large onion, halved and coarsely chopped

2 ribs celery, sliced

1 carrot, cut crosswise into thick slices

One 1-pound package frozen mixed vegetables

One 6-ounce package sliced fresh mushrooms or 1 to 2 cups rinsed spinach leaves, coarsely chopped

1 teaspoon dried thyme

One 15-ounce can chickpeas (garbanzo beans) or white beans, drained, or 2 cups cooked rice or pasta

14 1/2-ounce can stewed or diced tomatoes, with their liquid

About 3 cups strips of cooked turkey (dark or light meat or some of each)

2 teaspoons jarred curry sauce (optional)

Salt and freshly ground pepper, to taste

1. Combine broth, water, onion, celery, and carrot in a large saucepan. Bring to a boil. Cover and cook over medium heat 7 minutes. Add frozen vegetables and bring to a boil. Cover and cook 7 minutes. Add mushrooms or spinach and simmer 2 to 3 minutes or until all vegetables are tender.

2. Add thyme, chickpeas, tomatoes, and turkey and bring to a simmer. Stir gently. Add a few tablespoons boiling water if soup is too thick. Stir in curry sauce, if using, and return to a simmer. Season with salt and pepper. Serve hot.

Bok Choy and Turkey Soup with Bean Threads and Mushrooms

Makes 6 servings

Although there is evidence of an ancient practicing Jewish community in China, it has long since disappeared. However, the modern American Jewish love for Chinese cooking thrives and was the inspiration for this twist on chicken noodle soup. It uses thin transparent noodles called dried vermicelli or bean threads, as well as fresh bok choy, which cook in no time. In the Cantonese kitchen they are popular in soups made with just a little chicken or beef. Dried Chinese mushrooms, water chestnuts, and fresh ginger contribute interest to this version so it is delicate but not bland.

7 dried shiitake or black mushrooms

3^1/$_2$ ounces dried vermicelli (bean threads)

6 cups chicken or vegetable stock

3 cups water

1 tablespoon minced fresh peeled ginger

8 cups diced bok choy (^{1}/$_4$-inch cubes)

1^1/$_2$ cups strips of cooked turkey or chicken

12 to 18 canned water chestnuts, drained, rinsed, and sliced

2 tablespoons soy sauce

1 tablespoon rice wine or dry sherry

Salt and white pepper, to taste

3 tablespoons chopped green onions

1. Soak mushrooms in hot water to cover for 20 minutes or until tender. Drain well. Cut out and discard tough stems. Slice mushrooms.

2. Soak bean threads in hot water to cover for 10 minutes. Drain well.

3. Combine stock, water, mushrooms, and ginger in a large saucepan and bring to a boil. Add bok choy. Return to boil and add vermicelli. Cover and simmer over medium-low heat for 3 to 5 minutes or until bok choy is tender. Add turkey and water chestnuts and simmer 1 minute. Add soy sauce and rice wine. Adjust seasoning. Serve sprinkled with green onion.

Persian Split Pea Soup with Turkey and Rice

Makes 4 to 6 servings

Unlike most split pea soups, this recipe, favored by Iranian Jews, is not a thick puree. The peas, rice, and strips of turkey keep their distinct textures in the gently spiced broth flavored with garlic, dill, and cilantro.

^{3}/$_4$ cup split peas, sorted, rinsed, and drained

1 onion, sliced

About 2 quarts turkey or chicken stock, or stock mixed with water

Salt and freshly ground pepper, to taste

6 large cloves garlic, chopped

1 teaspoon ground turmeric

6 tablespoons chopped fresh dill

6 tablespoons chopped fresh cilantro

^{2}/$_3$ cup long-grain rice, preferably basmati

3 cups strips of cooked turkey

1. Cook peas with onion and 6 cups stock in large saucepan for about 1 hour and 15 minutes or until peas are tender. Season soup with salt and pepper.

2. Add 2 cups stock, garlic, turmeric, 4 tablespoons dill, and 4 tablespoons cilantro. Bring to a simmer. Add rice and bring to simmer. Cover and cook over low heat for 15 minutes or until rice is barely tender. Add turkey and heat through. If soup is too thick, add a little more stock and bring to a simmer. Stir in remaining dill and cilantro. Adjust seasoning. Serve hot.

🌿 *Meat Soups*

Meat and Vegetable Borscht

Makes 6 to 8 servings ⓜ

Popular in Poland, Russia, and Ukraine, this hearty soup gains an intriguing taste from beets and cabbage that cook in a beef broth. Some cooks add smoked meats, frankfurters, or salami for accent, while some prefer to make the soup with red cabbage. Still others add white beans or potatoes so the soup will be even more satisfying. The soup is good made ahead and reheated.

1 tablespoon vegetable oil

2 large onions, diced

4 large carrots, diced

1 parsnip or parsley root, diced (optional)

1¹/₂ pounds beef with bones, such as beef shank

6 cups water

1 bay leaf

3 medium beets, scrubbed thoroughly with brush

3 to 4 tablespoons tomato paste

¹/₂ small green cabbage, shredded

2 tablespoons chopped fresh parsley

1. Heat oil in large saucepan over medium heat, add onions, carrots, and parsnip, if using, and sauté about 10 minutes, stirring often. Transfer to a bowl. Put beef in same saucepan, cover with the water, and add bay leaf. Bring to a boil. Cover and cook over low heat 30 minutes. Add beets, cover and simmer 1 hour or until tender. Remove beets and slip off their skins under running water. Dice beets and return to saucepan.

2. Stir tomato paste into soup. Add sautéed vegetables. Cover and simmer 20 minutes. Add cabbage and simmer 15 minutes or until beef and vegetables are tender. Discard bay leaf. Skim excess fat from soup. (If preparing soup ahead, refrigerate, then skim off fat.) Adjust seasoning. Remove beef. Dice any meat, discarding bones, and add meat to soup. Serve hot, sprinkled with parsley.

Sephardic Beef and Bean Soup

Makes about 6 servings ⓜ

Garlic and plenty of Italian parsley lend good flavor to this warming soup. In some Sephardic families, this soup is served for Friday night dinner or for the Shabbat midday meal.

1 pound dried small or medium white beans (about 2¹/₂ cups)

2 tablespoons vegetable oil

3 medium onions, sliced

1¹/₂ pounds beef chuck, diced, or beef stew meat

6 cloves garlic, chopped

2 tablespoons tomato paste

1¹/₂ teaspoons paprika

6 cups water, plus more boiling water as needed

³/₄ cup chopped fresh Italian parsley

Salt and freshly ground pepper, to taste

1 teaspoon sugar (optional)

1. Sort beans, discarding any broken ones and any stones. If you like, soak beans generously covered in cold water in a large bowl, overnight, to slightly shorten their cooking time. Rinse beans and drain.

2. Heat oil in large saucepan, add onions and sauté over medium heat about 7 minutes or until golden. Add beef and sauté, stirring, 5 minutes. Add beans, garlic, tomato paste, paprika, water, and ¹/₄ cup parsley. Bring to a boil. Cover and cook over low heat 2 to 2¹/₂ hours or until meat and beans are tender; add boiling water from time to time if soup becomes too thick. Season with salt, pepper, and sugar, if using. Stir in remaining parsley. Serve hot.

Persian Chickpea Meatball Soup

Makes 4 or 5 servings

(M)

A favorite for Shabbat among Iranian Jews, this soup makes a substantial first course or a light main course.

1 small (8- or 9-ounce) can chickpeas (garbanzo beans), drained and rinsed

6 ounces lean ground beef

1 small onion, minced

1/4 teaspoon salt, or more if needed

1/4 teaspoon freshly ground pepper

2 tablespoons chopped fresh Italian parsley

6 cups beef broth

2 large boiling potatoes, peeled and diced

1 large carrot, diced

2 tablespoons tomato paste

1/2 teaspoon ground cumin

1/4 teaspoon ground turmeric

1/4 cup rice

1/4 teaspoon cayenne pepper, or to taste

1. Preheat oven to 350°F. To prepare meatballs: put chickpeas on a small baking sheet. Bake in oven 10 minutes to dry and toast them lightly. Let cool. Add chickpeas to food processor, chop them, and transfer them to a bowl. Add beef, onions, salt, pepper, and parsley. Shape tablespoons of mixture into small meatballs. Squeeze each to make it compact, then roll it between your palms to a smooth ball.

2. Bring broth to a boil in a medium saucepan. Meanwhile, peel and dice potatoes. Add potatoes and carrots to broth. Cover and simmer 15 minutes. Add tomato paste, cumin, and turmeric and stir to blend. Add rice and meatballs. Cover and simmer over low heat 30 minutes. Season with salt and cayenne. Serve hot.

❧ Bean and Grain Soups

Split Pea Soup with Egg White Matzo Balls

Makes 4 servings

(P)

Split pea soup is one of the most popular soups in Jewish homes as well as at deli restaurants. Jewish cooks often make their split pea soup meatless, although some do add sliced spicy sausages for extra zest. My mother likes to make her split pea soup very smooth, and for a special touch, garnishes it with matzo balls.

If you don't have time to prepare matzo balls, you can serve the soup with croutons—either light, baked, buttery or fried (pages 282–283).

1/2 pound split peas (1 1/4 cups), sorted and rinsed

5 cups water

1 medium onion, chopped

1 large carrot, diced

Salt and freshly ground pepper, to taste

1 large egg white or 1/4 cup egg substitute

2 tablespoons plus 1 teaspoon matzo meal, plus more if needed

Pinch of baking powder

1 tablespoon water

1. Combine peas, water, onion, carrot, salt, and pepper in a large saucepan and bring to a boil. Cover and cook over low heat, stirring occasionally for about 1 hour or until split peas are very soft. Puree soup in blender or with a hand blender.

2. Lightly beat egg white in a small bowl. Add matzo meal, baking powder, salt, and pepper and stir gently with fork until well blended. Stir in water. If mixture is too thin to form into soft balls, stir in another teaspoon matzo meal.

3. Bring a medium saucepan of salted water to a boil. Reduce heat so water does not bubble. With wet hands, take about 1/2 teaspoon of matzo ball mixture and roll it between your palms into a ball; mixture will be very soft. Add to saucepan of hot water. Continue shaping matzo balls and adding to pot of water, wetting your hands before making each. Cover and simmer over low heat about 30 minutes or until firm. Cover and keep them warm until ready to serve.

4. Serve matzo balls in hot soup.

Easy Split Pea Soup with Mushrooms

Makes 6 servings (P)

Packaged split pea soups are a pantry staple in many Jewish kitchens so that soups can be prepared without a trip to the market. I like to add the basic soup vegetables that I have on hand—onions, carrots, and celery. Mushrooms contribute a good flavor to the soup.

Use either split pea soup mix or vegetable soup mix that has split peas as the first ingredient.

2 quarts water

One 6-ounce package split pea soup mix

2 large onions, diced

3 large carrots, sliced

2 ribs celery, sliced, leafy tops reserved

6 to 8 ounces small mushrooms, quartered, or one 6-ounce package sliced mushrooms

1/4 cup chopped fresh parsley

Salt and freshly ground pepper, to taste

1. Bring water to boil in a large pot and add soup mix. Plan soup's cooking time according to package directions; 45 minutes before it is done, add onions. 15 minutes after that, add carrots and celery, so they have 30 minutes to cook. 20 minutes later, add mushrooms, so they'll have about 10 minutes to cook.

2. Just before serving, stir in parsley. Season with salt and pepper. Serve hot.

Moroccan Minestrone

Makes 3 main-course
or 4 or 5 first-course servings (M) or (P)

Italy is not the only place where you find minestrone-type soups. Hearty vegetable soups with beans and noodles are also popular in North Africa. Unlike Italian soups, they are fragrant with cilantro and cumin.

Recently I learned a tip for speeding up minestrone preparation from Nancy Eisman of Melissa's Specialty Foods in Los Angeles. Nancy, whose mother was born in Morocco, suggests using quick-cooking couscous in the classic soup. The soup turns out delicious and satisfying.

This soup is most attractive served in shallow bowls. Other favorite additions of mine to this North African minestrone are winter squash, zucchini, potatoes, turnips, and white beans. Adding cilantro in two portions gives the soup two different flavors—a mellow taste from cooked cilantro and a fresh punch from fresh cilantro added at the last minute. If you prefer Italian parsley, substitute it for the cilantro.

2 to 3 teaspoons olive oil or a little olive oil spray

1 large onion, chopped

2/3 cup coarsely chopped fresh cilantro or Italian parsley

One 14 1/2-ounce can vegetable or chicken broth (1 3/4 cups)

1 quart water

2 large carrots, diced

2 ribs celery, sliced

1 teaspoon ground cumin

2 cups small cauliflower florets

2 tablespoons tomato paste

One 15-ounce can chickpeas (garbanzo beans), drained, or an 11-ounce plastic tub of garbanzo beans (see Note)

1/2 cup couscous, plain or whole-wheat

Salt and freshly ground pepper, to taste

Cayenne pepper, to taste

1. Heat oil in a large saucepan, add onion and 1/3 cup cilantro and sauté 3 minutes over medium heat. Add broth, water, carrot, celery, and cumin and bring to a boil. Cover and simmer over medium-low heat for 5 minutes. Add cauliflower and cook 7 minutes or until vegetables are tender.

2. Stir in tomato paste, then chickpeas, and return to a boil. Stir couscous into soup and bring just to a boil. Remove from heat, cover, and let stand 5 minutes. Stir in remaining cilantro. Season with salt, pepper, and cayenne. Serve hot.

Note: If using a plastic tub of garbanzo beans, prepare them according to package directions.

Pareve Bean, Barley, and Vegetable Soup

Makes 6 to 8 servings

I prepare a flavorful vegetable soup as the base of this bean soup. It's quicker than other bean soups because I use canned or already cooked beans. Hearty and colorful, it makes a satisfying vegetarian entree but you can also serve it in smaller amounts as a first course.

I cook the pearl barley together with the vegetables. In pearl barley, the husk, bran, and germ have been removed. To save a little time, you can use quick-cooking barley, which is ready in ten minutes. You can find it at health-food stores.

6 cups water

1 quart vegetable broth

2 large onions, diced

2 bay leaves

4 sprigs fresh thyme or 1 teaspoon dried thyme

2 ribs celery, sliced, leafy tops reserved

1/2 cup pearl barley, rinsed and drained

1 medium turnip, peeled and diced

2 large potatoes, diced

Salt and freshly ground pepper, to taste

3 large carrots, cut into thick slices

6 large cloves garlic, chopped

8 ounces fresh mushrooms, cut into thick slices

2 zucchini, halved and sliced

Two 15-ounce cans white beans, drained

1. Bring water, broth, onions, bay leaves, thyme sprigs, and celery tops to a simmer in a large saucepan. Add barley. Cover and cook over low heat 10 minutes.

Add turnip, potatoes, and a pinch of salt and simmer 10 minutes.

2. Add celery slices, carrots, and garlic to soup. Cover and simmer 20 minutes. Add mushrooms, zucchini, and beans. Simmer 10 minutes or until all vegetables and barley are tender. Discard bay leaf, thyme sprigs, and celery tops. Season with salt and pepper.

Vegetarian Bean Soup with Meatless Sausages

Makes 6 main-course servings

To make this soup easy, I start with a package of bean soup mix, then add vegetables, herbs, and garlic as it cooks. To add zest to the soup, I like to finish it with slices of spicy meatless hot dogs or frankfurters. These soy-based sausages add a pleasant taste and many are low in fat or even fat-free.

If you prefer a meaty soup, you can stir in 1 or 2 cups diced cooked chicken or turkey or use chicken or turkey frankfurters.

10 cups water

One 6-ounce package bean soup mix (3/4 to 1 cup dry mix)

2 large onions, diced

3 large carrots, sliced

3 ribs celery, sliced

6 to 8 ounces meatless sausages or frankfurters, cut into
    1/2-inch slices

3 medium zucchini, halved and sliced

3 large cloves garlic, chopped

1/4 cup chopped fresh dill or Italian parsley

Salt and freshly ground pepper, to taste

Bring water to boil in a large pot and add soup mix. Plan soup's cooking time according to package directions; 45 minutes before it is done, add onions; 15 minutes after that, add carrots and celery, so they have 30 minutes to cook; 20 minutes later, add sausages, zucchini, and garlic so they'll have about 10 minutes to cook. Just before serving, stir in dill. Season with salt and pepper. Serve hot.

Pressure Cooker Bean and Vegetable Soup with Dill

Makes about 6 servings **P**

Along with the dill, this colorful bean soup features three other favorite Israeli soup flavorings—cumin, garlic, and tomato paste—which give the soup a rich taste and a warm reddish-brown hue. It's a good soup for winter and, of course, the pressure cooker shortens the cooking time. If you'd like to prepare it without a pressure cooker, see the note at the end of the recipe.

Served with multigrain, whole-wheat, or another hearty bread—either fresh or as Light Croutons (page 283)—this soup makes a satisfying main course. We like to begin the meal with a quick salad of lettuce, tomatoes, cucumbers, and jicama, or an Israeli salad with smoked cod.

1 cup bean soup mix or mixed white and red beans

10 cups water

2 ribs celery, sliced, leafy tops reserved

2 or 3 thick dill stems, feathery leaves reserved for sprinkling

1 bay leaf

1 large turnip, peeled and diced

3 potatoes, peeled and diced

1 large onion, diced

2 carrots, diced

Salt and freshly ground pepper, to taste

1/3 pound green beans, cut into 2-inch pieces

2 yellow squash, diced

4 cloves garlic, minced

2 tablespoons tomato paste

2 to 3 teaspoons ground cumin

1/2 teaspoon ground turmeric (optional)

1. Soak beans in a large bowl generously covered with cold water overnight. Drain beans and rinse.

2. Put beans in pressure cooker with 8 cups water, celery tops, dill stems, and bay leaf. Cook on low pressure 25 minutes or until beans are tender. Allow pressure to come down. Remove cover. Remove dill stems.

3. Add turnip, potatoes, onion, carrots, salt, pepper, and remaining water. Bring to a boil. Cover but do not use pressure. Simmer soup over low heat 20 minutes. Add green beans, squash, and sliced celery, and cook 15 minutes. Add garlic, tomato paste, cumin, and turmeric, if using. Cook 5 minutes or until vegetables are tender. Adjust seasoning. Chop reserved dill tops. Serve soup sprinkled with dill.

Note: To prepare the soup without a pressure cooker, cook the beans and flavorings as in the second step above for 1 to 1 1/2 hours or until just tender.

Hungarian White Bean Soup

Makes 4 servings **M**

Like Italian pasta e fagioli, *this bean soup is accented with pasta. Sausages, tomato paste, and paprika give it a rich color and flavor.*

This thick, substantial soup is made in Hungary with sour cream or yogurt, but Jewish versions omit the sour cream because the soup contains meat. Sometimes the soup is thickened by pureeing half of the beans and vegetables, as in this recipe. Old-fashioned versions call for a roux of flour and fat as well but it's easier and lighter if you omit it.

If you wish to make it pareve or vegetarian, use vegetable stock as the cooking liquid and meatless sausages or frankfurters.

1 tablespoon vegetable oil

1 small onion, chopped

1 medium carrot, diced

1/4 cup chopped parsnip or parsley root (optional)

One 15-ounce can white beans, drained (see Note)

1 quart beef or chicken stock or broth

1 teaspoon paprika

1 tablespoon tomato paste

2 beef or chicken frankfurters, sliced

1/4 cup square noodles or other small pasta shapes

Salt and freshly ground pepper, to taste

1. Heat oil in a heavy saucepan, add onion, and sauté until beginning to brown. Add carrot and parsnip, if using, cover, and cook over low heat, stirring often and adding 1 or 2 tablespoons water if needed, about 10 minutes or until softened and lightly browned.

2. Spoon about half the vegetables into a blender. Add half the white beans. Puree mixture and return to saucepan. Stir in stock, remaining beans, paprika, and tomato paste. Bring to a boil. Cover and cook over low heat 15 minutes. If soup is too thick, stir in a little boiling water. Add frankfurters and pasta and cook about 5 minutes or until pasta is tender. Season with salt and pepper.

Note: You can use 1/2 cup dried white beans. Soak them overnight or simply rinse them. Drain them and cook in water to generously cover about 1 1/2 hours or until tender.

Yemenite Lentil Soup

Makes 4 or 5 servings

I learned how to make this richly flavored soup from my mother-in-law, Rachel Levy. Whenever she prepared lentils, she first spread some in a single layer on a plate and inspected them very carefully to be sure no stones were mixed with them. She then removed them to a strainer for rinsing and added the next batch of lentils to the plate. It seemed like a lot of work, but the savory soup was worth it. Serve the soup with fresh, warm pita bread.

1 1/2 cups lentils (about 1/2 pound)

2 tablespoons vegetable oil

1 large onion, chopped

3 large cloves garlic, chopped

6 cups water

2 large carrots, diced

2 large potatoes, diced

Salt and freshly ground pepper, to taste

1 to 2 cups boiling water

3 zucchini, sliced

2 tablespoons tomato paste

2 large ripe tomatoes, coarsely grated

1 1/2 teaspoons ground cumin

1/2 teaspoon ground turmeric

1. Spread lentils on a plate, pick through them carefully, rinse, and drain.

2. Heat oil in a medium saucepan, add onion and sauté over medium-low heat 10 minutes or until

golden. Add garlic and sauté 1 minute, stirring. Remove to a bowl.

3. To pan add lentils and water and bring to a simmer. Add carrots, potatoes, salt, and pepper and return to a simmer. Cover and simmer over low heat 20 minutes. Gradually add boiling water if soup is too thick. Add zucchini and simmer 10 minutes.

4. Add onion mixture, tomato paste, tomatoes, cumin, turmeric, salt, and pepper. Simmer, covered, 15 minutes or until lentils are tender. Adjust seasoning; season generously with pepper.

Hungarian Mushroom-Barley Soup

Makes 4 to 6 servings

This delicious soup is an Eastern European Jewish favorite and a popular soup offering on deli menus. It's easy to make at home, especially if you have homemade meat or chicken soup or stock. Use any kind of dried mushrooms you like. I often find some in kosher shops labeled simply "Polish mushrooms." These mushrooms are from the boletus mushroom family; mushrooms called cèpes or porcini can be substituted.

1 ounce dried Polish mushrooms, cèpes, or porcini

1 cup hot water

1/2 pound carrots, diced

1 parsnip or parsley root, diced

1 medium onion, diced

1 quart beef, veal, or chicken stock

1 quart water

1/2 cup pearl barley

3 ribs celery, diced

2 teaspoons sweet paprika

Salt and freshly ground pepper, to taste

6 to 8 ounces small fresh mushrooms, quartered

1 1/2 cups thin strips of cooked beef or chicken (optional)

1/4 teaspoon hot paprika or cayenne pepper, to taste

2 to 3 tablespoons chopped fresh parsley

1. Rinse dried mushrooms and soak 20 minutes in hot water. Remove mushrooms, reserving liquid. Dice any large ones.

2. Combine carrots, parsnip, onion, stock, and water in a large stew pan and bring to boil. Skim foam from surface. Reduce heat to low. Add barley, celery, sweet paprika, salt, and pepper. Add fresh and dried mushrooms. Pour mushroom soaking water into another bowl, leaving behind and discarding the last few tablespoons of liquid, which may be sandy. Add mushroom liquid to soup. Cover and cook about 1 hour or until barley is tender. Add beef, if using, and heat through. Season with hot paprika, salt, and pepper.

3. Serve hot, sprinkled with parsley.

Fast Fat-Free Barley Soup

Makes 4 servings **P**

When I long for the homey feeling of old-fashioned Ashkenazic barley soup but I have little time to cook, this is the soup I prepare. I combine quick-cooking barley, which is ready in ten minutes, with fresh and frozen vegetables. The result is a healthful, hearty, warming soup in no time.

Look for quick-cooking barley at natural foods stores. If you can't find it, you can use quick-cooking brown rice; it's available at most supermarkets.

2 medium carrots, diced

1 medium onion, diced or 1/2 cup packaged diced onions

3 ribs celery, diced

3 1/2 cups vegetable stock or two 14 1/2-ounce cans broth

2 1/2 cups hot water

2 cups frozen mixed vegetables, including lima beans, corn, and green beans

1/2 cup quick-cooking barley

1 teaspoon dried dill

1/2 teaspoon dried thyme

Salt and freshly ground pepper, to taste

Cayenne pepper, to taste

Combine carrots, onion, celery, stock, and water in a large saucepan. Cover and bring to boil. Cook, covered, over medium-low heat 3 minutes. Add frozen vegetables and return to a boil. Add barley, dill, and thyme. Cover and simmer over medium-low heat for 10 minutes or until barley is tender. Season with salt, pepper, and cayenne. Serve hot.

Vegetable Soups

Velvet Vegetable Soup with Spiced Matzo Balls

Makes 6 servings

The striking orange hue of this soup makes it an enticing appetizer even before you savor its delicately sweet flavor. Pureeing rice along with the vegetables gives it a pleasing creamy texture. It makes a nice change of pace from chicken noodle soup for Shabbat. Use chicken stock for meat meals or vegetable stock to make it pareve.

This soup is low in fat. If you would like low-fat matzo balls, see Extra-Light Matzo Balls (page 280).

Spiced Matzo Balls (page 281)

1 tablespoon vegetable oil

2 medium onions, chopped

1 1/4 pounds butternut or banana squash, peeled and diced

1/2 pound carrots, diced

5 1/4 cups chicken or vegetable stock

3 tablespoons rice

Salt and freshly ground pepper, to taste

1/2 teaspoon dried thyme, crumbled

1 bay leaf

Pinch of sugar (optional)

1. Prepare matzo balls. Then, heat oil in a large, heavy saucepan. Add onions and sauté over medium-low heat, stirring often, 7 minutes or until soft but not brown. Add squash, carrots, 4 cups stock, rice, salt, pepper, thyme, and bay leaf. Stir and bring to a boil. Cover and cook over low heat about 30 minutes or until vegetables and rice are very tender. Discard bay leaf. Let soup cool 5 minutes.

2. Pour soup into blender and puree until very smooth. Return to saucepan. Bring to a simmer, stirring often. Add about 1 1/4 cups stock, or enough to bring soup to desired consistency. Bring to a boil, stirring. Adjust seasoning; add pinch of sugar, if using.

3. When serving soup, use slotted spoon to add 4 to 6 matzo balls to each bowl.

Quick Mushroom Soup with Rice

Makes 4 servings　Ⓜ or Ⓟ

This soup of Eastern European Jewish origin is made either with rice or with farfel, *a type of chopped pasta also known as egg barley. Make it with vegetable broth for pareve or dairy meals, or with chicken or beef broth for meat meals.*

The soup cooks fastest if made with white rice or with quick-cooking brown rice.

1 to 2 tablespoons vegetable oil

1 small onion, chopped

³/₄ pound small white mushrooms, halved and thinly sliced

1 teaspoon paprika

3 cups chicken or vegetable stock or broth

3 cups water

¹/₂ cup white or brown rice

2 tablespoons chopped fresh parsley

Salt and freshly ground pepper, to taste

Heat oil in a heavy saucepan. Add onion and sauté over medium heat 7 minutes, stirring often. Add mushrooms and paprika and sauté 5 minutes, stirring often. Add stock and water. Stir and bring to a boil. Add rice. Cover and simmer about 15 minutes, stirring occasionally, until rice is tender. Stir in parsley. Taste, and add salt and pepper if needed. Serve hot.

Creamy Potato Soup

Makes 4 servings　Ⓓ

This soup is popular for dairy meals in the kitchens of Jews of Polish origin. To turn it into a fleishig *(meat-based) soup, substitute chicken stock for the vegetable stock and the milk. You can heat sliced chicken or turkey frankfurters in the chicken version of the soup after you have pureed it.*

4 medium potatoes, peeled and diced (about 1 pound)

1 medium onion, diced

1 small carrot, diced

4 cups vegetable stock or broth

Salt and white pepper, to taste

¹/₂ cup milk, half and half, or whipping cream, or more if needed

1 tablespoon chopped fresh parsley

1. Combine potatoes, onion, carrot, and stock in a medium saucepan. Add salt and pepper and bring to a boil. Cover and cook over low heat about 25 minutes or until potatoes are very tender. Puree soup in a blender or with a hand blender.

2. Return soup to saucepan and bring to a simmer. Add ¹/₂ cup milk and heat through. If soup is too thick, stir in more milk or vegetable stock. Adjust seasoning. Serve sprinkled with parsley.

Sweet and Sour Cabbage Soup

Makes about 6 servings　Ⓜ or Ⓟ

Also known as cabbage borscht, this is a favorite of Jews from Poland. Traditionally it's made with beef bones and beef flanken, a cut of chuck with bones, or with brisket or stew meat cooked in water to make a rich broth. The beef is served in the soup. This is a much quicker, lighter version that can be vegetarian if you use vegetable broth. If you like, serve it with boiled potatoes.

6 cups beef or vegetable broth

1 onion, chopped

One 15-ounce can diced tomatoes, with their juice

1 small head green cabbage, shredded

Salt and freshly ground pepper, to taste

¹/₄ cup raisins

1 to 2 tablespoons sugar

2 to 3 tablespoons strained fresh lemon juice

Combine broth, onion, and tomatoes in a large saucepan. Bring to a boil, cover and cook over low heat 10 minutes. Add cabbage, salt, and pepper and bring to a boil. Cover and simmer 30 minutes or until cabbage is tender. Add raisins and sugar and simmer 5 minutes. Add lemon juice and heat through. Adjust seasoning. Serve hot.

Spicy Russian Cabbage Soup

Makes about 6 servings   M or P

Unlike many other Ashkenazic cabbage soups, this thick and hearty one gains its character from garlic, paprika, and hot pepper, and is not sweet and sour.

2 tablespoons vegetable oil

2 large onions, diced

6 large cloves garlic, chopped

1 teaspoon sweet paprika

6 to 8 cups beef or vegetable stock, or stock mixed with water

1 pound potatoes, peeled and diced

3 ribs celery, sliced

1 large head green cabbage, diced

Salt and freshly ground pepper, to taste

2 tablespoons all-purpose flour

2 to 3 tablespoons tomato paste

1/3 cup water

1/4 teaspoon hot paprika or cayenne pepper, or to taste

1. Heat oil in a large saucepan. Add onions and sauté over medium heat about 7 minutes or until beginning to turn golden. Add garlic and paprika and sauté 30 seconds.

2. Add 6 cups stock and potatoes and bring to a boil. Cover and cook over low heat for 10 minutes. Add celery, cabbage, salt, and pepper and bring to a boil. Cover and simmer 30 minutes or until cabbage is tender, adding stock or water if soup becomes too thick. Mix flour, tomato paste, and water in a small bowl until smooth. Gradually add to soup, stirring. Simmer 5 minutes, stirring often. Season with salt, pepper, and hot paprika. Serve hot.

Pareve Butternut Squash Soup with Dill

Makes about 6 servings P

When you want to have a satisfying soup in a hurry, it's good to remember the easy technique in this recipe: Cook a hard-shelled squash in the microwave while you prepare your soup base of onions cooked in broth. It saves lots of time in both cutting and cooking. All you need to do is scoop out the cooked pulp of the squash and add it to the soup.

Dill is a popular flavoring for soup among many Jewish communities, from Ashkenazic to Iraqi to Indian. For an extra special touch, serve the soup with Dill Matzo Balls (page 281).

If you are serving this soup at a meatless meal, top it with sour cream or yogurt of any degree of richness. Accompany it by good quality pumpernickel or whole-wheat bread.

2 tablespoon vegetable oil

3 large onions, halved and sliced

5 cups vegetable broth

1 cup hot water

1 butternut squash (about 1 3/4 to 2 pounds)

1/2 teaspoon ground allspice

3 tablespoons chopped fresh dill or 2 1/2 teaspoons dried

Cayenne pepper, to taste

Salt and freshly ground pepper, to taste

1. Heat oil in a Dutch oven or stew pan. Add onions and sauté over medium-high heat about 5 minutes or until beginning to brown. Add broth and hot water, cover, and bring to boil. Cook 10 minutes over medium-low heat.

2. Meanwhile, halve squash, cover with plastic wrap, and microwave on high for 10 minutes or until tender. Remove seeds. Scoop out flesh; it will be soft.

3. Add squash and allspice to soup. If using dried dill, add it now. Cook over low heat 7 to 10 minutes or until vegetables are tender. Stir in 2 tablespoons fresh dill if using. Add cayenne and adjust seasoning. Serve hot, sprinkled with remaining dill.

Sorrel Soup

Makes 4 servings

D

Sorrel is a popular soup green in the Polish-Jewish and Hungarian-Jewish kitchen. Often it is made into a sweet and sour soup called schav *and can also be purchased in bottles under that name. Sorrel is also made into a creamy soup with potato, so the cream and potato soften the sharp taste of the greens. If you prefer, you can add a dollop of sour cream to each bowl instead of stirring it into the pot of soup. Baked or Light Croutons (page 283) are a popular accompaniment.*

2 tablespoons butter

1 medium onion, chopped

4 medium boiling potatoes, diced

6 cups water

8 ounces fresh sorrel

1/3 to 1/2 cup sour cream, regular, low-fat, or nonfat

Salt and freshly ground pepper, to taste

1. Melt butter in a large saucepan, add onion, and sauté 5 minutes over medium heat. Add potatoes, water, and pinch of salt. Bring to a simmer. Cover and cook over low heat 30 minutes.

2. Remove stems of sorrel and wash leaves thoroughly. Chop leaves finely. Add sorrel to soup and cook 5 to 10 minutes or until very tender.

3. If you would like a smooth texture, puree soup in blender. Serve hot or cold. If serving hot, reheat just before serving, stir in sour cream, and heat through, stirring; do not boil. If serving cold, simply stir in sour cream. Adjust seasoning.

❧ *Cold Soups*

Polish Beet Borscht

Makes 6 servings

D

Borscht is made in many versions, some meatless, like this one, and some with beef broth. You can easily find it in bottles in the kosher products aisle of the market, but it's much fresher tasting if you make your own. My mother often made it when I was growing up, and she suggested adding the red stems of the beet leaves to give the soup more flavor.

This is a light rendition of borscht, made without the egg-yolk thickening typical of old-fashioned recipes. It's usually served cold with potatoes and sour cream, but you can also serve it hot with those same accompaniments. With cold borscht, you can also provide bowls of diced hard boiled eggs and diced cucumbers for sprinkling into each bowl of soup. Instead of sour cream, some serve borscht with meat-filled blintzes.

2 pounds beets, with leafy tops

1 large onion, diced

7 cups water

6 small boiling potatoes

Salt to taste

1 to 2 tablespoons brown or white sugar

2 to 3 tablespoons strained fresh lemon juice

2 teaspoons chopped fresh dill (optional)

Sour cream (optional)

1. Scrub beets completely clean with a stiff brush. Cut off leafy tops and reserve red stems for borscht. (Save green leaves for other dishes.) Rinse stems well and slice them. Leave beets whole.

2. Combine whole beets, onion, and water in a medium saucepan. Bring to a boil. Add beet stems. Cover and simmer over low heat about 1 hour or until beets are tender.

3. Put potatoes in another saucepan, cover with water, and add a pinch of salt. Bring to a simmer. Cover and simmer 30 minutes or until tender. Drain most of water. Cover to keep warm.

4. When beets are tender, remove from soup and slip off their skins under cool running water. Grate beets coarsely in food processor or with grater. Return to soup. Add salt and sugar. Cook 2 minutes, stirring, over low heat. Remove from heat and add lemon juice and dill, if using. Adjust seasoning; soup should be sweet and sour.

5. Serve cold or hot, with warm potatoes. Spoon a dollop of sour cream, if using, into each bowl.

Cucumber Yogurt Soup with Avocado

Makes about 6 servings

Cucumber yogurt soup seasoned with fresh garlic and mint is a summer favorite among Sephardic Jews. When an Israeli friend served it to me with avocado, I found its subtle flavor made it a perfect addition. Serve this soup for a light after-Shabbat supper when the weather is hot.

If you're preparing the soup ahead, you can mash all of the avocado and combine it with the soup; the yogurt will help keep the avocado from darkening. Otherwise you can mash half the avocado and use the rest as garnish.

1 large clove garlic, minced
1 teaspoon salt
1/4 cup chopped fresh mint
1 very ripe avocado (preferably Haas)
5 cups plain yogurt, regular, low-fat, or nonfat
1 long (hothouse) cucumber (about 1 pound)
Cayenne pepper, to taste
Strained fresh lemon juice, to taste (optional)
Small fresh mint sprigs

1. Mash garlic with salt and mint in a large bowl, using back of a spoon. Halve avocado and remove pit. Scoop all or half the avocado into the bowl and mash it. Add yogurt and mix thoroughly to blend with mixture.

2. Peel cucumber and quarter it lengthwise. Cut it into thin slices and add to yogurt mixture. Fold in gently. Add cayenne. Taste for seasoning and add lemon juice, if using. Refrigerate soup at least 15 minutes or up to 4 hours. If you have used only half the avocado, wrap the other half tightly in plastic wrap and refrigerate it.

3. If you have reserved half the avocado, slice or dice it and use it to garnish the soup. Serve soup cold, sprinkled lightly with cayenne, and garnished with small sprigs of mint.

Apple and Pear Soup

Makes 4 servings

When I lived in Israel, a friend gave me the recipe for this popular Polish fruit soup. It's served hot or cold as a first course but I also like it as dessert. Adding the prunes is a trick I learned from my mother to give the soup good color. If you like, use low-fat or nonfat sour cream, or omit it to make the soup pareve.

1 large apple
1 large pear
1 quart plus 1/4 cup water
2 pitted prunes, diced
2 to 4 tablespoons sugar
2 tablespoons cornstarch
1/4 teaspoon ground cinnamon, or to taste
Strained fresh lemon juice, to taste (optional)
3 to 4 tablespoons sour cream

1. Peel, halve, and core apple and pear, reserving peelings and cores in a medium saucepan. Add 1 quart water to saucepan and bring to a boil. Cover and simmer 20 minutes. Remove peels and cores with a slotted spoon.

2. Dice apple and pear and add to liquid. Add prunes and 2 tablespoons sugar and stir to blend. Bring to a simmer, stirring occasionally. Cover and cook over low heat about 10 minutes or until tender.

3. Mix cornstarch with 1/4 cup water in a small cup until blended. Slowly stir mixture into simmering soup. Return to a simmer, stirring. Combine cinnamon with 1/2 cup of the soup liquid in a small cup. Return to remaining hot soup, stirring. Remove from heat and add lemon juice, if using. Add more sugar if needed.

4. Spoon sour cream into a small bowl. Slowly stir in about 1/3 cup soup. If serving soup hot, bring it to a simmer at serving time. Remove from heat. Stir sour cream mixture into soup. Serve hot or cold.

Quick-and-Easy Fruit Soup with Red Wine

Makes 4 servings

Traditional fruit soup as made in Ashkenazic homes is usually cooked and thickened with flour or cornstarch, and that is how I learned to make it when I lived in Israel. This fast version needs no cooking or thickening. Vary the fruit according to the season, and serve the soup either as a first course or as dessert. Depending on the sweetness of the orange juice and the wine, you may want to add a little more sugar if you're serving the soup as dessert.

1 cup orange juice

1 cup dry red wine, such as Cabernet Sauvignon

1/4 cup water

1/3 cup sugar

3 ripe large peaches or nectarines

4 ripe apricots, sliced, or 2 kiwis, peeled, halved, and sliced (optional)

1 cup raspberries, blackberries, halved small strawberries, or halved baby kiwis

1 large orange

1. Mix orange juice, wine, water, and sugar in a medium glass bowl until sugar dissolves. Slice peaches or nectarines into wedges and add them to bowl. Add apricots, if using, and berries.

2. Peel orange, removing as much as possible of white pith. Cut into segments and cut segments in half. Add to bowl. Refrigerate 10 minutes or until ready to serve. Serve cold.

Matzo Balls and Croutons

My Mother's Matzo Balls

Makes 18 to 20 small matzo balls, 4 or 5 servings   Ⓜ or Ⓟ

These kneidelach *are light and easy to prepare. The secret to having them light, tender, and fluffy is to keep the batter soft by adding enough liquid. If the batter is easy to shape into neat balls, the matzo balls will be too firm.*

If making them ahead, you can refrigerate them for 2 days in the soup, or in their cooking liquid in a covered container in the refrigerator. Reheat them gently in cooking liquid or in soup.

2 large eggs

2/3 cup matzo meal

Pinch of salt

Pinch of freshly ground pepper

1/4 teaspoon baking powder

1 to 2 tablespoons chicken soup or water

About 2 quarts salted water

1. Lightly beat eggs in a small bowl. Add matzo meal, salt, pepper, and baking powder and stir with a fork until smooth. Stir in chicken soup, adding enough so mixture is just firm enough to hold together in rough-shaped balls.

2. Bring salted water to barely a simmer in a large saucepan. With wet hands, take about 1 rounded teaspoon of matzo ball mixture and roll it between your palms into a ball; mixture will be very soft. Gently drop matzo ball into simmering water. Continue making balls, wetting hands before shaping each one. Cover and simmer over low heat for 30 minutes or until firm. Cover and keep them warm in their cooking liquid until ready to serve, or refrigerate them in their liquid and reheat before serving. When serving, remove them with a slotted spoon, add them to soup bowls, and ladle hot soup over them.

Extra-Light Matzo Balls

Makes 18 to 20 small matzo balls,
4 or 6 servings

These matzo balls depend on whipped egg whites for their lightness. They are light in color, tasty, and fat-free. No chicken fat, oil, or egg yolks are needed to make them, but do serve them in flavorful chicken soup.

²/₃ cup matzo meal

¹/₄ teaspoon baking powder

Pinch of white pepper

4 large egg whites

¹/₂ teaspoon salt

About 2 quarts salted water

1. Stir together matzo meal, baking powder, and pepper in a small bowl. Combine egg whites and salt in large bowl with an electric mixer. Whip whites to soft peaks. Lightly fold in matzo meal mixture until blended. Cover and refrigerate 20 minutes.

2. Bring salted water to barely a simmer in a large saucepan. With wet hands, take about 1 rounded teaspoon matzo ball mixture and roll it between your palms into a ball; mixture will be soft. Drop ball into simmering water. Continue making balls, wetting hands before shaping each one. Cover and simmer over very low heat for 30 minutes. Cover and keep them warm in their cooking liquid until ready to serve, or refrigerate them in their liquid and reheat before serving. When serving, remove matzo balls with a slotted spoon, add them to soup bowls, and ladle hot soup over them.

Easy Cholesterol-Free Matzo Balls

Makes 16 small matzo balls, 4 servings

Made from egg substitute, which is composed primarily of egg whites, these matzo balls are very simple to make because you don't need to separate eggs or whip egg whites. They puff nicely and you'll find them surprisingly good. As with all kneidelach, *they'll be light and tender if you keep the batter soft by not adding too much matzo meal.*

¹/₂ cup egg substitute, or the equivalent of 2 large eggs

¹/₄ cup plus 2 teaspoons matzo meal, or more if needed

Pinch of salt

Pinch of baking powder

1 to 2 tablespoons chicken soup or water, if needed

About 2 quarts salted water

1. Lightly beat egg substitute in a small bowl with a fork. Use fork to lightly stir in matzo meal, salt, and baking powder. Batter should be just firm enough to hold together in rough-shaped balls. Add another teaspoon matzo meal or a little chicken soup if needed.

2. Bring salted water to barely a simmer in a large saucepan. With wet hands, take about 1 rounded teaspoon of matzo ball mixture and gently roll it between your palms into a ball; mixture will be very soft. Gently drop matzo ball into simmering water. Continue making balls, wetting hands before shaping each one. Cover and simmer over low heat for 30 minutes. Keep them warm in their cooking liquid until ready to serve, or refrigerate them in their liquid and reheat before serving. When serving, remove them with a slotted spoon, add them to soup bowls, and ladle hot soup over them.

Dill Matzo Balls

Makes 18 to 20 small matzo balls,
4 or 5 servings

Matzo balls with herbs are not traditional but, like flavored pastas and tortillas, they can be a tasty option for adding interest to old favorites. I like to serve these matzo balls with vegetable soups, such as Pareve Butternut Squash Soup with Dill (page 276).

Add the optional oil if you want slightly richer matzo balls. Baking powder helps make the matzo balls lighter but you can omit it if you're preparing these for Passover.

2 large eggs

1 teaspoon vegetable oil (optional)

²/₃ cup matzo meal

¹/₄ teaspoon salt

Freshly ground pepper to taste

¹/₄ teaspoon paprika

¹/₄ teaspoon baking powder (optional)

1 tablespoon snipped fresh dill or 1 teaspoon dried

1 to 2 tablespoons vegetable stock or water

About 2 quarts salted water

1. Lightly beat eggs with oil, if using, in a small bowl. Add matzo meal, salt, pepper, paprika, and baking powder, if using, and stir with a fork until smooth. Stir in dill. Stir in stock, adding enough so mixture is just firm enough to hold together in rough-shaped balls.

2. Bring salted water to barely a simmer in a large saucepan. With wet hands, take about 1 rounded teaspoon of matzo ball mixture and roll it between your palms into a ball; mixture will be very soft. Gently drop matzo ball into simmering water. Continue making balls, wetting hands before shaping each one. Cover and simmer over low heat for 30 minutes. Cover and keep them warm in their cooking liquid until ready to serve, or refrigerate them in their liquid and reheat before serving. When serving, remove matzo balls with a slotted spoon, add them to soup bowls, and ladle hot soup over them.

Spiced Matzo Balls

Makes 16 matzo balls, 4 servings

Curry powder adds an intriguing taste to these matzo balls. They are lightly, not aggressively, spiced. Green flecks of chopped parsley give them a colorful appearance so they liven up any soup, from chicken to vegetable.

¹/₄ cup packed sprigs fresh parsley

2 large eggs

2 teaspoons vegetable oil

¹/₂ teaspoon curry powder

¹/₂ teaspoon salt

¹/₂ cup matzo meal

2 tablespoons water

About 2 quarts salted water

1. Chop parsley in food processor. In a medium bowl, combine eggs, oil, curry powder, and salt in a bowl. Lightly beat until blended. Add matzo meal and beat until batter is well blended. Beat in 2 tablespoons water, then the chopped parsley. Transfer batter to bowl, cover, and refrigerate for 20 minutes.

2. Bring salted water to barely a simmer in a large saucepan. With wet hands, take about 1 rounded teaspoon matzo ball mixture and roll it between your palms into a ball; mixture will be soft. Set balls on a plate. With a rubber spatula, carefully slide balls one by one into simmering water. Cover and simmer over low heat about 30 minutes. Cover and keep them warm in their cooking liquid until ready to serve, or refrigerate them in their liquid and reheat them before serving. When serving, remove them with a slotted spoon, add them to soup bowls, and ladle hot soup over them.

Almond Matzo Balls

Makes 18 to 20 matzo balls,
5 or 6 servings

Chopped or ground almonds or other nuts are added to matzo balls in some Jewish homes. These are also delicately flavored with ground ginger, in the Alsatian-Jewish tradition. If you like, you can follow some cooks' custom and put an almond half in each kneidel. Serve them in clear chicken soup or vegetable soup.

2 large eggs

2 teaspoons vegetable oil

1/2 cup matzo meal

3 tablespoons ground blanched almonds

1/2 teaspoon salt

1/4 teaspoon ground ginger

1 tablespoon minced fresh Italian parsley (optional)

2 or 3 tablespoons clear chicken or vegetable soup or stock or water

12 to 15 whole blanched almonds (optional)

About 2 quarts salted water

1. Lightly beat eggs with oil in a bowl. Add matzo meal, ground almonds, salt, ginger, and parsley, if using, and stir until well blended. Stir in 2 tablespoons soup. Mixture should be barely firm enough to shape into rough balls; if it is too firm, gradually stir in more soup by teaspoonfuls. Let mixture stand for 20 minutes.

2. Cut each blanched almond, if using, in half lengthwise so it will be thin.

3. Bring salted water to barely a simmer in a large saucepan. With wet hands, take about 1 teaspoon of matzo ball mixture and roll it between your palms into a ball. Set balls on a plate. Push half a blanched almond into center of each, letting one end of almond show.

4. With a rubber spatula, carefully slide matzo balls into simmering water. Cover and simmer over low heat about 30 minutes or until they are firm. Cover and keep them warm in their cooking liquid until ready to serve; or refrigerate them in their liquid and reheat them before serving. When serving, use a slotted spoon to carefully remove them and add them to each soup bowl, with their almond halves showing.

Fried Croutons

Makes about 4 servings

This is the classic way to make croutons. They are rich and crunchy and are delicious with vegetable soups, bean soups, and creamy soups. You can make them up to 2 hours ahead.

4 slices white bread, crusts removed

About 6 tablespoons vegetable oil or 4 tablespoons oil and 2 tablespoons butter

1. Cut bread slices into 1/2-inch squares. Heat 4 tablespoons oil in a large, heavy skillet. Test oil by adding a bread square; when oil is hot enough, it should bubble vigorously around bread. Remove bread piece with slotted spoon.

2. Add enough bread squares to hot oil to make one layer in frying pan. Sauté them, tossing often or turning them over with a slotted spatula so they will brown evenly. Fry them until they are golden brown.

3. Transfer croutons to a strainer and drain them. Drain further on paper towels. If pan is dry, add another 2 tablespoons oil and heat thoroughly before frying more croutons. Serve warm or at room temperature.

Buttery Croutons

Makes about 4 servings

These flavorful croutons are great with creamy soups.

4 slices white bread

2 tablespoons butter, soft

Salt and freshly ground pepper, to taste

1. Preheat oven to 400°F. Butter a baking sheet. Cut crusts from bread. Spread bread with butter and sprinkle with salt and pepper. Cut each slice into about 1/2-inch squares and transfer to baking sheet.

2. Bake about 7 minutes or until bread becomes crisp. Serve hot.

Baked Croutons

Makes about 4 servings ⓅP

These easy croutons are good with Sorrel Soup (page 277) or with split pea soup (pages 267 and 269). Croutons are classically made with white bread with its crust removed, but I like whole-wheat bread also, and I often leave the crust on.

4 slices bread, with or without crusts

1 to 2 tablespoons vegetable oil

Salt and freshly ground pepper, to taste

1. Preheat oven to 400°F. Cut bread into about $1/2$-inch squares. Put them in a bowl, add oil, salt, and pepper and toss until thoroughly coated. Put them in 1 layer on a baking sheet with a rim.

2. Bake, stirring a few times, about 10 minutes or until browned on all sides.

Light Croutons

Makes about 4 servings ⓅP

This toasted alternative to baked croutons is fat-free, if you use bread that contains no fat. When I'm preparing a small amount of croutons, I often use a toaster oven and bake them on its tray.

Another way to prepare crisp croutons is to simply cut bread into cubes and let them dry. This works best with country-style white or whole-wheat bread, not with soft, rich bread. You can also use thin slices of baguette or of crisp rolls in this way.

4 slices bread, with or without crusts, or 12 thin slices of baguette or of thin crisp rolls

A little oil spray

Salt and freshly ground pepper, to taste

1. Preheat oven to 375°F. Cut bread into about $1/2$-inch squares; leave baguette or rolls in thin slices. Spray a little oil spray on a baking sheet with a rim. Put bread on baking sheet in 1 layer. Spray bread lightly with oil spray and sprinkle with salt and pepper.

2. Bake croutons, turning a few times, about 10 minutes or until browned on all sides.

Dairy Specialties, Blintzes, and Eggs

Appetizers
287

Vegetable and Goat Cheese
Lavosh Sandwiches

Potato and Cheese Salad
with Toasted Walnuts

Tomato-Cucumber Salad
with Yogurt and Mint

Polish Radish and Cottage
Cheese Salad

Vegetables
289

Zucchini with Onion Stuffing

Creamy Onion Compote

Gratin of Broccoli Rabe
and Brown Rice

Baked Eggplant with Herbed
Tomato Sauce and Ricotta

Spring Vegetable Blanquette

Milchig Mushroom-Barley Bake

Kugels
292

Double-Corn Kugel

Italian Pasta Shell and Cheese
Kugelettes

Whole-Wheat Noodle
Kugel with Vegetables and
Cottage Cheese

Chili and Cheese Spaghetti
Kugel

Provençal Zucchini and
Rice Kugel

Parmesan Potato Kugel

Pastries
295

Light Spinach Bourekas

Chard and Onion Pie

Pizza with Feta Cheese, Peppers,
and Mushrooms

Pita Pizza with Goat Cheese
and Tomato Sauce

Sauces
298

Cucumber-Dill Yogurt Sauce

Savory Orange Topping

Breakfast and Brunch
Dishes
298

Cottage Cheese Latkes

Potato Pancake Gratin
with Cheese

Couscous with Dates

 **P** = *Pareve* **D** = *Dairy* **M** = *Meat*

Blintzes
300

Basic Blintzes

Herb Blintzes for Meat Fillings

Pareve Buckwheat Blintzes

Whole-Wheat Blintzes

Savory Rye Blintzes

Light Blintzes

Filled Blintzes
304

Mushroom Stroganoff Blintzes

Blintzes with Duxelles

Blintzes with Spicy Onions

Rye Blintzes with Cabbage

Blintzes with Chard and Cheese

Blintzes with Creamy Greens

Sauces for Blintzes
307

Paprika-Herb Topping

Wild Mushroom Sauce
for Blintzes

Scrambled Eggs
and Omelets
308

My Mother-in-Law's Shakshuka

Light Leek Shakshuka

Lox and Eggs with Asparagus

Pastrami and Eggs with
Mushrooms

Scrambled Eggs with Exotic
Mushrooms

Israeli Onion Omelet

Flat Zucchini Omelet

Sephardic Spinach Fritada

Other Egg Dishes
312

Spicy Baked Eggs with Tomatoes

Brown Eggs
(Huevos Haminados)

Apple-Cinnamon Matzo Brei

Both dairy foods and eggs are important in Jewish customs and menus. This may be one reason that blintzes have become so popular, as they usually combine both of these foods.

Eggs are very useful in kosher menus because they are neutral and can be served with either dairy or meat foods. They are served at the Passover Seder because they symbolize fertility, an important theme of this springtime festival. Besides, they have been an important food during this season since ancient times—eggs weren't available year-round until modern days. In many Sephardic homes, Brown Eggs (page 313) appear on the Shabbat breakfast table or are part of the Shabbat meal-in-one-pot casserole known as *hamin* (pages 190 and 192).

Although dairy foods and eggs tend to be associated with casual meals, they are also featured prominently on many festive occasions. Dairy foods are central to Shavuot holiday menus and, in many families, for the meal that breaks the Yom Kippur fast.

Dairy foods and eggs gain special importance during the Nine Days—a period of sadness in July or August leading up to the Fast of Tisha B'av, which falls on the Ninth of Av on the Jewish calendar. Observant Jews consume no meat or wine for eight days and fast on the ninth day. The days of mourning and the fast are observed to remember the destruction of the Holy Temple in Jerusalem, first in 586 BC and again in 70 AD, which led to the exile of the Jews from the land of Israel.

As a child, these were days I enjoyed, however, because our dinner entrees were my favorite foods: homemade macaroni and cheese; scrambled eggs, or noodle kugels flavored with sour cream.

Specialties such as blintzes, kugels, cheese knishes, and bagels with cream cheese spreads often are served to celebrate a bar or bat mitzvah or a brit milah reception (circumcision of a newborn son). Israel produces excellent cheeses, sour cream, and other dairy foods. There, dairy dinners and buffets are such favorites for entertaining that I was asked to write a cookbook in Hebrew on the subject. It was published in Israel as *Aruhot Halaviot* (Dairy Meals).

Blintzes are the quintessential brunch treat. They resemble French crepes in that they are thin and usually enclose a filling. Many Americans are familiar with sweet cheese, blueberry, and cherry blintzes from deli menus, but in fact there is a great variety of other blintzes. The filling might be sweet or savory and may include tangy or mild cheeses, meats, vegetables, or fruit. Blintzes are of Ashkenazic origin but Sephardic Jews also have blintz-like pancakes of different names.

The batter for making blintzes resembles that of crepes, except that for meat blintzes, water replaces the milk in the batter. Unlike crepes, blintzes are sautéed on only one side before they are filled. Generally they are rolled in the shape of a fat cigar with the ends closed. The filled blintzes are sautéed or baked with their uncooked side facing outward, so they brown lightly when they are baked or fried.

Of course, both eggs and *milchig* (dairy) foods are the basis for light meals and for the entrees of the main meal in everyday cooking. Many dairy and egg dishes are quick and easy to prepare and are popular among adults and children alike. Cream cheese and sour cream flavor such terrific Jewish desserts as cheesecake and cinnamon coffeecake, and these are allowed on the menu only if no meat has been eaten.

Scrambled and poached eggs were frequently on our menus when I was growing up in the United States. Israelis most often prepare eggs as flat omelets sautéed in oil, and serve them as a supper or breakfast dish with Israeli salad and fresh pita bread.

❋ *Appetizers*

Vegetable and Goat Cheese Lavosh Sandwiches

Makes 2 or 3 servings

Lavosh, the thin, flat, soft bread that looks somewhat like a large square tortilla, is terrific for wrapping around cheeses and vegetables with savory seasonings and rolling into a delicious sandwich. Lavosh was originally a specialty of the region of Armenia and Iran; now, in America, it is available in many Israeli and Middle Eastern stores. If you can't find it, you can substitute thin flour tortillas.

1 roasted peeled green or red bell pepper (page 588), or roasted pepper from a jar

3 ounces soft mild goat cheese, or more if desired

1 tablespoon extra-virgin olive oil

1 teaspoon strained fresh lemon juice

1/4 teaspoon hot pepper sauce, or to taste

Salt and freshly ground pepper, to taste

2 or 3 sheets lavosh, 8- or 9-inch square

1 cup shredded lettuce, preferably green leaf or romaine

2 ripe small tomatoes, cut into thin slices or half slices

4 large white mushrooms, sliced thin

6 to 9 black olives, pitted and halved

1. Prepare pepper, if roasting.

2. Cut roasted pepper into strips. Cut goat cheese into thin slices. Whisk olive oil, lemon juice, hot pepper sauce, and a pinch of salt and pepper in a small bowl.

3. To make each sandwich, put cheese slices on lavosh, near one edge. Top with lettuce, tomato slices, and mushroom slices, spacing them evenly. Drizzle with olive oil mixture. Scatter pepper strips and olive halves over top. Roll up tightly and serve.

Potato and Cheese Salad with Toasted Walnuts

Makes 4 to 6 servings

I became familiar with this salad when I lived in Paris, where it is a favorite lunchtime salad served in the cafés. In France it is made with Gruyere cheese from the Alpine region or with Cantal or Roquefort cheese from central France. You can use any firm kosher cheese that can be cut into slices, or a crumbly cheese like feta or goat cheese. I love Israeli Kashkaval, as its assertive flavor stands up well to the potatoes. For a mild cheese that is also tasty, try American-made yogurt cheese, which is available sliced in many kosher markets.

2 pounds red-skinned potatoes, scrubbed and unpeeled

3 to 4 tablespoons white wine vinegar

Salt and freshly ground pepper, to taste

1/2 to 3/4 cup olive oil or vegetable oil

6 to 8 ounces Kashkaval, Swiss, or firm yogurt cheese, cut into thin strips

1 head romaine or other green leaf lettuce

2/3 cup walnut pieces

1. Put potatoes them in a saucepan, cover them generously with water, and add a pinch of salt. Cover and bring to a boil. Simmer for 25 minutes or until tender when pierced with a sharp knife.

2. Whisk vinegar with salt and pepper in a medium bowl; whisk in oil. Adjust seasoning.

3. When potatoes are tender, drain them and leave until cool enough to handle.

4. Peel potatoes, halve them lengthwise, and cut them into slices. Put them in a large bowl. Rewhisk dressing. Spoon 1/3 cup dressing over potatoes and mix gently.

5. Let cool to room temperature. Add cheese strips.

6. Rinse and dry lettuce leaves thoroughly. Tear large leaves in half.

7. A short time before serving, toss lettuce with 1/4 cup dressing. Arrange on a platter. Add enough of remaining dressing to potato mixture to lightly coat ingredients. Add all but 2 tablespoons of walnuts. Mix gently, adjust seasoning. To serve, spoon potato salad onto bed of lettuce. Garnish with remaining walnuts.

Tomato-Cucumber Salad with Yogurt and Mint

Makes 4 servings   Ⓓ

For milchig *meals Israeli salad is sometimes made in this mild and delicious way. In Israel* leben *or* eshel, *dairy products resembling mild yogurt, are used. This salad also makes an appealing complement for spicy dishes and for casseroles of beans or of grains, such as Curried Cabbage with Rice, Mushrooms, and Peas (page 430).*

2 cups plain yogurt

Salt and freshly ground pepper, to taste

Pinch of cayenne pepper

1 tablespoon chopped fresh mint or 1 teaspoon dried

1 green onion, chopped

1 long (hothouse) cucumber, finely diced

4 small or medium tomatoes, diced

Mix yogurt with salt, pepper, and cayenne. Lightly stir in mint, onion, cucumber, and tomatoes. Adjust seasoning and refrigerate. Serve cold.

Polish Radish and Cottage Cheese Salad

Makes 4 servings   Ⓓ

Radishes are very popular among Jews from Poland. A refreshing way to use them is in this very quick and easy salad along with cucumbers, cottage cheese, and chives. The mild cottage cheese is a pleasing foil for the sharpness of the radishes.

In some homes other fresh cheeses like pot cheese are used instead of cottage cheese. Sometimes the cucumber is halved and shaped into boats and stuffed with the cheese and radish mixture instead of being mixed in. For richer versions, some cooks add 1/2 cup sour cream and 2 chopped hard boiled eggs.

The salad is traditionally served with pumpernickel or rye bread. It's good for a Saturday night supper, which is usually light after all the hearty Shabbat specialties eaten during the day.

2 cups cottage cheese

Salt to taste

2 to 3 tablespoons snipped fresh chives

1 bunch small red radishes, thinly sliced

1/2 long (hothouse) cucumber, halved lengthwise and thinly sliced

Mix cottage cheese with salt and 1 to 2 tablespoons chives in a medium bowl. Lightly stir in radish and cucumber slices and refrigerate. Serve cold, sprinkled with about 1 tablespoon chives.

✿ *Vegetables*

Zucchini with Onion Stuffing

Makes 6 servings **D**

Meat stuffings are most often used for zucchini, but zucchini are also delicious with this French-inspired onion stuffing. Serve them as a festive side dish for Shavuot or for a meatless Sukkot meal. If you make the stuffing ahead, this dish is quick to assemble.

Creamy Onion Compote (this page)

2 to 3 tablespoons bread crumbs, fresh or dry

2 to 4 tablespoons freshly grated Parmesan or Swiss cheese (optional)

6 medium zucchini (about 1 1/2 to 2 pounds total)

1 tablespoon butter or vegetable oil

Salt and freshly ground pepper, to taste

1. Prepare compote. Stir in bread crumbs. If using cheese, reserve 1 tablespoon for topping; stir rest into stuffing.

2. Preheat oven to 400°F. Add whole zucchini to a large saucepan of boiling salted water. Boil 2 minutes and drain. Rinse with cold water and drain well. Trim zucchini ends. Cut each zucchini in half lengthwise. With a small sharp knife, carefully scoop out seed-filled centers of each half, leaving a boat-shaped shell; do not pierce the sides.

3. Generously butter or oil a shallow baking dish. Put zucchini in dish. Dot them with butter or sprinkle them with oil. Sprinkle with salt and pepper. Bake for 5 minutes.

4. Spoon onion stuffing into zucchini. Sprinkle with 1 tablespoon cheese, if using. Bake 10 minutes or until ends of zucchini are tender when pierced with a sharp knife. If you like, broil for about 30 seconds to lightly brown cheese; watch carefully so zucchini do not burn. Serve hot.

Creamy Onion Compote

Makes 4 to 6 servings **D** or **P**

In the Ashkenazic kitchen compote means stewed fruit, usually dried fruit. French chefs sometimes use the same word to apply to vegetables, especially onions, that cook slowly until they are sweet and tender. Depending on the sweetness of the onions, you might want to accent the compote with a little white wine vinegar or sugar. If you'd like to follow the French tradition, enrich the compote with crème fraîche. These onions make a tasty topping for Hanukkah latkes or brown rice, a delicious side dish with fish, or a flavorful butter alternative for spreading on bread.

3 to 4 tablespoons butter, olive oil, or vegetable oil

1 1/2 pounds white or yellow onions, halved and thinly sliced

Salt and freshly ground pepper, to taste

2 tablespoons crème fraîche or heavy cream (optional)

1 to 2 teaspoons white wine vinegar (optional)

1/4 teaspoon sugar (optional)

Heat butter in a heavy casserole. Add onions, salt, and pepper. Cover and cook over low heat, stirring often, 30 minutes. Uncover and cook, stirring very often, about 10 minutes longer, or until onions are tender enough to crush easily with a wooden spoon and are golden; do not let them burn. Stir in crème fraîche, if using, and cook until bubbling over high heat. Cook uncovered over very low heat, stirring often, about 2 minutes or until crème fraîche is absorbed. Just before serving, taste, and stir in vinegar and/or sugar if using. Heat until absorbed. Adjust seasoning. Serve hot.

Gratin of Broccoli Rabe and Brown Rice

Makes 4 servings

D

If you are serving a meatless feast for Purim to honor Queen Esther, for a vegetarian, or for another occasion, here is a tasty casserole to include. The slightly bitter taste of the broccoli rabe, also called broccoli raab or rapini, is good with the cheese topping, the creamy sauce, and the brown rice. If you don't have broccoli rabe, substitute Chinese or regular broccoli.

3 tablespoons butter
3 tablespoons all-purpose flour
1^1/2 cups milk
Salt and white pepper, to taste
Freshly grated nutmeg, to taste
2 tablespoons vegetable oil
1 large onion
3 cups cooked brown rice
1^1/2 pounds broccoli rabe
^{1}/4 to ^{1}/2 cup grated Swiss cheese

1. In a medium, heavy saucepan, melt butter over low heat, add flour, and cook, whisking constantly, about 2 minutes or until foaming but not browned. Remove from heat. Gradually whisk in milk. Bring to boil over medium-high heat, whisking. Add salt, white pepper, and nutmeg. Reduce heat to low and cook, whisking often, for 3 minutes. Adjust seasoning.

2. Heat oil in a large nonstick skillet. Add onion and sauté over medium heat, stirring often, about 7 minutes or until softened. Mix with cooked rice. Season with salt and pepper.

3. Preheat oven to 400°F. Cut ends off broccoli stalks. Cut stalks into 1- to 2-inch pieces. Add all of broccoli to a large saucepan of boiling salted water and boil uncovered over high heat 4 to 5 minutes or until crisp-tender. Drain in a colander, rinse with cold water, and drain well. Coarsely chop with a knife.

4. Butter a heavy 2-quart gratin dish or other shallow baking dish. Spoon rice into dish. Spoon ^{1}/4 cup sauce over rice. Top with broccoli. Spoon remaining sauce carefully over broccoli to coat completely. Sprinkle with cheese.

5. Bake until sauce begins to bubble, about 10 minutes if sauce was still hot, or about 15 minutes if ingredients were at room temperature. If you'd like to brown the top, broil just until cheese is lightly browned, about 1 minute, checking often and turning dish if necessary. Serve hot.

Baked Eggplant with Herbed Tomato Sauce and Ricotta

Makes 4 servings

D

Eggplant casseroles need not have greasy layers of fried eggplant. For this light and flavorful vegetarian entree, I bake the eggplant slices instead, then alternate them with layers of ricotta cheese and tomato sauce flavored with fresh basil. This makes a good entree for Shavuot, especially if you have rich blintzes or a hearty noodle kugel on the menu.

2 tablespoons olive oil
1 onion, finely chopped
2 cloves garlic, minced
2 pounds ripe tomatoes, peeled, seeded, and chopped, or two 28-ounce cans, drained and chopped
1 bay leaf
1 teaspoon dried thyme
Salt and freshly ground pepper, to taste
2 tablespoons chopped fresh basil or 2 teaspoons dried
1^1/2 pounds eggplant
1^1/4 cups low-fat ricotta cheese
2 tablespoons bread crumbs
Fresh basil sprigs

1. Preheat oven to 400°F. Heat 1 tablespoon oil in a saucepan, add onion, and sauté over medium heat until lightly browned. Add garlic, tomatoes, bay leaf, thyme, salt, and pepper. Cook 20 minutes or until thick. Stir in basil. Discard bay leaf.

2. Cut eggplant into round slices about ^{1}/2-inch thick. Arrange eggplant slices on 2 baking sheets. Brush very lightly with oil, using a total of ^{1}/2 tablespoon. Sprinkle with salt and pepper. Bake 5 minutes. Turn over and bake 5 more minutes. Reduce oven temperature to 350°F.

3. Lightly oil a shallow 2-quart baking dish. Arrange a layer of overlapping eggplant slices in dish. Spread eggplant with $^3/_4$ cup ricotta cheese, then with $^3/_4$ cup tomato sauce. Sprinkle with the bread crumbs. Add another layer eggplant, remaining ricotta cheese, another $^3/_4$ cup of tomato sauce, then a final layer of eggplant.

4. Cover baking dish with foil. Bake 40 minutes until eggplant is very tender. Heat remaining tomato sauce and serve as accompaniment. Serve garnished with basil sprigs.

Spring Vegetable Blanquette

Makes 4 servings

In classic French cooking, a blanquette *is a stew of veal or lamb with a creamy sauce. To make it kosher, I like to prepare the white stew with vegetables only. Feasting on this dish is a wonderful way to celebrate the arrival of beautiful spring produce, like baby carrots, fresh asparagus, and baby peas. Vegetable blanquette is delicious served for a meatless meal, with rice or pasta, and makes a rich, colorful side dish for baked or grilled salmon or other fish.*

12 pearl onions (about 3 ounces)

8 medium asparagus spears (8 ounces), peeled

1 cup vegetable stock

$^1/_2$ cup water

11 or 12 baby carrots (about 3 ounces) scrubbed if necessary, large ones halved crosswise

3 ounces small mushrooms, quartered

$^3/_4$ pound peas, shelled, or $^3/_4$ cup frozen

$^1/_2$ cup heavy cream

1 tablespoon minced fresh tarragon

1 tablespoon thinly sliced fresh chives

1 tablespoon minced fresh Italian parsley

A few drops strained fresh lemon juice

Salt and freshly ground pepper, to taste

1. Put onions in a saucepan, cover with water, and bring to a boil. Cook 1 minute, rinse under cold water, drain well, and peel. Cut off asparagus tips and cut stalks into 1-inch pieces, discarding about $1^1/_2$ inches of bases. Boil asparagus in a saucepan of boiling salted water for 2 minutes. Drain, rinse under cold water, and drain well.

2. Bring stock and water to a boil in a small saucepan. Add carrots, cover, and simmer over medium heat until they are just tender, about 12 minutes. Transfer with a slotted spoon to a strainer. Add mushrooms and onions, cover, and simmer over medium heat until onions are just tender, about 10 minutes. Transfer with slotted spoon to the strainer. Add peas and boil uncovered until just tender, 2 to 4 minutes. Transfer with slotted spoon to the strainer.

3. Bring vegetable cooking liquid to a boil. Boil until reduced to about $^1/_4$ cup. Whisk cream into cooking liquid and bring to a boil over medium-high heat, whisking. Boil, whisking often, until sauce is thick enough to coat spoon, about 4 minutes. Transfer to a shallow medium saucepan.

4. To serve, bring sauce to a simmer. Add vegetables and simmer over medium heat 2 minutes, stirring gently. Remove from heat. Add tarragon, chives, parsley, lemon juice, and salt and pepper. Toss gently. Adjust seasoning. Serve in a gratin dish or shallow serving dish.

Milchig Mushroom-Barley Bake

Makes 4 to 6 servings

D

Mushrooms and barley are such a popular pair in the Ashkenazic Jewish kitchen that they are used in other ways besides the famous soup. For this dairy-based casserole, the barley and mushrooms bake under a cheesy crust.

2 or 3 tablespoons butter or vegetable oil

2 large onions, sliced

Salt and freshly ground pepper, to taste

1 cup medium pearl barley

8 ounces mushrooms, sliced

2¹/₂ cups vegetable stock

¹/₂ cup shredded Swiss or mozzarella cheese or ¹/₄ cup freshly grated Parmesan

1. Preheat oven to 350°F. Melt butter in a heavy sauté pan over medium-low heat, and add onions, a pinch of salt, and pepper. Sauté, stirring often, 7 minutes or until onions begin to turn golden. Add barley and sauté, stirring, 1 minute. Add mushrooms and sauté, stirring, for 2 minutes.

2. Grease a 6-cup casserole. Spoon barley-mushroom mixture into casserole.

3. Add stock to the sauté pan and bring to a boil. Pour stock over barley mixture. Cover and bake, stirring 3 or 4 times, about 1 hour or until barley is tender. Remove from oven. Raise oven temperature to 400°F.

4. Fluff barley gently with a fork. Sprinkle with cheese. Bake uncovered for 10 minutes or until cheese melts. If you like, broil very briefly to brown cheese.

❧ *Kugels*

Double-Corn Kugel

Makes 8 to 9 servings

Sweet corn and cornmeal give this moist kugel its good flavor. Yogurt and sour cream contribute a tangy note that balances the sweetness, making the casserole good as a brunch or supper entrée or as a not overly sweet dessert. Serve it topped with yogurt or sour cream. Poached or baked apples or fruit compote is a good accompaniment.

1 cup cornmeal

1 cup all-purpose flour

1 teaspoon baking powder

¹/₂ teaspoon salt

1¹/₂ cups cooked or canned corn kernels, drained

¹/₂ cup cottage cheese

1 cup yogurt

1 cup sour cream, plus extra for serving

¹/₄ cup (¹/₂ stick) butter

¹/₂ cup plus 2 tablespoons sugar

3 large eggs, separated, or 2 large egg yolks and 4 large egg whites

1. Preheat oven to 350°F. Grease a square 9-inch baking dish. Mix cornmeal, flour, baking powder, and salt in a bowl. Mix corn kernels, cottage cheese, yogurt, and sour cream in another bowl.

2. Cream butter with ¹/₂ cup sugar in a large bowl with an electric mixer. Add egg yolks and beat until smooth. Stir in cheese mixture alternately with dry ingredients. Whip egg whites in a clean bowl until they form soft peaks. Beat in remaining 2 tablespoons sugar and beat until whites are stiff and shiny but not dry. Fold whites gently into corn mixture. Transfer to baking dish.

3. Bake 35 to 40 minutes or until a cake tester inserted in center comes out clean. Serve warm with sour cream.

Italian Pasta Shell and Cheese Kugelettes

Makes 4 servings

These rich and cheesy mini-kugels are delicious on their own, with Sephardic style Grilled Red Pepper Sauce (page 461), or with Fresh Tomato Sauce (page 585). You can either unmold them, or serve them in the ramekins in which they baked. If you are serving them unmolded, you can spoon a little sauce around or over them.

6 ounces small pasta shells (about 2 cups)

$^{1}/_{2}$ cup ricotta cheese

$^{3}/_{4}$ cup whipping cream

2 cups shredded Swiss cheese

$^{1}/_{3}$ cup chopped fresh Italian parsley

$^{1}/_{3}$ cup chopped green onions

1$^{1}/_{2}$ tablespoons chopped fresh thyme or 1$^{1}/_{2}$ teaspoons dried

Freshly grated nutmeg, to taste

Salt and freshly ground pepper, to taste

3 large eggs, beaten

Dry bread crumbs (for coating)

Boiling water (for pan)

Fresh parsley sprigs

1. Preheat oven to 375°F. Cook pasta uncovered in a large pot of boiling salted water over high heat, stirring occasionally, about 5 minutes or until nearly tender but firmer than usual. Drain, rinse with cold water, and drain well.

2. Mix ricotta with cream in a medium bowl. Add Swiss cheese, chopped parsley, green onions, and thyme and mix well. Add pasta and season with nutmeg, salt, and pepper. Stir in eggs.

3. Butter four 1- to 1$^{1}/_{4}$-cup ramekins. Cut 4 rounds of foil or wax paper to fit bases; line bases. Butter liner. Coat sides and lined bases of ramekins with bread crumbs.

4. Fill ramekins with pasta mixture. Put them in a roasting pan. Add enough boiling water to pan to come halfway up sides of ramekins. Set a sheet of buttered foil over ramekins. Bake about 1 hour or until firm when touched on top; top will feel oily but batter should not stick to your finger.

5. Heat serving plates. Remove kugels from water and let stand about 5 minutes. To unmold, run a thin knife carefully around each one. Unmold onto heated plates; hold mold with plate and tap together on towel-lined surface, then carefully lift mold straight up and remove foil. Serve garnished with parsley sprigs.

Whole-Wheat Noodle Kugel with Vegetables and Cottage Cheese

Makes about 4 servings

Using whole-wheat noodles gives kugel a different look but my relatives love to debate which type of noodle gives a tastier result. With plenty of vegetables, this casserole is a meal in one dish.

3 tablespoons vegetable oil

2 large onions, chopped

2 ribs celery, sliced thin

3 large carrots, coarsely grated

2 small zucchini, coarsely grated

Salt and freshly ground pepper, to taste

7 or 8 ounces medium or wide whole-wheat noodles

$^{1}/_{2}$ cup sour cream, regular, low-fat, or nonfat

$^{3}/_{4}$ cup cottage cheese, regular, low-fat, or nonfat

1 teaspoon caraway seeds (optional)

Cayenne pepper, to taste

2 large eggs, beaten, or egg substitute equal to 2 eggs

About $^{1}/_{2}$ teaspoon paprika (for sprinkling)

1. Preheat oven to 350°F. Heat 2 tablespoons oil in a large skillet. Add onions and sauté over medium heat, stirring, 5 minutes. Add celery and sauté about 5 more minutes or until onions begin to turn golden. Remove from heat. Add carrots and zucchini, sprinkle with salt and pepper, and mix well.

2. Add noodles to a large saucepan of boiling salted water and boil uncovered over high heat about 5 minutes; they should be nearly tender but firmer than usual. Drain, rinse with cold water, and drain well. Transfer to a large bowl. Add vegetable mixture and toss with noodles. Add sour cream, cottage cheese, and caraway seeds, if using, and mix well. Season with salt, pepper, and cayenne. Stir in eggs.

3. Lightly oil a 2-quart baking dish and add noodle mixture. Sprinkle with remaining tablespoon oil; dust lightly with paprika. Bake uncovered 40 minutes or until set. Serve from baking dish.

Chili and Cheese Spaghetti Kugel

Makes about 6 servings   Ⓓ

Chili with cheese is a popular American combination. To make it kosher, I prepare pareve chili, well flavored with onions, garlic, and tomatoes. Then, I pair it with another favorite chili partner, spaghetti, to make this rich and flavorful main-course kugel. If you like, serve it with sour cream, diced avocado, and extra shredded cheddar cheese.

3 tablespoons olive oil

2 large onions, chopped

6 large cloves garlic, chopped

2 teaspoons chili powder

1 tablespoon ground cumin

1 1/2 teaspoons dried oregano

1/2 teaspoon hot red pepper flakes, or to taste

Two 28-ounce cans diced tomatoes, drained

One 8-ounce can tomato sauce

Two 15- or 16-ounce cans white beans, drained

8 ounces spaghetti

1 cup shredded cheddar cheese

1. Preheat oven to 350°F. Heat 2 tablespoons oil in a wide stew pan or Dutch oven. Add onions and sauté over medium heat, stirring often, 7 minutes or until lightly browned. Add garlic, chili powder, cumin, oregano, and pepper flakes and stir over low heat for 30 seconds. Add tomatoes and tomato sauce. Stir and bring to a boil. Add beans and bring to a simmer. Simmer uncovered over medium heat, stirring often, for about 10 minutes or until chili is thick. Adjust seasoning.

2. Cook spaghetti uncovered in a large pot of boiling salted water over high heat, lifting occasionally with tongs, about 8 minutes or until tender but firmer than usual. Drain, rinse with cold water, and drain well. Transfer to a large bowl. Add 1 tablespoon oil and half the chili and toss to combine.

3. Lightly oil a 2-quart baking dish and add half of spaghetti mixture. Top with half the remaining chili and half the cheese. Top with the remaining spaghetti mixture, then the remaining chili. Sprinkle with the remaining cheese. Bake uncovered for about 30 minutes or until kugel is hot and cheese browns. Serve from the baking dish.

Provençal Zucchini and Rice Kugel

Makes 6 servings   Ⓓ

This dish is prepared in southern France with many different vegetables, such as pumpkin, spinach, chard, asparagus, and artichokes. Pareve versions are also made, with no cheese and more garlic. This type of kugel is light textured, as there is a high proportion of vegetables to rice. Usually the vegetables are sautéed in oil, but I cook them in water to keep the dish light.

2 cups water

1/3 cup long-grain rice

2 pounds zucchini, sliced 1/4-inch thick

3 tablespoons olive oil

2 large onions, halved and sliced thin

3 medium cloves garlic, chopped

Salt and freshly ground pepper, to taste

4 to 6 tablespoons freshly grated Parmesan cheese

3 tablespoons chopped fresh basil

3 large eggs, beaten

1. Bring water to a boil in saucepan. Add a pinch of salt and rice and boil uncovered for about 12 minutes or until just tender. Drain, rinse with lukewarm water, and drain well.

2. Cook zucchini slices uncovered in a medium saucepan of boiling salted water for 3 minutes or until just tender. Drain well. Chop coarsely.

3. Preheat oven to 350°F. Heat 2 tablespoons oil in a large skillet. Add onion and cook over medium-low heat, stirring often, about 7 minutes or until soft but not brown. Add garlic and cook 30 seconds. Add zucchini, salt, and pepper and cook, stirring often, about 2 minutes.

4. Oil a 6-cup baking dish. Mix zucchini mixture with rice. Add cheese, basil, salt, and pepper. Add eggs. Spoon into baking dish. Sprinkle with remaining tablespoon oil. Bake 15 minutes or until set. Raise oven temperature to 400°F. Bake for 10 more minutes or until top browns lightly.

Parmesan Potato Kugel

Makes 6 to 8 servings

Parmesan and Swiss cheese add a delicious flavor and richness to potato kugel. Serve this kugel as a side dish with a fish entree or as a partner for a vegetable stew at a vegetarian feast. It's great for Shavuot, Purim, or Shabbat, or for Hanukkah as a change from latkes.

2 tablespoons plus 1 teaspoon vegetable oil

1 large onion, chopped

³/₄ pound zucchini

1 large carrot, coarsely grated

3 large baking potatoes, peeled

3 large eggs, beaten

³/₄ teaspoon salt

¹/₂ teaspoon ground pepper, or to taste

1 teaspoon paprika

¹/₄ cup matzo meal

¹/₂ to 1 cup shredded Swiss cheese

6 tablespoons freshly grated Parmesan cheese

1. Preheat oven to 350°F. Heat 2 tablespoons oil in a skillet, add onion, and sauté over medium-low heat about 10 minutes or until just beginning to turn golden.

2. Coarsely grate zucchini, put in a large strainer, and squeeze out excess liquid. Transfer to a large bowl. Add grated carrot and sautéed onion. Coarsely grate potatoes, put in strainer, and squeeze out excess liquid. Add to bowl of vegetables. Add eggs, salt, pepper, paprika, and matzo meal and mix well. Add Swiss cheese and 3 tablespoons Parmesan and mix well.

3. Generously grease a 7-cup baking dish. Heat briefly in oven. Add potato mixture. Sprinkle with remaining 3 tablespoons Parmesan. Bake about 1 hour or until brown and set.

❧ *Pastries*

Light Spinach Bourekas

Makes about 32 turnovers,
or 10 to 16 appetizer servings

Sephardic pastries called bourekas *are said to have originated in Turkey and are favorite appetizers or holiday brunch dishes in Israel. Usually they are made with phyllo dough and have cheese or vegetable fillings. Phyllo dough is fat-free. If you are careful to dab the dough lightly with melted butter or oil rather than brushing it generously, these* bourekas *will be low in fat. They're also lighter-textured and crisper when they're not weighted down with too much butter.*

1 pound phyllo sheets (about 20 sheets)

1¹/₂ pounds spinach, stems discarded and leaves rinsed well

1 tablespoon olive oil

1 small onion, minced

¹/₂ cup ricotta cheese, low-fat or nonfat

2 to 4 tablespoons freshly grated Parmesan cheese

Salt and freshly ground pepper, to taste

Freshly grated nutmeg, to taste

2 large eggs, or 1 large egg and 1 large egg white, beaten

¹/₄ to ¹/₃ cup vegetable oil or melted butter or margarine

About 2 teaspoons sesame seeds

1. If phyllo sheets are frozen, thaw them in refrigerator 8 hours or overnight. Remove sheets from refrigerator 2 hours before using and leave them in their package.

2. Place spinach leaves in a large skillet with water clinging to them. Cover and cook over medium-high heat, stirring occasionally, about 4 minutes or until wilted. Drain, rinse, and squeeze to remove as much liquid as possible. Chop spinach finely.

3. Heat olive oil in a skillet, add onion, and cook over low heat, stirring, about 10 minutes or until tender. Add spinach and sauté 2 minutes. Remove from heat, transfer to a bowl, and let cool slightly. Add ricotta and Parmesan and mix well. Season with salt, pepper, and nutmeg; filling should be highly seasoned. Stir in eggs.

4. Lightly grease a baking sheet. Remove phyllo sheets from package and unroll them on a dry towel. With a sharp knife, cut stack in half lengthwise, to form 2 stacks of sheets of about 16 × 7 inches. Cover phyllo immediately with a piece of wax paper, then with a damp towel. Work with only one sheet at a time and always keep remaining sheets covered so they don't dry out.

5. Remove a pastry sheet from stack. Using a brush, dab it lightly with vegetable oil and fold it in half lengthwise, so its dimensions are about 16 × 3 1/2 inches. Place about 1 1/2 teaspoons filling at one end of strip. Fold end of strip diagonally over filling to form a triangle, and dab it lightly with oil. Continue folding it over and over, keeping it in a triangular shape after each fold, until you reach end of strip. Set filled pastry on greased baking sheet. Dab it lightly with oil. Sprinkle with sesame seeds. Shape more pastries with remaining phyllo sheets and filling.

6. Preheat oven to 350°F. Bake pastries 20 to 25 minutes or until golden brown. Serve warm (not hot) or at room temperature.

Chard and Onion Pie

Makes about 6 servings   Ⓓ

Jews in Italy and southern France make savory pies of greens and other vegetables. Chard and spinach are popular ingredients, sometimes mixed with artichokes or peas. They might be open-face or double-crust pies. Unlike quiches, they do not contain custard. Some, like this version, contain a sprinkling of cheese; others are pareve.

To save time, you can purchase the pie dough or use a ready-made shell.

One 8-inch tart or pie shell, unbaked (see Shell for Savory Tarts, page 40)

1 1/4 pounds Swiss chard

4 tablespoons olive oil

Salt and freshly ground pepper, to taste

3 large onions, halved and sliced

1 1/2 teaspoon fresh thyme or 1/2 teaspoon dried

4 large cloves garlic, minced

1/4 teaspoon hot red pepper flakes

4 to 6 tablespoons freshly grated Parmesan cheese

1. Prepare tart shell and refrigerate. Then, remove chard leaves from stems; reserve stems for soups or other dishes. Rinse leaves thoroughly. Pile leaves and cut into 1/2-inch-wide strips.

2. In a large skillet, heat 2 tablespoons oil. Add about half of chard and a pinch of salt and pepper. Cook over low heat, stirring often, about 6 minutes or until tender. Remove with tongs, add remaining chard and a little salt and pepper and cook it also until tender. Return all of chard to pan and heat, stirring, 1 minute. Transfer to a plate and cool to room temperature.

3. Heat 2 tablespoons oil in skillet. Add onions, thyme, and a pinch of salt and pepper. Cook over low heat, stirring often, about 20 minutes, or until very tender but not browned. Stir in garlic and pepper flakes and heat for 15 seconds. Adjust seasoning. Cool to room temperature.

4. Preheat oven to 400°F. Heat a baking sheet in oven. Spread onion mixture evenly in tart shell. Top with chard mixture. Sprinkle with Parmesan cheese.

5. Set tart on baking sheet in oven. Bake about 35 minutes, or until pastry is brown at sides and filling browns on top. Let cool on a rack for 10 minutes. Set tart on an upside-down flat-bottomed bowl and remove tart pan rim. Serve hot or warm.

Pizza with Feta Cheese, Peppers, and Mushrooms

Makes 3 or 4 servings **D**

Sephardic flavors, including the feta cheese, are popular on pizzas in Israel. This colorful pizza features sautéed peppers and mushrooms instead of the usual tomato sauce. Students in my pizza classes are pleased when they learn how simple it is to make.

1/4 cup olive oil

1 red bell pepper, halved lengthwise and cut into very thin strips

Salt and freshly ground pepper, to taste

2 ounces mushrooms (about 6 small mushrooms), halved and cut into thin slices

1/2 teaspoon dried oregano

Quick Pizza Dough (page 547)

3 ounces feta cheese, finely crumbled

1. Heat 1 tablespoon oil in a skillet, add pepper strips and a little salt and pepper and cook over low heat, stirring often, about 5 minutes or until tender. Remove and set aside. Add another tablespoon oil to skillet and heat. Add mushrooms, oregano, and a little salt and pepper. Sauté until mushrooms are lightly browned.

2. Make pizza dough and let rise. Then, oil a baking sheet. Knead dough briefly and put it on baking sheet. With oiled hands, pat dough out to a 9- to 10-inch circle, with a rim slightly higher than center.

3. Preheat oven to 400°F. Sprinkle crumbled feta evenly over dough. Arrange mushroom mixture on center of pizza. Arrange pepper strips around mushroom mixture. Sprinkle remaining oil on top, making sure to moisten rim of pizza. Let pizza rise for about 7 minutes.

4. Bake pizza about 20 minutes or until dough is golden brown and firm but not hard. Serve hot.

Pita Pizza with Goat Cheese and Tomato Sauce

Makes 4 servings **D**

When I lived in Israel, my friends and I often made pizzas on a pita bread base for a quick supper. If you don't have goat cheese or you're making these for children, substitute any grated cheese you like. If you're making only one or two servings, you can use a toaster oven.

4 pita breads

1 to 1 1/2 cups thick tomato sauce

3 or 4 ounces creamy goat cheese

8 small fresh mushrooms, halved and cut into thin slices

1 or 2 tablespoons olive oil

1/2 teaspoon dried oregano

Salt and freshly ground pepper, to taste

Fresh basil leaves

Preheat oven to 400°F. Split each pita bread into two rounds. Set them on baking sheets in 1 layer, crust side down. Spread a thin layer of tomato sauce. Dice or crumble cheese and scatter it over sauce. Top with sliced mushrooms. Sprinkle lightly with oil and with oregano, salt, and pepper. Bake for about 10 minutes or until heated through and cheese softens. Serve topped with basil leaves.

Sauces

Cucumber-Dill Yogurt Sauce

Makes 3 cups, about 8 servings **D**

This creamy sauce is good with patties and latkes made of all kinds of vegetables, but is particularly suited to Givetch (page 416), as it echoes the dill flavor of this Balkan vegetable entree. The sauce is much better with fresh dill but you can substitute dried dill.

¹/₂ long (hothouse) cucumber or 1 regular
2 cups plain yogurt
3 tablespoon chopped fresh dill or 2 teaspoons dried
1 tablespoon chopped fresh Italian parsley (optional)
1 green onion, white and green parts, finely chopped
Salt and freshly ground pepper, to taste
Cayenne pepper, to taste

1. Peel cucumber. If using a regular cucumber, cut it in half lengthwise and remove seed-filled center with a spoon. Coarsely grate cucumber.

2. Mix yogurt, dill, parsley if using, and onion in a medium bowl. Stir in grated cucumber. Season with salt, pepper, and cayenne. Mix well. Serve cold.

Savory Orange Topping

Makes about 1 cup, about 4 servings **D**

Serve this easy-to-make sauce with carrots, winter squash, and sweet potatoes, plain or in kugels or casseroles such as Tu Bishvat Sweet Potato and Fruit Casserole (page 415). Make it with regular, low-fat, or nonfat yogurt and sour cream.

¹/₂ cup plain yogurt
¹/₂ cup sour cream
¹/₄ teaspoon ground ginger
1 teaspoon grated orange rind
2 to 4 tablespoons orange juice
1 to 2 teaspoons honey or sugar (optional)

Mix yogurt, sour cream, ginger, and orange rind in a bowl. Slowly stir in enough orange juice to give sauce a thick, pourable consistency. Taste, and add honey or sugar, if using. Serve cold or at room temperature.

Breakfast and Brunch Dishes

Cottage Cheese Latkes

Makes 4 to 6 servings

Jews from Russia and Poland make delicate-flavored light-textured latkes out of cottage cheese and serve them sprinkled with cinnamon and sugar. For Hanukkah, they make a pleasant change from the usual potato latkes. They are also popular for Passover or for Shavuot. Creamed cottage cheese is traditional but you can use low-fat cottage cheese if you like.

2 to 3 teaspoons ground cinnamon
¹/₄ cup sugar
1 cup cottage cheese
4 large eggs, or 2 large eggs and 3 large egg whites, beaten
¹/₂ cup matzo meal
2 tablespoons butter or margarine, melted, or vegetable oil
Salt and freshly ground pepper, to taste
¹/₄ to ¹/₃ cup vegetable oil

1. Mix cinnamon and sugar in a small bowl.

2. Mix cottage cheese with beaten eggs, matzo meal, melted butter, and salt and pepper in a medium bowl.

3. Heat ¹/₄ cup oil in a large, heavy skillet. Add batter by tablespoonfuls and fry over medium heat about 2 minutes per side or until lightly browned; turn them carefully using 2 slotted spatulas. Continue frying remaining batter, adding more butter and oil as pan becomes dry and reducing heat if oil begins to brown. Serve hot, with bowl of cinnamon sugar for sprinkling.

Potato Pancake Gratin with Cheese

Makes 10 cakes, 10 servings

These super-rich potato cakes are incredibly delicious. You can serve them for Hanukkah, Shavuot, Purim, or for other festive occasions. French cooks devised them as a way to use up extra baked potatoes and they give the pancakes their delicate texture and flavor. After the pancakes are sautéed, they are baked in a coating of cream and cheese. When I studied at La Varenne Cooking School in Paris, we coated the cakes with crème fraîche, but whipping cream works fine. For this dish, do not substitute milk or light cream.

Because they are super-rich, it's best to serve one per person and to plan plenty of other light dishes on the menu, such as Broccoli and Carrot Salad with Water Chestnuts (page 177) and Easy Baked Salmon Fillet (page 317). (If guests can't eat just one, then figure on one recipe making five portions instead of ten.)

2 pounds baking potatoes, scrubbed but not peeled (about 3 large potatoes)

1/2 cup crème fraîche or whipping cream

Salt and white pepper, to taste

Pinch of cayenne pepper

Freshly grated nutmeg, to taste

About 1/3 cup all-purpose flour

3 tablespoons vegetable oil

1 tablespoon butter

2/3 cup grated Swiss cheese

1. Preheat oven to 425°F. Pierce potatoes with a fork. Bake on rack in preheated oven about 1 hour or until tender.

2. Halve hot potatoes, scoop out pulp and transfer it to a bowl, discarding skins. Mash pulp with a fork. Stir in 3 tablespoons cream. Season with salt, pepper, cayenne, and nutmeg. Mix well with fork.

3. Shape mixture into cakes, using 1/4 cup mixture for each and making them about 3/4-inch high and 2 inches in diameter. Put them on a plate in one layer.

4. Roll each potato cake in flour and pat so all sides are lightly coated.

5. Heat oil and butter in a medium, heavy skillet over medium heat. Add half the potato cakes and sauté lightly on both sides, turning very carefully with 2 pancake turners.

6. Transfer to a shallow 9-inch round baking dish or any baking dish in which the potato cakes fit snugly in 1 layer. Sauté remaining potato cakes.

7. Preheat oven to 450°F. Pour remaining 5 tablespoons cream over cakes and sprinkle with grated cheese. Bake 8 minutes or until bubbling. If top is not brown, broil briefly until cheese browns lightly. Serve immediately.

Couscous with Dates

Makes 4 servings

Couscous enriched with butter, moistened with milk, and garnished with luscious dates is the ultimate comfort food. When I lived in Paris, it was one of my favorite dishes to order at Moroccan restaurants specializing in couscous dishes. Serve it for Shavuot or any time you have excellent quality dates. I like it for breakfast, brunch, or dessert.

Traditionally, it's best to steam the couscous above boiling water, following the method for Traditional Steamed Couscous (page 76). However, this recipe is a quick and easy version.

1 1/2 cups water

2 1/2 cups milk

Pinch of salt

One 10-ounce package couscous (1 2/3 cups)

2/3 cup golden raisins

1 1/2 cups dates

6 to 8 tablespoons butter, room temperature, cut into small pieces

1. Bring water, 1/2 cup milk, and salt to a boil in a heavy saucepan. Stir in couscous and raisins. Remove from heat, top with dates, and cover pan. Cook over very low heat, without stirring, 1 minute. Remove from heat. Let stand 5 minutes or until couscous softens. Add more salt if needed.

2. Heat remaining milk to a bare simmer in a small saucepan or in microwave. Pour into a pitcher.

3. Remove dates from couscous and put on a plate. Add butter to couscous and mix lightly with a fork. Mound hot couscous on a platter or spoon into a serving bowl and arrange dates on top. Serve couscous in bowls. Serve hot milk separately, for pouring over couscous.

Blintzes

Basic Blintzes

Makes about 12 large or 15 small blintzes

One of the best-known and best-loved Ashkenazic foods, blintzes have become specialties in Jewish homes and Jewish delis throughout the United States. They can have a great variety of fillings, from sweet ones, like blueberry or apple for dessert, to mushroom or broccoli for appetizers or main courses. The most famous of all are cheese blintzes, which are served either as entrees or desserts.

Blintz batter is ready in a minute if you make it in a blender. You can keep prepared blintzes up to 3 days in the refrigerator if you wrap them tightly, or you can freeze them. To avoid tearing the delicate pancakes, bring them to room temperature before filling them.

Filling blintzes doesn't have to be an elaborate undertaking. Many cooks keep blintzes on hand because they are delicious with very simple fillings like good quality preserves or jam. When I was a child, a friend of mine often brought unfilled blintzes in her lunch box. That was just about the only item for which I would agree to trade my egg salad sandwich!

3 large eggs

About 1 1/3 cups milk, pareve rice milk, or water

3/4 cup all-purpose flour, sifted

1/2 teaspoon salt

2 to 3 tablespoons butter or margarine

Vegetable oil, for brushing pan

1. To prepare batter in a blender, combine eggs, 1 1/4 cups milk, flour, and salt in blender. Blend on high speed about 1 minute or until batter is smooth.

2. To prepare batter by hand, push flour to sides of medium bowl, leaving a large well in center of flour. Add eggs, salt, and 1/4 cup milk to well; whisk them briefly until blended. Using the whisk, gradually stir flour into egg mixture until mixture is smooth. Gradually whisk in 1 cup milk.

3. Cover and refrigerate about 1 hour or up to 1 day. (Strain batter if lumpy.)

4. When you're ready to sauté the blintzes, melt butter in microwave or in a small saucepan over low heat. Stir batter well. Gradually whisk melted butter into batter. It should have consistency of whipping cream. If it is too thick, gradually whisk in more milk, about 1 teaspoon at a time.

5. Sauté batter to make blintzes (see How to Cook Blintzes, below).

Herb Blintzes for Meat Fillings

Makes about 12 large
or 15 small blintzes

Blintzes don't usually have herbs but I find them a lively addition to the classic. Use these savory wrappers for preparing appetizer or main course blintzes with meat or poultry fillings, such as Turkey Blintzes with Leeks and Ginger (page 368) or for cutting into strips and serving in soups.

Blintzes are easiest to sauté in a nonstick crepe pan or skillet. I find smaller pans easier to handle so you can lift the pan and slide the blintz out onto a plate.

3 large eggs
1 cup chicken stock
3/4 cup all-purpose flour, sifted
3/4 teaspoon salt
Pinch of white pepper
1/2 teaspoon dried thyme
2 tablespoons vegetable oil, plus a few teaspoons for pan
2 teaspoons snipped fresh chives

1. To prepare batter in a blender, combine eggs, stock, flour, salt, pepper, and thyme in blender. Blend on high speed about 1 minute or until batter is smooth.

2. To prepare batter by hand, push flour to sides of medium bowl, leaving a large well in center of flour. Add eggs, salt, pepper, thyme, and 1/4 cup stock to well; whisk them briefly until blended. Using the whisk, gradually stir flour into egg mixture until mixture is smooth. Gradually whisk in 3/4 cup stock.

3. Cover and refrigerate about 1 hour or up to 1 day. Strain batter if it is lumpy.

4. When you're ready to sauté the blintzes, stir batter well. Gradually whisk 2 tablespoons oil into batter. Whisk in chives. Batter should have consistency of whipping cream. If it is too thick, gradually whisk in water, about 1 tablespoon at a time.

5. Sauté batter to make blintzes (see How to Cook Blintzes, below).

How to Cook Blintzes

1. Heat a 6- to 6 1/2-inch crepe pan or skillet over medium-high heat. Sprinkle pan with a few drops of water. If water immediately sizzles, pan is hot enough. Brush pan lightly with oil. Remove pan from heat and hold it near bowl of batter. Working quickly, add 2 tablespoons batter to pan; add batter to edge of pan and tilt and swirl pan until base is covered with a thin layer of batter. Immediately pour any excess batter back into bowl.

2. Return pan to medium-high heat. Loosen edges of blintz with a metal spatula, discarding any pieces clinging to sides of pan. Cook blintz until its bottom browns very lightly. Slide blintz out onto a plate, with uncooked side facing up. Top with a sheet of wax paper or foil if desired. Reheat pan a few seconds.

3. Continue making blintzes, stirring batter occasionally with whisk. Adjust heat and brush pan with more oil if necessary. If batter thickens on standing, very gradually whisk in a little more milk or water, about 1 teaspoon at a time. Pile blintzes on plate as they are done.

Large blintzes: Use an 8- to 9-inch skillet and 3 tablespoons batter for each blintz.

Pareve Buckwheat Blintzes

Makes about 12 large or 15 small blintzes

Buckwheat flour is popular for Russian blinis (yeast-raised pancakes) and French crepes. It also makes tasty blintzes. Use these blintzes for wrapping savory fillings such as Broccoli-Cheddar Filling (page 226) or mushroom duxelles.

$1/2$ cup buckwheat flour

$1/4$ cup all-purpose flour

$3/4$ teaspoon salt

3 large eggs

1 cup water, plus more if needed

3 tablespoons vegetable oil, plus a few teaspoons for pan

1. Sift together buckwheat flour, all-purpose flour, and salt in a medium bowl.

2. To prepare batter in a blender, combine eggs, water, and flour mixture in blender. Blend on high speed about 1 minute or until batter is smooth.

3. To prepare batter by hand, push flour mixture to sides of bowl, leaving a large well in center of flour. Add eggs and $1/4$ cup water to well and whisk them briefly. Using the whisk, gradually stir flour mixture into egg mixture until batter is smooth. Gradually whisk in $3/4$ cup water.

4. Cover and refrigerate about 1 hour or up to 1 day. (Strain batter if it is lumpy.)

5. When you're ready to sauté the blintzes, stir batter well. Gradually whisk 3 tablespoons oil into batter. Batter should have consistency of whipping cream. If it is too thick, gradually whisk in water, about 1 tablespoon at a time.

6. Sauté batter to make bintzes (see How to Cook Blintzes, page 301).

Whole-Wheat Blintzes

Makes about 12 large or 15 small blintzes

I like whole-wheat blintzes with all kinds of fillings, both sweet and savory, especially those made of vegetables or fruit.

For simple meals the blintzes are flavorful enough to be served with such basic accompaniments as sour cream, yogurt, or melted butter. To these you can add any cooked vegetables you happen to have for a tasty supper blintz. The blintzes are also terrific with preserves, apple butter, honey, or cinnamon and sugar.

$1/2$ cup whole-wheat flour

$1/4$ cup all-purpose flour

$3/4$ teaspoon salt

3 large eggs

$11/4$ cups milk, plus more if needed

3 tablespoons butter or vegetable oil

A few teaspoons vegetable oil for pan

1. Sift together whole-wheat flour, all-purpose flour, and salt in a bowl.

2. To prepare batter in a blender, combine eggs, $11/4$ cups milk, and flour mixture in blender. Blend on high speed about 1 minute or until batter is smooth.

3. To prepare batter by hand, push flour to sides of medium bowl, leaving a large well in center of flour. Add eggs and $1/4$ cup milk to well and whisk them briefly. Using the whisk, gradually stir flour mixture into egg mixture until batter is smooth. Gradually whisk in 1 cup milk.

4. Cover and refrigerate about 1 hour or up to 1 day. (Strain batter if it is lumpy.)

5. When you're ready to sauté the blintzes, melt butter in microwave or in a small saucepan over low heat. Stir batter well. Gradually whisk melted butter into batter. It should have consistency of whipping cream. If it is too thick, gradually whisk in more milk, about 1 teaspoon at a time.

6. Sauté batter to make blintzes (see How to Cook Blintzes, page 301).

Savory Rye Blintzes

Makes about 12 large or 15 small blintzes

These rye flour blintzes flavored with dill and paprika are good with hearty fillings like cabbage or onion.

²/₃ cup rye flour

¹/₃ cup all-purpose flour

³/₄ teaspoon salt

¹/₂ teaspoon paprika

3 large eggs

1¹/₄ cups milk, plus more if needed

¹/₂ teaspoon dried dill

Pinch of cayenne pepper

3 tablespoons butter or vegetable oil

A few teaspoons vegetable oil for pan

1. Sift together rye flour, all-purpose flour, salt and paprika in a bowl.

2. To prepare batter in a blender, combine eggs, milk, flour mixture, dill, and cayenne in blender. Blend on high speed about 1 minute or until batter is smooth.

3. To prepare batter by hand, push flour to sides of medium bowl, leaving a large well in center of flour. Add eggs, ¹/₄ cup milk, dill, and cayenne to well and whisk them briefly. Using the whisk, gradually stir flour mixture into egg mixture until batter is smooth. Gradually whisk in 1 cup milk.

4. Cover and refrigerate about 1 hour or up to 1 day. (Strain batter if it is lumpy.)

5. When you're ready to sauté the blintzes, melt butter in microwave or in a small saucepan over low heat. Stir batter well. Gradually whisk melted butter into batter. It should have consistency of whipping cream. If it is too thick, gradually whisk in more milk, about 1 teaspoon at a time.

6. Sauté batter to make blintzes (see How to Cook Blintzes, page 301).

Light Blintzes

Makes about 12 large or 15 small blintzes

Use these low-fat blintzes with savory or sweet fillings to make lighter versions of your favorite filled blintzes. I always use a nonstick pan and lower heat for sautéing these than for other blintzes to make sure they don't stick.

2 large eggs

2 large egg whites

1¹/₄ cups nonfat milk, plus more if needed

³/₄ cup all-purpose flour, plus more if needed

¹/₂ teaspoon salt

1 teaspoon vegetable oil, plus a little more for brushing pan

1. Combine eggs, egg whites, milk, flour, and salt in blender. Blend on high speed about 1 minute or until batter is smooth; scrape down once or twice. Cover and refrigerate about 1 hour or up to overnight.

2. Whisk 1 teaspoon oil into batter. Batter should have consistency of heavy cream. If it is too thick, gradually add more milk, about 1 teaspoon at a time. If batter is too thin, sift 2 tablespoons flour into another bowl and gradually stir batter into it.

3. Heat a nonstick crepe pan or skillet with 6- to 6¹/₂-inch base over medium heat. Sprinkle pan with few drops of water. If water immediately sizzles, pan is hot enough. Remove pan from heat and hold it near bowl of batter. Using a brush, dab pan very lightly with oil. Working quickly, add about 3 tablespoons batter to pan, add batter to edge of pan and tilt and swirl pan until base is covered with a thin layer of batter. Immediately pour any excess batter back into bowl.

4. Return pan to medium heat. Loosen edges of blintz with metal spatula, discarding any pieces of batter clinging to sides of pan. Cook until bottom browns very lightly. Slide blintz onto a plate, with uncooked side facing up. Top with a sheet of wax paper or foil if desired. Reheat pan a few seconds. Continue making blintzes, stirring batter occasionally with whisk. Adjust heat and brush pan with more oil if necessary. If batter thickens on standing, very gradually whisk in a little more milk, about 1 teaspoon at a time. Pile blintzes on plate as they are done.

Note: For large Light Blintzes, use a nonstick 8- to 9-inch skillet and about ¹/₄ cup batter for each blintz.

✤ Filled Blintzes

Mushroom Stroganoff Blintzes

Makes 5 to 6 servings   Ⓓ

Blintzes with a creamy mushroom filling began as an Ashkenazic specialty and now are a universal Jewish favorite. For a special touch, I love to add exotic mushrooms. If you like, serve these topped with sour cream.

10 to 12 small blintzes (any type)

1/4 pound fresh shiitake or other exotic mushrooms

1 tablespoon vegetable oil

4 or 5 tablespoons butter

1/2 small onion, minced

8 ounces small fresh mushrooms, halved and cut into
    thick slices

Salt and freshly ground pepper, to taste

1 teaspoon paprika

2 tablespoons all-purpose flour

1 1/4 cups milk

1/3 cup sour cream

Pinch of cayenne pepper

1. Prepare blintzes. Then, prepare filling: If using shiitake mushrooms, discard tough stems. Cut into bite-size pieces. Heat oil and 1 tablespoon butter in a large skillet. Add onion and sauté over medium-low heat about 3 minutes. Add all of mushrooms, salt, pepper, and paprika and sauté over medium heat, stirring often, for 5 minutes or until tender.

2. Melt 2 tablespoons butter in a medium, heavy saucepan. Add flour and cook over low heat, whisking constantly, about 2 minutes or until foaming but not browned. Remove from heat. Whisk in milk. Bring to boil over medium-high heat, whisking. Add a small pinch of salt and pepper. Cook over low heat, whisking occasionally, for 5 minutes or until thick. Whisk in sour cream and bring to a simmer. Add cayenne. Remove from heat and stir in mushroom mixture. Adjust seasoning.

3. Preheat oven to 400°F. Butter one large or 2 medium shallow baking dishes. Spoon 3 tablespoons filling onto cooked side of each blintz, across lower third of blintz. Fold sides over so that each covers part of filling. Roll up in cigar shape, beginning at edge with filling. Arrange blintzes in single layer in buttered dish. Dot blintzes with remaining butter.

4. Bake blintzes about 15 minutes or until heated through and lightly browned. Serve hot.

Blintzes in the Blink of an Eye

When I have a craving for blintzes but I'm pressed for time, I find that packaged fresh crepes are perfect. Technically, crepes are different from blintzes. Crepes are sautéed on both sides, while blintzes are sautéed on only one side before being filled. For a quick blintz, however, the prepared crepes fit the bill just fine for me.

Inside the blintzes, sweet fillings of sweet cheese or apples are favorites, but blintzes are also delicious wrapped around savory meat or vegetable fillings.

Some old-fashioned recipes call for frying blintzes. To keep them low in fat and to make their preparation easier, I bake them instead.

Following custom, you might like to top the blintzes with a dollop of sour cream. For a lean but luscious alternative for sweet fillings, substitute sweet, nonfat vanilla yogurt. (For blintzes in other chapters, see Broccoli Blintzes and Main Course Cheese Blintzes, page 38, and Quick-and-Easy Apple Blintzes, page 558.)

Blintzes with Duxelles

Makes 5 to 6 servings

Duxelles, which is made of chopped mushrooms sautéed with shallots, is a delicious French filling with intense mushroom flavor. It's perfect for blintzes. Make with oil to be pareve or use butter and add cream for a richer dairy filling.

10 to 12 small blintzes (any type)

1 pound mushrooms, rinsed, patted dry

2 tablespoons vegetable oil or butter

2 medium shallots, minced

Salt and freshly ground pepper, to taste

1/3 to 1/2 cup whipping cream (optional)

2 to 3 tablespoons chopped fresh tarragon

1. Prepare blintzes. Then, prepare the filling: Chop mushrooms in batches in food processor with brief pulses so they are chopped in fine pieces but are not pureed.

2. Heat oil in a large skillet, add shallots, and sauté over low heat about 30 seconds until soft but not brown. Add mushrooms, salt, and pepper. Cook over high heat, stirring, 5 to 7 minutes or until mixture is dry. Add cream, if using, and cook, stirring often, until it is absorbed. Stir in 2 tablespoons tarragon. Adjust seasoning.

3. Preheat oven to 400°F. Spoon 2 or 3 tablespoons filling onto cooked side of a blintz near one edge. Fold sides over so that each covers about half the filling; roll up, beginning at filling edge. Arrange them in one layer in a shallow oiled baking dish. Brush blintzes with remaining oil.

4. Bake blintzes about 15 minutes, or until heated through. Serve blintzes hot. If you like, top each with remaining chopped tarragon.

Blintzes with Spicy Onions

Makes 6 servings

This is a bit of Jewish fusion cuisine, with slow-cooked onions flavored with chiles and tomatoes in the North African style inside a Russian buckwheat blintz. The combination is terrific and these make great pareve blintzes, perfect for serving on Sukkot or Hanukkah. I also like this savory filling in whole-wheat or plain blintzes.

12 Pareve Buckwheat Blintzes (page 302)

1 1/2 pounds onions (3 large)

About 3 tablespoons olive oil

Salt and freshly ground pepper, to taste

1 or 2 jalapeño peppers, seeded if desired, minced

One 14 1/2-ounce can tomatoes, drained and chopped

1 teaspoon paprika

2 or 3 tablespoons chopped fresh Italian parsley

Cayenne pepper, to taste (optional)

1 tomato, finely diced (optional)

1. Prepare blintzes. Then, prepare the filling. Halve onions, and cut into thin slices lengthwise. Heat 2 tablespoons oil in a heavy Dutch oven, add onions and salt and sauté over medium heat 5 minutes. Cover and cook over low heat, stirring often, 15 minutes or until tender and beginning to brown. Stir in jalapeño peppers, then tomatoes, paprika, salt, and pepper. Cook uncovered over medium heat about 15 minutes or until mixture is thick. Stir in 2 tablespoons parsley. Adjust seasoning; add cayenne, if using.

2. Preheat oven to 400°F. Spoon 2 or 3 tablespoons filling onto cooked side of a blintz near one edge. Fold sides over so that each covers about half the filling; roll up, beginning at filling edge. Arrange them in one layer in a shallow oiled baking dish. Brush blintzes with remaining oil. Reserve any remaining filling in a pan.

3. Bake blintzes about 15 minutes, or until heated through. Reheat any remaining filling.

4. Serve blintzes hot. If you like, top each with a dollop of extra filling or with diced fresh tomatoes and remaining chopped parsley.

Rye Blintzes with Cabbage

Makes 6 servings   Ⓓ

Russian and Polish Jews use cabbage to make savory fillings for blintzes. Rye blintzes are the favorite for this recipe, but you can use plain, whole-wheat, or buckwheat blintzes if you prefer. I flavor my cabbage filling with caraway seeds, plenty of sautéed onions, and vegetarian sliced "deli meat." Serve these blintzes crowned with a spoonful of Paprika-Herb Topping (page 307) and a pinch of chives or simply with plain sour cream or yogurt.

12 Savory Rye Blintzes (page 303)

1/2 large head green cabbage (1 1/2 pounds), cored and rinsed

2 tablespoons vegetable oil

3 or 4 tablespoons butter

2 large onions, chopped

Salt and freshly ground pepper, to taste

1/2 teaspoon paprika

1 teaspoon caraway seeds

3 ounces vegetarian sliced "deli meat" (optional), cut into
    1/2-inch squares

1/2 cup sour cream, room temperature

1. Prepare blintzes. Then, prepare the filling: Finely shred cabbage. Put it in a large pan of boiling salted water and boil it for 3 minutes. Drain, rinse under cold water, and drain thoroughly. Squeeze out excess liquid.

2. Heat oil and 1 tablespoon butter in a large skillet. Add onions and cook over medium-low heat, stirring occasionally, about 15 minutes or until very soft but not browned. Add cabbage, salt, pepper, paprika, and caraway seeds. Cook 5 minutes, stirring often. Cover and cook, stirring occasionally, about 10 minutes or until tender. Add deli meat squares, if using, and stir over low heat 1/2 minute. Transfer mixture to a bowl. Cool to room temperature. Stir in sour cream. Adjust seasoning.

3. Preheat oven to 400°F. Spoon 2 or 3 tablespoons filling onto cooked side of a blintz near one edge. Fold sides over so that each covers about half the filling; roll up, beginning at filling edge. Arrange them in one layer in a buttered shallow baking dish. Cut remaining butter into small bits and use to dot blintzes.

4. Bake blintzes about 15 minutes, or until heated through. Serve hot.

Blintzes with Chard and Cheese

Makes 4 to 6 servings   Ⓓ

Creamy greens seasoned with grated cheese and fresh nutmeg make a delectable filling for blintzes. Chard is easy to prepare because it has large leaves, so there are not many to rinse. You can use either green Swiss chard or red chard for this recipe. If you like, substitute spinach for the chard. Serve blintzes plain, or with tomato or mushroom sauce.

8 to 12 small blintzes (any type)

Two 12-ounce bunches or about 1 1/2 pounds chard
    (leaves with stems)

2 tablespoons butter

1/2 cup whipping cream, crème fraîche, or sour cream

1/3 cup grated Swiss cheese

Salt and freshly ground pepper, to taste

Freshly grated nutmeg, to taste

1. Prepare blintzes. Then, prepare the filling: Pull chard leaves from stems and keep in separate piles. Rinse leaves well and soak in a large bowl of cold water if they're sandy. Cut stems into 1/2-inch slices. Coarsely chop leaves.

2. In a large saucepan of boiling water cook chard stems over medium heat 2 minutes. Add leaves and cook uncovered 3 minutes or until tender. Drain chard, rinse with cold water, and drain well. Squeeze by handfuls to remove excess liquid.

3. Melt butter in saucepan over medium heat, add chard, and cook, stirring, about 2 minutes. Remove from heat and stir in cream and cheese. Season with salt, pepper, and nutmeg.

4. Preheat oven to 400°F. Spoon 2 or 3 tablespoons filling onto cooked side of a blintz near one edge. Fold sides over so that each covers about half the filling; roll up, beginning at filling edge. Arrange them in one layer in a shallow oiled baking dish. Brush blintzes with remaining oil. Reserve any remaining filling in a pan.

5. Bake blintzes about 15 minutes, or until heated through. Reheat any remaining filling. Serve blintzes hot.

Blintzes with Creamy Greens

Makes 4 to 6 servings

Use spinach, Swiss chard, or turnip greens to make this luscious filling. You can use regular, low-fat, or nonfat milk and sour cream to make it.

12 to 15 small blintzes (any type)

3 pounds bunches of spinach or other greens or
     two 10-ounce bags rinsed spinach leaves

2 tablespoons butter

2 tablespoons all-purpose flour

3/4 cup milk

1/2 cup sour cream

Salt and freshly ground pepper, to taste

Freshly grated nutmeg, to taste

1. Prepare blintzes. Then, prepare the filling: If using bunches of greens, remove stems and wash leaves thoroughly.

2. Cook greens in a large saucepan of boiling salted water uncovered over high heat, pushing leaves down into water often, about 3 minutes or until tender. Rinse with cold water and drain. Squeeze by handfuls until dry. Chop coarsely.

3. Melt butter in a small, heavy saucepan. Add flour and cook over low heat, whisking, 1 minute. Remove from heat. Pour in milk, whisking constantly; be sure to whisk in any flour adhering to sides of pan. Bring sauce to a boil over medium heat, whisking. Cook over low heat, whisking often, 2 minutes.

4. Return chopped spinach to its pan and cook over medium heat, stirring, 1 minute, to evaporate any liquid. Remove from heat and stir in sauce. Mix well. Stir in sour cream. Season with salt, pepper, and nutmeg.

5. Preheat oven to 400°F. Spoon 2 or 3 tablespoons filling onto cooked side of a blintz near one edge. Fold sides over so that each covers about half the filling; roll up, beginning at filling edge. Arrange them in one layer in a oiled shallow baking dish. Brush blintzes with remaining oil.

6. Bake blintzes about 15 minutes, or until heated through. Serve blintzes hot.

Sauces for Blintzes

Paprika-Herb Topping

Makes about 6 servings

This topping is delicious on blintzes filled with cabbage or mushrooms. You could also serve it on potato latkes for Hanukkah.

3/4 cup sour cream

3/4 cup yogurt

1 teaspoon sweet paprika

1 tablespoon snipped fresh chives

1 tablespoon snipped fresh dill or 1 teaspoon dried

1 tablespoon chopped fresh parsley

Salt and freshly ground pepper, to taste

Hot paprika or cayenne pepper, to taste

Mix sour cream, yogurt, sweet paprika, chives, dill, and parsley in a bowl. Season with salt, pepper, and hot paprika. Refrigerate until ready to serve.

Wild Mushroom Sauce for Blintzes

Makes about 2 cups, 6 to 8 servings **D**

If you keep dried mushrooms in your pantry, you can make this creamy sauce on short notice. It's delicious spooned over any blintzes with a vegetable or mushroom filling, whether homemade or purchased. You can also serve it to accompany spinach or cheese bourekas or savory noodle kugels.

1 1/2 ounces dried morels, shiitake mushrooms, porcini or Polish mushrooms
1/4 cup (1/2 stick) butter
1/4 cup all-purpose flour
1/2 cup vegetable stock
1 1/2 cups milk, or 1 cup milk and 1/2 cup whipping cream or half and half, plus 2 tablespoons more milk if needed
Salt and white pepper, to taste
2 tablespoons chopped fresh chives or parsley (optional)

1. Soak mushrooms in hot water for 20 minutes. Remove mushrooms from water. Rinse mushrooms and cut into small pieces; if using shiitake mushrooms, discard stems.

2. Melt butter in medium saucepan, add flour, and cook over low heat, whisking, 2 minutes. Remove from heat and gradually pour in stock, then milk, whisking and making sure to whisk in any flour adhering to sides of pan. Bring sauce to a boil, whisking. Cook over low heat, whisking often, for 2 minutes. Add mushrooms, salt, and white pepper. Cook uncovered over low heat, stirring often, 5 minutes or until mushrooms are tender and sauce is well flavored.

3. Just before serving reheat sauce, stirring. If sauce is too thick, gradually whisk in 1 to 2 tablespoons milk and return to simmer. Stir in chives, if using. Adjust seasoning. Serve hot.

❧ Scrambled Eggs and Omelets

My Mother-in-Law's Shakshuka

Makes 3 or 4 servings **P**

Shakshuka is a dish of eggs and vegetables that is made in many different ways—scrambled, poached, baked, or as a flat omelet. In Israel it is a popular dish among Jews of North African and Middle Eastern origin and can be found on the menus of casual restaurants. Cooks make it at home for a quick supper and serve it with fresh pita.

My mother-in-law makes her shakshuka scrambled and adds plenty of fresh tomatoes, sautéed onions, and her favorite Yemenite spice mixture. You can either cook the tomatoes until they become a thick sauce, or simply heat them briefly so they keep their fresh texture.

3 tablespoons vegetable oil
1 medium onion, chopped
1 pound ripe tomatoes, diced small (about 4 medium)
Salt to taste
1/4 teaspoon freshly ground pepper, or to taste
1 teaspoon ground cumin
1/4 teaspoon ground turmeric
6 large eggs, beaten

1. Heat oil in a large skillet. Add onion and sauté over medium heat, stirring occasionally, about 7 minutes or until golden brown. Add tomatoes, salt, pepper, cumin, and turmeric and mix well. Cook for 1 minute.

2. Add beaten eggs and scramble over low heat until set. Adjust seasoning. Serve immediately.

Light Leek Shakshuka

Makes 3 or 4 servings   **P**

Leeks are a popular vegetable to include in the Middle Eastern Jewish egg dish called shakshuka. *For this light version, I use egg whites or egg substitute for half of the eggs and keep the oil to a minimum. The dish is easy to make for a quick supper, as the leeks need only a few minutes to cook. Serve leek* shakshuka *with a tomato-cucumber salad and pita or crusty French bread.*

1 tablespoon vegetable oil

3 cups chopped split and rinsed leeks

Salt and freshly ground pepper, to taste

3 large eggs

3 large egg whites or egg substitute to equal 3 eggs

1/2 teaspoon ground cumin

Cayenne pepper, to taste

2 tablespoons chopped fresh Italian parsley

2 ripe plum tomatoes, diced

1. Heat oil in a heavy nonstick skillet. Add leeks and sprinkle with salt and pepper. Sauté over medium heat 2 minutes. Cover and cook over low heat, stirring occasionally, for 3 to 5 minutes or until tender. Adjust seasoning.

2. Beat eggs with egg whites, cumin, salt, pepper, and cayenne in a bowl. Add egg mixture, parsley, and tomatoes to skillet and scramble over low heat until set. Serve immediately.

Lox and Eggs with Asparagus

Makes 4 servings   **D** or **P**

A popular brunch choice at delis is lox and eggs. Asparagus makes it even more festive. When it's not in season, I add small, lightly steamed broccoli florets.

12 to 16 medium asparagus spears

3 tablespoons butter or vegetable oil

3/4 cup chopped onion

1/2 teaspoon salt, or to taste

1/2 teaspoon white pepper, or to taste

8 to 10 large eggs

3/4 cup diced or thin strips of lox or smoked salmon

1. Lightly peel asparagus and discard tough ends (about 1 inch from base). Cut each asparagus spear into 3 or 4 pieces. Cook asparagus uncovered in a saucepan boiling salted water about 2 minutes or until just tender. Drain well.

2. Melt butter in a large skillet. Add onion and sauté over medium-low heat, stirring often, about 7 minutes or until tender and light golden. Add asparagus, sprinkle lightly with salt and pepper, and sauté 2 minutes. If you like, remove 8 asparagus tips and reserve for garnish.

3. Whisk eggs with 1/2 teaspoon salt and 1/2 teaspoon pepper in large bowl until well blended. Add to skillet and scramble over low heat, stirring often, until eggs are set to your taste. Remove from heat and gently stir in lox. Serve immediately, garnished with asparagus, if reserved.

Pastrami and Eggs with Mushrooms

Makes 4 servings

Pastrami and eggs is a perennial deli favorite that's easy to make at home. You can use turkey pastrami to cut the fat and still have plenty of flavor. Like many cured meats, pastrami should not be heated for too long, as prolonged heating makes it seem more salty. I find that fresh mushrooms are a terrific complement for the spicy flavor of the pastrami and the mild taste of the eggs.

2 to 3 tablespoons vegetable oil

6 to 8 ounces small mushrooms, quartered

1/4 teaspoon freshly ground pepper, or to taste

8 to 10 large eggs

2 tablespoon chopped fresh parsley (optional)

2 ounces thinly sliced beef pastrami or turkey pastrami, cut into thin strips

1. Heat oil in a large skillet. Add mushrooms and season with pepper. Sauté, stirring often, about 7 minutes or until tender and lightly browned.

2. Beat eggs with parsley, if using, and 1/4 teaspoon pepper in a bowl until blended. Reduce heat under skillet to low. Add eggs and scramble them, stirring often, until they are nearly set to your taste. Gently stir in pastrami and heat a few seconds. Serve hot.

Scrambled Eggs with Exotic Mushrooms

Makes 2 servings

Jews in Poland and Russia have long used wild mushrooms in their cooking. After all, in their native lands, these fruits of the forest were free! This is one of the most delicious ways to enjoy them.

8 ounces fresh exotic mushrooms, such as chanterelles or shiitake mushrooms

2 to 3 tablespoons vegetable oil, or half oil and half butter

1/2 small onion, finely chopped

Salt and freshly ground pepper, to taste

4 large eggs

2 tablespoons milk (optional)

1 or 2 tablespoons chopped fresh parsley

1. Clean mushrooms very gently with damp paper towel. If using shiitake mushrooms, cut off stems, which are tough. If mushrooms are large, cut into bite-size pieces.

2. Heat oil or butter in a heavy skillet. Add onion and sauté over medium heat 3 minutes. Add mushrooms, salt, and pepper. Sauté over medium-high heat, stirring often, about 3 to 5 minutes or until mushrooms are tender and any liquid in skillet has evaporated.

3. Beat eggs with milk, if using, salt, and pepper in a bowl. Reduce heat under skillet to low. Add eggs and scramble them, stirring often, until they are set to taste. Remove from heat and stir in parsley. Serve hot.

Israeli Onion Omelet

Makes 2 servings

Omelets in Israel are usually not folded but flat, like in southern France, and are sautéed on both sides. They are a favorite supper dish, with pita bread, Israeli salad, and leben, *a mild yogurt. Onions sautéed in vegetable oil or butter are a popular flavoring.*

2 to 3 tablespoons vegetable oil or half butter and half oil

1 medium onion, minced

4 large eggs

Salt and freshly ground pepper, to taste

Cayenne pepper, to taste (optional)

1. Heat 1 to 2 tablespoons oil in a heavy skillet. Add onion and sauté over medium heat, stirring occasionally, about 5 minutes or until tender and beginning to turn golden.

2. Thoroughly beat eggs with salt, pepper, and cayenne, if using, in a bowl. Add remaining oil to skillet and heat over medium heat. Swirl pan slightly so oil coats sides as well. Add egg mixture. Cook, without stirring, occasionally lifting edge of omelet and tipping skillet so uncooked part of egg mixture runs to edge of pan.

3. When top of omelet is nearly set, slide omelet onto a plate, turn it over onto another plate, and slide it back into pan. Sauté second side over medium-low heat 30 to 60 seconds or until set. Serve hot.

Flat Zucchini Omelet

Makes 2 to 4 servings

This Sephardic flat omelet of grated zucchini and onion is served at light meals. For a richer version, it is sometimes flavored with grated Kashkaval cheese or with ground meat. It's a favorite during Passover. During that holiday, some cooks stir in a few table-spoons matzo meal to make the omelet more substantial. You can serve it hot as a light entree or cool and cut in wedges as an appetizer.

If you're making omelets with the smaller amount of oil, it's best to use a nonstick skillet.

8 ounces zucchini, coarsely grated

1 medium onion, coarsely grated

4 large eggs

1/2 teaspoon salt

Freshly ground pepper, to taste

2 tablespoons chopped fresh Italian parsley

2 to 3 tablespoons olive oil

1. Put grated zucchini and onion in a colander. Squeeze them by handfuls to remove most of moisture.

2. Thoroughly beat eggs with salt and pepper in a bowl. Stir in zucchini, onion, and parsley.

3. Heat oil in a heavy skillet over low heat. Swirl pan slightly so oil coats sides as well. Add egg mixture. Cook about 5 minutes, without stirring, occasionally lifting edge of omelet and tipping skillet so uncooked part of egg mixture runs to edge of pan.

4. When top of omelet is nearly set, slide omelet onto a plate, turn it over onto another plate, and slide it back into pan. Sauté second side over low heat about 2 minutes or until set. Serve hot or cool.

Sephardic Spinach Fritada

Makes 2 to 4 servings

Fritadas, the Ladino name for flat omelets, are popular among Sephardic Jews. (Ladino was the Hebrew-influenced Spanish language spoken by Sephardic Jews who left Spain in 1492.) They are similar to Italian frittatas, although frittatas often have cheese while fritadas do not. They can be prepared like Israeli omelets—sautéed on both sides—but more often are sautéed on one side and finished by broiling or baking in the oven. This is a simple fritada flavored only with spinach and garlic; others contain ground meat in addition to the vegetables. You can cut the fritada into wedges and serve it as a holiday appetizer for Rosh Hashanah, when greens are favored on the menu, or at any festive occasion.

2 or 3 tablespoons olive oil

One 10-ounce bag rinsed spinach leaves, cut into thin strips

Salt and freshly ground pepper, to taste

4 large eggs

1 large clove garlic, finely chopped

1. Heat oil in a large, heavy skillet, with an ovenproof handle if possible. Add spinach and sauté over medium-high heat, stirring often, about 3 minutes or until just wilted. Season with salt and pepper.

2. Thoroughly beat eggs with garlic in a medium bowl. Add to skillet. Cook without stirring; occasionally lift edge of omelet and tip pan so uncooked part of egg mixture runs to edge of pan.

3. When top of omelet is nearly set, place pan in broiler. Broil until top is set and lightly browned. Serve hot, from pan.

❦ Other Egg Dishes

Spicy Baked Eggs with Tomatoes

Makes 4 servings

These Moroccan baked eggs are also called shakshuka, *although they are completely different in flavor from the scrambled egg dish of that name. They are often served at Middle Eastern restaurants in Israel as a lunch or supper dish.*

About 3 tablespoons olive oil or vegetable oil

1 medium onion, halved and sliced

3 large cloves garlic, minced

One 28-ounce can diced tomatoes, drained

1/2 teaspoon paprika

1/2 teaspoon dried oregano

Salt and freshly ground pepper, to taste

Harissa (page 592) or hot sauce, to taste

2 tablespoons chopped fresh cilantro or Italian parsley (optional)

4 large eggs

1. Preheat oven to 400°F. Heat 2 tablespoons oil in large, heavy skillet. Add onion and sauté over medium heat about 7 minutes or until golden. Add garlic and cook over low heat about 30 seconds. Add tomatoes, paprika, oregano, salt, and pepper. Bring to a boil. Cook over medium heat, stirring often, about 10 minutes or until mixture is thick. Add hot sauce and cilantro, if using. Adjust seasoning.

2. Grease a shallow 8- or 9-inch round baking dish. Spread tomato mixture in dish. With a spoon make 4 hollows in tomato mixture, each large enough to contain 1 egg. Break egg carefully into each hollow. Sprinkle a little oil over each egg.

3. Bake 12 to 15 minutes or until eggs are done to your taste. Serve immediately.

Brown Eggs

Huevos Haminados

Makes 10 servings

This time-honored Sephardic specialty is made by cooking eggs in the slow-cooked stew called hamin, *which explains their name. (The name comes from Ladino, a language spoken by descendants of Jews who left Spain in the fifteenth century.) The eggs in their shells are placed inside the pot of* hamin, *or* cholent, *and cook all night. They are served for Shabbat, along with the* hamin. *In Yemenite kitchens they might bake overnight with a Shabbat pastry such as* jahnoon.

These eggs are so popular, however, that they are made for other occasions as well, for serving with phyllo pastries such as bourekas. *They are simmered very slowly in seasoned water with skins of onions, which give the shells a brown hue. Simply save the peel from onions for a few days until you have enough.*

These eggs go against the usual culinary guidelines for cooking hard boiled eggs but they are delicious and have a slightly creamy texture.

Brown skins of 8 to 10 onions (about 4 to 5 cups)
10 large eggs that have no cracks
1 teaspoon salt
2¹/₂ quarts water
2 tablespoons olive oil or vegetable oil
¹/₂ teaspoon freshly ground pepper

Choose a medium, heavy saucepan in which eggs fit in a single layer. Put half the onion peels in the pan. Carefully set eggs on top. Add remaining ingredients and bring to a boil. Reduce heat as low as possible. Cover and cook eggs for 6 hours or overnight. Serve hot or warm.

Apple-Cinnamon Matzo Brei

Makes 4 or 5 servings

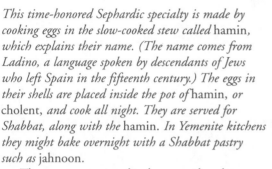

Matzo brei is a year-round treat, too good to be reserved only for Passover. If you like yours on the sweet side, sprinkled with sugar or topped with jam, you'll like this version made with butter-sautéed apples. Serve topped with sour cream and, if you like, sprinkled with more sugar.

5 plain, egg, or whole-wheat matzos
¹/₄ cup (¹/₂ stick) butter or vegetable oil
2 large apples, cored and sliced
2 tablespoons sugar
¹/₂ teaspoon ground cinnamon
5 large eggs
¹/₄ cup milk
¹/₄ teaspoon salt

1. Cover matzos in cold water and soak about 10 minutes.

2. Heat 2 tablespoons butter or oil in a large, heavy skillet. Add apples and sauté over medium-low heat, stirring occasionally, about 10 minutes or until tender. Sprinkle with sugar and cinnamon and sauté another minute, stirring and turning so apples are well coated.

3. Drain matzos, break them into bite-size squares, and place in a bowl. Beat eggs with milk and salt in a bowl and pour over matzos. Stir until matzos are coated. Add sautéed apples and stir.

4. Melt remaining butter in skillet. Add matzo mixture. Cook over low heat, stirring, until the eggs are set to your taste. Serve at once.

Fish

Baked, Grilled, and Broiled Fish
317

Easy Baked Salmon Fillet

Red Trout and Asparagus with Lemon-Parsley Sauce

Tovah's Trout with Paprika Oil and Cilantro

Baked Trout with Spinach Stuffing

Grilled Whole Salmon

Broiled Salmon with Walnut Sauce

Kosher Fish Tacos

Steamed and Poached Fish
321

Steamed Sole with Turkish Lemon-Dill Dressing

Cod in Green Olive–Tomato Sauce

Jewish Fish

Polish Sweet and Sour Fish

Blintzes with Fish and Morel Filling

Braised Fish
325

Moroccan Fish with Red Peppers, Cilantro, and Garlic (Hraimeh)

Yemenite Fish with Tomatoes and Spices

Sea Bass Steaks with Chickpeas

Sea Bass in Garlic Tomato Sauce

Sea Bass with Lima Beans

Fish Stews
327

Halibut with Green Beans and Black Beans

Salmon with Noodles and Leeks

Sephardic Fish Paella

Creole Fish Stew

Fish Jambalaya

Kosher California Cioppino

Sautéed Fish
331

Sole with Garlic Butter

Sole Schnitzel

Shavuot Sole with Spiced Butter and Basmati Rice

P = *Pareve*   D = *Dairy*   M = *Meat*

Gefilte Fish and Other Ground Fish Dishes
333

Salmon Gefilte Fish with Dill

Baked Gefilte Fish

French Gefilte Fish Loaf

Quick "Home-Cooked" Gefilte Fish from a Jar

Fish Falafel

Fish Latkes

Mati's Fish Balls in Tomato Sauce

Dishes Made with Cooked or Canned Fish
337

Salmon Casserole

Smoked Whitefish with Tomato Noodles and Herbs

Tuna Tabbouleh

Sauces
339

White Horseradish Sauce

Horseradish with Beets

Mustard-Dill Dressing

Garlic Sauce for Fish

Mushroom–Sour Cream Sauce for Fish

Mildred's Dill Sauce

Cilantro Salsa

Cucumber-Zehug Salsa

Moroccan Marinade

Red Pepper Vinaigrette

Caper-Lemon-Parsley Dressing

Hot Tomatillo Salsa

In the Jewish kitchen fish plays a special role because it can appear at kosher meals that include either meat or dairy foods. For traditional holiday meals, fish is often an appetizer that is then followed by a main course of meat. Quite a few Jewish fish appetizers are served cold or at room temperature, because of the prohibition of cooking on Shabbat. These make-ahead specialties are convenient for serving at festive meals.

Gefilte fish is the best-known Jewish fish dish. This Eastern European Jewish specialty is widely available in jars but for holidays, many people prefer to make it at home. Classically it is made of fresh-water fish like those available in the recipe's place of origin: carp, pike, and whitefish. Originally gefilte fish meant a stuffed whole fish. Today the term refers to ground fish poached in the form of balls, oval cakes, or long cylinders that are similar to classic French galantines. The seasoning of gefilte fish may be delicate, sweet, or peppery and usually includes onions and carrots.

Sephardic Jews also prepare fish appetizers for holidays, often whole fish or pieces, flavored with garlic, peppers, cilantro, and tomatoes.

Because today many Jews are health conscious or simply prefer fish, in many homes it has replaced meat as a holiday entree. Depending on the quantity served, most fish appetizer dishes can be transformed into main courses. Many people bake gefilte fish mixture in loaves and serve it during the week as a hot or cold entree. Fried fish are popular among all Jewish ethnic groups. Sephardic Jews also like grilled fish. Baked fish is also a frequent choice for entertaining because of its ease and convenience.

On menus for brunches and casual get-togethers, a variety of smoked and cured fish, notably lox, whitefish, and herring, are much esteemed, especially by Ashkenazic Jews. Traditionally they are served with bagels and cream cheese but might also be served as a salad—on a bed of greens. Smoked salmon or lox is also a popular ingredient in scrambled eggs and omelets on deli menus as well as at home.

🍁 Baked, Grilled, and Broiled Fish

Easy Baked Salmon Fillet

Makes 4 servings

With no fat added, this delicious salmon is perfect for light menus. We love it for Shabbat, with basmati rice and Rachel's Spiced Cauliflower with Chickpeas (page 109). I like to marinate the salmon with a dry rub of thyme, oregano, and cumin. After baking the salmon, I broil it very briefly to give it a tasty, attractive crust.

1¼ to 1½ pounds salmon fillet, preferably tail section, about 1 inch thick

½ teaspoon dried thyme

½ teaspoon dried oregano

½ teaspoon ground cumin

½ teaspoon paprika

Salt and freshly ground pepper, to taste

Lemon wedges

1. Preheat oven to 450°F. Line a heavy roasting pan with foil. Set fish on foil. Sprinkle fish evenly with thyme, oregano, cumin, and paprika. Refrigerate 10 to 15 minutes. Sprinkle fish evenly with salt and pepper.

2. Roast fish in oven about 10 minutes or until the thickest part of the fish is pink inside; check with a sharp knife. Broil fish 30 seconds to 1 minute to lightly brown top. Serve with lemon wedges.

Red Trout and Asparagus with Lemon-Parsley Sauce

Makes 4 servings

This colorful entree is perfect for Passover or other festive occasions in springtime. It is flavored with a Sephardic sauce of fresh lemon juice, olive oil, and an abundance of Italian parsley, and is quick and easy to prepare. Red trout fillets make this a beautiful dish but you can use any trout that is fresh at your market. The entree is also delicious with salmon fillets.

1 pound thin asparagus, thick bases removed

1¼ to 1½ pounds red trout fillets, 1-inch thick

2 tablespoons strained fresh lemon juice

1 or 2 tablespoons olive oil

Salt and freshly ground pepper, to taste

1 green onion, chopped

¼ cup chopped fresh Italian parsley

Cayenne pepper, to taste

Lemon wedges

1. Cut each asparagus spear into 3 pieces. Rinse asparagus. Put pieces in a saucepan of boiling water. Boil 2 minutes. Drain and rinse with cold water.

2. Preheat oven to 375°F. Lightly oil a baking dish in which fish and asparagus can fit easily in one layer. Put fish in dish and sprinkle it with 1 tablespoon lemon juice, 1 teaspoon olive oil, salt, pepper, and chopped green onion. Add 2 tablespoons water to dish.

3. Bake fish uncovered for 7 minutes. Add asparagus to baking dish around fish. Cover lightly with foil and bake 5 minutes or until asparagus is tender and the thickest part of the fish is opaque inside; check with a sharp knife. Cover fish to keep it warm.

4. In a small bowl combine remaining lemon juice, olive oil, and parsley and whisk to blend. Season with salt, pepper, and cayenne. Spoon sauce over fish. Garnish with lemon wedges.

Tovah's Trout with Paprika Oil and Cilantro

Makes 4 servings

This tasty trout, seasoned in the Moroccan-Jewish style, is easy to prepare. You use butterflied trout and season it with garlic, cilantro, and paprika oil, then bake it in foil.

The recipe is from Tovah Carmona, a friend who lives near Los Angeles. She served it as a first course at a Rosh Hashanah dinner at my brother-in-law's home and we all enjoyed it. If you would like it spicy, you can add minced jalapeño along with the garlic.

3 tablespoons olive oil or vegetable oil

2 teaspoons paprika

4 large cloves garlic, minced

1/4 cup chopped fresh cilantro

4 whole trout, butterflied

Salt and freshly ground pepper, to taste

1. Mix oil with paprika in a small bowl. Let stand at room temperature for at least 1 hour, preferably several hours. Stir it occasionally. Add garlic and cilantro to paprika oil and mix well.

2. If trout still has fins, snip them with sturdy scissors and trim tails straight. Rinse fish inside and out, removing any scales, and pat dry.

3. Put trout on a large tray. Sprinkle trout inside and out with salt and pepper. Set trout on tray skin side down. Using about half the garlic mixture, spoon it over the trout. Fold each trout in half, re-forming it. Set each trout on a piece of foil large enough to wrap it. Spoon remaining garlic mixture over trout and rub it in lightly. Wrap each trout tightly in foil. Set wrapped trout in a roasting pan.

4. Preheat oven to 400°F. Bake trout about 20 minutes or until a thin skewer inserted into thickest part of fish comes out hot to touch. Serve hot, in foil packets.

Baked Trout with Spinach Stuffing

Makes 4 servings **D** or **P**

Whole stuffed fish are traditional favorites on the Jewish menu, and in fact are the inspiration for gefilte fish, which in Yiddish means simply, stuffed fish. So this dish is, in fact, spinach gefilte fish. Buy butterflied trout so that they are easy to stuff.

2 pounds spinach, stems discarded, leaves rinsed thoroughly

1 tablespoon butter or vegetable oil

3 shallots, chopped

1 large egg

2 tablespoons matzo meal or bread crumbs

Freshly grated nutmeg

Salt and freshly ground pepper, to taste

4 small trout (each about 1/2 pound), butterflied

1/4 cup dry white wine or broth from a jar of unsweetened gefilte fish

4 lemon slices

1 tablespoon chopped fresh parsley

1. Boil spinach leaves in a large pan of boiling salted water about 1 minute until wilted. Rinse under cold running water and drain well. Squeeze out as much liquid as possible. Coarsely chop spinach.

2. Melt butter in a skillet or sauté pan, add 2/3 of chopped shallots, and cook over low heat, stirring often, about 3 minutes or until soft but not browned. Add spinach and stir over low heat for 1 minute. Transfer to a bowl and let cool slightly. Add egg and matzo meal and mix well. Add nutmeg, salt, and pepper.

3. Preheat oven to 425°F. Cut off trout fins and shorten tails. Remove heads if you prefer. Run your finger along trout about 3/4-inch from backbone line, on both sides of it, until you find a row of small bones running parallel to backbone. Run point of boning knife along both sides of each row of bones. Pull out bones with aid of tweezers. Sprinkle trout with salt and pepper inside and outside. Spoon stuffing into trout.

4. Lightly butter a shallow baking dish and add remaining shallot. Set stuffed trout in dish on their sides. Add wine. Bake uncovered about 15 minutes or until trout are just tender and a skewer inserted into fish and filling comes out hot. Top each trout with a lemon slice, and sprinkle lemon with chopped parsley.

Grilled Whole Salmon

Makes about 6 servings **P**

Whole fish cooked on the barbecue is a favorite entree of Israelis, both for home cooking and for dining out. A fresh fish cooked this way needs no sauce, just lemon halves for squeezing the fresh juice onto the fish just before eating it. If you would like a sauce, choose a simple one such as Caper-Lemon-Parsley Dressing or Red Pepper Vinaigrette (page 342). You can grill all sorts of whole fish this way.

One 4-pound whole salmon
Salt and freshly ground pepper, to taste
4 sprigs fresh thyme (optional)
3 lemons, halved

1. Clean barbecue well and preheat it. If it has a thermometer, heat it to 450°F.

2. Snip salmon fins with sturdy scissors and trim tails straight. Rinse fish inside and out, removing any scales, and pat it dry.

3. Put salmon on a large tray. Sprinkle it inside with salt and pepper. Put thyme sprigs, if using, in the fish. Measure thickest point of fish in inches and calculate the grilling time of 9 or 10 minutes per inch. (If the fish is 2¹/₂ inches thick, it will take about 22 to 25 minutes.)

4. Lightly oil barbecue. Put fish on barbecue on its side. Grill it for about half the time. Turn the fish over and grill it for the remaining time. Check if fish is done by inserting a skewer into its thickest part; the skewer should come out hot; or cut into the thickest part of the fish, near its backbone, it should be less pink. Remove thyme sprigs, if using.

5. To serve fish, slit skin along backbone. Use a broad spatula to remove portions of fish, putting spatula under a piece of fillet and lifting the piece off the bones. Serve with lemon halves.

Broiled Salmon with Walnut Sauce

Makes 6 servings **P**

Serve this tasty salmon and its rich sauce with basmati rice and briefly cooked broccoli florets. It will make a terrific Sukkot dinner or an easy entree for any festive occasion.

Walnut and Garlic Sauce (page 593)
2 pounds salmon fillet, preferably tail section, about 1 inch thick
2 tablespoons strained fresh lemon juice
2 teaspoons vegetable oil
2 teaspoons ground coriander
1 teaspoon dried oregano
Salt and freshly ground pepper, to taste
Lemon wedges
Fresh parsley sprigs

1. Prepare sauce. Sprinkle salmon with lemon juice and oil and rub over fillet. Sprinkle fish evenly with coriander, oregano, salt, and pepper.

2. Preheat broiler. Line broiler rack with foil if you like, or brush rack lightly with oil. Set fish on broiler rack and broil 4 minutes. Turn over and broil 4 to 5 more minutes or until the thickest part of fish is less pink inside; check with a sharp knife.

3. To serve, cut fish into 6 portions and top each with a small dollop of sauce. Garnish with lemon wedges and parsley sprigs.

Kosher Fish Tacos

Makes 4 servings

P

A variety of kosher tortillas are becoming available in more and more markets. Often these are low-fat or even fat-free, and some come with herb, spice, or vegetable flavorings and in different colors. Use them to prepare these savory tacos with a healthy new twist—I learned this from Chef James Boyce of the Azzura Point restaurant at Loews Coronado Bay Resort on Coronado Island near San Diego.

Instead of frying the tortillas, simply heat them briefly on the grill, or stuff room temperature tortillas with a hot filling. It's easier, quicker, lighter, and much more healthful than the usual tacos. Although this is a casual entree, it looks elegant when served, with platters of grilled salmon fillet, peppers, avocado, and tortillas and bowls of salsa. You can prepare your own salsa or purchase it ready-made.

2 tablespoons vegetable oil

1 large white onion, halved and sliced thin

4 red or green peppers, cut into 1/2-inch strips

1 1/2 pounds salmon fillet

2 teaspoons fresh lime juice

1/2 teaspoon ground cumin

Salt to taste

A few dashes cayenne pepper or pure chili powder

4 flavored or plain flour tortillas

1 or 2 ripe avocados (preferably Haas), sliced thin

1 cup shredded iceberg lettuce (optional)

1 1/2 cups tomato or tomatillo salsa, or some of each

1. Preheat broiler with rack about 4 inches from heat; or prepare grill. Line broiler pan with foil, if desired. Heat 1 tablespoon plus 1 teaspoon oil in a heavy skillet or sauté pan. Add onion and sauté over medium heat 5 minutes. Stir in peppers, cover and cook, stirring occasionally, about 7 minutes or until crisp-tender. Remove from heat and keep warm, covered.

2. Meanwhile, sprinkle fish with lime juice, remaining 2 teaspoons oil, cumin, salt, and cayenne. Grill or broil fish on oiled rack or on foil-lined broiler pan for 8 to 9 minutes or until thickest part of fillet is less pink inside; check with a sharp knife. Cut each piece into 4 to 6 crosswise slices. Transfer to pan of peppers. Cover to keep warm.

3. Either heat tortillas according to package instructions or serve them at room temperature. Serve platter of fish and pepper mixture with tortillas, avocado, lettuce if using, and salsa. To serve, spoon fish and pepper mixture onto a tortilla, top with avocado, lettuce if using, and salsa to taste, and roll up gently. Fold one end over to hold filling inside.

✻ Steamed and Poached Fish

Steamed Sole with Turkish Lemon-Dill Dressing

Makes 4 main-course
or 6 to 8 first-course servings

Jews from both Turkey and Greece serve fish with a sauce of lemon and dill. Usually the sauce is thickened with eggs but I prefer this lighter dressing. It is perfect with the delicate flavor and texture of steamed sole and makes a terrific opening to a Shabbat dinner. You can also serve the sole and its vegetables hot, accompanied by small boiled potatoes or cooked rice.

3 tablespoons olive oil

6 ounces small mushrooms, thinly sliced

1 red bell pepper, cut into 1/2-inch dice

1 small green bell pepper, cut into 1/2-inch dice

Salt and freshly ground pepper, to taste

1 1/2 tablespoons strained fresh lemon juice

1/2 tablespoon water

2 tablespoons chopped fresh dill

1 1/4 pounds sole fillets

2 tablespoons chopped fresh Italian parsley

1/4 cup chopped green onion

2 large cloves garlic, minced

1. Heat 1 tablespoon oil in a large, heavy skillet. Add mushrooms, peppers, salt, and pepper and sauté over medium-high heat for 7 minutes or until vegetables are just tender and any excess liquid evaporates; cover and reduce heat if vegetables begin to brown. Set aside.

2. Make vinaigrette: Combine remaining 2 tablespoons oil with lemon juice, water, and 1 tablespoon dill in a small bowl. Whisk until blended. Season with salt and pepper.

3. Run your fingers over fillets to check for bones; pull out any bones using tweezers or a sharp paring knife. Sprinkle sole on both sides with salt and pepper. Sprinkle lightly with about 1/2 tablespoon dill and 1/2 tablespoon parsley and fold each fillet in half. Sprinkle top with remaining dill and parsley. Set sole on top portion of a steamer over boiling water, cover, and cook over high heat about 2 minutes or until the thickest part of the fish is opaque inside; check with a sharp knife. Transfer to a platter and keep warm.

4. Reheat vegetables over medium heat. Stir in green onion and garlic and cook 1 minute.

5. To serve, transfer fish to plates, discarding liquid from their platter. Scatter vegetables over and around fish. Whisk vinaigrette, spoon it over fish, and serve.

Cod in Green Olive–Tomato Sauce

Makes 4 main course
or 6 first course servings

Fish cooked with Sephardic flavors makes a delectable opening for a Shabbat dinner. This dish is also terrific for Shavuot or Sukkot.

1 cup Fish Stock (page 600) or water

2 tablespoons extra-virgin olive oil

1 medium onion, chopped

4 large cloves garlic, coarsely chopped

1¹⁄₂ pounds ripe tomatoes, peeled and diced,
    or one 28-ounce can diced tomatoes, drained

Salt and freshly ground pepper, to taste

1 bay leaf

1 large sprig fresh thyme or ¹⁄₂ teaspoon dried thyme,
    crumbled

1¹⁄₂ pounds cod fillet, cut into 4 or 6 pieces

1 tablespoon tomato paste

1¹⁄₂ teaspoons fresh oregano or ¹⁄₂ teaspoon dried

²⁄₃ to 1 cup pitted green olives, drained well

1. Prepare stock. Then, heat oil in large deep skillet. Add onion and cook over medium-low heat, stirring often, about 5 minutes or until softened but not brown. Stir in garlic. Add tomatoes, fish stock, salt, bay leaf, and thyme. Bring to boil. Cover and cook over low heat 10 minutes. Add fish pieces. Cover and poach over low heat about 10 minutes or until fish can just be flaked with a fork. With a slotted spatula, carefully remove fish pieces. Discard bay leaf and thyme sprig.

2. Simmer uncovered over medium heat, stirring often, about 10 minutes or until it is thick. Stir tomato paste into sauce until well blended. Stir in oregano and olives and simmer 1 minute. Remove from heat. Adjust seasoning.

3. To serve hot, return fish to sauce in skillet, cover and reheat briefly; or refrigerate. Serve hot or cold.

Jewish Fish

Makes 4 servings

Carp prepared in several different Jewish styles became part of classic French cooking. Four formulas for this dish, named carpe a la juive *or Jewish carp, appear in Auguste Escoffier's* Guide Culinaire, *the definitive chefs' manual of haute cuisine, published in 1921. This recipe, inspired by a version flavored with aromatic vegetables and herbs, is still popular in French Jewish homes. I have followed the custom of many of today's cooks by reducing the amount of oil and eliminating the large quantity of flour.*

French cooks include the head of the carp to flavor the liquid and help it to jell. If you want a jelled liquid but don't have carp heads, you can instead use fish stock made with halibut. The dish is flavorful whether or not the liquid sets. Instead of carp, you can make this dish with trout or with tilapia, a fish that is popular in Israel and is becoming widely available in American markets.

2 cups Fish Stock (page 600) or water

4 small whole fresh fish, such as carp, trout, or tilapia,
    or 2 pounds halibut steaks

Salt and freshly ground pepper, to taste

1 or 2 tablespoons vegetable oil

2 medium onions, chopped

4 medium shallots, chopped

2 cups dry white wine

1 large sprig fresh thyme or 1 teaspoon dried thyme

1 bay leaf

8 sprigs fresh Italian parsley, stems separated from leaves

4 large cloves garlic, minced

Cayenne pepper, to taste

1. Prepare fish stock. Then, trim fish fins and tails. Rinse fish and set them on a plate. Season whole fish with salt and pepper inside and out; season steaks on both sides. Measure whole fish, or steaks, at thickest part in inches, and calculate 10 minutes cooking time per inch of thickness.

2. Heat oil in a wide stew pan and add onions. Cook over medium-low heat, stirring often, about 5 minutes or until soft but not brown. Add shallots and cook 1 minute. Add wine, fish stock, thyme sprig, bay leaf, parsley stems, garlic, salt, and pepper and bring to a boil. Cook over medium-low heat 5 minutes. Add fish, cover, and cook over low heat, 10 minutes per inch. Whole fish is done when a skewer inserted into its thickest part comes out hot; steaks are done when their thickest part is opaque inside when they are checked with a sharp knife. Remove fish carefully to a deep platter with a slotted spatula.

3. Simmer cooking liquid uncovered over medium heat until it is reduced to about 2 cups. Either strain liquid to remove pieces of onion, or leave them in and simply discard thyme sprig, bay leaf, and parsley stems. Chop enough of reserved parsley leaves to make 3 tablespoons. Add half the parsley to the fish cooking liquid. Season liquid with cayenne, and more salt and pepper if needed. Pour liquid over fish. Refrigerate at least 4 hours before serving.

4. Serve fish cold, with a few tablespoons of the cooking liquid. Sprinkle generously with remaining chopped parsley when serving.

Polish Sweet and Sour Fish

Makes 4 to 6 servings as first course

This traditional Polish Shabbat specialty calls for carp because the fresh water fish was readily available in that region. Indeed, carp is so popular among Jews of Eastern European extraction for gefilte fish and for dishes like this, that it is farmed in Israel in vast pools, although it is not native to the Middle East.

My mother uses carp or other firm fish and flavors the cooking liquid simply with carrots, onions, bay leaves, vinegar, and sugar. She notes that the fish gets a pickled flavor. Some people add spices like cloves or dried ginger. I like to add pickling spices, which

include bay leaves but also have coriander seeds, peppercorns, and cloves. Make the dish with carp if you like, or use halibut or pike. Dried cranberries are a new twist but go well with the flavors and give the fish a festive garnish.

This dish is served cold and is refreshing and low in fat.

1¹/₂ pounds carp or halibut steaks, 1 inch thick
Salt and freshly ground pepper, to taste
1 tablespoon pickling spices
1 onion, sliced
2 carrots, sliced into rounds
2¹/₂ cups water
2 or 3 tablespoons vinegar
2 to 3 teaspoons sugar
3 tablespoons dried cranberries (optional)

1. Sprinkle fish lightly with salt and pepper and set aside.

2. Wrap pickling spices in cheesecloth and tie ends together to make a spice bag, or put them in a tea ball. In a sauté pan or deep skillet in which fish can just fit, combine spice bag, onion, carrots, salt, pepper, and water. Bring to a boil. Cover and simmer 15 minutes. Add fish, cover and cook over low heat 10 to 12 minutes or until fish is tender and its thickest part is opaque inside; check with a sharp knife. Transfer fish carefully to a deep serving dish.

3. Boil cooking liquid 5 minutes or until it is reduced to 2 cups. Strain if you wish to remove onion slices, but reserve a few carrot slices for garnish and return liquid to pan; or simply discard pickling spices and leave all of vegetables in liquid. Add vinegar, sugar, and cranberries, if using, to liquid and simmer 1 minute. Adjust seasoning. Pour mixture over fish. Refrigerate.

4. Serve fish cold. When serving, spoon a little of the liquid over fish. Garnish with cranberries, if using, and carrot slices.

Blintzes with Fish and Morel Filling

Makes 4 servings Ⓓ

This lavish rendition of blintzes is worthy of the most festive occasions. Its richly flavored sauce is redolent of the exquisite perfume of morel mushrooms. Cook any fish that you like for the filling or use boneless cooked fish that you already have on hand in the refrigerator or freezer. If you don't have a chance to prepare fish stock, use prepared vegetable broth.

2 cups Fish Stock (page 600)

8 Basic Blintzes (page 300)

1/2 to 3/4 ounce dried morel mushrooms

Salt and freshly ground pepper, to taste

1 pound fish steaks or fillets, such as halibut, cod, sea bass, or salmon

2 tablespoons dry or semi-dry white wine

1/4 cup (1/2 stick) butter

3 tablespoons all-purpose flour

3/4 cup whipping cream

4 teaspoons snipped fresh chives

1. Prepare fish stock. Meanwhile, prepare blintzes. Then, rinse morels. Soak them in hot water to cover for 30 minutes.

2. Bring fish stock to simmer in a medium saucepan. Add salt and fish. Cover and poach fish over low heat, turning once, about 10 minutes or until the thickest part of the fish is opaque inside; check with a sharp knife. Transfer fish with slotted spatula to a plate, reserving cooking liquid. Strain cooking liquid and return to saucepan.

3. Rinse soaked morels, discarding soaking liquid, and drain well. Cut large morels into 2 or 3 pieces. Add morels and 2 tablespoons wine to fish cooking liquid. Bring to a simmer. Cover and cook over low heat 10 minutes. Remove morels with slotted spoon, reserving cooking liquid.

4. Preheat oven to 400°F. Melt 3 tablespoons butter in heavy medium saucepan. Whisk in flour. Cook over low heat, whisking, about 2 minutes or until mixture turns light beige. Remove from heat. Gradually whisk in morel cooking liquid. Bring to boil over medium-high heat, whisking. Whisk in cream and return to boil, whisking. Reduce heat to low, return morels to sauce and simmer uncovered, stirring often, about 7 minutes or until sauce heavily coats a spoon. Remove from heat. Leave morels in sauce. Set aside 1 cup sauce with a few morels for serving separately.

5. Discard any bones and skin from fish. Flake fish. Stir fish into remaining sauce, which will be used for filling. Stir in 2 teaspoons chives. Add pepper; Adjust seasoning.

6. Butter 1 or 2 shallow baking dishes. Spoon 3 tablespoons filling onto cooked side of each blintz, across lower third of blintz. Roll up in cigar shape, beginning at edge with filling. Arrange blintzes seam-side down in single layer in a buttered dish. Melt remaining tablespoon butter and brush lightly over blintzes.

7. Bake blintzes about 15 minutes or until hot. Bring sauce just to simmer in small saucepan, stirring. Remove from heat and stir in remaining 2 teaspoons chives. Add pepper; Adjust seasoning. To serve, transfer blintzes to plates and spoon a little sauce over each blintz.

❧ Braised Fish

Moroccan Fish with Red Peppers, Cilantro, and Garlic

Hraimeh

Makes about 4 main-course or 6 first-course servings

Hraimeh is one of the most popular fish dishes of Moroccan Jewish cooking and is made in numerous versions. Almost all include plenty of fresh garlic and cilantro and many add fresh sweet peppers as well. Other flavoring variations are cumin, lemon juice, and tomato paste. Some cooks make the dish very hot, adding plenty of chiles and accenting the dish with additional ground hot pepper. Others make it milder, especially when children are at the table. This version makes use of whole dried chiles to flavor the sauce. They are fairly hot but since they are removed before the sauce is served, the result is flavorful but not searing. If you want it hotter, add hot red pepper flakes or cayenne pepper to taste, or choose smaller, more fiery chiles such as chiles japones and add more of them. Traditionally, the fish simmers slowly in the sauce until it's very tender. If you're serving the fish as a main course, rice is a good accompaniment.

2 to 4 tablespoons extra-virgin olive oil

2 red bell peppers, cut into strips

10 large cloves garlic, chopped

1/2 cup chopped fresh cilantro

1 tablespoon tomato paste

1 1/2 cups water

2 long dried chiles, such as New Mexico chiles

2 pounds fish steaks or fillets, about 1 inch thick

Salt and freshly ground pepper, to taste

1 teaspoon paprika

1/4 to 1/2 teaspoon hot red pepper flakes, or cayenne pepper to taste (optional)

1. Heat oil in a large sauté pan. Add bell peppers, half the garlic, and 1/4 cup cilantro. Sauté over medium-low heat 2 minutes. Stir in tomato paste and water, add chiles, and bring to a simmer. Remove from heat. Add fish to pan and sprinkle it with salt, pepper, paprika, remaining garlic, and half the remaining cilantro. Return to a simmer. Cover and cook over very low heat 5 minutes. Turn fish over. Uncover and simmer about 5 more minutes or until fish just flakes but is not falling apart.

2. With a slotted spatula, transfer fish and pepper strips to a deep platter. Leave chiles in pan.

3. If sauce is too thin, simmer it over medium-high heat, stirring occasionally, until it reduces to about 3/4 cup. Taste liquid; if you like, add pepper flakes or cayenne and simmer 2 more minutes. Pour sauce over fish. Discard dried chiles. Serve fish sprinkled with remaining cilantro.

Yemenite Fish with Tomatoes and Spices

Makes 4 servings

My husband's aunt, Mazal Cohen of Rehovot, Israel, who was born in Yemen, taught me how to make this dish about ten years ago when we cooked together at my home in Santa Monica, California. For the sauce, she grates fresh tomatoes, so that most of their peels remain in the grater. She spikes the sauce generously with cumin, turmeric, and black pepper, and finishes the dish with fresh cilantro. In Israel, she makes this dish with mullet steaks and simmers them 20 to 30 minutes so that they are very tender. I use halibut or cod, which are more widely available in the United States and cook more quickly.

1 pound ripe fresh tomatoes or one 28-ounce can whole tomatoes, drained

2 tablespoons vegetable oil

1/2 large onion, diced

1 tablespoon ground cumin

1 1/2 teaspoons ground turmeric

1 teaspoon paprika

Salt, to taste

1/2 teaspoon freshly ground pepper plus more, to taste

1/4 cup chopped fresh cilantro

1 1/2 pounds halibut or cod steaks or fillets, about 1 inch thick

1. Grate fresh tomatoes using large holes of grater. If using canned tomatoes, chop them fine.

2. Heat oil in a large sauté pan, add onion, and sauté over medium heat until golden brown. Add tomatoes, cumin, turmeric, paprika, salt, and pepper. Bring to a boil. Cover and simmer 10 minutes.

3. Add 2 tablespoons cilantro to sauce. Add fish and sprinkle it with salt and pepper. Bring to a simmer. Cover and cook over low heat 7 minutes. Turn over and cook 7 to 10 more minutes or until flesh flakes easily.

4. Serve fish hot or at room temperature, sprinkled with remaining cilantro.

Sea Bass Steaks with Chickpeas

Makes 4 to 6 servings

Pairing delicate fish like sea bass with humble chickpeas might seem surprising but this match is traditional for festive dinners in the North African Jewish kitchen.

3 to 3¹/₂ cups cooked chickpeas (garbanzo beans) with 1 cup of their cooking liquid, or two 15-ounce cans chickpeas, drained

5 large cloves garlic, sliced

6 dried hot red peppers, such as chiles arbol or chiles japones

Salt and freshly ground pepper, to taste

3 or 4 tablespoons extra-virgin olive oil

¹/₄ cup chopped fresh cilantro

1 teaspoon paprika

¹/₂ teaspoon ground cumin

¹/₄ teaspoon ground turmeric

2 pounds sea bass steaks, about 1 inch thick

1. Combine chickpeas with garlic, chiles, pinch of salt, 2 tablespoons oil, and 2 tablespoons cilantro in sauté pan. Add 1 cup chickpea cooking liquid; if using canned chickpeas, add 1 cup water. Push chiles to bottom of pan. Bring to simmer. Cover tightly and cook over medium-low heat 5 minutes.

2. Mix paprika, cumin, and turmeric in a bowl. Set fish on chickpeas and sprinkle it with salt, pepper, and spice mixture. Drizzle with remaining oil. Bring to a simmer. Cover and cook over medium-low heat, turning fish once, 10 to 15 minutes or until the thickest part of the fish is opaque inside; check with a sharp knife. Adjust seasoning.

3. Serve hot, sprinkled with remaining cilantro.

Sea Bass in Garlic Tomato Sauce

Makes 4 servings

When you want a flavorful, easy-to-make fish dish for Shabbat, try this one from the kitchens of the Jews of Italy. It makes a savory cold appetizer or a tasty main course accompanied by bow-tie pasta or rice. For this fast-cooking, one-pan dish, the fish simmers right in its sauce. If you don't have sea bass, you can make it with cod or halibut.

1¹/₂ pounds ripe tomatoes, peeled and seeded, or one 28-ounce and one 14-ounce can tomatoes, drained

2 tablespoons olive oil

6 large cloves garlic, minced

Salt and freshly ground pepper, to taste

¹/₄ cup chopped fresh Italian parsley

1¹/₂ pounds sea bass fillets, about 1 inch thick

1. Puree fresh or canned tomatoes in blender or food processor. Heat oil with garlic in a large sauté pan over medium-low heat for 30 seconds. Add tomatoes, salt, and pepper and cook over medium-high heat, stirring often, 8 to 10 minutes or until thick.

2. Add half of parsley to sauce. Add fish in one layer and sprinkle with salt and pepper. Bring to a simmer. Cover and cook over medium-low heat, spooning sauce over fish from time to time, about 10 minutes or until the thickest part of the fish is opaque inside; check with a sharp knife. Adjust seasoning. Serve fish hot or cold, sprinkled with remaining parsley.

Sea Bass with Lima Beans

Makes 4 servings

In springtime, Jews from Morocco like to pair fish with fava beans. I usually substitute the more available lima beans, which also give a delicious result in this entree flavored with red pepper, garlic, and cilantro. If you like, substitute frozen fava beans and cook them 20 to 30 minutes.

One 10-ounce package frozen lima beans

1 red bell pepper, diced

1/3 cup water

6 large cloves garlic, chopped

1/4 cup fresh cilantro leaves, plus a few sprigs for garnish

1 1/2 pounds sea bass fillets, in 4 pieces, about 1 inch thick

1 tablespoon extra-virgin olive oil

Salt and freshly ground pepper, to taste

1/2 teaspoon sweet paprika

Pinch of hot paprika or cayenne pepper

1. Cook lima beans in a saucepan of boiling water about 5 minutes, or until tender. Drain well.

2. Choose a sauté pan wide enough for fish to fit in one layer. Put red bell pepper, water, half the garlic, and half the cilantro in the pan. Top with fish. Sprinkle fish with olive oil, remaining cilantro, and remaining garlic, then with salt, pepper, paprika, and hot paprika. Heat over high heat just until the liquid boils. Cover and cook over low heat, turning fish once, about 8 minutes.

3. Add lima beans and cook 2 minutes more or until lima beans are heated through and the thickest part of the fish is opaque inside; check with a sharp knife. Serve garnished with cilantro sprigs.

❧ *Fish Stews*

Halibut with Green Beans and Black Beans

Makes 4 servings

For a weekday supper, I like to cook this one-pot main course. Following the Sephardic tradition, I simmer the halibut with vegetables in a tomato sauce seasoned with cumin, oregano, and cilantro. It is easy to prepare, as it makes use of fresh, frozen, and pantry vegetables. The entree is so flavorful that it needs no oil. All you need to complete the dinner is good bread and a green salad.

Use cut green beans, rather than the slivered "French style."

12 ounces fresh or 8 ounces frozen green beans

One 15-ounce can low-salt black beans, drained

One 14-ounce can diced tomatoes, with their juice

3 zucchini, halved lengthwise and sliced

3 small cloves garlic, coarsely chopped

One 1 1/4-pound halibut steak, about 1 inch thick

Salt and freshly ground pepper, to taste

1 teaspoon ground cumin

1 teaspoon dried oregano

1/4 cup chopped fresh cilantro

1 teaspoon prepared curry sauce (optional)

1. Heat 1 cup water in a large, deep sauté pan. Add green beans and bring to a boil. If using fresh beans, cover and cook 3 minutes over medium heat. Add black beans and tomatoes and bring to a simmer. Add zucchini, cover, and return to a simmer. Add garlic.

2. Put halibut steak in center of pan, pushing vegetables to side. Sprinkle fish with salt, pepper, cumin, oregano, and half the cilantro. Stir curry sauce, if using, into vegetable mixture. Bring to a simmer. Cover and cook over medium-low heat for 7 minutes, then over low heat for about 5 minutes. It's done when the thickest part of the fish is opaque inside; check with a sharp knife. Serve sprinkled with remaining cilantro.

Salmon with Noodles and Leeks

Makes 4 servings **D**

Chicken with noodles is a popular pair but fish and noodles can be just as satisfying. I love salmon and noodles tossed in a creamy leek and dill sauce. To make it easy, I cook the salmon right in the sauce.

1/2 cup Fish Stock (page 600)

3 medium leeks, split and rinsed thoroughly (green part reserved for stock)

1 tablespoon vegetable oil

1 tablespoon water

Salt and freshly ground pepper, to taste

1 1/4 pounds salmon fillet

1/3 cup dry white wine

1/3 cup whipping cream

1 teaspoon dried thyme

2 tablespoons butter

8 ounces medium noodles

2 tablespoons snipped fresh dill

1. Prepare fish stock. Then, cut white part of leeks into thin slices. Heat oil in a large skillet. Add leeks, water, salt, and pepper. Cover and cook over low heat, stirring occasionally, about 5 minutes or until tender but not brown.

2. Remove skin and any bones from salmon fillet. Cut fish into small dice.

3. Add wine, fish stock, and cream to leeks and bring to a boil. Reduce heat to low, add fish, and sprinkle lightly with salt, pepper, and thyme. Cook uncovered, stirring often, about 3 minutes or until fish becomes less pink. Remove from heat.

4. Cut butter into pieces and put in a large heated bowl. Cook noodles uncovered in a large pot of water over high heat for about 5 minutes or until tender but firm to the bite. Drain well, transfer to bowl and toss with butter.

5. Reheat sauce if necessary. Stir in dill. Pour over noodles and toss. Adjust seasoning. Serve hot.

Sephardic Fish Paella

Makes 4 to 6 servings **P**

Sephardic means Spanish in Hebrew, indicating that the origin of many Sephardic Jews is in the Iberian Peninsula. Spain's national dish, paella, is made of saffron rice cooked with seafood, poultry, meat, or some combination, often with sausages as well. Naturally, paella became part of the Sephardic culinary repertoire but of course, theirs is made with only kosher ingredients. If you would like a sausage to flavor your paella, add a vegetarian one.

3 1/2 cups fish or vegetable stock, or stock mixed with water

1/2 teaspoon crushed saffron threads

2 to 3 tablespoons olive oil

1 medium onion, chopped

1 small red bell pepper, cut into 1/4-inch-wide strips

1 1/2 cups white rice, preferably short-grained

3 medium cloves garlic, minced

1 ripe medium tomato, peeled, seeded, and chopped, or 1 canned tomato, chopped

Salt and freshly ground pepper, to taste

1 1/2 pounds sea bass, cod, or halibut fillets, diced

1 cup frozen peas, thawed

1/2 pound vegetarian sausages (optional), cut into chunks

2 tablespoons chopped fresh Italian parsley

1. Bring stock to a simmer in a medium saucepan. Crush saffron threads in a small bowl and pour hot broth over them. Let mixture stand while continuing next step.

2. Heat oil in a large, deep, heavy skillet or sauté pan. Add onion and bell pepper and cook, stirring often, about 7 minutes or until softened. Add rice and sauté over low heat, stirring, 2 minutes. Stir in garlic, tomato, salt, pepper, and 3 cups hot saffron broth. Bring to a simmer. Cover and simmer over low heat 10 minutes.

3. Add diced fish, peas, vegetarian sausages if using, and any remaining saffron broth. Bring to a simmer. Cover and cook over low heat about 10 more minutes or until fish is opaque inside and rice is tender. Adjust seasoning. Serve sprinkled with parsley.

Creole Fish Stew

Makes 4 servings

Jewish cooks in the American South know that the tasty sauces used in Louisiana for cooking shellfish are fabulous for fish. This one makes use of a light brown roux and the traditional trio of aromatic vegetables used in Cajun and Creole dishes—peppers, onion, and celery. Serve this fish in its pepper-studded sauce with plenty of rice or linguine.

2 tablespoons vegetable oil or olive oil, or 1 tablespoon oil and 1 tablespoon butter

1 large onion, finely diced

3 ribs celery, diced

1 red bell pepper, diced

1 green or yellow bell pepper, diced

2 large cloves garlic, minced

1 tablespoon all-purpose flour

1 1/2 cups vegetable stock or water

1/2 teaspoon dried oregano

1/2 teaspoon dried thyme

Salt and freshly ground pepper, to taste

1/4 teaspoon cayenne pepper, or to taste

1 pound cod, halibut, or sea bass fillets, cut into cubes

1/3 cup chopped green onions

1/3 cup chopped fresh parsley

1. Heat oil in a large skillet. Add onion, celery, and peppers, and cook over medium-low heat about 5 minutes. Add garlic and cook 1 minute. Add flour and cook, stirring, 1 or 2 minutes or until it turns light brown. Remove from heat and gradually stir in vegetable stock. Bring to a boil over medium heat, stirring. Cook uncovered over low heat for 10 minutes. Add oregano, thyme, salt, pepper, and 1/4 teaspoon cayenne.

2. A short time before serving, bring sauce to a simmer. Add fish cubes and sprinkle with salt and pepper. Return to a simmer. Cover and cook over low heat, stirring occasionally, about 5 minutes or until larger fish pieces become opaque. Add green onions and parsley to sauce. Taste, and add more salt, pepper, and cayenne if needed. Serve hot.

Fish Jambalaya

Makes 6 servings

Here is a kosher adaptation of the hot and spicy Cajun specialty jambalaya. I like to make it with fish, spicy vegetarian frankfurters, and just a little olive oil, so that it is healthful too but it still makes a hearty helping. Serve it for Purim or Hanukkah. As a meal in one pan, it's great for entertaining. Cajuns like jambalaya with Louisiana hot sauce, but I serve Zehug (page 592).

1 1/2 to 2 tablespoons extra-virgin olive oil

1 large onion, chopped

1 green, red, or yellow bell pepper, chopped

1/2 cup chopped celery

4 large cloves garlic, chopped

2 jalapeño peppers, chopped (see Note)

1 cup tomato sauce

1 teaspoon oregano

1 bay leaf

3 cups vegetable stock

2 pounds sea bass or other fish fillets, cut into 6 pieces

Salt and freshly ground pepper, to taste

2 cups long- or medium-grain white rice

6 ounces spicy vegetarian frankfurters, cut into chunks

1/2 teaspoon cayenne pepper, or to taste

1/4 cup chopped fresh parsley

1. Heat oil in a large deep skillet. Add onion, bell pepper, and celery and sauté over medium heat, stirring often, for 5 minutes. Add garlic, jalapeño peppers, tomato sauce, oregano, bay leaf, and stock. Bring to a simmer. Add fish and sprinkle with salt and pepper. Cover and cook 10 minutes or until the thickest part of the fish is opaque inside; check with a sharp knife. Remove fish pieces to a plate.

2. Return sauce to a boil and stir in rice. Add frankfurter pieces, salt, pepper, cayenne, and 2 tablespoons parsley. Cover and cook over low heat 30 minutes, or until rice is tender. Do not stir often, to avoid crushing rice. Remove bay leaf. Return fish pieces to skillet, cover, and heat for about 5 minutes or low heat. Sprinkle with remaining parsley and serve.

Note: Wear rubber gloves when handling hot peppers.

Kosher California Cioppino

Makes 4 servings   Ⓟ

Cioppino, the pride of many fine California restaurants, is a garlic-scented seafood stew in tomato broth. Jewish cooks have developed their own delicious versions of cioppino using kosher fish.

This elegant dish had modest origins. It is thought to have begun in San Francisco in the early twentieth century as a way for fishermen to make use of their catch, especially the local rockfish. Cioppino is derived from an Italian Riviera fishermen's fish soup called "ciuppin," which is flavored mainly with tomatoes, olive oil, garlic, and white wine.

When I was a judge of a cioppino contest, in which prominent California restaurant chefs competed, I found it remarkable how much the dish can vary in seasoning. The only ingredients all the cioppinos had in common were tomatoes, garlic, and olive oil. Other flavors that entered their cioppino pots were porcini mushrooms, thyme, basil, oregano, rosemary, saffron, and even jalapeño peppers, cilantro, and orange juice. So once you taste this recipe, feel free to be as creative as those cioppino chefs!

Fresh-baked, crusty sourdough or Italian bread is the customary accompaniment.

1/2 cup Fish Stock (page 600), liquid from a jar of unsweetened gefilte fish, or water

1 1/2 to 3 tablespoons olive oil

1 large onion, sliced thin

2 large cloves garlic, chopped

One 28-ounce can diced tomatoes, undrained

One 8-ounce can tomato sauce

3/4 cup dry red wine, such as Cabernet Sauvignon

Salt and freshly ground pepper, to taste

Hot pepper sauce to taste

1 to 1 1/2 pounds good quality fish fillets, diced

1 teaspoon dried oregano

1 or 2 tablespoons chopped fresh Italian parsley

1. Prepare fish stock, if using. Then, in a large, heavy saucepan, heat oil, add onion, and sauté over medium-high heat, stirring often, 5 minutes. Stir in garlic, then tomatoes and their juice, tomato sauce, wine, and fish stock. Cover and bring to a boil. Simmer over medium-low heat 7 minutes. Season with salt, pepper, and hot pepper sauce.

2. Add fish and oregano to simmering cioppino base. Cover and simmer over low heat 2 minutes or until just tender and opaque. Serve cioppino in wide bowls. Sprinkle with parsley.

❧ Sautéed Fish

Sole with Garlic Butter

Makes 4 servings

French Jews make good use of garlic butter, pairing it with fish to make luscious dishes. It lends incomparable flavor to fish fillets, whether you choose rich ones like salmon or sea bass, or lean fish, such as sole or halibut.

³/₄ cup fresh fine white bread crumbs (see Note below)

Garlic Butter (page 593)

1 to 1¹/₄ pounds sole or flounder fillets, about ¹/₄-inch thick

Salt and freshly ground pepper, to taste

¹/₂ cup milk

2 to 3 tablespoons vegetable oil

2 tablespoons soft butter

Fresh parsley sprigs

Lemon wedges

1. Prepare fresh bread crumbs and Garlic Butter. If making garlic butter ahead, bring it to room temperature before serving. If you like, spoon it into a piping bag fitted with small star tip.

2. Run your fingers over fillets to check for bones. Gently remove any bones using tweezers or small sharp knife.

3. Preheat oven to 275°F. Spread bread crumbs in a large plate. Season fish with salt and pepper on both sides. Dip each fillet in milk; then dip on both sides in bread crumbs and press so they adhere. As each fillet is dipped, set it on a large plate; place fillets side by side.

4. Heat 2 tablespoons oil and 2 tablespoons butter in a skillet over medium-high heat. Handling fillets lightly, add enough to make one layer in skillet. Sauté fillets about 1 minute per side or until golden brown on both sides, using 2 slotted spatulas to carefully turn them. Place sautéed fillets side by side on an ovenproof platter and keep them warm in a 275°F oven while sautéing remaining fillets. Add remaining oil if needed so skillet remains coated. If butter begins to brown, reduce heat to medium.

5. To serve, pipe Garlic Butter in decorative line down center of each fillet; or spoon a few dabs of Garlic Butter onto each. Garnish plates with parsley sprigs and lemon quarters. Serve remaining Garlic Butter separately. (Diners spread butter so it melts into hot fish.)

Note: To prepare fresh white bread crumbs, slice French bread or other unsweetened white bread and let dry uncovered for 1 to 2 days. Remove crust and cut bread into pieces. Pulverize bread in food processor until very fine.

Sole Schnitzel

Makes 4 servings

Schnitzel made of sautéed chicken or turkey is one of the most popular entrees in Israel, especially with children. This cooking technique, which coats the meat in a crisp crust, is also perfect for fish fillets. In fact, it's a great recipe for encouraging young eaters to enjoy fish. For adults, serve this fish with Red Pepper Vinaigrette or Caper-Lemon-Parsley Dressing (page 342).

1 to 1¹/₄ pounds sole or flounder fillets

¹/₂ teaspoon salt, plus more to taste

¹/₂ teaspoon freshly ground pepper plus more to taste

¹/₃ cup all-purpose flour

³/₄ cup dry bread crumbs

1¹/₂ teaspoons paprika

2 large eggs or egg whites

¹/₃ cup vegetable oil

Lemon wedges

1. Run your fingers over fillets to check for bones. Gently remove any bones using tweezers or small, sharp knife. Cut each fillet into two pieces crosswise. Arrange them in one layer on plate. Sprinkle evenly with salt and pepper.

2. Spread flour in a large plate. Put bread crumbs in a shallow bowl or baking dish and mix evenly with paprika, ¹/₂ teaspoon salt and ¹/₂ teaspoon pepper. Beat eggs in a shallow bowl. Lightly coat a fish piece with flour on both sides. Tap and shake to remove excess flour. Dip piece in eggs. Last, dip both sides in bread crumbs so fish is completely coated; pat and press lightly so crumbs adhere. Repeat with remaining slices. Set pieces side by side on a large plate. Handle fish lightly at all stages.

3. Heat oil in large, heavy skillet over medium-high heat. Add enough fish to make one layer, leaving room to turn them over. Sauté until golden brown on both sides, about 1 minute per side. Turn carefully using two slotted spatulas. If oil begins to brown, reduce heat to medium. Set fish pieces side by side on ovenproof platter and keep them warm in a 275°F oven while sautéing remaining slices. Serve hot, with lemon wedges.

Shavuot Sole with Spiced Butter and Basmati Rice

Makes 4 servings   Ⓓ

My husband and I love using the Yemenite seasonings of his family in French-style sauces. In this easy dish, we make a flavored butter with fresh garlic, cumin, and turmeric, and use it to sauté sole fillets and to enhance its accompanying basmati rice. The rich, aromatic dish makes a wonderful Shavuot entree.

1¹/2 cups basmati rice

1 to 1¹/4 pounds sole fillets, patted dry

4 to 6 tablespoons butter, softened

2 large cloves garlic, minced

1 jalapeño pepper (optional), ribs and seeds discarded, minced

2 teaspoons ground cumin

¹/2 teaspoon ground turmeric

Salt and freshly ground pepper, to taste

2 tablespoons vegetable oil

¹/2 cup minced green onions

2 tablespoons chopped fresh parsley

1. Rinse rice in several changes of water. Drain well. Put rice in a large saucepan.

2. Run your finger over sole fillets to check them for bones; remove any bones carefully with tweezers or a small, sharp knife. Cut sole in thin diagonal strips about 1-inch wide and 3-inches long. Refrigerate sole until ready to cook it.

3. Add 2¹/₂ cups water and a pinch of salt to pan of rice. Bring to a boil. Cover and cook over low heat, without stirring, 18 to 20 minutes or until rice is tender and liquid is absorbed.

4. Combine butter, garlic, jalapeño if using, cumin, turmeric, salt, and pepper in a medium bowl; mix well.

5. Preheat oven to 275°F. Spoon 2 tablespoons spiced butter into a large, heavy skillet for sautéing sole; set aside. Spoon remaining spiced butter over cooked rice. Cover and let stand about 10 minutes or until ready to serve.

6. Just before serving, add oil to the spiced butter in the skillet. Cook over medium heat. Add half of sole to pan, sprinkle with salt and pepper, and sauté, stirring often, about 1¹/₂ to 2 minutes or until just cooked through and opaque. With a slotted spoon, transfer sole to a platter and keep warm in a 275°F oven. Sauté remaining sole and transfer to platter. Add green onions to skillet used to sauté sole and heat 30 seconds. Spoon over sole.

7. Fluff rice with a fork and blend in spiced butter. Spoon rice onto platter or plates. Serve sole over or alongside rice and sprinkle with parsley.

❀ Gefilte Fish and Other Ground Fish Dishes

Salmon Gefilte Fish with Dill

Makes about 8 servings (P)

Traditional Gefilte Fish (page 180) is made with carp, whitefish, and pike, but today's cooks don't limit themselves to these options. In recent years salmon has become popular and makes delicious gefilte fish with an attractive color. Serve the gefilte fish cold on lettuce leaves to accent the color. Accompany it with White Horseradish Sauce, Mustard-Dill Dressing, or Mildred's Dill Sauce (pages 339–340).

To make preparation easy, have the salmon filleted at the market.

4¹⁄₂ pounds salmon (including bones and head), filleted, bones and heads reserved for fish stock

Salmon Gefilte Fish Stock (page 601)

2 large eggs

2 medium onions, finely chopped

1¹⁄₂ teaspoons salt

¹⁄₂ teaspoon freshly ground pepper

¹⁄₄ cup chopped fresh dill or 1 tablespoon dried

3 tablespoons matzo meal

1. Using salmon head and bones, prepare fish stock. Pour strained stock into a large, deep pot.

2. To remove skin from salmon, set a fillet on a board, skin side down. Slip blade of a flexible knife between flesh and skin and use it to remove skin of fish, sliding knife away from you with one hand and pulling off skin with other. Run your fingers carefully over fillets and remove small bones remaining in flesh with tweezers or a small, sharp knife. Cut salmon into large pieces.

3. Grind salmon in 2 batches in a food processor until very fine. Return half the fish to food processor and add 1 egg, half the chopped onions, ³⁄₄ teaspoon salt, and ¹⁄₄ teaspoon pepper. Process to thoroughly mix. Transfer to a large bowl. Repeat with remaining fish, egg, onion, salt, and pepper. Transfer to bowl and mix with first batch. Stir in dill and matzo meal.

4. Bring strained stock to a simmer. With moistened hands, shape fish mixture into ovals or balls, using about ¹⁄₃ cup mixture for each. Carefully drop fish balls into simmering stock. If necessary add enough hot water to barely cover them, pouring it carefully into stock near edge of pan, not over fish. Return to a simmer, cover, and simmer over low heat for 1 hour. Let fish cool in stock. Refrigerate fish in stock for at least 4 hours before serving. Remove fish balls from stock and serve cold.

Baked Gefilte Fish

Makes about 6 servings (P)

Baking is a popular way to cook gefilte fish. It's easier because you don't have to poach it in fish stock. When baked, gefilte fish has a different texture, with a crusty top and a softer interior, unlike the traditional poached fish balls which are moist throughout. Some people shape the fish into patties and bake them in a tomato sauce; others shape it as a free-form loaf. Easiest of all is to spoon the fish mixture into a loaf pan or baking dish and serve the finished loaf in slices or squares. Baked gefilte fish is served hot or cold and often is a main course. If you serve it cold, you can top each serving with a cooked carrot slice and accompany it with horseradish.

We often ate baked gefilte fish when I was growing up. When my mother made poached gefilte fish, she saved part of the mixture to bake as a loaf. Some cooks enrich their baked gefilte fish mixture with oil. Some sprinkle it with paprika, while others spread ketchup on top for the last 5 minutes of baking so it will brown.

2 pounds halibut, sole, or sea bass fillets

2 large eggs

2 medium onions, finely chopped

1¹⁄₂ teaspoons salt

¹⁄₂ teaspoon ground pepper, preferably white

1 teaspoon sugar (optional)

2 ribs celery, finely chopped

2 medium carrots, grated

2 tablespoons vegetable oil (optional)

¹⁄₄ cup matzo meal

Paprika, to taste

1. Preheat oven to 350°F. Grease a 9-inch square baking pan.

2. Grind fish in 2 batches in a food processor until very fine. Return half the fish to food processor and add 1 egg, half the chopped onions, 3/4 teaspoon salt, 1/4 teaspoon pepper, and 1/2 teaspoon sugar, if using. Process to thoroughly mix. Transfer to a large bowl. Repeat with remaining fish, egg, onion, salt, pepper, and sugar. Transfer to bowl and mix with first batch. Stir in celery, carrots, oil if using, and matzo meal.

3. Spoon fish into prepared pan. Sprinkle with paprika. Cover and bake 15 minutes. Uncover and bake 30 more minutes or until set. Serve hot or cold, in slices.

French Gefilte Fish Loaf

Makes 5 or 6 servings

This is a delicate French style fish terrine that is enriched with cream. The fish loaf is made of sole and dotted with salmon. Unlike most gefilte fish loaves, this one is baked in a water bath so it will cook very gently.

Serve this loaf hot or cold on festive occasions. A salad of baby greens is a perfect accompaniment. Don't overpower the subtle taste of the fish with the strong type of horseradish usually served with gefilte fish. Instead, accompany it with creamy White Horseradish Sauce (page 339), Fresh Tomato Vinaigrette (page 595), or French spinach-watercress sauce (see Baked Halibut with French Spinach-Watercress Sauce, page 183).

1½ pounds sole fillets
½ pound salmon fillet
3 large egg whites
1 teaspoon salt
½ teaspoon white pepper
Freshly ground nutmeg, to taste
1 cup heavy cream

1. Remove any skin or bones from sole and salmon. Cut sole into 1-inch pieces. Cut salmon in thin strips and pat them dry.

2. Puree half the sole in a food processor until very fine. Add 1 egg white and process until blended. Remove to a bowl. Puree remaining sole and a second egg white. Leave mixture in processor. Return first mixture to processor. Add third egg white, salt, pepper, and nutmeg. Process until thoroughly blended and very smooth. Transfer to a bowl, cover, and refrigerate 30 minutes. Refrigerate work bowl of processor also.

3. Preheat oven to 350°F. Butter a 6-cup terrine mold or loaf pan. Line base of pan with wax paper or parchment paper, then butter liner. Butter another sheet and reserve.

4. Return cold fish mixture to cold food processor. With machine running, gradually pour in cream through feed tube in a slow, steady stream. Adjust seasoning; if adding more, process until mixed. Transfer mixture to a bowl.

5. Spoon about one third of sole mixture into mold. Pack mixture in mold well, pushing it into corners. Arrange half the salmon strips lengthwise on the mixture without letting them touch the edges of the pan. Top them carefully with another third of the sole mixture. Arrange remaining salmon strips lengthwise on top. Cover with remaining sole mixture. Smooth top. Tap mold on table to be sure mixture is packed down.

6. Cover with reserved buttered paper, then with 2 layers of foil, sealing top around edge of pan. Set mold in a larger pan and fill pan with very hot water about halfway up sides of mold. Bake about 35 minutes or until set; a skewer inserted into mixture and left in for 10 to 15 seconds should come out hot to touch. Remove mold from pan of water and leave about 10 minutes before unmolding; or refrigerate, if serving cold.

7. To serve, unmold loaf onto a platter or board; drain off any liquid. Cut carefully into 1/2-inch slices with a sharp knife.

Quick "Home-Cooked" Gefilte Fish from a Jar

Makes 6 to 14 servings,
depending whether you serve
1 or 2 patties per person

To make store-bought gefilte fish taste more like home-made, many cooks doctor up its flavor. My aunt Sylvia Saks first told me how to do this. You cook the fish patties in a tasty, quickly made, homemade vegetable broth.

Use any kind of gefilte fish you like. If you're using sweet gefilte fish, you can season the broth with a pinch of sugar, or more if you like. Serve it with its traditional partner, red horseradish made with beets.

2 large carrots, sliced

2 large onions, cut into thick slices

3 ribs celery, halved

Two 24-ounce jars gefilte fish (total 12 to 14 pieces)

Salt and white pepper, to taste

1. Combine carrots, onions, and celery in a large saucepan. Add liquid from gefilte fish. Bring to a simmer. Add gefilte fish patties and enough water to just cover them. Season with a pinch of salt and pepper. Bring to a simmer. Cover and cook over low heat 30 minutes. Adjust seasoning. Uncover and let cool.

2. If you're preparing fish for serving later, transfer patties carefully to a bowl or to clean jars and add enough carrot slices to garnish them. Strain remaining broth and pour it over fish. Cover and refrigerate. Serve fish patties garnished with carrot slices.

Fish Falafel

Makes about 8 to 10 servings

One of the lines in a popular, humorous Israeli song about falafel is that if it's made by an Ashkenazic Jew (instead of an "authentic" Yemenite Jew), it comes out tasting like gefilte fish! So my husband and I found it very funny when we saw a dish labeled "fish falafel"

on the menu of an Israeli eatery in a Jewish neighborhood in Paris. Curious, we ordered it. Soon we stopped laughing; they tasted really good! These "falafel" were basically fried gefilte fish balls seasoned like falafel and served in pita bread.

Serve these fish patties like falafel, with tahini sauce and hot sauce or with Cilantro Salsa (page 341).

2 pounds halibut or sea bass fillets

2 large eggs

1 large onion, chopped

6 large cloves garlic, chopped

$1/4$ cup small sprigs fresh cilantro, chopped

$2^1/2$ teaspoons ground cumin

1 teaspoon ground coriander

$1^1/2$ teaspoons salt

$1/2$ teaspoon freshly ground pepper

About $1^1/4$ cups dry bread crumbs

About 6 cups vegetable oil (for frying)

1. Remove any skin from fish. Grind fish in 2 batches in a food processor until very fine. Return half the fish to food processor and add 1 egg, half the chopped onions, garlic, and cilantro, $1^1/4$ teaspoons cumin, $1/2$ teaspoon coriander, $3/4$ teaspoon salt, and $1/4$ teaspoon pepper. Process to thoroughly mix. Transfer to a large bowl. Repeat with remaining fish, egg, onion, garlic, cilantro, and seasonings. Transfer to bowl and mix with first batch. Stir in 3 tablespoons bread crumbs. If mixture is wet, stir in more bread crumbs, 1 tablespoon at a time. Knead thoroughly to mix very well.

2. Put remaining bread crumbs in a dish for coating fish. To shape the fish falafel, take about $1/4$ cup of mixture and flatten it into smooth patty. Roll it in bread crumbs; pat them on if necessary so patty is evenly coated.

3. In a deep fryer, heavy saucepan, or large, deep skillet, heat oil to about 350°F. Add some of patties, leaving room to turn them. Do not drop them into oil from high up so oil won't splash. Fry 4 to 5 minutes, turning once, until they are deep golden brown. Drain on paper towels. Serve hot or warm.

Fish Latkes

Makes 4 servings

My cousin Mildred Greenberg gave me the idea for this recipe. She makes it using gefilte fish mixture. The fish has a completely different taste when it is sautéed instead of being poached. You can use any kind of fish. Either grind fillets yourself or buy ground fish if you will be using it right away. For quick fish latkes, Mildred thaws frozen, ready-to-cook gefilte fish mixture and adds eggs and matzo meal to it.

1 pound ground salmon, halibut, or other fish

1 large egg

1 medium onion, minced

1 teaspoon dried dill

3/4 teaspoon salt

1/4 teaspoon freshly ground pepper

About 1 1/4 cups matzo meal

About 1/2 cup vegetable oil

1. Mix fish, egg, and onion in a large bowl. Add dill, salt, pepper, and 2 tablespoons matzo meal and mix well. Mixture should be fairly firm. Add 1 or 2 tablespoons more matzo meal if needed; amount depends on how firm the fish is.

2. Line a tray with paper towels. Have a baking sheet ready for keeping latkes warm. Put 1 cup matzo meal on a plate for breading fish. Moisten your hands and shape fish mixture into balls, using about 1/4 cup for each. Flatten each to a patty and roll in matzo meal, coating it evenly.

3. Heat 1/2 cup oil in a deep, large, heavy skillet. Add a few latkes to pan; do not crowd them. Fry over medium heat 3 or 4 minutes per side, or until browned and cooked through. Use 2 slotted spatulas to turn them carefully so oil doesn't splatter. Transfer to paper towels. If necessary, add more oil to pan, and heat it before adding more latkes. Keep finished latkes warm on a baking sheet in a 250°F oven.

4. Pat tops of latkes with paper towels before serving. Serve hot.

Mati's Fish Balls in Tomato Sauce

Makes 4 main course
or 6 or 7 appetizer servings

My sister-in-law Mati Kahn prepares these savory Sephardic-style fish balls for Shabbat in the summer. You can serve them as a fish course but they also make a tasty main course when the weather is hot and many of us want a lighter meal.

If you're serving them as a hot entree, Israeli Rice Pilaf (page 499) garnished with pistachios is a good accompaniment.

2 slices stale white bread, crust removed

1 pound halibut or cod fillet, any bones removed,
      cut into pieces

1 teaspoon ground cumin

Salt and freshly ground pepper, to taste

1/4 teaspoon ground white pepper

1 large egg

1 large egg white

2 medium onions, minced

6 tablespoons finely chopped fresh Italian parsley

2 pounds ripe tomatoes or two 28-ounce cans whole tomatoes

2 or 3 tablespoons olive oil or vegetable oil

1 large clove garlic, minced

1 bay leaf

1 or 2 teaspoons strained fresh lemon juice

Lemon wedges

1. Put bread in food processor and grind to fine crumbs. Remove to a bowl.

2. Remove any bones from fish. Cut fish into pieces and put them in food processor. Pulse to chop fish finely. Add cumin, 1 teaspoon salt, white pepper, egg, egg white, and bread crumbs. Process until blended. Transfer to a bowl. Stir in half the minced onion and 4 tablespoons parsley. Moisten your hands and form mixture into small balls, using about 2 tablespoons mixture for each. Roll them between your palms until smooth. Put them on a plate.

3. Peel and seed fresh tomatoes, reserving juice; if using canned tomatoes, drain and reserve juice. Coarsely chop tomatoes. Heat oil in a medium saucepan, add remaining minced onion and sauté over medium-low heat 7 minutes. Add garlic, tomatoes, bay leaf, salt, and pepper. Bring to a boil. Cover and cook over low heat 20 minutes. Remove bay leaf. Transfer sauce to a sauté pan.

4. Measure reserved tomato juice, adding water if necessary to make 1 cup. Add measured juice to sauce. Bring to a simmer.

5. Gently add half the fish balls to the sauce. Cover and cook, without stirring, for 20 minutes or until they are firm. Carefully remove them with slotted spoon. Cook remaining fish balls in the same way. Add 1 or 2 teaspoons lemon juice to sauce, or to taste. Taste sauce and adjust seasoning. Return all fish balls to sauce. Serve hot or cold, sprinkled with remaining parsley and garnished with lemon wedges.

❧ Dishes Made with Cooked or Canned Fish

Salmon Casserole

Makes 8 servings ⓟ

This has long been a favorite entree in our family. I have been fond of it since I was a child. Now my mother finds that her grandchildren in Israel like it too. She prepares it for Shavuot and occasionally for a meatless Shabbat lunch.

3 large russet potatoes (1 pound), unpeeled and quartered

3 tablespoons vegetable oil

2 medium onions, finely chopped

2 to 4 tablespoons butter, cut into small pieces, or vegetable oil

One 15-ounce can red or pink salmon, drained and mashed

2 large eggs, or 1 large egg and equivalent of 1 egg in egg substitute

3/4 cup yogurt

Salt and freshly ground pepper, to taste

About 3/4 cup bread crumbs

Paprika, to taste

1. Put potatoes in a large saucepan with water to cover and a pinch of salt and bring to a boil. Cover and simmer over low heat about 25 minutes or until very tender. Drain and leave until cool enough to handle but still fairly warm.

2. Preheat oven to 350°F. Heat oil in a large skillet, add onions, and sauté over medium heat, stirring often, about 7 minutes or until golden.

3. Peel potatoes and cut each into a few pieces. Put in large bowl and mash with 1 tablespoon butter. Stir in onions. Stir in salmon, eggs, yogurt, and salt and pepper. Mix well.

4. Grease a 13 × 9-inch baking pan and sprinkle bottom and sides with bread crumbs. Add salmon mixture and smooth top. Sprinkle lightly with more bread crumbs and dot with remaining of butter. Lightly sprinkle with paprika. Bake for 45 minutes or until firm. Serve hot.

Smoked Whitefish with Tomato Noodles and Herbs

Makes 4 servings   **D**

Flavorful smoked whitefish is great not only with bagels and cream cheese, but with pasta as well. Instead of cream cheese, I like to make a quick cream sauce for the pasta and heat the fish in it. Tomato noodles make the fish the most colorful but you can use plain egg noodles also.

6 ounces smoked whitefish

1/3 to 1/2 cup whipping cream

1 tablespoon butter (optional)

12 ounces dried tomato noodles, egg noodles, or fusilli

2 tablespoons vegetable oil

4 teaspoons chopped fresh tarragon or 1 1/2 teaspoons dried

3 tablespoons snipped fresh chives

4 tablespoons chopped fresh parsley

Freshly ground pepper, to taste

1 cup diced fresh tomatoes, room temperature

1. Remove skin and any bones from whitefish. Cut fish into 1/2-inch dice.

2. Gently heat cream and butter, if using, in a small saucepan over low heat. Stir in diced smoked whitefish. Keep warm over very low heat.

3. Cook pasta uncovered in a large pot of boiling salted water over high heat 5 to 7 minutes or until tender but firm to the bite. Drain well. Transfer to a shallow heated serving bowl, add oil and toss.

4. Stir tarragon, chives, and 2 tablespoons parsley into sauce and add pepper. Add sauce to pasta and toss. Add tomatoes and toss again. Adjust seasoning. Serve immediately, sprinkled with remaining parsley.

Tuna Tabbouleh

Makes 4 to 6 servings   **P**

Tabbouleh, the mint-flavored Middle Eastern salad of bulgur wheat and chopped vegetables, is a favorite in Israel, especially among Jews of Lebanese extraction. Unlike many versions of tabbouleh in the United States, theirs is not mostly bulgur wheat, but is mostly parsley. It's very fresh and light and has lots of bright green flecks. Tuna adds good flavor and turns it into an easy, refreshing main course. It's perfect for a summer buffet and needs no cooking. The dish is especially delicious if you use tuna packed in olive oil.

1 cup bulgur wheat

3 cups boiling water

Three 6-ounce cans tuna, drained

3 tablespoons strained fresh lemon juice, or more to taste

Salt and freshly ground pepper, to taste

Cayenne pepper to taste

5 or 6 tablespoons extra-virgin olive oil

1/2 long (hothouse) cucumber or 1 medium cucumber, peeled and finely diced

3 green onions, sliced thin

2/3 cup chopped fresh Italian parsley

3/4 cup chopped fresh mint

5 plum tomatoes, finely diced

Lettuce leaves

1. Put bulgur wheat in a large bowl. Pour 3 cups boiling water over wheat and let stand until it is completely cool and tender, about 1 hour.

2. Meanwhile, combine tuna, 1 tablespoon lemon juice, salt, pepper, cayenne, and 3 tablespoons oil in a bowl. Cover and refrigerate while preparing remaining ingredients.

3. Drain wheat in a colander. Gently squeeze out excess water and return wheat to large bowl.

4. Gently mix diced cucumbers with onions, herbs, and wheat. Add tuna mixture. Gently fold in tomatoes and add remaining oil and lemon juice. Adjust seasoning, adding more lemon juice, oil, and cayenne if desired. Serve on a lettuce-lined platter, either cold or cool.

Sauces

White Horseradish Sauce

Makes about 1 cup, 6 to 8 servings

If you find that straight horseradish is too strong for you, here is a creamy sauce flavored with horseradish. You can serve it with gefilte fish or with simple poached, baked, or steamed fish. It's also good with poached beef.

1 tablespoon white wine vinegar

1 cup mayonnaise, regular or low-fat

2 to 3 tablespoons freshly grated or bottled white
    horseradish, or to taste

1 tablespoon chopped fresh parsley or dill

Salt and white pepper, to taste

2 to 3 teaspoons water

Whisk vinegar into mayonnaise in a bowl. Stir in horseradish and parsley. Add salt and white pepper, if needed. If sauce is too thick, gradually whisk in water. Refrigerate until ready to serve.

Horseradish with Beets

Makes about 2 cups

Horseradish is the classic accompaniment for gefilte fish and is popular in some homes with other fish and with boiled meats as well. When fresh horseradish roots are available, many Jewish cooks like to make red horseradish at home. It's easy if you use a food processor. Grating fresh horseradish on a hand grater makes your eyes sting and tear badly and must be done in a well-ventilated room. Even if you use a food processor, be sure to avert your face when you open the processor because of the strong fumes from the horseradish. Most people mix the horseradish with raw beets but you can use cooked beets for a softer texture.

The strength of horseradish roots varies greatly. Using the higher proportion of beets in this recipe helps

to tone it down. Some people make their horseradish very salty, sweet, or sour, and some use lemon juice instead of vinegar. This version has modest amounts of vinegar, salt, and sugar. Gradually add more if you like. Horseradish loses its strength the longer it stands.

1 pound horseradish

2 or 3 medium beets

1/4 cup cider vinegar, or to taste

1 teaspoon salt, or to taste

1 teaspoon sugar, or to taste

1/4 cup water

Peel and rinse horseradish and beets. Grate horseradish in a food processor with a shredding disk. Grate beets the same way. Averting your eyes, open food processor and transfer mixture to a bowl. Add vinegar, salt, and sugar. Mix well. If mixture is dry, add water. Add more vinegar, salt, and sugar, if needed. Spoon into jars and refrigerate.

Mustard-Dill Dressing

Makes about 1 1/2 cups, 8 to 10 servings

My mother often makes salad dressing with mayonnaise, ketchup, and mustard. If she prepares a salad without it, her grandchildren clamor for it. I find fresh dill is a terrific addition to her dressing, especially as an accompaniment for fish. Serve this dressing with salmon gefilte fish, baked or grilled salmon, or other baked fish.

1 cup mayonnaise, regular or low-fat

2 to 3 tablespoons mustard

1/4 cup ketchup

1 tablespoon vinegar or strained fresh lemon juice

2 to 3 tablespoons chopped fresh dill

Salt and freshly ground pepper, to taste

Mix mayonnaise with mustard and ketchup in a bowl. Stir in vinegar, dill, and salt and pepper. Refrigerate until ready to serve.

Garlic Sauce for Fish

Makes about 1 cup, about 6 servings

Terrific with grilled or broiled fish of distinctive character like tuna and salmon, this thick sauce made with olive oil is also delicious with cooked or raw vegetables as a sauce or dip. It is creamy without needing any dairy products and thus is convenient for pareve meals. In Israeli markets this popular Sephardic sauce resembling the alioli of Spain and the aioli of Provence is sold alongside the tahini and hummus.

Since the garlic is raw, be sure it is very fresh and not sprouting. If you are concerned about using uncooked eggs, buy pasteurized eggs for making this sauce. You can keep it up to 2 days in the refrigerator. If you prefer to make half a recipe, use a small food processor.

2 large cloves garlic, peeled
2 large egg yolks
1 tablespoon plus 1 teaspoon strained fresh lemon juice
1 cup olive oil, or 1/2 cup olive oil and 1/2 cup vegetable oil, room temperature
Salt and freshly ground pepper, to taste
Cayenne pepper, to taste
1 or 2 tablespoons warm water

Drop garlic cloves through feed tube of food processor with motor running, and process until finely chopped. Add egg yolks, 1 tablespoon lemon juice, 1 tablespoon oil, and a pinch of salt, pepper, and cayenne and process until thoroughly blended. With motor running, gradually pour oil through feed tube in a thin trickle. After adding 1/4 cup of the oil, you can pour in remaining oil a little faster, in a fine stream. With motor still running, gradually pour in remaining tablespoon lemon juice, 1 teaspoon at a time. Gradually add warm water to make sauce slightly thinner. Adjust seasoning. Refrigerate until ready to use.

Mushroom–Sour Cream Sauce for Fish

Makes 4 servings

This luscious, delicate sauce is wonderful with baked halibut, cod, salmon, or sole. The ideal side dish, to my taste, is fresh noodles.

6 to 8 ounces small mushrooms
2 tablespoons butter
Salt and freshly ground pepper, to taste
1/4 cup chopped green onion (mostly white part)
2 teaspoons all-purpose flour
1/4 cup milk
1/2 cup heavy cream
1 teaspoon sweet paprika
1/2 cup sour cream, room temperature
Pinch of hot paprika or cayenne pepper
2 tablespoons chopped fresh parsley

1. Quarter mushrooms. Melt 1 tablespoon butter in a large skillet. Add mushrooms, salt, and pepper and sauté over medium-high heat about 5 minutes or until tender and lightly browned. Remove from skillet.

2. Melt remaining butter in skillet. Add onions and sauté over medium heat for 2 minutes. Sprinkle with flour and cook over low heat, stirring, for 1 minute. Gradually stir in milk and cream. Add paprika and a little salt and pepper. Simmer over medium heat, stirring, until sauce is thick enough to coat a spoon. Add mushrooms and sour cream and heat gently, stirring, without boiling. Add hot paprika or cayenne. Adjust seasoning. Remove from heat. Add parsley.

Mildred's Dill Sauce

Makes about 1 cup, about 6 servings

My cousin Mildred Greenberg makes this sauce for serving with gefilte fish, for those who prefer a delicate dressing to a sharp condiment of horseradish. It's also delicious with poached trout, baked salmon, or boiled potatoes.

1 cup mayonnaise, regular or low-fat
1 tablespoon vinegar, any kind
2 tablespoons chopped fresh dill
Salt and freshly ground pepper, to taste

Mix mayonnaise with vinegar and dill in a bowl. Season with salt and pepper. Refrigerate until ready to serve.

Cilantro Salsa

Makes about 1¼ cups, 8 to 10 servings

This easy-to-make salsa is the perfect accompaniment for Fish Falafel (page 335). It's also good with gefilte fish balls as an alternative to horseradish and is a terrific pick-me-up for plain baked fish.

4 fresh jalapeño peppers (see Note)

4 large cloves garlic, peeled

3 cups sprigs fresh cilantro, medium-packed

2 tablespoon extra-virgin olive oil

2 tablespoon strained fresh lime juice

⅓ cup water

Salt, to taste

½ teaspoon ground cumin

Remove seeds and ribs from peppers if you want less heat. Cut peppers in a few pieces. Combine peppers and garlic in food processor and mince fine. Add cilantro and process until coarsely chopped. Transfer to a bowl and add remaining ingredients. Adjust seasoning. Refrigerate until ready to serve. Serve cold or at room temperature.

Note: Wear rubber gloves when handling hot peppers.

Cucumber-Zehug Salsa

Makes 4 servings

This lively fresh salsa is an ideal partner for grilled tuna or salmon. It is based on one I learned from Chef Brad Martin of Sea Grille in Palm Desert, California. The salsa is flavored with Chinese chile-garlic sauce, but I, instead, use Yemenite green or red zehug, which is also made of chiles and garlic. You can make your own Zehug (page 592) or buy it at Israeli or kosher markets. Whether you use Zehug or chile-garlic sauce, remember to add fiery condiments with caution, to make the salsa as hot as you like.

If you have a long hothouse cucumber, you can skip the step of removing the center, as its seeds are very small.

1 teaspoon sesame seeds

2 medium cucumbers

1 tablespoon rice wine vinegar

1 to 3 teaspoons zehug or chile-garlic sauce

1 teaspoon sesame oil

3 green onions, chopped

Salt and freshly ground pepper, to taste

1. Toast sesame seeds in a small dry skillet over medium heat 1 or 2 minutes or until light golden. Transfer immediately to a plate.

2. Peel cucumbers and cut in half lengthwise. With a teaspoon, remove seed-filled part center. Cut cucumber in small dice.

3. Mix cucumber with rice wine vinegar, 1 teaspoon chile garlic sauce, sesame oil, green onions, and toasted sesame seeds in a bowl. Taste, and add more chile garlic sauce if you like. Add salt and pepper. Refrigerate until ready to serve. Serve cold.

Moroccan Marinade

Makes about ½ cup, enough for
4 servings of fish or chicken

Called tchermela or chermoula, this wonderful marinade of cilantro, garlic, and cumin is a favorite flavoring for fish, whether fried or grilled. I thinks it's also delicious in other ways—for marinating chicken before grilling or roasting it, for marinating meaty vegetables like eggplant or mushrooms, or as a sauce or dressing on its own. When I use it as a marinade, I don't add salt as it draws moisture out of the food.

3 large cloves garlic, peeled

½ to ¾ cup cilantro leaves and fine stems

6 tablespoons olive oil or vegetable oil

1½ teaspoons ground cumin

1 teaspoon paprika

¼ teaspoon freshly ground pepper

⅛ to ¼ teaspoon cayenne pepper

Finely chop garlic in food processor. Add cilantro and chop fine. Transfer to a bowl. Add oil, cumin, paprika, black pepper, and cayenne. Mix well. Refrigerate until ready to use.

Red Pepper Vinaigrette

Makes about 1/2 cup, about 4 servings

This colorful, easy-to-make sauce is dotted with peppers and parsley. Serve it as a partner for Sole Schnitzel (page 331), or spoon it over broiled fish.

3 tablespoons white wine vinegar

Salt and freshly ground pepper, to taste

8 or 9 tablespoons vegetable oil or extra-virgin olive oil

1/4 cup diced red bell pepper

1 tablespoon chopped fresh Italian parsley

Whisk vinegar with salt and pepper in a small bowl. Whisk in oil. Stir in bell pepper and parsley. Adjust seasoning. Just before using, stir vigorously.

Caper-Lemon-Parsley Dressing

Makes about 1/2 cup, about 4 servings

This tangy dressing of capers, herbs, and finely diced lemon is a perfect foil for fried fish like Sole Schnitzel (page 331).

1 lemon

3 tablespoons strained fresh lemon juice

Salt and freshly ground pepper, to taste

5 or 6 tablespoons extra-virgin olive oil

1 tablespoon capers, rinsed and chopped

1 large hard boiled egg or egg white, chopped (optional)

1 tablespoon chopped fresh Italian parsley

Cayenne pepper to taste

1. Use a small serrated knife to cut rind and all bitter white pith from lemon. Hold lemon over a bowl to catch juice and cut inward on each side of membranes to free one section. Cut to release section from lemon. Fold back membrane. Continue with remaining sections. Cut lemon sections into tiny dice. Use juice as part of amount needed for dressing.

2. Whisk 3 tablespoons lemon juice with salt and pepper. Whisk in oil. Stir in capers, diced lemon, chopped egg if using, and parsley. Add cayenne. Adjust seasoning.

Hot Tomatillo Salsa

Makes about 1 1/3 cups

Fish Falafel (page 335) is great with hot salsa. I like it with this green one, made from tangy grilled tomatillos and grilled chiles. The salsa is also good with gefilte fish, as a change from horseradish. It is easy to make in the food processor. Because the heat of jalapeño chiles varies, taste carefully the first time you try it. Use a barbecue, broiler, or stove top grill to grill the tomatillos, onion, and chiles.

To speed up preparation, grill tomatillos, jalapeños, and onion at the same time if there is room on the grill.

1 pound tomatillos (husk tomatoes), husk removed

2 large jalapeño peppers (see Note)

1 small white or yellow onion, peeled

1/2 cup coarsely chopped fresh cilantro leaves and fine stems

1 tablespoon water

Salt, to taste

1. Preheat barbecue, broiler, or stove top grill. Grill tomatillos, turning occasionally, about 5 minutes until they are soft and their skin is charred in spots.

2. Put jalapeños on broiler rack or on grill about 2 inches from heat. Roast jalapeños, turning them often, 5 to 7 minutes or until their skin blisters and chars on all sides. Do not let them burn. Put them in a bowl and cover. Let stand 10 minutes. Peel using paring knife. Discard cap, seeds, and ribs.

3. Cut onion into thick slices. Grill about 5 minutes, turning once, or until lightly charred on both sides.

4. Cut hard stem ends from tomatillos. Put tomatillos, onion, and jalapeños in a food processor. Add cilantro, water, and a pinch of salt. Process until ingredients are pureed, with a few small chunks left. Add more salt, if needed. Refrigerate. Serve cold.

Note: Wear rubber gloves when handling hot peppers.

Poultry

Roasted, Baked, and Grilled Chicken
346

Old-Fashioned Roasted Chicken

Chicken with Challah Stuffing and Roasted Potatoes

Stuffed Chicken with Orzo and Apples

Chicken with Couscous Stuffing, Peppers, and Toasted Almonds

Roasted Chicken with Noodles, Mushrooms, and Toasted Walnuts

Glazed Sweet and Sour Chicken with Ginger

Israeli Baked Chicken with Potatoes and Onions

Baked Chicken Pieces with Orange and Soy Marinade

Aromatic Baked Chicken with Brown Rice

Baked Chicken with Orzo and Tomato Sauce

Baked Chicken with Apples and Prunes

Roasted Chicken from the Soup

Oven-Barbecued Chicken Breasts

Our Family's Favorite Grilled Chicken Legs

Chicken Kebabs from the East

Braised and Poached Chicken
354

Moroccan Jewish Chicken in Grilled Pepper Sauce

Tarragon Chicken

Braised Chicken with Eggplant and Couscous

Braised Chicken with Winter Vegetables

Moroccan Chicken with Prunes, Almonds, and Couscous

Chicken Thighs with Onions and Green Olives

Chicken Potée

Chicken Breasts in Pomegranate-Walnut Sauce

Poached Chicken Breasts

Chicken Livers and Gizzards
360

Broiled Chicken Livers

Chicken Livers and Mushrooms on a Bed of Rice

Livers in Lavosh

Chicken Gizzards in Tomato-Wine Sauce

As a holiday main course, chicken reigns supreme on the Jewish menu. It is loved by Jews everywhere and is prepared in numerous ways.

Kosher chickens, turkeys, and Cornish hens are easy to find at the supermarket. So are a variety of kosher poultry cold cuts and chicken and turkey frankfurters. At kosher grocery stores there also are kosher ducks and geese.

When I was growing up, a well-browned roast chicken was our favorite main course for Shabbat and holidays. Typical of Ashkenazic cooking, it was seasoned simply with pepper and paprika. No extra salt was needed because the chicken was plenty salty from the koshering process, which my mother did at home. Now the kosher chicken at the market has already been salted and so preparation is easier.

My mother often roasts her chicken whole, with or without a stuffing. At other times she bakes it in pieces in a sweet and sour or a barbecue sauce. Many Israeli cooks bake their holiday chicken with vegetables, especially onions and potatoes, and sometimes with carrots, cabbage, eggplant, peppers, or tomatoes. Another variation is baking the chicken in a spiced tomato sauce.

In my husband's family, the holiday chicken is more likely to be braised or poached in an aromatic broth flavored with cumin, turmeric, and pepper in the Yemenite manner. Jews from North Africa often stew the chicken with tomatoes, onions, and garlic. These chicken dishes that cook with liquid are convenient for Shabbat because they reheat easily. Besides, the tasty sauce is terrific on rice or couscous.

Another popular chicken dish prepared in many Jewish communities is a whole "chicken in the pot." The chicken is poached gently until it is very tender and the poaching water turns into a wonderful chicken soup. Traditional for the dinner preceding the Yom Kippur fast, it is also prepared for Shabbat in some families and might be embellished with noodles or matzo balls. I prepare it often with a great variety of seasonal vegetables. Indeed, this simple dish has become such a metaphor for good, old-fashioned home cooking that people who don't have a chance to prepare it, like to order it at Jewish deli-type restaurants, where it has become a standby on menus.

For quick suppers the most popular poultry dish is schnitzel, made of breaded and fried chicken or turkey breasts. Children adore it and therefore many mothers also prepare it for holiday dinners.

For hints on cooking kosher poultry, see Cooking Kosher Foods (page xxiii).

❧ Roasted, Baked, or Grilled Chicken

Old-Fashioned Roasted Chicken

Makes 4 servings

When I was growing up, this was the way my mother most often prepared chicken for our Friday night dinner. I still love the natural taste of chicken prepared this way.

If you like, fill the chicken with Dill and Onion Stuffing (page 374). After you stuff the bird, if you have extra stuffing, spoon it into a small greased baking dish. Bake it for the last 40 to 45 minutes of the chicken's roasting time. Remember that stuffed chickens take longer to roast, so allow another 20 minutes, and insert a skewer into the stuffing, then touch the tip to be sure it is hot. To emphasize the flavor, you can sprinkle the chicken and stuffing at serving time with snipped fresh dill.

One 3¹/₂- to 4-pound chicken
¹/₄ teaspoon salt (optional)
¹/₄ teaspoon freshly ground pepper
¹/₂ teaspoon paprika
2 to 3 teaspoons vegetable oil (optional)
¹/₂ cup chicken stock or broth

1. Preheat oven to 375°F. Trim excess fat around chicken cavity; remove giblets. Mix salt if using, pepper, paprika, and oil, if using, in a bowl. Rub chicken all over with spice mixture. Set chicken in a roasting pan.

2. Roast chicken 30 minutes. Add stock to pan. Roast another 45 minutes to 1 hour, basting chicken occasionally with pan juices. To check whether chicken is done, insert a skewer into thickest part of thigh; juices that run from chicken should be clear. If juices are pink, continue roasting chicken a few more minutes and check again.

3. Transfer chicken to a carving board or platter. Carve chicken and serve hot. If you like, serve with pan juices.

Chicken with Challah Stuffing and Roasted Potatoes

Makes 4 servings

Chicken roasted with potatoes seems to be a Shabbat favorite of Jewish mothers worldwide, probably because the whole family enjoys this dish so much. Filling the chicken with a savory challah stuffing makes it even more festive.

Challah Stuffing (page 373)
One 3¹/₂- to 4-pound chicken
2 teaspoons paprika
3 tablespoons vegetable oil or olive oil
¹/₂ teaspoon salt
¹/₄ teaspoon freshly ground pepper
2 pounds small new potatoes or medium red-skinned potatoes

1. Prepare stuffing. Then, preheat oven to 375°F. Trim excess fat around chicken cavity; remove giblets. Sprinkle chicken with 1 teaspoon paprika and rub it into chicken skin. Spoon stuffing lightly into chicken. Fold skin over stuffing; truss or skewer closed, if desired. Set chicken in a roasting pan large enough to hold potatoes. If any stuffing remains, spoon it into a small greased baking dish.

2. Mix oil with salt, pepper, and remaining paprika in a bowl. If potatoes are small, remove a strip of peel around center. If potatoes are over 1 inch in diameter, quarter them. Put them in a bowl. Add oil mixture and toss potatoes to coat them well. Put potatoes around chicken.

3. Roast chicken 30 minutes; baste chicken and potatoes once or twice. Turn potatoes over and roast 30 more minutes. If pan becomes dry, add ¹/₂ cup hot water. If you have a pan of extra stuffing, put it in oven. Roast chicken 15 to 30 more minutes or until tender. To check whether chicken is done, insert a skewer into thickest part of thigh; juices that run from chicken should be clear. If juices are pink, continue roasting chicken a few more minutes and check again. Also insert a skewer into stuffing inside chicken; it should come out hot. If potatoes are not yet tender, remove chicken, cover potatoes, and roast another 10 or 15 minutes or until tender. Stuffing in extra dish should be hot and firm on top.

4. Transfer chicken to a carving board or platter and remove any trussing strings. Carve chicken and serve hot, with stuffing and potatoes.

Stuffed Chicken with Orzo and Apples

Makes 4 servings

Ⓜ

Apples complement this entree in two ways—in the lemony orzo stuffing and lightly sautéed as an accompaniment for the roasted chicken. A green vegetable such as broccoli, green beans, or zucchini is a good partner for the bird.

Orzo, Lemon, and Walnut Stuffing (page 476)

3 large tart apples, such as Granny Smith or Pippin

One 3¹/2- to 4-pound chicken

Salt (optional) and freshly ground pepper, to taste

2 tablespoons vegetable oil

¹/2 teaspoon ground cinnamon

Fresh parsley sprigs

Lemon quarters

1. Prepare stuffing. Then, preheat oven to 400°F. Peel 1 apple. Grate it on large holes of grater. With a fork, lightly stir grated apple into stuffing.

2. Trim excess fat around chicken cavity, remove giblets. Sprinkle chicken with salt, if using, and pepper. Spoon stuffing inside chicken. Spoon extra stuffing into a baking dish or a microwave container for reheating.

3. Set chicken on a rack in a roasting pan. Roast chicken, basting occasionally, about 40 minutes. If you want to reheat extra stuffing in oven, cover it tightly and add it now. Roast chicken about 20 more minutes. To check whether chicken is done, insert a skewer into thickest part of thigh; juices that run from chicken should be clear. If juices are pink, continue roasting chicken a few more minutes and check again.

4. Meanwhile, peel remaining 2 apples. Core and cut them in eighths. Heat 3 tablespoons oil in a large skillet over medium heat. Add apples and sauté about 3 minutes on each side, or until nearly tender. Sprinkle lightly with about half the cinnamon and sauté 2 minutes. Turn apple pieces over, sprinkle with remaining cinnamon, and sauté 1 or 2 more minutes or until tender and lightly browned; reduce heat if necessary so cinnamon doesn't burn.

5. Transfer chicken to a carving board. Let stand 5 to 10 minutes before serving. Carve chicken.

6. Reheat apples if necessary. Arrange on platter with chicken. Spoon stuffing onto platter or into separate dish. Garnish chicken with parsley sprigs and with lemon quarters, for squeezing fresh lemon juice on stuffing or chicken.

Serving Roasted Chicken for Shabbat and Holiday Meals

Unlike French chefs, Jewish cooks often reheat roasted chicken. It is a particularly common practice for the Shabbat midday meal.

Here's the way I learned to do it from my mother: I often serve a whole roasted chicken for the Friday night dinner. After the meal, I cut what is left into pieces, put it in a baking dish, cover it with foil, and refrigerate it. Thus it's ready to be reheated. (The oven stays on low all night, because the oven shouldn't be turned on during Shabbat.)

The next day, I put the chicken in the oven. On low heat, it often takes an hour to reheat. Gently reheating the covered dish keeps it moist, though you can add a few tablespoons chicken soup or water to the bottom of the pan. (It's best not to reheat a whole bird this way, as it would dry out.)

If there is stuffing in the chicken, it must be removed before the bird is refrigerated, and stored and heated separately.

Chicken with Couscous Stuffing, Peppers, and Toasted Almonds

Makes 4 servings ⓂM

For this luscious dish, sweet peppers and toasted almonds embellish the chicken and appear in the Moroccan style stuffing as well. It's terrific for most holidays: Shabbat, Rosh Hashanah, Sukkot, Hanukkah, or Purim.

Couscous Stuffing with Peppers, Almonds, and Saffron (page 486)

1/3 cup whole unblanched almonds

One 3 1/2- to 4-pound chicken

Salt (optional) and freshly ground pepper, to taste

1 large onion, halved and sliced

2 red bell peppers, cored and quartered lengthwise

1 yellow or green bell pepper, cored and quartered lengthwise

1 tablespoon chopped fresh cilantro or Italian parsley

Fresh cilantro or parsley sprigs

1. Prepare stuffing. Then, preheat oven to 350°F. Toast whole almonds in oven 5 minutes; their color should not change much, but toasting will enhance their aroma. Transfer to a plate. Set oven temperature at 400°F.

2. Trim excess fat around chicken cavity; remove giblets. Sprinkle chicken with salt, if using, and pepper. Spoon stuffing inside chicken. If there is extra stuffing, spoon into a baking dish or a microwave container for reheating.

3. Set chicken in a roasting pan. Put onion slices and bell pepper pieces around chicken. Roast chicken, basting occasionally, about 40 minutes; check from time to time and add a few tablespoons water if pan becomes dry so onion and peppers don't burn. If you want to reheat extra stuffing in oven, cover it tightly and add it now. Roast chicken about 20 more minutes. To check whether chicken is done, insert a skewer into thickest part of thigh; juices that run from chicken should be clear. If juices are pink, continue roasting chicken a few more minutes and check again. Also insert a skewer into stuffing inside chicken; it should come out hot. Transfer chicken to a carving board. Let stand 5 to 10 minutes before serving.

4. Carve chicken and arrange on a platter. With a slotted spoon, remove pepper and onion mixture from roasting pan and add to platter. Sprinkle vegetables with chopped cilantro and top with toasted almonds. Spoon stuffing onto platter or into separate dish. Garnish chicken with cilantro sprigs.

Roasted Chicken with Noodles, Mushrooms, and Toasted Walnuts

Makes 4 servings Ⓜ

For Friday night or holiday dinners, this tasty dish is terrific and is a pleasant change from chicken and noodle kugel. It's much easier to prepare too, and doesn't need any eggs.

One 4-pound roasting chicken
2 to 3 tablespoons vegetable oil
Salt and freshly ground pepper, to taste
$^{1}/_{3}$ cup walnut halves
1 large shallot, minced
8 ounces mushrooms, halved and sliced
6 to 8 medium noodles or fettuccine
1 tablespoon walnut oil or olive oil
2 tablespoons chopped fresh Italian parsley plus a few sprigs for garnish

1. Preheat oven to 400°F. Trim excess fat around chicken cavity; remove giblets. Rub chicken all over with 1 tablespoon vegetable oil and sprinkle it lightly with pepper. Set chicken in a roasting pan just large enough to contain it. Roast chicken, basting it occasionally, about 1 hour. To check whether chicken is done, insert a skewer into thickest part of thigh; juices that run from chicken should be clear. If juices are pink, continue roasting chicken a few more minutes and check again.

2. Meanwhile, toast walnuts in a baking dish in oven, shaking it occasionally, about 7 minutes or until lightly browned. Transfer to a bowl and let cool.

3. Heat 1 or 2 tablespoons vegetable oil in a large skillet. Add shallot, mushrooms, salt, and pepper and sauté over medium-high heat about 3 minutes or until mushrooms brown lightly.

4. Bring a large pot of water to a boil; add salt, then fettuccine. Cook uncovered over high heat, separating strands occasionally with a fork, 2 to 5 minutes or until tender but firm to the bite. Drain well and transfer to pan of mushrooms. Add 1 tablespoon walnut oil, 3 tablespoons of toasted walnuts, and chopped parsley; toss mixture. Season it with salt and pepper.

5. To serve, set chicken on a heated platter and spoon pasta-mushroom mixture around it. Garnish with parsley sprigs. Sprinkle pasta with remaining toasted walnuts. Carve chicken at the table.

Glazed Sweet and Sour Chicken with Ginger

Makes about 6 servings Ⓜ

There are many theories on why Chinese recipes are so popular on Jewish menus. A friend of mine in St. Louis said that when she was growing up, once a week her mother wanted a break from cooking, so they went out to Chinese restaurants to taste food that was exotic and different. I think that with some families the opposite may be true, that the Chinese sweet and sour taste is familiar from Ashkenazic cooking. Still a third theory is that Chinese sauces do not contain dairy products and thus are perfect for serving with meats at a kosher meal.

No matter what theory you subscribe to, this chicken glazed in a ginger-flavored sauce is always a hit at dinner parties. Besides, it's easy to prepare.

One $3^{1}/_{2}$-pound chicken, cut into pieces, or 3 pounds drumsticks
Salt and white pepper, to taste
1 tablespoon minced peeled fresh ginger
$^{1}/_{3}$ cup ketchup
2 tablespoons soy sauce
2 tablespoons rice vinegar
2 tablespoons sugar
$^{1}/_{2}$ cup water
$1^{1}/_{2}$ teaspoons potato starch
Few drops hot pepper sauce (optional)

1. Preheat oven to 400°F. Lightly oil a roasting pan or spray it with oil spray. Put chicken in pan in 1 layer and sprinkle with salt and white pepper. Roast 45 minutes or until meat is no longer pink; cut in thickest part to check.

2. When chicken is nearly done, combine ginger, ketchup, soy sauce, vinegar, sugar, water, and potato starch in a small saucepan and mix well. Cook over medium heat, stirring constantly, until sauce thickens and comes to a simmer. Add hot pepper sauce, if using, to taste. Let cool 5 to 10 minutes before using.

3. Drain off fat from pan of chicken. Brush chicken with about half of sauce. Roast 5 minutes. Turn pieces over and brush with remaining sauce. Roast 5 to 10 more minutes or until glazed and browned. Serve hot.

Israeli Baked Chicken with Potatoes and Onions

Makes 8 servings

Every Jewish mother in Israel seems to make this dish. The reason is simple—the children always love it. And so do the adults. Besides, it's easy to make. Cumin and paprika are the most popular seasonings, and in some homes, turmeric as well, as it gives the chicken and potatoes a lovely orange hue. Serve the chicken with Everyday Israeli Salad (page 238) and with Zucchini in Israeli Tomato Sauce (page 74).

Most people leave the skin on the chicken pieces, but the recipe is still good if you remove the skin; since the chicken is covered as it bakes, the pieces stay moist. You can use chicken breasts but thighs remain more succulent because of the fairly long baking time.

4 pounds boiling potatoes, scrubbed

2 tablespoons ground cumin

1 tablespoon sweet paprika

1¹/₂ teaspoons ground turmeric (optional)

¹/₄ to ¹/₂ teaspoon hot paprika or cayenne pepper (optional)

³/₄ teaspoon freshly ground pepper, plus more to taste

¹/₂ to ³/₄ teaspoon salt, plus more to taste

1 tablespoon olive oil or a little oil spray

4 cloves garlic, chopped

4 pounds chicken thighs

1¹/₂ pounds onions, halved and sliced

1. Preheat oven to 400°F. Peel potatoes if you like. Slice them about ³/₈-inch thick. Mix cumin, paprika, turmeric, and hot paprika if using, ³/₄ teaspoon ground pepper, and ¹/₂ to ³/₄ teaspoon salt in a bowl.

2. Pour 1 tablespoon oil into a large roasting pan or spray it with oil spray. Add potatoes and sprinkle them evenly with salt and pepper. Toss to coat evenly.

Sprinkle potatoes with garlic. Top potatoes with chicken pieces and season them on both sides with spice mixture. Rub mixture into chicken. Top chicken with sliced onions. Cover tightly with foil and bake 1 to 1¹/₄ hours or until chicken is tender when pierced in thickest part with a knife. Potatoes should be tender as well.

3. A short time before serving, uncover chicken. Adjust broiler rack so pan of chicken will be about 4 inches from heat source. Uncover chicken and broil it about 5 minutes or until browned; do not let onions burn. Serve hot.

Baked Chicken Pieces with Orange and Soy Marinade

Makes 4 servings

Choose dark meat, white meat, or some pieces of each according to your family's preferences. This is a good way to prepare lean chicken breasts, as the marinade helps prevent them from drying out. Still, richer chicken legs will be even moister. If you like, garnish the platter of chicken with orange slices. I love this chicken with jasmine rice or brown rice and with cooked carrots and green beans.

¹/₄ cup orange juice

2 tablespoons strained fresh lemon juice

3 tablespoons soy sauce

1 tablespoon vegetable oil

1 tablespoon honey

1 teaspoon grated orange rind

1 medium shallot, minced

1 teaspoon ground ginger

¹/₄ teaspoon ground cloves

Pinch of freshly ground pepper

2³/₄ pounds chicken pieces

1. Mix orange juice, lemon juice, soy sauce, oil, honey, grated orange rind, shallot, ginger, cloves, and pepper in a shallow dish. Add chicken pieces and turn to coat both sides. Rub marinade into chicken. Cover and refrigerate chicken 2 hours or up to 24 hours, turning occasionally.

2. Preheat oven to 400°F. Put chicken with its marinade in a small roasting pan. Bake uncovered 20 minutes. Reduce oven temperature to 350°F. Turn chicken and baste with marinade. Bake 10 minutes; baste again, and cover with foil if chicken is deep brown. Continue baking about 20 more minutes or until chicken is tender. Leg and breast pieces should be tender when pierced in thickest part with a thin, sharp knife and juices that run out of leg pieces should be clear, not pink. Serve hot.

Aromatic Baked Chicken with Brown Rice

Makes 4 servings

I first learned to prepare this tasty Shabbat entree when I lived in Israel, and I have made it often over the years. What makes it delicious is that the rice gains so much taste from the chicken. For many years I used long-grain white rice and although it tasted great, it's texture was very soft. Recently I discovered that I like this dish better when I make it with brown rice, as its longer cooking time makes it the perfect partner for the chicken.

Serve this Sephardic-style chicken and rice with Zucchini in Israeli Tomato Sauce (page 74) or with Glazed Carrots (page 199).

1 or 2 tablespoons vegetable oil

1 large onion, chopped

1¹/₂ cups brown rice

¹/₂ teaspoon freshly ground pepper

2 teaspoons ground coriander

2 teaspoons ground cumin

1 teaspoon ground turmeric

1 teaspoon paprika

3¹/₃ cups cold water

1 teaspoon salt

One 3¹/₂-pound chicken, quartered, or 2¹/₂ to 3 pounds chicken pieces

Fresh cilantro or parsley sprigs

1. Preheat oven to 350°F. Heat oil in a heavy skillet. Add onion and sauté over medium heat, stirring often, about 10 minutes or until golden brown.

2. Transfer onion to a large shallow baking dish. Add rice and mix with onion.

3. Mix pepper, coriander, cumin, turmeric, and paprika in a small bowl. Set aside 2 teaspoons of spice mixture for seasoning chicken. Add remaining mixture to 3¹/₃ cups cold water. Add salt and mix well. Pour evenly over rice in baking dish. Top with chicken pieces, skin side up. Sprinkle chicken with reserved spice mixture. There will appear to be a lot of water but rice will absorb it as it bakes.

4. Bake uncovered about 1 hour and 15 minutes or until chicken is tender when checked with a knife, rice is tender, and water is absorbed. Serve garnished with cilantro or parsley.

Baked Chicken with Orzo and Tomato Sauce

Makes about 6 servings

This festive, simple casserole, pairing chicken thighs with orzo (rice-shaped pasta), is great for Sukkot because it's a portable one-dish meal. It's seasoned with allspice and ground coriander, in the Egyptian Jewish manner.

1 large onion, halved and thinly sliced

2¹/₂ pounds chicken thighs

1 tablespoon olive oil

¹/₂ teaspoon ground allspice

Salt and freshly ground pepper, to taste

2 teaspoons ground coriander

1 cup chicken stock

4 large cloves garlic, minced

1 cup smooth tomato sauce

2 cups boiling water

1 pound orzo or riso (rice-shaped pasta)

2 tablespoons chopped fresh Italian parsley

1. Preheat oven to 400°F. Put onion slices in a large baking dish or roasting pan and top with chicken. Sprinkle chicken with oil, allspice, and pepper and 1 teaspoon coriander. Turn to coat chicken evenly with flavorings.

2. Bake chicken 15 minutes, turning once. Reduce heat to 350°F. Add stock to pan. Bake 20 more minutes. Remove chicken thighs; they will not yet be done.

3. Add garlic, tomato sauce, remaining coriander, and 2 cups boiling water to pan. Season generously with salt and pepper. Add orzo and stir. Bake 15 minutes without stirring. Set chicken on top in 1 layer and press gently into orzo. Return to oven and bake 15 minutes or until chicken is tender when checked with a knife and orzo is tender but slightly firm to the bite. Serve sprinkled with parsley.

Baked Chicken with Apples and Prunes

Makes about 6 servings   **M**

"It is the interplay of tart apples and sweet prunes that makes this dish taste so good," Orit Knoller explained when she gave me this recipe. She brought this easy-to-make dish to a Rosh Hashanah pot-luck dinner, a popular custom these days among working people. With plenty of fruit, it helps symbolize our wish for a sweet year, but it's also a delicious choice for any dinner occasion.

3 pounds chicken thighs

Salt (optional) and freshly ground pepper, to taste

About $1/2$ teaspoon paprika

4 or 5 large tart apples, such as Granny Smith or Pippin

$1/2$ pound large pitted prunes

About $1^1/2$ cups chicken stock

1. Preheat oven to 375°F. Remove skin from chicken, if you like. Put chicken pieces in one layer in a large roasting pan. Sprinkle with salt if using, pepper, and paprika. Core and slice apples; leave peels on. Scatter apple slices and prunes around chicken. Pour stock into side of pan, not over chicken, adding enough to go about $1/4$-inch up sides of pan.

2. Cover and bake 1 hour; check from time to time and add a few tablespoons hot water to pan, adding just enough so juices do not burn but are not soupy. Uncover and bake, basting and checking juice level once or twice, about 15 more minutes or until chicken is tender and slightly brown. Serve hot; spoon juices over chicken and fruit.

Roasted Chicken from the Soup

Makes 4 servings   **M**

Resourceful cooks can make chicken do double duty: after it has simmered until nearly tender to flavor chicken soup, it is put in the roasting pan with spices and browned in the oven, so it can be served as a main course. I've seen both my Polish mother and my Yemenite mother-in-law do this, so it's definitely a widespread custom!

Use chicken and broth from Old-Fashioned Chicken Soup with Kreplach (page 68) or My Mother-in-Law's Spicy Chicken Soup (page 261).

4 cooked chicken legs or thighs, from chicken soup

About $1/2$ to 1 cup chicken soup broth

$1/2$ teaspoon paprika

$1/2$ teaspoon onion powder or ground cumin

Salt and freshly ground pepper, to taste

1. Preheat oven to 350°F. Put chicken pieces in a small roasting pan and add enough soup broth to just cover bottom of pan. Sprinkle chicken with paprika, onion powder or cumin, salt, and pepper.

2. Bake uncovered, basting once or twice, about 15 minutes or until chicken is brown and very tender.

Oven-Barbecued Chicken Breasts

Makes 4 servings

Baking chicken in barbecue sauce was a popular Shabbat dish in our family from the time I was a child. We called it barbecued chicken and for a while didn't realize that barbecue had a different meaning. We loved the chicken with noodle and mushroom kugel (Lukshen Kugel with Mushrooms and Onions, page 198) and with glazed carrots.

Now I like to make it with horseradish barbecue sauce for extra zip but of course you can use any barbecue sauce you like. I add the sauce when the chicken is half done so it won't burn. If you would like extra barbecue sauce to accompany the chicken, double the recipe.

2 medium onions, sliced

2¹/₂ pounds chicken breasts, with skin and bones

2 or 3 teaspoons vegetable oil

¹/₂ teaspoon paprika

Freshly ground pepper to taste

Cayenne pepper to taste

Horseradish Barbecue Sauce (page 375)

1. Preheat oven to 375°F. Lightly oil a roasting pan or spray it with oil spray. Put sliced onion in roasting pan. Lightly rub chicken with oil and sprinkle it with paprika, pepper, and cayenne. Set chicken pieces on onion slices in one layer. Bake chicken uncovered 20 minutes.

2. Prepare sauce while chicken is baking. Then, reduce oven temperature to 350°F. If you like, remove skin from chicken breasts.

3. Spoon about half of sauce over chicken. Bake 15 minutes; cover if chicken begins to brown too fast. Turn chicken pieces over and coat them with remaining sauce. Bake 15 minutes longer or until meat is no longer pink in thickest part; cut to check. Serve hot.

Our Family's Favorite Grilled Chicken Legs

Makes 5 or 6 servings

This may be the main course I make most often for family meals. The reason is simple: everyone in my family loves it, children, teenagers, and adults, no matter where they live—Israel or the United States—and no matter what style of cooking they grew up with—Ashkenazic, Moroccan, Yemenite, Indian, or a mix. The clean, simple tastes appeal to everyone. It's very easy to make. There's no marinade, just a spice rub that you can put on while the barbecue is heating.

3¹/₂ pounds chicken legs (drumsticks with thighs attached)

1 tablespoon olive oil (optional)

4 teaspoons ground cumin

1 teaspoon ground turmeric

¹/₂ teaspoon freshly ground pepper

¹/₄ teaspoon salt (optional)

1. Put chicken on a plate and rub lightly with olive oil, if using. Combine cumin, turmeric, pepper, and salt, if using, in small bowl and rub evenly all over chicken. You can season chicken up to 2 hours ahead and keep, covered, in refrigerator.

2. Heat barbecue or grill. Set chicken on rack 5 to 6 inches above glowing coals or other heat source. Cover and grill about 18 minutes per side, regulating heat to moderate so that chicken cooks through and does not burn. To check whether chicken is done, insert a skewer into thickest part of thigh; juices that run from chicken should be clear. If juices are pink, continue grilling chicken briefly and check again. Serve hot.

Chicken Kebabs from the East

Makes 4 to 6 servings

Perhaps the most common type of restaurant in Israel is known in Hebrew as a Misadah Mizrahit, *which literally means an "Eastern restaurant" and is often mistakenly translated on restaurant signs as "Oriental restaurant." From a culinary standpoint it refers to the food of Jews from Middle Eastern countries. A popular entree at such restaurants is kebabs of lemon-and-garlic marinated chicken, served sizzling on a skewer atop a bed of rice or accompanied by a pita and often by Israeli salad or fried potatoes.*

1/4 cup strained fresh lemon juice

1/4 cup extra-virgin olive oil

1 teaspoon ground white pepper

1 1/2 teaspoons dried oregano, crumbled

1 or 2 large cloves garlic, pressed

A few shakes of cayenne pepper

1 1/2 to 2 pounds boneless skinless chicken breasts or thighs

1 red, yellow, or green bell pepper

Salt, to taste

16 boiling onions, blanched and peeled

16 small or medium mushrooms, stems removed

1. For marinade: Mix lemon juice, oil, white pepper, oregano, garlic, and cayenne in a bowl. Cut chicken into 1 1/4-inch pieces. Put in a bowl. Reserve 2 tablespoons marinade in a ramekin. Add remaining marinade to chicken and mix well. Cover and marinate 2 to 6 hours in refrigerator. If using bamboo skewers, soak them in cold water 30 minutes so they won't burn.

2. Cut pepper into squares of about same size as chicken. Sprinkle chicken with salt, if using. Thread chicken on skewers, alternating with pepper pieces, onions, and mushrooms. Brush chicken and vegetables with marinade; discard any marinade remaining from bowl of chicken. If using bamboo skewers, put foil on ends to prevent burning.

3. Preheat barbecue, stovetop grill, or broiler. Put kebabs on oiled rack. Grill or broil, turning kebabs often and brushing them occasionally with marinade from ramekin. Total grilling time should be 10 to 12 minutes, or until meat is no longer pink; cut to check.

Braised and Poached Chicken

Moroccan Jewish Chicken in Grilled Pepper Sauce

Makes 4 servings

This spicy chicken in its colorful pepper tomato sauce is delicious with brown or white basmati rice, couscous, or potatoes. It's one of my favorite dishes for Rosh Hashanah or Sukkot, when peppers are at the height of their season. It's also good cold, with green salad and North African Carrot Salad With Peas and Corn (page 153).

Roasted Pepper Sauce with Tomatoes and Garlic (page 589)

2 1/2 to 3 pounds chicken pieces, patted dry

1 to 2 tablespoons olive oil

1 large onion, sliced

2 large cloves garlic, chopped

1/4 cup minced fresh cilantro

Salt and freshly ground pepper, to taste

1/2 teaspoon ground cumin

1/2 teaspoon paprika

1 cup water

Fresh cilantro sprigs

1. Prepare pepper sauce. Remove skin from chicken pieces if you like. Heat oil in a heavy stew pan or Dutch oven. Add onion, garlic, and cilantro and cook over medium-low heat, stirring, 5 minutes. Add chicken and sprinkle with salt, pepper, cumin, and paprika. Cover and cook 3 minutes. Pour water into side of pan, not over chicken, and bring to a boil. Cover and simmer over low heat, turning pieces over occasionally, 20 minutes, or until just tender. Transfer chicken pieces with tongs to a plate. Boil onion mixture uncovered until thickened and liquid is reduced to about 1/2 cup.

2. Return chicken to stew pan and add pepper sauce. Cover and cook over low heat, turning chicken pieces occasionally, 20 to 30 minutes, or until chicken is tender. Adjust seasoning. Serve hot or cold, garnished with cilantro.

Tarragon Chicken

Makes 4 servings

Like their countrymen, French Jews enjoy using fresh herbs to add a bright flavor to their cooking. This delicate, easy-to-make entree is great for Shabbat or for before the Yom Kippur fast. Serve it with white or brown rice or with egg noodles to soak up the delicious sauce. Remember to add the tarragon and parsley stems to the chicken's cooking liquid as they contribute good flavor.

6 large sprigs fresh tarragon, plus 3 tablespoons chopped
    fresh tarragon leaves

6 large sprigs fresh Italian parsley, plus 3 tablespoons
    chopped fresh parsley leaves

1 sprig fresh thyme or 1/2 teaspoon dried thyme

1 bay leaf

1 onion, quartered

1 large carrot, left whole

Salt and freshly ground pepper, to taste

2 cups chicken stock and 1 cup water, or 3 cups water

One 3 1/2-pound chicken, cut into 8 serving pieces,
    or 3 pounds chicken pieces

2 tablespoons vegetable oil

2 tablespoons plus 1 teaspoon all-purpose flour

A few drops strained fresh lemon juice (optional)

1. Remove tarragon and parsley leaves from stems; cover leaves and refrigerate. If you like, tie tarragon stems, parsley stems, thyme sprig (not dried thyme), and bay leaf together with string or wrap in cheesecloth to make them easy to remove. Put them in a stew pan. Add onion, carrot, salt, and chicken stock and water. Bring to a simmer.

2. Add chicken and more water if needed so chicken is just covered. Return to a simmer. Skim off foam from top of liquid. Add dried thyme, if using, and freshly ground pepper. Cover and cook over low heat 45 to 50 minutes or until chicken is tender. Remove chicken and discard skin. Skim fat from poaching liquid. Measure 1 1/2 cups cooking liquid to use in making sauce. Return chicken to remaining liquid.

3. Heat oil in a medium, heavy saucepan over low heat. Whisk in flour. Cook, whisking constantly, about 3 minutes or until mixture turns light beige. Remove from heat. Add measured liquid, whisking. Bring to a boil over medium-high heat, whisking. Add pinch of salt and pepper. Simmer uncovered over medium-low heat, whisking often, 5 minutes Add 2 tablespoons chopped tarragon and 2 tablespoons chopped parsley. Adjust seasoning, adding lemon juice, if using.

4. Reheat chicken in its cooking liquid to a simmer. Transfer to a platter, coat with sauce, and sprinkle with remaining herbs.

Braised Chicken with Eggplant and Couscous

Makes 4 servings

Sephardic Jews often cook meat or poultry with eggplant. Here the savory chicken juices enhanced with onion, garlic, and tomatoes give the eggplant and couscous a wonderful flavor. This makes a delicious entree for a Friday night dinner. It's fairly easy to prepare and makes use of the quick method of cooking couscous.

3 pounds chicken pieces

Salt and freshly ground pepper, to taste

2 or 3 tablespoons olive oil

1 large onion, cut into thin slices

4 large cloves garlic, chopped

One 1- or 1 1/4-pound eggplant, peeled, if desired, and diced

One 14 1/2-ounce can diced tomatoes, drained

1 bay leaf

2 sprigs fresh thyme or 1/2 teaspoon dried thyme

1/4 teaspoon hot red pepper flakes

1 1/3 cups chicken stock

1 1/4 cups quick-cooking couscous

1. Sprinkle chicken lightly with pepper. Heat 2 tablespoons oil in a large deep sauté pan. Add chicken in batches and brown lightly on all sides. Remove chicken to a plate.

2. Add onion to pan and cook over low heat about 7 minutes or until soft but not brown. Add garlic and cook 30 seconds. Stir in eggplant. Add tomatoes, bay leaf, thyme, and pepper flakes. Cook 3 minutes, stirring often. Return chicken to pan and add $1/3$ cup stock. Cover and simmer over low heat 35 minutes or until chicken is tender. Discard bay leaf and thyme sprigs. Taste sauce and adjust seasoning.

3. Combine 1 cup stock, 1 tablespoon olive oil, and a pinch of salt in a small saucepan. Bring to a boil. Stir in couscous, then remove from heat. Cover and let stand 5 minutes. Fluff couscous gently with a fork. If you like, gently blend in remaining tablespoon olive oil, using fork. Cover and keep warm.

4. Mound couscous in center of a platter. Arrange chicken and eggplant around it and moisten them with sauce. Serve remaining sauce separately.

Braised Chicken with Winter Vegetables

Makes 4 servings Ⓜ

Cooking chicken with such ordinary staples as cabbage, carrots, and onion might not seem glamorous but this Ashkenazic-style entree is most welcome during the cold weather months. Since it reheats beautifully, it's ideal for Shabbat.

To keep it a meal of comfort food, prepare simple boiled potatoes or Lukshen Kugel with Mushrooms and Onions (page 198) as an accompaniment. For a change of pace, serve Horseradish Mashed Potatoes (page 442) or Mamaliga (page 522).

If you prefer to make the dish as lean as possible, use chicken breasts on the bone, remove their skin, and skip the step of browning. Reduce the oil amount to 1 tablespoon and use it to sauté the onion.

4 medium carrots

1$1/2$ pounds green cabbage (1 fairly small head)

2$1/2$ pounds chicken pieces

Salt and freshly ground pepper, to taste

2 to 3 tablespoons vegetable oil

1 large onion, halved and thinly sliced

Pinch of sugar (optional)

1 to 1$1/4$ cups chicken stock

1 to 2 tablespoons chopped fresh parsley

1. Quarter carrots lengthwise and cut them into 2-inch pieces. Cut cabbage in slices, discarding core. Cut each slice into 3 or 4 strips.

2. Cook cabbage in a large saucepan in boiling water to cover, 2 minutes, or until just wilted. Drain in a colander, rinse under running cold water, and drain well. Gently squeeze cabbage by handfuls to remove excess water.

3. Pat chicken dry and sprinkle it with pepper. Heat 2 tablespoons oil in a large sauté pan or wide stew pan. Add chicken pieces in batches and brown them in oil over medium-high heat. Transfer chicken pieces with tongs to a plate.

4. Add remaining oil if pan is dry and heat it. Add onion and sauté over medium-low heat, stirring often, 7 minutes or until beginning to brown. Add cabbage, salt, and pepper and cook over low heat, stirring, 3 minutes. Return chicken pieces to pan and add juices from plate. Add carrots, sugar if using, and 1 cup stock.

5. Cover and cook over low heat 20 minutes or until chicken breasts are just tender. Transfer breasts with tongs to a plate. Add remaining stock if pan appears dry. Cover and cook remaining chicken 10 more minutes or until tender. Transfer chicken to plate.

6. Check carrots; if they are not yet tender, cover and cook 5 to 10 minutes longer. Taste cabbage mixture and adjust seasoning. Return chicken pieces to pan, cover, and heat through. Serve hot, sprinkled with chopped parsley.

Moroccan Chicken with Prunes, Almonds, and Couscous

Makes 4 or 5 servings Ⓜ

Braising chicken in a sauce that combines saffron with cinnamon, nutmeg, and honey might sound surprising but this is a delicious, spectacular dish. It is one of our favorites for Rosh Hashanah. The traditional way to prepare the almonds is to sauté them, but I toast them in the oven instead. Some people sprinkle the chicken with toasted sesame seeds as well.

3 pounds chicken pieces, patted dry

2 medium onions, minced

Salt and freshly ground pepper, to taste

1 cup chicken stock, broth, or water

A large pinch of saffron threads (about 1/8 teaspoon)

One 2-inch cinnamon stick

1 1/3 cups moist pitted prunes

2 tablespoons honey

Freshly grated nutmeg to taste

2 cups water

1 tablespoon vegetable oil

One 10-ounce package couscous (1 2/3 cups)

1/2 cup whole blanched almonds, toasted

1. Combine chicken, onions, salt, and pepper in a heavy stew pan. Cover and cook over low heat, turning chicken over occasionally, 5 minutes. Add stock, saffron, and cinnamon stick; push it into liquid. Bring to a boil. Cover and simmer over low heat, turning pieces occasionally, about 35 minutes or until breast pieces are tender when pierced with a knife. Transfer them to a plate. Cook remaining chicken, covered, 10 more minutes or until tender. Transfer chicken to plate.

2. Add prunes and honey to sauce and cook uncovered over medium heat 15 minutes or until prunes are just tender. Transfer prunes to a heated bowl, leaving most of onions in casserole. Cover prunes.

3. Discard cinnamon stick. Cook sauce over medium heat, stirring occasionally, about 5 minutes to thicken it slightly. Add nutmeg. Adjust seasoning.

4. Return chicken to stew pan and turn to coat pieces with sauce. Cover and heat over low heat 5 minutes.

5. Combine 2 cups water, oil, and a pinch of salt and pepper in a medium saucepan. Bring to a boil. Stir in couscous, remove from heat, and cover. Let stand 5 minutes.

6. Fluff couscous with a fork and mound it on a heated platter. Arrange chicken around couscous and spoon sauce and prunes over chicken. Garnish with almonds.

Chicken Thighs with Onions and Green Olives

Makes 4 servings

When chicken cooks with plenty of onions, the flavor combination is sensational. I learned this dish from Paule Tourdjman, a Moroccan friend of mine in Paris. She likes to serve it for Shabbat with couscous, and this is indeed a wonderful way to enjoy it, as the couscous absorbs the savory sauce.

2 1/2 pounds chicken thighs, patted dry

Salt and freshly ground pepper, to taste

1 1/2 teaspoons ground cumin

1 teaspoon paprika

2 tablespoons olive oil

1 1/2 pounds onions (about 3 large), halved and thinly sliced

1 cup chicken stock

2 large cloves garlic, chopped

1/4 teaspoon hot red pepper flakes

1/2 cup green olives, pitted

1 tablespoon strained fresh lemon juice, or to taste

2 tablespoons chopped fresh Italian parsley

1. Sprinkle chicken pieces with pepper on both sides. Mix 1 teaspoon cumin with 1/2 teaspoon paprika and sprinkle over chicken. Rub spices into chicken pieces.

2. Heat oil in large deep sauté pan. Add half the chicken thighs and lightly brown them over medium heat about 2 minutes per side. Remove to a plate. Brown remaining chicken pieces and remove.

3. Add onions to pan. Cook over medium-low heat, stirring often, about 15 minutes or until onions soften. If pan appears to be getting too dry, cover onions as they cook.

4. Return chicken to pan and add any juices from plate. Add stock, garlic, pepper flakes, remaining 1/2 teaspoon cumin, and remaining 1/2 teaspoon paprika. Cover and simmer, turning pieces once or twice, 30 minutes. Add olives, cover and simmer 5 to 10 minutes or until chicken is tender. Add lemon juice. Taste sauce and adjust seasoning. Serve hot, sprinkled with parsley.

Chicken Potée

Makes 4 to 6 servings (M)

When I was a student at La Varenne Cooking School in Paris, I learned about a classic French country dish of cooked meats in broth called potée, *which somewhat resembles New England "boiled dinner." Usually it has large chunks of pork and sausages poached with herbs and a variety of vegetables—carrots, turnips, cabbage, potatoes, and sometimes leeks.*

There are different versions of potée from diverse French provinces: potée savoyarde *from the Alpine area of Savoie, to which fresh chestnuts lend their delicate sweetness;* potée *from the region of Champagne, made flavorful with lots of leeks; and the substantial* potée *of Auvergne in central France, in which white beans cook with the meats and other vegetables. In springtime cooks from Lorraine add fresh green beans and peas to their potée.*

In my kitchen I make kosher potée by using chicken breasts and ready-to-eat chicken frankfurters; this also drastically cuts the cooking time and keeps the dish lean. I always add the customary French flavorings of fresh thyme sprigs, bay leaves, and onion. If you like, serve the potée French style in two courses— first the broth with crusty country bread, then a large platter of the meats and vegetables accompanied by hot Dijon mustard.

1³/₄ cups chicken broth

6 cups water

1 large onion, cut into large dice

1 bay leaf

4 sprigs fresh thyme or 1 teaspoon dried thyme

1 medium turnip, peeled and cut into 8 wedges

4 medium potatoes, quartered

4 large carrots, scrubbed and cut into 1-inch lengths

2 ribs celery, cut into 1-inch lengths

¹/₂ small cabbage, cored and cut into 4 wedges

4 chicken breast halves, with bones, skin removed

Salt and freshly ground pepper, to taste

8 ounces low-fat chicken or turkey frankfurters

1. Combine chicken broth, water, onion, bay leaf, and thyme sprigs in a stew pan or Dutch oven. Bring to a boil. Add turnip, potatoes, carrots, and celery. Return to a boil. Add cabbage, chicken, salt, and pepper. Bring to a simmer. Cover and cook over medium-low heat, so that liquid simmers, 20 minutes. Add frankfurters and cook 5 to 10 minutes or until chicken and vegetables are tender. Discard bay leaf and thyme sprigs. Skim fat from soup. Adjust seasoning.

2. To serve in two courses, remove a few of the vegetables from broth and dice. Then, remove chicken pieces, frankfurters, and remaining vegetables to a platter. As a first course, serve broth with diced vegetables. As a main course, serve poultry and whole vegetables in deep plates with a little broth spooned over the top to moisten the dish. To serve as one course, you may want to take the chicken off the bone and slice the frankfurters beforehand.

Chicken Breasts in Pomegranate-Walnut Sauce

Makes 4 to 6 servings (M)

Cooking chicken with walnuts and pomegranate paste is typical of both Persian (now Iran) and Georgian (south of Russia) cuisine. At first the flavors might seem very exotic but the combination makes perfect sense. From the walnuts, the sauce gains a creamy quality without any dairy products. The pomegranate paste gives a sweet and sour taste. The sauce is slightly pink but the dish is not colorful. You can perk up the color by sprinkling chopped parsley or by scattering fresh pomegranate seeds when the fruit is in season.

You can find pomegranate paste at Middle Eastern and Greek grocery stores. Sometimes it is labeled pomegranate molasses or pomegranate concentrate. Be sure that the walnuts are very fresh.

Duck is the traditional choice of Jews from Iran and many families cook meatballs this way. I prefer leaner chicken breasts in the rich sauce. Serve this dish with a generous mound of basmati rice.

2 cups walnuts

2 tablespoons vegetable oil

2 1/2 pounds chicken breasts with skin and bones, patted dry

1 large onion, halved and thinly sliced

1/3 to 1/2 cup pomegranate paste, molasses, or concentrate

1 cup water

1/2 teaspoon ground allspice

Salt and freshly ground pepper, to taste

1 tablespoon tomato paste (optional)

1 to 2 teaspoons sugar (optional)

1 to 2 teaspoons strained fresh lemon juice (optional)

1. Finely grind walnuts in food processor with brief pulses.

2. Heat oil in a wide casserole or Dutch oven. Add chicken in batches and sauté over medium-high heat until brown. Remove chicken to a plate. Discard all but 2 tablespoons oil from pan.

3. Add onion to pan and sauté over medium heat about 10 minutes or until golden. Add walnuts and stir a few seconds over heat. Mix 1/3 cup pomegranate paste with water. Add to pan and bring to a simmer. Add chicken and any juices on plate, allspice, salt, and pepper. Cover and cook over low heat, turning over occasionally, about 35 minutes or until chicken is tender. Sauce will not be smooth. Stir in tomato paste, if using. Taste; if you like, add another 1 to 3 tablespoons pomegranate paste mixed with 1/4 cup water and simmer 1 or 2 minutes. Adjust seasoning. Add sugar and/or lemon juice, if using, to enhance the sweetness or tartness. Serve chicken topped with sauce.

Note: If you prefer, remove chicken skin before cooking; instead of browning chicken, sauté it over medium heat only until meat changes color.

Poached Chicken Breasts

Makes about 8 servings,
or 3 to 4 cups diced chicken for salads

When you poach chicken breasts, add them to hot liquid to keep in their flavor, unlike chicken for soup, which you start in cold water to slowly draw out its flavor into the liquid. Poach chicken breasts on the bone so the meat will be more moist and flavorful. Chicken cooked this way makes delicious salads and sandwiches. You can also serve it hot with homemade tomato sauce or Mediterranean Green Sauce for Vegetables (page 462), which also happens to be wonderful with chicken.

Although the poaching liquid will not be concentrated, you can save it to use as a light stock or soup. If you want a more flavorful soup, return the chicken bones to the liquid after you remove the meat, and cook them 1 more hour.

1 onion, sliced

1 large carrot, sliced

2 ribs celery with leaves, sliced (optional)

2 bay leaves

1 large sprig fresh thyme or 1 teaspoon dried thyme

1/2 cup dry white wine (optional)

Salt and freshly ground pepper, to taste

4 to 6 cups water

7 or 8 chicken breast halves, with skin and bones

1. Combine onion, carrot, celery if using, bay leaves, thyme, wine if using, salt, and pepper in a sauté pan with 4 cups water. Bring to a simmer. Add chicken and more water if needed so chicken is just covered with liquid. Return to a simmer. Cover and cook over low heat about 25 minutes or until chicken is tender.

2. Remove skin before serving chicken. If using for salad or sandwiches, also remove bones and any visible fat. Reserve poaching liquid for other uses.

❧ Chicken Livers and Gizzards

Broiled Chicken Livers

Makes 2 to 4 servings, depending on recipe

Chicken livers are broiled or grilled over an open flame to kosher them. The process cooks the livers completely. Then they are ready to be used to make chopped liver or other appetizers or main courses.

¹/₂ to 1 pound chicken livers
Kosher salt

Preheat broiler with rack about 3 inches from flame. Rinse livers and pat dry on paper towels; cut livers in half. Cut off any green spots. Put livers on foil-lined broiler rack and sprinkle with kosher salt. Broil 3 minutes or until they are light brown on top. Turn livers over, sprinkle second side with kosher salt, and broil 3 or 4 more minutes or until cooked through; check to be sure their color has changed inside. Discard juices from foil.

Foie Gras, An Israeli Specialty

Many people will be surprised to learn that France, a country famous for its fine produce and ingredients, imports produce from Israel. Even more surprising is that one of the signature foods served at top French restaurants—foie gras—often comes from Israel.

For some years, Israel has been specializing in producing foie gras (fattened goose or duck liver). It used to be reserved just for export, but it has become a restaurant specialty in certain Mediterranean-style restaurants in Israel, too. It is prepared differently than in France. In Israel, it's grilled—a real treat, and kosher too.

Foie gras is not easy to obtain for home cooking. For those who like foie gras, in these Israeli restaurants it is a good value for its price, as it is not as expensive as in Europe and the United States.

Chicken Livers and Mushrooms on a Bed of Rice

Makes 4 servings

Sautéed livers with browned onions are a favorite among Jews of all origins, and they're even better with mushrooms. Following the rules of kashrut, the livers are first broiled, then only briefly sautéed to heat them through and blend them with the onions and mushrooms.

If you prefer a kebab-style presentation, you can thread the livers on skewers and grill or broil them until done and skip the step of sautéing. Serve the skewered livers on a bed of rice and accompany them with the mushroom mixture.

5 tablespoons vegetable oil
2 large onions, thinly sliced
Salt and freshly ground pepper, to taste
2 cloves garlic, chopped
12 ounces small mushrooms, quartered
1¹/₂ teaspoons sweet paprika
1 pound chicken livers
Kosher salt
¹/₂ cup canned tomato puree (optional)
¹/₄ teaspoon hot paprika or cayenne pepper
3 to 4 cups hot cooked rice

1. Heat 2 tablespoons oil in a large, heavy skillet. Add onions, salt, and pepper and sauté 2 minutes over medium heat. Cover and cook over medium-low heat, occasionally, about 10 minutes or until tender but not brown. Add garlic and mushrooms and sprinkle with salt, pepper, and 1 teaspoon sweet paprika. Sauté over medium-high heat, stirring often, about 3 minutes or until mushrooms are tender and onions begin to brown.

2. Preheat broiler with rack about 3 inches from flame. Rinse livers and pat dry on paper towels; cut off any green spots. Put livers on foil in broiler and sprinkle with kosher salt. Broil 3 minutes or until top is light brown. Turn livers over, sprinkle second side with salt, and broil 3 or 4 more minutes or until brown. Discard juices from foil. Cut livers in half.

3. Reheat mushroom mixture in skillet over medium heat. If you would like mixture to be more sauce-like, stir in tomato puree and bring to a boil. Adjust seasoning. Cover and keep warm.

4. In another skillet heat remaining 2 tablespoons oil over medium-high heat. Add livers and sprinkle with remaining sweet paprika and hot paprika. Toss over heat about 1 minute or until heated through.

5. To serve, mound rice on plates, spoon mushroom mixture over rice, and top with livers.

Livers in Lavosh

Makes 4 servings

This seemingly surprising combination is inspired by a modern Tel Aviv specialty—grilled foie gras that is served with a soft bread resembling fresh lavosh that Israelis call Iraqi pita. Israel is now a major producer of foie gras, or livers of fattened geese or ducks, and exports it to France. At restaurants in the Hatikvah Market district of Tel Aviv, the foie gras is served on skewers. The diners scoop the rich cubes into the pita bread and roll it up, for a melt-in-your-mouth delight.

For this recipe, broiled chicken livers are heated with browned onions and spices, then rolled in lavosh. If you don't have fresh lavosh, you can use thin flour tortillas.

2 or 3 tablespoons olive oil or vegetable oil

2 large onions, thinly sliced

Salt and freshly ground pepper, to taste

1 pound chicken livers

Kosher salt

1¹/2 teaspoons ground cumin

¹/2 teaspoon dried oregano

¹/4 teaspoon cayenne pepper

4 sheets fresh lavosh, about 8- or 9-inch square

1. Heat oil in a large, heavy skillet. Add onions, salt, and pepper and sauté over medium heat, stirring often, about 10 minutes or until tender and browned.

2. Cut livers in half. Cut out any green spots and discard. Rinse and pat livers dry with paper towels.

3. Preheat broiler with rack about 3 inches from flame. Put livers on foil-lined broiler rack and sprinkle with kosher salt. Broil 3 minutes or until they are light brown on top. Turn livers over, sprinkle second side with kosher salt, and broil 3 or 4 more minutes or until cooked through; check to be sure their color has changed inside. Discard juices from foil. Cut each liver into 2 to 4 pieces.

4. Reheat onions in skillet. Add livers and sprinkle with cumin, oregano, cayenne, and freshly ground pepper. Sauté over medium heat, stirring, 1 or 2 minutes or until mixture is hot and spices are blended in.

5. Serve livers immediately, with lavosh. Roll up and enjoy!

Chicken Gizzards in Tomato-Wine Sauce

Makes about 6 servings

Both Ashkenazic and Sephardic Jews make good use of all parts of the chicken. Those who have tasted slowly cooked, tender chicken gizzards prize them and the flavorful sauce they create as they simmer. Serve these with rice, egg barley, or pareve polenta.

2 tablespoons olive oil or vegetable oil

1 large onion, diced

3 large cloves garlic, chopped

2 pounds chicken gizzards, halved

2 tablespoons all-purpose flour

¹/2 cup dry red wine

1 cup chicken broth or water

One 14-ounce can diced tomatoes, drained

1 tablespoon tomato paste

1¹/2 pounds chicken wings, cut apart at joints and patted dry

1 bay leaf

Salt and freshly ground pepper, to taste

1 teaspoon dried oregano

2 tablespoons chopped fresh Italian parsley

Heat oil in a deep, heavy casserole. Add onion and sauté over medium heat 7 minutes or until golden. Stir in garlic and gizzards and sauté 2 or 3 minutes. Sprinkle with flour and sauté over low heat, stirring, 2 minutes. Stir in wine and bring to a boil. Stir in broth, tomatoes, and tomato paste. Add wings, bay leaf, pepper, and oregano. Bring to a simmer. Cover and simmer, stirring occasionally so flour won't stick, about 1 hour 15 minutes or until gizzards are tender. Discard bay leaf. Taste and add salt and more pepper if needed. Serve hot, sprinkled with parsley.

✿ Roasted Turkey

Roasted Turkey with Fruity Almond Rice Stuffing

Makes 6 to 8 servings Ⓜ

Festive and delicious, this roasted turkey is perfect for Rosh Hashanah or for Thanksgiving. Raisins and orange juice flavor the sauce, echoing the tastes in the stuffing. For a special touch, garnish the stuffing on the platter with whole toasted almonds.

Almond, Fruit, and Rice Stuffing (page 506)
One 10- to 12-pound fresh or thawed frozen turkey
Salt and freshly ground pepper, to taste
3 to 4 tablespoons vegetable oil
3 cups chicken stock
1/2 cup orange juice
4 teaspoons cornstarch dissolved in 3 tablespoons dry white wine or water
1/4 cup golden raisins

1. Prepare stuffing. Then, remove top rack from oven and preheat to 425°F. Sprinkle inside of turkey with salt and pepper. Spoon some stuffing into neck cavity. Fold neck skin under body and fasten with a skewer. Pack body cavity loosely with stuffing and cover opening with a crumpled piece of foil. Truss turkey if desired or close it with skewers. Spoon remaining stuffing into a greased 1-quart baking dish.

2. Put turkey, breast side up, on a rack in a large roasting pan. Spread turkey with oil and sprinkle with salt and pepper. Roast 30 minutes, basting twice.

3. Reduce oven temperature to 350°F. Roast turkey 1 1/2 hours, basting with pan juices every 15 minutes. If pan becomes dry, add 1/4 cup chicken stock.

4. Put dish of extra stuffing in oven and baste with 1 or 2 tablespoons turkey juices. Cover stuffing with foil; bake about 45 minutes. Cover turkey loosely with foil and continue roasting 20 to 45 minutes, or until meat thermometer inserted into thickest part of thigh registers 180°F, or until juices run clear when thickest part of thigh is pricked.

5. Transfer turkey carefully to platter or large board. Discard any trussing strings or skewers. Baste turkey once with pan juices, and cover turkey.

6. Skim excess fat from juices in pan. Add 1 cup stock to pan and bring to a boil, stirring and scraping to dissolve any brown bits in pan. Strain into a saucepan. Add remaining stock and orange juice. Bring to a boil. Set pan over medium heat. Whisk in cornstarch mixture. Return to boil, whisking. Add raisins. Simmer sauce until it is thick enough to lightly coat a spoon. Cook another 1 to 2 minutes or until raisins are tender. Adjust seasoning.

7. Carve turkey and arrange on platter. Spoon stuffing onto platter or into a serving dish. Serve reheated sauce in a sauceboat alongside turkey.

Turkey with Pecan and Mushroom Stuffing

Makes 8 to 10 servings Ⓜ

This turkey with its delicious bread stuffing flavored generously with nuts, vegetables, and herbs, is great for Thanksgiving, Sukkot, or Shabbat.

Pecan and Mushroom Stuffing (page 373)
One 14-pound turkey
Salt and freshly ground pepper, to taste
1/4 cup plus 3 tablespoons vegetable oil
3 cups turkey or chicken stock, more if needed for basting
1/2 cup dry white wine
1/4 cup all-purpose flour

1. Prepare stuffing. Then, remove top rack from oven and preheat to 400°F. Sprinkle inside of turkey with salt and pepper. Spoon some stuffing into neck cavity. Fold neck skin under body and fasten with a skewer. Pack body cavity loosely with stuffing and cover opening with a crumpled piece of foil. Truss turkey if desired or close it with skewers. Spoon remaining stuffing into a greased 1- to 1 1/2-quart baking dish.

2. Put turkey, breast side up, on a rack in a large roasting pan. Spread turkey with 3 tablespoons oil and sprinkle with salt and pepper. Roast 30 minutes, basting twice.

3. Reduce oven temperature to 325°F. Roast turkey 30 minutes, basting with pan juices or with stock every 15 minutes.

4. Cover turkey loosely with foil. Roast 1 hour, basting turkey with pan juices every 30 minutes. If pan becomes dry, add 1/4 cup wine.

5. Put dish of extra stuffing in oven and baste with 1 or 2 tablespoons turkey juices. Cover stuffing with foil; bake about 45 minutes. Meanwhile, cover turkey loosely with foil and continue roasting 20 to 45 minutes, or until meat thermometer inserted into thickest part of thigh registers 180°F, or until juices run clear when thickest part of thigh is pricked.

6. Transfer turkey carefully to platter or large board. Discard any trussing strings or skewers. Baste turkey once with pan juices, and cover turkey.

7. Skim excess fat from juices in pan. Add remaining wine and 1/2 cup stock to pan and bring to a boil, stirring and scraping to dissolve any brown bits in pan. Boil liquid until reduced to about 1/2 cup and strain into a bowl.

8. Heat 1/4 cup oil in a large, heavy saucepan over low heat. Whisk in flour. Cook, whisking constantly, about 3 minutes or until mixture turns light beige. Remove from heat and let cool slightly. Gradually pour remaining 2 1/2 cups stock into flour mixture, whisking. Bring to a boil over medium-high heat, whisking constantly. Whisk in strained wine mixture. Simmer uncovered over medium-low heat, whisking often, about 5 minutes or until sauce is thick enough to coat a spoon. Taste, and add salt and pepper if needed.

9. Carve turkey and arrange on platter. Spoon stuffing onto platter or into a serving dish. Serve reheated sauce in a sauceboat alongside turkey.

Spiced Roasted Turkey

Makes 6 to 8 servings

When I want a roast turkey that doesn't take too long to cook, I bake my stuffing in a separate dish and not inside the bird. Stuffings that are good with this turkey are Challah Stuffing, Pecan and Mushroom Stuffing, and Spicy Matzo Stuffing (pages 373–374).

This aromatic turkey is seasoned with our family's favorite spice mixture—cumin, turmeric, and black pepper. Kosher turkeys do not need salt as they have already been salted. The spices give the bird a delicate aroma and flavor. To reinforce the taste, I like to serve a separate tomato sauce accented with the same spices— Hot Cumin-Tomato Sauce (page 587). Sometimes I add some of the turkey roasting juices to the sauce.

5 teaspoons ground cumin

1 1/2 teaspoons ground turmeric

1 teaspoon freshly ground pepper

Salt, to taste (optional)

One 10- to 12-pound fresh or thawed frozen turkey

About 2 to 4 tablespoons olive oil

About 3/4 cup chicken or turkey stock or dry white wine

1. Preheat oven to 425°F and remove top rack. Mix cumin, turmeric, pepper, and salt in a small bowl. Rub turkey with olive oil. Rub it inside and out with spice mixture. Truss turkey if desired or close it with skewers.

2. Put turkey on a rack in a large roasting pan. Pour 1/2 cup stock into pan. Roast turkey 30 minutes.

3. Reduce oven temperature to 350°F. Roast turkey 1 1/2 hours, basting with additional olive oil or with pan juices every 30 minutes. If pan becomes dry, add 1/4 cup stock.

4. Cover turkey loosely with foil and continue roasting 20 to 30 minutes, or until meat thermometer inserted into thickest part of thigh registers 180°F, or until juices run clear when thickest part of thigh is pricked.

5. Transfer turkey carefully to platter or large board. Discard any trussing strings or skewers. Baste turkey once with pan juices, and cover turkey. Reserve juices if you want to add them to a sauce.

6. Carve turkey and arrange on platter. Serve hot.

❧ Braised Turkey

Middle Eastern Turkey and Rice Supper

Makes 4 servings

This is a turkey version of a favorite chicken dish of Sephardic Jews from Middle Eastern countries, who pair the bird with rice for a stove-cooked whole-meal casserole somewhat resembling the Latin American arroz con pollo. *Flavored with peppers, cumin, and turmeric, the aromatic yellow rice gains extra taste from the meat. Using turkey breast fillets makes this version low in fat and quick cooking.*

1¼ to 1½ pounds boneless turkey breast fillets,
    cut into 1-inch cubes

Salt and freshly ground pepper, to taste

½ teaspoon ground turmeric

1½ teaspoons ground cumin

1 or 2 tablespoons olive oil or vegetable oil

1 medium onion, halved and thinly sliced

2 red or green bell peppers or 1 of each, cut into thin strips

2 large cloves garlic, minced

1 cup long-grain white rice

¼ teaspoon hot red pepper flakes

2 cups hot turkey, chicken, or vegetable stock or water

3 canned tomatoes, chopped

    1. Sprinkle turkey pieces on both sides with pepper, turmeric, and a total of 1 teaspoon cumin. Rub seasonings into turkey.

    2. Heat oil in a large, deep, heavy skillet or sauté pan. Add turkey pieces in 2 batches and brown them lightly over medium-low heat, removing each batch as it changes color.

    3. Add onion to skillet and sauté over low heat 3 minutes. Add peppers and garlic and cook, stirring often, about 5 minutes. Add rice, a pinch of salt, pepper flakes, and remaining cumin and sauté over low heat, stirring, 1 minute. Add turkey pieces. Add stock and tomatoes and bring to a simmer. Cover tightly and

cook over low heat, without stirring, 25 to 30 minutes or until turkey and rice are tender and liquid is absorbed. If liquid is absorbed but rice is not yet tender, add a few tablespoons water and simmer a few more minutes. Serve hot.

Braised Turkey Drumsticks in Red Wine and Porcini Sauce

Makes 6 to 8 servings

Cooked gently in the Italian style, these turkey legs in their richly flavored, vegetable-thickened sauce are terrific for Purim or for Shabbat. Serve them with pasta. Plain egg noodles or fettuccine are fine accompaniments, or you might like to serve a savory noodle kugel or an Orzo, Lemon, and Walnut Stuffing (page 476). Rice or Mamaliga (page 522) are also good with this turkey.

4 large sprigs fresh thyme or 1 teaspoon dried thyme

2 fresh sprigs marjoram or ½ teaspoon dried marjoram

1 bay leaf

2 whole cloves

2 tablespoons olive oil

1 large onion, diced

1 rib celery, diced

2 large carrots, diced

6 large cloves garlic, chopped

1½ cups dry red wine

3½ pounds turkey drumsticks or thighs

1 pound ripe tomatoes, diced, or one 28-ounce can
    tomatoes, drained and diced

Salt and freshly ground pepper, to taste

2 cups turkey or chicken stock or water, or mixed stock
    and water

2 ounces dried porcini or shiitake mushrooms

1 tablespoon chopped fresh oregano or 1 teaspoon dried

2 tablespoons cornstarch or potato starch (optional)

4 tablespoons chopped fresh Italian parsley

    1. Wrap thyme, marjoram, bay leaf, and cloves in cheesecloth and tie ends together to form a seasoning bag. Heat oil in a large stew pan or Dutch oven. Add onion, celery, and carrot and sauté over medium heat, stirring often, about 10 minutes or until onion softens and begins to turn golden. Stir in garlic and sauté 30 seconds. Add wine, seasoning bag, and turkey. Bring to a boil and cook uncovered over medium heat, turning turkey from time to time, 5 minutes. Add tomatoes, salt, pepper, and stock. Bring to a boil. Cover and simmer over low heat, turning turkey pieces over from time to time, 2 hours or until turkey is very tender when pierced in thickest part with a knife.

2. Meanwhile, soak dried mushrooms in a bowl of enough hot water to cover them for 30 minutes. Remove mushrooms and rinse. If using shiitake mushrooms, discard stems. Cut mushrooms into bite-size pieces.

3. Remove turkey from liquid. Remove skin with a paring knife. Discard turkey bones, cartilage, and visible fat Pull or cut meat into wide strips. Discard seasoning bag. Skim fat from cooking liquid.

4. Puree vegetables with about 1 cup cooking liquid in a food processor or blender, or work vegetables through a food mill. Return to pan.

5. Add mushrooms to stew pan. Add dried oregano if using (but not fresh). Cook about 10 minutes or until mushrooms are tender. Season sauce with salt and pepper.

6. If you would like a thicker sauce, mix cornstarch with 1/4 cup water in small bowl until blended. Bring sauce to a simmer. Gradually whisk in about half of cornstarch solution and simmer 1 to 2 minutes or until thickened. Adjust seasoning. Return turkey to sauce and heat gently. Stir in 3 tablespoons parsley. Serve sprinkled with remaining parsley.

Turkey Franks and Beans in Tomato Sauce

Makes 4 to 6 servings

Both Ashkenazic and Sephardic cooks have long known that economical sausages do wonders to help perk up the bland taste of beans, even if the meat is used in small amounts. This combination, usually moistened with tomato sauce, is a standard weekday dish in many homes. My mother used mild beef frankfurters when I was growing up. Spicy sausages are favored in many Sephardic families. Today there is much greater choice. Alongside the old-fashioned beef franks you can buy reduced-fat versions as well as chicken and turkey wieners. There are even vegetarian hot dogs in case you want to prepare this as a pareve dish.

1 pound dried white beans (about 2¹/₃ cups)

1 bay leaf

2 onions, one whole and one chopped

2¹/₂ quarts water

1 to 2 tablespoons olive oil

1 small green bell pepper, diced

1 teaspoon paprika

¹/₄ teaspoon hot red pepper flakes, or cayenne pepper to taste

5 large cloves garlic, minced

Two 28-ounce cans diced tomatoes with their juice

2 teaspoons dried oregano

Salt and freshly ground pepper, to taste

³/₄ to 1 pound turkey frankfurters

2 tablespoons chopped fresh cilantro

1. Sort beans, discarding any broken ones and any stones. Rinse beans and drain. Put them in a large saucepan and add bay leaf, 1 whole onion, and water. Bring to a boil. Cover and simmer over low heat, adding hot water if necessary so that beans remain covered, about 1¹/₂ hours or until beans are tender. Discard onion and bay leaf.

2. Heat oil in a large skillet. Add chopped onion and green pepper and sauté over medium heat, stirring occasionally, about 5 minutes or until golden brown. Add paprika, pepper flakes, and garlic and sauté 30 seconds. Add tomatoes, oregano, salt, and pepper. Cook over medium heat, stirring often, about 20 minutes or until sauce is thick.

3. Cover frankfurters with water in a medium saucepan and bring just to a simmer. Cover and cook over low heat 5 minutes or according to package instructions. Drain well.

4. Reheat beans and drain well. Gently mix tomatoes with beans. Add sausages, cover, and cook over low heat 5 minutes to blend flavors. Add cilantro. Adjust seasoning.

✳ Ground Chicken and Turkey

Celery with Aromatic Chicken Stuffing

Makes 4 servings

A friend of mine born in Tunisia taught me how to make this tasty stuffed vegetable. She serves it for her Friday night dinner as part of her "grand couscous" along with other poached vegetables and braised meats. She uses ground beef for the stuffing. My chicken version is leaner.

6 large ribs celery plus 1 tablespoon chopped celery leaves

1 small onion, minced

2 slices white bread

1/2 pound ground chicken

3 tablespoons chopped fresh Italian parsley or cilantro

1 teaspoon dried oregano

1 teaspoon paprika

1/2 teaspoon freshly ground pepper

1/4 teaspoon cayenne pepper

3 large cloves garlic, minced

1/4 teaspoon salt (optional)

1 large egg

2 or 3 tablespoons olive oil

Quick Tomato Sauce for Vegetables (page 463)

1. Peel celery to remove strings. Cut celery into 3-inch lengths. Pat dry.

2. Put onion in a strainer and sprinkle lightly with salt. Let stand about 5 minutes. Dip each bread slice in a bowl of water to moisten. Rinse onions in strainer. Add soaked bread to onions in strainer and squeeze both dry.

3. Mix chicken with onions, bread, celery leaves, parsley, oregano, paprika, pepper, cayenne, garlic, and 1/4 teaspoon salt, if using, in a medium bowl. Add egg and mix well. Knead mixture briefly to be sure ingredients are evenly combined. Put chicken mixture inside celery pieces and press so it adheres well.

4. Heat oil in a large deep skillet, preferably nonstick, over medium heat. Add stuffed celery, filling side down, and fry 3 minutes. Carefully remove with slotted spatula.

5. Prepare sauce in same skillet. Bring sauce to a simmer. Carefully add celery, stuffing side up. Cover and cook over low heat 30 to 40 minutes or until celery is very tender, adding a little hot water occasionally if sauce becomes too thick. Taste sauce and adjust seasoning. Serve hot or at room temperature.

Sephardic Turkey Balls in Tomato Sauce

Makes 4 to 6 servings

Beef and lamb are the traditional meats used for meatballs but with ground turkey readily available, many people are opting for this lighter version.

To make these turkey balls leaner still, omit the step of browning them in oil. Instead double the tomato sauce and cook the turkey balls in it about 30 minutes.

Sephardic Tomato Sauce (page 375)

1 1/4 pounds ground turkey

3 tablespoons matzo meal

2 large cloves garlic, minced

2 tablespoons minced fresh Italian parsley

1 teaspoon ground cumin

1/2 teaspoon ground allspice

1/4 teaspoon ground cinnamon

1/2 teaspoon salt

1/2 teaspoon freshly ground pepper

4 tablespoons olive oil

1. Prepare sauce. Then, put turkey in a bowl. Mix matzo meal with garlic, parsley, cumin, allspice, cinnamon, salt, and pepper in a small bowl. Add to turkey and mix well. Make small meatballs, using 2 tablespoons of mixture for each, and roll them between your palms until smooth. Transfer to a plate. Refrigerate 5 minutes.

2. Heat oil in large, heavy skillet over medium heat. Add meatballs in 2 batches and brown them lightly on all sides. With slotted spoon, transfer to paper towels.

3. Heat sauce in a sauté pan or shallow saucepan just to a simmer. Add turkey balls. Cover and cook over low heat 20 to 25 minutes or until cooked through. Taste sauce and adjust seasoning.

Garlic-Scented Turkey Patties

Makes 4 servings

Lean turkey patties are a favorite in many kitchens. These are seasoned in the Israeli style, with cumin and plenty of garlic. You can grill them but they will remain more moist if you sauté them, as this recipe. Serve them in pita bread and top them with Sephardic Salsa (page 131) or Cilantro Salsa (page 341) and, if you like, Tahini Sauce (page 437). You might also wish to add some Israeli salad and a few pickle slices.

4 large cloves garlic, pressed

2 teaspoons ground coriander

1 teaspoon ground cumin

1/2 teaspoon freshly ground pepper

Pinch of cayenne pepper

1/4 teaspoon salt (optional)

1 1/4 pounds ground turkey

2 tablespoons olive oil or vegetable oil

1. Mix garlic with coriander, cumin, pepper, cayenne, and salt, if using, in a bowl. Add spice mixture to turkey and mix lightly to blend. Shape in 4 patties.

2. Heat oil in a medium skillet. Add burgers and sauté over medium heat about 3 minutes on each side or until they are springy when pressed. Serve immediately.

Whole Stuffed Zucchini with Turkey, Raisins, and Pecans

Makes 4 to 6 servings

For this festive version of stuffed zucchini, the turkey and rice filling has a tasty embellishment of nuts and raisins. By using ground turkey, you keep the filling lean and healthful. If your family prefers rich stuffings, you can make this stuffing with beef instead.

Jews from Middle Eastern countries love to form whole zucchini into tubes for stuffing; this way the stuffing is completely enclosed. The best zucchini for stuffing whole are the small, pale-green-skinned zucchini that are slightly thicker than the common dark-skinned zucchini. In some markets these are sold as

Mexican zucchini. If you are using the dark-green zucchini, the easiest way to prepare them is to first cut the vegetable in two crosswise, so you have two stuffed zucchini from each one.

1/2 cup long-grain white rice, rinsed and drained

4 tablespoons vegetable oil

1 medium onion, finely chopped

1/2 pound ground turkey

1/4 to 1/2 teaspoon salt, plus more to taste

1/2 teaspoon freshly ground pepper, plus more to taste

1/4 teaspoon ground allspice

2 tablespoons chopped fresh Italian parsley

3 tablespoons raisins

3 tablespoons pecans, lightly toasted

2 to 2 1/2 pounds zucchini, preferably pale-skinned variety

1 tablespoon tomato paste, or juice of 1 or 2 lemons

2 medium cloves garlic, coarsely chopped

1. Add rice to 3 cups boiling salted water in a medium saucepan and boil 10 minutes. Rinse with cold running water and drain well.

2. Heat 2 tablespoons oil in a skillet, add onion, and sauté over medium-low heat about 5 minutes or until softened. Let cool.

3. Combine turkey with sautéed onion in a medium bowl. Add 1/4 to 1/2 teaspoon salt, 1/2 teaspoon pepper, the allspice, and parsley and mix well. Add rice, raisins, and pecans and mix well.

4. If using dark-skinned zucchini, cut each into 2 pieces crosswise. Carefully scoop out pulp with a special zucchini hollowing gadget, a vegetable peeler, or an apple corer, leaving a hollow cylinder for stuffing. Put stuffing into zucchini.

5. Heat remaining 2 tablespoons oil in a deep sauté pan. Add stuffed zucchini and sauté on all sides, turning them carefully. Mix tomato paste (but not lemon juice) with 1/4 cup water and add to pan. Add enough water to pan to cover zucchini by one third. Add garlic. Sprinkle zucchini with salt and pepper. Cover and simmer about 45 minutes or until zucchini are very tender; add a little hot water from time to time so pan does not become dry. If using lemon juice, add it when zucchini are tender and cook over low heat 5 minutes. Serve hot.

❧ Chicken and Turkey Blintzes and Sandwiches

Turkey Blintzes with Leeks and Ginger

Makes 4 or 5 servings   Ⓜ

Garlic, sesame seeds, and sesame oil complete the Chinese-style seasoning of these tasty blintzes. You can make them with turkey or chicken.

8 to 10 Herb Blintzes for Meat Fillings (page 301)

1 pound leeks (white and light green parts only), halved lengthwise, rinsed, and cut into 1/4-inch slices

2 tablespoons vegetable oil

Salt and freshly ground pepper, to taste

2 tablespoons plus 1 teaspoon Asian sesame oil

1 tablespoon minced garlic

1 tablespoon minced peeled fresh ginger

1/4 cup dry white wine

11/2 cups shredded cooked turkey

2 tablespoons sesame seeds, toasted

1. Prepare blintzes. Then, soak sliced leeks in cold water 5 minutes to remove any sand. Lift into a colander, rinse, and drain well. Heat oil in medium, heavy skillet. Add leeks, salt, and pepper. Cook over medium heat, stirring often, about 10 minutes or until leeks are soft but not brown. If any liquid remains in pan, cook leeks over medium-high heat, stirring, until it evaporates. Add 1 teaspoon sesame oil, quickly stir in garlic and ginger, and sauté 30 seconds. Add wine and boil over high heat, stirring, until it is completely absorbed by leek mixture.

2. Transfer mixture to a bowl and let cool. Add turkey and mix well. Stir in 1 tablespoon sesame oil and pinch of pepper. Adjust seasoning.

3. Lightly oil 2 medium baking dishes. Spoon 3 tablespoons filling onto less attractive side of each blintz, across the third of the blintz nearest you. Slightly fold over each side of the blintz, to your right and left, then roll up in cigar shape, beginning at edge with filling and rolling away from you. Arrange blintzes seam-side down in one layer in oiled dish. Brush them with 1 tablespoon sesame oil. Sprinkle with toasted sesame seeds.

4. Preheat oven to 375°F. Bake blintzes about 20 minutes or until filling is hot. Serve immediately.

Deli Chicken Salad Sandwiches

Makes 4 servings   Ⓜ

Why are those chicken salad sandwiches so enticing at the deli? There's really no secret; the best ones are freshly prepared from good quality ingredients. Use your favorite mayonnaise, very fresh rye bread or swirled rye and pumpernickel from a good bakery, and chunks of Poached Chicken Breasts (page 359). At some delis they will add sliced avocado, and if you have perfectly ripe ones of the dark-skinned Haas variety, they make a terrific addition.

3 cups diced cooked chicken

1 large hard boiled egg, chopped (optional)

2 to 3 teaspoons mustard (optional)

6 to 8 tablespoons mayonnaise, or more to taste

Salt (optional) and freshly ground pepper, to taste

1 ripe avocado, preferably Haas

8 slices fresh caraway-seed rye bread or swirled rye and pumpernickel

1. Combine chicken and egg, if using, in a medium bowl. Mix mustard, if using, with 6 tablespoons mayonnaise and add to salad. Season with salt, if using, and pepper.

2. A short time before serving, halve avocado and remove pit. Scoop out flesh and cut it into thin slices.

3. If you like, spread a little mayonnaise on each slice of bread. Spread chicken salad on half the bread slices, top with avocado, and then with second bread slice. Cut in half and serve.

Tel Aviv Turkey and Eggplant Sandwiches

Makes 12 appetizer or 4 main-course servings

This was the sandwich I always ordered at my favorite Tel Aviv sandwich shop. It was made of a long, crisp-crusted roll that was hollowed out and filled with eggplant salad with mayonnaise. The eggplant was topped with thin slices of smoked turkey and a pickle slice. It's easy to prepare at home. You can make your own eggplant salad or purchase eggplant with tahini, which is sometimes sold as baba ghanouj. If you like, you can substitute turkey pastrami or thin slices roasted turkey or chicken for the smoked turkey.

At the sandwich shop you could choose between French rolls or dark, pumpernickel-type rolls. I usually opted for the French rolls but now I often use whole-wheat ones if I can find some that are not sweet. Often I add mild pickled red peppers or roasted peppers. The sandwiches are good cut in thirds as appetizers or left whole as hearty sandwiches.

2 roasted red bell peppers, homemade (page 588), or bottled, or pickled sweet red peppers

4 long French, sourdough, whole-wheat, or other fresh, crusty rolls

1/2 to 1 cup Creamy Eggplant Dip (page 216) or other eggplant salads or dips

8 to 12 thin slices smoked turkey breast, turkey pastrami, or roasted turkey

1. Prepare peppers. Then, cut roasted or pickled peppers into thick strips.

2. Halve rolls lengthwise and remove part of soft bread from bottom half of each one. Fill hollow in roll with eggplant dip. Top with turkey and pepper strips. Set top half of roll on sandwich.

3. To serve as appetizers, cut each sandwich in three pieces; or leave them whole as lunch or supper sandwiches. Serve them with napkins, because of the creamy dip.

Israeli Hot Turkey Sandwich

Makes 2 servings

Middle Eastern grilled meat turning slowly on a vertical spit is a fixture on the Israeli street food landscape. Although lamb is the classic meat in this specialty called shwarma, *in Israel it is often made of turkey. For the sandwich, the meat is very thinly sliced off the large chunk on the grill and is served hot in pita bread. Here is a quick, tasty alternative for the home kitchen, using sautéed turkey breast strips and similar Middle Eastern spices.*

3/4 pound boneless turkey breast slices

1 teaspoon ground cumin

1/2 teaspoon paprika

1/4 teaspoon cayenne pepper, or to taste

Salt and freshly ground pepper, to taste

3 tablespoons vegetable oil or olive oil

1 large onion, chopped

1/2 red or green bell pepper, diced

2 pita breads, warmed briefly and halved

2 plum tomatoes, sliced

Pickled hot peppers or other pickles (optional)

1. Cut turkey into strips about 1/4-inch wide. Mix cumin, paprika, and cayenne and sprinkle over turkey. Sprinkle lightly with salt and pepper.

2. Heat oil in a large, heavy skillet. Add onion and bell pepper and sauté over medium heat about 7 minutes or until onion begins to turn golden. Push vegetable mixture to side of skillet. Add turkey and sauté about 2 minutes. Stir in vegetable mixture from side of skillet and sauté about 1 more minute or until turkey is cooked through. Cut into a thick strip with a sharp knife to make sure the meat is opaque inside.

3. Spoon turkey mixture into halved pita breads. Add tomato slices and pickles, if using. Serve immediately.

✣ Other Birds

Spicy Roast Cornish Hens

Makes 2 to 4 servings

Jews from India prepare creamy tandoori-style marinades like this one without including any dairy products. The fresh garlic and ginger along with the dried spices produce outstanding flavored roast Cornish hens and helps them turn an appetizing reddish-brown.

Serve half or a whole bird per person. To carve a Cornish hen easily into two portions, cut it in half using poultry shears, cutting through the breast, then along the backbone. If desired, cut out the backbone when serving.

1 large clove garlic, peeled

1 tablespoon coarsely chopped peeled fresh ginger

1 tablespoon strained fresh lemon juice

2 tablespoons vegetable oil

2 teaspoons paprika

1¹/₂ teaspoons ground cumin

¹/₂ teaspoon ground turmeric

¹/₄ teaspoon cayenne pepper

¹/₄ teaspoon ground cinnamon

Pinch of freshly grated nutmeg

Pinch of ground cloves

2 Cornish hens (each about 1¹/₄ pounds)

1. Combine garlic and ginger in food processor. Process until finely chopped. Add lemon juice, oil, paprika, cumin, turmeric, cayenne, cinnamon, nutmeg, and cloves. Process until combined.

2. Place hens in a large bowl. Add marinade and rub it all over hens, inside and out. Cover and refrigerate 1 day or overnight, turning occasionally.

3. Preheat oven to 400°F. Set hens on a rack in a roasting pan and spoon marinade over them. Roast about 50 minutes or until juices run clear when a skewer is inserted into thickest part of leg; if juices are pink, continue roasting a few more minutes. Let stand 5 minutes before serving.

Cornish Hens in Saffron Tomato Sauce

Makes 4 servings

These Cornish hens are braised in a sauce that combines favorite flavors of Sephardic Jews, especially those from Morocco. They make a delectable entree for Shabbat or holidays. Unlike most Cornish hen dishes, this one is easy to serve because there's no last minute carving. Instead the hens are cut before cooking, so they absorb the delicious flavors as they simmer. If you would rather use chicken pieces in the sauce, remember that their cooking time is longer than that of Cornish hens.

I prefer to keep accompaniments very simple—plain white or brown rice or couscous and a cooked green vegetable such as zucchini or broccoli are my choices.

2 large Cornish hens (each about 1¹/₂ pounds), thawed if frozen

Salt and freshly ground pepper, to taste

2 or 3 tablespoons olive oil

1 small onion, minced

8 large cloves garlic, minced

2 pounds ripe tomatoes, peeled, seeded, and chopped, or two 28-ounce cans whole tomatoes, drained well and chopped

¹/₂ cup chicken stock

Scant ¹/₄ teaspoon crumbled saffron threads

1 bay leaf

Cayenne pepper to taste

1. Cut each hen in four: First cut off 2 leg-and-thigh pieces at the thigh joint, then 2 breast-and-wing pieces. Cut off backs and wing tips and reserve for making stock. (You can freeze them and add them to chicken pieces to make chicken stock.)

2. Pat hen pieces dry. Sprinkle them with pepper. Heat oil in a heavy skillet large enough to hold the hens in one layer. Add hen pieces and brown them well over medium-high heat about 3 minutes on each side. Transfer browned hens to a plate.

3. Discard all but 1 tablespoon fat from skillet. Add onion and cook over medium-low heat, stirring often, about 7 minutes or until softened. Stir in garlic, then tomatoes, stock, saffron, bay leaf, and pepper and bring to a boil.

4. Return hens to skillet with any juices from plate. Bring to a boil. Cover and simmer over low heat 10 minutes. Turn pieces over, cover, and simmer about 10 more minutes or until tender. Transfer pieces with tongs to a plate.

5. Cook sauce over medium-high heat, stirring often, about 5 minutes or until thick. Discard bay leaf. Season sauce with salt, pepper, and cayenne. Return hens to sauce. Cover, heat briefly over low heat, and serve hot.

Duck with Sauerkraut

Makes 6 to 8 servings

M

Roasted goose and duck used to be prepared more often in the Ashkenazic kitchen than they are now, and stuffed goose neck was a special treat. These birds are simply roasted with onions and garlic, then heated with a savory accompaniment like sauerkraut, braised cabbage, or cooked turnips. Occasionally they are filled with a bread stuffing or a dried fruit stuffing. Duck's rich meat makes a hearty winter entree that is good for Hanukkah, but not at a meal where you're serving latkes! Instead, serve this with plain boiled potatoes and hot mustard. If you prefer, prepare this dish with chicken instead of duck.

2 ducks (each about 4¹/₂ to 5 pounds), thawed if frozen and patted dry

4 large onions, 2 quartered, 2 halved and sliced

Salt and freshly ground pepper, to taste

1 bay leaf

6 peppercorns

8 large cloves garlic, peeled

4 pounds sauerkraut, rinsed thoroughly in cold water, drained, and squeezed dry

1 cup dry white wine

1 cup chicken stock

1. Preheat oven to 400°F. Trim excess fat around duck cavities. Put quartered onion inside ducks. Sprinkle them inside and out with pepper. Using skewer, pierce skin all over, at intervals of about ¹/₂ inch; do not pierce meat.

2. Set ducks on their breasts on rack in large, heavy roasting pan. Roast 30 minutes. Using bulb baster, remove fat from pan. Reserve a few tablespoons for cooking sauerkraut.

3. Heat 2 or 3 tablespoons duck fat in a large stew pan. Add sliced onions and cook over low heat, stirring, until soft but not brown. Wrap bay leaf, peppercorns, and garlic in cheesecloth and tie ends to form a seasoning bag. Add sauerkraut, seasoning bag, wine, and chicken stock to stew pan. Cover and simmer 1 hour, adding water if pan becomes dry.

4. After ducks have roasted 30 minutes, turn them on their backs and roast 30 more minutes. Remove from oven and leave until cool enough to handle. Carve each duck into 4 pieces. Reduce oven temperature to 350°F.

5. Discard seasoning bag from sauerkraut. Adjust seasoning. If mixture is soupy, simmer uncovered a few minutes to evaporate excess liquid. Set duck pieces skin side up on sauerkraut. Cover and bake about 30 minutes or until duck is hot.

Goose Cassoulet

Makes about 8 servings   (M)

Goose is a traditional bird on the winter menus of Jews in France and Eastern Europe. In the Alsatian Jewish pantry, goose fat is prized as much as schmaltz *(chicken fat in Yiddish) is among American Ashkenazic Jews.*

Cassoulet is one of the most treasured dishes of French cooking, and goose cassoulet may be its best-loved version. Some historians feel that cassoulet's roots must be in cholent, *as both dishes contain meat or poultry cooked slowly with beans. Its total cooking time is about 3¹/₂ hours but you can do certain steps in advance. You can cook the beans and keep them in their cooking liquid in the refrigerator for 2 to 3 days. If you prefer, you can assemble the entire cassoulet in its baking dish and refrigerate it, covered, for 2 days. Then, heat it as in step 6 for about 1¹/₂ hours, covering it after 1 hour if the bread crumbs are already brown.*

During cold months you can find goose in kosher meat markets. If it is not available, use two ducks to make the cassoulet.

1 pound dried medium white beans (about 2¹/₃ cups), sorted and rinsed

4 whole cloves

2 large onions, 1 whole and 1 chopped

1 whole carrot

2 bay leaves

2 large sprigs fresh thyme or 2 teaspoons dried thyme

Salt and freshly ground pepper, to taste

1 young goose (about 8 pounds), thawed if frozen, patted dry

3 pounds chicken pieces

8 large cloves garlic, chopped

Two 28¹/₂-ounce cans whole tomatoes, drained well and chopped

¹/₂ cup water

1 tablespoon tomato paste

Cayenne pepper, to taste

¹/₂ pound beef, chicken, or turkey frankfurters, sliced

¹/₄ cup bread crumbs

1. Put beans in a large saucepan. Add enough water to cover by at least 2 inches. Stick whole cloves into whole onion and add to pan. Add carrot, 1 bay leaf, and half the thyme. Bring to a boil. Cover and cook over low heat for 1¹/₂ hours or until beans are just tender, adding hot water if necessary so they remain covered. Season with salt and pepper. Keep beans in their cooking liquid. Discard onion, carrot, bay leaf, and thyme sprig.

2. Meanwhile, preheat oven to 450°F. Trim excess fat around goose cavity. With a skewer, pierce goose skin several times without piercing meat. Roast goose on a rack in a roasting pan for 30 minutes. Reduce oven temperature to 350°F. Roast 1 hour, basting and removing fat from pan occasionally; reserve 2 tablespoons fat for step 3. Cover goose and roast 30 minutes more or until drumstick meat no longer looks pink when pierced deeply with thin knife.

3. Heat reserved goose fat in a large, heavy stew pan. Add chicken pieces and brown lightly over medium-high heat. Transfer to a plate. Add chopped onion and sauté about 7 minutes. Add garlic and tomatoes and cook 2 minutes. Return chicken to pan and add water and remaining thyme and bay leaf. Bring to a boil. Cover and simmer over low heat, turning chicken pieces once, about 35 minutes or until they are tender. Discard bay leaf and thyme sprig. Skim excess fat from sauce. Add tomato paste and cayenne to sauce; adjust seasoning.

4. When goose is done, transfer it to a board. Let cool slightly. Cut off goose legs and breast pieces. Slice meat.

5. With a slotted spoon, put half of beans in a large heavy baking dish in an even layer. Top with chicken and goose pieces and frankfurter slices. Spoon remaining beans on top, reserving their liquid. Ladle tomato sauce from chicken over beans; add enough of reserved bean liquid to come nearly to top of beans.

6. Preheat oven to 350°F. Sprinkle cassoulet with bread crumbs. Bake about 50 minutes to 1 hour or until hot and golden brown. Serve from baking dish.

❧ Stuffings and Sauces

Challah Stuffing

Makes 4 to 5 cups, about 4 servings,
enough for 1 chicken

Leftover challah makes a delicious stuffing for chicken. I like to follow my mother's custom of adding a variety of vegetables.

6 slices stale challah

3 tablespoons vegetable oil or chicken fat

1 medium onion, chopped

1 red or green bell pepper, chopped

4 ounces mushrooms, chopped

2 medium carrots, coarsely grated

2 medium zucchini, coarsely grated

Salt and freshly ground pepper, to taste

1 large egg, beaten

1. Soak challah in water. Squeeze out water. Mash challah in a bowl.

2. Heat 2 tablespoons oil in a large skillet. Add onion, bell pepper, and mushrooms and sauté, stirring occasionally, about 7 minutes or until onion begins to turn golden. Add vegetable mixture to bowl of challah and mix well. Add carrots, zucchini, salt, and pepper. Adjust seasoning. Add egg and mix well. Cool completely before spooning into chicken.

3. If you would like to bake stuffing separately, preheat oven to 350°F and grease a 9-inch square baking dish. Spoon stuffing into dish. Drizzle with remaining oil. Bake about 30 minutes or until firm.

Pecan and Mushroom Stuffing

Makes 9 to 10 cups, 8 to 10 servings,
enough for a 12- to 14-pound turkey

Kosher stuffing for turkey is made without butter, of course. Toasted pecans give this one a wonderfully rich flavor. I like to add grated zucchini to help keep the stuffing moist.

1¹/₂ cups pecans

6 tablespoons vegetable oil

¹/₂ pound mushrooms, halved and cut into thin slices

Salt and freshly ground pepper, to taste

2 large onions, chopped

1 finely cup chopped celery

4 large cloves garlic, chopped

¹/₂ pound zucchini, coarsely grated

¹/₂ pound day-old French or country bread, cut into ¹/₂-inch cubes

¹/₄ cup chopped fresh parsley

1¹/₂ teaspoons dried thyme, crumbled

1. Preheat oven to 350°F. Toast pecans in a baking dish in oven 5 minutes. Transfer to a plate and let cool. Chop coarsely.

2. Heat 2 tablespoons oil in a large skillet over medium-high heat. Add mushrooms, salt, and pepper and sauté until lightly browned, about 3 minutes. Transfer to a bowl.

3. Heat remaining 4 tablespoons oil in a very large skillet over medium-low heat. Add onions and celery and cook, stirring, about 7 minutes or until softened. Add garlic and cook 30 seconds. Remove from heat.

4. Put grated zucchini in a colander and squeeze out excess liquid. Stir zucchini into onion mixture.

5. Combine bread cubes, vegetable mixture, mushrooms, pecans, parsley, thyme, and a pinch of salt and pepper in a large bowl. Toss using 2 tablespoons until ingredients are mixed thoroughly and bread is moistened. Add salt and pepper if needed.

6. Spoon stuffing into turkey just before roasting it.

Dill and Onion Stuffing

Makes 4 to 5 cups, about 4 servings,
enough for one chicken

This Polish-style stuffing is great in gently spiced roasted chicken or turkey, such as Old-Fashioned Roasted Chicken (page 346), so you can enjoy the dill's fresh flavor. I like to use French, Italian, sourdough, or country-style bread to make the bread cubes. Challah or whole-wheat bread is good too if they are not sweet. You can leave the crust on if you like.

4 cups of 1/2-inch cubes of stale or day-old bread

3 to 4 tablespoons vegetable oil

2 large onions, finely chopped

1 teaspoon paprika

Salt and freshly ground pepper, to taste

1 medium zucchini, coarsely grated

3 to 4 tablespoons snipped fresh dill

1 large egg, beaten

2 to 4 tablespoons chicken stock or broth

1. Put bread in a large bowl. Heat 3 tablespoons oil in a large skillet. Add onions, paprika, and a pinch of salt and pepper. Sauté over medium heat, stirring occasionally, about 10 minutes or until onions are very tender. Stir in zucchini and cook 2 minutes. Remove from heat.

2. Add vegetable mixture and dill to bread and toss lightly. Adjust seasoning. Add beaten egg and toss lightly until blended. Gradually add stock and toss lightly. Mixture may appear dry, but will become much moister from juices in bird. You can make stuffing 1 day ahead and keep it in a covered container in the refrigerator. Stuff chicken just before roasting it.

Spicy Matzo Stuffing

Makes 6 to 8 cups, 6 to 8 servings,
enough for a 10- to 12-pound turkey

A good partner for Spiced Roasted Turkey (page 363), this stuffing echoes the turkey's seasoning trio of cumin, turmeric, and black pepper and has plenty of spice but is not hot. It's also good with plain roast chicken, lamb, and beef. Usually I bake the stuffing in a separate dish—instead of inside a roast bird—because I like the matzo's texture. You can use plain or flavored matzos.

8 matzos, plain or flavored, crumbled

1 1/2 cups hot turkey, chicken, or vegetable stock

3 to 4 tablespoons olive oil

2 large onions, chopped

2 teaspoons ground cumin

1/2 teaspoon ground turmeric

Salt and freshly ground pepper, to taste

4 large cloves garlic, minced

3 large eggs or 1 large egg and 3 large egg whites, beaten

1/4 cup chopped fresh cilantro or Italian parsley (optional)

3 to 4 tablespoons chopped pecans (optional)

1. Put matzos in a large bowl and pour hot stock over them. Let stand to soften.

2. Heat 2 to 3 tablespoons oil in a large skillet. Add onions and sauté over medium heat, stirring often, about 7 minutes or until beginning to turn golden. Add cumin, turmeric, salt, and pepper. Remove from heat and stir in garlic. Add onion mixture to matzo mixture and let cool. Adjust seasoning. Stir in eggs and cilantro, if using.

3. If stuffing turkey, cool completely before spooning into bird.

To bake stuffing separately, preheat oven to 350°F. Lightly oil a 2-quart casserole dish. Spoon stuffing mixture into casserole. Sprinkle with 1 tablespoon oil, then with chopped pecans, if using. Bake uncovered 45 minutes or until firm.

Horseradish Barbecue Sauce

Makes about ¾ cup, about 4 servings

A jar of horseradish is a staple in the Ashkenazic Jewish pantry. Mostly it's served with gefilte fish but it is also used to flavor other dishes. It lends plenty of zip to this easy barbecue sauce, which is great with chicken or turkey. Be sure to add the horseradish gradually, to taste. Also keep in mind: As horseradish stands, it loses its potency.

Brush the sauce on the meat when it is nearly done, or serve it separately as an accompanying sauce. If you add it too soon, it is likely to burn on the grill.

1 tablespoon vegetable oil

½ small onion, finely chopped

½ cup ketchup

¼ cup chicken stock

1 tablespoon brown sugar

1 tablespoon white or red wine vinegar

1 teaspoon paprika

2 to 3 teaspoons horseradish, or to taste

Salt and freshly ground pepper, to taste

Heat oil in a small saucepan. Add onion and sauté over medium-low heat, stirring, 5 minutes. Stir in ketchup, chicken stock, brown sugar, vinegar, and paprika. Bring to a simmer. Cook over low heat, stirring often, about 5 minutes or until thickened to your taste. Remove from heat and gradually stir in horseradish. Season with salt and pepper.

Sephardic Tomato Sauce

Makes 4 to 6 servings

Use this aromatic sauce for simmering Sephardic Turkey Balls (page 366) or other meatballs. Many cooks add cumin, as it complements meat well. Add the sugar and lemon juice after cooking the meatballs, if you'd like a touch of sweetness or acidity.

If you would like to make it with fresh ripe tomatoes, use 2 pounds. Peel, seed, and chop them before adding to the sauce.

2 tablespoons olive oil

1 small onion, minced

4 large cloves garlic, chopped

Two 28-ounce cans whole tomatoes, drained well and chopped

1 tablespoon tomato paste

½ teaspoon dried oregano

Salt and freshly ground pepper, to taste

½ teaspoon ground cumin (optional)

½ teaspoon sugar (optional)

1 tablespoon strained fresh lemon juice (optional)

Heat oil in a large saucepan, add onion, and sauté 5 minutes over medium heat until softened. Add garlic, tomatoes, and tomato paste. Bring to boil. Add oregano, salt, pepper, and cumin, if using. Cook uncovered over low heat 15 minutes or until thickened. A short time before serving, add sugar and/or lemon juice if using. Season with salt and pepper.

Meats

Beef Stews
379

Brisket Stew with Tomatoes
and Mushrooms

Beef Stew with Chickpeas

Provençal Beef Daube
with Red Wine

Spicy Beef with Green Beans

Meat and Potatoes, Yemenite
Style

Sweet and Sour Brisket Stew
with Carrots and Dried Fruit

Beef and Butternut Squash Stew
with Prunes

Israeli-Hungarian Beef Goulash

Beef Stew with Okra

Pot-Roasted, Braised,
and Poached Beef
385

Old-Fashioned Brisket Pot Roast

Chuck Roast in Porcini
Mushroom Sauce

Barbecue-Sauced Brisket
with Onions

Brisket with Sauerkraut

Oven-Braised Short Ribs in
Hot and Sweet Tomato Sauce

Beef-in-the-Pot with Dill
Matzo Balls

Ground Beef
389

Indian Jewish Chili with
Chickpeas and Bulgur Wheat

Savory Meat Blintzes

Middle Eastern Meatballs

My Mother's Layered
Shepherd's Pie

Hungarian Jewish Stuffed
Peppers

Mexican-Israeli Stuffing
for Peppers

Meat-Stuffed Winter Squash

Beef, Rice, and Tomato
in Zucchini Boats

Spaghetti with Spicy Meat Sauce

Meat Loaf with Egg

Spicy Beef Patties

P = *Pareve*   **D** = *Dairy*   **M** = *Meat*

Deli Meats
395

Warm Corned Beef and Pasta
Salad with Mustard Vinaigrette

Kosher Reuben Sandwiches

Pastrami and Peppers with
Bulgur Wheat

Veal
396

Veal Chops in Tomato-
Mushroom Sauce

Veal Tajine with Zucchini
and Saffron

Marinated Veal Chops in
Spiced Orange Wine Sauce

Grilled Veal Chops with
Walnut Topping

Hungarian Braised Veal

Springtime Veal with Peas
and Baby Onions

Veal with Artichokes,
Tomatoes, and Dill

Veal and Lima Bean Casserole
with Chard, Dill, and Cilantro

Calves' Liver and Onions with
Porcini and Wine Sauce

Lamb
401

Middle Eastern Grilled
Lamb Chops

Grilled Lamb with
Argentinean Pesto

Garlic-Studded Roast Lamb

Lamb with Prunes and
Toasted Almonds

Lamb with Eggplant Slices

Lamb and Vegetable Casserole

North African Lamb Stew
with Celery

Lamb with Lima Beans

Lamb Navarin

Sephardic Moussaka

Lamb-Stuffed Onions

Slowly cooked meats are the hallmark of Jewish cooking. Whether it is braised brisket or short ribs in the pot, these succulent meats with their flavorful juices are time-honored staples on the menus of Jews from all over the world.

Long, gentle simmering is perfect for the kosher cuts of meat, which come from the fore quarter of the animal. As the meats cook with vegetables, they create a delicious broth or sauce and flavor each other. The meat remains moist and becomes very tender.

These types of dishes are not only delicious, but also easy to serve and convenient. Since they can be cooked ahead and reheated, and often benefit from this, they are in keeping with the rule of avoiding cooking during Shabbat and certain holidays. This also makes them very convenient for family meals and for entertaining. When vegetables are added, many of these dishes become a whole meal in a single dish.

The most famous of these one-pot dinners is the hearty Shabbat stew of meat with potatoes, beans, or both, called *cholent* in Yiddish and *hamin* in Hebrew. By using different beans, grains, and flavorings, numerous versions of this overnight casserole have been developed over the centuries. You can find these recipes in the Shabbat chapter (pages 173–203).

A great variety of flavorings is added to the meats as they are braised or stewed. Garlic and chiles are favorites in North African cooking, although some Moroccan cooks also like to prepare sweet and savory stews with dried fruit and cinnamon. Oregano is favored by some Sephardic cooks, and cilantro by Jewish cooks from southern Mediterranean and Middle Eastern countries as well as India. Other Middle Eastern flavors popular in Israel are cumin and turmeric. Ashkenazic Jews like meats that keep their natural flavor and season them simply with onions, carrots, bay leaves, and sometimes garlic. They also make sweet and sour braised dishes with tomato, fruit, and vinegar or lemon juice.

Potatoes, dried beans, and tomatoes are frequently added to simmer alongside the meat but almost any seasonal vegetable can be added, from squashes and leeks to green beans and okra.

Poaching meat with vegetables in liquid produces not only a savory entree, but also a rich tasting soup. Braised meats create a wonderful sauce, which many cooks serve separately for spooning over potatoes, rice, noodles, or couscous. When a thick sauce is desired, it is thickened with a roux of oil and flour, or with a slurry of flour or cornstarch mixed with water. For Passover, the slurry is made with potato starch.

Other meat cooking techniques used in the Jewish kitchen are roasting or baking, primarily for rack and shoulder of lamb and sometimes beef ribs or brisket. Tender lamb chops and sometimes veal chops are grilled or pan-fried.

Ground beef, veal, and lamb all are much loved in Jewish cuisine, especially for stuffing vegetables. Using them this way turns a relatively inexpensive type of meat into a wonderful holiday dish.

❧ Beef Stews

Brisket Stew with Tomatoes and Mushrooms

Makes 4 to 6 servings

(M)

Cooking brisket in cubes rather than in one piece makes serving easier. Here, brisket adds rich flavor to the tomato-mushroom sauce as it simmers gently. The aromatic stew is good with potatoes, noodles, or rice.

4 tablespoons vegetable oil

2 pounds beef brisket, trimmed of excess fat, cut into 1$\frac{1}{4}$- to 1$\frac{1}{2}$-inch pieces and patted dry

1 large onion, chopped

1 medium clove garlic, crushed

1 sprig fresh thyme or $\frac{1}{2}$ teaspoon dried thyme, crumbled

1 bay leaf

3 fresh parsley stems plus 1 tablespoon chopped leaves

1 tablespoon plus 1 teaspoon all-purpose flour

Four 14$\frac{1}{2}$-ounce cans diced tomatoes, drained

About 2 to 2$\frac{1}{2}$ cups water

Salt and freshly ground pepper, to taste

8 ounces pearl onions

8 ounces medium mushrooms, quartered

1. Heat 2 tablespoons oil in 4- to 5-quart stew pan or Dutch oven. Add beef in batches and brown cubes over medium-high heat on all sides. Transfer cubes to a plate as they brown.

2. Add chopped onion to stew pan and cook over low heat, stirring often, about 7 minutes or until softened. Meanwhile wrap garlic, thyme, bay leaf, and parsley stems in a piece of cheesecloth and tie ends to form a seasoning bag. Return meat to pan, reserving any juices on plate, and sprinkle meat with flour. Toss lightly to coat meat with flour. Cook over low heat, stirring, 5 minutes.

3. Pour juices from plate over beef. Stir in tomatoes and 2 cups water, or enough to just cover beef. Add cheesecloth bag, salt, and pepper and bring to boil, stirring often. Cover and cook over low heat, stirring occasionally and adding more water if pan becomes dry, about 3$\frac{1}{2}$ hours or until beef is tender when pierced with tip of a sharp knife. Discard cheesecloth bag.

4. Meanwhile, add pearl onions to medium saucepan of boiling water and boil 1 minute. Drain, rinse with cold water, and peel with aid of a paring knife. Heat 1 tablespoon oil in medium, heavy skillet over medium-high heat. Add pearl onions and sauté, shaking pan occasionally, about 4 minutes or until lightly browned. Remove with slotted spoon. Heat remaining tablespoon oil in skillet. Add mushrooms, salt, and pepper and sauté until lightly browned, about 3 minutes.

5. Add onions and mushrooms to stew and simmer about 25 minutes or until onions are tender. If sauce is too thick, stir in a few tablespoons water. If sauce is too thin, carefully remove beef and vegetables using slotted spoon; boil sauce, uncovered, stirring often, until lightly thickened, and then return beef and vegetables to stew pan. Adjust seasoning. Stir in parsley leaves. Serve stew from stew pan or deep serving dish.

Hints on Braising and Stewing

- Use a heavy pan for even heating during browning and simmering. An enameled cast iron casserole dish is best and is often attractive enough to bring to the table, but a stainless steel stew pan or Dutch oven is also suitable. The pan should have a tight-fitting lid so the liquid does not evaporate too quickly.

- Pat the meat dry before browning. Avoid crowding the pan, or the meat will steam instead of browning.

- When browning the meat, do not stir it continuously as this would inhibit browning.

- Prevent splatters when browning meat by covering the pan with a frying screen.

- Check on the amount of liquid from time to time. If the pan is becoming dry but the meat is not tender, add a little more liquid.

Beef Stew with Chickpeas

Makes 4 to 6 servings

Jews from North Africa often add chickpeas to their meat stews. In this one the chickpeas gain a wonderful flavor from the beef that simmers in a zesty tomato sauce with garlic and hot peppers. Serve the stew with green beans, cauliflower, or zucchini, or simply accompany it with pita bread and begin the meal with a salad of mixed greens, cucumbers, and tomatoes.

3/4 cup dried chickpeas (garbanzo beans), rinsed and sorted, or one 15-ounce can chickpeas, drained

3 cups cold water

3 tablespoons olive oil or vegetable oil

2 pounds boneless lean beef chuck, trimmed of excess fat, cut into 1¼- to 1½-inch pieces and patted dry

1 large onion, chopped

1 tablespoon plus 1 teaspoon all-purpose flour

Four 14½-ounce cans diced tomatoes, drained

2 to 2½ cups water

1 or 2 jalapeño or serrano peppers, seeds and ribs discarded, minced (see Note)

Salt and freshly ground pepper, to taste

6 large cloves garlic, minced

2 tablespoons tomato paste

1. Put dried chickpeas, if using, in a bowl with enough cold water to cover and soak in cool place 8 hours or overnight. Drain and rinse. Put chickpeas in medium saucepan and add 3 cups fresh water. Bring to boil. Cover and simmer over low heat about 1 hour and 15 minutes or until tender.

2. Heat oil in a stew pan or Dutch oven. Add beef in batches and brown cubes over medium-high heat on all sides. Transfer cubes to a plate as they brown. Add onion to pan and cook over low heat, stirring often, about 7 minutes or until softened. Return meat to pan, reserving any juices on plate, and sprinkle meat with flour. Toss lightly to coat meat with flour. Cook over low heat, stirring, 5 minutes.

3. Pour juices from plate over beef. Stir in tomatoes and enough water to just cover beef. Add jalapeño pepper, salt, black pepper, and garlic and bring to boil, stirring often. Cover and cook over low heat, stirring occasionally, 1 hour. Stir in tomato paste. If pan appears dry or sauce is too thick, stir in more water. Drain cooked chickpeas and add to stew. If using canned chickpeas, add them now. Continue cooking, stirring occasionally, 30 to 45 minutes or until beef is tender when pierced with sharp knife. Adjust seasoning. Serve stew from stew pan or deep serving dish.

Note: Wear rubber gloves when handling hot peppers.

Provençal Beef Daube with Red Wine

Makes 6 or 7 servings

This specialty of Provence in southern France is perfect for Shabbat. The long, slow cooking in red wine makes the beef wonderfully tender; the dish even improves from being made ahead. For greater depth of flavor, the beef is first marinated in the wine. The beef can either be cooked over low heat or baked at 325°F. Serve it spooned over a bed of noodles, which happens to be the favorite French way to serve this aromatic stew. It's also good with rice.

3 pounds beef chuck, trimmed of excess fat, cut into 1½-inch pieces

2 cups dry red wine

1 large onion, thinly sliced

4 sprigs fresh thyme or ½ teaspoon crumbled dried thyme

2 bay leaves

Two 3-inch strips of orange rind

2 whole cloves

2 tablespoons olive oil

6 large cloves garlic, chopped

One 14½-ounce can diced tomatoes, drained

Salt and freshly ground pepper, to taste

½ cup water

3/4 pound boiling onions

1¼ pounds carrots, cut into 1-inch slices

Pinch of sugar (optional)

1. Combine beef with wine, sliced onion, thyme, and bay leaves in a large ceramic or glass bowl. Cover and let it marinate in refrigerator 4 hours or overnight.

2. Remove thyme sprigs and bay leaves from marinade and place them on a piece of cheesecloth. Add orange rind strips and cloves to cheesecloth and tie ends to form a seasoning bag. Set beef cubes and onions on paper towels to dry. Reserve marinade.

3. Heat oil in 4- to 5-quart stew pan or Dutch oven. Add beef in batches and brown cubes over medium-high heat on all sides. Transfer cubes to a plate as they brown.

4. Add sliced onion to stew pan and cook it over low heat, stirring, 10 minutes. Add garlic and cook 1 minute, stirring. Add tomatoes and bring to a boil, stirring. Return beef to stew pan with any juices that have accumulated on plate. Add salt, pepper, seasoning bag, marinade, and water. Bring to a boil, stirring. Cover and simmer over low heat 1 hour, stirring occasionally.

5. Add boiling onions to medium saucepan of boiling water and boil 1 minute. Drain, rinse with cold water, and peel with aid of a paring knife.

6. After beef has cooked 1 hour, add carrots and onions. Cover and simmer 4 to 4$^{1}/_{2}$ hours until ingredients are very tender and sauce is well flavored. Discard seasoning bag. Adjust seasoning; add a pinch of sugar, if using. Serve daube from stew pan or deep serving dish.

Spicy Beef with Green Beans

Makes 4 servings Ⓜ

Jews from Libya are known for their hot, spicy dishes. This stew is flavored in that tradition. I like it with plenty of rice.

Traditionally, the green beans cook directly in the stew for at least 30 minutes so they become very tender and absorb flavor from the sauce. I prefer beans that are bright green so I cook them separately, then heat them 2 or 3 minutes in the sauce.

2 tablespoons vegetable oil

2 large onions, halved and sliced thin

2 pounds beef chuck, trimmed of excess fat, cut into 1-inch pieces, and patted dry

4 jalapeño or serrano peppers, seeds and ribs discarded, chopped (see Note)

6 cloves garlic, chopped

4 ripe tomatoes, diced, or one 14$^{1}/_{2}$-ounce can diced tomatoes with their juice

$^{1}/_{2}$ teaspoon ground cumin

$^{1}/_{2}$ teaspoon ground turmeric

Salt and freshly ground pepper, to taste

1 cup water

1$^{1}/_{2}$ to 2 pounds green beans, ends removed, halved

2 tablespoons tomato paste

Cayenne pepper, to taste (optional)

1. Heat oil in large stew pan or Dutch oven, add onions, and sauté about 7 minutes over medium-low heat. Add beef and sauté about 7 minutes, stirring often. Add hot peppers, garlic, tomatoes, cumin, turmeric, salt, pepper, and the water. Stir and bring to a boil. Cover and cook over low heat 2 hours or until beef is tender, adding a few tablespoons water from time to time if needed.

2. Meanwhile, cook beans in boiling salted water about 7 minutes or until tender. Rinse with cold water.

3. When beef is tender, add tomato paste to stew. Add beans and heat gently 3 to 5 minutes to blend flavors. Add cayenne, if using. Season with salt and plenty of pepper. Serve from stew pan or deep serving dish.

Note: Wear rubber gloves when handling hot peppers.

Meat and Potatoes, Yemenite Style

Makes 8 servings Ⓜ

I learned this easy-to-prepare dish from my mother-in-law, who was born in Yemen. The beef and potatoes bake slowly with tomatoes, garlic, cumin, and turmeric, and the resulting sauce is delicious. It's a great dish for Sukkot or for Shabbat.

2 tablespoons vegetable oil

2 large onions, chopped

6 large cloves garlic, chopped

2 tablespoons ground cumin

1¹/₂ teaspoons ground turmeric

¹/₄ teaspoon cayenne pepper

1 tablespoon tomato paste

1¹/₂ cups water

³/₄ pound ripe tomatoes, chopped, or one 14-ounce can diced tomatoes, with their juice

¹/₄ cup coarsely chopped fresh cilantro or Italian parsley

3¹/₂ pounds lean beef chuck, cut into 1- to 1¹/₂-inch pieces

8 medium boiling potatoes, peeled (about 2 pounds)

Salt and freshly ground pepper, to taste

1. Preheat oven to 300°F. Heat oil in a large stew pan or Dutch oven. Add onions and sauté over medium-low heat, stirring often, about 10 minutes or until golden. Remove from heat. Stir in garlic, cumin, turmeric, cayenne, tomato paste, and ¹/₂ cup water and mix well. Stir in tomatoes and cilantro. Last, add beef and potatoes and mix well. Sprinkle lightly with salt and pepper.

2. Cover tightly and bake about 3 hours or until beef is very tender; check occasionally and add liquid if necessary, so there is just a little sauce but meat does not get dry. Taste sauce and adjust seasoning. Serve from stew pan or deep serving dish.

Sweet and Sour Brisket Stew with Carrots and Dried Fruit

Makes 6 servings Ⓜ

Dried apricots, prunes, and ground ginger give this Ashkenazic-style brisket pizzazz. Potatoes and carrots cook in the savory juices and acquire a delicious flavor. Serve this one-pot meal for Sukkot, Hanukkah, or for a fall or winter Shabbat.

1 to 2 tablespoons vegetable oil

3¹/₂ pounds beef brisket, cut into 1¹/₄-inch pieces and patted dry

2 onions, coarsely chopped

1 quart water

1 bay leaf

Salt and freshly ground pepper, to taste

6 medium potatoes (about 1¹/₂ pounds)

4 large carrots, cut into 1-inch chunks

¹/₄ pound pitted prunes

¹/₄ pound dried apricots

1 teaspoon ground ginger

¹/₃ cup brown sugar

¹/₃ cup white vinegar

2 tablespoons all-purpose flour

1. Heat 1 tablespoon oil in a stew pan or Dutch oven over medium heat. Add meat in batches and brown on all sides. Remove from pan. Add 1 tablespoon oil if pan is dry. Add onions and sauté until deep brown, about 10 minutes. Remove half of onions. Return meat to pan and add water, bay leaf, and a pinch of salt. Bring to a boil. Cover and simmer over low heat 2 hours.

2. Peel potatoes, cut each into 3 or 4 chunks, and add to pan. Add carrots and remaining browned onions. Push vegetables into liquid. Bring to a boil. Cover and simmer 30 minutes. Put prunes and apricots in a bowl, cover with hot water, and let stand 30 minutes.

3. Add ginger, brown sugar, and vinegar to stew and stir gently. Remove prunes and apricots from their liquid, reserving liquid, and add fruit to pan. Simmer stew uncovered 30 minutes more or until meat is very tender. Shake pan occasionally; avoid stirring so ingredients do not break up.

4. Whisk flour gently with 2 tablespoons fruit soaking liquid in a bowl. Gradually stir in about 1 cup of meat cooking liquid; return mixture to pan. Stir gently. Simmer about 5 minutes. Season with salt and pepper. Serve from stew pan or deep serving dish.

Beef and Butternut Squash Stew with Prunes

Makes 4 to 6 servings

Ⓜ

A touch of honey makes this colorful entree perfect for Rosh Hashanah. I also like it for Hanukkah and Shabbat in fall and winter. With a small amount of oil and a generous portion of squash, it's lighter than most beef stews. Serve it with couscous, noodles, potato latkes, or white or brown rice.

1 tablespoon vegetable oil

2 pounds boneless lean beef chuck, cut into 1¼- to 1½-inch pieces, trimmed of fat, and patted dry

1 large onion, chopped

2 cups water

1 cinnamon stick, about 2-inches long, or a pinch of ground cinnamon

Salt and freshly ground pepper, to taste

2 to 2½ pounds butternut squash, halved

2 tablespoons mild honey

½ pound pitted prunes

1. Heat oil in a non-stick Dutch oven. Add meat in batches and brown lightly on all sides over medium heat. Remove from pan. Add onion and sauté until brown, about 10 minutes; cover if pan becomes dry. Return meat to pan and add water, cinnamon stick, salt, and pepper. Bring to a boil, stirring often. Cover and simmer over low heat, stirring occasionally, 2½ hours or until beef is tender.

2. Meanwhile, scrape off any stringy parts from center of squash with spoon. Cut squash in large pieces and cut off peel. Discard seeds and any stringy parts around seeds. Cut squash into 1-inch cubes.

3. When meat is tender, stir in honey. Add squash and prunes and push squash down into liquid. Cover and simmer 10 minutes. Turn squash pieces over, cover, and simmer about 15 minutes or until squash and prunes are tender. Discard cinnamon stick. Adjust seasoning. Serve from stew pan or deep serving dish.

Israeli-Hungarian Beef Goulash

Makes 4 or 5 servings

Ⓜ

Hungarian food in Israel is quite spicy, and so is goulash, which is a meat stew flavored with both sweet and hot paprika. Use good-quality Hungarian paprika for the best taste. If you like, follow the custom of some cooks and add a pinch of caraway seeds to the stew along with the green pepper. The secret to tasty goulash is to use plenty of onions and to brown them well. You can cook potatoes in the sauce of the goulash, as in this recipe, or boil them and serve them separately.

2 tablespoons vegetable oil

2 large onions, halved and cut into thin slices

2 pounds beef chuck, trimmed of excess fat, cut into 1-inch pieces, and patted dry

4 teaspoons sweet paprika

Salt and freshly ground pepper, to taste

4 large cloves garlic, chopped

1 cup water

¾ pound ripe tomatoes, peeled and diced, or one 14½-ounce can diced tomatoes, drained

1 large green or red bell pepper, diced

1 small carrot, diced

4 large potatoes, peeled and diced

1 tablespoon tomato paste

¼ teaspoon hot paprika or cayenne pepper, or to taste

1. Heat oil in a wide stew pan or Dutch oven. Add onions and cook over medium-low heat about 12 minutes or until softened and lightly browned. Remove with slotted spoon. Add meat in batches and sauté over medium heat about 10 minutes or until meat is lightly browned; remove each batch after browning it.

2. Return onions and meat to pan. Add sweet paprika, salt, and pepper and sauté, stirring, 5 minutes. Add garlic and 1 cup water. Cover and simmer over low heat, stirring occasionally, 1 hour; add a few tablespoons water if pan becomes dry. Add tomatoes and bell pepper and simmer 30 minutes. Add carrot and potatoes and simmer 30 minutes or until meat and vegetables are tender when pierced with knife. Blend tomato paste with 1 tablespoon water and stir gently into sauce. Add hot paprika or cayenne and heat 1 minute. Adjust seasoning. Serve from stew pan or deep serving dish.

Beef Stew with Okra

Makes 4 servings

M

Okra is a great favorite throughout North Africa. It is believed to have originated in Egypt, where it is often cooked in savory meat stews like this one. Egyptian Jews flavor the stew with ground allspice, plenty of garlic, and fresh lemon juice and serve it with cooked rice.

Choose small okra about 3 inches long or less. When fresh okra is not in season, you can use frozen. Cook it only about 10 minutes.

3 or 4 tablespoons vegetable oil

1 1/2 pounds beef chuck, trimmed of excess fat, cut into
    1-inch pieces, and patted dry

One 14 1/2-ounce can diced tomatoes with their juice

1 1/2 cups beef or chicken stock or water

1 to 1 1/4 pounds okra

1 red or green bell pepper, cut into thin strips

3 tablespoons tomato paste

6 large cloves garlic, chopped

1/2 teaspoon ground allspice, or to taste

Salt and freshly ground pepper, to taste

Juice of 1/2 to 1 lemon

1. Heat 1 tablespoon oil in large stew pan or Dutch oven, then add beef in batches and sauté over medium heat to brown, removing each batch with a slotted spoon to a plate as it browns; add more oil if necessary between batches and heat it before adding more meat.

2. Pour off any oil remaining in pan. Return beef to pan with any juices on plate. Add tomatoes and 1 cup stock and bring to a simmer. Cover and cook over low heat 1 1/2 hours, adding a few tablespoons boiling water from time to time if pan becomes dry.

3. Rinse okra, put on paper towels, and pat dry. Cut caps off without piercing okra. In a large deep sauté pan, heat 2 tablespoons oil. Add pepper strips and okra and sauté over medium heat, stirring often, 5 minutes.

4. Add tomato paste and remaining 1/2 cup stock to stew. Add okra and pepper mixture. Bring to a simmer. Add garlic, allspice, salt, and pepper. Cover and simmer without stirring about 20 minutes or until beef and okra are tender. Add lemon juice and heat through. Adjust seasoning. Serve from stew pan or deep serving dish.

Pot-Roasted, Braised, and Poached Beef

Old-Fashioned Brisket Pot Roast

Makes 8 to 10 servings

Succulent brisket cooked slowly with onions on top of the stove is a favorite in the Ashkenazic Jewish kitchen. Some cooks prepare the brisket with potatoes and carrots, as in the recipe below; others prefer the pure flavor of the meat and cook it only with the onions, garlic, and seasonings.

A convenient way to prepare this pot roast is to cook it ahead, slice the meat, and skim the fat from the sauce. Then reheat the sliced meat and vegetables in the savory sauce.

One 4-pound piece of brisket

1 teaspoon salt

3/4 teaspoon freshly ground pepper

1 tablespoon vegetable oil (optional)

3 large onions, sliced

4 large cloves garlic, chopped

1 teaspoon paprika

About 1 cup water

8 to 10 medium potatoes, scrubbed

5 medium carrots, cut into 2-inch chunks

2 ribs celery, sliced

1. Trim excess fat from brisket. Pat brisket dry. Sprinkle brisket with salt and pepper.

2. Heat oil in a large stew pan or Dutch oven; if pan is heavy or has a nonstick surface, no oil is needed. Add meat and brown on all sides over medium heat. Add onions and continue browning, stirring occasionally. Add garlic, paprika, and 1/2 cup water. Cover and cook over low heat 2 hours, adding a few tablespoons water occasionally if pan becomes nearly dry.

3. Peel potatoes if desired, cut them in half, and add to pan. Add carrots, celery, and 1/2 cup water. Cover and cook over low heat, adding more water if needed,

30 to 45 minutes or until meat and vegetables are tender. With thin, sharp knife, carve meat into thin slices crosswise, making sure to cut against the grain. Skim excess fat from sauce. Taste sauce and adjust seasoning. Serve meat and vegetables with sauce.

Chuck Roast in Porcini Mushroom Sauce

Makes 4 main-course servings

Serve this aromatic entree with plenty of rice or noodles to soak up the delectable sauce. It's also great for Hanukkah, accompanied by potato pancakes.

2 tablespoons olive oil

1 large onion, diced

2 ribs celery, diced

1 small carrot, diced

2-pound piece boneless beef chuck roast, trimmed of excess fat and patted dry

3 large cloves garlic, chopped

2/3 cup dry red wine

4 large sprigs fresh thyme or 1 teaspoon dried thyme

2 sprigs fresh marjoram or 1/2 teaspoon dried marjoram, crumbled

1 bay leaf

12 ounces ripe tomatoes, diced or one 14-ounce can diced tomatoes, drained

About 1 1/2 cups beef stock, or stock mixed with water

1 ounce dried porcini mushrooms or other dried mushrooms

1. Heat 1 tablespoon oil in a large stew pan or Dutch oven that fits meat snugly. Add onion, celery, and carrot. Sauté over medium heat, stirring often, about 7 minutes or until onion begins to brown. Transfer vegetables with a slotted spoon to a bowl. Add remaining tablespoon oil to stew pan and heat it. Add meat and brown it on all sides.

2. Return vegetables to stew pan. Add garlic and wine. Wrap thyme, marjoram, and bay leaf in cheesecloth, tie ends to form a seasoning bag, and add. Bring to a boil. Cook uncovered over medium heat, turning meat once or twice, until about half of wine evaporates. Add tomatoes and enough stock to cover meat by about half. Bring to a simmer. Cover and cook over low heat, turning meat over from time to time, about 1 1/2 hours or until beef is very tender.

3. Soak mushrooms in enough hot water to cover for 30 minutes or until tender. Remove mushrooms, rinse, and coarsely chop.

4. When meat is tender, remove it from stew pan. Cover it and keep warm.

5. Remove seasoning bag from sauce. Puree sauce in blender, food processor, or a food mill. Return sauce to stew pan. Add mushrooms, and 1/4 cup more stock if sauce is very thick. Cover and cook 5 minutes.

6. To serve, cut meat into thin slices. Spoon a little sauce over meat. Serve remaining sauce separately.

Barbecue-Sauced Brisket with Onions

Makes 5 or 6 servings (M)

Baked until very tender in homemade barbecue sauce, this savory brisket is great for Hanukkah or Shabbat dinners. Serve it with baked or boiled potatoes or latkes and with rye bread.

1 teaspoon paprika

3/4 teaspoon freshly ground pepper

1/2 teaspoon salt

1 tablespoon plus 1 teaspoon vegetable oil

One 3-pound piece of brisket, trimmed of excess fat and patted dry

1 small onion, finely chopped, plus 2 large onions, sliced

1 cup ketchup

2 tablespoons brown sugar

2 tablespoons red or white wine vinegar

2 teaspoons chili powder

2 tablespoons Dijon mustard

1/2 cup water, plus more if pan becomes dry

1. Mix paprika, pepper, salt, and 1 teaspoon oil in a bowl to a paste and rub into meat. Let stand about 30 minutes.

2. Heat 1 tablespoon oil in a medium saucepan. Add chopped onion and sauté over medium-low heat, stirring, 5 minutes. Stir in ketchup, brown sugar, vinegar, and chili powder and bring to a simmer. Remove from heat and stir in mustard. Cool to room temperature.

3. Preheat oven to 400°F. Put sliced onions in small roasting pan and top with brisket, fat side up. Cover with foil and roast 15 minutes. Reduce oven temperature to 325°F. Pour barbecue sauce over brisket and spread lightly. Add 1/2 cup water to pan, pouring it around, not over, meat. Cover tightly and bake about 3 hours, basting once or twice; occasionally add a few tablespoons water to pan if it becomes nearly dry. When done, brisket should be very tender when pierced with a fork.

4. Remove meat to board, sauce side up. With a slotted spoon transfer onions from roasting pan to a small saucepan for reheating.

5. With a thin sharp knife, carve meat into thin slices crosswise, making sure to cut against the grain. Skim excess fat from sauce. Serve sauce and onions separately.

Brisket with Sauerkraut

Makes about 6 servings

Sauerkraut, or pickled cabbage, is made by shredding cabbage and layering it with salt and seasonings, like juniper berries and bay leaves, and letting it sit for about a month.

Ashkenazic Jews like to cook sauerkraut with fresh cuts of beef that have a long cooking time like brisket or short ribs. This savory entree is seasoned in the sweet and sour Polish style.

1 teaspoon paprika

³/₄ teaspoon freshly ground pepper

One 3-pound piece of brisket

4 pounds uncooked sauerkraut

1 large potato

1 large onion, diced

2 tablespoons brown sugar

1 tablespoon caraway seeds

³/₄ cup apple juice

2 tablespoons cider vinegar, rice vinegar, or other mild vinegar

1 cup water

Salt to taste (optional)

1. Mix paprika and pepper in a bowl and rub into meat. Let stand about 30 minutes. Drain sauerkraut in a colander. Rinse sauerkraut thoroughly under cold running water. Drain and squeeze out excess liquid. Peel potato and grate on large holes of grater. Mix with sauerkraut. Add onion, brown sugar, and caraway seeds and mix well.

2. Put half the sauerkraut mixture in a heavy stew pan. Put brisket on top. Cover with remaining sauerkraut mixture. Add apple juice, vinegar, and water. Bring to a boil. Cover and cook over low heat about 3 hours or until brisket is very tender when pierced with a fork; check and add hot water from time to time if pan appears to be getting dry.

3. Remove meat to board. If sauerkraut is too soupy, cook it uncovered over medium-high heat, stirring, until it thickens to taste. Adjust seasoning.

4. With a thin sharp knife, carve meat into thin slices crosswise, making sure to cut against the grain. Serve it with sauerkraut.

Oven-Braised Short Ribs in Hot and Sweet Tomato Sauce

Makes about 6 servings

A standard "hot plate" on many deli menus is boiled beef short ribs in the pot, accompanied by potatoes and vegetables. Other popular ways to prepare this cut in the Jewish kitchen are in soups, in cholent, *and braised.*

Many people braise short ribs differently from other meats. Instead of browning them in fat and then simmering them on top of the stove, they brown them in the broiler and then braise them in the oven. This is more convenient and gives tasty results. Ketchup- or tomato-based sauces, usually with a sweet and sour accent, are the most widely used seasonings in Jewish-American homes. I like to combine both, with hot red pepper flakes and fresh ginger for extra zip.

3 pounds lean beef short ribs

1 large onion, diced

One 14-ounce can diced tomatoes, with their liquid

³/₄ cup ketchup

¹/₂ cup water

¹/₂ teaspoon hot red pepper flakes, or to taste

1¹/₂ tablespoons minced peeled fresh ginger

2 to 3 tablespoons brown sugar

2 tablespoons vinegar

Salt and freshly ground pepper, to taste

1. Preheat broiler. Cut off excess fat and gristle from ribs. Put ribs in broiler pan. Broil until brown.

2. Preheat oven to 400°F. Put onion in a large roasting pan and brown in oven 5 minutes.

3. Reduce oven temperature to 350°F. Put ribs in roasting pan with onions. Mix tomatoes with ketchup, water, pepper flakes, ginger, 2 tablespoons brown sugar, vinegar, salt, and pepper in a saucepan. Bring to a simmer. Adjust balance of hot and sweet flavors to your taste by adding more pepper flakes or brown sugar if needed.

4. Pour sauce over ribs in roasting pan. Cover and bake, basting occasionally and checking water level so pan does not get dry, about 2 hours or until meat is tender.

Beef-in-the-Pot with Dill Matzo Balls

Makes 6 to 8 servings

(M)

Beef-in-the-pot is a staple on deli restaurant menus. Often it's made with short ribs and includes potatoes and vegetables. It's quite similar to pot au feu, *a beloved standard of homey French cooking. I like beef-in-the-pot best with matzo balls, as they are so good in the rich, flavorful broth. As in the French version, I like to add leeks and to flavor my version with a bouquet garni. You can serve the meat the French way, accompanied by Dijon mustard, or the way a Romanian Jewish friend of mine does, with white or red horseradish.*

6 cloves garlic, peeled

1 bay leaf

1 large sprig fresh thyme

6 fresh Italian parsley stems (without leaves)

2 whole cloves

5 peppercorns

1 large onion

2 ribs celery

Salt and freshly ground pepper, to taste

4 quarts water, or more if needed

3 pounds lean beef short ribs

3 medium leeks, cleaned

1 1/2 pounds boneless beef chuck

Dill Matzo Balls (page 281)

4 medium carrots, halved crosswise

1 medium turnip, peeled and cut into 8 wedges

1. Put garlic, bay leaf, thyme, parsley, cloves, and peppercorns on a piece of cheesecloth and tie ends to form a seasoning bag.

2. Combine seasoning bag, onion, celery, salt, water, and short ribs in stock pot or other large pot of at least 7 quarts. Bring to a boil. Cover and simmer 30 minutes, skimming occasionally.

3. Cut off dark green tops of leeks. If you like, tie dark parts in a bundle with string and put in the pot to flavor the broth. Tie rest of leeks in another bundle, leaving them whole; set aside.

4. Add beef chuck to pot and bring to a simmer; skim froth from surface. Cover and cook over low heat, skimming froth and fat occasionally, 1 1/2 hours. Water should bubble very gently; if it boils hard, reduce heat to very low and cover pot only partially.

5. Meanwhile, prepare matzo balls. After chuck has simmered 1 1/2 hours, add carrots, turnip, and whole leeks to pot. Push vegetables into liquid. Add water, if necessary, so it barely covers vegetables. Bring to a simmer. Cover and cook about 1 hour or until beef and vegetables are very tender when pierced with a sharp knife. If cooking this ahead, refrigerate broth in one container and beef and vegetables in another. Before serving, remove fat from surface of broth.

6. Reheat beef and vegetables gently in broth. Reheat matzo balls in their cooking liquid. Remove beef and vegetables to serving bowls. Cover and keep warm. Discard celery, onion, dark green of leeks, and seasoning bag. Season broth to taste with salt and pepper.

7. Ladle broth into bowls. Add matzo balls with a slotted spoon. Serve meat and vegetables moistened with a little broth.

❋ Ground Beef

Indian Jewish Chili with Chickpeas and Bulgur Wheat

Makes about 6 servings

Seasoned in the fashion of Indian Jews—with garlic, cumin, and dill—and spooned over Bulgur Wheat Pilaf, this chili is tasty and simple to prepare. If you prefer, use ground chicken or turkey instead of beef.

1 tablespoon vegetable oil

1 medium onion, minced

3/4 pound extra-lean ground beef

4 large cloves garlic, minced

2 teaspoons ground cumin

1 pound ripe tomatoes, peeled, seeded, and chopped, or one 28-ounce can plum tomatoes, drained and chopped

1 bay leaf

Salt and freshly ground pepper, to taste

1/4 teaspoon hot red pepper flakes

One 15-ounce can chickpeas (garbanzo beans), drained

3 tablespoons tomato paste

1/4 cup water

1/4 cup chopped fresh dill

Bulgur Wheat Pilaf (page 511)

2 tablespoons chopped fresh Italian parsley

1. Heat oil in a sauté pan. Add onion and sauté over medium heat about 5 minutes. Add beef, garlic, and cumin and sauté, stirring often, about 7 minutes or until meat changes color. Add tomatoes, bay leaf, salt, pepper, and pepper flakes. Cover and cook 10 minutes. Add chickpeas, tomato paste, and water and stir until blended. Cook uncovered 5 minutes or until sauce is thick. Discard bay leaf. Stir in dill. Adjust seasoning.

2. Prepare Bulgur Wheat Pilaf. Then, transfer pilaf to a serving dish. Ladle 1/3 to 1/2 cup chili over the center of the pilaf and sprinkle with a little of the parsley. Spoon remaining chili into a serving dish and sprinkle with remaining parsley.

Savory Meat Blintzes

Makes 4 to 6 servings

Just a small amount of olives, capers, and raisins lift this meat filling beyond the usual mixture of meat and onions. Beef is the traditional choice for meat blintzes but you can make this filling with chicken or turkey if you like. Serve them with Sephardic Tomato Sauce (page 375), Tomato Sauce with Mild Chiles (page 587), or your favorite tomato sauce.

2 or 3 tablespoons vegetable oil

1 small onion, chopped

1/2 green bell pepper, chopped

1/2 pound lean ground beef (about 1 cup packed)

2 ripe medium tomatoes, peeled, seeded, and chopped, or canned tomatoes, drained and chopped

1/2 teaspoon dried oregano

Salt and freshly ground pepper, to taste

3 tablespoons raisins

1/3 cup diced green olives

1 tablespoon capers, rinsed and chopped

1 large hard boiled egg, chopped (optional)

10 to 14 Herb Blintzes for Meat Fillings (page 301)

1. Heat 1 or 2 tablespoons oil in a skillet. Add onion and pepper and sauté over medium heat 7 minutes or until softened. Add beef and sauté, stirring, until it changes color, 3 or 4 minutes. Add tomatoes, oregano, salt, pepper, and raisins and bring to boil. Cook over medium heat, stirring often, 5 minutes. Remove from heat. Stir in olives, capers, and chopped egg, if using. Adjust seasoning. Transfer to a bowl and let cool.

2. Prepare blintzes. Then, lightly oil 2 medium baking dishes. Spoon about 3 tablespoons filling onto less attractive side of each blintz, across the third of the blintz nearest you. Slightly fold over each side of the blintz, to your right and left, then roll up in cigar shape, beginning at edge with filling and rolling away from you. Arrange blintzes seam side down in one layer in oiled dish. Brush them with 1 tablespoon oil.

3. Preheat oven to 375°F. Bake blintzes about 20 minutes or until filling is hot. Serve immediately, with tomato sauce.

Middle Eastern Meatballs

Makes 4 or 5 servings

Meatballs in tomato sauce are popular among Jews from most parts of the world. Jews from Middle Eastern countries like to make them spicy, adding the lively flavors of cumin, turmeric, and fresh garlic. Serve these meatballs over rice.

1 pound ground beef

2 tablespoons bread crumbs

1/3 cup finely minced onion

4 large cloves garlic, minced

1 1/2 teaspoons ground cumin

1/2 teaspoon ground turmeric

1/4 teaspoon cayenne pepper, plus a pinch for sauce

1/4 to 1/2 teaspoon salt

2 tablespoons olive oil or vegetable oil

2 cups tomato sauce

1/2 cup water

1. Put beef in a bowl. Mix bread crumbs with onion, garlic, cumin, turmeric, cayenne, and salt in another bowl. Add to beef and mix well. Shape mixture into small balls, using 1 or 2 tablespoons for each. Roll them between your palms until they are smooth.

2. Heat oil in a heavy skillet. Add meatballs and brown them on all sides over medium-high heat. Transfer to paper towels with slotted spoon. Discard fat form skillet.

3. Heat tomato sauce and water in a medium saucepan. Simmer 2 minutes. Add meatballs, cover and cook over low heat 30 minutes. Taste sauce for seasoning, adding a pinch of cayenne, if desired.

My Mother's Layered Shepherd's Pie

Makes 4 to 6 servings

Traditional English shepherd's pie features meat topped with mashed potatoes and includes cheese and milk. My mother's savory kosher version includes no dairy products but instead is enhanced with tomato sauce. She uses two layers of potatoes and meat and adds additional vegetables inside her "pie" or casserole dish for good taste as well as nutrition.

2 pounds boiling potatoes, scrubbed and quartered

2 to 3 tablespoons vegetable oil

About 1/3 cup beef or chicken stock

Salt and freshly ground pepper, to taste

1 large onion, chopped

2 large cloves garlic, chopped

1 teaspoon paprika

1 pound ground beef

2 cups tomato sauce

1 cup diced cooked carrots

1 cup frozen peas, cooked 1 minute and drained

1. Cook potatoes in water to cover in a large saucepan about 25 minutes or until tender. Peel them, put them in a large bowl, and mash. Beat in 1 or 2 tablespoons oil. Gradually beat in stock, leaving potato mixture fairly stiff. Season with salt and pepper.

2. In large skillet heat 1 tablespoon oil. Add onion and sauté over medium heat 5 minutes. Stir in garlic, paprika, and beef and sauté, stirring to separate meat pieces, about 7 minutes. Stir in 1 cup tomato sauce. Simmer over low heat 5 minutes. Add carrots and peas. Adjust seasoning.

3. Preheat oven to 350°F and grease a 2-quart casserole dish. Spoon a little less than half the mashed potatoes into dish. Top with half the beef mixture. Spoon remaining mashed potatoes over top and spread lightly. Top with remaining beef mixture, then remaining tomato sauce.

4. Set baking dish on a baking sheet. Bake casserole 40 minutes or until bubbling. Let stand about 5 minutes before serving.

Hungarian Jewish Stuffed Peppers

Makes 4 or 5 servings

Jews from Hungary like to prepare peppers with a ground beef stuffing and to simmer them in a sweet and sour tomato sauce. Unlike the stuffed peppers of their countrymen, their stuffing uses kosher meat. Choose peppers that have squarish rather than pointed bottoms so they stand up straight. Green peppers are traditional but you can use red, yellow, or orange ones also. Stuffed peppers are a favorite for Sukkot, when plenty of peppers and tomatoes are in the markets.

1 medium onion

2 pounds ripe tomatoes, peeled, if desired, and diced, or two 14¹/₂-ounce cans diced tomatoes with their juice

2 tablespoons tomato paste

¹/₂ cup water

1 bay leaf (optional)

Salt and freshly ground pepper, to taste

¹/₃ cup long-grain rice, rinsed and drained

1 slice challah or white bread, day-old or stale

¹/₂ pound ground beef

¹/₄ chopped fresh parsley

1 teaspoon paprika (optional)

4 or 5 green bell peppers

1 to 2 tablespoons brown sugar, or to taste

1 to 2 tablespoons strained fresh lemon juice, or to taste

1. Slice half the onion and put it in a stew pan. Add tomatoes, tomato paste, water, bay leaf if using, and a pinch of salt and pepper. Mix well and bring to a boil. Cover and cook over low heat 15 minutes.

2. Boil rice in a saucepan of 2 cups boiling salted water 10 minutes. Rinse with cold water and drain well.

3. Soak bread in cold water and squeeze dry. Put in a bowl. Coarsely grate remaining onion half and add to bowl. Add beef, parsley, paprika if using, ¹/₂ teaspoon salt, and ¹/₄ to ¹/₂ teaspoon ground pepper and mix well. Add rice and mix again.

4. Cut a slice off top (stem end) of each pepper. Reserve slice; remove stem, core, and seeds. Spoon stuffing into whole peppers and cover with reserved slices. Stand them up in tomato sauce. Cover and simmer, adding boiling water from time to time if sauce becomes too thick, 45 minutes to 1 hour or until peppers are very tender.

5. Gently remove peppers. Discard bay leaf. If sauce is too thin, cook it uncovered over medium-high heat, stirring often, a few minutes or until thickened. Add sugar and simmer 1 minute. Add lemon juice. Adjust seasoning. Serve peppers hot, with sauce.

Mexican-Israeli Stuffing for Peppers

Makes 2 to 2¹/₂ cups, enough for 4 to 6 peppers

This stuffing recipe is inspired by a Mexican woman married to an Israeli whom I chatted with while waiting on line at a pharmacy. She takes her Ashkenazic mother-in-law's stuffed peppers and spices up the filling with the seasonings she grew up using: cumin, hot pepper, marjoram, and thyme. She also adds a pinch of the same spices to the sauce. The stuffing is aromatic and flavorful but not hot, and I love it.

¹/₂ cup white rice, short- or long-grain

1 to 2 tablespoons olive oil or vegetable oil

1 medium onion, minced

2 cloves garlic, minced

1¹/₂ teaspoons ground cumin

1 teaspoon sweet paprika

¹/₂ teaspoon dried marjoram

¹/₂ teaspoon dried thyme

¹/₂ pound lean ground beef

¹/₄ teaspoon salt

¹/₄ teaspoon freshly ground pepper

¹/₄ teaspoon hot paprika, pure chili powder, or cayenne pepper

1. Cook rice uncovered in a saucepan of boiling salted water 10 minutes; it should be partially cooked. Rinse with cold water and drain well. Transfer to a bowl.

2. Heat oil in a skillet and add onion. Cook over medium-low heat, stirring often, 7 minutes or until it begins to turn golden. Add garlic, cumin, and sweet paprika and cook, stirring, 1 minute. Add marjoram and thyme. Transfer mixture to bowl of rice. Let mixture cool completely.

3. When rice and onion mixture is cool, add beef, salt, pepper, and hot paprika. Knead by hand to blend ingredients thoroughly. Refrigerate in a covered container until ready to use.

Meat-Stuffed Winter Squash

Makes 4 servings   Ⓜ

Attractive, delicious stuffed winter squashes are always festive and are great for Sukkot, Thanksgiving, or for Friday night dinner. I love the sweet taste of the small zucchini-shaped striped Delicata squashes, but acorn squashes are also a great choice because of their lovely ridged shape.

2 Delicata or acorn squashes, halved lengthwise and seeded

1 large onion, minced

4 slices white bread

1 pound lean ground beef

1/4 cup chopped fresh parsley

1 teaspoon dried thyme

1 teaspoon paprika

1/4 teaspoon cayenne pepper

1/2 teaspoon freshly ground pepper

2 medium cloves garlic, chopped

1/2 teaspoon salt

2 large eggs

Quick Tomato Sauce for Vegetables (page 463)

1. Preheat oven to 375°F. Lightly spray a heavy roasting pan with oil spray. Add enough water to go about a 1/4-inch up sides of pan. Place squash halves cut-side down in pan. Bake about 35 minutes or until just tender when pierced with fork. Remove from oven.

2. Put onion in a strainer and sprinkle lightly with salt. Let stand about 5 minutes. Dip each bread slice in a bowl of water to moisten. Rinse onion in strainer. Add soaked bread to onion in strainer and squeeze both dry.

3. Mix beef with onion, bread, parsley, thyme, paprika, cayenne, ground pepper, garlic, and 1/2 teaspoon salt in a medium bowl. Add eggs and mix well. Knead mixture briefly to be sure ingredients are evenly combined.

4. Reduce oven temperature to 350°F. Turn squash halves cut-side up and fill them with stuffing. Reserve leftover stuffing for making meatballs. Add a little water to roasting pan. Cover squashes and bake 45 minutes. Uncover and bake 15 more minutes or until stuffing is hot.

5. Meanwhile, prepare tomato sauce. Then, roll remaining stuffing between your palms into small, walnut-size balls. Cook meatballs in quick tomato sauce 30 minutes. Serve meatballs in sauce separately.

Beef, Rice, and Tomato in Zucchini Boats

Makes 4 to 6 servings   Ⓜ

Stuffed zucchini are a most popular Sukkot specialty. In Israel they are one of the highlights of Sephardic cooking all year round. Zucchini are one of the easiest vegetables to stuff because they do not require pre-cooking. Simply cut them in half, remove their centers, fill them, and bake.

1/2 cup long-grain white rice, rinsed and drained

2 or 3 tablespoons vegetable oil or olive oil

1 medium onion, finely chopped

2 ripe plum tomatoes, peeled, or 2 canned plum tomatoes, drained

5 large cloves garlic, peeled

1/2 pound lean ground beef

1/2 teaspoon ground cumin

Salt and freshly ground pepper, to taste

2 tablespoons chopped fresh Italian parsley

2 to 21/2 pounds zucchini

1 tablespoon tomato paste

1/4 cup water

1. Add rice to 3 cups boiling salted water in a medium saucepan and boil 10 minutes. Rinse with cold running water and drain well.

2. Heat 1 or 2 tablespoons oil in a skillet. Add onion and sauté over medium-low heat until softened, about 5 minutes. Let cool. Finely chop fresh or canned tomato. Coarsely chop 3 garlic cloves and reserve for sauce. Mince remaining garlic.

3. Combine beef with sautéed onion and tomato in a medium bowl. Add minced garlic, cumin, $^1/_4$ to $^1/_2$ teaspoon salt, $^1/_2$ teaspoon ground pepper, and parsley and mix well. Add rice and mix well.

4. Preheat oven to 425°F. Cut zucchini in half lengthwise. Use a spoon to scoop out centers. Rinse zucchini shells and pat them dry. Put them in a baking dish. Fill them with stuffing.

5. Mix tomato paste with $^1/_4$ cup water and a pinch of salt and pepper and spoon mixture over zucchini. Add enough water to pan to cover zucchini by one third. Add coarsely chopped garlic to pan. Sprinkle remaining oil over zucchini. Cover and bake 15 minutes. Reduce oven temperature to 350°F and bake 15 more minutes. Uncover and bake, basting occasionally, 15 minutes or until zucchini is very tender. Serve hot.

Spaghetti with Spicy Meat Sauce

Makes 4 main-course servings   **M**

Yemenite spices brighten up any spaghetti sauce. Besides spaghetti, this sauce is good with bulgur wheat, kasha, or white or brown rice. If you have spicy Zehug (page 592) or another hot pepper-garlic sauce, you can serve it on the side, and omit the serrano peppers and garlic from the sauce.

2 or 3 tablespoons vegetable oil
12 ounces ground beef (about 1$^1/_2$ cups)
2 medium onions, minced
1 cup chopped celery
2 serrano peppers, ribs and seeds removed, minced (see Note)
Salt and freshly ground pepper, to taste
6 large cloves garlic, minced
1 tablespoon ground cumin
1 teaspoon ground turmeric
1 cup tomato sauce
12 ounces spaghetti
2 to 3 tablespoons chopped fresh cilantro

1. Heat 1 tablespoon oil in a large sauté pan. Add beef and sauté over medium heat, breaking up meat with a wooden spoon, about 7 minutes or until changes color. Transfer to bowl.

2. Add 1 or 2 tablespoon oil to pan. Add onions, celery, peppers, and a pinch of salt and ground pepper. Cook over medium-low heat, stirring occasionally, about 7 minutes or until onion begins to brown. Add beef, garlic, cumin, and turmeric and cook, stirring, 1 minute. Add tomato sauce and simmer 5 minutes. Cover and keep warm.

3. Cook spaghetti uncovered in a large pot of boiling salted water over high heat, lifting occasionally with tongs, 8 to 9 minutes or until tender but firm to the bite.

4. Drain spaghetti well. If there is room in pan of sauce, add it to pan; otherwise, put it in a large heated bowl and add sauce. Toss lightly until blended. Adjust seasoning. Bring some of sauce to top for serving. Sprinkle with cilantro and serve.

Note: Wear rubber gloves when handling hot peppers.

Meat Loaf with Egg

Makes 6 to 8 servings

My mother puts hard boiled eggs in her meat loaf to entice children to eat meat loaf. It worked in my case; for me the egg in the middle of my meat loaf slice was the best part. When I was growing up, this was a standard weekday entree. On the side, we always had pareve mashed potatoes.

You can bake the mixture in a loaf pan, as my mother does, or shape it free-form in one or several loaves and bake them in a roasting pan, as my aunt does. Some cooks bake individual meat portions in muffin tins.

Now my mother often makes meat loaf with ground turkey or chicken instead of beef so it will be leaner, and spices it up with garlic. Ketchup was the topping in my childhood home but as an adult I prefer to mix it with tomato sauce.

1¹⁄₂ pounds ground beef

1 medium onion, grated

2 large cloves garlic, pressed (optional)

2 large eggs, lightly beaten

2 slices challah or white bread, soaked in water and squeezed dry

¹⁄₄ teaspoon salt

¹⁄₂ teaspoon freshly ground pepper

4 tablespoons ketchup

2 large hard boiled eggs, shelled

1 cup tomato sauce or one 8-ounce can

1. Preheat oven to 350°F. Combine the beef, onion, garlic if using, beaten eggs, challah, salt, pepper, and 2 tablespoons ketchup very well in a medium bowl. Lightly oil a 9 × 5-inch loaf pan. Put half of beef mixture inside. Put whole hard boiled eggs lengthwise in center. Top with remaining meat loaf mixture, filling spaces well.

2. Mix remaining 2 tablespoons ketchup with tomato sauce in a bowl. Pour sauce over top of loaf. Bake 1 hour. Serve in fairly thick slices.

Spicy Beef Patties

Makes 6 to 8 servings

For Friday's lunch, in the midst of cooking the Shabbat meals, my mother-in-law often prepared beef patties when her five children still lived at home. My husband says the aromas of the dishes she was preparing for the Friday night dinner were so enticing that everyone seemed to become extra-hungry at lunchtime. She quickly sautéed these patties in a skillet but you can grill or broil them instead as hamburgers. She slipped them inside fresh pita bread, with diced tomatoes, cucumbers, and pickles. For those who wanted it, there was fiery Zehug (page 592) on the table as well.

2 medium onions, minced

About 1 teaspoon salt

4 slices stale white bread

1 pound lean ground beef

¹⁄₄ cup chopped fresh cilantro

1¹⁄₂ teaspoons ground cumin

1 teaspoon paprika

¹⁄₂ teaspoon ground turmeric

¹⁄₄ teaspoon cayenne pepper

¹⁄₄ teaspoon freshly ground pepper

2 large garlic cloves, chopped

2 large eggs

About 3 tablespoons vegetable oil

1. Put onions in a strainer and sprinkle with ¹⁄₂ teaspoon salt. Let stand about 5 minutes. Dip each bread slice in a bowl of water to moisten. Rinse onions in strainer. Add soaked bread to onions and squeeze both dry.

2. Mix beef with onions, bread, cilantro, cumin, paprika, turmeric, cayenne, ground pepper, garlic, and if you like, ¹⁄₂ teaspoon salt. Add eggs. Mix thoroughly but lightly. Shape mixture into patties, using about ¹⁄₃ cup mixture for each. Flatten them.

3. Heat 2 or 3 tablespoons oil in a large, heavy skillet. Add enough patties to make one layer and sauté over medium-low heat about 5 minutes per side or until cooked through. Sauté remaining patties in same way, adding oil to skillet if necessary and heating it before adding more patties. Drain patties on paper towels before serving.

Deli Meats

Warm Corned Beef and Pasta Salad with Mustard Vinaigrette

Makes 4 to 6 servings **M**

Corned beef is not just for sandwiches. Try it in this colorful salad, with pasta spirals, green beans, capers, and a spicy dressing. You can make it ahead and keep it in the refrigerator, then warm it slightly before serving.

Mustard-Caper Vinaigrette (page 596)
1 pound pasta spirals
6 to 8 ounces very thin slices corned beef, cut into thin strips
8 ounces green beans, ends removed, halved
1/3 cup chopped fresh parsley
1/2 cup cherry tomatoes

1. Prepare vinaigrette. Then, cook pasta uncovered in a large pot of boiling salted water over high heat about 8 minutes or until tender but firm to the bite. Drain, rinse with cold water, and drain well again. Transfer to a large bowl, add vinaigrette, and toss. Add corned beef and toss.

2. Cook green beans uncovered in a saucepan of boiling salted water over high heat about 5 minutes or until crisp-tender. Drain.

3. Add green beans to salad and toss. Cover and microwave or steam briefly until warm.

4. Add parsley to salad and toss. Adjust seasoning. Garnish salad with cherry tomatoes.

Kosher Reuben Sandwiches

Makes 2 servings **M**

Growing up in a traditional Orthodox home, I always found it strange that the Reuben sandwich, which features the nonkosher combination of meat with cheese, became a standard item on American kosher-style deli menus. I make a kosher version with nondairy tofu cheese instead of the usual Swiss cheese. It tastes good with sauerkraut and corned beef or pastrami.

4 slices rye bread or marbled pumpernickel and rye
Mayonnaise or mustard (for spreading)
2 to 4 ounces thinly sliced corned beef or pastrami
1/4 cup sauerkraut, drained
2 or 4 slices tofu cheese
2 to 3 teaspoons vegetable oil or a little oil spray

1. Preheat toaster oven to 450°F or preheat sandwich grill. Spread bread lightly with mayonnaise or mustard. Top 2 bread slices with the meat, then cover with sauerkraut and tofu cheese. Top with other slices of bread and press together.

2. Set sandwiches on tray of toaster oven or in sandwich grill. Brush top of each sandwich lightly with oil, or spray with a little oil spray. Bake or grill just until cheese melts, about 2 minutes.

Pastrami and Peppers with Bulgur Wheat

Makes 4 servings

Diced pastrami makes a tasty seasoning for grains, and fortunately, a little goes a long way. For a quick lunch or supper dish, you can combine it with bulgur wheat and with fast-cooking vegetables.

2 tablespoons vegetable oil

1 medium onion, chopped

2 red or green bell peppers, or 1 of each, cut into strips

1 1/2 cups bulgur wheat

3 cups beef, chicken, or vegetable stock or water

1/2 teaspoon dried oregano

Salt and freshly ground pepper, to taste

1 cup frozen or canned corn kernels

2/3 cup frozen peas

4 ounces thinly sliced pastrami, cut into short, thin strips (about 1 cup strips)

Cayenne pepper to taste (optional)

Heat oil in a large saucepan. Add onion and peppers and sauté over medium heat about 5 minutes. Add bulgur and sauté lightly. Add stock, oregano, salt, and pepper and bring to a boil. Cover and cook 10 minutes over low heat. Add corn and peas and stir lightly. Cover and cook 5 minutes or until bulgur wheat is tender and liquid is absorbed. Lightly stir in pastrami, cover, and cook 1 minute. Let stand about 5 minutes before serving. Adjust seasoning, adding cayenne, if using.

Veal

Veal Chops in Tomato-Mushroom Sauce

Makes 4 servings

When I was growing up, my mother often prepared veal chops by breading and sautéing them in oil, as you would for schnitzel, and then baking them in tomato sauce. For this lighter, easier version, I like to brown the veal without a coating and braise it in a savory sage-accented tomato-mushroom sauce.

4 veal chops, trimmed of excess fat and patted dry

Salt and freshly ground pepper, to taste

2 to 3 tablespoons olive oil

1 small onion, minced

8 ounces mushrooms, diced

3 large cloves garlic, chopped

One 28-ounce can tomatoes, drained and chopped

1 tablespoon chopped fresh sage or 1 teaspoon dried, crumbled

1 tablespoon chopped fresh parsley

1. Sprinkle veal on both sides with pepper. Heat oil in large, heavy sauté pan or skillet over medium-high heat. Add veal and brown it, in batches if necessary, about 2 minutes per side. Transfer to a plate. Add onion to pan and sauté about 5 minutes over medium heat. Add mushrooms and sauté 2 minutes. Stir in garlic, then tomatoes, and sauté 2 minutes. Add salt, pepper, and half the sage.

2. Return veal to skillet with any juices on plate and bring to a simmer. Cover and cook over low heat about 10 minutes per side or until veal is tender and cooked through; meat should be white. Add remaining sage to sauce. Adjust seasoning, and serve sprinkled with parsley.

Veal Tajine with Zucchini and Saffron

Makes 4 servings

A tajine is a Moroccan stew usually prepared with meat or chicken and is named for the serving dish with a cone-shaped lid that is traditionally used for cooking and serving the stew.

I like this light stew for Shabbat in late spring or summer. Couscous is the perfect accompaniment.

1/4 teaspoon saffron threads

1/4 cup hot water

2 tablespoons olive oil

2 large onions, sliced

4 large cloves garlic, chopped

2 pounds boneless veal shoulder or veal stew meat, cut into 1 1/2-inch pieces

Salt and freshly ground pepper, to taste

1 teaspoon ground ginger

2 teaspoons paprika

1/2 teaspoon ground cumin

2 cups water

1 1/2 pounds zucchini, halved and cut into 1/2-inch slices

3 tablespoons chopped fresh Italian parsley

1. Add saffron to hot water and leave to soften 20 minutes.

2. Heat oil in a large stew pan or Dutch oven. Add onions and garlic and cook over low heat, stirring often, 5 minutes. Add veal, salt, pepper, ginger, paprika, cumin, and saffron in its liquid and mix well. Add 2 cups water and bring to a boil. Cover and simmer over low heat, stirring occasionally, 1 hour and 15 minutes or until veal is tender.

3. Transfer veal with a slotted spoon to a plate, leaving most of onions in stew pan. Cover plate. Boil sauce, including onions, stirring occasionally, until it is reduced to about 1 1/2 cups. Adjust seasoning.

4. Add zucchini to sauce and sprinkle with salt and pepper. Cover and cook over medium-low heat about 5 minutes or until tender. Return veal to sauce and heat through. Serve sprinkled with parsley.

Marinated Veal Chops in Spiced Orange Wine Sauce

Makes 4 servings

This aromatic sauce of cumin, orange juice, and white wine accented with raisins was popularized in Israel by my friend and culinary mentor, cookbook author Ruth Sirkis. She serves it with chicken. I also love it with the delicate taste of veal. If you make the sauce with potato starch, you can serve this dish for Passover.

1 1/2 teaspoons ground cumin

1 teaspoon paprika

Pinch of cayenne pepper

4 veal chops

1 onion, sliced thin

1 small carrot, sliced thin

1 rib celery, sliced thin

1 cup orange juice

1 cup dry white wine

Salt and freshly ground pepper, to taste

2 tablespoons vegetable oil

2 oranges, divided into neat segments, with any escaped juice reserved

1/4 cup dark raisins

2 teaspoons potato starch or cornstarch

1. Mix cumin, paprika, and cayenne in a bowl, then rub mixture thoroughly into veal chops. Put them in a large bowl and add onion, carrot, celery, orange juice, and wine. Cover and refrigerate at least 2 hours or overnight.

2. Preheat oven to 350°F. Pat veal dry, reserving marinade. Sprinkle with pepper. Heat oil in a large, heavy skillet, add veal in 2 batches, and sauté over medium-high heat until lightly browned on both sides. Transfer to a shallow baking dish. Discard fat from skillet. Add marinade with vegetables to skillet and bring to a boil, stirring.

3. Pour mixture over veal. Cover and bake 30 minutes. Uncover and bake about 10 more minutes or until veal is tender. Remove veal and strain cooking sauce into a saucepan. Return veal to baking dish, cover, and keep warm.

4. To veal sauce, add reserved juice from oranges and raisins, and simmer over medium heat about 7 minutes or until raisins are tender and sauce is well flavored.

5. Put potato starch in a small cup and whisk in 2 tablespoons water until smooth. Add to simmering sauce, stirring, and bring just back to a boil. Adjust seasoning. Add orange segments, heat over low heat a few seconds, and pour sauce over veal. Serve hot.

Grilled Veal Chops with Walnut Topping

Makes 4 servings

These summertime veal chops are topped with a delectable kosher walnut "butter" made of walnut oil, chopped walnuts, and pareve (nondairy) margarine. Be sure the nuts and the walnut oil are fresh. Store walnuts in the freezer and walnut oil in the refrigerator to prevent rancidity. To keep the veal moist, it is marinated before it is grilled. I like this veal with orzo or couscous and fresh green beans.

4 veal chops, about 1 inch thick

2 tablespoons vegetable oil

1 tablespoon strained fresh lemon juice

$^1/_2$ teaspoon dried basil

3 tablespoons nondairy margarine, soft

$1^1/_2$ tablespoons ground or very finely chopped walnuts

1 tablespoon minced fresh Italian parsley

3 tablespoons walnut oil

Salt and freshly ground pepper, to taste

1. Put veal chops in a shallow dish in which it fits snugly in 1 layer. Mix vegetable oil, lemon juice, and basil in a bowl and pour over veal. Turn veal so both sides are well coated. Cover and refrigerate 2 to 8 hours.

2. Mix margarine with walnuts and parsley in a bowl. With fork, gradually beat in walnut oil. Season with salt and pepper to taste. Cover and refrigerate 2 hours so flavors blend. Bring to room temperature before serving.

3. Heat grill or broiler with rack 3 to 4 inches from heat. Lightly oil grill or broiler rack. Remove veal chops from marinade and sprinkle them with salt and pepper. Put veal chops on hot grill or hot broiler rack and grill or broil, brushing occasionally with remaining marinade, about 4 minutes per side or until cooked to desired doneness; check by piercing with a sharp knife—meat should be white, not pink.

4. Transfer to platter and top each with a spoonful of walnut "butter." Serve immediately.

Hungarian Braised Veal

Makes 5 or 6 servings

Braising is a favorite technique for cooking meat in the Jewish kitchen. It is especially good for veal as it helps keep the meat moist. Here the veal is braised in a flavorful sauce of sweet peppers, mushrooms, and sweet and hot paprika. Serve the veal with farfel (egg barley).

One 2-pound veal roast, rolled and tied

Salt and freshly ground pepper, to taste

3 tablespoons vegetable oil

2 large onions, sliced

1 green pepper, diced

1 red or yellow pepper, diced

4 ounces mushrooms, quartered

2 large cloves garlic, chopped

2 teaspoons sweet paprika

$^1/_4$ teaspoon hot paprika or cayenne pepper, or to taste

$1^1/_2$ cups veal, beef, or chicken stock

$1^1/_2$ tablespoons tomato paste

1 bay leaf

1. Preheat oven to 350°F. Sprinkle veal lightly with pepper. Heat oil in a large ovenproof stew pan or Dutch oven over medium heat. Add veal and brown lightly on all sides. Remove to a plate.

2. Add onions to pan and sauté over medium heat about 15 minutes or until browned. Stir in green and red peppers and mushrooms and sauté 3 minutes. Stir in garlic, sweet and hot paprika and sauté a few seconds. Add stock, tomato paste, and bay leaf and bring to a simmer.

3. Return veal to stew pan and add juices from plate. Cover and bake in oven, turning once and basting from time to time, about 1 hour or until tender. Transfer to a plate.

4. Discard bay leaf from sauce. Season sauce with salt and pepper; add more hot paprika if desired. Slice veal and serve with sauce.

Springtime Veal with Peas and Baby Onions

Makes 4 servings   Ⓜ

My Parisian friend Paule Tourdjman once served this memorable dish to my husband and me for a Friday night dinner, and it's worth sharing. Braised veal with seasonal vegetables is often her choice for a festive Shabbat meal. Born in Morocco, she likes to cook in the styles of both her native and her adopted country. For this French dish she adds glazed pearl onions and serves it with rice pilaf or with Moroccan couscous.

2 pounds boneless veal shoulder

Salt and freshly ground pepper, to taste

3 or 4 tablespoons vegetable oil

2 large cloves garlic, chopped

**1 tablespoon fresh rosemary, minced, or 1 teaspoon
     crumbled dried**

**2 pounds ripe tomatoes, peeled, seeded, and chopped, or
     two 28-ounce cans tomatoes, drained and chopped**

1/2 cup water

3 pounds fresh peas, shelled, or 3 cups frozen

3/4 pound pearl onions of uniform size

1 teaspoon sugar

1. Cut veal into 1¹/₂-inch pieces, trimming off any excess fat, and pat them dry. Season lightly with pepper.

2. Heat 2 tablespoons oil in a heavy stew pan or Dutch oven. Add veal in batches and brown it lightly over medium heat, transferring pieces as they brown to a plate. Add garlic and rosemary cook over low heat, stirring, 30 seconds. Stir in tomatoes. Return veal to pan with any juices on plate and add water. Bring to a boil, stirring. Cover and simmer over low heat, stirring occasionally, 1 hour and 15 minutes. Skim fat from cooking liquid.

3. Cook fresh peas (but not frozen ones) in a saucepan of boiling salted water 3 minutes. Drain peas. Add fresh or frozen peas to veal stew and simmer uncovered 10 minutes or until meat is very tender, peas are tender, and sauce thickens slightly.

4. Put unpeeled onions in a heavy saucepan in which they can fit in one layer. Cover with water and bring just to a boil. Drain onions, rinse with cold water, and peel them. Return onions to saucepan. Add a pinch of salt and pepper, 1 or 2 tablespoons oil, and ¹/₃ cup water. Cover and cook over low heat, shaking pan occasionally, 15 minutes, or until nearly tender. Sprinkle onions with sugar and cook, uncovered, over medium heat, shaking pan often, until liquid is reduced to a syrupy glaze. Add glazed onions to veal stew and heat through. Adjust seasoning. Serve hot.

Veal with Artichokes, Tomatoes, and Dill

Makes 4 servings   Ⓜ

Jews from Greece, Turkey, and Lebanon use artichokes in many ways, and not just as an appetizer. Cooking them with meat or chicken as a main dish is a popular way to use this vegetable when it's at the peak of its season. To save time, however, you can use frozen or canned artichoke hearts (see Note).

**2 pounds boneless veal shoulder, trimmed of excess fat,
     patted dry, and cut into 1-inch pieces**

Salt and freshly ground pepper, to taste

2 tablespoons extra-virgin olive oil

1 medium onion, chopped

1/2 cup dry white wine

**3/4 pound ripe tomatoes, peeled, seeded, and chopped, or
     one 14-ounce can tomatoes, drained and chopped**

1 bay leaf

4 tablespoons minced fresh dill

4 fresh large artichokes bottoms (see page 589)

1. Season veal lightly with pepper. Heat 2 tablespoons oil in a heavy stew pan or Dutch oven. Add veal in batches and brown it lightly over medium heat, transferring pieces as they brown to a plate.

2. Add onion to pan and sauté 7 minutes, stirring often. Add wine, tomatoes, bay leaf, and a pinch of salt and pepper. Bring to a boil. Simmer uncovered

5 minutes. Stir in 2 tablespoons dill. Return veal to pan and mix well. Bring to a simmer. Cover and cook over low heat 1 hour or until veal is tender.

3. Meanwhile, prepare and cook artichoke bottoms. Cut each into 4 pieces.

4. Gently stir artichoke pieces into stew and heat 2 to 3 minutes. Stir in remaining 2 tablespoons dill. Adjust seasoning. Serve hot.

Note: Instead of fresh artichokes, you can substitute a 9-ounce package frozen artichoke hearts or 8 canned artichoke bottoms. Cook frozen artichoke hearts according to package directions and drain. Drain canned artichokes and quarter them.

Veal and Lima Bean Casserole with Chard, Dill, and Cilantro

Makes 4 servings

For this entree flavored abundantly with herbs in the style of the Jews of Egypt, you can vary the taste by using different meats. I like it with the delicate taste of veal but it is also good with ground beef, chicken, turkey, or with soy "ground meat." The stovetop casserole is easy to make and is popular among my students.

The original versions of this dish call for fava beans but most often I use lima beans, which are more readily available and faster to prepare.

3 tablespoons olive oil or vegetable oil

1 medium onion, chopped

1 pound ground veal

6 tablespoons long-grain rice

2 cups veal, beef, or chicken stock

One 10-ounce package lima beans

1/3 cup chopped fresh dill

1/3 cup chopped fresh cilantro

7 large cloves garlic, chopped

2 cups coarsely chopped Swiss chard leaves

Salt and freshly ground pepper, to taste

1. Heat 2 tablespoons oil in a large, heavy saucepan or stew pan. Add onion and sauté over medium heat 5 minutes or until beginning to turn golden. Add meat and sauté, stirring to separate it, until meat's color changes. Stir in rice, then 1 1/2 cups stock, and bring to a simmer. Cover and cook over low heat 10 minutes. Add lima beans, half the dill, half the cilantro, and remaining 1/2 cup stock. Shake pan and bring to boil. Cover and cook 5 more minutes or until rice and beans are barely tender.

2. Heat remaining tablespoon oil in a medium, heavy skillet. Add garlic and sauté 15 seconds. Add chard and sauté over medium heat, stirring, 3 minutes. Puree mixture in food processor.

3. Add garlic-chard mixture to beans and stir gently. Add salt and pepper. Cook uncovered over medium heat 2 minutes or until beans, chard, and rice are tender. Add remaining dill and cilantro. Serve hot.

Calves' Liver and Onions with Porcini and Wine Sauce

Makes 4 servings

Liver with onions is a classic in the Jewish kitchen. For reasons of kashrut, the liver is grilled or broiled rather than sautéed. This is my favorite twist on the popular classic. I like to top the liver with porcini mushrooms that cook along with the browned onions, and to make a quick sauce with red wine and beef stock. You can prepare a variation with chicken livers and use chicken stock in the sauce.

1 ounce dried porcini mushrooms or other dried mushrooms

3 tablespoons vegetable oil

2 large onions, halved and sliced thin

Salt and freshly ground pepper, to taste

1 pound calves' liver slices, about 1/4-inch thick

3/4 cup Quick Brown Sauce (page 590)

1/4 cup dry red wine

1 tablespoon minced fresh parsley

1. Soak mushrooms in enough hot water to cover for 30 minutes. Remove mushrooms and rinse. Cut any large pieces in half.

2. Heat 3 tablespoons oil in a large, heavy skillet or sauté pan. Add onions and sauté over medium heat, stirring often, until soft and golden brown, about 15 minutes. Add mushrooms, salt, and pepper. Cover and cook over low heat 5 minutes.

3. Prepare brown sauce. Preheat broiler with rack about 3 inches from flame. Rinse livers and pat dry on paper towels.

4. Transfer onion mixture to a bowl and keep warm. Add wine to skillet from cooking onions and bring to a boil, stirring.

5. Add to skillet and simmer until thick enough to coat a spoon. Adjust seasoning. Cover to keep warm.

6. Put livers on foil in broiler and sprinkle with salt. Broil $1^{1}/_{2}$ minutes or until top is light brown. Turn livers over, sprinkle second side with salt, and broil $1^{1}/_{2}$ to 2 more minutes or until cooked through and color is no longer pink; cut to check. Remove liver to a plate and keep warm.

7. Spoon onion mixture over liver. Spoon sauce over onions. Sprinkle with parsley and serve.

✻ Lamb

Middle Eastern Grilled Lamb Chops

Makes 4 servings

The most popular type of restaurant in Israel is called "Misadah Mizrahit," which means a restaurant serving Middle Eastern cuisine, although sometimes the English translation reads "Oriental food." Grilled lamb is a favorite in such restaurants, served with rice or fried potatoes and a variety of salads. These lamb chops, accompanied by a slightly hot sauce of peppers and tomatoes, make a festive entree for a Sephardic menu. The sauce, which is also delicious with chicken or with grilled eggplant, is easy to prepare. You can make it ahead and keep it in the refrigerator or freezer.

1 jalapeño pepper

2 tablespoons vegetable oil

1 large onion, chopped

2 red bell peppers or 1 red and 1 green, diced

2 cloves garlic, chopped

$1^{1}/_{2}$ pounds ripe tomatoes, peeled, seeded, and chopped, or one 28-ounce and one $14^{1}/_{2}$-ounce can tomatoes, drained and chopped

Salt and freshly ground pepper, to taste

8 rib lamb chops, about $1^{1}/_{2}$ inches thick

1. Discard seeds and ribs from jalapeño pepper and finely chop it. Wash your hands, cutting board, and knife immediately.

2. Heat oil in a deep skillet over low heat. Add onion and cook over low heat, stirring often, 5 minutes or until soft but not brown. Add bell peppers and cook, stirring often, about 5 minutes or until peppers soften. Add garlic and jalapeño pepper and sauté 1 minute. Add tomatoes and a pinch of salt. Cook uncovered over medium heat, stirring often, 20 to 30 minutes or until sauce is thick. Adjust seasoning.

3. Heat barbecue or stovetop grill; or preheat broiler with rack about 3 inches from heat source.

4. Trim excess fat from lamb chops and sprinkle them with pepper. Put chops on hot grill or hot broiler rack. Grill or broil about 6 minutes per side or until done to your taste. To check for doneness, press meat with your finger; if lamb is fairly firm, it is medium to well done.

5. Meanwhile, reheat sauce in a saucepan over medium heat. Serve sauce alongside chops.

Grilled Lamb with Argentinean Pesto

Makes 4 servings

Like most of their countrymen, Jews from Argentina like to make chimichurri, *the dipping sauce that traditionally is served with grilled meat. It's rather like a parsley pesto with zip, as it has hot red pepper flakes and vinegar. I like to divide the chimichurri in two parts: half of it without the parsley, which I use as a marinade for the lamb, and the other half with plenty of fresh parsley, for dipping.*

2 medium cloves garlic, peeled

2 tablespoons wine vinegar, red or white

2 tablespoons strained fresh lemon juice

1¹/₂ teaspoons dried oregano

¹/₂ teaspoon hot red pepper flakes, or to taste

5 tablespoons extra-virgin olive oil

8 rib lamb chops, about 1¹/₂ inches thick, trimmed of excess fat

Salt and freshly ground pepper, to taste

¹/₄ cup minced fresh Italian parsley

1. Chop garlic in food processor. Add vinegar, lemon juice, oregano, pepper flakes, and oil. Process to blend. Pour into a bowl.

2. Put lamb in a shallow dish in one layer. Add about 3 tablespoons of garlic mixture. Turn to coat lamb on all sides. Cover and refrigerate 1 or 2 hours. Cover remaining garlic mixture and reserve in a separate bowl.

3. Heat barbecue or stovetop grill; or preheat broiler with rack about 3 inches from heat source.

4. Remove lamb chops from marinade; discard any marinade remaining in dish. Sprinkle chops with

pepper. Put chops on hot grill or hot broiler rack. Grill or broil about 6 minutes per side or until done to your taste. To check for doneness, press meat with your finger; if lamb is fairly firm, it is medium to well done.

5. Add parsley to remaining garlic sauce. Season it with salt and pepper. Serve as a dipping sauce for the lamb.

Garlic-Studded Roast Lamb

Makes about 8 servings

Ashkenazic and Sephardic Jews agree that lamb and garlic are a terrific combination. For this roast, use the French technique of inserting slivers of garlic in the meat to flavor it as it roasts. For ease in preparation and in serving, ask your butcher to trim the fat from the lamb and to bone it and tie it as a rolled roast. Serve this delicious lamb for Passover or for a Friday night dinner. Good partners for the lamb are Oven-Fried Potatoes (page 443) and Israeli Eggplant Stew (page 446).

6 large cloves garlic, peeled

One 3¹/₂-pound boned rolled lamb shoulder roast (5¹/₂ pounds lamb shoulder before boning)

Salt and freshly ground pepper, to taste

2 medium onions, sliced

²/₃ cup water

2 large tomatoes, peeled, seeded, and chopped (optional)

2 tablespoons chopped fresh Italian parsley (optional)

1. Preheat oven to 375°F. Cut 12 very thin, lengthwise slivers of garlic; chop remaining garlic. Pierce lamb with point of a sharp knife. With aid of knife, hold a slit open and insert a garlic sliver. Repeat with remaining garlic slivers; space them fairly evenly. Sprinkle lamb with salt and pepper. Set it on a rack.

2. Add sliced onions, remaining garlic, and water to pan.

3. Cover lamb with foil and bake 1 hour. Uncover and bake 30 minutes. Add tomatoes, if using, to juices and stir. Roast lamb, basting it occasionally and adding a few tablespoons water to pan if it becomes dry, about 1 more hour. Lamb should be very tender and an instant-read or meat thermometer should register 150°F for medium or 160°F for well done.

4. Let meat rest 10 to 15 minutes before carving. Remove strings. With a very sharp large knife, carve lamb into slices about $1/2$-inch thick. With a small knife, cut excess fat from slices.

5. Serve lamb sprinkled with parsley, if using. If you like, season juices with pepper and serve them separately.

Lamb with Prunes and Toasted Almonds

Makes 4 servings

A favorite among Jews from North Africa, this saffron-seasoned entree is perfect for festive occasions like Rosh Hashanah. Serve it with couscous or rice and with artichoke hearts, green beans, or zucchini.

2 pounds lamb shoulder

1 tablespoon vegetable oil

1 large onion, minced

1 cup water

A large pinch of saffron threads (about $1/8$ teaspoon)

Salt and freshly ground pepper, to taste

1 cup pitted prunes

1 to 2 tablespoons brown sugar

$1/3$ cup whole blanched almonds, toasted

1. Cut lamb into 1-inch pieces, trimming off any excess fat, and pat them dry.

2. Heat oil in a nonstick stew pan or Dutch oven. Add lamb in batches and brown lightly on all sides over medium heat. Remove from pan to a plate. Add onion and sauté until brown, about 10 minutes; cover if pan becomes dry. Return meat and any juices from plate to the pan. Add water, saffron, salt, and pepper. Bring to a boil, stirring often. Cover and simmer over low heat, stirring occasionally, 1 hour or until lamb is tender; add a few tablespoons water if pan becomes dry.

3. Add prunes to stew pan and cook uncovered over medium heat 15 minutes or until just tender. Add sugar and cook over medium heat, occasionally stirring very gently, 5 minutes. Adjust seasoning.

4. Serve stew hot, garnished with toasted almonds.

Lamb with Eggplant Slices

Makes 4 to 6 servings

Jews of Middle Eastern origin often add fried eggplant to meat stews so the vegetable gains flavor from the meat's savory sauce. A friend of mine in Jerusalem gave me this recipe long ago. She makes it with either lamb or beef. Now I usually broil the eggplant slices; it's easier and uses much less fat. The dish is plenty rich from the lamb.

Serve the lamb with Bulgur Wheat Pilaf (page 511), fine noodles, or rice pilaf.

2 pounds lamb shoulder

2 or 3 tablespoons olive oil or vegetable oil, or 1 tablespoon oil and a little oil spray

1 large onion, chopped

2 pounds ripe tomatoes, peeled, or one 28-ounce can tomatoes with their juice

4 large cloves garlic, chopped

1 cup water

$1/2$ teaspoon ground allspice, or to taste

Salt and freshly ground pepper, to taste

2 medium eggplants, sliced crosswise $1/4$-inch thick

1 tablespoon strained fresh lemon juice

1 or 2 tablespoons chopped fresh Italian parsley

1. Cut lamb into 1-inch pieces, trimming off any excess fat, and pat them dry.

2. Heat 1 tablespoon oil in a heavy stew pan or Dutch oven. Add onion and sauté over medium heat 5 minutes or until beginning to turn golden. Add lamb and sauté lightly until meat becomes very light brown.

3. Chop fresh or canned tomatoes and add them with their juice to the pan. Add garlic and bring to a simmer. Add water, allspice, salt, and pepper and bring to a boil, stirring often. Cover and simmer over low heat, stirring occasionally, 1 hour or until lamb is tender; add a few tablespoons water if pan becomes dry. Arrange eggplant slices in one layer on a foil-lined baking sheet or broiler pan. If eggplant doesn't fit, do it in 2 batches. Brush or spray eggplant lightly with oil and sprinkle with salt and pepper. Broil 7 minutes. Turn over, brush or spray again with oil, and broil about 7 minutes or until barely tender.

4. When lamb is tender, add lemon juice to sauce, taste, and adjust seasoning. Add eggplant slices to pan, spoon a little sauce over slices, cover, and cook over low heat 10 minutes. Serve hot, sprinkled with chopped parsley.

Lamb and Vegetable Casserole

Makes 4 to 6 servings   Ⓜ

Jews from eastern Mediterranean countries make entrees like this using a small amount of meat to flavor a variety of vegetables. The result is a sort of baked ratatouille seasoned with allspice and a touch of cinnamon. It is easy to assemble as all the ingredients are combined in a baking dish and do not require separate sautéing.

Use either boneless lamb shoulder or buy shoulder chops and cut off the bones and fat.

1 to 1 1/2 pounds boneless lamb shoulder meat or about
    2 pounds shoulder chops

1 pound small zucchini, cut into 1-inch slices

One 1 1/4-pound eggplant, unpeeled and cut into 1-inch dice

2 pounds ripe tomatoes, peeled and diced, or two
    14 1/2-ounce cans diced tomatoes, with their juice

2 large onions, halved and sliced

1 pound red-skinned boiling potatoes, unpeeled

3 large cloves garlic, coarsely chopped

1/2 teaspoon salt, or to taste

1/2 teaspoon freshly ground pepper

1/2 teaspoon ground allspice

1/4 teaspoon ground cinnamon

A pinch of cloves

1/3 cup water

1 to 2 tablespoons olive oil

1. Preheat oven to 350°F. Trim excess fat from lamb and remove bones if using chops. Cut meat into 3/4-inch cubes. Combine lamb, zucchini, eggplant, tomatoes with their juice, and onions in a large gratin dish or shallow, heavy baking dish. Cut potatoes into 3/4-inch dice and add to gratin dish. Add garlic.

2. Mix the salt, pepper, allspice, cinnamon, and cloves in a small bowl. Sprinkle spice mixture over vegetables and lamb and toss with clean hands to mix thoroughly. Add water to gratin dish. Cover and bake

40 minutes. Drizzle with the oil. Bake uncovered, stirring often, 1 1/2 hours, or until lamb and vegetables are very tender; occasionally add a few tablespoons hot water to dish if necessary to prevent burning. When casserole is done, there should be little liquid left.

North African Lamb Stew with Celery

Makes 4 servings   Ⓜ

Jewish cooks from North African countries like to use celery as a vegetable and not simply as a seasoning. In this stew, the celery and lamb are paired with another popular flavor of the region, saffron. Many cooks substitute turmeric when they don't have saffron. The taste is completely different but is still good.

2 pounds boneless lean shoulder of lamb

2 tablespoons vegetable oil

1 large onion, chopped

1 tablespoon all-purpose flour

2 cups water

1/4 teaspoon firmly packed crushed saffron threads

Salt and freshly ground pepper, to taste

1 tablespoon tomato paste

1 pound celery (5 large ribs), peeled, halved lengthwise,
    and cut into 2-inch pieces

2 tablespoons chopped fresh Italian parsley

1 to 3 teaspoons strained fresh lemon juice, or to taste

1. Cut lamb into 1 1/4- to 1 1/2-inch pieces, trimming off any excess fat, and pat them dry.

2. Heat 1 tablespoon of oil in large, heavy stew pan. Add lamb in batches and brown lightly on all sides over medium-high heat. Remove from pan to a plate.

3. Add onion to pan and sauté over low heat, stirring often, about 7 minutes or until softened. Return meat to pan, reserving any juices on plate, and sprinkle meat with flour. Toss lightly to coat meat with flour. Cook over low heat, stirring often, 5 minutes. Stir in water and bring to boil, stirring often. Add meat juices from plate, saffron, salt, and pepper. Cover and cook over low heat, stirring and turning lamb cubes over occasionally, about 1 1/2 to 2 hours or until lamb is very tender. Stir in tomato paste.

4. Heat remaining tablespoon oil in large skillet over medium-high heat, add celery, and sauté about 3 minutes; do not let it brown. Add celery to stew and push pieces down into sauce. Simmer 10 to 15 minutes or until celery is just tender.

5. Sauce should be thick enough to lightly coat spoon; if it is too thin, simmer uncovered over low heat, stirring occasionally very gently, 5 to 10 minutes until lightly thickened. Remove from heat. Stir in parsley and lemon juice. Adjust seasoning.

Lamb with Lima Beans

Makes 4 or 5 servings

A favorite in the Sephardic kitchen, braised lamb shoulder produces a flavorful sauce that enhances many vegetables. It's popular with white beans and, in France, with pale green flageolet beans. I like to use frozen lima beans, as they contribute a similar color to the entree and taste great with the lamb and its sauce.

2 pounds boneless lamb shoulder or lamb for stew, cut into
    1-inch pieces and trimmed of excess fat

1 to 2 tablespoons extra-virgin olive oil

1 large onion, chopped

6 large cloves garlic, chopped

1 pound ripe tomatoes, peeled, seeded, and chopped, or one
    28-ounce can tomatoes, drained and chopped

1 large sprig fresh thyme

1 bay leaf

6 fresh Italian parsley stems, leaves reserved for chopping

1 cup water

1 small carrot, halved lengthwise

Salt and freshly ground pepper, to taste

One 1-pound or two 10-ounce packages frozen lima beans

Cayenne pepper, to taste

2 tablespoons chopped fresh Italian parsley

1. Pat lamb dry. Heat oil in a large, heavy stew pan or Dutch oven. Add lamb in batches and brown lightly on all sides over medium-high heat. Remove from pan to a plate. If necessary, pour off excess fat from pan, leaving only about 1 tablespoon. Add onion and sauté over medium-low heat about 5 minutes or until softened. Add garlic and sauté 30 seconds. Stir in tomatoes and cook 2 minutes.

2. Wrap thyme, bay leaf, and parsley stems in cheese-cloth and tie ends to form a seasoning bag; add to stew pan. Return lamb to pan. Add water, carrot, and a little salt and pepper. Bring to a boil. Cover and simmer about 45 minutes or until lamb is tender. Discard carrot and seasoning bag.

3. Skim off excess fat from sauce. Add lima beans. If stew is too thick, add a few tablespoons water. Bring to a boil. Cover and cook over low heat about 7 minutes or until beans are tender. Add cayenne; adjust seasoning. Serve sprinkled with parsley.

Lamb Navarin

Makes 4 servings

Navarin is a French stew of lamb and vegetables. This classic dish is popular among the Jews of France, especially for springtime. A meal in one pot with plenty of colorful vegetables, it's easy to prepare and delicious when made with delicate, young lamb.

    I thicken the sauce with potato starch instead of the traditional roux *because it's easier. Besides, potato starch makes the dish suitable for Passover; omit the peas if it's your family's custom not to eat them during the holiday.*

1¹/₂ to 2 pounds boneless lamb shoulder

Salt and freshly ground pepper, to taste

1 to 2 tablespoons olive oil

2 medium onions, chopped

2 large cloves garlic, chopped

1 pound ripe tomatoes, peeled, seeded, and chopped, or one
    28-ounce can tomatoes, drained and chopped

Bouquet Garni (page 602)

1¹/₂ cups veal, beef, or vegetable stock or water

12 to 16 pearl onions (optional), unpeeled

8 to 12 baby carrots, peeled

1 tablespoon tomato paste

2 tablespoons potato starch

2 small turnips, quartered

1¹/₂ pounds small new potatoes, peeled, or 3 to 4 large,
    quartered

1¹/₂ pounds fresh peas, shelled, or 1¹/₂ cups frozen peas

2 tablespoons chopped fresh Italian parsley

1. Cut lamb into 1-inch pieces, trimming off any excess fat, and pat them dry. Sprinkle lamb with pepper.

2. Heat oil in a heavy stew pan or Dutch oven. Add lamb in batches and brown lightly on all sides over medium-high heat. Remove from pan to a plate. Add onions and sauté over medium heat, stirring, 3 minutes. Add garlic and sauté 30 seconds. Stir in tomatoes.

3. Prepare Bouquet Garni and add to pan. Return lamb to stew pan with any juices that have accumulated on the plate. Add 1 cup stock and bring to a boil, stirring. Cover and simmer over low heat, stirring occasionally, 1 1/2 hours. Skim the fat from cooking liquid.

4. Put unpeeled pearl onions, if using, in a saucepan. Cover with water and bring just to a boil. Drain onions, rinse with cold water and peel them.

5. Add carrots and 1/2 cup stock and simmer 10 minutes. Stir tomato paste into sauce. Mix potato starch and 3 tablespoons water in a bowl to form a paste. Bring sauce to a simmer and add potato starch mixture, stirring. Return to a simmer, stirring.

6. Add turnips, potatoes, and pearl onions to stew pan and simmer 10 min. Add peas and simmer 8 to 10 minutes or until lamb and vegetables are tender. Discard bouquet garni. Adjust seasoning. Serve hot, sprinkled with parsley.

Sephardic Moussaka

Makes about 6 servings Ⓜ

Moussaka is a traditional favorite among Jews from Greece and Turkey. It is made of layers of ground lamb in a flavorful tomato sauce alternating with sautéed eggplant slices. Unlike many Greek moussaka recipes, the Sephardic one is made without cheese or béchamel sauce so it will be kosher. Instead, it has an easy tomato topping.

Pine nuts add a festive touch to the meat layers but you can omit them if you like. If you prefer a leaner dish, broil the eggplant instead of sautéing it. Follow the method in Broiled Eggplant (page 445).

About 8 tablespoons olive oil
2 large onions, chopped
1 1/4 pounds lean ground lamb
1 teaspoon paprika, plus a little for sprinkling
Salt and freshly ground pepper, to taste
Four 14 1/2-ounce cans diced tomatoes, drained
1 1/2 pounds eggplant
1/3 cup pine nuts (optional)
1/3 cup chopped fresh Italian parsley
4 large cloves garlic, minced
2 tablespoons tomato paste
1 1/2 cups beef or chicken stock

1. Heat 1 tablespoon oil in a large, heavy sauté pan. Add onions and sauté over medium-low heat about 5 minutes. Cover and sauté over low heat, stirring occasionally, about 5 minutes or until tender. Add lamb and cook over medium heat, crumbling with a fork, about 5 minutes or until it changes color. Add paprika, salt, pepper, and tomatoes, and cook over medium heat about 35 minutes or until mixture is thick and quite dry.

2. Meanwhile, cut eggplant into slices 1/4-inch thick. Heat 2 tablespoons oil in a large skillet over medium-high heat. Quickly add enough eggplant slices to make one layer. Sauté 2 minutes per side or until tender when pierced with a fork. Transfer slices to paper towels. Add 2 tablespoons oil to skillet and heat it. Continue sautéing remaining eggplant in batches, adding oil as needed.

3. Add pine nuts, if using, to meat sauce and cook 2 more minutes. Add parsley and half the garlic. Adjust seasoning.

4. For sauce, whisk tomato paste with stock. Add remaining garlic. Season with salt and pepper.

5. Preheat oven to 350°F. Oil a 13 × 9 × 2-inch baking dish. Put enough eggplant slices in dish to make 1 layer. Cover with about half the lamb mixture. Cover with another layer of eggplant. Spread remaining meat mixture on top. Cover with remaining eggplant. Pour sauce over top.

6. Bake moussaka 45 minutes. Let stand about 10 minutes before serving. Serve from the baking dish.

Lamb-Stuffed Onions

Makes 6 large or 12 small servings

If you love stuffed onions, stuffing whole onions or onion halves is a quicker method for making them than removing individual onion layers, as in Sweet and Sour Stuffed Onions (page 108). The robust taste of these thicker shells is a good match for a hearty cinnamon-accented lamb filling. Serve the stuffed onions for Sukkot or as a Hanukkah dish accompanied by potato, sweet potato, or zucchini pancakes.

6 large white or yellow onions, peeled

1/3 cup long-grain rice, washed and drained

Quick Tomato Sauce for Vegetables (page 463)

2 to 4 tablespoons olive oil or vegetable oil

1/2 pound lean ground lamb

2 medium cloves garlic, minced

1/2 teaspoon ground cinnamon

1/4 teaspoon salt

1/2 teaspoon freshly ground pepper

2 tablespoons chopped fresh parsley

1. Boil onions in a large pan of boiling salted water 15 minutes or until they are partially tender when pierced with a small, sharp knife. Drain and let cool.

2. Boil rice in a saucepan of 2 cups boiling salted water 10 minutes. Rinse with cold water and drain well.

3. Prepare tomato sauce. Then, for whole stuffed onions: cut a thin slice off the top and carefully scoop out the center, leaving a fairly thick shell; reserve center. For half onions: halve them crosswise and scoop out the center; reserve center.

4. Finely chop removed onion centers. (If you like, sauté chopped onion: heat 1 or 2 tablespoons oil in a skillet, add onion and sauté over medium-high heat, stirring often, 3 to 4 minutes or until lightly browned. Cool completely before mixing with meat.)

5. Combine lamb, garlic, cinnamon, salt, pepper, and parsley in a bowl and mix well. Add rice and chopped onion and mix well.

6. Preheat oven to 350°F. Spoon stuffing into onion shells. Put onions in a baking dish, stuffing side up. Sprinkle a little oil over each. Spoon tomato sauce over onions. Cover and bake 30 minutes. Uncover and bake, basting occasionally, 30 more minutes or until onions are very tender; add a few tablespoons hot water from time to time if pan becomes dry. Serve onions topped with sauce.

Pareve and Vegetarian Main Courses

Latkes and Schnitzel
411

Easy Vegetable Latkes

Black Bean Latkes

Crunchy Eggplant Schnitzel

Tzimmes and Other Casseroles
412

Valerie's Potato Pashtidah

Tzimmes with Matzo Balls

Indian Vegetable Tzimmes

Yemenite Eggplant Casserole

Tu Bishvat Sweet Potato and Fruit Casserole

Baked Balkan Vegetable Casserole (Givetch)

Cholent and Other Bean Dishes
417

Easy Meatless Cholent

Low-Fat Pareve Chili

Bean Medley with Zucchini and Za'atar

Esau's Lentil Pottage

Lentils with Peppers and Rice

Chickpea and Spinach Stew

Black Beans with Corn and Peppers

Black Beans with Moroccan Dressing

Sofrito Lima Beans

Black-Eyed Peas with Green Beans and Red Onions

Sweet and Spicy Chickpea-Zucchini Stew

Beans in Tomato-Garlic Salsa

Summer Squash with White Beans, Tomatoes, and Dill

White Beans with Rice and Carrots

Maghreb Bean and Squash Stew

P = *Pareve*   D = *Dairy*   M = *Meat*

Vegetable Stews
424

Day-after-Shabbat
Vegetable Stew

Double Tomato-Eggplant Stew

Sephardic Succotash

Sweet-and-Sour Vegetables

Easy Ratatouille with Tofu

Low-Fat Ratatouille with
Coriander

Stuffed Vegetables
427

Turkish Stuffed Eggplant

Stuffed Small Squashes with
American Rice Pilaf

Stuffed Acorn Squash with
Bulgur Wheat and Figs

Stuffed Peppers with "Meaty"
Almond-Rice Stuffing

Tomatoes with Ginger-Soy
Brown Rice Stuffing

Grains and Pasta
430

Curried Cabbage with Rice,
Mushrooms, and Peas

Wild and Brown Rice with
Asparagus and Broccoli

Brown Rice with Black-Eyed
Peas and Cumin Tomato Sauce

Bulgur Wheat with Lentils

Sunday Couscous

Savory Vegetable Medley
over Couscous

Blintzes, Sandwiches,
and Pizza
434

Mexican Onion-Tomato Blintzes

Israeli-Iraqi Vegetable Sandwich

Grilled Portobello Mushroom
Sandwich with Tahini

Sesame Vegetables in Pita

Pareve "Pizza"

Sauces
437

Herbed Tahini Sauce

Chunky Avocado Sauce
with Zehug and Olives

All the recipes in this chapter are meatless, or vegetarian. They also are pareve and do not contain dairy products. Therefore they can be served as stars of vegetarian menus or alongside dairy foods, meat, or fish.

Although eggs are also pareve, many of the recipes here do not contain eggs and thus qualify as vegan. For other pareve egg dishes, see the index on page 608. Vegetarians who eat dairy products can find recipes using milk and cheese in the chapter on dairy foods and blintzes in the Shavuot and other chapters. Additional vegetarian dishes can be found in the chapters on noodles and grains as well as in the holiday chapters. (See the table of contents, or the index on page 608.)

Pareve meals are often served in the homes of Orthodox Jews who wait six hours after eating meat before partaking of dairy foods. If people are hungry for a meal before the required number of hours has passed, they opt for a pareve repast.

Vegetarian dishes have long been an important component of Jewish cooking. Some practice vegetarianism on religious grounds and find evidence in the sacred writings that it is preferable. Many Jews follow the example of Queen Esther in the Purim story (see page 151), and become vegetarians when they're away from home and cannot obtain kosher meat. Today many are vegetarian because of personal taste or because of the health benefits of a vegetarian diet.

Because I love vegetarian food, I cook it often. I find pareve menus flexible and satisfying in many ways. They can be based on a big bowl of hearty soup, a substantial salad, or a casserole of legumes such as black-eyed peas. It's easy to serve one or several vegetable side dishes in larger quantities, along with bread or a grain dish, and have a satisfying vegetarian meal.

Many Jewish specialties are naturally pareve entrees or can become pareve with little adaptation. Vegetable kugels (casseroles) as well as savory noodle kugels are perfect when you want a festive main course. Vegetarian versions of *cholent* (slow-cooked stew) are on many Shabbat menus, both in homes and in synagogues.

A terrific choice for a holiday entree is stuffed vegetables—favorites in all branches of Jewish cooking. Whether you stuff eggplants, zucchini, onions, peppers, celery, cabbage leaves, or grape leaves, they turn the dinner into a feast. They are not only delicious but also economical. In addition, they can be made ahead and reheated. Many cooks serve stuffed vegetables hot on one day and cold on another.

Rice and other grains are a good basis for vegetable stuffings and can be combined with soy ground meat substitute to give them a meaty quality. Many Israeli cooks flavor their stuffings with sautéed onions, garlic, Italian parsley, fresh dill, or cilantro. For festive occasions, many add toasted walnuts, almonds, or pine nuts, which are especially welcome in a meatless stuffing. Such spices as paprika, saffron, cumin, or curry also add a wonderful aroma. For a different flavor in the sweet direction, you can add raisins and a hint of cinnamon or other sweet spices. A savory homemade tomato sauce makes a great accompaniment.

Soy has become the ultimate pareve food. A great variety of foods are made from soybeans, and they are very useful for preparing pareve meals and as substitutes for both *milchig* (milk-based) and *fleishig* (meat-based) ingredients. This selection is expanding every day. Many of them are certified kosher and can be found at natural foods stores as well as kosher groceries.

Many soy foods can also be added as pareve ingredients to meat or dairy meals. There are soy "cheeses," which can be paired with meats, and soy ground "meats," which can be used in dairy meals. With the aid of these foods, people can even make such recipes as kosher cheeseburgers—something never before imagined. In fact, with a soy meat substitute and a soy dairy substitute, even pareve "cheeseburgers" are now possible.

❋ Latkes and Schnitzel

Easy Vegetable Latkes

Makes 2 or 3 main-course
or 4 or 5 appetizer or side-dish servings

Green peas peek out of these golden brown pancakes made of mushrooms, chickpeas, onions, and carrots. They are delicious on their own, or topped with sour cream, yogurt, chunky tomato sauce, or your favorite salsa. For other latke recipes, see the Hanukkah chapter.

You can sauté the latkes ahead and reheat them on a baking sheet in a 400°F oven about 10 minutes.

4 to 6 ounces mushrooms

4 to 5 tablespoons vegetable oil

1 medium onion, finely chopped

1 cup coarsely grated carrot (1 large carrot)

¹/₂ cup canned chickpeas (garbanzo beans), drained and coarsely chopped

¹/₂ cup frozen green peas, thawed and cooked

2 large eggs or 3 large egg whites, slightly beaten

Salt and freshly ground pepper, to taste

1 tablespoon snipped fresh dill or 1 teaspoon dried

2 to 3 tablespoons matzo meal or dry bread crumbs

1. Halve mushrooms and slice thin. Heat 1 tablespoons oil in a large skillet. Add onion and sauté over medium heat 3 minutes. Add mushrooms and sauté 2 to 3 minutes or until vegetables are tender. Transfer to a bowl. Add carrot, chickpeas, and green peas and mix well. Add eggs, salt, pepper, dill, and 2 tablespoons matzo meal. Mix well; if mixture appears watery, add another tablespoon matzo meal.

2. Heat 3 to 4 tablespoons oil in a deep, large, heavy skillet, preferably nonstick. For each latke, drop 1 or 2 heaping tablespoons of vegetable mixture into pan. Flatten them slightly with back of a spoon. Sauté over medium heat 2 to 3 minutes on each side, or until golden brown. Turn very carefully using two slotted spatulas so the oil doesn't splatter. Drain on paper towels. Stir mixture before sautéing each new batch. If all the oil is absorbed, add a little more to pan before cooking next batch. Serve hot.

Black Bean Latkes

Makes 4 main-course
or 6 or 7 appetizer servings

Black beans make for hearty, protein-rich latkes, suitable for serving as a main course. These corn-studded latkes are good with Sephardic Salsa (page 131), Onion Marmalade (page 133), or tomato sauce, or with dairy toppings such as spiced yogurt. If using canned black beans, use those that contain only water and salt.

3 to 3¹/₂ cups cooked black beans or two 15- or 16-ounce cans, drained

1 medium onion, chopped

4 large cloves garlic, minced

¹/₄ cup chopped fresh cilantro

¹/₂ small jalapeño pepper, finely minced, or hot sauce to taste

2 teaspoons ground cumin

¹/₄ teaspoon salt

¹/₂ teaspoon freshly ground pepper

1 or 2 large eggs or egg whites, lightly beaten

¹/₂ cup cooked corn kernels

2 tablespoons bread crumbs

About 3 or 4 tablespoons vegetable oil

1. Combine black beans, onion, garlic, and cilantro in food processor. Process with brief pulses, scraping down the sides occasionally, until beans are ground, leaving a few small chunks. Transfer to a bowl. Add jalapeño pepper, cumin, salt, pepper, and 1 egg. Mix well. Lightly stir in corn and bread crumbs. If mixture is crumbly, add second egg or egg white and mix well. Shape mixture into 8 smooth patties. Set them on a plate.

2. Heat 3 or 4 tablespoons oil in a deep, large, heavy skillet, preferably nonstick. Add 4 patties to pan. Sauté over medium heat about 3 minutes on each side, or until browned. Turn carefully using two spatulas. Drain on paper towels. Stir mixture before sautéing each new batch. If all the oil is absorbed, add a little more to pan before cooking next batch. Serve hot.

Crunchy Eggplant Schnitzel

Makes 4 to 6 servings

To make a vegetarian schnitzel (breaded cutlet), eggplant is a favorite choice because of its meaty texture. This one has a crunchy corn meal coating. Serve this eggplant on its own, or accompanied by Sephardic Salsa (page 131), Grilled Red Pepper Sauce (page 461), or Onion Marmalade (page 133).

1 to 1¹/2 pounds eggplant

Salt and freshly ground pepper, to taste

²/3 cup all-purpose flour

²/3 cup bread crumbs

¹/3 cup cornmeal

2 large eggs

About ¹/3 cup vegetable oil

Lemon wedges

Fresh parsley or cilantro sprigs

1. Peel eggplant if desired. Cut into slices about ³/8-inch thick. Sprinkle eggplant slices lightly with salt and pepper.

2. Spread flour in a large plate and mix it with a pinch of salt. Mix bread crumbs and cornmeal; spread mixture in second plate. Beat eggs in a shallow bowl. Lightly coat 1 eggplant slice with flour on both sides. Tap and shake to remove excess flour. Dip piece in egg. Dip in cornmeal mixture, completely coating both sides; pat lightly so crumbs adhere. Set on a large plate. Repeat with remaining eggplant. Set coated pieces on plate side by side.

3. Heat ¹/4 cup oil in a large, heavy skillet. Add enough eggplant to make one layer. Sauté over medium-high heat about 2 minutes per side or until golden brown. Turn carefully using two slotted spatulas. If oil begins to brown, reduce heat to medium. Set slices on paper towels to absorb excess oil.

4. Set fried eggplant slices side by side on ovenproof platter and keep them warm in a 275°F oven. Serve them with lemon wedges and herb sprigs.

❧ Tzimmes and Other Casseroles

Valerie's Potato Pashtidah

Makes 6 servings

A pashtidah is an Israeli-style baked casserole, usually of vegetables or noodles. My neighbor Valerie Alon in Los Angeles serves this delicious stovetop potato cake for festive occasions. It has appeared on her table for her oldest son's bar mitzvah, and for Shabbat and other holiday dinners. She learned it from her mother-in-law, who is Moroccan, and adapted it to her family's taste. Usually she serves it as a side dish with fish or chicken but I find it also makes a tasty entree, accompanied by Israeli salad. You can make it with or without eggs. It has a lighter texture with eggs, but it tastes good both ways.

2¹/2 pounds boiling potatoes, unpeeled

5 to 8 tablespoons olive oil

2 medium onions, chopped

1 large carrot, chopped fine

1 cup frozen peas

Salt and freshly ground pepper, to taste

1 teaspoon curry powder

¹/4 teaspoon cayenne pepper, or to taste

2 to 4 large eggs, beaten (optional)

1. Put potatoes in a large saucepan with water to cover and a pinch of salt and bring to a boil. Cover and simmer over low heat about 30 minutes or until very tender. Drain and leave until cool enough to handle.

2. Heat 2 tablespoons oil in a large nonstick skillet. Add onions and carrot and sauté over medium-low heat, stirring often, about 10 minutes or until tender.

3. Peel potatoes, cut each into a few pieces, and put them in a large bowl. Mash with a potato masher. Add peas and onion mixture. Season with salt, pepper, curry powder, and cayenne. Stir in beaten eggs, if using.

4. Add 3 tablespoons oil to skillet and heat it over medium heat. Add all of potato mixture for 1 thick cake or, for 2 thinner cakes add half of mixture now and save

half. Cover and sauté about 10 minutes or until bottom browns. Flip the potato cake and brown the second side. Put on an ovenproof serving dish and keep warm in a 300°F oven. If you are making a second potato cake, add 3 more tablespoons oil to skillet and heat it before sautéing potato mixture. Serve hot.

Tzimmes with Matzo Balls

Makes 4 servings

For a vegetarian Shabbat meal, my mother and I enjoy making this sweet-savory dish. It's satisfying, has a delicate sweetness, and, as my mother puts it, "feels like Shabbat."

1 pound orange-fleshed sweet potatoes (often called yams), peeled, halved, and sliced about 1/2-inch thick

1/2 pound boiling potatoes, halved and sliced about 1/2-inch thick

3/4 pound carrots, sliced 1/2-inch thick

1 cup pitted prunes

1 cup dried pears

2 tablespoons brown sugar

1 cinnamon stick (optional)

6 cups water

1 large egg

1/3 cup matzo meal

1/8 teaspoon baking powder

1/2 teaspoon ground ginger

Salt and freshly ground pepper, to taste

1. Put sweet potatoes and boiling potatoes in a large saucepan. Add carrots, prunes, pears, sugar, cinnamon stick if using, and water. Bring to a simmer. Simmer over low heat 5 minutes.

2. Beat egg in a small bowl with a fork. Stir in matzo meal, baking powder, ginger, salt, and pepper. Mixture should be just firm enough to hold together in roughly shaped balls. If mixture is too firm, gradually beat in 1 to 2 tablespoons liquid from the simmering tzimmes.

3. Turn heat under tzimmes to very low so liquid no longer bubbles. With moistened hands, take about 2 teaspoons matzo mixture. Shape it very gently into a soft ball, rolling it lightly from one hand to the other. Put ball in pan of sweet potato mixture. Make balls from remaining mixture, wetting your hands before shaping each one.

4. Preheat oven to 350°F. Bring sweet potato mixture to a simmer. Cover and simmer over low heat 15 minutes. Turn matzo balls over. Simmer 5 to 10 more minutes or until vegetables and prunes are tender.

5. Remove 3 cups of sauce from sweet potato mixture and spoon it into a sauté pan. Spoon matzo balls, vegetables, and fruit with all of remaining sauce into a 2-quart shallow baking dish. Bake uncovered 20 minutes.

6. Meanwhile, simmer reserved sauce over medium heat until it reduces to 1 cup. Add reduced sauce to baking dish. Bake 10 more minutes. Serve hot.

Indian Vegetable Tzimmes

Makes 4 to 6 servings

Jews from India use the bold flavors of their country—including fresh ginger, chiles, garlic, and a variety of spices—to create lively sauces. They are delicious with all kinds of vegetables, from sweet to cruciferous. This tzimmes has mostly sweet vegetables—sweet potatoes, carrots, and peas—but also includes some cauliflower which provides a pleasing balance of tastes. Serve it for Rosh Hashanah if you would like a change from Ashkenazic tzimmes or for Shabbat as an accompaniment for chicken or fish. It also makes a tasty vegetarian main course served over white or brown basmati rice.

2 tablespoons vegetable oil

1 medium onion, chopped

2 tablespoons minced peeled fresh ginger

6 large cloves garlic, minced

2 or 3 fresh jalapeño peppers, minced (see Note)

1 tablespoon ground cumin

1 teaspoon ground coriander

1/2 teaspoon ground turmeric

2 pounds ripe tomatoes, peeled, seeded, and chopped, or two 28-ounce cans tomatoes, drained

Salt and freshly ground pepper, to taste

3/4 pound orange-fleshed sweet potatoes (often called yams), peeled, halved, and sliced about 1/2-inch thick

3 cups small cauliflower florets

1/2 pound baby carrots

1 cup frozen peas

1/3 cup chopped fresh cilantro

1. Heat oil in a large, heavy saucepan. Add onion and sauté over medium heat, stirring, 5 minutes. Add fresh ginger, garlic, and jalapeño peppers and cook 1 minute. Stir in cumin, coriander, and turmeric, followed by tomatoes, salt, and pepper. Mix well. Bring to a boil. Cover and cook over low heat, stirring occasionally (and crushing canned tomatoes), about 20 minutes or until tomatoes are soft.

2. Put sweet potatoes in a medium saucepan and cover with water. Bring to a boil. Cover and cook

over medium heat 5 minutes. Add cauliflower and carrots and cook 3 minutes or until vegetables soften slightly.

3. Drain vegetables and add to sauce. Cover and cook over low heat 3 minutes. Add peas and bring to a simmer. Cover and cook over low heat about 4 minutes or until vegetables are just tender. Stir in half of cilantro. Adjust seasoning. Serve sprinkled with remaining cilantro.

Note: Wear rubber gloves when handling hot peppers.

Yemenite Eggplant Casserole

Makes 4 to 6 servings

This is a simplified version of a casserole I learned to make from my husband's aunt, who is from Yemen. She salts her eggplant slices and lets them dry in the sun for a few hours before making the dish. She then fries them in plenty of oil. I find the eggplant tastes good without being dried and deep-fried. I either sauté them in a little oil, as in this dish, or for a low-fat version, I broil the eggplant slices (see Broiled Eggplant, page 445) before baking them in the sauce.

1 1/4 to 1 1/2 pounds eggplant

Salt and freshly ground pepper, to taste

About 6 tablespoons olive oil or vegetable oil

1 large onion, minced

4 large cloves garlic, minced

1/4 cup chopped fresh cilantro (optional)

1 1/2 teaspoons ground cumin

1/2 teaspoon ground turmeric

1/4 teaspoon hot red pepper flakes, or to taste

Two 28-ounce cans tomatoes, drained and chopped

1. Peel eggplant if you like. Cut it into 3/8-inch slices crosswise. Sprinkle lightly with salt on both sides. Let stand while making sauce.

2. Heat 2 tablespoons oil in large saucepan. Add onion and sauté over medium-low heat about 7 minutes or until soft and light brown. Add garlic, 2 tablespoons cilantro if using, cumin, turmeric, and pepper flakes and cook, stirring, 30 seconds. Add tomatoes, salt, and pepper. Stir and bring to a boil. Cook uncovered over medium-low heat, stirring occasionally, about 15 minutes or until sauce is thick. Adjust seasoning.

3. Preheat oven to 350°F. Pat eggplant dry. Heat 2 tablespoons oil in large, heavy skillet. Quickly add enough eggplant slices to make one layer. Sauté over medium heat about 2 minutes. Turn over and sauté 2 minutes more; cover pan if it looks too dry. Remove to plate. Add 2 tablespoons oil to skillet, heat oil and sauté remaining eggplant in same way.

4. Lightly oil a shallow baking dish. Arrange alternate layers of eggplant and sauce, ending with sauce. Bake uncovered 30 minutes or until eggplant is very tender, basting occasionally. Serve garnished with remaining cilantro.

Tu Bishvat Sweet Potato and Fruit Casserole

Makes 4 servings   Ⓟ

Dried fruit has a place of honor on the menu of Tu Bishvat, the Israeli tree-planting holiday. This colorful casserole flavored with honey, fresh ginger, and orange juice is also great for Sukkot. It's delicious as the centerpiece of a meatless meal or as a partner for roasted or braised meat or poultry. If you like, garnish it with toasted pecans. For dairy meals, you might like to crown each serving with Savory Orange Topping (page 298).

1 cup dried apricots

1/2 cup dried figs, halved

2 tablespoons vegetable oil

21/2 pounds orange-fleshed sweet potatoes (often labeled yams)

Salt and freshly ground pepper, to taste

3 tablespoons honey or brown sugar

2 tablespoons margarine or additional oil

1/2 cup orange juice

1 tablespoon minced peeled fresh ginger

1. Put apricots and figs in a bowl and pour boiling water over them. Cover and let soak about 20 minutes or until softened.

2. Preheat oven to 400°F. Pour oil into 2-quart baking dish. Peel sweet potatoes, halve lengthwise, and cut into 1/2-inch slices. Put in baking dish, add small pinch of salt and pepper, and toss to coat slices with oil. Bake uncovered, stirring occasionally, about 25 minutes or until barely tender; if pan becomes dry during baking, add 1 or 2 tablespoons hot water.

3. Drain figs and apricots. Add to sweet potatoes and mix very gently.

4. Combine honey, margarine, orange juice, and ginger in a small saucepan. Bring to a simmer, stirring, and pour evenly over sweet potato mixture. Bake uncovered, basting twice, 15 minutes. Remove from oven and stir very gently. Bake, basting occasionally, about 15 more minutes or until most of liquid is absorbed. Serve hot or warm.

Baked Balkan Vegetable Casserole
Givetch

Makes 8 servings

Givetch, *which originated in the Balkan countries, is often prepared in Israel. When I lived there, a friend introduced me to this cousin of French ratatouille and I've been making it often ever since. Like ratatouille, it usually contains eggplant, peppers, tomatoes, and onions. Variations abound, and cooks might add green beans, carrots, celery, potatoes, mushrooms, okra, cauliflower, or celery root. Garlic is the favorite flavoring but other herbs and sweet and hot paprika are also popular. For Jews from Romania, the favorite accompaniment is Mamaliga (page 522), which is similar to polenta. Givetch is also popular with rice. When I'm including dairy products in the meal, I love it topped with Cucumber-Dill Yogurt Sauce (page 298).*

3 to 5 tablespoons olive oil

2 medium onions, halved and sliced thin

3 bell peppers, any color or a mixture, cut into strips

1 medium eggplant (1¼ pounds) cut into ¾-inch cubes

Salt and freshly ground pepper, to taste

2 pounds ripe tomatoes, chopped, or one 28-ounce can diced tomatoes with their juice

1 teaspoon paprika

¾ pound boiling potatoes, cut into ¾-inch cubes

4 ounces green beans, ends removed

1½ cups fresh shelled or frozen peas

6 ounces mushrooms, quartered

3 tablespoons tomato paste

½ cup vegetable stock or water

¼ teaspoon sugar

2 tablespoons chopped fresh dill or 2 teaspoons dried

1 teaspoon dried thyme

3 large cloves garlic, minced

½ teaspoon hot red pepper flakes (optional)

2 tablespoons chopped fresh Italian parsley

1. Preheat oven to 350°F. Heat 2 tablespoons oil in a large, heavy skillet, add onions and peppers, and sauté over medium heat about 7 minutes or until onions brown. Remove onions and peppers. Add remaining oil to skillet and heat. Add eggplant, salt, and pepper and sauté, stirring, 3 minutes. Remove eggplant. Add tomatoes and paprika to pan and cook about 10 minutes or until thick.

2. Oil two baking dishes and layer vegetables in dishes, sprinkling each layer lightly with salt and pepper: Use half of onion-pepper mixture on bottom of dishes, top with potatoes, then beans, peas, and mushrooms, then tomatoes, then eggplant, and finally add remaining onion mixture.

3. Mix tomato paste, stock, salt, pepper, sugar, dill, thyme, garlic, and pepper flakes, if using, in a small bowl. Pour sauce over vegetables. Cover and bake 30 minutes; check and add a little water to bottom of pan if it's becoming dry. Cover and bake 30 more minutes or until all vegetables are tender. (Casserole can be kept, covered, 2 days in refrigerator.) Serve hot or cold, sprinkled with parsley.

Cholent and Other Bean Dishes

Easy Meatless Cholent

Makes 4 servings

For those cold winter days when you wish for something warming like cholent—*the famous all-night Shabbat casserole—but don't have time for the long simmering, here is a quick-to-assemble version made of red and black beans. The wine and sautéed vegetables give the stew a deeper color, somewhat like that of "real"* cholent. *If you're in a rush, you can buy the mushrooms already sliced, the carrots shredded, and the onions diced. Because the beans are already cooked, you would not heat this overnight because they would fall apart.*

1 to 2 tablespoons vegetable oil

1 large onion, chopped

1¹/₂ cups diced or shredded carrots

2 ribs celery, sliced

¹/₃ cup dry red wine

6 to 8 ounces sliced mushrooms

Salt and freshly ground pepper, to taste

¹/₂ cup vegetable stock

1 bay leaf

¹/₂ teaspoon dried thyme

One 10-ounce package frozen pearl onions (optional)

One 15-ounce can red beans, drained

One 15-ounce can black beans, drained

2 tablespoons chopped fresh parsley

1. Heat oil in a heavy saucepan. Add onions, carrots, and celery and sauté over medium heat, stirring often, about 7 minutes or until onions begin to brown; add 1 to 2 tablespoons of the wine if necessary to prevent burning. Add mushrooms, salt, and pepper and sauté over medium-high heat 2 minutes.

2. Add remaining wine, stock, bay leaf, and thyme and bring to a boil. Add pearl onions, if using; cover and return to a boil. Simmer over low heat about 10

minutes or until onions are tender. Add red and black beans and bring to a simmer over medium-high heat. Simmer uncovered 3 minutes. Discard bay leaf. Adjust seasoning. Serve sprinkled with parsley.

Low-Fat Pareve Chili

Makes 4 to 6 servings

To flavor and deepen the color of this meatless version of the American classic, I add plenty of sautéed onions and sliced mushrooms as well as a touch of soy sauce. Because it's made with tofu and vegetables, it cooks faster than meat-based chili. I serve it with pita bread or hot tortillas, or over rice or spaghetti. It makes a hearty, low-fat vegetarian main course, perfect for winter. In our house we especially like it during the week of Hanukkah, and we find it's also delicious with latkes.

1 to 2 tablespoons olive oil or vegetable oil

2 large onions, chopped

8 to 12 ounces mushrooms, sliced

6 large cloves garlic, chopped

2 teaspoons chili powder

1 tablespoon ground cumin

1¹/₂ teaspoons dried oregano

¹/₂ teaspoon hot red pepper flakes, or to taste

Two 28-ounce cans diced tomatoes, with their juice

2 tablespoons tomato paste

Two 15- or 16-ounce cans red beans or pinto beans, drained

2 tablespoons soy sauce

One 12- to 16-ounce package tofu, drained and cut into cubes

2 tablespoons chopped fresh cilantro (optional)

1. Heat oil in a wide stew pan or Dutch oven. Add onions and sauté over medium heat, stirring often, 5 minutes; add 1 to 2 tablespoons hot water from time to time if pan becomes dry. Add mushrooms and garlic and sauté, stirring often, 2 minutes. Add chili powder, cumin, oregano, and pepper flakes and stir over low heat 30 seconds.

2. Add tomatoes and tomato paste. Stir and bring to a boil. Add beans and soy sauce and bring to a simmer. Simmer uncovered over medium heat 10 minutes. Add tofu and stir gently. Simmer uncovered 5 minutes or until chili is thick. Add cilantro, if using. Adjust seasoning. Serve hot.

Bean Medley with Zucchini and Za'atar

Makes 4 servings

Za'atar is a dried herb and sesame seed mix found in the spice section of Israeli and Middle Eastern markets. In Israel it's popular for sprinkling over pita (See Za'atar-Topped Pita Bread, page 545), or other fresh bread after the bread is lightly dipped in olive oil. I find za'atar also makes a delicious seasoning for cooked vegetables and salads, especially the basic Israeli chopped salad of tomatoes, cucumbers, and onions.

1/2 pound green beans, ends removed, cut in half

1/2 pound zucchini, quartered and cut into 2-inch lengths

1 tablespoon olive oil or vegetable oil

One 14 1/2-ounce can diced tomatoes, drained

Two 15-ounce cans white beans, drained

1 to 2 tablespoons za'atar, or to taste

Salt and freshly ground pepper, to taste

1. Cook green beans in a medium saucepan of boiling salted water uncovered over high heat 3 minutes. Add zucchini and cook 3 minutes or until vegetables are barely tender. With a slotted spoon, remove vegetables; you can save broth for adding to soups.

2. Combine oil and tomatoes in a medium saucepan. Stir and bring to a boil. Simmer uncovered over medium heat 3 minutes. Add white beans, cover, and heat through. Add green beans and zucchini and heat uncovered. Add za'atar. Season with salt and pepper. Serve hot or cold.

Esau's Lentil Pottage

Makes about 8 servings

Of course, we don't have the exact recipe for the famous lentil soup in the story of Jacob and Esau, but it may have been seasoned with coriander and cumin, as these spices were used in biblical times. So were onions, garlic, and olive oil. Use Egyptian, also called orange, lentils if you would like them to have a puree-like consistency, or use green lentils if you prefer that they stay separate. Serve with pita bread or with hot, cooked rice.

1 pound lentils (about 3 cups)

3 tablespoons olive oil

2 large onions, chopped

6 large cloves garlic, chopped

2 teaspoons ground coriander

1 tablespoon ground cumin

6 cups vegetable stock

5 or 6 cups water

1 dried hot pepper, such as chile japone (optional)

2 bay leaves

One 14-ounce can diced tomatoes, drained

2 tablespoons tomato paste

Salt and freshly ground pepper, to taste

1/3 cup chopped fresh cilantro

1. Spread lentils on a plate, pick through them carefully, rinse, and drain.

2. Heat oil in a large saucepan. Add onions and sauté over medium-low heat 7 minutes. Add garlic, coriander, and cumin and sauté 1 minute. Add lentils, stock, 3 cups water, hot pepper if using, and bay leaves. Bring to a boil. Cover and simmer over low heat 30 minutes.

3. Add tomatoes, tomato paste, salt, pepper, and 2 cups water to lentils and return to a boil. Simmer 15 more minutes or until lentils are tender. If soup is too thick, add remaining cup water and bring to a boil. Discard hot pepper and bay leaves. Add cilantro and salt, and season generously with pepper. Serve hot.

Lentils with Peppers and Rice

Makes 6 servings

Lentils have been a staple in the land of Israel since the biblical time of Esau, and have long been a favorite among Jews of all origins. In modern days, too, lentils have much to recommend them. They are a most healthful food and are the fastest cooking of all the legumes.

1¼ cups lentils, picked over and rinsed

1¾ cups vegetable stock or a 14½-ounce can broth

2 tablespoons vegetable oil or olive oil

1 large onion, chopped

1 large red bell pepper, diced

1 medium yellow or green bell pepper, diced

1 jalapeño pepper, seeds removed, chopped

1 teaspoon ground cumin

1½ cups long-grain white rice

1 teaspoon dried oregano

½ teaspoon ground turmeric (optional)

Salt and freshly ground pepper, to taste

3 tablespoons chopped fresh cilantro or Italian parsley

1. Combine lentils, stock, and ½ cup water in a large saucepan. Bring to a boil. Cover and cook over medium heat about 20 minutes or until lentils are just tender. Drain liquid into a measuring cup and add enough water to make 3 cups; reserve.

2. Heat oil in a heavy skillet. Add onion and bell peppers and sauté over medium heat, stirring occasionally, about 10 minutes or until onions begin to brown. Add jalapeño pepper and cumin and sauté 30 seconds.

3. Add measured liquid to pan of lentils and bring to a boil. Add rice, oregano, turmeric if using, salt, and pepper and return to a boil. Cover and cook over low heat without stirring 10 minutes. Spoon onion-pepper mixture over rice but do not stir. Cover and cook 8 to 10 more minutes or until rice is tender. Fluff with a fork and mix in onion-pepper mixture and 2 tablespoons cilantro. Season with salt and pepper. Serve hot, sprinkled with remaining cilantro.

Chickpea and Spinach Stew

Makes 4 to 6 servings

Greens and chickpeas are a beloved combination among Jews from Middle Eastern countries. This dish is very easy to make if you use rinsed spinach leaves and canned chickpeas and is surprisingly tasty for so little effort. Serve it as a vegetarian entree with rice or as an accompaniment for chicken, beef, or lamb. In some Lebanese families the tomatoes and tomato paste are omitted and the dish is served cold, with lemon wedges.

1 pound spinach or a 10-ounce bag rinsed spinach leaves

1 to 2 tablespoons olive oil

1 medium onion, chopped

4 large cloves garlic, chopped

1 teaspoon paprika

One 14-ounce can diced tomatoes, drained

2 tablespoons tomato paste

⅓ cup vegetable stock or water

Two 15- or 16-ounce cans chickpeas (garbanzo beans), drained

Salt and freshly ground pepper, to taste

Cayenne pepper, to taste

1. Discard thick spinach stems. Rinse leaves and small stems. Cut or tear into bite-size pieces.

2. Heat oil in a large saucepan. Add onion and sauté over medium heat 7 minutes. Add garlic and paprika and sauté 30 seconds. Add tomatoes, tomato paste, and stock and stir until blended. Bring to a simmer. Add chickpeas and return to a simmer. Add spinach, cover, and cook over medium-high heat, stirring often, about 3 minutes or until spinach is just wilted. Season with salt, pepper, and cayenne.

Black Beans with Corn and Peppers

Makes 4 servings

A Sephardic salsa of garlic, parsley, capers, lemon juice, and olive oil gives spirit to this colorful American bean and corn medley. You can serve it as a pareve entree any time, but it's festive enough for holiday meals, too. Try it for Purim, Shavuot, or a meatless Shabbat dinner.

1 small clove garlic, peeled

1/2 cup sprigs fresh Italian parsley

1 tablespoon capers, rinsed

1/4 cup diced onion

3 tablespoons plus 1 teaspoon extra-virgin olive oil

1/2 teaspoon anchovy paste (optional)

1/2 cup vegetable stock or water

2 cups fresh or frozen corn kernels

Two 15-ounce cans black beans, drained

1 large red bell pepper, diced

2 tablespoons chopped fresh cilantro (optional)

1 tablespoon strained fresh lemon juice, or more to taste

Salt and freshly ground pepper, to taste

1. Chop garlic in food processor. Add parsley and process together until finely chopped. Add capers and onion and chop together with brief pulses. Transfer to a large bowl. Stir 3 tablespoons oil into anchovy paste, if using, in a cup, until well blended. Add to parsley mixture.

2. Bring stock to a boil in a medium saucepan. Add corn, cover and simmer 2 to 3 minutes or until tender. Add beans and heat through. Drain and add to bowl of parsley-caper salsa. Add diced red pepper, cilantro if using, lemon juice, salt, and pepper. Serve hot or warm.

Black Beans with Moroccan Dressing

Makes 4 servings

A friend from Morocco uses a garlic-cumin-cilantro dressing on potato salads and green salads. I find the aromatic dressing is also delicious with beans. These savory beans are easy to prepare and festive enough to serve as a party dish. Make them spicier, if you like, with more jalapeño or omit it for a milder dish. Hot, cooked rice or couscous salad are good accompaniments.

1 1/3 cups dried black beans or two 15-ounce cans, drained

1 whole small onion, peeled (optional)

1 bay leaf (optional)

1 quart water

1 Grilled Bell Pepper (page 588) or jarred roasted red pepper

1 to 2 tablespoons strained fresh lemon juice

2 large cloves garlic, pressed or very finely minced

1 teaspoon ground cumin

1 teaspoon paprika

Salt and freshly ground pepper, to taste

Cayenne pepper to taste

2 to 4 tablespoons extra-virgin olive oil

1 jalapeño pepper, seeded and finely minced, or harissa or hot pepper sauce, to taste

1/2 medium red onion, finely chopped

4 plum tomatoes, diced

1/3 cup chopped fresh cilantro

Fresh cilantro sprigs

Lemon wedges

1. If using dried beans, rinse and sort them. Put them in a saucepan with whole onion and bay leaf if using, a pinch of salt, and 1 quart water. Bring to a boil. Cover and cook over low heat 1 to 1 1/2 hours or until tender. Discard onion and bay leaf.

2. Prepare grilled pepper, if using homemade. Cut pepper into thin strips and reserve. Whisk 1 tablespoon lemon juice with garlic, cumin, paprika, salt, cayenne, and 2 tablespoons oil in a medium serving bowl. Add jalapeño pepper.

3. With a slotted spoon, remove beans from their cooking liquid, drain them and put them in bowl of dressing; you can use cooking liquid in soups.

4. Mix cooked or canned beans gently with dressing. Add chopped red onion, roasted pepper strips, tomatoes, and cilantro and gently mix again. Adjust seasoning. Add more lemon juice and oil if needed. Serve hot or cold, garnished with cilantro sprigs and lemon wedges.

Sofrito Lima Beans

Makes 4 to 6 servings

Sofrito *is a Spanish flavoring for all sorts of foods. In the Spanish Caribbean islands, it is made of sautéed peppers, onions, garlic, and cilantro and often includes nonkosher meat. A man from Cuba, who grew up as part of the small Jewish community there, told me about this meatless version made in his family. It's quick and easy to make and spices up beans and vegetables. Serve with hot, cooked rice or baked potatoes.*

One 1-pound bag or two 10-ounce boxes frozen lima beans

2 tablespoons olive oil or vegetable oil

1 medium onion, finely chopped

1 small green or red bell pepper, finely diced

2 large cloves garlic, minced

1 teaspoon minced fresh or canned jalapeño or other chile

3 tablespoons chopped fresh cilantro

1/2 teaspoon ground cumin

Salt and freshly ground pepper, to taste

1. Cook lima beans according to package directions.

2. Heat oil in a medium, heavy skillet or sauté pan. Add onion and bell pepper and sauté over medium-low heat, stirring often, about 10 minutes or until tender. Add garlic, jalapeño, cilantro, cumin, salt, and pepper and sauté 1 minute, stirring.

3. Drain lima beans and combine with onion mixture. Heat 1 to 2 minutes over low heat to blend flavors.

Black-Eyed Peas with Green Beans and Red Onions

Makes 4 servings

Serving black-eyed peas for a new year of good luck is a popular Rosh Hashanah custom among Sephardic Jews and in the American South. As with all legumes, they are a nutritious way to start the year. Use them frozen, dried, or choose the fast-cooking type available in the produce section. Rice, bulgur wheat, orzo, or pasta shells are good accompaniments.

1³/4 cups or a 14¹/2-ounce can vegetable broth

One 1-pound package frozen black-eyed peas (2¹/2 cups)

2 cups fresh or frozen green beans

1 large carrot, sliced

1/2 red onion, chopped

1/3 cup chopped fresh Italian parsley

1 to 2 tablespoons extra-virgin olive oil

Salt and freshly ground pepper, to taste

1. Bring broth to a boil in a saucepan. Add black-eyed peas and return to a boil. Cover and simmer over low heat. When 7 minutes are left of their cooking time, add green beans and carrots and return to a boil. Cover and cook over low heat 7 minutes. Leave vegetables in broth if you will be serving them with grains or pasta, or drain if you like; broth liquid can be saved for soups.

2. Transfer mixture to a serving bowl. Add red onion, parsley, and olive oil and mix well. Season with salt and pepper. Serve hot.

Sweet and Spicy Chickpea-Zucchini Stew

Makes 4 servings

Raisins and carrots lend a touch of sweetness to this savory stew, the perfect accompaniment for a steaming bowl of couscous. It's reminiscent of the vegetable sauce served in some North African Jewish homes with the Friday night couscous dinner. Usually the dinner includes meat also, but I love this sauce with the couscous as a vegetarian entree.

1 cup vegetable stock or water

2 medium carrots, cut into thick diagonal slices

4 medium zucchini, halved and sliced

1 tablespoon olive oil or vegetable oil

4 large cloves garlic, chopped

One 14½-ounce can diced tomatoes, drained

One 8-ounce can tomato sauce

1½ teaspoons ground cumin

Salt and freshly ground pepper, to taste

Two 15-ounce cans chickpeas (garbanzo beans), drained

⅓ cup raisins

½ teaspoon bottled hot sauce, or more to taste

1. Combine stock and carrots in a medium saucepan and bring to a boil. Cover and cook over medium-low heat 5 minutes Add zucchini and cook 3 minutes or until barely tender. With a slotted spoon, remove vegetables; save broth for adding to soups.

2. Heat oil in a medium saucepan, add garlic and sauté 10 seconds over medium heat. Add tomatoes, tomato sauce, cumin, salt, and pepper. Stir and bring to boil over high heat. Simmer uncovered over medium heat 3 minutes. Stir in chickpeas and raisins. Bring to a simmer. Cook uncovered over medium-low heat 3 minutes. Add hot sauce, zucchini, and carrots and simmer 2 minutes. Adjust seasoning. Serve hot.

Beans in Tomato-Garlic Salsa

Makes 4 servings

The Sephardic standard, beans in tomato sauce, gains a new summertime twist in this recipe. The sauce turns into an easy, uncooked salsa for the beans so that the season's sun-ripened tomatoes retain all their fresh, luscious flavor. Use a mixture of fresh green or yellow beans and shell beans such as lima or fava beans if you find them. If you're serving them for a festive meal, for example for Shabbat or Shavuot, serve the bean medley with Saffron Basmati Rice (page 200). Rice pilaf or risotto are other good choices.

½ jalapeño pepper, very finely minced

1 large clove garlic, pressed

⅓ cup chopped sweet onion

3 tablespoons extra-virgin olive oil

1 tablespoon strained fresh lemon juice (optional)

¾ pound ripe tomatoes, cut into small dice

Salt and freshly ground pepper, to taste

2 pounds fresh fava or lima beans, shelled, or 2 cups frozen lima beans (about 10 ounces)

1 pound green beans, wax (yellow) beans, or a mixture, ends removed, broken into 2 or 3 pieces

¼ cup chopped fresh Italian parsley

1. In a bowl combine jalapeño, garlic, onion, oil, and lemon juice, if using. Add tomatoes, salt, and pepper. Let stand while preparing beans.

2. If using fresh fava beans, cook, drain, and peel them (see Fava Beans with Carrots and Zucchini, pages 246–247). Or, add lima beans to a large saucepan of enough boiling salted water to cover them generously and cook uncovered over medium-high heat until just tender, 15 to 20 minutes for fresh beans or about 10 minutes for frozen. Add green beans and wax beans the last 5 minutes of cooking. Drain well.

3. Put beans in a serving bowl and add salsa. Toss to combine. Add parsley. Adjust seasoning. Serve hot, cold, or at room temperature.

Summer Squash with White Beans, Tomatoes, and Dill

Makes 4 to 6 servings

Sephardic cooks like to pair dill with vegetables as it enlivens their flavor. Serve this summery dish as a meatless main course with rice or bulgur wheat or as a partner for grilled chicken or lamb.

3 tablespoons olive oil

2 large onions, finely chopped

2 pounds ripe tomatoes, peeled, seeded, and chopped, or two 28-ounce cans tomatoes, drained and chopped

1/2 teaspoon sugar

Salt and freshly ground pepper, to taste

1 1/2 teaspoons paprika

1 pound yellow crookneck squash or yellow pattypan squash

1 pound medium zucchini or other green summer squash

1/3 cup chopped fresh dill or 1 tablespoon dried

1/2 cup chopped fresh Italian parsley

Two 15-ounce cans white beans, drained

Cayenne pepper, to taste

2 or 3 teaspoons strained fresh lemon juice (optional)

1. Heat oil in a deep skillet or stew pan. Add onions and sauté over medium-low heat about 7 minutes or until just beginning to turn golden. Add tomatoes, sugar, salt, pepper, and 1 teaspoon paprika. Cook, stirring often, over medium-high heat 7 minutes or until thick.

2. Add yellow squash and zucchini to tomato sauce and sprinkle with salt and remaining paprika. Cover and cook over low heat, stirring occasionally, 20 minutes or until tender. If pan becomes dry, add a few tablespoons water during cooking. Reserve 1 tablespoon dill and parsley. Add remaining dill and parsley, white beans, and cayenne and heat through. Taste, adjust seasoning, and add lemon juice, if using. Serve warm, room temperature, or cold, sprinkled with reserved herbs.

White Beans with Rice and Carrots

Makes about 6 servings

Beans and rice are a popular pair in many lands, including India, the Middle East, Mediterranean countries, the American South, Latin America, and the Caribbean islands. They are also enjoyed by Sephardic Jews. This garlicky version is a specialty of the Jews of Bukhara, in Uzbekistan. They are very fond of rice casseroles, both vegetarian and with meat.

3/4 pound dried black beans (about 1 2/3 cups)

7 cups water

3 tablespoons vegetable oil

1 1/2 cups long-grain rice

4 large carrots, diced

8 large cloves garlic, minced

3 1/2 cups boiling water

Salt and freshly ground pepper, to taste

1 1/2 teaspoons paprika

1/4 teaspoon cayenne pepper, or to taste

1/4 cup chopped fresh Italian parsley (optional)

1. Pick over dried beans, discarding pebbles and broken or discolored beans. Rinse well. Put beans in a large saucepan and add water. Bring to a simmer. Cover and cook over low heat about 1 hour and 15 minutes or until nearly tender. Drain beans; you can reserve their cooking liquid for making soups.

2. Heat oil in a heavy saucepan. Add rice and sauté over medium-low heat, stirring, 1 minute. Add carrots, garlic, cooked beans, boiling water, salt, pepper, paprika, and cayenne. Bring to a boil. Cover and cook over low heat about 20 minutes or until rice is tender. Adjust seasoning, then stir in parsley, if using.

Maghreb Bean and Squash Stew

Makes 3 or 4 servings   (P)

If you have cooked white beans or chickpeas on hand or if you use canned ones, this is a quick and easy dish to make. Seasoned in the style of the region called Maghreb, or the northwest African areas of Morocco, Algeria, and Tunisia, it's good for Purim or for any vegetarian meal. Israeli Rice Pilaf (page 499) or Basic Quick Couscous (page 483) are perfect accompaniments. If you like, garnish each serving with chopped cilantro or Italian parsley.

$2/3$ cup dried or $1^1/2$ cups cooked white beans or chickpeas (garbanzo beans) or one 15-ounce can, drained

2 to 3 tablespoons olive oil or vegetable oil

2 large onions, sliced

1 teaspoon paprika

1 teaspoon ground cumin

4 large cloves garlic, chopped

$2^1/2$ cups bean cooking liquid or vegetable broth

3 medium carrots, sliced

Salt and freshly ground pepper, to taste

2 ribs celery, cut into thin slices (optional)

$3/4$ pound yellow squash or zucchini, halved and cut into thick slices

One $14^1/2$-ounce can diced tomatoes with their liquid

1 tablespoon tomato paste

Hot sauce or cayenne pepper, to taste

1. If using dried beans, soak and cook them. Then, heat oil in a large sauté pan. Add onions and cook over low heat, stirring, until soft but not browned. Add paprika, cumin, and garlic and sauté 30 seconds. Add $2^1/2$ cups bean liquid, if using freshly cooked beans, or broth, if using canned beans.

2. Add carrots, salt, and pepper and bring to a boil. Cover and simmer 10 minutes. Add celery if using, squash, tomatoes, and beans. Return to a boil. Cover and simmer 10 minutes. Stir in tomato paste. Add hot sauce or cayenne. Adjust seasoning. Serve in a deep serving dish.

❧ *Vegetable Stews*

Day-after-Shabbat Vegetable Stew

Makes 6 servings   (P)

Everyone seems to make "clean the refrigerator stew," even chefs of the top culinary temples. Indeed, when I studied at La Varenne Cooking School in Paris, I always looked forward to our chef's weekly habit of making up dishes from leftovers, as it was always an enjoyable learning experience. After Shabbat or holidays I like to make the vegetables in my refrigerator into a low-fat main-course stew flavored with tomatoes, thyme, and cumin.

1 large head cauliflower

1 tablespoon canola oil

2 large onions, quartered and sliced

1 cup hot water

3 sprigs fresh thyme or $1/2$ teaspoon dried thyme

Salt and freshly ground pepper, to taste

4 Chinese or Japanese eggplants, halved and sliced

$1/4$ pound green beans, trimmed

2 large zucchini, quartered lengthwise and sliced

One $14^1/2$-ounce can diced tomatoes with their liquid

2 tablespoons tomato paste

6 large cloves garlic, chopped

2 teaspoons ground cumin

One 15-ounce can chickpeas (garbanzo beans)

1. Divide cauliflower into fairly small florets. Cut peel from cauliflower stem; slice stem.

2. Heat oil in a large, heavy stew pan. Add onions and sauté over medium heat 3 minutes. Cover and sauté, stirring often about 5 minutes or until onions brown, adding a few tablespoons water if necessary to prevent burning.

3. Add hot water and thyme and bring to a boil. Add cauliflower, salt, and pepper and cook, covered, over medium heat 5 minutes. Add eggplants, green beans, zucchini, tomatoes, tomato paste, garlic, and cumin. Stir to blend in tomato paste. Cover and cook over medium heat, stirring occasionally, about 20 minutes or until vegetables are tender; add water occasionally if pan begins to dry. Discard thyme sprigs. Add chickpeas and heat through. Adjust seasoning. Serve hot.

Double Tomato-Eggplant Stew

Makes 4 servings

A combination of sun-dried and canned tomatoes makes this tasty stew easy to prepare. When I can find Chinese or Japanese eggplants I prefer them for this fat-free dish because their cooked texture is more creamy than that of the common eggplants. I serve this as a main course with brown rice or noodles but it's also a good accompaniment for chicken or turkey.

1 large onion, chopped

2 pounds Japanese eggplants, halved and sliced

Salt and freshly ground pepper, to taste

One 14^1/$_2$-ounce can diced tomatoes with their juice

6 to 8 dry-packed sun-dried tomatoes

1 large sprig fresh thyme or 1 teaspoon dried thyme

1 bay leaf

About ^{1}/$_4$ teaspoon hot red pepper flakes

4 large cloves garlic, chopped

2 tablespoons slivered fresh basil or chopped Italian parsley

1. Briefly heat a large, heavy sauté pan and add onion. Cover and sauté over medium heat, stirring often and adding hot water by tablespoons as necessary, about 7 minutes or until onion browns.

2. Add eggplant slices and mix well. Sprinkle with salt and pepper. Add diced tomatoes, dried tomatoes, thyme, bay leaf, and pepper flakes. Cover and cook over medium heat stirring occasionally, 10 minutes; add water if pan becomes dry. Add garlic. Cover and cook over medium heat 5 minutes, then over low heat 5 more minutes or until eggplant is tender. Discard thyme sprig and bay leaf. Serve hot or cold, sprinkled with basil.

Sephardic Succotash

Makes 4 servings

Sephardic seasonings lend zest to this colorful pareve succotash of beans, corn, and butternut squash. You can perk it up even more by topping it with Sephardic Salsa (page 131) or a touch of Zehug (page 592). For a milder complement that includes dairy products, crown each serving with a dollop of Mint-Yogurt Topping (see Zucchini and Red Beans with Mint-Yogurt Topping, page 450).

2 tablespoons olive oil

1 large onion, chopped

1 or 2 jalapeño peppers, minced (optional); See Note

4 large cloves garlic, chopped

1^1/$_2$ teaspoons ground cumin

1^1/$_2$ teaspoons paprika

One 28-ounce can tomatoes, drained and chopped

1^1/$_2$ teaspoons dried oregano

Salt and freshly ground pepper, to taste

One 1^1/$_4$-pound piece butternut, banana, or other winter squash, peeled and cut into 1-inch cubes

^{3}/$_4$ cup vegetable stock or water

1^1/$_2$ cups fresh or frozen corn kernels

One 15-ounce can white beans, drained

3 tablespoons chopped fresh cilantro or Italian parsley

1 or 2 tablespoons strained fresh lemon juice (optional)

1. Heat oil in a large sauté pan, add onion, and sauté over medium heat 5 minutes. Add jalapeño peppers if using, garlic, cumin, and paprika and sauté 2 minutes over low heat, stirring. Add tomatoes, oregano, salt, and pepper. Stir and cook over medium heat 5 minutes or until thickened.

2. Add squash and vegetable stock and bring to a simmer. Cover and cook over low heat 15 minutes, occasionally stirring gently. Add corn and cook 7 minutes or until corn and squash are tender. Add beans, salt, and pepper. Cover and cook over low heat about 2 minutes. Add 2 tablespoons cilantro, and lemon juice, if using. Adjust seasoning. Serve sprinkled with remaining cilantro.

Note: Wear rubber gloves when handling hot peppers.

Sweet-and-Sour Vegetables

Makes 4 or 5 servings

Vegetables cooked in a sweet-and-sour tomato sauce are popular in many Jewish homes as a side dish with braised meat or roasted chicken. I also like them as a colorful vegetarian entree, accompanied by kasha or brown rice. You can add a little ketchup to enhance the sweetness and sourness of the sauce. Raisins are often added to traditional Ashkenazic versions of the sauce but there are many other dried fruits readily available for variety, such as cranberries, blueberries, currants, diced prunes, pears, or apricots.

1/2 **pound yellow crookneck squash**

1/2 **pound zucchini**

3/4 **pound carrots**

3/4 **pound red-skinned potatoes, scrubbed**

3 **tablespoons vegetable oil**

2 **medium onions, chopped**

One 28-ounce can diced tomatoes, drained

Salt and freshly ground pepper, to taste

1/3 **cup dark or light raisins or other dried fruit, diced if large**

1 **tablespoon ketchup, or to taste (optional)**

2 **tablespoons vinegar, or more to taste**

4 **teaspoons sugar, or more to taste**

1. Cut thin "neck" part of squash into 1/2-inch slices. Quarter thick part lengthwise and cut into 1/2-inch slices, to form dice. Quarter zucchini and carrots and cut into similar dice. Dice potatoes.

2. Put potatoes and carrots in a medium saucepan and cover with water. Bring to a boil. Cover and cook over medium-low heat about 15 minutes or until just tender.

3. Heat oil in a heavy stew pan. Add onion and sauté over medium heat about 5 minutes or until golden. Add tomatoes and cook uncovered 5 minutes. Add zucchini, yellow squash, salt, and pepper. Stir and bring to boil. Cover and cook over medium heat, stirring occasionally, 7 minutes or until squash is crisp-tender.

4. With a slotted spoon, transfer carrots and potatoes to pan of squash in tomato sauce. Add raisins, ketchup if using, vinegar, and sugar and cook 1 minute. Adjust seasoning; add more ketchup, vinegar, or sugar if you like. Serve hot.

Easy Ratatouille with Tofu

Makes 4 servings

Tofu is popular in Jewish cooking because it's so versatile for making pareve dishes. I like this savory, colorful stew with white basmati or brown rice and with Israeli salad.

2 **to 3 tablespoons olive oil**

1 **small onion, chopped**

3 **large cloves garlic, chopped**

1 **pound Japanese or Italian eggplant, unpeeled and cut into** 3/4-**inch dice**

1 **small red or green bell pepper, cut into** 3/4-**inch dice**

Salt and freshly ground pepper, to taste

One 28-ounce can diced tomatoes, drained (juice reserved)

1 **bay leaf**

1/2 **pound zucchini, unpeeled and cut into 1-inch dice**

One 14- to 16-ounce package firm tofu, cut into 3/4-**inch dice**

1/2 **teaspoon dried thyme**

1 **tablespoon chopped fresh sage (optional)**

2 **tablespoons chopped fresh Italian parsley**

1. Heat oil in a heavy, wide stew pan or Dutch oven. Add onion and sauté 5 minutes over medium heat. Stir in garlic, then eggplant, bell pepper, salt, and pepper. Sauté, stirring, about 3 minutes. Add tomatoes and bay leaf and bring to a boil. Cover and simmer over low heat, stirring often, 10 minutes. Add zucchini and cook 10 more minutes or until vegetables are tender. If stew is too thick, add 1 tablespoon reserved tomato juice. Remove bay leaf.

2. Add tofu to stew, spoon a little of sauce over tofu cubes, and sprinkle them with salt, pepper, and thyme. Cover and heat gently, without stirring, about 3 minutes. Stir in sage, if using. Adjust seasoning. Serve sprinkled with chopped parsley.

Low-Fat Ratatouille with Coriander

Makes 6 to 8 servings

A favorite Egyptian Jewish combination for seasoning vegetable dishes is ground coriander, the seeds of the coriander plant, or cilantro, the fresh leaves, added to garlic. Often the mixture is sautéed but in this low-fat eggplant stew I omit the sautéing step. I use both leaves and seeds along with plenty of fresh garlic to give this dish its lively flavor. This makes a delicious side dish, or entree served with rice or potatoes.

2 to 3 teaspoons canola oil

2 large onions, halved and thinly sliced

2 to 4 tablespoons vegetable broth or water

1 green pepper, cut into strips

One 28-ounce can tomatoes, with their juice

2 pounds eggplant, unpeeled and cut into 1-inch cubes

Salt and freshly ground pepper, to taste

2 teaspoons ground coriander

5 to 6 tablespoons chopped fresh cilantro

1 pound zucchini or yellow crookneck squash or a mixture, halved and sliced about 3/8-inch thick

6 large cloves garlic, chopped

Heat oil in a large, heavy sauté pan. Add onions and sauté over medium heat about 10 minutes or until golden brown, gradually adding 2 to 4 tablespoons broth or water as necessary to prevent burning. Add green pepper strips and sauté about 5 minutes. Add tomatoes with their juice and eggplant cubes. Sprinkle with salt, pepper, and ground coriander and add 3 tablespoons chopped cilantro. Cover and cook over medium-low heat 15 minutes. Add zucchini slices. Cover and cook 10 minutes. Add garlic. Cover and cook 5 minutes or until vegetables are tender. Serve hot or at room temperature. To serve, add 2 to 3 tablespoons cilantro; either stir it in lightly or sprinkle it on top.

Stuffed Vegetables

Turkish Stuffed Eggplant

Makes 6 servings

Jews from Turkey flavor their eggplant stuffing with a generous amount of fresh garlic, which gives it a lively taste. When I first learned to prepare this dish, the recipe called for deep frying the eggplant. Like many old recipes, it came from a time when ovens were not common in homes. I find baking the eggplant much easier, and, of course, the dish is lower in fat. It is satisfying enough to make a meatless main course, and good for Passover or Sukkot. In fact, with eggplant available year round, you can serve it at any time. Be sure to use fresh, unblemished eggplants.

3 eggplants, each about 1 pound

Salt and freshly ground pepper, to taste

3 to 4 tablespoons olive oil

2 large onions, chopped

Two 28-ounce cans tomatoes, drained and chopped, or 2 1/2 pounds ripe tomatoes, peeled, seeded, and chopped

1 teaspoon dried oregano

1/2 teaspoon paprika

8 large cloves garlic, minced

1/3 cup matzo meal

1/3 cup chopped fresh Italian parsley

Cayenne pepper to taste

2 tablespoons tomato paste

1/4 cup water

1. Preheat oven to 450°F. Remove green caps and halve eggplants lengthwise. With a sharp knife, score flesh of each half lightly to make a border along skin, leaving a shell about 3/8-inch thick. Cut 3 or 4 shallow lines in center of each eggplant half. Place eggplants cut side up in a large lightly oiled roasting pan. Sprinkle them with salt and with half the oil. Bake 25 minutes, or until eggplant is tender when pierced with a knife.

2. Heat remaining oil in a large nonstick skillet. Add onions and sauté over medium heat 5 minutes, stirring often. Cover and cook over low heat, stirring often, about 7 minutes or until brown and tender; if pan becomes dry or onions turn too dark, add 1 or 2 tablespoons water. Remove onions from skillet. Add tomatoes, oregano, paprika, salt, and pepper. Cook uncovered, stirring occasionally, about 25 minutes or until mixture is thick. Remove half of tomato mixture and reserve as sauce.

3. Let eggplants cool slightly. Cut gently with a thin knife along border and remove pulp carefully with spoon; do not pierce eggplant skin. Drain pulp 5 minutes in colander. If shells are watery, drain them also. Return eggplant shells to shallow baking dish.

4. Chop eggplant pulp and add to tomato mixture in the skillet. Add onions, garlic, matzo meal, and parsley. Season mixture well with salt, pepper, and cayenne.

5. Spoon filling into eggplant shells. Bake about 15 minutes, or until eggplant is very tender and hot.

6. Reheat tomato mixture reserved as sauce. Add tomato paste and water, or more if needed to thin sauce to desired consistency. Adjust seasoning.

7. Serve eggplant hot, warm, or at room temperature, accompanied by tomato sauce.

Stuffed Small Squashes with American Rice Pilaf

Makes 4 servings (P)

This beautiful dish is perfect for Sukkot, when many winter squashes are at the markets, or for Thanksgiving, whether or not you are serving a turkey. After all, it's much easier to stuff a squash than a turkey. Besides, a turkey will roast much more quickly without stuffing. Here you have a stuffing and vegetable all in one dish.

If you are using your oven at a temperature between 325°F and 400°F, you can add the pan of squashes to bake. A quicker way to prepare one or two squashes is in the microwave; either follow squash label or see the following Note.

You can easily multiply this recipe by using a large roasting pan for the squashes and a stew pan for cooking the rice.

2 acorn or Delicata squashes, halved lengthwise and seeded
1/2 cup slivered almonds
2 or 3 tablespoons vegetable oil
1 small onion, minced
1 cup long-grain white rice
2 cups vegetable stock or water
1 bay leaf
Salt and freshly ground pepper, to taste
1/2 cup dried cranberries
1/4 teaspoon ground cinnamon
1 teaspoon finely grated orange rind

1. Preheat oven to 375°F. Lightly spray a heavy roasting pan with oil spray. Add enough water to go about 1/4-inch up sides of pan. Place squash halves cut side down in pan. Bake about 40 minutes or until tender when pierced with fork. Remove from oven. Toast almonds on a baking sheet in oven, stirring once or twice, for 5 minutes or until very lightly browned. Transfer to a plate.

2. Heat oil in a deep skillet or sauté pan, add onion, and sauté over low heat about 5 minutes or until soft but not brown. Add rice and sauté over medium heat, stirring, about 2 minutes. Add stock, bay leaf, salt, and pepper and bring to a boil. Stir once. Cover and cook over low heat 10 minutes. Add cranberries without stirring. Cover and cook about 8 minutes or until rice is just tender. Discard bay leaf. Fluff rice lightly with a fork and lightly stir in cinnamon, orange rind, and almonds. Adjust seasoning.

3. Fill squash halves with stuffing. Put in roasting pan, stuffing side up. Bake squashes about 10 minutes or until stuffing is hot. Serve remaining stuffing separately.

Note: To microwave one acorn squash, put the halved squash cut-side down in a baking dish containing about 1/4 inch of water. Cover and microwave about 12 minutes or until just tender. Remove from pan. Microwave second squash.

For a Delicata squash, follow the same instructions; you will need only about 8 minutes for each squash.

Stuffed Acorn Squash with Bulgur Wheat and Figs

Makes 4 main-course or 8 side-dish servings

Serve this festive stuffed squash for Purim or Sukkot, either as a side dish for chicken, turkey, or meat or as a meatless main course. For a change you can prepare a vegetarian Shabbat dinner and feature this dish as an entree. Use any color acorn squash. Orange ones are the most colorful but you can use green or pale yellow ones or more than one color.

4 acorn squashes, each about 1¹/₂ pounds
Fig, Bulgur Wheat, and Toasted Almond Stuffing (page 187)
1 large egg, beaten
Salt and freshly ground pepper, to taste
1 tablespoon vegetable oil
8 small sprigs fresh parsley

1. Preheat oven to 400°F. Have squashes lengthwise and remove the seeds. Cut thin slice from bottom of each squash half if necessary, so they will stand straight when stuffed. Oil a large nonstick roasting pan; or line pan with foil and oil the foil. Place squash skin side up in pan. Bake about 40 minutes or until tender when pierced with fork.

2. Prepare stuffing. Cool slightly. Adjust seasoning. Add egg, tossing lightly.

3. Reduce oven temperature to 350°F. Sprinkle squash halves with salt and pepper. Fill them generously with stuffing. Sprinkle oil over stuffing. Cover squashes and bake them 30 minutes or until stuffing is hot. Serve garnished with parsley.

Stuffed Peppers with "Meaty" Almond-Rice Stuffing

Makes 5 or 6 servings

Nobody will miss the meat in these pareve stuffed peppers. Soy-based ground "meat" stands in handily for it and makes a delicious stuffing with the toasted almonds, rice, and tasty Yemenite Jewish spicing. Choose peppers that are flat-bottomed rather than tapered so they can stand up during baking.

¹/₂ cup long-grain rice, rinsed and drained
3 to 4 tablespoons olive oil or vegetable oil
1 medium onion, finely chopped
6 to 8 ounces soy ground meat substitute
2 tablespoons tomato paste
1 teaspoon ground cumin
¹/₂ teaspoon ground turmeric
¹/₂ teaspoon salt
¹/₄ teaspoon freshly ground pepper
1 jalapeño pepper, seeds removed, minced, or hot sauce to taste
2 large cloves garlic, minced
2 tablespoons chopped fresh cilantro or Italian parsley
¹/₃ cup slivered almonds, toasted
5 or 6 red or green bell peppers
¹/₄ cup water

1. Boil rice in a saucepan of 3 cups boiling salted water 10 minutes. Rinse with cold water and drain well.

2. Heat 2 tablespoons oil in a skillet, add onion, and sauté over medium-low heat about 5 minutes or until beginning to turn golden. Add soy meat substitute and sauté 2 to 3 minutes, stirring to separate it into small pieces. Let cool slightly.

3. Transfer onion-soy mixture to a large bowl. Add 1 tablespoon tomato paste, cumin, turmeric, salt, pepper, jalapeño pepper, garlic, and cilantro. Mix well. Add rice and almonds and mix well. Adjust seasoning.

4. Cut a slice off stem-end of peppers. Reserve slice; remove stem, core, and seeds. Spoon stuffing into whole peppers and cover with reserved slices. Stand them in a baking dish in which they just fit. Mix remaining tomato paste with water and spoon mixture over peppers. Sprinkle them with remaining oil.

5. Bake peppers uncovered about 1 hour or until very tender. Serve hot or warm.

Tomatoes with Ginger-Soy Brown Rice Stuffing

Makes 6 servings

Flavors of Asia are popular in many Jewish kitchens today, in the Unites States as well as in Israel. Serve these meatless stuffed tomatoes as a light Sukkot or Shavuot main course; or use tomato halves or smaller tomatoes to turn this into an appetizer.

When I cook brown rice, I make a habit of cooking extra to use in dishes like this one. If you don't have any already cooked, you can save time by using quick-cooking brown rice.

2 tablespoons vegetable oil

2 ribs celery, chopped

1 large green onion, white and green parts, chopped

1 tablespoon minced peeled fresh ginger

3 large cloves garlic, minced

6 to 8 ounces soy ground meat substitute

1 to 2 teaspoons soy sauce, or to taste (optional)

1/4 teaspoon hot pepper sauce or chili oil (optional)

1/2 cup canned water chestnuts, drained and chopped

1 cup cooked brown rice

1/2 cup cooked fresh or frozen corn kernels

Salt, to taste

2 1/2 pounds tomatoes (about 6 large), ripe but firm

1. Preheat oven to 400°F. Heat oil in a skillet. Add celery, green onion, ginger, and garlic and sauté over medium-low heat 1 minute. Add soy meat substitute and sauté, stirring to separate it into small pieces, 2 or 3 minutes. Remove from heat and add soy sauce and pepper sauce, if using. Transfer to a bowl. Add water chestnuts, rice, and corn and mix well. Adjust seasoning.

2. Cut off a slice from smooth end of each tomato, cutting about 1/4 of the tomato; reserve slice as a "hat." Remove pulp and seeds from tomato with spoon. Sprinkle interior of tomatoes lightly with salt.

3. Put tomatoes in an oiled baking dish. Fill with stuffing, mounding slightly, and cover with hats. Bake uncovered 30 to 40 minutes or until tomatoes are tender. Serve hot.

❧ Grains and Pasta

Curried Cabbage with Rice, Mushrooms, and Peas

Makes 4 servings

Flavors of the Jews of India lend spirit to this hearty entree. White basmati rice is preferred but I often like to use either brown basmati or other brown rice for its extra nutrition. If you would like a dairy accompaniment, serve Tomato-Cucumber Salad with Yogurt and Mint (page 288).

1 to 2 tablespoons vegetable oil

1 large onion, halved and sliced

1 small head cabbage (1 to 1 1/4 pounds), shredded, or one 1-pound package shredded cabbage (7 or 8 cups)

1 teaspoon curry powder

1 teaspoon ground cumin

1/4 teaspoon hot red pepper flakes

Salt and freshly ground pepper, to taste

1 1/2 cups brown basmati or other brown rice

1 3/4 cups vegetable stock or one 14 1/2-ounce can

1 1/4 cups hot water

1 1/2 cups frozen peas, thawed; or 1 1/2 cups shelled fresh peas, blanched 2 minutes

8 ounces mushrooms, quartered

One 14 1/2-ounce can diced tomatoes, drained

1 or 2 tablespoons chopped fresh dill or 1 teaspoon dried (optional)

1. Heat oil in a large wide stew pan. Add onion and sauté over medium heat 3 minutes. Add cabbage and sprinkle with curry powder, cumin, pepper flakes, salt, and pepper. Cover and cook over low heat 3 minutes; cabbage will wilt. Mix well.

2. Add rice, stock, and hot water to pan. Stir once and bring to a boil over high heat. Cover and cook over low heat without stirring 35 minutes. Add peas and mushrooms without stirring. Cover and cook about 5 more minutes or until rice is tender. Add tomatoes and toss lightly with a fork. Add 1 tablespoon dill, if using. Adjust seasoning. Serve hot.

Wild and Brown Rice with Asparagus and Broccoli

Makes 6 to 8 servings

For a lovely meatless casserole suitable for a Shavuot or Purim feast, serve this dish as an entree or accompaniment. Wild rice and brown rice are convenient to cook together because both take about the same amount of time. If you prefer to add only asparagus or broccoli, simply double the amount.

2 quarts water

1 bay leaf

1 large sprig fresh thyme or 1 teaspoon dried thyme

1 cup wild rice, rinsed and drained

1 cup brown rice

Salt and freshly ground pepper, to taste

3/4 to 1 pound asparagus, peeled if thick

3/4 to 1 pound broccoli, divided into small florets

2 to 3 tablespoons vegetable oil or olive oil

1 large onion, chopped

3 tablespoons chopped fresh tarragon (optional)

1/3 cup chopped fresh Italian parsley

1. Combine water, bay leaf, and thyme in a large saucepan and bring to a boil. Add wild and brown rice and a pinch of salt and return to boil. Cover and cook over low heat about 50 minutes or until kernels of wild rice begin to puff open and brown rice is tender.

2. Cut asparagus tips from stems. Cut stems into 2 or 3 pieces, discarding tough ends (about 1/2-inch from end). Cut peel from broccoli stalk and cut into thin slices.

3. Boil enough water in a large sauté pan to cover vegetables. Add broccoli and boil uncovered 2 minutes. Add asparagus and return to a boil. Boil 2 to 3 more minutes or until vegetables are barely tender when pierced with a small sharp knife. Drain, rinse with cold running water until cool, and drain well.

4. Heat oil in sauté pan. Add onion and sauté over medium-low heat, stirring often, about 7 minutes or until soft but not brown.

5. Just before serving, reheat onion, add asparagus, broccoli, salt, and pepper and sauté about 2 minutes to heat them through.

6. Drain rice if necessary. Discard bay leaf and thyme sprig. Transfer to a shallow serving bowl, add vegetables, and toss to combine. Add tarragon if using, and all but 1 tablespoon parsley. Adjust seasoning. Serve hot, sprinkled with remaining parsley.

Brown Rice with Black-Eyed Peas and Cumin Tomato Sauce

Makes 4 to 6 servings

A favorite on Sephardic tables, black-eyed peas often appear in a tomato sauce. Traditional cooks pair them with white rice but today more and more people are serving brown rice, not only for its nutritional value but also for its good taste.

3/4 pound dried black-eyed peas or 4 cups frozen black-eyed peas, cooked according to package directions

7 cups water

3 cups vegetable stock or more water

1 1/2 cups long-grain brown rice

1 tablespoon olive oil

1 large onion, chopped

2 large cloves garlic, chopped (optional)

One 28-ounce can diced tomatoes, drained

1 tablespoon tomato paste

2 teaspoons ground cumin

1 1/2 teaspoons ground coriander

1 1/2 teaspoons paprika

Salt and freshly ground pepper, to taste

1/4 teaspoon cayenne pepper, or to taste

1/4 cup chopped fresh Italian parsley

1. Pick over dried peas, discarding pebbles and broken or discolored peas. Rinse well. Put peas in a large saucepan and add 7 cups water. Bring to a simmer. Cover and cook over low heat about 1 1/2 hours or until tender.

2. Bring stock to a boil in a large, heavy saucepan. Add rice, cover, and cook over low heat 40 to 45 minutes or until just tender. Transfer to a large bowl, fluff with fork, and cool.

3. Heat oil in a heavy nonstick skillet, add onion, and sauté over medium heat, stirring often, about 5 minutes; when onion begins to brown, add 1 tablespoon water and continue to sauté until deeply browned. Add garlic if using, then diced tomatoes, and bring to a boil. Cook over medium heat 5 minutes.

4. Drain peas, reserving cooking liquid, and return to saucepan. Add tomato sauce from skillet, tomato paste, cumin, coriander, paprika, salt, pepper, and cayenne. Bring to a simmer. Cover and heat gently 5 minutes. If you would like peas to be in a thinner sauce, add about 1/4 cup pea cooking liquid.

5. Fluff rice with a fork. Adjust seasoning and transfer to a serving dish. Add half the parsley. Serve hot, with about 1/4 cup of the black-eyed peas ladled over rice for garnish, and rest in a shallow serving bowl. Sprinkle rice with remaining parsley.

Bulgur Wheat with Lentils

Makes 4 servings   Ⓟ

Sephardic Jews cook lentils often, pairing them not only with rice but also with bulgur wheat. Like lentils with rice, lentils with bulgur is most enjoyed with plenty of well sautéed onions. If you shop at Israeli or Middle Eastern markets, you will most likely find coarse or large bulgur wheat, which is good for this dish. Otherwise, use the more commonly available medium bulgur wheat granules. Serve this as a hearty vegetarian entree, accompanied by one or more raw vegetable salads such as Israeli salad or red cabbage salad. It's also good with chicken dinners.

1 cup lentils, sorted

2 cups vegetable stock, or stock mixed with water

4 to 5 tablespoons vegetable oil

2 large onions, chopped

3 large cloves garlic, chopped

1 teaspoon ground cumin

Salt and freshly ground pepper, to taste

1/4 teaspoon hot red pepper flakes

1 cup bulgur wheat, large- or medium-grain

Cayenne pepper, to taste

2 tablespoons chopped fresh Italian parsley

1. Combine lentils and 2 cups stock in a medium saucepan. Bring to a boil. Cover and cook over medium heat about 20 minutes or until lentils are just tender.

Drain liquid into a measuring cup and add enough water to make 2 cups; reserve.

2. Heat oil in a heavy skillet over medium heat. Add onions and sauté, stirring occasionally, until they are well browned, about 15 minutes. Remove half of onion mixture and reserve.

3. Add garlic and cumin to onions in pan and sauté 1 minute. Add onion-garlic mixture to pan of lentils. Add measured liquid and bring to a boil. Add salt, pepper flakes, and bulgur wheat and return to a boil. Cover and cook over low heat about 15 minutes or until bulgur wheat is tender.

4. Add reserved onions to pot. Cover and let stand 5 or 10 minutes. Adjust seasoning, adding pepper and cayenne to taste. Serve hot, sprinkled with parsley.

Sunday Couscous

Makes about 4 servings   Ⓟ

Jews from Tunisia make this dish to use up leftovers from Shabbat. They simply spice up some cooked couscous and heat it with cooked vegetables. Traditionally, it's made from couscous that was already steamed but today it's easy to use quick-cooking couscous.

1 1/2 to 2 teaspoons harissa or bottled hot pepper sauce, or to taste

1/2 teaspoon caraway seeds

3 large cloves garlic, pressed or very finely minced

1 teaspoon paprika

Salt and freshly ground pepper, to taste

2 tablespoons water

2 to 4 tablespoons extra-virgin olive oil

2 1/2 cups vegetable stock or water

1 cup diced cooked carrots

1 cup diced cooked zucchini

1 cup chopped cooked cauliflower or broccoli

1 2/3 cups couscous or one 10-ounce package

1. Combine harissa, caraway seeds, garlic, paprika, salt, pepper, water, and 1 to 3 tablespoons olive oil in a bowl. Whisk to blend.

2. Bring stock to a simmer in a medium saucepan with remaining tablespoon oil. Add carrots, zucchini, and cauliflower and bring to a boil. Stir in couscous and bring to a simmer. Remove from heat and let stand 5 minutes. Add sauce to couscous, cover, and let stand until ready to serve. Fluff with a fork before serving. Adjust seasoning.

Savory Vegetable Medley over Couscous

Makes 4 servings

A popular dish in the North African kitchen is chicken with vegetables in a tomato broth, served with a steaming mound of couscous. Here is my pareve version that I make with tofu. It is much quicker and easier to prepare than the classic and is a favorite in our household. Homemade Harissa *(page 592) adds the best flavor but store-bought works well for this recipe.*

2 to 3 tablespoons olive oil or vegetable oil

1 large onion, cut into thin slices

1 small green pepper, diced (optional)

4 large cloves garlic, chopped

1¹/₂ teaspoons ground cumin

1 pound ripe tomatoes, peeled, seeded, and chopped, or one 28-ounce can tomatoes, drained and chopped

2 tablespoons tomato paste

¹/₂ cup vegetable stock

Salt and freshly ground pepper, to taste

¹/₄ to ¹/₂ teaspoon hot red pepper flakes

1¹/₂ pounds zucchini, cut into 1-inch dice

One 14- to 16-ounce package firm or extra-firm tofu, cut into ³/₄-inch dice

One 15-ounce can white beans or chickpeas (garbanzo beans), drained (optional)

Basic Quick Couscous (page 483)

2 tablespoons chopped fresh cilantro or Italian parsley

Bottled harissa, or other hot sauce or salsa

1. Heat oil in a heavy, wide stew pan or Dutch oven. Add onion and green pepper, if using, and sauté over medium heat 5 minutes. Stir in garlic, cumin, and tomatoes and bring to a boil. Cook uncovered, stirring often, 7 minutes.

2. Add tomato paste, stock, salt, pepper, and pepper flakes to stew pan and bring to a boil. Add zucchini and cook over medium heat 5 minutes. Add tofu, cover, and cook over low heat 5 minutes or until zucchini are tender. Add beans, if using, and heat through. Adjust seasoning.

3. Prepare quick couscous. Spoon couscous onto center of a large platter. Spoon tofu and some of zucchini around it. Sprinkle tofu and vegetables with chopped cilantro. Serve remaining vegetable sauce and harissa separately.

Blintzes, Sandwiches, and Pizza

Mexican Onion-Tomato Blintzes

Makes 6 to 8 servings

The filling for these easy-to-make blintzes is Mexican inspired, seasoned with jalapeño peppers, cumin, and cilantro. The blintzes are rolled in a tortilla instead of the usual blintz crepe. It's a pleasure to make them, now that several kinds of kosher tortillas are available. If you like, choose a tortilla flavored with tomato or herbs. Use tortillas that are thin, fresh, and pliable; they won't work if they're old and stiff.

This recipe is pareve. For dairy meals, you can sprinkle a little grated cheese on the blintzes before baking, and top each blintz at serving time with a dollop of sour cream or of Garlic-Yogurt Sauce (page 462).

2 cups Tomato Sauce with Mild Chiles (page 587), or your favorite tomato sauce

Sephardic Salsa (page 131) or Cilantro Salsa (page 341) (optional)

About 3 tablespoons olive oil or vegetable oil

1¹/₂ pounds onions, halved and sliced

2 jalapeño or serrano peppers, seeded if desired, minced (see Note)

One 14¹/₂-ounce can tomatoes, drained and chopped

1¹/₂ teaspoons ground cumin

Salt and freshly ground pepper, to taste

3 to 4 tablespoons chopped fresh cilantro

Cayenne pepper, to taste (optional)

8 to 12 flour tortillas, plain, whole wheat, tomato, or herb

Fresh cilantro sprigs

Avocado slices

1. Prepare tomato sauce, if using homemade. Prepare salsa, if using. Heat 2 tablespoons oil in a heavy stew pan. Add onions and sauté over medium heat 5 minutes. Cover and cook over low heat, stirring often, 15 minutes or until tender and beginning to brown. Stir in jalapeño peppers, then tomatoes, cumin, salt, and pepper. Cook uncovered over medium heat, stirring occasionally, about 15 minutes or until mixture is thick. Stir in cilantro. Adjust seasoning; add cayenne, if using.

2. Put tomato sauce in a sauté pan, bring to boil, and remove from heat.

3. Preheat oven to 350°F. Stack tortillas in 2 stacks in an oiled baking dish, spraying or brushing each lightly with oil as you stack them. Cover and bake 5 minutes just to warm tortillas slightly. Leave oven at 350°F.

4. To assemble, dip a tortilla in sauce on both sides; then put on a plate. Spoon 3 to 4 tablespoons filling in a strip near one end of a tortilla and roll up in cigar shape. Arrange side by side in a shallow oiled baking dish. Brush tortillas with remaining oil.

5. Bake blintzes about 10 minutes or until hot. Serve hot or warm, topped with salsa, if using, and garnished with cilantro sprigs and avocado. If you like, heat extra filling and extra tomato sauce and serve them on the side.

Note: Wear rubber gloves when handling hot peppers.

Israeli-Iraqi Vegetable Sandwich

Makes about 4 servings

This recipe is inspired by the Iraqi sandwich that I like to order at Shula and Esther, an Israeli restaurant in Los Angeles. It contains eggplant, tomato, and hard boiled egg slices and is moistened by tahini. You can enjoy the combination in a pita bread or a long crusty roll. The eggplant slices are fried but I broil mine to save on effort, time, calories, and clean-up. If you prefer it fried, follow the instructions for Fried Eggplant with Herbed Tomatoes (page 221).

The sandwich is best if you make your own tahini sauce, but you can purchase prepared tahini sauce as well. If you're buying the sauce to serve as is, read the label to be sure it is a ready-to-eat sauce, not the thick tahini paste or sesame butter which is designed to be diluted with water and lemon juice before you can eat it.

About ¹/₂ cup Herbed Tahini Sauce (page 437)

1 small eggplant, about ¹/₂ pound, cut into slices ¹/₄-inch thick

2 or 3 teaspoons olive oil, or a little oil spray

Salt and freshly ground pepper, to taste

4 fresh pita breads or crusty French rolls

1 or 2 ripe tomatoes, sliced

2 to 4 large hard boiled eggs, sliced

Tender lettuce leaves, such as butter lettuce, Boston lettuce,
    or green leaf lettuce (optional)

1. Prepare sauce. Then, arrange eggplant on a foil-lined baking sheet or broiler pan. Brush or spray lightly with oil and sprinkle with salt and pepper. Broil about 8 minutes. Turn over and broil about 7 minutes or until tender. Cover and keep warm.

2. Cut a strip from top of each pita to make a pocket; or split each pita bread in two. If using rolls, split them lengthwise. Spoon a little tahini sauce into each pita, or spread a little on each roll. Fill with slices of broiled eggplant, tomato, and hard boiled egg and sprinkle them with salt and pepper.

3. For roll sandwiches, top with lettuce, if using, then with top half of roll; or insert a few bite-size pieces of lettuce inside pita sandwiches. Serve more of the tahini sauce separately.

Grilled Portobello Mushroom Sandwich with Tahini

Makes 4 servings

Sandwiches of grilled vegetables and tahini in a pita are popular in Israel. With their meaty texture, portobello mushrooms make a scrumptious, satisfying sandwich. This is wonderful with homemade tahini sauce, but store-bought can work in a pinch.

Herbed Tahini Sauce (page 437)

Zehug (page 592) or bottled hot sauce

1 cup shredded romaine lettuce

1 green onion, chopped

¹/₂ small cucumber, diced

2 large ripe tomatoes, cut into small dice

4 large portobello mushrooms

2 teaspoons extra-virgin olive oil

Salt and freshly ground pepper, to taste

4 fresh or warmed pita breads

1. Prepare sauce and zehug, if fresh preferred. Flavor tahini sauce to taste with zehug. Mix lettuce, onion, cucumber, and tomatoes in a bowl.

2. Clean mushrooms with a damp towel. Heat a ridged stovetop grill pan over medium-high heat. Rub mushrooms with oil and sprinkle with salt and pepper on both sides.

3. Set mushrooms on hot grill. Grill about 3 minutes per side or until browned and done to your taste.

4. Cut mushrooms into thick slices. Cut a strip from top of each pita to form a pocket. Put mushroom slices inside and moisten with a spoonful of tahini sauce. Add vegetable salad and spoon a little more sauce over. Serve more zehug on the side.

Sesame Vegetables in Pita

Makes 4 servings

For this warm pareve sandwich, sautéed vegetables are flavored with sesame seeds. I often enhance the sesame taste by using a little sesame oil as well; or, if I have tahini sauce on hand, I follow the Israeli taste and spoon a little into each pita. The sandwich is especially enticing if you use good-quality pita bread from a bakery or an Israeli or Middle Eastern market. You can prepare the vegetable mixture ahead and reheat it before serving.

1 small eggplant (about ³/₄ pound)

4 tablespoons vegetable or olive oil

Salt and freshly ground pepper, to taste

1 medium onion, halved and cut into thin slices

1 large red bell pepper, cut into thin strips

1 small zucchini, cut into thin strips

1 tablespoon sesame oil or additional olive oil

4 large cloves garlic, minced

1 tablespoon sesame seeds

3 tablespoons chopped fresh oregano or 1 tablespoon dried

2 tablespoons chopped fresh Italian parsley

4 fresh or warmed plain or whole-wheat pita breads

1. Cut eggplant into strips of about 2 × ¹/₂ × ¹/₄-inch. Heat 2 tablespoons vegetable or olive oil in a large skillet over medium heat. Add eggplant, salt, and pepper. Sauté, tossing constantly, about 7 minutes or until just tender. Transfer to a bowl.

2. Add 2 tablespoons vegetable or olive oil to skillet. Add onion and pepper and sauté over medium heat, stirring often, about 7 minutes or until nearly tender. Add zucchini and return eggplant to pan. Sauté about 3 minutes, tossing often, until zucchini is crisp-tender. Transfer vegetables to a large bowl and keep warm. Wipe skillet clean and reserve.

3. Add sesame oil to skillet and warm over low heat. Add garlic and sesame seeds and cook about 30 seconds. Add oregano and parsley and heat 2 to 3 seconds. Pour mixture over vegetables and toss well. Adjust seasoning.

4. Serve vegetables spooned inside pita breads; or serve them in a bowl, with pita breads on a plate.

Pareve "Pizza"

Makes 2 pizzas, total 6 to 8 servings   **P**

Making pizza pareve is useful for many occasions, such as Saturday night suppers when people are often in the mood for casual food. If an Orthodox Jew has eaten a rather late Shabbat lunch that included meat or poultry, it's not always convenient to wait the six hours that would be required before cheese is allowed. A pareve pizza is a perfect solution.

Of course, a pizza made without cheese is also lighter. You can spread any vegetable topping you like on the pizza. This one has a flavorful, easy-to-make topping of mushrooms, tomatoes, and olives. If you prefer a cheese-like topping, you can scatter thin slivers of soy cheese over the top before baking.

Pizza Dough (page 546)

3/4 pound ripe tomatoes, peeled, seeded, and coarsely chopped, or one 14 1/2-ounce can tomatoes, drained and chopped

2 cloves garlic, finely chopped

1 teaspoon dried thyme

Salt and freshly ground pepper, to taste

1/4 teaspoon hot red pepper flakes, or to taste

1/2 pound mushrooms, sliced thin

1/3 to 1/2 cup pitted black olives, halved

2 or 3 tablespoons extra-virgin olive oil

1. Make dough and let rise. Then, put chopped fresh or canned tomatoes in a colander or strainer to drain.

2. Lightly oil 2 baking sheets or spray them with oil spray. Knead dough briefly, divide into 2 pieces and put each on a baking sheet. With oiled hands, pat each portion of dough into a 10-inch circle, with rims slightly higher than centers.

3. Mix tomatoes with garlic, thyme, salt, pepper, and pepper flakes. Spread tomato mixture over dough. Arrange mushroom slices on top and sprinkle them lightly with pepper. Garnish with olive halves. Drizzle olive oil evenly over topping, making sure that rim of dough is moistened with oil as well.

4. Preheat oven to 425°F. Let pizzas rise about 15 minutes. Bake pizzas about 18 minutes or until dough is golden brown and firm. Serve hot.

Sauces

Herbed Tahini Sauce

Makes about 1 cup, 5 to 6 servings

Israelis of Middle Eastern origin often prefer the taste of tahini sauce to mayonnaise and use it in the same ways—in salads, sandwiches, and with grilled vegetables and fish.

To make tahini sauce, buy tahini paste. It's easy to find in well-stocked supermarkets, as well as in Israeli, Middle Eastern, and natural foods stores. Tahini paste is sometimes called sesame butter and when you buy a jar, you'll see why; the oil often rises to the top, as in jars of natural peanut butter. Stir the tahini until well blended before measuring it; hold it away from you, as the oil splashes. Making the sauce in the blender is a favorite technique in Israel and is the easiest way. You can also stir the ingredients together in a heavy bowl.

1/2 cup tahini (sesame paste), stirred before measuring

About 1/2 cup plus 1 tablespoon water

1/4 teaspoon salt, or to taste

About 2 tablespoons strained fresh lemon juice

3 large cloves garlic, minced

1/4 cup small sprigs fresh Italian parsley

2 tablespoons chopped fresh cilantro

Pinch of cayenne pepper, or to taste

1. Combine tahini and 1/2 cup water in blender. Add salt, lemon juice, garlic, parsley, and cilantro. Blend until smooth and herbs are finely chopped.

2. Transfer to a bowl. If sauce is too thick, gradually stir in more water. Season with cayenne, and add more salt or lemon juice, if desired.

Chunky Avocado Sauce with Zehug and Olives

Makes 6 to 8 servings

In this sauce the pungency of the olives balances the rich, buttery character of the avocado, an Israeli favorite. The Yemenite hot pepper chutney called zehug gives it plenty of heat.

For meatless meals, I find this sprightly sauce adds great color and flavor to bulgur wheat, brown rice, kasha, and lentils. It's also delicious with grilled fish or chicken or, for an appetizer, atop slices of broiled eggplant. Or you can just scoop it into fresh pita bread or warm tortillas for a tasty sandwich.

2 teaspoons Zehug (page 592) or minced jalapeño peppers, or to taste

3/4 pound ripe tomatoes, finely diced

1/2 cup Kalamata or other good-quality black olives, pitted and diced

1/4 cup minced white onion

1/4 cup chopped fresh cilantro

1 tablespoon chopped fresh oregano or 1 teaspoon dried

1 ripe avocado, preferably Haas

2 to 3 tablespoons fresh lime juice

Salt and freshly ground pepper, to taste

1 to 2 tablespoons water, if needed

1. Prepare zehug, if using homemade. Then, combine tomatoes, olives, onion, zehug, cilantro, and oregano in a bowl. Refrigerate salsa in a covered container until ready to serve.

2. A short time before serving, halve avocado. Remove pit by hitting it with the heel of a heavy knife so knife sticks in pit; twist to remove pit. Scoop out avocado meat with a spoon and dice it. Add to bowl of sauce. Add lime juice. Season with salt and pepper. Add water if sauce is too thick. Serve cold.

Vegetable Side Dishes

Potatoes and Sweet Potatoes
441

Potato Kugel with Mushrooms and Peas

Bubble-and-Squeak Kugel

Mashed Potatoes with Garlic

Horseradish Mashed Potatoes

Oven-Fried Potatoes

Potato Kneidel with Duxelles Sauce

Savory Sweet Potato Kugel

Sweet Potato Tzimmes with Dried Pears

Mediterranean Vegetables
445

Artichokes with Easy Garlic Sauce

Broiled Eggplant

Baked Eggplant Slices

Israeli Eggplant Stew

Eggplant with Rice and Pine Nut Stuffing

Okra with Tomatoes, Garlic, and Cilantro

Savory Red Chard with Garlic

Fava Beans in Quick Tomato Sauce

Squashes and Pumpkins
449

Yellow and Green Squash, Hungarian Style

Syrian Squash with Carrots

Zucchini and Red Beans with Mint-Yogurt Topping

Tangy Tunisian Mashed Pumpkin

Cauliflower, Broccoli, and Cabbage
451

Hungarian Cauliflower and Peas in Dill Sauce

Cauliflower in Indian-Spiced Tomato Sauce

Broccoli Gratin with Cheese Sauce

Polish Cabbage with Raisins

Sauerkraut with Onions and Caraway Seeds

P = Pareve   **D** = Dairy   **M** = Meat

$\mathcal{O}$ne important theme of the three main biblical festivals on the Jewish calendar—Passover, Shavuot, and Sukkot—is the harvest. We express our appreciation for the produce of the past season and pray for success in the upcoming one. Thus vegetables and fruit are highlighted in celebrating these holidays. Serving an array of cooked and raw vegetable appetizers and salads to begin meals is one festive manner of presenting them. Jewish cooks often turn vegetables into special occasion dishes by filling them with a savory stuffing.

Vegetables are also important in everyday Jewish cooking, not only for reasons of health, economy, and variety in menus, but also because all vegetables are kosher and can be served with any other food, whether it is meat or dairy.

In addition to the usual cooking techniques for vegetables, Jewish cooks make them into kugels and latkes. We are most familiar with noodle kugels but in fact kugels are often made from vegetables. Israeli cooks are especially fond of vegetable kugels and casseroles called *pashtidot*. (See box on *Pashtidot*, page 507.)

A vegetable kugel can be made of one vegetable or from a combination of several. Most kugels are baked in casserole dishes, then cut into portions, but small ones can be baked in muffin pans or ramekins and make attractive individual servings. The texture varies enormously too. The vegetables can be mixed with eggs and a cream sauce or other sauce, then baked in a hot oven so the kugel resembles an airy soufflé, or pureed and baked gently in ramekins in a water bath like moist French timbales.

Latkes are cherished for their central role in Hanukkah parties, when potato latkes are most prominent. But latkes are made year-round out of all sorts of vegetables and served as accompaniments. I learned from my mother that latkes and kugels are related, because the same mixture can be either fried as latkes or baked as a kugel.

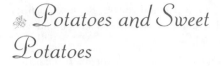

Potatoes and Sweet Potatoes

Potato Kugel with Mushrooms and Peas

Makes 6 servings

Mashed potato kugel has always been a favorite in our family, especially when it's flavored with plenty of sautéed onions and mushrooms, like this one. If you like, use a mixture of peas and carrots instead of peas alone. I love this kugel with baked fish, especially Red Trout and Asparagus with Lemon-Parsley Sauce (page 317). It's also good with roast chicken or beef.

1 cup frozen or shelled fresh peas

2¹/2 pounds boiling potatoes, unpeeled

3 tablespoons plus 1 teaspoon vegetable oil

2 medium onions, chopped

¹/2 pound small mushrooms, quartered

Salt and freshly ground pepper, to taste

2 large eggs, or 1 large egg and ¹/4 cup egg substitute, beaten

1. Remove frozen peas from freezer to thaw. If using fresh peas, cook them in boiling water 2 minutes and drain. Put potatoes in a large saucepan with water to cover and a pinch of salt and bring to a boil. Cover and simmer over low heat about 35 minutes or until very tender. Drain and leave until cool enough to handle.

2. Heat oil in a large skillet, add onions, and sauté over medium heat about 15 minutes or until light golden. Add mushrooms, salt, and pepper and sauté over medium-high heat about 7 minutes or until brown.

3. Preheat oven to 350°F. Peel potatoes while still fairly hot and cut each into a few pieces. Put in large bowl and mash with a potato masher. Season with salt and pepper (mixture should be seasoned generously). Stir in beaten eggs. Lightly stir in mushroom mixture and peas.

4. Generously oil a 2-quart casserole dish and add potato mixture. Smooth top. Sprinkle with 1 teaspoon oil. Bake uncovered about 40 minutes or until top is firm and light golden at edges.

Bubble-and-Squeak Kugel

Makes about 6 servings

Even the humble cabbage becomes festive when turned into a kugel. This one is inspired by the tasty British cabbage and potato sauté known as bubble and squeak. The kugel doesn't bubble or squeak, but it makes a tasty side dish with roast chicken for a winter Friday night dinner. Or bake it for Hanukkah, after you've had your fill of latkes.

2¹/4 pounds boiling potatoes (about 6 large), unpeeled

2 pounds cabbage

5 to 6 tablespoons vegetable oil

2 large onions, chopped

Salt and freshly ground pepper, to taste

1 teaspoon paprika, plus more for sprinkling

1 teaspoon caraway seeds (optional)

1 large egg, beaten

1. Put potatoes in a large saucepan with water to cover and a pinch of salt and bring to a boil. Cover and simmer over low heat about 35 minutes or until very tender. Drain and leave until cool enough to handle.

2. Core cabbage and shred or chop it. Boil cabbage in a saucepan of boiling salted water to cover 2 minutes or until barely tender. Drain and rinse with cold water. Drain well again.

3. Heat 3 tablespoons oil in a large skillet, add onions, and sauté over medium heat about 15 minutes or until light golden. Remove ¹/2 cup sautéed onions for mixing with potatoes. To onions in skillet add cabbage, salt, and pepper. Sauté 5 minutes, stirring often. Stir in paprika and caraway seeds, if using, mix well, and sauté another minute.

4. Preheat oven to 350°F. Peel potatoes while still fairly hot. Mash them with a potato masher or in a food mill, not in a food processor. Add remaining oil and stir until blended. Add reserved ¹/2 cup of sautéed onion. Add salt and pepper to taste; mixture should be seasoned generously. Add beaten egg and mix well.

5. Oil a 2-quart casserole dish. Spoon about half of potato mixture into casserole dish. Top with all of cabbage mixture, then with remaining potatoes. Smooth top. Sprinkle lightly with paprika.

6. Bake kugel uncovered about 50 minutes or until top is firm and light golden at edges. Let stand about 10 minutes before serving. Use a spoon to serve.

Mashed Potatoes with Garlic

Makes about 8 servings

Jewish cooks don't hesitate to serve mashed potatoes with their fleishig *(meat-based) meals. In many families they are a standard on holiday tables because children love them. By using chicken or meat broth to cook and moisten the potatoes, you can make them taste great without any butter, cream, or milk. If you want to make them pareve, you can use vegetable broth. For extra flavor, I simmer the stock with thyme and a bay leaf so their flavor infuses into the liquid, and I cook a few garlic cloves along with the potatoes and mash them together. The garlic becomes tender and mild-tasting and adds good flavor to the potatoes.*

Don't use a food processor to mash the potatoes or they will become gluey. If you like, leave the peel on the potatoes for a "country" look.

2¹/₂ pounds boiling potatoes or all-purpose potatoes such as Yukon Gold

4 large cloves garlic, peeled

1 large sprig fresh thyme or ¹/₂ teaspoon dried thyme

1 bay leaf

3 cups beef, veal, chicken, or vegetable stock or broth

Salt and freshly ground pepper, to taste

1 to 2 tablespoons vegetable oil or margarine

1. Cut each potato into 3 or 4 pieces. Put them in a large saucepan and add garlic, thyme, bay leaf, stock, salt, and pepper. Bring to a boil. Cover and simmer over medium-low heat about 25 minutes or until potatoes are very tender. Discard thyme sprig and bay leaf.

Remove garlic from pan and reserve. Remove potatoes with a slotted spoon, reserving the cooking liquid, and peel them if you like.

2. Puree potatoes in a food mill or mash them in a bowl with a potato masher. Chop garlic very fine or mash it with a fork.

3. Heat oil in saucepan. Add potatoes and cook 1 minute over low heat, stirring. Add garlic. Slowly stir in ³/₄ cup of the stock used to cook the potatoes. Heat over medium-low heat, stirring, about 3 minutes or until stock is absorbed. If you like, stir in a few more tablespoons stock. Adjust seasoning. Serve hot.

Horseradish Mashed Potatoes

Makes 6 servings P

Jewish home cooks have long used horseradish as a seasoning, and in recent years it has become "discovered" by restaurant chefs as well. It's great for adding zip to mashed potatoes, as in this pareve yet creamy version. Serve it with poached or braised chicken, such as Braised Chicken with Winter Vegetables (page 356).

2 pounds boiling potatoes

2 cups vegetable stock

¹/₂ cup nondairy soy milk or rice milk

2 to 3 teaspoons finely grated fresh horseradish or bottled white horseradish, or to taste

Salt and freshly ground pepper, to taste

1. Cut each potato into 3 or 4 pieces. Put in a medium saucepan and add 2 cups stock. Cover, bring to a boil, and simmer over medium-low heat 25 minutes or until potatoes are very tender. Remove potatoes with a slotted spoon and peel them. Mash with a potato masher in a bowl. Return puree to saucepan.

2. Slowly add nondairy milk, stirring with a wooden spoon. If you would like softer mashed potatoes, beat in a little of the cooking liquid, 1 tablespoon at a time. Add horseradish to taste. Season with salt and pepper. Serve hot.

Oven-Fried Potatoes

Makes 6 servings

Deep-fried potatoes are ubiquitous in restaurants in Israel, as accompaniments for meat, poultry, fish, and even omelets. In many home kitchens oven-fried potatoes are made more often than French fried potatoes, as they are easier to prepare and use less oil.

2 pounds boiling potatoes

1/3 cup vegetable oil

Salt and freshly ground pepper, to taste

2 large cloves garlic, minced (optional)

About 1/2 teaspoon paprika (optional)

1. Preheat oven to 375°F. Peel potatoes, if you like. Cut each into 8 lengthwise wedges. Heat oil in a heavy roasting pan in oven 5 minutes. Add potatoes and sprinkle them evenly with salt, using 1/2 to 3/4 teaspoon.

2. Bake potatoes uncovered, gently stirring and turning from time to time, 30 minutes. Sprinkle potatoes with garlic, if using, pepper, and paprika, if using, and toss to combine. Bake 5 to 10 more minutes or until potatoes are tender and lightly browned. Serve hot.

Potato Kneidel with Duxelles Sauce

Makes 4 servings

The Jews of Alsace are fond of all sorts of dumplings, not just matzo balls. They're not limited to soups either. These make a fine side dish, bearing a slight resemblance to Italian potato gnocchi, and are good with a savory mushroom duxelles sauce.

Duxelles Sauce for Savory Kugels (page 493)

2 medium baking potatoes (total 10 ounces)

1 cup matzo meal

2 large egg whites

1/2 cup water

1/2 teaspoon salt

Pinch of freshly ground pepper

Freshly grated nutmeg, to taste

1 teaspoon vegetable oil

1 tablespoon chopped fresh Italian parsley

1. Prepare sauce. Then, peel potatoes and grate them on a coarse grater; you will need 1 1/2 cups grated potato. Mix potato and matzo meal in a bowl. Add egg whites and mix well. Gradually mix in water. Add salt, pepper, nutmeg, and oil and mix well.

2. Bring 3 to 4 quarts salted water to a boil in a large saucepan or stew pan. With wet hands, take about 1 scant tablespoon of potato mixture and roll it between your palms into a ball. Set balls on a plate. Reduce heat so water in pan simmers. With a rubber spatula, carefully slide balls into water. Return to a simmer. Cover and cook over low heat about 1 hour or until firm. Cover and keep them warm until ready to serve.

3. Heat sauce. With slotted spoon, remove potato kneidelach from water and put them in a shallow serving dish. Coat with sauce. Sprinkle with parsley and serve.

Savory Sweet Potato Kugel

Makes about 6 servings   **P**

Unlike most sweet potato kugels, this one is flavored with sautéed onions instead of sugar. The onions are cooked slowly to develop their natural sweetness. I like the way they complement the natural taste of the sweet potatoes.

2¹/2 pounds orange-fleshed sweet potatoes
    (often labeled yams), unpeeled and cut into
    3-inch chunks if large
4 tablespoons vegetable oil
2 medium onions, chopped
¹/2 teaspoon ground ginger
Salt and freshly ground pepper, to taste
2 large eggs
¹/4 cup bread crumbs

1. Put sweet potatoes in a large saucepan with water to cover and a pinch of salt and bring to a boil. Cover and simmer over low heat about 30 minutes or until tender. Drain and let cool.

2. Heat 3 tablespoons oil in a large skillet, add onions, and sauté over medium-low heat, stirring often, about 15 minutes or until tender and golden brown.

3. Preheat oven to 350°F. Peel sweet potatoes and cut each into a few pieces. Put in large bowl and mash. Stir in sautéed onions with their oil. Add ginger. Season with salt and pepper. Beat in eggs, one at a time.

4. Grease a 6- or 7-cup casserole dish and add sweet potato mixture. Smooth top and sprinkle with bread crumbs. Drizzle with remaining oil. Bake uncovered about 45 minutes or until top is firm.

Sweet Potato Tzimmes with Dried Pears

Makes 4 to 6 servings   **P**

Flavored with orange juice, honey, and fresh ginger, this sweet casserole is great with roast chicken, brisket, or lamb. Serve it for Rosh Hashanah, Yom Kippur eve, Sukkot, or Shabbat.

3 tablespoons vegetable oil
1 cup dried pears
2¹/2 pounds orange-fleshed sweet potatoes (often labeled
    yams)
1 tablespoon minced peeled fresh ginger
Salt and freshly ground pepper, to taste
¹/2 cup raisins
¹/4 cup honey
1 tablespoon strained fresh lemon juice
¹/2 cup strained fresh orange juice
¹/2 teaspoon ground cinnamon
Pinch of ground cloves

1. Preheat oven to 375°F. Pour 1 tablespoon oil into a 10-cup casserole dish. Put pears in a bowl and pour boiling water over them. Let soak about 20 minutes or until nearly tender. Dice pears.

2. Peel sweet potatoes and cut into ³/4-inch dice. Put them in a saucepan and add water to cover. Bring to a boil. Cover and cook over low heat about 10 minutes or until nearly tender. Drain well.

3. Add 2 tablespoons oil to pan used to cook sweet potatoes. Add ginger and sauté over medium heat, stirring, 1 minute. Add sweet potatoes and a little salt and pepper. Cook over low heat, stirring, about 2 minutes. Remove from heat.

4. Dice pears and add to sweet potatoes. Add raisins. Transfer mixture to casserole dish.

5. Combine honey, lemon juice, orange juice, cinnamon, and cloves in small saucepan. Bring to simmer, stirring. Pour evenly over sweet potatoes. Bake uncovered about 30 minutes or until most of honey mixture is absorbed.

6. Serve casserole from baking dish.

❋ Mediterranean Vegetables

Artichokes with Easy Garlic Sauce

Makes 4 servings

Jews from Mediterranean lands make abundant use of artichokes—Roman Jews are famous for their deep-fried whole artichokes—and they are delicious with this rich garlic dipping sauce. If you prefer a milder garlic flavor, substitute 2 or 3 Roasted Garlic Cloves (page 456) for the raw garlic.

4 medium or 8 small artichokes

2 or 3 teaspoons strained fresh lemon juice

1/2 cup mayonnaise, any kind

1 small very fresh clove garlic, pressed

Salt and freshly ground pepper, to taste

Cayenne pepper, to taste

1. To trim artichokes, cut off top 1 inch of large artichokes or 1/2-inch of small ones. Trim spikes from tips of leaves with scissors. Put artichokes in a large saucepan of boiling salted water and cover with a lid of slightly smaller diameter than that of pan to keep them submerged. Cook over medium heat until a leaf can be easily pulled out; large artichokes will require 45 to 50 minutes and small ones 15 to 20 minutes. Using tongs, remove artichokes from water, turn them upside down, and drain thoroughly.

2. Either cover to keep warm; or let cool and serve at room temperature or chilled.

3. To make the sauce, gradually stir lemon juice into mayonnaise in a bowl. Stir in garlic. If sauce is too thick, beat in warm water by teaspoons until the sauce can just be poured. Season with salt, pepper, and cayenne. Refrigerate until ready to serve.

Broiled Eggplant

Makes about 4 servings

Instead of frying eggplant slices, you can broil or grill them. You use less fat, and it's quicker and easier, too. Broiled eggplant has a pleasing, slightly charred flavor and appearance that many enjoy in preparations of this vegetable. As in frying, you need to keep an eye on the eggplant so it won't burn.

Serve these eggplant slices as an appetizer, topped with roasted peppers (page 588), Zehug (page 592), or hot or cold Fresh Tomato Sauce (page 585), or serve Roasted Garlic Cloves (page 456) alongside.

1 large eggplant, (about 1 1/2 pounds), cut into 1/4-inch-thick slices

About 4 to 6 teaspoons olive oil

Salt and freshly ground pepper, to taste

Arrange eggplant on a foil-lined baking sheet or broiler pan. Brush lightly with oil and sprinkle with salt and pepper. Broil about 8 minutes. Turn over and broil about 7 minutes or until tender. Serve hot, warm, or room temperature.

Baked Eggplant Slices

Makes 3 or 4 servings

Many traditional Sephardic dishes call for fried eggplant slices as one step in their preparation, as in Fried Eggplant with Herbed Tomatoes (page 221). I often bake the eggplant instead. Baking requires less attention—and less oil. If you have a large amount of eggplant to cook, baking is also more convenient than broiling because you can bake more eggplant slices at a time than you can broil. (During baking the slices brown slightly.)

You can use the baked eggplant slices in casseroles or mix them with cooked rice or with pasta and tomato sauce. If you'd like to serve them as a quick appetizer or accompaniment, top them with Onion Marmalade (page 133) or with your favorite salsa.

1 medium eggplant (1 to 1¼ pounds), unpeeled and cut into ³/₈-inch-thick slices

1½ tablespoons vegetable oil

Salt and freshly ground pepper, to taste

Preheat oven to 450°F. Put eggplant slices on a large, lightly oiled baking sheet in 1 layer. Drizzle with oil, then sprinkle lightly with salt and pepper. Bake 10 minutes; turn slices over, sprinkle with salt and pepper, and bake about 10 more minutes or until tender. Serve hot or use in recipes.

Israeli Eggplant Stew

Makes 4 or 5 servings

Israelis love eggplant and prepare it in numerous ways. This is one of the easiest eggplant dishes to prepare. The eggplant cooks quickly in a savory tomato sauce that can simmer pretty much unattended. It keeps well, reheats beautifully, and you can serve it hot or cold. Serve it with roast lamb, chicken, or turkey, or at a vegetarian meal with rice or bulgur wheat.

If your eggplant is fresh and has a smooth, glossy peel, you can leave the peel on.

3 tablespoons olive oil

1 large onion, chopped

6 large cloves garlic, chopped

1½ pounds eggplants, unpeeled and cut into ¼-inch dice

Salt and freshly ground pepper, to taste

¼ cup chopped fresh Italian parsley or cilantro

One 28-ounce can diced tomatoes

2 tablespoons tomato paste

1 bay leaf

¼ teaspoon dried hot pepper flakes, or to taste

1 teaspoon dried oregano

1. Heat oil in a heavy stew pan or Dutch oven. Add onion and sauté over medium heat 5 minutes or until it turns golden. Stir in garlic, followed by eggplant, salt, pepper, and half the parsley. Stir over low heat 2 to 3 minutes or until eggplant is coated with onion mixture.

2. Add tomatoes with their juice, tomato paste, bay leaf, hot pepper flakes, and oregano. Cook over high heat, stirring, until bubbling. Cover and simmer over medium-low heat, stirring often, about 25 minutes or until eggplant is tender. Discard bay leaf. Adjust seasoning. Serve hot or cold, sprinkled with remaining parsley.

Eggplant with Rice and Pine Nut Stuffing

Makes 4 to 6 servings

Jews from Middle Eastern countries use this festive stuffing for pareve meals. Besides eggplants, it's used to make stuffed grape leaves, zucchini, and peppers.

2¹⁄₂ to 3 pounds small or medium eggplants

6 tablespoons olive oil

3 medium onions, finely chopped

³⁄₄ cup long-grain white rice

¹⁄₄ cup pine nuts

2 tablespoons raisins

2 teaspoons dried mint

¹⁄₄ teaspoon ground allspice

¹⁄₂ teaspoon sugar

Salt and freshly ground pepper, to taste

1¹⁄₄ cups water

2 plum tomatoes, chopped

2 tablespoons tomato paste

4 cloves garlic, halved

1. Cut stem ends from eggplants. Halve eggplants lengthwise. Peel if desired; if eggplant is fresh, there is no need to peel it. Use a spoon to scoop out centers, leaving boat-shaped shells. Sprinkle eggplant shells with salt. Put them in a colander upside down and leave to drain while making stuffing. Preheat oven to 425°F.

2. Heat 3 tablespoons oil in a sauté pan, add onions, and sauté over medium heat 10 minutes. Add rice and pine nuts and stir 5 minutes over low heat. Add raisins, mint, allspice, sugar, salt, and pepper; cook 2 minutes. Add water and bring to a boil. Cover and cook over low heat about 12 minutes or until liquid is absorbed; rice will not be cooked yet. Add tomatoes.

3. Chop flesh removed from eggplant. Heat 2 tablespoons oil in a skillet and add chopped eggplant, salt, and pepper. Sauté over medium-low heat, stirring often, about 10 minutes or until tender. Mix with stuffing. Adjust seasoning.

4. Rinse eggplant shells, pat them dry, and put them in a baking dish. Fill them with stuffing. Mix tomato paste with ¹⁄₄ cup water and spoon mixture over eggplant. Add enough water to dish to cover eggplant by one third. Add garlic to dish. Spoon 1 tablespoon oil over eggplant. Cover and bake 15 minutes. Reduce oven temperature to 350°F and bake 15 more minutes. Uncover and bake, basting occasionally, 30 minutes or until eggplant is very tender. Serve hot, warm, or room temperature.

Note: If you have any stuffing left, you can spoon it into a small baking dish, cover it, and bake it at 350°F 15 to 20 minutes or until rice is tender.

Okra with Tomatoes, Garlic, and Cilantro

Makes 4 servings

No longer liked only in the South, okra is becoming more popular throughout the United States and can now be found at many markets in other parts of the country, especially in the summer.

I first learned to appreciate it in Israel. Okra is loved by Jews from Lebanon and other eastern Mediterranean countries and I prefer their method of cooking the vegetable; first you sauté the okra, then add chopped tomatoes and seasonings, and finish cooking the vegetable in a covered pan. It makes a tasty accompaniment for grilled chicken or braised meat. Okra's meaty texture also makes this a satisfying vegetarian entree for serving with rice.

For the best okra, choose small, firm, deep green pods. If they are over 3 inches long, they are likely to be stringy and tough.

3 tablespoons olive oil

1 large onion, chopped

6 large cloves garlic, minced

¹⁄₂ jalapeño pepper, minced

²⁄₃ cup chopped fresh cilantro

2 pounds okra, stemmed

2 pounds ripe tomatoes, diced, or one 28-ounce can diced tomatoes, drained

¹⁄₂ teaspoon ground coriander

Salt and freshly ground pepper, to taste

1. Heat 2 tablespoons oil in a large, deep skillet or sauté pan. Add onion, garlic, jalapeño, and $1/3$ cup cilantro. Sauté over medium heat, stirring often, 7 minutes or until onions begin to turn golden. Add okra and sauté, stirring, 2 minutes.

2. Add tomatoes, coriander, salt, and pepper. Bring to a boil. Cook over medium-low heat 20 to 30 minutes or until tender. Stir in remaining tablespoon oil and remaining $1/3$ cup cilantro and remove from heat. Adjust seasoning. Serve hot or lukewarm.

Savory Red Chard with Garlic

Makes 2 to 4 servings

My friend Dvorah Alon, who was born in Morocco and lives in Israel, prepares this aromatic side dish for Shabbat. A colorful dish of red stems and green leaves, it's delicious with fish or chicken or as part of vegetarian meals.

1 bunch red chard

1 tablespoon olive oil

3 large cloves garlic, chopped

$1/2$ teaspoon ground cumin

$1/2$ teaspoon paprika

Salt and freshly ground pepper, to taste

1 tablespoon strained fresh lemon juice

1. Pull chard leaves from stems and keep each in a separate pile. Rinse chard well and soak it in a large bowl of cold water if it is sandy. Cut stems into $1/2$-inch slices. Coarsely chop leaves.

2. Cook chard stems in a medium saucepan of boiling water over medium heat 2 minutes. Add leaves and cook 3 minutes or until tender. Drain chard, reserving a few tablespoons of the cooking liquid.

3. Heat oil in the saucepan, add garlic, and sauté over low heat about 30 seconds. Add chard and heat about 3 minutes, adding 1 or 2 tablespoons cooking liquid if pan is dry. Add cumin, paprika, salt, and pepper and heat about 1 minute. Just before serving, add lemon juice and heat through. Adjust seasoning.

Fava Beans in Quick Tomato Sauce

Makes 2 or 3 servings

Fava beans are prized in the Sephardic kitchen and are used in all sorts of ways—in soups, in stews, in salads, and combined with rice. You can find them fresh at farmers' markets, especially in the summer months, and in Middle Eastern markets, where they are often available frozen as well. If you like, you can substitute lima beans (see Note).

Fava beans are shelled like peas. The large beans have thick skins and most people find them more attractive and more appealing to eat if the skin is removed. Some cooks prefer to leave them on.

2 pounds fresh fava beans

1 tablespoon olive oil

1 onion, chopped

One 14$1/2$-ounce can diced tomatoes, drained

Salt and freshly ground pepper, to taste

$1/2$ teaspoon ground allspice

Cayenne pepper, to taste

2 tablespoons chopped fresh cilantro or Italian parsley (optional)

1. Remove fava beans from pods. Put beans in a medium saucepan of boiling salted water and cook uncovered over high heat 5 to 7 minutes or until they are done to your taste; some people like to cook them only 2 minutes, while others prefer as long as 20 minutes. Drain well; peel off thick skins.

2. Heat oil in a medium saucepan. Add onion and sauté over medium-low heat 7 minutes or until beginning to turn golden. Add tomatoes, salt, pepper, and allspice. Cook uncovered over medium heat 5 minutes. Add fava beans and cook about 2 minutes or until heated through. Season with salt, pepper, and cayenne. Add half of cilantro, if using. Serve sprinkled with remaining cilantro.

Note: If fava beans are not available, use a 10-ounce package of frozen lima beans. Cook them according to package directions and add them to sauce.

✺ Squashes and Pumpkins

Yellow and Green Squash, Hungarian Style

Makes 4 to 6 servings

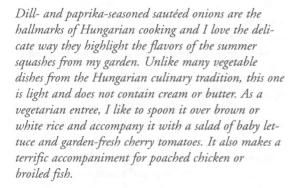

Dill- and paprika-seasoned sautéed onions are the hallmarks of Hungarian cooking and I love the delicate way they highlight the flavors of the summer squashes from my garden. Unlike many vegetable dishes from the Hungarian culinary tradition, this one is light and does not contain cream or butter. As a vegetarian entree, I like to spoon it over brown or white rice and accompany it with a salad of baby lettuce and garden-fresh cherry tomatoes. It also makes a terrific accompaniment for poached chicken or broiled fish.

1 pound crookneck squash (about 4)

1 pound zucchini (about 4)

1 tablespoon vegetable oil

1 large onion, halved and sliced

1½ teaspoons sweet paprika

Pinch of hot paprika or cayenne pepper

Salt and freshly ground pepper, to taste

2 to 4 tablespoons vegetable broth or water

2 tablespoons chopped fresh dill or 2 teaspoons dried

1. Cut off thin "neck" of each squash. Halve rest of squash lengthwise, place each half cut-side down, and cut it into 4 lengthwise slices to form sticks. Quarter each zucchini and cut each quarter into 3 crosswise pieces.

2. Heat oil in a nonstick sauté pan over medium heat. Add onion and sauté 5 minutes or until golden. Add squash necks and pieces, sweet paprika, hot paprika, salt, and pepper and sauté 1 minute, stirring to coat.

3. Add 2 tablespoons broth to pan. Cover and cook over medium-low heat, stirring occasionally, 8 to 10 minutes or until crisp-tender. If pan becomes dry during cooking, add 1 to 2 tablespoons broth. Add dill and toss. Adjust seasoning.

Syrian Squash with Carrots

Makes 4 or 5 servings

Jews from Syria like sour and sweet vegetables seasoned with a touch more lemon juice than sugar. Dried mint, garlic, and onion accent the sauce, which is a particularly good match for the sweetness of carrots and delicate zucchini.

½ pound carrots

½ pound yellow summer squash, either straight, crookneck, or pattypan

½ pound zucchini, cut into ½-inch slices

2 or 3 tablespoons vegetable oil

1 large onion, chopped

Salt and freshly ground pepper, to taste

About ½ cup water

1½ teaspoons dried mint

2 medium cloves garlic, minced

1 tablespoon sugar

2 tablespoons strained fresh lemon juice

1. Cut carrots into diagonal slices about ¼-inch thick. (There is no need to peel the squash.) Cut yellow squash and zucchini into ½-inch slices.

2. Heat oil in a sauté pan, add onion, and sauté over medium heat about 5 minutes or until golden. Add carrots, yellow squash, zucchini, salt, and pepper. Sauté, tossing, 2 minutes.

3. Add ½ cup water, mint, garlic, and sugar. Cover and cook over medium heat, stirring occasionally, 5 minutes. Add 1 tablespoon lemon juice. Cook about 5 more minutes or until vegetables are tender and absorb most of liquid; add a little more water during cooking if pan becomes dry. Add remaining lemon juice. Adjust seasoning. Serve hot or cold.

Zucchini and Red Beans with Mint-Yogurt Topping

Makes 4 servings **D**

Serve this quick and colorful medley of zucchini and red beans for an easy supper side dish, topped with its Sephardic-style topping of yogurt flavored with mint and a touch of garlic. Or turn it into a main course by serving couscous or brown rice as an accompaniment.

1 cup plain yogurt, regular, low-fat, or nonfat
1 medium clove garlic, pressed or finely minced
1 tablespoon chopped fresh mint or 1/2 teaspoon dried
Salt and white pepper, to taste
4 medium zucchini, halved and sliced 1/2-inch thick
One 15-ounce can red beans, drained

1. Mix yogurt with garlic and mint in a bowl. Season with salt and white pepper.

2. Boil enough water in a medium saucepan to just cover zucchini. Add zucchini and beans and bring to a simmer. Cover and cook over medium heat 3 to 5 minutes or until zucchini are tender. Drain well and serve hot. Serve yogurt sauce separately, for spooning over vegetables.

Tangy Tunisian Mashed Pumpkin

Makes 4 to 6 servings **P**

We in America tend to think of pumpkin for desserts but it's delicious as a savory starter or side dish too. Tunisian Jews serve this as one of an array of salads before the meal, but it's also good served warm as an accompaniment for chicken. You can make it with sugar pumpkin or any type of winter squash. I like mild acorn or banana squash or sweet butternut squash. If you are in a hurry for this dish, the squashes cook beautifully in the microwave.

1/2 teaspoon Harissa (page 592), Zehug (page 592), or bottled hot sauce, or to taste
One 3-pound acorn or butternut squash or sugar pumpkin
1 green onion, white and green parts, chopped
1 large clove garlic, pressed or finely minced
1/2 teaspoon paprika
1 teaspoon ground caraway seeds
2 tablespoons strained fresh lemon juice
1 to 3 tablespoons extra-virgin olive oil
Salt, to taste
1 tablespoon chopped fresh cilantro, plus sprigs for garnish

1. Prepare sauces, if fresh preferred. Then, to cook squash or pumpkin on stovetop: Cut squash or pumpkin in pieces and cut off peel. Remove seeds. Cut pumpkin meat in approximately 1 1/2-inch cubes. (You should have 5 to 6 cups.) Combine squash cubes in a medium saucepan with 2 cups water and a pinch of salt and bring to a boil. Cover and simmer over low heat, stirring occasionally so that all pieces come in contact with the water, about 25 minutes or until very tender when pierced with a sharp knife. Drain thoroughly.

2. To cook squash or pumpkin in microwave: cut squash or pumpkin in half and remove seeds. Put halved squash in glass baking dish cut-side down. Add 1/4 cup water to dish. Cover and microwave on high about 12 minutes or until tender; check by piercing meat in thickest part with fork.

3. Mash squash pieces with a fork; leave a few small chunks if desired. Transfer to a colander and let drain 1 hour.

4. Put pumpkin in a bowl and add green onion, garlic, harissa, paprika, caraway seeds, lemon juice, 1 tablespoon olive oil, and salt to taste. Mix well, cover, and chill.

5. Serve pumpkin in a shallow bowl. Sprinkle with chopped cilantro. If you like, drizzle olive oil over top. Garnish with cilantro sprigs.

✽ *Cauliflower, Broccoli, and Cabbage*

Hungarian Cauliflower and Peas in Dill Sauce

Makes 4 to 6 servings

Serving vegetables in a white sauce flavored with dill is popular among Jews from Eastern Europe, and those from Hungary often add sweet and hot paprika as well. Although the sauce is creamy, it does not contain dairy products. Serve the vegetables with baked salmon or trout, or with braised or poached chicken.

1¹/₂ cups Velouté Sauce (page 591)

2 pounds cauliflower, divided into medium florets

2 cups frozen peas

1 teaspoon sweet paprika

Salt and freshly ground pepper, to taste

Pinch of hot paprika or cayenne pepper, to taste

3 tablespoons snipped fresh dill or 3 teaspoons dried

1. Prepare sauce. Then, cook cauliflower uncovered in a large saucepan of boiling salted water 4 minutes. Add peas and return to a boil. Cook another 2 minutes or until cauliflower is crisp-tender. Reserve ¹/₃ cup of cooking liquid. Drain vegetables in a colander and rinse with cold water.

2. Bring veloute sauce to a simmer in saucepan, whisking. Stir in sweet paprika. If sauce is too thick, whisk in a tablespoon or two of reserved vegetable cooking liquid. Season sauce with salt, pepper, and hot paprika. Stir in 2 tablespoons fresh dill or all of dried dill. Add vegetables and heat through, gently turning cauliflower in the sauce. Serve sprinkled with remaining fresh dill.

Cauliflower in Indian-Spiced Tomato Sauce

Makes 4 to 6 servings Ⓟ

Cauliflower in tomato sauce appears on the tables of Jews of many different origins. In our family we loved it spiked with coriander, cumin, and fresh dill, as I learned from my sister-in-law Mati Kahn, who was born in India.

2 tablespoons vegetable oil

1 medium onion, chopped

4 large cloves garlic, minced

2 teaspoons ground coriander

2 teaspoons ground cumin

¹/₂ teaspoon ground turmeric

¹/₈ teaspoon cayenne pepper

2¹/₂ pounds ripe tomatoes, peeled, seeded, and chopped, or two 28-ounce cans tomatoes, drained and chopped

2 teaspoons tomato paste

1 bay leaf

Salt and freshly ground pepper, to taste

1 large head cauliflower, divided into medium florets

2 tablespoons chopped fresh dill or Italian parsley

1. Heat oil in a heavy stew pan. Add onion and cook over medium-low heat 7 minutes, or until it is soft and beginning to brown. Add garlic, coriander, cumin, turmeric, and cayenne and cook, stirring, 1 minute. Add tomatoes, tomato paste, 2 tablespoons water, bay leaf, salt, and pepper. Cook over medium heat, stirring often, about 20 minutes or until tomatoes are soft and sauce is thick. Discard bay leaf.

2. Cook cauliflower uncovered in a large pan of boiling salted water over high heat about 3 minutes or until nearly tender. Drain, rinse with cold water, and drain thoroughly.

3. Add cauliflower to sauce, cover, and simmer, gently turning florets over occasionally, about 5 minutes or until tender. Adjust seasoning. Serve sprinkled with dill.

Broccoli Gratin with Cheese Sauce

Makes 4 servings   **D**

A classic combination, this is the favorite way to eat broccoli for many people. It's a terrific accompaniment for a plain or tomato-sauced fish. For a vegetarian menu it's delicious with a simple grain dish such as Herbed Rice (page 500) or Israeli Rice Pilaf (page 499), and a fresh vegetable salad. The luscious sauce is rich but its texture is smooth and light, not sticky. You can prepare the gratin ahead and keep it in the refrigerator; simply cover it lightly so it won't dry out.

2 tablespoons butter

2 tablespoons all-purpose flour

1¹/₂ cups milk

Salt and white pepper, to taste

Freshly grated nutmeg, to taste

¹/₄ cup heavy cream, crème fraîche, or whole milk

Pinch of cayenne pepper, or to taste

¹/₃ cup freshly grated Parmesan cheese

1¹/₂ pounds broccoli

1. Melt butter in a heavy saucepan over low heat. Add flour and cook, whisking constantly, about 2 minutes, or until foaming but not browned. Remove from heat. Gradually whisk in milk. Bring to boil over medium-high heat, whisking. Add a small pinch of salt, white pepper, and nutmeg. Reduce heat to low and cook, whisking often, 5 minutes. Whisk in cream and bring to boil. Cook over low heat, whisking often, about 5 more minutes or until sauce thickens. Remove from heat and add cayenne. Adjust seasoning.

2. Before using, bring sauce to boil, whisking. Remove from heat. Whisk in half the cheese.

3. Preheat oven to 425°F. Divide broccoli into medium florets. Peel and slice stalk. Put broccoli in a saucepan with boiling salted water to cover. Return to boil. Cook uncovered about 4 minutes or until florets are just tender. Drain, rinse with cold water, and drain well.

4. Butter a heavy 5-cup gratin dish or other shallow baking dish. Arrange florets in one layer in prepared dish. Spoon sauce carefully over to coat completely.

Sprinkle evenly with remaining cheese. Refrigerate if necessary.

5. If gratin was cold, bring it to room temperature. Bake until sauce begins to bubble, about 7 minutes if sauce was hot, or about 10 minutes if gratin was at room temperature. If you like, brown the gratin lightly in broiler about 1 minute, checking often and turning dish so top browns evenly. Serve hot, from the gratin dish.

Polish Cabbage with Raisins

Makes 4 servings   **P**

Among Jews from Poland, raisins are a favorite partner for cabbage, whether it is braised for this simple dish, made into a soup, or stuffed with meat. Some prepare a stuffed cabbage variation of this dish by filling blanched cabbage leaves with a simple mixture of cooked rice, raisins, and cinnamon and placing a lump of sugar in each leaf before rolling it up.

Including raisins doesn't mean the dish has to be very sweet. Cooks balance the sugar by adding lemon juice or vinegar to taste. Serve this cabbage with Old-Fashioned Brisket Pot Roast (page 385) or Old-Fashioned Roasted Chicken (page 346).

1 small head green cabbage (1¹/₂ to 2 pounds)

1 or 2 tablespoons vegetable oil

1 large onion, chopped

Salt and freshly ground pepper, to taste

2 tablespoons tomato paste

¹/₂ cup water

¹/₃ cup raisins

1 to 2 tablespoons sugar

2 to 3 tablespoons strained fresh lemon juice

1. Coarsely shred or chop cabbage, discarding the core. Boil enough water to cover cabbage in a Dutch oven or large, heavy pot. Add a pinch of salt and the cabbage and boil about 3 minutes or until just tender. Drain in a colander, rinse under running cold water, and drain thoroughly. Gently squeeze cabbage by handfuls to remove excess water.

2. Heat oil in the same pan, add onion, and sauté about 5 minutes over medium heat. Add cabbage and sauté lightly 5 minutes. Sprinkle with salt and pepper. Mix tomato paste with ¹/₄ cup water and add to the pan. Add remaining water and raisins. Cover and cook over low heat, stirring often, about 15 minutes or until cabbage is tender.

3. Add sugar and simmer uncovered, stirring, 2 minutes. If cabbage is too soupy, simmer uncovered another 3 to 5 minutes or until excess liquid evaporates. Remove from heat and add lemon juice to taste. Adjust seasoning. Serve hot.

Sauerkraut with Onions and Caraway Seeds

Makes 4 servings (P)

Ashkenazic cooks developed a wealth of recipes using sauerkraut for times when not many fresh vegetables were available. It can be cooked with meat as a main course or without meat as an accompaniment. For hearty side dishes, it is simmered with potatoes, or mixed with white bean or green pea puree. Sauerkraut is also used to make soups and salads.

This quick, easy dish can be served with meats, poultry, or meatless meals. For meat or poultry dinners, you can substitute beef or chicken stock for the vegetable stock, and chicken fat for the oil.

4 cups sauerkraut, preferably from a jar

2 tablespoons vegetable oil

2 large onions, halved and sliced

1 cup vegetable stock

1 teaspoon caraway seeds

Salt (optional) and freshly ground pepper, to taste

1. Put sauerkraut in a colander and rinse with cold water. Drain well.

2. Heat oil in a heavy saucepan. Add onions and sauté over medium heat, stirring often, about 7 minutes or until golden brown. Add sauerkraut and stock. Bring to a boil. Cover and cook over low heat about 20 minutes or until sauerkraut and onions are tender; check from time to time and add a little hot water if pan becomes dry.

3. A short time before serving, stir in caraway seeds. Season with pepper; salt may not be needed.

❦ *Root Vegetables*

Kohlrabi Stew with Dried Mushrooms

Makes about 6 servings

This Eastern European style dish is popular among Jews from Russia, Ukraine, Poland, and Hungary, where kohlrabi, a green or purplish root vegetable, and dried mushrooms are plentiful. I first became familiar with kohlrabi in Israel, where it is easy to find and is used both cooked and raw. I love it in soups and stews like this colorful one, in which the kohlrabi cooks with carrots and potatoes. A light sauce forms as the vegetables cook.

This recipe includes the kohlrabi greens as an option; if you would rather use them for another dish, reduce the oil amount to 3 tablespoons and skip the steps that refer to the greens.

Serve this stew for Shabbat or Hanukkah.

1¹/₂ to 2 ounces dried mushrooms, such as porcini or cèpes

1 pound kohlrabi (2 medium), including greens (optional)

1 pound carrots

1 pound boiling potatoes

3 tablespoons plus 2 teaspoons vegetable oil

1 large onion, chopped

Salt and freshly ground pepper, to taste

1 teaspoon sugar

2¹/₂ tablespoons all-purpose flour

3 cups chicken or vegetable stock

¹/₄ cup chopped fresh parsley

1. Soak mushrooms in hot water to cover 30 minutes. Drain well. If using shiitake mushrooms, discard tough stems. Slice mushrooms.

2. Rinse kohlrabi greens, if using, and discard stalks. Peel kohlrabi bulbs and cut meat into ³/₄-inch cubes. Halve carrots lengthwise if they are large. Cut into ¹/₃-inch slices. Peel potatoes and cut in small dice.

3. If using, add kohlrabi leaves to a saucepan of boiling salted water and boil uncovered over high heat about 15 minutes or until crisp-tender. Drain in a colander, rinse with cold water and drain well. Chop fine.

4. Heat 3 tablespoons oil in a heavy stew pan. Add onion and sauté over medium heat 5 minutes. Add kohlrabi cubes, salt, and pepper. Sauté, stirring often, 5 minutes. Sprinkle with sugar and stir it in. Sprinkle with flour and sauté 30 seconds. Off heat, slowly stir in stock. Add carrots, potatoes, and mushrooms. Bring to a boil, stirring. Cover and cook over low heat, stirring often, about 15 minutes or until vegetables are tender.

5. In a small skillet heat kohlrabi leaves in 2 teaspoons oil. Season with salt and pepper. Stir into stew.

6. If you would like a thicker sauce, simmer stew uncovered 2 or 3 minutes so the excess liquid evaporates. Remove from heat. Add chopped parsley; season with salt and plenty of pepper.

Moroccan Beets

Makes 4 to 6 servings

Beets seasoned with garlic, lemon juice, and cumin are popular in many Israeli homes, whether or not the person doing the cooking is of Moroccan origin. Serve this flavorful vegetable as part of an array of appetizers or as a side dish with chicken, beef, or lamb.

8 to 10 beets of 1¹/₂-inch diameter (about 1 pound, without greens)

2 tablespoons strained fresh lemon juice

Salt and freshly ground pepper, to taste

1 teaspoon ground cumin

2 medium cloves garlic, pressed or very finely minced

5 tablespoons vegetable oil or olive oil

1. Rinse beets, taking care not to pierce their skins. Put in a pan, cover with water, and bring to a boil. Cover and simmer over low heat 35 to 40 minutes or until tender. Let cool. Run beets under cold water and slip off the skins. Slice beets.

2. Whisk lemon juice with salt, pepper, and cumin in a small bowl. Stir in garlic. Whisk in 5 tablespoons oil.

3. Put beets in a bowl and add enough dressing to moisten. Toss gently. Adjust seasoning. Serve cold or at room temperature.

Carrots and Green Beans Gremolata

Makes 4 servings

When my mother wants to prepare a very simple Friday night meal, it still "has to feel like Shabbat"; in other words, it must be festive. Her typical menu might include a salad, roast chicken, carrots, green beans, noodle kugel with onions, and cake or baked apple for dessert.

An easy way to give the carrots and beans a lively flavor is to sprinkle them with gremolata, an Italian seasoning blend of garlic, parsley, and grated citrus rind. Classically it's used on veal shanks in tomato sauce but it's great on vegetables. You can prepare the vegetables before sundown on Friday night and keep them warm on a hot plate, as my mother does, or simply reheat them for other occasions.

¹/₂ teaspoon finely grated or finely chopped lemon rind

1 small clove garlic, pressed or very finely minced (¹/₄ teaspoon)

2 tablespoons minced fresh Italian parsley

4 medium carrots, sliced

¹/₂ pound green beans

2 teaspoons vegetable oil

Salt and freshly ground pepper, to taste

1. For gremolata, combine lemon rind, garlic, and parsley in a small bowl and mix thoroughly with a fork. Cover and reserve at room temperature.

2. Put carrots in a saucepan, cover with water, and bring to a simmer. Cook 5 minutes. Add green beans and cook together about 5 more minutes or until vegetables are just tender. Drain, reserving cooking liquid.

3. If prepared in advance, reheat vegetables in a few tablespoons of their cooking liquid and drain again. Just before serving, sprinkle vegetables with oil and 1 tablespoon cooking liquid and toss until coated. Sprinkle with salt and pepper and toss again. Sprinkle with gremolata, cover and let stand 1 or 2 minutes before serving.

Carrot Kugel with Almonds and Orange

Makes 6 to 8 servings **P**

Carrot kugels appear often on the holiday tables of Ashkenazic Jews. Some are sweet, dense, and rich, almost like warm carrot cakes. This one is light and delicately sweetened with orange juice and brown sugar.

1/2 cup almonds

4 large eggs

1/2 cup brown sugar

6 medium carrots, coarsely grated (about 21/2 cups grated)

1 cup bread crumbs

Pinch of salt

1/3 cup orange juice

11/2 teaspoons grated orange rind

1. Preheat oven to 350°F. Oil a 6- to 7-cup baking dish. Finely grind almonds in food processor or nut grinder.

2. Beat eggs with sugar in a large bowl with an electric mixer until thick and light. Stir in grated carrots, almonds, bread crumbs, and salt. Add orange juice and rind and mix well.

3. Spoon carrot mixture into baking dish. Bake about 30 minutes or until firm and golden brown. Serve hot or warm.

Individual Carrot Kugels

Makes 4 servings

Made of pureed cooked carrots, these rich-tasting kugels lend an elegant note to dinners. Serve them in their baking dishes or turn them out onto plates. They're good as a side dish with any entree that you would pair with carrots.

You can make them dairy or pareve, according to whether you use butter and milk or pareve margarine and vegetable stock.

1 pound carrots, sliced

1 tablespoon butter or pareve margarine

Salt and freshly ground pepper, to taste

1/2 teaspoon sugar, or to taste

3 large eggs

1/2 cup milk or 1/3 cup vegetable stock

1. Preheat oven to 400°F. Generously grease four 2/3-cup ramekins. Put carrots in a saucepan, cover with water, and add a pinch of salt. Bring to a boil, cover, and cook over medium-low heat 15 minutes or until very tender. Drain well; you can reserve cooking liquid for vegetable stock. Puree carrots in food processor until smooth.

2. Melt butter in saucepan. Add carrot puree and cook over low heat, stirring often, about 3 minutes or until puree is fairly dry. Remove from heat. Season with salt, pepper, and sugar.

3. Whisk eggs with milk in a medium bowl. Gradually whisk in carrot puree. Divide mixture among ramekins. Tap each to pack down mixture. Smooth top. Set ramekins in a roasting pan in oven. Add enough boiling water to pan to come halfway up sides of ramekins. Bake 35 to 40 minutes or until firm; a cake tester inserted into mixture should come out clean. During baking add hot water to pan if most of it evaporates.

4. With a slotted metal spatula, remove molds from water. Cool 3 minutes. If you wish to turn kugels out of molds, run thin-bladed, flexible knife around edge of one mold. Set small plate atop mold and invert both. Holding them together, tap them on towel-lined counter. Gently lift up mold. Repeat with remaining kugels. Serve hot or warm.

Honey-Glazed Parsnips

Makes 4 servings

I sometimes follow the custom in some Ashkenazic kitchens and add parsnips to my chicken soup, as I like the flavor they contribute. Slowly cooked parsnips become sweet and, like many root vegetables, are good glazed. This dish is a good choice for Rosh Hashanah, especially if you're looking for a sweet vegetable to serve but you already have carrots on the menu in another dish.

1¹/₂ pounds parsnips
Salt, to taste
1 tablespoon sugar
1 tablespoon honey
2 tablespoons vegetable oil

1. Cut parsnips into 2-inch lengths. Quarter any wide pieces (over ³/₄-inch in diameter) lengthwise. Trim any woody centers from the pieces.

2. Put parsnips in a medium sauté pan and add 2¹/₂ cups water or enough to barely cover them. Add salt, sugar, honey, and oil. Bring to a boil. Reduce heat to medium and simmer uncovered about 30 minutes or until largest pieces are very tender; stir once or twice during first 5 minutes, but afterwards shake pan to stir.

3. When parsnips are tender, if too much liquid remains in pan, cook over medium-low heat, shaking pan often, 3 to 5 minutes or until liquid evaporates and parsnips become coated with a light glaze. Serve hot.

Roasted Garlic

Makes 4 servings (whole heads); individual cloves are for use in other recipes

If you've never tasted roasted garlic, you'll be amazed at its flavor. The garlic becomes mellow, creamy, and slightly sweet.

Roasting garlic is very easy because you don't need to peel the garlic. You can roast whole heads or individual cloves. When it's ready, you simply squeeze the garlic pulp out of the skin. You can squeeze each clove or whole or halved heads. It's important to use very fresh, firm garlic; old garlic will taste terrible. Generally you roast whole heads to keep some roasted garlic on hand. It will keep 4 or 5 days in a covered dish in the refrigerator, or the pulp can be frozen. Roast individual cloves when you need just a few for a specific recipe.

Roasted garlic pulp or individual peeled cloves makes a delicious, if unusual, topping for Hanukkah potato latkes or turkey schnitzel. For light appetizers, you can spread it on toasted pita wedges or use to make garlic-tomato toasts. It's also terrific for livening up pareve mashed potatoes.

There is plenty of flexibility on the roasting temperature of garlic. The range varies from 250°F to 450°F. Some people even use the barbecue. I usually roast garlic at 400°F while I'm baking eggplants and roasting chickens. If you're baking something at 350°F (but not a cake), you can roast garlic in the same oven for about an hour.

4 large fresh heads garlic, unpeeled, or 10 to 40 individual cloves, or as many as you need
1 to 2 teaspoons extra-virgin olive oil (optional)

1. Preheat oven to 400°F. Remove the loose layers of garlic peel.

2. To roast whole heads: Cut a thin slice off the top of each head of garlic, about ¹/₄-inch thick, removing the tips of the garlic cloves.

To roast individual cloves: Separate the cloves from the garlic head.

3. Put 2 sheets of foil in a small, heavy roasting pan. Set garlic heads or cloves on the foil in 1 layer. Sprinkle garlic with olive oil, if using. Leaving garlic in one layer, wrap it in the 2 layers of foil. Set wrapped garlic in the roasting pan. Bake individual cloves about 30 minutes and whole heads 40 to 45 minutes, or until garlic is very soft. Let cool.

4. To serve, you can separate garlic in cloves or serve garlic heads whole; each person will squeeze out his or her own garlic. You can squeeze the garlic pulp from the whole head, or cut the head in half horizontally and squeeze each half.

Glazed Onions

Makes 4 small servings

Baby onions are available in two varieties at the markets: small, white boiling onions and pearl onions with white, red, or yellow skins. Whichever ones you choose, this French dish will be a delicious accompaniment for meat or fish. In France the onions are glazed with butter. To keep them pareve for serving with meat, Jewish cooks use vegetable oil instead.

³/₄ to 1 pound small boiling onions or pearl onions of uniform size

2 tablespoons vegetable oil

¹/₃ cup water

Salt and freshly ground pepper, to taste

1 teaspoon sugar

1. Put unpeeled onions in a heavy saucepan in which they can fit in one layer. Cover with water and bring just to a boil. Drain, rinse with cold water until they cool completely, and peel them.

2. Return onions to saucepan. Add oil, water, and a pinch of salt and pepper. Cover and cook over low heat, shaking pan occasionally, 10 to 20 minutes, depending on size, or until they are tender. Sprinkle onions with sugar and cook uncovered over medium heat, shaking pan often, until liquid is reduced to a syrupy glaze. Serve hot.

❧ *Vegetable Medleys*

Basic Tzimmes

Makes 6 servings

Tzimmes is the Yiddish term for a casserole of sweet vegetables and dried fruit. It's a favorite for most holidays, especially Rosh Hashanah. Often it includes meat as well and is served as a main course. When prepared without meat, as in this version, it makes a tasty accompaniment for roast chicken or braised beef.

1 pound orange-fleshed sweet potatoes, peeled, halved, and sliced about ¹/₂-inch thick

1 pound boiling potatoes, halved and sliced about ¹/₂-inch thick

³/₄ pound carrots, diagonally sliced ¹/₂-inch thick

4 ounces pitted prunes

2 tablespoons brown sugar, or more to taste

¹/₂ teaspoon ground cinnamon (optional)

3 tablespoons cornstarch

Salt, to taste

1. Preheat oven to 350°F. Combine sweet potatoes, boiling potatoes, carrots, prunes, brown sugar, and cinnamon, if using, in a large saucepan. Add 1 quart water and bring to a simmer. Cover and cook over low heat 25 to 30 minutes or until vegetables and prunes are tender.

2. Mix cornstarch with ¹/₃ cup water. Add to simmering liquid, stirring gently. Cook over medium-low heat, stirring gently, until sauce comes to a simmer and thickens. Season it with salt and more brown sugar, if desired.

3. Spoon mixture into a lightly oiled 2-quart casserole dish. Bake 20 to 30 minutes or until bubbling.

Thanksgiving Tzimmes

Makes 4 servings   (P)

Dried cranberries lend a colorful note to this tzimmes of carrots and pineapple instead of the usual prunes. It's great with a holiday turkey, whether for Thanksgiving or for Purim. Since this tzimmes is so easy to prepare, it's good to serve with the Shabbat chicken too. Tzimmes often has oil or margarine but you won't miss them in this delicious, fat-free rendition.

You'll find packages or containers of diced fresh pineapple in the prepared fruit section of your supermarket's produce department.

4 cups diced fresh pineapple

2 tablespoons cornstarch

2 pounds carrots, sliced ¹/₂-inch thick

3 to 4 tablespoons honey

¹/₂ cup dried cranberries

1¹/₂ teaspoons ground ginger

Pinch of ground cloves

Salt and freshly ground pepper, to taste

1. Reserve ¹/₄ cup juice from the pineapple. Mix reserved juice with the cornstarch in a cup.

2. Combine carrots with 2 cups water and a pinch of salt in a large saucepan. Bring to a boil. Cover and cook over low heat about 12 minutes or until just tender. Remove carrots with slotted spoon. Add honey to carrot cooking liquid and bring to a simmer, stirring. Mix cornstarch solution to blend. Add to simmering liquid, stirring. Cook over medium-low heat, stirring, until sauce comes to a simmer and thickens. Stir in carrots, cranberries, pineapple, ginger, and cloves. Heat until bubbling. Season with salt and pepper. Serve hot.

Portobello Mushrooms with Asparagus and Toasted Walnuts

Makes 4 servings   (P)

Wild mushrooms have long been used by Jewish cooks from Eastern Europe because they were plentiful and inexpensive in that region. In America, wild mushrooms can be hard to find and costly, so I use flavorful portobellos in this and other mushroom dishes. If you want, substitute chanterelles or cèpe mushrooms. Whichever mushrooms you choose, they are a great substitute for meat, they're pareve, and they make this dish delicious! Serve it as an appetizer salad or a side dish with baked fish or roast chicken.

¹/₄ to ¹/₃ cup walnut halves

³/₄ pound medium asparagus

1 or 2 tablespoons vegetable oil

6 to 8 ounces portobello mushrooms, sliced

Salt and freshly ground pepper, to taste

2 tablespoons walnut oil

2 or 3 teaspoons wine vinegar or herb vinegar

6 cups mixed baby lettuces

1. Preheat toaster oven or oven to 350°F. Toast walnuts in oven 5 minutes. Transfer to a plate.

2. Peel asparagus by putting it on a board, holding it at the base, and peeling it towards you, turning it after each strip is peeled. Cut off thick bases. Rinse asparagus. Cut each spear into 3 pieces. Put asparagus in a medium sauté pan or deep skillet of boiling salted water and cook 3 to 5 minutes or until just tender. Drain gently.

3. Heat vegetable oil in a large nonstick skillet. Add mushrooms, salt, and pepper and sauté over medium-high heat about 5 minutes or until they are tender and browned. Add asparagus and toss over medium heat until heated through.

4. Whisk walnut oil, vinegar, salt, and pepper in a small bowl. In a serving bowl, toss lettuce with walnut oil dressing. Adjust seasoning. Serve lettuce topped with mushrooms and asparagus. Sprinkle with toasted walnuts.

Roasted Mediterranean Vegetables

Makes 4 to 6 servings

Roast these vegetables at the same time as the Friday night chicken and serve them with the bird as an easy accompaniment. They also make a good appetizer, topped with Sephardic Salsa (page 131) or Zehug Vinaigrette (page 463) or simply drizzled with a little olive oil, sprinkled with cayenne pepper, and served with a lemon wedge.

Although this is a Mediterranean recipe, I often use small, thin, Asian eggplants, either the deep purple Japanese or the pale-skinned Chinese variety. They cook quickly and have a delicate taste and pleasing, tender texture.

1½ pounds Japanese, Chinese, or small Italian eggplants

4 large red bell peppers, or 2 red and 2 green

1 head garlic

2 tablespoons extra-virgin olive oil (optional)

Salt and freshly ground pepper, to taste

Cayenne pepper or paprika, to taste

Lemons, cut into wedges

1. Preheat oven to 400°F. Rinse vegetables and pat dry. Separate garlic into cloves and wrap them tightly in foil. Line a roasting pan with foil if you like. Prick each eggplant a few times with a fork and put in roasting pan. Put peppers in pan and add foil-wrapped garlic. Bake peppers and garlic 35 to 40 minutes, and eggplants 40 to 60 minutes or until tender; turn vegetables once during roasting.

2. Transfer peppers to a bowl and cover tightly or wrap in a plastic bag. Let stand 10 minutes. Peel with aid of a paring knife. Halve peppers and drain liquid from inside. Remove core. Quarter lengthwise. Peel eggplant if you like. Quarter each eggplant lengthwise.

3. Alternate eggplant and pepper pieces on platter. Add garlic cloves. Sprinkle eggplant with oil if using, salt, pepper, and cayenne. Garlic can be squeezed out of cloves onto eggplant, or served on the side. Serve with lemon wedges.

Lecso

Makes 6 to 8 servings

This savory pepper stew is best known as a Hungarian dish but many say it originated in Serbia. It is a popular dish in Israel too.

Lecso (pronounced "letcho") is easy to make and keeps well. Many cooks like to keep it on hand to use as the base for a quick dish of scrambled eggs or to heat with frankfurters or sausages. Lecso is a good side dish on its own and accompanies beef, chicken, fish, or grains well. I find it also makes a terrific topping for a pareve pizza.

To make lecso you can use either the pale green peppers called Hungarian or Italian peppers or the common green bell peppers. Other colors of peppers are not traditional but you can mix peppers if you like.

3 pounds green bell peppers or Hungarian peppers

5 or 6 tablespoons vegetable oil

3 large onions, halved and sliced

2 cloves garlic, chopped (optional)

1½ tablespoons sweet paprika

2½ pounds ripe tomatoes, peeled, seeded, and coarsely chopped, or two 28-ounce can tomatoes, drained and chopped

Salt and freshly ground pepper, to taste

Hot paprika or cayenne pepper, to taste

1. Cut peppers into strips about ½-inch wide and 3 inches long.

2. Heat oil in a stew pan. Add onions and sauté over medium-low heat 12 minutes or until beginning to turn golden. Add peppers and sauté, stirring occasionally, 15 minutes. Add garlic, if using, and sweet paprika and sauté 1 minute, stirring.

3. Add tomatoes, salt, pepper, and hot paprika. Cover and simmer, stirring occasionally, 30 to 35 minutes or until peppers are tender and mixture is thick. If there is too much liquid in the pan, uncover and boil mixture 1 or 2 minutes, stirring often. Adjust seasoning, adding more hot paprika if desired. Serve hot or cold.

Vegetables with Spiced Yogurt

Makes 4 to 6 servings

A tangy yogurt topping with a touch of spice is a favorite among Sephardic Jews, especially those from eastern Mediterranean countries like Lebanon and Turkey. It's great with lentils and with fried eggplant. It also livens up any simply-cooked vegetable dish, such as this quick and easy vegetable medley, which is perfect for a light Saturday night supper on a hot day.

2 medium yellow crookneck squash

2 large carrots, sliced (¼-inch thick)

1½ cups frozen corn kernels

2 medium zucchini, halved and sliced ½-inch thick

1 cup nonfat yogurt

½ teaspoon ground cumin

Salt and white pepper, to taste

Cayenne pepper, to taste

2 tablespoons minced fresh Italian parsley

1. Slice neck part of yellow squash into ½-inch diagonal slices. Halve thicker part of squash lengthwise and slice about ½-inch thick.

2. Put carrots in a saucepan and add water to cover. Bring to a boil. Cook over medium heat 5 minutes. Add corn, zucchini, and squash and bring to a boil. Cover and cook over medium heat 3 to 5 minutes or until vegetables are tender. Drain well; you can save their cooking liquid as vegetable stock.

3. Mix yogurt with cumin, salt, white pepper, cayenne, and 1 tablespoon parsley. Serve vegetables warm or at room temperature, topped with spiced yogurt and sprinkled with remaining parsley.

Brussels Sprouts and Carrots in Creamy Parsley Sauce

Makes 5 or 6 servings

Serve this Ashkenazic-style dish in meatless meals, as it has a creamy sauce. The sauce has plenty of flavor from sautéed onions, grated lemon zest, and a generous amount of fresh parsley. If you prefer to serve the colorful vegetable medley with roast turkey or chicken, substitute Velouté Sauce (page 591) for the cream sauce.

1½ cups Cream Sauce (page 591)

1 pound small Brussels sprouts

1 pound carrots, diagonally sliced about ½-inch thick

2 tablespoons vegetable oil or butter

1 large onion, minced

2 teaspoons grated lemon rind

3 tablespoons chopped fresh parsley

Salt and white pepper, to taste

1. Prepare sauce. Meanwhile, rinse Brussels sprouts well. Trim brown bases of sprouts; do not remove so much of base that leaves come off.

2. Put carrots in a large saucepan and add water to cover. Bring to a boil, cover, and cook over medium-low heat 8 to 10 minutes or until carrots are just tender. Remove carrots with a slotted spoon, reserving liquid. Pour ¼ cup carrot cooking liquid into a bowl and set aside.

3. Add more water to carrot cooking liquid in saucepan so there is enough to cover Brussels sprouts. Bring to a boil and add a pinch of salt and the sprouts. Cook uncovered over high heat 8 to 10 minutes or until they are just tender; check by removing one with slotted spoon and piercing its base with a small sharp knife. Drain gently in a colander or large strainer, rinse with cold running water until cool and drain well.

4. Heat oil in saucepan. Add onion and sauté over medium-low heat, stirring often, 7 minutes or until tender but not brown. Add cream sauce and bring to a simmer, stirring.

5. Add cooked vegetables to sauce. Heat uncovered 2 to 3 minutes, gently stirring them occasionally; add 1 to 2 tablespoons of carrot cooking liquid if sauce becomes too thick. Remove from heat. Stir in grated lemon rind and parsley. Adjust seasoning. Serve hot.

Turnips with Spinach and Garlic

Makes 4 servings

We tend to overlook turnips, perhaps thinking they are too strong. They become mild and delicately sweet when cooked, however. This Egyptian dish is a tasty accompaniment for baked or roasted chicken, for Barbecue-Sauced Brisket with Onions (page 386) or a Bulgur Wheat Pilaf (page 511). It's easy to prepare and reheats beautifully.

2 pounds turnips, peeled

3^1/$_2$ tablespoons olive oil or vegetable oil

6 large cloves garlic, chopped

1 cup finely chopped spinach leaves

1 large onion, chopped

^{3}/$_4$ cup chicken, beef, or vegetable stock

Salt and freshly ground pepper, to taste

   1. Cut turnips into ^{3}/$_4$-inch dice. Heat 2 tablespoons oil in a stew pan. Add turnips and sauté over medium heat 3 minutes. Remove them with slotted spoon. Add ^{1}/$_2$ tablespoon oil to pan and heat it briefly. Add garlic and sauté 15 seconds. Add spinach and sauté about 30 seconds or until dry. Remove from skillet.

   2. Add remaining tablespoon oil to pan. Add onion and sauté over medium heat about 5 minutes or until beginning to brown. Add broth and bring to boil. Add turnips, cover, and simmer over low heat 15 minutes. Add spinach mixture and cook 5 minutes or until turnips are tender, adding a few tablespoons stock or water if pan becomes dry. Adjust seasoning. Serve hot.

❧ *Sauces*

Grilled Red Pepper Sauce

Makes about 6 servings

Grilling bell peppers was a traditional technique in the Sephardic kitchen long before it became trendy on restaurant menus. When they are in season, it's a good idea to grill plenty of peppers. You can freeze them and use them to make this easy sauce. If you don't have home-grilled peppers, you can use roasted sweet red peppers from a jar. This sauce has almost as many uses as tomato sauce. Use it to top broiled, baked, or fried eggplant to accompany vegetable kugels, or to liven up plain steamed vegetables.

3 large grilled red bell peppers, peeled (page 588)

2 tablespoons extra-virgin olive oil (optional)

3 large cloves garlic, chopped

About 1 cup vegetable stock

1^1/$_2$ teaspoons fresh thyme or ^{1}/$_2$ teaspoon dried

Salt and freshly ground pepper, to taste

1 to 2 teaspoons strained fresh lemon juice, or to taste

   1. Prepare peppers. Then, cut peeled peppers in half and discard seeds and ribs. Cut peppers in pieces. Puree in a food processor with oil, if using, until smooth, or leave it a little chunky if you prefer.

   2. Combine garlic and ^{1}/$_2$ cup stock in a medium saucepan and bring to a boil. Boil 2 minutes. Add thyme. Stir in pepper puree. Add enough of remaining stock to thin sauce to the consistency you like. Season with salt and pepper. Add lemon juice. Serve hot or cold.

Mediterranean Green Sauce for Vegetables

Makes 4 servings

Sephardic Jews in Italy and southern France serve this pareve cousin of pesto with cooked meats and chicken. It's also good with hard boiled eggs. But my favorite way to serve it is with cooked vegetables of all types, from cauliflower and broccoli to carrots, winter squash, and potatoes. It also does wonders for dried beans and instantly perks up canned ones.

1 medium clove garlic, peeled

1/2 cup sprigs fresh Italian parsley

1 tablespoon capers, drained and rinsed

1/4 cup diced mild onion, such as white or red onion

3 tablespoons extra-virgin olive oil

1 or 2 tablespoons chopped fresh basil

2 tablespoons strained fresh lemon juice, or to taste

Salt and freshly ground pepper, to taste

Chop garlic in a food processor, add parsley, and chop together finely. Add capers and onion and chop together with brief pulses. Transfer to a bowl. Stir in oil, basil, lemon juice, salt, and plenty of pepper. Taste, and add more lemon juice if needed.

Garlic-Yogurt Sauce

Makes 6 servings

Serve this easy-to-make sauce with Savory Zucchini Kugel (page 198) or with simply cooked vegetables such as green beans or grilled, baked, or fried eggplant slices. It's also good on lentils, bulgur wheat, and rice. You can serve it as a light dip for an assortment of vegetables; it's especially good with cucumber spears, jicama sticks, baby carrots, and toasted pita wedges. Use any kind of yogurt you like—regular, low-fat, or nonfat.

1 1/2 cups plain yogurt

1 medium clove garlic, pressed or finely minced

1/4 teaspoon paprika, plus a little more for sprinkling

1/4 teaspoon ground coriander

2 tablespoons chopped fresh parsley

Salt, to taste

Cayenne pepper, to taste

Fresh parsley sprigs

Mix yogurt with garlic, paprika, coriander, and chopped parsley in a bowl. Season with salt and cayenne. Serve sprinkled lightly with paprika and garnished with parsley sprigs.

Quick Tomato Sauce for Vegetables

Makes 4 servings

Israeli cooks use tomato paste, sautéed onions, and garlic to make this sauce in no time. It's popular for serving with vegetables in many ways, from simple canned or frozen vegetables that are heated in the sauce to cooked fresh ones. A sauce like this is also a favorite for keeping stuffed vegetables moist as they cook. To vary the sauce, you can try one of the herb-flavored varieties of tomato paste.

You can make this sauce in a sauté pan, a skillet, or a saucepan, depending on how you want to cook or heat the vegetable in it.

2 tablespoons olive oil or vegetable oil (see Note)

1 medium onion, chopped

2 large cloves garlic, minced

1 to 3 tablespoons tomato paste

1¹/₂ cups water

Salt and freshly ground pepper, to taste

1. Heat oil in a skillet, sauté pan, or saucepan. Add onion and sauté over medium heat 7 minutes or until beginning to brown. Add garlic and sauté a few seconds. Whisk tomato paste with water in a bowl and add. Add a little salt and pepper. Bring to a simmer.

2. Adjust the cooking time of the sauce according to how you will use it:

For stuffed vegetables that will cook with the sauce: Remove sauce from heat at this point.

For already cooked or canned vegetables that will heat in the sauce: Cook sauce about 10 minutes or until it thickens and the onions are tender.

For fresh uncooked vegetables that will simmer or bake in sauce: add raw or blanched vegetables and cook in sauce.

Note: If you are using oil to sauté the stuffed vegetable and enough oil remains in the pan, as in Celery with Aromatic Chicken Stuffing (page 366), you will not need this oil amount.

Zehug Vinaigrette

Makes about ¹/₂ cup, 4 to 8 servings

The Yemenite hot pepper chutney called zehug *adds delicious zip to salad dressings. Make your own Zehug (page 592) or purchase it in either its green or red version at Jewish or Middle Eastern markets. You can substitute Moroccan harissa or any hot chutney, relish, or salsa that you like.*

Serve this vinaigrette with vegetables. It's especially good with cauliflower, broccoli, eggplant, or with dishes like Roasted Mediterranean Vegetables (page 459). Add the zehug a short time before serving if you want it to keep its full strength; the lemon juice in the dressing seems to tone it down.

4 to 6 teaspoons Zehug (page 592) or hot salsa

2 to 3 tablespoons strained fresh lemon juice or vinegar

Salt and freshly ground pepper, to taste

6 tablespoons olive oil

Prepare zehug, if using homemade. Whisk lemon juice, salt, and pepper in a small bowl. Whisk in oil. Stir in zehug. Adjust seasoning. Serve at room temperature.

Chive Sour Cream

Makes 4 to 6 servings

This topping is delicious on potato or vegetable latkes, or plain baked or microwaved potatoes.

1 cup sour cream

Freshly ground pepper, if possible from white peppercorns

Salt, to taste (optional)

Cayenne pepper, to taste (optional)

Pinch of paprika

2 tablespoons snipped fresh chives

Season sour cream to taste with white pepper, and salt and cayenne, if using. Reserve 1 teaspoon chives; stir remaining into mixture. Refrigerate until ready to serve. Serve sprinkled very lightly with paprika and topped with remaining teaspoon chives.

Creamy Herbed Mustard Sauce

Makes about 1¼ cups, 6 to 8 servings **D**

For a tasty, no-cook sauce for topping cooked vegetables, combine mustard with fresh herbs, mayonnaise, and sour cream or yogurt. It's also good as an appetizer dip with raw vegetables, such as cauliflower and broccoli florets, quartered mushrooms, and cucumber, carrot, celery, jicama, and zucchini sticks. Use any type of mayonnaise and sour cream you like—regular, low-fat, or nonfat. To make it pareve, omit the sour cream or yogurt.

¾ cup sour cream or yogurt

½ cup mayonnaise

1 tablespoon mustard, or to taste

1 tablespoon strained fresh lemon juice, or more to taste

1 small shallot, minced, or 1 tablespoon minced green or red onion

1 tablespoon chopped fresh parsley

1 tablespoon thinly sliced fresh chives

1 tablespoon chopped fresh tarragon

Salt and freshly ground pepper, to taste

Mix sour cream with mayonnaise in a bowl until smooth. Stir in mustard, lemon juice, shallot, parsley, chives, tarragon, salt, and pepper. Adjust seasoning. Cover and refrigerate until ready to serve.

Basil Cream with Diced Tomatoes

Makes 8 servings **D**

Luscious French cream sauces are popular partners for fish or vegetable loaves called terrines. This one is a delicious complement for Striped Vegetable Terrine (page 43) and is very easy to prepare. It also tastes great on vegetable-filled kreplach or other pasta or on plain boiled potatoes. Since it's very rich, serve only a few tablespoons of sauce with each portion. You can serve it hot or cold.

To keep the color of the herbs bright, add them at the last minute. Be sure they are dry when you chop them, and use a dry board and a dry knife.

1 large shallot, minced

2 large cloves garlic, minced

⅓ cup dry white wine

1½ cups heavy cream or whipping cream

Salt and freshly ground pepper, to taste

2 ripe plum tomatoes

5 tablespoons chopped fresh basil

2 tablespoons chopped fresh parsley

A few drops strained fresh lemon juice

Cayenne pepper, to taste

2 to 3 teaspoons vegetable broth or water (optional)

1. Combine shallots, garlic, and wine in a large, heavy saucepan. Bring to a boil. Cook over medium-high heat, stirring often, until liquid is reduced to about 2 tablespoons.

2. Stir in cream, add a pinch of salt and pepper, and bring to a boil, stirring. Cook over medium heat, stirring often, about 7 minutes or until sauce is thick enough to coat a spoon.

3. Halve tomatoes and squeeze out their juice and seeds. Dice tomatoes. Just before serving, with the sauce off the heat, stir in the tomatoes, basil, and parsley. Add a few drops of lemon juice. Season with salt, pepper, and cayenne. If serving sauce cold, sauce will thicken. If you like, stir in vegetable broth or water to thin it.

Noodles, Couscous, and Other Pasta

Noodles with Chicken or Meat
468

Noodles and Chicken in Port and Portobello Sauce

Noodles and Chicken with Plum Sauce

Noodles with Zucchini and Meaty Mushroom Sauce

Noodles with Vegetables or Fish
471

Alsatian Noodles with Asparagus and Chanterelles

Spinach Noodles with Sephardic Vegetable Sauté

Pareve Noodles with Sesame–Peanut Butter Dressing

Noodles with Lox, Dill, and Cream

Egg Barley and Orzo
473

Toasted Egg Barley with Sautéed Onions

Egg Barley with Dill and Diced Vegetables

Pasta Farfel with Raisins and Pecans

Fast and Festive Low-Fat Orzo

Orzo with Spinach and Sesame Seeds

Orzo, Lemon, and Walnut Stuffing

Other Pastas
476

Italian Jewish Penne with Eggplant-Tomato Sauce

Angel Hair Pasta with Spicy Orange Sauce

Fusilli with Liver, Onions, and Red Pepper

Noodle and Other Pasta Kugels
478

Springtime Noodle Kugel

Jerusalem Kugel

Creamy Noodle Kugel with Three Cheeses

Linguine Kugel with Broccoli, Garlic, and Pine Nuts

Lasagne Kugel with Ricotta-Parmesan Filling and Rich Tomato Sauce

Macaroni and Eggplant Kugel with Swiss Cheese

Dairy Noodle Kugel with Pears, Lemon, and Golden Raisins

Low-Fat Sweet Noodle Kugel

Pasta is much loved in the Jewish kitchen, for both holiday and everyday cooking. Best known to us are golden egg noodles served in chicken soup or made into rich, sweet kugels (noodle casseroles). Yet there are many other types of traditional Jewish pastas and pasta specialties, from egg barley to bow-ties to couscous.

Noodles in chicken soup might sound like a very simple dish but when they are fresh egg noodles served in homemade soup, there is nothing better, and this is a wonderful holiday dish. The pure, delicate tastes of the tender noodles and the richly flavored soup make this the supreme comfort food. Other small pastas often served in soup are alphabet noodles, including Hebrew ones, which we always enjoyed as children because we liked to pick out the letters of our names.

Jewish cooks really use their noodle (I couldn't resist!) when it comes to creating delicious kugel recipes. There are countless variations, from savory noodle and vegetable kugels flavored with deeply browned onions to sweet, cinnamon-scented kugels in which the pasta is mixed with fruit.

For a dish so steeped in tradition, you would think it would involve a time-consuming process, but actually, kugels are not at all complicated to prepare. The noodles and other ingredients are simply mixed with eggs and baked. They can even be baked ahead and reheated. Kugels can be extremely rich in eggs, butter, cream cheese, or cream or can be low in fat when made with egg whites and moistened with a little oil. Noodle kugels are usually pareve or dairy but they can also contain chicken or meat, making them suitable only for *fleishig* meals. Traditionally, sweet kugels are served as accompaniments but today many people like them as a separate course or for dessert.

Egg barley, also called farfel, is pasta cut in small bits. Popular in Ashkenazic cooking, it might be yellow or brown, if it's toasted. Egg barley is cooked like other pasta and is often combined with sautéed onions as an accompaniment.

The Moroccan form of pasta is couscous, which seems like a grain but is more like little beads of spaghetti, as it is made of the same ingredients—semolina and water. Time-honored recipes call for making it at home by rolling semolina and water between your fingers and then steaming the resulting little grains of pasta several times above a simmering meat stew. Packaged couscous is pre-cooked. It needs only to be moistened with boiling water and is ready in five minutes. In natural foods stores you can also find whole-wheat couscous.

Couscous is the center of holiday feasts on the tables of Jews from North Africa. It is served with an array of braised vegetables and meat in a savory sauce, and sometimes with stuffed vegetables as well.

Because pasta is pareve, it is very versatile in kosher cuisine. It can be combined with any ingredient and is great for using up leftovers. I find it especially useful for stretching small amounts of cooked vegetables, chicken, or turkey left from Shabbat dinners. The cooked pasta can be mixed with the vegetables or meat, tossed with sautéed onions and garlic, and perhaps moistened with a little tomato sauce. Either I heat the mixture in a skillet or I mix it with eggs or egg whites and bake it as an easy kugel.

For more information and recipes on noodle kugels and couscous, see the table of contents or the index on page 608.

Noodles with Chicken or Meat

Noodles and Chicken in Port and Portobello Sauce

Makes 4 servings (M)

The perennial Jewish favorite, chicken and noodles, gains a French twist in this tasty dish. It combines exotic and white mushrooms with chicken breasts and port to make a luscious sauce for the noodles. You can also make this dish with fresh shiitake, oyster, or chanterelle mushrooms.

6 to 8 ounces portobello mushrooms
4 tablespoons vegetable oil
2 large shallots, minced
Salt and freshly ground pepper, to taste
6 to 8 ounces button mushrooms, sliced
$^{1}/_{2}$ cup port or sherry
1 pound boneless skinless chicken breasts
12 to 14 ounces medium noodles or fettuccine
2 tablespoons chopped fresh Italian parsley
1 tablespoon snipped fresh chives

1. Gently clean portobello mushrooms with damp paper towels. Cut them into bite-size pieces.

2. Heat 1 tablespoon oil in a large, heavy skillet over medium heat. Stir in shallots, then portobello mushrooms, salt, and pepper. Sauté, tossing often, about 4 minutes or until mushrooms are just tender. Remove from skillet. Add 1 tablespoon oil and heat it over medium-high heat. Add button mushrooms, salt, and pepper and sauté about 2 minutes or until light brown.

3. Return portobello mushrooms to skillet and reheat mixture until sizzling. Add $^{1}/_{4}$ cup port and simmer over medium heat, stirring, about 3 minutes or until it is absorbed by mushrooms. Remove from heat.

4. Sprinkle chicken with pepper on both sides. Heat 2 tablespoons oil in a large, heavy skillet over medium-high heat. Add chicken and sauté, pressing on chicken occasionally with slotted spatula, 4 to 5 minutes per side or until meat feels springy and is no longer pink inside; cut to check. Transfer to a cutting board.

5. Discard fat from skillet. Add remaining port and bring to a boil, stirring and scraping in pan juices. Pour into mushroom sauce. Cut chicken into thin strips and add to sauce.

6. Meanwhile, cook noodles in a large pot of boiling salted water uncovered over high heat about 5 minutes or until tender but firm to the bite. Drain well and transfer to a shallow serving dish.

7. Heat sauce gently. Adjust seasoning. Add parsley. Spoon sauce over noodles. Serve sprinkled with chives.

Cooking Noodles

Although old recipes often specify long cooking times, today's cooks boil pasta only briefly to keep its flavor and texture. Prepare any soups or sauces before you cook the pasta. You don't have to measure the pasta cooking water, but you can use these amounts as a guide:

For 8 to 12 ounces noodles or other pasta, boil 3 to 4 quarts water and add 1 tablespoon salt.

For 12 ounces to 1 pound noodles or other pasta, boil 5 quarts water and add 1½ tablespoons salt.

Use quantities above or simply fill a pasta pot or other large pot about $^{2}/_{3}$ to $^{3}/_{4}$ full of water. Cover and bring the water to a boil over high heat. When the water is boiling rapidly, add salt.

Add the noodles to the boiling salted water. Stir them from time to time, or lift the strands occasionally with a fork or with tongs to prevent sticking. Cook the pasta uncovered over high heat until it is tender but firm to the bite, or "al dente."

Noodle packages and containers provide cooking time guidelines, but make sure you check the noodles and cook to your taste. Check by removing 1 or 2 noodles with tongs and tasting them; fresh noodles may need as little as 1 minute of cooking. Although some cooks rinse noodles immediately after cooking, this is not necessary except if you want to cool the pasta fast or if you must cook it ahead, as in making kugels.

Noodles and Chicken with Plum Sauce

Makes 4 servings

This light and easy updated version of chicken chow mein, prepared in many Jewish homes when I was growing up (see box, "Chicken Noodle Nostalgia and Asian Inspiration," page 470), makes use of bottled condiments, many of which are available not only in the Asian section of the supermarket but also in the kosher products section.

12 ounces dried Chinese wheat noodles or spaghetti

³/₄ cup chicken broth

6 ounces fresh snow peas, ends removed, or frozen
    snow peas

1¹/₂ to 2 cups cooked chicken strips

One 5-ounce can baby corn, drained (optional)

2 to 4 tablespoons soy sauce

3 to 4 tablespoons Chinese plum sauce

A few drops Asian hot sauce, or to taste

¹/₄ cup chopped green onions (optional)

1. Cook noodles in a large pot of boiling salted water over high heat, separating strands occasionally with a fork, 7 to 8 minutes or until tender but firm to the bite. Drain well. Transfer to a large serving bowl and toss with oil.

2. Bring broth to a simmer in a medium saucepan. Add snow peas and return to a simmer. Add chicken, baby corn, if using, and 2 tablespoons soy sauce. Cover and cook over medium-low heat about 2 minutes or until chicken is hot. Stir in plum sauce and hot sauce. Add mixture to noodles and toss. Taste, and add more soy sauce if needed. Serve topped with green onions, if using.

Noodles with Zucchini and Meaty Mushroom Sauce

Makes 4 to 6 servings

When I braise chuck roast in porcini mushroom sauce, it makes a generous amount of delicious sauce. I like to save the extra sauce in the refrigerator or freezer and enjoy it at another meal with noodles and vegetables. This dish is very quick and easy to make. If you don't have the sauce, use your favorite spaghetti sauce and diced deli roast beef.

1¹/₂ cups sauce from Chuck Roast in Porcini Mushroom Sauce
    (page 385)

8 ounces zucchini

8 ounces yellow squash

3 tablespoons olive oil

Salt and freshly ground pepper, to taste

12 ounces to 1 pound noodles, medium shells or orecchiette
    (pasta discs)

4 to 6 ounces mushrooms, sliced

2 slices meat from the chuck roast, cut into small dice
    (optional)

¹/₄ cup chopped fresh Italian parsley

1. Thaw sauce if frozen. Halve zucchini and squash lengthwise and cut into ¹/₄-inch thick slices. Heat 2 tablespoons oil in a large skillet. Add half of squash, sprinkle with salt and pepper, and sauté over medium heat, turning occasionally, about 5 minutes or until tender. Transfer to a plate. Add remaining tablespoon oil to skillet, heat it and sauté remaining squash. Return reserved squash to skillet and turn off heat.

2. Cook noodles in a large pot of boiling salted water uncovered over high heat 5 to 8 minutes for noodles or shells or 10 minutes for orecchiette, or until tender but firm to the bite. Drain well and transfer to a shallow serving dish.

3. Combine sliced mushrooms and sauce in a medium saucepan. Bring to a simmer, stirring occasionally. Add meat, if using. Cook 2 minutes or until mushrooms are just tender.

4. Gently reheat squash. Drain pasta well and transfer to a large heated bowl. Add sauce and toss. Add squash and parsley and toss lightly. Adjust seasoning.

Chicken Noodle Nostalgia and Asian Inspiration

Chicken with noodles is a universal favorite. So many regional specialties come to mind, from Alsatian *coq au Riesling* with rich egg noodles, to Filipino chicken *pancit* with shiitake mushrooms, garlic, and soy sauce, to Pennsylvania Dutch chicken pot pie made not with pie dough but with fresh noodles.

For me, as a child this pairing meant homemade chicken noodle soup, which my family savored on Friday nights. This was the soup course of our festive Shabbat meals, repasts of ceremony and tradition.

For Sunday dinner my mother served us a casual version of chicken and noodles. She heated strips of chicken from the Shabbat soup with celery slices, canned button mushrooms, and a little of the chicken broth, then thickened the sauce with cornstarch and served the mixture over rice. I didn't like the mushrooms but my brother did, so I meticulously picked them out of my portion and gave them to him. There was one ingredient that we thought made the dish "Chinese": crisp chow mein noodles that came from a can and were sprinkled on top.

Thinking about our chicken chow mein dinner makes us smile today but it was fun food to our family. Somehow it struck a balance of the familiar with the foreign. Crisp noodles were not otherwise part of our menus, and neither were main courses of bite-size chicken and vegetables in a savory sauce.

This type of entree is still a favorite formula of mine for fast dinners. I mix cooked chicken or meat with a flavorful sauce and vegetables, then add noodles. When I want to give Far Eastern pizzazz to my noodles, I find an impressive array of choices, even at the supermarket. During my childhood my mother did not even have soy sauce in her cupboard. These days I can use hoisin sauce, rice wine vinegar, and sesame oil from my pantry. I can make Thai-inspired chicken and noodles with green curry sauce or Indian casseroles with tandoori sauce, simply by heating chicken or vegetables with store-bought sauces. Although these dishes are not classic Asian specialties any more than my mother's chow mein, the prepared condiments provide me with an effortless way to add authentic flavors to my noodles.

These quick and easy seasonings are a boon to all of us with busy schedules. I love using them, especially on those days when I have no time to shred fresh ginger or mince garlic. And they don't compromise my kosher meals at all.

Adding vegetables is just as easy. Instead of peeling and cutting fresh vegetables, when I'm in a hurry, I get frozen Asian mushroom medleys or mixed Chinese vegetables at the market. I sometimes add dried shiitake mushrooms or packaged rinsed fresh spinach. And yes, I do use canned vegetables from time to time, like water chestnuts and baby corn. Now and then I like to stir in some canned Chinese straw mushrooms.

Chow mein noodles are not a staple in my kitchen. However, like my mother, I enjoy combining chicken with Asian noodles. I use Chinese wheat or rice noodles, bean threads, or Japanese buckwheat noodles. When I want crisp noodles, I fry rice noodles, which instantly and dramatically puff in the oil and are very tasty.

For crispness I sprinkle a few toasted almonds, cashews, or peanuts on the finished entree. Occasionally I toss the hot chicken with crunchy vegetables, which I find in the supermarket's salad section. I usually add very fresh bean sprouts, thin sticks of jicama or broccoli slaw, a mixture of shredded broccoli stems with a little carrot, and red cabbage. Prepared in these ways, chicken and noodles is still one of my best-loved comfort foods.

Noodles with Vegetables or Fish

Alsatian Noodles with Asparagus and Chanterelles

Makes 4 servings **D** or **P**

The Jewish community of Alsace, France contributes to the province's wonderful cuisine known for its foie gras, its excellent noodles, and yeast-risen pastries. The Jews take advantage of the region's wonderful wild mushrooms to produce tasty meatless dishes. You can use any specialty mushrooms like chanterelles, portobello, shiitake, or porcini with great results. A good way to use them in springtime is to combine them with asparagus and serve them with fresh noodles, especially homemade Alsatian Egg Noodles as on page 489.

1 pound asparagus

12 ounces fresh exotic mushrooms

2 tablespoons vegetable oil

2 to 3 tablespoons butter or additional vegetable oil

Salt and freshly ground pepper, to taste

2 tablespoons minced shallots

1½ teaspoons chopped fresh thyme or ½ teaspoon dried

10 to 14 ounces fresh or dried egg noodles

¼ cup crème fraîche or whipping cream (optional)

2 tablespoons chopped fresh Italian parsley

1. Peel asparagus if it is thick. Cut asparagus tips from stems. Cut stems into 2 or 3 pieces, discarding tough ends (about ½-inch from end). Put all of asparagus in a medium saucepan of boiling salted water. Boil uncovered 2 to 3 minutes or until asparagus is just tender when pierced with a small sharp knife. Drain, rinse with cold water, and drain well again.

2. Clean mushrooms by rubbing them gently with damp paper towels; or gently rinse mushrooms and dry them on paper towels. Cut them into bite-size pieces if they are large, keeping their attractive shapes.

3. Heat oil and butter in a large skillet. Add mushrooms, salt, and pepper and sauté over medium heat about 3 minutes. Add shallots and thyme and sauté over medium-high heat, tossing often, about 3 more minutes or until mushrooms are browned and tender and any liquid they give off evaporates. Add asparagus. Season with salt and pepper.

4. Cook noodles uncovered in a large pot of boiling salted water over high heat, separating strands occasionally with fork, about 3 minutes for fresh or about 5 minutes for dried or until tender but firm to the bite. Meanwhile reheat mushrooms and asparagus, uncovered. Add cream, if using, and simmer uncovered 1 or 2 minutes.

5. Drain pasta well and transfer to a heated serving dish. Add mushroom mixture and toss. Adjust seasoning. Add parsley, toss again, and serve.

Spinach Noodles with Sephardic Vegetable Sauté

Makes 4 to 6 servings **P**

Garlic and olive oil give this zucchini and pepper sauté its Sephardic character and make it a colorful, tasty topping for pasta. To lend an Israeli or eastern Mediterranean accent, I season it with the herb blend called za'atar (a relative of thyme blended with other herbs and sesame seeds), which is available in Middle Eastern and Israeli markets.

3 to 4 tablespoons extra-virgin olive oil

1 red bell pepper, cut into thin strips

1 yellow bell pepper, cut into thin strips

1 green bell pepper, cut into thin strips

Salt and freshly ground pepper, to taste

4 small zucchini, cut into thin strips

⅓ cup chopped green onion, white and green parts

4 large cloves garlic, minced

1 teaspoon za'atar or dried thyme

12 ounces spinach noodles, plain noodles, or tri-color pasta

1. Heat 3 tablespoons oil in a large, heavy skillet. Add bell peppers, salt, and pepper. Cook over medium heat, stirring often, about 5 minutes or until peppers soften but remain slightly crisp. Add zucchini, green onion, and garlic and cook about 3 minutes or until crisp-tender. Add za'atar.

2. Add pasta to a large pan of boiling salted water. Cook uncovered over high heat 2 to 5 minutes, or until just tender but firm to the bite.

3. Drain pasta well and transfer to a shallow bowl. Add vegetable mixture, and remaining oil if desired. Toss until well combined. Taste for seasoning. Serve immediately.

Pareve Noodles with Sesame–Peanut Butter Dressing

Makes 4 to 6 servings   Ⓟ

Recently I enjoyed this noodle and fresh vegetable medley at a brit milah—*the celebration of the birth of a baby boy—catered by a Persian Jewish chef. It is truly a multicultural dish, beginning as a Chinese specialty with an Asian sesame paste dressing, then adapted by American cooks who substituted peanut butter. The delicious salad has become a favorite in American Jewish homes because it is pareve, satisfying, easy to make, and appeals to all tastes and all ages.*

The caterer added a fresh touch with favorite flavors of Jews from Iran—lime juice and plenty of cilantro and Italian parsley. If you can find small, sweet, thin-skinned Persian cucumbers, also known as Middle Eastern or Israeli cucumbers, use them for garnish.

12 ounces medium egg noodles or linguine
2 tablespoons Asian sesame oil
8 ounces green beans, ends removed, broken into 2 or 3 pieces
4 ounces white mushrooms
1 tablespoon strained fresh lime juice
3 ounces bean sprouts, (optional), ends removed
1 large carrot, coarsely grated
Peanut Butter Dressing (page 495)
2 to 4 tablespoons vegetable stock or broth (optional)
3 tablespoons chopped fresh cilantro, plus small sprigs for garnish
1/4 cup chopped fresh Italian parsley
Salt and freshly ground pepper, to taste (optional)
1/4 long seedless cucumber, cut into thin slices

1. Cook noodles in a large pot of boiling salted water for 5 to 8 minutes or until tender but firm to the bite. Drain, rinse with cold water, and drain well. Transfer to a large bowl and toss with sesame oil.

2. Meanwhile, add green beans to a large saucepan of enough boiling salted water to cover them generously and cook uncovered over high heat about 5 minutes or until crisp-tender. Drain, rinse with cold water, and drain well. Add to noodles.

3. Halve mushrooms and cut into thin slices. Sprinkle with lime juice, toss, and add to noodles. Reserve a few bean sprouts, if using, and a little grated carrot, for garnish. Add remaining bean sprouts and carrot to noodle mixture.

4. Prepare dressing. Then add to noodle mixture and toss to combine. If mixture is too thick, add stock by spoonfuls until noodles are moist. Add chopped cilantro and parsley. Add salt or pepper, if using.

5. Spoon into a serving bowl. Garnish with reserved bean sprouts, carrot, and cilantro sprigs. Arrange cucumber slices around edge. Serve at room temperature.

Noodles with Lox, Dill, and Cream

Makes 4 servings **D**

Lox, noodles, and cream make a terrific trio, as satisfying as lox, bagels, and cream cheese. When I developed this recipe for my pasta article in Gourmet *magazine, I was delighted that it was chosen for the magazine's cover. Use homemade or fresh egg noodles or fettuccine, or good-quality dried. Because this dish is rich, it's best served in small quantities, as a first course or to accompany baked fish or vegetables.*

4 or 5 ounces thinly sliced mild lox or smoked salmon

2 large shallots, minced

$\frac{1}{2}$ cup dry white wine

1 cup whipping cream

8 ounces fresh or dried egg noodles or fettuccine

2 tablespoons snipped fresh dill, plus a few small sprigs for garnish

Salt and freshly ground pepper, to taste

Cayenne pepper, to taste (optional)

1. Cut lox into lengthwise strips of about 2 × ³/₈-inch, cutting with the grain rather than crosswise so that strips hold together better.

2. Combine shallots and wine in a medium saucepan. Bring to a boil. Cook over low heat about 5 minutes or until liquid is reduced to about 3 tablespoons. Stir in cream and bring to a boil. Cook over medium heat about 6 minutes or until sauce is thick enough to lightly coat a spoon.

3. Cook noodles uncovered in a large pot of boiling salted water over high heat, separating strands occasionally with fork, about 2 minutes for fresh pasta or 2 to 5 minutes for dried or until tender but firm to the bite. Drain well. Transfer to a heated platter.

4. Bring sauce to a boil. Remove from heat and stir in snipped dill. Pour sauce over noodles and toss. Gently stir in salmon, using a large fork. Add a little salt, pepper, and cayenne, if using. Garnish with dill sprigs and serve.

❧ Egg Barley and Orzo

Toasted Egg Barley with Sautéed Onions

Makes 4 servings **M** or **P**

Egg barley is small, barley-size bits of pasta. It is a favorite in the Hungarian Jewish and Polish Jewish kitchen, especially to accompany goulash, other meat stews, and soups of all kinds. You can find it in the kosher products section of many supermarkets. Some kinds of egg barley are toasted.

4 cups chicken, meat, or vegetable stock, or half stock and half water

One 7-ounce package egg barley, plain or toasted

2 to 3 tablespoons vegetable oil

2 medium onions, chopped

1 teaspoon paprika (optional)

Salt and freshly ground pepper, to taste

1. Bring stock to a boil in a large saucepan. Add egg barley. Cover and cook over low heat for 15 to 20 minutes or until barley is tender.

2. Heat oil in a large sauté pan. Add onions and sauté over medium heat, stirring often, about 12 minutes or until tender and well browned. Add paprika, if using, and sauté, stirring, 1 minute.

3. If barley has not absorbed all the liquid, drain it. Add to pan of onions and toss over low heat, stirring very gently, 1 to 2 minutes. Season with salt and pepper. Serve hot.

Egg Barley with Dill and Diced Vegetables

Makes 4 servings

In many Jewish homes, egg barley is a traditional side dish for the Friday night chicken. I like to liven it up it with plenty of vegetables.

4 cups chicken or vegetable stock, or half stock and half water

One 7-ounce package egg barley, plain or toasted

2 medium carrots, diced

2 to 3 tablespoons vegetable oil

1 large onion, chopped

2 ribs celery, diced

4 ounces small mushrooms, halved and sliced

1 medium zucchini, diced

Salt and freshly ground pepper, to taste

1 tablespoon snipped fresh dill or 1 teaspoon dried dill

2 tablespoons chopped fresh parsley

1. Bring stock to a boil in a large saucepan. Add egg barley. Cover and cook over low heat for 5 minutes. Add carrots and return to a simmer. Cover and cook 10 to 15 minutes or until barley is tender.

2. Heat oil in a large sauté pan. Add onion and celery and sauté over medium heat, stirring often, for 7 minutes. Add mushrooms, zucchini, salt, and pepper. Sauté for about 3 minutes or until they are just tender.

3. If barley has not absorbed all the liquid, drain it. Add barley, carrots, dill, and 1 tablespoon parsley to pan of mushroom mixture and toss over low heat, stirring very gently, 1 to 2 minutes. Season with salt and pepper. Serve hot, sprinkled with remaining parsley.

Pasta Farfel with Raisins and Pecans

Makes 4 servings

Farfel is another name for egg barley. For Passover there is also matzo farfel, made of small squares of matzo. Pasta farfel is commonly flavored with browned onions but it also tastes good with dried fruits and nuts. Shallots and ground ginger are popular seasonings among Jews from Alsace, France.

For this dish I like to use fresh ginger instead of dried, for more punch. Serve this festive side dish with roast chicken, Cornish hens, duck, lamb, or brisket.

1/2 cup pecan pieces

2 tablespoons vegetable oil

3 tablespoons minced peeled fresh ginger

2 large shallots, chopped

One 7-ounce package egg barley, plain or toasted

1/3 cup dark raisins

3 1/2 cups hot chicken or vegetable stock, or half stock and half water

Salt and freshly ground pepper, to taste

1/4 cup chopped fresh parsley

1. Preheat oven or toaster oven to 350°F. Toast pecan pieces on a tray in oven about 4 minutes or until lightly browned. Transfer to a plate and let cool.

2. Heat oil in a medium saucepan. Add ginger and shallots and sauté over medium heat, stirring, 1 minute. Add egg barley and cook over low heat, stirring, 1 minute. Scatter raisins on top. Add hot stock, salt, and pepper and bring to a boil. Cover and cook over low heat 15 to 20 minutes or until barley is tender.

3. With a fork, gently stir in pecans and parsley. Adjust seasoning. Serve hot.

Fast and Festive Low-Fat Orzo

Makes 4 servings

Orzo is a quick pasta to prepare because you don't need a big pot of boiling water to cook it. Instead you can use just the amount of liquid it needs to absorb, like rice pilaf, and this liquid can be stock, for extra flavor. A topping of toasted nuts makes the orzo fit for a Shabbat or other holiday table. If you buy dry-roasted nuts, they will be lower in fat because no extra oil is added. Of course, you can also toast your own. This orzo is delicious with Low-Fat Ratatouille (page 427) or with Sea Bass in Garlic Tomato Sauce (page 326).

1 to 2 teaspoons nut oil or olive oil

1¹/₂ cups orzo or riso (rice-shaped pasta)

1³/₄ cups vegetable stock or a 14¹/₂-ounce can broth

1¹/₄ cups water

2 tablespoons dried onions

Salt and freshly ground pepper, to taste

2 tablespoons slivered fresh basil or chopped Italian parsley

¹/₄ to ¹/₃ cup dry-roasted pecans

Heat oil in a heavy, medium saucepan. Add orzo and sauté over low heat, stirring, 1 minute. Add stock, water, dried onions, salt, and pepper. Stir and bring to a boil. Cover and cook over low heat, without stirring, 15 minutes or until orzo is just tender. Adjust seasoning. Lightly stir in half the basil. Serve sprinkled with remaining basil and with pecans.

Orzo with Spinach and Sesame Seeds

Makes 4 servings

M or **P**

Greens with garlic and rice are popular in the kitchens of Jews from eastern Mediterranean countries such as Lebanon and Egypt. For this recipe, I substitute orzo, or rice-shaped pasta, for the rice. The dish is satisfying and seems rich but is actually healthful. Top it with toasted sesame seeds, pine nuts, or both for a festive touch.

10 to 12 ounces rinsed fresh spinach

1 or 2 tablespoons olive oil

1 medium onion, chopped

2 large cloves garlic, chopped

1¹/₂ cups orzo or riso (rice-shaped pasta)

1³/₄ cups chicken or vegetable stock or one 14¹/₂-ounce can

1¹/₄ cups water

Salt and freshly ground pepper, to taste

1 or 2 tablespoons sesame seeds, toasted

3 tablespoons pine nuts, toasted

Coarsely chop spinach. Heat oil in a heavy sauté pan. Add onion and sauté 5 minutes over medium heat, stirring often. Add garlic and orzo, and sauté over low heat, stirring, 1 minute. Add stock and water and bring to a boil. Add spinach, salt, and pepper. Cover and cook over low heat, without stirring, for 15 minutes or until orzo is just tender. Adjust seasoning. Serve sprinkled with toasted sesame seeds and pine nuts.

Orzo, Lemon, and Walnut Stuffing

Makes about 3¹/₂ to 4 cups, enough for
1 chicken or 4 side-dish servings

For this stuffing I like to cook the orzo as a pilaf, just like rice, by sautéing the orzo briefly before I add the liquid. The savory stuffing embellished with toasted nuts and lemon rind and juice is versatile. You can use it to stuff zucchini or chicken or use a double recipe to stuff a small turkey. This pilaf is also delicious as a side dish, on its own.

¹/₂ cup walnut pieces

6 tablespoons olive oil

1 large onion, finely chopped

1¹/₂ cups orzo or riso (rice-shaped pasta), about 12 ounces

3 cups hot chicken or vegetable stock or water

2 to 3 tablespoons strained fresh lemon juice

2 teaspoons grated lemon rind

¹/₃ cup chopped fresh Italian parsley

Salt and freshly ground pepper, to taste

1. Preheat oven or toaster oven to 350°F. Toast walnut pieces in oven about 4 minutes or until lightly browned. Transfer to a plate and let cool.

2. Heat 4 tablespoons oil in a medium saucepan. Add onion and sauté over medium heat, stirring often, 7 minutes or until it begins to turn golden. Add orzo and cook over low heat, stirring, 3 minutes. Add stock and bring to a boil Cover and cook over low heat, without stirring, about 14 minutes or until barely tender. If you wish to serve it as a side dish, cook it 16 to 18 minutes or until tender.

3. Fluff mixture with a fork to break up any lumps in orzo. Add 2 tablespoons lemon juice, the lemon rind, walnuts, and parsley and toss mixture to combine it. Season with salt and pepper. Add more lemon juice if you like.

4. Let stuffing cool before spooning it into chicken. If serving as a side dish rather than as stuffing, serve it hot.

❦ *Other Pastas*

Italian Jewish Penne with Eggplant-Tomato Sauce

Makes 4 servings

This tasty dish is inspired by a pasta entree I enjoyed at Tiramisu restaurant in Philadelphia, which has several specialties from the Italian Jewish kitchen on its menu. The sauce is made of grilled eggplant, which blends into the tomato sauce and lends an intriguing flavor. Eggplant is an Italian Jewish favorite. Some even credit the Jews with introducing the vegetable to Italian cooking. When Israel was under the rule of the Roman Empire dating back to 100 BCE, many Jews moved to Italy and established an important Jewish community in Rome that continued for centuries. Pellegrino Artusi, who codified Italian cooking, wrote that Jewish vendors brought eggplant to the Florentine market in the 19th century.

If you can't find slim eggplants, cut larger eggplants in half and place skin-side-down on broiler pan.

1 pound eggplant, slim enough to fit in broiler

2 pounds ripe tomatoes or two 28-ounce cans

2 to 4 tablespoons olive oil

1 onion, finely chopped

2 cloves garlic, minced

1 bay leaf

1 teaspoon dried oregano

Salt and freshly ground pepper, to taste

¹/₄ teaspoon dried hot pepper flakes, or cayenne pepper, to taste

2 tablespoons chopped fresh basil

12 ounces penne or mostaccioli

Fresh basil sprigs

1. Prick eggplant a few times with fork. Grill eggplant above medium-hot coals about 1 hour or broil about 40 minutes, turning often, until its skin blackens and flesh is tender. Leave eggplant until cool enough to handle. Remove eggplant skin and cut off cap. Halve eggplant and drain off any liquid inside. Chop eggplant very fine, either with a knife or in a food processor.

2. If using fresh tomatoes, peel, seed, and chop them, reserving juice. If using canned tomatoes, drain them, reserving juice, and chop them.

3. Heat 1 or 2 tablespoons oil in a large shallow saucepan, add onion and sauté over medium heat until lightly browned. Add garlic, tomatoes, bay leaf, oregano, salt, pepper, and pepper flakes. Cook 10 minutes, stirring occasionally. Discard bay leaf.

4. Add chopped eggplant to sauce. If sauce is too thick, stir in reserved tomato juice. Cook, stirring often, about 10 minutes or until sauce is thick and well flavored. Stir in basil.

5. Meanwhile, cook penne in a large saucepan of boiling salted water over high heat, stirring occasionally, 9 or 10 minutes until tender but firm to the bite. Pour into a colander and drain.

6. Transfer penne to a large shallow bowl and, if you like, toss with 1 to 2 tablespoons olive oil. Reserve about 1/2 cup sauce, and toss remaining sauce with penne. Serve topped with reserved sauce and garnished with basil sprigs.

Angel Hair Pasta with Spicy Orange Sauce

Makes 4 servings

I got this idea from an Israeli vegetarian I met at a food market. Our conversation, of course, led to our favorite subject: cooking. She adds orange juice to the popular Sephardic flavoring combination of garlic, hot peppers, and cilantro to make a quick sauce for pasta. It's a tasty combination, good for all sorts of pasta. Serve the pasta hot or at room temperature.

2 red or green jalapeño peppers, seeds and ribs discarded (see Note)

3 large cloves garlic, peeled

3 to 4 tablespoons extra-virgin olive oil

1/3 cup orange juice

8 ounces angel hair pasta or capellini

Salt and freshly ground pepper, to taste

1/4 cup sliced green onions

1/3 cup chopped fresh cilantro plus cilantro sprigs for garnish

Orange segments or slices

1. Remove seeds and ribs from jalapeño peppers. Mince peppers and garlic in a small food processor or with a knife.

2. Heat 2 tablespoons oil in a medium skillet. Add garlic and jalapeño peppers. Sauté them over low heat, stirring, about 1 minute or until they soften slightly. Remove from heat and add orange juice. Transfer to a serving bowl large enough for pasta.

3. Cook pasta uncovered in a large pot of boiling salted water over high heat, separating strands occasionally with fork, about 4 minutes or until tender but firm to the bite. Drain, rinse with cold water, and drain well.

4. Add pasta to bowl of orange juice mixture. Add remaining oil, salt, pepper, green onions, and cilantro. Mix well; Adjust seasoning; add more olive oil if desired. Garnish with cilantro sprigs and orange segments. Serve warm or at room temperature.

Note: Wear rubber gloves when handling hot peppers.

Fusilli with Liver, Onions, and Red Pepper

Makes 4 servings

M

Chicken livers and onions are such a popular pair in the Jewish kitchen that they are used in many ways. When I lived in Israel a friend gave me her recipe for chicken liver and onions baked in a noodle kugel. I find the combination tastes even better this way, and it's ready in minutes.

8 ounces Broiled Chicken Livers (page 360)

3 tablespoons vegetable oil

1 large onion, halved and cut into thin slices

1 large red bell pepper, seeds and ribs discarded, cut into 2-inch strips

1 teaspoon ground cumin

Salt and freshly ground pepper, to taste

12 ounces pasta fusilli, rotini, or spirals

2 tablespoons chopped fresh parsley

1. Prepare livers. Then, cut each liver half in 2 to 4 pieces.

2. Heat oil in a large, heavy, deep skillet or sauté pan. Add onion and bell pepper and sauté over medium heat, stirring occasionally, about 10 minutes or until vegetables are tender and onion browns lightly. Remove from heat. Add broiled livers and sprinkle with cumin and pepper.

3. Cook pasta in large pot of boiling salted water uncovered over high heat, stirring occasionally, 6 to 7 minutes or until tender but firm to the bite. Drain well.

4. Reheat onion-liver mixture over low heat about 1 minute or until it is hot. Add pasta to skillet and heat over low heat, tossing with a fork, about 1 minute. Add parsley and toss. Adjust seasoning. Serve on heated plates.

Noodle and Other Pasta Kugels

Springtime Noodle Kugel

Makes 8 to 10 servings

P

Asparagus, sweet onions, and carrots make this kugel delicious. For an elegant touch, you might like to garnish each plate with a few lightly cooked baby carrots and asparagus tips. Serve the kugel as an entree or as an accompaniment for fish or chicken.

3/4 pound asparagus

3/4 pound slim carrots

6 tablespoons vegetable oil

2 large sweet onions, sliced thin

2 teaspoons fresh thyme or 3/4 teaspoon dried thyme

Salt and freshly ground pepper, to taste

1 pound wide egg noodles

4 large eggs, beaten

1/4 cup chopped fresh parsley

Paprika, to taste

1. Peel asparagus if it is thick. Cut asparagus tips from stems. Cut stems into 3 pieces, discarding tough ends (about 1/2-inch from end). Quarter carrots lengthwise and cut them into sticks about the same length as the asparagus pieces.

2. Put carrots in a saucepan and cover with water. Add a pinch of salt. Bring to a boil. Cover and cook over medium-low heat 5 minutes. Add asparagus and bring to a boil. Cook uncovered over medium heat about 2 minutes or until carrots and asparagus are nearly tender. Remove vegetables to a colander with a slotted spoon, reserving their cooking liquid. Rinse vegetables with cold water and drain well.

3. Heat 3 tablespoons oil in a large skillet. Add onions and sauté over medium-low heat about 10 minutes or until very tender. Add carrots, asparagus, and thyme, toss with onions, and heat through. Season with salt and pepper.

4. Preheat oven to 350°F. Cook noodles in a large pot of boiling salted water uncovered over high heat, stirring occasionally, about 4 minutes or until nearly tender. Drain, rinse with cold water, and drain well. Transfer to a large bowl. Toss with 2 tablespoons oil and 1/4 cup cooking liquid from the vegetables. Season with salt and pepper.

5. Add vegetable mixture, eggs, and parsley to noodles and mix well. Oil a 3 1/2- to 4-quart baking dish or two 7- to 8-cup baking dishes and add noodle mixture. Sprinkle with remaining tablespoon oil and with a little paprika.

6. Bake 45 to 55 minutes or until set. Serve hot, from baking dish.

Jerusalem Kugel

Makes 8 to 10 servings

This dense, rich kugel is standard fare in Jerusalem synagogues for the kiddush snack after Shabbat morning services. The kugel has an intriguing peppery yet slightly sweet caramel flavor. It bakes all night in a very low oven, much like cholent *and other Shabbat dishes, and turns deep brown throughout.*

If you prefer to bake the kugel faster, you can bake it uncovered at 350°F for 1 hour. It will still taste good but its color will not be as deep. You can reheat any leftover kugel slices by wrapping them in foil and heating them in a toaster oven at 350°F.

12 ounces fine egg noodles

8 tablespoons vegetable oil

1/3 cup sugar

3 large eggs

1 teaspoon salt

1 teaspoon freshly ground pepper

1/4 cup raisins (optional)

1. Generously grease a round 2-quart baking dish. Cook noodles in a large pot of boiling salted water about 5 minutes or until nearly tender. Drain, return to pot, and toss briefly with 3 tablespoons of the oil. Keep on stove so noodles remain warm; do not cover.

2. Meanwhile, pour remaining oil into a heavy saucepan, then add sugar. Heat over low heat, shaking

pan gently from time to time; do not stir. Cook 15 to 20 minutes or until sugar turns deep brown. Gradually add mixture to noodles, mixing well with tongs.

3. Beat eggs with salt and pepper in a bowl. Add to noodles and mix well. Add raisins, if using, and mix well. Transfer to greased baking dish. Cover with foil and with a lid. Refrigerate kugel if not ready to bake it.

4. Put kugel in oven set at 200°F (or lowest numerical setting). Bake kugel about 10 hours or overnight. Run a knife around edge and turn out onto a round platter. Serve hot, in slices.

Note: If you want to present the kugel on a platter, it's best to use a round baking dish; the kugel will stick less to the sides. If you want to serve the kugel from the casserole dish, you can use any shape dish.

Creamy Noodle Kugel with Three Cheeses

Makes 8 servings

Unlike most kugels, this one features a cream sauce instead of eggs. It's a meal in a casserole, with a colorful medley of vegetables and two or three kinds of cheese.

1/4 cup butter or vegetable oil

1/2 cup minced onion

8 ounces mushrooms, sliced

Salt and freshly ground pepper, to taste

1/4 cup all-purpose flour

2 1/2 cups milk

Freshly grated nutmeg, to taste

Cayenne pepper, to taste

2 large carrots, cut into thin strips

One 10-ounce package frozen peas or 1 1/2 cup fresh peas

1 pound fine noodles

2 medium zucchini, cut into strips

2 cups chopped fresh spinach

2 cups cottage cheese

3/4 cup mozzarella cheese

1/4 cup freshly grated Parmesan cheese (optional)

1. Melt butter in a medium, heavy saucepan over medium heat. Add onion and cook, stirring occasionally,

3 minutes. Add mushrooms, salt, and pepper and sauté over medium-high heat, stirring often, 3 minutes. Remove from heat and stir in flour. Return to heat and cook over low heat, stirring constantly, 1 minute. Remove from heat. Stir in milk, scraping bottom of pan to thoroughly blend in flour. Cook over medium-high heat, stirring constantly, until sauce thickens and comes to a boil. Add a pinch of salt, pepper, and nutmeg. Simmer over low heat, stirring often, 5 minutes. Add cayenne. Adjust seasoning.

2. Preheat oven to 375°F. Add carrots, peas, and noodles to a large pot of boiling salted water. Cook uncovered over high heat, stirring occasionally, 3 minutes. Add zucchini and spinach and cook 2 to 3 more minutes or until noodles are nearly tender. Drain, rinse with cold water, and drain well. Transfer mixture to a large bowl.

3. Lightly butter a 2-quart baking dish. Add sauce to noodle mixture and stir. Add cottage cheese and mix well. Adjust seasoning. Spoon into baking dish. Sprinkle with mozzarella and Parmesan cheese, if using. Bake 20 to 30 minutes or until bubbling. Brown under broiler, about 1 to 2 minutes. Serve from baking dish.

Linguine Kugel with Broccoli, Garlic, and Pine Nuts

Makes about 6 servings Ⓟ

Although kugels are of Ashkenazic origin, there's no reason we can't make them with ingredients from the other branches of Jewish cooking. Combining broccoli, garlic, and pine nuts with linguine lends Italian flair to this kugel. It's terrific with Braised Turkey Drumsticks in Red Wine and Porcini Sauce (page 364) or with Chicken Thighs with Onions and Green Olives (page 357).

1 pound broccoli, divided into florets

8 ounces linguine

4 tablespoons olive oil

1 medium onion, chopped

6 large cloves garlic, chopped

1/4 teaspoon hot pepper flakes

Salt and freshly ground pepper, to taste

2 large eggs, beaten

1/4 cup pine nuts, toasted

1. Preheat oven to 350°F. Boil broccoli in a large pot of boiling salted water about 4 minutes or until crisp-tender. Remove with slotted spoon and transfer to a strainer. Rinse with cold water and drain well. Chop broccoli coarsely. Add linguine to the boiling water and boil uncovered over high heat about 7 minutes or until nearly tender. Drain, rinse with cold water, and drain well. Transfer to a large bowl.

2. In a large skillet heat 1 1/2 tablespoons oil. Add onion and sauté over medium heat, stirring, about 5 minutes or until beginning to turn golden. Remove from pan.

3. Add another 1 1/2 tablespoons oil to skillet. Add garlic and pepper flakes and sauté over low heat about 15 seconds. Add broccoli and sauté, stirring, about 1 minute. Remove from heat. Season with salt and pepper.

4. Beat eggs with 1/2 teaspoon salt and a pinch of pepper in a bowl. Add to linguine. Add onion and toasted pine nuts and mix well.

5. Lightly oil a 2-quart baking dish and add half of linguine mixture. Top with all the broccoli mixture, then with the remaining linguine. Sprinkle with remaining tablespoon oil. Bake uncovered for 50 minutes to 1 hour or until set. Serve from the baking dish.

Lasagne Kugel with Ricotta-Parmesan Filling and Rich Tomato Sauce

Makes 6 to 8 servings

Like lasagne, this sumptuous kugel is composed of layers of noodles, tasty filling, hearty sauce, and cheese. It's easier to make than lasagne because there is no need to dry the noodles individually. With its cheesy filling and robust flavored sauce, this kugel is sure to please. You can assemble it a day ahead, ready for baking, and keep it covered in the refrigerator.

Hearty Spaghetti Sauce (page 494)

2 cups ricotta cheese (about 1 pound)

3/4 cup freshly grated Parmesan cheese

1/4 cup minced fresh Italian parsley

Freshly grated nutmeg, to taste

Salt and freshly ground pepper, to taste

2 large egg yolks or 1 large egg

12 ounces wide noodles

3 tablespoons olive oil

2 large eggs, beaten

1/2 to 1 pound Swiss or kashkaval cheese, shredded
    (2 to 4 cups)

1. Prepare sauce and let cool. Then, mix ricotta, 1/2 cup Parmesan, parsley, nutmeg, salt, and pepper in a bowl. Adjust seasoning; mixture should be flavored generously with nutmeg. Add egg yolks and mix well.

2. Cook noodles uncovered in a large pot of boiling salted water over high heat, stirring occasionally, about 6 minutes or until nearly tender. Rinse with cold water and drain well. Transfer to a large bowl and toss with olive oil and salt and pepper. Add beaten eggs and toss to coat.

3. Preheat oven to 375°F. Grease a 13 × 9 × 2-inch baking dish. Spoon 1 cup tomato sauce on bottom of dish and spread evenly with spatula. Top with 1/4 of noodle mixture. Sprinkle with 1/3 of shredded Swiss cheese.

4. Top with another 1/4 of noodle mixture. Top with all of ricotta mixture by spoonfuls; carefully spread it evenly. Top with another 1/4 of noodle mixture, then with 1 cup tomato sauce. Sprinkle with another 1/3 of shredded Swiss cheese.

5. Top with remaining noodle mixture. Spoon remaining tomato sauce over top. Sprinkle evenly with remaining Swiss cheese, then with remaining Parmesan.

6. Bake kugel for 30 to 40 minutes or until bubbling and lightly browned. Let stand 5 minutes in a warm place before serving.

Macaroni and Eggplant Kugel with Swiss Cheese

Makes 4 to 6 servings

Tomato sauce is the perfect partner for this hearty kugel. Serve it as a main course for Shavuot or for any meatless meal. If your market carries Chinese or Japanese eggplants, choose them, as their more delicate taste is perfect for this kugel.

1 pound eggplant, preferably Chinese or Japanese

4 tablespoons vegetable oil

Salt and ground white pepper, to taste

2 tablespoons butter

1 small onion, minced

2 1/2 tablespoons all purpose flour

1 1/2 cups milk

Cayenne pepper, to taste

Freshly grated nutmeg, to taste

1 1/2 cups elbow macaroni

3/4 to 1 cup grated Swiss cheese

2 large eggs, beaten

1. Peel eggplant if you like. Cut in 1/2-inch dice. Preheat oven to 375°F. Butter a 5- to 6-cup soufflé dish or deep baking dish.

2. Heat 2 tablespoons oil in a skillet. Add half the eggplant cubes, sprinkle with salt, and sauté over medium heat for 3 minutes. Cover and cook over medium-low heat, stirring often, about 4 minutes or until eggplant is tender. Remove eggplant. Heat another 2 tablespoons oil in skillet and sauté remaining eggplant.

3. Melt butter in a medium, heavy saucepan. Add onion, and sauté over low for heat about 5 minutes, or until soft but not brown. Sprinkle with flour and cook, stirring, about 2 minutes. Remove from heat. Gradually whisk in milk. Bring to a boil, stirring constantly with a whisk. Add salt, white pepper, cayenne, and nutmeg. Cook over low heat, whisking often, for 5 minutes. Transfer to a large bowl.

4. Cook macaroni uncovered in a large pan of boiling salted water over high heat, stirring occasionally, about 9 minutes, or until nearly tender. Rinse with cold water and drain well. Add macaroni and eggplant to sauce and mix gently. Gently stir in cheese. Adjust seasoning. Stir in eggs.

5. Spoon macaroni mixture into buttered dish. Set dish in a roasting pan and put in oven. Add enough very hot water to roasting pan to come halfway up sides of soufflé dish. Bake kugel for about 40 minutes or until it sets. Remove from pan of water. Serve hot.

Dairy Noodle Kugel with Pears, Lemon, and Golden Raisins

Makes 6 servings **D**

This fruity kugel makes a wonderful cold-weather brunch dish or dessert. Serve it with fresh sliced pears and, if you like, sour cream or yogurt.

2 large ripe pears

2 tablespoons strained fresh lemon juice

8 ounces wide egg noodles

4 to 6 tablespoons butter, melted

1 cup cottage cheese

1¼ cups sour cream

4 large eggs, separated

6 tablespoons sugar

1½ teaspoons grated lemon rind

Pinch of salt

¼ cup golden raisins

1. Preheat oven to 350°F. Butter a deep 8- to 10-cup baking dish. Peel, halve, and core pears. Cut them in very thin slices and put them in a bowl. Sprinkle them with the lemon juice.

2. Cook noodles in a large pot of boiling salted water uncovered over high heat, stirring occasionally, about 5 minutes or until nearly tender. Drain, rinse with cold water, and drain well. Transfer to a large bowl.

3. Toss with 2 to 4 tablespoons melted butter. Stir in cottage cheese, sour cream, egg yolks, 4 tablespoons sugar, grated lemon rind, salt, and raisins. Gently stir in pear mixture.

4. Beat egg whites in a large bowl until soft peaks form. Add remaining 2 tablespoons sugar and beat 30 seconds or until stiff and glossy. Gently fold ¼ of whites into noodle mixture; fold in remaining whites.

5. Transfer noodle mixture to baking dish. Sprinkle with remaining melted butter. Bake about 50 minutes or until puffed and golden brown. Serve hot or warm.

Low-Fat Sweet Noodle Kugel

Makes 4 to 6 servings ⓓ

By using fat-free cottage cheese and sour cream, and flavoring the kugel with fresh lemon juice and grated rind as well as vanilla extract, you will have a tasty, cholesterol-free, almost fat-free kugel. I include just a little oil to moisten the noodles. Whipped egg whites give the kugel a pleasing, light texture. If you would like an accompaniment, serve this kugel with Easy Honey-Vanilla Sauce (page 494), Strawberry Sauce (page 580), Fresh Plum Sauce (page 81), or Pears in Vanilla Syrup (page 147).

8 ounces wide yolk-free noodles

1 to 2 tablespoons vegetable oil

3/4 cup nonfat cottage cheese

1 1/2 cups nonfat sour cream

6 tablespoons sugar

1 1/2 teaspoons grated lemon rind

1 tablespoon strained fresh lemon juice

2 teaspoons vanilla extract

5 large egg whites

1. Preheat oven to 350°F. Lightly oil a deep 8- to 10-cup baking dish or spray with oil spray.

2. Cook noodles in a large pot of boiling salted water uncovered over high heat, stirring occasionally, about 5 minutes or until nearly tender. Drain, rinse with cold water, and drain well. Transfer to a large bowl. Toss with vegetable oil. Stir in cottage cheese, sour cream, 4 tablespoons sugar, lemon rind, lemon juice, and vanilla.

3. Beat egg whites in a large bowl until soft peaks form. Add remaining 2 tablespoons sugar and continue beating 30 seconds or until stiff and glossy. Gently fold 1/4 of whites into noodle mixture; fold in remaining whites.

4. Transfer noodle mixture to baking dish. Bake about 50 minutes or until puffed and golden brown. Serve hot or warm.

Couscous

Basic Quick Couscous

Makes 4 to 6 servings Ⓜ or Ⓟ

Prepared this way, you can have a side dish of couscous on the table in no time. The taste of the couscous depends on the stock you use. It's a great accompaniment for fish, vegetables, chicken, or meat. It's also delicious spooned into chicken soup.

2 cups vegetable, chicken, or meat stock or water

1 tablespoon vegetable oil (optional)

One 10-ounce package couscous (1 2/3 cups)

Salt and freshly ground pepper, to taste

Combine broth and oil, if using, in a medium saucepan and bring to a boil. Stir in couscous, remove from heat, and cover. Let stand 5 minutes. Fluff with a fork before serving. Season with salt and pepper. Mix in seasonings lightly with a fork.

Quick Couscous with Cranberries and Toasted Almonds

Makes 8 servings Ⓜ

This colorful accompaniment is perfect with roasted turkey, for Purim or for Thanksgiving.

1/2 cup slivered almonds

5 1/2 cups turkey or chicken stock, or half stock and half water

Two 10-ounce packages couscous (3 1/3 cups)

1/2 cup dried cranberries

2 teaspoons chopped fresh rosemary or 1/2 teaspoon dried rosemary

Salt (optional) and freshly ground pepper, to taste

1. Preheat toaster oven or oven to 350°F. Toast almonds in oven about 5 minutes or until lightly browned. Transfer to a plate.

2. Bring stock to a boil in a medium saucepan. Stir in couscous, cranberries, and rosemary. Cover pan. Remove from heat and let stand 5 minutes. Adjust seasoning. Serve sprinkled with almonds.

Double-Walnut Couscous with Peppers and Basil

Makes 4 servings

(P)

Toasted walnuts along with intensely flavored walnut oil give this couscous dish a terrific taste. You don't need much of the oil because a little goes a long way. Sautéed mixed peppers and fresh herbs make the golden couscous a colorful and festive accompaniment for baked fish, roast chicken, or vegetable stews like ratatouille.

1/2 cup walnut pieces

2 or 3 tablespoons walnut oil

2 peppers of 2 different colors, seeds and ribs discarded, cut into 2 × 1/4-inch strips

One 10-ounce package couscous (1²/3 cups)

Salt and freshly ground pepper, to taste

2 cups boiling water

2 teaspoons strained fresh lemon juice

3 tablespoons chopped fresh parsley

3 tablespoons coarsely chopped fresh basil, plus a few small sprigs for garnish

1. Preheat oven or toaster oven to 350°F. Toast walnuts on a tray in oven about 5 minutes or until very lightly browned. Transfer immediately to a plate.

2. Heat 1 tablespoon oil in a large saucepan. Add pepper strips and sauté over medium-low heat, stirring often, about 5 minutes or until softened. Add couscous and a pinch of salt and pepper and stir mixture with a fork until blended. Pour boiling water evenly over couscous, return to a boil, and remove from heat. Cover and let stand for 5 minutes.

3. Fluff couscous with a fork. Drizzle lemon juice and remaining walnut oil over mixture and add parsley, chopped basil, and all but 2 tablespoons toasted walnuts. Toss mixture; adjust for seasoning. Transfer to a serving dish and garnish with remaining walnuts and with basil leaves. Serve hot or at room temperature.

Winter Vegetable Couscous

Makes 4 servings

(P)

Many of us associate summer cooking with Mediterranean countries but Jewish cooks from Morocco excel in creating cold weather dishes too. This dish is an easy-to-cook version of a complete entree called "couscous," that features couscous pasta (similar to lasagne that features lasagna noodles). Although yellow couscous is the usual choice of Moroccans and you can use it for this dish, I like the nutty taste and added nutrition of whole-wheat couscous. You can find whole-wheat couscous at natural foods stores. Serve hot sauce on the side.

2 tablespoons olive oil

1 large onion, diced

4 large cloves garlic, chopped

1¹/2 pounds small red potatoes, quartered

1 medium turnip, diced

1¹/2 cups hot water

3 large carrots, sliced

1¹/2 teaspoons ground cumin

1 teaspoon paprika

1/4 teaspoon hot pepper flakes, or more to taste

Salt and freshly ground pepper, to taste

2¹/4 cups vegetable stock, or stock mixed with water

One 10-ounce package whole-wheat or regular couscous (1²/3 cups)

1/4 cup currants or raisins

2 cups small cauliflower or broccoli florets

1/4 cup chopped fresh cilantro or Italian parsley (optional)

1. Heat oil in a large, heavy sauté pan. Add onion and sauté over medium heat 5 minutes or until it begins to turn golden. Stir in garlic. Add potatoes, turnip, and hot water and bring to a boil. Cover and cook over medium-low heat 5 minutes. Add carrots and bring to a boil. Reduce heat to medium-low and add cumin, paprika, pepper flakes, salt, and pepper. Cover and cook over low heat 20 minutes, occasionally stirring gently. Remove from heat.

2. Bring vegetable stock to a boil in a small saucepan. Stir in couscous and currants. Cover pan. Remove from heat and let stand 5 minutes. Season with salt and pepper. Cover and let stand until ready to serve.

3. Reheat vegetable stew. Add cauliflower and half the cilantro, if using. Cover and cook 6 minutes or until vegetables are tender. Adjust seasoning. Sprinkle with remaining cilantro. Mound couscous in shallow bowls and ladle vegetable mixture around it.

Fast and Festive Couscous with Currants, Apricots, and Pine Nuts

Makes 4 servings

This makes a lovely holiday side dish and can be made at a moment's notice. Serve it for Rosh Hashanah, Sukkot, or Friday night dinner. It's great with chicken, lamb, veal, and baked or stewed vegetables.

1/4 cup pine nuts
1³/4 cups chicken or vegetable stock
1/2 cup water
One 10-ounce package couscous (1²/3 cups)
1 green onion, white and green parts, finely chopped
1/4 cup currants
1/4 cup diced dried apricots
Salt and freshly ground pepper, to taste
Cayenne pepper, to taste

1. Toast pine nuts in a dry small skillet over medium-low heat about 2 minutes or until lightly browned. Transfer to a plate.

2. Bring stock and water to a boil in a small saucepan. Stir in couscous, green onion, currants, and apricots. Cover pan. Remove from heat and let stand 5 minutes. Taste for salt; add a little pepper and cayenne. Serve sprinkled with pine nuts.

Couscous with North African Chicken, Olive, and Lima Bean Sauce

Makes 4 to 6 servings

Couscous is wonderful with this aromatic chicken tomato sauce flavored with peppers, garlic, cilantro, and green olives. The sauce cooks quickly because it's made of ground chicken. Jewish cooks from Morocco and Tunisia use fava beans but I substitute the more widely available lima beans.

1 cup Fresh Tomato Sauce (page 585) or an 8-ounce can
2 or 3 tablespoons olive oil
1 large onion, chopped
1 large red or green bell pepper, diced
8 ounces ground chicken
4 large cloves garlic, minced
2 teaspoons ground cumin
2 teaspoons paprika
Salt and freshly ground pepper, to taste
One 28-ounce can diced tomatoes, with their juice
One 10-ounce package frozen lima beans, cooked
1/3 cup pitted green olives
2 tablespoons chopped fresh cilantro or Italian parsley
1/4 teaspoon hot sauce, or to taste
Basic Quick Couscous (page 483)

1. Prepare tomato sauce, if using homemade. Then, heat oil in a large saucepan. Add onion and bell pepper and sauté over medium heat, stirring often, for 5 minutes. Add chicken and cook over medium-low heat, stirring often, about 7 minutes or until it changes color. Add garlic, cumin, paprika, salt, and pepper. Cook over low heat, stirring, for 1 minute.

2. Add tomatoes and tomato sauce and bring to a boil, stirring. Cover and cook over low heat, stirring occasionally, for 15 minutes. Add beans and cook uncovered for about 5 more minutes or until sauce thickens to your taste. Sauce should not be dry, it will be spooned over couscous to moisten it. Add olives and cilantro to sauce and heat through. Add hot sauce to taste.

3. Prepare quick couscous. Then, spoon it into shallow bowls. Serve sauce in a separate bowl for spooning over couscous.

French-Style Couscous with Wild Mushrooms

Makes 4 servings

Instead of the usual North African seasonings, Jews in France sometimes flavor couscous the way noodles are in classic French cuisine. This couscous is flavored with shallots, thyme, chives, butter, and cheese, and topped with fresh chanterelle mushrooms. It's delicious for dairy dinners.

6 to 8 ounces fresh chanterelle or other exotic mushrooms

3 to 4 tablespoons butter

1 tablespoon vegetable oil

2 large shallots, minced

Salt and freshly ground pepper, to taste

1³/₄ cups vegetable stock

¹/₂ cup water

One 10-ounce package couscous (1²/₃ cups)

¹/₄ cup freshly grated Parmesan cheese

1¹/₂ teaspoons fresh thyme or ¹/₂ teaspoon dried

2 to 3 teaspoons snipped fresh chives

1. Gently rinse mushrooms and dry them on paper towels. If they are large, cut them lengthwise into pieces about ¹/₂-inch thick, keeping their shape.

2. Put 2 tablespoons butter in a skillet. Cut remaining butter into pieces and let soften at room temperature.

3. Add oil to butter in skillet and heat over medium heat. Add mushrooms and sauté about 3 minutes, or until mushrooms render their liquid. Add shallots, salt, and pepper and sauté over medium-high heat, tossing often, about 3 more minutes, or until mushrooms are browned and tender and liquid has evaporated.

4. Bring stock and water to a boil in a small saucepan. Stir in couscous and remaining butter. Cover pan. Remove from heat and let stand 5 minutes.

5. Reheat mushrooms if necessary. Fluff couscous mixture with a fork, tossing until butter is blended in. Add cheese, thyme, 1 teaspoon chives, and ²/₃ of mushrooms and lightly toss mixture. Adjust seasoning. Serve garnished with remaining chanterelles and sprinkled with remaining chives.

Couscous Stuffing with Peppers, Almonds, and Saffron

Makes about 3 cups stuffing,
enough for 1 chicken or 4 Cornish hens

Bake this savory, easy-to-make stuffing in chickens or Cornish hens or use it to fill zucchini boats.

2 pinches of saffron threads (about ¹/₄ teaspoon)

¹/₂ cup slivered almonds

2 to 3 tablespoons olive oil or vegetable oil

1 red bell pepper, diced

1¹/₄ cups couscous

1 teaspoon ground ginger

Salt and freshly ground pepper, to taste

3 tablespoons chopped fresh cilantro or Italian parsley

1. Crush saffron between your fingers. Add saffron to 1¹/₄ cups boiling water in a saucepan; cover and let stand 20 minutes.

2. Preheat oven or toaster oven to 400°F. Toast almonds on rimmed baking sheet or tray, stirring once or twice, for 4 minutes or until very lightly browned. Transfer to a plate and let cool.

3. Heat 2 tablespoons oil in a large saucepan. Add diced pepper and sauté over medium-low heat for 3 minutes. Add couscous, ginger, salt, pepper, and saffron flavored water. Stir once and bring to a boil. Cover and let couscous stand for 5 minutes.

4. Fluff couscous with a fork to break up any lumps. Drizzle remaining olive oil over couscous mixture and add cilantro and toasted slivered almonds. Toss the mixture and taste it for seasoning. Let stuffing cool completely before spooning it into a chicken.

Whole-Wheat Couscous with Sun-Dried and Fresh Tomatoes

Makes 4 to 5 servings

Whole-wheat couscous is a departure from tradition but it tastes great and is becoming popular on modern Jewish menus. It cooks as quickly as regular couscous and can be substituted for it in most recipes. Here is an easy, low-fat way to prepare it. It's good hot or cold, as an accompaniment for fish, chicken, or vegetarian entrees. You can find whole-wheat couscous at natural food stores and specialty markets.

1 to 2 tablespoons olive oil

1 medium onion, chopped

2¹/₂ cups chicken, beef, or vegetable stock or water

¹/₄ cup dry-pack sun-dried tomatoes, cut into bite-size pieces

Salt and freshly ground pepper, to taste

¹/₂ teaspoon dried oregano

1¹/₂ cups whole-wheat couscous

2 large ripe tomatoes, diced

2 tablespoons snipped fresh chives

2 tablespoons chopped fresh parsley

Heat oil in a medium saucepan, add chopped onion, and sauté over medium heat about 7 minutes or until tender. Add stock, sun-dried tomatoes, salt, pepper, and oregano and bring to a boil. Stir in couscous, remove from heat, and cover. Let stand 5 minutes. Fluff with a fork before serving. Lightly stir in tomatoes, chives, and parsley. Adjust seasoning. Serve hot or cold.

Whole-Wheat Couscous with Walnuts, Mushrooms, and Vegetables

Makes 4 to 5 servings

This dish is perfect for a casual family meal, like for autumn or winter evenings after Shabbat, but with its toasted walnuts and sautéed mushrooms, it's festive enough to serve when friends are coming for brunch or for a vegetarian lunch. I like to cook a few vegetables with the couscous, then embellish the mixture with the mushrooms and the nuts. I also use fresh peas and corn when they are available.

¹/₃ to ¹/₂ cup walnuts

2 medium carrots

2¹/₄ cups vegetable stock or water

1¹/₂ cups frozen peas or corn, or ³/₄ cup of each

1²/₃ cups whole-wheat couscous

Salt and freshly ground pepper, to taste

2 to 3 tablespoons vegetable oil or olive oil

1 large onion, minced

4 to 6 ounces mushrooms, halved and sliced thin

1. Preheat oven or toaster oven to 400°F. Toast walnuts in small baking pan or baking dish, stirring occasionally, for 5 minutes, or until they are aromatic and slightly darker in color. Transfer to plate and reserve at room temperature.

2. Cut carrots in half lengthwise and then into thin slices. Combine carrots with stock in a medium saucepan and bring to a boil. Cover and cook over medium-low heat for 4 minutes. Add peas and cook about 3 minutes until vegetables are just tender. Add couscous, salt, and pepper, stir, and return to a boil. Cover pan tightly, remove from heat, and let mixture stand for about 10 minutes.

3. Meanwhile, heat oil in a large skillet. Add onion and sauté over medium heat, stirring often, for 5 minutes. Add mushrooms, salt, and pepper, and sauté, stirring, for 3 minutes or until mushrooms and onions are tender and lightly browned. Adjust seasoning.

4. Fluff couscous with a fork. Add mushroom mixture and toss. Adjust seasoning. Serve garnished with walnuts.

Homemade Noodles and Kreplach

Homemade Egg Noodles

Makes about 12 ounces fresh pasta (P)

Egg noodles have long held a place of honor on the Jewish table, especially as fine noodles in the Shabbat chicken soup. Homemade fresh noodles have an incomparable flavor. It is best highlighted in simple dishes such as clear soup or simple medleys of pasta and vegetables.

Plain white flour is traditionally used for making noodles. I use a simple hand crank pasta machine to roll the dough and cut the noodles.

2¼ cups all-purpose flour, preferably unbleached

3 large eggs

½ teaspoon salt

1 tablespoon vegetable oil

About 1 tablespoon water, if needed

1. Combine flour, eggs, salt, and oil in a food processor. Process about 10 seconds or until ingredients are blended and dough holds together in sticky crumbs that can be easily pressed together. If crumbs are dry, sprinkle them with water, 1 teaspoon at a time, processing briefly after each addition; add enough water to make crumbs moist. Press dough together into a ball. Knead dough a few seconds on a work surface, flouring lightly if it sticks, until it is fairly smooth.

2. Wrap dough in plastic wrap, or set it on a plate and cover it with an inverted bowl. Let stand for 30 minutes, or refrigerate up to 4 hours; if refrigerating dough, let it stand about 15 minutes at room temperature before using.

3. Prepare a pasta rack; or generously flour 2 or 3 baking sheets for placing finished noodles. Cut dough into 6 pieces; leave 5 pieces wrapped.

4. Turn smooth rollers of a pasta machine to widest setting. Flatten 1 piece of dough to a 4-inch square and lightly flour it. Run it through machine. Fold dough in thirds so ends just meet in center, press seams together, and flatten slightly. Run dough through machine again. Fold and roll dough, lightly flouring if it feels sticky, about 7 more times or until smooth.

5. Turn dial of pasta machine 1 notch to next narrower setting. Without folding piece of dough, run it through machine. Turning dial 1 notch lower each time, repeat feeding dough without folding, flouring as necessary. Cut dough in half crosswise if it gets too long to handle. Stop when dough is ¹/₁₆-inch thick; usually this is on next to narrowest setting.

6. Hang dough sheet to dry on pasta rack or on back of a towel-lined chair. Roll remaining dough. Dry dough sheets about 10 minutes or until they are firmer and have a leathery texture; do not leave until brittle, or they will fall apart when cut.

7. To cut medium noodles: Move handle of pasta machine to wider noodle setting. Put 1 sheet of pasta through machine, holding it with 1 hand and catching noodles with other hand. If strands stick together, dough is too wet; dry remaining dough sheets a bit longer before cutting them. Separate strands. To cut fine noodles, move handle of machine to narrow noodle setting.

8. Let noodles dry on pasta rack or on floured baking sheet. Dry pasta at least 10 minutes to use immediately, or up to several hours. If noodles are on baking sheet, toss them occasionally to prevent sticking. Noodles can be refrigerated, covered loosely, on tray, or in large plastic bags up to 5 days; they can also be frozen.

Alsatian Egg Noodles

Makes about 10 ounces

These noodles are richer and more yellow than most. Jewish cooks in the French region of Alsace make them into fine noodles for serving in chicken soup, or into medium or wide ones for tossing with vegetables or accompanying stewed chicken.

2 large eggs

2 large egg yolks

1/2 teaspoon salt

1 3/4 cups plus 1 tablespoon all-purpose flour

1. Combine eggs, egg yolks, salt, and 1 1/2 cups flour in a food processor. Process about 10 seconds or until dough begins to form a ball. Add remaining flour 1 tablespoon at a time, processing briefly after each addition. Process 30 seconds or until dough forms ball. If not very smooth, knead dough a few seconds on a work surface, flouring lightly if it sticks, until it is fairly smooth.

2. Wrap dough in plastic wrap; or set it on a plate and cover it with an inverted bowl. Let stand for 30 minutes, or refrigerate up to 4 hours; if refrigerating dough, let it stand about 15 minutes at room temperature before using.

3. Prepare a pasta rack; or generously flour 2 or 3 baking sheets for placing finished noodles. Cut dough into 3 pieces; leave 2 pieces wrapped.

4. Continue from step 4 of Homemade Egg Noodles (page 488).

Whole-Wheat Noodles

Makes about 12 ounces fresh pasta

The dough for these noodles does contain some white flour, as it is much easier to handle than one made entirely of whole-wheat. (When using the pasta machine with this dough, cut these into medium rather than fine noodles; it's much easier.) I like these noodles in vegetable soups, kugels, dairy dishes, with herbed tomato sauce, and in noodle and vegetable medleys.

1 1/4 cups whole-wheat flour, preferably unbleached

1 cup all-purpose flour

3 large eggs

1 to 2 tablespoons water

1/2 teaspoon salt

1 tablespoon vegetable oil (optional)

1. Combine whole-wheat flour, white flour, eggs, 1 tablespoon water, salt, and oil, if using, in food processor. Process about 10 seconds or until ingredients are blended and dough holds together in sticky crumbs that can be easily pressed together. If crumbs are dry, sprinkle them with water, 1 teaspoon at a time, processing briefly after each addition; add enough water to make crumbs moist. Press dough together into a ball. Knead dough a few seconds on a work surface, flouring lightly if it sticks, until it is a fairly smooth ball.

2. Continue from Step 4 of Homemade Egg Noodles (page 488).

Curry Noodles

Makes 9 to 10 ounces noodles

Our relatives of Yemenite origin like these noodles as the flavors remind them of their mother's curry-like spice mixture. These noodles add a lively taste and color to chicken, turkey, and vegetable soups. They're also great with sautéed vegetables and with tomato sauce.

2 large eggs

1 tablespoon ground cumin

2 teaspoons ground turmeric

1 1/4 teaspoons ground ginger

1/2 teaspoon cayenne pepper

2 teaspoons ground coriander

1/4 teaspoon salt

2 teaspoons vegetable oil (optional)

1 1/2 cups all-purpose flour

1 to 5 teaspoons water, if needed

1. Combine eggs with cumin, turmeric, ginger, cayenne, coriander, salt, and oil, if using, in food processor; process to blend. Add flour. Process about 10 seconds until ingredients are well blended and

dough holds together in sticky crumbs that can be easily pressed together. If crumbs are dry, sprinkle with water, about 1 teaspoon at a time, processing about 5 seconds after each addition, adding enough to obtain moist crumbs. Press dough together into a ball. Transfer to a work surface and knead a few seconds, flouring lightly if dough sticks to surface, until it is fairly smooth.

2. Continue from Step 4 of Homemade Egg Noodles (page 488).

Herb-Garlic Noodles

Makes 9 to 10 ounces noodles

These tasty green-flecked noodles add an elegant touch to chicken and vegetable soups. They also make a lovely accompaniment for fish or for springtime vegetable stews.

3 medium cloves garlic, peeled

1/2 cup small sprigs fresh parsley

2 large eggs

1/4 teaspoon salt

1 tablespoon dried basil

1 tablespoon dried thyme

1 tablespoon dried oregano

2 teaspoons vegetable oil (optional)

1 1/2 cups all-purpose flour

1 to 5 teaspoons water, if needed

1. Mince garlic in food processor. Add parsley and process until it is minced. Add eggs, salt, basil, thyme, oregano, and oil, if using, and process until well blended. Add flour. Process about 10 seconds until ingredients are well blended and dough holds together in sticky crumbs that can be easily pressed together. If crumbs are dry, sprinkle with water, about 1 teaspoon at a time, processing about 5 seconds after each addition, adding enough to obtain moist crumbs. Press dough together into a ball. Transfer to a work surface and knead a few seconds, flouring lightly if dough sticks to surface, until it is fairly smooth.

2. Continue from step 4 of Homemade Egg Noodles (page 488).

Spinach Noodles

Makes 9 to 10 ounces noodles

The fresh, green color of spinach noodles makes them inviting. They are a pleasant change from plain noodles, especially in dairy dishes. They're also terrific in vegetable soups.

8-ounce bunch fresh spinach, 3/4 of a 10-ounce bag spinach leaves or one 10-ounce package frozen leaf spinach

1 large egg

1/4 teaspoon salt

2 teaspoons vegetable oil (optional)

1 1/2 cups all-purpose flour

1 to 5 teaspoons water, if needed

1. If using fresh spinach, remove large stems and rinse leaves well. Put fresh or frozen spinach in a saucepan containing enough boiling salted water to generously cover leaves. Boil uncovered over high heat, stirring, about 2 minutes or until wilted. Drain in a colander, rinse until cool, and squeeze dry. Puree spinach in food processor. Measure puree; return 1/2 cup to processor. (You can save extra puree for adding to sauces or soups.)

2. Add egg, salt, and oil, if using, to spinach and process until blended. Add flour. Process about 10 seconds until ingredients are well blended and dough holds together in sticky crumbs that can be easily pressed together. If crumbs are dry, sprinkle with water, about 1 teaspoon at a time, processing about 5 seconds after each addition, adding enough to obtain moist crumbs. Press dough together into a ball. Transfer to a work surface and knead a few seconds, flouring lightly if dough sticks to surface, until it is fairly smooth.

3. Continue from step 4 of Homemade Egg Noodles (page 488).

Basic Kreplach

Makes about 6 appetizer servings

Kreplach are a classic of the Ashkenazic kitchen. They are known as Jewish ravioli or tortellini because like these Italian pastas, they are filled pockets of egg noodle dough. They can be triangular, square, half moon, or ring shaped. Cooked chicken or beef are the usual fillings but kasha or potatoes are also used.

Kreplach are most often served in clear chicken soup. I cook them in water first so their starch doesn't cloud the soup, then add them to the soup. Other ways to enjoy kreplach is to toss them with fried onions or to simply drizzle them with oil and heat them in the oven.

Uncooked kreplach do not keep for long in the refrigerator. You can make them about 6 hours ahead and keep them in one layer on a floured baking sheet or tray, lightly covered. If you freeze them, they'll keep for longer. Once you've cooked them, they'll keep for 2 days in the refrigerator. Cooked kreplach can also be frozen.

2¹/4 cups all-purpose flour, preferably unbleached

3 large eggs

¹/2 teaspoon salt

1 tablespoon vegetable oil

About 1 tablespoon water, if needed

Chicken or Meat Filling for Kreplach (pages 492–493)

1. Combine flour, eggs, salt, and oil in a food processor. Process about 10 seconds or until ingredients are blended and dough holds together in sticky crumbs that can be easily pressed together. If crumbs are dry, sprinkle them with water, 1 teaspoon at a time, processing briefly after each addition; add enough water to make crumbs moist. Press dough together into a ball. Knead dough a few seconds on a work surface, flouring lightly if it sticks, until it is fairly smooth.

2. Wrap dough in plastic wrap, or set it on a plate and cover it with an inverted bowl. Let stand for 30 minutes, or refrigerate up to 4 hours; if refrigerating dough, let it stand about 15 minutes at room temperature before using.

3. Prepare a pasta rack; or generously flour 2 or 3 baking sheets for placing finished noodles. Cut dough into 6 pieces; leave 5 pieces wrapped.

4. Turn smooth rollers of a pasta machine to widest setting. Flatten 1 piece of dough to a 4-inch square and lightly flour it. Run it through machine. Fold dough in thirds so ends just meet in center, press seams together, and flatten slightly. Run dough through machine again. Fold and roll dough, lightly flouring if it feels sticky, about 7 more times or until smooth.

5. Turn dial of pasta machine 1 notch to next narrower setting. Without folding piece of dough, run it through machine. Turning dial 1 notch lower each time, repeat feeding dough without folding, flouring as necessary. Cut dough in half crosswise if it gets too long to handle. Stop when dough is ¹/16-inch thick; usually this is on next to narrowest setting.

6. Prepare dough through step 5. Prepare filling. Then, to form the kreplach, lay dough sheet on floured surface. Place filling in ¹/2 teaspoon mounds 1¹/2 inches apart on sheet of dough. Cut into 2¹/2-inch squares. Brush 2 adjacent sides of each square lightly with water. Fold over into a triangle, pressing moistened sides to dry sides; press edges firmly to seal. Put each on floured baking sheet as it is completed. Roll, shape, and fill remaining dough, one piece at a time.

7. To cook kreplach: Add half of kreplach to a large pot of boiling salted water. Bring to a boil, reduce heat so water simmers, cover, and cook over low heat 15 minutes or until pasta is tender. Remove kreplach with slotted spoon and drain in a colander. Bring cooking liquid to boil and cook remaining kreplach.

8. To serve, drain kreplach again if necessary and transfer to heated soup bowls or a shallow serving dish. Pour hot soup or sauce over kreplach.

Won Ton Kreplach

Makes about 25 small kreplach,
5 or 6 appetizer servings

These days it's easy to find won ton wrappers in kosher markets, and many shoppers know that they are good for making kreplach. Some of them even specify on the label that these wrappers are suitable for won tons or kreplach. They taste very good and certainly are faster than making and rolling your own noodle dough. Serve them in chicken soup, with tomato sauce, or with sautéed onions.

Chicken or Meat Filling for Kreplach (this page and page 493)

About 30 won ton wrappers, thawed if frozen

1. Prepare filling. Then, generously flour 2 or 3 trays or baking sheets. Keep won ton wrappers covered with a dampened towel or keep package closed to prevent drying, removing only the one you are shaping. Put 1 won ton wrapper on a work surface and mound 1¹/₂ teaspoons of filling in center. Moisten 2 adjoining edges with water. Fold in half to make a triangle, pressing dry edges to moistened ones. Pinch edges together, pressing out excess air and sealing them well. Transfer kreplach to floured baking sheet. You can keep them, covered loosely with plastic wrap, 1 day in refrigerator.

2. Oil a large baking sheet. To cook kreplach: Bring a large pot of water to a boil; add salt, then ¹/₃ to ¹/₂ of the kreplach. Reduce heat so water simmers and cook kreplach, stirring occasionally, about 2 minutes or until tender but firm to the bite. Remove with a large slotted skimmer or slotted spoon and drain very well. Transfer to oiled baking sheet.

3. To serve, drain kreplach again if necessary and transfer to heated soup bowls or a shallow serving dish. Pour hot soup or sauce over kreplach.

Meat Filling for Kreplach

Makes about 1 cup, enough for
6 appetizer servings of kreplach

Beef filling is the most traditional for kreplach but you can also use veal. Serve these kreplach in clear chicken soup or beef soup. To shape the kreplach, follow the instructions in Basic Kreplach (page 491).

1 or 2 tablespoons vegetable oil

¹/₂ large onion, minced

2 large cloves garlic, minced

2 teaspoons minced fresh rosemary or ¹/₂ teaspoon dried rosemary, crumbled

4 teaspoons minced fresh sage or 1¹/₂ teaspoons dried sage, crumbled

6 ounces ground beef

Salt and freshly ground pepper, to taste

¹/₄ cup dry white wine, beef or vegetable stock, or water

1 large egg yolk

3 tablespoons dry bread crumbs

1. Heat oil in a medium skillet. Add onion and cook over medium-low heat, stirring often, about 5 minutes or until softened. Add garlic, rosemary, and sage. Raise heat to medium and add beef and pepper. Cook, stirring to separate clumps of ground meat and to blend meat with onion mixture, about 5 minutes or until meat changes color.

2. Add wine and bring to a boil. Simmer over medium-low heat about 5 minutes or until wine is absorbed. Adjust seasoning. Transfer to a medium bowl. Cool to room temperature. Stir in egg yolk and bread crumbs. Cover and refrigerate 30 minutes before using, or up to 1 day.

Chicken Filling for Kreplach

Makes about 1 cup, enough for
6 appetizer servings

Traditional recipes for kreplach fillings often call for cooked meats left over from making soup. Generally they are blended with sautéed onions. Old-fashioned formulas call for chicken fat for sautéing them but I prefer vegetable oil.

To shape the kreplach, follow the instructions in Basic Kreplach (page 491).

2 cups chicken stock or broth

7 ounces boneless chicken thighs

2 tablespoons vegetable oil

1 large onion, chopped

1 small clove garlic, minced (optional)

2 teaspoons chopped fresh dill or 1 teaspoon dried

Salt and freshly ground pepper, to taste

Hot paprika or cayenne pepper, to taste

1 large egg, beaten

1. Bring stock to a simmer in a small saucepan. Add chicken and return to a simmer. Cover and poach over low heat 10 to 15 minutes or until tender. Remove chicken; reserve stock for soups. Cut chicken into large dice.

2. Heat oil in a medium skillet, add onion, and sauté over medium-low heat about 7 minutes or until beginning to brown. Add garlic, if using, chicken, dill, salt, pepper, and hot paprika. Sauté over low heat, stirring often, about 2 minutes so flavors blend. Transfer mixture to a bowl and let cool slightly.

3. Grind chicken onion mixture in food processor until fine. Transfer to a bowl. Taste, and add more salt, pepper, and hot paprika if needed. Thoroughly mix in egg. Cover and refrigerate 30 minutes before using, or up to 1 day.

❧ Sauces

Duxelles Sauce for Savory Kugels

Makes 4 servings

Serve this easy-to-make mushroom sauce with Springtime Noodle Kugel (page 478) and all sorts of other vegetable and nonsweet noodle kugels. It's also delicious with Potato Kneidel (page 443). Vary the stock you use according to the menu—meat or chicken stock for fleishig meals, vegetable stock for pareve or milchig ones. This is a convenient sauce to make when you happen to have mushrooms on hand in your freezer. An added bonus—it's tasty and healthful as well.

8 ounces mushrooms, rinsed and patted dry

1 tablespoon vegetable oil

1 small shallot or green onion, minced

Salt and freshly ground pepper, to taste

1/4 cup dry white wine

4 teaspoons tomato paste

1 1/2 cups beef, chicken, or vegetable stock

1 teaspoon dried thyme

1 tablespoon cornstarch dissolved in 2 tablespoons water

2 tablespoons chopped fresh parsley

1. Chop mushrooms in food processor with brief pulses so they are chopped into fine pieces but are not pureed. Heat oil in a medium skillet. Add shallot and sauté over low heat about 30 seconds or until soft but not brown. Add mushrooms and sprinkle with salt and pepper. Cook over high heat, stirring, 3 to 5 minutes or until mixture is dry.

2. Mix duxelles with wine, tomato paste, stock, and thyme in a medium saucepan. Bring to boil. Reduce heat to medium-low. Add dissolved cornstarch, stirring. Return to boil. Add parsley. Season with salt and pepper. Serve hot.

Creamy Tomato-Mushroom Sauce for Kugels

Makes about 4 servings

For noodle kugels served at dairy meals, this sauce makes a luscious accompaniment. It is enlivened by Provencal herbs.

2 to 4 tablespoons butter

8 ounces small mushrooms, quartered

Salt and freshly ground pepper, to taste

1 cup tomato sauce

2 tablespoons chopped fresh basil or 2 teaspoons
   dried basil

2 tablespoons chopped fresh sage or 2 teaspoons
   dried sage

1 tablespoon chopped fresh rosemary or 1 teaspoon
   dried rosemary

1/4 cup whipping cream

1. Melt 2 tablespoons butter in a medium skillet over medium heat. Add mushrooms, salt, and pepper and sauté over medium heat about 5 minutes or until lightly browned. Transfer mixture to a medium bowl. Add tomato sauce, basil, sage, and rosemary to skillet and bring to a simmer. Stir in cream and return to a simmer. Return mushroom mixture to skillet. Adjust seasoning.

2. Reheat sauce before serving. With sauce over low heat, add remaining 2 tablespoons butter if desired. Stir until blended into sauce; do not boil. Serve hot.

Hearty Spaghetti Sauce

Makes about 3 1/2 cups, 6 to 8 servings   **P**

The secret to this thick, rich, yet meatless sauce is to use vegetarian ground "meat" made of soy. Use it as a pareve spaghetti sauce, with or without cheese, or layer it with noodles and cheeses to make Lasagne Kugel with Ricotta-Parmesan Filling and Rich Tomato Sauce (page 481). You can keep it for 3 days in the refrigerator or store it in your freezer.

2 to 3 tablespoons olive oil

1 medium onion, minced

1/2 medium carrot, chopped

1 rib celery, chopped

12 ounces soy ground "meat"

2 pounds ripe tomatoes, peeled, seeded, and chopped,
   or two 28-ounce cans tomatoes, drained well

5 large cloves garlic, minced

1 bay leaf

1 teaspoon dried oregano, crumbled

1/4 to 1/2 teaspoon hot red pepper flakes, if desired

Salt and freshly ground pepper, to taste

3 tablespoons tomato paste

1. Heat oil in a medium, heavy stew pan or Dutch oven over medium heat. Add onion, carrot, and celery and cook, stirring, about 10 minutes or until onion is soft but not brown. Add soy meat and sauté over medium heat, crumbling with a fork, about 3 minutes.

2. Add tomatoes, garlic, bay leaf, oregano, pepper flakes, salt, and pepper and bring to a boil, stirring. Cover and cook over low heat, stirring occasionally, for 20 minutes; if using canned tomatoes, crush them with spoon a few times. Discard bay leaf. Stir in tomato paste and simmer uncovered medium heat for 15 minutes, stirring often, until sauce is thick. Adjust seasoning.

Peanut Butter Dressing

Makes about 1¼ cups, 4 to 6 servings

Flavored with fresh ginger, garlic, and chili oil, this rich, lively dressing is delicious with noodles, raw or cooked vegetables, chicken, and turkey. It's ready in no time.

¹/₂ cup creamy peanut butter

¹/₂ cup warm vegetable stock, or more if needed

2 or 3 tablespoons sesame oil

3 tablespoons soy sauce, or more if needed

1 tablespoon rice vinegar

1 teaspoon Asian chili oil or Tabasco sauce, or to taste

1 tablespoon minced garlic

1 tablespoon minced peeled fresh ginger

1 teaspoon sugar

Combine peanut butter, ¹/₂ cup stock, 2 tablespoons sesame oil, 3 tablespoons soy sauce, rice vinegar, chili oil, garlic, ginger, and sugar in a blender or food processor. Process until well blended. If dressing is too thick, add another tablespoon or two of vegetable stock. Taste and add more sesame oil, soy sauce, or chili oil if you like.

Easy Honey-Vanilla Sauce

Makes about 1½ cups, about 6 servings

Serve this creamy fat-free sauce with Low-Fat Sweet Noodle Kugel (page 483) or with fruit for dipping.

³/₄ cup nonfat yogurt

³/₄ cup nonfat sour cream

3 tablespoons honey

2 teaspoons vanilla extract

1 teaspoon grated lemon rind

2 to 3 teaspoons strained fresh lemon juice (optional)

Mix yogurt, sour cream, honey, and vanilla in a bowl. Stir in lemon rind. Taste, and add lemon juice if you like. Serve cold.

Rice and Other Grains

Basic Rice Dishes
499

Israeli Rice Pilaf

Molded Rice

Rice with Yemenite Flair

Herbed Rice

Dairy-Free Saffron Risotto

Rice with Vegetables
501

Rice with Stewed Mushrooms

Roman Rice with Eggplant

Lebanese Lentil and Rice
Casserole (Majadrah)

Red Chard with Rice

Basmati Rice with Fava Beans
and Dill

Rice with Fresh Peas

Lazy-Day Stuffed Cabbage

Mushroom Risotto with
Parmesan

Rice Kugels and Casseroles
506

Sephardic Rice Casserole
with Peppers

Springtime Rice Kugel with
Asparagus and Peas

Rice, Chicken, and Vegetable
Pashtidah

Roasted Pepper and Rice
Casserole with Olives

Rice with Fruit and Nuts
505

Valerie's Two-Way Shabbat Rice

Red Rice with Raisins

Almond, Fruit, and Rice
Stuffing

P = *Pareve*   **D** = *Dairy*   **M** = *Meat*

Brown Rice
509

Brown Rice Pilaf with Feta
Cheese and Onions

Brown Rice Pilaf with Peppers

Brown Rice Ring with
Curried Zucchini

Confetti Brown Rice with
Toasted Pecans

Savory Pilaf with Dried Fruit

Kasha
514

Kasha with Browned Onions

Egg-Free Kasha

Kasha with Smoked Turkey,
Mushrooms, and Ginger

Colorful Kasha and Bow-Tie
Pasta Medley

Kasha and Noodle Kugel

Kasha with Turkey Chili

Wild Rice
520

Wild Rice with Shiitake
Mushrooms and Leeks

Wild Rice with Pecans and
Winter Squash

Wild and White Rice with
Dried Fruit

Sephardic Wild Rice
with Almonds, Pine Nuts,
and Pistachios

Bulgur Wheat
511

Bulgur Wheat Pilaf

Bulgur Wheat with Sweet
and Sour Squash

Bulgur Wheat with Turnip
Greens and Red Pepper

Spicy Bulgur Wheat
with Vegetables

Bulgur Wheat with Green
Onions and Pecans

Bulgur Wheat with Chickpeas,
Tomatoes, and Coriander

Barley
518

Baked Barley with Aromatic
Vegetables

Barley with Herbs and
Roasted Peppers

Barley with Chicken
and Spinach Pesto

Cornmeal
522

Mamaliga

Oven-Toasted Mamaliga

Baked Mamaliga with
Kashkaval Cheese

Rice is so popular among Sephardic Jews that some include it in their menu every day to accompany whatever they are eating, whether it is meat, fish, or vegetables. It appears on Ashkenazic tables also but not as often.

The favorite Sephardic way of cooking rice, which has been adopted by most Israelis, is as pilaf. Pilaf is more richly flavored than boiled or steamed rice. People also like it because the rice grains stay separate and fluffy and do not stick together. First the rice is sautéed in oil, often with minced onion, then cooked with stock, broth, or water in a covered saucepan over very low heat. Kosher cooks generally use chicken broth for cooking the rice for *fleishig* meals; this way it gains an especially rich taste.

Besides the basic white rice pilaf, Sephardic Jews often prepare red and yellow pilaf. Red pilaf is flavored with tomato, and yellow with turmeric or saffron and sometimes cumin as well. Pilaf might be a simple accompaniment or might become a more substantial dish by being mixed with a variety of vegetables or sometimes meat. A popular holiday garnish is fried or toasted almonds or other nuts as well as raisins.

For festive menus, many people now cook with aromatic basmati rice, which has become widely available in Israel as well as in kosher grocery stores in the United States.

Another grain used often by Jews from eastern Mediterranean and Middle Eastern countries is bulgur wheat. This quick-cooking form of wheat is made into pilaf, just like rice. It is especially common in the cooking of Jews from Iraq, Kurdistan, and Lebanon.

Whole wheat berries also appear on the Jewish table. Because of their long cooking time, they are most often included in the overnight Shabbat stew called *cholent* (Yiddish) or *hamin* (Hebrew). During the long, slow cooking, they absorb the aromas of the meat in the stew.

Barley, like wheat, has been known since biblical times. It also is cooked in *cholent* and made into casseroles and side dishes. Its best-known use is in soups.

A favorite grain in the Ashkenazic kitchen is buckwheat, or kasha. This healthful grain is cooked with broth as an accompaniment for meat and chicken. Because kasha's flavor is assertive, many people mix it with pasta and with sautéed onions to balance its taste. Kasha is also used to fill pastries or is simmered in milk as a breakfast cereal.

❦ Basic Rice Dishes

Israeli Rice Pilaf

Makes 4 to 6 servings

Pilaf is the favorite way of cooking rice in Israeli homes as well as in restaurants. The Sephardic Jews brought this technique to Israel and it has been adopted by nearly everyone else. The reason it is so popular is that the rice grains stay separate and do not clump together. Most often the rice is left white but yellow and red versions also appear on many tables.

The principle of making rice pilaf is to sauté the rice. Some people sauté the rice until the grains turn milky white; others continue to sauté until it browns. Whether to flavor the rice with a sautéed onion depends on the family's taste.

2 to 3 tablespoons vegetable oil
1 medium onion, finely chopped (optional)
1¹/₂ cups long-grain white rice
3 cups hot chicken, beef, or vegetable stock or water
Salt and freshly ground pepper, to taste

1. Heat oil in a large sauté pan or wide casserole. Add onion, if using, and cook over low heat, stirring, about 7 minutes or until soft but not brown. Add rice and sauté, stirring, about 2 minutes or until the grains turn milky white, or a few more minutes if you want rice to brown.

2. Add stock, salt, and pepper. Stir once with a fork and cover. Cook over low heat, without stirring, for 18 minutes. Taste rice; if not yet tender, simmer 2 more minutes. Adjust seasoning. Cover and let stand for 10 minutes or until ready to serve. Gently fluff with a fork. Serve hot.

Molded Rice

Makes 6 to 8 servings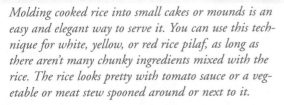

Molding cooked rice into small cakes or mounds is an easy and elegant way to serve it. You can use this technique for white, yellow, or red rice pilaf, as long as there aren't many chunky ingredients mixed with the rice. The rice looks pretty with tomato sauce or a vegetable or meat stew spooned around or next to it.

Israeli Rice Pilaf (page 499)
Sephardic Tomato Sauce (page 375)
6 to 8 small sprigs curly parsley (optional)

1. Prepare the pilaf and the sauce. Then, preheat oven to 350°F. Oil or butter six to eight 4- or 5-ounce ramekins. Spoon cooked pilaf into the ramekins. Press with a spoon so the rice is lightly packed, but do not crush grains.

2. Put molds in a roasting pan. Add enough simmering water to come halfway up sides of molds. Cover with buttered or oiled parchment paper. Bake for 10 minutes. Leave rice in mold in warm water until ready to serve.

3. Heat sauce in a saucepan. To serve, unmold the ramekins onto plates. Spoon a little sauce around rice. Top mound of rice with a parsley sprig, if using. Serve remaining sauce separately.

Rice with Yemenite Flair

Makes 7 or 8 servings

Although the traditional diet of the Jews of Yemen was based more on bread than on rice, my mother-in-law, who was born in Yemen, loved making this delicious golden rice. What makes it special is the cooking liquid—her spiced chicken or beef soup, a staple in her kitchen. (See My Mother-in-Law's Spicy Chicken Soup, page 261.) When I don't have this soup on hand, I use chicken or meat stock and season the rice with the same seasonings—garlic, cumin, turmeric, and black pepper. For meatless meals, I use vegetable stock.

2 or 3 tablespoons vegetable oil
1 large onion, chopped
4 large cloves garlic, chopped
2¹/₂ teaspoons ground cumin
1 teaspoon ground turmeric
¹/₂ teaspoon freshly ground pepper
2 cups long-grain white rice
4 cups chicken, beef, vegetable stock or broth, or stock mixed with water
Salt, to taste
3 tablespoons finely chopped fresh cilantro (optional)

1. Heat oil in a large saucepan. Add onion and sauté over medium heat, stirring often, about 7 minutes or until beginning to turn golden. Stir in garlic, cumin, turmeric, and pepper. Cook, stirring, for 1 minute. Add rice and sauté, stirring, for 3 minutes or until rice is well coated with onion and spices.

2. Add stock and salt. Stir once and bring to a boil over high heat. Cover and cook over low heat, without stirring, 18 to 20 minutes or until rice is tender. Remove from heat and let stand, covered, for 10 minutes. Adjust seasoning. Fluff rice with a fork just before serving, and add cilantro, if using. Serve hot.

Herbed Rice

Makes 4 to 6 servings

This simple dish is perfect with poached or baked chicken, with veal dishes, and with vegetable stews.

2 to 3 tablespoons vegetable oil or olive oil

1 medium onion, finely chopped

1¹/₂ cups long-grain white rice

3 cups hot chicken, beef, or vegetable stock or water

1 bay leaf

1 large sprig fresh thyme or ¹/₂ teaspoon dried thyme

Salt and freshly ground pepper, to taste

2 tablespoons chopped fresh Italian parsley

1 tablespoon chopped fresh chives

1 tablespoon chopped fresh basil or 2 teaspoons chopped tarragon or snipped dill (optional)

1. Heat oil in a large sauté pan or wide stew pan. Add onion and cook over low heat, stirring, about 7 minutes or until soft but not brown. Add rice and sauté, stirring, about 2 minutes or until the grains turn milky white.

2. Add stock, bay leaf, thyme, salt, and pepper. Stir once with a fork and cover. Cook over low heat, without stirring, for 18 minutes. Taste rice; if not yet tender, simmer 2 more minutes. Adjust seasoning. Cover and let stand for 10 minutes or until ready to serve. Remove bay leaf and thyme sprig. Fluff rice with a fork and gently stir in parsley, chives, and basil, if using. Serve hot.

Dairy-Free Saffron Risotto

Makes 4 to 6 servings Ⓜ

Although restaurant risotto tends to be full of cheese and butter, Jews in Italy make it without dairy foods so it can be served with meat. With a flavorful broth, the risotto is delicious. If you've never made risotto before, you'll discover that it's easier to prepare than you expected.

3¹/₂ cups chicken or veal stock

¹/₄ teaspoon saffron threads

2 to 3 tablespoons olive oil

1 medium onion, chopped

2 large cloves garlic, minced

1¹/₂ cups Arborio rice or other round risotto rice

¹/₂ cup dry white wine

Salt and freshly ground pepper, to taste

¹/₃ cup chopped fresh Italian parsley

1. Combine stock and saffron in a small saucepan and bring to a simmer. Cover and keep warm over very low heat.

2. Heat oil in a medium, heavy saucepan. Add onion and sauté over medium heat for 5 minutes or until soft but not brown. Add garlic and rice and sauté, stirring, 2 minutes or until rice is coated with onion mixture. Add wine and stir. Simmer over medium heat 1 to 2 minutes or until wine evaporates.

3. Add 2 cups of hot saffron-flavored broth and stir. Simmer uncovered, stirring occasionally, 9 to 10 minutes or until liquid is absorbed. Add remaining broth, stir, and cook 8 minutes or until rice is just tender but still a little firm, al dente. Remove from heat. Season with salt and pepper. Let stand 2 to 3 minutes. Add parsley. Serve in deep dishes.

✼ Rice with Vegetables

Rice with Stewed Mushrooms

Makes 4 servings

Rice and mushrooms is one of our family's favorite combinations, especially for Friday night dinners. We cook the mushrooms slowly with onions, garlic, cumin, and thyme so they absorb the seasonings, then toss the mixture with hot cooked rice. This dish is a good partner for just about any entree, from fish to meat to vegetables. We sauté the mushrooms in olive oil for meat or poultry dinners, and in half oil and half butter for fish or vegetarian meals.

3 to 4 tablespoons olive oil or half oil and half butter

1 large onion, chopped

3 large cloves garlic, chopped

1 pound small mushrooms, quartered

Salt and freshly ground pepper, to taste

1 teaspoon dried thyme

1 teaspoon paprika

1¹/₂ teaspoons ground cumin

Cayenne pepper, to taste

3 to 4 cups hot cooked rice, white or brown

3 tablespoons chopped fresh parsley

1. Heat oil in a large skillet. Add onion and sauté over medium heat about 10 minutes or until tender. Add garlic, mushrooms, salt, pepper, thyme, paprika, and cumin. Sauté, stirring often, about 15 minutes or until mushrooms are very tender and well flavored and any liquid in pan has evaporated. Reduce heat towards end of cooking time if necessary. Add cayenne.

2. Just before serving, toss hot rice with hot mushrooms in a serving dish. Add parsley and toss gently. Adjust seasoning.

Roman Rice with Eggplant

Makes about 6 servings

Lightly seasoned with garlic and parsley, this rice pilaf is traditional on menus of the Jews of Rome. It makes a convenient Shabbat side dish as it combines both a grain and vegetable in a single pot. For the cooking liquid you can use water or vegetable stock. If you wish to serve the rice with meat or poultry, use all or part chicken, beef, or veal stock.

1¹/₂ pounds eggplant

3 to 4 tablespoons olive oil or vegetable oil

Salt and freshly ground pepper, to taste

2 large cloves garlic, chopped

¹/₂ cup chopped fresh Italian parsley

1¹/₂ cups long-grain white rice

3 cups water or vegetable, beef, or veal stock

1. Peel eggplants if skins are tough. Cut eggplants into small dice. Heat 2 tablespoons oil in a large sauté pan or stew pan. Add eggplant, salt, and pepper, and sauté over medium heat for 5 minutes. Add garlic and half the parsley. Sauté, stirring often, 2 minutes. Cover and cook over medium-low heat, stirring often, about 7 minutes or until eggplant is nearly tender.

2. Add remaining oil and heat briefly. Add rice and sauté, stirring, about 5 minutes, so that rice absorbs flavors in pan. Add water or stock and bring to a boil. Cover and cook over low heat without stirring for 15 to 20 minutes or until rice is just tender.

3. Adjust seasoning. Use fork to fluff rice. Gently stir in 3 tablespoons of parsley. Serve hot, sprinkled with remaining tablespoon parsley.

Lebanese Lentil and Rice Casserole

Majadrah

Makes about 4 servings

I learned about this time-honored dish from Suzanne Elmaleh, who was born in Lebanon and spent most of her life in Jerusalem. When she lived in Beirut more than fifty years ago, this regional specialty, called majadrah *in Arabic, was a dish for the servants and the poor. In other homes it appeared on the table on laundry day, when there was little time to cook. Now the dish has become very popular in Israel, not only in homes but in restaurants too. Serve it as a vegetarian entree or as an accompaniment for chicken or meat.*

Majadrah is popular throughout the Middle East. The Lebanese version is the most delicately seasoned, relying on the natural flavor of the lentils, rice, and sautéed onions.

1 cup lentils

2 cups water

3 to 5 tablespoons vegetable oil

2 large onions, chopped

1¼ cups long-grain white rice

Salt and freshly ground pepper, to taste

Cayenne pepper, to taste

1. Combine lentils and water in a medium saucepan. Bring to a boil. Cover and cook over medium heat about 20 minutes or until lentils are just tender. Drain liquid into a measuring cup and add enough water to make 2½ cups; reserve.

2. Heat oil in a heavy skillet. Add onions and sauté over medium heat, stirring occasionally, about 15 minutes or until they are well browned. Add onions and their oil to pan of lentils. Add measured liquid and bring to a boil. Add rice and salt and return to a boil. Cover and cook over low heat without stirring about 20 minutes or until rice is tender. Adjust seasoning, adding pepper and cayenne. Serve hot.

Red Chard with Rice

Makes 4 servings

Chard and other greens cooked with rice is a popular dish in many eastern Mediterranean countries such as Egypt, Lebanon, Syria, Armenia, Turkey, and Greece. You can use green Swiss chard, but if you use red chard, the stems will add an attractive pink color. For a tasty Sephardic menu, serve this dish with roast chicken or grilled fish. If you like, sprinkle the rice with a few tablespoons toasted almonds or pecans for a festive touch.

One ³/₄-pound bunch red chard

1 to 2 tablespoons olive oil

1 large onion, chopped

1 cup long-grain white rice

Salt and freshly ground pepper, to taste

2 cups boiling water

1. Rinse chard thoroughly by placing leaves and stems in a large bowl of cold water, lifting them out and putting them in a strainer, then discarding water. Repeat several times until water is no longer sandy. Cut chard stems into ¹/₂-inch slices. Chop leaves.

2. Heat oil in a heavy sauté pan. Add onion and sauté over medium heat 5 minutes, stirring often. Add chard stems and sauté 2 minutes. Add leaves, cover, and cook over low heat, stirring occasionally, 5 minutes or until wilted. Add rice, sprinkle with salt and pepper, and mix with greens. Add boiling water, cover, and cook over low heat without stirring about 18 minutes or until rice is tender. Adjust seasoning. Serve hot.

Basmati Rice with Fava Beans and Dill

Makes 4 to 6 servings (P)

Rice with saffron is one of the best-loved dishes in the Iranian Jewish kitchen. The rice is varied in infinite ways. One popular way to prepare it for springtime is to dot the rice with fresh, bright green fava beans. If fava beans are not available, you can substitute lima beans (see Note).

2 pounds fresh fava beans

1/4 teaspoon saffron

1 1/2 cups basmati rice, rinsed well

2 tablespoons olive oil

4 large cloves garlic, minced

Salt and freshly ground pepper, to taste

1/3 cup chopped fresh dill

1. Remove fava beans from pods. Put beans in a medium saucepan of boiling salted water and cook uncovered over high heat for 3 to 5 minutes or until just tender. Drain the beans, rinse with cold water, and drain well. Peel off and discard the tough outer skins.

2. Soak saffron in 2 tablespoons warm water in a small bowl for about 15 minutes.

3. Bring 6 cups water to a boil in a large, heavy saucepan. Add rice and cook it over high heat for 12 minutes or until barely tender. Drain, rinse with luke-warm water, and drain well.

4. Heat oil in same saucepan, add garlic, and cook over low heat about 30 seconds. Add fava beans, salt, and pepper, and toss 1 to 2 minutes over heat. Add rice and toss very gently. Add saffron liquid. Cover tightly and cook over low heat for 5 minutes. Add dill, salt, and pepper and toss very gently. Serve hot.

Note: If fresh fava beans are not available, use a 10-ounce package of frozen fava beans or lima beans. Cook them according to package directions and add them to rice

Rice with Fresh Peas

Makes 4 servings **D** or **P**

This light, fresh side dish flavored with sautéed sweet onions is great for Shavuot or for other late spring or early summer dinners. It makes a terrific accompaniment for broiled salmon. When you can find fresh peas, I recommend them but if time is short, you can use frozen ones.

The rice is cooked like pasta, then rinsed. This is a technique I learned when I worked in a restaurant in Paris. It makes it easy to cook the rice ahead. All it needs is quick reheating with a little butter or oil.

1 cup long-grain white rice

1 pound fresh peas (about 1 cup shelled), or 1 cup frozen peas

2 to 4 tablespoons butter or vegetable oil

1/2 cup minced onion, preferably sweet onion

Salt and freshly ground pepper, to taste

2 tablespoons chopped fresh Italian parsley or basil

1. Bring about 6 cups water to a boil in a large saucepan and add a pinch of salt. Add rice, stir once, and cook uncovered over high heat about 12 to 14 minutes or until tender; check by tasting. Drain in a strainer, rinse with cold water until cool, and let drain for 5 minutes.

2. Cook peas uncovered in a pan of boiling salted water about 7 minutes for fresh peas or about 3 minutes for frozen ones, or until just tender. Drain thoroughly.

3. Melt 2 tablespoons butter in a large skillet over medium-low heat. Add onion and sauté about 5 minutes or until softened but not brown. Add peas, rice, and salt and pepper. Heat mixture over low heat, tossing lightly with a fork, until hot. Add remaining butter if desired. Cover pan and let rice stand about 2 minutes, or until butter melts. Add chopped parsley; toss again lightly. Adjust seasoning. Serve hot.

Lazy-Day Stuffed Cabbage

Makes 4 to 6 servings

When I would like the flavor of stuffed cabbage but I don't have time to stuff individual leaves, I use an old formula from my husband's Sephardic family. You simply cook the cabbage and its rice stuffing together. Their stuffing is enhanced with ground beef but I use chicken to make it leaner. When I want it pareve, I omit the meat or I make it with soy ground "meat."

2 tablespoons vegetable oil

2 medium onions, sliced

12 ounces to 1 pound ground chicken

1 small head cabbage (1 to 1¼ pounds), shredded
    (8 to 10 cups)

Salt and freshly ground pepper, to taste

4 large cloves garlic, chopped

1½ teaspoons ground cumin

1 teaspoon paprika

½ teaspoon ground turmeric

2 cups long-grain white rice

4½ cups chicken or vegetable stock or water

Heat oil in a large stew pan or Dutch oven. Add onions and sauté over medium heat 5 minutes until softened. Add chicken and sauté, stirring to separate it into small pieces. Add cabbage and salt, cover, and cook over low heat, stirring often, 5 minutes. Add garlic, cumin, paprika, turmeric, and rice and sauté about 2 minutes. Add stock, salt, and pepper. Stir and bring to boil. Cover and cook over low heat, without stirring, 20 minutes or until rice is tender. Adjust seasoning. Serve hot.

Mushroom Risotto with Parmesan

Makes 4 to 6 servings

Although risotto is generally served as a first course in restaurants, I like this one in smaller portions as an accompaniment for vegetable entrees or for a mild-flavored baked fish such as cod. It's a lovely dish to serve for Shavuot.

3 tablespoons olive oil

2 tablespoons butter (optional)

12 ounces mushrooms, quartered

Salt and freshly ground pepper, to taste

1 medium onion, chopped

3 large cloves garlic, minced

1½ cups Arborio rice or other round risotto rice

½ cup dry white wine

¼ teaspoon hot red pepper flakes

3½ cups hot vegetable stock

1 teaspoon dried thyme

½ teaspoon dried oregano

Freshly grated nutmeg, to taste

⅓ cup chopped fresh Italian parsley

⅓ cup freshly grated Parmesan cheese, plus more for serving

1. Heat 1 tablespoon oil, and if you like, 1 tablespoon butter, in a medium, heavy saucepan. Add mushrooms, salt, and pepper and sauté over medium-high heat for 5 minutes or until light brown. Transfer mushroom mixture to a bowl.

2. Add 2 tablespoons oil to saucepan and heat it. Add onion and sauté over medium heat 5 minutes or until soft but not brown. Add garlic and rice and stir 2 minutes until coated. Add wine and stir. Simmer over medium heat for 1 to 2 minutes until wine evaporates.

3. Add pepper flakes and 2 cups hot stock and stir. Simmer uncovered, stirring occasionally, 9 to 10 minutes or until liquid is absorbed. Add remaining stock, thyme and oregano. Stir and cook 5 minutes. Add mushrooms with their liquid and simmer 3 minutes or until rice is al dente and most of liquid is absorbed. Remove from heat. Add remaining tablespoon butter, if using, pepper, and nutmeg. Let stand 2 to 3 minutes. Add parsley and ⅓ cup Parmesan. Adjust seasoning. Serve with more Parmesan.

❧ Rice with Fruit and Nuts

Valerie's Two-Way Shabbat Rice

Makes 4 to 6 servings, about half
as white rice and half as yellow rice

*For her family's Friday night meal, my neighbor
Valerie Alon prepares two kinds of rice to please everyone in her family, as the younger children insist on
plain white rice, while the adults prefer her delicious
yellow rice with sautéed onions, pine nuts, and raisins.
She has a special technique for preparing both kinds
of rice from a single batch by dividing the white rice
in half.*

*Unlike many versions of yellow rice, this method
features onions with more of a sautéed flavor, as they
do not cook with the rice from the beginning and don't
come in contact with the water used to cook the rice.
Valerie uses a wok to heat the spiced onion mixture
with the rice, but you can use a deep skillet instead.*

1¹/₂ cups long-grain white rice or basmati rice

3 cups water

2 to 3 tablespoons vegetable oil

1 large onion, minced

¹/₂ teaspoon ground turmeric

¹/₄ cup pine nuts

¹/₄ cup raisins

Salt and freshly ground pepper, to taste

1. Combine rice, water, and a pinch of salt in a large
saucepan and bring to a boil. Cover and cook over low
heat 12 to 15 minutes or until rice is just tender.

2. Heat oil in a wok or deep skillet. Add onion and
sauté over medium heat, stirring often, about 7 minutes
or until it begins to turn golden. Add turmeric and pine
nuts and sauté over medium-low heat, stirring, 1 to 2
minutes to toast pine nuts lightly. Add raisins and heat 1
minute. Add 2 to 2¹/₂ cups cooked rice and sprinkle with
salt and pepper. Heat, tossing very gently, 2 to 3 minutes
or until ingredients are combined and rice is evenly colored; do not stir hard so rice grains don't stick together.

3. Serve white and yellow rice in separate bowls.

Red Rice with Raisins

Makes 4 servings

*Rice pilaf that gains a light red tint from the addition
of tomatoes or tomato paste is a popular dish in Israel.
Jews from Iraq and Kurdistan turn their red rice into
a tasty side dish by embellishing it with raisins and
often with toasted almonds. Some cooks add chickpeas
as well and garnish the rice with fried onions. Red
rice is delicious with roast chicken or braised beef,
lamb, or veal, as well as with vegetable dishes such as
eggplant stew, sautéed mushrooms, or turnips with
spinach and garlic.*

2 tablespoons vegetable oil

1 small onion, minced

1 cup long-grain white rice

1 tablespoon tomato paste

2 cups hot water

1 large ripe tomato, grated on large holes of grater

Salt and freshly ground pepper, to taste

Cayenne pepper, to taste

¹/₄ cup golden raisins, rinsed and drained

¹/₃ cup blanched almonds, toasted (optional)

1. Heat oil in a deep skillet or sauté pan, add onion,
and sauté over medium heat 5 minutes. Add rice and
sauté, stirring, about 2 minutes. Mix tomato paste with
hot water and add to pan. Add grated tomato, salt, pepper, and cayenne. Bring to a boil. Stir once. Cover and
cook over low heat without stirring about 20 minutes
or until rice is just tender. Add 2 tablespoons raisins
without stirring. Let rice stand off heat, covered, 10
minutes.

2. Fluff rice lightly with a fork. Adjust seasoning.
Serve rice topped with remaining raisins and almonds,
if using.

Almond, Fruit, and Rice Stuffing

Makes 6½ to 7 cups, enough for a
10- to 12-pound turkey, or 6 to 8 servings

*This delicious stuffing is wonderful for any holiday or
for Shabbat. If you wish to serve it with a 3- or 4-
pound chicken instead of a turkey, use half the ingredient quantities.*

1 cup slivered almonds

3 tablespoons vegetable oil

1 medium onion, minced

2 cups long-grain white rice

3 cups hot chicken stock or water

1 cup orange juice

Salt and freshly ground pepper, to taste

1 large apple

1 cup golden raisins

1½ teaspoons finely grated lemon rind

¼ teaspoon ground cinnamon

1. Preheat oven to 400°F. Toast almonds on rimmed
baking sheet in oven, stirring once or twice, 4 minutes
or until very lightly browned. Transfer to a plate and let
cool.

2. Heat oil in a deep skillet or sauté pan, add onion
and cook over low heat about 5 minutes or until soft
but not brown. Add rice and sauté over medium heat,
stirring, 2 minutes. Add hot stock, orange juice, salt,
and pepper and bring to a boil. Cover and cook over
low heat 10 minutes.

3. Meanwhile, peel, halve, and core apple and cut it
into small dice. Add apple and raisins to rice and stir
very lightly with a fork. Cover and cook 5 more minutes or until rice is nearly tender. Stir in lemon rind,
cinnamon, and almonds. Adjust seasoning. Let cool
completely before stuffing turkey.

Rice Kugels and Casseroles

Sephardic Rice Casserole with Peppers

Makes 4 servings

*Use this simple rice pashtidah ("casserole" in Hebrew),
to make use of cooked rice you have on hand. In a
Sephardic home, the rice is most likely to be pilaf of
white rice but you can use boiled white or brown
rice also.*

2 tablespoons olive oil

1 large onion, chopped

2 red, green, or yellow bell peppers, or mixed colors, diced

4 large cloves garlic, chopped

1 teaspoon paprika

One 14½-ounce can diced tomatoes, drained, juice reserved

3 cups boiled rice

Salt and freshly ground pepper, to taste

Cayenne pepper, to taste

1 large egg

1. Preheat oven to 350°F. Heat 2 tablespoons oil in
large, heavy skillet. Add onion and peppers and cook
over medium-low heat 5 minutes. Add garlic and
½ teaspoon paprika and sauté a few seconds. Add
tomatoes and cook over medium-high heat, stirring
often, until vegetable mixture thick. Remove from heat.
Add rice and mix well. Season with salt, pepper, and
cayenne.

2. Lightly oil a 2-quart baking dish. Add rice mixture. Beat egg with remaining ½ teaspoon paprika.
Add enough water to reserved tomato juice to make
¼ cup. Add to egg mixture and beat until blended.
Pour egg mixture over top of rice mixture. Pour ½ cup
water around the edges of the casserole. Bake 30 minutes or until top browns lightly. Serve hot.

2. Cut asparagus tips from stems. Cut stems into 3 or 4 pieces, discarding tough ends (about $1/2$-inch from end).

3. In a large saucepan, boil enough water to cover vegetables. Add asparagus and peas and return to a boil. Boil 2 or 3 minutes or until asparagus is barely tender when pierced with a small sharp knife. Drain, rinse with cold running water until cool, and drain well.

4. In a bowl lightly mix vegetables with cooked rice.

5. Preheat oven to 350°F. Heat 2 tablespoons oil in a large skillet. Add onion and cook over medium-low heat, stirring often, about 7 minutes or until soft but not brown. Add garlic and cook 30 seconds. Add onion mixture to rice and vegetable mixture and mix lightly.

6. Oil a 6-cup baking dish. Season rice mixture with salt and pepper. Add parsley and eggs. Spoon into baking dish. Sprinkle with remaining tablespoon oil. Bake 25 to 30 minutes or until kugel sets and top browns lightly.

Rice, Chicken, and Vegetable Pashtidah

Makes 4 servings **M**

If you have chicken and either white or brown rice left from the Shabbat meal, this pashtidah *("casserole" in Hebrew), is a good way to make use of them. To prepare it, you simply mix the chicken and rice with sautéed onions and any cooked or frozen vegetables you have on hand. Green beans, carrots, peas, spinach, cabbage, and broccoli are all good. If you like, serve the casserole with tomato sauce.*

3 tablespoons vegetable oil

1 large onion, chopped

1 teaspoon ground cumin

$1/2$ teaspoon ground turmeric

$1/2$ teaspoon paprika

1 large carrot, halved and sliced (optional)

1 cup frozen peas, lima beans, green beans, or mixed frozen vegetables

$1/2$ pound broccoli, divided into small florets

4 cups cooked white or brown rice

$1 1/2$ to 2 cups strips of cooked chicken

Salt and freshly ground pepper, to taste

$1/2$ cup hot chicken or vegetable stock or water

Springtime Rice Kugel with Asparagus and Peas

Makes 6 servings **P**

Flavored in the southern French style with sautéed onions and garlic, this kugel is a festive accompaniment for baked salmon or other fish or roast chicken.

$1/3$ cup long-grain white rice

1 pound asparagus, peeled if thick

2 cups frozen peas

3 tablespoons olive oil or vegetable oil

2 large onions, halved and sliced thin

2 medium cloves garlic, chopped

Salt and freshly ground pepper, to taste

3 tablespoons chopped fresh Italian parsley

3 large eggs, beaten

1. Bring 2 cups water to a boil in saucepan. Add a pinch of salt and rice and boil uncovered for about 12 minutes or until just tender. Drain, rinse with lukewarm water, and drain well.

1. Preheat oven to 350°F. Heat 2 tablespoons oil in large saucepan, add onion, and sauté over medium heat, stirring often, about 7 minutes or until beginning to brown. Add cumin, turmeric, and paprika and sauté 1 minute. Transfer to a large bowl.

2. In same pan bring 6 cups water to a boil with a pinch of salt. Add carrot, cover, and cook over medium heat 5 minutes. Add frozen vegetables and broccoli and return to a boil. Cook uncovered over medium-high heat 5 minutes or until vegetables are just tender. Drain, rinse with cold water, and drain well.

3. Add rice to bowl of onions and mix well. Add chicken and vegetables and mix again. Season with salt and pepper. Oil a 2-quart baking dish and spoon rice mixture into it. Spoon remaining 1 or 2 tablespoons oil over top. Pour 1/2 cup hot stock around edge of mixture. Cover and bake 45 minutes or until mixture is hot and water is absorbed.

Roasted Pepper and Rice Casserole with Olives

Makes 8 servings   Ⓥ

This autumn casserole is actually a rice kugel baked on a bed of roasted peppers, which give the rice a wonderful flavor. The kugel makes a good vegetarian entree, accompanied by feta or cottage cheese and a green salad, or is a good accompaniment for lamb chops or grilled chicken.

If you have roasted or grilled peppers on hand, this is a quick dish to make. Whenever I use the grill, I like to put some peppers on to grill also, so I have plenty ready to use in salads and casseroles.

8 bell peppers, red or green, or 4 of each, roasted or grilled (page 588)

3/4 cup long-grain white rice

3 to 4 tablespoons olive oil or vegetable oil

1/4 pound mushrooms, halved and sliced thin

Salt and fresh ground pepper, to taste

1 medium onion, minced

1 pound ripe tomatoes, peeled, seeded, and chopped, or a 28-ounce can tomatoes, drained well and chopped

2 teaspoons fresh thyme or 3/4 teaspoon dried thyme

1 tablespoon chopped fresh basil

1/2 cup pitted black olives, diced

1. Grill and peel peppers. Then, in a large saucepan, bring about 6 cups water to a boil and add a pinch of salt. Add rice, stir once, and boil, uncovered, 12 to 14 minutes, or until just tender; check by tasting. Rinse with cold water and drain in a strainer for 5 minutes.

2. Preheat oven to 400°F. Heat 1 tablespoon oil in a medium skillet over high heat, add mushrooms, and salt and pepper, and sauté, stirring, about 3 minutes or until lightly browned. Set aside.

3. Add another tablespoon oil to skillet and lower heat. Add onion and cook, stirring, about 10 minutes, or until soft but not brown. Add tomatoes and thyme and cook over medium-high heat, stirring often, about 12 minutes, or until dry.

4. Gently mix tomatoes, mushrooms, basil, and diced olives with rice. Adjust seasoning.

5. Oil two 8- or 9-inch shallow baking dishes or a large gratin dish. Put a layer of peppers in prepared dishes. Spoon half of rice mixture lightly over peppers. Top with remaining peppers, then remaining rice. Sprinkle with remaining oil. Bake about 15 minutes, or until very tender. Serve hot, warm, or at room temperature.

❧ Brown Rice

Brown Rice Pilaf with Feta Cheese and Onions

Makes 4 or 5 servings

For a dairy meal with a Bulgarian accent, I like to add feta cheese to rice, and to serve it with Grilled Eggplant and Red Pepper Salad (page 215), a favorite among Jews from that area. The cheese is particularly good with the nutty taste of brown rice, and not much is needed; feta is so flavorful that a little goes a long way.

1 Bouquet Garni (page 602)

3 tablespoons olive oil or butter

1 medium onion, minced

1¼ cups long-grain brown rice

2½ cups hot vegetable stock or water

¼ teaspoon salt, or to taste

Freshly ground pepper to taste

⅓ cup crumbled feta cheese

½ cup thinly sliced green onions (green and white parts)

1. Preheat oven to 350°F. Prepare bouquet garni. Then, heat oil in a medium ovenproof sauté pan or deep skillet. Add onion and sauté over medium-low heat, stirring, about 5 minutes or until soft but not brown. Add rice and sauté, stirring, about 4 minutes or until grains are well coated with onion mixture and change color slightly.

2. Bring stock to a boil over high heat. Pour over rice and stir once. Add bouquet garni and submerge it in liquid. Add salt and pepper. Bring to a boil. Cover tightly. Place in oven and bake for 35 minutes. Taste rice; if it is too chewy or if liquid is not absorbed, bake 5 more minutes. Discard bouquet garni.

3. Scatter feta over rice and add all but 2 tablespoons green onions. Cover and let stand 5 minutes. Fluff with fork. Adjust seasoning. Serve sprinkled with remaining onion.

Brown Rice Pilaf with Peppers

Makes 4 servings

I serve this savory pilaf with vegetarian meals as well as with roast chicken or baked salmon. It's easy enough for everyday cooking, yet festive enough for Shabbat. The pilaf keeps well and reheats beautifully, so I often make enough for more than one meal, and refrigerate or freeze some of it.

2 tablespoons olive oil or vegetable oil

1 large onion, finely chopped

1 red bell pepper, finely diced

1 yellow or green bell pepper, finely diced

1 cup long-grain brown rice

2 cups hot vegetable stock or water

1 bay leaf

1 sprig fresh thyme or ½ teaspoon dried thyme

Salt and freshly ground pepper, to taste

1. In large, heavy sauté pan, heat oil over low heat. Add onion, and sauté 3 minutes. Add peppers and cook, stirring occasionally, about 5 minutes, or until softened. Add rice and cook, stirring, about 4 minutes, or until evenly coated.

2. Add stock, bay leaf, thyme, salt, and pepper. Stir once, and bring to boil. Cover and cook over low heat, without stirring, about 35 minutes, or until rice is tender and liquid is absorbed. Let stand, covered, 5 minutes. Discard bay leaf and thyme sprig. Fluff rice with fork. Adjust seasoning.

Brown Rice Ring with Curried Zucchini

Makes 4 servings

(P)

If there will be both vegetarians and meat eaters at your table for a Shabbat or holiday meal, this dish is perfect for everyone.

Brown Rice Pilaf with Peppers (page 509)

3 tablespoons olive oil

2 tablespoons minced shallots

1 tablespoon minced peeled fresh ginger

2 large cloves garlic, minced

2 teaspoons curry powder

1 cup vegetable stock

1 bay leaf

Salt and freshly ground pepper, to taste

1 1/2 cups tomato sauce

1/4 teaspoon hot red pepper flakes

1 pound zucchini, unpeeled and cut into 3/4-inch dice

1. Prepare rice pilaf. Then, in medium, heavy saucepan, heat 1 tablespoon oil, add shallots, and cook over low heat, stirring, about 2 minutes or until soft but not browned. Add ginger and garlic and cook 1 minute. Add curry powder and cook, stirring, 30 seconds. Add stock, bay leaf, and a little salt and pepper. Stir well and bring to boil. Simmer, uncovered, over medium-high heat, stirring occasionally, until mixture is reduced to about 1/4 cup. Discard bay leaf.

2. Add tomato sauce and pepper flakes to sauce and bring to boil, stirring. Simmer over medium heat until sauce is thick enough to coat a spoon.

3. In a large skillet, heat remaining oil. Add zucchini, and sauté over medium heat, tossing often, about 5 minutes or until tender. Transfer to bowl and keep warm.

4. Preheat oven to 300°F. If rice is cold, microwave it in a covered container on high until it is just warm. Oil a 4- to 5-cup ring mold. Spoon rice into mold. Press it in gently so there are no holes; do not crush grains. Cover with foil and warm in oven 10 minutes.

5. Reheat sauce to simmer in medium, heavy saucepan, stirring. Adjust seasoning. Sauce should be quite sharply flavored. Cover and keep warm.

6. Unmold pilaf ring onto round platter. Add zucchini to tomato sauce. Spoon some zucchini with sauce into center of rice ring. Serve remaining zucchini in a separate dish.

Confetti Brown Rice with Toasted Pecans

Makes 4 servings

(P)

For a colorful and nutritious accompaniment for a Shabbat chicken or a Purim turkey, serve this brown rice casserole with its colorful diced vegetables. Perfect for make-ahead meals, it reheats beautifully.

3 tablespoons vegetable oil or olive oil

1 large onion, chopped

1 1/2 cups long-grain brown rice

3 cups hot vegetable stock or water

2 large carrots, diced

3 ribs celery, diced

Salt and freshly ground pepper, to taste

1 bay leaf

1 large sprig fresh thyme or 1/2 teaspoon dried thyme

1 1/2 cups shelled fresh or frozen peas

1 small green bell pepper, diced

1 red bell pepper, diced

2 tablespoons chopped fresh parsley

1/4 cup toasted pecans

1. Heat 2 tablespoons oil in a large sauté pan or wide stew pan. Add onion and cook over low heat, stirring, about 7 minutes or until soft but not brown. Add rice and sauté, stirring, about 2 minutes.

2. Add stock, carrots, celery, salt, pepper, bay leaf, and thyme. Stir once with a fork and cover. Cook over low heat, without stirring, 40 minutes. Taste rice; if not yet tender, simmer 2 more minutes.

3. Cook peas in a medium saucepan of boiling salted water 2 minutes. Add green and red peppers and cook 1 or 2 minutes or until peas are barely tender. Drain well.

4. When rice is done, discard bay leaf and thyme sprig. Spoon peas and peppers over rice; do not mix yet. Cover and let stand for 10 minutes.

5. Gently fluff rice with a fork and mix in vegetables. Stir in parsley. Adjust seasoning. Serve hot, garnished with pecans.

Savory Pilaf with Dried Fruit

Makes 4 or 5 servings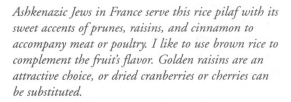

Ashkenazic Jews in France serve this rice pilaf with its sweet accents of prunes, raisins, and cinnamon to accompany meat or poultry. I like to use brown rice to complement the fruit's flavor. Golden raisins are an attractive choice, or dried cranberries or cherries can be substituted.

2 tablespoons vegetable oil

1 medium onion, minced

1¼ cups long-grain brown rice

2½ cups hot water

Salt and freshly ground pepper, to taste

½ to ¾ cup small pitted prunes

½ teaspoon ground cinnamon

⅓ cup golden raisins, rinsed and drained

1. Heat oil in a large sauté pan or stew pan. Add onion and sauté over medium-low heat for 5 minutes or until softened but not browned. Add rice and cook, stirring, about 4 minutes, or until coated.

2. Add hot water, salt, and pepper. Stir once, and bring to boil. Reduce heat to low and add prunes and cinnamon. Cover and cook, without stirring, about 35 minutes or until rice is tender and liquid is absorbed. Add raisins without stirring. Let rice stand off heat, covered, for 10 minutes. Fluff rice with fork and gently mix in raisins. Adjust seasoning.

Bulgur Wheat

Bulgur Wheat Pilaf

Makes 4 to 6 servings

A favorite in Sephardic cooking, bulgur is wheat that has been steamed, dried, and cracked into small pieces. This process makes the wheat fast and easy to cook. In Israeli and Middle Eastern grocery stores bulgur comes in several sizes—fine, medium, and coarse. Purists prefer fine bulgur for salads, medium size for pilafs, and large grains for soups. Medium works in all these types of dishes, and is the size most often available in natural foods stores and some supermarkets.

1 to 2 tablespoons olive oil or vegetable oil

1½ cups medium bulgur wheat

3 large cloves garlic, minced (optional)

3 cups vegetable or chicken stock or water

Salt and freshly ground pepper, to taste

Heat oil in a heavy saucepan. Add bulgur wheat and garlic, if using, and sauté over medium heat, stirring, for 1 minute or until bulgur grains are coated with oil. Add stock, salt, and pepper and bring to boil. Cover and cook over low heat 15 minutes or until water is absorbed. Adjust seasoning. Serve hot.

Bulgur Wheat with Sweet and Sour Squash

Makes 4 servings

I learned this delicious dish when I lived in Israel, where there is a sizable population of Jews from Kurdistan, the place of origin of this dish. It makes a terrific vegetarian entree in winter.

2¹/₂ pounds butternut or banana squash

4 to 5 tablespoons vegetable oil

2 medium onions, chopped

One 28-ounce can tomatoes, drained and chopped

²/₃ cup water

Salt and freshly ground pepper, to taste

1 tablespoon sugar, or to taste

³/₄ cup medium bulgur wheat

¹/₄ cup dark raisins

2 to 3 tablespoons strained fresh lemon juice, or to taste

1. Peel or cut off squash peel. Cut in half and remove seeds and strings. Cut squash meat into 1-inch pieces.

2. Heat 2 to 3 tablespoons oil in a large, heavy sauté pan, add half the chopped onions, and sauté over medium heat about 7 minutes or until golden. Add tomatoes and cook uncovered 5 minutes. Add squash, water, salt, pepper, and sugar. Stir and bring to boil. Cover and cook over low heat, occasionally stirring gently, 30 minutes.

3. Heat 2 tablespoons oil in medium, heavy saucepan over medium heat. Add remaining onion and cook, stirring often, about 5 minutes or until softened. Add bulgur wheat and sauté, stirring, 2 minutes. Add 1¹/₂ cups water, salt, and pepper and bring to boil. Cover and cook over low heat about 15 minutes or until water is absorbed. Adjust seasoning.

4. When squash is nearly tender, add raisins and 2 tablespoons lemon juice and cook 5 minutes or until squash and raisins are tender. Adjust seasoning, adding more sugar or lemon juice if needed. Serve squash stew spooned over bulgur wheat.

Bulgur Wheat with Turnip Greens and Red Pepper

Makes 4 servings

Jews from around the Mediterranean often cook grains with greens. The partnership is terrific for both taste and nutrition. If you don't have turnip greens, you can prepare this dish with mustard greens, chard, or spinach.

2 tablespoons olive oil

1 medium onion, chopped

1 red bell pepper

2 large cloves garlic, chopped

1²/₃ cups medium bulgur wheat

1³/₄ cups chicken or vegetable stock or a 14¹/₂-ounce can broth

1²/₃ cups hot water

1 teaspoon ground coriander

¹/₂ teaspoon dried oregano

1 bunch turnip greens (12 ounces), rinsed, drained, and cut into ¹/₂-inch–wide strips

Salt and freshly ground pepper, to taste

Heat oil in large, heavy saucepan. Add onion and bell pepper, and sauté over medium heat, 5 minutes. Add garlic and bulgur wheat and sauté, stirring, 2 minutes. Add stock, hot water, coriander, and oregano. Stir and bring to boil. Add turnip greens. Cover and cook over low heat about 15 minutes or until water is absorbed and bulgur wheat is tender. Season with pepper; season lightly with salt if needed.

Spicy Bulgur Wheat with Vegetables

Makes 5 or 6 servings **P**

Bulgur wheat is an important staple in the kitchens of many Jews of Middle Eastern origin. With its rich, nutty taste, this grain deserves more attention in American Jewish kitchens. In this nutritious salad it is combined with sautéed vegetables and a generous amount of parsley. Serve it warm or at room temperature on a bed of lettuce leaves and surround it with sliced radishes, cherry tomatoes, or tomato wedges.

2 cups boiling water

1 cup bulgur wheat, fine, or medium

3 to 5 tablespoons olive oil

1 medium onion, chopped

2 red bell peppers or 1 red and 1 green, finely diced

2 medium zucchini, finely diced

1 tablespoon tomato paste

3 to 4 tablespoons strained fresh lemon juice, or more to taste

Salt and freshly ground pepper, to taste

1 teaspoon ground cumin

1 teaspoon paprika

1/4 teaspoon cayenne pepper, or to taste

1 1/3 cups finely chopped fresh Italian parsley

4 green onions, white and green parts, sliced

1. Pour boiling water over bulgur wheat in a large bowl. Let bulgur wheat soak, stirring it from time to time, 45 minutes to 1 hour or until it is tender. Drain in a colander. Gently squeeze wheat dry. Put it in a large bowl.

2. Heat 2 tablespoons oil in a large skillet. Add chopped onion and peppers and sauté over medium heat, stirring often, 5 minutes. Add zucchini, cover, and sauté 5 minutes or until vegetables are tender.

3. Mix tomato paste with 1 tablespoon oil, 3 tablespoons lemon juice, salt, pepper, cumin, paprika, and cayenne. Add to wheat. Fold in sautéed vegetables with their oil. Add parsley and green onions and mix gently. Adjust seasoning; add more lemon juice or oil if desired. Serve at room temperature.

Bulgur Wheat with Green Onions and Pecans

Makes 4 to 6 servings

Bulgur wheat is one of the oldest convenience foods, and Sephardic cooks know that it comes in handy when they need a side dish in minutes. This quick, easy, and tasty pilaf goes well with just about any food, from vegetable stews to baked fish to braised meat.

5 green onions

1 tablespoon olive oil

1 1/2 cups medium bulgur wheat

3 cups vegetable or chicken stock or water

Salt and freshly ground pepper, to taste

1/4 cup chopped fresh Italian parsley

1/4 cup toasted diced pecans

1. Slice white and light green parts of onions. Chop dark green parts. Heat oil in a medium saucepan over medium heat. Add white and light green parts of onion and sauté 30 seconds. Add bulgur wheat and sauté, stirring, for 2 minutes.

2. Add stock, salt, and pepper and bring to boil. Reduce heat to low, cover, and cook over low heat for 10 minutes. Add dark green parts of green onions. Simmer over low heat for 5 more minutes or until bulgur wheat is tender and liquid is absorbed.

3. Gently stir in parsley. Adjust seasoning. Serve sprinkled with pecans.

Bulgur Wheat with Chickpeas, Tomatoes, and Coriander

Makes 4 to 6 servings

This dish combines two favorite staples of Jews from Middle Eastern countries—bulgur wheat and chickpeas. Pairing the grain and the legume makes the dish especially satisfying as a vegetarian entree. The flavorful, stovetop casserole also makes a fine accompaniment for braised, poached, or roasted chicken.

2 tablespoons olive oil

1 large onion, halved and sliced

1 small green pepper, diced

4 ripe plum tomatoes, peeled, seeded, and chopped, or 4 canned tomatoes, chopped

1 teaspoon ground coriander

1 teaspoon ground cumin

1½ cups medium bulgur wheat

3 cups vegetable or chicken stock or water

One 15-ounce can chickpeas, drained, or about 1½ cups cooked chickpeas

Salt and freshly ground pepper, to taste

2 to 3 tablespoons chopped fresh Italian parsley

1. Heat oil in a heavy saucepan. Add onion and green pepper and sauté over medium heat, stirring often, 5 minutes. Add tomatoes, coriander, and cumin and sauté, stirring, 5 minutes. Stir in bulgur wheat, stock, and chickpeas and bring to a boil.

2. Cover and cook over low heat 15 minutes or until bulgur wheat is tender. Season with salt and pepper. Stir in parsley. Serve hot.

✿ Kasha

Kasha with Browned Onions

Makes 4 servings

This is the basic recipe for cooking kasha, or roasted buckwheat, the favorite of Polish and Russian Jews. Serve it with brisket or with roasted or poached chicken. If you wish, omit the browned onions and serve the kasha as an accompaniment for chicken soup, for spooning into each bowl.

1 cup medium kasha (roasted buckwheat groats or kernels)

1 egg or 1 egg white, any size, beaten

2 cups beef, veal, chicken, or vegetable stock or water

2 to 3 tablespoons vegetable oil

2 medium onions, chopped

Salt and freshly ground pepper, to taste

1. Combine kasha with beaten egg in a wide bowl and stir with a fork until grains are thoroughly coated. Set a dry, heavy skillet over medium heat. Add kasha mixture and heat it over medium heat about 3 minutes, stirring to keep grains separate.

2. Meanwhile, bring stock or water to a boil in a small saucepan. Add boiling stock to kasha and stir. Cover and cook over low heat 15 minutes or until all of liquid is absorbed.

3. Heat oil in a skillet, add onions, and sauté over medium-low heat, stirring often, about 10 minutes or until soft and well browned. Stir kasha with a fork to fluff. Lightly stir onion into kasha. Taste for salt; season kasha generously with pepper. Serve hot.

Egg-Free Kasha

Makes 4 servings

Although kasha is traditionally cooked with egg to keep the grains separate, it can be prepared using oil instead, thus cutting out the cholesterol and saturated fat and making it suitable for vegan diets.

2 tablespoons canola oil

1 large onion, finely chopped

4 to 6 ounces sliced mushrooms (optional)

1/2 teaspoon paprika

Salt and freshly ground pepper, to taste

1 cup medium kasha (roasted buckwheat groats or
    kernels)

1 3/4 cups hot vegetable stock or one 14 1/2-ounce can broth

1/4 cup hot water

1/2 teaspoon dried marjoram

1. Heat 1 tablespoon oil in a heavy sauté pan. Add onion and sauté over medium-low heat, stirring often, about 7 minutes or until softened and beginning to turn golden; cover if pan becomes dry. Add mushrooms, if using, paprika, salt, and pepper and sauté uncovered over medium-high heat, stirring, 2 minutes. Transfer mixture to a bowl. Cover to keep warm.

2. Add 1 tablespoon oil to the pan and heat. Add kasha and sauté over medium heat about 1 minute, stirring. Add hot stock, hot water, salt, pepper, and marjoram. Stir once and bring to a boil. Cover and cook over low heat for 10 minutes or until kasha is just tender and all liquid is absorbed. Spoon onion mixture over kasha, cover, and cook over low heat for 2 minutes. Let stand off heat 5 minutes. Use fork to fluff kasha and to gently stir in onion mixture. Adjust seasoning. Serve hot.

Kasha with Smoked Turkey, Mushrooms, and Ginger

Makes 4 servings

Mushrooms are a popular partner for kasha, and smoked turkey adds a pleasing accent as well. Fresh ginger is not traditional but livens up the combination. Serve this dish for a quick, hearty, and nutritious supper. Onion Marmalade (page 133) makes a terrific topping. Glazed carrots are a tasty, colorful accompaniment.

2 or 3 tablespoons vegetable oil

2 teaspoons finely minced peeled fresh ginger

8 ounces mushrooms, halved and cut into thin slices

Salt and freshly ground pepper, to taste

2 large cloves garlic, minced

1 cup medium kasha (roasted buckwheat groats or kernels)

1 egg or 1 egg white, any size, beaten

2 cups hot chicken or vegetable stock or water

2 to 4 ounces thinly sliced smoked turkey, cut into
    3 × 1/4-inch strips

4 tablespoons chopped fresh parsley

1. Heat oil in a large skillet. Add ginger and mushrooms, sprinkle with salt and pepper, and sauté over medium-high heat 5 minutes or until mushrooms are tender and lightly browned. Add garlic and sauté 30 seconds. Remove from heat.

2. Combine kasha with beaten egg in a wide bowl and stir with a fork until grains are thoroughly coated. Set a dry, heavy skillet over medium heat. Add kasha mixture and heat it over medium heat about 3 minutes, stirring to keep grains separate. Add hot stock to kasha and stir. Cover and cook over low heat 15 minutes or until all of liquid is absorbed.

3. Add smoked turkey to mushroom mixture and heat through. Stir kasha with a fork to fluff. Lightly stir mushroom mixture into kasha. Add 3 tablespoons parsley. Adjust seasoning. Sprinkle with remaining tablespoon parsley and serve hot.

Colorful Kasha and Bow-Tie Pasta Medley

Makes 4 to 6 servings

Bow-tie pasta is a time-honored partner for kasha (roasted buckwheat) in the Ashkenazic kitchen but the customary dish is not particularly colorful. To liven it up and lend a fresh, sweet taste to balance the assertive nature of the kasha, I like to add lightly cooked carrots, zucchini, and peas. I cook them together with the pasta so there is no need for an extra saucepan.

2 to 3 tablespoons vegetable oil

2 large onions, sliced

1³/₄ cups vegetable, beef, or chicken stock or one 14¹/₂-ounce can broth

¹/₄ cup water

1 cup medium or large (whole) kasha

1 egg, any size, beaten

¹/₂ teaspoon dried thyme

Salt and freshly ground pepper, to taste

2 large carrots, sliced

8 ounces pasta, bow-ties or squares

1 cup frozen peas

2 medium zucchini, halved and sliced

1. Heat oil in a large, heavy skillet. Add onions and cook over medium-low heat, stirring often, about 15 minutes or until brown. Transfer to a bowl; cover to keep warm. Combine broth with water and bring to a simmer in a small saucepan or in a measuring cup in microwave; cover to keep warm.

2. Combine kasha with beaten egg in a wide bowl and stir with a fork until grains are thoroughly coated. Add mixture to the skillet and heat it over medium heat, stirring to keep grains separate, about 3 minutes. Add hot broth and stir. Add thyme, salt, and pepper. Cover and cook over low heat 10 to 15 minutes or until kasha is tender and water is absorbed. Stir with a fork to fluff. Add onions, stir lightly and cover.

3. Cook carrots and pasta uncovered in a large pot of boiling salted water over high heat, stirring occasionally,

3 minutes. Add peas and zucchini and return to a boil. Cook 4 to 5 more minutes or until pasta is tender but firm to the bite. Drain well. Toss pasta and vegetables with kasha mixture. Adjust seasoning. Serve hot.

Kasha and Noodle Kugel

Makes 5 or 6 servings

Kasha and noodles are a time-honored pair in the Eastern European Jewish kitchen. Flavored with plenty of well-browned onions, they make a hearty, tasty kugel, perfect with brisket or chicken. For a rich, old-world accent, add ¹/₂ cup of Grivenes (page 602), or crisp bits of chicken skin, to the kasha mixture before baking it.

4 to 5 tablespoons vegetable oil

2 large onions, halved and sliced

1 teaspoon paprika, plus a little more for sprinkling

7 to 8 ounces medium egg noodles

3 large eggs

1 cup medium or large kasha (roasted buckwheat groats or kernels)

Salt and freshly ground pepper, to taste

2 cups hot chicken, beef, or vegetable stock

1. Preheat oven to 350°F. Heat 3 tablespoons oil in a large, heavy skillet. Add onions and cook over medium-low heat, stirring often, about 15 minutes or until deep brown. Add paprika and sauté 1 minute. Transfer to a large bowl.

2. Cook noodles uncovered in a large pot of boiling salted water over high heat about 4 minutes or until nearly tender. Drain, rinse with cold water, and drain well. Add to bowl of onions.

3. Beat 1 egg in a wide bowl. Add kasha and stir with a fork until grains are thoroughly coated. Put mixture in a heavy skillet and heat it over medium heat about 3 minutes, stirring to keep grains separate. Add salt, pepper, and hot stock and stir. Cover and cook over low heat 15 minutes or until all water is absorbed. Fluff with a fork.

4. Add kasha to noodle mixture and mix lightly. Adjust seasoning; mixture should be seasoned generously. Beat remaining eggs and add to noodle mixture. Mix well.

5. Oil a 2-quart baking dish and add noodle mixture. Sprinkle with remaining oil, then dust with paprika. Bake uncovered 1 hour or until set. Serve from baking dish.

Kasha with Turkey Chili

Makes 4 to 6 servings

A great introduction to the earthy taste of kasha is to serve it as a bed for spicy chili. This novel use of the old-fashioned Ashkenazic favorite makes it enticing for eaters with a modern taste for highly seasoned food.

3 tablespoons olive oil or vegetable oil

1 large onion, chopped

12 ounces ground turkey or chicken

6 large cloves garlic, minced

3 or 4 fresh jalapeño peppers, seeds discarded, minced (see Note)

2 tablespoons chili powder

1 1/2 tablespoons ground cumin

1/2 teaspoon hot red pepper flakes or 1/4 teaspoon cayenne pepper, or to taste

Salt and freshly ground pepper, to taste

One 28-ounce can tomatoes, with their juice

2 teaspoons dried oregano

One 15-ounce can red beans, drained

Fresh Tomato Salsa (page 234)

1 egg, any size

1 cup kasha (buckwheat groats or kernels), preferably medium grains

2 cups boiling water

1 ripe avocado

1 cup chopped green, white, or red onion

Small fresh cilantro sprigs

1. Heat 1 tablespoon oil in a large saucepan over medium heat. Add onion and cook, stirring often, about 10 minutes or until tender. Transfer to a bowl.

2. Add remaining 2 tablespoons oil to saucepan and heat. Add turkey and cook, stirring often, until it changes color, about 7 minutes. Return onions to pan and add garlic, jalapeño peppers, chili powder, cumin, pepper flakes, salt, and pepper. Cook over low heat, stirring, about 3 minutes to coat meat with spices. Add tomatoes and bring to a boil, stirring and crushing tomatoes. Cook uncovered over low heat, stirring occasionally, 30 minutes. Add oregano and beans and cook 10 or 15 more minutes or until thick.

3. Meanwhile, prepare salsa. Then, beat egg with a pinch of salt. Combine kasha with beaten egg in a wide bowl and stir with a fork until grains are thoroughly coated. Add to a dry, heavy skillet and heat it over medium heat about 3 minutes, stirring to keep grains separate. Add boiling water and stir. Cover and cook over low heat 15 minutes or until all of water is absorbed. Stir with a fork to fluff.

4. Taste chili and adjust seasoning. If you would like it hotter, add more pepper flakes. Peel and dice avocado.

5. Serve kasha topped with chili. Surround with small bowls of avocado, salsa, chopped onion, and cilantro sprigs, for garnishing each serving.

Note: Wear rubber gloves when handling hot peppers.

❧ Barley

Baked Barley with Aromatic Vegetables

Makes 4 to 6 servings

Barley has long been a staple in the Jewish kitchen, and recent studies have shown that, like oatmeal, it is rich in healthful fiber. While you are roasting a chicken for Shabbat, you might like to put this hearty side dish in the oven. It bakes slowly, requires little preparation, and makes a pleasant change from the usual rice or noodles.

2 tablespoons vegetable oil or olive oil

1 large onion, chopped

3 ribs celery, diced

4 large cloves garlic, chopped

1 cup medium pearl barley

2 large carrots, diced

3 cups chicken or vegetable stock

Salt and freshly ground pepper, to taste

1 teaspoon dried oregano

1 teaspoon dried sage

2 tablespoons snipped fresh chives or dill or chopped Italian parsley (optional)

1. Preheat oven to 350°F. Heat oil in a skillet. Add onion and celery and sauté over medium heat for 5 minutes. Add garlic and barley and sauté 1 minute, stirring.

2. Oil a 2-quart casserole dish. Transfer barley mixture to casserole. Add carrots, stock, salt, pepper, oregano, and sage. Cover and bake, stirring 3 or 4 times, about 1 hour and 15 minutes or until barley is tender. Fluff with a fork before serving. Adjust seasoning. Serve topped with chives, if using.

Barley with Herbs and Roasted Peppers

Makes 4 to 6 servings **P**

Barley is popular not only with Ashkenazic Jews in soups and in cholent. *Jews from Mediterranean and Middle Eastern lands like it too, and use their favorite seasonings to flavor it. Serve this lively barley dish with roast turkey or chicken or with vegetable stews.*

2 to 3 tablespoons olive oil or vegetable oil

1 large onion, chopped

2 large cloves garlic, minced

1 cup medium pearl barley

2¹/₂ cups vegetable stock or water

1 bay leaf

Salt and freshly ground pepper, to taste

2 red or green bell peppers, grilled and peeled (page 588), or 4 roasted pepper halves from a jar

1¹/₂ teaspoons chopped fresh thyme or ¹/₂ teaspoon dried

1 tablespoon chopped fresh oregano or 1 teaspoon dried

¹/₄ cup chopped fresh Italian parsley

1. Heat 2 tablespoons oil in a large, heavy saucepan. Add onion and sauté over medium-low heat, stirring often, 7 minutes or until it begins to turn golden. Add garlic and barley and sauté, stirring, 1 minute. Add stock, bay leaf, salt, and pepper and bring to a boil. Cover and cook over low heat, about 40 minutes or until barley is tender. Discard bay leaf.

2. Meanwhile, grill peppers. Dice grilled or jarred peppers. When done, fluff barley gently with a fork. Add diced peppers, thyme, oregano, parsley, and another tablespoon oil if you like. Adjust seasoning. Serve hot.

Barley with Chicken and Spinach Pesto

Makes 4 to 6 servings

The popular Ashkenazic duo, chicken and barley, are good not only in soup but as a hearty entree as well. Poach your own chicken breasts and use the cooking broth to cook the barley; or use extra roast chicken from your refrigerator or freezer, or buy some from a deli, and use prepared chicken or vegetable stock.

Pesto is not traditional to Eastern European cuisine but it livens up the combination with color and flavor. This pesto of course is made without cheese so that it can be added to a chicken dish without violating the rules of kashrut.

3 or 4 Poached Chicken Breasts (page 359)

6 tablespoons olive oil

1 large onion, chopped

1 cup medium pearl barley

2¹/₂ cups Chicken Poaching Broth (from recipe above), or chicken or vegetable stock

1 bay leaf

Salt and freshly ground pepper, to taste

2 large cloves garlic, peeled

2 tablespoons walnuts

1 teaspoon dried basil

1¹/₂ cups packed spinach leaves, rinsed thoroughly, patted dry

1. Prepare chicken, reserving broth. Then, heat 2 tablespoons oil in a large, heavy saucepan. Add onion and sauté over medium-low heat, stirring often, 7 minutes or until it begins to turn golden. Add barley and sauté, stirring, 1 minute. Add broth, bay leaf, salt, and pepper, and bring to a boil. Cover and cook over low heat, about 40 minutes or until barley is tender. Discard bay leaf.

2. Meanwhile, prepare pesto: With blade of food processor turning, drop garlic cloves, one at a time, through feed tube and process until finely chopped. Add nuts, basil, and spinach and process until spinach is chopped. With blade turning, gradually add remaining 4 tablespoons olive oil. Scrape down sides and process until mixture is well blended. Add 1 tablespoon water if pesto is too thick. Season with salt and pepper. Transfer to a small bowl and set aside.

3. Cut chicken into strips. Fluff barley gently with a fork. Lightly stir in chicken. Gently stir in half of spinach pesto. Adjust seasoning. Serve hot; serve remaining pesto separately, in a small dish.

Wild Rice

Wild Rice with Shiitake Mushrooms and Leeks

Makes 4 to 6 servings

This luxurious dish is a perfect partner for Cornish Hens in Saffron Tomato Sauce (page 370) or a change-of-pace accompaniment for a Shabbat chicken.

5 cups water

1 cup wild rice, rinsed and drained

1/2 pound fresh shiitake mushrooms or 1 or 2 ounces dried

2 large leeks, white and light green parts only

2 to 3 tablespoons vegetable oil

1/2 teaspoon dried thyme

1/4 cup chicken or vegetable stock or water

Salt and freshly ground pepper, to taste

2 tablespoons chopped fresh chives or parsley

1. Bring water to boil and add a pinch of salt. Add rice, return to boil, cover, and cook over low heat about 50 minutes or until kernels begin to puff open.

2. If using dried mushrooms, soak them in hot water for 20 minutes. Remove mushrooms from water. Rinse mushrooms and cut into small pieces; discard tough stems.

3. Slit leeks twice lengthwise, from center of white part upward. Rinse quickly under running cold water, fanning layers to remove sand. Cut leeks into pieces about 1 1/2 inches long. Flatten each piece and cut into thin strips, using a sharp, heavy knife. If necessary, put strips in a bowl of cold water to rid them of any remaining sand. Remove them from bowl; sand will sink to bottom.

4. Heat oil in a large sauté pan. Add fresh shiitake mushrooms (but not dried) and sauté over medium heat for 3 minutes or until tender. Remove from pan. Add leeks, thyme, dried mushrooms, stock, and a pinch of salt and pepper. Cover tightly and cook over low heat, stirring often, about 20 minutes or until leeks are tender but not brown; if pan becomes dry, add a few tablespoons water. If any liquid remains in pan, uncover and cook over medium heat until it evaporates. Remove from heat; set aside.

5. Drain rice and add to pan of leeks. If using fresh shiitake mushrooms, add them to pan. Heat together briefly. Adjust seasoning. Serve hot, sprinkled with parsley.

Wild Rice with Pecans and Winter Squash

Makes 4 to 6 servings

M or P

The mild sweetness and bright orange hue of the squash combined with the wild rice and toasted nuts makes this a delightful treat. It's great for Rosh Hashanah or for the eve of Yom Kippur.

5 cups water

1 cup wild rice, rinsed and drained

1 to 1 1/2 pounds butternut or banana squash

2 tablespoons vegetable oil

1 medium onion, minced

1/3 cup chicken or vegetable stock or water

Pinch of sugar (optional)

Salt and freshly ground pepper, to taste

2 tablespoons chopped fresh parsley

1/4 to 1/3 cup pecans, toasted

1. Bring water to boil and add a pinch of salt. Add rice, return to boil, cover and cook over low heat 50 minutes to 1 hour or until kernels begin to puff open.

2. Cut squash into pieces and remove peel with a vegetable peeler or a heavy, sharp knife. Remove seeds. Cut flesh into about 1-inch cubes. Heat oil in a large, heavy saucepan, add onion, and sauté 5 minutes over low heat. Add squash, stock, sugar if using, salt, and pepper. Cover and cook over low heat, stirring occasionally, 25 minutes or until tender, adding hot water by tablespoons if pan becomes dry.

3. Drain rice and add to pan of squash. Heat together briefly, stirring very gently. Add parsley. Adjust seasoning. Serve hot, sprinkled with toasted pecans.

Wild and White Rice with Dried Fruit

Makes 6 to 8 servings (P)

Studded with colorful fruit and seasoned with shallots and fresh ginger, this festive dish is welcome at any celebration. Try it for Sukkot with roast chicken, turkey, or duck. For Rosh Hashanah, you might want to flavor the cooking liquid with a tablespoon of honey.

5 cups water

1 cup wild rice, rinsed and drained

2 tablespoons vegetable oil

2 medium shallots, chopped

1 tablespoon minced peeled fresh ginger

1 cup long-grain white rice

2 large carrots, diced small

2 cups hot water

Salt and freshly ground pepper, to taste

1/4 cup dried cranberries or cherries

1/4 cup diced dried apricots

1/4 cup golden raisins

1. Bring water to boil in a large saucepan and add a pinch of salt. Add wild rice, return to boil, cover, and cook over low heat 50 minutes to 1 hour or until kernels begin to puff open.

2. Heat oil in a large saucepan. Add shallots, ginger, and white rice and sauté over medium-low heat, stirring, for 2 minutes. Add carrots, hot water, and a pinch of salt and pepper. Bring to a boil. Cover and cook over low heat, without stirring, about 18 minutes or until rice is just tender. Remove from heat. Sprinkle dried cranberries, apricots, and raisins over rice but do not stir. Cover and let stand for 10 minutes.

3. Drain wild rice and add to saucepan of white rice and fruit. Toss very gently with a fork. Adjust seasoning. Serve hot.

Sephardic Wild Rice with Almonds, Pine Nuts, and Pistachios

Makes 4 to 6 servings

This lavish dish, shared with me by culinary historian Charles Perry, was inspired by a Sephardic recipe from the Middle Ages for a bread and meat stuffing for partridge. This is also wonderful when made with wild rice and no meat, and baked as a separate casserole instead of inside a bird. Serve this savory side dish with roasted turkey or chicken, baked fish, or stewed or baked vegetables.

1/3 cup almonds

1/3 cup pine nuts

13/4 cups chicken or vegetable stock or water

31/4 cups water

1 cup wild rice, rinsed and drained

2 tablespoons olive oil or vegetable oil

1 large onion, finely chopped

1/4 teaspoon ground cinnamon

1/4 cup chopped fresh cilantro or Italian parsley

Salt and freshly ground pepper, to taste

1/4 cup toasted pistachios, shelled

Fresh cilantro or parsley sprigs

1. Preheat oven to 350°F. Toast almonds and pine nuts in small baking dish in oven about 5 minutes or until lightly browned. Cool nuts on a plate. Reserve about 2 tablespoons almonds and pine nuts for garnish. Coarsely chop remaining almonds and pine nuts.

2. Combine stock, 31/4 cups water, and a pinch of salt in a large saucepan and bring to a boil. Add rice and return to a boil. Cover and cook over low heat for 50 minutes to 1 hour or until kernels begin to puff open.

3. Heat oil in a deep skillet or sauté pan. Add onion and sauté over medium-low heat about 7 minutes or until golden. Add cinnamon and sauté, stirring, 30 seconds.

4. Drain rice and add to pan of onions. Add chopped nuts and chopped cilantro. Heat together 2 to 3 minutes, stirring very gently. Season with salt and pepper. Serve hot, sprinkled with toasted pistachios and reserved toasted almonds and pine nuts. Garnish with cilantro sprigs.

❧ Cornmeal

Mamaliga

Makes 4 to 6 servings

Mamaliga is the Romanian version of polenta. Traditionally it is made of cornmeal cooked only with water and salt. It is pareve, so Romanian Jews serve it with milchig or fleishig dishes. Like polenta, it can be soft or it can be firm and cut into slices. Soft mamaliga is often served dotted with soft butter or margarine. Some cooks serve mamaliga slices plain; others bake or fry them. Mamaliga often accompanies saucy meat stews or vegetable casseroles like Baked Balkan Vegetable Casserole, or Givetch (page 416). In some families it's served with sugar and sour cream or mild cheese like pot cheese or cottage cheese for a casual supper.

Instead of water I sometimes use vegetable stock to give it a delicate background flavor.

1½ cups yellow or white cornmeal

1 cup cold water

1 teaspoon salt

3 cups vegetable stock, water, or a mixture of both

Soft butter or margarine (optional)

1. Put cornmeal in a bowl and slowly stir in cold water to make a smooth mixture. Stir in salt. Bring stock to a boil in a heavy saucepan. Gradually stir in cornmeal mixture. Reduce heat to low and simmer, stirring, 5 minutes; stir with a whisk if necessary to remove any lumps. Partially cover and cook, stirring very often, about 20 minutes or until mixture is thick.

2. Serve soft mamaliga with small pats of butter or margarine, if using; or pour mamaliga into a shallow bowl or baking dish, let it set, and cut it into small squares.

Oven-Toasted Mamaliga

Makes 4 to 6 servings

Mamaliga that is brushed with butter and baked gains a delicate crust. Either make hot mamaliga and bake it this way, or use cooled, sliced mamaliga. (If using slices, simply arrange them slightly overlapping or side-by-side on a greased baking sheet, then bake as in recipe.)

Mamaliga (this page)

2 tablespoons butter or margarine, melted, or vegetable oil

Salt and white pepper, to taste

Paprika to taste (optional)

Prepare mamaliga. Then, preheat oven to 400°F. Grease a baking sheet. Pour hot mamaliga onto sheet and use wooden spoon to pat it in a rough square about 1 inch high. Season melted butter with salt and pepper and use it to brush over mamaliga. Sprinkle lightly with paprika, if using. Bake about 10 minutes or until top browns lightly. Cut into slices or squares to serve.

Baked Mamaliga with Kashkaval Cheese

Makes 4 to 6 servings

You can use freshly cooked mamaliga for this dish, or use mamaliga that has cooled and has been cut into squares. Some people serve this rich dish with sour cream.

Kashkaval is a flavorful grating cheese that originated in the Balkans and is very popular in Israel. It is available in Israeli and some Middle Eastern and Eastern European grocery stores. If you cannot find it, substitute Swiss cheese.

Mamaliga (this page)

½ to 1 cup grated Kashkaval or Swiss cheese

2 tablespoons butter, cut into bits

Sour cream (optional)

1. Prepare mamaliga. Then, preheat oven to 350°F. If using hot, just-cooked mamaliga, butter a baking sheet. Spoon hot mamaliga onto baking sheet. Using wooden spoon or spatula, shape it into a rough square about 1-inch high. Sprinkle it with cheese and dot it with butter.

2. If using cold mamaliga squares, butter a shallow baking dish and add a layer of squares. Sprinkle them lightly with cheese. Continue layering, ending with cheese. Dot with butter. Bake uncovered about 20 minutes or until mamaliga is hot and cheese melts. Serve hot; accompany the mamaliga with sour cream, if using.

Breads and Yeast Cakes

Challah
525

Basic Challah Dough
Prepared By Hand
Prepared By Mixer
Prepared By Food Processor

Braided Challah

Large Challah

Round Rosh Hashanah Challah

Holiday Honey Challah

Apricot-Pecan Challah

Sweet and Fruity Challah

Macadamia-Cranberry Challah

Walnut Challah

Light Challah

Onion-Sesame Braid

Buttery Braid

Swiss Cheese Challah Loaf

Bagels
536

Egg Bagels

Water Bagels

Whole-Wheat Walnut Bagels

Garlic-Butter Bagels

Cinnamon-Raisin Bagels

Blueberry Bagels

Herbed Bagels

Parmesan Bagels

Citrus and Spice Bagels

Pita Breads and Pizza
543

Pita Bread

Sesame Pita Bread

Kurdish Spiced Pita Bread

Za'atar-Topped Pita Bread

Pizza Dough

Quick Pizza Dough

Sweet Breads and Babka
547

Overnight Shabbat Bread
(Kubaneh)

Rich Cinnamon Rolls with
Raisins

Creamy Cinnamon Filling

Chocolate Chip Sweet Rolls

Poppy Seed–Lemon Rolls

Poppy Seed Filling for
Sweet Rolls

Lemon Glaze

Blueberry-Orange Muffins

Babka with Cinnamon
and Raisins

Chocolate-Walnut Babka

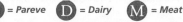

*J*ewish tradition dictates that every meal begin with a blessing over bread. Indeed, bread is so central to the Jewish culinary culture that its presence determines whether any other foods being eaten deserve to be considered a true meal, a *seudah*. If there is bread, it is a meal and a special blessing on the bread is recited before the meal, as well as a prayer of thanks afterwards. If there is no bread, any food eaten, no matter how substantial, is treated as a mere snack and a different, abbreviated prayer is said after eating it. A *seudah* is required by tradition for Shabbat and holidays. For Passover, matzo fulfills the function of the bread.

Jewish bakers have a reputation for their excellent bread. Challah, bagels, rye bread, pumpernickel, and more recently, pita bread, have been popularized by Jewish bakeries throughout the United States and in many European cities as well. Many of these are now available in supermarkets and kosher grocery stores. Of course, visiting bakeries ensures fresher, more delicious versions of these breads as well as special breads like bialys, flat onion breads called *pletzlach* in Yiddish, whole-wheat challah, and sweet breakfast breads and yeast cakes.

Challah (or *hallah*) is the Hebrew word for "egg bread" that is also used in Yiddish and English. With its beautiful brown crust and golden yellow crumb, challah is festive and delicious and is the traditional bread for Shabbat and holidays. It is usually braided, but for the Jewish New Year, it is shaped in a spiral or dome instead. When prepared for an everyday meal, challah is often rolled into a cylinder and baked in a loaf pan.

The delicately flavored bread is a good accompaniment for food, but most bakeries also feature sweet challah, which I prefer for breakfast or snacks. Challah is usually baked plain or with raisins. The crust might be smooth or sprinkled with poppy seeds, sesame seeds, or both. Plain or sweet challahs are more commonly eaten, but savory challahs and challah made with butter or dairy products are now being made also.

Baking bread for Shabbat and holidays is a custom in many Jewish families. Often this bread is braided challah but Moroccan cooks might bake smooth round breads flavored with anise seeds, and Yemenites often bake pita bread instead.

Making your own bread is one of the most joyful experiences in the kitchen. The aroma of the bread baking and its fresh flavor are incomparable. Although letting bread rise takes time, you don't need to hover over it. Yeast dough is very forgiving and even if you've never made bread, you will find it surprisingly easy to make. It is versatile and can be made in a food processor or mixer, or by hand. There is no doubt that serving homemade bread helps transform a meal into a feast.

You also have much more control over the quality of the bread when you make your own. Recently I was surprised to read on a grocery-store challah label that it contained unhealthful hydrogenated fat instead of the traditional vegetable oil. If you keep kosher, you also have to watch out for milk or whey listed in the ingredients, which makes them not kosher for accompanying meat meals.

Many time-honored Jewish cakes and pastries, such as babka and cinnamon rolls, are made with yeast rather than baking powder for a simple reason: baking powder is a relatively recent invention, and before it became available, all cakes were leavened with yeast or with beaten eggs. These cakes remain popular today because yeast-risen dough has an incomparable flavor and texture. There is no reason to hesitate to make yeast cakes at home. Like challah, they are not difficult to make, and nothing surpasses their wonderful fresh-baked taste.

✿ Challah

Basic Challah Dough

Makes enough dough for 1 medium loaf

Use these ingredients for preparing a basic challah dough by hand, by mixer, or by food processor, following the methods described below. The recipes that follow in this chapter use different quantities of ingredients but follow the same basic methods.

$^1/_2$ **cup plus 2 tablespoons warm water (105°F to 115°F)**

1 envelope dry yeast ($^1/_4$ ounce or 2$^1/_2$ teaspoons); see Note

1 tablespoon plus 1$^1/_2$ teaspoons sugar

About 2$^3/_4$ to 3 cups unbleached all-purpose flour

$^1/_4$ **cup plus 2 tablespoons vegetable oil**

2 large eggs

1$^1/_2$ teaspoons salt

Note: For these and all yeast dough recipes, you can use fresh yeast: 1 cake fresh yeast ($^3/_5$ ounce) is the equivalent of $^1/_4$-ounce envelope (2$^1/_2$ teaspoons) of dry yeast. Crumble the fresh yeast into the water, sprinkle 1 teaspoon sugar over the mixture, stir, then let stand for 10 minutes.

Prepared By Hand

Challah dough is fun and easy to mix and knead by hand. As with all yeast doughs, the amount of flour needed to absorb the liquid varies with the humidity, the flour's dryness, and the size of the eggs. But remember that bread dough is forgiving and works well in a wide range of flour to liquid ratios.

Do try to keep the dough soft. Although firm dough is easier to braid, soft dough gives the lightest, most delicious bread. Use this recipe or follow this method for any challah recipe.

1. Pour $^1/_4$ cup of the water into a small bowl. Sprinkle yeast over the water and 1 teaspoon sugar over yeast. Let yeast mixture stand about 10 minutes or until foamy. Stir if not smooth. Oil a large bowl.

2. Sift 2$^3/_4$ cups of the flour into a large bowl. Make large, deep well in center of flour. Add yeast mixture, remaining sugar, oil, eggs, remaining water, and salt to well. Mix ingredients in well with a wooden spoon until blended.

3. Mix in flour, first with a spoon, then by hand, until ingredients come together to form a dough. Dough should be soft and sticky. Knead dough vigorously on work surface until it is very smooth and elastic, about 7 minutes; during kneading, if it sticks to your fingers, add more flour 1 tablespoon at a time, until dough is no longer very sticky.

4. Put dough into oiled bowl and turn dough over to oil all surfaces. Cover with warm, slightly damp towel or plastic wrap and let rise in warm draft-free area about 1 hour 15 minutes or until doubled.

5. Remove dough with rubber spatula to work surface. Knead dough lightly again about 30 seconds to knock out air. Clean bowl if necessary. Return dough to bowl, cover, and let rise again until doubled, about 1 hour.

6. Shape and bake dough as desired (see recipes).

Prepared By Mixer

Use a heavy-duty mixer with a dough hook for this recipe. It is the best and most efficient way to mix and knead large amounts of dough and to prepare doughs that are very sticky.

1. Pour $^1/_4$ cup of the water into a small bowl. Sprinkle yeast into water, then sprinkle 1 teaspoon sugar into yeast water. Let stand about 10 minutes or until foamy. Oil a large bowl.

2. Sift 2$^3/_4$ cups flour into bowl of mixer fitted with dough hook. Make large, deep well in center of flour. Add yeast mixture, remaining sugar, oil, eggs, remaining water, and salt to well. Mix at medium-low speed, pushing flour in often at first and scraping dough down occasionally from bowl and from hook, until ingredients come together in a soft, sticky dough. Add remaining flour and beat until blended in.

3. Mix dough at medium speed to knead it, scraping down twice, about 5 minutes or until dough is smooth and almost cleans sides of bowl. Pinch dough quickly; if it sticks to your fingers, beat in more flour 1 tablespoon at a time until dough is no longer very sticky. If you add flour, mix at medium speed about 2 minutes. Dough should be soft, smooth, and elastic.

4. Put dough into oiled bowl and turn dough over to oil all surfaces. Cover with warm, slightly damp towel or plastic wrap. Let rise in warm draft-free area about 1 1/4 hours or until nearly doubled.

5. Knead dough lightly in bowl to knock out air. Cover and let rise again about 1 hour or until nearly doubled.

6. Shape and bake dough as desired (see recipes).

Prepared by Food Processor

I love making challah dough in the food processor because it is so quick and easy and produces very good results. In fact, the dough is mixed and kneaded in less than three minutes! Naturally, the amount you can make is limited by the size of your food processor.

I use a medium-size (10- to 12-cup capacity) food processor to mix this dough, which is enough for 1 medium loaf.

If you are in a hurry, you can skip the dough's second rising; the loaf won't be quite as light but it will still taste good.

1. Pour 1/4 cup of the water into small bowl. Sprinkle yeast over water. Sprinkle 1 teaspoon of sugar over yeast. Let stand about 10 minutes or until foamy. Stir if not smooth. Oil a large bowl.

2. Fit food processor with dough blade. Combine 2 3/4 cups flour and remaining sugar in food processor. Process briefly to mix. Add yeast mixture, oil, eggs, and salt. With blades of processor turning, pour in remaining water. Process until ingredients come together to form a soft dough; it will not form a ball. Process for about 30 seconds to knead dough. Pinch dough quickly; if it sticks to your fingers, add more flour 1 tablespoon at a time, until dough is no longer very sticky. Knead again by processing about 30 seconds or until smooth.

3. Remove dough from processor and shape it into a rough ball in your hands. Put dough into oiled bowl

---

Hand-Kneading Bread Dough

You can knead bread dough in a mixer with a dough hook or in a food processor. If you are making the dough by hand, there are two basic techniques for kneading it: the slapping method, used for soft doughs; and the conventional bread dough method, pushing with your palms.

Since challah dough is quite soft when I knead it by hand, I prefer the slapping method, which I learned in France. With this method, you end up adding less flour and the dough stays softer, resulting in a bread that is more moist. If you are used to the conventional method or feel more comfortable with it, however, you

can use it. Bagel dough is firmer than challah dough and works equally well by either method.

Slapping Method of Kneading
With the dough on the work surface, place your hands next to each other on top of the dough, holding it lightly in your fingertips. Pull up the dough and slap it vigorously onto the work surface. Grasp the dough again at a different place, and repeat. Continue slapping dough, lightly flouring the surface if necessary to prevent excessive sticking, until the dough is smooth and elastic and holds together in one piece. It's all right if the dough is

still slightly sticky but it should be much less sticky than it was before kneading. Be sure to handle the dough lightly and quickly so it does not stick much to your fingers.

Conventional Method of Kneading
Put the dough on the work surface. Push the dough away from you against the work surface with the palm of your hand. Turn the dough, fold its top third down toward you, and push it again. Continue kneading the dough, flouring the work surface as necessary to prevent excessive sticking, until the dough is smooth and elastic.

and turn dough over to oil all surfaces. Cover with warm, slightly damp towel or plastic wrap and let rise in warm draft-free area about 1 hour 15 minutes or until doubled.

4. Remove dough with rubber spatula to work surface. Knead dough lightly again about 30 seconds to knock out air. Clean bowl if necessary. Return dough to bowl, cover, and let rise again until doubled, about 1 hour.

5. Shape and bake dough as desired (see recipes).

Braided Challah

Makes 1 medium loaf

A challah braided from three strands of dough is the most popular shape. The dough is simple to shape; it's just like braiding hair. Prepare the dough by hand, by mixer, or by food processor (pages 525–527).

Basic Challah Dough (pages 525–527)

1 egg, beaten with pinch of salt (for glaze)

2 to 4 teaspoons sesame seeds, 1 to 3 teaspoons poppy seeds, or 2 teaspoons of each (optional)

1. Prepare dough. Then, lightly oil a baking sheet. After dough has risen twice in a bowl, knead it lightly on a work surface, flouring lightly only if dough sticks.

2. Shape dough into a rough cylinder. Cut cylinder into 3 equal parts.

3. Knead 1 part briefly and shape it into a cylinder. Roll cylinder back and forth firmly on the work surface until it forms a smooth rope about 20 inches long and about 3/4-inch wide; when rolling dough, press it with your hands held flat and elongate the cylinder from its center to its edges. Taper the rope slightly at its ends. Roll the other 2 parts into ropes.

4. To braid the dough, put the ropes side by side, with one end of each closer to you. Join the ends farther from you, covering the end of the rope on your right side with the end of the center rope, and on top of that, the end of the left rope. Press joined ends together. Bring the left rope over the center one. Then bring the right rope over what is now the center rope. Continue bringing the outer ropes alternately over the center one,

braiding tightly. Pinch each end. Tuck ends underneath loaf. Set the braided bread carefully on the oiled baking sheet.

5. Cover the challah with a warm, slightly damp towel and let rise about 1 hour or until nearly doubled. Preheat oven to 375°F.

6. Brush risen loaf gently with beaten egg and sprinkle with seeds, if using. Bake in center of oven about 40 minutes or until top and bottom of bread are firm and bread sounds hollow when tapped on bottom. (Remove bread from oven before testing.) Carefully transfer bread to a rack and let cool.

Large Challah

Makes 1 fairly large loaf

This beautiful challah is sprinkled with both poppy and sesame seeds. It is best baked on a baking sheet so the heat penetrates evenly. I like to shape the dough as a braid but you can also make it into a braided crown or a round challah. Because this is a large quantity of dough, a mixer is most efficient.

3 large eggs

2 to 3 teaspoons sesame seeds

2 to 3 teaspoons poppy seeds

1 cup warm water (105°F to 115°F)

2 tablespoons sugar

2 envelopes dry yeast or 2 cakes fresh yeast

About 4 cups unbleached all-purpose flour

1/2 cup vegetable oil

2 teaspoons salt

1. Set aside one egg for glaze and the sesame and poppy seeds for sprinkling. Using remaining ingredients above, prepare Basic Challah Dough, Prepared By Mixer (pages 525–526).

2. Lightly oil a baking sheet. Knead dough lightly on a work surface, flouring lightly only if dough sticks. Shape dough in a rough cylinder. Cut cylinder into 3 equal parts.

3. Knead 1 part briefly and shape it into a cylinder. Roll cylinder back and forth firmly on the work surface until it forms a smooth rope about 20 inches long;

when rolling dough, press it with your hands held flat and elongate the cylinder from its center to its edges. Taper the rope slightly at its ends. Roll the other 2 parts into ropes.

4. To braid the dough, put the ropes side by side, with one end of each closer to you. Join the ends farther from you, covering the end of the rope on right side with the end of the center rope, and on top of that, the end of the left rope. Press joined ends together. Bring the left rope over the center one. Then bring the right rope over what is now the center rope. Continue bringing the outer ropes alternately over the center one, braiding tightly. Pinch each end. Tuck ends underneath loaf. Set the braided bread carefully on the oiled baking sheet.

5. Cover the challah with a warm, slightly damp towel and let rise about 1 hour or until nearly doubled. Preheat oven to 350°F.

6. Beat remaining egg with a pinch of salt. Brush risen loaf gently with beaten egg. Sprinkle with sesame and poppy seeds. Bake in center of oven about 1 hour or until top and bottom of bread are firm and bread sounds hollow when tapped on bottom. (Remove bread from oven before testing.) Carefully transfer bread to a rack and let cool.

Round Rosh Hashanah Challah

Makes 1 medium loaf   **P**

The traditional challah to celebrate the Jewish New Year is often sweeter than usual and round in shape. Actually, it is a spiral mounded in a dome. The rounded loaves are made plain or with raisins and are popular also for Yom Kippur eve.

To make sure the challah has a light texture, you let the dough rise twice in a bowl and once after shaping the loaf. The challah tastes best on the day it is baked but you can wrap it and keep it 1 day at room temperature, or freeze it.

I like to make this sweeter, stickier dough in a mixer with a dough hook. You can also make it by hand (page 525).

3 large eggs
1/3 cup raisins (optional)
1/2 cup warm water (105°F to 115°F)
3 tablespoons sugar
1 envelope dry yeast (1/4 ounce or 2 1/2 teaspoons)
About 3 cups all-purpose flour
1/3 cup vegetable oil
1 1/2 teaspoons salt

1. Set aside 1 egg for glaze and raisins, if using. Using remaining ingredients above, prepare Basic Challah Dough, Prepared By Mixer (pages 525–526).

2. If you're adding raisins, rinse, drain, and dry them on paper towels. Oil a baking sheet.

3. Knead dough lightly on a floured work surface. Pat dough into about a 9-inch square on work surface. Sprinkle evenly with raisins, if using, and pat them into dough. Roll dough up tightly from one end to the other, lightly flouring work surface if dough begins to stick.

4. Roll dough back and forth on work surface, pressing with your palms, to form a smooth rope about 28 inches long. Wind rope around one of its ends in a spiral. Tuck other end underneath and pinch firmly to attach it to dough. Press whole loaf firmly with your hands to give it an even round shape. Carefully set loaf on oiled baking sheet.

5. Cover shaped loaf with a warm, slightly damp towel. Let rise about 1 hour or until nearly doubled. Preheat oven to 375°F.

6. Beat remaining egg with a pinch of salt. Brush risen loaf gently with egg. Bake 15 minutes. Reduce heat to 350°F. Bake about 30 more minutes or until top and bottom of bread are firm and bread sounds hollow when tapped on bottom.

7. Carefully transfer bread to rack and cool.

Holiday Honey Challah

Makes 1 medium loaf

Honey gives this challah a distinctive pleasing flavor. The dough is a little stickier than most bread doughs and takes a bit longer to rise. It's easiest to bake in a simple loaf pan, as in this recipe, but if you like, you can form it into a round, following the directions in Round Rosh Hashanah Challah (page 528) and bake it for the Jewish New Year. To emphasize the bread's sweetness, you can add raisins if you like. Honey makes the dough easiest to make in a mixer. You can also make it by hand (page 525).

3 large eggs

$1/3$ to $1/2$ cup raisins (optional)

$1/2$ cup warm water (105°F to 115°F)

1 teaspoon sugar

1 envelope dry yeast ($1/4$ ounce or $2^1/2$ teaspoons)

About 3 cups unbleached all-purpose flour

$1/4$ cup plus 2 tablespoons vegetable oil

$1/4$ cup liquid honey

$1^1/2$ teaspoons salt

1. Set aside 1 egg for glaze and raisins, if using. Using remaining ingredients above, prepare Basic Challah Dough, Prepared By Mixer (pages 525–526) through step 5, adding honey after oil.

2. Put raisins, if using, in medium bowl. Add enough warm water to cover and soak them for 15 minutes. Thoroughly oil or grease an 8 × 4-inch loaf pan. Drain raisins well, put on paper towels, and pat dry. Sprinkle about half of raisins over dough and knead in lightly by slapping dough in bowl. Repeat with remaining raisins. Turn dough out onto work surface. Knead thoroughly until raisins are well distributed.

3. Pat dough to rough 8 × 4-inch rectangle. Roll up from longer side into a cylinder, pressing firmly. Pinch ends and seam tightly. Then roll cylinder again on work surface to press seam further. Place in pan seam-side down.

4. Cover loaf with a warm, slightly damp cloth and let rise until nearly doubled, about 1 hour. Preheat oven to 375°F.

5. Beat remaining egg with a pinch of salt. Brush top of risen loaf gently with beaten egg. Bake bread 15 minutes. Reduce oven temperature to 325°F. Bake about 35 minutes or until top and bottom of bread are firm and bread sounds hollow when tapped on bottom; if loaf browns too quickly, cover loosely with brown paper or foil. Turn out of pan; if bread appears to be sticking, run a metal spatula or a thin knife carefully around bread. Cool on rack.

Keeping Homemade Breads

Since homemade breads do not contain preservatives, they taste best when served fresh. This is true for challah, rolls, bagels, and pita bread, but if they are well wrapped in plastic wrap and kept at room temperature, they also taste very good the following day. After two days their quality is acceptable if they are toasted or heated slightly, but if you know you're not going to eat them after one day, freeze them.

The smaller a bread is, the faster it dries out. Naturally, sliced breads dry much faster than whole loaves.

I slice whole loaves before freezing them so they can be heated easily in the toaster.

Apricot-Pecan Challah

Makes 1 medium loaf

Braiding a challah, then curving it and joining the two ends makes it into a beautiful braided crown or wreath. This one contains pecans and apricots and is sure to please. Prepare the dough by hand, by mixer, or by food processor (pages 525–527).

Basic Challah Dough (pages 525–527)

1/2 cup dried apricots

1/2 cup chopped pecans

1 egg, beaten with a pinch of salt (for glaze)

2 teaspoons sesame seeds (optional)

1. Prepare dough. Then, put apricots in a bowl, add enough warm water to just cover, and soak 5 minutes. Drain well, put on paper towels, and pat dry. Chop apricots. Mix them with pecans. Lightly oil a baking sheet.

2. After dough has risen for second time, sprinkle about 1/2 of apricot mixture over dough and knead in lightly by slapping dough in bowl. Repeat with remaining apricot mixture. Turn dough out onto work surface. Knead thoroughly until apricots and pecans are well distributed.

3. Cut dough into 3 equal parts. Knead each to distribute fruit evenly and to coat fruit with dough so that there are not many pieces of fruit on surface. Roll each piece of dough to rope about 25 inches long and about 5/8-inch wide and tapered slightly at ends, lightly flouring surface only if dough sticks.

4. To braid the dough, put the ropes side by side, with one end of each closer to you. Join the ends farther from you, covering the end of the rope on your right side with the end of the center rope, and on top of that, the end of the left rope. Press joined ends together. Bring the left rope over the center one. Then bring the right rope over what is now the center rope. Continue bringing the outer ropes alternately over the center one, braiding tightly. Pinch each end. Tuck ends underneath loaf.

5. Set braided bread carefully on prepared baking sheet. Bring the 2 opposite ends of braid together, curving braid into a wreath, and pinch ends tightly together.

6. Cover with a warm, slightly damp cloth and let rise about 1 hour 15 minutes or until nearly doubled. Preheat oven to 375°F.

7. Brush risen loaf gently with beaten egg. Sprinkle with sesame seeds, if using. Bake 35 minutes or until top and bottom of bread are firm and bread sounds hollow when tapped on bottom. Cool on a rack.

Sweet and Fruity Challah

Makes 1 medium loaf

Sugar not only makes a challah sweeter. It also gives it a more cakelike texture and rises a bit less and a bit more slowly than a challah with little sugar. This challah is enhanced with dried pears, dates, and golden raisins. The dough is made quickly in a food processor. If you prefer, prepare it in a mixer or by hand (pages 525–526). Baking this challah in a loaf pan protects the sweet dough with fruit from burning because the dough stays slightly more moist in the pan.

3 large eggs

1/3 cup diced dried pears

1/3 cup diced dates

1/2 cup golden raisins

1/2 cup plus 2 tablespoons warm water (105°F to 115°F)

1 envelope dry yeast (1/4 ounce or 2 1/2 teaspoons)

3 tablespoons plus 1 teaspoon sugar

About 2 3/4 cups unbleached all-purpose flour

1 1/2 teaspoons salt

1/4 cup plus 2 tablespoons vegetable oil

1. Set aside 1 egg and dried fruit. Using remaining ingredients above, prepare Basic Challah Dough, Prepared By Food Processor (pages 525 and 526–527) through step 4.

2. Put diced pears, dates, and raisins in a bowl, add enough warm water to just cover them, and soak 5 minutes. Drain well, put on paper towels, and pat dry. Sprinkle about 1/3 of fruit mixture over dough and knead in lightly by slapping dough in bowl. Repeat with remaining fruit mixture in 2 batches. Turn out onto work surface. Knead thoroughly until fruit is well distributed. If dough is very sticky, knead in enough flour, 1 tablespoon at a time, so that it can be shaped into ropes.

3. Cut dough into 3 equal parts. Knead each to distribute fruit evenly and to coat fruit with dough so that there are not many pieces of fruit on surface.

4. Oil or grease 8 × 4-inch loaf pan. Knead dough lightly on a work surface, flouring lightly only if dough sticks. Shape dough into a rough cylinder. Cut cylinder into 3 equal parts.

5. Knead 1 part briefly and shape it into a cylinder. Roll cylinder back and forth firmly on the work surface until it forms a smooth rope about 10 inches long and about ³/4-inch wide; when rolling dough, press it with your hands held flat and elongate the cylinder from its center to its edges. Taper the rope slightly at its ends. Roll the other 2 parts into ropes in the same way.

6. To braid the dough, put the ropes side by side, with one end of each closer to you. Join the ends farther from you, covering the end of the rope on right side with the end of the center rope, and on top of that, the end of the left rope. Press joined ends together. Bring the left rope over the center one. Then bring the right rope over what is now the center rope. Continue bringing the outer ropes alternately over the center one, braiding tightly. Pinch each end. Tuck ends underneath loaf. Slip loaf into prepared pan.

7. Cover the challah with a warm, slightly damp towel and let rise about 1 hour or until nearly doubled. Preheat oven to 375°F.

8. Beat remaining egg in a small bowl. Brush risen loaf gently with beaten egg. Bake loaf in center of oven 15 minutes. Reduce oven temperature to 325°F. Bake about 35 more minutes or until top and bottom of bread are firm and bread sounds hollow when tapped on bottom; cover last 15 minutes so top doesn't brown too much. Run metal spatula or knife around bread to unmold it. Carefully transfer bread to a rack and let cool.

Macadamia-Cranberry Challah

Makes 1 medium loaf ⓟ

Toasted macadamia nuts, dried cranberries, and a touch of honey give this new challah a festive appearance and a scrumptious taste. You can make the dough in a mixer or by hand (page 525–526), but I prefer the food processor to save time.

3 large eggs

²/3 cup dried cranberries

³/4 cup toasted macadamia nuts, unsalted or lightly salted

¹/2 cup warm water (105°F to 115°F)

1 envelope dry yeast (¹/4 ounce or 2¹/2 teaspoons)

1 teaspoon sugar

About 2³/4 cups unbleached all-purpose flour

1¹/2 teaspoons salt

¹/4 cup plus 2 tablespoons vegetable oil

2 tablespoons (liquid) honey

1. Set aside 1 egg, cranberries, and nuts. Using remaining ingredients above, prepare Basic Challah Dough, Prepared By Food Processor (pages 525 and 526–527) through step 4, adding honey after oil.

2. If cranberries are dry, put them in a bowl, add enough warm water to just cover, and soak 5 minutes. Drain well, put on paper towels, and pat dry.

3. Coarsely chop nuts evenly into small pieces but not into a powder. Mix nuts and cranberries. Lightly oil a baking sheet.

4. After dough has risen for second time, sprinkle about ¹/3 of cranberry mixture over dough and knead in lightly by slapping dough in bowl. Repeat with remaining cranberry mixture in 2 batches. Turn out onto work surface. Knead thoroughly until nuts and cranberries are well distributed. If dough is very sticky, knead in enough flour, 1 tablespoon at a time, so that it can be shaped into ropes.

5. Cut dough into 3 equal parts. Knead each to distribute fruit evenly and to coat fruit with dough so that there are not many pieces of fruit on surface. Roll each piece of dough into rope about 15 inches long and about 1¹/4-inches wide, lightly flouring surface only if dough sticks.

6. To braid the dough, put the ropes side by side, with one end of each closer to you. Join the ends farther from you, covering the end of the rope on right side with the end of the center rope, and on top of that, the end of the left rope. Press joined ends together. Bring the left rope over the center one. Then bring the right rope over what is now the center rope. Continue bringing the outer ropes alternately over the center one, braiding tightly. Pinch each end. Tuck ends underneath loaf. Set the braided bread carefully on the oiled baking sheet.

7. Cover with a warm, slightly damp cloth and let rise about 1 hour 15 minutes or until nearly doubled. Preheat oven to 375°F.

8. Beat remaining egg with a pinch of salt. Brush risen loaf gently with beaten egg. Bake 15 minutes. Reduce oven temperature to 325°F. Bake about 25 more minutes or until top and bottom of bread are firm and bread sounds hollow when tapped on bottom. Cool on a rack.

Walnut Challah

Makes 1 medium loaf　Ⓟ

Walnuts are a favorite accent in Ashkenazic yeast doughs, and this rich challah contains plenty of them. Taste a few walnuts before using them in this bread to be sure they are fresh. The walnut oil really enhances the bread's flavor, but it will still taste great without it. A food processor whips up this dough in no time.

3 large eggs

1 to 1¹/₂ cups walnut pieces, coarsely chopped

¹/₂ cup plus 2 tablespoons warm water (105°F to 115°F)

1 envelope dry yeast (¹/₄ ounce or 2¹/₂ teaspoons)

1 tablespoon sugar

About 2³/₄ cups unbleached all-purpose flour

1¹/₂ teaspoons salt

¹/₄ cup vegetable oil

2 tablespoons walnut oil or additional vegetable oil

1. Set aside 1 egg and walnuts. Using remaining ingredients above, prepare Basic Challah Dough, Prepared By Food Processor (pages 525 and 526–527) through step 4.

2. Grease a 9 × 5-inch loaf pan. After dough has risen for second time, pat out dough into a 9-inch square. Sprinkle evenly with all the walnuts. Press them into dough. Roll up tightly in a cylinder, pressing firmly. Pinch ends and seam tightly. Then roll cylinder again on work surface to press seam further. Place in pan seam-side down.

3. Cover loaf with a warm, slightly damp cloth and let rise until nearly doubled, about 1 hour. Preheat oven to 375°F.

4. Beat remaining egg with a pinch of salt. Brush risen loaf gently with beaten egg. Bake about 45 minutes or until top and bottom of bread are firm and bread sounds hollow when tapped on bottom. Run a metal spatula or a thin knife carefully around bread. Turn out of pan and cool on a rack.

Light Challah

Makes 1 medium loaf　Ⓟ

This challah contains less oil than most and egg whites in place of two of the eggs. If you wish, you can use only egg whites. Since challah slices traditionally have a yellow color, use a traditional trick followed for years by Jewish bakers—add a pinch of powdered saffron to the water when you make the dough. Baking the challah in a loaf pan helps keep it moist. I like to braid it before putting it in the pan, so the top has an attractive, slightly braided appearance. I prefer to make this somewhat sticky dough in a mixer, but you can also prepare it by hand or in a food processor (pages 525 and 526–527).

³/₄ cup warm water (105°F to 115°F)

2 tablespoons sugar

1 envelope dry yeast (¹/₄ ounce or 2¹/₂ teaspoons)

About 3 cups unbleached all-purpose flour

3 tablespoons vegetable oil

1 large egg and 2 egg whites, or equivalent of 2 eggs in egg substitute

1¹/₂ teaspoons salt

1 egg or equivalent in egg substitute, beaten (for glaze)

2 teaspoons poppy seeds or sesame seeds

1. Using ingredients above, prepare Basic Challah Dough, Prepared By Mixer (pages 525–526) through step 5.

2. Oil or grease 8 × 4-inch loaf pan. Knead dough lightly on a work surface, flouring lightly only if dough sticks. Shape dough into a rough cylinder. Cut cylinder into 3 equal parts.

3. Knead 1 part briefly and shape it into a cylinder. Roll cylinder back and forth firmly on the work surface until it forms a smooth rope about 10 inches long and about ³/₄-inch wide; when rolling dough, press it with your hands held flat and elongate the cylinder from its center to its edges. Taper the rope slightly at its ends. Roll the other 2 parts into ropes in the same way.

4. To braid the dough, put the ropes side by side, with one end of each closer to you. Join the ends farther from you, covering the end of the rope on right side with the end of the center rope, and on top of that, the end of the left rope. Press joined ends together. Bring the left rope over the center one. Then bring the right rope over what is now the center rope. Continue bringing the outer ropes alternately over the center one, braiding tightly. Pinch each end. Tuck ends underneath loaf. Slip loaf into prepared pan.

5. Cover the challah with a warm, slightly damp towel and let rise about 1 hour or until nearly doubled. Preheat oven to 375°F.

6. Beat remaining egg in a small bowl. Brush risen loaf gently with beaten egg. Sprinkle with poppy seeds. Bake loaf in center of oven about 50 minutes, or until top and bottom of bread are firm and bread sounds hollow when tapped on bottom. Run thin-bladed knife around bread to unmold it. Carefully transfer bread to a rack and let cool.

Onion-Sesame Braid

Makes 1 medium loaf

Savory onion bread is a favorite at many Jewish bakeries. This one is made with challah dough and is delicately flavored with sautéed onions and a touch of oregano. The food-processor method is fastest, but you can also make the dough in a mixer or by hand (pages 525–526).

3 large eggs
³/₄ pound onions, minced (2 cups minced)
2 teaspoons dried oregano, crumbled
5 teaspoons sesame seeds
¹/₂ cup plus 2 tablespoons warm water (105°F to 115°F)
1 envelope dry yeast (¹/₄ ounce or 2¹/₂ teaspoons)
2 teaspoons sugar
About 2³/₄ cups unbleached all-purpose flour
1¹/₂ teaspoons salt
¹/₄ cup plus 2 tablespoons vegetable oil

1. Set aside 1 egg for glaze, and the onions, oregano, and sesame seeds for filling and garnish. Using remaining ingredients above, prepare Basic Challah Dough, Prepared By Food Processor (pages 525 and 526–527) through step 4.

2. Pat minced onion dry with several changes of paper towels. Heat 2 tablespoons oil in large, heavy skillet. Add onion and oregano and cook over medium-low heat, stirring often, about 10 minutes or until soft but not brown. Continue cooking over low heat, stirring occasionally, about 20 minutes or until mixture is dry. Add 2 teaspoons sesame seeds and cook 2 more minutes. Transfer mixture to a shallow bowl and cool.

3. Lightly oil a baking sheet. Knead dough lightly on work surface, adding flour 1 tablespoon at a time only if necessary so that dough can be rolled out; it should still be soft and slightly sticky so it can be easily pinched around onions.

4. Roll dough into 13 × 9-inch rectangle. Cut dough into three 13 × 3-inch strips. Spoon onion mixture evenly down center of each strip. Spread onion mixture over strip, leaving a ¹/₂-inch border of dough on each side. Join long sides of strips by pinching together

borders of dough to form ropes enclosing onions. Pinch ends and edges to seal very well. Turn over so that seams face down. Roll lightly on surface to smooth seams.

5. To braid the dough, put the ropes side by side, with one end of each closer to you. Join the ends farther from you, covering the end of the rope on right side with the end of the center rope, and on top of that, the end of the left rope. Press joined ends together. Bring the left rope over the center one. Then bring the right rope over what is now the center rope. Continue bringing the outer ropes alternately over the center one, braiding tightly. Pinch each end. Tuck ends underneath loaf. Set the braided bread carefully on the oiled baking sheet.

6. Cover with warm, slightly damp cloth and let rise about 1 hour or until nearly doubled in size. Preheat oven to 375°F.

7. Beat remaining egg with a pinch of salt. Brush risen loaf gently with beaten egg and sprinkle with remaining 3 teaspoons sesame seeds. Bake about 40 minutes or until top and bottom of bread are firm and bread sounds hollow when tapped on bottom. Cool on a rack.

Buttery Braid

Makes 1 medium loaf

Challah has become exceedingly popular in America, and some bakeries are making it with dairy products. Enhanced with milk and butter, this rich loaf tastes something like French brioche. It makes a wonderful breakfast or brunch treat or a good complement for meatless meals. Because this dough is rich, I prefer to make it in a mixer, but you can also prepare it by hand or by food processor (pages 525–527).

3 large eggs
¼ cup warm water (105°F to 115°F)
1 tablespoon plus 1½ teaspoons sugar
1 envelope dry yeast (¼ ounce or 2½ teaspoons)
About 3 cups unbleached all-purpose flour
6 tablespoons (¾ stick) butter, melted and cooled
¼ cup plus 2 tablespoons warm milk
1½ teaspoons salt

1. Set aside one egg to glaze. Using remaining ingredients above, prepare Basic Challah Dough, Prepared By Mixer (pages 525–526) through step 5, adding butter and milk to well along with the yeast mixture in step 2.

2. Lightly oil a baking sheet. Knead dough lightly on a work surface, flouring lightly only if dough sticks. Shape dough into a rough cylinder. Cut cylinder into 3 equal parts.

3. Knead 1 part briefly and shape it into a cylinder. Roll cylinder back and forth firmly on the work surface until it forms a smooth rope about 20 inches long and about ¾-inch wide; when rolling dough, press it with your hands held flat and elongate the cylinder from its center to its edges. Taper the rope slightly at its ends. Roll the other 2 parts into ropes in the same way.

4. To braid the dough, put the ropes side by side, with one end of each closer to you. Join the ends farther from you, covering the end of the rope on right side with the end of the center rope, and on top of that, the end of the left rope. Press joined ends together. Bring the left rope over the center one. Then bring the right rope over what is now the center rope. Continue bringing the outer ropes alternately over the center one, braiding tightly. Pinch each end. Tuck ends underneath loaf. Set the braided bread carefully on the oiled baking sheet. Cover the challah with a warm, slightly damp towel and let rise about 1 hour or until nearly doubled. Preheat oven to 375°F.

5. Beat remaining egg in a small bowl. Brush risen loaf gently with beaten egg. Bake loaf in center of oven about 40 minutes, or until top and bottom of bread are firm and bread sounds hollow when tapped on bottom. Carefully transfer bread to a rack and let cool.

Swiss Cheese Challah Loaf

Makes 1 medium loaf

Serve this rich, cheesy bread at brunches, parties, festive dairy meals, or for Shavuot. I like to make this challah less sweet than usual so its flavor complements the cheese. You can use other kosher grating cheeses if you like, such as mozzarella or kashkaval. Because the dough is rich, I make it in a mixer. You can also prepare it by hand or with a food processor (pages 525–527).

3 large eggs

1¹/2 cups grated Swiss cheese (about 5 ounces)

2 teaspoons sesame seeds

¹/2 cup plus 2 tablespoons warm water (105°F to 115°F)

1 envelope dry yeast (¹/4 ounce or 2¹/2 teaspoons)

1 teaspoon sugar

About 2³/4 cups unbleached all-purpose flour

6 tablespoons (³/4 stick) butter, softened

1¹/4 teaspoons salt

1. Set aside 1 egg for glaze, cheese for filling, and sesame seeds for sprinkling. Using remaining ingredients above, prepare Basic Challah Dough, Prepared By Mixer (pages 525–526) through step 4, adding butter to well along with the yeast mixture in step 2.

2. Remove dough with rubber spatula to work surface. Knead lightly. Clean bowl if necessary. Return dough to bowl, cover, and let rise again until doubled, about 1 hour.

3. Grease a 9 × 5-inch loaf pan. Sprinkle about ³/4 cup grated cheese over a 5-inch square area on work surface. Pat dough out over cheese. Sprinkle remaining cheese over dough. Knead cheese lightly into dough. Pat out dough into 9-inch square. Roll up tightly into a cylinder, pressing firmly. Pinch ends and seam tightly. Then roll cylinder again on work surface to press seem further. Place in pan seam-side down.

4. Cover loaf with a warm, slightly damp cloth and let rise until nearly doubled, about 1 hour. Preheat oven to 375°F.

5. Beat remaining egg with a pinch of salt in a small bowl. Brush loaf gently with beaten egg. Sprinkle with sesame seeds. Bake about 45 minutes or until top and bottom of bread are firm and bread sounds hollow when tapped on bottom. Run thin flexible knife carefully around bread. Turn out of pan and cool on rack.

✿ Bagels

Egg Bagels

Makes 18 bagels

Homemade bagels are easy to make. They taste great and have a wonderful aroma as they bake. They will not be as perfectly shaped as commercial ones but you can be sure they will disappear quickly. Use either a mixer with a dough hook or mix dough by hand. If you're baking them ahead, you can wrap them in plastic and keep them 2 days at room temperature. You can also freeze them and reheat them before serving. (This recipe yields more bagels than other recipes to keep ingredients easier to measure.)

6 cups bread flour

1 cup plus 2 tablespoons lukewarm water

2 envelopes dry yeast (¹/₂ ounce or 5 teaspoons)

2¹/₂ tablespoons sugar

¹/₃ cup vegetable oil

4 large eggs

2¹/₂ teaspoons salt

2 or 3 teaspoons sesame, poppy, or caraway seeds, or a mixture (optional)

1. Sift flour into mixer bowl or another large bowl. Make a well in center of flour. Pour in ¹/₂ cup lukewarm water. Sprinkle yeast on top and add 1 teaspoon sugar. Leave 10 minutes until yeast is foamy. Add another 2 teaspoons sugar, oil, 3 of the eggs, remaining ¹/₂ cup plus 2 tablespoons water, and salt to well in center of flour. Mix with dough hook or with a wooden spoon until ingredients begin to come together into a dough. If using mixer, beat dough until smooth. If mixing with a spoon, when adding flour becomes difficult, mix in remaining flour with your hands.

2. Knead dough vigorously on a work surface about 10 minutes or until very smooth and no longer sticky. Put dough in a clean oiled bowl, cover with a damp cloth, and let rise in a warm place about 1 hour or until light but not doubled.

3. Shape bagels (see Shaping Bagels, page 538). Then, preheat oven to 400°F. To boil bagels, bring 2 quarts water and 1¹/₂ tablespoons sugar to a boil in a

large saucepan. Add 3 or 4 bagels and boil 1 minute. Turn them over and boil 1 minute. If holes begin to close, force them open with handle of a wooden spoon. With a slotted spoon, transfer them to a cloth or to paper towels. Repeat with remaining bagels.

4. Put bagels on 2 or 3 lightly floured or greased baking sheets. Beat remaining egg with a pinch of salt. Brush egg over bagels. Sprinkle with seeds, if using.

5. Bake bagels about 20 minutes or until browned; if baking sheets don't fit on center rack, bake them one above the other and switch their positions after 10 minutes. If not serving them right away, cool them on a rack and wrap them.

Water Bagels

Makes 12 bagels

Water bagels are made of a dough moistened with water rather than egg. This makes them chewy. One reason for their increasing popularity is that they are cholesterol free and fairly low in fat. I love them sprinkled with seeds, as in this recipe. You can make them in a variety of flavors by adding the same amount of onion, garlic, cheese, nuts, or fruit as in egg bagel recipes. But they also taste very good plain and make tasty sandwiches.

About 4¹/₄ cups bread flour

1 cup plus 3 tablespoons lukewarm water

1 envelope dry yeast (¹/₄ ounce or 2¹/₂ teaspoons)

1¹/₂ tablespoons plus 1 teaspoon sugar

4 or 5 tablespoons vegetable oil

1³/₄ teaspoons salt

1 large egg or egg white, beaten with a pinch of salt (optional)

2 or 3 teaspoons sesame, poppy, or caraway seeds (optional)

1. Sift 4 cups flour into a large bowl. Make a well in center. Pour in ¹/₄ cup lukewarm water. Sprinkle yeast on top and add 1 teaspoon sugar. Leave 10 minutes until yeast is foamy.

2. Add oil, remaining ³/₄ cup plus 3 tablespoons water, and salt to well in flour. Mix with a wooden spoon until ingredients begin to come together into a dough. Mix in remaining flour with your hands.

3. Knead dough vigorously on a work surface about 10 minutes or until very smooth and no longer sticky. Flour lightly during kneading if dough is very sticky. Put dough in a clean oiled bowl and cover with a damp cloth or plastic wrap. Let rise in a warm place about 1 hour or until light but not doubled.

4. Shape bagels (see Shaping Bagels, page 538). Then preheat oven to 400°F. Set out a cloth for draining boiled bagels. To boil bagels, bring 2 quarts water and 1^1/$_2$ tablespoons sugar to a boil in a large saucepan. Add 3 or 4 bagels and boil 1 minute. Turn them over and boil 1 minute. If holes begin to close, force them open with handle of a wooden spoon. With a slotted spoon, transfer bagels to a cloth or to paper towels. Repeat with remaining bagels.

5. Lightly flour 2 or 3 baking sheets. Transfer bagels to the sheets. Brush them lightly with beaten egg, if using. Sprinkle with seeds, if using. Bake bagels about 20 minutes or until browned; if baking sheets don't fit on center rack, bake sheets one above the other and switch their positions after 10 minutes. If not serving them right away, cool them on a rack and wrap them.

Whole-Wheat Walnut Bagels

Makes 12 bagels

(P)

Unlike many whole-wheat bagels, these are not very sweet so they are good with both savory and sweet accompaniments. I like them with mozzarella or goat cheese and with sliced red onions, tomatoes, and roasted red peppers.

2 cups whole-wheat flour

2 cups bread flour

^{3}/$_4$ cup lukewarm water

1 envelope dry yeast (^{1}/$_4$ ounce or 2^1/$_2$ teaspoons)

2 teaspoons brown sugar or honey

3 tablespoons vegetable oil

2 or 3 large eggs

1^3/$_4$ teaspoons salt

^{1}/$_2$ cup chopped walnuts

1^1/$_2$ tablespoons sugar (for boiling)

1. Sift both types flour into a large bowl. Make a well in the center. Pour in ^{1}/$_4$ cup lukewarm water. Sprinkle yeast on top and add 1 teaspoon brown sugar. Leave

---

Bagels: From Jewish Treat to Global Delight

Fresh bagels with lox and cream cheese are the quintessential Jewish brunch treat. In our family, we have always loved this wonderful combination.

Bagels were brought to the United States by Ashkenazic Jews. In the old days they were served with a little butter, as lox was too expensive. Bagels used to be available only in American cities with substantial Jewish populations—at bagel bakeries and some supermarkets. *Bon Appètit* magazine presented bagels as a top trend in 1997, and now they have moved past a trend; they are loved and available everywhere.

And it's not just in the United States. In France, for example, poppy seed bagels with cream cheese and smoked salmon are now sold at Fauchon's, Paris' showcase delicatessen.

Bagels are easy and fun to make at home. They taste great, often better than the ones you buy. When you bake your own, you don't add artificial flavorings, which I find mar the flavor of some commercially available bagels.

Because of their brief rising and baking time, bagels are one of the fastest yeast breads to make. What is unique about bagels is that they are boiled before they are baked. This gives them their special texture and enables them to bake quickly.

Bagel spreads of cream cheese mixed with chopped lox, chives, or other herbs are easy to make at home and, of course, much more economical. Besides, you can use the type of cream cheese you prefer and the amounts of seasonings to your own taste.

With bagels' new-found popularity, they have become available in numerous new flavors, from herbs to garlic to nuts to blueberry to chocolate chip. Although lox and cream cheese remains the favorite topping, today there is a much greater choice of spreads or "shmears," as they are called in Yiddish. Many of these spreads are now made with ingredients not at all associated with Ashkenazic cooking, like sun-dried tomatoes, spinach, and goat cheese.

---

10 minutes until yeast is foamy. Add remaining brown sugar, oil, 2 eggs, remaining water, and salt. Mix with a wooden spoon until ingredients begin to come together into a dough. When mixing with a spoon becomes difficult, mix in remaining flour using your hands.

2. Knead dough vigorously on a work surface until very smooth and no longer sticky, about 10 minutes. Sprinkle dough with walnuts and knead dough to mix them in. Put dough in a clean oiled bowl, cover with a damp cloth, and let rise in a warm place about 1¹/₂ hours or until light but not doubled.

3. Shape bagels (see Shaping Bagels, below). Then, preheat oven to 400°F. To boil bagels, bring 2 quarts water and 1¹/₂ tablespoons sugar to a boil in a large saucepan. Add 3 or 4 bagels and boil 1 minute. Turn them over and boil 1 minute. If holes begin to close, force them open with handle of a wooden spoon. With a slotted spoon, transfer them to a cloth or to paper towels. Repeat with remaining bagels.

4. Put bagels on 2 or 3 lightly floured or greased baking sheets. If you want to glaze bagels, beat remaining egg with a pinch of salt. Brush egg over bagels.

Bake about 20 minutes or until browned; if baking sheets don't fit on center rack, bake them one above the other and switch their positions after 10 minutes. If not serving them right away, cool them on a rack and wrap them.

Garlic-Butter Bagels

Makes 12 bagels

These savory bagels gain a special flavor from garlic butter that bakes inside them. They're good plain, or split and sandwiched with cream cheese, tomatoes, and grilled vegetables.

4 cups bread flour

³/₄ cup lukewarm water

1 envelope dry yeast (¹/₄ ounce or 2¹/₂ teaspoons)

1¹/₂ tablespoons plus 1 teaspoon sugar

6 tablespoons (³/₄ stick) butter

4 large cloves garlic, minced

3 large eggs

1³/₄ teaspoons salt

Shaping Bagels

1. Make bagel dough and let it rise. (If you prefer, you can make the dough 1 day ahead, let it rise 30 minutes and punch it down. Then cover it with a damp cloth or plastic wrap so it doesn't dry out and refrigerate it overnight. Let it come to room temperature before shaping bagels.)

2. Knead the risen dough lightly. Roll dough into a thick log. For every cup of flour, cut into 3 pieces with a floured knife to make 3 bagels.

(4 cups of flour yields 12 pieces.)

3. Roll each piece of dough into a very smooth ball by holding it under your cupped palm on an unfloured surface, and rolling it over and over while pressing it firmly on the surface. The more the dough is rolled, the more evenly shaped and smooth the final bagel will be.

4. Flatten one ball slightly. Make a hole by flouring your index finger and pushing it

through the center of the dough ball. Twirl the dough around your finger on the work surface to stretch the hole; then insert 2 fingers and continue twirling until hole is about 1 inch in diameter and evenly round.

5. Gently pull the edges to even out the shape of the bagel. Transfer the bagels to a floured board. Cover and let rise 15 minutes. Boil and bake them as directed in each recipe.

1. Sift flour into a large bowl. Make a well in center. Pour in $^1/_4$ cup lukewarm water. Sprinkle yeast on top and add 1 teaspoon sugar. Leave 10 minutes until yeast is foamy.

2. Melt butter in a medium saucepan. Add garlic and cook over low heat, stirring, about 1 minute or until softened but not brown. Let cool slightly.

3. Add garlic butter mixture, remaining water, 2 of the eggs, and salt to well in flour. Mix with a wooden spoon until ingredients begin to come together into a dough. When mixing with a spoon becomes difficult, mix in remaining flour with your hands.

4. Put dough in a clean oiled bowl, cover with a damp cloth, and let rise in a warm place about 1 hour or until light but not doubled.

5. Shape bagels (see Shaping Bagels, page 538). Then, preheat oven to 400°F. To simmer bagels, bring 2 quarts water and $1^1/_2$ tablespoons sugar to a boil in a large shallow saucepan. Add 3 or 4 bagels and simmer them over medium heat 1 minute. Turn them over and simmer 1 minute. If holes begin to close, force them open with handle of a wooden spoon. With a slotted spoon, transfer them to a cloth or to paper towels. Repeat with remaining bagels.

6. Put bagels on 2 or 3 lightly floured or greased baking sheets. Lightly beat remaining egg with a pinch of salt. Brush bagels with beaten egg. Bake bagels about 20 minutes or until browned; if baking sheets don't fit on center rack, bake them one above the other and switch their positions after 10 minutes. If not serving them right away, cool them on a rack and wrap them.

Cinnamon-Raisin Bagels

Makes 12 bagels

Ⓟ

These sweet bagels are made with some whole-wheat flour and are flavored with honey. They're good on their own when you want a bit of a sweet taste with a cup of coffee but you would rather not eat rich cakes or cookies. I also like them spread with cream cheese or cottage cheese.

2$^1/_2$ cups bread flour

1$^1/_2$ cups whole-wheat flour

$^1/_2$ cup plus 2 tablespoons lukewarm water

1 envelope dry yeast ($^1/_4$ ounce or 2$^1/_2$ teaspoons)

$^1/_4$ cup honey

1$^1/_2$ teaspoons ground cinnamon

$^1/_4$ cup vegetable oil

2 or 3 large eggs

1$^3/_4$ teaspoons salt

$^1/_2$ cup raisins, coarsely chopped

1$^1/_2$ tablespoons sugar (for boiling)

1. Sift both types flour into a large bowl. Make a well in the center. Pour in $^1/_4$ cup lukewarm water. Sprinkle yeast on top and add 1 teaspoon honey. Leave 10 minutes until yeast is foamy. Add remaining honey, cinnamon, oil, 2 eggs, remaining water, and salt. Mix with a wooden spoon until ingredients begin to come together into a dough. When mixing with a spoon becomes difficult, mix in remaining flour using your hands.

2. Knead dough vigorously on a work surface until very smooth and no longer sticky, about 10 minutes. Sprinkle dough with raisins and knead dough to mix them in. Put dough in a clean oiled bowl, cover with a damp cloth, and let rise in a warm place about 1$^1/_2$ hours or until light but not doubled.

3. Shape bagels (see Shaping Bagels, page 538). Then, preheat oven to 375°F. To boil bagels, bring 2 quarts water and 1$^1/_2$ tablespoons sugar to a boil in a large saucepan. Add 3 or 4 bagels and boil 1 minute. Turn them over and boil 1 minute. If holes begin to close, force them open with handle of a wooden spoon. With a slotted spoon, transfer them to a cloth or to paper towels. Repeat with remaining bagels.

4. Put bagels on 2 or 3 lightly floured or greased baking sheets. To glaze bagels, beat remaining egg with a pinch of salt. Brush egg over bagels. Bake 20 to 25 minutes or until browned; watch them carefully so raisins don't burn. If baking sheets don't fit on center rack, bake them one above the other and switch their positions after 10 minutes. If not serving them right away, cool them on a rack and wrap them.

Blueberry Bagels

Makes 12 bagels

Bagels studded with blueberries are now easy to find at bagel bakeries as well as many supermarkets. Often I have been disappointed by them, however, as they had artificial flavors. When you bake your own, you can flavor them the way you like. I like them gently spiced and sweetened to complement the blueberries.

4 cups bread flour

³/4 cup lukewarm water

1 envelope dry yeast (¹/4 ounce or 2¹/2 teaspoons)

2 tablespoons brown or white sugar

¹/2 teaspoon ground ginger

¹/2 teaspoon ground cinnamon

¹/4 cup vegetable oil

2 or 3 large eggs

1³/4 teaspoons salt

²/3 cup dried blueberries

1¹/2 tablespoons sugar (for boiling)

1. Sift flour into a large bowl. Make a well in the center. Pour in ¹/4 cup lukewarm water. Sprinkle yeast on top and add 1 teaspoon sugar. Leave 10 minutes until yeast is foamy. Add remaining sugar, ginger, cinnamon, oil, 2 eggs, remaining water, and salt. Mix with a wooden spoon until ingredients begin to come together into a dough. When mixing with a spoon becomes difficult, mix in remaining flour using your hands.

2. Knead dough vigorously on a work surface until very smooth and no longer sticky, about 10 minutes. Sprinkle dough with blueberries and knead dough to mix them in. Put dough in a clean oiled bowl, cover with a damp cloth, and let rise in a warm place about 1¹/2 hours or until light but not doubled.

3. Shape bagels (see Shaping Bagels, page 538). Then, preheat oven to 375°F. To boil bagels, bring 2 quarts water and 1¹/2 tablespoons sugar to a boil in a large saucepan. Add 3 or 4 bagels and boil 1 minute. Turn them over and boil 1 minute. If holes begin to close, force them open with handle of a wooden spoon. With a slotted spoon, transfer them to a cloth or to paper towels. Repeat with remaining bagels.

4. Put bagels on 2 or 3 lightly floured or greased baking sheets. To glaze bagels, beat remaining egg with a pinch of salt. Brush egg over bagels. Bake 20 minutes or until browned; watch them carefully so blueberries don't burn. If baking sheets don't fit on center rack, bake them one above the other and switch their positions after 10 minutes. If not serving them right away, cool them on a rack and wrap them.

Herbed Bagels

Makes 12 bagels ·P·

Some bakeries bake bright green bagels; they're intriguing, but their color usually looks unnatural to me. I much prefer these water bagels, which are delicately flecked with the natural green of fresh parsley and chives and flavored with dried herbs as well. They're good with lox and cream cheese or with sliced ripe tomatoes and cottage cheese.

4 cups bread flour

1 cup plus 2 tablespoons lukewarm water

1 envelope dry yeast (¹/4 ounce or 2¹/2 teaspoons)

1¹/2 tablespoons plus 1 teaspoon sugar

¹/3 cup vegetable oil

1¹/2 teaspoons dried oregano

¹/2 teaspoon dried thyme

¹/4 cup finely chopped fresh Italian parsley

2 tablespoons snipped fresh chives

1³/4 teaspoons salt

1 large egg or egg white, beaten with a pinch of salt (optional)

2 or 3 teaspoons sesame or poppy seeds (optional)

1. Sift flour into a large bowl. Make a well in center. Pour in ¹/4 cup lukewarm water. Sprinkle yeast on top and add 1 teaspoon sugar. Leave 10 minutes until yeast is foamy.

2. Add oil, remaining water, oregano, thyme, parsley, chives, and salt to well in flour. Mix with a wooden spoon until ingredients begin to come together into a dough. Mix in remaining flour using your hands.

3. Knead dough vigorously on a work surface until very smooth and no longer sticky, about 10 minutes.

Put dough in a clean oiled bowl, cover with a damp cloth, and let rise in a warm place about 1 hour or until light but not doubled.

4. Shape bagels (see Shaping Bagels, page 538). Then, preheat oven to 400°F. To boil bagels, bring 2 quarts water and 1¹/₂ tablespoons sugar to a boil in a large, shallow saucepan. Add 3 or 4 bagels and boil 1 minute. Turn them over and boil 1 minute. If holes begin to close, force them open with handle of a wooden spoon. With a slotted spoon, transfer them to a cloth. Repeat with remaining bagels.

5. Lightly flour 2 or 3 baking sheets. Transfer bagels to the sheets. Brush them lightly with egg glaze, if using. Sprinkle them with seeds, if using.

6. Bake bagels about 20 minutes or until browned. If baking sheets don't fit on center rack, bake them one above the other and switch their positions after 10 minutes. If not serving them right away, cool them on a rack and wrap them.

Parmesan Bagels

Makes 12 bagels

Most bagels are firm textured, but those made with cheese are more delicate and should be simmered instead of being boiled. Using a food processor eases preparing the sticky dough. These savory bagels are good spread with a little bit of light cream cheese and sandwiched with sliced ripe tomatoes, red onions, and arugula.

1 envelope dry yeast (¹/₄ ounce or 2¹/₂ teaspoons)

³/₄ cup lukewarm water

1¹/₂ tablespoons plus 2 teaspoons sugar

4 cups bread flour

²/₃ cup freshly grated Parmesan cheese, plus 2 or 3 teaspoons for sprinkling

1¹/₂ teaspoons dried oregano

1 teaspoon salt

¹/₄ cup olive oil or vegetable oil

3 large eggs

1. Sprinkle yeast over ¹/₄ cup lukewarm water in a bowl, add 1 teaspoon sugar and leave 10 minutes until yeast is foamy. In a food processor, briefly process flour, teaspoon sugar, ²/₃ cup Parmesan cheese, oregano, and salt to mix them. Add oil and 2 of the eggs and process with a few brief pulses to mix. Add remaining water to yeast mixture. With blades of processor turning, gradually pour in yeast-liquid mixture. If dough is too dry to come together, add 1 tablespoon water and process again. Process for 1 minute to knead dough.

2. Put dough in a clean oiled bowl, cover with a damp cloth, and let rise in a warm place about 1 hour or until light but not doubled.

3. Shape bagels (see Shaping Bagels, page 538). Then, preheat oven to 400°F. To simmer bagels, bring 2 quarts water and 1¹/₂ tablespoons sugar to a boil. Add 3 or 4 bagels and simmer them over medium heat 1 minute. Turn them over and simmer 1 minute. If holes begin to close, force them open with handle of a wooden spoon. With a slotted spoon, transfer them to a cloth or to paper towels. Repeat with remaining bagels.

4. Put bagels on 2 or 3 lightly floured or greased baking sheets. Beat remaining egg with a pinch of salt for glaze. Brush bagels with beaten egg and sprinkle lightly with Parmesan. Bake about 20 minutes or until browned. If baking sheets don't fit on center rack, bake them one above the other and switch their positions after 10 minutes. If not serving them right away, cool them on a rack and wrap them.

Citrus and Spice Bagels

Makes 12 bagels

Marmalade and cream cheese are the perfect accompaniment for these bagels, which blend the flavors of orange, lemon, cinnamon, ginger, and allspice. They're great for tea time.

4 cups bread flour

³/4 cup lukewarm water

1 envelope dry yeast (¹/4 ounce or 2¹/2 teaspoons)

2 tablespoons plus 2 teaspoons brown or white sugar

2 tablespoons frozen orange juice concentrate

1 teaspoon ground cinnamon

¹/2 teaspoon ground ginger

¹/2 teaspoon ground allspice

¹/4 cup (¹/2 stick) butter, melted, or vegetable oil

2 teaspoons grated orange rind

2 teaspoons grated lemon rind

2 or 3 large eggs

1³/4 teaspoons salt

1¹/2 tablespoons sugar (for boiling)

1. Sift flour into a large bowl. Make a well in the center. Pour in ¹/4 cup lukewarm water. Sprinkle yeast on top and add 1 teaspoon sugar. Leave 10 minutes until yeast is foamy.

2. Gradually stir remaining water into frozen orange juice concentrate until blended; set aside. Add remaining sugar, the cinnamon, ginger, allspice, melted butter, orange rind, lemon rind, and 2 of the eggs to well in flour. Add orange juice mixture and salt. Mix with a wooden spoon until ingredients begin to come together into a dough. When mixing with a spoon becomes difficult, mix in remaining flour using your hands.

3. Knead dough vigorously on a work surface until very smooth and no longer sticky, about 10 minutes. Put dough in a clean oiled bowl, cover with a damp cloth, and let rise in a warm place about 1¹/2 hours or until light but not doubled.

4. Shape bagels (see Shaping Bagels, page 538). Then, preheat oven to 375°F. To boil bagels, bring 2 quarts water and 1¹/2 tablespoons sugar to a boil in a large saucepan. Add 3 or 4 bagels and boil 1 minute. Turn them over and boil 1 minute. If holes begin to close, force them open with handle of a wooden spoon. With a slotted spoon, transfer them to a cloth or to paper towels. Repeat with remaining bagels.

5. Put bagels on 2 or 3 lightly floured or greased baking sheets. Beat remaining egg with a pinch of salt. Brush egg over bagels. Bake 20 to 25 minutes or until browned. If baking sheets don't fit on center rack, bake them one above the other and switch their positions after 10 minutes. If not serving them right away, cool them on a rack and wrap them.

Pita Breads and Pizza

Pita Bread

Makes 8 or 10 pita breads

In Israel pita appears on the table frequently in just about every home. Originally a specialty of Middle Eastern Jews, these tasty breads have been embraced by everyone. Fresh, good-quality pita bread is available everywhere but many people love to bake it at home. Some of my husband's relatives in Israel who came from Yemen still bake it the traditional way, in a round clay oven. Others buy a special electric pita baking pan, with heat elements above and below the dough, or bake theirs in a very hot oven.

In the United States good quality pita bread (which is thicker, softer textured, and fresher tasting than standard supermarket types) can be found at Israeli, Middle Eastern, and some fine foods stores. Pita is also popular in natural foods stores and restaurants because it's usually fat-free or low in fat.

Pita is one of the fastest breads to make at home, as its rising and baking times are shorter than other breads. The dough is easy to make and resembles pizza dough. Don't worry if a few don't puff and form pockets; they'll still taste good. Like fresh pita bread that you buy, you can keep these a day or two tightly wrapped in plastic wrap at room temperature, or you can freeze them.

2 envelopes dry yeast (¹/₂ ounce or 5 teaspoons)

About 1¹/₄ cups lukewarm water

¹/₂ teaspoon sugar (optional)

4 cups bread flour

2 teaspoons salt

1 teaspoon vegetable oil (optional)

1. Sprinkle yeast over ¹/₂ cup lukewarm water in a bowl. Sprinkle with sugar, if using, and leave 10 minutes. Stir to dissolve yeast.

2. Briefly process flour and salt in a large food processor to mix them. Add oil, if using, and remaining ³/₄ cup water to yeast mixture. With blades of processor turning, gradually pour in yeast-liquid mixture. If dough is too dry to come together, add 1 tablespoon water and process again. Process 1 minute to knead dough. Add another tablespoon of water if needed and process again 1 minute.

3. Transfer dough to an oiled bowl and turn dough over to oil its entire surface. Cover with a damp towel and let rise in a warm place 1 to 1¹/₂ hours or until doubled.

4. Knead dough briefly on a lightly floured surface until smooth. Roll dough back and forth with your hands into a thick log.

5. With a floured knife, cut dough into 8 or 10 equal pieces. With cupped palms, roll each piece into a smooth ball, flouring only if dough begins to stick. Put balls on a floured board or other surface. Cover and let rise about 30 minutes or until doubled. Preheat oven to 500°F.

6. Lightly flour 2 baking sheets. Using a floured rolling pin, roll 4 balls of dough on a lightly floured surface to 6-inch circles about ¹/₄-inch thick. Transfer 2 rounds to each baking sheet.

7. Bake about 3 minutes or until beginning to brown. Turn them over and bake 2 to 3 minutes or until firm. Repeat with remaining dough.

8. If not serving pita breads immediately, cool them on racks. Wrap them tightly in plastic wrap or plastic bags.

Sesame Pita Bread

Makes 8 or 10 pita breads

Traditional pita breads are generally made of flour, water, yeast, and salt but there are a few variations. Following the Yemenite tradition, my mother-in-law adds about a tablespoon of black caraway or nigella seeds (also known simply as "black seeds") to the dough. They add a delightful taste to the bread. These seeds are available at some Israeli and Middle Eastern grocery stores and can be ordered from baking supply houses.

Today pita bakeries in Israel and some in the United States are making pita in all sorts of flavor variations, just like with bagels. They also bake stuffed pita breads, which resemble Italian calzones.

Sesame seeds are another time-honored seasoning for pita bread and are a simple way to give pita plenty of flavor. As the pita bakes, the seeds become toasted.

3 cups bread flour

1 cup whole-wheat flour or additional bread flour

2 envelopes dry yeast ($^1/_2$ ounce or 5 teaspoons)

1$^1/_3$ cups lukewarm water

$^1/_2$ teaspoon sugar (optional)

2 teaspoons salt

About 3$^1/_2$ tablespoons sesame seeds

1. Sift bread flour and whole-wheat flour into a bowl and make a well in center. Sprinkle yeast into well. Pour $^1/_2$ cup water over yeast and sprinkle with sugar. Let stand 10 minutes.

2. Stir to dissolve yeast. Add remaining water and salt to well and mix with ingredients in middle of well. Stir in flour and mix well, to obtain a fairly soft dough. When dough becomes difficult to mix with a wooden spoon, mix in remaining flour using your hands. If dough is dry, add 1 tablespoon water. Knead dough by slapping it vigorously on a lightly floured working surface until dough is very smooth and elastic. If it is very sticky, flour it occasionally while kneading.

3. Transfer dough to an oiled bowl and turn dough over to oil its entire surface. Cover with a damp towel and let rise in a warm place 1 to 1$^1/_2$ hours or until doubled.

4. Knead dough briefly on a lightly floured surface until smooth. Roll dough back and forth with your hands into a thick log.

5. With a floured knife, cut dough into 8 or 10 equal pieces. With cupped palms, roll each piece into a smooth ball, flouring only if dough begins to stick. Put balls on a floured board or other surface. Cover and let rise about 30 minutes or until doubled. Preheat oven to 500°F.

6. Lightly flour 2 baking sheets. Roll each ball of dough in 1 teaspoon sesame seeds. Using a floured rolling pin, roll 4 sesame-coated balls of dough on a lightly floured surface to 6-inch circles about $^1/_4$-inch thick. Transfer 2 rounds to each baking sheet.

7. Bake about 3 minutes or until beginning to brown. Turn them over and bake 2 to 3 minutes or until firm. Repeat with remaining dough. Serve pita breads warm, or cool them on racks and wrap them tightly in plastic wrap or plastic bags.

Kurdish Spiced Pita Bread

Makes 8 pita breads

A student in one of the classes I taught on Jewish and Israeli breads gave me this delicious recipe. It was from a friend of hers, a Jewish woman who was born in Kurdistan. The pita bread is topped with oil, grated onions, coriander, and paprika and could be considered a Middle Eastern version of focaccia.

2 envelopes dry yeast ($^1/_2$ ounce or 5 teaspoons)

About 1$^1/_4$ cups lukewarm water

$^1/_2$ teaspoon sugar (optional)

4 cups bread flour

2$^1/_2$ teaspoons salt

2 teaspoons ground coriander

1$^1/_2$ teaspoons paprika

1 cup grated onion

1 to 2 tablespoons vegetable oil

1. Sprinkle yeast over $^1/_2$ cup lukewarm water in a bowl. Sprinkle with sugar, if using, and leave 10 minutes. Stir to dissolve yeast.

2. Briefly process flour and 2 teaspoons salt in a large food processor to mix them. Add remaining ³/₄ cup water to yeast mixture. With blades of processor turning, gradually pour in yeast-liquid mixture. If dough is too dry to come together, add 1 tablespoon water and process again. Process 1 minute to knead dough. Add another tablespoon of water if needed and process again 1 minute.

3. Transfer dough to an oiled bowl and turn dough over to oil its entire surface. Cover with a damp towel and let rise in a warm place 1 to 1¹/₂ hours or until doubled.

4. Knead dough briefly on a lightly floured surface until smooth. Roll dough back and forth with your hands into a thick log. With a floured knife, cut dough into 8 equal pieces. With cupped palms, roll each piece into a smooth ball, flouring only if dough begins to stick. Put balls on a floured board or other surface. Cover and let rise about 30 minutes or until doubled. Preheat oven to 450°F.

5. Lightly flour 2 baking sheets. In a small bowl mix coriander, paprika, and remaining ¹/₂ teaspoon salt.

6. Using a floured rolling pin, roll 4 balls of dough on a lightly floured surface into 6-inch circles about ¹/₄-inch thick. Transfer 2 rounds to each baking sheet. Sprinkle each round with about 2 tablespoons grated onion. Pat lightly so onions adhere. Sprinkle with ¹/₂ teaspoon spice mixture. Drizzle lightly with oil.

7. Bake pita breads about 10 minutes or until firm. Transfer to racks. Repeat with remaining dough. If not serving pitas immediately, cool them on racks. Wrap them tightly in plastic wrap or plastic bags.

Za'atar-Topped Pita Bread

Makes 8 pita breads

Za'atar is a tasty herb and sesame mixture that is sprinkled over pita breads or served with olive oil for dipping soft bagels. You can buy za'atar at Israeli grocery stores. The main herb in the mix is hyssop, which is related to thyme. If you don't have za'atar, you can substitute a mixture of thyme and sesame seeds.

2 envelopes dry yeast (¹/₂ ounce or 5 teaspoons)

About 1¹/₄ cups lukewarm water

¹/₂ teaspoon sugar (optional)

4 cups bread flour

2 teaspoons salt

1 to 2 tablespoons olive oil

About 4 teaspoons za'atar, or 2 teaspoons dried thyme and 2 teaspoons sesame seeds

1. Sprinkle yeast over ¹/₂ cup lukewarm water in a bowl. Sprinkle with sugar, if using, and leave 10 minutes. Stir to dissolve yeast.

2. Briefly process flour and salt in a large food processor to mix them. Add remaining ³/₄ cup water to yeast mixture. With blades of processor turning, gradually pour in yeast-liquid mixture. If dough is too dry to come together, add 1 tablespoon water and process again. Process 1 minute to knead dough. Add another tablespoon of water if needed and process again 1 minute.

3. Transfer dough to an oiled bowl and turn dough over to oil its entire surface. Cover with a damp towel and let rise in a warm place 1 to 1¹/₂ hours or until doubled.

4. Knead dough briefly on a lightly floured surface until smooth. Roll dough back and forth with your hands into a thick log. With a floured knife, cut dough into 8 equal pieces. With cupped palms, roll each piece into a smooth ball, flouring only if dough begins to stick. Put balls on a floured board or other surface. Cover and let rise about 30 minutes or until doubled. Preheat oven to 450°F.

5. Lightly flour 2 baking sheets. Using a floured rolling pin, roll 4 balls of dough on a lightly floured surface into 6-inch circles about ¹/₄-inch thick. Transfer 2 rounds to each baking sheet. Brush each round lightly with oil. Sprinkle each round with about ¹/₂ teaspoon za'atar. Bake pita breads about 10 minutes or until firm. Repeat with remaining dough. If not serving pitas immediately, cool them on racks. Wrap them tightly in plastic wrap or plastic bags.

Pizza Dough

Makes enough for two 10-inch pizzas,
about 6 to 8 servings

You can make this dough in a large food processor, in a mixer, or by hand. Use it for Lecso Pizza (page 104) or with your favorite pizza topping.

1 cup plus 2 tablespoons warm water (105 to 115°F)

**1 envelope dry yeast (¹/₄ ounce or 2¹/₂ teaspoons)
    or 1 cake fresh**

3 cups unbleached all-purpose flour

1¹/₂ teaspoons salt

2 tablespoons vegetable oil or olive oil

1. If using food processor or mixer, pour ¹/₃ cup warm water into a small bowl. Sprinkle dry yeast over water or crumble fresh yeast into water. Let stand 10 minutes until foamy. Stir until smooth.

2. To make dough in a food processor: Combine flour and salt in food processor with dough blade or metal blade. Process briefly to mix. Add remaining ²/₃ cup plus 2 tablespoons water to yeast mixture. Add oil. With blades of food processor turning, gradually pour in yeast mixture. If dough is too dry to come together, add 1 tablespoon water and process again. Process about 1 minute to knead dough.

To make dough in a mixer: Sift 2³/₄ cups flour into bowl of mixer fitted with dough hook. Make large deep well in center of flour. Add yeast mixture, remaining ²/₃ cup plus 2 tablespoons water, oil, and salt to well. Mix at medium-low speed, pushing flour in often at first and scraping dough down occasionally from bowl and from hook, until ingredients come together to a soft, sticky dough. Add remaining ¹/₄ cup flour. Mix at low speed 2 minutes. Continue mixing, adding flour if dough is too wet, until dough clings to dough hook and cleans the side of the bowl. Knead at medium speed for 5 minutes.

To make dough by hand: Sift flour into a bowl and make a well in center. Sprinkle dry yeast or crumble fresh yeast into well. Pour ¹/₃ cup water over yeast and let stand 10 minutes. Stir until smooth. Add remaining water, oil, and salt to well and mix with yeast mixture. Stir in flour and mix well, to obtain a fairly soft dough. If dough is dry, add 1 tablespoon water. Knead dough vigorously on work surface until it is smooth and elastic. If it is very sticky, flour it occasionally while kneading.

3. Lightly oil a medium bowl. Add dough; turn to coat entire surface with oil. Cover with plastic wrap or a lightly dampened towel. Let dough rise in a warm draft-free area about 1 hour or until doubled. At this point you can roll the dough to make pizzas; or knead dough again, cover it, and refrigerate overnight.

Quick Pizza Dough

Makes enough for one 9- to 10-inch pizza **P**

Use this fast, easy dough made with quick-rising yeast to make Pizza with Feta Cheese, Peppers, and Mushrooms (page 297). You can make the dough in a food processor, in a mixer, or by hand.

1¹/₂ cups unbleached all-purpose flour

1 envelope quick-rising dry yeast (¹/₄ ounce or 2¹/₂ teaspoons)

³/₄ teaspoon salt

¹/₂ cup water

1 tablespoon olive oil

1. To make dough in a food processor: In food processor fitted with dough blade or metal blade, process ³/₄ cup flour with yeast and salt briefly to mix them. In small saucepan heat water and olive oil until hot to the touch (about 125°F). With blades of the processor turning, gradually pour in liquid mixture. Add remaining flour and process until combined with other ingredients. If dough is too dry to come together, add 1 tablespoon water and process again. Process 1 minute to knead the dough.

To make dough in a mixer: Mix ³/₄ cup flour with salt and yeast in bowl of mixer fitted with dough hook. Heat water and olive oil until hot to the touch (about 125°F). With mixer on low speed, gradually add liquid mixture. Add remaining flour. Mix at low speed 2 minutes. Continue mixing, adding flour if dough is too wet, until dough clings to dough hook and cleans the side of the bowl. Knead at medium speed for 5 minutes.

To make dough by hand: Mix ³/₄ cup flour with salt and yeast in a bowl. Heat water and olive oil until hot to the touch (about 125°F). Stir liquid into flour mixture. Stir in remaining flour. Knead dough vigorously, slapping it on the working surface, until it is smooth and elastic. If it is very sticky, flour it occasionally while kneading.

2. Transfer dough to a clean bowl and sprinkle it with a little flour. Cover with a damp towel and leave to rise in a warm place about 30 minutes or until doubled.

3. Use with any topping. After adding the topping, let pizza rise 7 minutes.

✿ *Sweet Breads and Babka*

Overnight Shabbat Bread

Kubaneh

Makes 8 servings

I learned to prepare this Yemenite Shabbat yeast bread from my mother-in-law. Like the pastry called jahnoon, kubaneh *bakes slowly all night and is served warm for breakfast on Shabbat. The enticing aroma of* kubaneh *baking permeates the house on Friday night, so you can't wait to wake up the next morning and savor it. Also like* jahnoon, *this slightly sweet bread is served either with sugar for sprinkling or with Fresh Tomato Salsa (page 234).*

Although its baking technique is unusual, the flavor of this bread appeals to everyone. One student of mine said it reminds her of a Polish cake called babka *because it's also a sweet, rich, cake-like bread.*

1 envelope dry yeast (¹/₄ ounce or 2¹/₂ teaspoons)

¹/₃ cup lukewarm water

3 tablespoons sugar

3 tablespoons honey or additional sugar

1¹/₂ teaspoons salt

¹/₂ to ³/₄ cup (1 to 1¹/₂ sticks) margarine or butter, cut into pieces

³/₄ cup very hot water

3 cups all-purpose flour

8 large eggs (optional)

1. Sprinkle yeast over lukewarm water and add 1 teaspoon sugar. Leave 10 minutes until yeast is foamy.

2. In a mixing bowl, combine remaining sugar, honey, salt, ¹/₄ cup margarine, and hot water. Stir until sugar and margarine are completely dissolved. Stir in yeast mixture. Add flour and mix with a wooden spoon until dough becomes difficult to stir. Knead in remaining flour.

3. Knead dough vigorously on a lightly floured work surface, adding flour by tablespoons if necessary, until dough is very smooth but still soft, about 10 minutes.

Put dough in a clean, oiled bowl, cover with a damp cloth, and let rise in a warm place 1 hour or until nearly doubled.

4. Punch down dough, knead it briefly in bowl, cover and let rise again in a warm place about 1 hour; or refrigerate 3 to 4 hours.

5. Let remaining ¹/₄ to ¹/₂ cup margarine stand at room temperature until it is very soft. Generously rub a deep 2-quart baking dish with margarine or butter. Divide dough into 8 pieces. With a lightly oiled rolling pin, roll out one piece on a lightly oiled surface into a rectangle about ¹/₈-inch thick. Spread with about 2 teaspoons of soft margarine. Roll up like a jelly roll. Flatten resulting roll by tapping it with your knuckles and spread it with about 1 teaspoon margarine. Then roll up into a spiral and place it in baking dish so that spiral design faces up. Continue with remaining pieces of dough, placing them one next to other and touching each other in dish. If any margarine remains, put it in small pieces on top. If using, rinse eggs in their shells and add to baking dish on top of dough. Cover dough with greased paper or foil placed on surface of dough and with a tight lid.

6. Preheat oven to 225°F. Bake 3 hours or until golden brown. Remove eggs. Turn bread out onto a plate, then onto another plate and back into baking dish, so it is now upside down. Return eggs to baking dish. Cover dough. Reduce oven temperature to 180 to 200°F and bake overnight. Serve warm.

Rich Cinnamon Rolls with Raisins

Makes 15 cakes

D

Unlike most cinnamon rolls, these delicious yeast-risen cakes are flavored with a creamy cinnamon filling instead of the usual sprinkling of cinnamon and sugar. They are great for breaking the Yom Kippur fast or make a superb brunch treat.

1 envelope dry yeast (¹/₄ ounce or 2¹/₂ teaspoons)
2 tablespoons warm water (110°F)
1 tablespoon sugar
2 cups all-purpose flour
1 teaspoon salt
4 large eggs
1 large egg yolk
¹/₂ cup (1 stick) butter, cut into 16 pieces, room temperature
Creamy Cinnamon Filling (page 549)
¹/₂ cup light raisins

1. Sprinkle yeast over water in a small bowl; add ¹/₄ teaspoon sugar. Let stand 10 minutes or until foamy. Stir yeast mixture.

2. Put flour into bowl of mixer; make a well in center. Add salt, remaining 2³/₄ teaspoons sugar, and 3 whole eggs. (Keep fourth egg in refrigerator to use as glaze.)

3. Mix ingredients in center of well briefly with dough hook of mixer. Add yeast mixture. Mix at low speed until mixture comes together into a dough, pushing in flour occasionally. Scrape down mixture. Add egg yolk; beat until blended. Continue beating on medium speed about 12 minutes or until dough is very smooth. Add butter pieces. Beat on low speed, scraping down dough often, just until butter is blended in. Dough will be soft.

4. Lightly oil a medium bowl. Place dough in oiled bowl; turn dough over to oil surface. Cover with damp towel or plastic wrap; let dough rise in a warm draft-free place about 1¹/₂ hours or until nearly doubled. Gently turn dough over several times to knock out air. Return to bowl. Cover and refrigerate at least 4 hours or overnight.

5. Prepare filling. Refrigerate 1¹/₂ hours to overnight.

6. Lightly butter 2 baking sheets. Beat 1 egg with a pinch of salt in a small bowl to use as glaze.

7. On a cool floured surface, roll out dough into a 10 × 15-inch rectangle, flouring often. Whisk filling. Spread it over dough, leaving a 1-inch border on one long side. Sprinkle raisins evenly over filling. Brush plain border with egg glaze. Roll up dough from opposite long side like a jelly roll. Press roll of dough along egg-brushed border to seal.

8. Trim ends. Cut a 1-inch slice of rolled dough. Using rubber spatula, set slice on buttered baking sheet, with more narrow side of slice (side that was pressed with knife) facing down. Slice remaining dough; set slices about 2 inches apart on sheet. Work quickly so dough will not become too soft. Press any uneven slices into an even round shape.

9. Let rolls rise uncovered in a draft-free area about 30 minutes. Preheat oven to 400°F.

10. Bake rolls on center rack of oven. If there is room for only 1 baking sheet on center rack, bake in 2 batches. Bake them at 400°F 12 minutes. Reduce oven temperature to 350°F. Bake 10 to 12 more minutes or until rolls are golden brown. Transfer to a rack; cool slightly. Serve warm or at room temperature.

Creamy Cinnamon Filling

Makes about 1³/₄ cups

Spread this on a yeast dough or challah dough and roll it up to make luscious sweet rolls, such as Rich Cinnamon Rolls with Raisins (pages 548–549). You can use it to fill cream puffs and it's good in fruit tarts or pies too, especially those made with apples or pears. Spread this filling in a tart or pie shell, then top with the fruit. You can keep this filling for 2 days in the refrigerator.

5 large egg yolks
6 tablespoons sugar
³/₄ teaspoon ground cinnamon
2 tablespoons plus 2 teaspoons cornstarch
1¹/₂ cups milk

1. Whisk egg yolks in a medium bowl. Add sugar and cinnamon; whisk until blended. Lightly whisk in cornstarch.

2. Bring milk to a boil in a heavy medium saucepan. Gradually whisk hot milk into yolk mixture. Return to

saucepan. Cook over medium-low heat, whisking constantly, until mixture is very thick and barely comes to a boil; it will be too thick to bubble. Cook over low heat, whisking constantly, 1 minute. Do not overcook or yolks will curdle. Remove from heat. Transfer to a bowl; dab with a small piece of butter to prevent a skin from forming. If not using immediately, cover with a piece of plastic wrap directly on the surface of the filling. Let cool slightly, then refrigerate.

Chocolate Chip Sweet Rolls

Makes about 15 sweet rolls

The recipe for these scrumptious pastries came about as a result of a request from several students at a class I taught on Jewish breads. The filling is simply a sprinkling of chocolate chips, cinnamon, and sugar, and the dough comes together easily in a mixer. Make them pareve or dairy, according to how you'd like to serve them. They're great for breakfast, brunch, or coffee breaks.

1 envelope dry yeast (¹/₄ ounce or 2¹/₂ teaspoons)
¹/₄ cup warm water (110°F)
5 tablespoons plus 1 teaspoon sugar
2 cups all-purpose flour
1 teaspoon salt
3 large eggs
¹/₂ cup (1 stick) butter or margarine, 8 tablespoons cut into 12 pieces, room temperature, or vegetable oil
2 teaspoons ground cinnamon
1 cup semisweet or bittersweet chocolate chips

1. In a small bowl sprinkle yeast over water; add 1 teaspoon sugar. Let stand 10 minutes or until foamy. Stir yeast mixture.

2. Put flour into bowl of mixer; make a well in center. Add salt, 1 tablespoon sugar, and 2 of the eggs. (Keep third egg in refrigerator to use as glaze.)

3. Mix ingredients in center of well briefly with dough hook of mixer. Add yeast mixture. Mix at low speed until mixture comes together into a dough, pushing in flour occasionally. Scrape down mixture. Continue beating on medium speed about 12 minutes or until dough is very smooth. Add butter pieces or 6 tablespoons oil. Beat on low speed, scraping down dough often, just until butter is blended in. Dough should be soft; if it is dry, beat in 1 tablespoon water.

4. Lightly oil a medium bowl. Place dough in oiled bowl; turn dough over to oil surface. Cover with damp towel or plastic wrap; let dough rise in a warm draft-free place about 1¹/₂ hours or until nearly doubled. Gently turn dough over several times to knock out air. Return to bowl. Cover and refrigerate at least 4 hours or overnight.

5. Lightly butter 2 baking sheets. In a small bowl beat 1 egg with a pinch of salt to use as glaze.

6. Mix cinnamon with remaining 4 tablespoons sugar. Melt remaining 2 tablespoons butter. On a cool floured surface, roll out dough into a 10 × 15-inch rectangle, flouring often. Brush dough lightly with melted butter or oil. Sprinkle evenly with cinnamon-sugar, then with chocolate chips. Brush plain border with egg glaze. Roll up dough from opposite long side like a jelly roll. Press roll of dough along egg-brushed border to seal.

7. Trim ends. Cut a 1-inch slice of rolled dough. Using rubber spatula, set slice on buttered baking sheet, with more narrow side of slice (side that was pressed with knife) facing down. Slice remaining dough; set slices about 2 inches apart on sheet. Work quickly so dough will not become too soft. Press any uneven slices into an even round shape.

8. Let rolls rise uncovered in a draft-free area about 30 minutes. Preheat oven to 400°F with rack in center of oven.

9. When baking rolls, set baking sheet on center rack; if necessary, bake in 2 batches. Bake them 12 minutes. Reduce oven temperature to 350°F. Bake 10 to 12 more minutes or until rolls are golden brown. Transfer to a rack; cool slightly. Serve warm or at room temperature.

Poppy Seed–Lemon Rolls

Makes 15 sweet rolls **D** or **P**

These lemon-glazed sweet rolls make a welcome treat on Shabbat morning or at a festive brunch. You can bake them ahead and freeze them.

1 envelope dry yeast (¹/₄ ounce or 2¹/₂ teaspoons)

3 tablespoons warm water (110°F)

1 tablespoon sugar

2 cups all-purpose flour

1 teaspoon salt

3 large eggs

1 large egg yolk

2 teaspoons grated lemon rind

7 tablespoons butter or margarine, cut into 14 pieces, room temperature, or vegetable oil

Poppy Seed Filling for Sweet Rolls (page 551)

Lemon Glaze (page 551)

1. In a small bowl sprinkle yeast over water; add ¹/₄ teaspoon sugar. Let stand 10 minutes or until foamy. Stir yeast mixture.

2. Put flour into bowl of mixer; make a well in center. Add salt, remaining 2³/₄ teaspoons sugar and whole eggs.

3. Mix ingredients in center of well briefly with dough hook of mixer. Add yeast mixture. Mix at low speed until mixture comes together into a dough, pushing in flour occasionally. Scrape down mixture. Add egg yolk; beat until blended. Continue beating on medium speed about 12 minutes or until dough is very smooth. Add lemon rind and butter pieces. Beat on low speed, scraping down dough often, just until butter is blended in. Dough will be soft.

4. Lightly oil a medium bowl. Place dough in oiled bowl; turn dough over to oil surface. Cover with damp towel or plastic wrap; let dough rise in a warm draft-free place about 1¹/₂ hours or until nearly doubled. Gently turn dough over several times to knock out air. Return to bowl. Cover and refrigerate at least 4 hours or overnight.

5. Prepare filling. Refrigerate 1 hour to overnight.

6. Lightly grease 2 baking sheets. On a cool floured surface, roll out dough into a 10 × 15-inch rectangle, flouring often. Spread filling over dough, leaving a

1-inch border on one long side. Roll up dough from opposite long side like a jelly roll. Pinch roll of dough along edges to seal.

7. Trim ends. Cut a 1-inch slice of rolled dough. Using rubber spatula, set slice on baking sheet, with more narrow side of slice (side that was pressed with knife) facing down. Slice remaining dough; set slices about 2 inches apart on sheet. Work quickly so dough will not become too soft. Press any uneven slices into an even round shape.

8. Let rolls rise uncovered in a draft-free area about 30 minutes. Meanwhile, prepare glaze.

9. Preheat oven to 400°F. Bake rolls in center rack of oven 12 minutes. Reduce oven temperature to 350°F. Bake 10 to 12 more minutes or until rolls are golden brown. Transfer to a rack; cool slightly. Spread with glaze while still warm. Serve warm or at room temperature.

Poppy Seed Filling for Sweet Rolls

Makes about 1²/₃ cups

Lemon zest and juice add a fresh tang to this sweet filling. Your poppy seed rolls will taste even better than the ones you can buy at the bakery.

1¹/₄ cups poppy seeds

³/₄ cup water

³/₄ cup sugar

2 tablespoons butter, margarine, or vegetable oil

¹/₃ cup finely chopped candied orange peel

2 tablespoons strained fresh lemon juice

2 teaspoons grated lemon rind

Grind poppy seeds in a spice (or coffee bean) grinder. In small saucepan combine poppy seeds, water, and sugar and bring to a simmer. Cook over low heat, stirring often, 15 minutes. Add butter, candied orange peel, and lemon juice. Stir over low heat about 5 minutes or until filling is thick and well blended. Remove from heat. Stir in grated lemon rind. Refrigerate before using.

Note: If you don't have a spice grinder or two separate coffee grinders, you can use one coffee grinder. When finished grinding spices, clean out thoroughly and run dried bread pieces through it to absorb lingering odors.

Lemon Glaze

Makes enough for 15 sweet rolls

Spread this glaze on sweet rolls, especially those with citrus flavors in the dough or filling, such as Poppy Seed Lemon Rolls (pages 550–551). It's best to spread it on the rolls while they are still warm. You can reheat the rolls after glazing them.

³/₄ cup powdered sugar

2 tablespoons butter or margarine, softened

1 to 2 tablespoons strained fresh lemon juice

1¹/₂ teaspoons grated lemon rind

1. Sift powdered sugar in a bowl. Beat butter until very soft and smooth in a bowl. Gradually beat in powdered sugar. Beat in 1 tablespoon lemon juice. If glaze is too thick to spread, add a little more juice, 1 teaspoon at a time. Stir in grated lemon rind.

2. Glaze becomes firm if refrigerated; bring back to room temperature before spreading. If it's still too thick, set bowl of glaze above a pan of hot water until it softens.

Blueberry-Orange Muffins

Makes 12 muffins

American-Jewish bakeries feature a variety of muffins and they're a favorite for home baking too. These are made with orange juice rather than milk, so they are pareve. They make a fairly light, not overly sweet dessert or a terrific, dairy-free breakfast bread.

2 cups all-purpose flour

1 tablespoon baking powder

¹/₄ teaspoon baking soda

¹/₄ teaspoon salt

1 large egg

³/₄ cup plus 2 tablespoons strained fresh orange juice

1 teaspoon finely grated orange rind

¹/₃ cup vegetable oil

¹/₃ cup sugar

1¹/₂ cups blueberries, rinsed and patted dry

1. Preheat oven to 400°F. Line 12 muffin cups of 2½-inch diameter with cupcake papers; or lightly brush muffins cups with oil or spray with oil spray.

2. Sift flour, baking powder, baking soda, and salt into a large bowl. Combine egg, orange juice, orange rind, oil, and sugar in a medium bowl; whisk to blend. Add orange juice mixture to flour mixture and stir gently with wooden spoon until just blended. Do not beat or overmix. Gently stir in blueberries.

3. Divide batter among muffin cups, filling each about ⅔-full. Bake about 20 minutes or until golden brown. Cool about 5 minutes in pan on a rack before removing. Serve warm or cool.

Babka with Cinnamon and Raisins

Makes about 10 servings

A staple of Jewish bakeries, babka is of Polish origin and is made in many versions: as light airy batters, streusel-topped cakes, or swirled with a cinnamon filling, like this one. Some French bakers consider babka to be the origin of their batter yeast cake specialty, babas.

¼ cup warm water (105°F to 115°F)

1 envelope dry yeast (¼ ounce or 2½ teaspoons)

¼ cup plus 1 teaspoon sugar

About 2¾ to 3 cups unbleached all-purpose flour

1 teaspoon salt

½ cup (1 stick) butter or margarine, melted, or vegetable oil

3 large eggs

½ cup plus 2 tablespoons warm milk or water

1 tablespoon ground cinnamon

⅓ to ½ cup white or brown sugar (for sprinkling)

½ cup raisins

1. Pour ¼ cup of water into small bowl. Sprinkle yeast over water. Sprinkle 1 teaspoon sugar over yeast. Let stand about 10 minutes or until foamy. Stir if not smooth. Oil a large bowl.

2. Fit food processor with dough blade. Combine 2¾ cups of flour, ¼ cup sugar, and salt in food processor. Process briefly to mix them. Add yeast mixture, 6 tablespoons melted butter, and 2 of the eggs. With blades of processor turning, pour in milk. Process until ingredients come together into a soft dough. It will not form a ball. Process about 30 seconds to knead dough. Pinch dough quickly; if it sticks to your fingers, add more flour 1 tablespoon at a time until dough is no longer very sticky. Knead again by processing about 30 seconds or until smooth.

3. Remove dough from processor and shape it into a rough ball in your hands. Put dough in oiled bowl and turn dough over to oil all surfaces. Cover with warm, slightly damp towel or plastic wrap and let rise in warm draft-free area about 1 hour 15 minutes or until doubled.

4. Grease a 9 × 5-inch loaf pan. Mix cinnamon with ⅓ to ½ cup sugar. Roll or pat out dough into a 9 × 11-inch rectangle. Brush with 2 tablespoons melted butter. Sprinkle evenly with cinnamon-sugar mixture, then with raisins. Press so raisins adhere to dough. Roll up tightly into a cylinder. Put dough in prepared loaf pan.

5. Cover loaf with a warm, slightly damp cloth and let rise about 1 hour or until nearly doubled. Preheat oven to 375°F.

6. Beat remaining egg with a pinch of salt. Brush risen loaf gently with beaten egg. Bake about 40 minutes or until top and bottom of loaf are firm and loaf sounds hollow when tapped on bottom. (Remove bread from oven before testing.) Run a metal spatula or a thin knife carefully around loaf. Turn out of pan and cool on a rack.

Chocolate-Walnut Babka

Makes about 8 servings

Babka is made by Jewish bakers with several different fillings. Cinnamon is the most popular, with chocolate a close second. Some people fill their babkas with a mixture of sweetened cheese and raisins. This babka is made with a rich dough resembling brioche, made by a similar technique to the classic recipe, but because the dough is soft, the best way to make it is in a mixer with a dough hook.

1 envelope dry yeast (¼-ounce or 2½ teaspoons)

3 tablespoons warm water (110°F)

1 tablespoon sugar

2 cups all-purpose flour

1 teaspoon salt

4 large eggs

½ cup (1 stick) butter or margarine, cut into 16 pieces, room temperature

⅓ cup brown sugar

¼ cup cocoa

1 tablespoon butter or margarine, melted

½ cup chopped walnuts

1. Sprinkle yeast over water in a small bowl; add ¼ teaspoon sugar. Let stand 10 minutes or until foamy. Stir yeast mixture.

2. Put flour into bowl of mixer; make a well in center. Add salt, remaining 2¾ teaspoons sugar, and 3 eggs. (Keep fourth egg in refrigerator to use as glaze.)

3. Mix ingredients in center of well briefly with dough hook of mixer. Add yeast mixture. Mix at low speed until mixture comes together into a dough, pushing in flour occasionally. Scrape down mixture. Continue beating on medium speed about 12 minutes or until dough is very smooth. Add butter pieces. Beat on low speed, scraping down dough often, just until butter is blended in. (Dough will be soft.)

4. Lightly oil a medium bowl. Place dough in oiled bowl; turn dough over to oil surface. Cover with damp towel or plastic wrap; let dough rise in a warm draft-free place about 1½ hours or until nearly doubled. Gently turn dough over several times to knock out air. Return to bowl. Cover and refrigerate at least 4 hours or overnight.

5. Grease an 8 × 4-inch loaf pan. Thoroughly mix brown sugar and cocoa in a bowl for filling.

6. On a cool floured surface, roll out dough to an 8 × 12-inch rectangle. Brush with melted butter. Sprinkle evenly with cocoa mixture, then with walnuts. Press so walnuts adhere to dough. Roll up tightly in a cylinder. Put dough in prepared loaf pan.

7. Cover loaf with a warm, slightly damp cloth and let rise about 1 hour or until nearly doubled. Preheat oven to 375°F.

8. Beat remaining egg with a pinch of salt in a small bowl. Brush risen loaf gently with beaten egg. Bake about 30 minutes or until top and bottom of loaf are firm and loaf sounds hollow when tapped on bottom. Run a metal spatula or a thin knife carefully around loaf. Turn out of pan and cool on a rack.

Desserts, Cakes, and Cookies

Fruit Desserts

Sweet Kugels and Baked Puddings

Simple Cakes

P = Pareve   D = Dairy   M = Meat

Cakes with Frosting
569

Lemon Meringue Cheesecake

Sweet Sour Cream Pastry

Meringue Topping

My Mother's Orange Chiffon
Cake

Easy Orange Frosting

Chocolate-Pecan Chiffon Cake

Chocolate Glaze

Sabrinas

Sabrina Syrup

Pies
573

Streusel Apple Pie

Low-Fat Strawberry Cheese Pie

Sweet Cheese Tart

Dessert Tart Pastry

Rugelach and Other Cookies
576

Cream Cheese Dough for
Rugelach or Knishes

Pareve Dough for Rugelach
(or Knishes)

Traditional Cinnamon-Walnut
Rugelach

Strawberry Rugelach

Chocolate-Pecan Rugelach

Orange Mandelbrot

Tu Bishvat Date Bars with
Macadamia Nuts

Sauces, Toppings, and Garnishes
579

Bittersweet Chocolate Sauce

Raspberry Sauce

Blueberry Sauce

Strawberry Sauce

Mango Sauce

Kiwi Sauce

Vanilla Whipped Cream

Vanilla Custard Sauce

Streusel Topping

Apricot Glaze

Raspberry Brandy Syrup

Chocolate-Dipped Oranges

Candied Orange Peel

*J*ewish home cooks and bakeries are well known for their delicious cakes, cookies, and desserts. Cakes and other desserts are part of every holiday celebration, including the weekly Shabbat. Even people who are busy try to bake homemade cakes for these occasions. Getting together for coffee or tea and cake during holidays remains a popular custom.

In the United States, Jewish bakers from Russia, Poland, and Hungary have popularized such treats as cheesecake, strudel, and rugelach. Thus these treats now have a Jewish identity, although, like bagels, they are widely available in supermarkets. But they are even better when made at home.

In the kosher kitchen, many desserts are pareve. After all, festive meals traditionally feature meat as the main course. Sponge cakes, nut and chocolate tortes, honey cakes, chiffon cakes, and Sephardic nut-filled phyllo pastries are some popular pareve desserts. Blintzes often have blueberry or other fruit fillings, hamantaschen are filled with prunes or poppy seeds, and sweet noodle and rice kugels are flavored with raisins or apples rather than cream or cheese.

When a kosher cook reads new cake recipes, substitutions for making them pareve come easily to mind. Orange juice or applesauce replaces milk and buttermilk in cake and pastry recipes, and pareve margarine or vegetable oil are used instead of butter. These alternative ingredients create variations of flavor and texture, leading to two versions of many recipes instead of one. Fruit juices and purees are used to make pie fillings, puddings, and ice creams instead of milk-based custards. Today, with soy milk and rice milk widely available, they are being used to develop an even greater variety of pareve desserts with a creamy consistency.

✤ Fruit Desserts

Garden-of-Eden Fruit Plate

Makes 2 servings Ⓓ

Dates are considered by some Bible scholars to have been the fruit of the Tree of Life in the story of Adam and Eve. Some say that figs were the fruit of the Tree of Knowledge—the forbidden fruit that Adam and Eve tasted and that led to their banishment from the Garden of Eden. Dates and figs have long been favorite fruits of the Land of Milk and Honey. Here they are matched with a dollop of soft, white cheese drizzled with honey and sprinkled with pine nuts. For a richer treat, substitute mascarpone or crème fraîche for the cheese.

This is a fitting dessert for Sukkot, when fresh figs and dates are in season. Use fine dates, such as Barhi or Medjool, and ripe figs. My husband and I like to make this dish with sweet, delicious Brown Turkey or Black Mission figs that we pick from our tree as we imagine ourselves in the Garden of Eden.

4 fresh figs, halved

4 plump dates

6 tablespoons soft, white cheese, such as ricotta, regular, low-fat, or nonfat

1 teaspoon liquid honey

2 teaspoons toasted pine nuts

On each of two dessert plates, near rim of plate, put 3 fig halves cut-side up, and one half cut-side down. Add dates to plate between fig pieces. Mound 3 tablespoons ricotta in center of each plate. Drizzle ricotta with honey, then sprinkle with pine nuts.

Bananas and Strawberries in Orange-Honey Sauce

Makes 4 servings

Serve this colorful fruit as an accompaniment for sweet noodle kugels and dessert casseroles, such as Pareve Challah Pudding (page 563) or Matzo Kugel with Apples, Almonds, and Raisins (page 20). After a substantial dinner, the fruit makes a light, appealing dessert on its own.

1 to 2 tablespoons honey

2 to 3 tablespoons orange juice

¹/₂ teaspoon grated orange rind

2 bananas

1 large orange

2 cups sliced strawberries

Mix 1 tablespoon honey, 2 tablespoons orange juice, and orange rind in a serving bowl. Peel and slice bananas; add to bowl. Cut peel from orange. Divide orange into segments and cut them in half. Add orange segments and strawberries to bowl. Mix gently. Add remaining honey and orange juice if you like. Refrigerate until ready to serve.

Quick-and-Easy Apple Blintzes

Makes about 6 servings   D or P

Apple blintzes rival cheese blintzes as our family favorites. These take very little time or effort because you make use of ready-made crepes or blintz wrappers that are available in many markets. Of course, if you have homemade blintzes in your refrigerator or freezer, they'll be much better. Keep in mind that because purchased crepes are thicker than homemade blintzes, they usually need more filling.

Many traditional apple blintz recipes call for grating apples and mixing them with sugar as the filling. To my taste, sautéing sliced apples with cinnamon makes a much more delicious filling. The apple flavor becomes more intense and their texture becomes buttery. I consider the few minutes needed to cook a filling as time well spent.

I generally use Golden Delicious, Gala, or Fuji apples. Since these apples are sweet, I don't need to add much sugar. If you prefer tart apples like Granny Smith, you'll probably want to add the larger amount of sugar.

Serve these blintzes for dessert or as a brunch treat. You can make them dairy or pareve, as you please. Depending on the rest of the meal, serve one or two blintzes per person.

12 Basic Blintzes (page 300) made in an 8- or 9-inch pan, or 6 purchased 9-inch crepes

2 pounds Golden Delicious or other apples

2 to 3 tablespoons unsalted butter, margarine, or vegetable oil

2 teaspoons ground cinnamon

2 small pinches of ground cloves (optional)

6 to 8 tablespoons sugar

2 to 3 tablespoons butter or margarine, or 1 to 2 teaspoons vegetable oil (for baking)

Sour cream or plain or vanilla yogurt (optional)

1. Prepare blintzes, if fresh is preferred. Then, preheat oven to 375°F. Let blintzes or crepes soften at room temperature so they don't tear when you roll them. Peel and halve apples. Core them and cut them into thin slices.

2. Heat butter in 2 large, heavy skillets or sauté pans; use nonstick pans to use less fat. Divide apples between the pans. Sprinkle each with $1/2$ teaspoon cinnamon and a small pinch of cloves, if using. Cover and cook over medium-low heat, stirring often, for 8 minutes or until apples are tender. Add about $2^1/2$ tablespoons sugar to each pan. Heat uncovered, stirring, just until sugar dissolves.

3. Combine apples in one pan and heat briefly, tossing. Remove from heat. Taste and add more sugar if necessary; heat, tossing apples gently, about 1 minute.

4. If using homemade blintzes, spoon about $2^1/2$ tablespoons filling onto brown side of each blintz near edge of blintz closest to you. If using purchased crepes, spoon $1/4$ to $1/3$ cup filling onto either side of crepe near edge closest to you. Fold over edges of blintz or crepe to right and left of filling so that each covers about half of filling; roll up, beginning at edge with filling.

5. Grease a shallow baking dish or spray it with oil spray. Arrange blintzes in one layer in dish. Dot blintzes with small pieces of butter or brush very lightly with oil. Bake about 15 minutes, or until hot. Meanwhile, mix 1 teaspoon cinnamon with 1 tablespoon sugar. Serve blintzes hot, sprinkled with cinnamon sugar. Top them with sour cream or yogurt, if using.

Basic Baked Apples

Makes 3 to 6 servings

This easy, fat-free way to bake apples is favored by my mother and me. Because it's wonderful comfort food, it's the dessert my neighbor Valerie Alon serves at the break-the-fast meal after Yom Kippur. Baked apples also make a light dessert after a filling Shabbat dinner. We like to use large Jonathan or Jonagold apples but it's also good with Golden Delicious or Macintosh. When I have very sweet Gala or Fuji apples, I bake them without sugar.

3 large apples (1 1/2 pounds)

1 teaspoon ground cinnamon

2 1/2 teaspoons sugar

1. Preheat oven to 350°F. Do not peel apples. Core them but not quite all the way to the bottom. Put apples in an 8-inch baking pan or any baking dish in which they fit snugly. Mix cinnamon and sugar and spoon a little of mixture into each apple. Pour enough water into bottom of dish so it is about 1/2-inch deep. Bake apples 1 hour to 1 hour 15 minutes or until very tender.

2. Serve hot, warm, or cold, in dessert dishes. If apples are really large, you may want to serve half an apple per person. Spoon a little juice from the pan over each serving.

Prune-Filled Baked Apples

Makes 4 servings

Bite-size pitted prunes are easiest to use because they fit inside the cored apples. If you have large prunes, use a half of a prune in each apple. I learned this easy dessert from my mother. We both like it for Shabbat in the winter.

4 sweet, medium apples (2 pounds)

4 bite-size pitted prunes

1/2 teaspoon ground cinnamon

2 teaspoons sugar

4 teaspoons orange juice

1. Preheat oven to 350°F. Do not peel apples. Core them thoroughly but not quite all the way to the bottom.

Put apples in a baking dish in which they fit snugly, such as an 8-inch round dish. Put a prune in each apple and push it as far down inside as you can.

2. Mix cinnamon and sugar and spoon about 1/2 teaspoon mixture into each apple. Pour 1 teaspoon orange juice into each apple. Pour enough water into bottom of dish so it is about 1/2-inch deep. Bake apples uncovered about 1 hour or until very tender.

3. Serve hot, warm, or cold in dessert dishes. Spoon a little juice from the pan over each serving.

Pecan Streusel Pears

Makes 6 servings

Pears baked with a crumbly streusel topping is an easy-to-make, pareve dessert that always pleases. I find that nuts and oatmeal contribute good flavor and appealing texture to the topping. Many Jewish bakers keep streusel on hand—not just for cakes, but as a topping for baked fruit. Ripe pears are best but you can also make this dessert with underripe, less than perfect ones.

2 pounds pears

1 tablespoon cornstarch

1/2 cup light brown sugar

1 tablespoon strained fresh lemon juice

1/4 cup all-purpose flour

2 tablespoons unsalted butter or margarine, chilled and cut into bits

1/4 cup chopped pecans

1/2 cup rolled or quick-cooking oats (not instant)

1. Preheat oven to 350°F. Peel and slice pears and put them in a bowl. Mix cornstarch and 1/4 cup brown sugar in a small bowl. Add to pears. Add lemon juice and toss to combine. Spoon into a shallow, square 9-inch baking dish.

2. Mix remaining 1/4 cup brown sugar with flour in a small bowl. With 2 knives, cut butter into mixture until coarse crumbs form. Add pecans and oats and stir lightly with a fork. Sprinkle mixture evenly over fruit. Bake about 30 minutes or until topping is golden and pears are tender. Serve warm or cool, in bowls.

The Cantor's Compote

Makes 4 to 6 servings

Cantor Yossi Knoller brought this tasty compote of apples and prunes cooked with sweet wine and cinnamon one year when we celebrated Rosh Hashanah at my brother-in-law's house near Los Angeles. Light and flavorful, it was an instant hit. The compote is good on its own, or with simple cookies or ice cream. You can use pitted or unpitted prunes; those with pits will take a few more minutes to cook.

1/2 pound prunes

4 cups sweet wine

2 cups water

1 1/2 pounds Golden Delicious apples

2 cinnamon sticks

2 to 4 tablespoons sugar

1. Combine prunes, wine, and water in a large saucepan. Let soak 45 minutes.

2. Peel apples and cut them into thick wedges. Add to saucepan. Add cinnamon sticks and 2 tablespoons sugar. Heat 2 minutes, stirring gently to dissolve sugar. Bring to a boil. Simmer about 15 minutes or until apples and prunes are tender when pierced with the point of a knife. Taste syrup, and add more sugar, if needed. Stir very gently to dissolve sugar. Pour compote into a glass bowl and let cool.

Fresh Raspberry Sorbet

Makes 3 to 4 cups sorbet, 6 to 8 servings

This is the way intensely flavorful raspberry sorbet is made in the finest restaurants. It makes a fabulous accompaniment for Pareve Almond Cake (page 564) or Toasted Hazelnut Cake (page 21). Use frozen raspberries when fresh ones are not available. Sorbet is best when served on the day it is made but can be kept up to 4 days.

1 1/2 cups sugar

1 cup water

6 cups raspberries (about 1 1/2 pounds) or two 12-ounce packages unsweetened frozen raspberries

1 tablespoon strained fresh lemon juice, or to taste (optional)

1. Combine sugar and water in medium, heavy saucepan. Cook over low heat, stirring gently, until sugar dissolves completely. Stop stirring. Bring to full boil over medium-high heat. Boil 30 seconds. Pour into heatproof bowl and cool completely. Cover and refrigerate 1 hour or up to 2 weeks.

2. Gently rinse berries and drain. Puree in food processor until very smooth. Pour puree into large bowl. Add 1 2/3 cups syrup and mix thoroughly.

3. Strain mixture into a bowl, pressing on pulp in strainer. Use rubber spatula to scrape mixture from underside of strainer. Stir in lemon juice, if using.

4. Taste, and add more syrup or lemon juice, if needed. (Mixture should taste quite sweet; the sorbet will seem less sweet when frozen.)

5. Chill a medium metal bowl and an airtight container in freezer. Transfer sorbet mixture to an ice cream machine and process until mixture has consistency of soft ice cream; it should not be runny but will not be very firm. Spoon sorbet as quickly as possible into chilled bowl; sorbet melts very quickly. Cover and freeze until ready to serve. If keeping sorbet longer than 3 hours, transfer it when firm to airtight container and cover tightly.

6. Soften sorbet slightly before serving. Serve sorbet with chilled utensils in thoroughly chilled dessert dishes or wine glasses.

Orange Sorbet

Makes about 3 cups, about 6 servings **P**

This delicious dessert is a favorite on kosher menus as it is perfect after any meal, whether meat or dairy. It's fat-free, light, and refreshing and has an intense, natural orange flavor. Be sure to use fine-quality orange juice. Squeezing your own is best.

Sorbet is best when served on the day it is made but can be kept up to 4 days. If your homemade sorbet becomes too hard after a few days in the freezer, puree the sorbet, 2 cups at a time, for a few seconds in the chilled container of a food processor. You can return the softened sorbet to the freezer and it will remain soft for an hour or two.

1 medium orange, rinsed and patted dry

3/4 cup sugar

1/2 cup water

2 1/3 cups strained fresh orange juice

1 tablespoon strained fresh lemon juice, or to taste

1. Using a sharp vegetable peeler, pare the orange peel in strips, removing only the thin orange rind and not the thick, bitter white pith. Put the orange strips in a small, heavy saucepan. Add sugar and water. Cook over low heat, stirring gently to avoid splashing syrup on the sides of the pan, until sugar dissolves completely. Stop stirring. Bring to full boil over medium-high heat. Boil 30 seconds. Remove from heat. Pour into a heat-proof bowl, leaving the strips of orange peel in it. Let it cool completely. Cover and refrigerate for 4 hours or up to 1 week.

2. Remove orange strips from syrup with a slotted spoon. Pour 3/4 cup syrup into a bowl. Stir in orange juice and lemon juice. Taste, and add more syrup or lemon juice if needed. (Mixture should taste quite sweet; the sorbet will seem less sweet when it is frozen.)

3. Chill a medium metal bowl and an airtight container in freezer. Transfer sorbet mixture to an ice cream machine and process until mixture has consistency of soft ice cream; it should not be runny but will not be very firm. Spoon sorbet as quickly as possible into chilled bowl; sorbet melts very quickly. Cover and freeze until ready to serve. If keeping sorbet longer than 3 hours, transfer it when firm to airtight container and cover tightly.

4. Soften sorbet slightly before serving. Serve with chilled utensils in thoroughly chilled dessert dishes or wine glasses.

❧ Sweet Kugels and Baked Puddings

Creamy Hazelnut Noodle Kugel

Makes 6 servings ⓓ

Golden raisins and hazelnuts give a delicious taste to this dessert kugel. The technique of cooking very thin noodles directly in milk makes the kugel exceptionally creamy. As soothing, warm comfort food, it's especially welcome during Hanukkah or on any cold winter day.

2¹/₂ cups milk

1 cup very fine noodles

Pinch of salt

¹/₃ cup sugar

2 tablespoons unsalted butter

¹/₄ cup golden raisins

¹/₄ cup chopped hazelnuts

1 teaspoon grated lemon rind

2 large eggs, separated

1. Bring milk to a boil in a medium-heavy saucepan. Add noodles and salt and cook over low heat, stirring occasionally, 20 to 30 minutes or until noodles are tender and absorb most of milk.

2. Meanwhile, preheat oven to 350°F. Butter a 4- to 5-cup baking dish and sprinkle a little sugar on sides of dish. Set baking dish in a roasting pan.

3. Stir 3 tablespoons sugar into hot noodle mixture. Cool several minutes. Stir in butter, raisins, hazelnuts, lemon rind, and egg yolks.

4. Beat egg whites until soft peaks form. Beat in remaining sugar at high speed and whip until whites are stiff. Fold whites, in two portions, into noodle mixture. Transfer to baking dish.

5. Add enough hot water to roasting pan to come halfway up sides of dish containing noodle mixture. Bake kugel uncovered about 40 minutes or until a small knife inserted into its center comes out dry. Serve hot or warm.

Low-Fat Vanilla Rice Kugel

Makes 6 servings ⓓ

Using Arborio rice ensures that this rice kugel will be creamy even if made with low-fat or nonfat milk. I love the flavor that a vanilla bean gives to the kugel as the rice simmers in the milk.

1 cup Arborio or other short-grain rice

5 cups low-fat or nonfat milk

1 vanilla bean, split

Pinch of salt

6 tablespoons sugar

Cinnamon

1. Bring 2 quarts water to a boil in a large, heavy saucepan and add rice. Boil uncovered 7 minutes; drain well.

2. Preheat oven to 350°F. Bring 4 cups milk to a boil in same saucepan over medium-high heat, stirring occasionally. Add vanilla bean, rice, and salt. Cook uncovered over medium-low heat, stirring often, about 15 minutes or until rice is very soft and absorbs most of milk. Remove from heat and stir in sugar. Remove vanilla bean.

3. Spoon rice mixture into a buttered 2-quart baking dish. Bake uncovered 30 minutes or until firm. Serve warm, sprinkled with cinnamon.

Ginger-Raisin Rice Kugel

Makes 6 servings ⓓ

My husband, Yakir, and I love candied ginger and enjoy adding it to creamy desserts. The sweet ginger gives this kugel its unique spicy taste.

1 cup Arborio or other short-grain rice

5 cups milk

Pinch of salt

¹/₃ cup sugar

¹/₂ cup raisins

2 to 3 tablespoons finely diced candied ginger

2 teaspoons ground cinnamon, plus more for sprinkling

¹/₂ teaspoon freshly ground nutmeg

2 tablespoons unsalted butter, cut into small pieces

1. Bring 2 quarts water to a boil in a large, heavy saucepan and add rice. Boil uncovered 7 minutes; drain well.

2. Preheat oven to 350°F. Bring milk to a boil in same saucepan over medium-high heat, stirring occasionally. Add rice and salt. Cook uncovered over medium-low heat, stirring often, about 15 minutes or until rice is very soft and absorbs most of milk. Remove from heat and stir in sugar. Add raisins, candied ginger, 2 teaspoons cinnamon, and nutmeg.

3. Spoon the rice mixture into a buttered 2-quart baking dish. Dot with butter. Bake uncovered 30 minutes or until firm. Serve warm, sprinkled with cinnamon.

Apple-Challah Bread Pudding

Makes 6 servings

Bread pudding made with challah is a scrumptious dessert. This one is studded with apples and flavored with cinnamon and vanilla. It rises slightly and, like a soufflé sinks when cool. For special occasions you might like to accompany the pudding with Vanilla Custard Sauce (page 581) or Apples in Spiced Wine (page 172).

4 ounces challah (1/4 of a 1-pound challah), day-old or stale

1 1/4 cups milk

1 pound sweet apples such as Golden Delicious

6 tablespoons sugar

2 large eggs, separated

1 teaspoon vanilla extract

1 1/2 teaspoons ground cinnamon

2 tablespoons butter, cut into small pieces

1. Preheat oven to 375°F. Generously butter a 5-cup baking dish. Remove crust and cut challah into chunks. Put it in a large bowl. Bring milk to a simmer in a small saucepan. Pour it over bread and let stand about 5 minutes to soften.

2. Peel, halve, and core apples. Slice them very thin.

3. Mash challah with a fork. Add 4 tablespoons sugar, egg yolks, vanilla, and 1 teaspoon cinnamon and mix well. Add apples and mix well.

4. Whip egg whites until they form soft peaks. Gradually beat in remaining 2 tablespoons sugar and beat until stiff and shiny. Gently fold whites, in 2 batches, into bread mixture. Transfer mixture to baking dish. Sprinkle with remaining 1/2 teaspoon cinnamon and scatter butter pieces on top. Bake about 50 minutes or until a thin knife inserted in pudding comes out dry.

5. The pudding is best served warm. Although it sinks when cool, it still tastes good.

Pareve Challah Pudding

Makes about 6 servings

Jewish homemakers originally designed challah puddings or kugels to use up stale challah, but they turned into such popular desserts that modern cooks buy extra challah to be sure there is enough left for pudding. This one is flavored with dried cherries, kirsch, and lemon zest. If you like, substitute golden raisins or chopped candied citrus peel for the cherries. You can also use orange juice for soaking the cherries instead of kirsch.

3/4 cup dried cherries

1/4 cup kirsch or cherry brandy

8 ounces challah or egg bread (1/2 of a 1-pound challah), day-old or stale

1/2 cup sugar

1/4 cup chopped walnuts

3 large eggs

1 tablespoon strained fresh lemon juice

2 teaspoons grated lemon rind

3 to 4 tablespoons vegetable oil or melted margarine

1. Preheat oven to 350°F. Oil a 6-cup baking dish. Combine cherries and kirsch in a jar; cover, shake, and let stand about 10 minutes.

2. Remove crust and cut challah into chunks. Soak it in cold water until softened. Squeeze out excess water. Put challah in a large bowl and mash it with a fork.

3. Mix 1 tablespoon sugar with walnuts; set aside. Add remaining sugar to challah. Add eggs, lemon juice, lemon rind, and oil. Mix well. Add cherries with their kirsch and mix well. Transfer mixture to baking dish. Sprinkle with walnut-sugar mixture. Bake about 50 minutes or until set. Serve hot or warm.

❀ Simple Cakes

Pareve Almond Cake

Makes 8 servings

This easy-to-make French-style cake makes a lovely Shabbat dessert on its own, or with a fresh fruit sauce like Kiwi Sauce (page 581) or Mango Sauce (page 580). If you don't need it to be pareve, make it with butter. If wrapped well, the cake keeps up to four days at room temperature or in the refrigerator.

5 tablespoons pareve margarine

³/₄ cup whole blanched almonds

¹/₂ cup plus 1 tablespoon sugar

2 tablespoons cornstarch

2 tablespoons all-purpose flour

¹/₂ teaspoon baking powder

3 large eggs

2 tablespoons orange liqueur or orange juice or 1 teaspoon vanilla extract

1. Grease an 8-inch round cake pan, about 2 inches deep. Line base with a round of wax paper or foil; grease liner. Preheat oven to 375°F.

2. Melt margarine in a small saucepan over low heat; let cool. Grind almonds with sugar in a food processor to a fine powder. Sift cornstarch with flour and baking powder.

3. Beat 1 egg with almond mixture at low speed of mixer until blended, then at high speed for 2 minutes or until mixture is thick and smooth. Add remaining eggs one by one and beat at high speed about 3 minutes after each. Beat in liqueur. Sprinkle cornstarch mixture over almond mixture and fold it in gently. Gently fold in margarine in a fine stream.

4. Transfer immediately to cake pan. Bake 28 to 30 minutes or until cake comes away from pan and a cake tester inserted into center of cake comes out clean. Carefully turn cake out onto a rack. Gently remove paper. Turn cake over again so smooth side is down. Let cool. Wrap it and keep it at room temperature or in the refrigerator.

Cherry-Vanilla Pound Cake

Makes about 12 servings **D** or **P**

A simple pound cake is many people's favorite dessert. This scrumptious tea time cake is featured prominently at Jewish bakeries but is very easy to make at home. This one is dotted with dried cherries. For a different flavor, try dried cranberries.

One advantage of pound cakes is that they keep very well. Wrap this cake in plastic wrap or foil, and it will keep 3 days at cool room temperature or up to 1 week in refrigerator; or you can freeze it for about 2 months.

1¹/₃ cups all-purpose flour

1¹/₄ teaspoons baking powder

²/₃ cup dried cherries

³/₄ cup unsalted butter or margarine, room temperature

1 cup plus 2 tablespoons sugar

3 large eggs, room temperature

2 teaspoons vanilla extract

5 tablespoons whipping cream, half and half, milk, or water

Powdered sugar (optional)

1. Preheat oven to 350°F. Butter and flour a nonstick 9 × 5-inch loaf pan, tapping pan to remove excess flour. Sift flour with baking powder. Sort through cherries to be sure there are no pits. Rinse cherries and pat them dry.

2. In a large bowl with an electric mixer, cream butter until it is soft, smooth, and most of it clings to side of bowl. Gradually beat in sugar. Beat at medium speed until mixture is very pale, smooth, and fluffy. Beat in 2 eggs one at a time at medium speed, beating thoroughly after each addition. Beat third egg in small bowl. Gradually add it to batter, beating well.

3. With mixer at low speed, add about ¹/₄ of flour mixture. Blend in vanilla and 1 tablespoon cream. Blend in remaining flour in 3 batches, alternating with remaining cream. Stir at low speed just until blended. Lightly stir in cherries until blended.

4. Spoon batter carefully into pan. Smooth top with spatula. Tap pan a few times on work surface to level batter. Set pan in oven with a short side of loaf pan facing back of oven.

5. Bake about 50 minutes or until cake tester inserted in center of cake comes out clean. Cool cake in pan on rack 10 minutes. Run metal spatula or thin knife around edges of cake. Turn cake out onto rack. Carefully turn cake back over and cool it completely.

6. Serve cake at room temperature. Sift powdered sugar over it, if using. Cut cake into $^1/_2$-inch slices with serrated knife.

Chocolate Marble Cake

Makes about 12 servings

When I was growing up, my mother often made marble cake. This simple but really appealing cake entices with its swirled appearance and then delivers a delicious chocolate and vanilla taste.

4 ounces semisweet chocolate, chopped

1³/₄ cups cake flour, sifted

1 teaspoon baking powder

1 cup unsalted butter or margarine, room temperature

1¹/₄ cups sugar

4 large eggs, room temperature

2 teaspoons vanilla extract

1. Preheat oven to 350°F. Butter and flour 9 × 2¹/₂-inch springform pan, tapping pan to remove excess flour.

2. Melt chocolate in medium bowl over a pan of simmering water. Stir until smooth. Remove bowl from pan and let cool. Sift flour with baking powder.

3. In a large bowl with an electric mixer, cream butter until it is soft, smooth, and most of it clings to sides of bowl. Gradually beat in sugar. Beat at medium speed until mixture is very pale, smooth, and fluffy. Beat in 3 eggs one at a time at medium speed, beating thoroughly after each addition. Beat fourth egg in small bowl. Gradually add it to batter, beating well.

4. With mixer at low speed, add about ¹/₄ of flour mixture. Blend in 1 teaspoon vanilla. Blend in remaining flour in 3 batches. Stir at low speed just until blended. (Be sure flour is completely mixed into batter.) Transfer 2¹/₄ cups batter to a bowl and stir in remaining teaspoon vanilla. Stir cool melted chocolate into batter remaining in bowl of mixer.

5. Spoon about ¹/₂ of chocolate batter into prepared pan without spreading. Spoon about ¹/₂ of vanilla batter over chocolate batter. Spoon remaining chocolate batter on top. Spoon remaining vanilla batter over chocolate batter. Tap pan several times on work surface to level batter. Draw knife through batters several times with swirling motion to marble slightly; chocolate batter should show only slightly at top. Tap pan again several times on work surface to level batter.

6. Bake about 50 minutes or until cake tester inserted in center of cake comes out clean. Cool in pan on rack 10 minutes. Release spring and remove sides of pan. Cool cake to lukewarm. Turn over onto another rack. Carefully remove base of pan with aid of metal spatula. Serve cake at room temperature.

Upside Down Prune Cake

Makes about 16 servings

This simple cake is composed of lemon pound cake baked with a layer of moist prunes, which come out on top when you turn the cake over. It's easy to make and is a welcome treat for Tu Bishvat, the tree-planting holiday, which takes place in late January to early February. For this holiday, dried fruits and the desserts made with them are the time-honored treats because fresh fruit was not available during this season before the age of refrigeration and imports. This cake is terrific with tea any time of the year.

16 moist pitted prunes (about 6 ounces or 1¹/₄ cups)

1³/₄ cups cake flour

1 teaspoon baking powder

1 cup (2 sticks) unsalted butter or margarine, at room temperature

1 cup plus 2 tablespoons sugar

4 large eggs

2 teaspoons finely grated lemon rind

1. Put prunes in bowl and cover with hot water. Let stand 30 minutes until softened. Remove prunes from water, set them on paper towels, and cover with more paper towels. Thoroughly pat them dry.

2. Preheat oven to 350°F. Butter a 9- to 9½-inch square pan. Line its base with parchment or foil. Generously butter liner. Flour pan, tapping it to remove excess flour.

3. Set prunes on paper at equal intervals, with their more attractive side downwards. Sift flour with baking powder.

4. In a large bowl with an electric mixer, cream butter until it is soft, smooth, and most of it clings to side of bowl. Gradually beat in sugar. Beat at medium speed until mixture is very pale, smooth, and fluffy. Beat in 3 eggs, one at a time, at medium speed, beating well after each. Beat fourth egg in small bowl. Gradually add it to batter, beating well. Stir in lemon rind.

5. With mixer at low speed, add about ¼ of flour mixture. Blend in remaining flour in 3 batches. Stir at low speed just until blended.

6. Spoon batter carefully into pan without moving prunes. Spread smooth with rubber spatula. Tap pan once on work surface to level batter. Bake about 40 minutes or until cake comes away from sides of pan and cake tester inserted in center of cake comes out clean. Cool in pan on rack 5 minutes. Turn cake out onto rack, carefully remove paper, and cool completely. Serve at room temperature.

Plum Cake

Makes 8 servings **D**

I first became aware of how delicious plums can be in cakes when I lived in Israel. When plum season came in late summer, everyone seemed to be baking plum cakes. Later I learned that the recipes were brought to Israel by Ashkenazic Jews coming from a broad area that ranges from Hungary to Alsace, France. Small oval plums, sometimes called Italian plums or prune plums, are best for this cake. For a rich crumbly topping, you can sprinkle the cake with Streusel Topping

(page 582) before baking it. If you wish, dust the cake with powdered sugar before serving it. You can make the cake ahead and keep it for 1 to 2 days in the refrigerator.

1½ cups cake flour

1 teaspoon baking powder

4 ounces cream cheese, softened

¼ cup plus 2 tablespoons sour cream

4 large eggs, separated

¾ cup sugar

1 teaspoon vanilla extract

1 teaspoon grated lemon rind

¾ pound small fresh plums, halved lengthwise and pitted

1. Preheat oven to 350°F. Thoroughly grease a 9-inch springform pan. Sift flour with baking powder.

2. Beat cheese until soft and creamy. Add sour cream and beat until blended. Transfer mixture to a small bowl.

3. Whip egg yolks with ½ cup sugar until thick and light. Beat in cheese mixture. Stir in vanilla and grated lemon rind.

4. Whip egg whites in a large bowl until they form soft peaks. Gradually beat in remaining ¼ cup sugar. Beat whites for another 30 seconds at high speed until stiff and shiny but not dry. Fold about half of flour mixture into cheese mixture, followed by half of whites. Repeat with remaining flour and remaining whites, folding lightly and quickly.

5. Transfer batter to pan and smooth it lightly. Top with plum halves with their cut-side up, nearly touching each other. Bake about 45 minutes or until a cake tester inserted in cake comes out clean and dough browns lightly. Let stand 5 minutes. Run metal spatula or knife around cake and release spring. Remove pan sides but leave cake on base. Cool slightly on a rack. Serve warm or at room temperature.

Low-Fat Chocolate Applesauce Cake

Makes 12 to 16 servings   (P)

When I adapted my mother's chocolate applesauce cake to be lowfat, I was very pleased with the result. It's hard to believe this flavorful cake is low in fat. Basically I replace part of the oil with applesauce. This gives it an appealing, light texture and helps it stay moist for 3 or 4 days. When I want an accompaniment, I serve the cake with Apples in Spiced Wine (page 172) or with nonfat vanilla yogurt or frozen yogurt.

Oil spray

1 1/2 cups all-purpose flour

1/3 cup unsweetened cocoa

1 1/4 teaspoons ground cinnamon

1/4 teaspoon ground ginger

Pinch of ground cloves (optional)

1 teaspoon baking soda

3 tablespoons vegetable oil

1 cup sugar

1 large egg

1 1/3 cups applesauce

1. Preheat oven to 350°F. Grease a 9-inch square baking pan with oil spray; flour pan. Sift flour with cocoa, cinnamon, ginger, cloves, if using, and baking soda into a bowl. Beat oil, sugar, and egg in a large bowl at medium speed until pale in color and fluffy. On low speed, stir flour mixture alternately with applesauce into egg mixture; mix well.

2. Bake in prepared pan 25 to 30 minutes, or until a cake tester inserted in cake comes out clean. Turn out onto a rack or leave in the pan; cool completely. Serve at room temperature.

Honey Fruitcake

Makes 10 to 12 servings   (P)

In my local Jewish bakeries fruitcake has become popular in recent years for Rosh Hashanah. Unlike many American and English fruitcakes, these are studded with fruit instead of being dense with fruit. I like to flavor mine with a little honey and to use dried rather than candied fruit. This cake is so much better than typical fruitcake that I enjoy making and eating it at other times of the year.

1/2 cup chopped mixed dried fruits, such as pears, apricots, and prunes

3/4 cup raisins

1/4 cup rum or orange juice

1 3/4 cups all-purpose flour

1/2 teaspoon baking powder

1/2 cup vegetable oil or margarine

2 tablespoons honey

1/2 cup plus 1 tablespoon sugar

3 large eggs

Grated rind of 1 orange

1/4 cup apricot preserves (optional)

1. Put chopped fruits and raisins in a container, add rum, and mix well. Cover tightly and let stand 1 hour; or refrigerate up to overnight.

2. Preheat oven to 325°F. Grease an 8 1/2 × 4 1/2-inch loaf pan, line with parchment paper or wax paper, and grease liner.

3. Drain fruits, reserving rum in a covered container. Pat fruits dry with paper towels. Toss fruits with 1/4 cup of flour with your fingers, carefully coating each piece. Sift remaining 1 1/2 cups flour with baking powder.

4. Beat oil, honey, and sugar in a bowl until smooth. Add eggs one at a time, beating thoroughly after each addition. Stir in flour mixture. Stir in the grated rind, then fruit mixture. Stir until no trace of flour remains.

5. Transfer to pan and bake about 1 hour, or until a cake tester inserted in center of cake comes out clean. Cool in pan about 15 minutes. Turn out onto a rack and cool completely. If not serving immediately, wrap cake in foil and keep it at room temperature.

6. To finish with preserves, if using, heat with 2 tablespoons of reserved rum until warm. Strain, pressing on mixture. Brush it over top and sides of cakes. Serve at room temperature.

Fruitcake for the Tree-Planting Holiday

Makes 10 to 12 servings **D** or **P**

Tu Bishvat is a wonderful holiday that celebrates planting trees. It occurs in late winter, when traditionally there wasn't much fresh fruit, and so is honored by cooks who include dried fruit in their meals. Good-quality dried fruit makes a scrumptious fruitcake, which is perfect for the holiday.

¹/₂ cup chopped dried dark figs

¹/₂ cup chopped dried apples

¹/₂ cup golden raisins

¹/₄ cup orange juice

1³/₄ cups all-purpose flour

¹/₂ teaspoon baking powder

¹/₂ cup plus 2 tablespoons unsalted butter or margarine, softened

³/₄ cup light brown sugar

3 large eggs

Grated rind 1 lemon

¹/₂ cup chopped pecans (optional)

1. Put chopped figs, apples, and raisins in a container, add orange juice, and mix well. Cover tightly and let stand 30 minutes.

2. Preheat oven to 350°F. Grease an 8¹/₂ × 4¹/₂-inch loaf pan, line with parchment paper or wax paper, and grease paper.

3. Drain fruits, reserving juice. Pat fruits dry with paper towels. Toss fruits with ¹/₄ cup of flour with your fingers, carefully coating each piece. Sift remaining 1¹/₂ cups flour with baking powder.

4. Cream butter and sugar in a large bowl with an electric mixer until smooth. Add eggs one at a time, beating thoroughly after each addition. Stir in half of flour mixture. Stir in 2 tablespoons orange juice and the lemon rind. Stir in remaining flour. Stir in the fruit mixture and pecans, if using. Stir until no trace of flour remains.

5. Transfer to pan and bake about 50 minutes or until a cake tester inserted in center of cake comes out clean. Cool in pan about 15 minutes. Turn out onto a rack and cool completely. Wrap cake in foil and keep it at room temperature.

❧ Cakes with Frosting

Lemon Meringue Cheesecake

Makes 8 to 10 servings

The filling of this cheesecake is delicately flavored with lemon and beautifully complements the light meringue topping. Crowning cheesecakes with meringue is a trick that Ashkenazic bakers brought from Eastern Europe to Israel, where it has been adopted by home cooks. Serve this cake for Shavuot or for brunch, with strawberry or raspberry sauce.

Sweet Sour Cream Pastry (this page)

1 pound (1 pint) whole-milk cottage cheese

1 pound cream cheese, softened

³/₄ cup plus 2 tablespoons sugar

4 large eggs, separated, plus 1 large egg yolk

2 teaspoons strained fresh lemon juice

2 teaspoons grated lemon rind

1 teaspoon vanilla extract

Meringue Topping (page 570)

1. Prepare pastry. Then, lightly butter a 9- or 10-inch springform pan. Pat pastry into pan to line it 2 inches up side. Prick base and sides lightly. Freeze 20 minutes.

2. Preheat oven to 375°F. Bake pastry shell 15 minutes, until very light golden. Remove from oven. Reduce oven temperature to 350°F. Let pastry cool while making filling.

3. Push cottage cheese through a strainer. Beat cream cheese with ³/₄ cup sugar in a large bowl with an electric mixer until smooth. Beat in 5 egg yolks, one at a time. Stir in cottage cheese, lemon juice, lemon rind, and vanilla. Whip 4 egg whites in a large, dry bowl with mixer until soft peaks form. Beat in 2 tablespoons sugar, and whip until stiff but not dry. Fold into cheese mixture. Transfer to pastry shell. Bake 50 minutes to 1 hour or until top is light brown, set, and beginning to crack. Remove from oven, set pan on rack, and let cool 30 minutes. Leave oven at 350°F.

4. Prepare meringue topping. Then, spread it over filling with a metal spatula. Use spatula to decorate it in waves. Return cake to oven and bake 8 to 10 minutes or until meringue is light beige.

5. Cool completely on a rack. Stick a toothpick in center of cake and 5 or 6 at edges, then cover loosely with paper towel. (Toothpicks keep towel from sticking to meringue.) Refrigerate about 2 hours before serving. Serve cake cold, in slices.

Sweet Sour Cream Pastry

Makes enough for a 9- to 10-inch pan

Make this dough for a delectable pastry base for cheesecakes, dessert tarts, and single-crust pies. It's easy to make in a food processor and easy to use as well— you simply pat it in the pan. You can use a springform, tart, or pie pan.

2 large egg yolks

2 tablespoons sour cream

1 teaspoon grated lemon rind

1¹/₃ cups all-purpose flour

1 teaspoon baking powder

¹/₃ cup sugar

Pinch of salt

7 tablespoons cold unsalted butter, cut into bits

Beat egg yolks with sour cream and lemon rind in a small bowl with a whisk. Combine flour, baking powder, sugar, and salt in a food processor and process briefly to blend. Scatter butter pieces over mixture. Process with brief pulses until mixture resembles coarse meal. Pour sour cream mixture evenly over mixture in processor. Process with brief pulses, scraping down occasionally, until dough forms sticky crumbs that can easily be pressed together and dough just begins to come together in a ball. If mixture is dry, add ¹/₂ teaspoon water and process briefly again.

Meringue Topping

Makes enough for a 9- to 10-inch cheesecake or pie

Prepare this topping just before you're ready to spread it. It's great on cheesecakes and sweet pies. Whipping it over hot water helps to slightly stabilize it and makes it smoother.

3 large egg whites

¹/₄ teaspoon cream of tartar

6 tablespoons sugar

Combine egg whites, cream of tartar, and sugar in a large bowl with an electric mixer. Set bowl in a pan of hot water over very low heat and stir whites with whisk about 3 minutes or until mixture is slightly warm and sugar dissolves. Remove from pan of water and whip at high speed of mixer until whites are stiff.

My Mother's Orange Chiffon Cake

Makes 12 to 16 servings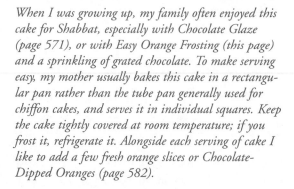

When I was growing up, my family often enjoyed this cake for Shabbat, especially with Chocolate Glaze (page 571), or with Easy Orange Frosting (this page) and a sprinkling of grated chocolate. To make serving easy, my mother usually bakes this cake in a rectangular pan rather than the tube pan generally used for chiffon cakes, and serves it in individual squares. Keep the cake tightly covered at room temperature; if you frost it, refrigerate it. Alongside each serving of cake I like to add a few fresh orange slices or Chocolate-Dipped Oranges (page 582).

2 cups cake flour

1 tablespoon baking powder

¹/₂ teaspoon salt

1¹/₄ cups sugar

3 large eggs, separated, plus 2 large egg whites

¹/₂ cup vegetable oil

¹/₂ cup orange juice

Grated rind of 1 large orange (about 1 tablespoon)

1 to 2 teaspoons vanilla sugar or 1 teaspoon vanilla extract

Easy Orange Frosting (optional) (this page)

Grated semisweet or bittersweet chocolate (optional)

1. Preheat oven to 350°F. Have ready a 13 × 9 × 2-inch pan. Sift flour, baking powder, and salt into a large bowl. Add ³/₄ cup sugar; stir until blended. In another bowl combine egg yolks, oil, and juice; beat until smooth. Beat in orange rind and vanilla.

2. Make a large well in bowl of dry ingredients; pour in egg yolk mixture. Gently stir dry ingredients into yolk mixture, using a wooden spoon.

3. Beat 5 egg whites in a large bowl with an electric mixer until soft peaks form. Gradually beat in remaining ¹/₂ cup sugar. Beat at high speed until whites are stiff and shiny but not dry. Fold about ¹/₄ of whites into yolk mixture until nearly blended. Gently fold yolk mixture into remaining whites. Transfer batter to prepared pan. Bake about 30 minutes or until a cake tester inserted in cake comes out clean. Cool in pan on a rack.

4. Spread cake with frosting and grate some dark chocolate over the top, if using.

Easy Orange Frosting

Makes enough frosting for a 13 × 9-inch rectangular cake, 12 to 16 servings

This quick frosting is made by the usual method of confectioners' sugar icings but is not as sweet. It's good on orange cakes like My Mother's Orange Chiffon Cake (this page), simple chocolate cakes, and white or yellow cakes, as well as on cupcakes.

¹/₂ cup unsalted butter or margarine, softened

1 cup powdered sugar, sifted

3 to 4 tablespoons orange juice

1 tablespoon grated orange rind

Cream butter until light. Add sugar a little at a time, alternating with 3 tablespoons juice. Beat until well blended. Beat in another tablespoon orange juice if needed, so that frosting is spreadable but still thick. Stir in orange rind. When frosting is ready, spread it over cake in a thin layer.

Chocolate-Pecan Chiffon Cake

Makes 14 to 16 servings P

This tall, dark chocolate cake tastes so rich it's hard to believe it contains no dairy products. Serve it for a festive meal for Sukkot or Shabbat. The cake doesn't really need embellishment but if you like, pour a little chocolate glaze over the top and garnish the cake with toasted pecan halves.

3 ounces semisweet or bittersweet chocolate, chopped

2 ounces unsweetened chocolate, chopped

1 cup pecans

1 1/2 cups sugar

2 cups cake flour

1 teaspoon salt

1 tablespoon baking powder

6 large eggs, separated, plus 2 large egg whites

1/2 cup vegetable oil

3/4 cup cold water

1/2 teaspoon cream of tartar

Chocolate Glaze (optional) (this page)

8 to 10 pecan halves, lightly toasted (optional)

1. Preheat oven to 325°F. Have ready a 10 × 4-inch tube pan with a removable tube, but not a nonstick pan; do not grease it. Combine chocolates in a medium bowl and melt them over a pan of simmering water. Stir until smooth. Remove bowl from pan, and let cool.

2. Combine pecans and 1/2 cup sugar in food processor. Process until finely ground.

3. Sift flour, salt, and baking powder into a large bowl. Add 1/2 cup sugar; stir until blended. In another bowl combine egg yolks, oil, and water; beat until smooth.

4. Make a large well in bowl of dry ingredients; pour in yolk mixture. Gently stir dry ingredients into yolk mixture using a wooden spoon. Add melted chocolate, stirring gently just until there are no lumps.

5. Beat 8 egg whites with cream of tartar in a large, dry bowl with an electric mixer until soft peaks form. Gradually beat in remaining 1/2 cup sugar. Beat at high speed until whites are stiff and shiny but not dry. Fold about 1/4 of whites into chocolate mixture until nearly blended. Gently fold chocolate mixture into remaining

whites. When nearly blended, sprinkle pecan mixture over batter and fold in lightly.

6. Transfer batter to prepared pan. Bake about 1 hour 10 minutes or until a cake tester inserted in cake comes out clean. Invert pan on its "feet" or on a heatproof funnel or bottle; let stand about 1 1/2 hours or until completely cool. Run a metal spatula gently around side of cake. Push up tube to remove side of pan. Run a thin-bladed knife around tube. Run metal spatula carefully under cake to free it from base; turn out carefully onto a platter.

7. If glazing the cake, first brush any crumbs gently from top of cake. Prepare glaze. Slowly spoon glaze over top of cake, letting it run down outer sides a little. Garnish with toasted pecans, if using. Let cake stand in a cool place at least 30 minutes before serving so glaze can set; refrigerate if necessary, but glaze will be shinier if it cools outside the refrigerator.

Chocolate Glaze

Makes enough for a 10 × 4-inch
tube or bundt cake

This easy-to-make glaze turns any simple cake into something festive. It's especially delicious on Chocolate-Pecan Chiffon Cake (this page).

Use good-quality chocolate for best flavor. If you're spooning the glaze over an orange-flavored cake, you can substitute orange juice for the water. Before using glaze, be sure to remove any crumbs from the top of the cake. The glaze remains shiny if you let the glazed cake cool at room temperature instead of in the refrigerator.

8 ounces semisweet or bittersweet chocolate, chopped

3 tablespoons vegetable oil

3 tablespoons water

1 teaspoon vanilla extract

Melt chocolate with oil and water in a medium bowl set over a pan of simmering water. Stir until smooth. Remove bowl from pan. Stir in vanilla. Let glaze cool slightly before spooning it over cake; it should still be pourable. If it becomes too thick, set it over warm water again to soften it.

Sabrinas

Makes 16 individual cakes   Ⓓ

These rich, flavorful cakes have long been a favorite in Israel. Derived from the French savarin, *which is usually ring-shaped, these are individual cakes baked in fluted molds. The dough is a light, yeast-risen batter. The cakes are then soaked in a syrup flavored with spirits and frosted with apricot jam. As a luxurious final touch, they are split and filled generously with whipped cream.*

Instead of using fluted brioche molds, I use muffin pans, as these are already in most kitchens. You can buy individual brioche molds in specialty kitchen equipment shops and use them to bake these in the same way; be sure to butter the flutes of the molds carefully before adding the batter.

1 envelope dry yeast (1/4 ounce or 2 1/2 teaspoons)

1/4 cup warm water (110°F)

1 tablespoon plus 1 teaspoon sugar

2 cups all-purpose flour

4 large eggs

1 teaspoon salt

1 1/2 teaspoons grated orange rind

7 tablespoons unsalted butter or margarine, cut into
   14 pieces, room temperature

1 cup apricot preserves

About 1/2 cup orange liqueur

Sabrina Syrup (page 573)

1 cup heavy cream or whipping cream

1 tablespoon powdered sugar

16 candied cherries (optional)

1. Sprinkle yeast over warm water in a small bowl and add 1 teaspoon sugar. Let stand 10 minutes or until foamy. Sift flour into bowl of a mixer fitted with a dough hook. Add 2 eggs, salt, 1 teaspoon grated orange rind, and remaining tablespoon sugar. Mix at low speed until a few tablespoons of flour are drawn into egg mixture. Add yeast mixture and remaining 2 eggs. Mix at low speed, occasionally scraping down dough, about 10 minutes or until dough is soft and smooth. Beat at medium speed about 12 minutes or until dough is very smooth and most of it comes away from sides of bowl. (Dough will be soft and very sticky.)

2. Lightly oil a medium bowl and place dough in it. Put butter pieces in one layer on dough. Cover with slightly damp towel or plastic wrap. Let dough rise in a warm, draft-free place about 1 hour or until doubled in bulk. Transfer to clean mixer bowl. Beat in butter with dough hook at low speed, scraping down often, about 3 minutes or until blended.

3. Generously butter 16 muffin cups. Add about 2 tablespoons dough to each cup. Cover with plastic wrap and let rise in warm, draft-free place 20 minutes. Remove covering; let dough rise to top of molds, about 5 more minutes.

4. Preheat oven to 400°F. Put a little water in any empty muffin cups. Bake sabrinas about 12 minutes or until dough comes away from sides of pan, top is browned, and cake tester inserted into a cake comes out clean; test 2 or 3 to be sure. Unmold onto a rack. Cool completely.

5. Combine preserves and 2 tablespoons orange liqueur in a medium saucepan. Cook over low heat, stirring, until preserves melt completely. Strain into another saucepan, pressing on pieces. Stir in remaining 1/2 teaspoon orange rind. Reserve to use as glaze.

6. Prepare syrup. Set a cake rack above a rimmed tray. Put one sabrina in hot syrup and leave a few seconds. Ladle syrup over cake repeatedly until it is moist but not soggy. Roll sabrina quickly around to encourage it to absorb more syrup. Cake should absorb plenty of syrup so no part of it remains dry, but if left in syrup too long, it may fall apart. Lift cake with slotted spoon. Touch it to check that it is well moistened and softened; if there are any firm parts, ladle syrup over cake a few more times. Remove carefully with slotted spoon and set on prepared rack. Dip remaining cakes; reheat syrup occasionally. If any syrup remains, slowly spoon it over cakes. Let cakes drain 30 minutes.

7. Put sabrinas on a tray with their tops facing down. A short time before serving, slowly spoon orange liqueur over each one, rolling cake so it absorbs liqueur evenly.

8. Set sabrinas on rack with their tops facing up. Heat glaze in a small saucepan until it just begins to bubble. If glaze is very thick, stir in 1 more tablespoon liqueur. Brush glaze on all sides of cakes. Let stand about 10 minutes if serving soon; or refrigerate at this point.

9. Just before serving, whip cream with powdered sugar in a chilled bowl with an electric mixer until stiff. Put cream in a piping bag with a star tip. Carefully split each sabrina almost in two horizontally, so the top and bottom are still joined at one end. Pipe cream generously inside sabrina. Garnish with a candied cherry, if using. Serve any remaining cream separately.

Sabrina Syrup

Makes about 2 cups

Use this syrup for moistening Israeli cakes called Sabrinas (page 572) after baking them.

1¼ cups sugar

2 cups water

Combine sugar and water in a medium, heavy saucepan. Cook over low heat, stirring gently to avoid splashing syrup on sides of pan, until sugar dissolves. Once sugar has dissolved, stop stirring. Bring syrup to a boil over high heat. Remove from heat. Use syrup while hot to brush or pour over cakes.

❧ *Pies*

Streusel Apple Pie

Makes 8 servings

Streusel makes a delightful topping for fruit pies with moist fillings, such as this one of vanilla- and lemon-flavored apples. The contrast of textures of the delicately crisp crust, the smooth filling, and the buttery crumbly topping is the reason for its charm. Bake this as a tart, using Dessert Tart Pastry as a base, or make it a pie with your favorite homemade or purchased pie shell. Refrigerating the shaped pie shell before baking helps prevent it from shrinking.

Dessert Tart Pastry (page 575), refrigerated, or a 9-inch pie shell, unbaked

2 pounds Golden Delicious apples

3 tablespoons butter or margarine

½ teaspoon strained fresh lemon juice

Grated rind of ½ lemon

1 vanilla bean

4 to 5 tablespoons sugar

Streusel Topping (page 582)

Powdered sugar (optional)

1. If making your own tart pastry, grease an 8- or 9-inch metal tart pan with fluted edges. Let dough soften 1 minute at room temperature. Roll out dough on a lightly floured surface until about ¼-inch thick. Roll up dough loosely around rolling pin and unroll it over pan. Gently ease dough into pan. Using your thumb, gently push dough down slightly at edge of pan, making top edge of rim thicker than remaining dough. Roll rolling pin across pan to cut off dough. With your finger and thumb, press to push up edge of dough around pan, so it is slightly higher than rim of pan. Prick dough all over with a fork. Refrigerate 1 hour; or cover with plastic wrap and refrigerate overnight.

2. Peel, core, and thinly slice apples. Melt butter in a large sauté pan. Add apples, lemon juice, lemon rind, and vanilla bean. Cover and cook over low heat, stirring occasionally, about 20 minutes or until apples are very tender. Uncover and cook, stirring often, about 5 minutes or until any excess liquid has evaporated. Remove vanilla bean. Add 4 tablespoons sugar. Cook over high heat, stirring, until sugar dissolves and apple mixture is very thick. Taste and add more sugar if you like. Let cool completely.

3. Prepare streusel topping. Then, preheat oven to 400°F and heat a baking sheet in oven.

4. Spread cool apple mixture in tart shell. Top with streusel in an even layer.

5. Bake tart on hot baking sheet 30 minutes. Reduce heat to 350°F and bake 20 more minutes. Let tart cool a few minutes. Remove tart from pan and cool it on a rack. Serve warm or at room temperature, sprinkled with powdered sugar, if using.

Low-Fat Strawberry Cheese Pie

Makes 6 servings

This glazed strawberry pie has a no-bake cheesecake layer on the bottom and a crunchy graham cracker crust. Enjoy it as a Shavuot treat or whenever you want a tasty dessert that's quick and easy to prepare. It's hard to believe it's low in fat.

5 ounces graham crackers, preferably low-fat

6 tablespoons sugar

3 tablespoons vegetable oil

One 8-ounce bar nonfat cream cheese

1/4 cup nonfat sour cream

1 teaspoon vanilla extract

1/2 teaspoon grated lemon rind

3 cups small strawberries, rinsed and hulled

1/3 cup strawberry jelly

1. Preheat oven to 350°F. Process crackers in a food processor to fine crumbs. Mix crumbs with 1 tablespoon sugar in a bowl. Add oil and mix well. Lightly oil a 9-inch pie pan. Press crumb mixture in an even layer in pan. Bake 8 minutes. Let cool completely.

2. Cut cream cheese into a few pieces and let soften slightly. Beat cream cheese in a large bowl with an electric mixer, until smooth. Beat in remaining 5 tablespoons sugar, followed by sour cream, vanilla, and lemon rind. Pour into crust. Refrigerate, uncovered, while preparing strawberries.

3. Pat strawberries dry. Halve them lengthwise. Arrange them cut side down on top of cheese filling, beginning at outer edge of pie.

4. Melt jelly with 2 teaspoons water in a small saucepan over low heat, stirring often. Cool slightly. Brush or spoon jelly over berries; spoon any remaining jelly in spaces between them. Refrigerate uncovered about 30 minutes or until ready to serve. If there is any leftover pie, refrigerate it uncovered.

Sweet Cheese Tart

Makes 6 to 8 servings

A cheesecake filling baked in a buttery pastry crust— what could be better? To save time, you can use refrigerated pie pastry dough or a ready-made unbaked pie shell (begin with step 2). But I have to admit, they don't rival the taste of homemade pastry. Baking the tart shall briefly with dried beans helps prevent the filling from making the pastry soggy and also helps minimize shrinkage in the dough.

Dessert Tart Pastry (page 575)

6 ounces bar cream cheese

1/2 cup heavy or whipping cream

1/3 cup sugar

2 large eggs

2 teaspoons strained fresh lemon juice

1 teaspoon grated lemon rind

1 teaspoon vanilla extract

2 teaspoons all purpose flour

1. If making your own tart pastry, grease an 8-inch metal tart pan with fluted edges. Then, let dough soften 1 minute before rolling it. Roll out dough on a lightly floured surface until about 1/4-inch thick. Roll up dough loosely around rolling pin and unroll it over pan. Gently ease dough into pan. Using your thumb, gently push dough down slightly at edge of pan, making top edge of rim thicker than remaining dough. Roll rolling pin across pan to cut off dough. With your finger and thumb, press to push up edge of dough around pan, so it is slightly higher than rim of pan. Prick dough all over with a fork. Refrigerate 1 hour, or cover with plastic wrap and refrigerate overnight.

2. Preheat oven to 425°F and heat a baking sheet in oven. Line dough with parchment paper or aluminum foil and fill it with dried beans. Bake tart on hot baking sheet 10 minutes. Remove paper and beans. Bake 7 more minutes or until base is beginning to brown. Remove tart pan from oven but leave baking sheet in oven. Let pastry shell cool. Reduce oven temperature to 325°F.

3. Beat cream cheese with cream in a large bowl with an electric mixer at low speed. Gradually beat in sugar. Add eggs one at a time and beat after each addition. Stir in lemon juice and rind, vanilla, and flour.

4. Return tart shell, still in its pan, to hot baking sheet. Pour filling into shell. Bake about 35 minutes or until filling is firm. Let tart cool in oven, with door slightly open. Refrigerate and serve cold.

Dessert Tart Pastry

Makes enough for an 8- to 10-inch tart shell

This pastry is only lightly sweetened and so is great with sweet fruit fillings or for Sweet Cheese Tart (page 574). I like to make the dough in the food processor. It's very quick and easy and the results are terrific.

2 large egg yolks

2 tablespoons ice water

1¹/₂ cups all-purpose flour

³/₈ teaspoon salt

3 tablespoons powdered sugar

¹/₂ cup unsalted butter or margarine, cold, cut into bits

1. Beat egg yolks with ice water in a small bowl. Combine flour, salt, and powdered sugar in a food processor. Process briefly to blend. Scatter butter pieces over mixture. Process with brief pulses until mixture resembles coarse meal.

2. Pour egg yolk mixture evenly over mixture in processor. Process with brief pulses, scraping down occasionally, until dough forms sticky crumbs that can easily be pressed together but dough does not come together in a ball.

3. If crumbs are dry, sprinkle ¹/₂ teaspoon water and process with brief pulses until dough forms sticky crumbs. Add more water by ¹/₂ teaspoons if crumbs are still dry, and process briefly each time.

4. With a rubber spatula, transfer dough to a sheet of plastic wrap. Wrap it and push it together. Shape dough into a flat disc. Refrigerate dough 1 hour or up to 2 days in refrigerator.

❧ Rugelach and Other Cookies

Cream Cheese Dough for Rugelach (or Knishes)

Makes enough for 4 to 6 dozen
bite-size pastries, depending on shape

Rugelach are delectable, small filled pastries with a flaky, rich dough wrapped around a sweet filling. This dough is very easy to roll out and makes great-tasting pastry. You can also use it to make knishes.

6 ounces block cream cheese
1 cup (2 sticks) unsalted butter, cold
2 cups all-purpose flour
1/4 teaspoon salt
1/3 cup sour cream

1. Cut cream cheese into tablespoon-size pieces and let it soften at room temperature. Cut butter into small pieces of about 1/2 tablespoon; refrigerate them until ready to use.

2. Combine flour, salt, and butter in a food processor and process with brief pulses until mixture resembles coarse meal. Add cream cheese and sour cream, distributing them evenly over mixture. Process with brief pulses until dough just holds together. If dough is too dry, add 1 to 2 teaspoons water. Wrap dough in plastic wrap, press it together into a ball, and flatten into a disk. Refrigerate dough 4 hours before rolling, or up to 2 days.

Pareve Dough for Rugelach (or Knishes)

Makes enough for 4 dozen rugelach
or about 20 knishes

The egg in this dough makes it flexible and easy to shape and helps the finished pastries hold together well as they bake. Use it for making rugelach or knishes.

You can also use it as pie dough, but it won't be as flaky as the kind made without egg.

1 large egg
3 tablespoons ice water, plus more if needed
2 cups all-purpose flour
3/8 teaspoon salt
3/4 cup (11/2 sticks) pareve margarine, cold, cut into bits

1. Beat egg in a small bowl. Beat in 3 tablespoons ice water.

2. Combine flour and salt in a food processor. Process briefly to blend. Scatter margarine pieces over mixture. Mix using brief pulses until mixture resembles coarse meal. Pour egg mixture evenly over mixture in processor. Process with brief pulses, scraping down occasionally, until dough forms sticky crumbs that can easily be pressed together but dough does not come together in a ball. If crumbs are dry, sprinkle 1/2 teaspoon water and process with brief pulses until dough forms sticky crumbs. Add more water in same way, 1/2 teaspoon at a time, if crumbs are still dry.

3. With a rubber spatula, transfer dough to a sheet of plastic wrap, wrap it, and push it together. Shape dough into a flat disk. Refrigerate dough at least 1 hour, or up to 2 days.

Traditional Cinnamon-Walnut Rugelach

Makes 48 bite-size cookies

Until recently, rugelach were a well-kept secret of regular shoppers at Jewish bakeries, where these delicious, not-too-sweet pastries are one of the most popular items. But the word is out. Rugelach have captured America's attention when it comes to a tasty snack. They appear in fancy food mail-order catalogs, in gourmet shops, and in many supermarkets.

People debate whether rugelach are cookies or pastries. Actually, they're sort of both. They're made of pastry and are served like cookies, with coffee, tea, or milk.

These traditional home-baked rugelach are scrumptious. Like croissants, they are rich, tender, and flaky, but they demand less effort. In fact, they're easier than pie! You don't need to worry about dough that tears, cracks, or doesn't hold together. They bake quickly too. And you can freeze them, either baked or unbaked, or keep the baked ones about 4 days in airtight containers.

The rugelach filling couldn't be easier—you scatter chopped nuts, cinnamon, and sugar over the dough. Be sure the walnuts are very fresh. For another time-honored rendition, add light or dark raisins to the filling along with the nuts.

Cream Cheese Dough for Rugelach (page 576)

1/4 cup plus 3 tablespoons sugar

1 tablespoon ground cinnamon

3/4 cup chopped golden or dark raisins (optional)

1 cup finely chopped walnuts

1. Prepare dough. Then, lightly butter 2 or 3 baking sheets. Mix sugar and cinnamon in a bowl. If using raisins, mix them with walnuts in another bowl.

2. Divide dough into 4 pieces. Press one fourth of dough into a round, then flatten it. Roll it on a lightly floured surface into a 9-inch circle about 1/8-inch thick. Sprinkle 2 tablespoons cinnamon mixture all over circle of dough. Sprinkle either 1/4 cup nuts or a scant 1/2 cup raisin-walnut mixture near outer edge of circle. Press lightly with rolling pin so nut mixture adheres.

3. With a heavy, sharp knife, cut circle into 12 wedges, making each cut with a sharp downward movement of heel of knife. Roll up tightly from wide end to point, making sure filling is enclosed.

4. Put rugelach on baking sheets, with points of triangles facing down, spacing them about 1 inch apart. Curve each into a crescent, if desired. Refrigerate while shaping more cookies. Refrigerate all at least 20 minutes before baking.

5. Preheat oven to 350°F. Bake cookies 22 to 25 minutes or until light golden. Cool on racks.

Strawberry Rugelach

Makes 48 bite-size cookies

Rugelach are made with a variety of fruit fillings by using jams or preserves. Strawberry, raspberry, and apricot are the most popular but rugelach are also made with fillings of blackberries, dates, and orange. You can use any jam you like. Some people fill rugelach with poppy seed fillings like those used in hamantaschen.

Jam fillings taste good in rugelach because the dough is not sweetened. To balance the jam's sweetness, I like to add chopped nuts and grated lemon rind.

Cream Cheese Dough for Rugelach (page 576)

1/2 cup strawberry jam

1 teaspoon grated lemon rind

1/2 cup finely chopped pecans or walnuts

1. Prepare dough. Then, lightly butter 2 or 3 baking sheets. Mix jam and lemon rind in a bowl. Stir in chopped nuts.

2. Divide dough into 4 pieces. Press one fourth of dough into a round, then flatten it. Roll it on a lightly floured surface into a 9-inch circle about 1/8-inch thick. Lightly spread 1/4 cup filling over circle of dough. With a heavy, sharp knife, cut circle into 12 wedges, making each cut with a sharp downward movement of heel of knife. Roll up tightly from wide end to point.

3. Put rugelach on baking sheets, with points of triangles facing down, spacing them about 1 inch apart. Curve each into a crescent, if desired. Refrigerate while shaping more cookies. Refrigerate all at least 20 minutes before baking.

4. Preheat oven to 350°F. Bake cookies 22 to 25 minutes or until light golden. Cool on racks.

Chocolate-Pecan Rugelach

Makes 72 small cookies

With rugelach's new popularity, many filling variations have been developed, such as chocolate, apricot, cheese, and raspberry. Rugelach are often shaped into little cushions instead of crescents, as in this recipe, in which the dough is cut into slices.

Cream Cheese Dough for Rugelach (page 576)
1 cup mini semisweet chocolate chips
1/2 cup finely chopped pecans

1. Prepare dough. Lightly butter 2 or 3 baking sheets. Mix chocolate chips and pecans in a bowl.

2. Divide dough into 4 pieces. Press one fourth of dough into a square, then flatten it. Roll it on a lightly floured surface into a 9- to 9 1/2-inch square. Trim edges. Cut into 3 equal strips, then cut each strip into 3 squares. You will have 9 squares.

3. Put 1 1/2 teaspoons chocolate-pecan mixture on a square about 1/2-inch from edge nearest you, arranging chips close together in one row along the edge. Press lightly with rolling pin so filling adheres to dough.

4. Fold over edge of dough nearest you to cover filling. Roll up dough tightly towards other side, like a jelly roll. It will look like a thin cylinder. Cut cylinder in two, with the heel of a heavy knife. Put cookies on baking sheet. Shape remaining squares into cookies. Refrigerate while shaping more cookies. Refrigerate all cookies at least 20 minutes before baking.

5. Preheat oven to 350°F. Bake cookies about 22 minutes or until light golden. Cool on racks.

Orange Mandelbrot

Makes about 36 cookies

Mandelbrot bring back memories of my grandmother, Goldie Kahn, who used to dip them in her tea—my favorite way to enjoy them today.

Mandelbrot, also spelled mandelbroit, *translates from Yiddish as almond bread but it is best described as Ashkenazic biscotti. Like biscotti, mandelbrot are baked twice, once as a loaf and once in slices. Also, like biscotti, they are meant to be dunked so they soften a bit before being eaten. Because of the double baking, they keep well, for about two weeks.*

3 large eggs
1 1/4 cups sugar
3/4 cup vegetable oil
1 tablespoon grated orange rind
1 teaspoon vanilla extract
4 cups all-purpose flour
1 1/2 teaspoons baking powder
1/4 teaspoon salt
1 cup slivered almonds, chopped
1 tablespoon sugar mixed with 1 teaspoon ground cinnamon

1. Preheat oven to 350°F. Grease a baking sheet. Beat eggs, sugar, and oil in a large bowl with an electric mixer until blended. Beat in orange rind and vanilla. Sift flour with baking powder and salt into a bowl. Add to egg mixture. Stir on low speed of mixer just until blended. Stir in almonds on low speed.

2. Shape dough into 4 log-shaped rolls, each about 2 inches. Place on baking sheet. Refrigerate 30 minutes. Use spatula to smooth dough and to push again into log shape if it has spread a bit. Sprinkle top with cinnamon sugar and pat to make it adhere to sides as well.

3. Bake 30 minutes or until lightly browned and set. Transfer carefully to a board and let stand until cool enough to handle. With a sharp knife, carefully cut into diagonal slices about 1/2-inch thick; dough will be slightly soft inside. Return slices in one layer to 2 or 3 cleaned baking sheets.

4. Bake about 7 minutes per side or until lightly toasted so they are beige and dotted in places with golden brown; side of cookie touching baking sheet will brown first. Watch carefully so cookies don't brown throughout or they will be too hard and dry. Cool on a rack. Keep in airtight containers.

Tu Bishvat Date Bars with Macadamia Nuts

Makes 16 or 20 bars

When I was growing up, my school, the Hebrew Academy of Washington D.C., celebrated Tu Bishvat by having a tree planted in Israel in each child's name, for which my classmates and I received a tree-decorated certificate. At school we ate dried fruit on the holiday, usually carob, a sweet tropical fruit common in Israel (and the source of the chocolate substitute of the same name).

You can honor this holiday by planting a tree in your own yard and baking these scrumptious bar cookies studded with diced dates and plenty of nuts. You can vary the nuts and dried fruit to your taste, or even replace half the nuts with chocolate chips.

1 cup plus 2 tablespoons all-purpose flour

1 teaspoon baking powder

1/4 teaspoon salt

1/2 cup (1 stick) plus 2 tablespoons unsalted butter
    or margarine, slightly softened

3/4 cup packed light brown sugar

1/4 cup granulated sugar

2 large eggs

1 teaspoon vanilla extract

1/2 cup to 2/3 cup chopped unsalted macadamia nuts or
    blanched almonds

1 cup finely diced dates

1. Position rack in center of oven and preheat to 350°F. Butter a square 9-inch baking pan. Sift flour, baking powder, and salt into a medium bowl. Cream butter in a large bowl with an electric mixer. Add sugars; beat until smooth and fluffy. Add eggs, one at a time, beating very thoroughly after each addition. Beat in 2 tablespoons of flour mixture at low speed. Add vanilla; beat to blend. With a wooden spoon, stir in flour mixture. Stir in macadamia nuts and dates.

2. Spread batter evenly in prepared pan. Bake 30 to 35 minutes or until cake is brown on top, pulls away slightly from sides of pan, and a cake tester inserted into center comes out nearly clean. Cool in pan on a rack. Cut into 16 or 20 bars, using the point of a sharp knife.

✿ *Sauces, Toppings, and Garnishes*

Bittersweet Chocolate Sauce

Makes about 2 cups, 8 to 10 servings

This sauce is wonderful with Toasted Hazelnut Cake (page 21) or with any white cake, nut cake, or chocolate cake. I prefer to serve it with unfrosted cakes but the choice is yours. The sauce is also good with ice cream and for dipping strawberries, bananas, and cookies.

For Passover make the sauce with Passover chocolate and substitute vanilla sugar for the vanilla extract. For the rest of the year, you can use any bittersweet or semisweet chocolate that you like. If you want to serve it after a meat entree in a kosher menu, use pareve margarine and pareve chocolate. You can make it ahead and keep it for a week in the refrigerator in a covered container.

12 ounces bittersweet or semisweet chocolate, chopped

6 tablespoons (3/4 stick) unsalted margarine or butter, cut
    into pieces

2/3 cup water, or half strained fresh orange juice and half
    water

2 teaspoons vanilla extract or vanilla sugar

1. Melt chocolate with margarine and water in a medium bowl set over a pan of simmering water. Stir until smooth. Remove bowl from pan and cool 10 minutes. Stir in vanilla.

2. If preparing sauce ahead, reheat it above a pan of hot water. If desired, cool it to room temperature.

Raspberry Sauce

Makes about 2 cups, 8 to 12 servings

This ruby-red classic sauce is the favorite sweet sauce of European chefs. It is wonderful with cheesecake, such as White Chocolate Cheesecake (page 57), or with cheese or fruit blintzes, vanilla ice cream, or fruit salad. Accent it with raspberry brandy or raspberry liqueur just before serving, if you like.

6 cups (about 1¹/2 pounds) fresh raspberries; or two 10- to 12-ounce packages frozen unsweetened or lightly sweetened raspberries, thawed

About 1¹/2 cups powdered sugar, sifted

About 1 to 2 tablespoons strained fresh lemon juice (optional)

1. Puree raspberries in a food processor or blender. Add 1¹/2 cups powdered sugar. Process until very smooth. Taste and add another tablespoon or two powdered sugar if desired.

2. Strain sauce in batches into a bowl, pressing on pulp in strainer; use rubber spatula to scrape mixture from underside of strainer. Continue straining remaining sauce.

3. Cover and refrigerate up to 2 days. Stir sauce before serving and add lemon juice, if using. Serve cold.

Blueberry Sauce

Makes about 1 cup sauce, 4 to 6 servings

When blueberries are in season, this sauce of a deep Bordeaux color is great with cheese blintzes, such as Cheese Canneloni Blintzes (page 53). For a variation, you can flavor it with crème de cassis. *The sauce thickens if chilled for more than an hour, so stir it very well to make it smooth before serving.*

3 cups (about 12 ounces) fresh blueberries, rinsed

About ²/3 cup powdered sugar, sifted

1 teaspoon strained fresh lemon juice (optional)

1. Puree blueberries in food processor or blender. Add ¹/2 cup powdered sugar. Process until very smooth. Taste and add more powdered sugar if desired.

2. Strain sauce into a bowl; press gently while straining but avoid pushing through too much of skins. Use

rubber spatula to scrape mixture from underside of strainer.

3. Cover and refrigerate 30 minutes or up to 1 day. Stir sauce well before serving and add lemon juice, if using. Serve cold.

Strawberry Sauce

Makes about 1¹/2 cups, about 6 servings

Bright red strawberry sauce livens up a multitude of desserts, from fruit salads to blintzes to cheesecakes to sweet kugels.

3 cups (about 12 ounces) fresh strawberries or thawed frozen strawberries

¹/4 cup sugar, or to taste

1 to 2 teaspoons strained fresh lemon juice

1 or 2 tablespoons strawberry or raspberry liqueur (optional)

1. If using fresh strawberries, rinse them, hull them, and pat dry.

2. Puree strawberries in a food processor or blender with ¹/4 cup sugar until smooth. Add lemon juice, and more sugar if desired. Cover and refrigerate up to 2 days. Stir before serving and add liqueur, if using. Serve cold.

Mango Sauce

Makes about 2¹/2 cups, 8 to 10 servings

When mangoes are at the height of their season, this is one of the best and easiest recipes to make from them. Even if a mango turns out to be stringy, the sauce will be fine, since it is strained anyway. The sauce is a perfect complement for Pareve Almond Cake (page 564) and for plain sponge cakes. It's also lovely with ice cream and with fruit salads.

2¹/2 pounds ripe mangoes

About ¹/2 cup powdered sugar, sifted

4 teaspoons strained fresh lemon or lime juice

1. Peel mangoes, cut flesh around pits, and cut flesh into chunks. Puree mangoes in food processor or blender. Add ¹/2 cup powdered sugar. Process until very smooth. Taste and add more powdered sugar if desired. Strain puree into a bowl, pressing on pulp in strainer.

Use rubber spatula to scrape mixture from underside of strainer.

2. Cover and refrigerate 30 minutes or up to 2 days. Stir sauce before serving, adding lemon juice. Serve cold.

Kiwi Sauce

Makes about 1³/4 cups unstrained,
about 8 servings

Serve this easy-to-make sauce with simple unfrosted cakes such as Pareve Almond Cake (page 564) or My Mother's Orange Chiffon Cake (page 570). You can leave the kiwi seeds in the sauce if you like them, or strain the sauce if you want it smoother.

1¹/2 pounds kiwi

About ³/4 cup powdered sugar, sifted

1. Peel and quarter kiwi. Puree kiwi with ³/4 cup powdered sugar in food processor or blender until smooth. Taste and add more powdered sugar if desired.

2. For a smooth sauce, strain sauce without pressing on pulp, or leave sauce unstrained if you like texture of seeds.

3. Cover and refrigerate 30 minutes or up to 2 days. Stir sauce before serving. Serve cold.

Vanilla Whipped Cream

Makes about 2 cups

This is known in France as Chantilly cream. It is lightly sweetened and is delicious with just about any dessert, especially those made with a generous proportion of fruit or chocolate.

In many stores heavy cream is a little richer than whipping cream; both give good results. Unlike in ice cream, black specks of vanilla are not desirable in whipped cream. Therefore it's flavored with vanilla extract or vanilla sugar, not vanilla bean. If you prefer vanilla sugar, simply use 2 teaspoons and omit the sugar.

1 cup (one ¹/2-pint container) heavy cream or whipping cream, well chilled

2 teaspoons sugar

1 teaspoon vanilla extract

Chill electric mixer bowl and beater in refrigerator about 20 minutes. Whip cream with sugar in the chilled bowl with the chilled beater until soft peaks form. Add vanilla and beat until just stiff. Do not overbeat, or cream may turn to butter.

Vanilla Custard Sauce

Makes 6 to 8 servings

This luscious vanilla bean sauce turns even a simple dessert into a fancy finale like those served at the finest restaurants. It is perfect with challah bread pudding, sweet noodle kugels, and cakes that are not frosted. If you want to make it pareve, you can substitute a nondairy rice milk, soy milk, or multigrain drink. You can discard the vanilla bean after using it—or you can rinse, dry, and reuse it.

1¹/2 cups milk or nondairy milk

1 vanilla bean, split lengthwise

5 large egg yolks

¹/4 cup sugar

1. Bring milk and vanilla bean to a boil in a medium, heavy saucepan. Remove from heat. Cover and let stand 15 minutes. Reheat to a boil. Remove the vanilla bean.

2. Whisk egg yolks lightly in a large bowl. Add sugar; whisk until smooth. Gradually whisk in hot milk. Return mixture to saucepan, whisking. Cook over medium-low heat, stirring mixture and scraping bottom of pan constantly with a wooden spoon, about 5 minutes or until mixture thickens slightly and reaches 170°F to 175°F on an instant-read or candy thermometer. To check whether sauce is thick enough without a thermometer, remove pan from heat. Dip a metal spoon in sauce and draw your finger across back of spoon. Your finger should leave a clear path in mixture that clings to spoon. If it does not, cook 30 seconds more and check again. Do not overcook sauce or it will curdle.

3. Immediately strain sauce into a bowl. Stir about 30 seconds to cool; cool completely. Refrigerate at least 30 minutes before serving, or up to 2 days.

Streusel Topping

Makes enough for a 9-inch pie or cake

Cakes and pastries topped with rich, sweet crumbs known as streusel are a favorite in Jewish bakeries. Hungarian desserts are especially well known for this topping. Streusel is also well loved by Polish Jewish cooks, who use it to top even yeast cakes, such as some versions of babka. You can also try this sprinkled on Plum Cake (page 566) or baked fruit desserts before putting them in the oven.

¹/₃ cup brown sugar

¹/₃ cup granulated sugar

²/₃ cup all-purpose flour

³/₄ teaspoon ground cinnamon

¹/₄ cup (¹/₂ stick) unsalted butter or margarine, chilled and cut into bits

Mix brown sugar, white sugar, flour, and cinnamon in a small bowl. With 2 knives, cut butter into sugar mixture until coarse crumbs form. If not ready to use, refrigerate, covered, up to 2 days; or freeze for longer.

Apricot Glaze

Makes about 1 cup, enough for
16 cupcakes or 1 fruit tart

Bakers use this traditional European glaze more than any other jam or jelly glaze because its flavor and color are perfect with so many desserts. Use this for brushing on Baba Cupcakes (page 170) or fruit tarts. It makes them shiny and adds good flavor as well.

1 cup apricot preserves

2 tablespoons water

Heat preserves and water over low heat in medium saucepan, stirring, until preserves are completely melted. Strain into another saucepan, pressing on pieces.

Raspberry Brandy Syrup

Makes about ¹/₃ cup

Brushing a flavorful syrup like this on sponge cakes or other light cakes before filling or frosting them helps keep them moist. You can vary the flavor with other spirits or juices such as orange liqueur, orange juice, or any that you like.

¹/₄ cup sugar

¹/₄ cup water

2 tablespoons clear raspberry brandy

Heat sugar and water in a small, heavy saucepan over low heat, stirring very gently, until sugar dissolves. Increase heat to medium-high and stop stirring. Bring to a boil. Pour into a bowl; cool completely. Stir in raspberry brandy.

Chocolate-Dipped Oranges

Makes 12 to 16 dipped orange segments

Serve these delightful treats with chocolate cakes or orange cakes or for a luscious garnish for fruit salads, orange sorbet, or vanilla ice cream. You can dip tangerines the same way. Try to choose citrus fruit that is seedless. It's best to serve chocolate-dipped orange segments within an hour or two of making them but you can keep them uncovered up to 4 hours in the refrigerator.

2 small oranges

4 ounces fine-quality bittersweet or semisweet chocolate, chopped

1. Line a rack with paper towels. Cut a thin slice from top and bottom of each orange. Score orange with a knife and remove peel. Using a small serrated knife, cut off all bitter white pith from orange. Cut orange into segments. Put them on lined rack. Let dry about 30 minutes, patting them often with paper towels. (A small amount of moisture can make the melted chocolate solidify and make it impossible to use in dipping.)

2. Line a tray with waxed paper. Melt chocolate in a medium bowl set over a pan of simmering water. Stir until smooth. Remove bowl from pan; cool to 88°F to 90°F, or until it feels neither warm nor cold to the touch.

3. Dip ¹/₂ of one orange segment in chocolate. Let excess chocolate drip into bowl. Transfer orange section to wax paper. Dip remaining sections, setting on wax paper with chocolate-half of all oranges pointing in same direction. Refrigerate about 30 minutes or until chocolate sets. Remove from refrigerator about 10 minutes before serving.

Candied Orange Peel

Makes enough candied peel to garnish
10 to 12 servings of dessert

This is a quick version of candied orange peel, a very popular sweet in Israel. Unlike commercially candied peel, it needs to be refrigerated and keeps only about a week, but it tastes good and adds a festive touch to desserts. Use these candied peel strips (peel is the same as rind) to garnish fruit salads, such as Citrus Salad with Home-Candied Orange Peel (page 147), chocolate cakes, and ice creams. Use organically grown oranges for the freshest flavor and to avoid pesticides in the rind.

2 large oranges
¹/₂ cup sugar
2 cups water

1. Rinse oranges and pat completely dry. Using a sharp vegetable peeler with a flexible blade, pare colored part of orange rind into long strips, without including any white pith. With a large sharp, sturdy knife, cut the rind into very thin strips, about ¹/₈-inch wide.

2. Put the strips of rind in a small saucepan and cover with water. Bring to a boil and boil 3 minutes. Drain, rinse with cold water, and drain well again.

3. Combine sugar and 2 cups water in a medium, heavy saucepan. Heat mixture over low heat, gently stirring from time to time, until sugar dissolves. Increase heat to high and bring to a boil. Add strips of rind to syrup. Shake pan very gently to submerge the strips. Cook uncovered over medium heat, without stirring, 10 minutes. Reduce heat to low and cook 5 to 10 more minutes or until orange rind is very tender and syrup thickens. Cool rind completely in syrup. You can keep candied orange peels in their syrup in a covered container up to 1 week in the refrigerator.

4. To use candied orange peel, remove strips from syrup with a fork and drain briefly on paper towels. Use them as long strands or cut them into smaller pieces, to garnish desserts.

Note: Don't use this candied orange for dipping in chocolate. It is too moist for this purpose.

Basics

P = *Pareve*   **D** = *Dairy*   **M** = *Meat*

This chapter is composed of basic recipes that are served with many foods or that are used as ingredients in a variety of other recipes.

Homemade stocks and sauces make the difference between a dish that tastes good and one that is really memorable. Making them at home is a tradition in Jewish cooking because making your own ensures that they are kosher.

Although meat stocks have a long cooking time, they are easy to put together and can simmer virtually unattended.

Vegetables and Vegetable Sauces

Fresh Tomato Sauce

Makes about 3 cups

P

Good tomato sauce plays a major role in fine Jewish cooking, especially in the Sephardic branch, where it accompanies most vegetables as well as many entrees and grain dishes. When tomatoes are at the height of their season, this thick, chunky sauce is a real treat. It does not cook for a long time so it captures the tomatoes' wonderful sun-ripened flavor. Not many seasonings are needed, so the accent is on the tomatoes.

I especially love making the sauce with different varieties of tomatoes from my garden and from farmers' markets, including yellow and orange ones. I freeze the sauces in the summer and enjoy them throughout the year.

3 pounds ripe tomatoes, any color

3 tablespoons olive oil or vegetable oil

1 medium onion, minced

2 large cloves garlic, minced

1 bay leaf

1 large sprig fresh thyme or 1/2 teaspoon dried thyme or oregano

Salt and freshly ground pepper, to taste

3 to 4 tablespoons chopped fresh herbs: Italian parsley, dill, cilantro, basil, tarragon, or oregano (optional)

1. Peel, seed, and chop the tomatoes (page 586). Then, heat oil in a large, heavy, shallow stew pan. Add onion and sauté over medium-low heat, stirring occasionally, about 7 minutes or until it begins to turn golden. Add garlic and sauté 30 seconds. Add tomatoes, bay leaf, thyme, salt, and pepper and bring to boil. Cook uncovered over medium heat, stirring often, 20 to 25 minutes or until tomatoes are very soft and sauce is fairly thick, reducing heat as sauce begins to thicken; tomatoes burn easily. Discard bay leaf and thyme sprig. Adjust seasoning.

2. At serving time, reheat sauce and stir in herbs, if using.

Peeling and Seeding Tomatoes

To Peel Tomatoes:

1. Bring a saucepan full of water to boil. Meanwhile, cut green cores from tomatoes.

2. Turn each tomato over and slit skin on bottom of tomato in an X-shaped cut.

3. Fill a large bowl with cold water.

4. Put tomatoes in the boiling water. Boil tomatoes 10 to 15 seconds or until their skin begins to pull away from their flesh.

5. Immediately remove tomatoes from water with a slotted spoon and put them in the bowl of cold water. Leave for a few seconds so they cool.

6. Remove tomatoes from water and pull off their skins. (You can add the tomato skins to vegetable or meat stocks.)

To Seed Tomatoes:

1. Cut tomatoes in half horizontally.

2. Hold each tomato half over a bowl, cut side down. Squeeze tomato to remove the seeds and juice.

3. You can chop the tomatoes with a knife or pulse them in a food processor to chop them.

4. If you like, strain the juice and refrigerate it for drinking.

Basic Tomato Sauce from Canned Tomatoes

Makes about 2 cups

During much of the year, when sun-ripened tomatoes are not available or are too expensive, most cooks use canned tomatoes. Although I sometimes use canned diced tomatoes for quick sauces, I find that whole canned tomatoes tend to have more substance and produce a finer sauce. Generally, I season this sauce more than I would one of fresh tomatoes.

Two 28-ounce cans whole tomatoes

3 tablespoons olive oil or vegetable oil

1 medium onion, minced

4 large cloves garlic, minced

1 bay leaf

1 large sprig fresh thyme or $1/2$ teaspoon dried thyme

1 teaspoon dried oregano

$1/4$ teaspoon hot pepper flakes (optional)

Salt and freshly ground pepper, to taste

1. Drain tomatoes in a strainer, reserving juice.

2. Heat oil in a large, heavy skillet. Add onion and sauté, stirring, over medium-low heat about 7 minutes or until it begins to turn golden. Add garlic and sauté 30 seconds. Add tomatoes, bay leaf, thyme, oregano, pepper flakes if using, salt, and pepper and bring to boil. Cook uncovered over medium heat, stirring often, about 15 minutes or until sauce is fairly thick, reducing heat as sauce begins to thicken; tomatoes burn easily. Discard bay leaf and thyme sprig. Adjust seasoning.

Tomato Sauce with Lemon and Garlic

Makes 4 to 6 servings

Lemony sauces are especially popular among Jews of Greek and Turkish extraction. The garlic is added when the sauce is nearly ready so its taste is more prominent, although it is not raw. This refreshingly tangy sauce is most welcome in summer as an accompaniment for baked or grilled fish. It's also good with pasta and rice salads.

2 pounds ripe tomatoes or two 28-ounce cans whole tomatoes

3 tablespoons olive oil or vegetable oil

1 medium onion, minced

2 tablespoons chopped fresh oregano or 1 teaspoon dried

Salt and freshly ground pepper, to taste

3 large cloves garlic, minced

2 teaspoons tomato paste (optional)

1 to 3 tablespoons strained fresh lemon juice

Pinch of cayenne pepper

2 tablespoons chopped fresh Italian parsley

1. Peel and seed fresh tomatoes (page 586), reserving their juice and straining it; if using canned tomatoes, drain and reserve juice. Coarsely chop tomatoes.

2. Heat oil in a medium saucepan. Add onion and sauté over medium-low heat 7 minutes or until soft but not brown. Add tomatoes, dried oregano (but not fresh), salt, and pepper. Bring to a boil. Cover and cook over low heat 20 minutes.

3. Add reserved tomato juice and garlic to sauce. Cook uncovered over medium heat, stirring often, about 10 minutes or until sauce thickens to your taste. Add tomato paste, if using, mix well, and simmer 1 minute.

4. A short time before serving, add fresh oregano and 1 tablespoon lemon juice. Taste before adding more lemon juice. Add a pinch of cayenne. Adjust seasoning. Add parsley. Serve hot or cold.

Tomato Sauce with Mild Chiles

Makes 4 to 6 servings　Ⓟ

This tasty tomato sauce recipe is from Sara Boni, a cousin of my husband who lives in Rehovot, Israel. When she visited us in Los Angeles, she made this recipe, adapting it with local ingredients. She flavored it with the long chiles called Anaheim chiles (milder than jalapeños) that are usually pale green but are sometimes available red; they reminded her of mild Israeli chiles.

Bell pepper, garlic, and sometimes cilantro complete the fresh flavorings. You can sauté the chiles and bell pepper before peeling them, as in this recipe, or broil or grill them if you prefer. Serve the sauce cold as a dip alongside hummus, or hot or cold as a side dish for meat. You can also poach eggs in the sauce or mix the sauce with beaten eggs and scramble the mixture.

2 pounds ripe tomatoes
2 tablespoons vegetable oil
3 mild chiles (Anaheim chiles), green or red
1 green or red bell pepper
3 large cloves garlic, chopped
Salt and freshly ground pepper, to taste
1 teaspoon paprika
1/4 cup chopped fresh cilantro (optional)
1/4 teaspoon cayenne pepper, or to taste

1. Peel and seed tomatoes (page 586), reserving their juice for other uses. Dice tomatoes.

2. Heat 1 tablespoon oil in a heavy skillet. Add chiles and bell pepper and sauté over medium-high heat, turning often, until their peels blister and begin to blacken in spots. Put all peppers in a plastic bag and close bag. Let stand 10 minutes.

3. Peel chiles and pepper, discarding seeds. Cut into small dice.

4. Combine diced tomatoes, chiles, garlic, salt, pepper, paprika, and remaining oil in skillet. Bring to a simmer. Cook over low heat, stirring often, about 30 minutes or until sauce is thick. Add cilantro, if using, and cook 5 more minutes. Season with cayenne.

Hot Cumin-Tomato Sauce

Makes about 8 servings　Ⓟ

This spicy sauce is delicious with Spiced Roast Turkey (page 363) or roast chicken. If you like, stir a little of the cooked bird's roasting juices into the sauce. For meatless meals, the sauce gives a lift to beans, brown rice, or couscous.

3 to 4 tablespoons olive oil
1 large onion, minced
4 large cloves garlic, chopped
2 or 3 jalapeño peppers, ribs and seeds removed, minced (see Note)
Three 28-ounce cans tomatoes, drained and chopped
1 tablespoon tomato paste
2 1/2 teaspoons ground cumin
1 teaspoon ground turmeric
1/2 teaspoon freshly ground pepper, plus more to taste
1/4 teaspoon hot red pepper flakes (optional)
Salt, to taste

Heat oil in a large saucepan, add onion, and sauté over medium heat about 7 minutes or until beginning to brown. Add garlic and jalapeño peppers and sauté 30 seconds. Add tomatoes and tomato paste and bring to a boil, stirring. Add cumin, turmeric, black pepper, pepper flakes if using, and salt. Cook uncovered over medium-low heat 20 minutes or until thickened to taste. Season with salt and pepper.

Note: Wear rubber gloves when handling hot peppers. If not using gloves, always wash your hands after touching hot peppers.

Grilled Bell Peppers

Makes 8 servings

As a young newlywed in Israel, I saw my neighbor putting peppers on her gas burners and wondered what she was doing. I learned she was charring the skins, and that this was a common technique in Israel for getting the smoky flavor found often in grilled foods. You can use a burner to get this effect if you line the base with foil first to keep it clean. Instead, I generally use the outdoor grill or broiler.

Grilled peppers are one of the most useful culinary preparations to have. They make a delightful first course or accompanying vegetable but they are also the basis for numerous appetizers, salads, and sauces. I generally grill red, orange, or green ones. Yellow ones tend to get brown spots on the meat if you grill them even a bit too much. This doesn't harm the taste, only the presentation.

Another way to get delicious smoky flaver is to roast the peppers. (The similarity in flavor often causes grilled peppers to be called "roasted red peppers.") If you like, preheat the oven to 450°F, roast them, and peel them the same way; they will take a few minutes longer and will become softer than grilled peppers.

8 large bell peppers

1. Preheat grill or broiler. Put peppers on grill or broiler rack about 4 inches from heat. Grill or broil peppers, turning every 4 to 5 minutes with tongs, about 15 minutes total, or until their skins are blistered and charred. Transfer to a bowl and cover tightly, or put in a bag and close the bag. Let stand 10 minutes.

2. Peel peppers using a paring knife. Halve peppers; note that there may be hot liquid inside. Discard caps, seeds, and ribs. Pat dry if desired; do not rinse.

3. Serve in halves or in wide strips. Serve warm, cold, or at room temperature.

Roasted Chile Strips

Makes 8 servings

My Moroccan friends prepare these for festive meals and serve them along with the main course, rather like a hot chutney.

I like to use heart-shaped dark green poblano chiles, which have a good flavor. (The names for these aren't uniform; they are labeled pasilla chiles in California.) Chile experts describe them as mild to medium-hot, but most of those I have tried have been hot to my palate. If you would like a milder chile, use Anaheim chiles, which are long and light green or red. If you want even hotter ones, use green or red jalapeño peppers. Whichever you choose, do let your guests know that these are not bell peppers.

4 fresh poblano or 8 jalapeño peppers (see Note)
About 1 tablespoon extra-virgin olive oil
Salt, to taste

1. Preheat broiler or grill. Put chiles on broiler rack or on grill about 2 inches from heat. Roast chiles, turning them often, until skin blisters and chars on all sides, 5 to 7 minutes. Do not let them burn.

2. Transfer to a bowl and cover tightly, or put in a bag and close bag. Let stand 10 minutes. Peel using paring knife. Discard cap, seeds, and ribs. Be careful; there may be hot liquid inside. Drain well and pat dry.

3. Cut chiles lengthwise into strips about 1/4-inch wide. Transfer to a shallow dish. Sprinkle lightly with oil and salt. Serve at room temperature.

Note: Wear rubber gloves when handling hot peppers. If not using gloves, always wash your hands after touching hot peppers.

Roasted Pepper Sauce with Tomatoes and Garlic

Makes 4 servings

This wonderful sauce is redolent of the favorite flavors of North African Jews—cumin, garlic, cilantro, and hot peppers. Serve it with just about any dish, from vegetarian entrees to fish to chicken, or use it to lend a lively touch to rice or couscous. You can also use it as a sauce for cooking veal or chicken, as in Morroccan Jewish Chicken in Grilled Pepper Sauce (page 354). If you like, prepare a double recipe and keep some on hand in the freezer.

2 green bell peppers

1 large red bell pepper

2 jalapeño peppers (see Note)

1 tablespoon olive oil

One 28-ounce can tomatoes, drained and chopped

3 large cloves garlic, minced

¹⁄₄ cup minced fresh cilantro

2 teaspoons paprika

1 teaspoon ground cumin

Salt, to taste

Pinch of cayenne pepper

1. Preheat broiler or grill. Broil green and red bell peppers, turning every 5 minutes, until their skins are blistered and charred, a total of about 20 minutes. Broil jalapeño peppers, turning often, about 5 minutes. Transfer peppers to bowl and cover; or put in a plastic bag and close bag. Let stand 10 minutes.

2. Peel bell peppers and jalapeño peppers using paring knife. Halve peppers; discard seeds and ribs. Cut bell peppers into ¹⁄₂-inch dice. Chop jalapeño peppers.

3. Heat oil in a large skillet. Add tomatoes, bell peppers, jalapeño peppers, garlic, cilantro, paprika, cumin, and salt. Cook uncovered over medium heat, stirring often, about 20 minutes or until sauce is thick. Season with cayenne. Serve hot or cold.

Note: Wear rubber gloves when handling hot peppers. If not using gloves, always wash your hands after touching hot peppers.

Artichoke Bottoms and Stems

Makes 4 servings

Artichoke bottoms are favorites in the Sephardic kitchen for salads, appetizers, and stuffings.

Many people prepare them by cooking whole artichokes and removing the leaves. Here is the way that chefs prepare them; the cooking time is shorter and the artichoke bottoms remain firmer. It does involve shaping the artichoke bottoms with a knife. Chefs use a sharp, sturdy knife. In the home kitchen, I find a serrated knife is easiest.

One adaptation I make to the chef's technique: I don't throw out the artichoke stems. I cook them along with the artichoke bottoms. Once you remove their skins, they are tender inside and taste like the artichoke bottoms.

2 lemons, halved

4 large artichokes

1. To shape the artichokes: Squeeze the juice of ¹⁄₂ lemon into a bowl of cold water. Break off the stem of 1 artichoke and the large leaves at bottom. Put one artichoke on its side on board. Holding a very sharp knife or serrated knife against the side of the artichoke (parallel to the leaves), cut the lower circle of leaves off, up to edge of artichoke heart, turning the artichoke slightly after each cut. Rub cut edges of artichoke with cut lemon. Cut off leaves under artichoke's base. Trim all dark green areas from base. Rub again with lemon. Cut off central cone of leaves just above artichoke bottom. Put artichoke in the bowl of lemon water. Repeat with remaining artichokes. Keep artichokes in lemon water until ready to cook them. Discard the removed leaves.

2. To cook artichoke bottoms: Add 1 tablespoon lemon juice to a medium saucepan of boiling salted water. Add artichoke bottoms and stems. Cover and simmer over low heat 15 to 20 minutes or until tender when pierced with a knife; the stems may take a few minutes longer. If serving cold or making ahead, cool to lukewarm in liquid.

3. Using a teaspoon, scoop out hairlike "choke" from center of each artichoke. Pull thick skin from stems.

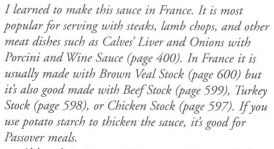

Brown and White Sauces

Quick Brown Sauce

Makes about 1 cup

I learned to make this sauce in France. It is most popular for serving with steaks, lamb chops, and other meat dishes such as Calves' Liver and Onions with Porcini and Wine Sauce (page 400). In France it is usually made with Brown Veal Stock (page 600) but it's also good made with Beef Stock (page 599), Turkey Stock (page 598), or Chicken Stock (page 597). If you use potato starch to thicken the sauce, it's good for Passover meals.

Although it simmers 30 minutes, it's a quick alternative to traditional brown sauce, which simmers for hours and is made with a heavy roux of fat and flour.

If you like, prepare a double or triple quantity of this sauce and keep it on hand. You can keep this basic sauce 2 days in the refrigerator or several months in the freezer. Often the sauce is finished with a splash of dry or semi-dry wine and a little salt and pepper.

2 teaspoons vegetable oil

1/2 onion, diced

1/2 carrot, diced

1 1/2 cups Brown Veal Stock (page 600), Beef Stock (page 599), Turkey Stock (page 598), or Chicken Stock (page 597)

2 ripe medium fresh tomatoes or 4 canned plum tomatoes, coarsely chopped (optional)

1 large sprig fresh thyme or 1/2 teaspoon dried thyme, crumbled

1 bay leaf

2 tablespoons cold water

1 teaspoon potato starch, arrowroot, or cornstarch

1 teaspoon tomato paste (optional)

1. Heat oil in a medium, heavy saucepan. Add onion and carrot and sauté over medium-high heat, stirring often, until well browned. (Do not let them burn.) Add stock, tomatoes, if using, thyme, and bay leaf. Bring to a boil, stirring. Simmer uncovered over very low heat about 20 minutes.

2. Strain into another saucepan, pressing on vegetables. Skim as much fat as possible from surface. Simmer uncovered over medium heat until reduced to 1 cup.

3. Whisk cold water and potato starch in a small bowl to form a smooth paste. Whisk in tomato paste, if using. Gradually pour paste into simmering sauce, whisking constantly. Bring back to a boil, whisking constantly. Simmer 1 to 2 minutes if necessary, until thickened. If not using immediately, dab surface of warm sauce with small piece of margarine to prevent skin from forming; or simply stir the sauce as it cools. Reheat over medium heat before using, stirring often.

Quick Turkey Gravy

Makes about 3 cups, 8 to 10 servings

When you have roasted a turkey, use the pan juices and turkey or chicken stock to make this rich, savory sauce. It takes only a few minutes. You can make it with any turkey roast, whether a whole bird or just part of one, no matter how it is seasoned.

Roasting pan with the pan juices from 1 roast turkey

1/2 cup dry white wine

3 cups Fast Turkey Stock (page 598), Brown Turkey Stock (page 599), or Chicken Stock (page 597)

1/4 cup vegetable oil or margarine

1/4 cup all-purpose flour

1 tablespoon tomato paste (optional)

Salt and freshly ground pepper, to taste

1. After roasting the turkey, transfer the bird carefully to platter or large board. Cover turkey and let it rest while making the sauce.

2. Skim fat from pan juices. Add wine and 1/2 cup stock to pan and bring to a boil, stirring and scraping to dissolve any brown bits in pan. Boil liquid until reduced to about 1/2 cup. Strain into a bowl.

3. Heat oil in a large, heavy saucepan over low heat. Whisk in flour. Cook, whisking constantly, about 3 minutes or until mixture turns light beige. Remove from heat. Gradually pour in remaining 2 1/2 cups stock, whisking. Bring to a boil over medium-high heat, whisking. Add strained turkey pan juices. Simmer uncovered over medium-low heat, whisking often, about 5 minutes or until sauce is thick enough to coat a spoon. Whisk in tomato paste, if using, and simmer 1 minute. Season with salt and pepper.

4. Reheat gravy just before serving. Pour into a sauce boat and serve alongside turkey.

Velouté Sauce

Makes about 1¹/₂ cups,
about 6 servings   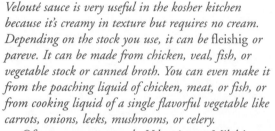 **M** or **P**

Velouté sauce is very useful in the kosher kitchen because it's creamy in texture but requires no cream. Depending on the stock you use, it can be fleishig or pareve. It can be made from chicken, veal, fish, or vegetable stock or canned broth. You can even make it from the poaching liquid of chicken, meat, or fish, or from cooking liquid of a single flavorful vegetable like carrots, onions, leeks, mushrooms, or celery.

Of course, you can make Velouté sauce Milchig too, by using butter and by choosing fish or vegetable stock. If you like, you can whisk ¹/₄ to ¹/₃ cup whipping cream into the finished sauce and simmer it another few minutes or until it thickens.

Velouté sauce takes just a few moments to prepare and is great for adding interest to plainly cooked foods like poached fish, chicken, meat, or vegetables. Of course, you can enhance its flavor by adding spices like curry powder or paprika to the sauce along with the flour, or adding chopped herbs to the finished sauce. Just about any herb is good—tarragon, thyme, chervil, chives, cilantro, dill, or parsley.

2 tablespoons vegetable oil or margarine
2 tablespoons plus 1 teaspoon all-purpose flour
1¹/₂ cups cup chicken, veal, fish, or vegetable stock or canned broth
Salt and white pepper, to taste
A few drops strained fresh lemon juice (optional)
Cayenne pepper, to taste (optional)

1. Heat oil in a medium, heavy saucepan over low heat. Whisk in flour. Cook, whisking constantly, about 3 minutes or until mixture turns light beige. Remove from heat.

2. Add stock, whisking. Bring to a boil over medium-high heat, whisking. Add a small pinch of salt and white pepper. Simmer uncovered over medium-low heat, whisking often, 5 minutes. Adjust seasoning, adding lemon juice and cayenne if using. If not using sauce at once, dab top with margarine to prevent a skin from forming. Whisk sauce when reheating. Serve hot.

Cream Sauce

Makes 1³/₄ to 2 cups, 6 to 8 servings   **D**

Cream sauce is popular for milchig meals, especially in the Ashkenazic kitchen. It's great with fish and with vegetables. You can also use it to moisten cooked noodles, mix them with cooked vegetables or cooked fish, and bake the mixture in the oven as a casserole. Be sure to season the sauce well so it won't be bland. Embellish it with herbs if you like, such as dill, chives, or parsley, as in Brussels Sprouts and Carrots in Creamy Parsley Sauce (page 460).

3 tablespoons butter
3 tablespoons all-purpose flour
2¹/₄ cups milk
Salt and white pepper, to taste
Freshly grated nutmeg, to taste
¹/₃ cup whipping cream (optional)
Cayenne pepper, to taste (optional)

1. Melt butter in medium, heavy saucepan over low heat. Whisk in flour and cook, whisking constantly, until foaming but not browned, about 2 minutes. Remove from heat. Gradually whisk in milk. Bring to boil over medium-high heat, whisking. Add a small pinch of salt, white pepper, and nutmeg. Reduce heat to low and cook, whisking often, 5 minutes.

2. Whisk in cream, if using, and bring to boil. Cook over low heat, whisking often, until sauce thickens and coats a spoon heavily, about 7 minutes. Remove from heat and add cayenne, if using. Adjust seasoning. Dab surface of sauce with butter if not using immediately. Whisk sauce when reheating. Serve hot.

Spicy Sauces and Other Uncooked Sauces

Yemenite Hot Pepper Chutney
Zehug

Makes about 1 cup, 8 to 12 servings

Ⓟ

Zehug is a fiery Yemenite chutney made of fresh hot peppers and garlic. Some cooks add spices as well. It's made in two basic versions: red zehug made from hot red chiles and green zehug from green ones. Green zehug often has cilantro, which helps to balance the heat somewhat. You can buy it in markets that sell Israeli products but it's easy to make and is fresher if you make your own.

For many Jews of Yemenite origin, whether or not they were born in Yemen, a meal without zehug has no taste. Usually it is placed on the table in a very small dish when the meal begins. The usual way to eat it is to spread it on bread as an appetizer. Many people also like it as an accompaniment for the soups and main courses.

This chutney is really hot. The only way I can eat it is to use relatively mild chiles like jalapeños. But you can use any hot green chiles that you like. I remove the seeds and ribs so it will be less hot but my mother-in-law and most other Yemen-born cooks leave them in.

¼ pound hot green chiles, such as jalapeño or serrano (see Note)

1 cup garlic cloves, peeled (¼ pound)

4 to 5 tablespoons water, if needed

1 cup fresh cilantro

1 teaspoon salt

¼ teaspoon freshly ground pepper

2 tablespoons ground cumin (optional)

1. Remove stems from peppers. Put garlic and peppers in food processor and puree until finely chopped and well blended. If necessary, add a few tablespoons water, just enough to enable food processor to chop mixture. Add cilantro and process until blended. Add salt, pepper, and cumin, if using.

2. Keep zehug in a jar in refrigerator. It keeps about 1 week. Take only a small amount from the jar for serving, reserving the rest in the refrigerator. You can also freeze it.

Note: Wear rubber gloves when handling hot peppers. If not using gloves, always wash your hands after touching hot peppers.

Hot Pepper Sauce, North African Style
Harissa

Makes about ½ cup

Ⓟ

Jews from North African countries love hot sauce, made with dried hot peppers. It has two Arabic names: Tunisians call it harissa, *the more common name in the United States. Moroccans refer to it as* sahakeh, *but they are quite similar. Made basically with dried chiles, oil, and salt, it might also include garlic, vinegar, or spices like cumin or caraway. It is used for seasoning soups, stews, and salads of cooked vegetables, and for spreading on bread.*

The sauce is thick, more like a paste. To make it more sauce-like, it is sometimes mixed with tomato paste, water, and chopped green onions.

If you use a blender or mini chopper, the ingredients will blend to a more uniform paste than in a food processor.

½ cup small or medium dried red chiles (see Note)

About ⅓ cup water

½ teaspoon salt

2½ tablespoons olive oil or vegetable oil

3 or 4 large cloves garlic (optional)

1 teaspoon ground cumin (optional)

1. Put dried chiles in a bowl and cover with lukewarm water. Soak 2 hours. Remove chiles; discard soaking liquid. Slit chiles and remove seeds. Cut chiles into pieces.

2. Put chile pieces in a blender or mini-food processor. Add water, salt, 2 tablespoons oil, and garlic and cumin, if using. Process until blended to a paste; a few pieces may remain. (Avert your face when you open the blender—the fumes can be overpowering!) If necessary, add another tablespoon water so mixture will blend more easily. Transfer to a jar and pour a little oil over the top. Cover and keep in refrigerator up to 1 week.

Note: Wear rubber gloves when handling hot peppers. If not using gloves, always wash your hands after touching hot peppers.

Walnut and Garlic Sauce

Makes 6 servings

Sauces of walnuts and herbs are made by cooks from Georgia, Turkey, Iran, as well as by other Sephardic Jews. This garlic-flavored walnut sauce is usually served with chicken but I also like it with flavorful fish like salmon, sea bass, and tuna. Be sure the walnuts and the garlic are very fresh. You can keep the sauce in a covered container up to 2 days in the refrigerator.

3 large cloves garlic, peeled

1/3 cup sprigs fresh parsley

2/3 cup walnuts

Salt and freshly ground pepper, to taste

2 tablespoons cold water

1/2 to 2/3 cup vegetable oil

Cayenne pepper to taste

1. Finely chop garlic in food processor. Add parsley sprigs and chop together. Add walnuts, salt, and pepper and process until walnuts are finely ground. Add water and puree to a smooth paste. With blades turning, add oil in a very fine stream. Stop adding oil occasionally and scrape down sides and bottom of work bowl. Transfer to a bowl. Add cayenne. Adjust seasoning.

2. Serve sauce at room temperature. Stir it before serving.

Garlic Butter

Makes about 1/2 cup, enough for
4 to 6 servings

This scrumptious butter has a multitude of uses, from spreading on hot toasted bagels to spooning over fish fillets before you bake them or after you grill or sauté them. It also adds a lovely flavor to hot cooked noodles and green vegetables.

1/2 cup (1 stick) butter, softened

4 large cloves garlic, finely minced

1/4 cup finely minced fresh Italian parsley

Salt and freshly ground pepper, to taste

Thoroughly beat butter, garlic, and parsley in a small bowl with a wooden spoon; or mash them together with a fork until blended. Season with salt and pepper. Spoon into a small bowl, cover, and refrigerate; or, form into a rough log shape onto wax paper, then roll into a log to enclose, wrap in plastic wrap, and freeze. Bring to room temperature before using.

 # Dressings

Sephardic Salad Dressing

Makes about ¹/₂ cup dressing

This makes terrific dressing for Israeli Salad (page 239). Actually, it's an all-purpose dressing great with any raw or cooked vegetable. It also makes a pleasant, light-textured alternative to mayonnaise for chicken or tuna salads. If you like, make a larger quantity and keep it in a jar, so you have your own homemade dressing ready. If you are making it ahead, it's best to add the parsley just before you use it so it stays fresh and bright green.

3 tablespoons strained fresh lemon juice

Salt and freshly ground pepper, to taste

Cayenne pepper, to taste

6 to 7 tablespoons extra-virgin olive oil

3 to 4 teaspoons chopped fresh Italian parsley (optional)

Whisk lemon juice with salt, pepper, and cayenne in a small bowl. Whisk in oil. Adjust seasoning. Just before using, whisk again and add parsley, if using.

Israeli Garlic-Cumin Dressing

Makes about ¹/₃ cup, about 4 servings

Use this easy-to-make dressing with cooked or raw vegetables, chicken, or fish. It makes for a pleasant, zesty potato salad.

2 to 3 tablespoons strained fresh lemon juice

2 large cloves garlic, pressed or very finely minced

1 teaspoon ground cumin

Salt and freshly ground pepper, to taste

Cayenne pepper, to taste

¹/₄ cup extra-virgin olive oil

Whisk 2 tablespoons lemon juice with garlic, cumin, salt, pepper, and cayenne in a small bowl. Whisk in olive oil. Taste, and add more lemon juice if you like. You can multiply the quantities and keep the dressing 3 to 4 days in a jar in the refrigerator. Shake well or whisk to blend before using.

Chive-Caper Vinaigrette

Makes about ¹/₂ cup

This lively dressing is great with cooked potatoes, cauliflower, or green beans, or with mixed green salads. It's also delicious on fish or chicken.

2 tablespoons white wine vinegar

Salt and freshly ground pepper, to taste

6 tablespoons extra-virgin olive oil

1 tablespoon drained capers, rinsed and chopped

1 tablespoon chopped fresh chives

Whisk vinegar with salt and pepper in a bowl. Whisk in oil. Stir in capers and chives. Adjust seasoning.

Lemon-Mint Vinaigrette

Makes about ¹/₂ cup

Serve this refreshing vinaigrette with fish, such as Sole Salad for Shabbat (page 180), with cucumbers, or with raw or cooked carrots.

1 tablespoon white wine vinegar

1 tablespoon strained fresh lemon juice

Salt and freshly ground pepper, to taste

6 tablespoons extra-virgin olive oil

1 tablespoon chopped fresh mint

¹/₂ teaspoon grated lemon rind

Whisk vinegar with lemon juice, salt, and pepper in a bowl. Whisk in oil. Stir in mint and lemon rind. Adjust seasoning. Whisk again before using.

Lemon-Herb Dressing

Makes about 1/2 cup

This Sephardic-style dressing is delicious with cooked fish, chickpeas, and cooked vegetables, as well as all sorts of salads. I like to keep it for only a few days so the flavor of the lemon juice remains fresh. You can blend the dressing with a whisk, or follow this easy shake-and-store jar method.

6 tablespoons extra-virgin olive oil

3 to 4 tablespoons strained fresh lemon juice

1 teaspoon fresh thyme or 1/4 teaspoon dried

2 teaspoons chopped fresh oregano or 1/2 teaspoon dried

1 teaspoon finely grated lemon rind

Salt and freshly ground pepper, to taste

Pinch of cayenne pepper

Combine ingredients in a screw-top jar. Close jar and shake to blend. Keep in the refrigerator. Before using, shake again. Adjust seasoning.

Fresh Tomato Vinaigrette

Makes about 1 1/2 cups sauce, 6 to 8 servings

This light, summery sauce is perfect with French Gefilte Fish Loaf (page 334). It's also delicious with hot or cold poached fish or vegetables and can perk up delicate types of gefilte fish from a jar, such as white-fish and pike or pure whitefish gefilte fish. Use very ripe, flavorful tomatoes that are red inside.

1 pound ripe large tomatoes

2 tablespoons white wine vinegar

Salt and freshly ground pepper, to taste

6 to 10 tablespoons extra-virgin olive oil

2 tablespoons chopped fresh basil, tarragon, or Italian parsley

1. Peel and seed tomatoes (page 586), reserving their juice for other uses. Finely chop tomatoes. Put them in a bowl.

2. Add vinegar, salt, and pepper to tomatoes and whisk until smooth. Very gradually whisk in the olive oil; sauce should remain thick and emulsified. Add herbs and taste for seasoning.

3. If you want sauce to stay thick, serve it immediately, at room temperature.

Lebanese Garlic Dressing

Makes about 1/2 cup, 4 to 6 servings

I have learned from Lebanese-Jewish friends how to make low-fat salads by seasoning vegetables with equal amounts of oil and lemon juice. This results in a dressing that is much lower in calories than the classic vinaigrette, which has 3 tablespoons oil for every tablespoon of lemon juice or vinegar. The dressing tastes good on green vegetables like green beans, spinach, Swiss chard, and zucchini, as well as sweet vegetables like beets and carrots. It's also popular with potatoes.

It's very important to use fresh garlic. If the garlic is old and a little dry or beginning to sprout, it gives the dressing a bitter flavor.

3 small cloves garlic, peeled

Salt, to taste

1/4 cup strained fresh lemon juice

Freshly ground pepper (optional)

1/4 cup extra-virgin olive oil

Crush garlic, sprinkle with salt, and chop very fine, almost to a puree. Put garlic in a bowl and add lemon juice and pepper, if using. Gradually whisk in olive oil. Adjust seasoning. If you would like a more mellow garlic flavor, refrigerate 30 minutes before using.

Mustard-Caper Vinaigrette

Makes ³/₄ cup dressing, 4 to 6 servings Ⓟ

Serve this dressing with salads containing meat or poultry, such as Warm Corned Beef and Pasta Salad with Mustard Vinaigrette (page 395). It's also delicious with potato salad and with salads of spicy greens.

5 teaspoons Dijon mustard

3 tablespoons white wine vinegar

Salt and freshly ground pepper, to taste

¹/₂ cup vegetable oil, plus 1 tablespoon if needed

3 tablespoons chopped green onion

¹/₄ cup chopped fresh Italian parsley

2 tablespoons finely chopped drained capers

1 large clove garlic, pressed or finely minced

Whisk mustard in a small bowl with vinegar, salt, and pepper. Whisk in ¹/₂ cup oil. Stir in green onion, parsley, capers, and garlic. Adjust seasoning. Add another tablespoon oil if needed.

Oregano–Red Onion Dressing

Makes about 1 cup, 4 to 6 servings Ⓟ

Use this dressing for chicken, turkey, and pasta salads.

¹/₄ cup strained fresh lemon juice

Cayenne pepper, to taste

1 teaspoon dried oregano, crumbled

Salt and freshly ground pepper, to taste

²/₃ cup extra-virgin olive oil

¹/₄ cup minced red onion

Whisk lemon juice with cayenne, oregano, salt, and pepper in a medium bowl. Gradually whisk in olive oil. Stir in onion. Adjust seasoning. If making ahead, keep in a covered jar in refrigerator.

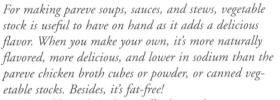

✤ *Stocks*

Vegetable Stock

Makes about 1 quart Ⓟ

For making pareve soups, sauces, and stews, vegetable stock is useful to have on hand as it adds a delicious flavor. When you make your own, it's more naturally flavored, more delicious, and lower in sodium than the pareve chicken broth cubes or powder, or canned vegetable stocks. Besides, it's fat-free!

Vegetable stock is almost effortless and very economical to make, as it's made of inexpensive vegetables. You can use the ones in this recipe or whatever you have on hand. Resourceful cooks save parsley stems and trimmings of onions, leeks, carrots, mushrooms, and celery in the freezer to make stock. You can refrigerate the stock for 3 days or keep it in the freezer.

2 large onions, diced

1 large carrot, diced

2 ribs celery with leafy tops, sliced

1 large, soft tomato, halved (optional)

Dark green part of 1 leek, rinsed thoroughly and sliced (optional)

6 cups water

1 bay leaf

2 sprigs fresh thyme or ¹/₂ teaspoon dried thyme

5 parsley stems (optional)

2 large garlic cloves, peeled and crushed (optional)

1¹/₂ cups mushroom stems (optional)

Pinch of salt (optional)

Combine all ingredients in a medium saucepan. Bring to a boil. Cover and cook over low heat 1 hour. Strain stock, pressing on ingredients in strainer; discard ingredients in strainer. Refrigerate or freeze stock until ready to use.

Quick-and-Easy Vegetable Broth

Makes about 1 quart

Tasty broth is a by-product of cooking many vegetables. I save the cooking liquid of most vegetables in a jar in the refrigerator and so I always have pareve broth for making soups or stews. When I need a very fast vegetable dish, I like to cook carrots and zucchini together. They're ready in a few minutes, and they produce a flavorful broth.

2 large carrots, sliced

4 cups water

1 bay leaf (optional)

Pinch of salt (optional)

2 medium zucchini, halved and sliced

Combine carrots, water, and bay leaf and salt, if using, in a medium saucepan. Bring to a boil. Cover and cook over low heat 10 minutes. Add zucchini cook over low heat 5 minutes or until tender. Discard bay leaf. Serve carrots and zucchini as an easy side dish. Refrigerate or freeze broth until needed.

Chicken Stock

Makes 3 to 3¹/₂ quarts

Chicken soup or broth from cooking a whole chicken or meaty chicken pieces is a staple in the Jewish kitchen. In my home, however, chicken soup disappears fast! There rarely seems to be any left over for me to keep on hand in the freezer when I need a base for quick soups. Stock is a more economical but still flavorful alternative made from chicken bones, necks, wing tips, other trimmings, and giblets. Use it to make soups, sauces, and as a cooking liquid for rice and vegetables for fleishig *meals. You can refrigerate the stock for 2 to 3 days or keep it in the freezer.*

4 pounds chicken wings, bones, backs, necks, and giblets (except livers)

2 onions, quartered

2 carrots, quartered

2 ribs celery, with leaves (optional)

Dark green parts of 2 or 3 leeks, cleaned (optional)

2 bay leaves

12 parsley stems, without leaves (optional)

About 5 quarts water

2 sprigs fresh thyme or ¹/₂ teaspoon dried thyme (optional)

1. Combine chicken, onions, carrots, celery and leeks, if using, bay leaves, and parsley, if using, in a large pot. Add enough water to cover the ingredients. Bring to a boil, skimming froth. Add thyme, if using.

2. Reduce heat to low so that stock bubbles very gently. Partially cover and cook 2 hours, skimming foam and fat occasionally with a large metal spoon or a slotted spoon. Strain stock into large bowls. If not using immediately, cool to lukewarm. Refrigerate until cold and skim fat off top.

Turkey Stock: Substitute turkey wings or wing tips, turkey bones, and giblets (except livers) for those from chicken. Cook the stock 3 hours.

Roast Turkey Stock

Makes about 3 quarts

There are four ways to make turkey stock. Roasting turkey stock, as in this recipe, is probably the most common technique. It makes use of the bones left from a roast turkey; it's surprising what good turkey flavor the stock has even when made from cooked bones. The second, Fast Turkey Stock (this page), is the most rapidly made of the turkey stocks and makes use of turkey giblets and trimmings. A third way is atypical for poultry but provides delicious flavor: turkey neck and giblets are sautéed with seasonings and then simmered with chicken stock. See Brown Turkey Stock (page 599). Finally, a fourth way is to use whole turkey wings or uncooked bones from a turkey to make turkey stock the way you make chicken stock. (See variation, Chicken Stock, page 597.)

No matter how it's made, turkey stock has the same uses as chicken stock. You can refrigerate the stock for 2 to 3 days or keep it in the freezer.

Bones and carcass of 1 roast turkey

2 onions, whole

2 carrots, whole

3 ribs celery, with leaves

1 parsnip or parsley root, whole (optional)

12 parsley stems, without leaves (optional)

2 bay leaves

About 4 to 5 quarts water

2 sprigs fresh thyme or 1/2 teaspoon dried thyme (optional)

1. Chop roast turkey bones and carcass into manageable pieces. Put in a stock pot or other large pot. Add onions, carrots, celery, parsnip, and parsley stems, if using, and bay leaves. Add enough water to cover the ingredients. Bring to a boil, skimming froth. Add thyme.

2. Reduce heat to low so that stock bubbles very gently. Partially cover and cook, skimming foam and fat occasionally with a large metal spoon or a slotted spoon, 3 hours or until well flavored. Strain stock into large bowls. If not using immediately, let cool. Refrigerate until cold and skim fat off top.

Fast Turkey Stock

Makes about 1 quart

Make this fairly quick stock from turkey neck and giblets while the bird is roasting. Then you can use it to make Quick Turkey Gravy (page 590). Use water as the cooking liquid, or, for a more concentrated taste, begin with chicken stock.

1 turkey neck and giblets (except liver)

1 large onion, quartered

1 small carrot, cut into thick slices

1 rib celery (optional)

2 large cloves garlic, crushed

1 bay leaf

1 sprig fresh thyme or 1/2 teaspoon dried thyme

6 cups chicken stock, mixed stock and water, or water

1. Combine turkey neck and giblets, onion, carrot, celery, if using, garlic, bay leaf, thyme, and stock in medium saucepan. Bring to a boil, skimming foam and fat occasionally with a large metal spoon or a slotted spoon. Cover and simmer over very low heat for 1 to 1 1/2 hours.

2. Strain stock into a bowl. Use at once, refrigerate, or freeze. Skim fat from surface before using.

Fast Duck or Goose Stock: Substitute duck or goose neck and giblets for those of turkey.

Brown Turkey Stock

Makes about 1 quart (M)

In classic European cooking, brown stock is made primarily from veal or beef. Today many cooks also make it with chicken or turkey stock. It gives soups and sauces a deeper flavor and richer color. You can refrigerate it for 2 or 3 days or keep it in the freezer.

1 turkey neck and giblets (except liver)

2 tablespoons vegetable oil

1 onion, diced

1 carrot, diced

1 rib celery, diced (optional)

4 to 5 cups chicken stock, or stock mixed with water

1 large tomato, quartered

1 tablespoon tomato paste

1 bay leaf

1 large sprig fresh thyme or $1/2$ teaspoon dried thyme

1. Chop turkey neck into a few pieces. Dice turkey giblets. Heat oil in a medium, heavy saucepan. Add giblets and sauté over medium-high heat, stirring often, about 7 minutes or until browned. Add onion, carrot, and celery, if using, and sauté over medium heat, stirring often, about 5 minutes or until onion browns. Keep stirring and reduce heat if necessary. Turkey pieces tend to stick; do not let them burn.

2. Add stock, tomato, tomato paste, bay leaf, and thyme to saucepan. Bring to a boil, stirring often to dissolve brown bits. Cover and simmer over very low heat, skimming foam and fat occasionally with a large metal spoon or a slotted spoon, $1^1/2$ hours or until well flavored. Strain stock. Use at once, refrigerate, or freeze.

Beef Stock

Makes about 2 quarts (M)

To give a meaty flavor to soups, stews, and sauces, keep this stock in your freezer. You can use it interchangeably with beef broth, the liquid from poaching beef. Homemade stock tastes much better than broth made from powders or cubes and is much lower in sodium. Although the stock needs several hours to simmer, it cooks on its own with virtually no attention on your part. To cut the cooking time to 2 hours instead of 6, you can use a pressure cooker. Beef stock is very economical to prepare and provides good flavor for little effort. Use beef soup bones or any inexpensive cut of beef with bones. You can refrigerate the stock for 2 to 3 days or keep it in the freezer.

For French style beef stock, which has a richer flavor and deeper color, follow the recipe for Brown Veal Stock (page 600), substituting beef bones.

5 pounds beef soup bones, chopped into pieces by the butcher

2 onions, rinsed but not peeled, root-end cut off

2 carrots, scrubbed but not peeled

2 ribs celery, cut into 3-inch pieces (optional)

2 bay leaves

10 parsley stems (save leaves for chopping)

4 large cloves garlic, unpeeled

About 4 quarts water

1. Preheat oven to 450°F. Roast bones in a large roasting pan in oven, turning them over once, about 30 minutes or until they begin to brown. Add onions and carrots and roast about 30 minutes or until browned.

2. Combine bones, onions, carrots, celery, if using, bay leaves, parsley stems, and garlic in a stock pot or other large pot. Add enough water to cover ingredients. Bring to a boil, skimming froth. Partially cover and cook stock over very low heat, so it bubbles very gently, skimming foam and fat occasionally with a large metal spoon or a slotted spoon. During first 2 hours of cooking, add hot water occasionally to keep ingredients covered. Cook stock a total of 6 hours. Strain stock. Cool, refrigerate until cold, and skim solidified fat off top.

Brown Veal Stock

Makes about 2 quarts

This flavorful stock, prepared in the French style, makes delicious sauces for meat. To make brown beef stock, simply substitute beef soup bones for the veal bones. You can refrigerate the stock for 2 to 3 days or keep it in the freezer.

5 pounds veal knuckle bones, chopped into pieces by butcher if possible

2 onions, rinsed but not peeled, root-end cut off, quartered

2 carrots, scrubbed but not peeled, quartered crosswise

2 ribs celery, cut into 3-inch pieces (optional)

1 ripe large tomato (optional)

2 bay leaves

10 parsley stems (optional)

4 large cloves garlic, unpeeled

About 4 quarts water

2 sprigs fresh thyme or $1/2$ teaspoon dried thyme, crumbled

1. Preheat oven to 450°F. Roast bones in a large roasting pan in oven, turning them over once, about 30 minutes or until they begin to brown. Add onions and carrots and roast about 30 minutes or until browned.

2. With a slotted metal spatula, transfer bones and vegetables to a stock pot or other large pot. Discard any fat from roasting pan. Add 1 cup hot water to roasting pan and heat over low heat, stirring to dissolve the roasting juices in the water. Add to the stock pot.

3. Add celery and tomato if using, bay leaves, parsley stems, if using, and garlic to the pot, and enough water to cover ingredients. Bring to a boil, skimming froth. Add thyme. Partially cover and cook stock over very low heat, so it bubbles very gently, skimming foam and fat occasionally with a large metal spoon or a slotted spoon. During first 2 hours of cooking, add hot water occasionally to keep ingredients covered. Cook stock a total of 6 hours. Strain stock. Cool, refrigerate until cold, and skim solidified fat off top.

Fish Stock

Makes about 5 cups

Prepared fish stock is not widely available, but it's easy to make at home. Use it to poach fish or gefilte fish or to make fish soups or sauces for fish. The fish frames of halibut are perfect for stock, but you can use the heads, tails, and bones of any kosher fish except strong-flavored ones like tuna and mackerel. You can also use fish trimmings or fish pieces for chowder, which are available at some markets.

Fish stock is usually made without salt so that any sauces you make by boiling the stock to concentrate it won't become too salty. You can refrigerate the stock for 2 days or keep it in the freezer.

$1^{1}/2$ pounds fish tails, heads, and bones, rinsed thoroughly

1 tablespoon vegetable oil

1 onion, diced small

1 bay leaf

1 sprig fresh thyme

5 sprigs fresh parsley

7 cups water

1. Rinse fish bones under cool, running water, 5 minutes.

2. Heat oil in a large saucepan. Add onion and sauté 7 minutes over low heat until softened but not brown. Add bay leaf, thyme, parsley, and water to cover and bring to a boil; skim off foam. Simmer uncovered over low heat, 20 minutes, skimming foam and fat occasionally with a large metal spoon or a slotted spoon. Strain into a bowl. Refrigerate or freeze until ready to use.

Fish Stock for Gefilte Fish

Makes 6 to 8 cups   Ⓟ

This stock is very easy to make and it gives gefilte fish a great flavor. It is more delicate than the usual fish stock because traditionally it is made with fresh water fish.

Some old-fashioned recipes call for cooking the gefilte fish in unstrained fish stock so that the fish bones and other ingredients continue to add flavor during the hour that the gefilte fish cooks. I prefer to strain the stock before adding the gefilte fish so there's no problem separating it from the stock elements later.

You can prepare the stock a day ahead and keep it in a covered container in the refrigerator, or you can freeze it.

Bones and head of fish used to prepare gefilte fish

2 to 3 pounds additional fish bones and heads (optional)

2 onions, sliced

1 small carrot, sliced

3 sprigs fresh parsley

1 teaspoon salt

2 quarts water, or enough to just cover bones

Rinse bones and heads of fish under cold water at least 5 minutes. Combine all ingredients for stock in a large, deep saucepan or pot. Bring to a boil. Skim off foam as it accumulates with a large metal spoon or a slotted spoon. Cover and simmer over low heat 30 to 40 minutes or until well flavored. Strain and return to pan. Taste for seasoning. Strain stock. If not using right away, cool and refrigerate up to 2 days.

Salmon Gefilte Fish Stock: Add 2 large sliced carrots to pot with other ingredients.

❧ *Flavorings*

Yemenite Soup Spice

Makes about 1/2 cup   Ⓟ

This spice blend is the hallmark of Yemenite Jewish cooking. Known in Yemenite Arabic as hawaij marak *(soup spice), it sometimes includes cardamom seeds in addition to the spices below. I learned to make it from my mother-in-law, who used to pound the cumin seeds in a mortar with a pestle. I agree with her that freshly grinding the cumin seeds is the best way to enjoy the spice, but I use an electric spice grinder. She uses this spice mixture with a liberal hand to season not only soups, but also fish, chicken, meat, and most vegetables, no matter how she intends to cook them.*

This spice mixture used to be available only at special spice stores in areas in Israel with a substantial Yemenite population, but now can be found in supermarkets. I have even found it in Israeli grocery stores in the United States.

6 tablespoons freshly ground cumin seeds

2 tablespoons ground turmeric

1 or 2 tablespoons freshly ground pepper

Mix spices in a small bowl. Store mixture, tightly covered, in a jar or airtight container in a dark cupboard for up to 6 months.

Bouquet Garni

Makes enough for about 2 quarts of soup

This bundle of herbs—traditionally parsley, thyme, and bay leaves—is added by French cooks to almost all soups and stews as it adds a lovely subtle flavor and aroma. A bouquet garni adds the flavor of the herbs without leaving pieces of herb in the final dish. I love this technique and I use it often with many different herb and spice combinations. Bouquet garni is also very economical. Only the stems of the parsley enter the bouquet garni—the leaves are reserved for chopping and adding to the finished dish. If you have tarragon, chervil, or leafy celery sprigs, you can do the same with them. I've also used the stems of cilantro in a bouquet garni, when its flavor is appropriate for the dish.

If you keep kitchen twine on hand, a bouquet garni is very simple to make; if you don't have it, use cheesecloth. Some cooks tie one end to the handle of the pot for easy removal.

6 stems of Italian or curled parsley

2 large sprigs fresh thyme

1 bay leaf

Dark green part of 1 leek (optional), cleaned

1. Remove leaves from parsley and reserve for other uses. Hold thyme, bay leaf, and parsley together. Open the piece of leek flat, if using, and enclose the herbs in it. Wrap it with kitchen twine and tie a knot. Or wrap it in cheesecloth and tie ends together to form a seasoning bag.

2. Add a bouquet garni to any soup, stew, or sauce that will simmer more than 10 minutes.

Chicken Fat

Schmaltz

Makes about 1 cup

Food flavored with chicken fat is one of the hallmarks of traditional Ashkenazic Jewish cooking. It's used for general sautéing for fleishig *dishes and to flavor such foods as matzo balls and potato kugel.*

Before being used, chicken fat is cooked, or "rendered." It is available in jars at kosher markets but many people prefer to make their own. You can save the fat from chickens in the freezer until you have enough to render. You can also make this with goose fat. The schmaltz keeps for several months in the refrigerator.*

Fat from 4 or more chickens

Salt, to taste

¹/₂ cup water

1 onion, chopped

Rinse the fat, cut it into pieces, and sprinkle it with salt. Heat a heavy skillet over low heat, add the fat and water, and cook until water evaporates and fat melts. Add onion and sauté about 10 minutes or until golden. Strain fat. Pour it into a clean jar, cover, and keep in the refrigerator.

Chicken Cracklings

Grivenes

Makes about 1 cup cracklings
and about 1¹/₂ cups chicken fat

Chicken cracklings, or grivenes *in Yiddish, are made of crisp bits of chicken skin. They are popular in the old-fashioned Ashkenazic kitchen as snacks and as flavorings for noodles, savory kugels, and chopped liver.*

When you make grivenes, you also get plenty of chicken fat, which you can save in jars for sautéing.

Fatty portions of skin of 4 or more chickens

Fat from 4 or more chickens

Salt to taste

¹/₂ cup water

2 onions, chopped

1. Rinse the chicken skin and fat. Cut them into pieces and sprinkle with salt. Heat a heavy skillet over low heat. Add the skin, fat, and water and cook until the water evaporates and the fat melts. Add onions and sauté about 15 minutes or until golden. Continue to sauté, stirring occasionally, until chicken skin is crunchy. Strain fat, reserving onion and skins. Put onion and skins in refrigerator in a covered container. Pour the fat into clean jars, cover, and keep in the refrigerator.

2. Reheat grivenes before serving.

Appendix A:

The Jewish Calendar

The first Jewish calendar year began 5,760 years ago and is said to have started from the day of the birth of Adam—the sixth day of the biblical creation.

The Jewish calendar is a lunar one, based on the cycles of the moon. Each lunar month begins with the New Moon and lasts 29 or 30 days. There are 12 months in the lunar calendar and the lunar year has 354 days. Because the solar Gregorian calendar has 365 days, the discrepancy between the two calendars causes holidays that were established based on the lunar calendar to occur on different dates each year on the solar calendar. For example, Rosh Hashanah, the Jewish New Year, occurs in the month of Tishrei, which can begin in September or October.

To keep each Jewish holiday in its right season, a thirteenth month called Adar 2 is added every two or three years.

The New Moon is considered a festive day on the Jewish calendar and is known as Rosh Hodesh. In ancient Israel, religious leaders established the dates of the major Jewish holidays based on a set number of days from the New Moon of a designated month.

When all the Jews lived in ancient Israel, the start of each month was declared by the high court in Jerusalem when eyewitnesses observed that the New Moon had appeared in the sky (which could be one of two days). After the Jews were dispersed to other countries, it was hard for religious leaders to convey what the exact date was. Thus, Jewish people would not know when to celebrate each holiday. To solve this dilemma, two days were set for many holidays. Jews outside Israel observed both days, while those in Israel continued to celebrate as before. This custom continues today.

The Months on the Jewish Calendar are:

Jewish Month	Gregorian Month	Holidays and Important Days
Tishrei	September–October	Rosh Hashanah, Yom Kippur, Sukkot
Heshvan	October–November	
Kislev	November–December	Hanukkah
Tevet	December–January	
Shevat	January–February	Tu Bishvat (Tree Holiday)
Adar	February–March	Purim
Adar 2(leap month)	March–April	
Nissan	March–April	Passover
Iyar	April–May	Israeli Independence Day
Sivan	May–June	Shavuot
Tamuz	June–July	
Av	July–August	Fast of Tisha B'av
Elul	August–September	

Glossary—Cooking, Customs, and Kashrut

afikoman—a piece of matzo that is hidden during the Passover Seder ritual. Hebrew and Yiddish.

Ashkenazic—Jews of eastern or central European origin. Hebrew.

bar mitzvah—a celebration of a 13-year-old boy's passage into adulthood. Hebrew.

bat mitzvah—a celebration for 12-year-old girls, similar to a boy's bar mitzvah; traditional among Conservative and Reform Jews. Hebrew.

bechamel—a smooth, nutmeg-flavored white sauce. French.

beitza—egg; also, a roasted hard-boiled egg for the Passover Seder. Hebrew.

blanquette—a stew with a creamy sauce. French.

bletels—crepe-like wrappers for blintzes. Yiddish.

blintz(es)—filled crepe-like dishes with savory or sweet fillings; also, the crepe-like wrappers. Yiddish.

boureka(s)—savory Sephardic pastries, similar to Spanish empanadas, often made with phyllo dough and cheese or vegetable fillings. Turkish.

bouquet garni—herb bundle for flavoring. French.

bsari—made of or containing meat. Hebrew. Same as *fleishig*.

challah—Jewish egg bread, often braided. Hebrew and Yiddish.

chimichurri—spiced parsley dipping sauce from Argentina served with grilled meat.

cholent—slow-cooking meat stew prepared for the Sabbath. Yiddish.

cioppino—California seafood stew. Italian.

couscoussier—a couscous steamer. French.

duxelles—a savory mushroom mixture, often used as a filling or topping. French.

etrog (sukkot)—a citron used in Sukkot prayers. Hebrew.

fleishig—made of or containing meat. Yiddish.

genoise—a classic French sponge cake. French.

gremolata—Italian garnish of garlic, parsley, and grated citrus rind for meat. Italian.

grivenes—cracklings made of chicken skin. Yiddish.

halavi—made of or containing dairy products. Hebrew. Same as *milchig*.

halvah—a sesame sweet. Hebrew, Yiddish, and Turkish.

hamantaschen—triangular pastries with sweet fillings for the holiday of Purim. Yiddish.

hametz—not kosher for Passover. Hebrew and Yiddish.

hamin—see *cholent*. Hebrew.

Hanukkah gelt—coin-shaped chocolates for Hanukkah. *Gelt* means money in Yiddish.

haricots verts—very thin French green beans. French.

harira—Moroccan lentil, chickpea, and meat soup. Arabic.

harissa—a North African hot pepper paste. Arabic.

hummus—a golden chickpea puree served as an appetizer or dip. Arabic.

jahnoon—Yemenite Shabbat breakfast pastries made with a flaky dough. Yemenite Arabic.

karpas—a celery stalk or parsley sprig, a ritual food for the Passover Seder. Hebrew.

kasha—buckwheat. Yiddish and Russian.

kashrut—the rules of keeping kosher. Hebrew.

kebab—food grilled on a skewer. Turkish.

kiddush—a blessing over wine; also, a light meal in the synagogue after services. Hebrew.

kishke—stuffed beef casings. Yiddish.

kitniyot—legumes; also, a variety of grains, legumes, and other foods avoided by many Jewish communities during Passover. Hebrew.

kneidel (plural kneidelach)—dumpling, usually made from matzo meal and eggs, and served in chicken soup; matzo ball. Yiddish.

knish—Ashkenazic pastry with meat or vegetable filling. Yiddish.

kreplach—Ashkenazic tortellini; or stuffed, often ring-shaped pasta. Yiddish.

kubaneh—Yemenite Shabbat breakfast bread made from a yeast dough. Yemenite Arabic.

kubeh—savory pastries made of a crunchy case, often of bulgur wheat, and a meat or chicken filling, popular among Jews from Middle Eastern countries. Arabic.

kugel—a casserole, usually baked, often of potatoes, other vegetables, or grains but can be made from any food. Yiddish.

kugelhopf—a delicate, yeast-leavened cake usually studded with raisins and almonds. Yiddish and German.

latke—pancake, especially a potato pancake for Hanukkah. Yiddish.

leben—mild yogurt-like dairy product. A similar but richer product is called *eshel*. Hebrew.

lecso—a Hungarian pepper stew. Hungarian.

lekvar—prune jam. Hungarian.

majadrah—lentils cooked with rice. Arabic.

malawah—Yemenite skillet bread made from rich, flaky dough. Yemenite Arabic.

mamaliga—cornmeal porridge, similar to Italian polenta. Romanian.

mandelbrot—"almond bread"; twice-baked Ashkenazic cookies resembling Italian biscotti. Yiddish.

mandeln—baked soup nut-like croutons; almonds. Yiddish.

maror—bitter herbs for the Passover Seder ritual, usually fresh horseradish or bitter greens. Hebrew.

matzo—unleavened cracker-like bread made of flour and water for Passover. Hebrew and Yiddish.

matzo farfel—little squares of matzo, used for stuffings and as breakfast cereal; available packaged. Yiddish.

milchig—made of or containing dairy products. Yiddish. Same as *halavi*.

moussaka—a Greek layered casserole often made of eggplant and meat sauce also popular in a kosher version among Sephardic Jews.

nigella—black seeds, often incorrectly called "black cumin," added by Yemenite Jews to breads. Latin. They are called *haba sauda* in Arabic.

oznei haman—*hamantaschen*. Hebrew.

pareve—neutral food from a kosher standpoint, neither dairy nor meat. Yiddish.

pashtidah—a baked casserole, or skillet cake, sometimes with a pastry base. Hebrew.

pâte sucrée—rich, sweet pie pastry. French.

pepitas—Mexican pumpkin seeds. Spanish.

phyllo—very thin flaky dough used to make savory and sweet Sephardic pastries. Now also used for strudel. Greek.

piroshki—savory Russian turnovers. Russian.

pistou—a Provençal version of pesto that often is made without cheese. French.

pot-au-feu—meat and vegetables poached slowly in water with herbs. French.

povidl—plum jam. Yiddish.

pletzlach—flat breads, often flavored with onion. Yiddish.

sahakeh—see *harissa*. Moroccan Arabic.

samneh—clarified butter. Yemenite Arabic.

schav—sorrel soup. Yiddish.

schmaltz—chicken fat. Yiddish.

schnitzel—pan-fried cutlets. German.

Sephardic—Jews of Mediterranean or Middle Eastern origin. Hebrew.

seudah—meal (with bread). Hebrew.

Shabbat—Sabbath; the weekly "day of rest," from sundown on Friday to nightfall on Saturday. Hebrew.

shakshuka—eggs cooked with vegetables. Arabic.

shul—synagogue. Yiddish.

sofrito—Spanish aromatic vegetable mixture for flavoring stews, often including onions and peppers. Spanish.

soofganiyot—doughnuts without holes, traditional for Hanukkah. Hebrew.

tahini—sesame paste, used to make sauce. Arabic.

tajine—aromatic Moroccan stews, usually of meat or poultry. Moroccan Arabic.

tayglach—an Ashkenazic confection of pastry balls and nuts simmered in honey, usually made for Rosh Hashanah. Yiddish.

tchermoula/chermoula—Moroccan cilantro-garlic marinade for fish. Moroccan Arabic.

tzimmes—an Eastern European Jewish casserole that often includes carrots, prunes, sweet potatoes, honey, or sugar, and sometimes beef. Yiddish.

zehug—Yemenite hot pepper chutney with garlic. Yemenite Arabic and Hebrew.

zeroah—neck; also, a roasted lamb bone or poultry neck that appears on the Passover Seder plate. Hebrew.

Index

About the Author

Faye Levy has lived in the capitals of the United States, Israel, and France, the countries with the world's largest Jewish communities. She has thoroughly enjoyed and wholeheartedly studied cooking in each of these countries, and has contributed to its culinary literature. Levy is a four-time award-winning cookbook author and has the outstanding achievement of writing and publishing fine cookbooks in three languages—English, Hebrew, and French. She has written other major volumes on Jewish cooking: *Faye Levy's International Jewish Cookbook* and *The Low-Fat Jewish Cookbook,* and she contributed to *The New York Times Passover Cookbook.*

Faye Levy's *International Vegetable Cookbook* won the James Beard Cookbook Award in 1994 for the best book of the year in the category of fruits, vegetables, and grains. Levy also won awards from the International Association of Culinary Professionals for her books *Vegetable Creations, Chocolate Sensations,* and *Classic Cooking Techniques.*

Levy received her Jewish education at Midrasha Hebrew High School and at the Hebrew Academy of Washington, D.C., and as an adult received the Academy's Eishet Hayil, or Woman of Valor, award. She attended college at the Hebrew University in Jerusalem and Tel Aviv University, where she graduated magna cum laude in sociology and anthropology. Levy trained as a professional chef at the Parisian cooking school La Varenne in Paris, where she spent six wonderful years.

Levy has been the main cooking columnist for the *Jerusalem Post* for ten years, covering all aspects of Jewish and kosher cooking. She has written articles on Jewish holiday cooking for major newspapers throughout the United States, as well as for *Gourmet* and *Bon Appétit* magazines. For four years she was the culinary columnist of Israel's foremost women's magazine, *At.*

For the last ten years Levy has been a nationally syndicated cooking columnist for the *Los Angeles Times* Syndicate. In her biweekly column she emphasizes fast, easy, nutritionally sound dishes that taste delicious. From the numerous letters she receives from her readers and from discussions with her students in her cooking classes, Levy knows how much this kind of light, fresh food is appreciated. She and her husband-associate Yakir Levy enjoy cooking, eating, and celebrating—holidays and everyday—in their home in Woodland Hills, California.